*Encyclopedia of the*

# AMERICAN LEGISLATIVE SYSTEM

## ASSOCIATE EDITORS

*Encyclopedia of the*

# AMERICAN LEGISLATIVE SYSTEM

Studies of the Principal Structures, Processes, and Policies
of Congress and the State Legislatures
Since the Colonial Era

## JOEL H. SILBEY

*Editor in Chief*

**Volume III**

CHARLES SCRIBNER'S SONS/NEW YORK
MAXWELL MACMILLAN CANADA/TORONTO
MAXWELL MACMILLAN INTERNATIONAL/NEW YORK OXFORD SINGAPORE SYDNEY

Charles Scribner's Sons     Maxwell Macmillan Canada, Inc.
Macmillan Publishing Company    1200 Eglinton Avenue East

866 Third Avenue    Suite 200
New York, New York 10022    Don Mills, Ontario M3C 3N1

Macmillan Publishing Company is part of the Maxwell Communication Group of
Companies.


**Library of Congress Cataloging-in-Publication Data**


Encyclopedia of the American legislative system / Joel H. Silbey,
  editor in chief.
     p.  cm.
    Includes bibliographical references.
    ISBN 0-684-19243-8 (set)—ISBN 0-684-19601-8 (vol. 1)—ISBN 0-684-19602-6
    (vol. 2)—ISBN 0-684-19600-X (vol. 3)
    1. Legislative bodies—United States—Encyclopedias.  I. Silbey,
Joel H.
JF501.E53  1994
328.73'003—dc20                  93-35874
                                    CIP


1  3  5  7  9  11  13  15  17  19  V/C  20  18  16  14  12  10  8  6  4  2

PRINTED IN THE UNITED STATES OF AMERICA

The paper used in this publication meets the minimum requirements
of American National Standard for Information Sciences—Permanence
of Paper for Printed Library Materials. ANSI Z3948-1984. ∞™

# CONTENTS

## Volume III

# CONTENTS

# CONTENTS

# Part V

# LEGISLATURES AND PUBLIC POLICY

# LEGISLATURES AND AMERICAN ECONOMIC DEVELOPMENT

## *Harry N. Scheiber*

One of the abiding preoccupations of Congress and the state legislatures throughout American history has been the formulation of policies designed to promote economic growth and welfare. Indeed, in his first annual presidential message, George Washington called upon Congress to assist enterprise and bolster the new nation's economy. The Senate's prompt response was that it would advance "by all proper means in our power" the interests of commerce, manufacturing, and agriculture; and the House of Representatives similarly promised to extend "legislative protection" to domestic economic interests.

There soon emerged, of course, deeply rooted sectional, interest-group, and ideological differences in the First Congress about what measures in aid of the economy were appropriate and how far they should go. Many leaders of the new nation, especially those in the Jeffersonian political camp, paid homage in a general way to the precepts of laissez-faire doctrine. Still, there proved to be wide agreement that it was Congress's responsibility to develop policies that, as the Federalist Pelatiah Webster said, would "most enrich, strengthen, and happify a nation." Even political leaders who were most hostile to active governmental intervention in general acknowledged that it was important to extend "the fostering hand of government" (as James Madison termed it) to some degree, to build up the young nation's economic base in a competitive international environment.

In the state legislatures as well, from the Republic's earliest beginnings there was a commitment to mobilization of government's coercive authority and deployment of its resources—though both in the state arena and in Congress there were deeply rooted differences as to how far intervention should go—in order to protect and advance economic interests. One of the most compelling arguments for ratification of the Constitution in the 1787–1789 debates was that the states' legislative activism on behalf of localized interests since the end of the Revolution had severely undermined national unity and economic strength. To establish a single national authority over trade and commerce, to protect against the arbitrary betrayal of contract obligations by populistic legislatures, and to lay the foundations for a more unified national economy were thus among the principal stated objectives of the nationalists in the great ratification debates. Nonetheless, inherent in the concept of limited "enumerated" powers for the national government (a core element of the constitutional bargain) was the assurance of continued decentralization of significant authority over economic institutions and policies. And so when the government commenced its operations in 1789 under the new Constitution, it was fully expected on all sides that the states—even though now constrained by the commerce clause and other constitutional provisions—would continue to exercise a very wide-ranging authority in economic policy matters. And, as events proved, significant decentralization of power did in fact prevail in the nineteenth century.

## THE COLONIAL HERITAGE IN ECONOMIC POLICY

A strong positive role by government was entirely consistent, moreover, with the role that the provincial governments had played during the colonial era, as well as the role the states had played during the short life of the Articles of Confederation. Throughout the colonial period, Parliament and the British administrators of the empire had given the governing authorities in the colonies ample room for pursuit of economic policies suited to their own needs and ambitions.

Parliament established the basic legal framework with imperial trade regulations beginning in the 1620s, but especially after enactment of the Acts of Trade and Navigation in 1660. These measures were at the core of what became in the eighteenth century a fully developed system of British mercantilist regulation, requiring the colonists to ship specified goods (termed "enumerated articles") exclusively to the mother country and placing strict limits on the role of foreign-flag shipping in English imperial trade. Parliament elaborated the system as time went on, adding commodities such as rice, ocean products, furs, and lumber to the "enumerated" list. The British also kept firm control over imposition of duties, deriving revenues for imperial administration from tariffs and tonnage fees. Interventions by the imperial government beneficial to the colonies included subsidies of the trans-Atlantic mails and the development of a domestic colonial postal service (headed by Benjamin Franklin in 1751); in addition, the Royal Navy guarded the commercial sea-lanes that were so vital to American trade.

Some of the British trade policies bore hard on colonial economic interests, and they had the effect of constraining the reach of the colonial legislatures' autonomous control over their provincial economies. Notable in this regard was a series of British statutes including one in 1699 banning export of woolens from the colonies or even in intercolonial trade, one in 1732 prohibiting any exports of hats, and another in 1750 imposing restrictions on the manufacture of iron and the trade in iron products. Such measures were designed, of course, to protect important manufacturing interests in the home country, a fact not lost on the Americans. The British government also viewed with concern the numerous experiments of colonial legislatures with creation of land banks, currency offices, and other institutions authorized to issue paper money; and in 1764, Parliament moved against these practices by invalidating any provincial statutes giving legal-tender status to such currency.

Within these broad limits, however, the colonial legislatures still found significant room for the autonomous pursuit of their provincial and localized interests. Every colony developed a policy of making land available to purchasers seeking to establish new farms, either directly through sale or grant, or else indirectly through privileged grantees (including, often, royal governors themselves) or land companies. Some of the legislatures gave free land in small tracts to all new arrivals or newly freed indentured servants. Varied policies were pursued with respect to immigration, usually to encourage it but in a few instances with a view toward limiting the entry of excessive numbers of transported convicts or other "undesirables."

More generally, the colonial legislatures all engaged in the fashioning of labor policies, ranging from the notorious laws in Virginia and then other colonies binding blacks and their descendants into a permanent legalized slavery, to the great variety of laws that defined the rights and obligations of indentured servants, minors, apprentices, and masters. Regulation of commercial and industrial activities was commonplace. Virginia and Maryland, for example, at several junctures required the warehousing, inspection, and official grading of tobacco, as a means of assuring quality of exports and also—in times of weak markets and falling prices—holding back the product from trade.

In the seventeenth century the Massachusetts Bay Colony, consistent with its bent toward paternalism in the Puritan quest for a "well order'd society," acting through statutes enacted by its legislature (the General Court) and, by devolution of authority, by its town governments, imposed detailed wage scales for many of the crafts and banned what was termed "oppression" of wages by employers and of prices by sellers of basic commodities. Port regulations and tonnage fees, some of them successfully advantaging local shippers over London shipowners (much to the anger of the latter), were imposed by all the colonial legislatures. Common to almost every province were regulations of livestock fencing and other farm operations that impinged on the public; laws granting special franchises for construction of mills and other facilities required to advance the local economies; supervision of fisheries and navigation on inland and coastal waters; and statutes requiring labor services, or commutation in money taxes, of all residents of the colony.

In addition, the legislatures voted funds for improvement of harbors and roads; and both through statutes and the common law, as interpreted by the colonial courts, the concept of the "public interest" was stoutly reaffirmed by licensing traders and town and rural markets and by regulating mills, ferries, bridges, inns, and other facilities that were considered quasi-public rather than strictly private in their "use," regardless of whether they were private in their ownership.

The common thread running through this record of legislation in the colonial era was the persistence of an interventionist approach, along mercantilistic lines. Not only were the colonial legislatures activist—pursuing interventions involving both the promotional and the regulatory powers of government—in their quest to advance localized interests, they were also conscious of operating in a milieu of intercolonial competitiveness, as they vied with one another for immigrants, for capital, and for trade advantage. This heritage of particularism and localism, with rivalry among the colonies and later among the states, carried forward into the early decades of the new Republic.

## ESTABLISHING THE ECONOMIC FRAMEWORK

State-based particularism and the continuing strength of interstate economic rivalries served after 1789 to reinforce ideological, constitutional, and sectional cleavages that militated against an all-powerful centralized role for Congress in shaping the nation's economic policies. The record of the First Congress, however, demonstrates clearly that the new nation's leaders approached the task of shaping policies to govern international economic relations squarely within the terms of the eighteenth-century mercantilist tradition.

Thus, among the earliest statutes enacted were tonnage and navigation acts that effectively excluded foreign-flag vessels from the American coastal trade (i.e., commerce between American ports) and reserved this important sector of the shipping trade for American enterprise. Many of the southern members of Congress objected to provisions that would levy discriminatory tonnage fees favoring the U.S. merchant fleet even in the export-carrying trade, fearing that it would cut into the profits enjoyed by exporters of tobacco, forest products, wheat, and other staples. The tonnage measure was successfully championed, however, by James Madison of Virginia, among other influential leaders from all regions of the country, on the grounds that it would serve not only the economy but also the cause of building up American naval power for national defense.

Like control of navigation, the structuring of foreign trade and protection of domestic manufacturing interests were key elements of traditional mercantilism. The Constitution empowered Congress to "lay and collect Taxes, Duties, Imposts and Excises" (Article I, Section 8) so long as such measures were not imposed on exports and were uniformly applied. When national party organizations emerged in later years, the discipline imposed by the party leadership on tariff policy became a major factor in shaping debates. But in the First Congress there was a surpisingly broad consensus on the need for some level of protective tariff so as to foster nascent American manufacturing interests. Accordingly, a tariff on imported goods became one of the earliest measures that Congress considered.

The first tariff became law on 4 July 1789, and it provided for a wide range of rates, with significant protection over the 15-percent level on a number of manufactured articles in trade. Like all tariff measures, both in that day and later, the debate of the first national tariff bill evoked political divisions (albeit within a broader consensus favoring a protective policy) that revealed complex fragmentation and cleavages—some of them sectional in nature, some highly localized, and others reflecting the opposing views of functional interests (agricultural, industrial, commercial) that cut across state lines.

Under terms of Article I, Section 8, of the Constitution, which gave Congress authority "to promote the Progress of Science and useful Arts" by granting patents and copyrights, it also enacted a patent law to protect the rights of inventors. It was a badly conceived measure, leading to extensive litigation in the ensuing decades; but still, the law did set in place the conceptual foundations of the nation's patent system. As the industrialization of the country gathered strength in later years, Congress returned to the subject, revising the basic law in 1836 so as to make the administration of patents more efficient and clarifying the requirements of novelty and usefulness.

Turning to the domestic economy and its needs, the First Congress soon ventured into much more controversial political terrain. The terms of controversy were laid out by Secretary of the Treasury Alexander Hamilton's well-known bold proposals for funding of the state debts remaining from the Revolutionary and Confederation era, as a way of establishing national public and private credit; for an excise tax, which would give the national government additional resources independent of the states; and for chartering by Congress of a Bank of the United States to provide a uniform currency and handle the government's fiscal operations. All three of these measures were adopted after intense and bitter debate. But an additional element of Hamilton's program, calling for a broad range of national subsidies to infant industries, did not carry.

When, after a bitter debate that did much to advance the formation of a formally organized opposition party, Congress finally adopted the funding measure, it was a stunning victory for the Federalist champions of what their opponents denounced as "consolidated government." No less controversial was Hamilton's and the Federalist leadership's sponsorship of the Bank of the United States. Whether Congress had constitutional authority to charter a banking institution (modeled on the Bank of England in vital respects) that would enjoy a monopoly position in the handling of federal receipts and disbursements became the central issue in a heated political battle that pitted Thomas Jefferson and his followers against the Federalist majority. The Federalists won the day, and the bank measure was approved; the Bank of the United States was successfully launched in 1791 and for the next twenty years operated as the government's fiscal agent and as a clearinghouse bank whose branches checked the operations of state banks in many areas of the country.

One of the major issues in economic policy in the early Congresses was the question of policy for management of the vast landed domain under its control as the result of land cessions by the original states. (Later, of course, the Louisiana Purchase and land acquired by purchase, conquest, and treaty expanded westward to the Pacific the public domain under control of Congress. Almost two-thirds of the land area of the present continental United States was once in the federal public domain.) Above all, Congress needed to establish the priorities that would be given to revenue maximization and to the conflicting goal of promoting rapid and extensive settlement. Also, Congress needed to decided whether to permit speculators and companies to acquire land or, instead, to deal only with individual settlers and whether—and how much—land ought to be granted to the new western states as they formed.

Congress early set in place three fundamental elements of land policy that would endure throughout the antebellum era. First was its commitment to removing Native American title to the lands under federal control—indeed, to do so by virtually any means necessary, including acceptance of blatantly corrupt treaties or the pursuit of merciless warfare against resistant Native American nations. Second was acceptance and extension of a policy that predated the Constitution itself under terms of the 1787 Northwest Ordinance—the granting of rights of self-government and eventual statehood to the Euro-American populations that settled the western country. Third, Congress instituted in the 1790s the basic policy of alienation of land and other resources on the public domain—that is, the policy of transferring (by terms that would change, indeed radically in some respects, over time) from public to private ownership not only land itself but the water, mineral, and timber resources of the public domain.

Perhaps no other policy of the founding period expressed so succinctly and accurately as did the public land policy the basic consensus in the new nation that private economic interests should enjoy the support of government's "fostering hand" on the basis of selective interventionism. Certainly no other policy, except perhaps the tariff, revealed in such stark form the potential redistributive effects that might result from policy choices about what interests should be advantaged and at what other interests' expense.

Another major area of federal legislative influence on economic development concerned immigration. Although Congress did briefly regulate naturalization for citizenship by the notorious 1798 Alien Acts, in general the new nation's immigration policy was one of an open door to all immigrants. This policy would prevail throughout the antebellum period, and in its essence (except for exclusion of Asians) until World War I. The open door meant that immigration would make a large contribution to national population growth and consequently to economic and territorial expansion in the nineteenth century.

## CONGRESS AND ECONOMIC POLICY, 1800–1861

Although the American mercantilist measures of the 1790s were of dramatic importance, they did not add up to a program of truly comprehensive intervention in the domestic economy. Enormous areas of economic policy were scarcely touched by Congress; among them were nearly all the elements of regulatory authority exercised by governments in the European and Anglo-American traditions, in what in the law is designated the "police power" for advancement of the health, welfare, and safety of the community. With the exception of laws for the return of fugitive slaves and for the protection of merchant seamen on the high seas, the record of Congress in the Federalist period and ensuing decades amounted to only a feeble and attenuated federal police power. Insofar as the regulatory authority of government was extended to constraint of institutions and dynamic relationships of the domestic economy, it would be done mainly by the legislatures and courts of the states. In several major areas of policy, however—most notably in transportation, banking, tariff, and land-disposal policy—Congress did make continuing, if sometimes sporadic and often inconsistent, contributions to the promotion of economic development during the pre–Civil War years.

### Internal Improvements

The cause of what nineteenth-century Americans commonly termed "internal improvements"—that is, the development of transportation facilities—was constantly before Congress in the antebellum era. Petitions for federal projects or aid to private enterprises were commonplace in every session of the national legislature. Pressure to obtain the national government's support for roads, river and harbor improvements, canal projects, and railroads tended to be local or regional in their organization or to come from specific economic interest groups and communities of investors; seldom was aid for a specific project made a party issue. There was often an element of partisan ideological division as well, however, and it grew stronger as the decades passed and slavery-focused sectionalism came to dominate congressional and national partisan divisions. Particularly from the South, throughout the pre–Civil War era, came principled objections to government subsidizing or direct promotion of transportation. Even the southern antigovernmental ideologues in Congress, however, often voted for river or harbor bills and various types of subsidies for projects that would benefit their own districts.

Few specific proposals could win votes enough to overcome the burden of constitutional, sectional, and conflicting interest-group opposition. Nonetheless, during the period 1800–1833, Congress did authorize the construction of the National Road as a federal project (though its extension in the Midwest was later turned over to the states), as well as other "military roads" in all regions of the country. A series of stock subscriptions and other subsidies to some major canal projects on the eastern seaboard was also approved, as were land grants in 1824 and 1827–1828 to Ohio, Indiana, and Illinois in aid of their state canal projects. With the help of expanded representation for the western states after the 1820 census, Congress also passed the General Survey Act of 1824, under which the Army Corps of Engineers was loaned out to state projects and private canal and railroad companies. Each year, moreover, old-fashioned "logrolling" (vote trading) resulted in river and harbor appropriations, as well as some federal road projects.

Following President Andrew Jackson's 1830 veto of the Maysville Road project because it would have benefited only one state, the dominant Jacksonian Democratic party aligned itself with increasing rigidity against a major federal role in internal improvements. Repeated efforts in the 1850s to gain support for aid to a transcontinental railway line to the Pacific foundered on sectional rivalries; no majority coalition could be mobilized in favor of any route that was recommended. In the 1850s, except for large land grants to the Illinois Central Railroad and the Sault Sainte Marie Canal project in Michigan, only minimal federal aid was extended for transport. As American promoters constructed the world's largest national railroad network in the pre–Civil War decade, the locus of action was almost wholly in the state legislatures and private corporate boardrooms.

## Banking

Although sectionalism and localistic ambitions played a part in shaping congressional banking policy, the dominant influence came to be partisan and ideological—more so than in the politics of most other aspects of federal economic policy. Ironically, although the antibanking creed of the Jeffersonian opponents of the first Bank of the United States in 1791, with its opposition to "monopoly" privileges, paper money, and credit, was taken up wholesale by the Jacksonians in the 1830s, the object of this later attack was the second Bank of the United States, chartered by a Jeffersonian Democratic-Republican Congress in 1816. The second bank had won its charter in the aftermath of the War of 1812, when rampant inflation and fiscal disruption persuaded the Democratic-Republicans that the central banking functions of a national institution were indispensable to the country's economic stability.

Once Andrew Jackson turned upon the bank, however, opposition to an activist federal role in banking became a central element of Jacksonian orthodoxy—so much so, in fact, that it drove many prominent business leaders who had been active Democrats out of the party and into the Whig opposition. The new orthodoxy became institutionalized in the "independent Treasury" policy, which was adopted by Congress during Martin Van Buren's administration, reinstated in 1846 after a four-year lapse during a period of Whig control of the government, and then kept in effect until the Civil War. Under the Independent Treasury scheme, the national government's finances were entirely divorced from banking operations, and both commercial banking functions and provision of paper money for the market economy were left

entirely to the state-chartered banks. Although the divorce of banks from government has been interpreted as a laissez-faire measure by Jackson and his successors responding to pressure from state bankers, as argued by Bray Hammond and others, it applied only to the national government; in fact, in many states the Jacksonian parties were favorable to banking charters and extended bank operations.

The Democrats' success in withdrawing the federal government from the field as regulator, promoter, or participant in banking operations stimulated the expansion of state banks from seven hundred in 1844 to more than fifteen hundred in 1861, while their capitalization rose in the same period from $75 million to $207 million. Whether the instability associated with the lack of central banking was offset or overbalanced by the stimulative impact of such rapid state banking expansion on investment and economic growth is a subject of continuing debate among economic historians.

## Land Policy

The consistent policy of Congress with respect to the public domain, despite shifts in emphasis and in some important substantive aspects, was to "privatize" federal resources—not only arable land but also minerals, forests, and water—through a congeries of statutes that amounted to a "development policy" for the West. Debates centered on how quickly the lands should be surveyed and brought to market; on limits, if any, as to price and size of allowable purchases; on special advantages that might be devolved on actual settlers seeking to gain ownership; on the proper role of speculators and companies as middlemen; and, not least, on the extent to which lands should be transferred to the western state governments (which would themselves sell to private owners, as a way of subsidizing internal improvements, education, and other state governmental operations) or to railroad corporations and other projects as direct subsidies.

Sectional and regional differences dominated in the land-policy debates from 1800 to 1861. Party-based differences were also sometimes evident, most dramatically in the 1830s when the Whig party took a stand on the need to protect the flow of revenues by maintaining minimum prices for purchasers of the public land, and in the 1850s, when the emergent Republican coalitional party made "free land" through homestead rights a core party commitment, one that would result in passage of the Homestead Act of 1862, which granted 160 acres of land to any actual settler on the public domain. More generally, however, the western states pressed for rapid survey and sales at ever-lower prices, with adjustments downward in minimum price for wetlands or lands that had been on the market for a long period. Congress responded in the 1840s and 1850s with legislation that instituted a series of such price adjustments; in addition, increasingly generous grants of acreage were given to new states upon their admission to the Union.

The land policies adopted in the nineteenth century added up to something very different from systematic resource management by government. Such management was never attempted, even when valuable mineral lands were involved, as in the California gold rush after 1849.

## The Tariff

As with internal-improvements policy, tariff questions typically evoked complex interest-group divisions and coalition building. After the plantation economy became firmly established in the South in the 1820s, however, sectionalism became a powerful force in tariff debates; this reflected the dual concerns of southern representatives, first, to support the agricultural interests of their region against trade barriers and, second, to defend the institution of slavery against potential attacks from a powerful central government controlled by a dynamic industrial North. Beginning in the mid-1840s, moreover, the impact of sectional influence in determining tariff questions was reinforced by the southern-oriented Jacksonian Democratic party's opposition to protectionism.

From 1846, when Congress passed the Walker Tariff, embodying the so-called "revenue-only principle" (though in fact steep duties were retained on luxury goods and selected goods in the nonluxury category), until 1857, the Democrats maintained the lower tariff. In 1857 a new bill brought U.S. tariff policy closer to free trade than it had been since the

War of 1812 or would be again until well into the twentieth century.

## STATE LEGISLATURES AND THE ECONOMY, 1789–1861

Although Congress undertook programs of sometimes intensive intervention in the nation's economic life, there was a great deal of room remaining for the states to define and pursue their own economic-policy agendas. Indeed, national policy was virtually absent with respect to the basic aspects of commercial law, and corporation law, the definition of property rights (except insofar as the contract clause was at issue), and labor law all remained under jurisdiction of the state legislatures and courts.

To a remarkable degree, the state legislatures were also the principal arena for policymaking in regard to transportation development, most aspects of agriculture, and even banking after the successful Jacksonian assault on the Bank of the United States in 1833. As a practical matter, the states also enjoyed wide discretion in taxation, since federal levies were at such a low level—about 2 percent of national income.

Although the U.S. Supreme Court did give extensive force in the Republic's first quarter century to the contract clause and to the nationalistic implications of the commerce clause, the sphere of action left to the states by federal law was remarkably extensive. The states' area of constitutional discretion and autonomy became even more extended in the period 1836–1861, during the Supreme Court's dominance by a Jacksonian majority that adhered to the concept of "dual federalism"—the idea that the states had their "separate sphere" of legitimate authority, with an assurance of freedom from interference by Congress or the national executive.

## Common Law and Public Law

Before turning to the matters in which the legislatures took an activist stance, one must recognize that legislatures deferred to the judicial branch of government in many areas of law important in their economic effects. The state courts developed an elaborate set of "common-law" doctrines—that is, rules that were built up over time on the basis of accumulated precedent—which served to define many of the most basic rights, immunities, and obligations of private property. In general, the state judiciary adopted and modified, when it seemed appropriate to the peculiar geography of America or indeed seemed required by the imperatives of republican governance, the doctrines of property rights, torts (that is, civil, rather than criminal, injury to property and persons), and contracts. Comfortable with this traditional reliance on the judiciary and the common law, legislatures only occasionally led or reformed lawmaking in these realms. The basic doctrines of capitalism were thus shaped in the early nineteenth century to a great degree by judges rather than by legislators.

This is not to say that the doctrines advanced by the state courts were never given general direction or were left entirely unmodified by the legislatures. Development of the law of eminent domain, for example, was in many states established in broad outline by statutes that gave governmental authorities engaged in state canal construction, road building, and other public works broad discretion in taking property. Most state legislatures also sought to define by statute the rules of compensation for private owners who lost property through takings. More dramatic still was the tendency of the legislatures by the 1840s to devolve the types of legal privilege and subsidization advantages upon enterprises in the private sector that had already been given to public agencies in takings for state-built works—most of them to the advantage of the railroad companies, which were favored in a great variety of ways by the legislatures in a nation eager to apply new steam-transport technology as extensively as possible.

In shaping the rules of the eminent-domain power, the state legislatures and courts routinely made choices that gave priority to certain types of economic interests (for example, the railroads) over other interests (such as agricultural landowners). The same kind of conscious priority-setting was typical of legislative debates over bankruptcy and debtors' imprisonment measures, taxation laws, and rules of commercial and insurance law. Although some scholars have tried to argue that the "dynamic" investment sectors that were advancing

new industrial enterprises and railroads consistently had the advantage everywhere over farming interests—and that the wealthiest elements of society uniformly had the advantage over the poorer elements—in fact the evidence suggests a very mixed picture. The only well-founded generalization that one can venture may be that the costs and benefits of lawmakers' setting of priorities did not fall into uniform patterns, either across the nation or even within individual states as policy goals and prevailing political alignments changed over time.

## The Regulatory Power

Of greater political salience than property or eminent-domain questions was the question of how actively the states should exercise their general regulatory authority under the rubric "police powers." In a society devoted to protection of private-property rights with a legal system biased in favor of enterprisers, as the United States clearly was, the state courts might have been expected to erect doctrinal barriers to the effective regulation of economic interests. In fact, the courts generally exhibited a broad deference to the judgment of legislatures in regard to economic-policy issues.

Thus, unsurprisingly, the southern state courts gave wide latitude to the legislatures in establishing the rules of slavery and manumission; only on rare occasions did a southern state judge invoke humane principles to modify some of the harshest elements of slave law, but in general the legislatures had full discretion in maintaining the racial caste system of the plantation region. Similarly, the state courts throughout the country upheld the validity of legislative efforts to assert and protect the "common good" with regard to removal of privately owned obstructions of navigable streams and coastlines or to assure public access to, and continued productivity of, fisheries in lakes and streams. Laws intended to protect public health by authorizing the destruction of homes in which smallpox or other diseases were present or to limit the movements of newly arrived immigrants during a period of quarantine were similarly upheld by the courts.

In many states, liquor-prohibition statutes were challenged by owners of distilleries or stocks of liquor that were to be destroyed without compensation; here too, with a few exceptions, the state judiciary generally upheld the police power. The courts also validated a considerable discretion in the legislatures with regard to debtor laws, bankruptcy, and mechanics' liens. Therefore, the legislatures exercised a powerful prerogative in determining which private interests were to have priority and which must yield when the legal rules created winners and losers in cases of economic conflict.

Still, whatever the broad legal foundations for the police power in that era, the legislatures did not establish the kind of intensive regulatory policies that earlier mercantilist regimes had imposed on their domestic economies in Europe—or in colonial America, for that matter—let alone the kinds of regulatory regimes that would become commonplace in the states in the twentieth century. And when regulatory interventions were undertaken, it was done selectively and without the kind of bureaucratic administrative apparatus that characterizes regulatory regimes of the modern industrial era.

## Transportation, Banking, and Corporations

How dominant the role of state legislatures was in fashioning the nation's economic policy before 1861 is well illustrated by the range and variety of interventions they successfully undertook. Every state legislature distributed public largess to individuals, groups, and localities. Some of this largess was in the form of land sales on favorable terms to companies and individuals; some, in the form of privileges and immunities granted by special charters to companies formed for internal improvements, banking, and manufacturing; and some, in cash, through subscriptions to stock of corporations, or in tax exemptions for favored enterprises. The pressures from special interests for such largess tended to be highly localistic and particularistic, especially because if the legislature favored one local district or enterprise with largess, it could generally devolve similar favors on rival localities or companies. Moreover, "have-not" regions disadvantaged by earlier distributions of largess typically argued—to

good effect—for "equality of benefits" as a principled matter of basic fairness in a republican scheme of government.

Equally important in many states, though not all, was the policy of promoting and operating public works. Direct capital investment and public operation of this sort became widespread after New York—the pioneering state in this regard—made a spectacular success of its Erie Canal project. Typically, in the states that followed New York's lead, there was a strong element of planning and some movement toward bureaucratization and professionalization in the operation of canals and other state enterprises. To this degree, the "public-enterprise states," as they may be termed—with their reliance on the expertise of engineers as planners and with the manifest need to proceed by stages with giant programs that required unprecedented long-term borrowing of funds—legislated in a style that contrasted with the pattern of what has been termed the ad hoc, almost random responses to interest-group pressure that characterized economic policy-making in states that eschewed major public-enterprise investments. (Hurst, in *Law and the Conditions of Freedom,* used the phrase "drift and default" in describing the latter, ad hoc style of weak government yielding to the complex and proliferating demands of private and localized special interests.)

Even the states initially committed to well-conceived plans typically overextended their state projects in a reckless way; meanwhile, the legislatures in many states yielded to local pressures by also approving state aid or local government assistance, or both, to private railroad corporations. The economic losses suffered in consequence by many state governments during the post–1839 depression became a major factor in turning public opinion against such policies in later years. Indeed, in the 1850s, numerous state constitutions were amended to bar the incurring of such massive public debts, or even to prohibit the legislatures from extending public aid to private corporations such as railroad companies.

The impact on development of these legislative initiatives was far-reaching, even in the states with policies that proved financially disastrous. In the southern states, for example, more than half the capital for railroads built before 1861 came from government: of $144 million in public funds, 56 percent was from the state coffers, 39 percent from local government, and 5 percent from Congress. Similarly, in the Old Northwest states (Ohio, Indiana, Illinois, Michigan, and Wisconsin), the state governments contributed the vast preponderance of funding for canal projects that were vital to regional development from 1831 to the 1850s, and local and state aid to railroads played a key role in building the region's rail network and connections with export centers on the eastern seaboard.

The flow of public money was not matched with regulatory policies to protect the public interest in oversight of the rate systems and operating practices of the private railroads. Laws enacted by the legislatures of New York, Ohio, and a few other states to protect consumers and shippers from discriminatory rate practices were poorly designed and went largely unenforced; by 1861, most of even these inadequate efforts had been abandoned in the face of pressure from local districts that as yet were not served by railroad lines and so feared the effects of regulation on investment—a clash of interests that would become a major theme in transport-regulation debates of the post–Civil War era. Ironically, moreover, in the 1830s and 1840s, the state legislatures in the public canal states had pursued discriminatory rate policies: they had authorized canal-toll scales that were designed to favor in-state producers or consumers at the expense of out-of-state interests.

Policies regarding the charter of corporations illustrated with equal vividness the pattern of special-interest pressures in legislative debate and action in this era. Until the late 1830s, the preponderance of charters granted by the legislatures to bridge, turnpike, canal, railroad, banking, and manufacturing corporations were in the form of "special legislation"—statutes setting out the terms of the charter, specifically designed for the project in question. Gradually, political pressure gathered strength against the practice of special charters. Entrepreneurs who felt shut out, along with ideological opponents of "corporate privilege" and other reformers concerned with growing business influence over the legislatures, demanded enactment of "general corporation laws" to set uniform terms and conditions for obtaining the corporate privilege (a privilege that in most states included the vitally important element of limited stockholder liability).

By the 1850s the granting of special charters had begun to give way in most states to a preference for incorporation under general laws. The shift from special to general status for corporations also marked, many historians have argued, abandonment of a once-powerful concept of the corporation as an agency of the state that performed a public function and only for that reason was worthy of special privileges and immunities. If the reform movement had its democratic and antimonopoly side, however, it also had its entrepreneurial side, for it bespoke the emerging interest of business firms in operating free of the obligations that might be inferred from a quasi-public status.

How the state legislatures handled the banking question provides vivid evidence of how American federalism, with the autonomy its early-nineteenth-century constitutional version afforded the states, encouraged extraordinary diversity of policy and practice. Some legislatures approved through special and general charter acts the incorporation of scores of privately operated banks that could issue paper money and engage in commercial or agricultural banking virtually without regulation. Others chartered banks, but subjected them to common safety-fund requirements or imposed strict limits on operations with respect to specie reserves, circulation of paper, and interest rates. In some western and southern states, chartered bank operations were altogether prohibited; their economies were reliant on out-of-state and federal bank operations for their money supply and credit. Some legislatures created banking regulatory commissions with power to engage in oversight of specified operating practices and to ensure probity. And in Louisiana and a few other states, the legislatures created mixed public-private or else entirely state-owned and state-run banking institutions.

Most historians of antebellum economic policy conclude from this record that the legislatures were incapable of pursuing coherent policies that would be well administered. With pitifully small tax bases, impossible to reform in the face of popular antitax biases; with high turnover and political organizations that were not focused on coordination or sustaining of policy goals; and with private interests typically arrayed in powerful coalitions to influence the course of legislation, the typical state legislature of this era did not stand up well to interest-group or localistic pressure. The legislatures did contribute in a variety of vitally important ways to the fostering and promotion of the economy, but they did so while relying largely on ad hoc responses to particularistic pressures for action. And more generally, they failed to embrace the objective of developing government's independent competence to formulate and implement programs effectively—something that required bureaucratization, permanence of state organizations, and professional expertise. The reforms that moved in this direction awaited a much later era of state legislative and political development.

## INDUSTRIAL POLICIES FROM THE CIVIL WAR TO 1929

The Civil War and Reconstruction era (1861–1877) brought dramatic changes both in the nation's basic economic policies and in the constitutional balance of power between the states and the national government. It is not too much to say that Congress's wartime legislation produced a fundamental transformation in political economy, a transformation that involved a shift in the locus of policy innovation and regulatory power from the state capitals to Washington. Moreover, this shift in authority in economic policy-making carried forward into later years, so that the entire period from 1861 to the late 1920s was one of fairly continuous centralization of power. At the same time, the constitutional system also underwent basic change as the result of the war, for the adoption of the Thirteenth and Fourteenth Amendments abolished slavery and held state legislation to the standard of "equal protection."

Secession in 1861 and withdrawal of the South's representatives from Congress gave the newly ascendant Republican party an opportunity as great as the Federalists had enjoyed seventy years earlier to establish new foundations for an American political economy. There were some serious intraparty differences as to primacy of objectives and interests; indeed, the historian Richard Bensel contended that the party was in fact a "hegemonic coalition" of banking, manufacturing, and agrarian interests. All the party's factions were dedicated in common, however, to the fostering of modernization through integration of the national market, transportation growth that would link agricultural with industrial and commercial centers, a protective tariff policy to support vigorous growth of the manufacturing sector, and a reformed and more centralized banking system that would give the country uniform currency and reduce the autarky represented by state control of banks. From this coalition, then, quickly came a series of measures in pursuit of industrialization and related developmental objectives.

First, Congress voted lavish grants of public land and cash aid for transcontinental railroad companies that were chartered by Congress as national corporations. Second, the long-debated homestead principle was enacted in the 1862 land law, providing for 160 acres to settlers—a measure that, together with the railroad bills, was designed to stimulate western agricultural development as industrialization went forward. Third, Congress instituted high protective tariffs covering a broad range of imports and, in subsequent years, despite repeated attacks on the protective system, raised even further the duties on many key imported products. Fourth, a national banking system was adopted, providing for nationally chartered banks, a tax on state bank notes (designedly high enough to drive the state notes out of circulation), and the reestablishment of the functional connection between government's fiscal operations and banking that had been destroyed by the Jacksonians.

In addition, the wartime Congress established a system of land-grant subsidies for agricultural and mechanical colleges (which became the basis of the modern land-grant universities), and it changed the immigration laws to permit industrialists to contract for labor in foreign countries. New excise and income taxes, which soon displaced the customs and land-sale revenues as the chief sources of funds for the federal Treasury, were also adopted. After the war, moreover, the excise tax, which was regressive, was continued, but the mildly progressive income tax was abandoned—a shift in policy that probably further favored investment and certainly disadvantaged consumers and the poorer classes.

After the Civil War, even as the extreme radical faction of the Republican party was losing influence, the process of transforming the basic political economy went forward apace. Civil rights acts, appropriations of federal funds to aid former slaves, and extended military occupation of several former Confederate states all worked for a time—until the end of Reconstruction and the Republicans' virtual abandonment of the African Americans' cause after 1877—to advance the reintegration of the South into the national process of industrially driven development.

In later decades, Congress moved toward a further centralization of authority at the expense of the states by imposing national controls over railroad operating practices. In the Interstate Commerce Act of 1887, not only was national power asserted, but also Congress devolved important discretionary authority upon an appointive commission; this marked the modern beginnings of the federal administrative agency as a "fourth branch" of the government. Centralization went still further in 1890, as reform pressures generated by factions within both the Republican party and the reemergent Democratic organization led to enactment of the Sherman Antitrust Act—the first federal legislation that amounted to a national corporate regulatory policy.

Withal, power was shifting decisively to the federal government, and the transformation of basic policy had proven to be enduring; but still, Congress was not seeking to intervene in the economy in ways that constituted anything like systematic, comprehensive control or planning. A key example of the limitations on the reach of congressional power was the history of post–Civil War land policy. Despite its making the Homestead Act the land system's keystone, Congress continued to dispose of land by approving grants to railroads and increasingly large grants to individual western states, with all such lands placed on sale on terms often highly disadvantageous to actual settlers. Even special legislation in the 1870s designed to encourage settlement and the use of timbered or desert lands proved to be a boon to speculators and fraudulent operators, as Congress never established a bureaucratic administrative system with sufficient resources to withstand the pressures of aggressive private exploitation. Similarly, during the gold and other mineral booms in the West, Congress simply validated the local and state mining codes, rather than adopting uniform national rules, and it never sought to recapture through royalties any significant portion of the rich yields of precious metals and other minerals.

The national government thus remained administratively underdeveloped; neither Congress nor the bureaucracy was an equal match for the well-focused pressures that could be generated by private interests eager to feed at the public trough. "The halls of Congress and the executive departments became annexes to the market place," as Wallace Farnham has written. Lobbyists easily prevailed in the halls of Congress when largess was to be had or a regulatory program was to be formulated; consequently "ineffective government was the rule rather than the exception for much of the nineteenth century" (Farnham, pp. 666, 669). Willard Hurst, Farnham, and other historians have argued persuasively, too, that the electorate got what it deserved: it wanted government to subsidize development and was heedless, at least until the conservation movement took hold in the 1890s, of long-term social costs and the loss of irreplaceable natural resources for future generations.

## The Persistence of State Authority

Despite the shift of authority to the center, the states retained important areas of autonomy in setting their economic agendas. American federalism was a mosaic of sorts, with each state representing a piece of the whole and each piece colored or patterned individually. Every legislature had its own set of policy preferences—a mixture of promotional and regulatory laws, with increasing evidence of concern by the late nineteenth century for social legislation that carried the potential for significant redistribution of society's benefits.

In the South, from the end of Reconstruction until the beginning of the Progressive Era, the autonomy of the legislatures generally meant above all a recommitment to white supremacy. The region remained behind the rest of the nation in public education, even for whites; social-welfare legislation was largely absent; and as a strategy for development, welcomed and encouraged by the large-scale corporate interests as well as the entrenched old-line plantation elite, the South built up its industry on the basis of low-wage scales, absence of protective legislation even for child workers, and generous tax exemptions to investors from outside. The paradox of southern industrialization perpetuating, not ameliorating, poverty and underdevelopment—as a price of perpetuating segregation and discrimination—is often interpreted by southern historians as evidence of the perfidious "colonialism" of northern financiers and industries. It might more accurately be seen, instead, as evidence of the shortsighted way in which southern legislators consciously eschewed creation of a more open society designed to advance the welfare of poor whites and blacks alike.

In states outside the South, a variety of patterns prevailed. Some of the pre–Civil War trends and emphases in legislation continued to be seen, most notably the policy in many states of handsome public subsidies for railroad construction; indeed, the subsidy policy was extended to various manufacturing enterprises in some states. The states also promoted their agricultural interests, not only through support of their land-grant colleges but also through research and extension programs; North Dakota even experimented with state ownership and operation of flour mills and terminal elevators.

One of the most important issues before the legislatures in this period was the question of "home rule" for the emerging industrial cities, whose municipal governments had to confront problems that were unique within most states. Devolution of special authority on the city governments—for example, for operation of river or harbor wharves or for construction of water-supply systems—helped to provide vital infrastructure for their commercial and industrial development. Similarly important was the power, often vested in urban government, to issue and control franchises for public transportation, electrical or gas production and supply, and sanitation facilities. Often the legislatures stalemated on these issues, so that urban interests sought expansion of their home-rule powers through a constitutional-revision process instead.

Meanwhile, some important elements of decentralized power of the states survived in substantial ways from the earlier era. This was true, for instance, in regard to their nearly entire control of family law, commercial law, criminal law, and law enforcement generally. The states also enjoyed wide-ranging practical discretion in taxation, as the national government revenues constituted only about 2 percent of national income. The state courts, too, continued to establish through common law the basic rules of commercial transactions, contract, and torts.

## Regulation and Progressivism

In both Congress and the state legislatures, the traditional emphasis in economic policy on promotion and subsidy began to give way by 1890 to a new preoccupation with regulatory legislation. Even before adoption of the Interstate Commerce Act and the Sherman Antitrust Act, many states had taken a strong lead in regard to regulation of both railroad practices and the anticompetitive practices referred to as the "trust" or "monopoly" problem. Moreover, the growing importance of the regulatory component of legislation persisted, despite the constitutional obstacles presented by a conservative, property-minded Supreme Court and despite the continued adherence to the laissez-faire ideas of many business leaders, lawyers, and academics of the day.

Regulatory legislation won support in many states, in part because farmer, merchant, and other producer groups sought protection against predatory railroad rates or corporate anticompetitive conspiracies. As David Thelen and other historians have shown, however, the pressure for regulation also came from organized labor and, more generally, a citizenry with a rising consciousness of consumer needs and interests that had finally found expression in urban and state politics. Reform impulses were rooted in popular outrage over the way in which some state legislatures had become almost reflexively subservient to powerful business interests, such as the mining industry in Colorado and Pennsylvania, the Southern Pacific Railroad in California, and the cattle-grazing interests in Wyoming.

The result of reform demands from various quarters was, first, to produce significant new regulatory legislation and constitutional reforms in the states. One major area of reform concerned railroad regulation, beginning with the so-called Granger Laws in the midwestern states in the 1870s; in these and other states, commissions were established that were empowered to oversee operating practices and mandate maximum rates on specified routes. After enactment of the Interstate Commerce Act, the state commissions continued to be active in regulation of intrastate operations of their railroad companies. In addition, there was a parallel extension of state regulatory power over the operations of grain elevators and other business facilities deemed in law to be "affected with a public interest" and thus different from ordinary business firms.

Labor legislation, including some far-reaching laws that regulated hours and conditions of work, and related accident and safety laws, constituted a second important area of action by the state legislatures. A related area of law taken up by many legislatures was employers' liability and workers' compensation reform. Both before and after federal authority was asserted under the Sherman Act in 1890, moreover, many states also legislated actively to curb restraint of trade by business corporations. Many statutes were enacted throughout the period 1865–1910 regarding public health, sanitation, tenement-house regulation in cities, and standards for food and drugs in intrastate sales. In the states with large urban centers, the home-rule movement also embraced demands, successful in most areas of the country, for professionalization of the public-health and other bureaucracies that developed in the administration of the new social and regulatory programs.

In sum, business enterprise generally—not only the railroad corporations, on which the strongest spotlight of publicity was cast—was caught in an increasingly wide net of regulatory legislation. The economy was by no means "managed," and it remained a quintessentially capitalist system, with the center of power in the private sector; but in its relationship with government, enterprise could no longer expect supportive and subsidizing legislation without accompanying assertions of the public interest through law.

How far this shift toward regulation had gone became evident in the Progressive Era after 1900, when not only many individual states but Congress as well, during the presidencies of Theodore Roosevelt, William Howard Taft, and Woodrow Wilson, responded in bold ways to the rising demands for reform. Legislative initiatives from the White House became increasingly common, unlike in earlier periods of American history, and both through political horse-trading and appeals to the public, all three presidents successfully pushed Congress in the direction of new reform measures. Some of the measures adopted represented further progress in directions already marked out; prime examples were the various antitrust initiatives of Roosevelt and Taft and a series of bills that strengthened the rate-making powers of the Interstate Commerce Commission. Other initiatives of this period, however, were of an entirely different order.

Among the most important results of the Progressive ascendancy were four measures that would lay the foundations for more sweeping change in political economy in the years ahead. One was the Pure Food and Drugs Act of 1906, which differed from most earlier regulatory legislation in that it required the establishment of a large-scale expert bureaucracy capable of carrying out inspections in the many thousands of processing plants throughout the United States. This measure was significant, in the view of some historians, because it was representative of many reform efforts that "nationalized" regulation formerly left to the states, which had often regulated at a disadvantage to the processors. Perhaps the act's greatest importance was that it established a powerful precedent for the safety, health, and environmental agencies whose elaborate bureacracies are prototypical of the modern-day regulatory role of government.

A second measure of enormous precedential importance was the Owen-Glass Act of 1913, which, in its creation of the Federal Reserve System, was a true departure from precedent in the sense that it provided for detailed, continuous management of fiscal and monetary matters by a permanent federal agency (albeit one that gave the private sector a central decision-making role). The new banking regulatory structure was elaborated in 1916 to provide federal intermediate farm credit facilities—a measure that looked toward the more comprehensive farm marketing and credit programs of a later day. The Federal Reserve also provided a model for latter-day securities markets regulation, national utilities regulation, and the structure of New Deal program administration under the National Industrial Recovery Act of 1933.

Conservation and resources policy was a third area of Progressive Era innovation that bespoke a major change in government's economic role. Land policy had traditionally been geared almost solely to privatization of the public domain. In the Progressive Era, policy shifted dramatically with Congress's approval of new programs of forest conservation, irrigation and reclamation, waterpower-site development, and increased supervision of mining and grazing operations on the public domain. Not only did these programs represent a shift of policy responsibility from the states (which continued to act in these areas) to Washington, but the agencies established to oversee them again represented a modernization of government's administrative capacity—and, consequently, an enhancement of government's ability to evaluate on a more competent basis the demands on it from the private sector.

Finally, among the landmark departures was the decision in Congress in 1916 to undertake (through the Federal Aid Road Act) a program of cash grants-in-aid to the states for the building of public roads. The main impetus had come from rural areas that suffered from unpaved highways and lack of access to urban marketing and buying centers. But in the longer run, this cash-grant program, providing for the distribution of funds from federal revenues to states on a formula basis, was significant as the precedent for a vast proliferation of such federal grant-in-aid programs (for public health, education, urban renewal, agricultural support, and other purposes) in later years. Indeed, the cornerstone of what came to be called "cooperative federalism" was, for the modern era at least, provided by this first major road-grant program.

Republican dominance of national politics in the 1920s slowed the pace of reform and to some extent reversed the Progressive initiatives. In Congress the decade witnessed abandonment of the Democratic Underwood Tariff of 1913, which had involved significant retreat from protectionism; high tariffs were now reinstituted. Another major shift in the 1920s occurred in immigration policy when restrictive laws, culminating in the Johnson-Reed Act of 1924, provided for numerical quotas by country and total immigration of 154,000 annually—a reversal of historic policies. Congress also moved on several fronts to carve out exceptions to the competitive business regime that the Sherman Act had mandated. With the Transportation Act of 1920, the railroads were effectively organized as a cartel and exempted from antitrust imperatives, and two years later, under

pressure from the Republican party's progressive midwestern and western farm bloc, Congress also exempted agricultural cooperatives. These exceptions augmented an earlier one in the Clayton Antitrust Act of 1914 to protect labor unions from antitrust prosecution (which proved to be little more than a paper guarantee). Another modification of competition policy was embodied in the Webb Export Act of 1918, which had permitted cartel-style cooperation in marketing goods overseas.

A leading feature of economic change in the 1920s was an accelerating merger and consolidation movement, abetted by the proliferation of holding companies, in virtually every industry. Neither Congress nor the executive exhibited much concern, and the Federal Trade Commission, the agency created in 1914 to oversee such developments, was packed with probusiness members little interested in enforcing antitrust policies. In sum, attitudes of conservatism and retrenchment were dominant throughout the decade, until the Great Crash. The great exception was in taxation policy, for adoption of the Sixteenth Amendment in 1913 opened the way to federal income taxation. A sharply progressive tax, ranging as high as 60 percent, was instituted during World War I. Although the progressive scale was cut back significantly after the war, corporate and personal income taxation had become a permanent feature of the policy landscape—what Elliot Brownlee has termed "one of the most significant victories in American history" for the cause of "social democracy," with its commitment to redistribution of wealth and advantage (p. 1278).

In the states as well, there were significant changes in taxation policy as revenues increased from sales, income, and user taxes—most important of all from gasoline taxes, the yield from which underwent dramatic increase as automobile use steeply rose and demands on state budgets for road construction and improvement soared. State legislatures also proved amenable to investment in human capital, and appropriations for education further fueled an increase in overall state expenditures. Per capita spending by the states, in constant 1926 dollars, rose 60 percent during 1922–1929 alone. State debt also soared, however, lending to the economy an element of instability that proved extremely dangerous when the great stock-market crash occurred in 1929 and states confronted a sharply declining revenue base.

Most of the impetus for progressive reform policies in the states seemed to dissolve after World War I. Legislatures in many states did consolidate insurance regulation, industrial-safety laws, home-rule reforms (including authorization for municipal government to institute land zoning, an important innovation of the era), support of agricultural cooperation, and expansion of resource research programs, irrigation, and reclamation. In some areas of the country there was also progress in upgrading technical expertise in state governments. The hallmark in most states, however, even some with strong progressive traditions, was continuing weakness of the legislatures in the face of interest-group influence, outright corruption, and hostility (or at least indifference) to proposals for advancing redistributive or regulatory programs.

## FEDERALISM AND THE MODERN POLITICAL ECONOMY

The response to the Great Depression that followed the 1929 crash involved a set of far-reaching changes in the distribution of power within American federalism, bringing a profound new centralization of authority in Washington. Paradoxically, Congress occupied a vast range of new policy areas that formerly had been left largely to the states, and yet this was accompanied by what Willard Hurst termed the growth of "an array of presidential, departmental, and independent-agency power of such unprecedented sweep as to put into question Congress's capacity to determine national public policy" (1977, p. 147).

Agriculture, for example, was made a managed sector, and manufacturing, including corporate prices and wage setting, was brought under governmental supervision. New legislation also placed banking, securities markets, and transportation under new types of strong federal control. Regional planning and economic development were embodied in the Tennessee Valley Authority, and for the first time in American history the federal government guaranteed certain rights of labor organization, collective bargaining, and free speech in the workplace. In all these instances,

however, responding to President Franklin Roosevelt's calls for emergency powers, the new policies were implemented through the creation of independent regulatory or administrative agencies. Thus, Congress in effect assented to a wholesale devolution of decision-making authority to commissions—many of them required by law to be balanced according to political affiliations of appointees, with commissioners made immune from arbitrary removal by the executive—which, it was hoped, would rise above the contending forces of politics to ascertain and enforce the "public interest" in their decisions.

Even the extensive programs of relief and welfare, prior to creation of the national Social Security system in 1935, devolved substantial discretionary authority on federal administrative officials. A burgeoning of federal grants-in-aid to state and local governments also occurred in the New Deal decade, with grants rising from $193 million in 1933 to almost $2.4 billion in 1940 and with emergency relief accounting for nearly 80 percent of the overall increase. These programs, too, were administered by large bureaucracies and fostered the development of civil service organizations in the states, but because the terms of eligibility for funding were set entirely by Congress, these programs of "cooperative federalism" also involved a centralization of real power of decision-making—again with federal administrative agencies left with broad discretionary power, albeit in the context of administration "shared" with the states.

In its budget decisions of the late 1930s, Congress accepted an equally important initiative, extending federal influence over the economy by accepting the Roosevelt administration's commitment to Keynesian anticyclical fiscal policy. The impact of federal fiscal operations was vastly enhanced by the massive rise in federal expenditures, both absolutely and as a proportion of national production that came with the New Deal. On the revenue side of the fiscal debates, however, the issue of federal taxes inspired some of the most bitter divisions in Congress during the 1930s, in response to Roosevelt's successful appeals for progressive personal and corporate income taxes and high levels of inheritance taxation.

The New Deal policies set in place the modern political economy, in which the national government leads in establishing basic economic policy, imposes a comprehensive regulatory structure on individual sectors of the economy (banking and finance, securities marketing, transportation, communications), and sets basic labor-relations policy, including minimum national wages. Other key elements of the new order were the disability, retirement, and dependents' support system mandated by the Social Security program after 1935 and a new fiscal role for the national government, including the so-called automatic stabilizers, ranging from bank-deposit and farm- and home-mortgage insurance to unemployment benefits.

The role of the state legislatures in the first decade of this transformation was relatively minor; the states spent more and did more in 1940 than in 1930, but as the historian James Patterson has demonstrated, this was so largely because of the flow of grants-in-aid from Washington. Not until the post–World War II era did state governmental functions expand anew, though even then in part because of the impetus of federal aid programs.

Both Congress and the state legislatures, however, were given much greater room to exercise legislative powers impinging on property rights and entrepreneurial operations. A series of Supreme Court decisions in the late 1930s established a virtually plenary congressional police power and knocked down the Tenth Amendment and Fourteenth Amendment interpretations the Court had invoked from the 1890s to 1935 to place strong restrictions on the scope of state regulatory actions. This change in legal interpretation established the constitutional foundation for further expansion of both state and federal regulatory regimes in the modern era.

In the years since World War II, the modern political economy has undergone still further change, affecting profoundly the balance of the congressional and state legislative roles in the federal system. First, Congress has authorized a significant expansion, accelerated beginning in the mid-1960s, in the scope and cost of federal social-welfare and medical-care programs. Meanwhile, Social Security taxation levels have been sharply increased, in contrast with a long series of federal corporate and individual income tax cuts; these changes have created a major shift in the income-redistributive effects of federal programs.

Second, whereas the regulatory regimes of the New Deal era remained focused mainly on market operations and prices in individual sectors of the economy (transport, agriculture, etc.) and regulation of terms of entry and competition, since 1965 there has been a dramatic broadening of federal regulation. The states had long regulated public health and safety, but the inadequacy of state regulation had become widely noticed and controversial, even before a series of environmental disasters. New public concern about the dangers of the pesticide DDT and other commonly used chemicals, and the disappearance of numerous fish and animal species all converged in the mid-1960s to produce irresistible political demands on Congress to act. There followed a decade of new legislation that brought the national government into a broad range of social regulatory areas formerly occupied almost exclusively by state authority: worker-and consumer-safety protection, air-pollution and water-quality regulation, control of pesticides and other chemicals, and protection of endangered species and habitats. Most remarkably, the new legislation placed important controls on government itself, and not only private industry, as federal agencies were required to file environmental-impact reports before proceeding with major projects that could harm sensitive habitats or affect patterns of human community life. Many state legislatures followed suit, introducing new legislation or making existing regulatory laws tougher. The role of the states was confined in some instances by Congress, however, under terms of the important doctrine of "preemption," by which, courts have held, regulations mandated in federal law can preclude the states from acting.

In the administrations of Ronald Reagan and George Bush, a conservative counterthrust, with powerful support from the White House, focused intensively on the new programs of social and industrial regulation. Despite conservative Republican claims that these programs discouraged new investment and harmed the competitive position of American business, the basic legal and administrative structures were largely preserved by a series of Congresses under Democratic control.

Yet another feature of the new order since the 1930s is the place of civil rights law in the regulation of private-sector interests. Attention focused initially on the discriminatory policies that disadvantaged African Americans, especially in the South. But with the passage of the Civil Rights Act of 1964 and subsequent legislation, Congress—following the lead established by the federal courts in school desegregation and political rights cases since the 1940s—broadened the reach of federal authority to act against discrimination against women, the disabled, the elderly, and all racial minorities. Affirmative-action programs for integration of work forces and of educational and other institutions carried the process a step further, again with a major impact on private economic institutions and virtually all their operations.

To some extent, the state legislatures have responded only reflexively to these overarching changes in the national context of economic policy. There have also been important reforms, however, both in the state governments' institutional structures and in their assertions of authority as they seek to maintain some meaningful control over their own economic policy agendas. One vitally important area of continuing state autonomy is taxation: after several decades of reform that expanded and shored up state finances, many states experienced popular voter reactions that led to sometimes devastating cutbacks in the taxation powers of their legislatures. The tax revolt occurred simultaneously with the astonishing acceleration of growth in the national debt in the Reagan-Bush years, caused by unprecedented peacetime military buildups combined with rising entitlement-program costs in the domestic sphere, leading to a diminution of federal grants-in-aid for general state programmatic purposes. The resulting squeeze on many state budgets in the early 1990s left open the question of what portion of the expanded state role in economic and social regulation, provision of educational facilities and student aid, welfare, and other areas of policy can be maintained in future years. Should the state role in these areas diminish significantly, it would have a telling effect on the balance of federal and state influence on the national economy. In economic hard times, moreover, there is a tendency in state policy to engage in a "race to the bottom" in regard to regulations; that is, every state, with an eye toward attracting business investment, is tempted to set regulatory standards lower and lower—and hence with less cost transferred to private firms for provision of social goods, such as clean water and air—in order not to be outdone by other states competing for the same investment and business in a national market.

Since the mid-1980s the state governments have also become increasingly sensitive to the possibilities of promoting in direct ways both new foreign investment in plant facilities and the export of their products to foreign markets. Hence, the kind of local development programs that many states have long supported, granting tax exemptions and other special benefits to firms making new investments from other parts of the United States, have been extended aggressively to Japanese and German automobile manufacturers, British and other European chemical and petroleum companies, and other foreign firms. Many states also have opened export promotion offices in foreign capitals. To promote research and development, with concomitant industrial investment possibilities, nearly all states have also adopted special subsidy programs and written exceptions to their competition laws to authorize cartel-style research and technology transfer; many have also authorized their state university campuses to form close commercial ties with private industry for research purposes.

In these and other respects, the state legislatures continue to be important actors in establishing the basic conditions of investment, enterprise, and economic change in the United States. Their continuing importance has to be understood, however, in the context of a severe attenuation of their autonomy since the nineteenth century and especially since the emergence of the modern, post–New Deal political economy. In this new order, the key policy decisions are made in Washington. Although the congressional arena of policy-making continues, of course, to be at the vital center of the system, there has also been a significant attenuation of power in the halls of Congress as a powerful executive—the "imperial presidency"—and an enormous congressionally mandated structure of independent regulatory and administrative agencies press their own claims to autonomous decision-making against inherited constitutional and political boundaries.

## BIBLIOGRAPHY

### General Studies

The classic work by JAMES WILLARD HURST, *Law and the Conditions of Freedom in the Nineteenth-Century United States* (Madison, Wis., 1956), provides critical analysis of legislative performance and of the content of public policies. Hurst carried his analysis of legal development forward into the modern period in *Law and Social Order in the United States* (Ithaca, N.Y., 1977); and in *The Growth of American Law: The Law Makers* (Boston, 1950), he dealt on a broad canvas with legal and governmental institutions, including legislatures. See also WALLACE D. FARNHAM, "'The Weakened Spring of Government': A Study in Nineteenth-Century American History," *American Historical Review* 68 (1963); and GENE M. GRESSLEY, *West by East: The American West in the Gilded Age* (Provo, Utah, 1972), a brilliant essay on regionalism and national policy.

In two important works, *Affairs of State: Public Life in Late Nineteenth-Century America* (Cambridge, Mass., 1977) and *Regulating a New Economy: Public Policy and Economic Change in America, 1900–1933* (Cambridge, Mass., 1990), MORTON KELLER offered an interpretation of policy process that stresses the impact of pluralism and fragmented governmental structure. Keller's work also constitutes an insightful commentary on American exceptionalism as evidenced in such policies as antitrust and labor relations law. DONALD PISANI, "Promotion and Regulation: Constitutionalism and the Economy," *Journal of American History* 74 (December, 1987), is a thorough analysis of scholarly writings on economic policy history. Two articles by HARRY N. SCHEIBER, "State Law and Industrial Policy in American Development," *California Law Review* 75 (January 1987), and "Public Economic Policy and the American Legal System: Historical Perspectives," *Wisconsin Law Review* 6 (1980): provide reappraisals of historic economic-policy process, content, and impacts.

The emphasis in the present essay is on the output of legislatures as they sought to influence American economic development or, alternatively, as they stayed their hand in that process. Political inputs and context are also important, however, and are treated more fully in LAWRENCE M. FRIEDMAN, *A History of American Law,* 2d ed. (New York, 1985), a broad-ranging interpretive history of law and society. SIDNEY FINE, *Laissez-Faire and the General-Welfare State: A Study of Conflict in American Thought, 1865–1901* (Ann Arbor, Mich., 1956), is unique for its breadth of scope in dealing with late-nineteenth-century intellectual, political, and legal developments. Also valuable are various articles in JACK P. GREENE, ed., *Encyclopedia of American Political History,* 3 vols. (New York, 1984), most notably RICHARD M. ABRAMS, "Business and Government"; W. ELLIOT BROWNLEE, "Taxation"; and NAOMI R. LAMOREAUX, "Regulatory Agencies." A unique analysis in depth of the relationship of politics to economic legislation and institutional behavior of a state legislature is L. RAY GUNN, *The Decline of Authority: Public Economic Policy and Political Development in New York, 1800–1860* (Ithaca, N.Y., 1988).

On economic policy and the legislative function in the colonial era, a long-standard work by RICHARD B. MORRIS, *Government and Labor in Early America* (New York, 1946), remains exceptional for its scope of coverage and detail, with respect to both policy and the law. RICHARD B. SHERIDAN, "The Domestic Economy," and other essays in JACK P. GREENE and J. R. POLE, eds., *Colonial British America: Essays in the New History of the Early Modern Era* (Baltimore, 1984) place legislative intervention in its broad social, political, and economic contexts.

HARRY N. SCHEIBER, "Federalism and the American Economic Order, 1789–1910," *Law and Society Review* 10 (Fall 1975), is a monograph that examines federal-state relations and economic policy issues in the context of constitutional and economic change. Studies of Congress's interventionism and legislative behavior in the nineteenth century include E. A. J. JOHNSON, *The Foundation of American Economic Freedom: Government and Enterprise in the Age of Washington* (Minneapolis, 1973); CARTER GOODRICH, *Government Promotion of American Canals and Railroads, 1800–1890* (New York, 1960), a work that also treats the individual states; and CURTIS P. NETTELS, *The Emergence of a National Economy, 1775–1815*

(New York, 1962). RICHARD FRANKLIN BENSEL, *Yankee Leviathan: The Origins of Central State Authority in America, 1859–1877* (New York, 1990), combines penetrating analysis of political coalitions in national politics with discussion of substantive policy outcomes.

### The Regulatory Function

Corporate chartering and public policy and, in later years, the relationship of antitrust to larger economic policy questions are dealt with in JAMES WILLARD HURST, *The Legitimacy of the Business Corporation in the Law of the United States, 1780–1970* (Charlottesville, Va., 1970); CHARLES McCURDY, "Justice Field and the Jurisprudence of Government-Business Relations," *Journal of American History* 61 (December 1975), and "The *Knight* Sugar Decision of 1895 and the Modernization of American Corporation Law," *Business History Review* 53 (Autumn 1979); JAMES MAY, "Antitrust in the Formative Era: Political and Economic Theory in Constitutional and Antitrust Analysis," *Ohio State Law Journal* 50:2 (1989); and RONALD SEAVOY, *The Origins of the American Business Corporation, 1784–1855* (Westport, Conn., 1982).

MARTIN J. SKLAR, *The Corporate Reconstruction of American Capitalism, 1890–1916: The Market, the Law, and Politics* (New York, 1988); and GABRIEL KOLKO, *The Triumph of Conservatism: A Re-interpretation of American History, 1900–1916* (Glencoe, Ill., 1963), contend that industrial regulation and antitrust policies were shaped under strong influence of the dominant business corporations, often in coalitions with skilled-labor union leaders and political Progressives.

The history of regulatory policies, the beginnings of deregulation, and the theme of "capture" of regulatory agencies is ably considered by THOMAS McCRAW "Regulation in America: A Review Article," *Business History Review* 49 (1975). Essays in JAMES Q. WILSON, *The Politics of Regulation* (New York, 1980), deal in detail with specific regulatory initiatives and agencies, also offering a useful typology of regulation in modern America.

### Federalism and State Policy

Several studies of individual states illustrate well the ideology and dynamics of interventionism and antigovernmentalism in the antebellum era. LOUIS HARTZ, *Economic Policy and Democratic Thought: Pennsylvania, 1776–1860* (Cambridge, Mass., 1948); OSCAR HANDLIN and MARY F. HANDLIN, *Commonwealth: A Study of the Role of Government in the American Economy: Massachusetts, 1774–1861*, rev. ed. (Cambridge, Mass., 1969); and MILTON HEATH, *Constructive Liberalism: The Role of the State in the Economic Development of Georgia to 1860* (Cambridge, Mass., 1954), deal with three states that pursued strikingly different policies. JAMES WILLARD HURST, *Law and Economic Growth: The Legal History of the Lumber Industry in Wisconsin, 1836–1915* (Cambridge, Mass., 1964), is a massive study, unusual because it focuses on a single industry as law and policy in all their aspects affected its development; Hurst carries the Wisconsin history forward to the Progressive Era. HARRY N. SCHEIBER, *Ohio Canal Era: A Case Study of Government and the Economy, 1820–1861*, rev. ed. (Athens, Ohio, 1987), examines the history of internal-improvements promotion, legislation, finance, administration, and economic impact in a western "public enterprise" state.

Post–Civil War, state-centered historical studies are few in number, but California has been well served. A comprehensive overview is in GERALD D. NASH, *State Government and Economic Development: A History of Administrative Policies in California, 1849–1933* (Berkeley and Los Angeles, 1964). A more penetrating study that, in the style of Hurst's account of Wisconsin lumbering and the law, uses a single industry as a lens through which to view major analytical issues is ARTHUR McEVOY, *The Fisherman's Problem: Ecology and Law in the California Fisheries, 1850–1980* (New York, 1986). Continuities from 1850 through the Progressive Era and later are illuminated in a model policy study by DONALD PISANI, *From the Family Farm to Agribusiness: The Irrigation Crusade in California and the West, 1850–1931* (Berkeley and Los Angeles, 1984).

BALLARD CAMPBELL, *Representative Democracy: Public Policy and Midwestern Legislatures in the Late Ninteenth Century* (Cambridge, Mass., 1980), deals briefly but insightfully with economic policy-making. An important study of pluralism, constitutional reform, and legislative innovation in the 1860s and 1870s is GEORGE H. MILLER, *Railroads and the Granger Laws* (Madison, Wis., 1971).

# LEGISLATURES AND AMERICAN ECONOMIC DEVELOPMENT

ELLIS HAWLEY, *The New Deal and the Problem of Monopoly* (Princeton, N.J., 1966), deals with competition policy and politics. A detailed analysis of 1930s politics and federal-state relations is JAMES T. PATTERSON, *The New Deal and the States: Federalsim in Transition* (Princeton, N.J., 1969). For the modern era of federalism and public policy, the best introduction is DAVID WALKER, *Toward a Functioning Federalism* (Cambridge, Mass., 1981).

## Sectorial Studies

The definitive comprehensive account of land policy, speculation, and administration is in PAUL W. GATES, *History of Public Land Law Development* (Washington, D.C., 1968). On the farm sector, see HARRY N. SCHEIBER, "Law and American Agricultural Development," *Agricultural History* 52 (October 1978). Despite its importance, tariff history lacks a comparable history of equal authoritativeness and breadth, but specialized studies of special value on legislative and political process include ROBERT A. PASTOR, *Congress and the Politics of U.S. Foreign Economic Policy, 1929–1976* (Berkeley, 1980); and J. J. PINCUS, *Pressure Groups and Politics in Antebellum Tariffs* (New York, 1977).

Studies of banking that stress public policy include BRAY HAMMOND, *Banks and Politics in America from the Revolution to the Civil War* (Princeton, N.J., 1957); and EUGENE N. WHITE, *The Regulation and Reform of the American Banking System, 1900–1929* (Princeton, N.J., 1983). American labor policy in relation to unionization and labor relations more generally are reappraised in IRVING BERNSTEIN, *The Lean Years: A History of the American Worker, 1920–1933* (Boston, 1960); BERNSTEIN, *Turbulent Years: A History of the American Worker, 1933–1941* (Boston, 1970); WILLIAM E. FORBATH, *Law and the Shaping of the American Labor Movement* (Cambridge, Mass., 1991), a work that emphasizes ideology in relation to the law; and CHRISTOPHER L. TOMLINS, *The State and the Unions: Labor Relations, Law, and the Organized Labor Movement in America, 1880–1960* (Cambridge, England, 1985), a deeply researched and broad new synthesis.

Studies in recent policy history that give attention to legislatures in the context of political change include STEPHEN BAILEY, *Congress Makes a Law: The Story Behind the Employment Act of 1946* (New York, 1950); the essays in JOHN BRAEMAN et al., *The New Deal*, 2 vols. (Columbus, Ohio, 1975); LOUIS GALAMBOS and JOSEPH PRATT, *The Rise of the Corporate Commonwealth: U.S. Business and Public Policy in the 20th Century* (New York, 1988); OTIS GRAHAM, JR., *Toward a Planned Society: From Roosevelt to Nixon* (New York, 1976); HURST, *Law and Social Order*, mentioned earlier; essays in THOMAS MCGRAW, ed., *Regulation in Perspective: Historical Essays* (Cambridge, Mass., 1981); and DAVID VOGEL, *Fluctuating Fortunes: The Political Power of Business in America* (New York, 1989).

## Law and the Policy Process

HARRY N. SCHEIBER, "Technology and American Legal Development, 1790 to the Present," in STUART W. BRUCHEY and JOEL COLTON, eds., *Technology, the Economy, and Society* (New York, 1988), deals with issues of law and technical innovation and diffusion. PETER K. EISINGER, *The Rise of the Entrepreneurial State: State and Local Economic Development Policy in the United States* (Madison, Wis., 1988), is an exhaustive account of modern-day subnational programs to attract investment and foster localized development. A classic study that identifies states that lead in policy initiatives and others that tend to follow is by JACK WALKER, "The Diffusion of Innovations Among the American States," *American Political Science Review* 63 (1969); unfortunately, no comparable study exists for the nineteenth century.

Finally, the reader will find invaluable, for establishing the full economic context of major policy issues, many of the essays in GLENN PORTER, ed., *Encyclopedia of American Economic History*, 3 vols. (New York, 1980).

SEE ALSO Congress, Sectionalism, and Public-Policy Formation Since 1870; Legislatures and the Environment; AND Legislatures and the Judiciary.

# LEGISLATURES AND SLAVERY

## *Phyllis F. Field*

American lawmakers often grapple with difficult and controversial issues, but the struggle to end slavery led not only to political confrontation but the dismemberment of the country and the bloodiest war in American history. Legislatures were at the heart of the slavery controversy. Required first to define and ultimately to abolish it, they received the brunt of pressure from those determined to protect or destroy the institution. Reactions to lawmakers' actions on slavery issues often shaped public responses to legislative power generally.

Slavery was never a simple issue. The political problems it caused varied according to the time and place. Only in the last decades before the Civil War did it emerge as a distinct moral issue in politics and then only to a dedicated minority in the North. For years the federal system shielded slavery from national political scrutiny while the national political parties focused attention on other issues. The path that in December 1865 led to the final abolition of slavery through the Thirteenth Amendment to the Constitution proved to be long and tortuous.

### THE LAW OF SLAVERY

English colonists needed neither laws nor legislatures to establish chattel slavery in Britain's North American colonies. Historians speculate that the first black people brought to Virginia in 1619 may have been treated as indentured servants, unfree laborers who worked for a master for several years to pay the costs incurred in bringing them to America. Yet within two decades, county courts in Virginia permitted sales of Africans for lifetime service and included their offspring in the sale. Another two decades elapsed before Virginia passed laws acknowledging slavery's existence.

Slavery emerged without legal sanction on the British-American mainland because by the seventeenth century African slavery was already a familiar institution throughout the Western Hemisphere. The developing sugar colonies of the Caribbean and Brazil showed that profits could be made from exploiting African labor. Also, as Winthrop D. Jordan has argued, the English were culturally disposed to fear and want to control dark-skinned peoples more than other laborers. These anxieties eventually led to the need to regularize the institution of slavery through legislation.

The first slavery laws responded to specific constituent concerns voiced in petitions to lawmakers. The eventual number of slavery laws and the frequency with which assemblies codified them varied with the importance of slavery to the community. For most of the seventeenth century, slaves were a relatively unimportant source of labor in all the mainland colonies. Legislation was haphazard and unsystematic. As long as sugar colonies in the Caribbean and Brazil continued to bring in the greatest profits, few slave ships visited North American ports. Slavery developed a solid foothold only in the late seventeenth century when the North American colonies became more settled and developed specific labor needs that slaves could fill. The supply of indentured white labor simultaneously fell off, and British ships took over the slave trade to North America. In the southern and middle colonies, slaveowners valued slaves as workers on large farms and plantations growing grain, tobacco, rice, or indigo. In northern urban areas slaves became a cheap and dependable source of household labor. While every colony recognized slavery, only in the South did slaves become a primary part of the labor force; slave codes there became the most elaborate as a result.

Imposing slavery on a previously free society created the same legal problems everywhere. Since slavery became important later in North America than elsewhere, early lawmakers eased the transition by selectively borrowing codes already developed in Britain's Caribbean colonies: South Carolina in 1712 virtually duplicated the code of Barbados, for example. The practice of copying slave codes continued throughout the history of slavery in North America and accounts for the overall similarity that developed among slave codes over time.

Regardless of when or where they were adopted, slave codes dealt with common issues. They had to define departures from traditional English legal procedures. The child of a slave, for instance, followed the condition of his or her mother, not father. The children of white men by slave women could thus be enslaved. Neither criminal penalties nor legal protection were the same for slaves as for freemen. For minor offenses (some of which, such as preaching, would not even have been crimes for freemen) slaves faced summary punishment without trial. In other cases, property considerations weighed heavily in assigning penalties. To punish a slave's serious offense by death was to deprive the owner of property. Some jurisdictions compensated owners for their loss or allowed the slave to be sold in another colony. White property-holding elites, often slaveholders themselves, dominated colonial assemblies and the laws clearly reflected their respect for private property and indifference to the slaves' welfare.

Only in New England, where from the outset relatively few individuals owned slaves, did some laws jeopardize property interests. The overriding desire to establish a community based on biblical principles led to treating slaves according to the Mosaic laws of bondage. These principles regarded slaves as victims of misfortune who merited the protection of the laws. Slaves could own property, sue for their freedom, testify against whites in court, and receive jury trials. Masters received no compensation if a slave was executed, and some owners chose to defend slaves accused of crime. The lack of sympathetic laws weakened slavery in New England although the institution itself remained unchallenged until the American Revolution in 1775.

Lawmakers were more likely to argue over slaves as property than as human beings. In most situations (sale, rental, security for loans) slave-owners considered slaves as personal (chattel) property. At other times, when a plantation might be ruined by the seizure of its slaves to pay a debt, for example, it would benefit slaveowners if the laws treated slaves as part of the estate. Colonies, and later states, wavered between the different designations, though generally preferring to consider slaves chattels. Virginia considered slaves real property from 1705 to 1792 but chattels before and after that period. Yet even in chattel states, laws often considered slaves real property for some specified purposes. One of the reasons for periodic attempts to codify slave laws was to identify laws that were contradictory in their assumptions about slavery and bring all laws into harmony. Even then, lawmakers, attempting to complete their task quickly during short legislative sessions, frequently created compendiums of old laws rather than true codes based on common legal principles.

By their resistance to slavery, slaves influenced the content of slave codes. Whenever the white population felt insecure—after a slave insurrection in New York in 1741 or South Carolina in 1739, during wartime, or when slavery came under attack—lawmakers faced demands to control independent behavior by slaves. Common prohibitions emerged in virtually all slave systems. Slaves could not assemble on their own, carry weapons, own means of communication like horns or drums, or travel anywhere without written permission. Slaves who disobeyed commands from whites, set fires, stole goods, ran away, or otherwise resisted their enslavement faced severe punishment.

Slave codes often sought to control free blacks as well as slaves on the grounds of their probable sympathy with slaves. Even whites faced restrictions. They could not sell alcohol to slaves, trade, or gamble with them, for example. In communities with many slaves, white males had to patrol the roads to enforce slave laws. The first such law was passed in South Carolina in 1690, the last in Kansas in 1855. Laws ordered slave-owners not to teach their slaves to read or allow them to work without white supervision. Still, the passage of laws rarely brought a lasting sense of security. As late as the Civil War the Texas legislature was threatening whites who left slaves unsupervised with harsher penalties.

One reason insecurity remained was the symbolic rather than practical nature of most legislative decrees. Problems of enforcement came from many sources. Slaves constantly sought personal autonomy, and governments had to rely on the cooperation of the white population to enforce laws. Despite the need for security whites resented limitations on their own freedom, especially compulsory service on slave patrols. Except in times of panic, lax enforcement was normal. Often owners preferred to judge for themselves whether a security problem existed. When Virginia's General Assembly in 1804 prohibited religious meetings of slaves at night, Pietist slave-owners, who often sponsored such meetings, were outraged. The law was subsequently modified to permit meetings if conducted by white ministers. More commonly, slave-owners simply ignored laws with which they disagreed. Although whites faced fines for violating slave laws, courts rarely considered such cases. The influence that went with slaveholding inhibited prosecution.

The wishes of legislative bodies could be countered in still other ways. Since laws were often inexpertly drawn, courts could draw on different legal precedents to circumvent existing legislation. In southern states before the Civil War, legislative attempts to limit slave manumissions, or formal release from slavery, by testators in wills, for example, were sometimes overturned. The South Carolina legislature had to revise its slave code in 1841 because judges had found loopholes to permit voluntary manumissions. Even with their revisions, the courts still ruled on these cases. In criminal cases those administering the laws sometimes relied on abstract notions of justice rather than strictly following the letter of the law. In 1834 the North Carolina Supreme Court refused to punish a slave who had killed a brutal overseer. Yet justice for slaves was rarely color-blind.

Voting on slave laws suggests that lawmakers understood the lack of societal consensus on the specifics of slave control. While a general lack of roll calls, especially in the early years, hinders analysis, we do know that votes on slave laws were sometimes close, and some restrictive measures failed.

As American society changed, some changes in slave codes did occur. Early criminal laws assumed that some people were naturally evil and only draconian punishments could deter them. The eighteenth-century Enlightenment brought more charitable assumptions about humankind. Maiming, branding, castration, and dismemberment as specified punishments declined although not so rapidly for slaves as for freemen. Slaves' humanity was more readily admitted. Laws and sometimes constitutions stated that they had rights to adequate food, clothing, and shelter. They could not be abandoned in old age or ill health (thus to become a burden on the public) or made to work excessive hours or on Sunday. After the Revolution some southern states began to treat the malicious murder of slaves the same as other murders; eventually all southern states did so. While laws changed to conform to new concepts of humanity, few prosecutions of whites actually occurred, and there is little evidence that slaves as a whole received substantially different treatment because of laws. They served instead to assure slave-owners that slavery did not compromise their values. In districts committed to slavery no laws emerged that seriously interfered with property interests in slaves. Despite their humanity, slaves could not legally marry, own property, make contracts, use the courts, or prevent the sale of family members.

Although slave codes consistently placed white property rights over black human rights, the future of slavery was by no means assured. Between 1777 and 1804 every northern state took steps to end slavery, and, as William W. Freehling has shown, even the commitment of the border South to slavery remained uncertain until the Civil War. The enslavement of labor represented a choice not only for the purchasers of slaves but for the communities that upheld it. The eagerness to support slave labor varied. Over time, new purchases and population shifts tended to concentrate slaves in those areas most suited to growing high-demand agricultural staples. Such crops could change. In the late-eighteenth century, the greater availability of white labor and the decline of tobacco as a profitable staple left only the Deep South with a strong economic commitment to slavery. Even with the rise of the Cotton Kingdom after the invention of the cotton gin in 1793, some areas of the South with short growing seasons or with less-fertile or worn-out soils saw a decline in the importance of slave labor.

## EARLY ANTISLAVERY EFFORTS IN THE STATES

While important cultural values as well as economics were considerations in making decisions about slavery, a greater diversity of opinion was possible in areas not directly dependent on slavery. The American Revolution and a crisis among the country's Quakers (Society of Friends) coincided with the economic weakening of slavery to produce the first ideological reconsideration of slavery. In 1775, Pennsylvania Quakers formed the world's first antislavery society. This act culminated a religious revival stressing self-renunciation and the need to be less worldly. Slaveholding Friends, to remain in good standing, were soon required to free their slaves. They emerged as an important interest group favoring laws making manumission easier and compensating slave-owners for emancipation. Over time more broadly based emancipation societies emerged that assisted in freedom suits, protested the slave trade, and watched over the operation of early emancipation statutes.

The American Revolution's emphasis on freedom, personal independence, and the rights of man drew attention to the inconsistency of slavery in a society that valued freedom. As Edmund S. Morgan has shown, some revolutionaries rationalized the presence of slaves, even claiming that slavery fostered greater equality among whites. Yet others such as Thomas Jefferson admitted slavery's evils, and manumissions increased, facilitated by laws such as Virginia's Manumission Act of 1782. Manumissions and other wartime changes produced enough free blacks to form independent communities that further invigorated the struggle against slavery.

Structural political changes also accompanied the Revolution. Many states created new constitutions. New patterns of representation gave relatively more influence to western areas that sometimes were less committed to slave labor. As poorer people, some of whom felt that slave labor lowered wages, gained the right to vote and became less deferential to the wishes of elites, another potential antislavery constituency emerged. Because of the belief that power should come from the people, constituents increasingly expected representatives to follow their will. Political rhetoric, aimed at new constituencies, acknowledged the contributions that free white laborers made to society that slaves could not: military service, payment of taxes, settlement of the frontier. Free labor began to be described as a more rational alternative to slave labor. Some states like Pennsylvania made their legislatures the most powerful branch of government. The ability to protect vested interests through other branches of government declined.

Greater diversity of opinion now existed on the subject of slavery. The institution of slavery, not just the mechanics of its operation, was in dispute. A new era had begun for lawmakers dealing with slavery. Since slavery was more likely to be questioned in the North than in the South, conflict could easily become sectional, destroying the effort to create a new nation. Ultimately federalism allowed states to follow their own courses on slavery while nationally lawmakers tried to stand aloof.

Yet even in states with few slaves, ending slavery proved difficult. Constitutional changes still left most legislatures controlled by white propertied elites, for whom slavery was first a question of property, not of humanity. In general, individual slave-owners continued to regard slavery as wise, moral, and personally profitable, and pressured legislators to protect it.

Politicians handled the diversity of views in a variety of ways. In several New England states, emancipation took place circumspectly. Mountainous Vermont, with only a few slaves, abolished slavery in its 1777 constitution without public discussion. The Massachusetts legislature twice postponed action; then in 1780 the state adopted a new constitution containing a declaration of rights affirming personal freedom and equality. A slave, Quok Walker, claimed freedom under the constitution and won in court. Fearing that similar decisions might free their own slaves, Massachusetts slave-owners reluctantly took steps either to free their slaves or to sell them in other states.

New Hampshire slave-owners, after a similar constitution was adopted in 1783, may have feared a similar fate. Without any known law or court decision, the number of slaves declined from several hundred to none. Only in 1857 did the state officially outlaw slavery.

In 1780, Pennsylvania, home of the first abolition society, became the first government in the world to end slavery by legislative act. The Act for the Gradual Abolition of Slavery, as it was called, proposed to eradicate slavery gradually, over a period of several decades. The state's radically democratic constitution weakened propertied opposition. Yet the emancipation statute was radical only in conception. Taking the position that enslavement made a person unfit for citizenship in a republic, legislators freed only the children of slaves born after 1 November 1780; true freedom would begin only after an apprenticeship that lasted until the age of twenty-eight. Apprenticeship served both to delay actual emancipation and to compensate masters for their property losses through the labor of the slaves rather than public expenditures. Even this compromise encountered substantial resistance. The measure passed 34–21 but divided the Constitutionalist Party in the unicameral, all-powerful legislature. Some slaveholders refused to register their slaves as the act required despite threats of immediate emancipation if they failed to do so. The turnover in the legislature in the following election was an unusually high 60 percent. The next, more conservative legislature tried to smooth matters over by extending the time for slave registration. Meanwhile, some slaveowners began to transfer their slaves out of state.

The remaining northern states followed Pennsylvania's example of gradual abolition. Usually acts encouraging manumission or weakening legal protection for slave property preceded and prepared the way for full emancipation. Incentives included exemption (during the Revolution) from military service for masters if their former slaves enlisted (in Connecticut, Rhode Island, and New York) and partial or full exemption from the need to post bonds to guarantee support of newly freed slaves (in Rhode Island, New York, and New Jersey). New York and New Jersey weakened the role of the state in slave discipline by moving toward similar treatment of slave and free offenders. After passage of its first emancipation act in 1799, New York guaranteed its remaining slaves the right to marry, own property, testify, and have jury trials. Connecticut, thirteen years after its gradual emancipation act of 1784, repealed its entire colonial slave code. Manumission societies, meanwhile, protested slave auctions and urged newspapers not to accept advertising regarding slaves. Some judges openly expressed belief in the natural right to freedom. This weakening of public support for slavery made slaveowners anxious about the future value of their slave property and encouraged them to reexamine slaveholding itself.

All northern emancipation laws followed the common pattern of freeing slaves' newborn children who were then apprenticed until ages ranging from eighteen to twenty-eight. Legislatures, often at the urging of manumission societies, made some effort to prevent sale of slaves out of state but minimal penalties (except in Pennsylvania) and poor enforcement everywhere meant many slaves were denied actual freedom. Lawmakers apparently saw little need to extend themselves to protect voteless blacks.

States with more slaves were slower to enact emancipation. New York delayed until 1799. New Jersey with the highest percentage of slaves in the North did not move until 1804, but when it finally did, the institution had been so undermined that the vote was nearly unanimous. Northern legislatures usually considered emancipation several times before eventually passing it. In Connecticut gradual emancipation was slipped through by subterfuge in 1784: a provision for ending slavery was added to a general codification of the laws and passed without special notice. Neighboring Rhode Island, however, enacted gradual emancipation openly the same year.

States with substantial slaveholding eventually offered additional financial incentives to slaveowners. New York and New Jersey allowed masters to "abandon" their slaves to the overseers of the poor and then receive compensation from the state for reemploying them. New Jersey annually paid one-third of its budget to its slaveowners. In 1811 the state ended the practice noting that payments had far exceeded the value of the slaves. Once gradual emancipation was well established, legislatures generally acted to free the remaining slaves outright.

New York, the first to act, passed a statute in 1817 to free all remaining slaves in 1827. Only New Jersey, which converted its remaining slaves to apprentices in 1847, still had unfree residents in 1860. By 1830, 98 percent of the blacks in the North were free.

Voting on the issue of slavery was rarely along party lines. Indeed, party itself was a vague concept in this era of political turmoil and redefinition. Usually representatives of areas with many slaveholders confronted those with few slaveholding constituents. Some representatives, however, followed their own judgment. A number of prominent northern emancipationists—Benjamin Franklin, Alexander Hamilton, John Jay—gave respectability to the cause and encouraged independent action.

Rather than tout the advantages of slave labor in a society increasingly indifferent to it, opponents of emancipation stressed the importance of respecting private property, the danger posed by free blacks, and the possible weakening of southern state loyalty to the infant union. Since Quakers were visible supporters of emancipation, and particular ethnic groups like the New York Dutch included many slaveholders, cultural values and attitudes toward other cultures also influenced positions on slavery.

The significance of northern emancipation could be viewed in different ways. Northern legislatures made the transition to free labor while upholding the idea of the legitimacy of property in slaves and racial inferiority. Indeed, most free states, except for a few in New England, quickly established laws that left free blacks second-class citizens deprived of educational opportunities, equal access to the courts, and the right to vote. Lawmakers had deliberately avoided bankrupting slaveholders or undermining the economy. But despite the limitations for blacks and obvious concern for property interests, northern emancipation demonstrated that a slaveholding society could become nonslaveholding through political acts, regardless of the wishes of slave-owners. That gradual emancipation would end with New Jersey was by no means foreordained. In the aftermath of the Revolution several other states considered but rejected gradual emancipation. Many states liberalized manumission laws, historically the first step toward gradual emancipa-

tion. As late as 1847 the Delaware legislature came within one vote in its upper chamber of passing a gradual emancipation bill. As usual, representatives from areas with more slaveholding confronted those with less.

Southern legislatures reacted to northern emancipation. Since slaveholders were a minority everywhere, some believed they must act at once to forestall emancipation in their own states. Yet not all slaveholders saw the issue this clearly. Lawmakers had successfully attacked slavery only in areas with relatively few slaves and only with great difficulty. Many years would pass before most southerners would be convinced that slavery was in imminent danger.

Where concern was high, states took steps to strengthen protection for slaveholders. The South participated in the national trend in the early nineteenth century toward broader suffrage and the removal of property qualifications for officeholding. Yet two states, North Carolina and South Carolina, retained the latter and, as a consequence, had disproportional numbers of planters (those owning twenty slaves or more) in their legislatures. A few states also employed representational formulas for their legislatures that favored slaveholding areas. In most—the exceptions being mainly on the frontier—a majority of legislators owned slaves. Perceived favoritism of planters or plantation areas could backfire, however, as poorer areas blamed their poverty on slaveholders' manipulation of power.

Perhaps because the South developed a tradition of vigorous political conflict, it became important to some to establish that slavery as an institution was not part of the disagreement. After a flirtation with more liberal manumission laws during the revolutionary era, a reaction set in. Increasingly legislatures passed laws demanding that owners wishing to free their slaves pay high bonds and settle their former slaves out of state. Rhetoric stressed the dangers posed by free blacks. The revolt by slaves in Santo Domingo in 1794 and slave coachman Gabriel Prosser's attempted insurrection in Richmond, Virginia, in 1800 were constantly cited to create hysteria against emancipation. In 1841, South Carolina, followed by Louisiana, Georgia, Mississippi, and Alabama, went so far as to outlaw all private manumissions. In the upper South, constitutional conventions in Virginia, Maryland, Tennessee, and Arkansas in the 1850s decreed that legislatures could never act to emancipate slaves.

Slavery's defenders did not stop with laws and constitutions. Just as manumission societies had questioned the legitimacy of slavery in the North, proslavery supporters questioned the legitimacy of such societies in the South, making their activities in some cases criminal offenses. As a result, constituencies that historically had disliked slavery (Quakers, some Methodist and Baptist groups) fled the region.

## SLAVERY AND NATIONAL POLITICS TO 1830

Despite the effort to address slavery at the state level and pursue different approaches to the institution based on different political contexts, from the beginning slavery had implications for national politics as well. Defenders of slavery from the Deep South conditioned their support for the union on protection for the peculiar institution. Other representatives, valuing union above free labor, were less demanding and allowed basic concessions to slavery. Indeed, the discrediting of the pacifist Quakers during the revolutionary war had left antislavery political activity largely in the hands of rationalist politicians who lacked a moral commitment to the cause and were all too willing to balance rights to freedom against rights to property.

When Thomas Jefferson's draft of the Declaration of Independence listed support for the "execrable" and "piratical" slave trade among King George III's crimes, the Continental Congress, in deference to the strong opposition of the Deep South's representatives, removed the passage. The proslavery bloc was equally effective at the Constitutional Convention in 1787. Although the national compact never once used the word "slavery," slave states secured disproportional power in Congress by counting slaves as three-fifths of a person for representation in the House of Representatives, the so-called three-fifths clause. Congress was also empowered to return fugitive slaves and use military power to put down slave revolts. It could not halt the slave trade for twenty years. William Wiecek argues that the delegates to the Constitutional Convention had, in essence, accepted a "federal consensus" that left the future of slavery in the hands of the states.

This consensus had important implications for the way Congress treated slavery. Slavery became a minor issue: only 1 or 2 percent of congressional roll calls in the 1790s dealt with it. Other issues shaped party formation in Congress. While representatives from the Deep South usually responded immediately to any implied threat to slavery, other congressmen looked to a variety of cues including perceptions of party benefit in making decisions. The Deep South, thus, rarely faced united opposition.

The First Congress in 1790 reconfirmed the federal consensus. As had been true in earlier representative bodies, petitions and executive reports set the agenda for a noninstitutionalized Congress. Manumission societies in the North petitioned to outlaw the foreign slave trade (the American-run trade in slaves to foreign countries) and take what action Congress constitutionally could to end or ameliorate slavery. Suspecting an anti-Federalist plot to heighten sectional antagonisms, senators refused to even consider the petitions. Despite solid opposition from the Deep South states, however, the House voted 43–11 to create a special committee to consider Congress's power over slavery. The committee, which contained only one southern member, issued a report that claimed Congress could tax slave importation even if it could not abolish the slave trade until 1808. It could stop the foreign slave trade and regulate the treatment of slaves sold in the U.S. and abroad. While Congress could not regulate slavery itself (decided by one vote in the committee), it could recommend humane treatment to the states.

The response from South Carolina and Georgia was quick and angry. Their representatives defended slavery without apology and suggested that disunion would quickly follow interference. For other congressmen to pursue the matter was to risk delay of pending legislation on the assumption of state debts. No prominent congressman stepped forward to champion the report. Instead, James Madison (R.-Va.) led an amendment process which established that Congress had no authority over emancipation or treatment of slaves, could not tax slave imports, but could regulate the foreign slave trade. The amended report passed

29–25, with the Deep South unanimously opposed and the rest of the country divided. The outcome demonstrated that an adamant proslavery minority could modify laws it disliked.

Having decided that most issues regarding slavery were best left alone, congressmen rarely touched them unless they expected general agreement. Rudolph Bell describes voting patterns on slavery in the first six Congresses as essentially nondivisive. For example, the House in 1800 rejected a petition of free blacks seeking a way to end slavery by a vote of eighty-five to one. Antislavery in the early years of the Republic had a few dedicated congressional supporters such as James Sloan (R.-N.J.) and George Thacher (Fed.-Mass.), but they accomplished little. Congress did outlaw the foreign slave trade in 1794 (which affected few Americans) but most proposals on slavery were clearly limited or self-serving. Federalists, for example, proposed in 1794 to deny citizenship to alien slaveholders, a move intended to show that southern Republican efforts to deny citizenship to titled aristocrats was hypocritical.

Congress did take some important actions, but to strengthen slavery. In 1793 Congress formulated the first fugitive slave law, giving slaveholders, not accused slaves, the upper hand. Owners or their representatives needed only to provide proof to satisfy a magistrate or judge of their claims to remove an alleged slave to the South. Anyone interfering with the process could be sued. The House passed the bill 48–7 with two southerners, more alarmed about federal power than the protection of slavery, among the dissenters. (The Senate vote was unrecorded.) Ironically, the bill had originally been precipitated by a manumission society's complaint about the illegal capture and sale of a man supposedly freed under Pennsylvania's emancipation statute.

While Congress acted quickly and with apparent unity in terminating the slave trade in 1808, the positions on slavery revealed in the episode were complex. The trade had long been associated with issues other than the future of slavery itself. Throughout the colonial period assemblies had attempted to regulate, even ban it. The importation of slaves affected white security by increasing the number of blacks, drained money from cash-scarce economies, changed the value of existing slaves by affecting supply, and affected white social mobility by establishing the cost of owning slaves. To cease importing slaves was not to define slavery as undesirable. But by the same token the slave trade was economically important to some. At the outset of the Revolution, the Continental Congress banned the slave trade to exert pressure on the British government. Even with this patriotic motivation the slave-hungry Deep South states had been reluctant to comply.

After the Revolution, despite general agreement on continuing the ban, full cooperation occurred only between 1798 (when Georgia ended the trade) and 1803 (when South Carolina, declaring the impossibility of enforcement, reopened it). South Carolina's decision was controversial even within the state. The measure passed 53–46, supported by the labor-scarce western counties. Although several bills were introduced in Congress to punish South Carolina by taxing the trade, unity quickly evaporated as other southerners argued that the moment was inopportune to act. Meanwhile, speculators imported forty thousand new slaves. Indeed, the era of near total restriction between 1780 and 1810 saw more importations than at any other time in history.

Since American experience amply demonstrated the difficulties of restricting slave imports, the key decision lawmakers faced in 1807 was not whether to stop the trade but how to enforce a ban. Peter Early's (R.-Ga.) original bill would have sold at auction all slaves illegally imported and punished purchasers only if they were aware of the slaves' origin. Thus, an increase in the number of slaves would result and the national government would be forced to conduct slave auctions. While this proved unacceptable even to some southerners, southern representatives generally were opposed to the alternative of freeing the captives, even when this was coupled with resettlement in free states under an apprenticeship plan. While freeing the captives in the South would have provided the strongest incentive for enforcement, Congress chose to resolve its dilemma by turning over illegally imported blacks to state governments to handle as they saw fit, usually by immediate sale.

When some southerners also argued that the death penalty was too harsh a penalty for slave trading, the House by a 63–53 vote lowered the punishment to ten years' imprisonment. This version passed the House 113–5. The final bill, which incorporated a Senate effort to improve enforcement by regulating the coastwise slave trade in small vessels, drew more southern fire and only passed the House, 63–49. The delegations from Virginia, South Carolina, and Georgia were almost unanimously opposed.

Since British abolitionists had earlier documented the horrors of the slave trade in an effort to get Parliament to ban it, Americans debating the issue in 1807 could draw on powerful indictments. The debate in America was more impassioned than any previous one on slavery, which may account for the greater southern solidarity at the end. But while imports of slaves to America decreased after 1 January 1808, the day the act took effect, they did not cease. It took twelve years for Congress to agree to send ships to intercept slavers off Africa, and the U.S. enforcement effort was by all accounts the weakest of any country pledged to halt the trade. During the Missouri Compromise debates in 1820 Congress agreed (with the slave states divided) to define the slave trade as piracy punishable by death. But the only execution ever to take place under the law occurred years later during the Civil War. Congress's action on the slave trade was frankly ambiguous. It signaled that the country wished to control its importation of slaves but not enough to make the ban truly effective.

Territorial expansion proved to be the issue that eventually changed slavery from a minor to a major issue on the congressional agenda. Yet for thirty years congressional overview of slavery in territories caused little stir. In 1787 the Confederation Congress meeting in New York unanimously passed the Northwest Ordinance, one article of which (added by a Massachusetts representative) provided that "there shall be neither slavery or involuntary servitude in the said territory, otherwise than in the punishment of crimes whereof the party shall have been duly convicted." Most historians believe that southern states expected something in return for the concession, but they disagree on what it was: the enactment of the three-fifths clause by the Constitutional Convention meeting nearby in Philadelphia or an alliance between South and West. In any case, slavery was only moderately stymied. Territorial officials allowed slaves already in the territory to remain and did little to check the importation of new slaves as apprentices. Indeed, Ohio, Indiana, and Illinois all considered legalizing slavery when they entered the union.

Congress made no serious attempt to restrict the spread of slavery in other territories. In 1798 a Federalist, upset at Republican claims of being democratic, suggested making Mississippi territory free, but most Federalists rejected the strategy as divisive to their own party. In 1804, James Hillhouse (Fed.-Conn.), who was trying to impede western expansion, suggested freeing after one year slaves brought into Louisiana, but his fellow party members showed no enthusiasm and helped kill the amendment.

In 1819 when Missouri applied for admission as a slave state, the situation had changed. The antislavery movement had organized nationally with the formation of the American Colonization Society on 28 December 1816, which encouraged African Americans to emigrate. While the organization was small and committed to racial separation through resettlement, it was still committed to ending slavery. Many prominent individuals (Henry Clay, John Marshall, James Madison) belonged to it, including some from the upper South. It was a reminder that even white southerners disagreed on the future of slavery.

The rapid decline of the Federalist party after the War of 1812 left party lines in Congress in disarray. The Republican caucus even opened its doors to Federalists if they cared to come. Yet the large number of first-termers in Congress and the absence of a strong committee structure created a pressing need for a new way to organize differences over goals and priorities. If regional blocs were to emerge as the new defining mechanisms, then the admission of Missouri as a state with ties to the West (and to the South if it became a slave state) was highly significant. In the evenly divided Senate it would give either the slave or free states an edge. Slavery's defenders might also find a way to increase southern support for the institution with the issue.

Toward the close of the Fifteenth Congress (1817–1819), James Tallmadge (R.-N.Y.) proposed amendments to the Missouri statehood bill banning the introduction of more slaves and gradually freeing those there. The latter proposal would permit Congress to emancipate slaves in a state for the first time. This threat united the slave states in opposition. The free states supported the amendments with only a few defections. The House passed but the Senate rejected the Tallmadge amendments, thus killing statehood temporarily.

In the Sixteenth Congress the same issue and the same sectional alignments carried over in the organization of Arkansas as a territory. Finally the Missouri statehood bill (including slavery) was joined with one for Maine (providing freedom). Senator Jesse Thomas (R.-Ill.) added an amendment from the floor to prohibit slavery in the remainder of the Louisiana Purchase territory north of 36° 30′ latitude, or the southern boundary of Missouri. This compromise divided southerners between those who would or would not accept congressional restrictions on the expansion of slavery. This enabled restrictions to pass. Enough northern Republicans concerned about a sectional resurgence of the Federalist party voted with a united South to admit Missouri as a slave state. After first resisting, the House accepted the Missouri Compromise with voting patterns mirroring those in the Senate. A second issue emerged when Missouri submitted a constitution for approval that excluded free blacks from the state. Only when the state's legislature made a nonbinding pledge not to discriminate against citizens of other states was Missouri finally admitted as a state in 1821.

The Missouri crisis showed that southern lawmakers were as determined to prevent Congress from becoming an agent of emancipation as northern lawmakers in 1807 had been to keep Congress from authorizing slave auctions. Clearly a renewed emphasis on states rights and limited government might reduce this conflict. Soon after the Missouri debate, Martin Van Buren (D.-N.Y.) wrote to southern politicians proposing an alliance along such lines. States rights and a racism that attempted to make poorer whites anxious about their status vis à vis blacks became the hallmarks of the Democratic party that emerged within the next decade.

Yet the Missouri Compromise also revealed that the concerns expressed in Congress were not broadly felt in the electorate. Between the meetings of the Fifteenth and Sixteenth Congresses, northern emancipation societies, often headed by Federalists, circulated antislavery speeches from Congress and demanded support for Tallmadge. In response, eight northern state legislatures passed resolutions against Missouri's admission unless slavery was excluded. Yet when it became clear to Republicans that Federalists were using the issue to reorganize, northern political unity evaporated. Both in the North and South, newspapers complained that more attention should be given to the financial crisis in the country following the panic of 1819 than to Missouri. Politicians could easily conclude that those who could deal successfully with the economy would win more plaudits than those who argued over slavery in a distant corner of the nation.

In the next decade as lawmakers grappled with banks, tariffs, and the expansion of the transportation system, the slavery issue receded into the background. The new alignments of the second party system as it emerged in the 1830s were national, not sectional. Most states by 1840 (and many even earlier) witnessed vigorous two-party competition between Whigs and Democrats over a variety of issues.

But there remained places in the South in which the echoes of the Missouri debates continued to reverberate. The South's division over slavery's expansion seemed ominous. In South Carolina, with its 56-percent slave population, the highest in the South, the fear of outside interference with slavery was intense. Fears heightened when the British Parliament suddenly voted to emancipate West Indian slaves in 1831. Nat Turner's slave rebellion in Virginia in 1832 was another jolt. For some southerners the absolute defense of slavery superseded all other values including party loyalty. South Carolina's favorite son, John C. Calhoun, illustrated this concern as he shifted from a mild nationalism to a strong sectionalism in the 1820s. Only in southern unity inside—or even outside—the Union did such southerners see security.

## THE ABOLITIONIST MOVEMENT AND POLITICS

During the 1820s the antislavery movement in the North began to change. Free blacks in the North rejected colonization. One, David Walker, perhaps America's first black nationalistic ideologue, even called for slave revolt in a pamphlet in 1829. The gradualist approach to abolition stood condemned as hopelessly ineffective. In attempting to reconcile slave-owners to gradual emancipation while respecting their property rights, abolition itself had been eviscerated. The number of slaves in America was growing, not declining. Meanwhile, evangelical revivals stirred the masses across America in the 1820s, persuading converts to free themselves from sin. A similar strategy seemed to hold promise for antislavery. If slaveholders could be convinced of the evil of slavery, they too might renounce it. Reasonably, they could neither demand compensation for giving up sin nor quibble about its economic or social consequences. The obstacles to antislavery would diminish. But for this great work to be accomplished abolitionists would have to ceaselessly agitate to create a moral climate in which all Americans recognized slavery to be a sin.

In the 1830s, new-style abolition societies emerged in the North dedicated to reforming the consciences of white Americans regarding slavery. Abolition proved most popular in New England and the region to its west settled by New Englanders. By 1840, 160,000 belonged to such societies. In their efforts to create a new moral atmosphere, abolitionists sought to convert religious and governmental leaders, moral arbiters of society, to their side. By 1838 they had sent half a million petitions to Congress demanding the abolition of slavery in the District of Columbia, the abolition of the interstate slave trade, the revocation of the three-fifths clause and an end to the admission of slave states. Abolitionists were enthusiastic lobbyists, but both in politics and in the churches they brought divisions instead of a unified antislavery vision.

The political world too was changing. The broadening of the suffrage and improved communications and education encouraged more people to participate in politics actively. To maintain political coalitions among an ever more diverse population, politicians stressed organization, loyalty, and discipline. Southern sectionalists and northern abolitionists represented problems to such coalitions because of their greater loyalty to their causes than to party. Legislative bodies became the battlegrounds where parties, interests, and ideologies clashed. Party increasingly became the dominant force in lawmaking.

In the new political environment the actions of state legislatures and Congress were linked in important ways. In theory the state legislature communicated the will of the state's electorate to its representatives in Washington through the passage of resolutions. In practice such communications were essential to make the party system itself work effectively. Managing parties in the antebellum era was difficult. The fear of despotism had stripped most governmental and party posts of decisive power. Effective party leadership resided in individuals—whether businessmen, editors, or officials—who could win the trust of others. To keep this trust required being able to create an image of the party that was satisfying to its many constituents. Most of the matters with which legislatures dealt on a daily basis were inconsequential to most voters. Some state issues that were important were also divisive to existing coalitions. Taking positions on national issues, however, enabled party leaders to define what great principles their party represented and how it differed from the opposition. It was also a way to pressure an opposition—whether a faction in the party or the other party—to conform to a position that represented the "will of the people" or face the consequences. Studies of state legislative voting show that resolutions on national policies were among the most partisan.

But while the local interpretation of national issues could strengthen a party locally, it could also lead to different interpretations of a party's position in different parts of the country. In the South, parties differed over how best to defend slavery and in the North the same parties differed over whether slavery should be attacked. When a party was out of power nationally, as the Whigs frequently were, differences were less crucial. But presidential elections could bring conflict into the open.

Slavery rarely dominated the congressional agenda, but it achieved a symbolic importance, suggesting the responsiveness of the national government to regional concerns. For example, in 1836 Democratic president Andrew Jackson, a slaveholding Tennessean, recommended the New Yorker, Martin Van Buren, as his successor. Jackson's southern opponents saw this as the perfect opportunity to raise questions about

Van Buren's loyalty to slavery and so engineer his defeat. Disturbed by the abolitionist petition campaign, James Henry Hammond, a slave-owner from South Carolina, introduced a gag rule in the House to refuse receipt of such petitions. The seeming infringement on the right of petition offended some northerners who saw it as an attack on democratic processes. Attempting to reassure the South about Van Buren, northern Democrats modified the gag to accept but automatically table antislavery petitions. In this form the gag passed the Senate 34–6 and the House 117–68. The Democrats generally supported the gag while the Whigs divided sectionally.

State legislatures joined the fray. Mississippi circulated resolutions calling on the free states to prevent agitation that endangered the property and "domestic repose" of slave states. The responding resolutions in northern legislatures gave Whigs and Democrats an opportunity to define their differences with the upcoming presidential election in mind. Democrats linked Whigs to the radical abolitionist minority while Whigs associated Democrats with indifference to democracy. Lawmakers agonized over wording, and resolutions varied from state to state. Partisanship shaped the final outcomes as representatives tried to find positions acceptable to their national parties and local constituents.

The gag rule was renewed many times before it was finally voted down in 1844. The presidential election years brought the hottest debates. In 1840 Waddy Thompson (Whig-S.C.), determined to split the Democrats, succeeded in passing a total gag (nonacceptance of petitions). He divided the Democrats sectionally as he had hoped but his own party as well. The last vote in 1844, a 108–80 defeat in the House, saw 79 percent of the northern Democrats and 98 percent of the northern Whigs voting against 87.5 percent of the southerners. Prolonging the dispute had increased sectional divisions. Strong partisans were unhappy and some southerners argued that gags did not stop the discussion of slavery.

Such sectional voting was largely confined to slavery issues. The panic of 1837 had solidified partisan differences on most other matters. But some hoped to use sectional differences to weaken partisan coalitions. Abolitionists de-spised any concessions to slavery. They formed their own Liberty party in 1840, weak in numbers but capable of affecting which major-party candidate won in some districts. Since Whigs in general had more antislavery constituents, they were the most vulnerable. Whigs introduced 95 percent of the abolitionist memorials in Congress. When northern Whigs deferred to abolitionists, it created problems for southern Whigs. On slavery-related roll calls in the early 1840s Whigs were usually divided more severely than Democrats. But many also resisted such division. Southern Whigs generally took more moderate positions than did southern Democrats and defined the overzealous defenders of slavery as traitorous disunionists.

Treating slavery as an issue of states' rights brought greater harmony to the Democrats, but they too experienced sectional strains. Strong southern sectionalists constantly tested the Democratic party for signs of weakness on slavery, making it ever more difficult for northern Democrats to appear responsive to their own section's needs. Explaining rifts as a plot of partisan opponents was a common way to handle this dilemma. Congressmen in both parties argued that their parties offered the best protection for sectional interests.

Territorial expansion in the 1840s tested such assumptions and raised the visibility of the slavery issue. Although Texas had desired annexation upon its successful revolution from Mexico in 1836, fears of war and the problem of slavery expansion delayed its admission for nearly a decade. Following President William Henry Harrison's untimely death in 1841, most Whigs rejected the leadership of his successor, states'-rights Whig John Tyler of Virginia. In a final effort to develop a winning issue, Tyler proposed the annexation of Texas in 1844. His secretary of state, John C. Calhoun, described annexation as a way to protect southern slavery (by forestalling British-sponsored abolition in Texas).

Southern Democrats welcomed this sectional reasoning because it would force southern Whigs to appear unsupportive of slavery if they opposed annexation. Despite their dilemma southern Whigs helped defeat Tyler's treaty in the Senate, 16–35. It was northern Democrats, fearing to appear submissive to the South in an election year, who split. The Democrats recovered by generalizing expansion in their 1844 platform to include expansion northward into Oregon Territory, occupied jointly with Great Britain. Following the Democratic victory, Congress, in a virtual party-line vote, annexed Texas by joint resolution. State legislatures echoed the views on Texas in similar partisan votes. But their understandings of annexation were different. Using tortured reasoning, New Hampshire Democrats applauded annexation as a way to increase free territory. Antislavery "Conscience" Whigs in Massachusetts warred with their conservative "Cotton" brethren to adopt resolutions that flayed annexation for perpetuating the evils of slavery. Meanwhile southern Whigs focused only on the unconstitutionality of annexation.

Because the Mexican war of 1846–1848 quickly followed Texas's annexation, sectional differences over the implications of expansion for slavery could not simply die down. Instead, for almost four years congressmen struggled to define those implications. To abolitionists in the North and sectionalists in the South the central issue in expansion was the enlargement of slave territory and the strengthening or weakening of that institution. But others also saw partisan implications or issues of power and oppression of whites, not slaves. America's republican political philosophy sensitized the politically aware to watch for attempts by the selfish to seek privileges for themselves. Northerners perceived slave-owners whom they labeled the "Slave Power" (because of the increased power granted them by the three-fifths clause of the Constitution) as such a selfish elite, just as some southerners saw attempts to restrict slavery as insulting deprivations of their equal rights as Americans. Astute sectionalists could use the language of republicanism to enlarge support for their causes.

The viability of such sectional strategies depended on the health of the party system. Economic recovery from the panic of 1837 lowered the saliency of traditional economic issues from the mid-1840s on. More seriously, a host of new issues arose. A modernizing economy, spurred on by a vast influx of Irish and German workers, stimulated the growth of towns and cities across the North and border South. With growth came problems of crime, poverty, social integration, and labor discontent. Congress did not deal with such matters but local and state government did. As change brought discontent, the task of creating satisfying images of party competence became more difficult.

The Mexican war put some northern Democratic congressmen in a tight position in 1846. As Whigs had predicted, Texas's annexation strengthened the slave states and caused a war that was unlikely to materially benefit northerners. Resentful that Democratic President James K. Polk, a southern slaveholder, pursued legislative and patronage policies that ignored northern interests, David Wilmot (D.-Pa.) introduced an amendment to an administration appropriations bill in 1846. The Wilmot Proviso copied the wording of the Northwest Ordinance in prohibiting slavery in any territory acquired from Mexico. The proviso passed, 83–64, with an almost unanimous South confronting a nearly unanimous North. The Senate adjourned without a vote.

As the sectional vote on the Wilmot Proviso indicated, politicians found it difficult to resist favoring their own section in a clear contest. In the next four years antislavery and southern sectionalist congressmen took advantage of this to introduce measure after measure that tested sectional loyalties. Not only was the Wilmot Proviso reintroduced but Calhoun in 1847 proposed resolutions that asserted the constitutional right of southerners to take their property into any territory of the union. Other proposals related to the future of slavery or the slave trade in the federal district, the right of Congress to abolish the interstate sale of slaves, and the revision of the fugitive slave law. The latter issue was particularly abrasive. Free states assumed all residents to be free and accorded them the rights of habeas corpus and jury trial. Slave states assumed blacks to be rightless slaves unless they could document their freedom. In the 1840s antikidnapping statutes in the North came into conflict with southern efforts to return accused fugitives to create charges of unfair behavior. New state legislation on kidnapping (personal liberty laws) was only one way that the sectional dispute spilled over into state politics. Negative sectional stereotyping related to slavery developed a broader base than it had had during the Missouri crisis.

Yet partisanship continued to thwart sectional unity. Initially secure in their opposition to territorial expansion, Whigs fanned the flames of sectionalism, hoping to consume the Democratic party. Fearing precisely this result, three-fourths of the northern Democrats took positions on slavery less extreme than northern Whigs in the Twenty-ninth Congress (1845–1847). Most northern legislatures passed resolutions in favor of the Wilmot Proviso, but often Democrats, lamenting the sectional division of their party, divided.

When the Mexican war ended with the annexation of New Mexico and California, Whig security ended. If Whigs elected their presidential candidate, Zachary Taylor, in 1848, they would be responsible for solving the territorial dilemma and their sectional differences would be exposed. If southern Democrats like Calhoun defined the southern stance on territorial slavery, southern Whigs might lose their own identity. Partisan pressures inched southern Whigs toward more moderate positions. The North Carolina legislature in 1848 passed resolutions (as did most southern legislatures) opposing the Wilmot Proviso, but for Whigs it was unjust, to Democrats unconstitutional. And Whigs deplored disunion; Democrats threatened it. In early 1849 congressional Whigs torpedoed an effort by Calhoun to create a common southern stance in an address to the southern people. Whigs in southern legislatures also resisted sending delegates to a Calhoun-inspired southern rights convention in Nashville in 1850, designed to pressure Congress in its deliberations on slavery.

Partisans grasped for solutions, coming up with four possibilities: extension of the 36°30′ line, reference of the question to the courts (the unsuccessful Clayton Compromise of 1848), admission of new territories immediately as states, and reference of the decision to territorial inhabitants (popular sovereignty). In 1848, encouraged by the new interest in slavery, some Liberty party politicians sought to form a new sectional party pledged to freedom in the territories. Offering a national ticket of former Democrat Martin Van Buren and former Whig Charles Francis Adams, the Free Soil party appealed to both antislavery Whigs and Democrats. Confronted by this threat, northern congressmen showed understandable reluctance to retreat from the Wilmot Proviso. The inability to find a solution kept sectional bills constantly before Congress and prolonged bitter sectional debates.

In 1850, near the end of the longest session in congressional history, Senator Stephen A. Douglas (D.-Ill.) devised a way to allow most congressmen to uphold their section's principles while ending the deadlock. The Compromise of 1850 consisted of a series of measures, some favoring the North, others the South. California would be a free state. New Mexico and Utah would invoke popular sovereignty. Texas, long viewed as a source of multiple slave states, would be reduced in size but its debt assumed by the federal government. The District of Columbia would no longer import slaves for sale but the abolition of slavery there would be contingent on the joint approval of Maryland and the District's voters. The fugitive slave law would be amended to deny jury trials and compel cooperation from northern citizens. Voting separately on the measures allowed a small group of compromisers to join with whichever section favored a measure to enact each proposal. Key abstentions enabled particularly controversial measures (the fugitive slave law) to pass. Border-state Whigs and northern Democrats made up the bulk of the compromisers.

Most congressmen—the exceptions being mainly northern Whigs—seemed content with the compromise on slavery. In the states, only Vermont in 1850 passed a personal liberty law to challenge the fugitive slave law. But politics as usual did not return. Voting on economic issues no longer showed the clear party differences present in the mid-forties. Voting cues now came from no sustained source, a sure sign that party redefinition was near.

With no great principle or issue dividing parties, voter enthusiasm waned and outsiders increasingly condemned politicians as corrupt opportunists. In response, politicians sought new, galvanizing issues. Nativists, those who favored the native-born over immigrants, addressed many of the social problems of the North, blaming them on foreign immigration. For most of the 1850s they were a major factor in politics. But Senator Douglas saw western development as the key future issue. In 1854 he introduced a bill organizing Nebraska Territory. Although the area was supposed to be free under the Missouri Compromise, Douglas felt that the 1850 debates proved that Democrats now preferred popular sovereignty. Hoping to unite all Democrats plus southern Whigs behind territorial organization, he proposed repealing the Missouri Compromise. Instead, his actions became a galvanizing issue for northern sectionalist Whigs. Although President Franklin Pierce, a northerner, urged all Democrats to support the Kansas-Nebraska bill, half of the northern House Democrats failed to comply. The combination of weak Democratic partisanship and strong southern sectionalism enabled the bill to pass 37–14 in the Senate and 113–100 in the House. But anti-Nebraska meetings across the North brought together those angered by the repeal, regardless of party. This became the first step in replacing the failing Whig party with a new organization committed to limiting slavery's growth, the Republican party.

Realignment put new pressures on lawmakers. Needing to rebuild coalitions, they appealed to vocal minorities. Northern legislatures rushed to enact new personal liberty laws, defying the South on the fugitive slave law, and to pass carefully worded resolutions on Kansas-Nebraska that might define new political groupings.

The defeat or defection of northern Democrats left their party in Congress with a distinct southern cast. The southern wing could now be more aggressive on slavery to entice southern Whigs vulnerable because of their party's collapse nationally. At first new coalitions were ill-defined and shifted as issues changed. But as Kansas's progress toward statehood brought bloodshed and charges of election tampering, coalitions reflecting opposing views on slavery began to gel. In the Thirty-fifth Congress (1857–1859) northern Democrats were in the middle on slavery roll calls, divided both from Republicans and southern Democrats. By the Thirty-sixth Congress (1859–1861) those northern Democrats who remained were voting with the South. Republicans benefited not only from continued problems in Kansas, but also began to draw nativist support as they learned how to affix blame on the Slave Power for economic and social strains.

Extreme southern sectionalists (the fire-eaters) portrayed Republicans not just as partisan foes but as wild-eyed fanatics for whom constitutional and legal guarantees of slavery were immoral and thus unsupportable. Republican victory in 1860 signified to them an offensive act against slavery, regardless of what the Republican party officially proclaimed. Following the election, seven Deep South states seceded and formed a Confederacy pledged to uphold slavery.

With partisan lines echoing sectional differences on slavery, compromise in Congress was nearly impossible. Although both houses in the secession winter of 1860–1861 had committees devoted to arranging a settlement, the perceived need to appease seceding states outraged Republicans. Senator John J. Crittenden (Whig-Ky.), for example, proposed six constitutional amendments and four resolutions offering the South, among other things, federal protection of slavery in all territories south of 36°30′. The only compromise measure to pass, and then with only minority support (40 percent) from Republicans, was an amendment forbidding any future amendments interfering with slavery in the states. Two states ratified the amendment before the Civil War broke out in 1861.

## THE CIVIL WAR

The Republican division on this amendment—and the later Crittenden resolution defining the war's goal as saving the union, not interfering with slavery—prefigured later Republican divisions on slavery. Indeed, no issue divided Republicans more during the war. Although all Republicans preferred free to slave labor, radical Republicans regarded slavery as a moral issue that could not be compromised (especially when Republicans—owing to the secession of eleven of the fifteen slave states—had large majorities in both houses). A persistent minority, however, pointed out that alienating Democrats, border-state unionists, and lukewarm Republicans would endanger the entire war effort and the party's future. Although Republicans usually united on final votes on slavery-related issues, squabbles over compensation, colonization, and constitutional law marked any bill's progress.

Republicans addressed slavery piecemeal as they searched for common ground. One set of laws deprived slavery of protection by repealing the fugitive slave law, enforcing the ban on the slave trade, and forbidding military officers to return escaped slaves. Others used war necessity to confiscate rebels' slaves and free slaves who served the Union cause and their families. In 1862 Congress abolished slavery in the District of Columbia (with slaveowners compensated) and the territories (uncompensated). President Abraham Lincoln also sought to emancipate the slaves in the border states by proposing financial compensation, gradual freedom, and colonization. But border-state representatives resented outside coercion while radicals disliked Lincoln's concessions to slaveholders. Only Missouri cooperated but the House and Senate could not agree on a bill to help the state. In the end two border states (Missouri and Maryland) and four reconstructing states (West Virginia, Tennessee, Arkansas, Louisiana) ended slavery during the war, all by irregular means. Each wrote a new constitution and excluded from the political process those likely to disagree with the results.

During the war hundreds of thousands of slaves fled to the Union lines. With the implementation of Lincoln's Emancipation Proclamation (freeing slaves in rebel-held territory as of 1 January 1863), more slaves claimed freedom. Confusion over status abounded. What would happen when the war ended was unclear. By 1864 a simple constitutional amendment abolishing slavery seemed attractive to most Republicans in Congress. Following his reelection, Lincoln was able to persuade eighteen House Democrats and Unionists to join with the unanimous Republican party to enact the Thirteenth Amendment abolishing slavery. To reassure the public about the dimensions of freedom, the amendment, which passed 31 January 1865, followed the familiar wording of the Northwest Ordinance. Congressional Democrats had defended slavery up to this point. Historians attribute the change of heart of the eighteen to strategic considerations (and possibly bribes) rather than a new understanding of the issue. In the northern legislatures party-line voting, with a minor number of Democratic crossovers, characterized the ratification process, which was completed by 18 December 1865. Southern states had to adopt the amendment as part of their reconstruction.

After almost 250 years, party politics in the legislative arena brought an end to slavery, but the moral vision of slavery's wrong was not universalized. From the beginning lawmakers faced slavery's contradictions: its definition of slaves as both human beings and property, its victimization of blacks while the society increasingly valued independence and equal rights, its challenge to the shibboleths of free labor. Yet to resolve the contradictions and end racial slavery was to threaten the privileges afforded a propertied elite and white skin. One might consider it remarkable that lawmakers, uniformly white and nearly always privileged, challenged slavery to the extent they did. They did so, however, on their own terms, maintaining the possibility of racial and propertied hierarchies even as they eliminated slavery. Evidence suggests that the virtually all-white northern electorate would have tolerated little more. Without agreement on the wrongs of racism as well as of slavery, America's lawmakers could not fulfill the expectations of former slaves. A politics of race was destined to follow the politics of slavery in American legislatures.

## BIBLIOGRAPHY

*The Law of Slavery*
The evolution of laws regarding slavery may be traced in the following: A. LEON HIGGINBOTHAM, JR., *In the Matter of Color: Race and the American Legal Process* (New York, 1978); WINTHROP D. JORDAN, *White Over Black; American Attitudes Toward the Negro, 1550–1812* (New York, 1965); EDGAR J. MCMANUS, *Black Bondage in the North* (Syracuse, N.Y., 1973); KENNETH M. STAMPP, *The Peculiar Institution: Slavery in the Antebellum South* (New York, 1956); MARK V. TUSHNET, *The American Law of Slavery, 1810–1860: Considerations of Humanity and Interest* (Princeton, N.J., 1981); and WILLIAM M. WIECEK, "The Statutory Law of Slavery and Race in the Thirteen Mainland Colonies of British

America," *William and Mary Quarterly,* 3d ser., 34:2 (April 1977).

### Politics and Slavery to 1830
The best works that explain the broader context in which antislavery developed are RUDOLPH M. BELL, *Party and Faction in American Politics: The House of Representatives, 1789–1801* (Westport, Conn., 1973); DAVID BRION DAVIS, *The Problem of Slavery in the Age of Revolution, 1770–1823* (Ithaca, N.Y., 1975); HOWARD A. OHLINE, "Slavery, Economics, and Congressional Politics, 1790," *Journal of Southern History* 46:3 (August 1980); DONALD ROBINSON, *Slavery in the Structure of American Politics* (New York, 1971); and WILLIAM M. WIECEK, *The Sources of Antislavery Constitutionalism in America, 1760–1848* (Ithaca, N.Y., 1977).

GLOVER MOORE, *The Missouri Controversy, 1819–1821* (Lexington, Ky., 1958), and ARTHUR ZILVERSMIT, *The First Emancipation: The Abolition of Slavery in the North* (Chicago, 1967), detail particularly important episodes in the history of antislavery.

### Politics and Slavery, 1830–1860
The following works provide an introduction to the politics of slavery in state and nation from the Jacksonian era to the Civil War: THOMAS B. ALEXANDER, *Sectional Stress and Party Strength: A Study of Roll-Call Voting Patterns in the United States House of Representatives, 1836–1860* (Nashville, Tenn., 1967); WILLIAM J. COOPER, JR., *The South and the Politics of Slavery, 1828–1856* (Baton Rouge, La., 1978); HERBERT ERSHKOWITZ and WILLIAM G. SHADE, "Consensus or Conflict: Political Behavior in the State Legislatures During the Jacksonian Era," *Journal of American History* 58:3 (December 1971); ROBERT WILLIAM FOGEL, *Without Consent or Contract: The Rise and Fall of American Slavery* (New York, 1989); WILLIAM W. FREEHLING, *The Road to Disunion,* vol. 1, *Secessionists at Bay, 1776–1854* (New York, 1990); HOLMAN HAMILTON, *Prologue to Conflict: The Crisis and Compromise of 1850* (Lexington, Ky., 1964); MICHAEL F. HOLT, *The Political Crisis of the 1850s* (New York, 1978); THOMAS D. MORRIS, *Free Men All: The Personal Liberty Laws of the North, 1780–1861* (Baltimore, Md., 1974); CHAPLAIN W. MORRISON, *Democratic Politics and Sectionalism: The Wilmot Proviso Controversy* (Chapel Hill, N.C., 1967); DAVID POTTER, *The Impending Crisis, 1848–1861* (New York, 1976); JOEL H. SILBEY, *The Shrine of Party: Congressional Voting Behavior, 1841–1852* (Pittsburgh, 1967); and GERALD W. WOLFF, *The Kansas-Nebraska Bill: Party, Section, and the Coming of the Civil War* (New York, 1977).

### The Civil War
ALLAN G. BOGUE, *The Congressman's Civil War,* (Cambridge, Mass., 1989); and ALLAN G. BOGUE, *The Earnest Men: Republicans of the Civil War Senate* (Ithaca, N.Y., 1981), are excellent accounts of the workings of Congress on many issues including slavery. JOEL H. SILBEY, *A Respectable Minority: The Democratic Party in the Civil War Era, 1860–1868* (New York, 1977), explains the strategy of congressional Democrats during the Civil War.

SEE ALSO The U.S. Congress: The Era of Party Patronage and Sectional Stress, 1829–1881.

# LEGISLATURES AND POLITICAL RIGHTS

## Marc W. Kruman

Throughout American history, colonial assemblies and state and national legislatures have profoundly influenced the nature and breadth of political rights. At the beginning of the colonial era, the legislatures determined the contours of the electorate, with little interference from England. They established who could vote and who could not. But after the English Revolution of 1688–1689, colonial officials imposed a relatively uniform constitutional order. During the American Revolution, constitutions, written by provincial congresses or constitutional conventions, determined the extent of the franchise. Thereafter legislatures influenced the right to vote through interpretation of constitutional provisions, the formal amendment of the federal and state constitutions, and election laws.

Since the Revolution, legislative power over political rights has shifted from the state legislatures to Congress, and Congress has dramatically broadened access to those rights. During the Revolutionary years, political leaders assumed that the determination of suffrage rights rested in the states. Accordingly, the Constitutional Convention created no national suffrage policy. But the Civil War transferred substantial control over suffrage policy from the state to the federal government, where it has generally remained. Congressional Reconstruction policies and the Fourteenth and Fifteenth amendments all established federal authority over black suffrage. Congress expanded its superintendence of the suffrage in subsequent voting-rights amendments to the Constitution, including enfranchising women and eighteen-year-old citizens, and prohibiting states from imposing poll taxes. The amendments, federal laws, and Supreme Court decisions have effectively established a national political community.

War has shaped legislative decision-making regarding political rights. The Revolution, the Civil War, World War I, and the Vietnam War all sparked dramatic changes in suffrage qualifications: property, religious, and sex limitations during the Revolution, racial restrictions after the Civil War, sex qualifications after World War I, and age requirements during the Vietnam War. But even when the United States was not at war its state and national legislatures have heeded Baron de Montesquieu's admonition that "the laws establishing the right to vote are fundamental" in a democracy.

## THE COLONIAL PERIOD

The laws and practices of medieval England, although initially ignored by the colonial assemblies, ultimately shaped suffrage policy in the colonies. In medieval England, the king—through Parliament—bestowed an office-holding or suffrage franchise on specific persons or groups of persons. The grant of a franchise conveyed privileges but also the obligation to participate. Until 1429, apparently all freemen could participate in their county's election of knights to Parliament. But in that year, Parliament restricted the vote in those elections to persons holding land that generated an annual income of forty shillings. The original law severely restricted participation to a few freemen by ridding the polity of a "very great, outrageous and excessive number of people, of which most part was people of small substance and of no value, whereof every of them pretended a voice equivalent as to such election with the most worthy knights and esquires."

In the boroughs, voting qualifications varied; charters typically required burgage tenure (permanent association with an "ancient property" in the borough), but when charters said nothing boroughs followed common law and enfranchised "inhabitant householders." Although some boroughs extended the suffrage to men who paid scot and lot (i.e., local taxes), others were "close boroughs," which limited the suffrage to the few governors—known as freemen—of the corporation.

The first North American colonies ignored English law when fashioning their own suffrage qualifications and adopted qualifications congruent with the rationale for founding a particular colony. In Massachusetts the royal charter limited governance to the Massachusetts Bay Company's few freemen, in the manner of the close borough. But the General Court, which attempted to create and sustain a Puritan commonwealth ruled by the "visible saints," admitted to freemanship all congregational church members in full communion. Voting by non-church members, in John Cotton's words, would "turn the edge of all authority and laws against the church and the members thereof."

In the colonies south of New England, legislatures expected that all freemen would vote. In Maryland, despite Lord Baltimore's desire to found a manorial society, all white freemen could participate directly in the first assemblies' deliberations. When representative elections replaced direct democracy, all white freemen could still vote for assemblymen. Similarly, all Virginia freemen could vote until 1670.

But from the 1650s through the 1670s, the colonial legislatures imposed property qualifications of varying amounts for voting. Before, they had identified the political community with freedom; now they distinguished between the propertied and propertyless. The initiation of property qualifications may also have reflected the colonial legislator's desire to emulate the English political system. Virginia, Maryland, Massachusetts, and Connecticut all established property qualifications. In 1658–1659 the Connecticut legislature justified its initiation of property qualifications for freemanship on the grounds that it would "p$^r$vent tumult and trouble at the Court of Election." Moreover, all of the colonies created after the restoration of the Stuart monarchy in 1660 demanded property qualifications for voting. New York, for one, in 1683 simply replicated the forty-shilling freeholder qualification.

The diversity in property qualifications lasted until the English Revolution of 1689 altered systems of government from New England to New Jersey. In new charters, King William III imposed rough conformity to the English county norm. The new charters for the New England colonies and New York reproduced the forty-shilling freehold; in the South, ownership of a freehold of a certain size (often fifty acres) or a freehold worth usually forty or fifty pounds approximated the English county rule. The New England colonies, where town government was so important, made special allowance for town dwellers. Unlike the chaos of English borough suffrage regulations, the New England colonies enfranchised men who owned a personal estate worth at least forty pounds.

The colonies also replicated English religious restrictions. Until 1689, New England colonies disfranchised most non-Congregationalists; elsewhere, legislatures excluded dissenting Protestant groups. Thereafter, the disfranchised comprised only non-Protestants: eight colonies disfranchised Catholics; seven excluded Jews.

As in England, custom and common law disfranchised most women in colonial America. Only the legislatures of Pennsylvania, Delaware, and South Carolina legally excluded them. Women, generally property-owning widows, voted occasionally in several colonies, among them New Hampshire, Rhode Island, New York, Maryland, and Pennsylvania.

Unlike in England, where racial distinctions were unknown at law, the colonial legislators considered the eligibility of free blacks. Northern assemblies established no formal restrictions on free black voting, but in the slave South, lawmakers usually disfranchised such men. South Carolina banned free blacks in 1716, Virginia in 1723, and Georgia in 1761. North Carolina equivocated, sometimes granting the suffrage to black freemen, and sometimes denying it.

Men otherwise eligible often had to meet residency requirements, which ranged from six months in Georgia to two years in Pennsylvania. For most of the colonial era, Virginia, New Hampshire, and New York had no residency requirement (although New York added one in 1769). Like the medieval Parliament, colonial assemblies obliged members to reside in the districts they represented. They maintained those restrictions despite England's departure from tradition. As a result, the colonists developed an understanding of representation that differed markedly from that in England.

In a society that included few Catholics, Jews, or free blacks, property qualifications comprised the primary restrictions on political participation. And unlike in England, where land was scarce and land tenure encumbered with varying degrees of obligation to one's superiors, in the colonies, where land was plentiful, most freemen (from 50 to 80 percent, depending on the colony) possessed the requisite estate. In many colonies, the property requirement acted as an age requirement because most freeborn men eventually obtained property.

## THE REVOLUTIONARY ERA

Classical republican thought shaped colonial suffrage theory. Republican theorists had long contended that membership in the political community required economic independence. Only those independent of others for their livelihood could make autonomous political decisions. Economic independence freed men to act for the public good and gave them a stake in society's well-being.

The disfranchisement of propertyless males developed from two partly contradictory beliefs: that their economic dependence made them susceptible to coercion or that such people might pursue their own self-interest and jeopardize the security of property rights. During the pre-Revolutionary years, the American political elite discovered that they often could not control crowds drawn from society's lower ranks. At different times, such people threatened not only English or pro-English targets, but also apparently unrelated economic targets. Whig leaders feared that the propertyless might easily turn against propertied patriots.

The centrality of the voting issue in the imperial conflict ("no taxation without representation") excited new interest in the suffrage. During the colonial era, many men could vote but few bothered; rarely did the disfranchised publicly complain. But in the first months of 1776, as citizens heatedly debated the form of their state governments, they made the right to vote a primary issue. The provincial congresses —ad hoc assemblies with legislative, executive, and judicial powers—and constitutional conventions reconsidered the relationship between property and voting in the new state constitutions. Five states, including Vermont, permitted all male (in some states only white males) adult taxpayers to vote for all or some popularly elected officials. Another four narrowly defeated similar clauses in their constitution.

The taxpayer suffrage qualification reveals how the Revolution altered thinking about the relationship between the people and their government. Colonial assemblies required property ownership as proof of a man's independence to act uncoerced by others and his allegiance to the community. Paying taxes— especially poll taxes—symbolized neither a man's economic independence nor his attachment to his community.

Rather the taxpayer qualification expressed a new American understanding of representation, the absorption of radical Whig ideas, and the logical conclusion of the conflict over English taxation of the colonies. In the taxation dispute, Americans had argued that Parliament could not tax them because they were unrepresented in it. Their argument partially repudiated the concept of virtual representation, which assumed that parliamentary members represented the interests of the entire empire, not merely those of their constituents. Because American and English interests differed, the Americans claimed, their concerns were unrepresented in Parliament. They assumed that a representative directly expressed the views of his constituents.

Although they rejected virtual representation in the imperial context, congresses and conventions restricted voting rights at home on the grounds that qualified voters shared the entire community's interests. Delegates assumed that the local assembly represented the entire colony, even though only a small fraction of the populace elected legislators. Because the legislator lived in the community, whatever helped or hurt the community helped or hurt him too. But the revolutionaries' belief that the colonists needed to consent directly to their own taxation implied that all taxpaying citizens needed the suffrage.

The taxpayer qualification marked the emergence of a new conception of the right to vote. It divorced the suffrage from property holding. Instead of property serving as a measure of one's personal independence and attachment to the community, the taxpayer qualification signified that citizens needed the vote to protect themselves against the oppression of a rapacious assembly. Taxpayer suffrage, which assumed an adversarial relationship between the voter and the legislator, thus subverted the classical ideal of the independent citizen participating actively in the politics for the common good. Yet it retained the traditional belief in the importance of contribution as a basis for political participation.

The growing reliance upon taxpaying qualifications violated the traditional emphasis on the ownership of property (especially real estate) as the only proof of permanent devotion to the community. As an alternate test, states used residency requirements of one to two years. Such a requirement could prove meaningless, for men could and did move frequently. But without a substantial real-estate qualification, residency offered the best evidence of attachment.

The act of revolution itself and the subsequent domestic turmoil compelled provincial congresses to alter the contours of their political communities. Congressmen generally required potential voters to take an oath renouncing allegiance to Great Britain and asserting fidelity to the American cause. They never enfranchised all patriots, but by using loyalty oaths to disfranchise those of doubtful allegiance (regardless of their wealth), they wrenched the right of suffrage further from its traditional economic moorings. At war's end, residency requirements replaced oaths.

During the Revolution, legislators and convention delegates also reconsidered understandings of attachment and independence. When the war began, a large minority of the colonists ardently supported independence. The delegates hoped that reduced suffrage requirements would attract the allegiance of those formerly excluded, for such men would have a political and personal stake in the Revolution's success. The congresses thereby inverted the traditional relationship between personal attachment and political competence. Whereas allegiance to the community once legitimized a citizen's claim to political rights, now the expansion of political rights legitimized the state's claim to the citizen's allegiance.

The states, except Rhode Island and South Carolina, also ended religious restrictions on voting. It appears that as Protestant citizens came to view the suffrage as a means of defending their rights, they easily accepted the right of Catholics and Jews to vote. But they often resisted constitutional provisions allowing non-Protestants to hold office. In 1780, numerous Massachusetts towns objected to constitutional provisions allowing all Christians to hold office. Greenwich asserted that for "the preservation of a free Government and security of the Protestant Cause that no Papist should be admitted to a Seat in the Legislative and Judicial Departments." Virtually all states limited office-holding to Protestants (New Hampshire), Christians (Massachusetts), or those who believed in God (Pennsylvania).

The Revolutionary provincial congresses and conventions also advertently and inadvertently expanded the electorate. States with a poll tax and a taxpayer franchise (like North Carolina and New Hampshire) established nearly universal male adult suffrage. In states (such as New Jersey) where the monetary value of an estate determined suffrage qualifications, wartime inflation expanded the numbers eligible to vote. As a result the electorate burgeoned, ranging from 60 to 90 percent of free adult males, with most states edging closer to the high end of the range.

Although the Revolutionary congresses and conventions expanded the electorate, they disfranchised more than half of the adult population, including many propertyless men, women, slaves, some free black men, apprentices, indentured laborers, felons, and the mentally impaired. Slaves, wives, indentured servants, children, and apprentices, as dependents of a master, were by definition excluded from the political community, and statutes barred felons and the insane, one for damaging the community's best interests and the other for incompetence.

Lawmakers generally assumed that children and women possessed insufficient "discretion" to vote, children "from their want of years and experience," and women, as Theophilus Parson asserted in 1778, "from the natural tenderness and delicacy of their minds, their retired mode of life, and various domestic duties." As a result, women presumably knew too little of the world to vote.

Only New Jersey's provincial congress transcended the Western tradition excluding women from the electorate. Delegates enfranchised "all inhabitants ... worth" £50 who resided in their place of voting for one year, and for thirty years propertied single women voted. Although the provision affected a small minority of women (mostly widows), the formal enfranchisement of women signified the radical potential of the American Revolution. New Jersey was unique; no other state considered women—no matter how much property they owned—politically competent.

When the Constitutional Convention assembled in 1787, most of the delegates deplored the democratic politics of the Revolutionary states and concluded that the people had insufficient virtue to maintain a republic. Nevertheless, the Constitution largely left the states in control of the suffrage. For elections to the House of Representatives, it established that "the electors in each State shall have the qualifications requisite for electors of the most numerous branch of the State Legislature." The delegates feared that more restrictive criteria would trigger considerable opposition. Instead, they hoped that enlarged districts in the House, the establishment of a powerful executive, and a vastly stronger central government would counterbalance popular and state power.

## THE EARLY REPUBLIC

During the decades between the Revolution and the Civil War, legislators and delegates to constitutional conventions elevated gender and race in place of property as the benchmarks of capacity for republican citizenship. They reduced or eliminated property requirements. At the same time, political capacity remained, as it long had been, linked to gender and became increasingly identified with African Americans. Most legislators continued to think of women as politically incapable and thus persisted in connecting civic virtue with masculinity (or what many called "manly independence"). In 1807 the New Jersey legislature disfranchised economically independent women by reinterpreting the suffrage clause in that state's constitution.

Legislators and constitutional convention delegates also absorbed the racist ideology then emerging triumphant in Europe and the United States and linked civic virtue to race. They believed that blacks were incapable of civic virtue and conversely that white men, by their nature, were sufficiently independent and prudent to be reliable citizens. Responding to these changes in thinking, between 1790 and 1840 virtually every state from North Carolina northward excluded free blacks from the electorate and included almost all white adult male citizens. The newer states of the West followed suit disfranchising black voters and enfranchising unpropertied white men.

Although historians have rejected Frederick Jackson Turner's contention that the frontier was more democratic than the East, real differences in suffrage requirements divided the West and East. Congress recognized that settlers' problems in securing land titles in newly settled territories when it replaced a fifty-acre property requirement with taxpayer suffrage. The western states went further. Beginning with Kentucky in 1792, all but two western states embraced white male suffrage; in the East, all but two states retained either a property or taxpaying qualification for all or part of the period 1820–1860. Between 1817 and 1821 eight states held constitutional conventions. Of the three eastern states, New York and Massachusetts substituted a taxpayer for a property qualification; the third, Connecticut, retained but reduced its property requirement. Meanwhile, four of the western states—Illinois, Indiana, Missouri, and Alabama—opened the suffrage to white male citizens who met the state-residency requirement. Mississippi included a taxpayer provision but soon eliminated it. Only one western state (Tennessee) required officeholders to believe in God, but North Carolina (to 1835), New Jersey (to 1844), and New Hampshire (through the Civil War) required that officeholders be Protestants, and North Carolina excluded Jews until the Civil War. In addition to insecure land titles, the relatively greater social equality of the frontier and the hope that it would entice new settlers encouraged western creation of a more democratic polity.

In the West and East, political conflict encouraged legislatures and constitutional conventions to expand suffrage rights for white men. In New York, for example, pressure from the

Bucktails' faction led the state convention in 1821 to replace the property qualification with payment of taxes or militia service. Opponents then compelled Bucktails to support a legislative initiative adopted in 1826, for a constitutional amendment enfranchising nearly all white men.

As the second party system emerged in the 1820s and 1830s, legislators and convention delegates reflected their new parties' disagreement about the democratization of political rights. Democrats saw the suffrage as the citizens' weapon against possible governmental tyranny. In most states, Jacksonians combined Revolutionary natural-rights ideology and nineteenth-century racism and concluded that the suffrage belonged to all white males as a natural right. In legislative halls and on the stump, they endorsed white male suffrage (including, in the midwestern states, aliens who established residency and planned to become citizens), free black disfranchisement, and the elimination of property-holding stipulations for officeholders. The Whigs largely accepted republican notions of an organic hierarchical society within which voting was a privilege. Thus, they rejected alien suffrage, but they were more receptive to ballots for free blacks. But by 1850, pressure from Democrats, and the popularity of suffrage expansion as a political issue among the country's already broad electorate, obliged Whigs to celebrate white male democracy during campaigns and to vote for it in the state legislatures. For example, New Jersey's Revolutionary constitution formally required that prospective voters be worth at least £50. In 1807, the legislature had decided that any white male citizen taxpayer was worth £50. Then in 1844, the assembly's Democratic majority dismissed Whig objections and redefined the value of £50 to include all white male citizens who lived in the state for one year. Whigs capitulated; later that year they supported universal white male suffrage at the state's constitutional convention.

Rhode Island's legislature defied the movement toward greater democracy. During the Revolution, the state assembly modified and reenacted its colonial charter as its new constitution. As a consequence, the colonial suffrage qualification of ownership of a freehold worth $134 persisted into the nineteenth century. It became increasingly restrictive as the Rhode Island economy shifted from agriculture toward industry. By the early 1840s possibly more than half of the state's male population could not vote. Rhode Islanders, led by Thomas Dorr (the son of a wealthy merchant), established the Constitutional party in 1834 to campaign for a constitutional convention that would, among other things, grant taxpayer suffrage. Dissension over the presidential election of 1840 shattered the party, but in its place emerged the more radical Rhode Island Suffrage Association, whose goal was white male suffrage. In 1841, in an effort to stem the reform movement, the legislature summoned a constitutional convention elected by freeholders. Dorr in turn invited all male adult residents to elect delegates to an extralegal convention in October. The resulting People's Charter enfranchised white male citizens but limited participation in local financial referenda. The freeholders' convention quickly undermined the Dorrites by democratizing suffrage provisions.

The conflict soon collapsed. In April 1842, Dorr claimed election to the governorship, but he failed to secure control of the state government or support in Washington. When his followers lost a few minor skirmishes, he fled the state, and the Dorr rebellion ended. The rebellion had spurred the democratization of suffrage rights for natives but not immigrants. The new constitution enfranchised native-born Americans, including black men (whom the legislature had disfranchised in 1821), who either paid a dollar tax or participated in the militia and resided in the state for two years (longer than the usual one year). But it retained the $134 freehold for naturalized citizens. The eligible electorate increased by 50 percent and included nearly 70 percent of the adult male population, but Rhode Island still maintained the most-restrictive voting requirements in the country.

## THE CIVIL WAR AND RECONSTRUCTION

The Civil War profoundly influenced thinking about the suffrage and who should possess it, and the locus of responsibility for shaping the electorate. Before 1861 individual states determined suffrage qualifications and required men to vote where they lived. When the war wrenched men from their homes it endangered their voting rights as well as their lives. In response, nineteen Northern and some Southern state legislatures passed laws enabling soldiers to vote in the field. These laws represented the culmination of the antebellum trend that severed the suffrage from its communal moorings and made it a right assumed by the individual and relinquished only by establishing permanent residence elsewhere. The Northern voting acts also had partisan ramifications, for both Republicans and Democrats assumed correctly that soldiers would vote Republican.

After the war, Congress confronted demands for enfranchisement by Southern freedmen. In a society where white men venerated the suffrage, blacks recognized that the right to vote represented the attainment of full citizenship. In the United States, Frederick Douglass observed, "universal suffrage is the ... fundamental idea of the Government, to rule us out is to make us an exception, to brand us with the stigma of inferiority" (Foner, p. 75). Similarly, after the state legislatures ratified the Thirteenth Amendment in December 1865, the American Anti-Slavery Society (instead of disbanding) demanded "No Reconstruction Without Negro Suffrage." And both abolitionists and especially blacks themselves pressured Congress to enfranchise the freedmen.

Partisanship and the struggle over the fruits of victory also induced Congress to enfranchise blacks. Emancipation had ironically threatened to increase white Southern strength in Congress. Until the Civil War, the Constitution's three-fifths clause (counting every five slaves as three inhabitants for purposes of representation and taxation) enhanced Southern representation in the House of Representatives. The Thirteenth Amendment effectively voided the three-fifths clause; therefore, still-disfranchised blacks would increase even further the disproportionate power of white Southerners. Northern Republicans refused to reward the white South (which would surely elect Democratic representatives) for rebellion.

To resolve this dilemma, implement a Republican plan for Reconstruction, and nip in the bud Southern evasion of the implications of the Thirteenth Amendment, congressional Republicans promulgated a Fourteenth Amendment. The apportionment provision offered white Southerners the choice of enfranchising free black men and obtaining greater representation or excluding them and shrinking their congressional delegations. The article prescribed a proportional reduction of representation based upon the percentage of disfranchised male adult citizens. The amendment also barred from public office antebellum officeholders who had sworn loyalty to the United States and subsequently aided the Confederacy.

The convoluted article on suffrage and representation took a halting first step toward black male suffrage, but it antagonized some reformers because it permitted states to disfranchise blacks. It angered Republican women and their allies because it introduced the word "male" into the Constitution and formally excluded women from federal citizenship. And it infuriated Southern legislators, who rejected the amendment. But few whites complained of the exclusion of Native Americans from citizenship, or congressional legislation in 1871 asserting the federal government's right to govern Native American tribes without their direct consent. Not until 1924 did Congress accord Native Americans full citizenship.

Compelled to devise a new Reconstruction plan, Congress passed the Military Reconstruction Act of 2 March 1867. The act placed ten Southern states under military rule and ordered the states to write new constitutions. Congress (overriding President Andrew Johnson's veto) permitted black men to vote for delegates to the state constitutional conventions, required that the new constitutions enfranchise black men, and disfranchised men excluded from office by the Fourteenth Amendment. Enfranchisement, Republican congressmen believed, would enable blacks to defend their other rights, shield themselves from white violence, and create a Republican majority in the South.

The law was enormously important. For the first time, Congress asserted federal authority over suffrage qualifications. The law also made the United States the world's first post-emancipation society to enfranchise and grant political power to newly freed slaves.

Just as the Republican party enfranchised black men in the South, it also sought to remove the political disabilities of the North's small black population. Whereas congressional Reconstruction policy enfranchised blacks in the South, Republican state legislators acted in the North. In 1865, only the New England states (outside of Connecticut) enfranchised black men who met the same requirements as those for whites. New York permitted blacks to vote if they owned a considerable $250 worth of property and met a three-year residency requirement. That year, Republican-dominated legislatures authorized special referenda on black suffrage in Connecticut, Minnesota, and Wisconsin. Voters defeated those referenda and similar proposals in Colorado Territory and in the District of Columbia. Those losses convinced Republicans to retreat; in 1866 only one referendum was held (a narrow defeat in Nebraska Territory). During the 1866 elections Democrats concentrated their campaign upon racist anti–black suffrage appeals; therefore, the Republicans' overwhelming victories persuaded them that white opposition to black suffrage was abating.

Thus, in 1867, Republicans embraced black suffrage in the North and South. All but two state party conventions endorsed black suffrage, and Republican-controlled legislatures authorized referenda in seven Northern states. In addition, Congress made black suffrage a precondition for Nebraska's admission to the Union. Although a large majority of Republican voters supported black suffrage, a minority combined with nearly unanimous Democrats to defeat all of the referenda. Not until November 1868 did voters in Northern states—Minnesota and Iowa—enfranchise black men.

Those defeats forced Republicans to turn to Congress. But they proposed no federal action in 1868 for fear of weakening their presidential candidate, Ulysses S. Grant. After the election of Grant and substantial Republican majorities in Congress, Republicans advocated a constitutional amendment enfranchising black men.

Why did Republican congressmen support a constitutional amendment when a majority of Northern voters opposed black suffrage and when black men already voted in the South? First and foremost, white terrorism of Southern black voters aroused concern about the permanency of the political rights of black men if Southern whites regained power. Furthermore, Republicans believed that if Democrats gained control of Congress they might subvert black-voting rights and that only a constitutional amendment would permanently protect Southern black voters. Second, Republican congressmen recognized that many of their constituents

championed universal suffrage for men. Anything less than a constitutional amendment might alienate the party's core supporters. Third, some Republicans endorsed black suffrage partly because they assumed that newly enfranchised blacks would enhance Republican majorities in the Northern and border states. Of course, Republicans also risked losing racist Republicans to the opposition. Fourth, a constitutional amendment would remove the vexing suffrage issue from the political scene. Every time Republican legislators approved suffrage referenda, their party lost votes. If Republicans could enfranchise blacks in one fell swoop, the question could be settled quickly and permanently.

Representatives and senators debated the language of the amendment throughout December 1868 and January 1869. Radical congressmen sought fundamental suffrage reform. Senator Henry Wilson (R.-Mass.) proposed a comprehensive amendment prohibiting states from restricting voting or office-holding rights because of "race, color, nativity, property, education, or religious belief." More conservative members sought to prohibit states from disfranchising men because of their race or status as former slaves. Such proposals rested on the assumption that voting requirements would remain the domain of the states, but that the federal government would intervene if states devised race-specific laws.

The most conservative version, supported by the party's moderates, succeeded. The proposed Fifteenth Amendment declared: "The right of citizens of the United States to vote shall not be denied or abridged by the United States or by any State on account of race, color, or previous condition of servitude." It also empowered Congress "to enforce this article by appropriate legislation."

By limiting the amendment to voting and race, congressmen hoped to facilitate ratification. But Southern Republicans worried that the amendment's loopholes allowed future Southern white legislators to disfranchise blacks through property and literacy requirements. The negative first section would prevent Democrats, if they regained power, from using the national government or the army to disfranchise blacks on account of race. The affirmative second section provided Republican congressmen with a means of protecting the black vote in the South and scrutinizing voting in urban Democratic strongholds in the North. In sum, the Fifteenth Amendment enfranchised Northern black men, helped protect Southern black men from disfranchisement, and (after its speedy ratification) removed black suffrage as a partisan issue.

The ratification of the amendment produced euphoria throughout the Republican North. Like virtually all Americans, Republicans imputed extraordinary value to the suffrage, seeing it as the linchpin preserving all individual rights and as the acknowledgment of full citizenship in the United States. No wonder that President Ulysses Grant proclaimed that the amendment "completes the greatest civil change and constitutes the most important event that has occurred since the nation came into life."

But the right to vote was meaningless without the ability to exercise it; that required federal intervention. In 1870 and 1871, Congress passed bills prohibiting interference with a man's voting rights on account of his race and provided mechanisms for enforcement in congressional and urban elections. The Enforcement Act of April 1871 banned organizations such as the Ku Klux Klan, who obstructed the exercise of suffrage rights. It enabled the president to declare martial law and suspend the writ of habeas corpus. The Enforcement Act of 1872 authorized electoral supervision in rural areas but gave no enforcement powers to those supervisors.

The enforcement acts applied to local election officials and private citizens as well as the states. But the funds and staff that Congress provided were insufficient for effective enforcement, and the Justice Department was unprepared for its massive task. Even before the U.S. Supreme Court invalidated crucial sections of the acts in 1876, the laws had failed to safeguard black voting rights. Indeed, the federal government spent most of its funds overseeing elections in urban Democratic strongholds.

During the debates over the Reconstruction amendments, Congress considered the voting rights of women as well as of blacks. The woman suffrage movement—founded on the assumptions that the right to vote was the measure of full citizenship, the ultimate right in a republican society, and the means for protecting all other rights—had grown gradually since its inception at Seneca Falls, New York, in 1848. Before the war, suffragists had blamed female disfranchisement for women's many legal disabilities and sought state legislative redress of their grievances. The most receptive assembly, New York's, permitted suffragist Susan B. Anthony to testify before a joint judiciary committee but ignored her plea.

During and after the Civil War, suffragists, who believed that all citizens were entitled to equal rights, had supported emancipation and black civil rights. In 1866, they had formed the Equal Rights Association to promote the voting rights of women and blacks. Suffragists testified before the New York and New Jersey legislatures and persuaded the Kansas legislature to authorize woman and black suffrage referenda the following year. But the New York and New Jersey assemblies rejected their demands, and Kansas voters crushed both suffrage proposals. Thereafter, suffragists looked to Congress in the hope that as Elizabeth Cady Stanton put it, "when the constitutional door is open," women would avail themselves of the "strong arm and blue uniform of the black soldier to walk in by his side."

Republican congressmen disagreed. The Senate initially debated woman suffrage in 1866, when several members unsuccessfully attempted to add women to a bill enfranchising black men in Washington, D.C.; it was the first of many defeats. The Fourteenth Amendment explicitly excluded women from the political community (it reduced representation only if a state deprived "male citizens" of the right to vote); and the Fifteenth Amendment prohibited disfranchisement based on race, color, or previous condition of servitude, but not sex.

The amendments had several profound consequences. First, they spurred a division in the suffrage movement. One group, headed by Anthony and Stanton, rejected the Republican party and its compromise on woman suffrage. In 1869, they formed the National Woman Suffrage Association (NWSA). Others, who acquiesced in the constitutional amendments and worked for woman suffrage within the Republican party, founded the American Woman Suffrage Association (AWSA).

While the AWSA sought state legislative approval for popular referenda to accomplish the same goal, the NWSA took the natural-rights argument to its logical conclusion. Based on the belief that political rights antedated all constitutions and governments and that such rights were inalienable, they reasoned that (despite the language of the recent amendments) female citizens already possessed the right to vote. At the same time, they asserted that the Fourteenth Amendment established the supremacy of national citizenship (which included women) and that the Fifteenth Amendment made the suffrage an attribute of national citizenship. Supported by those arguments, numerous women attempted to vote. Rebuffed by election officials, they sued the officials. Their interpretation of the amendments was rejected by the Republican congressmen who had drafted the amendments and by the Supreme Court in *Minor* v. *Happersett,* 21 Wall. 162 (1875).

## WOMAN AND BLACK SUFFRAGE: AFTER RECONSTRUCTION

Thereafter, Congress and the state legislatures became the main battlegrounds for woman suffrage. The NWSA turned once again to Congress and urged a new constitutional amendment. It also gradually repudiated the natural-rights argument by endorsing and extending the prevalent domestic ideology. The NWSA explained to congressmen that because women differed from men, women voters would make a special contribution to the republic. Thus it now argued that "as woman . . . is now the conservator of private morals, so woman in public life . . . will become the conservator of public morals" (Flexner).

Congress responded, although not the way that the NWSA wished. In 1878, Senator A. A. Sargent (R.-Calif.) introduced the constitutional amendment that would be adopted forty-two years later: "The right of citizens of the United States to vote shall not be denied or abridged by the United States or by any state on account of sex." In 1882, the House and Senate created special committees on woman suffrage, both of which reported favorably. In 1884 and 1886, the Senate repeated the process, and a full debate took place in early 1887, but each time the Senate overwhelmingly rejected it. Committees generally reported out the amendment until 1893, when it disappeared for twenty years.

Meanwhile, state legislatures, responding to pressure from the AWSA, permitted referenda in Michigan (1874), Colorado (1877), Nebraska (1882), Oregon (1884), Rhode Island (1887), Washington (1889), and South Dakota (1890). Supporters were few and poorly financed. They also faced opposition from liquor interests, which feared female temperance activism. None of the referenda succeeded.

Nevertheless, territorial and state legislatures gave the woman-suffrage movement some victories. The Wyoming and Utah territorial legislatures enfranchised women. Wyoming's Assembly apparently thought it would attract female settlers, and Utah's used it to disprove the contention that Mormon polygamy oppressed women.

In many states, legislatures granted women a partial right to vote, especially on matters perceived as extensions of the domestic sphere. The Kentucky legislature enfranchised widows with children in school elections in 1838; the Michigan legislature gave it to all women in 1875, a year after voters defeated a woman-suffrage referendum. In 1880 the New York legislature conferred the local-school suffrage upon women rearing children or paying taxes. Eleven years later the Illinois legislature, after defeating broad suffrage reform, permitted school suffrage. The experience in Michigan and Illinois suggests that some legislatures offered women school suffrage as a sop to the defeated suffragists. By 1890, nineteen states granted women the school suffrage.

The impact of partial suffrage has not yet been gauged by historians, but it surely undermined beliefs about women's incapacity for public life. The logic behind school suffrage could easily be extended to suggest that women, because they were unlike men, could make a special contribution to the polity. Furthermore, because school suffrage represented a legislature's assertion of its power to determine voter qualifications for offices it had created, school suffrage provided the foundation for legislative debates over other partial-suffrage laws. In the 1890s, the Illinois legislature debated but defeated bills to enfranchise women in township, bond, and some city elections. In 1901 the New York legislature permitted women taxpayers to vote in local tax-related elections.

As western and northern legislatures allowed women a toehold in the polity, their southern counterparts devised ways to exclude black men and poor whites, as well as women. The state laws played a crucial role. By themselves, laws restricted voting in many states (five southern legislatures disfranchised blacks without changing their constitutions). Furthermore, the laws facilitated suffrage restriction by limiting the electorate before referenda on constitutional revisions or the election of delegates to constitutional conventions.

Democratic legislators acted for several reasons, virtually all of which revolved around the desire to destroy biracial, anti-Democratic coalitions. Black Belt Democrats, who wrote and vigorously supported the various disfranchising measures, felt most threatened by potential opposition because they represented counties with black majorities. Their apprehensions about a Republican resurgence intensified in 1890, when Senator Henry Cabot Lodge proposed a bill to provide federal oversight of national elections in the South. The bill's introduction frightened southern legislatures into cleaning up their elections by disfranchising blacks legally. The bill's narrow defeat convinced them that northerners would allow them to proceed without congressional interference.

The fears of Democratic legislators escalated as the deepening depression of the 1890s alienated farmers. Dissident Populists, revived Republicans, or often a fusion of the two, attracted more than 40 percent of the popular vote in seven southern states in the early and mid-1890s. In North Carolina a Populist-Republican coalition gained control of the assembly in 1894 and the governorship in 1896. Two years later, massive Democratic violence restored Democrats to power, but to guarantee future victories, the legislature temporarily restricted the electorate to ensure popular ratification of its proposed constitutional restrictions of suffrage rights. The North Carolina experience was only the most extreme; in all of the southern states, no matter how remote the threat to their power, worried Democrats disfranchised blacks and many poor whites.

Southern state legislatures initially utilized discriminatory election laws to exclude potential Republicans—particularly blacks and poor whites—from the electorate. The South Carolina election law of 1882, for instance, required voter registration and reregistration if a voter moved (a situation common among rural blacks). It also established the eight-box provision, with a label on each ballot box revealing the office contested, and enabled election officials to move the boxes around during election day. The provision disfranchised illiterate voters. By allowing local registrars to add the names of men who had failed to register and to read the election-box labels on request, the legislature provided a loophole for poor whites. The successful implementation of the South Carolina system persuaded four other legislatures to enact stiff registration laws and two to adopt multiple-box balloting.

Southern states also imposed both formal and informal literacy tests, through either legislation or constitutional amendment. When the Australian, or secret, ballot was introduced in the United States, proponents advanced it primarily as an anticorruption measure. Seven southern legislatures also enacted the complex secret ballot to disfranchise illiterate and marginally literate blacks and whites. Seven states, through constitutional revisions, also adopted formal literacy requirements (in five states potential voters could substitute property ownership), which usually specified that the applicant read (and, in Virginia, understand) a portion of the state or federal constitution. With local white Democratic registrars implementing the tests, few blacks passed. All but one southern state adopted either a literacy test or a secret ballot; four employed both.

Further, every state, through legislation or constitutional amendment, imposed a poll tax. Unlike the poll taxes of the Revolution and the early Republic, which raised revenue for state and local governments and which inadvertently enfranchised many, Democrats designed the poll tax to bar poor blacks (and sometimes whites) from the polls. Several states magnified the impact of the poll tax by making the tax cumulative for two or three years or, as in Georgia and Alabama, letting it accrue indefinitely. In addition to disfranchising most blacks (who were almost invariably poor) the poll tax in some states also disfranchised as many as 25 percent of the white men.

The states also established small and temporary loopholes for poor, illiterate white men, which were designed to forestall opposition to disfranchisement, not to protect the political rights of poor white men. The grandfather clause (which enfranchised men whose direct ancestors could vote before 1867) and the understanding clause (which theoretically enabled a potential illiterate voter to prove that he understood a section of the state or federal constitution) provided only brief special registration periods ranging from several months to several years. And no state exempted poor whites from paying their poll taxes.

Southern laws and constitutional amendments together successfully circumvented the Fourteenth and Fifteenth Amendments. By disfranchising virtually all black men and many poor whites, they established Democratic hegemony in the region for more than a half century. For those few blacks who could still vote, the right became meaningless when the primary of the dominant state Democratic party became the state's de facto election and when the party (supported by state laws) restricted the primary to white men. In any case, few blacks before the New Deal wanted to support the party of Jefferson Davis.

As southern legislatures and conventions removed many blacks and poor whites from the polity, northern legislators passed laws that aimed to exclude persons deemed undesirable. Just like southern disfranchisers, northern ballot reformers thought of themselves as progressives. Both sought to purify and improve governance and the election process, not broaden democracy. They wanted better, not more, voters. They also yearned to rid the country of ignorant, incompetent, and (often) poor voters (the last of whom were presumed ignorant and incompetent). In the South that group included all blacks and many poor whites; in the North it consisted of urban immigrants and workers.

Therefore, legislatures established ballot laws intended both to purify and to disfranchise. The secret ballot, which eliminated vote buying, also eliminated from the polls illiterates and those who could only read a foreign language. Formal literacy tests, adopted in a dozen northern states by the early twentieth century, disfranchised many more. Legislatures also passed voter-registration laws—as early as 1800 in Massachusetts and in most northern states by 1880—to identify eligible voters, but rendered them ineffective by requiring the state to contest a man's eligibility. New state laws created highly restrictive systems that obliged voters to prove their eligibility.

The theory of disfranchisement—with its emphasis on intelligent voters and clean elections—revealed common ground between the disfranchisers and woman suffragists and encouraged the reunification of the suffrage movement. Many woman suffragists had resented the enfranchisement of illiterate and presumably incompetent voters while women remained disfranchised. Suffragists also shared the disfranchisers' desire for a better electorate, and came to argue (particularly in the South) that white women's votes would neutralize the effects of black suffrage and help clean up the polity. Leaders of both national organizations held these conservative views; only tactical disagreements and lingering personal animosity divided them. After several years of negotiations, the two groups merged to form the National American Woman Suffrage Association (NAWSA) in 1890.

Tactical disagreements quickly resurfaced. In 1893, over the objections of NAWSA president Susan B. Anthony, convention delegates voted to hold the annual meeting in Washington only in alternate years. NWSA regularly lobbied Congress during the annual meeting, and Anthony feared that its convention decision would ease pressure on lawmakers. She was right. Congress continued to hold formal hearings, but no committee made a favorable report after 1893.

Meanwhile, state legislators faced pressure from the NAWSA to approve franchise referenda. Between 1870 and 1910, legislators, the object of some 480 campaigns, authorized seventeen referenda. Woman suffrage triumphed in Wyoming (without a special referendum) in 1890, Colorado in 1893, and Idaho in 1896. Despite the apparently meager results from such great effort, the campaigns provided suffragists with an opportunity to educate legislators about woman suffrage and to keep the issue in the forefront of political discussion.

Legislators found woman suffrage less threatening to men, just as it appeared more important to women. At the turn of the century, women expanded their public roles as domestic demands shrank. More women worked outside of the home, attained an education (increasingly at the college level), bore fewer children, and spent less time rearing those children. Educated middle-class women sought intellectual stimulation outside of the home. They founded innumerable clubs that usually began as literary societies but often turned to social or political activism. They also joined other organizations, especially the Women's Christian Temperance Union, which wove together women's domestic and civic responsibilities. The WCTU's leader Francis Willard declared that women needed to play a public role in order to protect the home and that the domestic experience of women gave them fresher insight than men into many social issues. By portraying the vote as an extension of a woman's domestic obligations, woman suffrage seemed less menacing to those fearful of change. By the early twentieth century, as Nancy Cott has observed, suffragists argued that the vote was "part of women's duties as wives, mothers, and community members."

The legislative triumph of the suffrage movement also resulted from new militant and effective organizations (first at the local and then at the national levels). The tactics of the movement were profoundly influenced by the English suffragettes, especially the Women's Social and Political Union. The WSPU taunted politicians, incited police violence, sought arrest, and conducted hunger strikes in prison. American women then living in England, such as Harriet Stanton Blatch and Alice Paul, compared the vigorous English crusade to the comparatively listless American effort. Upon returning home, in a successful effort to broaden the social base of the middle-class suffrage movement, Blatch founded the Equality League of Self-Supporting Women in New York in 1907. It established strong ties to working-class women and their unions. The League also borrowed English tactics (such as parades and outdoor rallies) and contested the reelection of New York legislators opposed to woman suffrage.

Similarly, Carrie Chapman Catt's Woman Suffrage party of Greater New York (organized in 1909) broke through class and ethnic barriers. In the state referendum campaign of 1915, it directly contacted 60 percent of the registered voters, organized "suffrage days" for different occupational groups, held thousands of meetings, and distributed millions of leaflets. Catt's meticulous and vigorous organization of the New York campaign reflected the dynamism of grass-roots organizations throughout the country. They persuaded numerous legislatures to hold woman-suffrage referenda and won campaigns in Washington in 1910; California in 1911; and Kansas, Arkansas, and Oregon in 1912. Also in 1912 the Illinois legislature enfranchised women for presidential elections. Despite defeats in several states, the movement was building substantial legislative momentum in the states.

Congressmen, too, confronted a newly energized effort for a constitutional amendment. For nearly two decades, Congress had buried the amendment in committees, but congressmen could ignore the issue no longer. NAWSA's Congressional Committee, led by Alice Paul and Lucy Burns, jolted the national organization by adopting British tactics and renewed NAWSA's commitment to a national amendment. But the committee's militancy (it held a widely publicized suffrage march in Washington, D.C., on the eve of Woodrow Wilson's inauguration) soon antagonized the cautious national leadership. In response, Paul and Burns founded the Congressional Union, which formally separated from NAWSA in 1914.

The Union threatened Democratic congressmen. Drawing again upon English methods, the Union held the party in power (in this case the Democrats) responsible for the suffrage and opposed all Democrats—even suffrage supporters—when woman suffrage failed. It organized the National Woman's party (composed only of women voters) in 1916 to challenge Democratic congressional candidates in states where women voted. The fluidity of American party coalitions and the constitutional requirement of a two-thirds majority of both houses compelled bipartisan support for a suffrage amendment therefore thwarted Paul's political strategy. But Paul radicalized the debate, placed significant pressure on Democratic congressmen, energized NAWSA's interest in the amendment, and made NAWSA appear moderate to state and national politicians.

Congressmen and state legislators now became the object of NAWSA's "Winning Plan," a strategy articulated by its new president, Carrie Chapman Catt, in 1916. The plan urged suffragists to keep up the pressure for state referenda. That would increase the numbers of women voters, which would magnify their congressional influence. Already enfranchised women would push their congressmen to support the amendment. And in states where the movement was weakest, suffragists would seek partial suffrage.

The plan worked. In 1916, the Democratic and Republican parties and presidential candidates endorsed woman suffrage (though their state-by-state plan antagonized the suffragists). In 1917, referenda passed in New York, the most populous state, and Arkansas, the first southern suffrage state. The constitutional amendment received a further boost with the entry of the United States into World War I and from Woodrow Wilson's eleventh-hour decision to lend his support. NAWSA's leaders immediately and conspicuously supported the war effort, which allowed them to identify suffrage with American patriotism. Congressional resistance disintegrated. In 1918 the amendment passed in the House but fell one vote short in the Senate. NAWSA then campaigned successfully against several senators opposed to woman suffrage. In 1919 Congress passed the amendment and three-quarters of the state legislatures ratified the Nineteenth Amendment in time for the presidential election of 1920.

During the woman-suffrage struggle, NAWSA largely excluded black women. In response, African American women had founded the National Association of Colored Women in 1896. Exclusion from NAWSA symbolized the double disfranchisement of black women because of their race and sex. Consequently, NACW pointedly advocated political rights for all women and black men.

## THE REENFRANCHISEMENT OF BLACKS IN MODERN AMERICA

Indeed, as white women of the South gained the right to vote, black men sought the restoration of theirs. In 1903 black activist and academic W. E. B. Du Bois had demanded: "Negroes must insist continually that voting is necessary to modern manhood." This insistence influenced the formation and subsequent policies of the National Association for the Advancement of Colored People (NAACP), which Du Bois helped found in 1909. The NAACP

pursued reenfranchisement through federal courts, not in southern state legislatures or Congress, where southerners wielded great power. The NAACP closed loopholes in southern disfranchisement—particularly the grandfather clause—that had permitted some poor, illiterate whites to vote.

But the NAACP gained further opportunities for black participation in 1943 when the Supreme Court (following the NAACP's argument) invalidated the white primary. Because Texas legislators had incorporated the party primary into the public electoral process; therefore white primaries violated the Fifteenth Amendment. The courts also voided southern legislative efforts to circumvent the decision by repealing all laws relating to primaries. Southern blacks, who had identified increasingly with the Democratic party since the Great Depression, now had an incentive to vote; still, in 1947 only about 12 percent of southern adult blacks had registered.

Congress indirectly considered black reenfranchisement when it debated the abolition of poll taxes. U.S. Representative Lee Geyer (D.-Calif.) introduced a bill in 1939 to abolish the poll tax in national elections. Conceived as an effort to enfranchise the poor, not just blacks, the movement gained some success when Congress passed the Soldier Vote Act of 1942, which permitted soldiers to vote in national elections without paying a poll tax. The House also passed bills in 1942, 1943, and 1946 to extend the act to civilians, but southern senators defeated them either by filibuster or successful opposition to cloture. In 1948, President Harry S. Truman called for a national repeal law. Although the House passed the bill, the Senate never considered it. A substantial majority in both houses persistently supported poll-tax repeal; but unlimited debate in the Senate (which permitted the filibuster), the difficult two-thirds requirement to impose cloture shutting off debate, and southern control of key committees, delayed poll-tax repeal for more than a decade.

In the postwar years members of Congress accelerated the drive for black voting rights. Protection of voting and other civil rights would prove that the United States was sincere in its crusade against Soviet Communism. More important, over the previous several decades, millions of southern blacks had moved to northern cities, where they could vote. Northern black voters, in turn, pressured their congressmen to reenfranchise black southerners. But because Democrats also wanted to keep white southerners loyal and Republicans tried to attract them, the civil rights acts of 1957 and 1960, both of which dealt exclusively with voting rights, were weak and largely ineffectual.

President Dwight Eisenhower accepted the federal government's constitutional obligation to safeguard the right to vote. He supported a law permitting the attorney general to seek court injunctions prohibiting state and local officials from illegally interfering with the registration of qualified black voters. An enjoined official who persisted in discriminatory practices could be punished by a judge without a jury trial. The absence of a jury trial was crucial because white-dominated juries would not convict officials for such violations.

Southern senators weakened the law through amendment, not filibuster. They obtained a jury-trial provision in cases where the maximum jail term was greater than forty-five days and the fine more than $300. The act, shepherded through the Senate by majority leader Lyndon B. Johnson (D.-Tex.), also established both the Civil Rights Division of the Justice Department and the independent Civil Rights Commission. The latter became a fierce supporter of black enfranchisement. The Justice Department, hoping to goad southern election officials into compliance by gaining a favorable Supreme Court ruling on the law's constitutionality, pursued only three voting-discrimination cases. The courts accepted the law's constitutionality. Enforcement netted few additional voters, but a registration drive in southern cities increased the proportion of enfranchised black adults slightly, from 25 percent to 28 percent.

Dissatisfaction with the act convinced President Eisenhower to propose additional legislation. Once again, Johnson marshaled the same coalition behind the Civil Rights Act of 1960, which permitted the attorney general to seek injunctions prohibiting discrimination against black voters. If the court found a pattern of discrimination, the judge would allow an attempt to reregister. If rejected again, a court-appointed referee would evaluate black qualifications and oversee registration and voting. Because implementation was cumbersome,

southern judges usually hostile, and county officials still in charge of registration, even vigorous enforcement by the Kennedy administration enfranchised few southern blacks.

The Kennedy administration and Congress also focused their attention on the poll tax, still used by only a handful of states and with few white southern defenders. Congress proposed and the state legislatures ratified the Twenty-fourth Amendment outlawing the poll tax as a requirement in federal elections.

After Kennedy's assassination, his successor, Lyndon B. Johnson, pushed through Congress the Civil Rights Act of 1964, which dealt only incidentally with voting rights. Upon his own election in 1964, Johnson initiated plans to protect voting rights. But massive efforts to enfranchise blacks in Dallas County, Alabama (that included Selma), prodded the administration into early action. When the protests led by Rev. Martin Luther King, Jr., began, only 2.1 percent of Dallas County's eligible blacks were registered to vote. Out of jail and on bail, King met with President Johnson on 9 February to press for voting-rights legislation. He urged protection of blacks in federal and state elections, an end to literacy tests, the weakening of local registrars, and the appointment of federal registrars. The Johnson administration plan generally followed King's recommendations.

The pace of executive and congressional action quickened after Selma police used cattle prods on protesters and a state trooper killed a civil rights marcher in a neighboring county. In response, King announced the Freedom March from Selma to Montgomery on to be held 7 March. State troopers and county police assaulted the marchers as they left Selma and ignited a popular outcry that persuaded Johnson to address Congress on voting-rights legislation.

His bill established an automatic formula for federal intervention. It temporarily prohibited the use of "all educational qualifications" in states with literacy tests and where less than 50 percent voted in the presidential election of 1964 (i.e., Alabama, Georgia, Louisiana, Mississippi, South Carolina, Virginia, and parts of North Carolina). Then, if the Justice Department received twenty complaints or decided independently that intervention was necessary, the attorney general could ask the Civil Service Commission to assign federal registrars. If a state had passed discriminatory election laws in the previous five years, then the state and its localities had to clear all changes in electoral procedure with a three-person court in Washington, D.C.; Congress also required the attorney general to bring suit in federal court to prohibit the poll tax in state elections. The attorney general won the suit the next year.

In early August, both the House and Senate passed the bill by overwhelming margins. On 6 August, a jubilant President Johnson signed the bill into law. By 1 November the Civil Service Commission had appointed federal examiners in thirty-two counties. In Dallas County itself, some 8,000 blacks registered in the first few months after the act's passage.

Five years later, a bipartisan congressional coalition rejected the Nixon administration's effort to enfeeble the act by eliminating the preclearance provision and by nationalizing the act's coverage. The final bill preserved the Voting Rights Act unimpaired, but it also enfranchised eighteen-year-olds, established a national ban on literacy requirements, extended coverage to about ten northern counties, and limited residency requirements for federal elections to thirty days (a maximum extended to all elections in 1972 by the U.S. Supreme Court).

In the midst of the Vietnam War and the vigorous popular protests against it, members of Congress hoped that the enfranchisement of eighteen-year-olds would renew the confidence in the political system that America's alienated youth had lost. Congress therefore revived the long-standing claim that those old enough to fight should be eligible to vote. After the U.S. Supreme Court limited the act's application to federal elections, Congress proposed, and the state legislatures swiftly ratified, a constitutional amendment guaranteeing the eighteen-year-old vote in all elections.

In 1975, President Gerald Ford recommended to a receptive Congress a five-year extension of the Voting Rights Act. Since 1965 the gap between white and black registration had narrowed appreciably, but most members of Congress believed that black-voting rights would not survive without federal supervision. Moreover, they saw enfranchisement as a hedge against a renewal of the black urban violence of the late 1960s. Some members of Congress agreed with Eddie Williams, director of the Joint Center for Political Studies, who said that extension announced to blacks: "Cast a ballot,

not a brick." As if testifying to the legislation's efficacy, many southern legislators endorsed the act; after all, many of their constituents were African Americans. Despite a temporary retreat by the president, Congress extended the act for seven years (to include the legislative reapportionment after the 1980 census), permanently abolished literacy tests, and included language minorities (which added Texas and Arizona to the list).

Whereas objections to the act's extension in 1970 and 1975 stressed discrimination against the South and the preclearance requirement, in 1982 Republican president Ronald Reagan argued that government action had to be discriminatory in intent and not just in effect. In the end, the Congress backed Senator Robert Dole's (R.-Kans.) compromise proposal, which extended preclearance for twenty-five years and reestablished tests for discrimination that existed before the Supreme Court's *Mobile* decision, which required proof of intention to discriminate. The Dole compromise required the examination of the "totality of circumstances" when assessing discrimination. The passage of the extension bill affirmed the late-twentieth-century consensus that the suffrage was a right to which virtually all adult citizens were entitled and which the federal government was obliged to guarantee.

## CONCLUSION

From the founding of the Republic until the Civil War, legislators assumed that the states would determine membership in the political community. During the Revolution, quasi-legislative provincial congresses wrote the constitutions that prescribed suffrage and office-holding requirements. State legislatures remained crucial in the nineteenth century, even as the Civil War nationalized part of the debate over political rights. State legislatures successfully defended the exclusion of women from full citizenship, authorized referenda on black and woman suffrage, granted women partial suffrage, and ratified various voting-rights amendments to the U.S. Constitution. They also helped disfranchise blacks and many poor whites in the South, and numerous working-class natives and, especially, immigrants in the North.

Nevertheless, the Civil War moved the debate over political rights into the congressional arena, where it has remained ever since. By initiating constitutional amendments or passing legislation, Congress was primarily responsible for enfranchising and reenfranchising African Americans, enfranchising women, eliminating the poll tax, and lowering the voting age to eighteen. Although the constitutional amendments prohibited particular kinds of congressional and state legislation (e.g., race- or sex-specific rules), over time Congress has restricted so severely the scope of state legislation that it has effectively made the amendments into grants of rights. Combined with Supreme Court decisions, congressional action has established virtually uniform suffrage qualifications across the nation.

The national and state legislatures and state constitutional conventions did not march along a preordained path to greater democracy. They disfranchised and enfranchised free black men twice, restricted the political rights of many poor native and immigrant white men, and long resisted woman suffrage. When legis-

lators and constitutional convention delegates broadened the political community, they often did so in response to war. During the Revolution many or all of the provincial congresses reduced or eliminated property requirements adopted taxpayer suffrage, disfranchised Loyalists, and enfranchised Jews, Catholics, and (in New Jersey) some women. The political "warfare" of Democrats and Whigs stimulated the adoption of universal white male suffrage. The Civil War nationalized suffrage policy and spurred the enfranchisement of freed black men. World War I accelerated congressional and state adoption of woman suffrage, and the Vietnam War ensured legislative approval of the eighteen-year-old vote. Finally, the Cold War gave urgency to the congressional reenfranchisement of blacks, and warfare in the city streets helped persuade members of Congress to maintain protection of black voting rights. As a consequence, Congress effectively created a political democracy where almost all citizens over the age of eighteen possess the right to vote.

## BIBLIOGRAPHY

### General Studies
It is remarkable that in a country where citizens have long viewed the suffrage as the foundation of American political democracy there is neither a general history of political rights nor a history of legislatures and political rights. The closest modern scholars have come to a general history are two studies, both of which terminate before the Civil War: MARCHETTE CHUTE, *First Liberty: A History of the Right to Vote in America, 1619–1850* (New York, 1969), which is especially valuable for the colonial era, and CHILTON WILLIAMSON, *American Suffrage from Property to Democracy, 1760–1860* (Princeton, N.J., 1960), which studies property qualifications and their demise. JAMES KETTNER's superb *The Development of American Citizenship, 1608–1870* (Chapel Hill, N.C., 1978), places suffrage legislation in the context of a broader history of American citizenship. JUDITH N. SHKLAR, *American Citizenship: The Quest for Inclusion* (Cambridge, Mass., 1991), offers a stimulating, if nonhistorical and partial, analysis of voting rights in America.

### Colonial and Revolutionary Periods
An older work, ALBERT EDWARD McKINLEY, *The Suffrage Franchise in the Thirteen English Colonies in America* (New York, 1905), thoroughly canvases suffrage statutes. ROBERT E. BROWN, *Middle-Class Democracy and the Revolution in Massachusetts, 1691–1780* (Fenwick, W.Va., 1955), argues a doubtful thesis but has stimulated wide-ranging research by others on colonial suffrage. J. R. POLE, *Political Representation in England and the Origins of the American Republic* (Berkeley, Calif., 1966), brilliantly examines suffrage and representation in colonial and Revolutionary America. For a superb analysis of the colonial electorate, see JACK P. GREENE, "All Men Are Created Equal: Some Reflections on the Character of the American Revolution," in GREENE, *Imperatives, Behaviors, and Identities: Essays in Early American Cultural History* (Charlottesville, Va., 1992). ROBERT J. DINKIN, *Voting in Provincial America: A Study of Elections in the Thirteen Colonies, 1689–1776* (Westport, Conn., 1977) and his *Voting in Revolutionary Amer-*

*ica: A Study of Elections in the Original Thirteen States, 1776–1789* (Westport, Conn., 1982), offer much useful information about election practices and laws. WILLI PAUL ADAMS, *The First American Constitutions: Republican Ideology and the Making of State Constitutions in the Revolutionary Era* (Chapel Hill, N.C., 1980), ably summarizes property qualifications for office-holding and voting. Revolutionary legislation on political rights cannot be studied without GORDON S. WOOD, *The Creation of the American Republic, 1776–1787* (Chapel Hill, N.C., 1969), but that work may underestimate the significance of voting rights in Revolutionary America.

### The Early Republic

The fullest account of legislative and constitutional changes is Williamson's *American Suffrage,* listed above, which traces the political struggle to eliminate property qualifications. Also see ROBERT J. STEINFIELD's insightful essay on pauper suffrage, "Property and Suffrage in the Early Republic," *Stanford Law Review* 41 (1989): 335–376. JOHN ASHWORTH, *"Agrarians" and "Aristocrats": Party Political Ideology in the United States, 1837–1846* (London, England, 1983), illuminates party disagreement over the suffrage, and KENNETH J. WINKLE, *The Politics of Community: Migration and Politics in Antebellum Ohio* (New York, 1988), sheds new light on residency requirements. IRA BERLIN, *Slaves Without Masters: The Free Negro in the Antebellum South* (New York, 1975), and LEON LITWACK, *North of Slavery: The Negro in the Free States, 1790–1860* (Chicago, 1961), trace free black male disfranchisement. On the Dorr insurrection, see especially GEORGE M. DENNISON, *The Dorr War: Republicanism on Trial, 1831–1861* (Lexington, Ky., 1976).

ERIC FONER assesses the impact of the Civil War and Reconstruction on suffrage legislation in *Reconstruction: America's Unfinished Revolution, 1863–1877* (New York, 1988). The best study of congressional Reconstruction policy, voting-rights legislation, and the Fifteenth Amendment is MICHAEL LES BENEDICT, *A Compromise of Principle: Congressional Republicans and Reconstruction, 1863–1869* (New York, 1975). WILLIAM GILLETTE, *The Right to Vote: Politics and the Passage of the Fifteenth Amendment* (Baltimore, 1965), the only modern study of the amendment, oversimplifies Republican motivation in his contention that the

party was primarily concerned with gaining black votes in the northern and border states. Gillette's interpretation was first challenged in LAWANDA COX and JOHN H. COX, "Negro Suffrage and Republican Politics: The Problem of Motivation in Reconstruction Historiography," *Journal of Southern History* 33 (1967): 303–330, which emphasizes the moral commitment of Republicans but which rests upon weak evidence. Benedict's *Compromise of Principle,* listed above, briefly but effectively examines how Republicans' moral and partisan commitments shaped the framing of the amendment. See also WILLIAM GILLETTE's able study of congressional efforts to enforce the Fifteenth Amendment, *Retreat from Reconstruction: A Political History, 1869–1879* (Baton Rouge, La., 1980).

### Woman Suffage

A full, analytical legislative history of woman suffrage remains to be written, although JOAN HOFF, *Law, Gender, and Injustice* (New York, 1991), provides a welcome, if controversial, framework for such a history. A good brief introduction to the subject is ANNE FIROR SCOTT and ANDREW MACKAY SCOTT, *One Half the People: The Fight for Woman Suffrage* (Champaign, Ill., 1982). The only comprehensive book, ELEANOR FLEXNER, *Century of Struggle: The Woman's Rights Movement in the United States,* rev. ed. (Cambridge, Mass., 1975), is dated but still useful. ELLEN CAROL DUBOIS, *Feminism and Suffrage: The Emergence of an Independent Women's Movement in America, 1848–1869* (Ithaca, N.Y., 1978), carefully examines the early years of the movement. More insightful is her excellent essay, "Outgrowing the Compact of the Fathers: Equal Rights, Woman Suffrage, and the United States Constitution, 1820–1878," *Journal of American History* 74 (1987): 836–862. For the early twentieth century, see AILEEN S. KRADITOR, *The Ideas of the Woman Suffrage Movement, 1880–1920* (New York, 1965) and especially, NANCY F. COTT, *The Grounding of Modern Feminism* (New Haven, Conn., 1987). STEVEN M. BUECHLER, *The Transformation of the Woman Suffrage Movement: The Case of Illinois, 1850–1920* (New Brunswick, N.J., 1986), offers an important analysis of one state. CHRISTINE A. LUNARDINI, *From Equal Suffrage to Equal Rights: Alice Paul and the National Woman's Party, 1910–1928* (New York, 1986), assesses the history of an organization that had a significant impact on Congress. See also Mari Jo Buhle and Paul Buhle, eds., *The Concise History of Woman Suffrage: Selections from the Classic Work of Stanton, Anthony, Gage, and Harper* (Champaign, Ill., 1978), an abridgement of the notable work by Elizabeth Cady Stanton et al., *The History of Woman Suffrage,* 6 vols. (New York, 1881–1922).

### Black Disfranchisement

C. Vann Woodward, *The Strange Career of Jim Crow,* 3d rev. ed. (New York, 1974), is the starting point for the study of post–Civil War black disfranchisement. But the seminal study of partisan motivations for suffrage restriction is J. Morgan Kousser, *The Shaping of Southern Politics: Suffrage Restriction and the Establishment of the One-Party South, 1880–1910* (New Haven, Conn., 1974). See the two careful studies of national suffrage policy-making by Steven F. Lawson: *Black Ballots: Voting Rights in the South, 1944–1969* (New York, 1976), and *In Pursuit of Power: Southern Blacks and Electoral Politics, 1965–1982* (New York, 1982).

See also Congress in the Federalist-Republican Era, 1789–1828; Federalism and American Legislatures; Legislatures and Civil Rights; Legislatures and Gender Issues; The Modernizing Congress, 1870–1930; and Representation.

# LEGISLATURES AND SOCIAL WELFARE POLICY

## Glenn C. Altschuler

Promoting the general welfare has always been recognized as a basic responsibility of legislatures in the United States. Welfare, of course, is a broad term that can include public education, restrictions on the use of alcohol, agricultural subsidies, and even highway construction. As economist, sociologist and Yale professor William Graham Sumner put it more than a century ago, "In truth, the human race has never done anything else but struggle with the problem of social welfare. That struggle constitutes history, or the life of the human race on earth."

In one approach to social welfare, legislators often prescribed norms of behavior in order to promote order, virtue, and industry. Temperance bills, restrictions on pornography, and compulsory attendance in public schools were designed to prevent individuals from developing self-destructive habits that, sooner or later, would be costly to society. Advocates of these measures believed that morality could be legislated for and that moreover, a more wholesome environment was the best guarantee of equality of opportunity.

Of course, legislators accepted responsibility for material as well as moral needs. Less clear was who qualified for relief, what goods and services they should receive, and what impact assistance would have on self-reliance. Equally controversial was the level of government—local, state, or federal—deemed most appropriate to provide assistance to the poor.

If direct relief and cultural regulation were the social welfare programs of choice in the seventeenth, eighteenth, and nineteenth centuries, social insurance has been the policy preferred by many legislators in more recent times. Formulated in response to industrialization, the national integration of the economy, and a growing sense that unemployed workers were often casualties of business cycles, social insurance sought to prevent people from becoming impoverished rather than rescue them from destitution. Unlike means-tested programs—which single out the poor—social insurance has recommended itself as an earned entitlement, conferred on a worthy clientele— the involuntarily unemployed, the disabled, the retired, widows, mothers with dependent children—all of whom are eligible because they (or their spouses) paid taxes or made financial contributions to the system.

The political, economic, and ideological context in which debates over social welfare legislation occurred have remained remarkably stable over time. Behind welfare were humanitarian concerns, often rooted in religious faith. But self-reliance, an American axiom, suggested that few people deserved to feed at the public trough. Any able-bodied persons willing to submit themselves to the discipline of the market could make it, and children, the elderly, and the disabled should be cared for by their families, with assistance, if necessary, from private charity. In providing access to public education, a social welfare responsibility they accepted, many legislators believed they had made it possible for any hardworking American to succeed; to do more was neither prudent nor wise.

Constituent pressure tended to reinforce these ideological considerations. Legislators were loathe to antagonize tax-conscious voters from the middle class, who had far more political power than the poor. During depressions, poor people took to the streets, demanding food and jobs. Typically, legislators responded to this political pressure, which was largely absent during normal economic times, but the expansion in relief was temporary. By and large, political considerations prompted penury, and policies designed to regulate the behavior of the poor, whose plight, most Americans believed, was their own fault.

Impossible to ignore, moreover, was the view that relief might weaken the economy by removing workers from the labor force. Welfare policy, the business community argued, should push the poor toward gainful employment; relief should never be more than subsistence. It may well be an oversimplification to assert that legislators consciously expanded relief programs in times of mass unemployment to preserve order and then, when outbreaks of labor turmoil subsided, contracted welfare, expelling those needed to populate the labor market. But it is the case that to ensure that able-bodied workers would not choose welfare, legislators used the principle of "less eligible": the conditions of relief must be less desirable than the conditions of the lowest paid work. In the South, fear of social unrest added force to the argument for laissez-faire: public welfare might weaken control over a subservient African American labor force. Throughout the country, well-organized groups representing these economic interests have had substantial influence over social welfare legislation.

In the United States, then, legislators have been more reluctant than their counterparts in Western Europe to appropriate funds for direct relief and to adopt social insurance. By invoking traditions of local responsibility and states' rights, they intended not only to limit federal involvement in welfare, but to restrict eligibility, retain incentives to work, and keep benefits low. To be sure, the balance has shifted to some extent. With the New Deal the initiative for welfare legislation passed to the federal government. Advocacy groups, for social insurance and to a lesser extent relief, press legislators to do more. Nonetheless, self-reliance, cost and social control, expressed in the metaphor of local political responsibility, set the terms of the legislative deliberations, much as they have for three centuries.

## THE COLONIAL ERA

Inside the intellectual baggage that English colonists brought to North America was an assumption that government should play an active role in promoting the general welfare. Colonial assemblies supported the efforts of town meetings and selectmen (chief administrative authorities) to punish Sabbath-breaking,

blasphemy, and to remove children from the homes of irresponsible parents. Massachusetts in 1647 required the establishment of a grammar school in every town with one hundred or more households; acting on behalf of the common good the colony also saw fit to punish usury and define a just price for goods in the marketplace. Legislators in every colony believed, moreover, that individuals in distress had a claim on public assistance, and government was obliged to supplement private charity.

Between the late sixteenth and early seventeenth centuries, the British Parliament set out principles to deal with dependency in the Elizabethan Poor Law, which became the model for welfare legislation in the English colonies. In directing local authorities to discriminate between the worthy and unworthy, the statute established three categories of paupers: children, the incapacitated, and the able-bodied. The first two including the elderly and the physically disabled were to be assisted in their homes, while the able-bodied were to be given degrading tasks that would encourage them to seek employment. The poor law defined relief as a local responsibility, to be funded by a tax on householders. This provision encouraged magistrates to see to it that parents provided for their children and vice versa. Not surprisingly, the harshest treatment was reserved for those not settled in the community: vagrants could be committed to a house of correction, or whipped, branded, stoned, and even put to death if they refused to work.

The English poor laws seemed particularly relevant in the colonies, which had isolated, self-contained communities and lacked well-endowed private institutions to dispense charity. Among the legislatures to acknowledge responsibility for the poor in the seventeenth century were Plymouth in 1642, Virginia in 1646, Connecticut in 1673 and Massachusetts Bay in 1692. Assemblies, it is important to note, passed enabling legislation: the administration and financing of poor laws remained with the towns.

Although a monetary inconvenience, the poor seemed to many colonists an inevitable component of a hierarchical society and were therefore not wholly responsible for their condition. Great care was taken, for example, to board the mentally ill at public expense with relatives and to apprentice pauper children to families who would teach a trade. Less sympathetic to outsiders, legislators and magistrates conspired to prevent an influx of indigent strangers. In Plymouth, the poor-relief statute applied only to those who lived in a community for three months or more. The Rhode Island Assembly authorized town officials to expel nonresident vagrants, and virtually every colonial legislature permitted the "warning out" of strangers.

By the middle of the eighteenth century, as economic depression swelled the ranks of the unemployed, and a series of wars left widows and orphans in their wake, poor-law expenses increased alarmingly, especially in the cities where relief climbed to between 10 and 35 percent of municipal expenditures, the largest single item in the budget. A few legislatures responded by approving the construction of poorhouses, where presumably, costs would be easier to control than with outdoor relief. For this reason, the Pennsylvania Assembly in 1756 allowed officials in Philadelphia to build such a facility.

## THE ANTEBELLUM ERA

When the American Revolution ended and depression receded, however, local government again seemed able to handle poor law expenses. Despite the general welfare clause of the United States Constitution (Article I, Section 8), the federal government played a limited role in social welfare. In the Northwest Ordinance of 1787, and then in legislation establishing new territories, Congress set aside land that could be sold to endow a school fund. And by the early nineteenth century, the national government took over from the states financial support for disabled veterans, and the widows and orphans of men in the armed forces. With these exceptions, most congressmen regarded welfare as the domain of local government.

So too did state legislators, who were nonetheless compelled by the movement of people in the aftermath of the Revolution to care for indigent Americans who were not settled in any community. In New York, a state body called the Committee on Superintendence of the Poor assisted people dislocated by

war, and in 1796 the legislature allocated funds to New York City "for the maintenance and support of such persons as shall not have gained settlement in the state." Although these appropriations were extended to other cities as well, they constituted an episodic response to the problem of the "strolling poor," and one not adopted outside of New York.

Between 1820 and 1850, momentum built for comprehensive changes in many institutions in the United States, including the system of government relief. Reformers drew on the Enlightenment and Romanticism to argue that God was benevolent and planned for the salvation of all people; that Nature was beneficent, providing the pattern which people could use to structure their society; and that human beings were virtuous, unless corrupted by their environment. Using instinct and reason, men and women could control their destiny. With this optimistic worldview, reformers scrutinized political, social, and economic institutions in order to liberate individuals. They pushed for legislatures to enact penal reform, extend the right to vote, liberalize divorce laws, allow women to own property and to use the asylum as the means to reduce or even eliminate pauperism.

No longer convinced that poverty was inevitable or the poor innately depraved, reformers argued that, given the favorable position of labor and abundance of land in the United States, no healthy person need be dependent. In the wholesome environment of a poorhouse, the poor could rediscover the will and acquire the skills for self-reliance. Since poverty was a social problem, a social solution was required.

The legislatures of Massachusetts and New York became the pioneers in the institutionalization of poor relief, but, in effect, subordinated the reform agenda to traditional concerns about expenses and distinctions between worthy and unworthy paupers. In 1821, the Massachusetts Assembly asked an investigative committee, chaired by the lawyer and political leader Josiah Quincy, to report on the condition of the poor and the administration of relief. New York followed suit with a committee under Secretary of State John N. V. Yates. In seeking to relieve rather than reclaim the poor, Quincy and Yates insisted that public and private charity encouraged vice. Only in the controlled setting of a poorhouse could the disabled, insane, and elderly receive humane treatment, and the able-bodied be removed from temptations and taught discipline.

In response to Yates's report the New York legislature mandated that one or more poorhouses be constructed in each county and that all recipients of public relief, except those too ill or infirm to move, be sent to these institutions. By 1835, all but four of the state's fifty-five counties had complied. In Massachusetts sixty towns built new almshouses between 1820 and 1840 and many others refurbished existing buildings. By 1850, states in New England, the Middle Atlantic, the Middle West and even parts of the South made incarceration the main, if not the only, component of relief.

Although the desire to rehabilitate was sincere, legislators clearly supported institutional care because it was economical. In poorhouses, inmates could grow their own food and sell the surplus. Expensive litigation between counties over nonresident poor would also be eliminated. It is important to remember that state legislatures made no financial commitment to poor relief nor did they set standards for care. Left to their own devices, local officials rarely erected well-ordered establishments or hired professional staff. Poorhouses became custodial facilities keeping chronic paupers out of sight and mind, or clearinghouses, where strangers could be encouraged, in violation of state law, to leave the county. Occasionally legislative committees documented the deplorable conditions in state institutions, where inmates suffocated in summer and froze in winter, but these reports did not result in another round of reforms.

Unwilling to take money from the state treasury to aid able-bodied paupers, legislators in the antebellum era did appropriate funds for specialized institutions for indigent mentally ill, blind, and orphans. Local government did not have the resources to address their needs, many recognized, nor were there enough of them in any single community to make an institution cost-effective. Nonetheless it took the indefatigable advocacy of philanthropist and reformer Dorothea Dix to persuade lawmakers that neither private philanthropy nor local government could adequately treat the mentally ill. Pleading passionately that the number of dependent insane was more than twice as large as the total capacity of the three mental institutions in Massachusetts, Dix won approval of a bill to enlarge the state's facilities. She then took her show on the road to a dozen other states, including Kentucky, Georgia, Virginia, Mississippi, Louisiana, and South Carolina. In the "decade of victory," between 1843 and 1853, nine legislatures founded state hospitals.

In fact, she almost succeeded in getting the national government involved. Some precedents did exist. In 1819 Congress granted 23,000 acres of public land to the Connecticut Asylum for the Deaf and Dumb, a private institution, which realized $300,000 when the land was sold. In 1826, the state-run Kentucky Deaf and Dumb Asylum received a similar appropriation. Dix pressed Congress to use this approach in all the states and mobilized support from religious leaders, journalists, and organizations such as the Association of Medical Superintendents of the Insane. After six years of delay, Congress passed a bill—only to have President Franklin Pierce veto it. A strict constructionist, Pierce articulated the theory of limited government associated with the Democratic party throughout the nineteenth century. The President argued that in making grants to the Connecticut and Kentucky asylums, Congress had overstepped its authority: "If Congress has the power to make provision for the indigent insane . . . it has the same power for the indigent who are not insane." The Constitution did not make the federal government "the great almoner of public charity throughout the United States." Congressional Democrats helped sustain Pierce's veto, keeping the federal government to a limited role in social welfare.

The same concern for local autonomy and fiscal prudence constrained legislative provisions for public education. No colonial assembly, not even Massachusetts', mandated that towns provide free schools for anyone who wished to attend them. Thus, a crazy quilt of district schools, charity schools, denominational institutions, and private academies persisted well into the nineteenth century. Proposals for a national university, and for free common schooling (introduced into the Virginia legislature by Thomas Jefferson and the Pennsylvania Assembly by the physician and educator Benjamin Rush), failed to pass. The legislature of New York in 1795 appropriated

$50,000 per year for common-school committees that agreed to match at least half the allotment with local funds, but did not renew the law five years later, when doing so involved levying a property tax.

In the 1830s and 1840s, common-school reformers, usually with ties to the Whig party, appealed to state legislators for funds for district schools, a longer school term, consolidated school districts, new high schools, and an office of superintendent of education to establish standards for schools throughout the state. They argued that public support of education was necessary to guarantee an informed citizenry and unify a diverse nation of immigrants, many of them Irish and Catholic. An engine of social mobility for the talented, education also provided discipline for men and women who would be engaged in wage labor, either in farms or factories.

Opponents of state funding, invariably Democrats and or rural representatives, praised local schools for meeting the educational needs of young men and women, while encouraging thrift as well as parental participation. Skeptical of the argument that because they provided social insurance, public schools should be supported from general taxation, they preferred rate bills (i.e., parental fees). Centralization, they predicted, would be expensive, elitist, and authoritarian.

The reformers prevailed, except in the South, but only after a long struggle. In Massachusetts, the legislature in 1840 barely defeated a bill to abolish the Board of Education and dismiss its secretary, Horace Mann. Legislators recommended the abolition of districts in 1853, required their abolition in 1869, permitted their reestablishment in 1870 and abolished them again in 1883. When Democrats controlled the legislature in Connecticut in 1842 they abolished the board, dismissed its secretary Henry Barnard and repealed district consolidation. In New York and Vermont, lawmakers created the position of county superintendent in the 1840s, then reversed their decision amidst criticism that it was an unnecessary expense.

The seesaw dipped and rose in the Midwest as well. Ohio Whigs in 1838 succeeded by one vote in creating the office of state superintendent of education, but when in 1847 the legislature recommended centralization, few counties complied. Only in 1853 did Ohio enact a comprehensive school-reform law that required establishing free schools which were to be funded through local taxes. In Michigan the territorial legislature required towns to maintain schools, but did not prohibit them from charging fees to parents. Any town, moreover, could opt out of the law by a two-thirds majority vote. The Michigan constitution provided tax-supported free schools, but the legislature reauthorized rate bills in 1839. As late as 1860 a local district system survived in Michigan.

Throughout the South the legislatures were controlled by localists. Mass education there seemed to many to be social dynamite, exploding the natural hierarchy of plantation society. Even Whigs were unenthusiastic about common schools. An uncertain economy, resistance to taxes, sparse population, and preoccupation with tariffs and slavery, contributed to legislative apathy. Thus, despite vigorously attacking Virginia, "the banner state of ignorance," the legislature satisfied itself in the 1840s with a voluntary system of taxes for schools in counties where two-thirds of the voters approved. In Georgia, the legislature established a fund for pauper schools and academies and in 1837 passed a common-school law, albeit without mandating local taxation, only to repeal it following the depression late in the decade. Between the 1840s and 1850s, lawmakers permitted counties to found schools and tax them; only 18 of 132 counties did so. As elsewhere in the South a majority of Georgia legislators remained convinced that learning brought the masses more anxiety than enjoyment because it encouraged them to view their stations in life differently.

Although by no means universally accepted, public education was the great exception of the nineteenth century, the one social welfare program that passed muster in most state legislatures. Many Whigs, Know-Nothings, and Republicans tried to supplement classroom instruction in morality and discipline, not by spending more money, but by prescribing and enforcing norms of behavior. As bourgeois individualism began to replace republicanism in nineteenth-century America, colonial legislation punishing blasphemy and Sabbath-breaking seemed, to some, anachronistic. Two events gave new life to proponents of moral legislation. In emphasizing the immediate eradication of sin, the religious revivals known as the "Second Great Awakening" challenged the faithful to fight alcohol, slavery, and war. When attempts at moral persuasion failed, Protestant zealots turned to the legislatures. The immigration of millions of Germans and Irish, many of them Catholic, between the 1840s and 1850s galvanized others to seek statutes to preserve democratic institutions and Protestant values. In fact, the threat was cited by common-school reformers, who promised that schools could assimilate foreigners, and Know-Nothings, who tried to restrict immigration through congressional legislation.

With the exception of slavery, which could be acted upon only by Congress or the legislatures in the South, regulation of the liquor traffic was the politically salient moral issue of the nineteenth century. Supporters of restrictions on the sale and consumption of liquor pressed legislators with petitions and testified to the devastating social impact of drink on families, the workplace, and crime-ridden cities. In 1851, the legislature of Maine acted and within four years Massachusetts, Vermont, Connecticut, Rhode Island, New Hampshire, Michigan, Indiana, Iowa, Pennsylvania, New York, New Jersey, Delaware, and the territories of Minnesota and Nebraska passed temperance bills of some sort. In these states, where Whigs, Know-Nothings, and later, Republicans dominated, there were leaks-in-the-dike, concessions to the Democratic minority or the principle of local option. Even in Maine, which threatened three-to six-month jail sentences, towns could appoint bonded agents to sell liquor for medicinal purposes and beverages in the original packages were exempt from prosecution. Elsewhere legislation had yet more loopholes. As the temperance crusaders prepared their next campaign, however, Southern states seceded and legislatures prepared for war.

## THE CIVIL WAR AND ITS LEGACY

For a time the Civil War seemed likely to break the hold of localism on social welfare legislation. A consensus developed around the needs of families of disabled or deceased veterans, that the states should appropriate funds on their behalf. In the North, Republican-dominated legislatures set up permanent boards of state charities to coordinate welfare programs. Massachusetts led the way in 1863, followed by Ohio, New York, Illinois, Wisconsin, Michigan, Kansas, and Connecticut.

Even more important, a war to establish the supremacy of the national government was certain to alter Congress's role in social welfare, especially when the removal of Southerners from the House and Senate between 1861 and 1865 gave Republicans a working majority. They moved quickly to promote public education. The Morrill Act of 1862 granted to each loyal state 30,000 acres for each senator and representative then in Congress for the purpose of endowing at least one agricultural college. When the war ended Republicans pushed through a bill establishing a federal department of education.

Radical Republicans tried to go further. They proposed but could not pass federal aid for public schools based on the percentage of the population that was literate; thus, in effect, redistributing funds from more-wealthy to more-impoverished states. Charles Sumner (R.-Mass.) sought not only to prohibit segregation in schools but to require Confederate states to establish free public schools. However, Democrats and some Republicans balked at legislation by the bayonet, and in 1867 Sumner's amendment failed by a 20–20 vote. Although the Radicals failed to secure a congressional commitment to education as a basic civil right, their message was not lost on Southern politicians, who inserted provisions for free schools in state constitutions and appropriated funds for them in Reconstruction legislatures.

The most pressing problem facing Congress, of course, was the welfare of the several million African Americans, recently freed from slavery. The Thirteenth, Fourteenth, and Fifteenth Amendments to the Constitution, Republicans believed, constituted protection against state discrimination and the denial of voting rights. To help in the transition to freedom, Congress in 1865 set up the Bureau of Refugees, Freedmen and Abandoned Land. Authorized to dispense relief for one year, the Freedmen's Bureau had its life extended for six, despite fierce opposition from President Andrew Johnson, a Democrat, who deemed welfare a local matter. A magnet for hatred in the South, the bureau distributed rations, leased abandoned land to African American farmers, maintained hospitals, and provided financial aid for African American schools. As the influence of the Radical Republicans declined and Southerners returned to Congress the bureau lost favor in Washington. In 1872 it was liquidated.

The most ambitious federal welfare program in the nineteenth century was the provision of pensions to Civil War veterans and their families. Pension legislation depended on Republican control of the House and Senate. Able to raise tariffs on woolen and cotton goods, the Republicans had a budgetary surplus, which they swiftly applied to soldiers and their dependents.

For the next four decades Congress considered bills to extend benefits, as veterans' families who had missed filing deadlines, made claims. Despite unanimous opposition from southern representatives, Congress in 1879 passed the Arrears of Pension Act that granted back payment to all claimants based on their discharge date. The Grand Army of the Republic, boasting 215,000 members in 1885, became a pension lobby, pressing Republicans to do more. In 1886, Democratic president Grover Cleveland vetoed a bill granting pensions to all veterans who could not work, regardless of the source of their disability, but the Grand Army of the Republic and its congressional allies responded with more-ambitious legislation, which made pensions available to all 62-year-old veterans, whether they were disabled or not, and their families. By this time pensions cost $92 million or 27 percent of the federal budget, and some northern manufacturers also fearful of the impact of even higher tariffs on the export market, withdrew from the old-age pension coalition. In 1890, Congress passed the Dependent Pension Act, a compromise measure (still opposed by every southerner), that extended eligibility to every veteran who was unable to do manual labor. Only in 1906, when veterans were dying out and costs declining, did Congress define sixty-two as the age for permanent disability.

At its peak the Civil War pension system assisted 60 percent of the dependent elderly, all in the North, and this experiment in social welfare, conducted under unusual political circumstances, confirmed southern antipathy to the nationalization of relief.

With the exception of Civil War pensions, Congress's interest in social welfare receded between 1870 and 1900. Assistance to African Americans was not politically advantageous to Republicans in the North, where racial indifference or hostility was the norm, or in the South, where Democrats regained control as Reconstruction ended. As Radicals Charles Sumner and Thaddeus Stevens (R.-Pa.) died, Republicans turned their attention to economic growth. Tariffs and grants of land to railroads constituted their welfare program, as self-reliance, local responsibility, and even states' rights achieved bipartisan consensus, especially with reference to relief. When Grover Cleveland, in the midst of the depression of the 1890s, insisted that it was the business of the people to support the government, not of the government to support the people, he articulated the party line of Republicans as well as Democrats.

In this climate of laissez-faire individualism, even guardianship of Native Americans, the federal government's most venerable welfare policy, changed dramatically. To open up western land to white settlers, while making Native Americans self-reliant, Senator Henry Dawes (R.-Mass.), proposed to set aside 160 acres of tribal land for every Native American family, 80 acres for every single person and sell the rest, the proceeds to be held in trust by the government. The Red Homestead Act of 1887 conferred United States citizenship on those who opted for allotment, separated from their tribes and "adopted the habits of civilized life." Congress, however, was not fully prepared to relinquish guardianship. To prevent Native Americans from precipitously disposing of their land, the bill made title to it inalienable for twenty-five years. Moreover, a House-Senate conference committee eliminated a requirement that a majority of the adult male population consent to the destruction of a reservation. In essence the Dawes Act of 1887 was an eviction notice, a land grab, and "a mighty pulverizing engine to break up the tribal mass." In time, the bill's advocates promised that education and the responsibilities of property ownership would teach Native Americans to care for themselves. Despite its defects and delays, the Dawes Act celebrated itself as self-liquidating legislation, the best kind of welfare program.

As the federal government removed itself from social welfare, state legislators groped for ways to protect citizens, especially when put at risk by the impersonal forces of industrial capitalism, without destroying individual or entrepreneurial initiative or spending large sums of money. The answer, as William R. Brock has shown, was an expansion of state agencies, charged to investigate conditions related to the health and safety of the population. Agencies in many states deflected criticism, but in others they built support for legislation to protect the deserving poor. In the area of public health, the acclaim given the United States Sanitary Commission, a voluntary organization, for its work in army camps and field hospitals during the Civil War, helped persuade Massachusetts legislators in 1869 to create the first state board of health; by the end of the century almost every other state had followed suit. More controversial were laws regulating the workplace. In 1867 the Massachusetts legislature removed children under ten from the labor force. Other states were reluctant to pass a blanket prohibition. Throughout the North and Midwest, before 1900, laws regulating work hours for women and children, safety and fire rules, factory inspection, employer/employee liability, and sanitation in the workplace, were introduced and, more often than not, were defeated or diluted.

Legislators had to navigate between two powerful arguments before voting on these bills. Reformers argued that in an industrial society the invisible hand of the law did not adequately protect workers or consumers; under its police powers, which were recognized in common law, the state had the authority to weigh property rights against the public welfare. This proposition was challenged in the nineteenth century, by legislators and judges who claimed that the Fourteenth Amendment to the Constitution protected the economic liberty of corporate persons. Long before the case of *Lochner* v. *New York,* (1905), freedom of contract held a privileged place in legislative assemblies. Since business interests had greater influence in state capitols than unions or consumers, reformers focused on bills to protect women and children, seeking a consensus around the importance of the family, and hoping that even businessmen would not resist appeals to patriarchy.

Less amenable to compromise, however, were bills to prescribe values and control behavior. Labor strife and the influx of immigrants from Asia and southern and eastern Europe in the last third of the century ignited fears of class conflict, race suicide and the end of Protestant hegemony. These concerns contributed to a movement to control the undesirable elements in the United States. An army of organizations ranging from the American Protective Association to the Women's Christian Temperance Union endorsed laws to outlaw the sale of liquor, restrict the distribution of pornographic materials, control the curriculum of the public schools, criminalize abortion and sterilize the mentally handicapped.

In important ways, moral legislation complemented health and safety bills. Both fed on anxiety about the future of the family. To combat the influences of urban, industrial America, purity crusaders, led by Anthony Comstock, secretary of the Society for the Prevention of Vice, sought to ban sexually suggestive materials from general circulation. In 1873, Congress made it a federal offense to sell or give away any indecent book, pamphlet or drawing. Many states restricted the activities of minors. In Connecticut children under the age of sixteen were barred from dance halls, concert saloons, and roller-skating rinks, unless accompanied by an adult. (Restrictions on social behavior, it should be added, were not always limited to minors. Debates on whether to allow Sunday baseball grew so fierce in Illinois and Iowa, that legislative wags in each state, in a futile effort at *reductio ad absurdum,* offered amendments to add draw poker to the list of Sabbath-breaking activities.)

The most effective way to superintend the moral health of children, of course, was through the schools. To counter the seductive evils of the city and the tendency of parents to send their children to work, many legislatures passed truancy laws. More controversial were school bills aimed at immigrant children, such as the Bennett Law in Wisconsin of 1890, which ordered that instruction be given in English. Before 1917, seventeen state legislatures passed English language statutes, but it took the xenophobia generated by World War I to raise the number to thirty-five. Some legislatures delved into the curriculum prescribing courses in civics or Bible reading while Arkansas, Florida, Mississippi, Oklahoma, and Tennessee banned Darwin from the classroom. Behind all this legislation was the conviction that the state had a special obligation to provide children with the material and spiritual tools in which to become productive members of American society.

Restrictions on abortion were also justified as legitimate exercises of the state's power to regulate health and safety. Usually initiated by state medical societies, antiabortion bills sailed through state legislatures, aided considerably by high-profile comparisons of the declining birthrates of Protestants and the prolific performance of Catholics. Between 1866 and 1877 alone, thirty state and territorial legislatures passed restrictive abortion statutes; by 1900 every state but Kentucky had a law on the books. In Illinois, for example, a bill with a penalty of between two and ten years in prison (and trial for murder if the woman died) for anyone performing an abortion, unanimously passed both houses of the legislature in 1867.

More controversial were measures to restrict the sale and consumption of alcohol. Prone to compromise, legislators recognized that virtually no bill short of prohibition would satisfy the purists, while any statute energized the opposition. The politics of avoidance, however, did not work either. In Missouri, zealots sent 47 prohibition petitions to the legislature in 1881, 245 in 1883 and 761 in 1887. When no action occurred, they joined the Prohibition party—and got the attention of mainstream politicians.

As with other moral legislation, Republicans carried the spears for temperance. In Illinois, Wisconsin, and Iowa according to one study, GOP lawmakers supported a stringent policy on liquor, while 16 percent of Democrats took this position. Elsewhere, however, especially in rural areas and among Fundamentalists, temperance cut across the political parties. In the Solid South, alcohol, Darwin, and pornography led Democratic legislators to make exceptions to the precept—stateways do not make folkways.

Temperance advocates, many of them women, framed the issue as a social welfare as well as a moral imperative, pointing to the impact of drink on the family and the community, while opponents stressed the threat to individual liberty and local autonomy. In most sections of the country neither side could quite prevail. Illinois and Wisconsin revised their saloon laws in the 1870s but remained local option states. In

each session between 1887 and 1895, Illinois legislators debated license laws, while in Wisconsin, in the "most sensational floor fight" of the year, assemblymen who had recently banned state aid to agricultural fairs where liquor was sold, battled in 1895 over laws prohibiting sales of intoxicants in asylums for disabled veterans. Even an amendment to the Constitution did not end the conflict over prohibition, as events following the ratification of the Eighteenth Amendment in 1919 demonstrated. Until its repeal in 1933, Prohibition divided legislators in many states.

## THE PROGRESSIVE ERA

During the first two decades of the twentieth century, Progressives addressed the social welfare issues raised by industrialization and urbanization. Although Progressives differed sharply with one another, especially over moral legislation, and probably did not come together in a movement, they did have several ideas in common. Progress was possible, they believed, because human beings were shaped at least as much by environment as by heredity. Thus antisocial behavior could be reduced by improving schools, getting rid of ghettos and providing jobs. In order to cope with the economic interdependence of industrial capitalism, Progressives believed that an ethic of cooperation, stressing mutual interests, must replace competition. To bring about this change, the tasks of government must perpetually increase. To Progressives, government worked best as an umpire, acting on behalf of the common welfare, by mediating disputes between contending interests. Reluctant to interfere too much with free enterprise, Progressives were willing to use government to offset the most flagrant excesses of predatory capitalism. Although motivated in part by fears that class warfare would erupt if there was not some attempt to improve conditions, Progressives were cautious, sometimes conservative reformers.

Well represented in both political parties and throughout the country, except the South, Progressives, like their predecessors in the late nineteenth century, concentrated on laws to protect the health and safety of workers and consumers. The Public Health Law of 1913 in

New York State, for example, gave a public health council the power to devise a sanitary code for the state and enforce it.

With reforms that impinged directly on the economy, Progressives moved more slowly than their counterparts in western Europe. Compelled to seek alliance with large corporate interests, who were sufficiently concerned about stability in their industries to accept additional costs associated with regulation, Progressive legislators overcame opposition from small businesspeople and enacted bills to outlaw child labor and require minimum safety standards in most states in the North, the Midwest, and the Far West. Much more bitterly contested was minimum-wage and maximum-hours legislation, even when Progressives limited themselves to women and other groups in need of protection.

Workman's compensation was also shaped to meet concerns raised by employers. In introducing the issue in state legislatures, Progressives cited a report detailing accident rates among steel, railroad, and mine workers in Allegheny County, Pennsylvania between 1907 and 1908. Of 526 deaths and 509 injuries, few could be attributed to employee carelessness. The report and others like it resulted in a public outcry for protection for injured workers. As court settlements increasingly favored employees, employers supported compensation legislation that would control costs and deflect negative publicity. Between 1909 and 1920, forty-three states enacted compensation, but every legislature rejected Progressive proposals that full health-care costs and two-thirds of their former wages be included in the package, along with suggestions by union leaders that the injured employee be given a choice to accept low but fixed compensation or sue. Compensation statutes, according to one observer, established payment schedules covering no more than one-fourth of the costs actually incurred. Progressives succeeded in establishing the principle of social insurance, but they were hostages to the power of business interests in the legislatures.

That legislators were wary of the economic impact of social legislation becomes clear in an examination of health insurance and unemployment compensation. In Massachusetts an unemployment-insurance bill, requiring contributions from employers, employees, and the state government, was introduced into the legislature in 1916, but quickly died when the business community lined up to denounce compulsory action. A similar bill in Illinois failed even to reach a legislative committee. With the participation of the U.S. in World War I, the problem of unemployment was less of an issue. After the war, opposition from employers, commercial insurance companies, and some unions (opposed to government taking over a service they provided), as well as the decline of the political power of Progressives led to the question of unemployment compensation being taken off the legislative table. Not until the Great Depression did Wisconsin enact the first unemployment bill.

Health insurance faced the same formidable phalanx of opponents—insurance companies, employers, labor unions—and a new and increasingly powerful foe, the American Medical Association, which vilified the proposals as a form of socialized medicine that was made in Germany during World War I, and made in Russia in the postwar era. In 1920, health-insurance bills were defeated in New York and California, bringing an end to the momentum for other forms of social insurance as well. A few senior citizen pension bills were enacted in the 1920s, but they lacked any real substance.

A different coalition surfaced against mothers' pension bills which were the centerpiece of Progressive social welfare legislation. A White House conference, convened by President Theodore Roosevelt in 1909, provided the impetus for mothers' pensions, by recommending that public aid be given to fatherless families. While considerable support developed for aid to widows, many charitable organizations and individual social reformers denounced pensions for impoverished divorced, deserted, and unmarried women. Government money, it was argued, should not go to the undeserving poor nor should it be unaccompanied by supervision through home visits; moreover, the program might provide an incentive for single motherhood. It was also argued that the proposed legislation constituted an intrusion into local responsibility for relief. Thus, although forty states enacted legislation of some sort that pertained to this issue, by 1919, with only Georgia and South Carolina failing to act by 1935, many bills limited their coverage to widows only. Delegated judges and county administrators were empowered to decide who was worthy of assistance. The programs remained quite small, both in benefit levels and in the percentage of female households assisted (less than 5 percent by one estimate). Once they passed the law, mothers'-pension advocates paid little attention to administration or adequate financial support.

At the national level, as well, the legislative achievements were largely symbolic. That Progressives had to fight fiercely to fashion majority support in Congress for legislation is testimony to the power of localism and the ideology of self-reliance. It took them twelve years to overcome the resistance of business interests and persuade Congress in 1912 to create the United States Children's Bureau. With an initial appropriation of $25,000, and no administrative powers, the bureau collected data on the nation's youth. Its chief, Julia Lathrop, aware of the difficulty of persuading Congress to restrict child labor, concentrated on collecting data on infant mortality. One of its major studies found shocking rates of infant mortality and the number of women who died in labor.

The report led to a proposal, introduced into Congress in 1918, for government grants-in-aid to states promising a matching contribution to be applied to public-health nursing and education, outpatient clinics, and examination of maternity homes. The Sheppard-Towner bill was criticized by business groups and medical organizations as an attempt to subject youth to communist principles. Thomas Reed (D.-Mo.) charged on the floor of the Senate that if passed, "female celibates would instruct mothers on how to bring up their babies" and would receive the authority "to look over the nation's birth lists, check some off and say 'let's take charge of this or that baby.'" The opposition bottled up the bill for three years, but in 1921 the Infancy and Maternity bill passed, providing an annual appropriation of $1,252,000 (and an additional $50,000 to the Children's Bureau to administer the program). During the depression, Congress cut off the funds for the program but, in a modest way, the federal government had entered the field of child welfare and public health.

In addition to mothers and children, Progressives sought protection for consumers, arguing that in the age of industrial capitalism the principle of let the buyer beware was inade-

quate. Consumers had no way of discerning the contents of a can of food and there were no meaningful state laws to protect them. National standards for food, including labeling, actually appealed to some corporate executives who thought legislation might drive their less scrupulous competitors out of business, and boost the export trade by reassuring Europeans that they were purchasing wholesome products. Many food processors and distributors, however, opposed any legislation or preferred bills that banned poisonous ingredients but exempted other ingredients from labeling requirements. The Wholesale Growers of Chicago, for example, testified at a Senate hearing that the public deemed glucose "something vile and unfit for food" and would not buy products that contained the sweetener if it appeared on a label. The National Association of Retail Grocers, the Cream of Tartar Baking Company, and the blended-whiskey industry agreed at committee hearings that labeling was a mistake. During the period 1902–1905 a powerful trio of Republicans, Nelson Aldrich of Rhode Island, Orville Pratt of Connecticut and John Spooner of Wisconsin, used a variety of parliamentary maneuvers to block consideration of William Hepburn's (R.-Iowa) bill, which they deemed "imperfect," "ill-considered," in need of "revamping in the interest of the liberty of the citizen."

States'-rights Democrats in the South joined conservative Republicans in opposing a pure-food bill. Pretty soon, Ezekial Candler (D.-Miss.) guessed, a secretary of agriculture "will say what kind of clothing we shall wear in summer or winter, what kind of horse you should drive. . . ." Why burden the federal government "with little police matters all the local communities can better attend to," William Adamson (D.-Ga.) asked. "The federal government was not created for the purpose of cutting your toe nails or corns."

Twice a bill passed the House only to die in the Senate, and it took the public furor aroused by the publication of Upton Sinclair's *The Jungle* (New York, 1906), a devastating indictment of the meat-packing industry, to get pure-food legislation to the desk of President Roosevelt. The bill passed by Congress in 1906 was considerably weaker than the one proposed by Hepburn, but it did require the labeling of food, including alcohol, and drugs, and contained branding specifications that constituted a "complete knock-out" for patient medicines.

The Jungle had an even more-direct impact on legislation to insure that meat products were fit for human consumption. Interested in the issue before Sinclair's book appeared, Albert Beveridge (R.-Ind.), moved quickly to capitalize on the aroused sentiments of the public by introducing legislation requiring that all meat products be inspected and dated. According to the senator, the measure was "the most pronounced extension of federal power in every direction ever enacted."

Although a few of the largest producers welcomed inspection as essentially a government-sanctioned advertisement that would assure domestic and European customers that American meat was safe, most packers and livestock owners opposed the Beveridge bill. They claimed that to fund inspectors from a fee levied on packers for every animal examined was to add financial injury to insult. With the knowledge that some legislation was inevitable, the meat barons lobbied members of the House of Representatives, who succeeded in eliminating the requirement that canned meat be dated and stipulated that the government pay the inspection bill. In conference, House members refused to yield, and, eventually, the Senate relented. "We have met the enemy and we are theirs," Porter McCumber (R.-N.Dak.) glumly concluded, "indemnity, $3,000,000." Nonetheless, both the pure-food and meat packing bills were significant first steps in establishing national standards to protect the welfare of consumers.

When the United States declared war on Germany in 1917, the reach of government grew longer, at home as well as abroad, prompting some Progressives to prepare a more ambitious list of social welfare legislation, including an insurance program for soldiers and some experiments in public housing. However, the Progressive coalition split on the issue of civil liberties during wartime was, by the 1920s, weakened by and, in some cases, defeated as a result of factionalism. In the anti-Bolshevik, laissez-faire climate of the Harding and Coolidge presidencies, social legislation in Congress tended to take the form of immigration restriction. When agricultural interests, after several tries, mustered majorities for the McNary-Haugen bill, whereby the government would purchase surplus commodities to stabilize prices, President Coolidge vetoed the measure. In the "prosperity decade," if Congress kept out of the way, there might just be a chicken in every pot and two cars in every garage.

In state legislatures the 1920s was not an inactive period for social welfare. During the period 1920–1931, state and local appropriations for education increased from $1,705 to $2,311 million, on highways from $1,294 to $1,742 million and, even more dramatically, on hospitals from $200 to $349 million, and on public welfare from $119 to $444 million. In many areas of concern New York led the way. The legislature passed a minimum-wage law for women. One of three states (California and Wyoming were the other two) with a mandatory senior citizen pension, the Empire State by 1931 assisted more than 34,000 elderly citizens. Even more far-reaching was New York's Public Welfare Law of 1929, which replaced one hundred fifty overlapping "poor" laws with a statute that attempted to remove some of the stigma attached to relief. Under the 1929 law, wherever possible, relief helped people remain in their homes. Although welfare remained the financial responsibility of towns and counties, the state set the standards for care and replaced elected overseers of the poor with appointed public welfare professionals. New York was in the vanguard, but reformers hoped that legislators in other states would assist the indigent in other ways.

## THE NEW DEAL AND THE GREAT SOCIETY

During the Great Depression unemployment rates of 25 percent or more overwhelmed the public welfare capacity of the states. In most legislatures, representatives from agricultural areas, which were more insulated from unemployment than metropolitan centers, had enormous political influence. They recognized that voting for higher taxes to pay for relief or public works jobs was political suicide; and in any event taxes could not yield sufficient revenue without damaging the recovery. Even those legislatures that consented to borrow at high rates quickly exhausted the resources available to them to meet the crisis.

# LEGISLATURES AND SOCIAL WELFARE POLICY

As in previous years, New York committed more public funds than any other state. In 1931, with an appropriation of $20 million, the legislature established a Temporary Emergency Relief Administration (TERA). Mandating that home relief be sufficient to cover food, fuel, clothing, and shelter, the bill allowed localities to recover 40 percent of outlays for relief, while committing the state to pick up all the expenses for approved public works projects. Cities and counties could only refuse to comply with state standards if they refused aid; if a county opted for state funds, every town within it was obliged to go along and a grant of discretionary power to TERA officials, finally, helped to pressurize local welfare officials into responding more adequately to the needs of the poor.

By the end of 1931, twenty-five legislatures had set up state agencies to administer funds, but more often than not relief efforts floundered for want of money and a commitment to usurp local authority. In Pennsylvania, the legislature appropriated some money for relief but levied no new taxes, forcing governments to choose between borrowing or reducing other expenditures. It gave the Department of Public Welfare the authority to distribute money, but did not invest it with the power to regulate its use. Thus local overseers continued to administer relief. Governor Gifford Pinchot concluded that the bill was "about the worst and most slipshod measure I have ever had to handle." In Illinois, to allow rural townships to avoid having to support poor people concentrated in urban areas, the legislature passed the Finn Act in 1931, ending county contributions to general relief. When assembly members from Chicago and Cook County, Ill., pressed for more funds, the legislature voted to adjourn. Only after the governor called them back into session, did both houses pass a bill creating the Illinois Emergency Relief Commission. In California and Michigan as well, legislatures accepted centralism piecemeal, invariably attaching terms like temporary and emergency to relief bills.

However, as they did so they looked to the federal government, with its broad power to tax and borrow, for help. Congressional initiatives, however, contended with the certainty of a presidential veto. Although Hoover approved $45 million for livestock, he opposed an additional $25 million to feed farm families. He vetoed a $2.6 billion federal public works program sponsored by Representative John Nance Garner (D.-Tex.) and Senator Robert Wagner (D.-N.Y.). In 1932 the president agreed to a bill to create a Reconstruction Finance Corporation, but since it provided loans rather than grants, state participation was minimal. However, for the most part opposition from Republicans and southern Democrats kept social welfare legislation far short of majority support. During the 1930–1931 session ten bills, many of them grants of relief to areas hardest hit by the depression, sank without a trace.

With the election of Franklin D. Roosevelt in 1932, the equation changed. With a heavily Democratic Congress, the president seized the legislative initiative in his first hundred days in office. Widespread disorder, in the form of rallies, marches, food riots, rent strikes, occupation of vacant buildings, and looting increased the pressure for government action. Deferring to Roosevelt's popularity and the severity of the crisis, Congress passed virtually all New Deal relief proposals, sometimes only hours after they rolled off the presses. The most significant welfare bills of the first New Deal were: the Federal Emergency Relief Act (FERA), a $500-million unemployment relief package of grants to states, which empowered federal officials to make discretionary appropriations, demand improvements in state and local practices, withhold money if compliance did not follow and, under extraordinary conditions, seize control of relief operations in a state. The Civilian Conservation Corps was set up to employ young men on reforestation and fire control. Also established under Roosevelt's leadership were the Public Works Administration, to provide jobs in depressed industries; the Civil Works Administration (CWA), a broadly based public works program (employing more than four million people by 1934), with relatively high wages set according to skill and geographical area; the National Youth Administration, to create part-time jobs for students; and the Farm Security Administration, to assist farmers and migratory workers.

That this avalanche of legislation passed both houses of Congress underscores the political impact of the depression. This legislation's subsequent fate demonstrates that the triumph of centralization was, at best, temporary. To keep the unemployed from suffering the stigma of relief, the CWA eschewed a means test for employment. Within two months Congress compelled CWA administrators to hire only those who could demonstrate dire need. The program's insistence on wages negotiated through collective bargaining and its assumption of administrative control over the projects it funded, principles that were disliked in the extreme by southern Democrats, contributed to a severe cutback of funding in early 1934. The Federal Emergency Relief Act (FERA) experienced similar problems. Its controversial 30 cents per hour minimum wage, which was higher than many private-sector rates, especially in the South, was rescinded in November 1934. Moreover, throughout the country, state governments refused to proceed with the FERA regulations. In North Carolina, the legislature refused to spend state money on relief, even in the face of an ultimatum from Harry Hopkins, the director of the FERA: no appropriation, no discretionary grant. Reluctant to impose any taxes, the Illinois legislature agreed, under pressure, to a gross-receipts levy on public utilities, one-third of it set aside for relief. Although the amount was woefully inadequate, FERA grants resumed because Hopkins was unwilling to punish the poor in order to get a state to cooperate. Few states joined with Massachusetts in refusing to set up a separate emergency-relief agency or acquiesce to FERA control of relief, but the agency met fierce opposition almost everywhere, and Roosevelt's decision to phase it out in 1935 was a bow to political realities. The Works Progress Administration (WPA), which replaced the FERA, was a grants-in-aid program that allowed state and local government to plan and administer projects, ban public works that competed with local business, target wages below private-sector rates and, in effect, abandon national minimum standards for relief. Throughout the depression, Congress cut the WPA and tried to force workers into the private sector. Despite the "alphabet" relief agencies (referring to agency acronyms), the New Deal brought no permanent changes to the public welfare system.

The most enduring legislative achievement of the New Deal was the Social Security Act of 1935. The bill combined contributory insurance and public assistance, directed at retired workers, the unemployed, senior citizens who were not eligible for pensions, and the blind. Initiated by President Roosevelt, who was pushed toward social insurance by the popular Townshend Plan and the Share the Wealth platform of Senator Huey Long (D.-La.), the legislation was developed by the Committee on Economic Security, a group convened by executive order. Sponsored in the Senate by Robert Wagner (D.-N.Y.) and in the House by David Lewis (D.-Md.), Social Security prevailed by votes of 77–76 and 371–333.

Although the final tallies were lopsided, the Social Security Act was a compromise measure designed to placate southern Democrats and business-minded conservatives. Financed for the most part through a regressive payroll tax, the unemployment-compensation provision contained benefits for a relatively short period (usually sixteen weeks), that were aimed primarily at stable long-term participants in the workforce. In most areas the maximum pay was set at $15 per week. The statute through its exclusion of agricultural workers and domestics, mollified southerners, who feared that federal law would be used to compel equal treatment of African Americans. Most importantly, unemployment compensation ceded control to the states in setting benefit levels, conditions, and administrative practices.

Although taxes for senior-citizen insurance were uniform throughout the country, the statute (at the insistence of Senator Harry Byrd, D.-Va.) allowed states to set eligibility requirements that were more exclusive than those implied by the "guidelines" in the statute. Businesses, however, were less concerned than with unemployment compensation about the impact of old age insurance on labor markets, and so resistance to it by the business community was minimal. Both provisions were sold to the public as contributory insurance and not relief in order to preserve the appearance that the scheme would cover all expenses, not funded by Congress, through general tax revenues.

Although social insurance was the cornerstone of this legislation, the direct-relief provisions commanded more of the attention of legislators. After all, benefits from senior citizen insurance and unemployment compensation would not be available for years, while provisions for Old Age Assistance and Aid to Dependent Children (ADC) would be implemented immediately. Thus the House Ways and Means Committee elevated these provisions to Title I of the long bill and not a single legislator spoke against the grant of funds to the states (a matching federal dollar for each state dollar, up to a maximum of 15). Southerners, however, succeeded in protecting states' rights in the legislation. They eliminated requirements that states provide a "reasonable subsistence compatible with decency and health" as well as a provision that relief be administered through a single state authority. State and local government set eligibility standards and benefit levels as they always had. With ADC, Congress insisted that states rather than localities administer funds, but did not encourage participation. As late as 1939, ten states did not utilize ADC appropriations. In addition, Congress permitted states to use "suitable home" and "employable mother" regulations to restrict eligibility.

During the depression, then, Congress did make the federal government responsible for several categories of poor or potentially poor people, thus creating the framework for social welfare legislation over the next half century. However, built into that framework was considerable latitude for states and localities to distinguish between the deserving and undeserving poor, and to set benefits in accordance with the prevailing market for low-skill labor. With the exception of some retired workers, recipients of aid or "the dole" continued to be stigmatized, and the dole scorned in Franklin Roosevelt's terms, as a "narcotic, a subtle destroyer of the human spirit."

In the three decades following the passage of the Social Security Act, the Congress consolidated and cautiously expanded social welfare programs. To be sure, by paying the tuition of World War II veterans, the G.I. Bill of Rights revolutionized access to higher education, but as we have seen, soldiers were considered a special class entitled to exceptional treatment by the federal government. Opposition to health care and food stamps exemplified the limits of legislative tolerance for relief and social insurance. In 1945, President Truman proposed compulsory sickness insurance, despite objections from the American Medical Association that the bill marked the first step toward

fascist totalitarianism. Fearful of postwar recession, federal deficits, and constraints on free enterprise, Congress shredded Truman's health-care proposals. It was only slightly more receptive to food stamps. Distributed at the beginning of World War II in Europe, when export markets collapsed and surplus commodities were available, food stamps disappeared in 1943. The next year Senators Robert La Follette (R.-Wisc.) and George Aiken (R.-Vt.) proposed a new program, aimed at millions of nutritionally deprived Americans. Denounced by southern Democrats and conservative Republicans the bill was defeated by a 29–46 vote. Despite repeated efforts by urban liberals in the 1950s, food-stamp proponents did not overcome opposition in Congress and the Eisenhower administration. Even the initiatives of John F. Kennedy encountered a farm bloc insistent that food stamps boost agricultural demand and that recipients pay an amount equal to the average monthly food expenditure for their income level.

Unwilling to extend the New Deal, Congress between the 1940s and 1950s forged a bipartisan consensus to retain existing social insurance programs. In 1950, it voted to bring into the Social Security system eight million workers, most of them self-employed, and boosted benefits by about 80 percent. By making Social Security a nearly universal program, Congress insured not only that recipients would not be stigmatized, but that taxpayers would support a plan from which they expected to draw benefits. Social Security was well on the way to becoming an enormously successful antipoverty program for senior citizens as well as a sacred trust, invulnerable to swings in the economy or party politics. Significantly, under the Republican President Eisenhower, Congress passed further amendments which lowered the minimum age for benefits to sixty-two, and created insurance for permanently disabled people between the ages of fifty and sixty-four.

With the Great Society programs of the 1960s the responsibilities of the federal government for social welfare took a quantum leap forward. The centerpiece of the Great Society was the civil rights legislation of 1964 and 1965, which outlawed discrimination on the basis of race in places of public accommodation, provided equal opportunity for workers in firms employing more than twenty-five people, and guaranteed federal government enforcement of the right to vote. As part of the "war on poverty," Congress also passed an Economic Opportunity Act, aimed at illiteracy and unemployment, a Mass Transportation Act, the first large scale grant of aid to elementary and secondary schools, the first federal government scholarships to college undergraduates, Medicaid grants to states for health services for the poor, Medicare for senior citizens, and a Model Cities Act to rehabilitate the slums. Whereas representatives in the 1950s had felt constrained to defend the use of federal funds for an interstate highway as crucial to the national defense, supporters of the Great Society insisted that the national government played the essential role in providing justice and equal opportunity for all.

Lyndon Johnson had unique advantages in guiding Great Society legislation through Congress, benefiting from the goodwill bestowed upon him after John F. Kennedy's assassination. He was also a brilliant tactician, an expert on the procedures and personnel of the House and Senate, as well as compellingly persuasive in one-on-one meetings. "Lyndon got me by the lapels and put his face on top of mine and he talked and talked and talked," one representative recalled. "I figured it was either getting drowned or joining." Most telling, however, was the political climate of the mid-1960s. The civil rights movement discredited states' rights, and ignited a brief period of liberal activism. In the landslide election of 1964, moreover, Johnson brought huge Democratic majorities to the House, 294–140, and the Senate, 68–32. Southerners could no longer block legislation without nearly unanimous support from Republicans. Urban liberals seized the moment, changing the rules of the House to make it possible to dislodge bills from the Rules Committee after twenty-one days. Equally significant, the traditional ratio of three members of the majority party to two of the minority on each committee was abandoned in favor of a ratio reflecting the strength of each party in the House as a whole. Johnson exploited these opportunities, which he knew would not last, to build a welfare state not only "for the desperate but for those who are already capable of helping themselves."

Most popular with Congress were the social insurance programs of the Great Society, although deference to business lobbies continued to express itself in amendments to administration bills. Medicare is the best example. Unable to secure passage of national health insurance for the working population, liberal Democrats settled for Medicare to cover people who had already retired and Medicaid for all those on social welfare. In both programs, the government reimbursed doctor and hospitals according to their "reasonable costs." Thus, as Edward Berkowitz has pointed out, Congress purchased medical care without trying to control it.

Like Social Security, Medicare was popular with middle-class voters. Legislators supported programs which spread benefits among these constituents, sometimes at the expense of the poor. Far more money was spent on social insurance in the Great Society than the means-tested relief programs of the war on poverty. That the two could be in conflict is evident in the Elementary and Secondary School Education Act (ESEA) of 1965, which was originally aimed at children from families with annual incomes below $2,000. Since 80.6 percent of low-income children lived in 31.8 percent of the nation's public school districts, aid might have been targeted to those districts. Instead Congress agreed on a formula that made 95 percent of the school districts eligible for federal funds and allowed local officials to define the educationally deprived students who needed help. Under ESEA two-thirds of the children who received assistance were not economically disadvantaged, one-half were not low academic achievers, and 40 percent were neither.

Although the political payoff for supporting social insurance was substantial, reservations about welfare programs persisted. With the experiments in "maximum feasible participation," slipped into the Economic Opportunity Act, congressional support evaporated almost immediately. Community action produced the popular Headstart program, but also the more controversial Welfare Rights Organization, legal services and birth control clinics. Local politicians complained that they were bypassed in favor of ad hoc, radical minority groups in the neighborhoods. Tenant unions and voter registration drives brought "Karl Marx to Syracuse," the mayor charged. Occurring at the same time as urban riots, Black Power rhetoric and a white backlash, this struggle to control funds was resolved in 1967 by a combination of administrative fiat and congressional directives which ensured that elected officials of government take over community action programs.

At the same time, Congress attempted to adjust welfare benefits to encourage the poor to return to basic values. In 1967, grants to Aid to Families with Dependent Children (AFDC) where the father had died or was unemployed remained open-ended, but Congress froze the appropriation for cases attributed to desertion or illegitimacy. To make sure that welfare did not become a way of life, Congress used a carrot as well as a stick. Before 1967, for each dollar welfare recipients earned, their government check was reduced by one dollar. By legislating for a so-called "earnings disregard provision," Congress allowed mothers on welfare to keep the first $30 they made each month, and one-third of the remainder of their earnings.

By the late 1960s and for the next two decades the perception that relief discouraged individual initiative dominated legislative debates. Congress set up the Work Incentive Program (WIN) in 1967. Under WIN, every able-bodied adult was given an opportunity to acquire vocational skills and work experience. When the voluntary approach failed to produce results, Congress passed the amendment of Aid to Families with Dependent Children (AFDC). Drafted by Senator Herman E. Talmadge (D.-Ga.), the amendment required that all able-bodied AFDC recipients, except those responsible for children under six, register for Work Incentive Program (WIN) services. In order to qualify for continued funding, AFDC program administrators had to spend at least one-third of their budget on training and placement. Although WIN's impact was limited, Congress continued to tie federal aid to systematic efforts to obtain work. In breaking the cycle of poverty, Senator Russell Long (D.-La.) insisted, "You can't put a value on those children seeing a mother get up at 5:30 A.M. to go to work."

Congress's emphasis on "workfare," however, should not obscure the fact that the war on poverty institutionalized federal funding for goods and services for the needy that were supplemented by state and local appropriations. In addition to well-known programs like the Jobs Corps, school lunches, and subsidies for low-rent housing, Congress established health centers for migrant workers, and nutrition programs for senior citizens. As if to demonstrate the validity of Lyndon Johnson's iron triangle, moreover, community action caseworkers, legal services, subcabinet level bureaucrats, and congressional subcommittee members formed a cadre of federally financed advocates of the poor. Thus between 1968 and 1973, despite an electorate increasingly hostile to welfare, congressional spending on means tested programs grew at a whopping average of 12.9 percent per year. Although appropriations for the AFDC leveled off, funding for food stamps and Medicaid continued to increase. Congressional grants-in-aid encouraged activity in many state legislatures, which were in any case responding to the stress on liberating personal and collective selves so characteristic of the 1960s (with implications, of course, for abortion, equal rights for women, and gay rights). Restrictions on eligibility for welfare were relaxed and benefits raised, in some states far in excess of federal standards. By the end of the decade, proponents of the view that welfare was the exclusive responsibility of local government were clearly on the defensive.

That Richard Nixon initiated an extraordinary expansion of social welfare, while denouncing Great Society "big spenders" and "welfare frauds," is one of the more intriguing mysteries of recent years. Not surprising, certainly, was the bidding war between the president and Congress over Social Security benefits. In 1972 benefits went up by 20 percent; two years later Congress boosted them by another 11 percent, while "indexing" the program with an automatic cost of living adjustment whenever the annual rate of inflation rose by 3 percent or more.

More puzzling was endorsement of programs aimed directly at the poor. Although Nixon vetoed a Comprehensive Child Care Act that appropriated billions of dollars for preschool, day care and nutritional programs, bipartisan support led to the passage of the Local Fiscal Assistance Act, which provided block grants to local governments for low-income housing and job training, an Earned Income Tax Credit, allowing poor families with dependent children a refund of 10 percent of their earnings, a Comprehensive Employment and Training Act, that subsidized public service jobs for the unemployed, and a liberalization of eligibility for food stamps, which also made state participation mandatory. In a dramatic reversal of Nixonian New Federalism, moreover, Congress in 1972 assumed complete financial responsibility for Old Age Assistance, Aid to the Blind, and Aid to the Permanently Disabled programs of Social Security, while establishing uniform eligibility standards and a fairly adequate monthly income. The Supplemental Security Income Program in essence nationalized public assistance to the unemployable poor.

Several factors may account for the receptivity of the president and Congress to this legislation. In many ways the 1960s continued throughout the Nixon era. Demanding assistance as a right and not a privilege, organizations like the National Coordinating Committee of Welfare Rights Groups kept the pressure on with protest marches, sit-ins, and school and rent boycotts. With sympathetic liberals bringing their case to a Democratic House and Senate, Richard Nixon may have pressed Republicans in Congress to cooperate, both to broaden the electoral base of the GOP and to preempt more far-reaching legislation. Most of the president's proposals, it is important to note, were grants of money to states and individuals that bypassed (and were designed to weaken) the Washington welfare bureaucracy. Nixon, often called the American Disraeli, may have intended to remove social welfare as a Democratic issue, while breaking one side of the iron triangle.

It was Congress, however, that balked at the most ambitious of Nixon's welfare initiatives, the Family Assistance Plan (FAP), whose defeat underscores the fact that the Great Society had not overcome hostility to assistance to the able-bodied poor. Under the plan, drafted in 1969 by Daniel P. Moynihan, executive secretary of the Council on Urban Affairs and special assistant to the president, every unemployed family of four would have an income floor of $1,600 per year. The working poor would be entitled to this sum as well, until the family income reached $4,000. An array of regulations to compel recipients to work accompa-

nied the establishment of this guaranteed annual income, no doubt to mollify skeptical representatives and more affluent voters. Indeed, in introducing the Family Assistance Plan (FAP), President Nixon mentioned work incentives sixty times in a 35-minute speech.

For very different reasons conservatives and liberals in Congress denounced FAP. To the Right the idea of guaranteeing an income was anathema, and the proposal to shift responsibility from states and localities an abandonment of federalism. Estimated to cost $4 billion per year, the proposal was a budget-buster. To those on the Left, FAP was woefully inadequate ($2,000 below the official poverty line), and significantly less than the welfare allotment in most states outside the South. If it passed, state legislatures might reduce their payment scales to conform to the federal standard. FAP's emphasis on work, liberals argued, ignored the fact that the vast majority of poor people were young, old, or sick, already employed at subsistence wages, or were single mothers. At a time when unemployment was 6 percent and rising, the Family Assistance Plan seemed paltry and punitive, likely to reinforce stereotypes; thus, not worth supporting even to establish the principle of a national guarantee of income.

Although FAP passed the House, it stalled in the Senate. During Finance Committee hearings in the spring of 1970, John Williams (R.-Del.) used charts prepared by the Department of Health, Education, and Welfare to demonstrate that under FAP a welfare mother in Chicago who earned $720 per year ended up with $6,128 in cash, public housing, food stamps, and medical care, while a mother who earned $5,560 received a total of only $6,109. In short the initiative left a working mother $19 behind her lazy counterpart. That FAP might encourage a man to refuse work infuriated Senator Talmadge: "So he could do a little casual labor on somebody's yard from time-to-time and maybe sell a little heroin or do a little burglary and he would be in pretty good shape, wouldn't he." The "people's hearings" chaired by Eugene McCarthy (D.-Minn.) in the fall turned into a public relations disaster for FAP proponents, when militant welfare mothers assailed the work requirement and the inadequate annual allotment. The Finance Committee did not send FAP to the Senate floor.

The Family Assistance Plan represents the peak of support in Congress for aid to the able-bodied poor. Efforts by Abraham Ribicoff (D.-Conn.) to revive the proposal failed to elicit any support from either the Republicans or southern Democrats, who could by the 1970s combine to defeat legislation. And Jimmy Carter's Better Jobs and Income Program—to replace AFDC, SSI, and food stamps with a federally funded system of jobs for those who could work and an annual allotment for those who could not—was summarily rejected by conservatives who thought it too costly (while complaining that public-sector jobs would compete with private industry) and liberals who deemed payments too low and "workfare" too harsh.

## THE REAGAN REVOLUTION

With the election of Ronald Reagan in 1980 opponents of congressional involvement in social welfare found a champion. The president regularly railed at "welfare cheats" and "freeloaders": more important, he was a reflection of and stimulus to political, economic, and ideological forces hostile to expanded benefits, especially for the poor. With the civil rights movement leaderless (and bogged down defending affirmative action), and liberals blamed for encouraging social disorder and an ethic of entitlement that blunted the nation's competitive edge, neoconservatives seized the social policy agenda. In *Losing Ground* (New York, 1984), Charles A. Murray argued that the Great Society actually hurt the poor by providing incentives for unemployment and single parenthood. The president, in fact, had anticipated Murray's argument. "In the war on poverty," he announced, "poverty won." In a series of proposals, Reagan asked the Congress to eliminate social welfare programs—or return them to the states.

Recession, massive budget deficits, and the president's plan to increase defense spending without raising taxes, added force to the arguments of advocates of cuts in domestic spending. Significantly the administration quickly climbed down from a trial balloon that Social Security should not be exempt from cuts. In fact, following the report of a bipartisan commission, Congress authorized a rescue plan that included new taxes for the financially troubled Social Security system. With social insurance off the table, the Congress of the 1980s generally acquiesced in chipping away at the far more vulnerable, if much smaller, welfare programs. A few were eliminated (most notably CETA, the job-training initiative), while others —AFDC, child care, school lunches, family planning, legal aid, Job Corps, subsidized housing, mass transit, and food stamps—were slashed.

Although Congress declined to return the financing of AFDC and food stamps to the states, the Reagan revolution succeeded in moving toward what might be called the old federalism. In the Omnibus Budget Reconciliation Act of 1981, Congress permitted states to adopt several options, including a single agency to administer WIN; requiring AFDC recipients to join a community work-experience program or lose their eligibility; and using AFDC funds to subsidize on-the-job training. The federal government still provided 90 percent of WIN funding, while the other options received AFDC administrative funds for which the federal share was only 50 percent. Between 1981 and 1987, moreover, WIN funds were cut by 70 percent; states had to replace federal funds (or not) and develop new program options. Even the much praised Family Support Act (FSA) of 1988 put a premium on state discretion, workfare and "learnfare" (educational requirements for teenage welfare recipients), without a substantial infusion of federal funds so that the Job Opportunities and Basic Skills (JOBS) Program of FSA states, in essence, decide which recipients will participate, what constitutes participation (including whether it is voluntary or mandatory) and who is assigned to the educational, job training, job placement, or wage-supplementation component. Although FSA requires states to guarantee child care if necessary for an adult's participation, states may choose to pay below the market rate. Federal funding for JOBS is relatively limited ($600 million in 1989) and will be capped at $1 billion in 1996.

In essence, then, the key social welfare decisions in the 1980s and 1990s reside in the state legislatures, where, as some observers argue, amid considerable variation, workfare remains the rule. In Massachusetts, a coalition of trade unions, churches, human services, and legal advocacy groups persuaded the legislature to defeat a mandatory program for all welfare recipients with children above the age of three, that consisted of a five-week job search and twenty-six weeks of community work for those who failed to find a job. At the urging of Governor Dukakis, the legislature passed a voluntary employment and training program replete with offers of educational and child-care services to induce welfare recipients to participate. A prosperous state in the mid-1980s, with an unemployment rate of only 3.9 percent, Massachusetts could afford a relatively generous program. By contrast California, with an unemployment rate of 8.7 percent in 1985, required participation in appraisal, remedial education, job search, and work for relief. Significantly, as the state confronted budget deficits, the legislature slashed its allocation for this program. In the 1990s legislators in most states, traumatized by both budget deficits and an electorate in revolt against taxes, have had to decide where to cut social welfare spending. Since workfare has not substantially reduced welfare rolls, no program is popular among legislators.

With the consolidation of the Reagan revolution, programs for the poor remain politically unpalatable in Washington. Democrats have carefully chosen a few social insurance programs—national health care, day-care services, extended benefits for the unemployed—that have appeal for middle-class voters. The promise of a presidential veto and, more importantly, the size of the federal deficit, however, loom as powerful obstacles to social welfare legislation in the 1990s. But the contours of legislative debate are likely to remain much as they have been for more than two centuries: which poor people deserve assistance; what impact social welfare is likely to have on labor markets, self-reliance, and the family; which unit of government is responsible for the moral and material needs of the nation's most vulnerable citizens; and, of course, what the political payoff is for support for a particular program.

## BIBLIOGRAPHY

### General Accounts
The most useful and comprehensive history of social welfare is WALTER TRATTNER, *From Poor Law to Welfare State: A History of Social Welfare in America,* 3d ed. (New York, 1984). For a detailed case study see DAVID M. SCHNEIDER, *The History of Public Welfare in New York State, 1609–1866* (Chicago, 1938) and ALBERT DEUTSCH and DAVID M. SCHNEIDER, *The History of Public Welfare in New York State, 1867–1940* (Chicago, 1941). More analytical and controversial treatments of welfare policy include MICHAEL B. KATZ, *Poverty and Policy in American History* (New York, 1983); FRANCES FOX PIVEN and RICHARD H. CLOWARD, *Regulating the Poor: The Functions of Public Welfare* (New York, 1971); and PIVEN and CLOWARD, *Poor People's Movements: Why They Succeed, How They Fail* (New York, 1977).

### Education
DAVID TYACK, *Law and the Shaping of Public Education, 1785–1954* (Madison, Wis., 1987), examines education as a public-policy issue;

CARL KAESTLE, *Pillars of the Republic: Common Schools and American Society* (New York, 1983), provides a superb survey for the period between the American Revolution and the Civil War.

### The Nineteenth Century
MARK E. LENDER and JAMES K. MARTIN, *Drinking in America* (New York, 1987), surveys temperance legislation; JAMES MOHR, *Abortion in America: The Origins and Evolution of National Policy, 1800–1900* (New York, 1978), covers the twist and turns of legislation; JILL QUADAGNO, *The Transformation of Old Age Security: Class Politics in the American Welfare State* (Chicago, 1988), examines Civil War pension, an issue treated definitively in THEDA SKOCPOL, *Protecting Soldiers and Mothers: The Political Origins of Social Policy in the United States* (Cambridge, Mass., 1992); DAVID J. ROTHMAN, *The Discovery of the Asylum: Social Order and Disorder in the New Republic* (Boston, 1971), is the classic work on the institutional approach to poverty, insanity, and crime

in the antebellum era; BALLARD CAMPBELL, *Representative Democracy: Public Policy and Midwestern Legislatures in the Late Nineteenth Century* (Cambridge, Mass., 1980), sees social welfare in the context of ethnocultural politics; WILLIAM R. BROCK, *Investigation and Responsibility: Public Responsibility in the United States* (Cambridge, Mass., 1984), evaluates government social welfare at the end of the century.

## The Twentieth Century

General accounts of the evolution of the welfare state are examined in EDWARD BERKOWITZ and KIM MCQUAID, *Creating the Welfare State: The Political Economy of Twentieth Century Reform,* 2d ed. (New York, 1988); ROBERT BROWNING, *Politics and Social Welfare Policy in the United States* (Knoxville, Tenn., 1986), and JOEL HANDLER and YEHESKEL HASENFELD, *The Moral Construction of Poverty: Welfare Reform in America* (Newbury Park, Calif., 1991). A useful chronology of government programs to ameliorate and or eliminate poverty is JAMES T. PATERSON, *America's Struggle Against Poverty, 1900–1980* (Cambridge, Mass., 1981).

## The Progressive Era

THEDA SKOCPOL, *Protecting Soldiers and Mothers,* provides a revisionist account of the role of women's organizations in shaping welfare reform; JAMES HARVEY YOUNG, *Pure Food: Securing the Federal Food and Drugs Act of 1906* (Princeton, N.J., 1989), examines the legislative history of this archetypal progressive reform; DAVID NELSON, *Unemployment Insurance: The American Experience, 1915–1935* (Madison, Wis., 1969), examines reform proposals at the state and federal level.

## The New Deal

WILLIAM R. BROCK, *Welfare, Democracy and the New Deal* (Cambridge, Mass., 1988) is especially useful in examining state implementation of federal policies. Accounts of Social Security reform by two men who were there are ARTHUR J. ALTMEYER, *The Formative Years of Social Security* (Madison, Wis., 1966), and EDWIN E. WITTE, *Development of the Social Security Act* (Madison, Wis., 1962). The best account by a professional historian remains ROY LUBOVE, *The Struggle for Social Security, 1900–1935,* 2d. ed. (Pittsburgh, 1986).

## The Post–World War II Era

A useful general account is EDWARD BERKOWITZ, *America's Welfare State from Roosevelt to Reagan* (Baltimore, 1991); DAVID PATRICK MOYNIHAN, *The Politics of a Guaranteed Annual Income: The Nixon Administration and the Family Assistance Plan* (New York, 1973), provides the assessment of the man who proposed the policy. Savage but well-informed indictments of recent policy are MICHAEL B. KATZ, *The Undeserving Poor: From the War on Poverty to the War on Welfare* (New York, 1989) and FRANCES FOX PIVEN and RICHARD CLOWARD, *The New Class War: Reagan's Attack on the Welfare State and Its Consequences* (New York, 1982). A superb analysis of Medicare is THEODORE R. MARMOR, *The Politics of Medicare* (Chicago, 1973). A careful and convincing evaluation of late-twentieth-century social welfare is THEODORE R. MARMOR, JERRY L. MASHAW, and PHILIP HARVEY, *America's Misunderstood Welfare State, Persistent Myths, Eduring Realities* (New York, 1990).

SEE ALSO The Contemporary Congress, 1930–1992; Legislatures and Gender Issues; AND The Modernizing Congress, 1870–1930.

# LEGISLATURES AND CIVIL LIBERTIES

## *Athan G. Theoharis*

Congress shall make no law . . . abridging the freedom of speech, or of the press; or the right of the people peaceably to assemble, and to petition the government for a redress of grievances. (First Amendment, U.S. Constitution)

Every citizen may freely speak, write, and publish his sentiments, on all subjects, being responsible for the abuse of that right; and no law shall be passed to restrain, or abridge the liberty of speech, or of the press. (New York State Constitution)

Despite explicit constitutional prohibitions, both Congress and state legislatures periodically enacted laws restricting speech, publications, and organizational activities. Ostensibly these laws were enacted to avert foreign threats to national or state security. Although the individuals who framed these laws may have distinguished between mere dissent and dissent that could promote violence, intending to restrict only those activities directed by or benefiting foreign governments or foreign movements, invariably these measures restricted civil liberties. To a great extent this is because their underlying purpose stemmed from an antipathy toward change.

It was not the case, moreover, that Congress and state legislatures enacted broadly worded and potentially repressive laws. In addition, congressional and state committees conducted highly publicized hearings focusing on radical ideas and movements. Often, the purpose of these hearings was not to develop legislation but, rather, to expose and discredit the political activities of specific organizations and activists, and thereby heighten popular insecurities about them. Because these hearings rarely led to legislation restricting speech or publications, their impact on civil liberties was transitory, dependent on continued public anxieties about internal security.

Legislative threats to civil liberties assumed yet another dimension. Confined almost exclusively to the Cold War period, members of Congress and congressional committees were covertly provided derogatory information about radical activists and organizations by officials of the Federal Bureau of Investigation (FBI). Increasingly after 1936, the focus of FBI investigations was on "subversive activities." Because such activities violated no federal statute, the acquired information could not be used for prosecutive purposes. Dating from the 1940s, FBI officials secretly disseminated information about "subversives" as part of a broader political attempt to contain radical activists, and their sources included members of the media and legislative bodies. If the FBI had shifted from law enforcement to political containment, the congressional recipients used this information to influence public opinion, and in the process ensure that public acceptance of security interests would override either privacy rights or democratic principles.

## THE COLONIAL AND EARLY NATIONAL ERA

Until the 1760s and 1770s, the relatively benign and permissive character of British colonial policy enabled colonial legislatures to exercise an unprecedented degree of autonomy over the affairs of the colony. The exigencies of creating order in a wilderness and of ensuring respect for authority in a society characterized by occupational and geographic mobility created tensions that invited legislative attempts to curb dissent. The *Zenger* case of 1734, the most famous freedom of the press case of the colonial era, had been brought by New York royal governor William Cosby, who sought Peter Zenger's arrest and prosecution because Zenger had libeled him in the press. Colonial legislatures shared this antipathy toward harmful dissent.

Colonial practices, moreover, were wholly consistent with the principle of seditious libel that condoned limiting dissent whenever speech or publications were either false or could undermine respect for constituted authority. Freedom of the press meant the absence of censorship and not an untrammeled right to speak or publish ideas intended to undermine authority. As early as 1635, the Virginia House of Burgesses not atypically sought to curb "newe and dangerous opinions." Indeed, the historian Leonard Levy, in his 1985 book, refers to Mary Clarke's study of colonial America in which she concludes that: "Literally scores of persons, probably hundreds, throughout the colonies were tracked down by the various messengers and sergeants and brought into the house to make inglorious submission for words spoken in the heat of anger, or for writings which intentionally or otherwise had given offense" (Levy, p. 18). Not confined to intemperate speech, these legislative restrictions also extended to criticisms of the legislature. In 1754, for example, the General Court of Massachusetts condemned a pamphlet criticizing an unpopular excise bill for having perpetuated "a false, scandalous libel reflecting upon the proceeding of the House in general, and on many worthy members in particular" (quoted in Levy, p. 33).

The outbreak of the American Revolution sustained this tradition of limited tolerance for dissent insofar as the former colonists were deeply divided between revolutionaries and those who remained loyal to Britain. In 1776, for example, the Continental Congress urged state legislatures to prevent their citizens from being "deceived and drawn into erroneous opinion." By 1778, all of the former colonies required loyalty oaths and some penalized libelous criticisms of the Continental Congress or state legislatures. The Virginia legislature, for example, prohibited "crimes injurious to the Independence of America, but less than treason," while the New York legislature created a committee to detect and defeat Loyalist conspiracies.

Nonetheless, resistance to British colonial policy and the quest for independence had altered the political landscape, producing a more democratic approach that valued dissent. In consequence, many state constitutions prohibited governmental regulation of political conduct. Virginia's constitution, for example, stipulated "that the freedom of the press is one of the greatest bulwarks of liberty, and can never be restrained but by despotic governments" (quoted in Levy, p. 184)—a rationale that, to ensure ratification of the U.S. Constitution in 1787, ultimately led to the drafting and ratification of the Bill of Rights.

Because this new constitutional system had been forged in the wake of a tenuously gained independence, with a citizenry deeply divided over independence, and with state governments suspicious of other states' and the federal government's powers, dissent and the prospect of disorder continued to worry the leadership of the new nation. These divisions gave rise to a two-party system, torn apart by divisions over "strict" and "loose" construction, over federal/state powers, and influenced by competing notions of the value of dissent. The international crisis precipitated by the French Revolution of 1789 and the subsequent military efforts of other European states, notably Great Britain, to contain that revolution further compounded these underlying ideological divisions—and provided the impetus for the domestic political crisis that resulted in the enactment of the Alien and Sedition Acts of 1798.

Ostensibly intended to protect the nation from foreign-inspired threats, the ancillary purpose of these acts was to contain dissent where it threatened to undermine respect for elected national leaders. They proscribed a variety of actions, some of which were legitimately directed at a perceived foreign threat—authorizing the president to expel or imprison "all such aliens as he shall judge dangerous to the peace and safety of the United States and shall have reasonable grounds to suspect are concerned in any treasonable or secret machinations against the government" (quoted in Smith, p. 438). Other provisions of the Sedition Act were directed at untrammeled dissent— either penalizing "any person" who

> shall unlawfully combine or conspire together with intent to oppose any measure or measures of the government of the United States which are or shall be directed by proper authority, or to impede the operation of any law

of the United States, or to intimidate or prevent any person holding a place or office in or under the government of the United States from undertaking, performing or executing his trust or duty" [or criminalizing any attempt to] "write, print, utter or publish, or shall cause or procure to be written, printed, uttered or published . . . any false, scandalous and malicious writings against the government of the United States, or either house of Congress of the United States, or the President of the United States with intent to defame. (quoted in Smith, pp. 441–442)

Based on the principle of seditious libel and an undemocratic philosophy of authority, the Alien and Sedition Acts had a leavening effect. The discretionary powers, which empowered the president to imprison aliens, combined with the attempts to proscribe speech and writing which challenged the wisdom, and character, of national leaders, brought forth a counterresponse, articulated in the Kentucky and Virginia resolutions. In effect, challenging the constitutionality of the Federalists' broad interpretation of federal powers, these resolutions reaffirmed the principle that when ratifying the Constitution the various states had formed a national government of limited powers. At the same time, the debate over the Alien and Sedition Acts effected a political revolution of sorts, resulting in Thomas Jefferson's election to the presidency in 1800 and Republican majorities in the new Congress. These successes ensured that the Sedition Act (which was due to expire in March 1801) would not be renewed.

The controversy provoked by these acts ushered in a new period in U.S. politics, one governed by principles that state and federal legislatures derived their powers from popular consent, and that citizens had the right to challenge the actions and motives of elected officials. In the 1820s, this democratic ferment brought about a second round of constitutional revisionism to amend state constitutions, to repeal property and religious qualifications for voting, and to reduce the powers of governors. Thus, until the outbreak of the Civil War, it was the divisive issue of slavery that comprised the principal legislative threat to the concept of civil liberties.

Responding to petitions to abolish slavery, the House in 1836 adopted the so-called Gag laws to file such resolutions without consideration by the House and its constituent committees, and restricted the circulation by mail of abolitionist literature. In addition, many Southern legislatures, notably South Carolina, required loyalty oaths of their residents while all Southern legislatures, excepting Kentucky, limited speech, press, and assembly. In 1849, for example, Virginia prohibited "speaking or writing [which] maintains that owners have no right of property in slaves" and Louisiana prohibited conversation "having a tendency to promote discontent among free couloured people, or insubordination among slaves" (Emerson et al., p. 42).

Nor was the North wholly immune to this antilibertarian virus. Some northern legislatures responded to the upsurge of abolitionism by enacting laws to curb efforts toward possible racial equality, notably in the case of Connecticut in 1833 prohibiting the operation of a private school for nonresidential blacks. The vast majority, notably in New York, Ohio, and Pennsylvania, rebuffed southern appeals to curb abolitionist publications. Nonetheless, the influx of immigrants duing the 1840s predominantly Catholic in religion, gave rise to the anti-Catholic and anti-immigrant Know-Nothing movement (and to the American party), centered principally in northeastern states. To preserve their religion, Catholic leaders responded by founding privately financed parochial schools and charitable institutions. Reacting to this challenge to a dominant Protestant culture, in 1855 the Massachusetts legislature created a special committee to visit such "theological seminaries, boarding schools, academies, nunneries, convents, and other institutions of like character as they may deem necessary" (Taylor, p. 37), and to report its findings. Adverse publicity about the extremism of the committee's members, however, led to abandonment of this special inquiry.

## THE CIVIL WAR AND THE EMERGENCE OF AN INDUSTRIAL SOCIETY

Because of its unique character and attendant military and internal security problems, the Civil War invited limitations on civil liberties.

While the more egregious restrictions resulted from President Lincoln's suspension of the writ of habeas corpus and proclamation of martial law, Congress also placed limitations on civil liberties. Following the outbreak of military hostilities in April 1861, the House created a special committee to "ascertain the number of persons . . . now employed" by the federal government "who are known to entertain sentiments of hostility to the Government . . . and who have refused to take the oath to support the Government." Congress eventually required that all federal employees take an oath of loyalty to the Constitution and to the Union. Similar oaths were demanded of former Confederate officials at the end of the Civil War as preconditions for holding federal office. Indeed, loyalty oaths became the standard adopted during the Reconstruction Era, having as their precedent the Wade-Davis Bill of 1864 requiring former Confederates to take iron-clad oaths of personal loyalty to the Union as conditions for holding elective and appointive office (a bill pocket-vetoed by President Lincoln, but one which signaled an ensuing executive-legislative conflict over what conditions the Northern-controlled Congress should impose prior to readmitting the former Confederate states to full status).

Eventually adopting a punitive approach with military Reconstruction, Congress limited the political rights of Southerners until their loyalty could be ensured, including drafting the Fourteenth and Fifteenth Amendments and enacting civil rights laws to preclude Southern attempts to reimpose slavery or to limit the civil rights of the recently emancipated slaves. Reconstruction, however, did not usher in a new era of race relations and, thus, with the formal end of Northern military occupation and political supervision in 1877, Southern legislators renewed efforts to preserve a social system of racial inequality by enacting, between the 1890s and early 1900s, a variety of so-called Jim Crow laws which in effect disfranchised African Americans living in the South and enforced a system of racial segregation.

The triumph of Jim Crow also represented a reaction to federal supremacy. While adversely affecting civil rights, this reaction proved to be a major constraint against restricting civil liberties. In combination, this antipathy toward political loyalty tests and revelations of corruption (identified as the result of basing federal appointments on partisan patronage) led to congressional enactment of the Civil Service Reform Act. This 1883 Act instituted the merit system for federal appointments, and prohibited federal officials from questioning any applicant for federal appointment about "political or religious opinions or affiliations." Antipathy toward the federal government's use of troops for policing purposes also developed following revelations that private corporations had recruited Pinkerton detectives for strike-breaking purposes, leading Congress in 1892 to prohibit the expenditure of any federal funds to contract for the temporary services of Pinkerton detectives. (Since the creation of the Department of Justice in 1870, department officials had turned to the Pinkerton agency for investigative assistance.) In addition, in 1893 many state legislatures prohibited the importation of armed nonresidents for police work (in effect, barring a practice whereby many corporations had contracted with the Pinkerton agency to break strikes and contain labor unions).

The defeat of Southern secession had also resulted in a political and economic climate that brought about a more industrialized society which, combined with the sharp increase in immigration after the 1880s, precipitated new challenges to civil liberties. Industrialization and immigration from eastern and southern Europe fundamentally changed the character of U.S. society, giving rise to an ethnically and religiously diverse social system and an impersonal and centralized economic system. Accordingly, many Americans were attracted to movements (trade unionism, socialism, anarchism) that sought the radical transformation of an economic system of private property. Responding to popular concerns over this specter of radicalism, Congress and state legislatures endorsed legislation to contain change.

In the aftermath of the 1877 national railroad strike, many state legislatures enacted laws directed at labor unions. By 1886, twenty-five states restricted labor-organizational activities. The Illinois legislature in 1887 made boycotting an illegal conspiracy, and five other states broadened the definition of conspiracy to limit coordinated action by workers.

Attributing radicalism to alien ideas and influence, Congress during the years 1903–1918 first prohibited the admission and then authorized the deportation of immigrants who were attracted to radical movements. The Immigration Act of 1903 banned the admission of those who "believe in or advocate" anarchism or violent revolutionary change, advocate the assassination of public officials, or are "a member of or affiliated with any organization entertaining and teaching such disbelief in or opposition to all organized government" (Preston, p. 32). By 1917, Congress extended this exclusionary principle to authorize the deportation of any alien who "at any time after entry shall be found advocating or teaching the unlawful destruction of property . . . anarchy or the overthrow by force or violence of the government of the United States or of all forms of law or the assassination of public officials" and then in 1918 authorized deportation if the alien had merely joined an organization that the Secretary of Labor ruled was anarchist or revolutionary.

Beginning with New York in 1902, state legislatures also prohibited the advocacy of "criminal anarchy" (defined as "the doctrine that organized government should be overthrown by force or violence") or belonging to any organization which taught or advocated criminal anarchy. In 1909, the Washington legislature even criminalized the circulation of any publication having a tendency to encourage illegal conduct, or disrespect for any law or court ruling, while the New Jersey legislature in 1908 criminalized the advocacy of the unlawful destruction of property, or criticism of the methods employed by the police to limit strikes by labor unions. In 1917, the Idaho legislature extended New York's restrictions on anarchists to bar personal advocacy by or membership in groups that advocated "crime, sabotage, violence or other unlawful methods of terrorism as a means of accomplishing industrial or political ends" (quoted in Goldstein, p. 101). Seeking to limit the appeal of the radical Industrial Workers of the World and of the Socialist party, state legislatures limited the right of assembly and the display of certain symbols, such as the red flag of socialism. Indeed, by 1921 thirty-three state legislatures banned the display of a flag in any public assembly or parade as "a symbol or emblem of any organization or association, or in furtherance of any political, social, or economic principle, doctrine or propaganda" (quoted in Walker, p. 43).

## THE CRISES OF WORLD WAR I, THE GREAT DEPRESSION, AND WORLD WAR II

Following U.S. entry into World War I in April 1917, efforts to curb radical movements were intensified. Both Congress and state legislatures, ostensibly to curb espionage and sedition, indirectly targeted the fledgling radical trade union and socialist movements.

The Espionage Act, enacted in June 1917, initiated such legislative restrictions on civil liberties. Limited to the period "when the United States is at war," this act prohibited anyone to "willfully make or convey false reports or false statements with intent to interfere with the operation or success of the military or armed forces [of the United States], or to promote the success of its enemies" or "willfully cause or attempt to cause insubordination, disloyalty, mutiny, or refusal of duty" in the armed forces (quoted in Chafee, p. 39). Publications violating the above provisions or "advocating or urging treason, insurrection, or resistance to any law of the United States" were also declared unmailable.

Because the Espionage Act confined prosecution to specified wartime activities (enforcement of conscription), additional changes were sought that culminated in the Sedition Act of May 1918. This act criminalized the publication or expression of "any disloyal, profane, scurrilous, or abusive language about the form of government of the United States, . . . or any language intended to encourage resistance to the United States, or to promote the cause of its enemies, or any language intended to bring the form of government of the United States . . . into contempt, scorn, contumely, or disrespect." Speech or publications "urging any curtailment of production of any things necessary to the prosecution of the war with intent to hinder its prosecution" were prohibited as were any "attempt to obstruct" the sale of wartime Liberty Bonds (quoted in Preston, p. 145). Internal security concerns also led to other legislative restrictions, whether congressional approval of the Eighteenth Amendment between 1917 and 1918 that instituted Prohibition (as a wartime measure to conserve grain), or a June 1920 amendment extending deportation to those advising (as opposed to the 1917 and 1918 acts' provisions of advocacy or membership) or "giving, loaning, or promising monies or anything of value to be used for advising, advocating or teaching" anarchism or revolutionary change (quoted in Preston, p. 228).

In 1919, U.S. Representative Frederick Dallinger (R.-Maine) led a successful effort to bar the seating of Socialist Congressman Victor Berger. Berger thereupon won reelection in a special race held later that year, but was once again barred. His subsequent defeat in the November 1920 congressional elections made this denial of the right of citizens to select their own representatives moot.

In contrast, the Senate in February 1919 authorized a special subcommittee of the Judiciary Committee, chaired by Lee Overman (D.-N.C.), to investigate Bolshevik propaganda. In highly publicized hearings held between April and May of 1919, the Overman committee provided a forum for impugning the loyalty of both radical and liberal activists. The committee then recommended peacetime-sedition legislation prohibiting advocacy of revolutionary change, destruction of private property, and the display of red flags, and also demanded the vigorous enforcement of exclusionary and deportation immigration laws and a heightened anti-Bolshevik propaganda campaign. However, the adverse reaction to the "Palmer Raids" of January 1920, inspired by Alexander Mitchell Palmer, who served as President Wilson's attorney general between 1919 and 1921 and who was determined to purge America of all left-wing radicals, discredited such efforts and instead precipitated congressional repeal, in 1921, of the 1918 Sedition Act.

Until then, the Espionage and Sedition acts had provided the model for similar state legislation. The Minnesota, Montana, South Dakota, and Nebraska legislatures, between 1917 and 1918, criminalized the advocacy of "the doctrine that organized government shall be overthrown by force or violence, or by assassination . . . or by any unlawful means" (Murray, p. 232). They were followed by an additional thirty-one

state legislatures who by 1921 had enacted similar restrictions that focused less on whether such speech aided the nation's military adversaries than on its anticapitalist intent. The Ohio legislature, for example, condemned any "doctrine which advocates crime, sabotage . . . violence or unlawful methods of terrorism as a means of accomplishing industrial or political reform" (Murray, p. 233). California prohibited speech or writing that advocated violence "as a means of accomplishing change in industrial ownership or control, or effecting any political change;" Montana prohibited any language "calculated to incite or inflame resistance to any duly constituted federal or state authority"; and Texas proscribed groups "whose principles include any thought or purpose of setting aside representative form of government and substituting thereafter any other form of government" (Biddle, pp. 19–21).

State legislators also initiated hearings to proscribe political liberties. Paralleling the action of the House, first in January and then again in April 1920, the New York Assembly barred the seating of five elected Socialist representatives on the grounds that the Socialist party was revolutionary, unpatriotic, and disloyal. The New York legislature also created a special committee in March 1919, chaired by Republican Senator Clayton Lusk, to investigate the "scope, tendencies, and ramifications . . . of seditious activities" (quoted in Murray, p. 98).

The resulting inquiry, which began on 12 June, had been based on documents acquired by Justice Department and state police agents through raids of the offices of the Russian Soviet Bureau, the Socialists' Rand School, the Industrial Workers of the World (IWW) and other unions, and radical publications. The committee's purpose, Lusk declared at the onset of the hearings, was to "find out . . . just what these radicals are advocating and just what they propose to accomplish" (quoted in Chamberlain, p. 14). Lasting until 1920, the hearings focused on radical influence among African Americans, trade unions, and the teaching profession. Five of the six teachers who were identified as Communist party members by the committee were dismissed and, based on the committee's findings, the New York legislature required loyalty oaths of all teachers, prohibited anyone from conducting "any school, institution, class or course of instruction in any class whatsoever" without being licensed by the state, and authorized the denial of a license "where it shall appear that the instruction proposed to be given includes the teaching of the doctrine that organized government shall be overthrown by force, violence, or unlawful means" (quoted in Chafee, p. 307). Although Democratic governor Al Smith vetoed this bill in 1920, the legislature reenacted it in 1921, and it was signed by Smith's Republican successor, Nathan Miller. Regaining the governorship in 1922, Smith successfully lobbied for the law's repeal in 1923. Five other states, moreover, adopted similar loyalty-oath requirements of teachers between 1919 and 1920 as did another twenty-four by the end of the 1920s. Other state legislatures initiated investigations of school textbooks and, in particular, scrutinized history teachers for any "unpatriotic" statements.

Concerns about "subversive" ideas continued throughout the 1920s. On the one hand, in 1925 the Minnesota legislature prohibited newspapers and other periodicals from printing "malicious, scandalous, and defamatory" stories, banned obscene periodicals, and limited claims to truth during libel proceedings only if "published with good motives and for justified ends." On the other hand, Nebraska prohibited teaching in any language other than English, while Tennessee in 1925 (followed by other southern states) prohibited the teaching in public schools or universities of "any theory that denies the story of the Divine Creation of man as taught in the Bible" (quoted in Walker, p. 72).

The crisis of the Great Depression and the expansion of the federal government's regulatory and relief roles that followed Roosevelt's New Deal, contributed to the emergence of more militant union and radical movements, which, in turn, rekindled federal and state actions affecting civil liberties.

On the one hand, reflecting the shift in public policy represented by the principle of federal responsibility to address social and economic inequities, the New Deal years ushered in a new era in federal labor policy that, among other changes, expanded civil liberties safeguards to labor organizers and union members. With the Norris-LaGuardia Act of 1932, Con-

gress recognized the right of workers to "full freedom of association, self-organization and designation of representatives" of their own choosing, and to negotiate the "terms and conditions" of their employment. Furthermore, workers and unions were safeguarded "from the interference, restraint, or coercion of employers of labor, or their agents" (quoted in Bernstein, p. 398). Congress extended the right of workers to join unions with the National Labor Relations Act of 1935. Employers were barred from forming so-called company unions and from discriminating against union members in their hiring and promotional practices. Further highlighting this concept of labor's right to organize unions as a civil liberties issue, in 1936 the Senate approved Senate Resolution 266 authorizing a subcommittee of the Committee on Education and Labor, chaired by Robert La Follette (Prog.-Wis.), to investigate "violations of the rights of free speech and assembly and undue interference with the right of labor to organize and bargain collectively" (quoted in Auerbach, p. 63). In highly publicized hearings between 1936 and 1941, the committee exposed various corporate abuses of labor's organizational rights. The committee's proposed legislative remedy, introduced in 1939, however, fell victim to the more conservative mood of World War II.

Nonetheless, Congress did enact other measures to safeguard the liberties of unpopular minorities. For one, Section 605 of the Communications Act of 1934 prohibited wiretapping. This ban, interpreted by the Supreme Court in rulings of 1937 and 1939 as it applied to federal investigators, safeguarded privacy rights and indirectly immunized dissident political activities from governmental surveillance. And, as highlighted by its recognition of the right of workers to organize unions as a civil liberties issue, the Senate sought to limit corporate lobbying by creating, in 1934, a special committee, chaired by Hugo Black (D.-Ala.), to investigate utility corporations' efforts to block enactment of proposed legislation regulating utility holding companies.

On the state level, the New Jersey legislature responded in 1935 to the upsurge in anti-Semitism, first kindled by the reorganization of the Ku Klux Klan in 1915 and then by the rise of fascist movements in Europe and the United

States during the 1930s, by prohibiting speech "advocating hatred, abuse, violence, or hostility against any group or groups of persons by reason of race, color, religion, or manner of worship" (a law that the New Jersey Supreme Court found unconstitutional in 1941).

These attempts to curb speech (whether corporate lobbying or anti-Semitism) highlighted the repressive side of the legislative politics of the 1930s. Responding to allegations of New York City police commissioner Grover Whalen that the Soviet Amtorg Trading Corporation was disseminating propaganda in the United States, the House, in 1930, created a special committee, chaired by Hamilton Fish (R.-N.Y.), to investigate "all entities, groups or individuals who are alleged to advise, teach or advocate the overthrow by force or violence of the Government of the United States, or attempt to undermine our representative form of government by inciting riots, sabotage or revolutionary disorder" (quoted in Goodman, p. 6).

The Fish committee failed to uncover any such foreign-inspired plot and brought about no legislative change. The triumph of Nazism in Germany, however, intensified an underlying conservative aversion to radicalism, heightened further by the prominent role played by Communist party activists in organizing industrial and migrant farm workers and the unemployed. To curb Nazi activities and allegedly "subversive propaganda," the House in 1934 created another special committee, chaired by John McCormack (D.-Mass.). In contrast to the Fish committee, the McCormack committee did help effect legislation, the Foreign Agents Registration Act of 1938, requiring "any person who acts or agrees to act . . . [as] a public-relations counsel, publicity agent, information-service employee, servant, agent representative, or attorney for a foreign principal" to register with the secretary of state and file information concerning this relationship (quoted in Emerson, p. 177).

The creation of the Special House Committee on Un-American Activities in 1938, the so-called Dies committee (named after its chairman Martin Dies [D.-Tex.]), provided greater impetus to the anti-New Deal antiradicalism which came to dominate U.S. politics during the Cold War years. Authorized to investigate the extent and effectiveness of "subversive and un-American propaganda" in the

United States "instigated from foreign countries or of a domestic origin and [that] attacks the principle of the form of government as guaranteed by the Constitution," the committee ranged far afield (quoted in Goodman, p. 16). Its targets included federal bureaucrats (notably officials of the Federal Theatre and Writers Project), the Campfire Girls, the trade-union movement, and a host of antiwar, civil liberties, and civil rights organizations. Moreover, when initiating public hearings in 1938, Congressman Dies conceded that he did not know whether the committee "can legislate effectively" but nonetheless claimed that exposure could prove to be "the most effective weapon . . . in our possession" by serving to publicize un-American activities and allowing "public sentiment to do the rest" (quoted in O'Reilly, p. 38). This tactic, as well as the unfairness of committee proceedings and disinterest in constitutional niceties (symbolized by its seizure in 1940 of records of radical organizations through raids of their offices, which the committee photocopied before complying with a court order to return these illegally seized documents), rendered it a controversial agency drawing support and criticism for its efforts to arrest social and economic change.

The committee's hearings did give impetus for the enactment of a series of antiradical laws during the period 1939–1941, preceding U.S. military involvement in World War II. In January 1939, Congress adopted a rider to the Relief Appropriation Act barring payment of funds to "any person who advocates or who is a member of an organization that advocates" the violent overthrow of the government and in June 1940 authorized the Navy and War departments to fire summarily, without the right of appeal, any employee when such action was "warranted by the demands of national security." When approving the so-called Hatch Act in 1939, Congress barred federal employment to anyone holding "membership in any political party or organization which advocated" the violent overthrow of the government. Then, on 28 June 1940, through the Alien Registration (or Smith) Act, Congress made it illegal to "knowingly or willfully advocate, abet, advise or teach the duty, necessity, desirability or propriety of violently overthrowing" the government, or assassinating any government official, or printing, writing, or disseminating publications advocating such doctrines, or organizing such groups. Moreover, aliens could be deported if they violated the act's provisions or if they ever participated in such activities even if subsequently discontinuing or repudiating such conduct.

These legislative restrictions were only slightly extended following U.S. involvement in World War II. On 18 December 1941, Congress created an Office of Censorship with broadly defined powers to control the flow of news to and from the United States. Then, in the most serious overt violation of civil liberties, on 19 March 1942, through Public Law 503, President Roosevelt's executive order 3066 of 19 February 1942, instituting the Japanese internment program, was granted legislative authorization.

The wartime crisis also provided the rationale to curb trade unionism and political radicalism. Thus, when enacting the War Labor Dispute Act in 1943, the so-called Smith-Connally Act, the encouragement of strikes in industries engaged in wartime production was criminalized and, in addition, union contributions to political campaigns were outlawed (a restriction which union officials circumvented by forming political action committees ostensibly to promote voter education). That same year the House responded to a Dies committee report attacking thirty-nine federal employees as "irresponsible, unrepresentative, crackpot radical bureaucrats" and calling for withholding their salaries. A special committee, chaired by John Kerr (D.-N.C.), was set up to inquire into the published writings and speeches of these employees who allegedly criticized government policy and capitalism. Disturbed by the political activities of three senior federal employees (Gordon Watson, William Dodd, Jr., and Robert Morrs Lovett), the committee proposed an amendment to the Deficiency Appropriation Act of 1943 to withhold their salaries unless reappointed by the president and confirmed by the Senate. However, in 1946, the Supreme Court overturned this restriction as an unconstitutional bill of attainder.

State legislative restrictions paralleled federal antiradicalism. The Fish committee alleged that New York City teachers were joining Soviet-sponsored tours and returning to "serve as valuable propagandists, some consciously, some unconsciously." In 1934,

Assemblyman Irving Ives (R.-N.Y.) introduced legislation to require loyalty oaths of all New York teachers as a needed antidote to "too much teaching of various 'isms in the schools." Vetoed by Democratic governor Herbert Lehman, Ives's bill was reintroduced and passed in 1935. In 1936, Senator John McNahoe (R.-N.Y.) demanded an investigation of a broad range of "un-American" activities allegedly being carried out by students and faculty in New York schools, pointing out that "students are being daily exposed to seditious or treasonable utterances in literature openly circulated in school rooms, assembly halls, on the campus, and in official school publications, as well as from the lips of faculty members" (quoted in Chamberlain, p. 56). The New York legislature did not approve McNahoe's 1936 resolution, but in 1940 it did authorize an investigation of New York City teachers, triggered then by the invitation of City College to the agnostic British philosopher Bertrand Russell and the avowedly radical activities of teachers-union activists. The resulting investigation of the Rapp-Coudert committee proposed to ascertain the "extent to which, if any, subversive activities may have been permitted to be carried on in the schools and colleges" (quoted in Schrecker, p. 76). No legislation was drafted by the committee, but its publicity led to the dismissal of twenty teachers and the resignation of eleven others.

Fifteen other states also enacted loyalty-oath requirements between 1935 and 1936, while in 1935 a Wisconsin legislative committee investigated allegations of subversive activities at the University of Wisconsin–Madison. Although the committee found no supporting evidence, it criticized university administrators for permitting the evolution of "an ultra-liberal institution and one in which communistic teachers were encouraged, and where avowed communists were welcome and allowed to spread their doctrines upon the campus" (quoted in Schrecker, p. 69). Similarly, responding to the complaints of drugstore magnate Charles Walgreen that his niece had been subverted by her teachers at the University of Chicago, the Illinois legislature in 1935 investigated this private university's "subversive communistic teachings and ideas."

Concerned about the threat of communism, in 1935 the Tennessee, Indiana, Arkansas, and Delaware legislatures barred from the ballot any political party which advocated revolutionary change (by 1941, nine other states adopted similar laws).

The outbreak of war in Europe in 1939 intensified this fear of communism. That year, the New York legislature barred persons from state employment who espoused forcible overthrow of government (five other states adopted similar laws in 1941), while in 1940 the Washington legislature refused to seat an elected state senator who had been a former member of the Communist party, and the California legislature in 1941 barred from participation in primaries and elections any party which "uses . . . as part of its party designation the word 'communist' or any derivative" or which is "directly or indirectly affiliated by any means whatsoever" (Chafee, p. 490) with the Communist party, the Third International, or any foreign organization or government.

And in what became the model for other states during the Cold War period, the California legislature in 1940 created a standing committee to investigate "un-American activities." Chaired by Democratic Senator Jack Tenney, this Fact-Finding Committee on Un-American Activities investigated alleged communist infiltration of state universities and relief agencies, tenant groups, left-wing unions, and certain right-wing patriotic groups. Although its stated purpose was to investigate the use of state funds or if foreign powers "dominated or controlled" (Gelhorn, p. 7) any organization, the committee instead developed a list of those organizations and individuals it deemed subversive and un-American. Its criteria centered on speech and propaganda, not illegal conduct—and included advocacy of sex education courses and progressive causes.

## THE COLD WAR YEARS

Legislative politics had been fundamentally altered by the political crisis of the Great Depression and the perceived internal security threat of the appeal of fascism and communism. One legacy, with the onset of a far more serious confrontation between the United States and the Soviet Union after 1945, was a wholesale abandonment of former libertarian principles and a political climate tolerant of restrictions on civil liberties, ostensibly to safeguard internal security. Moreover, increasingly after 1945, legislative hearings assumed a life of their own having the purpose to expose suspect ideas and associations and thereby influence public opinion (and not necessarily to draft legislation). In addition as part of this broader educational purpose, key legislators and legislative committees forged covert relationships with the FBI with the most prominent role in such efforts played by the House Committee on Un-American Activities (HUAC).

Created as a special committee in 1938, HUAC (renamed the House Internal Security Committee in 1969) became a permanent standing committee in 1945 and thereafter sought, through hearings held both in Washington, D.C., and in carefully planned settings around the country, to expose those individuals whom it concluded were subversive. A dominant political force during the 1950s, the committee's influence waned during the 1960s until formally dissolved in January 1975.

Relying on publicity, the committee pointedly questioned subpoenaed witnesses about their past conduct and insisted that they name other individuals with whom they had associated in communist or alleged communistic activities. This intention to stigmatize radical politics as subversive is highlighted by HUAC chair John Wood's (D.-Ga.) 1949 request of seventy colleges for lists of "textbooks and supplementary reading, together with authors" currently being used "in the fields of sociology, geography, economics, government, philosophy, history, political science, and American literature" (quoted in Biddle, p. 134).

No longer relying on its own resources, the committee sought the FBI's assistance in its efforts to influence public opinion. Indeed, the two most publicized cases which catapulted the committee into national prominence—involving Hollywood in 1947 and Alger Hiss–Whittaker Chambers in 1948—highlight the nature of this covert relationship.

The committee's decision in 1947 to investigate the film industry reflected an appreciation of the publicity value of an inquiry into Hollywood. Significantly, its target was the private-entertainment industry which, although having no access to national secrets, influenced popular values. When first considering convening hearings into Hollywood, the committee was stymied by the inability of its staff investigators to acquire needed information. To repair this deficiency, committee chair J. Parnell Thomas (R.-N.J.) requested the FBI's assistance. Recognizing the political value of the planned hearings, FBI director J. Edgar Hoover ordered his aides to "expedite" action on this request. In response FBI officials identified those "friendly" witnesses who could then be invited to testify about communist activities in Washington (including Ronald Reagan), those who were or had been members of the Communist party who could be interrogated about their membership, as well as preparing a general summary report on the problem of "communism in the film industry." When ten of the subpoenaed Hollywood writers, producers, and actors refused to testify on First Amendment grounds, the committee both benefited from this highly publicized confrontation and then secured their conviction for contempt of Congress. Far more importantly, this adverse publicity led cautious Hollywood executives to institute an informal blacklist, denying employment to anyone refusing to testify if subpoenaed by the committee.

The FBI provided similar assistance in the case of the Hiss-Chambers hearings of August and December 1948. Anxious in the heated presidential campaign of 1948 to establish the existence of a serious internal security threat to which the incumbent Truman administration was allegedly indifferent, HUAC investigators were alerted to the possible corroborative value of then *Time* magazine editor Whittaker Chambers's testimony. During the resulting hearings, Catholic priest John Cronin served as an intermediary between the FBI and committee member Richard Nixon (R.-Calif.), forwarding information from FBI files which proved helpful during Nixon's questioning of Hiss. During this same year, Nixon also worked closely with FBI assistant director Louis Nichols in a common effort to lend credence to Chambers's testimony about Hiss.

The FBI's assistance proved essential at this critical period in HUAC's history. Thereafter, the FBI-HUAC relationship waxed and waned, influenced both by the committee's publicity seeking (which alarmed the FBI director who suspected any rivals in the internal security field) and its members' tendency to compromise the FBI's assistance (rendered on the strict condition that this assistance not be disclosed). The level of the FBI's assistance (which included identifying former FBI agents for recruitment as staff investigators, providing background information on prospective committee witnesses, and locating friendly witnesses whose testimony could impugn the loyalty of trade union, civil rights, and progressive activists) depended on whether FBI interests would be advanced. Two cases illustrate this: one involved FBI authorship of a HUAC report impugning the loyalty of the National Lawyers Guild—timed to rebut Guild criticisms of FBI abuses disclosed during the Judith Coplon trial—and the second involved helping prepare and publicize a film, *Operation Abolition,* disparaging the loyalty of HUAC critics. (Coplon had been indicted for attempting to deliver FBI documents to a Soviet agent. During her resulting trial, however, questions were raised as to the targets of FBI investigations and the scope of FBI wiretapping activities.)

HUAC might have initiated the politics of exposure, but Senator Joseph McCarthy (R.-Wis.) was the most infamous congressional practitioner; indeed, his name came to describe the anticommunist politics of the Cold War years. McCarthy had burst from oblivion to notoriety in February 1950, following a series of speeches in which he claimed to have evidence identifying "known Communists in the State Department." Impugning the loyalty of federal employees but in fact targeting high level officials of first the Truman and then the Eisenhower administrations for tolerating the employment of subversives in sensitive policy positions, McCarthy directly or indirectly dominated national politics until December 1954.

McCarthy was not an effective legislator and played no role in drafting or effecting passage of even the one internal security measure enacted in 1950, the so-called McCarran Act. Instead, whether as a member of the Republican minority between 1950 and 1952 or as chair of the Government Operations Committee during the period 1953–1954, he sought to expose communist influence in the federal government: whether the State Department, the Justice Department's failure to prosecute the *Amerasia* case, or army security procedures at Fort Monmouth. McCarthy, moreover, depended on the covert assistance of senior FBI officials, which ranged from providing information (not files, allowing FBI officials to deny that McCarthy had received FBI reports) to recommendations on staff appointments and strategy. FBI assistance, ironically, terminated in July 1953 following McCarthy's appointment of FBI supervisor Frank Carr as chief counsel to his Senate committee. Should McCarthy's committee thereafter release any FBI-related information, FBI director Hoover pointed out, this would raise questions about the existence of a "pipeline" (Theoharis, *Secret Files,* pp. 261, 263).

The FBI, however, had never (nor was it capable of) providing McCarthy with information documenting the existence of a communist conspiracy at the highest levels of government. This did not matter since McCarthy's appeal derived from his ability to tap into public anxieties and belief that existing internal security procedures were inadequate. This politics of anticommunism continued long after McCarthy's condemnation in 1954. Indeed, the Senate vote to condemn McCarthy in December 1954 for conduct unbecoming a member of the Senate was based on the senator's methods, and not congressional concern about civil liberties.

Concurrent with McCarthy's "Communist in the State Department" accusations, conservative Republicans had raised another internal security issue of "homosexuals in the State Department." Responding to these charges, the Senate created a special committee, chaired by Clyde Hoey (D.-N.C.). Releasing its report in December 1950, the Hoey committee concluded that the employment of gays constituted a serious internal security problem despite its failure to document one case where gays had been forced to commit espionage as a result of blackmail. Following up on this report, the House Appropriations Committee in April 1951 invited FBI director Hoover's testimony and was informed that there were more than four hundred gay federal employees. Propelled by Congress's demonstrated concern but absent explicit legislative authorization, in June 1951 the FBI Director instituted a formal "Sex Deviates" program, whereby FBI information about alleged homosexuals was disseminated to officials in the executive, judicial, and legislative branches and, in time, to private universities and police agencies.

The FBI's "Sex Deviates" program indi-

rectly highlights McCarthy's marginality in the forging of a more repressive politics during the Cold War years. Indeed, the most serious Senate threat to civil liberties was posed by the Senate Internal Security Subcommittee (SISS). Created in 1951 as a subcommittee of the Judiciary Committee, SISS's purpose was to oversee the enforcement of the Internal Security Act of 1950. In fact, SISS investigations ranged well beyond the federal bureaucracy from the privately funded Institute of Pacific Relations to United Nations employees, the newspaper and publishing industries, trade unions, and civil rights organizations. SISS also relied on the FBI's covert assistance—in this case formally authorized by the attorney general.

Far more thorough in planning hearings, SISS (until it was terminated in 1978, only to be reconstituted as the renamed Senate Subcommittee on Terrorism in 1981) promoted a politics repressive of civil liberties. One example of the FBI-SISS relationship during the period 1951–1953 highlights this best.

Disturbed by the publication in 1950 of Max Lowenthal's critical history of the FBI, published by William Sloane, and entitled *The Federal Bureau of Investigation,* FBI officials in 1951 urged that SISS look into "the matter of Communist infiltration into the book publishing industry" in order to "counteract the left-wing element in the publishing business, which has been the source of attacks on the Bureau—particularly the Max Lowenthal book, William A. Sloan[e] Associates, Merle Miller's *The Sure Thing,* and others." SISS did not honor this request in 1951, owing to its preoccupation with planning hearings on the Institute of Pacific Relations and United Nations employees. In 1953, however, SISS counsel Ed Duffy recontacted the FBI to convey the committee's interest in "holding hearings concerning the general subject matter of Communist infiltration and domination of the publishing industry . . . [since] some of the men who are strongly anti-Communist are experiencing difficulty in getting their books published . . . [and] there seems to be some collusion among book reviewers to give favorable reviews to liberal writers and either refuse to review or give unfavorable reviews of individuals who are attacking Communists and Communist activities" (quoted in Theohavis, *Secret Files,* pp. 311–312). FBI officials were hesitant to cooperate in 1953, having serious doubts that the committee had developed a "plan of action" and also having concluded that there was no longer any need to discredit Lowenthal or his publisher. The committee did initiate hearings into the book publishing and newspaper industries in 1955, interrogating reporters and book reviewers of the *New York Times* about their past "subversive" activities.

This concern about political ideology also underlay a special House committee investigation initiated in 1952 into whether "foundations and organizations are using their resources for un-American or subversive activities or for purposes not in the interest and tradition of the United States." Heads of foundations were interrogated about the political philosophy and associations of grant recipients. Moreover, in 1954, B. Carroll Reece (R.-Tenn.), by then chair of the committee, admitted that the committee's concern was "not so much with subversion as it is the extent to which money of the tax-exempt foundations is used for propaganda and to influence public opinion for the support of certain types of ideologies that tend to the left" (quoted in Barth, *Government by Investigation,* p. 147).

In a companion action, in 1962, Senate Judiciary Committee chair James Eastland (D.-Miss.) characterized recent Supreme Court rulings as "pro-Communist" and as threatening "fundamentally the basic security of our country from the onslaught of the Communist conspiracy." Eastland then outlined his evaluation methodology: "If the decision of the individual justice was in favor of the position advocated by the Communist Party, or the Communist organization involved in the particular case, it was scored as pro, meaning pro-Communist. If the judge's position was contrary to this position, he was scored as con—or contrary" (quoted in *Frontiers of Civil Liberties,* p. 119).

The senator's effort to impugn the Court culminated a concerted (if ultimately unsuccessful) congressional effort to limit the impact of Supreme Court rulings in the area of civil liberties and national security. Responding to Court rulings between 1956 and 1957 involving the loyalty program, the Internal Security Act of 1950, state sedition legislation, congressional investigative activities, and FBI files, Senator William Jenner (R.-Ind.) introduced legislation in 1957 to curb the Supreme Court's jurisdiction over internal security cases. Senate majority leader Lyndon Johnson (D.-Tex.) prevented floor debate on Jenner's bill and steered through a narrowly focused bill that restricted the scope of the Supreme Court's ruling in *Jencks* v. *United States,* 353 U.S. 657 (1957). (The Court had ordered the release of FBI reports to defense attorneys because of questions about the veracity of an FBI informer.) The so-called Jencks law limited disclosure of FBI reports to only when an informer's grand jury and trial testimony conflicted with reports prepared contemporaneously by the FBI.

These efforts to curb Court review highlighted the priority which Congress assigned to internal security over civil liberties considerations. Thus, as part of the Labor Management Reforms Act of 1947, also known as the Taft-Hartley Act, any union officer bringing a dispute before the National Labor Relations Board was required to file an affidavit that he or she does "not believe in, and is not a member or support any organization that believes in or teaches" the violent overthrow of the government. Rejecting earlier legislative proposals to outlaw the Communist party, in 1950 Congress enacted the Internal Security (or McCarran) Act. Communist and communist action organizations were required to register with the specially created Subversive Activities Control Board; members of a "registered 'Communist organization'" could not "hold any nonelective office or employment under the United States or any office or employment with any labor organization," nor could any member of a "registered 'Communist action' organization" be employed in a defense industry; individuals "known or having reason to believe" to be members of Communist action organizations were denied passports; Communist and Communist action organizations could neither mail nor broadcast unless identifying their communications as Communist material; and anyone about whom there "is reasonable ground to believe . . . probably will engage in, or probably will conspire to engage in, acts of espionage or of sabotage" could be interned.

However, the McCarran Act's authorization of an internment program did not govern federal detention policy. Attorney General Tom Clark had secretly (in 1948) authorized the FBI to compile a list of individuals who should be detained in the event of war or national emergency. Because the department's earlier standards for detention were far more permissive, FBI and Justice Department officials decided in 1950 to ignore those mandated by this act—and drafted a proposed amendment and presidential proclamation to be introduced in the event of war to conform the McCarran Act's standards with those of this department portfolio. Then, in 1971 in response to protests precipitated by the disclosure in 1970 that certain facilities had been prepared to hold internees, Congress repealed the McCarran Act's preventive detention section. FBI and Justice Department officials nonetheless decided to continue compiling this list, renamed an Administrative Index. Fearful, in the wake of the more skeptical climate emerging in the aftermath of Watergate, that Congress might discover that they had ignored the rescission of legislative authorization for a preventive detention program, in 1973, FBI officials terminated this indexing program.

Ironically, at the time Congress had deemed the McCarran Act insufficiently restrictive and, thus, in 1954 enacted the Communist Control Act characterizing the Communist party as "in fact an instrument of a conspiracy to overthrow" the government whose policies and programs "are secretly prescribed for it by the foreign leaders of the world communist movement." Having concluded that the Communist party "should be outlawed" but aware that this might not be constitutional, Congress instead denied to the Communist party and its successors "any of the rights, privileges, and immunities" of legitimate political parties. Anyone who "knowingly or willfully becomes a member of the Communist party" also had to comply with the provisions of the McCarran Act and "Communist-infiltrated" unions were denied the rights provided under the National Labor Relations Act of 1935. In companion legislation, the Immunity Act, Congress denied the right to claim the Fifth Amendment during grand jury or congressional testimony relating to "national security or defense of the United States by treason, sabotage, espionage, seditious conspiracy" or violent overthrow of the government.

Earlier, in 1950, Congress enacted Public Law 733. Specified government officials were authorized in their "absolute discretion and when deemed necessary in the interest of national security" to dismiss any federal employee without the right to appeal such dismissal and the president could "from time to time" extend this summary dismissal authority to other departments and agencies when "in the best interest of national security" (quoted in Emerson, pp. 286–287).

In 1952, Congress also barred the admission and authorized the deportation of any alien who at any time belonged to proscribed totalitarian organizations. Then, in 1958, applicants for student loans and grant recipients under the National Defense Education Act were required to affirm that they did not belong to or support organizations advocating the overthrow of the government; and in 1959 any person who "is or had been a member of the Communist party" during the preceding five years was prohibited from serving as an officer or employee of "any labor organization."

The political crisis of the Vietnam War precipitated both legislative restrictions on civil liberties and a climate more supportive of civil liberties and skeptical of government surveillance. On the one hand, in 1965 Congress prohibited the destruction of draft cards and in 1968 criminalized travel across state lines or use of the mails or telephone by any person intending to encourage, organize, or participate in a riot or "any other overt act" of violence. On the other hand, in 1974, Congress enacted the Privacy Act and substantially amended the Freedom of Information Act of 1966 to curb government surveillance, information collection and dissemination practices. Then, in 1975, special House and Senate committees were created to investigate the federal intelligence agencies—in 1976, Congress created permanent intelligence-agency oversight committees. Responding to revelations of abuses of power, based either on the unwillingness of attorneys general to ensure adherence to the law or presidential interest in secrecy and deniability, Senators Edward Kennedy (D.-Mass.) and Frank Church (D.-Idaho) proposed legislation to specify the scope and responsibilities of the intelligence agencies. The election of the Reagan administration and Republican control of the Senate in the 1980 elections, however, buried these proposals.

State legislative actions paralleled those of the Congress. Despite the fact that counterintelligence was a federal responsibility, state legislatures nonetheless sought to curb "subversive activities," focusing particularly on public school and college teachers.

Thus, between 1945 and 1953, thirty-nine states criminalized either advocating or joining organizations seeking revolutionary change. The model for such legislative restrictions was Maryland's Subversive Activities Act of 1949, known as the Ober Law. This act made it a crime for any person "knowingly and willfully" to "commit, attempt to commit or aid in the commission of any act intended to overthrow, destroy or alter or to assist" in the violent overthrow or to attempt to "advocate, abet, advise, or teach by any means" the overthrow of the U.S. or state governments or to "assist in the formation and participate in the management or to contribute to the support of any subversive or foreign subversive organization knowing said organization to be a subversive organization or foreign subversive organization." All public employees were defined as "civil defense workers" under California's Levering Act of 1950, and were required to swear that during the preceding five years they had neither advocated nor belonged to any organization advocating the violent overthrow of the government. In contrast, the Texas legislature in 1951 required the filing of an affidavit by an applicant for a pharmacy license to prove that "he is not a member" or "affiliated" with the Communist party and "does not believe in, further, or teach" the violent overthrow of government, while Connecticut prohibited the printing of any "scurrilous, or obscene matter, concerning the form of government of the United States, its military forces, flag or uniform" or advocating anything "intended to injuriously affect the government." Earlier, in 1947, the Washington legislature created a special committee, chaired by Republican senator Albert Canwell, to investigate "Communist and subversive activities" in all state agencies, and as well those activities which "affect the conduct of the state, the functions of any state agency, unemployment relief and any form of public assistance, educational institutions of the state . . . or any political program."

In addition, by 1952 more than twenty states barred from the ballot both individuals and organizations advocating sedition, revolution, or a foreign-dominated government. Elected officials were required under a Washington statute to file a notarized affidavit that they did not belong to any organization listed as subversive by the attorney general; the Pennsylvania legislature required affidavits to be filed by all candidates for state elective office affirming that they were not a "subversive" person; Georgia required all public employees to disavow "sympathy" for communism; and Indiana required that the platforms of all political parties contain a plank that they did not advocate communism or revolution and authorized election boards to "determine the character and nature of the political doctrines" of candidates for state elective office. The Massachusetts, Indiana, Pennsylvania, Georgia, Texas, and Washington legislatures went further in 1951 to outlaw the Communist party while, in addition, Indiana required loyalty oaths of all those seeking a license to wrestle or box in the state.

California legislators, moreover, sought to promote cooperation among the state and public officials in this campaign against "subversive activities." Thus, in September 1948, the chair of California's Un-American Activities Committee, Jack Tenney, organized a Conference of State Un-American Activities to improve "liaison and coordination" among the states. Nine states sent representatives to this conference. No permanent liaison system evolved although Tenney's successor as chair of California's Un-American Activities Committee, Hugh Burns, in 1952 did establish a liaison relationship with representatives of California's public and private universities. Intended to effect "a cooperative plan to combat Communist infiltration," the committee's "contact" (former FBI or police officers) briefed university officials on the "subversive" background of incumbent and applicant faculty in order to "eliminate Communist party members from the faculties . . . and to take steps to prevent infiltration of the faculties by Communist party members, or those whose documentable record of Communist activities were so formidable as to raise a serious question concerning their ability to engage in objective teaching" (quoted in Iverson, pp. 270–271).

Other state legislatures shared California's interest in purging state colleges of "subversive" faculty. Special hearings were initiated by the Illinois, Washington, Michigan, and California legislatures into subversive influence in public education, while in 1949, New York enacted the Feinberg Law to eliminate "subversive persons from the public school system" by empowering the state's Board of Regents to develop a list of those organizations which "advocate, advise, teach or endorse" revolutionary doctrines, membership of which would be grounds for dismissal. Loyalty oaths of public school teachers were required by twenty-two states; in addition, the Alabama legislature required as a condition for school use that all textbooks and printed instructional material carry a statement indicating whether the author is or had been a member of the Communist party, an adherent of Marxist socialism, or a member of a Communist-front organization.

Nor was the effect of state legislative hearings confined to enacting legislative restrictions on civil liberties. In 1947, at the instigation of the American Legion, the Illinois legislature created the so-called Broyles Commission, chaired by Republican senator Paul Broyles, to investigate subversive activities in the state. In highly publicized hearings focusing on two private universities—Roosevelt University and the University of Chicago—the committee investigated the political orientation and teaching of selected faculty and sought to pressure university officials into purging their faculties, student bodies, and instructional material. In 1951, Senator Broyles attempted to capitalize on this publicity and introduced a bill to assign to a special attorney general the responsibility of ferreting out subversives from any private or state university. Democratic governor Adlai Stevenson, however, vetoed Broyle's bill.

Eager to avert similar legislative measures in the future, Stevenson and other governors, later that year, sought the FBI's assistance. In response, FBI director Hoover agreed to identify for governors or designated officials any "subversives" employed in state agencies or colleges, but on the strict condition that the FBI's assistance not be disclosed. When some governors did not honor this condition and at

times attributed their dismissal of specific employees to information obtained from the FBI, in 1955 Hoover reluctantly terminated this code-named "Responsibilities Program."

As the obsession over internal security threats waned, state legislatures and their federal counterparts responded during the 1970s to revelations of abuses of power by local and state-police "red squads" and of the misuse of school, police arrest, and credit records. To protect privacy rights and preclude police surveillance of political activities, state legislatures enacted privacy and freedom of information laws and ordered the destruction of police red-squad files. By the 1980s, controversy over abortion, pornography, and racist speech opened a new arena affecting civil liberties. While reflecting social (in contrast to earlier economic or political) tensions, state legislatures debated whether or not to restrict a woman's right to an abortion or to prohibit the publication and dissemination of offensive sexual or racial remarks (so-called hate speech, which was either prejudiced or intended to denigrate racial or sexual minorities).

Despite the wall created by constitutional prohibitions, then, both state and federal legislatures have periodically sought to restrict "dangerous" speech, publications, and other associational activities. Invariably these restrictions were imposed during periods of perceived crisis, triggered for the most part by international conflict but also by the emergence of radical movements seeking to effect societal change. As these international and domestic tensions subsided, the resulting more-libertarian political climate led to the repeal of legislative restrictions or the termination of either special legislative investigative committees or the covert relationship between public officials and federal and state police agencies. In striking contrast to the activist role that legislatures have assumed to promote civil rights, civil liberties, as the underlying premise of the First Amendment suggests, have historically been safeguarded through legislative inaction.

# LEGISLATURES AND CIVIL LIBERTIES

## *BIBLIOGRAPHY*

### General Surveys

Most of the literature on legislatures and civil liberties focuses on the twentieth century, consistent with the recency of such legislative activities. The best overall surveys include ZECHARIAH CHAFEE, *Free Speech in the United States* (Cambridge, Mass, 1941), which stops at World War II; FRANK DONNER, *The Age of Surveillance: The Aims and Methods of America's Political Intelligence System* (New York, 1980), which focuses on the twentieth century; ERNEST EBERLING, *Congressional Investigations: A Study of the Origin and Development of the Power of Congress to Investigate and Punish for Contempt* (New York, 1973), which is most useful for the 1790s and early nineteenth century; THOMAS EMERSON, DAVID HABER, and NORMAN DORSEN, *Political and Civil Rights in the United States,* 3d ed., 2 vols. (Boston, 1967), a law casebook that reprints the texts of various statutes and court rulings and identifies relevant articles and books; ROBERT GOLDSTEIN, *Political Repression in Modern America: From 1870 to the Present* (Cambridge, Mass., 1978), which surveys the various legislative efforts to curb trade union and radical activities from the general railroad strike of the 1870s through the Cold War years; and HAROLD W. HYMAN, *To Try Men's Souls: Loyalty Tests in American History* (Berkeley, Calif., 1959), which surveys the uses of loyalty oaths from the colonial era through the Cold War.

### Civil Liberties Issues Through World War II

LEONARD W. LEVY, *Emergence of a Free Press* (New York, 1985), and EDMUND S. MORGAN, *Inventing the People: The Rise of Popular Sovereignty in England and America* (New York, 1989), are insightful surveys of the colonial era, while JAMES M. SMITH, *Freedom's Fetters: The Alien and Sedition Laws and American Civil Liberties* (Ithaca, N.Y., 1956), is a solid survey of the Alien and Sedition Acts controversy of the 1790s. ROBERT K. MURRAY, *Red Scare: A Study of National Hysteria, 1919–1920* (Minneapolis, 1955), and WILLIAM PRESTON, *Aliens and Dissenters: Federal Suppression of Radicals, 1903–1933* (Cambridge, Mass., 1963), provide insights into legislative restrictions on civil liberties during the Progressive Era and

World War I, while LAWRENCE CHAMBERLAIN, *Loyalty and Legislative Action: A Survey of the Activity by the New York State Legislature 1919–1949* (Ithaca, N.Y., 1951), and ROBERT IVERSEN, *The Communists and the Schools* (New York, 1959), survey the post–World War I era, the 1920s and 1930s, World War II, and the early Cold War years. JEROLD AUERBACH, *Labor and Liberty: The LaFollette Committee and the New Deal* (Indianapolis, 1966), focuses more narrowly on the New Deal era, and RICHARD POLENBERG, *War and Society: The United States, 1941–1945* (Philadelphia, 1972), surveys the World War II period.

### The 1950s to the Present

The most extensive literature, however, details the role of the House Committee on Un-American Activities, Senator Joseph McCarthy, and various state legislative committees during the Cold War era. The most useful studies include ALAN BARTH, *Government by Investigation* (New York, 1955); FRANCIS BIDDLE, *The Fear of Freedom* (New York, 1951); DAVID CAUTE, *The Great Fear: The Anti-Communist Purge Under Truman and Eisenhower* (New York, 1978); WALTER GELHORN, ed., *The States and Subversion* (Ithaca, N.Y., 1952); WALTER GOODMAN, *The Committee: The Extraordinary Career of the House Committee on Un-American Activities* (New York, 1968); ROBERT GRIFFITH, *The Politics of Fear: Joseph R. McCarthy and the Senate,* 2d ed. (Amherst, Mass., 1987); TELFORD TAYLOR, *Grand Inquest: The Story of Congressional Investigations* (New York, 1955); and SAMUEL WALKER, *In Defense of American Liberties: A History of the ACLU* (New York, 1990). More recently, scholars have shifted the focus from the highly publicized hearings of the various federal and state legislative committees and have explored the covert liaison relationships between the Federal Bureau of Investigation and legislators and governors, as well as federal loyalty/security programs. Such works include RALPH S. BROWN, JR., *Loyalty and Security: Employment Tests in the United States* (New Haven, Conn., 1958); SIGMUND DIAMOND, *Compromised Campus: The Collaboration of the Universities with the Intelligence Community, 1945–1955 (New York,*

1992); Kenneth O'Reilly, *Hoover and the Un-Americans: The FBI, HUAC, and the Red Menace* (Philadelphia, 1983); Ellen Schrecker, *No Ivory Tower: McCarthyism and the Universities* (New York, 1986); Athan Theoharis, ed., *From the Secret Files of J. Edgar Hoover* (Chicago, 1991); and Athan Theoharis and John Stuart Cox, *The Boss: J. Edgar Hoover and the Great American Inquisition* (Philadelphia, 1988).

**See also** The Contemporary Congress, 1930–1992; Legislatures and Civil Liberties; Legislatures and Corruption from Colonial Times to the Present; Legislatures and Gender Issues; Legislatures and the Media; **and** The U.S. Congress: The Era of Party Patronage and Sectional Stress, 1829–1881.

# LEGISLATURES AND CIVIL RIGHTS

## *Hugh Davis Graham*

The concept of civil rights is applied here in its traditional, historic meaning as rights that are customarily exercised by the majority of adult citizens, but that are abridged or denied to other groups of citizens on account of their race, religion, ethnicity, or national origin. In the latter twentieth century in the United States the traditional definition was expanded to include groups sharing other attributes, such as language or some forms of disability, that are not immutable but that led to claims of discrimination and demands for civil remedies. Civil rights include the equal freedom to vote and to participate in the political process; equal access to the courts and the protections of the judicial process, to schools and other public facilities and accommodations, and to opportunities for employment and advancement.

### MINORITY DISCRIMINATION AND CIVIL RIGHTS

Historically, such rights were first extended to a minority of white propertied males in the early American republic and were most commonly denied to African Americans, Native Americans, and immigrants from non-Protestant countries—especially those from Roman Catholic, Jewish, and Asian cultures. African Americans constitute the most prominent historic exception to the American creed of equal rights, and the transition from slavery toward equal citizenship provides the most dramatic theme of evolving democracy. Because the rights of Native Americans were established by the colonial and national U.S. authorities in the diplomatic metaphor of treaty rights among nations, they fall beyond the constitutional and legislative scope of this essay. Women, not technically a minority group, constitute the most numerous and prolonged exception to the doctrine of equal citizen rights. Despite parallels between the drives for racial and gender equality in the U.S., especially the campaign for the right to vote, the historic uniqueness and complexity of gender-based law and family law require separate treatment. With the exception of some comparison of rights policies for minorities and women following the 1960s, this essay primarily discusses the struggle of minorities in the U.S. to achieve civil rights and equal protection in law where denial of these rights reflects historic discrimination based on race, religion, or ethnicity.

### MINORITY RIGHTS AND LEGISLATURES: THE HISTORIC TENSION

The group-based definition of civil rights, which rests on a history of prejudice and discrimination against certain minorities, poses the central dilemma of civil rights policy in the legislative arena. Legislatures in a democracy are likely to reflect the social views of majorities. The Founding Fathers of the American republic designed a constitutional structure of separated powers and internal checks and balances, including the Bill of Rights directed against the national government, to protect against the potential tyranny of popular majorities. The chief beneficiaries of this protection in the early republic, however, were not racial or ethnic minorities, but rather minorities of property and geography—of class and region. In a constitutional regime where owning slaves was protected under property rights, and representatives were selected by a franchise limited to white male freeholders, there was small incentive for legislatures to enlarge the rights of minorities.

For these reasons the champions of minority rights in nineteenth-century America sought to influence the behavior of legislatures in three ways. The first and broadest approach was to change public opinion itself through education and moral persuasion. The second was to create incentives for coalition politics within legislatures and political parties by extending the franchise to previously excluded groups. Appeals to fairness were reinforced by offering as a bargaining chip the future partisan loyalty of newly enfranchised voters. The third strategy was judicial: an appeal to judges who were theoretically insulated from popular passions, to strike down discriminatory laws and practices.

All three strategies carried risks, especially the last one, because the federal bench was predominantly conservative during its first century and a half, and so attempts to use the judiciary to invoke civil rights were largely ineffective until World War II. The foundering of the Whig party and the relative failure of Reconstruction testified to the volatility of ethnocultural issues and the precariousness of minority rights in an era of popular sovereignty. Nonetheless, the history of civil rights policy in American legislatures since the founding of the republic is a story of remarkable expansion.

## SLAVERY AND THE "FREE NEGRO"

Because chattel slavery is inconsistent with any coherent theory of republican rights, the legal status of African Americans historically referred to as "free Negroes" in antebellum America provides a more revealing benchmark of evolving rights than legislative changes regarding the institution of slavery. In 1860 there were approximately four million African American slaves, all of them in the southern and border states, while 488,000 blacks were free—250,000 in the South and 238,000 in the North. Southern free blacks were required by law to carry "free papers," and in many counties they were obliged to register annually and (in Alabama, Florida, and Georgia) to report periodically to white guardians. Free blacks were typically barred from serving on juries or testifying in court against whites. Evidence of gainful employment was often required and travel was restricted. Free blacks represented an anomaly that threatened the legal and racial symmetry of slavery and southern laws governing their emancipation and behavior remained strict.

Although northern blacks were less re-stricted by law than their "free" southern counterparts, they nonetheless remained narrowly circumscribed by customs and statutes that reflected the racist assumptions in the larger white society. African Americans were denied the right to vote except in New England, where only 6 percent of northern blacks resided. Illinois, Indiana, and Ohio, all sharing borders with slave states, had laws barring the entry of African Americans. These three states, along with Iowa and California, outlawed blacks from testifying against whites. As the commitment to public schooling began to spread throughout the North in the 1830s, most northern state legislatures passed laws requiring segregated schools for black children. Only in Massachusetts, in 1855, did a legislature end the requirement of school segregation.

In the federal system the U.S. Congress played no policy-making role in areas of state responsibility, which included voting, education, and most matters of civil and criminal law. In *Dred Scott* v. *Sandford,* 19 How. 393 (1857), the U.S. Supreme Court ruled that no black person descended from slaves was or could be a citizen of the U.S., and that consequently blacks could not sue in federal courts to defend their constitutional rights. On the eve of the Civil War, antislavery convictions had swept the northern states, but there was little public support for equal civil rights for African Americans, and racial classifications that limited their rights were common throughout the nation.

## THE CIVIL WAR AND RECONSTRUCTION IN THE SOUTH

When the Union armies crushed the Confederate rebellion at Appomattox in 1865, Congress, with the southern delegations absent since 1861, approved the Thirteenth Amendment and constitutionally buried the institution of human ownership that the Civil War had destroyed. To replace the elaborate slave codes, southern state governments between 1865 and 1866 enacted "Black Codes," or statutes aimed at improving the civil protections of the newly freed slaves to a level approximating that of the South's antebellum free blacks. African American marriages were legally recognized and blacks were allowed to own property and to sue and be sued. However, these statutes also functioned as instruments of social control to govern four-million illiterate freedmen. Because they were linked to the vagrancy laws, where the inability to pay fines made the freedmen vulnerable to manipulation by landowner and county elites, the new statutes sought to bind black farm labor to the land through a system of travel restrictions and mandatory labor contracts, licenses, and bonds.

Northern opinion was offended by the Black Codes, and Republicans especially resented the prospect of readmitting to Congress a delegation of refractory southern officeholders whose ranks were ironically swollen by the abolition under the Thirteenth Amendment of the Constitution's original three-fifths compromise. Slaves had only been counted as three-fifths of a person in the apportionment of seats in the U.S. House of Representatives, so the destruction of slavery increased the South's strength in the House by two-fifths. In response to resurgent southern defiance Congress, under the leadership of Radical Republicans, refused to seat the southern congressmen, and in the spring of 1866 Congress passed the first civil rights law of Reconstruction. The Civil Rights Act of 1866 sought to secure for the freedmen the "full and equal benefit of all laws and proceedings for the security of person and estate." It stipulated the rights to make and secure contracts; to buy, sell, and own real and personal property; and to bring suit and give evidence in court. To protect these rights, blacks were authorized to sue in federal court, with legal assistance available from the Department of Justice and from the agents of the Freedmen's Bureau, which Congress created in 1865 and extended through 1872.

Fearing that such controversial guarantees for the freedmen might be repealed by subsequent Congresses, where southern members might combine with northern Democrats, Radical Republican leaders in Congress in the summer of 1866 proposed the Fourteenth Amendment to the Constitution. It was designed to give a constitutional guarantee to the statutory commitments of the Civil Rights Act of 1866. The first section contained three powerful charters of freedom for citizens of the United States, phrased in the tradition of classical liberalism, as prohibitions against the state:

No State shall make or enforce any law which shall abridge the privileges or immunities of citizens of the United States; nor shall any state deprive any person of life, liberty, or property, without due process of law; nor deny to any person within its jurisdiction the equal protection of the laws.

For the first time, the Constitution carried a commitment to equality.

When Congress sent this language to the states for ratification, however, ten of the eleven Confederate states refused to ratify the Fourteenth Amendment. President Andrew Johnson, a Tennessee Democrat who as Lincoln's vice president had supported the war against slavery but had opposed racial equality, defended lenient policies toward southern state governments seeking readmission to the Union. In response, Radical Republicans charged that the bloody sacrifices of war were being squandered, and the Republicans swept the autumn elections of 1866. The following year Congress enacted, over Johnson's vetoes, a series of Reconstruction laws that imposed military rule on the South. With 150,000 Confederate leaders barred from the polls and 700,000 southern freedmen newly empowered to vote, the militarily reconstructed state governments in the South wrote new reform constitutions and ratified the Fourteenth Amendment as a price of readmission.

The forced enfranchisement of blacks in the South during the late 1860s, however, was paralleled by white voter rejection of black enfranchisement in the North. Between 1865 and 1869, referenda in Connecticut, Kansas, Michigan, New York, and Wisconsin all rejected extending the vote to black men. Public opposition to black suffrage in northern states seems to have declined under the impact of the abolitionist debate and the mobilization of the Republican party.

In New York State, where the black proportion of the population never exceeded 3 percent after 1820, popular referenda rejected black suffrage by 72.4 percent in 1846, by 63.6 percent in 1860, and 53.1 percent in 1869; only white males were allowed to vote in these referenda. However, this gradual erosion in the opposition to black suffrage was not accompanied by more-generalized support for equal rights within the northern states.

To secure the vote of 700,000 loyal black Republicans in the South and small but potentially decisive numbers of black Republicans in the North, while still not offending widespread "anti-Negro" sentiment, the Republican leaders in Congress in 1869 fashioned a compromise voting-rights amendment to the Constitution. It would leave voting policy under customary state control, and not attempt to confer the franchise on black men as a positive national act. But it would prohibit the states from denying the vote for racial reasons. Ratified in 1870, the Fifteenth Amendment held simply that "the right of citizens of the United States to vote shall not be denied or abridged by the United States or by any State on account of race, color, or previous condition of servitude."

In 1870, when Ku Klux Klan terrorism had spread through the South in an attempt to intimidate black citizens from exercising their rights, Congress began to enact a series of enforcement acts. Passed under the implementing authority that Congress gave itself in the final sections of all three Civil War amendments, the enforcement laws created penalties to deter violations of the Fourteenth and Fifteenth Amendments. Their effectiveness depended on prosecution by the U.S. attorney general and conviction by federal judges. In 1875, Congress passed its final major reform in civil rights law. The Civil Rights Act of 1875 guaranteed to all Americans regardless of race or color "the full and equal enjoyment of the accommodations . . . of inns, public conveyances on land or water, theatres and other places of amusement" and prohibited disqualification for jury service because of "race, color, or previous condition of servitude."

## THE RETREAT FROM RECONSTRUCTION

By the mid-1870s the national mood was tiring of the struggle of Reconstruction. When Senator Charles Sumner of Massachusetts drove through the last reform of Reconstruction in 1875, he was forced to abandon an attempt to ban racially segregated schools throughout the nation. Congress as early as 1862, when it voted to fund African American schools in the District of Columbia, had stipulated that the schools be racially segregated. The following year, the new state of West Virginia, breaking away from secessionist Virginia, created a school system that required racial segregation.

Despite the small size of the black population in the North, dominant white sentiment continued to be hostile to equal participation by blacks in political life or in public education. Radical reform of race relations in the South was supported in the North partly out of punitive sentiment against the Confederacy, and partly out of a desire to keep the bulk of the nation's black population south of the Mason-Dixon line.

In some northern areas, particularly in the New England states and in New York, Republican legislatures during the Reconstruction period strengthened civil rights protections for black constituents. By 1877, however, when the last federal troops were withdrawn from the South, most Republican leaders in the North were losing interest in civil rights issues, concentrating instead on programs to boost the nation's industrial economy. The Civil Rights Act of 1875, which barred racial discrimination in public accommodations, had been imposed from Washington on a nation where property rights were respected and the authority of proprietors to control entry to their premises was widely assumed. By 1883, more than one hundred test cases from all over the nation were bubbling up in the federal courts to challenge the open-accommodations provisions of the 1875 law.

The Supreme Court consolidated five of these challenges in several civil rights cases and ruled on them in 1883. The plaintiffs, supported by the U.S. Justice Department, were blacks who had been refused entry to a restaurant in Kansas, a hotel in Missouri, an opera in New York, a theater in San Francisco, and a "ladies car" on a railroad in Tennessee. In an 8–1 decision, the Supreme Court ruled that the Civil Rights Act of 1875 unconstitutionally infringed on the liberty of private proprietors, who were not officials of the state, to discriminate among their customers.

The judicial assault on Reconstruction started as early as 1873. In the Slaughterhouse Cases, which did not directly involve race relations, a narrowly divided Supreme Court ruled that the Fourteenth Amendment protected citizens from state denial of the "privileges and immunities" only of their national rights of citizenship. These included rights defined by the Constitution, such as the writ of habeas corpus, and such rights as access to federal buildings, navigable streams and seaports, the right to passports, and to protection abroad. However, the broader rights of person and property, which characterize republican civil liberty generally, were held in the Slaughterhouse decision to be state-protected and hence were not covered by the Fourteenth Amendment. The Supreme Court further narrowed the scope of Reconstruction rights by ruling in *United States* v. *Cruikshank,* 92 U.S. 542 (1876), that intimidation of blacks by private persons (white mobs) did not constitute the state action required by the Fourteenth Amendment. Similarly, the Court held in *United States* v. *Reese,* 92 U.S. 214 (1876), that the states retained control over the franchise and that the Fifteenth Amendment protected blacks only from proven racially motivated offenses.

## THE ERA OF RACIAL DISFRANCHISEMENT AND SEGREGATION

During the 1880s, conservative state governments in the South, "redeemed" by white Democrats from control by "Black Reconstruction" regimes, began to reassert local control over the electoral process. By the early 1890s, when rural distress led to economically radical populist coalitions of black and white dirt farmers, landowners raised the cry of racial corruption to split the biracial coalitions of the poor. Black disfranchisement was proposed as a reform to remove electoral corruption. Led by Mississippi in 1890, the South witnessed a wave of constitutional conventions and legislative revisions in which race-neutral methods, required by the Fifteenth Amendment, were devised to disfranchise black voters. The new poll taxes, residency requirements, and literacy tests were written in racially neutral language, but southern blacks were disproportionately affected. Most devastating was a racially nonneutral device: the all-white primary election. The spring and summer primaries nominated Democratic candidates for office in an increasingly one-party region, where Republicans tended to be hopelessly outnumbered in the autumn general elections. The federal courts agreed that although the Fifteenth Amendment prohibited

racial discrimination in elections to office, the political parties were private, nongovernmental organizations whose nominating processes were not bound by the Fifteenth Amendment.

By 1910, the black vote had been decimated throughout the South, where 90 percent of the nation's African Americans still resided. In 1896, for example, 130,000 African Americans were registered as voters in Louisiana. By 1900, however, following the constitutional convention of 1898, only 5,000 black men remained on Louisiana's voter rolls. In Alabama, only 2 percent of voting-age black men were registered by 1906, compared to 83 percent of voting-age white men. In the wake of disfranchisement, politically defenseless African Americans were subjected to waves of violence. The lynching of blacks in the South, which had been rare under slavery because the slave codes protected valuable property, soared in the 1890s. Between 1892 and 1902, 77 percent of the 1,455 southerners who were lynched were black—although they constituted only a third of the South's population.

After World War I, lynching dropped off substantially. But the terror had effectively subdued a black population that had been largely stripped of its judicial and political defenses. The reign of disfranchisement and racist terror was accompanied by the rapid maturing of a formal, legal structure of biracial caste—the "Jim Crow" system of racial segregation. Southern legislatures in the 1890s and the early 1900s enacted elaborate codes to separate the races in schools, transportation, hotels, restaurants, and places of entertainment, including racially segregated public restrooms and drinking fountains. The U.S. Supreme Court, in *Plessy* v. *Ferguson,* 163 U.S. 537 (1896), ruled 8–1 that the equal-protection clause of the Fourteenth Amendment did not prohibit state requirements that facilities be racially "separate but equal." *Plessy,* a case involving railroad segregation, was soon followed by rulings that upheld segregation in public and private schools and in virtually every realm of public life. During the presidency of Woodrow Wilson, a southern-born Democrat, segregation practices spread through the federal government itself.

By World War I the federal judiciary, always racially conservative and staffed by white men, had neutralized most but not all of Reconstruction's constitutional and legislative protections for black civil rights. In three significant rulings the Court struck down one traditional form of racial discrimination and two novel ones. The Supreme Court ruled in *Strauder* v. *West Virginia*, 100 U.S. 303 (1880), that citizens could not be excluded from juries because of their race; in *Guinn* v. *U.S.*, 238 U.S. 347 (1915), the Court awarded an early (and rare) victory to the new National Association for the Advancement of Colored People (NAACP), organized in 1909, by ruling unconstitutional the "grandfather clause," a southern device of the disfranchising era designed to limit voting to citizens (necessarily white) whose grandfathers had voted; and in *Buchanan* v. *Warley*, 245 U.S. 60 (1917), the Court struck down municipal zoning ordinances that required racial segregation by residential blocks.

The effect of all three victories for equal rights, however, was minimal. The ban on racial exclusions from juries had been largely nullified by the disfranchisement of 1890–1910, which effectively removed blacks from the voter rolls from which juries were chosen. The grandfather clause was a bizarre device whose termination had almost no discernible impact on black voting. The housing victory halted a potentially pernicious practice, but it had little relevance for the rural and small-town South, where most African Americans still lived in 1917 and where housing had historically been racially mixed. With the exception of the famous Scottsboro Cases of 1932 and 1935, which strengthened rights to counsel and protections against racially exclusive juries, the Supreme Court continued its conservative judicial stance until 1937. After that watershed year, the more liberal justices appointed by President Franklin Roosevelt fundamentally altered the judicial philosophy of the federal bench.

## THE PARALYSIS OF CONGRESS, 1875–1957

The retreat from Reconstruction after 1875 reflected a sectional reconciliation that by 1900 had effectively removed civil rights from the legislative agenda of Congress. The healing of the wounds of the Civil War among white Americans coincided with the popularity of the survival-of-the-fittest doctrine of conservative

Darwinism, and also with the formal creation of a racial caste system in the southern third of the nation. Segregationist regimes in the southern and border states were entrenched by the development of one-party systems based on disfranchisement of black (and many poor white) voters and by malapportioned legislatures that favored rural interests and county-seat elites.

Nationally, because Democratic nominees for the presidency could not win without southern electoral votes, southern delegates at nominating conventions exercised an implicit veto over candidates whose civil rights policies threatened party harmony and southern caste arrangements. As the political scientist V. O. Key, Jr., demonstrated in *Southern Politics in State and Nation,* the southern system of racial subordination, Democratic dominance, social stasis, and economic stagnation showed remarkable stability through the first half of the twentieth century. During the years from Woodrow Wilson to Harry S. Truman, white elites in the segregated South in effect held the national Democratic party hostage to its veto over civil rights policy.

In Washington southern Democrats, insulated from two-party competition in general elections, accumulated disproportionate seniority in the congressional committee system. When the Great Depression of the 1930s and Franklin Roosevelt's New Deal led to Democratic control of Congress, southerners came to dominate the committee chairmanships of both chambers. In the House, southern Democrats in coalition with Republicans gained control of the powerful Rules Committee. In the Senate the filibuster provided a defensive weapon with which a minority of senators could paralyze the chamber with almost unlimited debate until objectionable bills were withdrawn.

As a result of these southern defenses, no civil rights bills of any consequence passed the Congress between 1875 and 1957. On three occasions—in 1922, 1937, and 1940—the House passed bills designed to make lynching a federal crime. The legislative purpose was to bring Justice Department authority into southern jurisdictions where segregated systems of criminal justice failed to indict or convict the lynchers of blacks. During the 1920s and 1930s a federal antilynching bill was the top legislative priority of the NAACP and the northern civil rights coalition. Senate filibusters, however, doomed all such attempts. The anti-lynching campaign functioned primarily as an outlet for symbolic politics in an era of congressional paralysis in civil rights policy.

## ROOSEVELT'S WARTIME COMMITTEE ON FAIR EMPLOYMENT PRACTICE

With policy development blocked in Congress, policy innovation shifted to the wartime presidency. In the summer of 1941, President Roosevelt, responding to demands that black workers share jobs in the war industries boom, issued Executive Order 8802 creating the Committee on Fair Employment Practices (FEPC). As a small advisory body created under the president's authority to prepare adequately for national defense, the FEPC lacked the political legitimacy that accompanied agencies established through normal congressional authorization and appropriations. The FEPC's power to set and enforce the terms of federal contracts was drawn from presidential authority. But the committee's public hearings during the war and its policing role in job discrimination were resented by employers and unions and stirred little enthusiasm in the federal contracting agencies.

The FEPC struggled through World War II with a tiny staff, successfully resolving through voluntary negotiations almost a third of the 14,000 job-discrimination complaints it received. But by the war's end the FEPC had accumulated powerful enemies. With the conclusion of the war emergency, the committee was terminated by congressional conservatives under the leadership of Senator Richard Russell (D.-Ga.), chairman of the Senate Armed Forces Committee, and Representative Howard Smith (D.-Va.), a senior member of the Rules Committee and chairman of a House wartime committee to investigate federal agencies.

The FEPC experience was instructive both for civil rights reformers and for their opponents. Conservatives learned to tighten legislative scrutiny of presidential authority, especially when the executive bureaucrats lacked statutory approval and were not subject to congressional purse strings. In 1944, Senator Russell sponsored an appropriations rider that required congressional approval and budgeting after one year for presidentially created agencies. This forced the termination of FEPC in 1946. Through the Administrative Procedures Act of 1946, Congress imposed judicial procedures on the federal regulatory agencies, such as the Federal Trade Commission (FTC) and the National Labor Relations Board (NLRB), in order to control the actions of appointed bureaucrats by requiring more painstaking (and expensive) courtlike processes. After World War II the conservative bloc in Congress, centered around a coalition of Republicans from the Midwest and the Rocky Mountain region and Democrats from the South, remained alert to protect employers from the overreaching of New Deal agencies like the NLRB and to nip any new FEPC in the bud.

## THE PROBLEM OF CIVIL RIGHTS ENFORCEMENT

The paralysis of Congress in civil rights policy, as well as the retrenchment of segregationist southern and border-state legislatures, did not extend to all the states. The retreat from Reconstruction had been a national phenomenon, but the more urban and industrial states in the North did not entirely abandon the Reconstruction vision of equal civil rights. After the Supreme Court in 1883 had struck down the open-accommodations sections of the Civil Rights Act of 1875, New York State in 1895 reenacted most of the stricken national provisions into state law. By World War II, several states in the northern industrial tier, stretching from Massachusetts to Wisconsin to the West Coast, had passed similar antidiscrimination laws to cover employment, schooling, and public accommodations like theaters and restaurants. Indeed, even Congress itself as early as 1933 had included occasional, boilerplate prohibitions against discrimination by "race, color, or creed" in the New Deal's relief and recovery legislation. Such statutory language, however, whether in Washington, D.C., or even in states like New York, appeared to have little impact. The explanation for this lay in the nature of antidiscrimination law itself, and especially in its provisions for enforcement.

Discrimination by race, creed, color, or national origin had historically been understood in Anglo-American law to mean deliberate conduct motivated by hostility and based on prejudice. Although the concept of discrimination in the law was inherently neutral, the concept of invidious discrimination was based on the intent to harm individuals. In the American civil law of tort as it evolved in the nineteenth century, civil wrongs required blameworthiness, and there could be no liability without fault. Antidiscrimination law in the United States evolved from the traditions of the civil law rather than criminal law, wherein the right to be free from harm is a public right. In criminal law, the right of citizens to be free from robbery and murder is enforceable by public authority and does not require private complaints or lawsuits. Police and prosecutors are provided by the state, and defendants are criminally charged as the People versus John Doe.

In civil law, however, citizens bring private cases against one another, employing private attorneys to represent them before a magistrate. The historic sanctity of property rights in Anglo-American law, when combined with the traditional presumption of innocence and the consequent burden of proof on the accusing party, had made antidiscrimination claims both expensive and unpromising. The proof needed to convict alleged discriminators was often in the unique possession of the accused—commonly an employer or other official who commanded institutional authority and had access to the resources necessary for self-defense. Additionally, plaintiffs claiming discrimination could rarely afford sustained legal fees. Moreover, the rewards for conviction were modest, traditionally taking the form of "make-whole" relief, and the penalties against offenders were relatively light. In job-discrimination suits, remedies commonly required hiring or reinstatement with back pay but without compensatory or punitive damages. Thus even in the few jurisdictions where antidiscrimination law was on the books, the pursuit of litigation was risky and hence rare.

After the end of World War II, the United Nations was founded under U.S. leadership on principles of universal human rights. This inspired a bipartisan coalition of liberals in the northeastern cities to begin a campaign for new laws to enforce equal rights more effectively. The reformers sought to resolve what Gunnar Myrdal called *An American Dilemma,* in his classic study of 1944 of "The Negro Problem and Modern Democracy," by ending minority discrimination in the North as well as racial segregation in the South.

To deal with the problem of unenforced private rights, the reformers found a promising model of enforcement in the federal regulatory commissions. These quasi-judicial boards embodied at least a partial *public* right. The Federal Trade Commission, for example, protected consumers from false advertising; the Securities and Exchange Commission protected investors from investment fraud; the NLRB protected workers from the unfair labor practices of employers or unions. Congress had thus created regulatory agencies with the intention of avoiding slow and costly litigation, by streamlining the administrative resolution of disputes. The investigations of these agencies were mostly as a result of complaints against a particular body and their methods encouraged voluntary negotiation. Unlike the criminal justice system, they did not employ battalions of police and prosecutors. But their investigators were public officials armed with the authority to compel evidence and summon witnesses. Most important was their trump card: their ability to act as judges by issuing, following public hearings, cease-and-desist orders that were enforceable in the federal courts and could require "make-whole" relief.

## STATE ANTIDISCRIMINATION COMMISSIONS

Not surprisingly, New York was the first state to establish the new model. In 1945, Republican Governor Thomas E. Dewey signed into law the Ives-Quinn bill, which established the State Commission Against Discrimination—New York's legislatively authorized FEPC. New York's commission, which became a widely emulated model for state and municipal FEPCs, emphasized education and conciliation, while simultaneously keeping in reserve the threat of punitive sanctions.

Within five years the New York model was adopted by state legislatures throughout the urban-industrial tier of the country: New Jersey in 1945, Massachusetts and Connecticut in 1946; and then New Mexico, Oregon, Rhode Island, and Washington in 1947. By 1960, state commissions had been adopted in eight other states: Michigan, Minnesota, and Pennsylvania in 1955; Colorado and Wisconsin in 1957; California and Ohio in 1959; and Delaware in 1960. The urban-industrial base of the civil rights coalition also produced municipal FEPCs. Many of these arose predictably in the major cities of industrial states, such as Chicago, Cleveland, Philadelphia, and Pittsburgh. But a surprising number were in nonindustrial states where rural-dominated legislatures provided no state model, inspiring cities such as Louisville and Oklahoma City to create their own.

During the period 1945–1965 the state and municipal FEPCs earned respect from civil rights organizations, labor unions, and even employers who wanted greater work efficiency. New York's commission during its first twenty years received a total of 8,973 complaints. The commission found probable cause of discrimination against minorities in 1,753 charges, and successfully conciliated all but thirty-four of them. Full public hearings in these particular cases led to only seven cease-and-desist orders; the potential for punitive sanctions proved to be a successful deterrent.

Nonetheless, congressional conservatives remained adamant in opposing a national FEPC. During the late 1940s the national civil rights coalition created the Leadership Conference on Civil Rights. An umbrella organization formed to coordinate the lobbying efforts of minority, labor, and church groups—such as the NAACP, the Congress of Industrial Organizations, and the National Council of Churches—the Leadership Conference on Civil Rights set as its top legislative priority a national FEPC. In 1949 the House passed a voluntary FEPC bill that, although it lacked cease-and-desist authority, was killed by Senate conservatives in a filibuster. During the 1950s, public attention on civil rights shifted from Congress to the Supreme Court's school desegregation initiative in *Brown* v. *Board of Education,* 347 U.S. 483 (1954), and also to the black protest movement in the South, sparked in 1955 by a boycott led by Rev. Martin Luther King, Jr., against segregated buses in Montgomery, Alabama.

## THE CIVIL RIGHTS ACT OF 1957: A JUDICIAL STRATEGY

Following the *Brown* decision, northern disapproval of southern segregation, together with international pressure in the Cold War competition, produced a consensus in Washington, even among conservatives, that continued congressional silence on civil rights policy was politically insupportable. The most promising area of policy agreement was voting rights. The Eisenhower administration had proposed a voting-rights bill in 1956, and as a consequence the Republican ticket in that year's congressional elections was strongly supported by black voters in strategic northern states. In 1960, when the popular Eisenhower would be ineligible to run for reelection, the black vote could easily decide a close-run contest. In the South only 25 percent of voting-age blacks were registered to vote in 1957, and although this represented a sharp increase from 3 percent in 1940, it was a clear sign of continuing electoral abuse.

In 1957 a bipartisan coalition in Congress, led by Senate Majority Leader Lyndon Johnson (D.-Tex.), passed the nation's first significant civil rights bill since Reconstruction. The Civil Rights Act of 1957 was essentially a voting-rights law. In order to avoid a Senate filibuster by conservatives, the Eisenhower administration and congressional Democrats led by Johnson in the Senate and in the House by his fellow Texas Democrat, Speaker Sam Rayburn, agreed to adopt a judicial model that would enforce voting-rights violations through the federal courts rather than through administrative agencies. The 1957 bill established a temporary and advisory Civil Rights Commission to make investigations and reports, and a Civil Rights Division was created in the Justice Department. But the only enforcement action authorized was for the attorney general to bring suits for injunctions against local electoral jurisdictions on behalf of individuals claiming denial of their voting rights. Most blacks claiming voter discrimination would have to initiate and fund their own private suits, a process that was inherently time-consuming and expensive. For conservatives, however, the judicial approach avoided the danger of a federally controlled voter-registration machinery under the control of appointive officials in Washington.

In 1959 the Civil Rights Commission reported that in sixteen majority-black counties in the South not a single black was registered to vote, yet the Justice Department had filed only three franchise cases. In 1960, on the eve of the presidential election, Congress hastily passed another voting-rights bill. But the 1960 law changed the judicially enforced mechanisms of the 1957 legislation only marginally. The Justice Department, for all its prestige and visibility, remained a small, elite agency of legal professionals. Unlike large program-running and contracting agencies like the departments of Health, Education, and Welfare or the Pentagon, which shaped government policy through massive spending and its accompanying regulations, the Justice Department had historically performed its mission by carefully selecting a small number of test cases and pressing them through the federal courts, seeking precedents that would guide the long-range evolution of policy. Even under the more vigorous direction of Attorney General Robert Kennedy between 1961 and 1964, the judicial approach to civil rights enforcement from the Justice Department was unlikely to yield dramatic change.

## THE CIVIL RIGHTS MOVEMENT AND THE CIVIL RIGHTS ACT OF 1964

During the first two years of his administration, President John F. Kennedy, despite his campaign promises of 1960, proposed no significant civil rights legislation to Congress. By the 1960s, Congress, under Democratic control since 1933 with only two brief exceptions, was disproportionately influenced by the seniority of its southern members. When Kennedy entered the White House in 1961, southern and border-state Democrats chaired thirteen of the nineteen standing committees in the House and twelve of the sixteen in the Senate. Like Roosevelt before him, Kennedy was unwilling to risk his economic and international initiatives by provoking the conservative coalition in a civil rights battle. This static equilibrium was overturned not by events in Washington, but by the accelerating momentum of the civil rights movement in the South.

In 1960 the sit-in demonstrations against segregated restaurants led to the creation of the Student Nonviolent Coordinating Committee (SNCC). In 1961 the Congress of Racial Equality (CORE) sponsored the freedom-ride campaign to desegregate interstate bus lines and terminals in the Deep South. In the spring of 1963, the Southern Christian Leadership Conference (SCLC) under the direction of Martin Luther King, Jr., spearheaded the drive against segregation in Birmingham, Alabama. The civil rights movement had learned to select its targets strategically, and the violent repression by white police authorities in Birmingham captured a national television audience. Angry northern voters demanded effective national action. In response, President Kennedy in the summer of 1963 proposed a civil rights bill that would force all restaurants, hotels, stores, and other enterprises open to public business to admit all citizens irrespective of race, color, or creed.

The desegregation of public accommodations became Title 2 of Kennedy's civil rights bill of 1963. A radical proposal by historical standards, Title 2 would infringe on traditional property rights and interpose federal authority between proprietors and their customers. The televised violence in Birmingham had changed the national mood, politically mobilizing a nationwide constituency that was determined to punish and reform the white South. Like the voting-rights provisions of 1957, Title 2 would be enforced primarily by private citizens going to court, and secondarily by the attorney general's targeted suits for federal court injunctions against organizations that discriminated by race, religion, or national origin. Unlike the ineffective voting-rights machinery of 1957, however, Title 2 destroyed its target with devastating speed.

The reasons for Title 2's rapid success are several. By the fall of 1963, public opinion in the United States, including even much of the white South, seemed to have reached a consensus that segregated public accommodations were no longer defensible. And although southern business leaders conformed to local laws and customs, fearing the consequences of desegregating in isolation, they also recognized that segregation excluded paying customers and increasingly invited demonstrations and disruption. In private, many southern business leaders preferred a simultaneous overturning of Jim Crow policies that long had been imposed on them by segregation ordinances. Unlike voting-rights litigation, where technically race-neutral requirements like literacy tests complicated judgments about impermissible voting discrimination, the open-accommodations command of Title 2 simply required the dropping of barriers to entry. Questions of intent were scarcely relevant. There was little question about who would win in court if minorities contested their exclusion from premises normally open to the public.

By November of 1963, when President Kennedy was assassinated in Dallas, Texas, controversy over Title 2 had begun to recede. By the fall of 1964, after President Johnson had signed the civil rights bill into law, racial segregation in public accommodations was dead.

## JOB DISCRIMINATION AND THE EQUAL EMPLOYMENT OPPORTUNITY COMMISSION

Congressional liberals between 1962 and 1964 were not content merely to enact legislation granting blacks equal access to restaurants and hotels in the South. Nationally unemployment among African Americans was twice as high as among whites. In 1960, African American family income was only 55 percent of white family income. Long frustrated by their inability to create a national FEPC, the civil rights coalition in Congress in the late summer of 1963 inserted into Kennedy's civil rights bill a job-discrimination section, Title 7, that would establish a new enforcement agency, the Equal Employment Opportunity Commission (EEOC). The name was new, but to congressional conservatives the specter of FEPC was familiar.

In the House, moderate Republicans negotiated a compromise with the Kennedy administration and with the Democratic leadership in Congress that would deny cease-and-desist authority to the new agency. The EEOC, however, would retain *prosecuting* authority to file suits in court—a power traditionally reserved to the Justice Department. The EEOC would thus rely primarily on individuals filing their own suits as a means of processing citizen complaints and negotiating voluntary conciliations. Unlike the state FEPCs, the new agency would lack the quasi-judicial authority to issue cease-and-desist orders. But under the House compromise the EEOC would retain a prosecutor's role in protecting a public right to nondiscrimination in employment by filing suit in federal court against selected employers or unions.

In the winter of 1964 the civil rights bill passed the House in this form, but with the significant addition of sex discrimination to Title 7, an amendment that was adopted on the House floor without committee hearings. In the Senate, Minority Leader Everett McKinley Dirksen (R.-Ill.) held the key to passage because he controlled the Republican votes necessary to break the southern filibuster. The compromise negotiated by Dirksen stipulated that the new law would ban discrimination. It would therefore prohibit the use of minority preferences of any kind—a provision that found no dissent in either chamber. The bill's floor leader in the Senate, Majority Whip Hubert Humphrey (D.-Minn.), repeatedly attacked the "bubaboo" of racial quotas, and promised to "eat my hat" if the bill led to such abuses. "Title 7 prohibits discrimination," Humphrey explained. "In effect, it says that race, religion, and national origin are not to be used as the basis for hiring and firing."

In addition to banning the use of minority preferences, the Dirksen compromise stripped the EEOC of the prosecutor's role that it had been given in the House. Thus the new EEOC, scheduled to open in the summer of 1965, would be essentially a voluntary, complaint-processing agency. A major study of employment discrimination and the law, completed the year the EEOC opened for business, called the new agency a "poor enfeebled thing."

## THE VOTING RIGHTS ACT OF 1965

The Civil Rights Act of 1964 was a complex law of many titles, but it included no significant provision for voting rights. Despite the landslide Democratic victory in the elections of 1964, the once solidly Democratic Deep South voted massively for the conservative Republican nominee, Senator Barry Goldwater of Arizona, who had voted against the Civil Rights Act. In 1964, nine out of ten blacks voted for Johnson, but 65 percent of the South's voting-age blacks remained unregistered. Early in 1965, protestors led by Martin Luther King, Jr., once again commanded a national television audience—this time by demonstrating in Selma, Alabama. Selma was the seat of government for Dallas County, where blacks constituted 57.6 percent of the population but only

2.1 percent of registered voters. The voter-registration rolls listed 9,542 of the county's 14,410 whites but only 335 of its 15,115 blacks.

As in Birmingham in 1963, King's protesting marchers drew a nationally televised violent response from Alabama police forces. National opinion demanded that Congress guarantee the vote to southern blacks. In response, the Johnson administration sent Congress a voting-rights bill that was at once traditional and yet novel. The traditional core element was the commitment to nondiscrimination. Like the Civil Rights Act, the Voting Rights Act was grounded in a Constitution that was color-blind. Classic liberalism's commands were couched negatively: citizens and voters may not be treated differently on account of immutable attributes like race, color, or ethnicity.

The novel, even radical, elements of the administration's bill concerned enforcement. Rejecting a proposed new agency to register voters for federal elections, Johnson insisted that all elections, including state and local contests, be covered immediately. He required further that the unprecedented federal program to enfranchise black southerners be confined to an emergency intervention that would force black registration, provide guarantees against electoral backsliding, then return to normal federal-state relationships in electoral governance. The new law's operative provisions would expire in five years if successful, and in the meantime would provide for bailout from coverage on good behavior by local electoral districts.

The operational heart of the Voting Rights Act was section four. It contained a racially neutral, two-part statistical "trigger" to identify discriminating districts. If a voting jurisdiction used a literacy test or similar device, and if fewer than half of the adult population was registered or voted in the 1964 elections, then federal examiners could be dispatched to the county to ensure that election officials registered voters without discrimination. If local election officials were uncooperative, federal registrars could enroll the new voters themselves.

The second novel component was designed to prevent covered jurisdictions from playing dirty electoral tricks, such as switching offices from elective to appointive status or gerrymandering voting district lines. The "preclearance" provision in section five was designed to prevent such electoral backsliding. It required electoral officials in covered jurisdictions, which included Alabama, Georgia, Louisiana, South Carolina, Virginia, and twenty-eight counties in North Carolina, to obtain prior approval from the Justice Department or the federal district court in Washington, D.C., for any changes in local electoral arrangements.

The Voting Rights Act was a stunning success. By 1970, almost a million new black voters had been added to the rolls in the South. As the new black voters swelled the ranks of the Democratic party, suburban southern whites increasingly voted Republican. Two-party competition similar to national patterns replaced the South's one-party tradition of racial demagoguery. The unprecedented achievement was the fruit of the triggering and enfranchising functions of section four. Preclearance was rarely denied under the insurance function of section five. Like cease-and-desist authority in the state FEPCs, section five's preclearance was effective because it was available in reserve. So enthusiastic was Congress over the results of the Voting Rights Act that it was renewed for another five years in 1970, despite complaints by the Nixon administration and southern critics that the law was unfairly directed against the South.

## NONDISCRIMINATION, THE FEMINIST MOVEMENT, AND THE EQUAL RIGHTS AMENDMENT

The 1960s represented the high-water mark of the classic liberal tradition of nondiscrimination, especially on behalf of African Americans, and the ideal of a color-blind Constitution. The victories for nondiscrimination in 1964 and 1965 were rounded out in 1968 when the Fair Housing Act made open housing a national policy. Given the political volatility of the fair-housing issue among the nation's white voters, who feared the racial integration of white neighborhoods, Congress avoided creating an EEOC-style enforcement agency for housing. Instead, Congress in 1968 provided for voluntary conciliation through the Department of Housing and Urban Development, with Justice Department intervention only against patterns of noncompliance rather than single violations.

By the late 1960s the waves of urban rioting that began in Los Angeles in 1965 had alarmed national policymakers. Congress shied away from further race-centered legislation. But the urban turmoil during the period 1965–1968 accelerated the development by government agencies of affirmative action programs for racial minorities. Color-blind enforcement policies began to be displaced by requirements for minority preferences based on racial and ethnic status. National civil rights policy for women, however, was headed in the opposite direction.

With the chief exception of the suffrage issue, Congress and the state legislatures prior to the 1960s had based their policies for women not on nondiscrimination and the idea of a sex-blind Constitution, but rather on its opposite: the centrality of gender differences. State laws sought to protect women by regulating their working conditions and restricting them from dangerous or physically taxing work. Congress in 1920 established the Women's Bureau in the Department of Labor to monitor the special needs of women. The Equal Rights Amendment (ERA) was first proposed in Congress in 1923 by radical feminists who opposed special treatment for women, but Congress during the next four decades either ignored or buried the ERA or encumbered it with nullifying amendments. Opposition to the ERA was strongest among liberal Democrats like Eleanor Roosevelt, Adlai Stevenson, and the leaders of organized labor, who saw ERA as a threat to the liberal-progressive legacy of special laws to protect working women from the dangers of industrial labor.

The feminist movement of the 1960s rapidly overturned these traditions. Led by highly educated white women, the new feminists helped pass the Equal Pay Act of 1963, lobbied successfully for the ban on sex discrimination in the Civil Rights Act of 1964, and battled the new EEOC over equal enforcement on behalf of women as well as blacks. By 1969, with Republican Richard Nixon in the White House, the leaders of both Republican and Democratic women's groups had united behind the ERA. In the wake of the equal rights victories of the 1960s for African Americans, Congress by 1970 was unwilling to vote against equality for women. In 1971 the House approved the ERA by a vote of 354 to 23, and early in 1972 the Senate, by a similarly lopsided vote of 84 to 8, sent the ERA to the states for ratification.

Also in 1972, feminist forces won enactment of Title 9 of the Education Amendments of 1972. This required equal treatment for women in all educational programs that received federal financial assistance; it covered virtually all of the nation's public school systems and both private as well as public institutions of higher education, including graduate and professional schools. In the same year, Congress extended EEOC coverage to educational institutions and to state and local governments—two major areas of employment that had been excluded in 1964 in order to ease the passage of the Civil Rights Act.

Feminists after 1972 faced a decade of frustration and ultimate defeat in the drive to ratify the ERA. But the dominant goal of organized feminist groups remained equal treatment, and Congress continued to support this principle. After the Supreme Court in 1976 ruled in *General Electric Co.* v. *Gilbert,* 429 U.S. 126, that pregnant workers did not enjoy the same job-disability protections as men under the Civil Rights Act, Congress in 1978 passed legislation that reversed the *Gilbert* ruling and affirmed that women were equally protected from job discrimination.

## AFFIRMATIVE ACTION AND MINORITY PREFERENCES

In the civil rights legislation of the 1960s, Congress had affirmed a national commitment to nondiscrimination. By the early 1970s, however, the combined pressures of urban riots and intensified lobbying by organized minority groups had shifted the thrust of federal policy from nondiscrimination toward minority preferences in jobs and other government benefits. Affirmative action in civil rights policy had originated in President Kennedy's 1961 executive order on fair employment. It directed federal contractors to "take affirmative action to ensure that applicants are employed, and that employees are treated during employment, without regard to their race, creed, color, or national origin." Affirmative action in the Kennedy and Johnson administrations meant aggressive recruiting to maximize the presence of minorities in the applicant pool, and to ensure nondiscrimination thereafter. Congress in the civil rights legislation of the 1960s continued to require nondiscrimination in a similar manner.

The shift toward minority preferences came not from Congress but from the new federal enforcement agencies, with the support of the federal courts of the Warren era. Despite conflict with the nondiscrimination required by the Civil Rights Act, the development by federal agencies during the late 1960s of numerical employment requirements for minorities was approved by the federal courts, which during the same period began to require desegregating school districts to bus students and assign teachers by race. By 1970 most of the federal government's new enforcement offices for civil rights were controlled by officials, often minority members themselves, who regarded nondiscrimination as ineffective against the institutionalized racism built up by generations of prejudice and discrimination. To these officials the cumulative effects of past discrimination could be erased not by an equal-treatment standard, but only by an equal-results approach. The results-centered standard assumed that in the absence of discrimination, jobs and promotions and other social benefits would be distributed in society in proportion to racial and ethnic populations.

In 1969 the Office of Federal Contract Compliance (OFCC)—established in the Department of Labor in 1965 to enforce the Civil Rights Act in federal contract work—devised a new model of affirmative action in Philadelphia. The Philadelphia Plan required construction contractors to hire skilled minority workers until their numbers on the job approximately equaled their percentage in the metropolitan work force. The proportional standard of the Philadelphia Plan required that if 30 percent of a city's work force was black, then 30 percent of the plumbers, electricians, and sheet metal workers should also be black.

In response the Contractors Association of Eastern Pennsylvania brought suit, claiming that minority preferences in hiring violated the Civil Rights Act. But the Philadelphia Plan was upheld by the lower federal courts in *Contractors Association of Eastern Pennsylvania* v. *Secretary of Labor,* 311 F. Supp. 1002 (E.D. Pa. 1970). Similarly, the EEOC began to identify

employment discrimination not by the standards of traditional intent as set out in the Civil Rights Act, but rather by statistical tests of "disparate impact." By this standard, hiring and promotion standards were discriminatory if they selected fewer minorities than were proportionally available in the labor pool. In *Griggs* v. *Duke Power Co.,* 401 U.S. 424 (1974), the Supreme Court ruled that the EEOC's fair employment regulations expressed the intent of Congress.

In response to the ratchet effect of these policy interpretations by the civil rights enforcement agencies and the federal courts, congressional conservatives attempted to reaffirm the original standards of 1964. Their efforts failed, however. This was partly because the Nixon administration, despite the hostility of the civil rights coalition, defended from congressional attack the executive agencies that were enforcing the new minority-preference standards. More important, the conservatives failed because the logic and successes of the black civil rights movement was creating an expanding "Rights Revolution." The group-rights approach of affirmative action for racial minorities provided a model for other groups—the elderly, youth, the disabled, Hispanics, and other ethnic minorities—who formed activist organizations to lobby Congress for programs that served their members' interests.

## THE "RIGHTS REVOLUTION" OF THE 1970S

Congressional expansion of a rights-based legislative program of group claims and entitlements during the 1970s was partly obscured by the attention paid by the media and by contemporary political commentators to the politics of the white "backlash." Public resentment grew over the urban riots, the "Black Power" movement, and the perception that minorities were receiving preferential treatment. This backlash manifested itself in the 1968 vote for Nixon and for third-party candidate George Wallace of Alabama; in Nixon's nomination of conservative southerners to fill Supreme Court vacancies in 1969 and 1970; in his 1972 proposal for a constitutional amendment against school busing for racial balance; in the violent resistance by Boston working-class whites to court-ordered busing during the period 1974–1975; and in the prominence of "reverse discrimination" suits like the *DeFunis* and *Bakke* cases during the latter 1970s. In these cases, white applicants denied admission to professional school charged racial discrimination because minority applicants with weaker standard credentials were admitted under minority preference programs. In Congress, backlash politics was seen in the enactment of antiriot statutes during the late 1960s and in antibusing amendments during the 1970s.

Of more lasting significance, however, was the congressional extension of statutory rights and program entitlements from the traditional New Deal constituencies of interest-group pluralism (farmers, veterans, organized labor, homeowners, and pensioners) to the politically mobilized new constituencies making civil rights claims. Congress passed the Age Discrimination Act in 1967, and in 1975 Congress significantly strengthened protections for workers between the ages of forty and sixty-five. In response to the political mobilization of youthful Americans, Congress in 1970 lowered the voting age to eighteen by statute, and in 1972 Congress constitutionalized the eighteen-year-old franchise by approving the Twenty-sixth Amendment. The following year Congress allowed the selective service to expire, thus ending military conscription for young males. In section 504 of the Rehabilitation Act of 1973, Congress created a right to special assistance for the people with disabilities, especially the physically disabled. The disability legislation of the 1970s required large expenditures by governments, employers, and educational institutions to provide more equal access for disabled Americans in education, jobs, transportation, and housing. In the Civil Rights of Institutionalized Persons Act of 1980, Congress extended these protections to the mentally disabled.

During the 1970s, rights organizations for Latinos, such as the Mexican American Legal Defense and Education Fund, following the model of the NAACP, intensified their lobbying and litigation. In 1968 a federal subagency, the Office of Bilingual Education, was established within the Department of Health, Education and Welfare to administer a new program of federal aid for bilingual education primarily for Latino constituencies. The Supreme Court ruled in *Lau v. Nichols,* 414 U.S. 563 (1974), that school districts must provide special instructional programs for children whose native language was not English. Shortly thereafter, in a repeat of the development of group-based remedies at the OFCC and the EEOC, the Office of Bilingual Education issued regulations requiring school districts to provide native-language instruction for children with limited English proficiency. For most federally mandated bilingual programs, this meant Spanish.

Congress in 1974 significantly increased the authority and appropriations for an expanded Office of Bilingual Education and Minority Language Affairs (OBEMLA). The following year Congress amended the Voting Rights Act to extend the special protections of the Justice Department to selected language minorities. Signed by President Gerald Ford, the voting amendments of 1975 designated four new beneficiary groups: persons of "Spanish heritage," "American Indians," Asian Americans, and Alaskan natives. This added to the attorney general's original jurisdiction of 1965 for voting-rights enforcement, which included seven southern states; the entire state of Texas; twenty-nine counties with large Latino populations in Arizona, California, Colorado, Florida, New Mexico, and New York; and also sixteen counties in eight states with substantial Native American populations.

Congress responded in two ways during the 1970s to the proliferating demands of organized groups for designated protections and benefits. In addition to stipulating new rights for specific groups, Congress in its regular authorizations and appropriations for federal departments and programs added increasingly detailed requirements for policies concerning race, sex, age, disability, and selected ethnicity. Feminist pressure provided the cutting edge between 1972 and 1976 for extending nondiscrimination requirements to all fields of education and also to the commercial fields of credit, home mortgages, and insurance.

Black organizations took the lead in lobbying for minority-targeted "set-asides" in public works contracts. Only designated minorities or women were eligible to compete for set-aside contracts. Congress created the minority set-aside program in the Public Works Employment Act of 1977. It required that 10 percent of Commerce Department grants be allocated to business enterprises controlled by blacks, Spanish-speakers, Asian Americans, Native Americans, and Aleuts. Voting without any committee hearing or reports, Congress in 1977 enacted the first statute in modern American history creating a racial classification.

In a 6–3 ruling in 1980, the Supreme Court in *Fullilove* v. *Klutznick,* 448 U.S. 448, upheld the minority set-aside program, and minority lobbying groups were quick to exploit its potential. By 1980, the Leadership Conference on Civil Rights included almost 150 organizations in a national network of considerable lobbying sophistication. By 1985 more than 230 state and local legislative bodies had established contract set-aside programs for designated minorities and also for women.

## DIVIDED GOVERNMENT IN THE 1980S

In 1980, when former California governor Ronald Reagan defeated the reelection bid of President Jimmy Carter, the two elected branches of the national government returned to a pattern of partisan split that prior to the Civil War had paralyzed the national government and that had reappeared with the election of Richard Nixon in 1968. Democratic dominance on Capitol Hill was counterbalanced by Republican dominance in the White House.

Holding the potential balance of decision was the federal judiciary. During the 1970s the federal courts under Chief Justice of the Supreme Court Warren Burger had hedged but not fundamentally changed the civil rights rulings of the Warren era. No Democratic president, however, had appointed a Supreme Court justice since 1967. As a consequence the federal bench by 1980 was becoming more Republican and its rulings were shifting toward a more conservative interpretation of the Constitution. In 1980 the Supreme Court ruled in *City of Mobile, Ala.* v. *Bolden,* 446 U.S. 55, that the Voting Rights Act required a showing of intent and was not violated by a mere demonstration of discriminatory effect in electoral results. Statistical demonstration of disproportionate representation by groups in electoral politics was a simple task—African Americans in 1980, for example, accounted for 12 percent of the population but held only 17, or 4 percent, of the 435 seats in the House. But proving discriminatory intent was more difficult.

The *Mobile* decision galvanized the Leadership Conference on Civil Rights, which had been effective in influencing Congress during the debates over voter-rights renewal in 1981 and 1982. Significantly, no organized groups spoke in opposition to the Leadership Conference. With little resistance from the Reagan administration, Congress in 1982 reversed the Supreme Court's ruling in *Mobile* by stipulating an effects test rather than an intent standard. This meant that the results of elections, not the motives of legislators, would determine whether discrimination had occurred. Further, the voting-rights amendments of 1982 extended until 1997 the preclearance provisions of section five, under which local electoral changes in nine states and portions of more than a dozen others required prior approval from the Justice Department.

Similarly, Congress in 1988 reversed the 1984 decision of the Supreme Court in *Grove City College* v. *Bell,* 104 Sup. Ct. 1211. The Court had held in 1984 that private colleges that refused federal aid were not subject to regulation by federal civil rights officials merely because the colleges received federal funds indirectly through student fees. Congress amended the Civil Rights Act in 1988 to stipulate that even indirect financial assistance brought federal regulatory oversight. During the 1980s the conservative Reagan administration, despite Republican control of the Senate between 1981 and 1985, was generally unable to persuade Congress to retreat from equal-results standards and reaffirm the equal-treatment standard of 1964.

By the 1990s, American society was polarized by civil rights issues. On one side were the Democratic majorities in Congress and legislative majorities in many city councils and urban state legislatures, who were committed to the compensatory principle that equal justice required preferential treatment for minorities crippled by past discrimination. The legislators were joined in coalition with partners in the "iron triangles" of civil rights policy—the officials in federal and local enforcement and program agencies, and leaders of the minority lobbies, especially the African American and

Latino organizations. On the other side, critical of minority preferences in rights policy, was a rough alignment of the Republican presidency, the trend of judicial rulings on the federal bench, and the opinion of a majority bloc of white and Asian Americans of both sexes, as reflected in national polling data.

## CIVIL RIGHTS POLICY AND THE AMERICAN REGULATORY STATE

The period of the 1960s was the great watershed for civil rights policy in modern American legislative history. Prior to the 1960s, civil rights reform was an act of inclusion and a correction of past discrimination against minority groups that looked forward to equal rights for everyone. The great campaigns of the 1960s were fought to provide equal access to public goods where minority gains entailed no implicit losses by the larger society—access to schoolrooms, restaurants, parks, hotels, and the voting booth. Legislators, in the simpler era of nondiscrimination, nourished a spirit of bipartisan majorities, and journalists described votes as being "for" or "against" civil rights. The classic definition endowed civil rights reform with high moral content, and it implied a point of principled termination; civil rights reform would be completed when all individuals enjoyed the same rights.

The 1960s broke sharply with the past in a dual sense. First, the breakthrough laws during the period 1963–1968 etched equal treatment into national policy. Second, the rights revolution of the 1970s and 1980s transformed the definition of civil rights itself. From a contest waged over the morality of unequal treatment in a positive-sum game, policy-making on civil rights issues evolved into a complex process of political bargaining among multiple parties. In an increasingly zero-sum environment, winners and losers were determined by the lobbying skills of interest groups.

Civil rights debates increasingly featured the clash of legitimate but conflicting claims—minorities against whites, women against men, the disabled against the able-bodied, fetuses against mothers, children against parents, and students against school authorities. Like monetary or environmental or health policy, modern civil rights policy required from government a complex balancing of interests. In the American regulatory state of the late twentieth century, civil rights policy had become a tangled thicket of human need and conflicting morality; policy-making required balancing fetal rights against the rights of raped mothers, or balancing the rights of people with AIDS to be protected from discrimination against the rights of uninfected citizens to avoid danger. The post-1960s rights revolution thus redefined civil rights into a permanent policy process of interest-group adjustment, where distinctions between rights and entitlements were blurred, and the neutral principle of equal treatment for individuals no longer governed the boundaries of policy.

Debate over civil rights policy in the twenty-first century, however, will likely continue to differ in two respects from policy-making debate over other major issue areas, such as foreign affairs, the economy, or health policy. First, for historical reasons the civil rights label continues to carry unique symbolic and emotional weight, much as the "bloody shirt" issue fueled partisan hostilities until long after the Civil War. Second, civil rights policy, more than most other major policy fields, carries distinctive constitutional claims. As in the past, Americans will continue to pursue their civil rights beyond the halls of legislatures and the offices of agency officials and into the halls of justice.

## *BIBLIOGRAPHY*

*Antebellum America*
The civil status of free blacks in the nonslave states is surveyed in LEON F. LITWACK, *North of* Slavery (Chicago, 1961). Patterns of racial politics in mid-nineteenth-century America are analyzed in PHYLLIS F. FIELD, *The Politics of Race in*

*New York: The Struggle for Black Suffrage in the Civil War Era* (Ithaca, N.Y., 1982). On the Reconstruction, see ERIC FONER, *Reconstruction: America's Unfinished Revolution, 1863–1877* (New York, 1988); MICHAEL LES BENEDICT, *A Compromise of Principle: Congressional Republicans and Reconstruction, 1863–1869* (New York, 1974); WILLIAM E. NELSON, *The Fourteenth Amendment* (Cambridge, Mass., 1988); and WILLIAM GILLETTE, *The Right to Vote: Politics and the Passage of the Fifteenth Amendment* (Baltimore, Md., 1965). The development of racial segregation in the southern states is treated in C. VANN WOODWARD, *The Strange Career of Jim Crow,* 3d ed. (New York, 1974); J. MORGAN KOUSSER, *The Shaping of Southern Politics: Suffrage Restrictions and the Establishment of the One-Party South, 1880–1910* (New Haven, Conn., 1974); and V. O. KEY, JR., *Southern Politics in State and Nation* (New York, 1949). Key's modern classic followed the publication of GUNNAR MYRDAL's two-volume study, *An American Dilemma: The Negro Problem and Modern Democracy* (New York, 1944).

**Post–World War II**
General histories of the black civil rights movement and the development of public policy are STEVEN F. LAWSON, *Running for Freedom* (Philadelphia, 1991), and ROBERT WEISBROT, *Freedom Bound* (New York, 1990). The development and effectiveness of state antidiscrimination laws are studied in MORROE BERGER, *Equality by Statute* (Garden City, N.Y., 1967). The federal role in school desegregation is surveyed in J. HARVIE WILKINSON III, *From Brown to Bakke* (New York, 1979). On federal civil rights policy for both blacks and women, see HUGH DAVIS GRAHAM, *The Civil Rights Era: Origin and Development of National Policy, 1960–1972* (New York, 1990). On voting rights, see STEVEN F. LAWSON, *Black Ballots: Voting Rights in the South, 1944–1969* (New York, 1976), and his *In Pursuit of Power: Southern Blacks and Electoral Politics, 1965–1982* (New York, 1985); and ABIGAIL THERNSTROM, *Whose Votes Count? Affirmative Action and Minority Rights* (Cambridge, Mass., 1987).

**Feminist Movement and Women's Rights**
See JO FREEMAN, *The Politics of Women's Liberation* (New York, 1975); CYNTHIA HARRISON, *On Account of Sex* (Berkeley, Calif., 1988); and SUSAN M. HARTMAN, *From Margin to Mainstream* (New York, 1989). PAUL BURSTEIN, *Discrimination, Jobs, and Politics* (Chicago, 1985), studies equal employment policy for minorities and women since the New Deal.

**Legal and Constitutional Issues**
The standard case-law text is DERRICK A. BELL, JR., *Race, Racism and American Law,* 3d ed. (Boston, 1992). A critical analysis of affirmative action and the law is HERMAN BELZ, *Equality Transformed* (New Brunswick, N.J., 1990). For legal-historical interpretations of the "rights revolution," see CASS R. SUNSTEIN, *After the Rights Revolution* (Cambridge, Mass., 1990), and MARY ANN GLENDON, *Rights Talk* (New York, 1991).

SEE ALSO Legislatures and Gender Issues; Legislatures and Political Rights; Legislatures and Slavery; The Modernizing Congress, 1930–1992; and The U.S. Congress: The Era of Party Patronage and Sectional Stress, 1829–1881.

# LEGISLATURES AND THE ENVIRONMENT

## *Thomas R. Huffman*

Historians and political scientists have initiated the scholarly study of environmental issues only recently, beginning in the 1960s. Nevertheless, environmental policy-making has been a persistent feature of the political history of the United States from the early national period to the modern era, pervading all levels of government and society. Along with the courts and the executive branch, the legislative system has long been an arena of environmental conflict and change for politicians, officials, and citizens.

Given the expansive boundaries of the topic, a chronology of the environment and the legislative system must distinguish among several periods and their characteristic patterns of lawmaking. During most of the nineteenth century, legislators in Congress and in state capitols, eager to exploit "natural resources," approached the "environment" from an economic viewpoint. From the late nineteenth century through World War II, legislators applied various principles of "conservation," embodying utilitarian, preservationist, or egalitarian goals. The 1950s through 1980 witnessed an explosion of environmental activity at both state and federal levels. And during the administration of President Ronald Reagan, legislators responded to broader political and legal considerations and strengthened the centralization of administrative power.

Legislative environmental action in the United States entailed four developments: the idea of federalism, as Congress and the states argued about precedent and responsibility in environmental management; the influence of regional political cultures in determining environmental policy; the degree to which state and federal legislatures moved from economic promotion in the nineteenth century to environmental reform and innovation by the early 1970s; and the wide-ranging impact of a subject that has been continually redefined in technical, scientific, and legal terms, confronting legislative leaders with complicated policy problems impinging on the whole of the human experience. Furthermore, regardless of their environmental attitudes, legislators were required to sanction or reject all major natural-resource programs and thus had substantial input into the implementation of the administrative process. The history of these emerging legislative methods requires a clear, if abbreviated, explanation.

## NATURAL RESOURCES, LEGISLATURES, AND THE GREAT BARBECUE

The earliest legislative efforts to manage the environment involved support for westward land settlement and state building during the early- to mid-nineteenth century. Statutory law undergirded the "Great Barbecue," as some historians called the westering movement of white Europeans across the North American continent and their attendant use of natural resources. Up to 1900, lawmaking in the United States was characterized by dual federalism: members of Congress and state legislators shared equal power in supporting the "private will," in the terms of James Willard Hurst, the preeminent historian of American law, to release the "energy" of these westering entrepreneurs in the market place. In doing so, nineteenth-century lawmakers advanced the European American belief in economic growth and national progress. As the foremost policy-making arm of government, nineteenth-century legislatures were active in distributing public largess. Legislative action mirrored the common assumptions that natural resources were abundant, inexhaustible, and there to be used to encourage national development.

This ethic of environmental exploitation was most apparent in the policies concerning the disposal of the public domain. In a multitude of statutes, lawmakers in Congress and in western and midwestern state legislatures granted rights to use water, timber, agricultural, wildlife, and mineral assets. In so doing, legislators merely expressed the tenets of resource development found among all walks of nineteenth-century life; everyone wanted to make a killing. From his vantage point in the House of Representatives in June 1838, John Quincy Adams (Nat.Rep.-Mass.) commented that the "thirst of a tiger for blood is the fittest emblem of the rapacity with which the [congressional] members of all the new states fly at the public lands."

Laws advancing the transfer of public lands, from the preemption acts of the 1830s and 1840s, through the Homestead Act (1862), to the Mining (1872), Timber Culture (1873) and Timber and Stone (1878) acts, opened natural resources in regions west of the Appalachians as "property" to be used for almost any purpose. Members of Congress and state legislators were leading advocates of confiscating lands from Native Americans and, along with business barons, they profited from environmental exploitation. Western senators' disproportionate strength and direct relations with economic development illustrated this legislative environmental intent. Many western senators rose to political power on the force of timber, land, or water investment. They had the advantage of representing few major economic interests and were in a position to trade votes advantageously in order to pass the measures desired by the business groups they supported.

Congress did provide a policy framework for the conduct of natural-resource use in the nineteenth century. And, under the property clause of the Constitution, it had the power to further set the terms of public domain disposal. For instance, the white migration to the arid regions of the Great Plains during the generation after the Civil War compelled legislative leaders to adjust federal statutes to suit the new environment. Among other laws, Congress passed the Desert Land Act (1877) that offered larger tracts of land to settlers who would commence irrigation projects. Yet, federal resource policies remained vague and disunified, and members of Congress avoided the hard environmental questions, giving scant attention to concrete choices, values, and costs.

Environmental decision-making during the mid- to late-nineteenth century often devolved to state legislatures. Affected by the unique environmental situation of the region and the impact of agriculture and mining, western water law was one field where state legislators set new directions in natural resource policy and thereby pushed Congress to respond. Territorial and state lawmakers, particularly in California and Colorado during the 1870s, established irrigation districts, advanced reclamation projects, and developed an emerging paradigm of water rights known as "prior appropriation" (under the doctrine of prior appropriation, the one first in time to ownership of a water resource is the one first in right to its use). These efforts began the increasingly disputatious and controversial involvement of western state legislators in the crucial issue of water-resource management.

State legislatures in the nineteenth century, especially in the West and Midwest, became sectional enclaves, providing an open field for the maneuver of the major economic powers of the region (such as timber, water use, or mining). In many state legislatures prior to the 1890s, lawmakers also gave business associations quasi-governmental standing, allowing their representatives immunity from the oversight of reformers or supporters of the public interest. Consequently, state capitols were crowded with bills of minute detail and the narrowest local application, granting privileges to private concerns to exploit natural resources. In his monumental study of the Wisconsin lumber industry during the nineteenth century, James Willard Hurst detailed the hundreds of statutes passed by state lawmakers as they awarded water-power and transport franchises and gave timber-rich public lands to business entrepreneurs. In a pattern found among nearly all the states, Wisconsin legislators made it easy for business organizations to incorporate, giving these firms special advantages and rights in the expanding use of natural resources. In Hurst's view, such lawmaking exemplified the "booster theory of public investment," affirming the axioms of individualism and "bringing the land to market," regardless of the eventual effect on the environment.

## LEGISLATURES AND THE ORIGINS OF CONSERVATION

Despite the preponderance of developmental attitudes in the American legislative system, a nascent conservation consciousness helped fuel the fires of legislative action at the state and federal levels in the late nineteenth century. Scholarly examination of the origins of the conservation movement in the nineteenth century, however, is a miscellany of interpretation and argument for different precedents. Historians participating in this debate have pointed to parks, forestry, fish and wildlife concerns, water-resource management, land-use controls, urban-sanitation reform, or public-health impulses as the true sources of the conservation movement in the United States. Overall, though, three ideas current in the public-policy and intellectual discourse of the period contributed to the growth of the conservation movement: efficiency values emphasizing the sustained wise use of resources; equity values underlining the notion that natural resources belonged to all the "people" and thus required public control; and aesthetic values stressing the importance of preserving natural beauty.

Generally, when confronted by the rise of the conservation movement, legislators remained recalcitrant and rejected innovation. But, at the same time, there were noteworthy changes in the patterns of lawmaking. Two individuals, George Perkins Marsh and John Wesley Powell, exemplified the influence that intellectuals began to have on natural-resource policy-making in state legislatures and Congress.

A journeyman diplomat and scientist, Marsh was also elected to four terms in Congress as a Whig representative from Vermont (1843–1849). Marsh had long been interested in conservation—in 1857 the Vermont legislature had commissioned him to study the feasibility of restoring the state's depleted fish stocks. In 1864 Marsh completed *Man and Nature; or Physical Geography as Modified by Human Action,* the foremost conservation tract of the nineteenth century. Marsh's "revolutionary thesis," in the words of Roderick Nash, was that "the condition of the environment has more to do with human than with natural forces." Employing ecological analysis, he described the shortsighted land policies of Europe and the Near East and argued that Ameri-

cans must accept a policy of conservation, particularly in forestry, to deal with similar environmental problems emerging in the United States. Marsh's book provided the backbone for a growing conservation movement at the national level during the 1870s as Congress passed some inaugural measures, such as the Timber Culture Act (1873) and appointed a federal forestry administrator in the Department of Agriculture (1876). *Man and Nature* also stimulated the formation of forest conservation programs among the states. For example, Wisconsin legislators, lobbied by concerned citizens who had read Marsh, created a forestry commission in 1867. This commission issued a report that led to the first forest conservation laws in the Badger State in 1868. Other state legislators, in New York, Maine, Iowa, Nebraska, Massachusetts, and Illinois, began similar investigations into the forestry situation and promoted forest regeneration through "tree bounties" during the late 1860s and 1870s.

On 1 April 1878, John Wesley Powell, one of the eminent explorers and natural scientists of the day, presented the *Report on the Lands of the Arid Region of the United States* to Secretary of the Interior Carl Schurz. Secretary Schurz then passed the report to the House of Representatives where it was referred to the Committee on Appropriations and ordered printed. In the report, Powell evaluated the system of land laws and patterns of settlement west of the 100th meridian; it was a "model of ecological realism in an unsympathetic age of unbounded expectations," according to Donald Worster, a leading proponent of the new field of environmental history. Powell advocated a revolution in the approach to western land use, stressing the need to examine assumptions about water use in the East, where water was abundant, and adapt them to western aridity by surveying and classifying the irrigation and watershed potential of the West before settlement could proceed. Although his proposals were rejected and modified, Powell spent the next two decades soliciting Congress, testifying before hearings, and tutoring a coterie of scientists and federal bureaucrats, while advancing his "blueprint for a dryland democracy." Eventually, American lawmakers would accept as practical policy some of the central ideas of Marsh and Powell, although both men were initially considerd crackpot fanatics by most political leaders.

## State-Level Preservation

At the state level, the growth of conservation as a feature of government management was manifest by the late 1860s and expanded through the 1880s. In facing the burgeoning social, economic, and political problems that accompanied the industrial revolution, legislators sanctioned the impetus for regulatory government control that was increasingly centralized in state governments in all areas of action by the 1880s; environmental affairs were part of this process.

State environmental regulation in the late nineteenth century first involved the "fish-culture" movement. As overharvesting and pollution depleted the fisheries in New England streams and along the West and East coasts, sporting groups and other concerned citizens asked state politicians to intervene. This environmental and political situation impelled state legislatures to create fish commissions dedicated to the administration, restoration, and preservation of piscatorial resources. Maine lawmakers established the first in 1867; New York followed in 1868 and Massachusetts, California, New Jersey, and Rhode Island all set up commissions in 1870. Legislators from Massachusetts and Rhode Island also persuaded Congress to authorize a federal fish commission in 1871. By 1880 more than twenty-five states had these executive agencies.

The fish-culture movement was linked to other environmental trends in state legislative activity during the two decades after the Civil War. State lawmakers initiated water pollution control laws and formed boards of health to regulate water problems as well as to manage public-health issues related to urban sanitation. Massachusetts organized the first board of health in 1867, and other states soon followed suit.

In addition, state legislators pushed new conservation laws in game protection. In advance of federal efforts, and as the inaugural game laws for most states, these statutes frequently were omnibus in character and included stipulations on fishery preservation and logging or land-use practices along with hunting and commercial harvest regulations for deer, waterfowl, and predators, and protection of songbirds, for example. Minnesota's comprehensive "Act for the Preservation of Game," passed by legislators on 9 March 1874 as Chapter thirty-eight of the state laws illustrated this trend among the states in the 1870s. According to John Reiger, these state game regulations proliferated "into a tangled mass of confusing and often contradictory statutes."

For the most part, state efforts to protect game, fisheries, water, and public health for several decades after the Civil War were ambitious and idealistic but weakly enforced and underfunded. Moreover, some of the efforts had little to do with the principles of conservation. Such was the case with the California Board of Fish Commissioners, who spent their first years of work during the 1870s driving Chinese immigrants out of the state fishing industry, at the behest of white Europeans, and attempting to maintain, not conserve, the supply of a valuable economic commodity.

## Parks Become Environmental Battleground

The political struggle to establish state and national parks encouraged the growth of environmental policy-making in American legislatures prior to 1890. Congress played a direct role in the park preservation movement of the nineteenth century, as the creation of national parks depended upon congressional sanction. From the start, because parks were first shaped from public lands, Congress was more involved with the states concerning this issue than in forestry, game management, or public health.

The best and earliest example of the intermixing of congressional and state legislative policy-making with regard to the parks movement began when Yosemite Valley in California was designated a "state park" in 1864. Influenced by the ideas of the painter George Catlin, the landscape architect Frederick Law Olmsted, and the geologist Josiah Dwight Whitney, a group of citizens asked U.S. senator John Conness (R.-Calif.) to introduce a bill granting to the state of California a tract of land that included Yosemite Valley and the Mariposa Grove of Sierra Redwoods. A federal land grant of this variety was not unusual. But, in drafting the bill, Senator Conness had the General Land Office append a clause declaring that the ceded territory "be held for public use, resort and recreation . . . [and] shall be held inalienable for all time." Speaking before Congress, Senator Conness maintained that it was a patriotic duty and in the national interest to protect the scenic wonders of Yosemite, thus outlining the precepts of cultural nationalism and monumentalism that, according to Alfred Runte, were central to the nineteenth-century parks movement. Supported by Speaker of the House Schuyler Colfax (R.-Ind.), the bill slipped through Congress with limited opposition and was signed by President Abraham Lincoln on 29 June 1864. The legislation established a major precedent for the permanent preservation of land for a nonutilitarian undertaking. Furthermore, Congress retained ultimate rights of control over Yosemite, although never enforced, that made the area the first "national" park as well.

The 1864 act started a long dispute over the use of Yosemite Valley. Again, the Yosemite debate highlighted the circumstances of legislative participation in the parks movement. The valley was managed by a park commission that reported to the California legislature. Eventually, California lawmakers and park commissioners allied with grazing, farming, mining, and logging interests who wanted Yosemite to remain open for economic exploitation. By 1889 the declining environmental condition of the valley spurred the naturalist John Muir and Robert Underwood Johnson, editor of *Century Magazine,* to advocate the expansion of the park to 1,500 square miles under federal control. Muir and Johnson, backed by the tourist-minded Southern Pacific Railroad, lobbied the House Public Lands Committee to make this change. After some compromise, an act forming a "federal reserve" in the Yosemite Valley passed with little resistance on 30 September 1890, the last day of the legislative session. It was the "first preserve consciously designed to protect wilderness," in the words of Roderick Nash.

The controversy did not end there, however. California retained authority over the initial Yosemite "state park," including the valley itself, so state and federal parks existed side by side. For more than a decade a battle raged in Congress and in the California legislature as members of the newly formed conservation organization, the Sierra Club (1892), and executives from the Southern Pacific Railroad fought a "recession campaign" to have the state park merged with the federal reserve. Conversely, farmers, ranchers, land speculators, and California lawmakers, led by U.S. Representative Anthony Caminentti (D.-Calif.), sought to restrict and even annul the federal park. After a camping trip hosted by Muir in 1903, President Theodore Roosevelt became receptive to Muir's proposal that California retrocede the valley to the federal government for inclusion in the adjacent national park. Eventually, the Sierra Club won the struggle in the California legislature when nine state senators "controlled" by the railroad interests voted in favor of recession. California retroceded its section to the federal government in 1905, and Congress accepted it on 11 June 1906, thus completing the creation of Yosemite National Park. This course of debate mirrored the process that formed what is generally considered the first national park—the preservation in 1872 of the Yellowstone region in northwest Wyoming.

Influenced by efforts to safeguard Yosemite and Yellowstone, state legislators and concerned citizens moved to establish state parks. Aside from Yosemite, many states claim the first state park, but the most notable example appeared in New York. In 1872, New York lawmakers organized a park commission to study the Adirondacks, the great wilderness in the northern regions of the state that had long been a popular recreation ground. By the 1880s, bills to protect the Adirondacks were under consideration in the New York legislature. A strong advocate of this preservation was the young state-assembly member Theodore Roosevelt. Events culminated in 1885 when New York lawmakers set aside the Adirondacks as a preserve to remain "as wild forest lands." In 1892 the area became a state park and in 1894 its conservation was provided for in the New York constitution. The "first" state park actually was Niagara Falls, also created by the New York legislature in 1885; in 1891 Minnesota lawmakers apparently instituted the second at Lake Itasca, securing the headwaters of the Mississippi River.

Recent studies make clear, however, that economic considerations were often the chief stimulus behind the formation of state and national parks. Legislators accepted the idea of park preservation, particularly in the West, because the lands had monumental or symbolic value only and little economic worth. Indeed, many park statutes included utilitarian provisions. Furthermore, the history of the park movement from the mid-nineteenth to the mid-twentieth centuries is replete with examples of recidivist ventures in Congress and in state legislatures as representatives of special interests attacked preservation by redrawing boundaries, opening up key areas for economic exploitation, and even proposing to revoke the statutory authorization of particularly irksome parks.

The preeminent legislative conservation achievement in the nineteenth century was Section 24 of the General Revision Act, passed on 3 March 1891. As an obscure rider attached to a bill reforming the land laws, Section 24 stipulated that the president could create "forest reservations" in any state or territory having public lands bearing timber. Spurred by the efforts of Interior Secretary Carl Schurz, the American Forestry Congress, and later the Boone and Crockett Club, an organization of wealthy hunters was formed by Theodore Roosevelt, and forest conservation proposals were introduced by sympathetic members of Congress beginning in the 1870s. In 1887 Senator Eugene Hale (R.-Maine) offered the first bill that recommended permanent forest reserves, elements of which were incorporated into the 1891 statute. In March 1890 Representative Mark Hill Dunnell (R.-Minn.) submitted a more comprehensive forest-reserve bill, but it was deferred until completion of the land-revision law. Under pressure from Interior Secretary John W. Noble, proconservation legislators buried the forest-reserve clause in the land-law bill during a conference committee meeting. Subsequently, Representative Lewis E. Payson (R.-Ill.), chair of the Committee on Public Lands, rushed the bill through crucial votes in an inattentive House at the close of the Fifty-first Congress (1889–1891). Immediately after its passage, President Benjamin Harrison set aside several hundred thousand acres surrounding Yellowstone National Park as the nation's first forest reserve, commencing the federal government's immersion into centralized environmental management. By the time he left office in 1893, Harrison had proclaimed fifteen reserves of approximately thirteen million acres throughout the West.

The national forest-reserve system was forced upon an unwilling Congress. Moreover, Section 24 in the 1891 act did not provide for the protection or administration of the incipient forest reserves. Consequently, business leaders and western politicians challenged the reserve idea during the 1890s as they strove to reject federal control and protect economic concerns dependent on access to natural resources in the public domain. Resistance to the forest reserves was particularly strong in western state and territorial legislatures, with lawmakers from California, Colorado, New Mexico, and Arizona leading the charge under the banner of "states' rights." This political turmoil culminated in the Forest Management Act of 1897, a compromise that permitted private lumbering, mining, and grazing in the forest reserves when regulated by federal officials. The federal-forest-reserves debate of the 1890s fixed a pattern of legislative maneuvering and argument that became commonplace in the environmental lawmaking and policy implementation of the mid- to late-twentieth century.

Even though the underlying attitudes of most congressional leaders to natural-resource use had not altered much by 1900, the conservation movement was realigning legislative approaches in the federal body. Many lawmakers acknowledged the relevance of regulation as a positive force in integrating the administration of property with broader social values, such as conservation. This increasingly complex calculation of policy-making, as evident in the national parks and forestry disputes, helped temper the often one-sided advocacy of natural-resource exploitation that dominated environmental politics during the nineteenth century. A striking aspect of the trend toward formal regulation in Congress by the 1890s was the growth of authority related to natural-resource management centered in the committee system. Several committees composed of powerful individuals specializing in different areas of environmental policy controlled conservation decision-making. The first "environmental" committees were the House and Senate Public Lands committees, formed in 1805 and 1816, respectively. But by 1900 there was a wider range of permanent standing committees in both chambers involved in environmental management, including Rivers and Harbors (1883), Merchant Marine and Fisheries (1887), and Interior and Insular Affairs (1899).

## LEGISLATURES AND PROGRESSIVE CONSERVATION

Conservation as a public movement and as a focus of legislative enterprise at both state and federal levels intensified during the Progressive Era, from 1900 to 1920. Federal lawmakers debated, passed, and implemented an immense number of conservation laws at this time—in forestry, parks, wildlife preservation, water development and reclamation, land use, and bureaucratic management. Concurrently, many state legislators discussed similar issues, particularly the conservation-department idea —consolidating and standardizing state administration of natural resources. States with strong progressive traditions, such as New York and Wisconsin, were among the first to form conservation departments during this period.

Progressive conservation at the national level was identified prominently with the administration of President Theodore Roosevelt (1901–1909) and the intellectual and managerial prowess of chief forester Gifford Pinchot.* Particularly in the federal legislative arena, as described by Samuel Hays, the movement was characterized by the "gospel of efficiency" pushed by Pinchot and other professionals. Members of Congress were motivated by either one of two ideologies: utilitarianism, emphasizing wise and efficient use of physical resources; or, an anticonservation response based on a belief in states' rights and fear of executive-branch control without legislative oversight.

During the Roosevelt administration, Congress and the executive branch debated whether

conservation experts alone should disseminate natural-resource policy. Roosevelt and Pinchot believed that the president must have the power to administer conservation, and that Congress should only promulgate a broad policy framework. They therefore assumed legislative powers after Congress blocked a series of conservation proposals generated by the conservation professionals. The field of battle was the financial appropriations for forestry, water development, and administrative reorganization programs as congressmen, mainly from western states, challenged executive-branch authority.

The emergence of nationwide pressure groups for commercial natural-resource users (agricultural, timber, grazing, and mining interests) was central to the Progressive Era phase in legislative environmental politics. Cooperating with congressional committees, these groups organized lobbies to advance single-purpose resource policies such as dam building, public land use, etc. By making these policy decisions on a case-by-case basis, Congress protected itself to a degree from executive-branch scrutiny and the machinations of conservation experts, while allowing business interests to contribute to natural-resource legislation. This approach formed the characteristic pattern of environmental lawmaking at the federal level.

Two other developments underlined the close relationship between conservation and Progressive Era legislation. One was the rise of key proconservation congressional leaders, who became specialists in a natural-resource subject and could influence the statutory intent of important bills, such as Representative John F. Lacey (R.-Iowa) and Representative (later Senator) Francis G. Newlands (D.-Nev.). Chair of the Committee on Public Lands, Lacey was known as the "father of federal game legislation"; among many endeavors, he pushed through Congress the Lacey Act (1900) prohibiting interstate shipment of wildlife taken illegally. Newlands was the prototype for legislators concerned with conservation "efficiency" and the problems of managing water resources in the West. He drafted the landmark Reclamation Act (1902) and was an ardent proponent of federally sponsored water-resources planning, leading to the Water Power Act of 1920. These lawmakers laid the groundwork for other legis-

---

* The National Forests Division was created in 1891 and was managed by the chief of the Division of Forestry in the Department of the Interior. In 1898, Pinchot became chief of the division as chief forester. In 1905, the National Forests Division was transferred to the Bureau of Forestry in the Department of Agriculture, and its name was changed to the U.S. Forest Service. Pinchot was chief forester until 1910. As a member of Roosevelt's "Kitchen Cabinet" he wielded considerable power.

lators to establish themselves as experts in conservation policy.

The second trend indicative of new directions in legislative activity vis-à-vis conservation was the growing significance of Congress as a forum in which opposing groups debated natural-resource issues before the national press. Congressional hearings and investigations increasingly served as a vehicle for public environmental decision-making. The Hetch Hetchy Valley incident (1901–1913), resulting in a dam being built in Yosemite National Park to supply the water needs of San Francisco, exemplified this process. Resistance to the dam at Hetch Hetchy became the cause célèbre of the early conservationists. Through three sets of committee hearings, several sessions of floor debate, and dramatic late-night votes, Hetch Hetchy defined the future of environmental lawmaking in Congress: it illuminated the regional and nonpartisan character of natural resource disputes (West versus East); it revealed a split between utilitarians (Gifford Pinchot) and preservationists (John Muir) within the conservation movement; and it delimited the inchoate techniques of environmental lobbying. For the first time in American history, Roderick Nash maintains, substantial numbers of citizens used the political process to argue against development. And, for the first time, the evidence and rhetoric of science was employed by both sides as a weapon in an issue of conservation policy. Controversies similar to the Hetch Hetchy struggle would reappear many times in American environmental politics.

## LEGISLATIVE ACTION AND CONSERVATION, 1920–1945

The ethos of efficiency in the management of natural resources distinguished conservation lawmaking from the 1920s to the end of World War II. Despite the ideology of economic growth and individualism expressed by three Republican presidents, Congress charted an independent course supporting an increased federal role in natural-resource management throughout the 1920s. Congressional leaders passed policies fostering scientific research, bureaucratic efficiency, land-use reforms in soil conservation and grazing, multiple purpose re-

source planning—based on watersheds for power development and flood control—and park and wildlife-refuge preservation. These statutes anticipated the direction of New Deal environmental programs. For example, the creation of the Upper Mississippi River Wildlife and Fish Refuge along three hundred miles of the waterway in June 1924, in the words of the conservationist William T. Hornaday, marked "the birth of a virile, militant, uncompromising wild-life-defending Congress, and darn the expense!" Guided through Congress by Representative Harry B. Hawes (D.-Mo.), who later resigned from a Senate seat to devote his life to wildlife conservation, the Upper Mississippi Refuge Act signaled a notable departure in legislative activity. It challenged the traditional assumption that wildlands should be conquered in the cause of economic progress.

The leadership of President Franklin D. Roosevelt (1933–1945), Secretary of the Interior Harold L. Ickes, and other liberal intellectuals in the executive branch provided support for the New Deal conservation programs through the 1930s and 1940s. Their efforts led to laws forming the Civilian Conservation Corps (1933), the Tennessee Valley Authority (1933), a public-lands-management policy (Taylor Act 1934), a soil-conservation program (1935), and a wildlife-management financing system (Pittman-Robertson 1937), among others. Confronted by the ecological disaster of the Dust Bowl and the economic consequences of the Great Depression, a receptive Congress acquiesced to a conservation approach that greatly strengthened the federal role in environmental planning and administration.

The New Deal years also represented a shift from "dual" to "cooperative" federalism in which the centralized power of Washington came to dominate relations between state and federal governments. Congress began to approve comprehensive environmental programs, and it expanded the fiscal component of cooperative federalism, significantly increasing grants-in-aids to supplement state revenues, as in fish and wildlife conservation. Aside from the emphasis on planning, however, New Deal officials primarily emphasized traditional conservation issues: parks, forestry, fish and wildlife, and proper agricultural land use. State governments, and ultimately state legislators as the chief policymakers, were forced to fend for themselves in important areas of environmental concern such as air and water pollution and problems of urban origin (population growth, public health, and sewage and sanitation management). Yet, state lawmakers generally avoided dealing with the broader environmental questions. Conservation in most states, and in most state legislatures, before the 1950s remained a subject of local and pork barrel policy-making, favoring political cronyism, especially in the administration of fish and game programs, and stressing economic development over preservation or efficiency reforms.

## LEGISLATURES AND THE ORIGINS OF THE ENVIRONMENTAL ERA, 1950–1972

A crucial transformation in legislative action on the environment took place between the end of World War II and the beginning of the 1970s. The old methods and beliefs of conservation merged with the issues, laws, politics, and institutions of environmentalism. In his pioneering study of environmental politics in the United States, Samuel Hays outlined two components in this process: first, there was a dramatic strengthening in public attitudes among the middle classes emphasizing consumer, or quality-of-life, values; second, there was the rapid growth of an "organizational society" in which the control and dissemination of scientific, technical, economic, and legal knowledge was paramount, whether in institutions of government, academia, business, or in the incipient environmental and public-interest groups. The centralization and upward shift in power to large-scale institutions sustained the new dimensions of American environmental politics. Issues influencing these changes formed two successive phases in the conservation movement. The first, from the mid-1950s to 1965, entailed concern about outdoor recreation, wilderness preservation, and land use. The second phase, from the mid-1960s to the early 1970s, comprised interest in controlling water and air pollution and the related environmental impact of industrial development.

During this era of reform in environmental politics and policy, federal and state legislators were divided between two approaches: innova-

tion or reaction. The increasing power of regulatory and fiscal federalism, the emerging professionalization of legislative political culture at the state level, and the nascent strength of environmental lobby groups, drawing from shifts in public opinion, forced lawmakers to consider and implement reform measures. On the other hand, the enduring ability of the executive branch to challenge and supplant Congress and the states in the environmental field, and the intrinsic patterns of traditional policy-making, remained a major theme in most of the conservation debates held in legislatures during this period.

One episode in the 1950s demonstrated the growing complexity of postwar environmental issues and the degree to which they were shaped and defined in the congressional forum. Like the Hetch Hetchy controversy earlier in the century, the struggle to halt the construction of a dam at Echo Park in the Dinosaur National Monument along the Colorado-Utah border was a turning point in the history of American environmental politics. In the case of Echo Park, a strident coalition of conservation organizations joined with sympathetic members of Congress to remove the dam proposal from a bill authorizing the Colorado River Storage Project. The crucial showdown occurred during a series of hearings held before the Senate and House Subcommittees on Irrigation and Reclamation in 1954 and 1955, and in several votes in the House during the Eighty-fourth Congress (1955–1956). Unlike Hetch Hetchy, the Echo Park dam was stopped, despite the customary dominance of western members of congress in directing water legislation. The Echo Park incident suggested that conservation sentiments might gain equal consideration with economic concerns in congressional discussion as environmental disputes became a prominent aspect of American politics in the 1960s.

The promulgation of new environmental programs still depended upon the influence of the traditional policy-making apparatus within Congress. Political science literature stresses the significance of a powerful committee system before 1970, guided by entrenched western and southern conservatives and favoring narrow economic interests and "developmental missions." Several reorganization procedures after World War II strengthened committee-oversight prerogatives and further permitted appropriations and authorizing committees to thwart environmental action or to dictate the terms of the natural-resource legislation that did pass. This was so, especially in the House where committees were more autonomous.

The careers of two committee chairs typified this situation: Representative Jamie L. Whitten (D.-Miss.), head of the House Subcommittee on Agricultural Appropriations beginning in 1947, and chair of the Appropriations Committee starting in 1979; and Representative Wayne N. Aspinall (D.-Colo.), head of the House Committee on Interior and Insular Affairs from 1959 to 1973. Known as the "permanent secretary of agriculture," Whitten essentially determined the composition of farm programs, and proved to be a strong anti-environmentalist and an ardent supporter of integrating the interests of the pesticide industry with federal agricultural policies. Whitten was an outspoken leader in the attack on the popular naturalist Rachel Carson following the publication of her strong warning against pesticide use, *Silent Spring* (1962). For a time, in the early 1970s, his subcommittee also had jurisdiction over the Environmental Protection Agency and consumer protection appropriations. Whitten lost much of his environmental oversight power during the liberal reforms of the Ninety-fourth Congress (1975–1976).

A vigorous advocate of western economic interests, Wayne Aspinall once claimed that "mother earth is actually one of the worst environmentalists." Aspinall was a master of committee work and rules, and of the "trade-off." He wielded absolute dominion over natural-resource legislation during the sixties and early seventies, forcing proconservation legislators and environmental activists to negotiate with him on the issues. For example, he single-handedly stalled ratification of the Wilderness (1964) and Wild and Scenic Rivers (1968) acts for years until they contained compromise stipulations. During his tenure as Interior Committee chair, no environmental bill passed without Aspinall's stamp of approval and the appropriate concessions as it was funneled through the House of Representatives.

Regardless of the reactionary forces marshaled against environmental reform, federal legislators were dragged into a flurry of conservation policy-making during the 1960s by the changing nature of public opinion and a group of astute political leaders. By the turn of the decade, this activity led to a series of laws that distinguished the "new conservation," named after a phrase used by President Lyndon B. Johnson in 1965. It represented the beginning of environmentalism. Congress enacted statutes advancing wildlands preservation, outdoor recreation, water- and air-pollution control, and consumer protection, among others. The motivation for this strengthened emphasis on regulatory federalism and centralized federal management came chiefly from executive leadership. The Kennedy and Johnson administrations, under the aegis of Interior Secretary Stewart Udall, furnished support for environmental innovation; the Nixon administration, mainly following political expediency, also backed environmental reforms. Many of these new programs, however, remained underfunded because of the drain from the Vietnam War and restrictions secured by stalwart appropriations committees in Congress.

Unlike the earlier periods of reform—the Progressive and New Deal phases—and despite the continuing power of traditional ideology in Congress, federal legislators during the late 1960s and early 1970s embraced environmental innovation more prominently than reaction. The obvious shift in public opinion was foremost in convincing members of Congress that the time had come to reinforce environmental policy-making. The parallel rise of the consumer-oriented public-interest movement, led by Ralph Nader, and the revitalization of environmental lobby groups, exemplified by the Sierra Club, provided lawmakers with ammunition in the battle to mitigate the strength of economic interests in defining the boundaries of conservation legislation.

The fusion of these elements produced two important changes in the patterns of environmental decision-making in Congress by the early 1970s. The first was the appearance of a group of environmentally aware legislators willing to promote emerging conservation and ecological issues, and simultaneously to exploit them for political ends. Scholars debate whether these reformers were following public opinion or striking out on their own as advocates of policy innovation. Lawmakers had specialized in promoting either the development or preservation of environmental assets since the creation of congressional committees focused on different areas of natural-resource management in the nineteenth century. By the 1950s and early 1960s congressional leaders, such as Senator Clinton P. Anderson (D.-N.Mex.) and Representative John P. Saylor (R.-Pa.), were establishing themselves as ardent conservationists in the cause of national parks and wilderness preservation.

The ethos of environmental and consumer reform changed by the late 1960s, however. During this period, a number of lawmakers, particularly northern Senate Democrats, became zealous proponents of environmental and consumer regulatory reform. They were eager to slug it out on the floor and in committees—contesting status quo administrative policies that supported the power of business. Three senators embodied this approach: Henry M. Jackson (D.-Wash.), Edmund S. Muskie (D.-Maine), and Gaylord A. Nelson (D.-Wis.). As chair of the Committee on Interior and Insular Affairs beginning in 1963, Jackson amassed remarkable control over federal resource policy-making, leading an array of land use, energy, and preservation debates. As chair of the Public Works Subcommittee on Air and Water Pollution starting in 1962, Muskie became the principal environmental figure in Congress, and perhaps the nation, sponsoring a succession of benchmark pollution-control measures. He was a leader in turning the congressional committee process into a platform for environmental activism, drawing from the creed of new conservation. Nelson argued for both environmental and consumer reforms, along with colleagues like Senator Abraham A. Ribicoff (D.-Conn.). Senator Nelson centered his career on an environmental appeal; he was the first national politician to call for a ban on the pesticide DDT (1966). Among other endeavors, he inaugurated the movement that culminated in Earth Day (22 April 1970), a national celebration of ecology, emphasizing education of the public in environmental issues.

The second transformation in federal environmental lawmaking was a trend that had intensified since the days of Hetch Hetchy and Echo Park: the increased influence of citizens' organizations in shaping environmental legislation. At the cutting edge of the public interest movement, citizen environmentalists, by the early 1970s, had opened up the legislative process in Congress, defying the established authority of large corporations and conservative politicians in the field. Skilled in legal techniques, coalition-building, and the methods of pragmatic legislative compromise, and well-versed in science and economics, environmentalists received equal consideration in congressional hearings, at times even dominating them. Environmental groups successfully adopted many conventional strategies of political maneuvering. Furthermore, members of Congress soon recognized the power of the environmental lobby in electoral action and the emotional potency of grass-roots environmental politics. Therefore, as David Vogel argues, the new environmental and public-interest organizations constituted a permanent and effective presence on the Washington scene after the late 1960s, eventually replacing organized labor as the central countervailing force to American business. Environmentalists became, in a sense, a professional class of activists, representative of a broad and sustained public political force.

Three noteworthy federal laws symbolized the prevailing legislative tone of this period and the nature of statutory environmentalism: the National Environmental Policy Act, or NEPA (signed 1 January 1970); the Clean Air Act of 1970; and the Federal Water Pollution Control Act (Clean Water) of 1972. Guided by Senator Henry Jackson, NEPA passed Congress unanimously at a time when public interest in environmental issues was rising. The act declared environmental protection a national priority, created a Council on Environment Quality in the executive office, and furnished an "action forcing mechanism" (Section 102) requiring all federal agencies to consider the environmental impact of their projects. NEPA also gave impetus to the formation of the Environmental Protection Agency (December 1970 by executive order) and underscored the growing importance of legal and scientific procedures in environmental administration.

The Clean Air and Water acts ostensibly were reauthorizations of existing pollution control statutes. Drawing upon the work of Senator Edmund Muskie and other environmental activists, however, they encompassed directives of a scope comparable to NEPA. The 1970 air-pollution law was one of the strictest, most controversial, and bitterly fought pieces of legislation enacted by the federal government; the 1972 water act represented one of the most sweeping environmental statutes ever considered by Congress. These laws departed from earlier federal efforts in several respects: they included nationally uniform effluent standards and specific timetables and deadlines for pollution abatement, and the cleanup goals were to be met regardless of economic or technical considerations. The air and water statutes confirmed unequivocally the dominant role of the federal government in advancing environmental protection.

For twenty years prior to the 1970s, Congress had pursued an "incremental" approach to environmental lawmaking, slowly building upon small policy adjustments and emphasizing state and local action. The Clean Air and Water acts of the early 1970s signified an unprecedented means of policy-making. As defined by the political science literature, they were "speculative" laws, ordering policy mandates that leapt well beyond proven technology, existing scientific research, and past regulatory experience, to prescribe what was theoretically attainable. Although speculative policy-making lasted for only a short period in Congress during the 1970s, it was continued by laws like the Endangered Species Act (1973), which gave unique legal protection to nonhuman beings and assimilated ecology into policy. Speculative policy-making in Congress set precedents that continue to affect the conduct of environmental affairs in the United States.

## STATE LEGISLATURES AND THE ENVIRONMENTAL ERA, 1960–1980

Generally, environmental lawmaking in state legislatures between 1950 and 1980 lacked the obvious and rapid changes in congressional action occurring during the same period. The states, however, were as significant a setting for environmental policy-making as the federal government, even though the greater emphasis on national politics and the ubiquitous context of science and technology often obscured the local level of action. Furthermore, the environmental procedures of state legislatures involved increasingly progressive and professional responses. In fact, most environmental

lawmaking in the United States in the modern era has been done at the state level, either as provisions conforming to federal statutes like the Clean Air and Water acts, or as stipulations reflecting efforts by state legislators to direct state programs or to address environmental problems in different ways.

Regionalism was a crucial determinant of environmental policy-making among the states after World War II. Environmental legislation at this time depended on the traditions of political culture in each state, its variety of natural assets, and its institutional capacity. Some states distinguished themselves as areas of environmental strength, others as areas of weakness. The Pacific West (especially California and Oregon), New England, New York, Florida, and the Upper Midwest (Wisconsin, Minnesota, Michigan) all evinced environmental strength into the 1970s, whereas the Plains, the Southwest, the South, and midwestern states such as Ohio, Illinois, Pennsylvania, and Indiana revealed patterns of environmental weakness. Regional or state environmental culture, a "sense of place," proved essential to the character of state legislative action, often more so than partisan affiliation.

State legislatures and natural-resource policy after 1950 demonstrated the primary influence of urban-rural conflict. Growing urbanization in many states meshed with the movement to reapportion state legislatures. This climaxed with the Supreme Court decisions of the early 1960s, opening up statehouses to greater metropolitan representation and consequently stronger environmental sentiment in the political process. Urbanization, reapportionment, and the professionalization of state legislative activity compelled rural and suburban lawmakers to move to the environmental opposition by the late 1960s as they defended the developmental perspective in debates about tourism, land use, facility siting, cleanup of hazardous waste, and agency appropriations, for example. As at the federal level, state legislative committees became a battleground, pitting conservative rural and suburban lawmakers against the urban-based lawyers, activists, and other full-time legislators arguing for the preservationist or ecological point of view. Following Congress, the state legislatures emerged as public forums in which opposing groups debated environmental issues.

Another feature of environmental policy-making at the state level during the thirty years following World War II was the relationship between the executive branch and the legislature. State legislatures had evolved from institutions of economic promotion to ones incorporating both retarding and harmonizing forces when faced with reform measures. Governors had always maintained substantial control over environmental policy-making. As state legislatures modernized during the 1960s, so too did the executive; the status of governors strengthened and the chief executive became a key institutional contact for federal environmental programs and policies, often without legislative participation. Drawing on, and at times leading, public opinion, governors from both parties appeared as environmental advocates between 1960 and the end of the 1970s, presenting the subject as a reform issue integral to administrative ideology. This induced animosity between the governor and lawmakers in the environmental field as legislatures acted as a check on policy innovations, disputed directives emanating from the executive, and mediated the myriad demands of interest groups reacting to the governor.

The history of state legislative activity between 1950 and the end of the 1970s matched the same sequence of issues originating in Congress. However, state environmental policy-making at times preceded and thus influenced the federal legislature; many pioneering actions also spread from one state to others. Concern for outdoor recreation, as it related to urbanization, open-space preservation, and land-use planning, constituted the first impulse at the state level in the late 1950s. By the late 1960s and early 1970s, the issue of water-pollution control of industrial and municipal waste had supplanted the first state phase. Concurrently, state political leaders participated in a movement stressing reorganization and efficiency in government management. The centralization and consolidation of state environmental administration in superagencies, or "little EPAs," entailing an enhanced focus on the need for environmental protection, was one outcome of this trend in many states. States leading in these efforts included New York, Wisconsin, California, Minnesota, and Oregon.

By the late 1970s, state decisionmakers generally agreed that an integrated approach to administrative management could solve environmental problems, although many found this ideal impossible to implement. In the context of federalism, particularly the strictures of the Nixon administration's New Federalism, state legislators worked to align state functions with the requirements of federal mandates, often interceding between local governments and Washington in such controversial subjects as hazardous-waste disposal and wilderness preservation, and striking out on their own into new policy domains such as recycling and "green" issues of consumer rights. During the 1970s, state expenditures in the environmental realm increased dramatically, as did their heavy dependence on federal financing for natural-resource administration. Although the methods, intent, and rationale varied from state to state, and among regions, state environmental programs were institutionalized and politically popular by 1980; state legislatures were taking on a conservation conscience as lawmakers of all ideological perspectives recognized that environmental quality was important to a state's image and its potential for economic progress.

## CONGRESS AND THE ENVIRONMENT DURING THE 1970S

Congressional policy-making in the 1970s underlined the themes manifest in Samuel Hays's third stage of postwar environmental politics. Congress took a leading role in environmental affairs, dealing with issues of toxic- and solid-waste control, ecology, and energy use, among others. Several developments typified federal environmental legislation during this period. The increasing fragmentation of policy-making authority and the complexity of incipient environmental problems affected congressional action concerning such issues as acid rain and risk management.** Watergate-era attitudes brought an influx of liberals into the Capitol in the mid-1970s, distributing power more evenly

---

** An increasingly important feature of environmental policy-making in which politicians are required to determine (or assess) the magnitude of risk inherent in an environmental hazard—what amount of risk is acceptable?—based on the interpretation of and debate over scientific data.

and permitting legislators to consider a greater range of viewpoints. Environmental committees became decentralized and less predictable; it was harder for an exclusive group to control the policy-making process. Furthermore, Congress had passed by the end of the decade most of the definitive environmental statutes that set in place the basic regulatory direction of an environmental asset (such as water, air, solid waste). Legislative activity thus shifted back to incrementalism, concentrating on administrative oversight, investigation, mediation, and efforts to refine the major laws as Congress faced the demands of state governments, and the burgeoning power of the Environmental Protection Agency and the environmental lobby.

Studies of congressional voting, particularly in the House, have established that a national pattern of environmental lawmaking gradually emerged during the 1970s and intensified by the 1980s. Reinforcing earlier interpretations, the analysis of these votes demonstrated that environmental values were spreading throughout the United States among groups from across the ideological spectrum. This process was gradual and tentative, however. Some regions remained stronger in environmental support, and local environmental cultures proved crucial in determining the attitudes and approaches of members of Congress. Essentially, urban liberals from the Northeast, Pacific West, and Upper Midwest appeared as environmental advocates, and rural and suburban conservatives from the South, Plains, and Mountain West coalesced as environmental opponents. Despite attempts at bipartisanship, Democrats, with a few exceptions, became the recognized national proponents of environmental reform; Republicans divided on the issue along regional, demographic, and ideological lines.

A new and difficult environmental issue of the 1970s involved energy use and conservation. During the oil crises of 1973 and 1978, when the price of gasoline was raised precipitously by the Organization of Petroleum Exporting Countries (OPEC), Congress was propelled into the midst of the political argument about energy policy. A widely publicized investigation of the oil industry and its "obscene profits" in 1974, spearheaded by Senator Henry Jackson, exemplified Congress's initial approach to the subject. Later in the decade, Congress considered deregulation versus centralization and economic controls as the administration of President Jimmy Carter contested the energy problem with business and environmental groups. President Carter's ambitious policy proposals failed, but energy had become a permanently controversial topic of legislative affairs by 1980.

Two important laws represented the end of the environmental decade and presaged the future direction of federal environmental policy-making: the Comprehensive Environmental Response, Compensation, and Liability Act, or Superfund, and the Alaska National Interest Lands Act, both passed by a lame duck Congress in December 1980. Superfund formed a $1.6-billion emergency account to clean up toxic contaminants spilled or dumped into the environment. The Alaska act, called "the greatest single piece of legislation respecting parks and wilderness in world history" by Roderick Nash, preserved 104 million acres in national-park or wildlife-refuge units. Both laws were approved after years of legislative dispute and indicated the enduring power of environmental sentiment in challenging the onrushing force of the Reagan revolution.

## LEGISLATURES, THE ENVIRONMENT, AND THE REAGAN REVOLUTION, 1981–1988

In July 1979 the Nevada state legislature ratified a resolution demanding the transfer of forty-nine million acres of federal land in Nevada to state control; however, no public land returned to the states. This symbolic act of defiance initiated the "Sagebrush Rebellion," an insurrection of western states against federal environmental supremacy, which eventually became a vital part of the anti-environmental revolution pursued by the administration of President Ronald Reagan (1981 to 1989). Riding on a wave of apparent public support after the 1980 election, the Reagan administration challenged the principles of federal environmental management set by Congress from the mid-1960s to 1980. The Reagan administration, led by conservative radicals like EPA director Anne Gorsuch, a former Colorado state legislator, attacked the structure of environmental decision-making in American government, attempting to circumvent Congress and the courts. Labeled "The New Federalism," this doctrine emphasized conservative ideology, a return to the prerogatives of the business community, and executive power in promoting deregulation, budget cuts, and executive-branch control of policy implementation.

These efforts motivated Congress to respond. Congressional action moved away from the creative approach of the 1970s; instead, environmentally concerned lawmakers tried to protect existing policy and to defer the structural changes advocated by the president and his followers. The conflict between Congress and the executive branch was the crucial battleground in environmental politics during the 1980s. Congress emerged as the chief defender of environmental objectives. Congressional leaders employed their oversight powers as their chief means of defying the Reagan program. Backed by public opinion and a reinforced environmental lobby, House Democrats were the primary congressional champions of the environment. But a coalition of moderate Republicans, led by Senators Robert T. Stafford (R.-Vt.) and John H. Chafee (R.-R.I.), soon joined congressional resistance to the environmental retrogression. As early as 1982, when it overwhelmingly supported the extension of the Endangered Species Act and contested the administrative and budgetary enervation of the EPA and the Interior Department, Congress had launched a new direction in legislative strategy. The Ninety-ninth Congress (1985–1986), in fact, proved one of the strongest environmental sessions of all time, despite opposition from the Reagan administration: Congress reauthorized Superfund, the Clean Drinking Water Act, and the Clean Water Act, overriding a presidential veto. Federal legislators also passed important laws promoting energy-efficiency standards, soil conservation, and wild-rivers preservation. By the end of the Reagan presidency, Congress and the executive branch had reached a standoff in environmental policy-making.

A dominant theme in Reagan's New Federalism was the return of environmental authority to the states. The circumstances of federal-state relations were too complex for this plan to work, however. Indeed, states formed a major source of resistance to the Reagan administration's environmental policies; even western lawmakers ultimately rejected the arguments made previously by Sagebrush Rebel factions within their own states. Generally, state officials and legislators desired more federal money, stricter federal environmental regulations, and the expansion of all varieties of federal programs. Environmental values were institutionalized and popular in most states by the 1980s, thus less vulnerable to New Federalist inducements. Moreover, the connections between the federal government and the states were so firm that a sundering of the ties was impossible. In air- and water-pollution control, and especially toxic-waste management, the laws enjoined integration and coordination of policy-making, financing, and implementation under federal supervision. Hazardous-waste control, subject to the stipulations of Superfund and the Resource Conservation and Recovery Act (1976), became the paramount environmental issue at the state level. Demonstrating the depth of public concern, many states passed and implemented their own "superfund" laws between 1980 and 1986 to supplement the federal program. The disposal of radioactive by-products generated from nuclear power production was linked to this same problem after the 1982 Nuclear Waste Policy Act began a controversial search for permanent waste repositories that would be imposed upon the "host" states. These and other waste-management issues forced state legislatures to referee the volatile "not in my backyard" conflicts.

The uncertain course of federal policy in the 1980s further encouraged the development of new environmental programs among the states. Governors tended to champion reform, while legislators often remained in opposition or followed reluctantly. Yet, the overall professionalization of state lawmaking, the traditions of regional environmental cultures, and the rapid demographic growth and resulting ecological changes occurring in the largest states frequently pushed the legislature to the forefront. This trend was obvious in California, which had assumed the undisputed mantle of the leading environmental state by the 1980s. Almost a country unto itself, California had a strong institutional capacity, a vital citizen's movement, and was relatively free from dependence on federal money. California's lawmakers participated in the creation of divers innovative policies, especially in air-pollution control, recycling, energy use, and land preservation.

Three tendencies in state legislative action were prevalent by the end of the 1980s. In a pattern more clear-cut than in Congress, Democrats and urban representatives supported environmental objectives, and Republicans and rural legislators resisted them. State lawmakers also increasingly relied upon initiatives and referenda to gather popular approval before embarking on ambitious environmental schemes that necessitated raising revenues. In addition, state legislators turned to a wider assortment of financing measures to fuel incipient environmental programs, commencing special taxes and fees, bond issues, and lotteries with natural-resource provisions.

## CONCLUSION

The environmental politics of the 1980s revealed that the Reagan administration had underestimated the power of the environmental movement and the social values and public attitudes that underlay it. Environmental objectives, when potent enough, could break the bonds of partisanship. And, indeed, the Republican presidency of George Bush (1989–1993) revealed much the same pattern. Candidate Bush promised to be the "Environmental President" during the 1988 campaign. He appointed several prominent environmentalists to his administration: most noteworthy was William Reilly as head of the Environmental Protection Agency. But President Bush and his followers tended to carry on the same natural-resource policies as those from the Reagan years; this approach was especially manifest in the efforts to ease environmental regulation, promulgated by the Council on Competitiveness under Vice President Dan Quayle. Consequently, the Bush administration encountered bipartisan resistance from Congress and citizen groups in the environmental field. Nevertheless, the debates of the period demonstrated the importance of the executive branch in influencing environmental lawmaking and, as a consequence, challenging state and federal legislatures.

By the start of the 1990s, the complexity of natural-resource issues and the fragmentation of policy-making in the field at the state and federal levels signaled the arrival of a new era in environmental concern. Science, law, technology, economics, and international relations were all intertwined with emerging global ecological problems such as the greenhouse effect, airborne pollutants, ozone depletion, deforestation, drought, population growth, habitat destruction, nuclear hazards, and energy consumption. As a result, the legislative system was torn between the specialized focus on detail and the broader long-range vision demanded by the nascent environmental policy. For example, the complicated and disputatious nine-year battle to reauthorize the Clean Air Act, culminating in November 1990, foreshadowed the future direction of legislative activity in environmental affairs. So did the efforts of congressional policy entrepreneurs, allied with environmentalists, to compel the executive branch to cooperate with the international community in solving the greenhouse-effect and ozone-depletion crises. The election to the presidency of Democrat William Clinton in 1992, as well as the success of a throng of environmentally aware legislators from both parties, portended another shift in environmental policy-making. President Clinton's selection of Senator Albert Gore (D.-Tenn.) as vice president underscored the avowedly environmentalist stance taken by the new leaders in the executive branch, and was eagerly followed by many members of Congress. Senator Gore's best-selling book, *Earth in the Balance: Ecology and the Human Spirit* (1992), demonstrated an unusual cognizance of the specifics and far-reaching ramifications of environmental lawmaking. Conservatives would characterize Gore as an "extremist"; eco-radicals claimed the vice president did not go far enough. This political dialogue continued the endless controversy prompted by the debate over the development and implementation of environmental policy that had become so prevalent in the United States by the 1990s. Regardless of the ultimate outcome of these events, the American legislative system had moved far beyond its predominant interest in economic promotion during the nineteenth century to become an important institutional player in the environmental age.

## *BIBLIOGRAPHY*

Scholarship pertaining to legislatures and the environment is divided into two categories: history and political science. Historians tend to interpret the American legislative experience in terms of the larger intellectual, political, social, and ecological patterns of environmental history. Political scientists chiefly analyze the particulars of environmental policy-making after World War II; political science literature is particularly rich from the late 1960s onward. A combined reading of the two fields offers the best overview of the topic.

### *History*

CRAIG W. ALLIN, *The Politics of Wilderness Preservation* (Westport, Conn., 1982), provides detail on congressional debates about wilderness to 1980. RICHARD A. BAKER, *Conservation Politics: The Senate Career of Clinton P. Anderson* (Albuquerque, 1985), discusses a leading conservation figure in Congress after World War II. MICHAEL P. COHEN, *The History of the Sierra Club, 1892–1970* (San Francisco, 1988), summarizes the political-lobby efforts of a major environmental organization. WILLIAM CRONON, *Nature's Metropolis: Chicago and the Great West* (New York, 1991), is an important work by a leading environmental historian on the key role of Chicago in the westward movement. THOMAS R. COX, *The Park Builders: A History of State Parks in the Pacific Northwest* (Seattle, 1988), analyzes the politics of the state-parks movement from the nineteenth century to the 1970s.

ROBERT G. DUNBAR, *Forging New Rights in Western Waters* (Lincoln, Nebr., 1983), covers the changes in western water law in the nineteenth and early twentieth centuries. PAUL WALLACE GATES, *History of Public Land Law Development* (Washington, D.C., 1968), is an influential study of the evolution of American land use. WILLIAM L. GRAF, *Wilderness Preservation and the Sagebrush Rebellions* (Savage, Md., 1990), integrates and assesses the relative effects of John Wesley Powell, the Forest Reserve Act of 1891, the Wilderness Act of 1964, and the Reagan years for public-lands policy. The work of SAMUEL P. HAYS is central to the historiography of American environmental politics and should be the starting point for inter-

ested readers: his *Conservation and the Gospel of Efficiency: The Progressive Conservation Movement, 1890–1920* (New York, 1969, originally 1959), recounts the origins of Progressive conservation; his *Beauty, Health, and Permanence: Environmental Politics in the United States, 1955–1985* (New York, 1987), is a landmark study offering a broad and trenchant interpretation of the subject; his "The Politics of Environmental Administration," in LOUIS GALAMBOS, ed., *The New American State: Bureaucracies and Policies Since World War II* (Baltimore, 1987); his "The New Environmental West," *Journal of Policy History* 3 (1991): 223–248; and his "Environmental Political Culture and Environmental Political Development: An Analysis of Legislative Voting, 1971–1989," *Environmental History Review* 16 (Summer 1992), present syntheses of key ideas.

JAMES WILLARD HURST, *Law and Economic Growth: The Legal History of the Lumber Industry in Wisconsin, 1836–1915* (1964; repr. Madison, Wis., 1984), a pioneering environmental work by an influential legal historian, focuses on one state, but the model is generally applicable to most states in the nineteenth century. CLAYTON R. KOPPES, "Efficiency, Equity, Esthetics: Shifting Themes in American Conservation," in DONALD WORSTER, ed., *The Ends of the Earth: Perspectives on Modern Environmental History* (New York, 1988), offers a review of the ideas that have sustained the conservation movement, in a book summarizing the growing field of environmental history. PATRICIA NELSON LIMERICK, *The Legacy of Conquest: The Unbroken Past of the American West* (New York, 1987), is an important revisionist analysis of the westward movement. ARTHUR F. McEVOY, *The Fisherman's Problem: Ecology and Law in the California Fisheries, 1850–1980* (New York, 1986), supplies information on early legal efforts in conservation in California. MARTIN V. MELOSI, "Lyndon Johnson and Environmental Policy," in ROBERT DIVINE, ed., *The Johnson Years, Volume Two: Vietnam, the Environment, and Science* (Lawrence, Kan., 1987), outlines the environmental politics of the 1960s.

RODERICK FRAZIER NASH, *Wilderness and the American Mind* (1967; repr. New Haven,

Conn., 1982) and his *The Rights of Nature: A History of Environmental Ethics* (Madison, Wis., 1989), provide discussion of the intellectual history of environmentalism; his *American Environmentalism: Readings in Conservation History* (1968; repr. New York, 1989) is a good compilation of environmental-history readings. DONALD J. PISANI, "Fish Culture and the Dawn of Concern Over Water Pollution in the United States," *Environmental Review* 8 (1984): 117–131, describes early efforts by states to control water pollution in the nineteenth century; and PISANI, "Forests and Conservation, 1865–1890," *Journal of American History* 72 (September 1985), provides an excellent overview of the connections between an emerging conservation ethic and the state and federal forestry legislation of the period. JOHN F. REIGER, *American Sportsmen and the Origins of Conservation* (New York, 1986), discusses political lobbying by sporting groups in the nineteenth century. MARC REISNER, *Cadillac Desert: The American West and Its Disappearing Water* (New York, 1986), interprets the politics of water use in the West through the 1980s. ALFRED RUNTE, *National Parks: The American Experience* (1987; rev. ed., Lincoln, Nebr., 1979), supplies comprehensive background on the parks movement from the nineteenth century to the present; RUNTE's *Yosemite: The Embattled Wilderness* (Lincoln, Nebr., 1990), supplies a good overview of the struggle to create the park after 1864 and is one of the best studies of the conflict over management objectives in national parks since the 1860s. PHILIP V. SCARPINO, *Great River: An Environmental History of the Upper Mississippi River, 1890–1950* (Columbia, Mo., 1985), details congressional efforts to conserve the Mississippi during the 1920s and 1930s. SUSAN R. SCHREPFER, *The Fight to Save the Redwoods: A History of Environmental Reform, 1917–1978* (Madison, Wis., 1983), studies a specific conservation issue and covers state and congressional political debates. PHILIP SHABECOFF, *A Fierce Green Fire: The American Environmental Movement* (New York, 1993), is a recent and well-written general history of environmentalism in the United States by an environmental writer for the *New York Times*.

HERBERT A. SMITH, C. R. TILLOTSON, and CATHERINE M. O'DONNELL, "State Accomplishments and Plans," in *A National Plan For American Forestry*, Report of the U.S. Forest Service, U.S. Senate Doc. 12, Seventy-third Congress (Washington, D.C., 1933), is obscure but furnishes otherwise unobtainable information on state conservation efforts in the nineteenth century. MICHAEL L. SMITH, *Pacific Visions: California Scientists and the Environment, 1850–1915* (New Haven, 1987), analyzes the political role of science in California's conservation controversies. MICHAEL WILLIAMS, *Americans and Their Forests: A Historical Geography* (New York, 1989), is a superb treatment of the ecology and politics of North American forestry through time. DONALD WORSTER, *Rivers of Empire: Water, Aridity and the Growth of the American West* (New York, 1985), interprets the importance of water for the American West and its political institutions. DANIEL YERGIN, *The Prize: The Epic Quest for Oil, Money, and Power* (New York, 1991), a comprehensive survey of oil in world history, includes congressional debates concerning energy policy.

### Political Science

CHRISTOPHER J. BOSSO, *Pesticides and Politics: The Life Cycle of a Public Issue* (Pittsburgh, 1987), analyzes patterns of congressional debate about pesticides from the 1940s to 1980s. LYNTON K. CALDWELL, *Environment: A Challenge for Modern Society* (Garden City, N.Y., 1970), is an early work by one of the leaders in promoting the study of environmental issues in the field of political science. CONGRESSIONAL QUARTERLY, INC. (Washington, D.C.), publishes abundant materials on state and federal environmental politics. RICHARD A. COOLEY and GEOFFREY WANDESFORDE-SMITH, eds., *Congress and the Environment* (Seattle, 1970), is dated but supplies interesting information about policy debates in Congress. COUNCIL OF STATE GOVERNMENTS (Lexington, Ky.), publishes material on state environmental politics and policymaking. RICHARD F. FENNO, *Congressmen in Committees* (Boston, 1973), analyzes the work of the congressional Interior and Insular Affairs committees. BOB HALL and MARY LEE KERR, *1991–1992 Green Index: A State-by-State Guide to the Nation's Environmental Health* (Washington, D.C., 1991), is a good analysis of state environmental-policy initiatives and programs, including a chapter on congressional leadership in the field for each state. ROYCE HANSON, *Tribune of the People: The Minnesota*

*Legislature and Its Leadership* (Minneapolis, 1989), is a trenchant discussion of patterns of lawmaking in one state legislature after World War II, including analysis of the battle over a state superfund law in 1983.

MICHAEL E. KRAFT, BRUCE B. CLARY, and RICHARD J. TOBIN, "The Impact of New Federalism on State Environmental Policy: The Great Lakes States," in PETER K. EISINGER and WILLIAM GORMLEY, eds., *The Midwest Response to the New Federalism* (Madison, Wis., 1988), discusses the influence of the Reagan philosophy on state environmental management. MARC K. LANDY, MARC J. ROBERTS, and STEPHEN R. THOMAS, *The Environmental Protection Agency: Asking the Wrong Questions* (New York, 1990), furnishes a description of environmental policymaking in Congress in the modern era.

JAMES P. LESTER, ed., *Environmental Politics and Policy: Theories and Evidence* (Durham, 1989), is an excellent summary of recent political science literature, including the role of Congress and state legislatures. ARTHUR J. MAGIDA, "The House and Senate Interior and Insular Affairs Committees," in *The Environment Committees: A Study of the House and Senate Interior, Agriculture, and Science Committees* (New York, 1975), details the environmental policy-making process in crucial congressional committees during the 1960s and 1970s. ROBERT J. MASON and MARK T. MATTSON, *Atlas of United States Environmental Issues* (New York, 1990), presents comprehensive statistics relating to major environmental issues in clear visual form as well as a brief narrative about the politics of each. RALPH NADER, *Vanishing Air: Ralph Nader's Study Group Report on Air Pollution* (New York, 1970) and *Water Wasteland: Ralph Nader's Study Group Report on Water Pollution* (New York, 1971), are both influential studies of environmental politics in Congress during the 1960s. ROBERT C. PAEHLKE,

*Environmentalism and the Future of Progressive Politics* (New Haven, Conn., 1989), is a political science interpretation of environmental politics. BARRY G. RABE, *Fragmentation and Integration in State Environmental Management* (Washington, D.C., 1986), describes new methods of environmental administration and lawmaking in key states from the late 1960s through the early 1980s. WALTER A. ROSENBAUM, *Environmental Politics and Policy* (Washington, D.C., 1991), and his *Energy, Politics, and Public Policy* (Washington, D.C., 1987), provide good overviews of the history and patterns of modern environmental and energy use policy-making.

DANIEL P. SELMI and KENNETH A. MANASTER, *State Environmental Law* (New York, 1990, annual update), presents a broad discussion of the relationship between evolving federal and state environmental statutes. NORMAN J. VIG and MICHAEL E. KRAFT, eds., *Environmental Policy in the 1980s: Reagan's New Agenda* (Washington, D.C., 1984), summarizes federal environmental policies from the 1970s to the beginning of the 1980s. NORMAN J. VIG and MICHAEL E. KRAFT, eds., *Environmental Policy in the 1990s* (Washington, D.C., 1990), is a thorough compilation of current political science thinking about environmental politics, including surveys of congressional and state policy. DAVID VOGEL, *Fluctuating Fortunes: The Political Power of Business in America* (New York, 1989), is an incisive interpretation of business power and national politics, emphasizing the influence of the modern environmental movement. WORLDWATCH INSTITUTE (Washington, D.C.), offers an annual publication, *State of the World,* that discusses the key aspects of environmental policy-making in the United States and other nations, and its relation to the future of growing environmental problems around the world.

SEE ALSO Legislatures and American Economic Development.

# THE CONGRESSIONAL BUDGET PROCESS AND FEDERAL BUDGET DEFICIT

## *John F. Cogan*

Several times per day the telephone operators at the White House receive inquiries from well-meaning citizens asking, "What can I do to help get this country out of debt?" Imagine their astonishment if they were told the truth: "Send a check made out to the U.S. Treasury for $40,000." This is, in fact, how much every family in the United States would have to pay to dissolve the national debt as it stands in 1993. This extraordinary amount is a result of sixty years of persistent federal budget deficits.

As a historical matter, the deficits of the 1930s and 1940s were not unusual. Budget deficits, the amount by which annual federal spending exceeds annual revenues, have been a recurring phenomenon during years of economic contractions, and the Great Depression of the 1930s was the worst and most prolonged economic contraction in the nation's history. Likewise, the government has always run budget deficits during armed conflict, and World War II was no exception to this rule. But the almost continuous string of peacetime deficits since World War II is not so easy to understand.

Many observers believe these deficits persist because the American public demands more in government benefits than it is willing to pay for in taxes. Although this explanation has intuitive appeal, it fails to explain why the American public's preferences have changed. Why were Americans previously willing to settle for the same amount of benefits as they were paying for in taxes?

Others claim these deficits suddenly emerged as a result of unique policy decisions made during the 1980s, such as the simultaneous reduction in taxes and increase in defense spending. Although tax and spending policies pursued in the 1980s certainly exacerbated the deficit problem, this explanation ignores the reoccurring budget deficits of the three decades

prior to the 1980s. It also ignores the fact that, since 1981, expenditures on nondefense programs have grown almost as rapidly as those on defense programs, and that the average federal tax claim on the country's gross national product (GNP) during the 1980s was higher than it has averaged during any preceding decade.

Although the budget deficits of the 1980s and 1990s are much larger than those of prior decades, they nevertheless represent a continuation of previous trends. Deficit-producing forces have been operating for at least the entire post–World War II period and possibly longer. The last time the budget was balanced was in 1969, and the last time before that was in 1960. Each decade the federal budget deficit problem has worsened, rising from about one-half of 1 percent of the nation's income in the 1950s to more than 4 percent of the nation's income in the 1980s.

## A THEORY BEHIND THE DEFICITS

What accounts for this modern flow of red ink that, from all indications, seems to be here to stay? What deficit-causing forces do the federal budgets of the past four decades share in common? One strong theory is that the institutional rules by which Congress makes its budget decisions have had a profound impact in contributing to budget deficits. Two institutional forces have been particularly important. The first and most important institutional factor is the splintered structure of the congressional spending committees, which has been largely responsible for increasing spending pressure compared to available revenues. The second is that the creation of trust funds has reduced the availability of general revenues.

It is important to recognize that the congressional committees charged with the responsibility of drafting legislation have extraordinary influence over a final bill. The strength of their power is perhaps best illustrated by Woodrow Wilson's often-cited statement that the congressional committees operate as "little legislatures." Although committee bills are often amended on the House and Senate floors, they usually emerge from the floor debate without significant modification.

Widely dispersed decision-making among a host of these little legislatures has been the central feature of the congressional budget process for some time. In 1993, seventeen different committees in the House of Representatives and fifteen Senate committees share jurisdiction over spending. Dispersal of spending authority among these powerful committees is a recipe for excessive spending and persistent budget deficits. Under such a system, the total level of spending is beyond any single committee's control, and political accountability to the electorate for total spending is diminished.

The deficit spending caused by this decentralized committee system can be thought of as what Garrett Hardin called a "tragedy of the commons." The problem occurs any time there are several competing claimants for a commonly owned resource. Imagine, for example, a publicly owned forest open to all logging companies that desire access to it. No individual company would have any reason to restrain its logging activities. In fact, each company would have every incentive to cut down as many trees as it could before a competitor did so. Eventually, the forest would become bare. The depletion would probably not occur, however, were only one logging company given access to the forest. A single logging company would be more inclined to preserve some of the existing trees for later use and to establish a reforestation program to ensure an adequate supply of timber in the future.

In the case of the federal budget, the common resource, or "forest," is revenue raised primarily from corporate and individual income taxes, known as general-fund revenue. When many congressional committees have authority to spend general-fund revenue, each committee is less inclined to restrain its spending because the political blame for increased taxes or deficit spending is shared by all committees. In fact, the opposite of restraint occurs. Pres-

sured by interest groups to maintain their fair share of total spending, each committee becomes an advocate for the programs under its jurisdiction. As the committees observe one another dipping deeper and deeper into the pool of money they all must share, they begin to see the futility of practicing fiscal restraint and the wisdom of raising expenditures on programs within their jurisdiction. Competition among the separate committees soon develops. The result is that each committee reaps the full political rewards of higher expenditures on its programs, but bears only a portion of the adverse political consequences of financing higher expenditures. In the end, the available revenue pool is exhausted and the government must resort to borrowing from the public.

The commons theory helps explain the persistent budget deficits that have occurred since the 1930s, and the absence of persistent deficits during most prior U.S. history. As Table 1 indicates, during periods when spending jurisdiction was centralized in one committee, as it has been during the majority of Congress's history, deficits have been rare or nonexistent. In contrast, during periods when spending jurisdiction has been spread out over several committees, as is the case today, deficits become a regular feature of the federal budget.

A second factor operating since the 1930s that has exacerbated the effects of the commons has been the creation of programs funded by trust funds, such as Social Security, federal highway aid, and Medicare. Trust-fund programs are financed by specific taxes levied on the public. The proceeds of the tax flow

**Table 1**
**FEDERAL BUDGET DEFICITS**

| Time Period | Average Deficits |
|---|---|
| *Centralized Budgeting* | (Percent of GNP) |
| 1799–1885 | 0.26% |
| 1922–1931 | −0.77% |
| | |
| *Decentralized Budgeting* | |
| 1886–1921 | 0.69% |
| 1932–1991 | 3.67% |

*Source:* U.S. Office of Management and Budget, *Budget of the United States Government, Fiscal Year 1993 (Supplement)* (Washington, D.C., 1992); U.S. Department of the Treasury, *Report of the Secretary of the Treasury on the State of Finances* (Statistical Appendix), (Washington, D.C., 1980).

into the trust fund, and program expenditures are made by withdrawing money from the fund.

Creating trust funds and placing jurisdiction for them in the tax-writing committees created a bias in favor of raising trust-fund taxes and against other taxes. Trust-fund taxes finance programs that provide well-identified benefits, while general-fund taxes, such as income taxes, finance a diffuse array of programs. Moreover, the tax-writing committees decide how most trust-fund revenue is spent. These factors make it easier for the tax-writing committees to raise trust-fund taxes. Given the public's willingness to accept only a certain total tax burden, increases on trust-fund taxes that have been matched by increases in trust-fund expenditures have come at the expense of income taxes.

Thus, during the post–World War II years, two forces have been at work. The decentralized committee structure, operating with the incentives of the commons, has created upward pressure on expenditures from the general fund, while the establishment of trust funds has created downward pressure on general-fund revenues. The two forces have combined to produce the record string of postwar budget deficits.

## A CONSOLIDATED BEGINNING

For the first ninety years of the nation's history, almost all spending authority was concentrated in a single committee in each house. The alternative to this single-committee system was to allocate jurisdiction for spending legislation among several standing "expert" committees. This alternative has the advantage that spending decisions would be made by committees with a detailed knowledge of programs under their jurisdictions. However, this advantage was outweighed by two severe disadvantages. First, spending decisions would lack coordination and coherency. Second, there would be a risk that each standing committee would become an advocate for programs under its jurisdiction with little regard for the more general interests of the budget.

Faced with these trade-offs, each chamber initially chose to concentrate jurisdiction for spending legislation in one committee. Begin-

ning in 1789, the Ways and Means Committee in the House of Representatives had jurisdiction over all appropriations. In 1816, after briefly experimenting with select committees to handle appropriations, the Senate created the Finance Committee as a standing committee with jurisdiction over appropriations. Since these two committees were also the tax-writing committees, the institutional arrangement in these early years actually consisted of a single "budget" committee in each house responsible for virtually all taxing and spending matters.

These two committees carried out their responsibilities by dividing general appropriations into individual legislative bills. In 1794, appropriations were passed in the form of two legislative bills: a military establishment bill and a general government bill. By the 1850s, the number of appropriations bills had expanded to ten. Although the large number of bills did create coordination problems, they did not create incentives for excessive spending because a single committee in each house remained in charge of all spending legislation.

In 1865 the House voted to move appropriations jurisdiction from the Ways and Means Committee to a newly created Appropriations Committee. The Senate followed suit two years later and shifted jurisdiction from the Finance Committee to its Appropriations Committee. The shift of jurisdiction over appropriations still left a single congressional committee in each house in charge of all appropriations. This institutional arrangement continued in both houses until 1877. Throughout this period, the new House and Senate appropriations committees continued the practice of enacting appropriations through many individual bills.

From 1790 to 1835, this highly centralized budget process, along with the desire to eliminate the debt, produced a string of almost continuous annual budget surpluses until the Revolutionary War debt was fully extinguished in 1835. After the debt was repaid and before the Civil War began, neither surpluses nor deficits persisted for any significant length of time. During this early period, the longest string of consecutive budget deficits, from 1840 to 1843, was due to a severe economic recession in the first three of these four years. The longest string of consecutive budget surpluses was the eight-year period from 1850 to 1857, inclusive. These surpluses were used to reduce the national debt, which had increased greatly during the Mexican-American War.

Following the Civil War, the House and Senate appropriations committees continued the fiscal restraint practiced by their predecessors. Expenditures related to the war effort were cut back sharply; enough so that the income tax was allowed to expire, tariffs were cut, and the war-related debt was reduced by a third. Unfortunately, the year 1877 would mark the beginning of the end for this stretch of fiscal well-being.

## FIRST PERIOD OF DECENTRALIZATION

The year 1877 was the start of a period of radical change in the House of Representatives' spending procedures. The House, in a series of rule changes during the next eight years, stripped the Appropriations Committee of its authority over eight of the fourteen appropriation bills. In each instance, appropriations authority was transferred from the Appropriations Committee to the standing committee that had jurisdiction over the programs contained in the appropriations bill. Beginning in 1877, the House Committee on Commerce was given temporary responsibility for reporting rivers and harbors appropriations directly to the floor, bypassing the Appropriations Committee completely. In 1880, the Agriculture and Forestry Committee gained responsibility for the Agriculture Department's appropriations, and in 1883, appropriations for rivers and harbors were formally transferred to a newly created Rivers and Harbors Committee.

The most drastic action occurred in 1885. In that year, responsibility for the Army, Consular and Diplomatic Affairs, Indian Affairs, Military Academy, Navy, and Post Office and Postal Roads appropriations bills was transferred from the Appropriations Committee to the various legislative committees. Fourteen years later, the Senate divided appropriations jurisdiction along the same lines. The 1885 dispersal of spending authority was without historical precedent. Taken together, the appropriations transferred from the Appropriations Committee constituted almost one-half of all appropriations.

In the midst of these changes, many members of Congress predicted that a wide distribution of spending authority would inevitably lead to increased spending and budget deficits. Perhaps the most forceful of such arguments was made by one of the House of Representatives' most distinguished members, Samuel Randall (D.-Pa.). During his career, Randall had been both Speaker of the House and chair of the Appropriations Committee. In 1885, responding to a proposal that initiated this activity, Randall offered the following warning: "If you undertake to divide all these appropriations and have many committees where there ought to be but one, you will enter upon a path of extravagance you can not foresee the length of or the depth of, until we will find the Treasury of the country bankrupt" (U.S. Congress, House, *Congressional Record*, 4 December 1917, p. 23). Randall was not alone in his view. The *Congressional Record* and other historical documents of the period from 1877 to 1885 contain numerous similar statements by other national leaders, including James Garfield (R.-Ohio), who served as Speaker of the House prior to becoming president in 1881.

The reasons the House of Representatives chose to strip the Appropriations Committee of much of its budget-making responsibility are complex. One important consideration was that, at the time, the federal budget was running large surpluses. Throughout the late 1870s and the first half of the 1880s, revenues exceeded expenditures by almost 40 percent. The principal revenue source came from tariffs levied on imported goods. Tariffs had been lowered earlier and further reductions were hotly opposed by manufacturers. Additional reductions would increase the manufacturing sector's exposure to foreign competition. The Appropriations Committee, under the tight-fisted control of Randall, was unsympathetic to calls for the committee to "spend the surplus." Rather than depose Randall from his chairmanship, his committee was stripped of a large portion of its power.

## CONSEQUENCES OF DECENTRALIZATION

The shift in committee responsibility for spending had a direct effect on spending. In the five years following the transfer of responsibility for rivers and harbors funding, its appropriations increased by 60 percent. In the five years following the transfer of responsibility for Department of Agriculture funding, its appropriations doubled. And in the five years following the 1885 transfer of responsibility for the six remaining appropriations bills, funding for departments in these bills grew by 14 percent, twice the growth for departments that continued to be funded through the appropriations committees. The combined effect of these increases in spending sharply reduced the size of the budget surplus by the beginning of the 1890s.

The increase in spending did not stop at this point. As the powerful forces of the commons theory took hold, federal spending continued to rise sharply for the next three decades. More important, spending rose independently of revenues. By 1893, federal spending, excluding interest payments, was 50 percent larger than it had been in 1886. By the end of the century, it was 100 percent larger. The spending growth transformed the 40-percent budget surplus, which had existed during the period 1881–1885, into a deficit by 1894. The budget deficit persisted each year throughout the decade of the 1890s. From the turn of the century until the United States' entry into World War I, government spending increased another 45 percent. During half the years of this period, the federal budget was in deficit.

Virtually all of the increase in government spending during the thirty-year period from 1886 to 1916 occurred in programs no longer under the jurisdiction of the Appropriations Committee. Programs under the jurisdiction of committees that were the recipients of appropriations jurisdiction in 1885 grew 50 percent faster than GNP. Programs that were the responsibility of the Rivers and Harbors Committee grew 20 percent faster than GNP. And agriculture programs grew over 1000 percent faster than GNP. Spending on programs that remained under the jurisdiction of the Appropriations Committee declined slightly relative to GNP.

The thirty years from 1887 to 1916 represent a remarkable period in U.S. fiscal history. The size of federal spending grew at a rate that, at the time, was unprecedented in the nation's experience. Growth in spending outstripped growth in revenues. Budget deficits became chronic, occurring more frequently and in larger amounts than in prior history. In almost one out of every two years the budget was in deficit.

## RETURN TO CENTRALIZED SPENDING

As a result of this rapid growth in the budget, the issue of budgetary-process reform gained momentum in the years immediately preceding World War I. The issue soon became ripe for the campaign trail. Both political parties recognized the source of the problem and promised to do something about it. The Democratic party platform of 1916 called for a return to the pre-1865 single-committee regime: "We demand careful economy in all expenditures and to that end favor a return by the House of Representatives to its former practice of initiating and preparing all appropriation bills through a single committee."

The Republican party platform was less explicit. It called for enactment of former President Taft's "oft-repeated and earnest proposal efforts to secure economy and efficiency through the establishment of a single and business-like budget system."

President Wilson, himself a student of Congress, joined those calling for reform in his 1917 State of the Union message following his election to a second term. In his address Wilson stated:

> And I beg that the members of the House of Representatives will permit me to express the opinion that it will be impossible to deal in any but a very wasteful and extravagant fashion with the enormous appropriations of the public moneys . . . unless the House will consent to return to its former practice of initiating and preparing all appropriation bills through a single committee. (U.S. Congress, House, *Congressional Record*, 4 December 1917, p. 23)

World War I temporarily diverted attention from the issue of budget-process reform. But as soon as the war ended, the reform effort was immediately taken up again. In October of 1919, the House of Representatives created a select committee on the budget. The committee submitted its report to the Congress later in the year. The centerpiece of the report was a recommendation that the House adopt a resolution that "centers in one Committee on Appropriations . . . the authority to report all appropriations." According to the committee, effective control over the budget could not be achieved without consolidating spending jurisdiction. As the committee report summarized: "Without the adoption of this resolution true budgetary reform is impossible."

The select committee knew it was proposing a dramatic step. Never before in the history of Congress had authority been stripped away from so many committees. However, the committee also knew that the wide distribution of spending jurisdiction was not in the general interest.

> While it [the resolution] means the surrender by certain committees of jurisdiction which they now possess and will take from certain members on those committees certain powers now exercised, we ought to approach the consideration of the big problem with a determination to submerge personal ambition for the public good. (U.S. Congress, House, *Congressional Record*, 66th Cong., 1st sess., H. Rept. 373)

In one day, the House Select Committee on the Budget submitted its recommendations and reported out a bill to implement them. The bill, authored by the select committee's chair, James W. Good (R.-Iowa), sent shock waves reverberating through legislative committee hearing rooms. It proposed that the House wrench appropriations authority from seven powerful legislative committees.

More than seven months elapsed before the resolution was brought to the House floor. By that time, a majority had been marshaled in its favor and the resolution passed by a vote of 200 to 117.

There were undoubtedly many reasons for the House's action. The overriding one was a belief that without it, fiscal restraint could not be achieved. Still, it is not clear whether budget economy arguments alone would have carried the day in the House. The fact that the resolution had previously been embraced in almost identical form by the Democratic party platform and was consistent with the thrust

of the Republican party's platform was also important.

During the floor debate on the consolidation bill, several members reminded the Democratic members of this fact, but none as forcefully as James Good. In a powerful statement, Good began by invoking the words of former party leader William Jennings Bryan on the importance of adhering to the platform:

> The Representative who secures office on a platform and then betrays the people who elected him is a criminal worse than he who embezzles money.

Good then reminded his fellow Democrats that an election was five months away:

> A real test has come, vote to repudiate your platform or vote to carry out its provisions. But I want to assure you that those Democrats who vote to repudiate their platform in this respect will, I believe, live to regret that action, and your deserts may come sooner than you think. (U.S. Congress, House, *Congressional Record*, 1 June 1920, p. 8116)

The Senate followed the House lead two years later. On 6 March 1922, the Senate amended its rules to provide that all appropriation bills be considered by one committee instead of many.

## REWARDS OF CENTRALIZED SPENDING

The years following the consolidation of spending authority in the House and Senate were marked by considerable fiscal restraint. During the 1920s, the almost unbroken upward march of government spending of the preceding three decades was halted. The budget was brought into surplus each year from 1920 to 1930, and the size of the budget surplus actually increased from the beginning of the decade to its end.

This eleven-year string of consecutive budget surpluses was the longest since the 1880s, before spending authority was dispersed in the House. But the federal government's fiscal restraint of the 1920s would not be carried far into the 1930s. A string of budget surpluses and the centralized budget process were brought to an end by the Great Depression. The collapse of the economy greatly reduced the flow of annual revenues to the federal government and thereby produced budget deficits beginning in 1931.

In addition to a weakened economy, the decade of the 1930s witnessed two separate phenomena that would fuel a pattern of deficit spending for the next sixty years. First, the centralized committee structure achieved in the 1920s slowly unraveled, resulting once again in a splintered power structure vulnerable to the effects of the commons problem. And second, the emergence of trust funds exerted an extra force to widen the gap continually between revenues and expenditures.

## SECOND PERIOD OF DECENTRALIZATION

Unlike the decentralization of the 1880s, the broadening of spending authority that has occurred since the 1930s did not occur all at once, but has evolved over time. Rather than simply transfer appropriations jurisdiction, Congress devised new methods of financing government programs that gave an ever-increasing number of congressional committees spending authority. The new methods, including borrowing authority and entitlements, have become known as backdoor spending authority. And, the back door of the U.S. Treasury has proven much harder to close than the front door regular appropriations bills.

If there is any single legislative activity that marks the beginning of the modern process of broadening spending authority, it is the creation of the Reconstruction Finance Corporation (RFC) in 1932. In creating the RFC, the appropriations process was circumvented by permitting the corporation to borrow directly from the U.S. Treasury. The Treasury could, in turn, borrow the necessary funds from the public. Never before had such a funding technique been used. For the first time, the decision of how much to spend on a particular program was isolated from the rest of the decision-making process for the federal budget. Soon borrowing authority would come to be used to finance numerous agencies and programs.

Within the next five years, the Commodity Credit Corporation, the Tennessee Valley Authority, the Homeowners' Loan Corporation, the Rural Electrification Administration, and the Federal Public Housing Authority were created and allowed to obtain financing through the same mechanism.

By the early 1950s, seventeen different programs located in nine executive-branch agencies had been given borrowing authority. By the late 1950s, when its use peaked, borrowing authority had been extended to more than thirty programs, including farm, housing, civil defense, and college housing loans, area development projects, and the Export-Import Bank.

In the 1960s the use of borrowing authority by the legislative committees declined. It was replaced, however, by the widespread adoption of another form of legislation that further dispersed spending authority among congressional committees: entitlement programs. These are programs that provide eligible recipients with a legal right to certain payments or services from the federal government.

The number of eligible recipients receiving these government payments and services were significantly expanded by this new wave of entitlement activity. Prior to the 1930s, major entitlements were limited to payments to individuals who had performed some specified service in government: disabled veterans, and retired military and civilian personnel. During the economic emergency of the 1930s, entitlements were expanded to include persons who had not previously performed any direct government service, and to other private and public institutions.

Deposit insurance legislation, for example, was an entitlement enacted in 1933 that provided a federal government guarantee for certain deposits in banks and savings and loan institutions. Social Security legislation, enacted a year later, provided pensions to persons sixty-five years of age and older. These pensions were soon extended to widows and survivors. In the same legislation, state governments were guaranteed a federal matching payment to cover a portion of their costs of operating welfare programs for single mothers, the elderly poor, and the blind.

The 1930s were followed by about twenty

years of little new entitlement legislation. Most legislation focused on expanding existing entitlements. Only two new entitlements were created. In 1950, state governments were provided with federal matching payments for the cost of programs for poor persons suffering from disabilities. And in 1956 the Social Security disability program was created to provide cash assistance to all disabled persons.

In the 1960s and early 1970s a second wave of new entitlement legislation was enacted. But these entitlements differed from previously enacted programs. Earlier entitlements provided assistance in the form of cash. The entitlements of the 1960s, for the most part, provided assistance in the form of specific services known as in-kind benefits. The 1964 food stamp program provided low-income persons with vouchers to purchase food. In 1965, Medicare guaranteed acute health-care services to the elderly. In the same law, the federal government under Medicaid provided matching payments to states for a portion of the cost of health-care services to the poor. The federal government guaranteed bank loans to higher-education students in 1965. In 1974, states were guaranteed general assistance federal aid through the general revenue sharing program, and the costs of their child-support programs were matched by the federal government.

Each new entitlement weakened the control of the Appropriations Committee and widened the dispersal of spending authority among other congressional committees. In 1932 the Appropriations Committee in each chamber had responsibility for 90 percent of federal program spending. By the late 1980s its share had fallen to about 40 percent.

By dividing spending jurisdiction among so many committees between 1930 and 1980,

Congress reestablished the forces of the commons theory, creating a new trend of excessive spending and uncontrollable budget deficits.

This trend is described in Table 2, which displays the average level of federal government spending, revenues, and the budget deficit as a percentage of GNP for each decade since World War II. As the table indicates, the budget deficit has deepened each succeeding decade through the 1980s as the committee decision-making structure has gradually become more decentralized. Government spending, driven by the inexorable focus of the commons, has risen in each decade while government revenues have grown far less rapidly.

Thus far in the 1990s, federal government spending and the budget deficit have continued upward along their previously established trends. Both federal spending and the budget deficit are higher now than they have averaged during any post–World War II decade. Revenues, at 18.6 percent of GNP, are at about the level that they averaged during the preceding forty years. The slight reduction from their average level does not reflect a tax cut—taxes were in fact raised in the first two years of the Bush administration. Instead the reduction reflects the effects of the economic slowdown that began in 1990.

## THE COMPOUNDING PROBLEM OF TRUST FUNDS

During this same fifty-year period, a second change in the congressional budget process aggravated the deficits caused by splintered spending jurisdiction: the creation of tax-financed trust funds. It is important to under-

Table 2
FEDERAL BUDGET, 1950–1992 (PERCENT OF GNP)

|  | Spending | Revenues | Deficit |
|---|---|---|---|
| 1950–1959 | 18.0% | 17.6% | 0.5% |
| 1960–1969 | 19.0% | 18.2% | 0.8% |
| 1970–1979 | 20.5% | 18.3% | 2.1% |
| 1980–1989 | 23.0% | 19.0% | 4.3% |
| 1990–1992 | 23.9% | 18.6% | 5.3% |

*Source*: United States Office of Management and Budget, *Budget of the United States Government, Fiscal Year 1993, Supplement* (Washington, D.C., 1992), part 5, table 1.3.

stand the essential differences between trust funds and the general fund.

Trust-fund programs are financed by a specific tax levied on the public, such as the payroll tax, which funds the Social Security trust fund, and the federal gas tax, which funds the federal highway construction trust fund. Trust-fund tax revenues can only be used to support the activities of a specific trust-fund program and, therefore, are called dedicated revenues.

General-fund programs, on the other hand, are not financed by any specific revenue source. Instead, revenues from a multitude of sources such as corporate and individual income taxes, are pooled together in a common fund that is used to finance a broad array of government activities ranging from national defense to grants to study the migratory patterns of certain types of birds.

Prior to 1936, no major tax-financed trust funds existed in the federal budget. In that year, the Congress put the financing of the railroad retirement program on a trust-fund basis. Three years later, the Social Security program for old-age and survivors pensions, which had been created in 1935, was placed on a trust-fund basis. The Social Security program has grown into the largest of all the trust funds. Its revenues account for about 25 percent of all federal government revenues and its expenditures account for more than 20 percent of the federal government's total, excluding interest payments on the national debt. After World War II additional trust funds were added to the budget. In 1956 a trust fund for the federal highway program was established and the Social Security disability insurance trust fund was created. In 1965 the Medicare hospital insurance fund was created and financed by a payroll tax similar to the tax used to finance Social Security pensions and disability payments. In 1970 a trust fund for grants for airport facilities

was established and financed by an airline ticket tax, an airplane fund tax, and other minor excise taxes. In the 1980s Superfund was created to finance environmental cleanup.

The creation of tax-financed trust funds did not have a neutral effect on the budget deficit as one might expect. Quite the contrary. Trust-fund taxes are directly tied to very identifiable benefits, such as a monthly Social Security check, or a highway. On the other hand, general-fund taxes are spread among a diffuse array of programs, some more popular than others. Faced with the choice of raising trust-fund revenues or general-fund revenue, the tax-writing committees naturally faced less of a protest from constituents when they chose to increase the former. This revenue bias, in favor of trust-fund taxes and against general-fund taxes, resulted in significant downward pressure on general-fund revenues. Moreover, because the tax-writing committees had jurisdiction over trust-fund expenditures, they determined how the trust-fund tax proceeds were spent. Decisions regarding the expenditure of general revenues, on the other hand, were made primarily by other congressional committees. Responding to the incentives provided by the jurisdictional assignment, the tax-writing committees substituted trust-fund revenues for general-fund revenues.

Table 3 shows the combined impact of the tax bias on trust-fund and general-fund revenues during the post–World War II years. The table displays revenues as a percent of GNP for five-year intervals during each decade. From each decade to the next, trust-fund revenues rise and general-fund revenues decline. Each decade, the growth in the former is only slightly greater than the decline in the latter. It is as if there exists a dollar-for-dollar substitution of trust-fund for general-fund revenues relative to GNP.

Table 3
**TRUST-FUND TAXES VS. GENERAL-FUND TAXES (AS A PERCENT OF GNP)**

|  | 1950–1954 | 1960–1964 | 1970–1974 | 1980–1984 |
| --- | --- | --- | --- | --- |
| Trust Funds | 1.2 | 3.0 | 4.7 | 5.8 |
| General Fund | 16.0 | 14.5 | 13.2 | 12.7 |

*Source: U.S. Budget,* various years. Trust-fund taxes include Old-age and Survivors Insurance Program, Disabled Insurance, Medicare, highway trust fund, and airport trust-fund taxes. General-fund taxes include all other taxes except state unemployment-insurance taxes.

This substitution systematically reduced general-fund revenues at the same time the decentralization of committee jurisdiction over spending increased pressures to spend from the general fund. The result has been large deficits in the general fund. In fact, as Table 4 shows, in an accounting sense the entire source of the overall budget deficit lies in the general fund. Both the time path and the magnitude of the general-fund deficit match those of the total budget deficit.

The data in Table 4 raise a related paradox of the modern budget: While the Congress has been willing to open up cavernous deficits in the general fund, it has strictly adhered to the principal of a balanced budget (in fact, consistently showing a surplus over each decade) in the trust funds.

Furthermore, what applies to the trust funds in the aggregate applies to each of the trust funds individually. Each fund, with the exception of the railroad retirement fund, which has been plagued by deficits because of declining employment in the industry, has avoided running persistent deficits. Deficits, when they do occur, are caused mainly by economic recessions. In recessions, the decline in economic activity produces a reduction in revenues. When the economy recovers, so do revenues, and each of the funds returns to surplus. This financial behavior closely resembles the behavior of the entire federal budget during the nineteenth century, when spending jurisdiction was highly concentrated.

The paradox can be understood by contrasting the institutional structures that govern decision-making in the trust funds with those that govern decision-making over the general fund. For each of the trust funds, a single committee has jurisdiction over expenditures from the fund. The Ways and Means Committee in the House and the Finance Committee in the Senate have exclusive jurisdiction over the Social Security program for the elderly, Medicare, and the Social Security program for the disabled. Currently, the Appropriations Committee has exclusive jurisdiction to control expenditures from the highway and the airport and airway trust funds. For the trust funds, no commons problem is present.

## THE BUDGET PROCESS TODAY

The consequence of this fifty-year evolution which produced numerous entitlement programs as well as other avenues for bypassing the appropriations process is a budget system that produces the deficits decreed by the commons theory. Tax-financed trust funds compound the problem.

With spending authority dispersed among seventeen committees in the House and fifteen in the Senate, one might imagine that they would at least coordinate a spending ceiling for each annual budget. However, at no point in the current budget process is a comprehensive decision made on the total amount the federal government will spend. Instead, total federal spending is determined by the enactment of many legislative bills formulated by several different committees during the course of the year.

Congress begins this legislative process when the president submits a proposed budget for the upcoming fiscal year, which begins on October 1 and ends the following September 30. The president's budget proposes an amount of money to be spent for each program the federal government operates. The budget also proposes to raise an amount of revenue, through taxation, to finance expenditures for that fiscal

Table 4
FEDERAL BUDGET DEFICITS, 1950–1992 (PERCENT OF GNP)

|  | Total Budget | General Fund | Trust Fund |
|---|---|---|---|
| 1950–1959 | 0.5% | 0.8% | −0.3% |
| 1960–1969 | 0.8% | 1.0% | −0.2% |
| 1970–1979 | 2.1% | 2.4% | −0.3% |
| 1980–1989 | 4.3% | 4.7% | −0.4% |
| 1990–1992 | 5.3% | 5.7% | −0.4% |

Source: Budget of the United States Government (1950–1994).

year. When the amount of revenues is insufficient to cover expenditures, the president's budget also proposes to borrow the difference from the public.

Upon receiving the president's budget proposal, each chamber of the Congress parcels out the budget's individual programs to separate standing committees. The Appropriations Committee is responsible for drafting legislation that provides funding for nonentitlement programs—about 40 percent of the budget. These programs encompass most of the Department of Defense, the general operating expenses of most nondefense government agencies, and a wide variety of nondefense programs, such as those for education, job training, and basic research.

The Appropriations Committee carries out its responsibility by dividing itself into thirteen subcommittees. Each subcommittee is delegated the responsibility of drafting an individual appropriation bill. These thirteen bills move through the congressional lawmaking process as separate legislative bills. Most appropriations provide program funding for only one year. An annual appropriations process ensures that the performance of federal programs and agencies are reviewed and scrutinized on an annual basis.

The remaining 60 percent of the budget consists of entitlements. The eligibility rules and the amount of any payment or services are written into the entitlement law. Because the law obligates the government to make payments or to provide services, the only way to affect an entitlement program's spending level is to change the entitlement law's provisions through legislation. Responsibility for changing entitlement spending resides therefore not with the Appropriations Committee, but instead with other standing committees. Jurisdiction for entitlement programs rests with sixteen different committees in the Senate and fifteen committees in the House of Representatives. For example, in the House, the Ways and Means Committee is responsible for Social Security, Medicare hospital care, and certain welfare programs; the Agriculture, Forestry, and Nutrition Committee

handles food stamps, the school lunch program, and farm price-support subsidies; the Veteran's Affairs Committee has jurisdiction over disability payments to veterans and old-age veterans pensions; and the Energy and Commerce Committee is responsible for Medicare physician care and Medicaid, which provides health benefits for low-income families.

Unlike appropriations, most entitlement payments are not subject to annual review by congressional committees. Some entitlements, such as Social Security, are permanently authorized to operate and have a permanent funding source. For these programs, payments can continue to be made without any annual congressional action. Other entitlements are often authorized to operate for four years at a time. Although annual appropriations may be required, the appropriation is a formality since the government is obligated to make entitlement payments.

It is no wonder that today's budget process results in a deficit equal to almost 6 percent of GNP when so many committees are given access to the general fund.

## SUMMARY AND CONCLUSION

This two-hundred-year review of the relationship between the congressional budget process and the existence of structural budget deficits has demonstrated the critical role that institutional rules in the Congress play in determining specific policy outcomes. Although other factors, such as a defense buildup or a savings-and-loan crisis, may have importance at specific moments in contributing to deficits, it is the institutional rules that have the most influence at all times by creating incentives for particular forms of behavior, such as those defined by the commons theory, which drive decision-making over the long run. An understanding of these rules and the way in which they affect behavior is a necessary first step, therefore, toward correcting the structural problem of the budget deficits.

## BIBLIOGRAPHY

**Official Sources**
For the president's budget, see *Budget of the United States Government* (Washington, D.C.), which is published annually. In addition, each year the CONGRESSIONAL BUDGET OFFICE publishes a review of the president's budget called *An Analysis of the President's Budgetary Proposals* (Washington, D.C.). Both of these documents contain useful information on the level and distribution of federal government revenues and expenditures. In addition, both contain historical data on government spending for various categories of programs and various sources of revenues and on the national debt. Also, at various times during the year, the Congressional Budget Office publishes studies of individual government programs.

**On Federal Budgetary Decisions**
A most useful source of contemporary information is the *Congressional Quarterly Weekly Reports*. These reports summarize all congressional activities. The *Congressional Quarterly Almanac* summaries the major congressional events of the year. Both documents provide excellent descriptions of the history of individual government programs, the politics that influence decision making, and the process used to reach budget decisions.

The CONGRESSIONAL RESEARCH SERVICE regularly publishes studies that describe the congressional budget process. Most comprehensive of these is the *Manual on the Federal Budget Process*. A number of books have been written on individual components of the process. The seminal work on the appropriations process is RICHARD F. FENNO, *The Power of the Purse: Appropriations Politics in Congress* (Boston, 1966). DENNIS IPPOLITTO, *Congressional Spending Power* (Ithaca, N.Y., 1981), examines each of the individual components of the process. ALLEN SCHICK, *Congress and Money: Budgeting, Spending, and Taxing* (Washington, D.C., 1980), is an excellent study of the budget process established under the 1974 Budget Control and Impoundment Act; SCHICK's monograph *Reconciliation and the Congressional Budget Process* (Washington, D.C., 1981), is a short description of that process. LOUIS FISHER, *Presidential Spending Power* (Princeton, N.J., 1975) examines budgeting within the executive branch.

**On U.S. Fiscal History**
There are numerous general histories of the nation's fiscal history but none of them covers the entire period. CHARLES BULLOCK, *The Finance of the United States from 1775 to 1789, with Reference to the Budget* (Madison, Wisc., 1895) and ELMER JAMES FERGUSON, *The Power of the Purse* (Chapel Hill, N.C., 1961), provide excellent descriptions of the finances during the period of the Confederacy. DAVIS RICH DEWEY, *Financial History of the United States* (London, 1920), and ALBERT S. BOLLES, *The Financial History of the United States,* 3 vols. (reprint, New York, 1969), are general histories of the nineteenth-century government finances. LEWIS KIMMEL, *Federal Budget and Fiscal Policy, 1789–1958* (Washington, D.C., 1959), and MARGARET G. MYERS, *A Financial History of the United States* (New York, 1970), extend the historical period covered into the years immediately following World War II.

**Other Sources**
JAMES SAVAGE, *Balanced Budgets and American Politics* (Ithaca, N.Y., 1988), provides a comprehensive historical treatment of the role of the balanced budget in the nation's fiscal history. ROBERT HIGG, *Crisis and Leviation: Critical Episodes in the Growth of American Government* (New York, 1987), presents a fascinating discussion of the growth in government during American crisis periods from the 1890s to World War II.

E. E. NAYLOR, *The Federal Budget System in Operation* (Washington, D.C., 1941), and W. F. WILLOUGHBY, *The National Budget System, with Suggestions for Its Improvement* (Baltimore, 1927) provide excellent treatments of the events leading to the passage of the Budget and Accounting Act of 1921, which created the president's budget.

JAMES M. BUCHANAN and RICHARD E. WAGNER, *Democracy in Deficit: The Political Legacy of Lord Keynes* (New York, 1977), presents an examination of the impact of Keynesian economics on post–World War II government finances.

R. KENT WEAVER, *Automatic Government: The Politics of Indexation* (Washington, D.C., 1988), is the major comprehensive work on the growth of entitlements.

The "commons" problem was popularized by GARRETT HARDIN in "The Tragedy of the Commons," *Science* 162 (December 1968). For applications of his argument, see HAROLD DEMSETZ, "Toward a Theory of Property Rights," *American Economic Review* 57 (May 1967). JOHN F. COGAN, "A Tale of Two Budgets," in ANNELISE ANDERSON and DENNIS L. BARK, eds., *Thinking About America: The United States in the 1990s* (Stanford, Calif., 1988), applies the commons problem to explaining the current federal budget imbalance. THEODORE LOWI, *The End of Liberalism: The Second Republic of the United States* (New York, 1979), provides an informative look at the role of interest groups in the congressional process.

For an insightful anecdotal account of the way in which budgets are made see DAVID A. STOCKMAN, *The Triumph of Politics: Why the Reagan Revolution Failed* (New York, 1986).

MICHAEL J. BOSKIN and AARON WILDAVSKY, *The Federal Budget: Economics and Politics,* (San Francisco, 1982), contains an excellent set of articles on contemporary budget problems.

JOSEPH CANNON, "The National Budget," *Harper's* (October 1919), gives a description of the politics behind the 1885 decision by the House of Representatives to strip the Appropriations Committee of its jurisdiction. An examination of the consequences of the decision for government spending is provided by DAVID BRADY and MARK MORGAN, "Reforming the Structure of the House Appropriations Process: The Effects of the 1885 and 1919–1920 Reforms on Money Decisions," in MATHEW McCUBBINS and TERRY SULLIVAN, *Congress: Structure and Policy* (New York, 1987).

SEE ALSO The Congressional Budget Process AND Legislatures and American Economic Development.

# STATE LEGISLATURES AND POLICY INNOVATORS

## *Virginia Gray*

The fifty states have long been innovators in our federal system. From woman's suffrage and workers' compensation in the early twentieth century to economic development and public school reform in the late twentieth century, states have shown a penchant for experimentation. State legislatures are the institutions that adopt these new policies and programs. This essay examines their role in policy innovation. It also examines the diffusion process, in which new ideas spread from one state to another.

## HISTORICAL SKETCH

In the 1800s, state legislatures met every other year in short sessions, which were as brief as six to eight weeks in some states. The business of the day had to be conducted speedily, resulting in poorly drafted bills and inconsistent amendments. Membership turnover was high, and lobbyists were already crucial to getting anything done. To get the attention of busy legislators, they dispensed drinks and small favors such as railroad passes.

Despite this unpromising forum for deliberation, much significant legislation was passed, many new state agencies were established, and state spending mounted. This expansion of "public responsibility," as historian William Brock termed it, occurred in the states between 1865 and 1900. The national governmental expansion would come later. There is evidence, even then, of interstate diffusion, especially regional diffusion. Albert Shaw, writing in 1887, said that "laws find their way verbatim" from one state to another. "The spirit, aims, and methods" of statutes are the same throughout a group of neighboring states, he argued (p. 698).

Great changes took place in the public's attitudes toward collective welfare. By the turn of the century, thirty-two states had commissions regulating railroads, thirty-eight had boards regulating health, and twenty-nine had labor bureaus. Many states had boards regulating the private charities that constituted the nineteenth century's welfare system. Legislatures in Michigan, Ohio, Minnesota, Wisconsin, Illinois, and New York were leaders in this expansion of state capacity.

In the early twentieth century the lively climate of policy innovation continued. Child labor laws were reformed; workers' compensation laws were enacted in forty-three states; aid to the blind was provided in ten states; minimum wage legislation was passed in several states. The Progressive movement was instrumental in achieving many of these reforms.

In a 1940 study of diffusion, Edgar McVoy considered twelve social innovations adopted by states between 1869 and 1931. He ranked the states according to whether they were early or late adopters. His rankings were very similar to later rankings of the states on innovativeness. McVoy's first ten states included New York, Wisconsin, California, Michigan, Illinois, Minnesota, Colorado, Ohio, Massachusetts, and Pennsylvania. Seven of the ten ranked in the top ten in a study conducted thirty years later. Thus early traditions of innovation linger on.

Early successes at the state level, and failures in Washington, D.C., motivated Progressive reformers to try more new ideas in state capitals. They were particularly fond of using uniform state legislation as a mechanism for achieving social ends, while eliminating competitive economic disadvantages for states adopting such statutes. Supreme Court Justice Louis Brandeis, in particular, saw virtue in the federal structure. He saw the states as "laboratories of democracy." In *New State Ice Co.* v. *Liebmann,* 285 U.S. 262, 311 (1932), he wrote: "It is one of the happy incidents of the federal system that a single courageous State may, if its citizens choose, serve as a laboratory; and try novel social and economic experiments without risk to the rest of the country."

Two examples illustrate the spread of policy innovations in the early part of this century: the passage of woman's suffrage and Mothers' Aid legislation. Winning the right to vote took women fifty-three years, beginning with a Kansas referendum in 1867 which failed and culminating in the Nineteenth Amendment's ratification in 1920. The western states led the way in this battle. As territories, Wyoming and Utah had granted women the suffrage and retained that right when they became states, in 1890 and 1896 respectively. They were joined by Colorado and Idaho in the early 1890s. Then there was a fourteen-year hiatus in which no more states extended female suffrage.

In 1910 the state of Washington extended full suffrage and was quickly joined by four other western states. Not until 1917 were the South and East cracked. Thus, from 1867 to 1917 only eleven states had extended full suffrage. But the movement picked up momentum as World War I broke out; in 1918, the Nineteenth Amendment passed the U.S. House of Representatives. The Senate agreed in 1919, and the next year ratification by the states was accomplished.

The second example comes from the welfare area. The United States did not enact major social welfare legislation until 1935, when the Social Security Act was approved. But several states had experimented with Mothers' Aid, a forerunner to today's Aid to Families with Dependent Children program. Mothers' Aid shifted the care of neglected and dependent children from institutions to the home. In contrast to woman's suffrage, this law diffused rapidly: by 1926, forty-two states had adopted some version of Mothers' Aid legislation. Illinois pioneered the concept in 1911; eighteen states adopted similar programs in 1913, mostly because legislators anticipated it would cost no more than institutionalization. Another factor was the force of the Progressive movement. The earliest adopting states tended to be those where the Progressives had greater electoral strength. The authors of the 1935 Social Security Act relied on the states' experiences in writing the new national legislation.

These two historical examples show the dynamism of the federal system at work. In both cases the states were the first to try novel ideas; their experiences showed that the ideas could work. Following experimentation, the national government then picked up the idea and adopted it. In the welfare example, the states had tried different versions of Mothers' Aid, which meant that Congress could adopt the most successful version. It would have been much more difficult for a national welfare policy to be enacted in the 1930s without the states' paving the way. Similarly, the fear of the female vote was dissipated by the states' experiences.

These examples clearly illustrate the concept of laboratories of democracy. This pragmatic conception of federalism continues into the 1990s.

## THE STATES AS POLICY LABORATORIES

The states continued their tradition of innovation throughout the twentieth century. Such actions have tended to be in the areas in which state governments have sole legal responsibility, such as education and forms of local government, or in which they share responsibility with the federal government, such as welfare and the environment. This division of responsibility is spelled out in the United States Constitution, though it has been greatly modified in practice.

Modern innovations are enacted in legislative bodies that look very different from their nineteenth-century predecessors. Nearly all legislatures meet every year; as of 1990, only seven were still on biennial schedules. And the number of days in session has risen, too. At least nine legislatures are virtually full-time, like Congress. Consequently, legislators have more time to consider bills, to study problems, and so forth. Legislative work is organized much more effectively through a stronger committee system. These committees allow members to specialize in a few policy areas. Furthermore, the expansion of professional staffing since the 1960s has provided individual members and committees with professional bill drafting, fiscal analysis, and policy research. These and other improvements have enhanced state legislative capacity for innovation. This essay will highlight the role of state legislatures in the innovation process.

We begin by looking at some patterns policy innovation takes and how the state legislatures have been involved. Their experimentation takes several forms. One pattern is *interstate innovation:* a state tries a new idea; other states imitate it. But the federal government is not involved. For example, many states have adopted the lottery as a new revenue source but the federal government has not. Several policies stand out as cogent examples of interstate innovation: economic development, public school reform, and divorce law reform. These will be described below.

Another pattern is *federal innovation:* one or more states try a new idea; if it succeeds, then the federal government picks up the program. For example, the 1988 Family Support Act was modeled on successful state welfare programs.

Still another pattern is *disinnovation:* a state tries an idea, and it fails. But other states and the federal government learn from this failure. Or a state tries an idea that is so unusual or controversial that it does not spread very far. The failure of the Equal Rights Amendment to spread to enough states (discussed below) is a particularly interesting case of disinnovation.

## Interstate Innovation

*Economic Development*     In the 1980s the states adopted a number of bold new policies aimed at improving economic growth and performance. These policies represented an unprecedented degree of intervention in the market economy. Interestingly, they were undertaken at the same time that free-market orthodoxy reigned in Washington. What were these bold efforts? What role did state legislatures play in their creation?

More than half the states have become venture capitalists. That is, they have invested public funds—from employee pension funds, tax revenues, or bond proceeds—in new businesses. States commonly take an ownership share in the business, and then share in the profit or loss. As one observer said, this is called socialism anywhere else.

Nearly every state's economic strategy emphasizes high-tech industry as the key to the future. Biotechnology and microelectronics are particularly hot tickets. States compete to attract high-tech companies: hundreds of millions of dollars have been spent on research centers, incubators, and universities under the guise of "chip chasing." In 1989, for example, the Utah legislature appropriated $5 million to support cold fusion research (the nuclear reaction in a jar); unfortunately, this technique has now been discredited.

International trade and investment is the third area in which the states have rapidly increased their activity. More states now have overseas trade offices than have offices in Washington, D.C. In order to lure auto manufacturers and other foreign companies, states have improved roads and sewer systems, purchased land, and funded worker training.

Who was responsible for this outpouring of state entrepreneurial activity? In most states, governors were the catalysts. But they could not have done anything without the legislature's approval; the legislature had to adopt new laws, approve budgets, and authorize new agencies. In some states, such as California, legislators were the initiators.

Overall, enhanced institutional capacity in the legislature and the governorship allowed the states to innovate. A 1990 study by Virginia Gray and David Lowery showed that states adopting more of the then-new economic policies had certain similarities. They had experienced severe economic stress, had more-balanced interest group and political-party systems, and had strong governmental capacity in both executive and legislative branches. Legislative capacity was measured by the availability of professional staff, length of time in session, committee structure, and other features characteristic of the reformed, professionalized legislature. The authors concluded that the legislature's reaction to economic problems was critical, as was its capacity for action.

*School Reform*     Public education was the other area of major innovation by states during the 1980s. School reform was sparked by reports showing that American students were not performing as well as students in other countries. State legislatures and governors were squarely in the forefront of this reform movement. In a number of states the initiative for educational reform came from the legislature; Alan Rosenthal, in his book *Governors & Legislatures: Contending Powers* (1990), cited Florida, California, and Arizona as singular examples. In other states—for example, Arkansas and Minnesota—the governor initiated the reforms or shared the leadership role with the legislature. The National Governors' Association was particularly instrumental in formulating a series of measures designed to improve educational quality, which were then adopted by many state legislatures.

These measures were directed at students and teachers. Forty-four states increased the courses required for graduation; half of the states instituted minimum competency tests for graduation from high school; thirteen states established minimum grade point averages for participation in extracurricular activities. Most states now require people entering the teaching profession to pass a standardized test; nearly half have adopted some form of merit pay for teachers.

The diffusion of educational quality innovations was still underway in the early 1990s, but an early study of this movement is instructive. In 1988, Don C. Shinn and Jack R. Van Der Slik found that characteristics of the state legislatures were the most important determinants of adoption of school reform. Legislative bodies characterized by professionalism (for example, long sessions or large staffs) adopted the most school-reform legislation. Like economic development, educational improvements depended upon the capability of the legislatures.

*Divorce Law*    In the early 1970s state legislatures quietly achieved a revolution in divorce law, the so-called *no-fault divorce*. Generally, this means that adultery is not grounds for divorce, marital property is equally divided between partners, alimony is of shorter duration and depends upon each partner's income, and child custody is shared more equally between mother and father. The spread of this innovation is interesting because of its rapidity, its noncontroversiality, and its revolutionary importance to family law. This reform was entirely in the hands of state legislatures—although of course the governor in each state had to sign the bill into law.

In 1966, New York became the first state to reform its divorce law, but it remained for California to adopt an explicitly no-fault law in 1970. By 1974, forty-five states possessed no-fault provisions in their divorce laws, and in 1985 the last state, South Dakota, joined in.

Herbert Jacob, in his book *Silent Revolution: The Transformation of Divorce Law in the United States* (1988), examined the rapid spread of the no-fault divorce concept. He found that in each state the legislature, rather than the governor, was the key institutional actor. Within that body, committee chairs and other policy champions were often the catalysts for passage. Significantly, the innovation carried very little cost, so it engendered little organized opposition. Its adoption was accomplished through a routine process that provoked little public visibility. Such laws should diffuse more rapidly than laws stirring up conflict.

*Summary*    These three innovations illustrate the range of interstate innovations. Some were rapid in their diffusion, like economic development and divorce law; others, such as school reform, slowed down after an initial flurry of activity. The legislature played a role in all three. In economic development, the legislature backed up the governor; in school reform, the legislature initiated almost as often as the governor; in divorce law, the legislature was always the driving force. In all three cases the policy change was within the state's purview so that the federal government was not involved.

## Federal Innovation

Other policy areas in which both levels of government have some responsibility illustrate federal innovation. As stated earlier, one of the advantages of having a federal system is that the states may experiment with an idea before it is tried on a national scale. Some policies will be deemed successful and will be picked up by the federal government; others will die mercifully at the state level. Recent reforms in the welfare area illustrate forcefully the value of state experiments.

In 1988, Congress produced the most significant overhaul of the welfare system since 1935. Called the Family Support Act, it offered recipients more-extensive services, such as transportation and child care, in exchange for work effort. Its purpose was to move welfare recipients into full-time jobs, thereby reducing long-term welfare dependency.

Previous efforts at welfare reform had foundered on arguments between liberals and conservatives about workfare, child care, and cost. The major difference this time was convincing evidence from the states that a new plan would work. During the 1980s a number of states had tried workfare programs; among the best known were Massachusetts's Education and Training (E.T.) program and California's Greater Avenues for Independence (GAIN) program. But at least twenty-six other states instituted required work-and-training programs of some sort. By demonstrating that workfare programs were feasible and cost-effective in a variety of settings, a major barrier to national reform was removed. This example illustrates well how state actions can influence national policy. Success at the state level paved the way for a major innovation at the national level.

## Disinnovation

Discussion of innovation often focuses on the success stories but fails to mention that the landscape is also littered with policy failures. Many ideas start out with promise but never spread beyond a few states. For example, the unicameral legislature has never spread beyond the boundaries of Nebraska. Other ideas were initially adopted by many states but later disadopted.

Perhaps the most interesting instance of failed innovation in the late twentieth century was the failure of the Equal Rights Amendment (ERA). This was a constitutional amendment proposed by Congress in March 1972. Within the hour it was ratified by Hawaii; within the week five more states joined in. By early 1973, twenty-four more states had ratified, almost all without controversy. Opinion polls showed that a majority of the American public supported it. The amendment appeared headed toward ratification in the thirty-eight states required. However, the ERA never made it. What happened?

By late 1973 an opposition movement led by Illinois activist Phyllis Schlafly began to be effective. As head of STOP ERA, she appeared before many state legislatures considering ratification. At first Schlafly merely slowed down passage, but after 1977 approvals ceased. Four states were persuaded to rescind their approval, although the second decision was probably not legally binding. Despite the fact that Congress extended the ratification deadline to 1982, no more states passed the amendment.

Those states refusing to ratify the ERA had several things in common. Except for Illinois, they were either Mormon states or southern states with many religious fundamentalists and traditional political cultures. Also, legislatures in these states had been slow to adopt other women's rights legislation, such as the suffrage amendment, and slow to adopt innovations in general. Thus, Schlafly had only to play on these legislators' general fear of change. Strong opposition, effectively organized in fifteen states, stopped a constitutional amendment which would have affected the entire nation.

## Summary

In this section we have seen contemporary examples of the major types of innovation. We first examined innovations that began in one state and traveled to many others. Economic development, school reform, and divorce law are recent examples of interstate innovation. The state legislature played a major role in reforming divorce law; it also played an important role in the other two examples. We next examined federal innovation, where an idea starts at the state level and travels to the national level. Welfare reform is a particularly cogent example of this trend. In this case governors initiated the process, and state legislatures joined in. Finally, we examined disinnovation, where the idea fails to spread fully or is disadopted. The ERA was used as an example in this category. Now that we have examined the variety of innovations adopted by the states, we are ready to consider more systematically the innovation and diffusion processes.

## INNOVATION AND THE POLICY PROCESS

First, some definitions are needed. An innovation is commonly defined as an idea or practice perceived as new. In the state legislative context, an *innovation* is a program or policy which is new to the state adopting it, no matter how many other states may have adopted the idea. For example, the lottery was an innovation to Minnesota in 1986, even though New Hampshire had first adopted the idea in 1964. Moreover, the term *innovation* is not reserved just for good ideas. Any new program is termed *innovative* whether it turns out to be a great program or a poor one. Thus, the first states to adopt lotteries are labeled innovative even if some people believe that the lottery is sinful.

The process by which new ideas are communicated is called *diffusion,* the method by which ideas spread from one person or state to another. Diffusion researchers typically focus on the *rate of adoption*—that is, the relative speed by which ideas travel and are adopted—and distinguish between *innovative states* and *laggard states.* The output of the diffusion process, in our context, is a state legislature's adoption or rejection of new laws, programs, or practices.

The invention and diffusion of new policies occur at the beginning of the policy process, before enactment and implementation of the policy. Someone recognizes a problem that should be addressed; for example, medical costs may be dramatically increasing. Sometimes data already collected indicate the magnitude of the problem; at other times a particular crisis focuses attention on the problem. Or legislators may discover problems when they are evaluating an ongoing program.

After the problem is recognized, someone then has to propose a solution; that is, to formulate a policy that will fix the problem. Policy formulation is usually in the hands of experts, perhaps people from outside of government such as academics, consultants, or interest-group leaders. Or proposals may come from bureaucrats or legislators with experience in the policy area. Then a political coalition must be marshaled behind the proposed policy so that it can be enacted. This is the adoption stage, which is the province of the legislature. If all three steps are successful, then the innovation will be adopted. Our discussion below will combine these three steps—problem recognition, policy formulation, and adoption—as we describe innovation. As will become clear, state legislatures are key institutions in the innovation process, from invention of ideas, to formulation of policy proposals, and especially in adoption of the proposals.

## Diffusion Process

A substantial amount of research has been conducted on the diffusion of innovations across cities, states, and nations. Research at the political system level is modeled on similar research conducted on innovation in organizations. Such research seeks to explain the adoption of innovations, particularly the rate of adoptions. When ordered by time of adoption, political systems that are among the first to adopt a new idea rank high on innovativeness; those that adopt later, or never, score low. The terms *leaders* and *laggards* are often used to label the two ends of the spectrum, although this is not intended to be a value judgment about the worth of the innovation. Researchers then try to explain why some political systems are consistently among the first to adopt new ideas and why other systems are usually among the last.

Scholars have found two sets of explanations to be helpful. First, a set of *internal determinants*—factors within the adopting unit that either facilitate or deter adoption of innovations—is often critical. For states, the internal factors include the economic situation, the political forces present, and the capacity of governmental institutions such as the state legislature. Second, a set of *external determinants* is often significant in securing adoption of new ideas. These include professional networks and associations, the experiences of neighboring states, and federal incentives to innovate. Finally, in some circumstances, researchers may find that both sets of factors—internal and external—are important in explaining the rate of innovation.

Besides the studies at the system level, researchers have also focused on the agenda-setting stage of the policy process, typically using a case study approach. That is, for a single policy innovation they ask where the idea came from, who formulated the policy proposal, and how it got adopted. These investigators focus on the particular individuals involved in getting the problem on the agenda and in making the decision. Their findings about legislative champions, policy entrepreneurs and so forth, are helpful in fleshing out the results obtained from the system-level studies. Also, their findings often provide insight into particular states and how they operate. In the discussion below both types of studies will be integrated—system-level and case studies—into the discussion. We begin with the internal determinants and the role they play in innovation.

## Internal Determinants

*Economic Resources*     Of all the internal determinants, economic resources have received the most attention. It seems plausible that the financial resources of a state can permit or limit certain kinds of policy decisions. But it is a bit harder to decide exactly how a state's wealth affects its rate of innovation. The most common theory is that of *slack resources*: organizations with resources left over after attending to pressing business can afford to be more innovative than organizations with *tight resources.* Wealthy organizations tend to be larger and more professional; their personnel have time to think up new ideas and to try them out. If the new ideas fail, the relative cost is not so great. They have an organizational capacity to innovate which is missing in poorer organizations. This theory applies to legislatures as well: those with more staff, longer sessions, and so forth should have more resources to devote to initiating and discussing new ideas.

This theory has been shown to be valid in relation to the fifty states. Jack Walker, in his 1969 study of eighty-eight program innovations, found that larger, wealthier states adopted programs faster than smaller and poorer states. He reasoned that such states as New York and California had more slack resources to devote to policy experimentation than did poorer states like Mississippi. Virginia Gray, in 1973, reported a similar finding in a study of twelve innovations. Many other scholars have since come to the same conclusion.

But a counter-theory says, "Necessity is the mother of invention." Organizations are motivated to innovate when times are bad. This theory is based upon a model of organizational inertia: change doesn't occur unless a crisis develops in the organization's environment. According to this theory, states should innovate during recessions, wars, and other crises.

Some types of innovations—tax policy, for example—can be explained by this theory. Mississippi was the first state to adopt the sales tax in the 1930s, but is not otherwise known for

being innovative. Similarly, a 1990 study by Frances Stokes Berry and William D. Berry found that the lottery was adopted when states experienced severe budgetary shortfalls. But most policy innovations cost more money, not less, and hence are not likely to be adopted in times of financial hardship. Thus, wealth rather than poverty is most likely to facilitate innovation. This means that when sudden crises develop—the 1990–1991 recession, for example—wealthier states will have built up a capacity to respond, whereas poorer states will not have the personnel in place to come up with creative solutions. Thus, the necessity theory is not automatically antithetical to the slack resources theory. A state's economic resources and immediate budgetary climate are both important conditions affecting patterns of adoption.

*Political Factors*     In addition, researchers have focused upon the political conditions in the state at the time of the adoption. In the broadest sense, the political culture of a state makes a difference in its receptivity to new ideas. Scholars have divided the country into three political cultures or amalgams of religious, ideological, and attitudinal factors: moralistic, individualistic, and traditionalistic. Politics in moralistic subcultures revolves around the public interest, which is pursued through governmental intervention. Politics in individualistic subcultures revolves around private interests, restricting government to a narrow sphere. In traditionalistic subcultures, politics is an elite activity, and government is devoted to preserving the elite's dominant position. Numerous studies have found a state's political culture to be associated with innovativeness, presumably because cultures vary both in their willingness to embrace new ideas and to accept change, and in their beliefs about the appropriate scope of government. The moralistic subculture, which emphasizes governmental intervention, is the most innovative. It includes states such as Wisconsin, Michigan, Oregon, and Colorado, all of which ranked in the top ten on Walker's index. The traditionalistic culture, embracing the southern states, is the least innovative.

Another political factor examined by researchers is electoral competition. The assumption here is that when political parties compete for office they advance a number of new ideas;

once the parties are in office, some of these new ideas are adopted and put into practice. When party leaders know that the next election will be closely contested, they are motivated to accomplish something. Notice, for instance, how many governors have sought to make a mark in education or economic development so that they have a record of innovation on which to campaign. Both Walker and Gray, in fact, found that politically competitive states were the most innovative. But this effect was less important than the state's wealth in bringing about innovation.

A related theory is that turnover in office leads to more innovation. A change in administration—a new governor or a different party in control of the legislature—allows new ideas to surface. John W. Kingdon, in *Agendas, Alternatives, and Public Policies* (1984), calls this period the "policy window," a window of opportunity through which political actors push their pet ideas. Legislators wait until their party is in the majority and then present their favorite solutions, knowing they will get a more favorable reception. Experts outside of government seize the opportunity to press their case to a new gubernatorial administration. In fact, Walker's study found that states with higher turnover in office were more innovative. Thus, both turnover and political competition result in more innovation.

*Institutional Capacity*    Another set of internal determinants has to do with the capacity of state governmental institutions, principally the legislature, the bureaucracy, and the governor and his or her staff. In the case of the state legislature, capacity usually refers to the professionalization of the legislative body. Professional legislatures are fairly apportioned, have longer sessions, pay higher salaries to their members, and supply more staff personnel, computers, offices, and other support services to members. In essence, professionalized bodies have more slack resources to devote to information gathering and problem analysis.

In such institutions it is easier for legislators to learn about solutions that other states are trying, or to research new solutions their own state might try. Walker's study found that states with fairly apportioned legislatures and higher legislative professionalism did adopt innovations more rapidly. However, these fac-

tors paled in comparison to economic factors. Studies in the 1980s showed legislative professionalization to be important in the adoption of consumer-protection legislation and in deinstitutionalization of the mentally retarded. Such bodies adopted more laws protecting the consumer and relied more on residential placement for the retarded.

The capability of the legislative staff is particularly important. They are the persons most involved in analyzing policy problems, generating possible solutions, and drafting bills. They are critical links in transmitting new ideas from the outside world to legislators. In 1985, Paul Sabatier and David Whiteman studied the transmission process in the California legislature. They believed their findings could be applied to other well-staffed, professionalized legislatures.

They found a three-stage model that fit California: policy information first flows from outsiders—such as academic experts, interest groups, or staffers in other states—to committee staff; then from staff to legislators who are expert in a particular subject; and finally from these specialists to ordinary legislators. For example, a bill to solve a pollution problem might begin with environmental affairs staffers talking with outsiders. Then the staff person presents possible solutions to the interested legislator serving on the environmental affairs committee, who then introduces a bill on the subject. Next, the specialist legislator talks to his or her legislative colleagues outside the committee about the problem and the bill. In this way the staffers and specialist legislators are the gatekeepers for new information, translating novel ideas for their nonspecialist colleagues.

This three-stage translation process probably works best where there are slack resources —that is, where there is enough committee staff to devote time to searching for information, to translating this information for the expert member, and to transmitting the results to nonexpert members. In states with poorly staffed legislatures, the translation process appears to have one, or at most two, stages. Outsiders, usually from interest groups, talk directly to legislators about new ideas. These legislators may not have the time or the expertise to draft a bill embodying the new idea. Legislators may depend on blind copying of other states' laws, on carrying bills for interest groups, or they may do nothing. These states tend to be the followers, not the leaders, in policy innovation.

In addition to the legislature's role in the innovation process, we also need to consider the bureaucracy. Bureaucrats, after all, are experts in the particular subject matter of their agencies. They are expected to be sources of new ideas, of information about what other states are doing, and of suggestions for how a problem might be solved. A 1990 study by Keon S. Chi and Dennis O. Grady gives some insight into how innovation is achieved by bureaucrats. Chi and Grady surveyed the persons instigating three-hundred model innovations. The innovators were more educated, more experienced, and more active in professional organizations than the typical state employee. In short, professionalized bureaucracies, like professionalized legislatures, are likely to be more innovative.

Lastly, we consider the governor and his or her staff. No systematic study has assessed the governor's role in innovation, but it can be observed in a number of specific cases. For example, the economic development and welfare reforms already described were initiated by governors. The National Governors' Association was instrumental in pushing these changes, illustrating its new role in the diffusion of innovations.

***Policy Entrepreneurs*** Thus far, in our discussion of internal determinants, we have mentioned economic, political, and institutional factors that affect the rate of innovation among states. Most comparative state studies have emphasized these broad patterns in shaping innovation. But, as mentioned earlier, scholars who do case studies find that certain individuals are also important in instigating change. Particularly important are *policy entrepreneurs*. These are people outside of government who advocate particular ideas or policy proposals. They may be found in universities, think tanks, consulting firms, or interest groups. They are willing to invest their time and energy in advocating pet ideas. They enjoy participating in policy discussions and like being part of the action. When a new administration comes into power, they are ready with ideas for it to pursue.

As Kingdon said, one can nearly always pinpoint a specific person, or group, who was central in moving a subject up on the agenda. Policy entrepreneurs are especially crucial for innovative ideas, because usually stiff resistance must be overcome. In an interesting study, Paula King focused on the role of policy entrepreneurs in a Minnesota innovation. She studied a group of nine people who formulated the Minnesota open school-enrollment plan, the first in the nation. The plan, enacted in 1988, allowed students within certain constraints to attend any public school in the state.

Of the nine policy entrepreneurs King studied, only one was in government at the time; none were in the educational establishment. They met frequently as a group to thrash out their ideas and to consolidate their view that the educational system needed a complete overhaul, not just minor tinkering. They were responding to the sense of crisis expressed in national reports on the decline of America's schools. Given the crisis atmosphere, it was relatively easy to identify a performance gap and to overcome resistance to change. In late 1984 their ideas were embraced by Governor Rudy Perpich, who had been looking for new educational proposals. This was their window of opportunity. Perpich and several key legislators pushed the plan through the Minnesota legislature in 1988. Several other states have now adopted similar school-choice plans.

Policy entrepreneurs invent, create, and market ideas to policy champions in the legislative or executive branch. The champions accept ideas, give them legitimacy, and refine them before putting them on the formal agenda. The policy champions are in formal governmental positions, whereas the policy entrepreneurs are not. For example, a legendary policy champion in the California legislature was Frank Lanterman. He was responsible for a total reform in California's treatment of the mentally ill. His 1969 bill guaranteed their civil liberties and transferred much of their treatment from state hospitals to community facilities. Other states imitated California's law soon thereafter.

An interesting study of policy champions in the North Carolina legislature was written in 1990. The author, Carol Weissert, concentrated on legislators who introduced bills on salient issues and who had pushed them over several years. She discovered that these long-time policy champions were rated by their peers and others as highly effective legislators. Thus, persistence and hard work, while waiting for the policy window to open, garner the respect of others.

*Summary*    All of these internal elements feed into the innovation process. A state's wealth and professional institutions allow room for innovation. Its political culture and policy entrepreneurs foster the emergence of new ideas. Particular crises and office turnover create opportunities for policy champions to push those new ideas toward adoption. But, as we have continually noted, the fifty states are not isolated entities. They are part of a federal system in which they compete and cooperate with one another. These external dynamics are also critical to the innovation process. We turn now to their discussion.

## External Determinants

A substantial amount of research has been conducted on the external determinants of innovation in the states. Rather than focusing on the internal characteristics of a state, these diffusion models focus on how ideas spread from one state to another. Among the external influences are the emulation of other states' actions, the influence of professional associations, and the impact of the federal government.

*Copying Other States*    First, we will look at the *regional diffusion* models. Such models assume that state leaders look to other nearby states for ideas and solutions to policy problems, rather than searching within their own boundaries. Leaders often look for an analogy to their own situation; they find it in another state, most often a nearby state that is economically and culturally similar. If the neighboring state has adopted a program that successfully solved the problem, then the first state is more likely to adopt the same solution. Reference to a successful experiment in Wisconsin is likely to diminish resistance to change in Illinois, for example.

A number of scholars have documented this regional diffusion effect. Walker's 1969 study was the first to find a regional clustering pattern, indicating that states in the same geographic region adopted programs in a similar order. A later analysis of Walker's data separated the regional leaders more clearly from the national leaders. Several states lower in innovativeness can serve as regional leaders; for example, Colorado was a regional leader among the western states, while higher-rated California was both a regional leader and a national leader.

Cue-taking does not have to take place only through emulation of one's neighbors; a state can emulate any state that it takes as an appropriate referent. New York, Massachusetts, and California set a national standard that many other states outside their immediate regions follow. The impact of national policy leaders can overwhelm the effect of regional leaders in the diffusion process.

In the 1980s and early 1990s, much of the comparative state research tried to sort out the relative magnitude of regional diffusion versus national diffusion. Several case studies of specific policies also shed light on this question. Scholars have found that regionalism is present for some innovations but not for others. For example, the lottery evinces a clear regional pattern in its diffusion while technological innovations do not. Presumably the possibility of citizens traveling across state lines in order to gamble motivates states to start their own lotteries, thus accounting for the regional effect. Technology transfer, in contrast, is accomplished more through national professional associations or through federal incentives.

Scholars have discovered that regionalism in diffusion has declined over time. Innovations that diffused early in the twentieth century displayed more of a regional pattern than did innovations that diffused afterward, according to James M. Lutz. Policy contagion can be seen in the diffusion of child seat-belt laws. The first such law was passed in 1981; by 1984, forty-nine states had such restraints in place. In such rapid diffusion, regionalism is washed out.

*Professional Networks*    One reason that a broader, national pattern of emulation is emerging is because national professional associations are serving as conduits for the diffusion of innovations. These are associations that public officials join, such as the National Conference of State Legislatures, the National Governors' Association, the National Association of State Budget Officers, and so forth. These groups are sources of information about policies in other states. They organize conferences and publish newsletters so that officials are aware of the latest developments in their field. These organizations also serve to pressure laggard states to conform to national standards. Officials, from states like Mississippi and Nevada, learn what is happening in other states and bring these new ideas back to their states.

Interstate communication is especially important to state legislators. In less professionalized legislatures, members often have difficulty in obtaining information because they lack extensive staff, computers, or other organizational resources for information gathering. As a consequence, legislators frequently take cues from what other state legislatures are doing. Sometimes they copy bills introduced in other states, even to the extent of reproducing mistakes contained in the original bill. Patricia Freeman found that 90 percent of legislators interviewed in a six-state study had examined energy legislation from other states or had consulted with professional organizations. Their cue-taking behavior was directed most often at neighboring states, and secondarily at national leaders in the field of energy policy. Thus, Freeman's findings are consistent with the regional diffusion model.

Her study also examined the factors that predispose legislators toward a cosmopolitan stance; that is, toward support for innovation. Legislators who held leadership positions, and possessed expertise or a high educational level, were more cosmopolitan and more interested in cue-taking from other states. Freeman found that legislators in California and Massachusetts, the states ranking high in innovativeness, engaged in more cue-taking behavior than did other legislators. This finding suggests that states are innovative because their legislators support cue-taking and are more active in gathering information from external sources.

Interstate communication among state bureaucrats is also critical to the diffusion process. Again, scholars have attempted to find out if bureaucrats key on their neighboring states or upon states perceived as national leaders in innovation. The answer is that bureaucrats engage in both types of cue-taking, but national emulation is more important. The pattern of cue-taking seems to depend upon the degree of consensus in the policy area. In some policy areas—for example, transportation or land resources—there is a high degree of consensus

on which states are the leaders, according to a 1978 study by Alfred Light. Where bureaucrats share a consensus, national leaders are consulted first. In other policy areas, such as welfare, there is less consensus about agency prestige, and consequently less national emulation and more copying of one's neighbors.

*Policy Networks*     National diffusion has become more important because of *policy, or issue, networks* across governmental boundaries. Policy networks are loose collections of governmental and nongovernmental participants in a particular policy area. They include policy entrepreneurs plus professional associations, mass media, academics, and formal governmental actors such as legislators and bureaucrats.

One study by Michael Kirst, Gail Meister, and Stephen Rowley examines the rapid diffusion of educational innovations and attributes it to an active policy network in education. For example, the requirement of minimum competency testing for high-school graduates became law in thirty-eight states without any centralized support and without any single agency or interest group advocating it. This solution was popularized by the media and picked up by individual legislators who served as policy champions, by legislative staff, and by educational testing services. The authors believed that the existence of an education policy network enabled this relatively simple idea to diffuse rapidly throughout the states.

*The Federal Government*     A final external factor affecting the rate of diffusion is the role of the federal government. If the federal government provides an incentive for states to adopt a program, then diffusion is speeded up. A study by Susan Welch and Kay Thompson finds that federally assisted policies diffused in thirty years, while state-only policies took an average of fifty years. Thus, the federal government's financial incentives can be a powerful external catalyst for the spread of innovations.

*Summary*     In sum, the diffusion of innovations does not depend entirely upon the internal characteristics of states. Rather, several external forces facilitate the diffusion process. States emulate national leaders and imitate other states in their region. They do so because it shortens their search process for a solution to their policy problem. In general, the influence of neighboring states has decreased over time as policy networks, professional associations, and federal interventions have increased. All of these mechanisms reinforce national diffusion, a top-to-bottom process where new ideas travel from the leading states to others.

Most scholars have observed that today's innovations diffuse more rapidly than earlier ones. Rapid dissemination of information means that state leaders share more knowledge about new policy options. State legislators serving in the more professionalized bodies are especially knowledgeable about what other states are doing. When many states have adopted a particular innovative solution, then it is harder for other states to resist.

Clearly, scholars cannot explain every innovation's diffusion pattern. In some cases, the best explanation that can be offered was that "it was an idea whose time had come." The educational reforms of the mid-1990s are a cogent example; in state after state, leaders agreed that the time had come to reform education. And their solutions were remarkably similar— longer hours, more requirements, better teachers, and incentives for quality outcomes. The diffusion process is working even if we cannot observe it at every juncture.

## CONCLUSION

In this essay we have discussed policy innovation in the states, highlighting the important role of state legislatures. States have long served as the laboratories of democracy envisioned by Justice Brandeis. In the nineteenth century they enacted new regulations and programs long before the federal government did. The granting of woman suffrage and Mothers' Aid legislation are apt examples from the early twentieth century. Since then, more professionalized and careerist state legislative bodies have become even more capable of performing the laboratory function for our federal system. In the 1980s, states pioneered in economic development, public school reform, no-fault divorce law, and welfare reform. None of these innovations could have been accomplished without state legislative action.

One set of states has consistently been the first to adopt new legislation. Since the late nineteenth century, states such as New York, Wisconsin, Massachusetts, Minnesota, and Michigan have been pacesetters in policy innovation. What makes these states stand out? Why are they risk-takers? Such questions have attracted many scholars to the study of innovation. Those who conduct case studies of particular innovations have highlighted the role of policy entrepreneurs and legislative champions in the invention and adoption of new programs. Other scholars, who conduct aggregate studies of the fifty states, have identified sets of internal and external factors influencing the rate of adoption of new programs. Economic resources, political opportunities, and professionalism of state governmental institutions are the major internal determinants. Wealthier states with capable legislators and bureaucrats tend to be the first to try new ideas. The timing of innovation also depends on turnover in office, political competition levels, and a political culture which values change. The states that consistently lead in innovation are blessed with a confluence of these forces.

States and their leaders are also influenced by forces outside their boundaries. State policymakers—legislators, governors, and bureaucrats—often turn to neighboring states for answers to their problems. Or they use their professional networks and associations as information-gathering mechanisms. Over time, cue-taking from national leaders has increased so that innovations diffuse more rapidly than they did in the past, and their spread is less tied to regional boundaries. These trends mean that states' exposure to new ideas will become more similar over time. The lag time between the first and last adopters will shrink.

State legislatures play a critical role in the policy innovation process. Legislative leaders and legislative staff are involved in generating new ideas for legislation and in disseminating them to other states. Legislative capacity, often associated with early adoption of new legislation, has been strengthened through the reforms of the 1960s and 1970s. Consequently, state legislatures will be more effective innovators in the future.

What does the future hold for innovation? In the immediate future the states will be most influenced by the "necessity is the mother of invention" theory. Federal cutbacks, increased service loads, and the 1990–1991 recession strained the budgets of nearly every state. State legislators are contemplating all sorts of cost savings. Perhaps there is no better illustration than the area of health care. Here a major difficulty is the cost of medical care for the poor, typically funded by the federal-state Medicaid program. This is one of the fastest growing parts of states' budgets.

Oregon has come up with the most radical solution to the Medicaid cost containment problem. Oregon's policymakers decided to ration its medical services for the poor. Each medical procedure was prioritized in terms of its cost and effectiveness. If the money allocated by the legislature is not sufficient to cover all of the medical expenses of the poor, then the lowest priority services will not be offered. For example, prenatal care for pregnant women was rated higher than organ transplants. When money is tight, then transplants won't be funded. The Oregon plan was approved by the Clinton administration in early 1993, after having been rejected by the Bush administration.

Other states have grappled with the problem of the uninsured. In the early 1990s, over thirty million individuals did not qualify for medical coverage from their employers or from the government. Many states considering universal health-care access have found it too expensive, though in the early 1990s Minnesota and Florida expanded citizen access and regulated health-care costs simultaneously. The states' experiences in this area will undoubtedly influence the federal government in its future consideration of national health insurance.

This example, as well as others mentioned earlier, demonstrates how states lead in our federal system. The consequences of states' policy decisions are profound in several respects. Walker has asserted that the emulation and cue-taking process largely determines the pace and direction of social and political change. These changes are not necessarily in the direction of conservatism, as is often alleged in discussion of states' rights. Noting that state initiatives in the 1920s were the models for federal New Deal programs in the 1930s, Richard P. Nathan argued that state innovations in conservative periods often become the basis for national policy actions in liberal periods. The early months of the Clinton administration confirmed Nathan's observation. Former governor Bill Clinton brought to Washington, D.C., many ideas already tested in the laboratories of the states. We can expect state innovation to continue to be important in the future.

## BIBLIOGRAPHY

FRANCES STOKES BERRY and WILLIAM D. BERRY, "State Lottery Adoptions as Policy Innovations: An Event History Analysis," *American Political Science Review* 84 (1990): 395–415, is a sophisticated methodological examination of the determinants of lottery adoption by states. This is one of the few studies of the diffusion of revenue policy. WILLIAM R. BROCK's *Investigation and Responsibility: Public Responsibility in the United States, 1865–1900* (Cambridge, England, 1984), is an excellent treatment of the expansion of state government from 1865 to 1900. KEON S. CHI and DENNIS O. GRADY, "Innovators in State Governments: Their Organizational and Professional Environment," in THE COUNCIL OF STATE GOVERNMENTS, *The Book of the States: 1990–91 Edition* (Lexington, Ky., 1990), is based on an extensive survey of state bureaucrats regarding their role in successful innovations. PATRICIA K. FREEMAN, "Interstate Communication Among State Legislators Regarding Energy Policy Innovation," *Publius* 15 (Fall 1985): 99–111, surveyed legislators in six states regarding their cross-state cue-taking in energy policy. VIRGINIA GRAY, "Innovation in the States: A Diffusion Study," *American Political Science Review* 67 (1973): 1174–1185, is an early study of diffusion patterns in three policy areas. Interaction patterns are found to differ by policy area—in contrast to Walker, who found innovativeness to be a general trait of states. VIRGINIA GRAY and DAVID LOWERY, "The Corporatist Foundations of State Industrial Policy," *Social Science Quarterly* 71 (1990): 3–24, shows how governmental capacity affects adoption of economic development policies. HERBERT JACOB, *Silent Revolution: The Transformation of Divorce Law in the United States*

(Chicago, Ill., 1988), analyzes the diffusion of no-fault divorce. He argues that it was a routine decision as are most other agenda items. PAULA KING, *Policy Entrepreneurs: Catalysts in the Policy Innovation Process,* Ph.D. diss., University of Minnesota (1989), is an in-depth case study of nine policy entrepreneurs responsible for Minnesota's open-enrollment law.

JOHN W. KINGDON, *Agendas, Alternatives, and Public Policies* (Boston, Mass., 1984), is an insightful study of how issues get on the national agenda. It also makes a theoretical contribution. MICHAEL W. KIRST, GAIL MEISTER, and STEPHEN R. ROWLEY, "Policy Issue Networks: Their Influence on State Policymaking," *Policy Studies Journal* 13 (December 1984): 247–263, is a case study of four education policy reforms in the states. ALFRED R. LIGHT, "Intergovernmental Sources of Innovation in State Administration," *American Politics Quarterly* 6 (April 1978): 147–166, is based upon a mail survey of state administrators. He measures consensus about prestige and how it relates to emulation. JAMES M. LUTZ, "Regional Leadership Patterns in the Diffusion of Public Policies," *American Politics Quarterly* 15 (July 1987): 387–398, reanalyzes Walker's data. He shows that regional cue-taking has become less pronounced over time. EDGAR C. MCVOY, "Patterns of Diffusion in the United States," *American Sociological Review* 5 (1940), did one of the first quantitative studies of the diffusion of innovations among states. LAWRENCE B. MOHR, "Determinants of Innovation in Organizations," *American Political Science Review* 63 (March 1969): 111–126, is a major theoretical contribution to the study of innovation. RICHARD P. NATHAN, "The Role of the States in American Federalism," in CARL E. VAN HORN, ed., *The State of the States* (Washington, D.C., 1989), elaborates his cyclical theory of federalism. *New State Ice Co.* v. *Liebmann,* 285 U.S. 262, 311 (1932), is the case in which Justice Brandeis touted the virtues of state experimentation.

EVERETT M. ROGERS and F. FLOYD SHOEMAKER, *Communication of Innovations: A Cross-Cultural Approach,* 2d ed. (New York, 1971), is the bible of innovation research, summarizing more than 1,500 studies. ALAN ROSENTHAL, author of *Governors and Legislatures: Contending Powers* (Washington, D.C., 1990), is the preeminent observer of state legislatures. Here he argues that as governors and legislatures have become more powerful, tension between the two bodies has grown. PAUL SABATIER and DAVID WHITEMAN, "Legislative Decision Making and Substantive Policy Information: Models of Information Flow," *Legislative Studies Quarterly* 10 (August 1985): 395–421, contains a rather complicated model of information flow and legislative decision-making. ALBERT SHAW, "The American State and the American Man," *The Contemporary Review* 51 (January–June 1887): 695–711, describes state legislatures in the late 1800s, focusing on Minnesota's legislature. DOH C. SHINN and JACK R. VAN DER SLIK, "The Plurality of Factors Influencing Policymaking: School Reform Legislation in the American States, 1982–84," *Policy Studies Review* 7 (Spring 1988): 537–562, analyzes the determinants of school reform and credits state legislatures with much influence. JACK L. WALKER, "The Diffusion of Innovations Among the American States," *American Political Science Review* 63 (September 1969): 880–899, was the first empirical study of innovations in the states. It is the basis for all other studies of diffusion among the states. CAROL S. WEISSERT, "Policy Entrepreneurs, Policy Opportunists, and Legislative Effectiveness," *American Politics Quarterly* 19 (April 1991): 262–274, studies the effect of policy entrepreneurship upon perceived effectiveness. SUSAN WELCH and KAY THOMPSON, "The Impact of Federal Incentives on State Policy Innovation," *American Journal of Political Science* 24 (November 1980): 715–729, assess the impact of federal incentives upon the rate of diffusion.

SEE ALSO Reform in State Legislatures, AND State Legislatures in the Twentieth Century.

# CONGRESS, SECTIONALISM, AND PUBLIC-POLICY FORMATION SINCE 1870

### Richard Franklin Bensel

Formally defined, *sectionalism* describes political competition in which regional alliances are the principal organizing features. In the United States, sectionalism can be traced to the uneven development of regional economies, particularly those of the rapidly industrializing Northeast and the export-oriented, cotton-producing South in the nineteenth century. American sectionalism is, for that reason, distinct from most other national experiences in that ethnic and religious conflict has not been the primary basis of regional political competition.

From 1789 onward, sectional divisions frequently appeared on the floor of Congress. Antagonism between the settled East and the frontier West and, subsequently, the free North and the slave South fueled legislative struggles over economic development and the expansion of slavery. Sectional jealousy and competition were important barriers to the growth of the federal government in the United States. Paradoxically, however, the position of Congress within the federal government was probably strengthened by persistent efforts to craft legislative compromises between increasingly divergent sectional ambitions. These efforts left Congress, when the Civil War broke out in 1861, as the preeminent branch of the national state. While the executive branch regained some ground during the war, Congress reemerged after 1865 as both the formative institution for national policy-making and the central arena of sectional competition.

Aside from fundamental differences in the position of the various regions within the national political economy, much of the impetus to sectional political competition can be traced to attempts by the North to remake the southern political economy during Reconstruction. One outcome of the Civil War was, for example, the strong alignment of the national party system along a North-South cleavage, with the Democratic party anchored in the white South and the Republicans dominating the urban manufacturing regions of the North.

## POLITICAL RAMIFICATIONS OF SECTIONALISM

### The Post–Civil War Party System

With some qualifications, this Civil War alignment can be said to have provided the general framework around which the national party system was organized between 1870 and 1930. Working through the party system, sectional political competition was the primary factor shaping policy formation in several areas over these six decades. The most important of these policy areas concerned resolution of the serious and sustained threats to national unity posed by southern separatism. Northern victory in the war eliminated the most basic separatist demand, secession, by forcing the South back into the Union. That victory, however, left much of the population in the former Confederacy openly hostile to federal rule. In response, northern Republicans embarked upon a program of reconstructing the southern political economy in order to strengthen the position of loyalists in southern politics. On the whole, the wide variety of programs that constituted Reconstruction failed to establish loyalists (primarily black freedmen) as a competitive force in southern politics. During the late nineteenth century, the last remaining vestiges of the Reconstruction era were eliminated as the federal government withdrew from an active interventionist role in southern politics.

At the same time, the United States pursued a heavily contested policy of economic development that featured the creation of a national market largely imposed by central state juridical authority and rapid, unhindered capital consolidation into huge industrial trusts. By the turn of the century, active expansion of the United States into the international system brought on a new round of sectional competition over imperialism and American intervention in World War I. During the decade following the Versailles peace conference, sectional competition continued to revolve around the balance between unregulated economic development and federal protection for those sectors of society (particularly agriculture and labor) that were often victimized by unhindered corporate expansion. Compared with other periods since 1870, this was an era of (1) strong political parties, both within and outside Congress; (2) close executive-legislative cooperation, primarily but not exclusively due to the close connection between electoral fates of members of Congress and the president in the North; and (3) a very strong, even at times dominant, Congress that often set the policy agenda of the executive branch.

## The Democratic New Deal Coalition

The Great Depression brought the Civil War alignment of the party system and policy-making to a close. During the 1930s, Franklin D. Roosevelt's election and the New Deal remade the northern wing of the Democratic party even as the South became even more loyal to the party. The resulting New Deal coalition of northern labor and ethnic minorities with southern whites dominated both Congress and national politics for the next third of a century. Even though the New Deal coalition depended on a highly politicized brokering of interests by party leaders in Congress and the executive branch, this period witnessed a large expansion of the central state bureaucracy and a sweeping extension of federal power in both domestic and foreign affairs. While some scholars have viewed World War II as a conflict in which the demands of the war mobilization allowed conservative Democrats and Republicans to scale back or eliminate the most radical features of the New Deal revolution, the extensive use of bureaucratic controls on industrial production and labor relations also served to consolidate and even expand federal power in other areas. Political struggles over the course of the war mobilization, including the impact of federal controls on the future position of the most important sectors of the national political economy, ultimately produced a postwar détente between the southern agrarian and northern labor wings of the Democratic party.

The highly pragmatic and conditional nature of this intersectional alliance can be seen in the hard bargaining that accompanied the passage of agricultural commodity programs in the 1950s and the evasive attitude the party assumed toward civil rights until the early 1960s. The three and a half decades in which the New Deal coalition dominated American politics were characterized by (1) a slow decline in the strength of national political parties, including an increase in ticket-splitting between congressional and presidential races; (2) the consolidation of a strong committee system in Congress that decentralized legislative policy-making into groups of members whose constituencies often benefited directly from the federal programs controlled by those committees; and (3) a corresponding increase in legislative delegation as these committees combined wide bureaucratic discretion with close congressional oversight of the decisions of federal agencies under their jurisdiction. The net result of all these trends was the emergence of the so-called imperial presidency. However, the full realization of the latent authority embedded within the agencies and bureaus created by the New Deal coalition did not come until the collapse of that coalition during the mid-1960s.

## The Imperial Presidency and Post–New Deal Era

The most important factors in the demise of the New Deal coalition were the Civil Rights Act of 1964 and the Voting Rights Act of 1965. The first of these measures initiated, among other things, a very lengthy period of active bureaucratic support for primary- and secondary-school desegregation. In contrast, the Voting Rights Act enfranchised most southern blacks within a matter of months as federal registrars suspended restrictive suffrage provisions and enrolled hundreds of thousands of voters throughout the region. One immediate result of these civil rights measures was the exodus of southern whites from the Democratic party in presidential elections, although many remained loyal to the party in congressional races. Another result was the breakdown of the New Deal coalition in legislative voting as southern conservatives openly coalesced with Republicans. Over the long term, however, many of these conservatives were replaced by either southern Republicans or moderate-to-liberal Democrats as a more competitive two-party system emerged in the South. Over time, in fact, Democratic cohesion in congressional roll calls significantly increased as the growing southern wing of the Republican party absorbed many middle- and upper-class whites alienated by civil rights and other liberal measures associated with the national Democratic party.

A third result of the end of the New Deal coalition was the partial abandonment of the trilogy of authorization, appropriation, and revenue acts that had characterized the federal budget-making process for more than a century. Under the reign of the New Deal coalition, this process had allowed congressional committees to control federal expenditures and taxation within their respective policy jurisdictions with little or no central coordination or reconciliation of spending and revenue. During the weak party–strong committee era between 1932 and 1965, this decentralized process consistently produced a logrolling, pork barrel form of politics in which one outcome was small but persistent budget deficits. The collapse of the New Deal coalition severely undermined the strength of the committee system on which this budget process had come to depend. Several trends in the formerly routine consideration of legislation on the floors of the House and Senate accompanied a loss of committee power. One was a rapid rise in recorded roll calls on amendments to legislation sponsored by committees. A second was the increasing frequency with which the distributive decisions (such as the formulas that allocated federal subsidies to states and counties) of committees were challenged, often successfully, on the floor.

Another development that weakened the traditional budget process was the Vietnam War. That conflict aggravated budgetary strain because the Johnson administration chose to pursue both "guns and butter"—military and domestic spending. In addition, the unpopularity of the war ultimately encouraged Congress to attempt to recapture some of the power it had lost to the executive branch over war-making and budgetary decisions. Aside from the War Powers Resolution of 1973, which sought to reassert congressional authority over military intervention abroad, the most significant attempt to reclaim legislative authority was the Congressional Budget and Impoundment Control Act of 1974. Ironically, however, the most striking result of this new articulation of legislative power was a dramatic enhancement of executive influence over a now-unified budget accompanied by the extension of presidential bargaining leverage throughout the legislative process.

Aside from the growing dominance of the executive branch, several other trends have characterized American politics since the 1960s. One has been the strengthening of congressional party organizations and leadership which has partially replaced the committee system as the locus of policy-making and agenda coordination. Another has been an increasing disjunction in the national electoral base of presidents and members of Congress. This pattern possibly reflects a radical shift in the sectional alignment of the two-party system, as Republican presidential candidates continue to strengthen their hold on the white South while Democrats have become stronger in much of the East and Midwest. If so, the now-common explanation for these trends—that they merely reflect a nationalization of party competition in which the strength of the two parties will be more or less evenly distributed throughout the nation—may only describe an interim stage in a much more fundamental realignment of the party system, both nationally and in Congress. Since this would, in effect, reverse the partisan regional and socioeconomic bases of the Civil War party system, this realignment would constitute the most thoroughgoing change in the structure of party competition in American history.

This broad overview of the influence of

sectionalism on the party system, policy-making, and the institutional organization of Congress sets the stage for a closer look at some of the most important policy decisions between 1870 and 1990. This review will illustrate the historical impact of sectional competition on policy formation through an examination of several policy areas that were strongly embedded within well-established institutional structures and prevailing alignments within the party system. In chronological order, we will consider (1) Reconstruction and late-nineteenth-century monetary policy; (2) protective tariffs and military pensions; (3) antitrust measures and other regulation of economic activity; (4) the New Deal and national mobilization during World War II; and (5) civil rights and budget politics. Although this sampling conveys, of necessity, only a partial picture of the impact of uneven development on policy formation in the United States, it is hoped that the breadth and historical interrelationship between these major policy areas will compensate for the equally serious omissions in the analysis.

## SECTIONAL COMPETITION, INSTITUTIONAL STRUCTURE, AND POLICY FORMATION

### Reconstruction and Monetary Policy in the Late Nineteenth Century

"Reconstruction" is a general label for a wide variety of policies through which northern Republicans attempted to establish an indigenous loyalist group within the former states of the southern Confederacy in the decades following the end of the Civil War. Although Republican plans often included attempts to attract the political allegiance of upland, poor white yeomen, in practice Reconstruction policies targeted former black slaves (freedmen) as the group most likely to represent loyalist interests in the southern political economy. Except for a brief flirtation with southern whites during and immediately after the war, Reconstruction policies thus conflated black allegiance to the Republican party, federal protection for the rights and interests of southern freedmen, and the attempted establishment of a freestanding loyalist group in the South. In the first wave of

Reconstruction-related legislative activity, many congressional Republicans proposed a sweeping redistribution of southern wealth, particularly land, from landowning former Confederates to freedmen. These proposals foundered, in part, because these plans proposed a distribution of land to impoverished freedmen without delivering similar benefits to either (largely disloyal) poor southern whites or northern workers, many of whom had fought for the Union during the Civil War. The political base for such a redistribution was too narrow for implementation and, in addition, would have intensified the already highly charged racial divisions generally associated with Reconstruction.

With the abandonment of proposals to redistribute wealth in the South, congressional Republicans turned to policies that attempted to protect the suffrage rights of loyalist freedmen through the use of federal troops and marshals. The enforcement of these policies depended upon the continued presence of federal troops within southern states. As these troops were withdrawn from the region and civilian governments replaced military rule, direct federal enforcement of black suffrage rights became impossible. Although this was a gradual, drawn-out process, the final abandonment of direct military intervention in southern politics came as part of the negotiated settlement of the disputed 1876 presidential election between the Republican Rutherford B. Hayes and the Democrat Samuel J. Tilden in which the former assumed the presidency. At that point, congressional Republicans turned their attention to the readmission of the Southern states into the Union and proposed to set extraordinary preconditions protecting the political position of freedmen as part of the terms under which these states would resume, among other things, representation in Congress. These proposals all failed. For the remainder of the nineteenth century, the only national attempts to protect freedmen involved either proposals to send federal troops into the South once more (under the 1890 "Force Bill"), or case by case review of contested congressional elections in which one of the candidates, almost always the Republican, complained of flagrant disregard for state or federal election laws. Even these last vestiges of Reconstruction disappeared with the formal disfranchisement of southern blacks and poor whites at the turn of the century. The sectional alignment on all these Reconstruction policies closely followed the partisan and regional divisions that characterized disputes over slavery and economic development in the late antebellum and Civil War years. The major difference was the postwar incorporation of southern freedmen into the Republican party.

In many respects, Reconstruction was coterminous with the major economic policy of the immediate postwar era, resumption of the gold standard in domestic and international commerce. The federal government had abandoned the gold standard in December 1861, substituting irredeemable paper money, greenbacks, for gold-backed dollars. The value of these greenbacks, measured in gold, had subsequently inflated over the course of the war as the Union issued vast amounts of paper currency, along with equally vast amounts of bonded debt, to pay for the northern war effort. One consequence of this financial policy was the creation of a new class of financial capitalists dependent on the success of central state fiscal policy. Located for the most part in New York City, these finance capitalists traded federal debt securities, provided a foreign exchange market for greenbacks, and extended credit to brokers on the nation's major commodity and stock exchanges. Their dependence on federal fiscal policy and the often incompetent manner in which the Treasury conducted open market operations led these finance capitalists to advocate a return to conservative restraints, including a return to the gold standard, on central state power over the nation's financial system.

After peace came in April 1865, Congress narrowly chose to pursue resumption of the gold standard at prewar parity (as opposed to an immediate devaluation of the dollar to match the much lower, depreciated level of the postwar period). Strongly supported by both Democratic and Republican members of Congress from eastern financial centers and industrial districts, this resumption policy ultimately entailed a fourteen-year regimen of currency contraction, bond purchases, and federal budget surpluses that, in combination with a robust economic expansion in the domestic economy, deflated the American dollar to a point at which redemption in gold could take place.

This extremely conservative monetary policy was consistently supported in the executive branch. Congressional backing, however, was interspersed with more than a sprinkling of legislative initiatives and resolutions that would have prevented resumption and thus continued American reliance on irredeemable greenbacks. These attempts by southern and western members to prevent resumption later merged with agrarian insurgency and produced the third-party campaigns of the Greenbackers in 1880 and 1884, the Populists in 1892, and, finally, William Jennings Bryan's capture of the Democratic presidential nomination in 1896 and 1900. Throughout this period, American adhesion to the gold standard was firmly supported by presidential administrations, regardless of party, while congressional majorities either provided merely symbolic backing for administration policy or, in many instances, supported policies that would have forced the United States off the gold standard. The continuing struggle over the basis of the monetary system produced sectional alignments as stark as those that accompanied Reconstruction but, unlike the battles over federal protection for freedmen, monetary policy produced deep divisions within the two national parties.

## Tariff Protection, Civil War Pensions, and Economic Development

If the integration of the American dollar into the international gold standard can be called one of the two most contentious economic policies of the late nineteenth century, the other was the protective tariff. Tariff protection for infant American industry, particularly iron and steel producers, was one of the highest policy priorities of the Republican party when it assumed power in 1861 and remained a central plank in the party's program for national economic development throughout the late nineteenth century and well into the twentieth. In fact, tariff protection transformed iron and steel producers into one of the most important factions of the Republican party and clientele groups of the American state. (Among the other major factions and clients were southern freedmen, with respect to Reconstruction policy, and finance capitalists, with respect to postwar monetary policy and Treasury operations.) Industrial and manufacturing producers who benefited from the tariff were never powerful enough to impose protection as a national policy without making alliances with other major groups in the American political economy.

During the Civil War era, the first such alliance was with western farmers and led to the Homestead Act of 1862. Passage of the act, along with the Morrill Tariff, solidified the sectional coalition between West and Northeast as the basis of the Republican party. The second alliance emerged in the postwar period when tariff revenue began to produce substantial and persistent surpluses in the federal budget. Because free-trade advocates used these surpluses to buttress their arguments for a reduction in duties, protectionists sought to spend federal revenue in ways that would both reduce the surplus and strengthen resistance to tariff reform. Through the Republican party, which already had close ties to hundreds of thousands of Union veterans in the North and West, protectionists developed a close alliance with veterans' groups, particularly the Grand Army of the Republic (GAR). This alliance linked federal revenue from customs duties to expenditures on pensions for Union veterans and, in practice, extended support for the tariff well into the agrarian Midwest and West. After passage of the 1879 Arrears of Pensions Act, federal expenditures on Civil War pensions never dropped below 20 percent of the budget until World War I, peaking at almost 40 percent during the years between 1890 and 1894. In 1885 alone, 345,000 veterans or their survivors were drawing benefits. Tariff revenue averaged just over half of all federal income between 1880 and 1914. Not only were the political connections between pensions and production tariffs strong, but these terms comprised very sizable fractions of all federal expenditures and revenue.

As a central feature of American development, tariff protection and military pensions strongly accelerated northern expansion by systematically redistributing wealth from the commodity-exporting South to the industrializing North. Because almost all the manufacturing sectors that benefited from the tariff were centered in the Northeast and Midwest, tariff protection redistributed wealth from southern agrarian consumers to northern industrial producers in the form of higher prices for manufactured goods. Because the tariff also produced revenue for the federal Treasury and because that revenue was, in large part, spent on pensions for which Confederate veterans were ineligible, that part of the tariff responsible for higher prices on imported goods also redistributed wealth from South to North. Throughout this period, then, both pensions and protection aided American industrial expansion while, at the same time, accentuating the already wide disparity between northern and southern economic development. For all these reasons, the southern-based Democratic party strongly opposed both pensions and protection while northern Republicans supported both with equal fervor. As was true of party divisions over Reconstruction programs, this party alignment closely followed and fortified the prevailing Civil War alignment of the party system. Also like Reconstruction, both tariffs and pensions were policies primarily created and articulated through extremely specific legislation that positioned congressional party members, usually Republicans, as the dominant force in these areas of federal policymaking.

These highly sectional policies were often hammered out in freewheeling party caucuses and sometimes delicate negotiations between factions but, once sent from legislative committee to the floor, they almost always became major tests of partisan loyalty and doctrinal orthodoxy. Because passage of these highly conflictual policies constituted the major business of the late-nineteenth-century Congresses and because party strength was often closely balanced, many institutional changes during this period had as their major purpose the strengthening of parliamentary rules facilitating more expeditious passage of legislation sponsored by the majority party (e.g., the Reed Rules of 1890). While the president could assist or hamper execution, chief executives exercised much less influence in these areas than they did in, for example, foreign policy or Treasury operations in financial markets, including American adhesion to the international gold standard.

## Regulation of Markets, Trusts, and Capital in the Progressive Era

Although the developmental engine composed of intersectional wealth redistribution, Union pensions, and tariff protection drove both northern industrial expansion and national party politics for many decades after the end of Reconstruction, both the Civil War pension system and protectionism became less important after the turn of the century. In the first instance, Union veterans began to die off in increasingly large numbers and, even though eligibility was extended to survivors and dependents in 1890, pension recipients became a less important factor in both Republican party politics and the federal budget. A second trend behind the decline of this policy coalition was the increasing maturity and international competitiveness of American industry, which made, in many industrial sectors, tariff protection an unnecessary anachronism. While it lasted, this developmental engine also included within its scope both American adhesion to the international gold standard and (hitherto unmentioned) creation of a national market for capital and commercial distribution. This national market was largely the product of the federal judiciary, which struck down congressional attempts to regulate corporate competition and manufacturing conditions as unconstitutional extensions of the commerce clause and voided individual state legislation to regulate interstate corporate activity as impermissible violations of property rights and freedom of contract.

Those judicial decisions that struck down state statutes, such as *Wabash, St. Louis & Pacific Railway Co.* v. *Illinois,* 118 U.S. 557 (1886), encouraged southern and western agrarians to support more aggressive federal regulation of corporate competition and antitrust enforcement. For southern agrarians, many of whom were veterans who had served in the Confederate army, this support for central state expansion represented a considerable change in attitude toward American state authority. The *Wabash* case, for example, sparked a successful congressional effort to impose federal regulations upon railroad rates that resulted in establishment of the Interstate Commerce Commission in 1887. In the House of Representatives, John Reagan (D.-Tex.), former postmaster general of the Confederacy, was the most important proponent of strong federal regulatory powers over the nation's railroads. In his role as chair of the House Commerce Committee, Reagan offered the committee's version of what became the Interstate Commerce Act as a substitute for a much weaker

Senate bill. When the dust settled, Reagan's victorious substitute had drawn the unanimous support of all fifty-two voting representatives who had previously served in the Confederate military, while almost two-thirds (forty-three to twenty-two) of all Union veterans had opposed adoption of the stronger committee proposal. The origins of much of the legislation commonly associated with the expanding administrative capacity of the American state in the late nineteenth and early twentieth centuries follows a similar pattern: southern and western agrarians, many of whom were veterans of Confederate service, supported the extension of central state regulatory authority over national markets and corporations against the opposition of northeastern and midwestern Republican stalwarts. Put another way, the least nationalist region of the nation, the South, contributed most of the congressional votes for the erection of an administrative state apparatus over the opposition of the most nationalist elements within the American polity, Republicans from the industrial heartland.

Southern Democrats did not carry out their sporadic campaign for economic regulation because they were enamored of the then-prominent British model of national state authority with its strong centrist characteristics and professionally trained civil service. In fact, when looking at Britain, southern Democrats most commonly identified with Ireland, one of the most obvious victims of the British state. Instead, southern Democrats backed central state expansion as the only alternative, given Supreme Court decisions blocking defensive initiatives by local governments, to unrestrained predation by northeastern corporations and finance capital. Much more positive attitudes toward central state power were expressed by the comparatively small band of western Populists and, later, progressive Republicans who split with their party's regulars in the first decade of the new century. With respect to the international gold standard, the western wing of the Republican party had parted ways with the East even before the end of Reconstruction, but an enduring break did not come until 1910 and the revolt against Speaker Joseph G. Cannon in the House of Representatives. This revolt marked the end of centralized party rule in the House and initiated a twenty-year process that culminated in the emergence of a strong committee system as the central feature of legislative deliberation. At the time, the Cannon revolt signaled the rapidly increasing western opposition to protectionism and the unrestrained growth of corporate power.

Backed by this congressional alliance of Democrats and midwestern Republicans, the agrarian drive for central state expansion pushed for the creation of regulatory controls upon corporate trusts, the railroads, the national financial system, and the distribution and sale of agricultural commodities. In addition, these representatives proposed the substitution of an income tax for customs duties as the foundation of federal revenue, a move that, among other things, would transfer the primary burden of the tax system from the South and West to the Northeast. In addition to the Interstate Commerce Act and the Sherman Antitrust Act in 1890, the major policy enactments associated with agrarian insurgency came after the Cannon revolt. These included, in the transportation sector, the Mann-Elkins Act (1910), the Valuation Act (1913), and the Shipping Act (1916). In federal regulation of commodity distribution and marketing, the most important legislative accomplishments were the Cotton Futures Act (1914), the Warehouse Act (1916), and the Grain Standards Act (1916). Judicial emasculation of the Sherman Act was partially redressed by passage of the Clayton Antitrust Act in 1914. Congressional approval of the Underwood Tariff (1913), the income tax (1913), and the 1916 Revenue Act went a long way toward reforming regional inequities, as agrarians perceived them, of the federal revenue system. The creation of the Federal Reserve system (1913) and passage of the Federal Farm Loan Act (1916) increased the availability of credit in agricultural regions and reduced the dominant position of New York institutions within the national financial system while imposing federal participation upon the private banking network. Southern and western opposition to American entry into World War I produced deep divisions within Progressive ranks, particularly between congressional southern Democrats and President Woodrow Wilson. These divisions and Democratic losses in the North in the 1918 election brought an end to Progressive state expansion.

During the following decade, the United States renewed the rampant industrial expansion that characterized most of the 1870–1930 period. The Democratic party returned to its now traditional minority role in national politics and the southern wing continued to dominate congressional party caucuses. While congressional Democrats in the 1920s still resembled their predecessors in the late nineteenth century, congressional Republicans—even while in the majority—were chronically divided by Progressive insurgency and western agrarian resistance to eastern party leaders. As a result, Congress was potentially more favorable to central state expansion than any other branch of the federal government. However, the election of a series of conservative Republican presidents (Harding, Coolidge, and Hoover) eliminated the possibility of any renewal of Progressive state expansion and, in fact, deadened much of the activist potential of previous reforms through conservative appointments to commission panels and administrative positions. Through all of this period, northern industrial workers played only minor roles in national politics, now allying with conservative Republicans on the gold standard and tariff protection, now finding common cause with agrarian Democrats over national regulation of the length of the working day and the use of court injunctions against strike activity. With the stock market crash in 1929 and the beginning of the Great Depression the following year, industrial labor finally broke with the Republican party and forged permanent ties with the national Democratic party.

## The New Deal and World War II

The Democratic party took control of the House of Representatives in 1931 and, with the exception of only four intervening years, has organized the chamber ever since. Since the party already held almost all southern seats in the House before the pivotal 1930 elections, it was Democratic victories in the North, particularly urban industrial centers, that brought the party to power. Unlike the ephemeral northern expansion of the party during the Progressive Era, a number of new factors enabled the Democrats to secure these northern gains: (1) the political and economic prostration of northern industrial and finance capitalists during the Great Depression; (2) the utilization of the latent potential of the congressional committee system as the basis for brokering intraparty disputes between southern agrarians and northern labor; and (3) the enactment of decentralized federal programs that redistributed wealth between regions and classes, neither disturbing the dominant position of landed elites in the South nor weakening federal policies to protect industrial labor in the North. The result of all these factors was the institutionalization of the New Deal coalition between southern agrarians and northern labor both within the legislative organization of Congress and as the fundamental axis around which the national Democratic party operated.

The prostration of northern industrial and finance capitalists was recorded most clearly in the utter collapse of the Republican party during the six years following Franklin Roosevelt's election in 1932. The low point was reached in the 1936 elections, after which only seventeen Republicans sat in the Senate and eighty-nine were returned to the House. The dominant position of the Democratic party in national politics and Congress, combined with emergency conditions created by economic distress, brought on the erection of a new political economy in which central state power regulated, subsidized, or replaced private activity in almost every important sector of production. In many ways, this expansion of federal authority helped buttress the position of agricultural producers and organized labor as political interests that could later withstand the onslaught of resurgent capitalist wealth in the 1940s and 1950s. In other ways, the piecemeal manner in which federal authority was enlarged enticed one industrial sector after another to abandon a theoretically monolithic and philosophical hostility to government controls for the pragmatic benefits of subsidies and regulation of market competition. After the first decade of the New Deal era, the sectional implications of central state expansion were usually much more ambiguous compared to the stark, almost naked transfers of wealth involved in late-nineteenth-century economic development.

The central state that emerged from the New Deal possessed a number of strongly decentralizing characteristics. One was a frequent reliance on a "cooperative federalism" in which the central government merely provided monetary subsidies and local or individual state governments controlled most aspects of policy formulation and implementation. Another was the multiplication of bureaus and independent agencies whose mission was to regulate and/or subsidize a multitude of narrowly defined economic sectors or class interests. Congress conferred substantial bureaucratic autonomy on these agencies which, in practice, often insulated them from presidential influence while enabling congressional committee chairs to use their legislative influence over operations and budgetary authorizations to pressure federal officials. Congressional delegation of legislative authority to bureaucratic agencies cloaked divisive policy implications in broadly worded statutes that minimized the political costs of intersectional logrolling. As one product of this method of conflict avoidance, the New Deal thus encouraged the emergence of "iron triangles" in which political cooperation between influential private groups, congressional committees, and bureaucratic agencies blurred the boundary between private interest and public responsibility and made the purpose of federal policy the organized pursuit of political economic advantages for discrete regulated interests.

The congressional committee system contributed to the institutionalization of the New Deal coalition in many ways. In the first instance, the availability of the committee system in 1933 provided a legislative counterpart to the explosion of administrative capacity that accompanied central state expansion. The institutional position of the system both within Congress and the American state generally was reinforced by the almost exclusive reliance on seniority rules in committee-assignment decisions and the codification of committee jurisdictions (in the House by Asher Hinds [R.-Maine] and Clarence A. Cannon [D.-Mo.], in 1907 and 1936, respectively). These jurisdictions were later simplified and strengthened in the reforms effected by the 1946 Legislative Reorganization Act.

Seniority rules gave committee chairs to those members of the majority party who had continuously served on that committee for the longest period of time. They also guaranteed reappointment to that committee for as long as the member wished to serve. In combination, these rules insulated the dominant positions within the committee system from the influence of the majority-party leadership and caucus. The detailed and explicit rules that outlined committee jurisdictions and that highly privileged their role in the referral of bills gave individual committees fairly secure monopolies over legislative policy-making within their respective jurisdictions. The influence of seniority norms in allocating committee chairs had been increasing since the last decades of the nineteenth century, and exclusive committee jurisdictions accompanied the very emergence of the first standing committees in Congress. During the New Deal, the weak speakership (a legacy of the 1910 Cannon revolt), the vast expansion of legislative policy-making, and deep divisions between the two wings of the Democratic party dramatically reinforced the insulating impact of seniority rules and exclusive committee jurisdictions. The result was the strong committee system that dominated Congress throughout the life of the New Deal coalition.

The decentralization of legislative activity into congressional committees weakened the congressional floor and party caucuses as alternative policy-making arenas. In addition to shielding policy-making from public view and party responsibility, this decentralization also made possible the survival of the New Deal coalition, an otherwise quite heterogeneous and, on a national level, highly incompatible alliance. In practice, congressional Democrats divided up policy influence through an assignment process primarily combining seniority norms and self-selection as means of recruitment to legislative panels. The members of these committees then participated in distinct and, in terms of the interests they served, parochial policy arenas. The function of the party leadership within this system was to minimize intraparty conflict through the transformation of policy disputes into procedural questions and jurisdictional rights and, when all else failed, to use parliamentary power over scheduling to prevent open clashes between southern agrarians and northern labor.

For all these reasons, much of the New Deal can be viewed through the political lens of the modern committee system as well as the policy optics of bureaucratic implementation.

To the Committee on Public Works, for example, went the Tennessee Valley Authority and federal subsidies for highway construction and regional development. To the Committee on Ways and Means the New Deal assigned social security old-age benefits, unemployment insurance, and reciprocal trade agreements. The Agriculture Committee was given federal supports for commodities, soil conservation, crop insurance, and rural electrification. The Committee on Education and Labor, on the other hand, won oversight of federal regulation of the wages and hours of labor and the National Labor Relations Board. To the Committee on Banking and Currency was assigned federal insurance on bank deposits, public and private housing, and the foreign exchange value of the dollar. These examples, which have been described under the committee titles used after 1946, provide only a small sampling of the legislative agenda of the New Deal and the tight jurisdictional boundaries of the committee system during its halcyon years between 1933 and 1965. Even so, the division of legislative power in these few cases perhaps suggests some of the ways in which the strong decentralization of congressional power into legislative panels enabled the agrarian and labor wings of the Democratic party to divide federal power into a number of distinct spheres of influence peacefully.

The northern and southern wings of the Democratic party, of course, wanted different things from the New Deal. For northern labor, the New Deal represented an opportunity to install federal protection for the formation of unions in the nation's industrial sectors, government regulation of corporate competition, and a general redistribution of wealth from owners to workers. For southern agrarians, this agenda was more or less acceptable so long as it was limited to the North. Southerners were much more concerned with federal subsidization of regional development, including highways and waterways, and a government solution to chronic overproduction of agricultural commodities. Both of these regional programs targeted northern capital as the source of wealth for interclass (in the North) and intersectional (in the South) redistribution. As the New Deal decade wore on, southern Democrats became increasingly wary of their northern allies as the Roosevelt administration proposed more ambitious expansions of central state authority. Many of these proposals suggested the creation of permanent agencies staffed by ostensibly neutral civil servants as replacements for the temporary executive offices and patronage recruitment that characterized the early years of the emergency. In addition, many New Deal officials began to view the South, including the entrenched system of segregation that shaped black-white social and economic relations, as a potential area of expansion for an activist federal government and as an obstacle, in the form of southern congressional conservatives, to further social reform. The result of this growing New Deal activism was an increasingly effective alliance of southern Democratic and northern Republican conservatives in both the House and Senate that had almost brought the New Deal to a halt even before the beginning of World War II.

In some respects, mobilization for the war was a replay of state expansion during the early years of the New Deal; temporary emergency offices and agencies with overlapping, even contradictory, missions mushroomed in number and size, exploding federal authority over production and labor relations and overriding formal constitutional constraints. In addition, the federal bureaucracy created by the mobilization was staffed by presidential appointees recruited outside the civil-service system. In setting up these agencies, the most important legislation passed by Congress was the Second War Powers Act and the Emergency Price Control Act of 1942. The first granted the War Production Board sweeping, almost unlimited power over the allocation of materials or the utilization of production facilities throughout the nation and conferred statutory legitimacy on a board that had previously been established by presidential order. The Emergency Price Control Act similarly enhanced the bureaucratic authority of the Office of Price Administration. As was the case during the New Deal, activist proponents of central state power again tried to turn these and other temporary agencies with their sweeping regulatory authority into permanent bureaucratic structures.

In other respects, the mission assigned to this mobilization, defeating the Axis powers in war, was different from the domestic economic recovery that was the most widely accepted goal of the New Deal. This mission, most Americans accepted, entailed a temporary submission to federal authority and a sternly imposed but equally distributed "sacrifice" on the part of all classes in society. But this near consensus on the general goal of the war effort did not eliminate political conflict over practical implementation. In fact, the war effort came to encompass a much more state-centered, vast federal intervention into economic and social relations than the New Deal had entailed—an intervention that threatened, even when led by temporary agencies and volunteer "dollar-a-year" officials, to reshape the domestic political economy permanently.

Seen from the broadest perspective, federal intervention most directly implicated the interests of three major groups in the national political economy: industrial labor, industrial corporations, and the producers of agricultural commodities. The first of these was, by 1940, a major pillar of the Democratic party. The second group had become wary of, even alienated from, the Roosevelt administration and was the single most influential group within the Republican party. Agricultural producers were deeply split between the two parties; southern cotton and tobacco planters along with many western grain growers aligned with the Democrats and many, if not most, corn and truck (vegetable) farmers adhered to the Republicans.

As the war entered its third year, the impact of federal controls could be seen from several very different perspectives. From one vantage point, the war mobilization had finally brought the nation out of the Great Depression after all other purely domestic policies had apparently failed to produce sustained economic growth. In that perhaps narrow sense (e.g., ignoring battlefield casualties), the mobilization benefited all major sectors in American society. But, viewed from another angle, some groups benefited far more than others. In fact, the war appeared likely to raise these sectors permanently into much more advantageous positions, vis-à-vis the other sectors, within the postwar political economy than would have been the case without the war mobilization. Northern industrial labor, in this sense, was the clear victor in the tripartite conflict over which of the three major sectors would bear the brunt of the war effort. Business and industry also prospered under the mobilization as the federal government poured capital into productive capacity under cost-plus war-related contracts and direct investment. Because agriculture was an equally clear laggard in the contest for position in the postwar political economy, the southern wing of the Democratic party consistently pushed for the creation of new federal powers that would constrain the gains of the other sectors, particularly labor, and even proposed that emergency authority be extended into the postwar era in order to impose, from their perspective, a readjustment of "equitable sacrifice." The most important measures in this area include southern support for an administration proposal to extend the selective-service system to industrial labor and regional opposition to repeal of the 1943 War Labor Disputes Act. This southern campaign carried over into the postwar period with passage of the Taft-Hartley Act in 1947. In the ensuing Eisenhower administration, northern labor and southern agrarian Democrats uneasily coexisted but, with John F. Kennedy's election in 1960, the civil rights movement reopened conflict between the two great wings of the party.

## The End of the New Deal Coalition, 1965–1990

Abandonment of federal protection of black suffrage rights in the South in the late nineteenth century coincided with the rapid imposition of formal barriers to black voting across the region. During this period, every southern and many northern states copied one or more features of the Mississippi Plan, enacted in that state's 1890 constitutional convention. The plan included the imposition of stringent residency requirements, cumulative poll taxes, and literacy tests in which, for example, prospective voters were required to read and "understand" the text of federal and state constitutions. These revisions of suffrage eligibility effectively disfranchised almost all blacks and many poor whites and were accompanied by the rapid extension of segregationist arrangements in education, public accommodations, and marriage. The net result of the formalization of black exclusion in electoral politics and race segregation in social institutions was a regional political system in which power was concentrated in the hands of a small, wealthy white

minority. This system persisted despite sporadic rulings by the U.S. Supreme Court that struck down individual electoral arrangements as unconstitutional. In 1915, for example, the Supreme Court struck down the so-called grandfather clause, which had exempted many poor whites from literacy tests by excusing prospective voters who had been eligible to vote under the electoral laws in effect prior to 1867 or were the first- or second-generation descendants ("grandsons") of those who had been eligible. In additional decisions handed down between 1927 and 1948, the Court also abolished the "white primary," which had used party regulations to exclude blacks from participation in southern Democratic nominating elections. Like the civil rights acts of 1957 and 1960, however, these decisions did little to alter social and economic segregation in the South.

Between the end of World War I and the Voting Rights Act of 1965, Congress repeatedly considered legislation hostile to segregation under several headings (in rough chronological order): antilynching measures, anti–poll tax bills, omnibus civil rights acts, and authority for the establishment and renewal of the federal Civil Rights Commission. Attempts to pass a federal antilynching statute began in 1922 and continued for almost two decades. During this period, the number of southern lynchings declined to the vanishing point, but regional opposition to federal legislation remained monolithic. Serious efforts to eliminate the poll tax began during World War II and continued, as separate initiatives, through the early 1960s. Lynchings were finally made a federal crime with passage of the 1964 Civil Rights Act. The poll tax was invalidated, in federal elections, by a subsequent Supreme Court decision that was the result of a Justice Department suit authorized by the same act. Almost all of these measures focused exclusively on segregationist institutions in the South. The 1965 Voting Rights Act, for example, targeted states and counties in which a literacy test had been imposed as a voting qualification and fewer than half of the voting-age population voted in the 1964 presidential election. The areas covered by the act encompassed the entire states of Alabama, Georgia, Louisiana, Mississippi, South Carolina, and Virginia, and twenty-eight counties in North Carolina, three in Arizona, and one in Idaho.

Almost all of the above measures were considered between 1933 and 1965, when the New Deal coalition controlled Congress. During this period, passage of civil rights legislation threatened a fundamental precondition for intersectional peace within the Democratic party. At the same time, defeat or emasculation of civil rights proposals was difficult to reconcile with the public ideology of New Deal liberalism. In a rare attempt at reconciliation, Senator Claude Pepper (D.-Fla.) argued in 1938 that a proposed federal antilynching statute could never be a part of the New Deal because it contradicted the principles of "progressive democracy as it has been given expression and application in later days by the great humanitarian of our generation, Franklin D. Roosevelt" (quoted in Bensel, 1984, p. 231). Pepper's comments gave tacit recognition to the fact that maintenance of segregationist institutions in the face of northern opposition embodied, along with federal aid to regional development and agriculture, one of the primary claims on the loyalty of the white electorate for southern Democrats. For northern Democrats, public backing for proposals to use federal power to dismantle segregation represented one of their strongest claims on a "liberal" identity and a further enlargement of federal social-welfare programs and responsibilities. Recognizing the vulnerability of the Democratic New Deal coalition on civil rights issues, northern Republicans regularly offered bills to expand federal intervention in southern race relations. Northern Democrats, particularly those willing to put at risk their party's majority control of Congress in return for a more ideologically coherent national platform, also introduced their own or cosponsored Republican proposals. Just as regularly, the congressional leadership of the Democratic party disposed of these bills by arranging for their failure in one part or another of the legislative process. For this purpose, the procedural intricacies of the committee system proved to be an extremely effective killing ground.

Because of its control over the scheduling of legislation for consideration on the floor of the House of Representatives, the most important hurdle for civil rights bills during the heyday of the New Deal coalition was the House Committee on Rules. For contentious measures for which fewer than two-thirds of all members were likely to support passage, the Rules Committee controlled access to the floor by issuing "special orders." Without these special orders, bills could only be brought up on the floor under "suspension of the rules," which required a two-thirds majority, or almost unanimous consent. Most civil rights bills, however, never even reached Rules because they were bottled up in the House Committee on the Judiciary and were never reported out of that committee. The Senate's Committee on the Judiciary was equally, if not more, hostile to civil rights bills. In the Senate, however, the filibuster was the most effective barrier to legislative assault on segregation. Without the extraordinary majorities required to bring debate to an end (two-thirds of the entire membership between 1949 and 1959, two-thirds of those voting between 1917 and 1949 and between 1959 and 1975), civil rights measures were either "talked to death" or emasculated in an attempt to gain the marginal support necessary to invoke cloture. With the posting of southern Democrats on each of these committees and, of course, the Senate floor, the party leadership rarely had to coordinate opposition to major civil rights initiatives, although arranging for more or less symbolic roll calls on the House and Senate floors—permitting demonstrations of public support by northern Democrats and public opposition by southern Democrats—required more care.

The civil rights revolution in Congress began with passage of the 1964 Civil Rights Act and the 1965 Voting Rights Act. A major reason for the passage of these measures was the continuing migration of southern blacks from farms and plantations to northern urban centers. While bringing hundreds of thousands of blacks into the North, this migration also, in effect, franchised them for the first time since the last decade of the nineteenth century and dramatically strengthened those political forces for whom federal enforcement of civil rights was more than just a political football. In the middle years of the 1960s, this continuing migration coincided with the appearance, following the Johnson landslide in 1964, of extraordinarily large Democratic congressional majorities. These majorities contained, for the first time since the 1930s, regional Democratic majorities in the North as well as in the South. Northern party leaders, always uncomfortable with the racial implications of their alliance with southern Democrats, could now promote federal enforcement of suffrage rights and integration with, apparently, less risk to their legislative majorities in Congress from cross-party defections or strengthening Republican competition in the South. With the civil rights revolution came the end of the New Deal coalition and a rapid decline in the primacy of the committee system in the congressional legislative process. These developments, in turn, undercut the institutional supports for the logrolling, reciprocal politics that had both insulated spending decisions from revenue income and distributed legislative influence to small groups of members with a strong constituency interest in specific sets of federal policies. One immediate result was the outbreak of a kind of parochial, cost-benefit politics in which political support or opposition for specific policies turned solely on the size of federal payments to constituencies.

In the 1970s, the most regionally divisive policy decisions were those that either allotted federal funds among the major sections according to specific mathematical formulas or involved regulatory standards that threatened to retard southern or western economic development. Under the first heading, for example, extremely stark sectional coalitions formed over formulas allocating community block grants, public works jobs, and federal education funds, and the targeting of civilian contracts from the Department of Defense under the so-called Maybank amendment. Although Congress had used formulas to allocate federal spending and payments to state and local governments since at least the middle of the nineteenth century, the construction of the formulas had rarely been contested on the floor of Congress before the 1970s. With the declining authority of the congressional committee system and the onset of an era of declining budgetary freedom, however, these formulas, along with many other aspects of policy formation, were no longer among the legitimate, unchallenged prerogatives of legislative committees. They were increasingly challenged by floor-based regional groups such as the New England Congressional Caucus, the Northeast-Midwest Economic Advancement Coalition, and the informally organized southern "Boll Weevils."

These regional groups were also heavily involved in congressional decisions that imposed or removed federal regulations that had, as one of their implications, a strong impact on southern and western economic development. Such decisions included discretionary federal authority to ban the use of natural gas as a boiler fuel, congressional approval for decisions withdrawing public lands from mineral production, the section of the 1970 Clean Air Act that enjoined the "prevention of significant deterioration" in air quality, the rationing of oil supplies in order to protect the availability of home heating oil, and use of federal highway trust funds for mass transit projects. In addition to the institutional factors already cited, the context in which these formula and regulatory decisions erupted onto the floor of Congress was set by the explosion of energy prices following the 1973 oil embargo and the subsequent collapse in the competitive position of American industry in the world economy. On the one hand, rising oil and natural gas prices radically altered the terms of trade within the domestic economy between the energy-consuming states of the Northeast and Midwest and the producing states of the Southwest and West. On the other hand, the rapidly declining competitiveness of heavy industrial production imposed a painful reduction in the overall size of the sector, reduced payroll and dividend income to workers and shareholders throughout the manufacturing belt, and encouraged a relocation of manufacturing activity from the union-shop states of the North (where wages and work rules resisted adaptation to changing conditions in international competition) to the "right to work" states of the South and West (where wages and working conditions were more easily controlled by corporate management). In different ways, then, both rising energy prices and industrial decline dramatically redistributed wealth from the older urban centers of the Northeast and Midwest to the so-called Sun Belt cities of the South and West. With the degenerating role of the congressional committee system and the demise of the New Deal coalition, political conflict over this redistribution of wealth could not be kept off the House and Senate floors and thus ensued one of the most nakedly parochial periods of policy formation in American history.

The declining prestige of congressional committees, including such major panels as Appropriations and Ways and Means, combined with open floor battles over regulation and the regional allocation of federal expenditures to throw the traditional budget process of separate authorization, appropriation, and revenue bills into chronic disarray. The inability of Congress to achieve even a minimum of coordination between spending, revenue, and programmatic design provided an opening for aggressive executive intervention which, under President Richard Nixon, took the form of impoundment orders preventing agencies and departments from spending duly appropriated funds. In reaction to the growth of presidential power over spending and, separately, war making, Congress passed the War Powers Resolution of 1973 and the Congressional Budget and Impoundment Control Act of 1974. By 1981 it was clear that the budget act—far from reclaiming legislative influence over the federal budget —had in fact further enhanced the ability of the executive branch to penetrate congressional cloakrooms and committee rooms. By creating a process in which decisions over policy design and expenditures became combined into one omnibus resolution, the budget act made president-led bargaining the primary focus of congressional policy-making and forced majority-party leaders and committee chairs to the sidelines. Since the first year of the Reagan administration, floor consideration of budget resolutions has been, in most years, far and away the most important annual legislative event. As a result, the congressional committee system has been further weakened by the inability of committees to protect their policy jurisdictions from incursions by wide-ranging budget resolutions and by a legislative environment in which preoccupation with annual budget decisions has drastically reduced opportunities for the consideration of separate, more narrowly framed legislative initiatives. In addition, the fiscal constraints imposed by this new legislative environment have prevented congressional committees from proposing new programs or effectively protecting pet projects under existing ones.

These budget battles have had significant regional overtones since southern Democrats have proved most susceptible to the influence of Republican presidents. However, the most important regional implications lay in the secondary impact of budget-centered legislative politics on the increasing importance of party leaders and organizations in Congress. Just as the decentralizing features of the strong committee system made possible the ongoing reconciliation of the competing interests and social bases of the New Deal coalition, the accumulation of formal authority in the hands of the majority leadership and party caucus since the 1970s has encouraged the expression and pursuit of general policy principles that will, over time, reduce diversity within the party membership. Almost certainly this reduction in diversity will move the congressional membership of the two major parties into a closer alignment with the electoral pattern of late-twentieth-century presidential contests. The geographical distribution of candidate support in these elections, in which general party principles have played out across the entire terrain of the national political economy, suggests a further shift in the South toward the Republican party while historical trends toward the Democrats in much of the Northeast and Midwest should also continue. However, until party discipline is more effectively enforced in congressional voting and/or a crucial, regionally sensitive issue emerges and is taken up by the major parties, this rolling realignment of the social bases will probably involve small incremental shifts in sectional party strength.

## CONCLUSION

The alignment of sections within the American political system has persisted more or less unchanged since the Civil War. During this time, however, the party system has almost reversed its regional bipolarity, with the Republicans, at least in presidential elections, now the dominant party in the South and the Democrats at least competitive in most of the North. This necessarily broad and incomplete overview of sectionalism and policy formation in Congress can only suggest the many ways in which institutional structure, policy conflict, and the social bases of party competition have been intertwined in the nation's history. Contemporary commentators often argue that sectionalism has ceased to be an important factor in American politics. In support of that position, they cite a growing "nationalization" of American political life in response to national television programming and decreasing differences between the primary productive bases of regional economies. By most formal measures of sectional conflict, these observers are correct; sectional divisiveness in congressional party membership and roll-call voting have been declining since the 1920s and, as the flip side of these trends, legislative conflict has appeared to involve important party cleavages within each of the nation's sections as well as ever weaker divisions between the regions. On the other hand, the nation may very possibly be involved in one of the most important political realignments in its history. As long as the American political system is within this transition period, lower scores on formal measures of sectional conflict in Congress would be expected to lag behind this fundamental realignment, as long-standing institutional structures such as the committee system lose ground to the reemergence of party-centered legislative processes and the two parties switch their respective social bases within the national political economy. From this perspective, presidential election returns, which show a persistent and striking sectional cleavage between the parties, may be one leading indicator of the future of congressional politics.

## BIBLIOGRAPHY

A very broad synthesis of regionalism and American political development can be found in JOHN AGNEW, *The United States in the World-Economy: A Regional Geography* (Cambridge and New York, 1987). Treatments of the South as a distinct political region include JACK BASS and WALTER DeVRIES, *The Transformation of Southern Politics: Social Change and Political Consequence Since 1945* (New York, 1976) and EARL BLACK and MERLE BLACK, *Politics and Society in the South* (Cambridge, Mass., 1987). Interpretations that link sectional conflict more precisely to policy formation include RICHARD FRANKLIN BENSEL, *Yankee Leviathan: The Origins of Central State Authority in America, 1859–1877* (Cambridge and New York, 1990), and *Sectionalism and American Political Development, 1880–1980* (Madison, Wis., 1984). On historical changes in policy-making coalitions in Congress, see DAVID W. BRADY, *Critical Elections and Congressional Policy Making* (Stanford, Calif., 1988). On the characteristics of national party coalitions in the late nineteenth century, see WALTER DEAN BURNHAM, "Periodization Schemes and 'Party Systems': The 'System of 1896' as a Case in Point," *Social Science History* 10 (Fall 1986). For an analytical account of the congressional politics surrounding American entry into World War I, see JOHN MILTON COOPER, JR., *The Vanity of Power: American Isolationism and the First World War, 1914–1917* (Westport, Conn., 1969). There is a vast selection of texts on Reconstruction. Among the many strong possibilities, the best general works are, perhaps, ERIC FONER, *Reconstruction: America's Unfinished Revolution, 1863–1877* (New York, 1988) and WILLIAM GILLETTE, *Retreat from Reconstruction, 1869–1879* (Baton Rouge, La., 1979). For an excellent analysis of domestic economic policy formation during the New Deal, see ELLIS W. HAWLEY, *The New Deal and the Problem of Monopoly* (Princeton, N.J., 1966). A more than serviceable account of congressional politics during the Cannon revolt can be found in KENNETH W. HECHLER, *Insurgency: Personalities and Politics of the Taft Era* (New York, 1964).

One attempt to conceptualize the nature of sectionalism in the United States is V. O. KEY, JR., *Politics, Parties, and Pressure Groups,* 5th ed. (New York, 1964). The classic work on the distinctive nature of politics in the states of the South is V. O. KEY, JR., *Southern Politics in State and Nation* (New York, 1949). For a study of growing party competition in the South, see ALEXANDER P. LAMIS, *The Two-Party South* (New York, 1984). On the characteristics of the "imperial presidency" and the origins of unrealizable popular expectations with respect to the performance of modern presidents, see THEODORE J. LOWI, *The Personal President: Power Invested, Promise Unfulfilled* (Ithaca, N.Y., 1985). The best account of the early years of the "conservative coalition" is JAMES T. PATTERSON, *Congressional Conservatism and the New Deal: The Growth of the Conservative Coalition in Congress, 1933–1939* (Lexington, Ky., 1967). RICHARD POLENBERG provides a narrative account of one attempt to turn chaotic and temporary New Deal administrative arrangements into a permanent, rationalized bureaucracy in his *Reorganizing Roosevelt's Government, 1936–1939: The Controversy over Executive Reorganization* (Cambridge, Mass., 1966).

For general overviews of sectional and party politics during the Progressive Era that demonstrate the overwhelming dependence of Progressive forces in Congress on agrarian votes from the South and West, see ELIZABETH SANDERS, "Farmers and the State in the Progressive Era," in EDWARD S. GREENBERG and THOMAS F. MAYER, *Changes in the State: Causes and Consequences* (New York, 1990) and "Industrial Concentration, Sectional Competition and Antitrust Politics in America, 1880–1980," in KAREN ORREN and STEPHEN SKOWRONEK, eds., *Studies in American Political Development,* vol. 1 (New Haven, Conn., 1986). A good description of executive-congressional conflicts over the budget, including the pivotal 1981 struggle, can be found in BARBARA SINCLAIR, *Majority Leadership in the U.S. House* (Baltimore, 1983). The seminal work on American state authority is STEPHEN SKOWRONEK, *Building a New American State: The Expansion of National Administrative Capacities, 1877–1920* (New York, 1982). FREDERICK JACKSON TURNER, *The Significance of Sections in American History* (New York, 1932), is the most important early treatment of sectionalism as a fundamental theme in American history. On the intersectional and interparty bargaining that ultimately resolved the contested presidential election involving Rutherford Hayes and Samuel Tilden, see C. VANN WOODWARD, *Reunion and Reaction: The Compromise of 1877 and the End of Reconstruction* (Boston, 1966).

# LEGISLATURES AND GENDER ISSUES

## Lori D. Ginzberg

The legal and political system of the United States was established by men; the authors of the Declaration of Independence hardly intended its famous decree, "all men are created equal," to include women. Laws concerning marriage and family, property and employment, as well as those concerning the control of women, children, servants, laborers, people of color, criminals, and "deviants" were constructed, imposed, and interpreted by men. Thus the question of legislatures' relationship to gender issues is an especially complicated one, for it involves the content of the law, on the one hand, and the process by which women of different groups, denied direct access to the electoral process until the twentieth century, sought to articulate their own political agendas, on the other.

There is a gender component to virtually every issue that legislators confront; implicit assumptions about the "proper place" and rights of women inform legislation about social welfare, military personnel, court appointments, labor relations, the development of new technology, and so forth. Such assumptions are revealed as well in questions—many of which lie beyond the scope of this essay—ranging from black male suffrage to gay rights to AIDS funding. Nor should one assume that there has been historically a single women's perspective or experience that would unify women around a particular legislative program. Just as issues of family relationships, property, work, and sexuality have pervaded legislatures' actions, so too have gender issues been inseparable from issues of class and race and their legal construction and regulation. From colonial legislation regulating families to the nineteenth-century transformation of laws regarding property and employment, to more recent statutes on sexuality and reproduction, legislatures have reflected the fears,

prejudices, and hopes of their own historical and regional contexts.

The content of legislation is an important measure of our society's values regarding women. Also important, however, are the ways in which women expressed themselves as citizens and the ways in which legislators have responded to the wishes of their female constituents. Until 1920, legislators in most states did not need to care about a woman's vote, though they frequently heard women's voices. At least from the 1830s, middle-class women have routinely marched into legislative halls as if they assumed they would be welcome. There, though voteless, they lobbied for new laws, gained corporate status for their organizations, and sought funds to operate the charitable enterprises of their day. The question of women's political activism and of lawmakers' responses prior to women's enfranchisement—and of how women of different groups understood and acted upon their relationship to the state—pervade the history of legislation and gender issues.

This dynamic between the content of the law and women's efforts to influence it is epitomized by legislation regarding sexuality. In many ways, the relation between sexuality and the state offers a window into society's deepest concerns about gender and, especially, about changes in gender relations. Anxieties about social change frequently find expression in laws regarding sexual behavior, laws that historically have ranged from those regulating abortion or the age of consent to those prohibiting homosexuality. In addition, efforts to institutionalize in the law particular views of sexuality has been one way in which women have directly confronted men's legal dominion. Through their support of legislation that many others have condemned as "repressive," some women have helped to shape the legislative record by articulating their own critique of men's behavior, which itself was and remains codified in law. Thus the relationship among legislatures, sexuality, and female activists distills a long history of legal content, activism, and conflicts among women themselves.

## THE COLONIAL SETTING: THE WELL-ORDERED HOUSEHOLD

Historian Michael Grossberg notes as "one continuing reality" that "the family is in many ways a legal creation" (p. ix). The ways in which gender served to establish, order, and regulate families (and their property) made it a most salient category in colonial legislation. Indeed, family law can be seen as exemplifying colonists' ideals for their society and for the place of white women within it. Colonies varied in their specific legislation and in their adaptations of the British legal tradition, yet the dynamic among the English common law, new colonial statutes, and the practice of equity jurisprudence (judges' discretionary amelioration of statutory law) characterized colonial efforts to articulate women's legal place.

According to the common law tradition, which was adopted either expressly or implicitly by colonial legislatures, married women assumed feme covert ("covered woman") status. As the British jurist Sir William Blackstone put it, "the very being or legal existence of the woman is suspended during the marriage, or at least is incorporated . . . into that of the husband" (Blackstone, *Commentaries,* quoted in Beard, p. 89). Commonly referred to as "civil death," coverture forbade wives from owning or inheriting property, suing, making contracts, or assuming guardianship of their children. Although husbands' legal obligations to support their wives, the law of dower (the minimal right of a widow to a life interest in her husband's estate), and equity rulings tempered women's common law status to a certain extent, this status, combined with women's political powerlessness, remained the law of the land until well after the Revolution.

This simple truth is more complex than it might seem at first, for colonies differed in the extent to which they sought to enforce the common law ideal. Marylynn Salmon has noted, "rather than offering only mouth service to the patriarchal ideal, the Puritans created a social and legal system in America that personified it"; in other words, the Puritan legal system did not merely reflect certain abstract ideals; it was the mechanism by which these ideals were expressed as practical realities. In strict conformity with the tradition of marital unity, New Englanders insisted on clear patriarchal control over property; in Connecticut, until 1723, a husband could control absolutely all of his wife's property, even, as the statutes about widows made clear, after his death. In contrast, in the southern colonies, with their greatly skewed sex ratio, laws to protect women from coercion remained strong; women in those colonies could not easily forfeit their control over inherited property or their dower rights. Yet in all colonies wives had extremely limited access to property. There were also differences among the colonies in matters of divorce. Only Massachusetts and Connecticut, which viewed marriage as a civil contract rather than as an inviolable sacrament, allowed absolute divorce, thus permitting the "innocent party" to remarry.

This said, the common law understanding of feme covert status was largely an abstract "ideal"; its practical consequences were mitigated in part by special contracts for separate estates under equity, a distinct system of civil law, which was inherited from English tradition. Even colonial legislators, when confronted with the absence of male spousal support, occasionally recognized that common law disabilities severely limited married women in certain circumstances—and that the law threatened the community with the real possibility of having to support such women. In 1718 in Pennsylvania, "An Act Concerning Feme Sole Traders" declared that "where any mariners and others are gone . . . to sea, leaving their wives at shopkeeping, or to work for their livelihood at any other trade in this province, all such wives shall be deemed, adjudged and taken, and are hereby declared to be, as feme sole traders. . . ." In 1744 the South Carolina legislature similarly protected married women who acted as sole traders, and thereby protected their *creditors,* who might otherwise be defrauded as a result of the women's coverture. (South Carolina legislators were still trying to control frauds perpetrated by married women acting as sole traders eighty years later, when they passed a law in 1823 detailing how a married woman must publish her intention to operate as a sole trader.) Increasingly, as courts gradually expanded women's control over settlement property, legislators began to accept and ratify wives' independent activity.

In addition to passing laws about free families, legislators enacted their beliefs about gender and sexuality into laws intended to control unfree labor. In 1705, for example, Virginia passed its laws on "bastardy," declaring that women servants who bore a child would "repay" their master with an extra year of indenture, unless the master were the father, in which case the woman owed a year of work to the community. If any white woman, free or indentured, had a child with a black man, the punishment was more extreme, ranging from fines to banishment from the colony to incarceration; the child of a free white woman and a black man was bound out as a servant until age thirty-one.

In the colonial South, laws about sexuality were inextricably tied to laws that institutionalized racial control in the emerging slave system. As early as 1662, with Virginia's first law stating that children's status—whether slave or free—followed the mother's legal status, legislators implicitly condoned white men's sexual exploitation of their black female slaves and placed under the control of the slave system their mixed-race children. At the same time, colonial governments sought to restrict fornication (nonmarital heterosexual relations) between consenting adults of different races, applying stricter consequences for those convicted under these circumstances. Significantly, legislatures reserved their most severe, and uniquely American, noncapital punishment— castration—for the rarest of crimes: rapes by black men of white women.

Anxiety over interracial sex—and, more strikingly, interracial marriage—persisted in the nation's laws. Legal bars to interracial marriage emerged first in Maryland in 1661, in Virginia in 1705. By the first half of the eighteenth century, every southern colony, and Massachusetts and Pennsylvania as well, had barred interracial marriage and proscribed interracial sex (what became known by 1864 as "miscegenation").

Intense anxiety about interracial sex outlived slavery, however, and seems to have followed periods of widespread popular alarm over changing moral standards; the persistence of legislation proscribing the practice reflects the ongoing interconnectedness of racial and sexual control. Between 1880 and 1920, for example, twenty states and territories strengthened or added antimiscegenation laws. As Peggy Pascoe has shown, the laws against interracial marriage underscore the extreme attention legislators paid to a fairly rare practice in order to regulate sexuality and control race relations. Although legislators attacked both interracial sex and interracial marriage, the latter drew the strongest prohibitions, most elaborately articulated in the West, where a complicated system of categorization of "race"— including Chinese, Japanese, Filipino, Hawaiians, Hindus, Native Americans, Mongolians, and others—expressed white Americans' anxieties over the complex interrelation of their age's racial and sexual issues. It was not until 1967 that the Supreme Court prohibited such laws.

## THE IMPACT OF REVOLUTION

American independence had little effect on the legal status of free white women and virtually none on women who remained enslaved. The new nation upheld feme covert status for married women and denied citizenship to all women. Indeed, some unmarried women with property *had* voted in the early years after the Revolution but lost that right with the advent of white manhood suffrage; in 1807, New Jersey legislators inserted the word "male" into the new state constitution, making that state the last to rescind propertied women's voting privileges.

Other changes did occur; with the decisive collapse of primogeniture (inheritance of the father's estate by the eldest son), daughters gained increased property rights vis-à-vis their brothers, while widows may have lost some rights with the decline of dower. Dissolving a marriage became simpler after the Revolution, for all the new states except for South Carolina liberalized their divorce laws. Pennsylvania, for example, ruled in 1785 that the "innocent and injured person" might obtain a separation "not only from bed and board, but also [an outright divorce] from the bond of matrimony itself" provided that the complaint was "not made out of levity, or by collusion between said the husband and wife, and for the mere purpose of being freed and separated from each other." In general, states permitted divorces for adultery and often for impotence, bigamy, and desertion. Absolute divorce also ended the husband's obligation to support his wife; women, not surprisingly, tended to sue for divorces that would allow them to get support but weren't absolute. Although these statutes may have simply formalized traditional practices under equity, these changes overall reflected the growing acceptance of New England's view of marriage as a civil contract.

## THE NINETEENTH CENTURY: WOMEN'S VOICES, WOMEN'S VOTES

The early nineteenth century saw a fundamental shift in the relationship of white, middle-class women to legislatures. With the advent of men's mass electoral activity, women's organized benevolent activity, and especially the antislavery movement, women increasingly turned to petitioning as the tool most available to the disenfranchised. Petitioning legislators reflected a different form of "influence" from that previously ascribed to women; it represented the onset of women's mass politics and their growing understanding of the centrality of legislative change. Indeed, the assumption that progressive legal change occurs through judicial initiative is a relatively recent one; throughout the nineteenth century it was state legislatures that most often provided an avenue through which white women could address their concerns.

Property—its ownership, use, and inheritance—continued to concern legislatures throughout the post-Revolutionary period, and it was by petitioning for changes in property laws that women first entered legislative halls on their own behalf. As stated earlier, under the common law doctrine of coverture, women lost control of their property, whether inherited or earned, when they married. In a number of ways, the common law tradition—and the cumbersome equity process by which propertied individuals could circumvent it—was anachronistic by the early nineteenth century. As legal scholar Deborah Rhode has noted, "the legal disabilities of married women . . . impeded

land and credit transactions. . . . Married women's statutes were a means of regularizing equitable principles and extending them to the general public" (pp. 24–26). With the codification of American law in the early nineteenth century came the first small steps toward expanding women's property rights.

The first, rather tentative Married Women's Property Act was passed in Mississippi in 1839, but it is the history of the acts in New York that most clearly shows women's early involvement with state legislatures. Beginning in 1836, when six women signed a petition for a law protecting married women's separate property, an increasing number of women and men, including the bill's original sponsor, freethinker Thomas Herttell, pressured the legislature to pass such a bill. It took twelve years until the Married Women's Property Act passed in New York, declaring that "the real and personal property of any female who may hereafter marry, and which she shall own at the time of marriage . . . shall continue her sole and separate property, as if she were a single female" (quoted in Basch, p. 233). (Other states followed suit, although the Connecticut legislature waited until 1877 to do so.) The final version of the law was the result not so much of feminist agitation as of a recognition among legislators that a father's wealth might be protected from sons-in-law, and debtors would be protected from creditors by keeping married women's wealth separate. The Married Women's Property Acts were therefore the result of several forces: the move toward regulating and codifying equity practices that had been the province of the wealthy, the needs of the expanding market economy, debtor-protection laws, and the emergence of American voices on behalf of women's rights.

To early woman's rights activists such as Ernestine Rose and Elizabeth Cady Stanton, the passage of the Married Women's Property Acts signaled wealthy men's efforts to protect their daughters' inheritance as well as the "emancipat[ion] [of] wives from the slavery of the old common law of England . . ." (Stanton, et al., vol. 1, p. 63). Many women petitioners understood the limitations of a revolution that denied all citizens their rights, and they warned that since women's consent had never been sought in the current government, "it is evident that in justice no allegiance can be claimed for them" (quoted in Basch, p. 156). Thus armed with Republican rhetoric ("Is the principle of taxation without representation less oppressive and tyrannical, than when our fathers expended their blood and treasure, rather than submit to its injustice?" asked an Ohio memorialist [quoted in Stanton et al., vol. 1, p. 109]), women began to speak to legislatures directly about their legal disabilities in general and about married women's problems under coverture in particular. Legislators' responses were less than respectful; in 1854, Stanton addressed a joint judiciary committee of the New York legislature, the first woman to do so in that state. The committee report was argued by the "married gentlemen" of the committee (the bachelors, "with becoming diffidence," and a need still to gain "the favors of the gentler sex," had excused themselves), and it considered Stanton's carefully reasoned arguments in favor of a broad legislative program of women's rights to be absurd. Questioning the masculinity of those men whose names appeared alongside their wives', the committee report suggested, in a tone that would become characteristic of many legislative remarks about women, that the petitioners "apply for a law authorizing them to change dresses" (quoted in Flexner, pp. 87–88).

However, legislative opinion did change, as did that of the voters. In 1860, having again been addressed by Stanton in a joint session of both houses, the legislators of New York granted married women the right, in addition to owning property (a right granted in 1848), to keep "that which she acquires by her trade, business, labor or services, carried on or performed on her sole or separate account" (quoted in Basch, p. 234), to sue in court, and to have other protections similar to those of men. Furthermore, reflecting society's growing glorification of motherhood, women gained joint guardianship of their children. Twenty-nine states had passed some married women's property legislation by 1865.

Legislators heard increasingly from women on a wide range of issues. Women drew on religious, domestic, and republican rhetoric to petition state and federal legislatures on matters ranging from antislavery to temperance to working conditions to suffrage. Sometimes they spoke to legislators directly, as in the case of an early Investigation of Labor Conditions by the Massachusetts House of Representatives in the spring of 1845. There, a special committee, faced with over two thousand signatures protesting the hours of labor in the textile mills, heard from young female laborers about their employment. Aside from providing the historian with a vivid look at the conditions under which young women labored in the early industrial revolution, the report testifies to the women's rather naive faith in the legislative hearing—a faith that lessened when the committee concluded that no restriction of the hours of labor was justified, and that, although some abuses no doubt existed, it was better in a free market to trust to "the progressive improvement in art and science, in a higher appreciation of man's destiny, in less love for money and a more ardent love for social happiness and intellectual superiority for a remedy" (quoted in Wortman, ed., p. 231).

Although Congress occasionally debated women's right to petition at all (most notably when faced with antislavery petitions), state legislators were generally willing to respond sympathetically to the concerns of women whose causes seemed to accord with their own concerns. In a society that understood gender roles to be profoundly divided and fundamental to people's identity, legislators expressed some willingness to accede to women who demanded change "as mothers," especially regarding sexual matters. When, for example, middle-class moral reformers asked legislators to take children from "dissipated and vicious parents" and to place them in their own benevolent hands, legislators did so. And it was with a swell of popular, middle-class support that Massachusetts and New York passed legislation in the 1840s that allowed single women (significantly, of "previous chaste character") to sue their seducers. In New York, in 1848, the year the law passed, the "lady managers" of the Female Moral Reform Society made "repeated visits to Albany" until they achieved various legislative goals, including a corporate charter for their organization. Through the next decade they continued to lobby a supportive legislature for financial assistance, insisting throughout that their activity had been pursued "discreetly" and "with scrupulous regard to woman's sphere." Although moral reformers were occasionally subjected to "those licentious insinuations with which . . . legislative bodies never fail to greet petitions from women, upon the subject of marriage, or of crimes against their sex," legislators were somewhat more willing to view women's concerns about sexual behavior through the prism of "domestic," rather than partisan, interest. In 1842, when more than one thousand Ohio women petitioned for laws punishing adultery, a legislative committee warned that "no question about the propriety of the interference of women in these affairs will justify the slightest levity toward the petitioners."

Throughout the nineteenth century, most women remained reluctant to demand a vote for themselves. Still, growing numbers sought legislative solutions to a wide range of social problems. Temperance reformers, for instance, appealed increasingly for legislative aid as midcentury approached. By the 1850s, the so-called Maine law (abolishing liquor sales in that state as of 1851) had drawn many women toward legislative solutions. Many of these women would increasingly recognize the limitations of their political work and would demand suffrage after the Civil War. It is no coincidence that when the Woman's Christian Temperance Union, the largest women's organization of its time, organized in 1874, it did so by congressional district, and replaced the once-ubiquitous "temperance pledge" with a "voters' pledge," signaling the increasingly political aspect of a work once considered exclusively "moral." Indeed, by the late nineteenth century, temperance legislation—and the related laws criminalizing wife beating—were viewed by both friends and foes as the central "woman's issues" of their time.

Not surprisingly, over the course of the antebellum period, women reformers—those involved in temperance, moral reform, and antislavery in particular—developed a more acute sense of the importance of electoral change. Although most continued to believe that a moral position superseded electoral victories, many came to feel, as a Wisconsin legislative committee report on woman suffrage put it, that "there is *no reality in any power that can not be coined into votes*" (quoted in Stanton, et al., vol. 1, p. 868).

It was with this emerging recognition of the frustrations of votelessness in an electoral age that in 1848 a few women organized a convention at Seneca Falls, New York, at which they boldly demanded suffrage as a right of free citizens. The convention's "Declaration of Sentiments" stressed that "the law, in all cases, [goes] upon a false supposition of the supremacy of man." It left no doubt that the women were living in a legislative age, and that they demanded legislated solutions.

The history of the movement that emerged from the convention is well known. Although historians have tended to focus on the achievement of the Nineteenth Amendment as suffragists' only victory, the history of women's access to legislatures is longer and more complex. It is, to a certain extent, a history of legislative disappointments; most notable among them was that of woman's rights leaders after the Civil War when, in the face of congressional hostility (and Republican party priorities), they were forced to choose between black male suffrage and universal suffrage—a choice that split the movement for decades to come (and which saw the introduction of the word "male" to the U.S. Constitution). Some suffragists, frustrated by their experience with the federal government, soon turned to activism on behalf of partial suffrage (whether permitting women to vote on certain *issues* or granting the vote only to particular *women*); through the 1870s and 1880s, this more moderate demand resulted in school board suffrage, temperance suffrage, and/or suffrage for women with property from many munipalities and nineteen states. In 1869, Wyoming became the first territory to grant full woman suffrage (and to permit women to serve on juries), followed by the territory of Utah (1870). From 1870–1910, there were 480 campaigns in thirty-three states just to get the issue of woman suffrage submitted to voters; seventeen resulted in referenda, although only two (Colorado in 1893, and Idaho in 1896) were successful.

Congress moved far more slowly than the western states in granting woman suffrage. A woman suffrage amendment was first introduced to that body in 1868, but ten years passed before the bill whose exact wording would become the Nineteenth Amendment was proposed. In 1882 both houses appointed select committees on woman suffrage; both reported on the measure favorably. In the winter of 1886–1887 the bill was discussed on the Senate floor, where, as was characteristic of debates over women's rights, legislators expressed more about their own fears than about the issue at hand; much of the opposition focused on their dread of black women voting in the South, the threatened end of American femininity, and the warning that American women would descend to the "bloodthirsty mobs" that characterized the French Revolution. The amendment was introduced in nearly every session until 1896, when it disappeared from the agenda until 1913.

After 1911, though, pressure began to mount again, and public opinion became increasingly clear to legislators. With a victory in California that year, the voting states in the West now numbered six. In early 1917, seven states granted woman suffrage (including Arkansas, thereby breaching the antisuffrage south). In New York, with the decision of the Democratic machine to bow to the strongly prowoman suffrage wishes of immigrant and working-class voters, the referendum passed. On 10 January 1918, the House voted 274–136 in favor of the federal amendment, exactly the two-thirds needed. "The New York delegation of more than forty representatives, with a stinging mandate from its constituents fresh in mind, voted in favor, with only four exceptions." Nay votes came from the South and from "the still unregenerate and largely industrial states of Massachusetts, Pennsylvania, New Jersey, and Ohio" (Flexner, pp. 292–293). Still, the Senate came up one vote short in 1918 and again in early 1919, with many of the "no" votes coming from senators whose state legislatures had explicitly asked them to pass it. In June 1919 the amendment finally passed. Three states (Wisconsin, Illinois, and Michigan) ratified the amendment that same day; passage was not complete, however, until August 1920.

The history of the suffrage movement is not, however, one simply of male legislators moving inexorably, if sluggishly, toward what now seems an unquestionable position; it is also very much the story of the most sustained lobbying effort on behalf of Americans who were excluded from electoral politics. As Carrie Chapman Catt, the onetime president of the National American Woman's Suffrage Association, put it

> To get the word "male" in effect out of the Constitution cost the women of the country fifty-two years of pauseless campaign. During that time they were forced to conduct fifty-six campaigns of referenda to male voters; 480 campaigns to get legislatures to submit suffrage amendments to voters; 47 campaigns to get State constitutional conventions to write woman suffrage into state constitutions; 277 campaigns to get State party conventions to include woman suffrage planks; 30 campaigns to get presidential party conventions to adopt woman suffrage planks in party platforms, and 19 campaigns with 19 successive Congresses. (quoted in Flexner, p. 173)

## WOMEN AS CITIZENS, WOMEN AS WORKERS

Issues of property and citizenship for women came together in the early twentieth century around the question of regulating women's paid labor. As a growing number of women—mostly young, unmarried immigrants—entered the industrial labor force at the end of the nineteenth century, their working conditions and organizing efforts gradually brought about the passage of "protective" legislation, which regulated their working hours, physical conditions, and, less frequently, wages. (Such legislative efforts never touched on the working conditions experienced by African American women, though, whose agricultural and domestic work remained the lowest paid and least subject to any legislative protection.) In addition to bringing to public attention the harsh conditions faced by many industrial workers, protective legislation exemplified what would become an ongoing debate among feminists: whether legislation should "protect" women who suffered from the differences between the sexes or whether so recognizing women's "double burden" merely reinforced sexual inequality.

Sanctioned by the Supreme Court's 1908 ruling in *Muller* v. *Oregon,* the allied forces of the Women's Trade Union League, the National Consumers' League, and working-class women themselves brought about the passage of protective legislation and/or minimum wage laws for women in nineteen states. (Legislators were far more reluctant to regulate wages than hours, arguing as had earlier opponents of the ten-hour day, that market forces must not be impeded; to the extent that they resolved this in favor of minimum wage laws, Alice Kessler-Harris argues, they did so by exaggerating women's weakness and therefore their inability to bargain effectively.) Reflecting Progressive era assumptions that the state bears some responsibility for preventing starvation, such laws were intended, as the District of Columbia act noted, "to protect women and minors from conditions destrimental to their health and morals, resulting from wages which are inadequate to maintain decent standards of living" (quoted in Kessler-Harris, p. 35). According to the logic behind making such laws gender specific, lengthy working hours in industry posed a special danger to "childbirth and female functions."

The support for these "protective" laws among most women's rights activists and union members (female and male) suggests that such laws seemed to promise short-term alleviation from the double work load and specific hardships of wage-earning women. As Deborah Rhode put it, "the issue was whether women would gain more by recognition of their equal entitlements or their different needs, and whether emphasis on securing formal rights was adequately responsive to social realities" (p. 35). Indeed, some feminists argued at that time that women's labor laws were needed to remove women's economic disabilities which prevented women and men from being treated equally. Only when it became apparent that unions and employers would use such laws to prevent women from filling "men's jobs" (and when factory owners were pressured to improve industrial working conditions for men as well) did feminists demand that legislators approve the gender-neutral Equal Rights Amendment for a solution to workplace inequities. And it was not until the 1970s that labor unions followed suit.

Legislative efforts—and feminist lobbying—on behalf of women, defined through their traditional roles as wives and mothers, peaked with Congress's passage of the Sheppard-Towner Maternity and Infant Protection Act in 1921, one year after woman suffrage became the law of the land. The act was intended to improve maternal and infant health through federal subsidies of health education; in its very conception, it went against the concept of legal gender-neutrality that would gain ground in the 1960s and 1970s. In the meantime, for most feminists, socialists, and other progressives, any legislation that defined women as a group with specific needs seemed more appropriate than the blanket Equal Rights Amendment, which was supported only by a small group of elite and professional women.

While wage-earning women and their advocates directed most of their lobbying efforts at improved working and health conditions, legislatures, backed by both female and male "purity reformers," expressed their distress about laboring women by focusing on sex, especially prostitution. Throughout much of American history, legislators had paid little explicit attention to this common form of female labor and sexual exploitation, preferring instead, generally, to legislate their concern about "nightwalkers" in terms of vagrancy and public order. By the post–Civil War period, however, public anxiety over prostitution and the possibilities of legislating morality led to the enactment of municipal codes to regulate dance halls, brothels, and solicitation "on the public streets." Following efforts by self-proclaimed purity (anti-prostitution) reformers, by 1917 thirty-one states had passed some form of the so-called Iowa Abatement Act (1909), which closed red-light districts by regulating the use of private property. Congress's adoption of the Mann Act in 1910, which prohibited the interstate transport of women "for immoral purposes," further highlighted legislators' awareness of public hysteria over the rumored "white slave trade."

Through their efforts either to regulate or to abolish prostitution, state and municipal governments closely linked sexual, race, and class issues, associating degeneracy with poverty and passing laws that tried to control the sexual behavior of the poor. By 1913, for example, twelve states had passed laws that permitted the sterilization of "criminals, idiots, the feeble-minded, imbeciles, syphilitics, moral and sexual perverts, epileptics, and rapists." With the advent of World War I, the federal government moved into the business of "social hygiene" with an increasing willingness to regulate sexual behavior and sexual morality through federal legislation.

## THE MIDDLE TWENTIETH CENTURY

By the 1920s, white women looked upon the legislative system through the eyes of nearly full citizens; northern black women, too, increasingly turned to electoral politics to express their hopes and concerns. In 1924 the League of Women Voters surveyed the legal status of women in the United States and found that in most states women had the right of contract, even though great inequalities in wives' rights to family income, right to choose the family home, or jointly head the family remained. In many cases, husbands had far greater control over supposedly joint property than did wives. Furthermore, as the report noted, "in no state may a wife collect for services performed in the home" (quoted in Wortman, ed., p. 377).

In custody arrangements, the situation was less bleak for advocates of maternal prerogatives. Thirty-seven states had passed equal guardianship laws, replacing older laws that gave preference to paternal custody. And in twenty-one states women were permitted to serve as jurors—a major victory for suffrage advocates. (Still, as late as 1942, only twenty-eight states permitted women to serve as jurors; it was not until 1975 that all states were forced by the Supreme Court to accept women on juries.)

However, the depression of the 1930s demonstrated how tenuous were women's gains, even as it revealed legislators' reluctance to pass drastic legislation in the face of a popular panic. Although the hard-won rights of citizenship were never revoked, women's position in the paid labor force came under attack, as did any concern with women's legal equality. Indeed, much New Deal legislation institutionalized traditional conceptions of sex roles (as it did of racial hierarchies)—married women's economic dependence on wage-earning husbands was presumed to be both an accurate and a preferred depiction of reality. As women's status in professional occupations dropped, and as white married women increasingly entered the labor force, legislators grappled with their (seemingly contradictory) beliefs in a free labor market and in an extremely gendered understanding of labor and family. The mandate from the American public was clear; a 1936 poll showed that 82 percent of Americans believed that if a husband had a job, his wife should be discriminated against in employment. That same year, *Fortune* magazine found that 85 percent of men and 79 percent of women thought that no wife (even if her husband were unemployed) should receive wages. Legislators responded quickly to this rare evidence of public agreement. On the federal level, Section 232 of the 1932 National Economy Act, the "married persons clause," mandated that federally employed spouses of government employees lose their jobs. State legislators, arguing that wage-earning wives failed to fulfill their social obligations as mothers when they competed with men for scarce employment (New York Assemblyman Arthur Swartz called them "undeserving 'parasites'" [quoted in Scharf, p. 45]), also considered a variety of acts that would prohibit the wives of employed men from keeping their own jobs. At the start of the 1939 legislative sessions, twenty-six state legislatures prepared to debate "married persons clauses." Opposition from the Federation of Business and Professional Women's Clubs, the YWCA, and the League of Women Voters stopped the laws' passage, but ongoing hostility restricted women's employment and salaries in government, teaching, and other white-collar occupations. National Woman's Party leader Gail Laughlin noted that, during a depression, "the first impulse seems to be to 'wallop the ladies'" (quoted in Scharf, p. 47).

## THE 1960s AND BEYOND: ATTEMPTING EQUALITY

From the passage of suffrage in 1920 to the 1960s, there was virtually no congressional legislation that addressed sexual equality per se, even though the focus of legislation had shifted in many other respects to the national arena. On both state and national levels, a legacy of unequal legislation remained, however much the conditions that spurred it were changed. In 1960, thirty-nine of forty-two state statutes that restricted working hours applied only to women; nineteen states had gender-specific night-work rules. About half of the states had minimum wage laws, but only four applied equally to men. Using language about health and morals, states banned women from employment in bars, shoeshining, legislative services, and the legal profession. In some cases, in the decades before the reemergence of feminism in the mid-1960s, state legislatures acted to correct obvious anachronisms in the law. These changes, which occurred with little fanfare, hinted at a far more sweeping transformation of American law yet to come.

The years from 1963 to the present have seen an explosion of legislative enactments on a wide range of gender issues—as well as a concomitant rise in women's participation in all levels of political activism. Although some laws were passed before the rise of the second wave of feminism—and others with little feminist action or intent—the changes in American law in the past thirty years can only be understood in the context of both the expansion of women's wage-earning and their role in raising feminist concerns. If the feminist insight that the "personal is political" cannot claim credit for every legislative foray into new domains, it nevertheless legitimized and expanded these excursions.

The concept of gender neutrality shaped important state and federal legislation in the 1960s. By the early 1960s, after years of Congressional debate and inaction, a growing national consensus on "equal pay for equal work" had become impossible to ignore. The issue of pay inequities was resolved on the national level with the Equal Pay Act of 1963. Although a similar bill, which included the controversial "comparable worth" standard (guaranteeing equal pay for work of equal value), was first proposed immediately after World War II, it took several decades—and the passage of equal pay legislation by sixteen states by 1955—to achieve congressional passage. Government policy now prohibited employers from offering women lower wages than those offered men for the same work.

But it was a quirk of legislative bickering that led to the broadest change in the legal status of women's employment. The addition of the word "sex" to Title VII of the 1964 Civil Rights Act—which the *New York Times* referred to only as one among the "unexpected amendments" that the civil rights forces had to accept, and the *Congressional Quarterly Weekly Report* barely mentioned—was proposed as a joking effort by those opposed to racial equality in hiring. However, it established the legal mechanism by which women could sue (namely, the Equal Employment Opportunity Commission) and raised both the federal and state governments' awareness of the extent of sex discrimination in the workplace. By 1969, all fifty states had created commissions to study women's status in the law. In many cases, the state laws that resulted are broader than the federal Title VII; for example, of the thirty-nine states with equal-pay laws, fifteen specifically refer to "comparable" work (although much of this language has been disregarded thus far). Later efforts to gain comparable worth standards in state legislation achieved some success, reflecting a growing sense that job market segregation is structural rather than a matter of individual "choice." In addition, with the addition in 1972 of Title IX to the Civil Rights Act, the government put its weight behind the enforcement of nondiscrimination in education as well—at least in theory.

Most important to the advocates of gender neutrality in law was the Equal Rights Amendment, a constitutional measure that "would ensure that 'Equality of rights under the law shall not be denied or abridged . . . on account of sex.'" Introduced in 1923, the ERA had gained enough popular support to pass Congress in 1972. Within months, twenty state legislatures had ratified it. However, amidst a nationally organized and hugely emotional battle over issues that were largely symbolic, fifteen states, mostly but not entirely southern, never endorsed the measure, and five tried to rescind; between Indiana's ratification vote in January 1977 and the congressionally imposed deadline in 1982, no state ratified the measure. However, state legislators saw ERA—as for instance another sign of their declining status vis-à-vis the federal government—the amendment's defeat signaled that core conservative attitudes about women, family, and sexuality had won out. Nevertheless, sixteen states passed their own constitutional prohibitions against sex discrimination. And in North Carolina (home of Democratic Senator Sam Ervin, the ERA's main opponent), by 1979 thirty-three pieces of legislation dealing with sex discrimination had been discussed in the assembly; nineteen were enacted, and eight others were amended to delete sexist language.

The concept of gender neutrality also framed various pieces of legislation about domestic concerns which gained pace through the 1960s and 1970s—in some cases prior to the re-emergence of feminist activism on those same issues. Divorce reform is a significant example, for, as Deborah Rhode notes, "policies concerning marital dissolution have always given important signals about gender roles and cultural priorities" (p. 49). While the differences among the state laws varied wildly (in New York, for example, adultery was the only ground for divorce until 1966), in following decades a number of states established gender-neutral family laws (including those involving alimony, child custody, and the ages of marriage and of consent). Divorce law changed dramatically, as every state moved toward more lenient regulations; some, beginning with California in 1970, established no-fault divorce, which shifted legislation from moral questions about family dissolution to economic questions about support and autonomy. By the early 1980s, two-thirds of the states had some kind of joint custody legislation. Ironically, these gender-neutral laws may actually have penalized some women, who tended as a result of their economic dependence on men to have less bargaining power in a divorce, and for whom less contentious divorces may have meant diminished alimony, child support, and long-term financial settlements. In addition, the "best interests of the child" standard, which replaced the onetime feminist ideal of maternal preference with gender-neutral criteria for child custody, has meant that increasing numbers of women have had either to fight for custody or to relinquish financial support in order to prevent such a battle.

In the early 1970s, some state legislatures dealt with entire packages of feminist-sponsored bills, which covered a range of issues—for example, the sexist content of textbooks, child care in state universities, and equalizing the proportions of men and women in various schools and places of employment. Yet on both the state and federal levels, much legislation with unambiguous feminist intent continued to fail or to be vetoed. Karen DeCrow notes that in 1971–1972 almost one hundred bills were introduced into Congress that would have, in her view, benefited women; all but eight died. One of the eight, a compre-hensive child care bill, was vetoed by President Richard Nixon, who argued that day care ran counter to the stated goal of the federal government to "bring the family together." The Ninety-third Congress (1973–1975) did pass a number of important bills intended to ameliorate discrimination against women, notably the Equal Credit Opportunity Act, the Women's Educational Equity Act, and the creation of the National Center for the Control and Prevention of Rape; however, much more progressive action occurred in these same years by dint of the case law developed by the Supreme Court under Chief Justice Warren Burger.

In some cases, notably in the laws about rape and sexual harassment, feminist lobbying provoked major changes on the state level. By advocating a liberal legal framework that understood rape as a crime of *violence* as opposed to a matter of sexual behavior, feminists were successful in convincing about half the state legislatures to revoke the common law definition of rape as simply "illicit carnal knowledge of a female by force and against her will" and adopted a definition based on sexual assault and battery. The 1974 Michigan law, which is seen by many as a model criminal sexual conduct statute, defines rape in gender-neutral terms and includes degrees of assault along a spectrum of violent acts; it further prohibits defense attorneys from inquiring into victims' sexual pasts, repeals arbitrary and extreme standards for resistance and consent, and extends the law's protection to male victims of sexual violence. Similarly, many states passed rape shield laws, which were intended to protect the victim from additional intrusion into her personal life. Some feminists have become increasingly critical of the liberal approach to legal reform, though. Defining rape exclusively as a violent, rather than a sexual crime, for example, may explain legislators' reluctance to abolish the marital exemption in rape laws; as of 1985, twenty-seven states still did not permit the prosecution of a husband for raping his wife. More broadly, the revised rape statutes have failed to prevent courts from blaming women for rape; the doctrine of consent has not erased from legal practice ancient prejudices about women and sexual violence. Although new statutes against rape, sexual harassment, and wife beating provide examples of the ways in which the law has "validated women's sense of violation," it is the reality of prosecution, more than the statutes themselves, that has limited feminist successes in the area of sexual exploitation and violence.

The election of Ronald Reagan in 1980 signaled a new era of federal government, one that would actively undermine women's gains over the previous decades. In addition to its conservative, "profamily" program against women's rights, reproductive freedom, gay and lesbian rights, and other progressive causes, the federal government also scaled down the New Deal social welfare programs that disproportionately assisted women and children. Funding became a major issue for those who wished to restrict abortions, further limiting lower-income women's alternatives; with its passage of the so-called Hyde Amendments (1977–1980), which denied federal funding to poor women who wanted abortions, Congress had already made clear its intention to use its funding power to enter national debates about appropriate sexual and reproductive behavior. Although Congress tried to modify some of its own more restrictive abortion and civil rights laws during the administration of George Bush, his insistent use of the veto sustained the conservative character of the Reagan years in virtually all areas of feminist concern, including abortion funding and parental leave, as well as amendments to, and enforcement of, the Civil Rights Act. Legal remedies seemed few and far between, although innovations in this regard included the 1984 Child Support Enforcement Amendments and the Family Support Act of 1988, which required state cooperation in wage withholding from fathers who are delinquent in child support payments. More recent proposals included the Women's Health Equity Act of 1991, which sought to redress the gender imbalance in health research and treatment.

Feminists were frustrated by the increasingly conservative turn taken by the very federal government in which they had placed their hopes for change in the 1960s and 1970s; as a result, they turned again to the state legislatures and the courts for redress. By the 1990s, state legislative attention to women's issues had expanded exponentially, although not necessarily in coherent or progressive ways—and with few feminist victories. The Winter 1992 issue of just one state's (Pennsylvania's) legislative report, *Womenews,* described legislation then under consideration ranging from funding for abortion, to grading offenses of prostitution, to sexual harassment and family leave, to a proposal to honor women in the military. The list demonstrated both the greater focus by women on local legislative bodies and the perception that, despite vocal right-wing and religious women's organizations, a large number of women continued to identify with progressive causes.

## REGULATING SEX

Throughout American history, the issues of sexuality and sexual behavior have fallen within the purview of state legislatures; Congress has been willing to regulate such matters only through its powers to regulate interstate commerce and immigration—and even then reluctantly, at least until the 1950s. Although sexuality has generally been categorized as a "private" matter, governments have over time nevertheless addressed wide-ranging social concerns through their promotion and restriction of certain forms of sexual behavior, expression, and identity. Laws about sexual behavior—which range from colonial sodomy and fornication laws, to vagrancy laws intended to control prostitution, to laws against birth control, abortion, "obscenity," and childhood sexual behavior—have reflected American society's fluctuating and inconsistent views of sexuality and gender, and of women themselves. As Leo Kanowitz put it in 1969, "in sexual matters, the law, as does society at large, often appears ambivalent, vacillating between a view of woman as an object to be protected . . . and an object of scorn, distrust and aversion" (p. 201).

A law that passed Congress (with little debate) in 1873 to suppress "immoral" literature from flowing through the U.S. mail set the tone for much of the political regulation of sexuality in the late nineteenth and early twentieth centuries. The so-called Comstock Law—named for postmaster and anti-vice crusader Anthony Comstock—included in its purview "any obscene book, pamphlet, paper, writing, advertisement, circular . . . or other article of an immoral nature, or any drug or medicine, or any article, whatever, for the prevention of conception, or for causing unlawful abortion, or shall advertise the same for sale." This was the single greatest victory of the social purity movement of the late nineteenth century; along with other obscenity laws that the Social Purity Alliance persuaded twenty-two state legislatures to enact, it remained for decades to come the most severe impediment to the dissemination of birth control and other sexual information.

Laws directed against providing information about sex and reproduction have little to do with concerns about the U.S. mail; rather, they underscore popular opinion about sexual matters and demonstrate legislators' willingness to express these widespread anxieties through regulations regarding sexual behavior. More than other kinds of legislation, these laws have been unenforceable—indeed, enforcement may never have been the issue. As in the case of statutes forbidding interracial marriage, laws regulating sexual behavior often seem to be entirely out of proportion to the incidence of the proscribed behavior. Part of a larger effort to define women's and men's (and, as we have seen, blacks' and whites') roles in society, "moral panics" about sexuality seem to fuel legislators' concerns about the state of family life and American virtue. The proposed federal Family Protection Acts of 1979 and 1981, for instance, would have banned federal funds for school materials that could "denigrate, diminish, or deny the role of the sexes as it has been historically understood in the United States."

Legislative activity in several areas highlights these concerns among voters and, therefore, legislators—namely, abortion, gay and lesbian rights, teenage sexual behavior, and pornography. All have raised fundamental questions about the relationship between public power and "privacy," sexual expression and the state, morality and politics. All demonstrate the range of views among women themselves, including many powerful voices claiming, in quite contradictory ways, to represent women's best interests. These debates reveal the enduring tension between gender equality and gender difference, between women's right to personal autonomy and their all-too-frequent experience as victims in need of the law's protection.

The history of abortion law offers an important lesson on how anxieties about sexual behavior are written into law—and, indeed, how legislatures have shaped the law to reflect

public attention to previously "private" concerns. Over the course of the nineteenth century, as the practice of birth control became more common and accepted, abortion became increasingly associated with "deviant" sexuality. Although it took some time for the laws on birth control to catch up with public realities (not until 1965, in *Griswold* v. *Connecticut,* did the Supreme Court prevent states from prohibiting married couples from using it), the laws regulating abortion moved ahead of changing practices in a prescriptive—and, for a time, largely successful—fashion.

In 1800 no jurisdiction had enacted any statutes on abortion. Throughout the 1830s and 1840s, middle-class women commonly turned to abortion for an end to early pregnancy; to the extent that any concept of a fetus existed, it was not recognized until the woman experienced "quickening," or movement, usually around the fourth month of pregnancy. In 1821, members of the General Assembly of Connecticut first passed a revised Crimes and Punishments law, which provided up to life imprisonment for causing an abortion; other states soon followed. An 1828 New York criminal code, which banned abortion after quickening, actually legalized therapeutic abortion, that is, abortion to preserve the woman's life, thus establishing in law the priority of the woman's health. As the preeminent historian of abortion, James Mohr, writes, these laws were passed in the context of criminal codes and laws about medical regulation, not out of a specific concern for abortion itself; he notes, "no legislator took a political stand on abortion; no legislator cast a recorded vote for or against abortion as a question by itself" (p. 42).

Through the 1840s and 1850s, states began to legislate more specifically against abortion. The American Medical Association (AMA), founded in 1847, led the battle for more restrictive laws, such as New York's in 1845, laws that increasingly held women responsible for an act now defined as criminal. At the same time, the AMA—with the assistance by the 1870s of Anthony Comstock—sought to redirect public opinion toward its view that abortion was a crime perpetrated by untrained quacks. In addition, they lobbied successfully to challenge the quickening doctrine; in 1869, New York established a new pattern by removing quickening—and, in fact, proof of pregnancy itself—from the evidence needed by prosecutors.

As Michael Grossberg argues, "the transformation of the quickening doctrine . . . signalled the end of legalized abortion, save for the therapeutic exemption. . . . By the end of the century American abortion law codified the role of women as child bearers. . . . [The law made] the womb part of the public domain" (p. 186). By the late nineteenth century, all states but one had made abortion a crime. Only the 1973 *Roe v. Wade* decision, which legalized abortion in the United States, reversed that trend on a national level. But the *Roe* decision did not come about in a legislative vacuum; in the years preceding *Roe,* more than a dozen states and the District of Columbia, lobbied vigorously by the emerging feminist movement, had taken steps to liberalize abortion laws. Nor did *Roe* end legislative activity: within nine months of the decision, nearly two hundred bills were introduced in forty-one states to restrict abortion. Legislative efforts to restrict abortion since *Roe* underscore the emergence of the idea of "fetal rights" and the role of technology in defining abortion as a crime. According to the Pennsylvania Abortion Control Act of 1989, the "age of the unborn child" is to be calculated "from the first day of the last menstrual period of the pregnant woman"; the law requires that women receive "counseling" that includes "pictures representing the development of unborn children at two-week gestational increments" (in *Laws of the General Assembly of the Commonwealth of Pennsylvania* (Harrisburg, 1989, pp. 592–595). Laws in several states requiring women who seek abortion to get their male partners' and/or parents' permission, proscriptions against abortions and/or abortion counseling in public facilities, and so-called fetal protection legislation further indicated that some legislators sought not simply to limit the number of abortions performed in the United States but to regulate the ways in which women (and men) view female sexual (heterosexual, that is) behavior and its consequences.

Closely tied to these ideas about appropriate reproductive behavior is the issue of homosexuality. Just as the development of the birth control pill and the emergence of new ideas of sexual liberation frightened many Americans into a new campaign against abortion, so the growing visibility of gay men and lesbians gripped a public already defensive of traditional "family values." Fear and hatred of homosexuality, of course, is not a recent phenomenon. Colonial law made sodomy (which can include heterosexual oral sex as well as all homosexual sex) a capital offense, although sex between women seems not to have been a concern of early lawmakers. Most states abolished the death penalty for sodomy after the Revolution, but it remained a felony in all but two states until the 1950s. As a result of the gay liberation movement, more than half the states reformed or repealed sodomy laws (although the first to do so, Illinois, repealed its sodomy law in 1961, prior to the movement). As of 1993, sodomy remained a crime in twenty-four states. Some of these laws refer simply to "the infamous crime against nature" or "the abominable and detestable crime against nature," which is assumed to suffice as a definition of a criminal act. As with many laws about sexuality, these were rarely enforced, though they expressed deeply held beliefs about appropriate sexual behavior. As legal scholar Stephen Schnably argues, "laws banning homosexual conduct are an integral part of a social effort to channel all sexual expression into one of two distinct outlets. . . . [N]o one is untouched by the constitutive effects of such laws . . ." (p. 898).

Beginning in the 1960s, with the expansion of the concept of "privacy" in such matters as birth control and that of civil rights, gay liberation activists have grasped new ways of achieving particular legislative ends. Since discrimination against individuals because of their sexual orientation has been considered outside the purview of Title VII, gay rights groups had urged Congress to pass the Civil Rights Amendment Act of 1981, which would amend the Civil Rights Act of 1964 to include sexual orientation as a protected category. On the state and local level, as of early 1993, gay rights organizations had achieved the passage of gay civil rights legislation in eight states (California, Hawaii, Minnesota, New Jersey, Massachusetts, Vermont, and Wisconsin), approximately sixty-five municipalities, seventeen counties, as well as the District of Columbia. They had also lobbied to add gay men and lesbians to those groups counted in, and protected by, hate crimes statistics. So-called hate crimes bills had passed in numerous states, as well as in such disparate municipalities as Lexington, Kentucky, Ithaca, New York, and Stamford, Connecticut. Congressional advocates, though, were able to pass only a mild hate crimes statistics bill in the early 1990s, and chances of a sweeping gay and lesbian rights bill seemed minuscule.

Owing in part to the AIDS crisis and the increased visibility of lesbian parenting, so-called "family issues" had come to the fore of gay and lesbian legislative activism. About a half dozen localities had recognized gay and lesbian families through ordinances that allowed individuals to register as domestic partners and thus receive most of the benefits granted to married couples, including health care and bereavement leave. In the absence of federal support on these issues (and in the face of the Supreme Court's 1986 decision in *Bowers* v. *Hardwick,* which found that sodomy laws were constitutional), most of these legal changes have taken place on the level of the lower courts.

Another area of sexuality that has provoked some panic among Americans is that of teenage sexuality. In 1978 Congress amended a family-planning bill to provide federally funded birth control services (although not abortion) to adolescents. In contrast, the 1981 Adolescent Family Life Act encouraged "sexual self-discipline" and banned federal funds for abortion counseling. Particularly fervent in the face of the AIDS crisis, strong moral language appeared in much of the public debate about teenage sexual behavior, although far less legislative attention was paid to the social and economic conditions under which teenagers, especially lower-income, black, and female teenagers, experience and make choices about their sexuality.

Questions about choice, sexual freedom, and female equality have been most glaring—and most fiercely debated among feminists—around the issue of pornography. Although rarely dealt with in early American statutes, the 1873 Comstock law illegalized the use of the mails to distribute obscene printed material. With the decline of the social purity movement, however, First Amendment advocates have increasingly treated the publication and dissemination of pornographic materials as a central test for free speech standards. Feminists expressed concern about pornography from the early days of the movement, arguing that its portrayal of violent sex as pleasurable objectifies women, that is to say, treats women, in both theory and practice, as objects of male fantasy, desire, and aggression. Recently, some feminists have moved the legal discussion about pornography out of the terrain of free speech and into that of civil rights.

In 1983 writer and activist Andrea Dworkin and legal scholar Catharine A. MacKinnon drew up an ordinance for the Minneapolis city government (later adopted in Indianapolis) which redefined pornography, civil rights, and equality for women by declaring certain kinds of pornographic materials harmful to women and therefore a form of sex discrimination. The law's authors argued that pornography (which they defined as "the graphic sexually explicit subordination of women through pictures or words that also includes women dehumanized as sexual objects, things, or commodities..." [MacKinnon, p. 176]) is a civil rights issue, not a first amendment issue. In some ways, MacKinnon harkened back to the debate over protective legislation (indeed, she refers to the cases surrounding that debate), by arguing that the legal system's purported neutrality could not constitute justice between groups that were situated differently in a relationship of power. By eroticizing hierarchy and women's pain, she argues, society's decision to permit or prohibit pornography is not about moral judgments but about a practice of sex discrimination that harms women. This analysis of pornography emerged later in several proposals, notably in the form of a Massachusetts Act to Protect the Civil Rights of Women and Children, which would allow lawsuits against the makers and producers of pornography by anyone who could demonstrate harm.

MacKinnon and Dworkin's analysis of pornography as a civil rights issue epitomizes a new focus by many feminist legal theorists and lobbyists, one that encompasses far more than the hotly contested issue of pornography itself. Although there is serious disagreement among feminists about the efficacy and appropriateness of the particular ordinance, many have concluded with Deborah Rhode that "the law's traditional focus on equal treatment cannot cope with situations where the sexes are not equally situated" (p. 319). This insight is especially pointed in an area related to sexual activity, where feminists have long disagreed about the best way to use the law to protect women from male coercion. Some have argued that traditional liberal categories of equality, contract, and individual rights fail to confront the concreteness and specificity of women's status in contemporary society. In Rhode's view, these categories emphasize not gender difference but gender disadvantage, and she goes on to argue that law should treat women not simply as the same as men but, rather, should explain and correct a situation in which men's experience acts as the standard for fairness itself. In employment discrimination and sexual harassment cases, for instance, an employer's intention to discriminate would matter less than his (or her) various actions. The debate about pornography is especially complicated, since Americans experience neither "pure" free speech nor, in the case of women, "pure" victimization: legislation that reinforces the view of women as victims, Rhode writes, "risks perpetuating sexist stereotypes." Resolving and, indeed, redefining various dichotomies—free contract versus special protection, gender neutrality versus gender hierarchies, free speech versus group censure—remains an ongoing challenge to our political system.

## CONCLUSION

The history of American legislatures and gender issues is not one of inexorable progress toward women's "emancipation"; nor is it one of unmitigated failure. Indeed, the definition of progress itself is subject to debate, and women themselves have disagreed on what constitutes "emancipation" and equality. Legislatures were not uniformly or consistently deaf to women's appeals for greater freedom, access, and rights—nor were they, in a system dependent on judicial action to interpret and implement statutes, solely responsible for the laws' successes and failures. At the same time, laws that often appeared as gains for women—or, at least, for certain women—were frequently passed not with any benevolent or, certainly, feminist intent, but because of other considerations, such as the needs of debtors, or simply because current laws were not feasible to maintain or enforce. In these and other cases, legislators responded to sometimes contradictory forces, including changing economic circumstances, interest group activity, legal experts and reformers, personal prejudices, and women themselves.

Historical debates over women's and men's "difference" and "sameness," and over the law's allegedly equal treatment of unequal groups, will no doubt continue to inform legislative debates. Seen first in the dispute between supporters of protective legislation and the advocates of the ERA, these disagreements continue in the controversy over whether to legislate for maternity leave—thus recognizing the realities of wage-earning women's current responsibility for children—or to hold out for nongendered parental leave, thus expressing the hope that men too will care for small children and other family members. Feminist legal scholars, greatly influenced by Carol Gilligan's work on female moral development, have argued from a variety of positions that the law needs to take both perspectives into account, that it needs to emphasize context, and that gender neutrality has been an insufficient legal protection for women situated unequally in society at large.

When the participants in the Seneca Falls woman's rights convention met in 1848, it was indeed "self-evident" that "all men and women are created equal" and that women should thus demand "immediate admission to all the rights and privileges which belong to them as citizens of the United States." To feminists and liberal male legislators of their generation, the promise of a state that might afford all its citizens equal treatment was a radical solution to women's grievances. More recently, legal scholars, faced with the legacy of three centuries of unequal treatment of women and with the ambiguous history of three decades of attempted gender neutrality, have reconsidered the very terms of that equality. For many, the liberal notion of equality itself is insufficient, even as the "protection" granted by sex-based statutes is anachronistic and discriminatory. These debates find their parallel in legislative hearings and debates over specific concerns: whether the issue faced by legislators is comparable worth, gay and lesbian rights, abortion and reproductive freedom, health care or day care, it is clear that providing women with the rights of male citizens is not enough. It is also clear that legislation, for all its real and symbolic importance in articulating women's status, cannot alone transform it.

## BIBLIOGRAPHY

The historical scholarship that relates to the subject of legislatures and gender issues is extensive. Almost universally, however, works treat all aspects of the law—the judicial as well as the legislative—as a coherent whole. Two recent, exceptionally valuable scholarly treatments are JOAN HOFF, *Law, Gender and Injustice: A Legal History of U.S. Women* (New York, 1991) and DEBORAH L. RHODE, *Justice and Gender: Sex Discrimination and the Law* (Cambridge, Mass., 1989). A useful collection of laws and essays is MARLENE STEIN WORTMAN, *Women in American Law,* vol. 1, *From Colonial Times to the New Deal* (New York, 1985). For a discussion of the English common law and equity traditions as established in America, see MARY R. BEARD, *Woman as Force in History: A Study in Traditions and Realities* (New York, 1971 [1946]). An excellent overview of American law that includes some information about women is LAWRENCE M. FRIEDMAN, *A History of American Law* (New York, 1973).

### The Colonial Period

Of course, much literature exists on specific topics and periods covered here, see especially MARYLYNN SALMON, *Women and the Law of Property in Early America* (Chapel Hill, N.C., 1986), and A. LEON HIGGENBOTHAM, *In the Matter of Color: Race and the American Legal Process—The Colonial Period* (New York, 1978).

### The Nineteenth Century

On Married Women's Property Acts, women's changing relationship to politics, and changing family law, see NORMA BASCH, *In the Eyes of the Law: Women, Marriage, and Property in Nineteenth-century New York* (Ithaca, 1982); ELEANOR FLEXNER, *Century of Struggle: The Woman's Rights Movement in the United States* (rev. ed., Cambridge, Mass., 1975 [1959]); LORI D. GINZBERG, *Women and the Work of Benevolence: Morality, Politics, and Class in the Nineteenth-Century United States* (New Haven, 1990); MICHAEL GROSSBERG, *Governing the Hearth: Law and the Family in Nineteenth-century America* (Chapel Hill, N.C., 1985); PEGGY RABKIN, *Fathers to Daughters: The Legal Foundations of Female Emancipation* (Westport, Conn., 1980); MARY P. RYAN, *Women in Public: Between Banners and Ballots, 1825–*

*1880* (Baltimore, 1990); AMY DRU STANLEY, "Conjugal Bonds and Wage Labor: Rights of Contract in the Age of Emancipation," *Journal of American History* 75 (Sept. 1988): 471–500. The classic history of the woman suffrage movement compiled by some of its participants is ELIZABETH CADY STANTON, SUSAN B. ANTHONY, and MATILDA JOSLYN GAGE, *History of Woman Suffrage,* 6 vols. (reprint, New York, 1969 [1881–1922]).

On the legal issues surrounding women's employment see, in addition to FLEXNER (cited above), ALICE KESSLER-HARRIS, *A Woman's Wage: Historical Meanings and Social Consequences* (Lexington, Ky., 1990) and, on the 1930s, LOIS SCHARF, *To Work and to Wed: Female Employment, Feminism, and the Great Depression* (Westport, Conn., 1980).

### Sex Discrimination in the Law

Several dated but very useful discussions are BARBARA ALLEN BABCOCK, ANN E. FREEDMAN, ELEANOR HOLMES NORTON, and SUSAN C. ROSS, *Sex Discrimination and the Law: Causes and Remedies* (Boston, 1975); BARBARA BROWN, ANN E. FREEDMAN, HARRIET N. KATZ, and ALICE M. PRICE, *Women's Rights and the Law: The Impact of the ERA on State Laws* (New York, 1977); KAREN DeCROW, *Sexist Justice* (New York, 1974) and LEO KANOWITZ, *Women and the Law: The Unfinished Revolution* (Albuquerque, 1969). An excellent study of the Equal Rights Amendment is DONALD G. MATHEWS and JANE SHERRON DE HART, *Sex, Gender, and the Politics of ERA: A State and the Nation* (New York, 1990).

### On Divorce Reform

See especially MARTHA FINEMAN, *The Illusion of Equality: The Rhetoric and Reality of Divorce Reform* (Chicago, 1991), and LENORE J. WEITZMAN, *The Divorce Revolution: The Unexpected Social and Economic Consequences for Women and Children in America* (New York, 1985).

### History of Sexuality and Reproduction

See JOHN D'EMILIO and ESTELLE B. FREEDMAN, *Intimate Matters: A History of Sexuality in America* (New York, 1988); JAMES C. MOHR, *Abortion in America: The Origins and Evolution of National Policy, 1800–1900* (New York, 1978); PEGGY PASCOE, "Race, Gender, and Intercultural Relations: The Case of Interracial Marriage,"

*Frontiers* 12:1 (1991): 5–18; ROSALIND POLLACK PETCHESKY, *Abortion and Woman's Choice: The State, Sexuality, and Reproductive Freedom* (Boston, 1985) and STEPHEN J. SCHNABLY, "Beyond *Griswold:* Foucauldian and Republican Approaches to Privacy," *Connecticut Law Review* 23:4 (Summer 1991): 861–954. On prostitution, see RUTH ROSEN, *The Lost Sisterhood: Prostitution in America, 1900–1918* (Baltimore, 1982).

*Feminist Legal Theory*
The most useful are ZILLAH R. EISENSTEIN, *The Female Body and the Law* (Berkeley, 1988); MARTHA ALBERTSON FINEMAN and NANCY SWEET THOMADSEN, eds., *At the Boundaries of the Law: Feminism and Legal Theory* (New York, 1991) and CATHARINE A. MACKINNON, *Feminism Unmodified: Discourses on Life and Law* (Cambridge, Mass., 1987).

SEE ALSO Legislatures and Civil Liberties AND Legislatures and Political Rights.

## Part VI

# LEGISLATURES WITHIN THE POLITICAL SYSTEM

# LEGISLATIVE-EXECUTIVE RELATIONS

## Cary R. Covington
## Ross E. Burkhart

Legislative-executive relations have been at the core of governmental relations within the United States throughout its history. The relationship has seen dramatic ebbs and flows of the powers exercised by both participants. This essay reviews the history of the relationship, identifying events and trends that have affected the balance of power and nature of interaction between the two branches at the national and state levels of government. It concludes with a discussion of recent scholarly research.

## THE PRE-CONSTITUTIONAL ERA

Legislative-executive relations in the pre-Constitutional era can be divided into the colonial and confederal periods. Each period exhibited distinctive features that influenced the contents of the Constitution and the future conduct of legislative-executive relations.

### The Colonial Period

Colonial governors exercised executive authority in the colonies. They were appointed by the British crown (with the exception of Rhode Island and Connecticut, which elected their governors). Governors were expected to protect the interests of the crown and of English commercial enterprises from potential colonial threats and so were perceived by the colonists to be responsive to British interests, at the expense of the colonists'.

Colonial leaders viewed centralization of power in the executive as the most serious threat to colonial affairs. They advocated the Whig philosophy of government, which mistrusted executive power in favor of legislative supremacy (Schwartz, p. 25). The colonists viewed the legislature as the most legitimate channel of political representation. Their preference for popular representation appears, for example, as an integral part of the joint stock companies that formed the economic base of the first expeditions into the New World. Moreover, the colonies were quick to create legislatures. Virginia, for example, established its House of Burgesses in 1619.

Colonial assemblies commonly used their powers to loosen the executive's grasp. They used their appropriations power to limit governors' influence over the administrative process and could refuse to fund services or pay governmental officials they opposed. The assemblies also contested executive power by creating administrative commissions to perform executive duties and thereby circumvent the governors. The success of their efforts strengthened colonial enthusiasm for legislative governance.

### The Confederal Period

From 1781 to 1789, the United States was governed under the Articles of Confederation, in which fear of executive power was clearly evident. Thomas Paine's radical view of governmental power based on dominating legislatures had prevailed (in Foner, vol. 1). As a consequence, the scope of legislative power was left essentially undefined and the executive power was invested in the Continental Congress. The office of president possessed no formal powers. It was a part of the legislative branch: the president had the same voting powers as did the other legislators and was chosen annually by the legislators. Presidents were not completely powerless, but they did not possess the resources needed to fulfill the executive functions of government (Morris, p. 674).

Support for strong legislatures weakened as people realized that minorities could be exploited by popular majorities in the state legislatures. Fears of legislative tyranny brought about efforts to impose checks on the legislatures' powers. John Adams, among others, called for a bicameral legislature with an upper house indirectly responsive to the people, an executive power, balanced duties among branches of government, and checks on all sources of power. Eventually, dissatisfaction with the ineffectiveness and abuses of legislatures at the state and national levels, along with many other complaints (e.g., the confederal system's imbalance of power in favor of the states over the national government), culminated in the Constitutional Convention in 1787.

## PROVISIONS OF THE CONSTITUTIONAL CONVENTION

The U.S. Constitution significantly shifted the distribution of powers and duties between the legislature and executive. As the convention began, the founders knew they wanted to balance the relationship, but lacked agreement on how to do so. By the end of the convention, they had ended legislative dominance by creating a more balanced though ambiguous relationship between the two branches.

Consider the convention's debate over the legislature. The founders' long experience with legislatures enabled them to give concrete definitions to Congress's powers. Their consensus is evident in Article I, which contains the longest and most specific set of provisions in the Constitution. The powers granted to Congress are impressive, ensuring its ability to play an independent role in the formulation of government policy. However, the same experiences had also revealed the administrative inefficiency and the potential for trampling individual rights inherent in a purely legislative government. The convention resolved the dilemma over the proper role of the legislature by dividing power among separate branches of government. To improve governmental efficiency while minimizing the risks of legislative tyranny, the founders created an executive branch separate from the legislative branch, with powers of its own.

Agreement was less forthcoming concerning the executive. Disputes over how it should be organized and related to the legislature divided the founders. Many were reluctant to give the executive too much power or independence. Both the Virginia and New Jersey Plans, for example, empowered the legislature to elect the president. However, the founders' mistrust of the executive was countered by their desire for more-effective executive action and greater governmental efficiency.

The states' legislative-executive arrangements provided potential models for the U.S. Constitution. Most states employed the "weak executive" model, which reserved to the legislatures most of the important executive powers while leaving the governors, according to James Madison, "mere ciphers." New York and Massachusetts adopted a "strong executive" model. Their governors were popularly elected and exercised powers of appointment and/or veto, as well as responsibilities for the executive branch.

The constitutional provisions adopted by the Convention of 1787 empowered the presidency in a number of ways. First, they established the office as a separate branch with its own inherent powers. Second, they minimized Congress's role in electing the president. Both of these features helped establish the presidency's independence. Third, the founders provided only a vague definition of "executive power." The convention was unable to agree on the proper boundaries of presidential power. In the face of division, the founders left the powers unspecified. This created the potential for expansive definitions of presidential power under assertive presidents, who claimed that the absence of an explicit definition implied that the president could establish the office's limits.

However, the Constitution's failure to provide a specific enumeration of the powers of the executive also left the division of powers between the two branches unclear. James Sundquist identified five areas of constitutional ambiguity: (1) which branch would provide the initiative in the legislative process; (2) on what grounds and with what frequency the veto power would be exercised; (3) what the scope of authority encompassed within the meaning of "executive power" would be; (4) how much control Congress would exercise over the administrative process; and (5) what the proper balance would be between the executive's right to privileged information and the legislature's right to information about the executive (1981, pp. 16–19). These uncertainties have been sources of conflicts between the two branches throughout the nation's history.

The Constitution created a structure of relationships that can best be characterized as "separated institutions sharing power" (Neustadt, 1960, p. 33). The Constitution gives neither branch a clear mandate to lead, nor can either branch accomplish its goals without at least the acquiescence of the other. This ambiguous state of interdependence leaves the two branches free to compete for the initiative. That is why the history of their relationship reveals periodic shifts in the balance of power between them.

## THE FEDERALIST AND JEFFERSONIAN ERAS

Throughout the forty years of the Federalist and Jeffersonian eras, presidents lacked the resources and legitimating mandate needed to force Congress to treat them as peers in the legislative process (Young, pp. 193–194). Instead, presidents were concerned with showing, at least in their official actions, proper respect for Congress's independence. Under such circumstances, presidential leadership depended on a willingness by the executive to exert influence and a willingness by Congress to accept such leadership.

Presidents of this era varied significantly in their inclinations to initiate and advocate policy goals. Some presidents (or their representatives) actively sought to lead. Others saw their role as requiring them to respond passively to congressional initiatives, not to pressure Congress in its deliberations.

During this period, Congress grew increasingly independent of the executive. In the early years of George Washington's administration, Congress was disorganized and desired executive guidance. As conflicts emerged, so too did congressional cleavages. Over time, these cleavages gave rise to two opposing coalitions: the loyalist Federalists and the Republicans. Later in this era, when a president's coalition was in the minority in one or both houses, Congress was much more likely to resist the president. Congress also developed its own committee structure to formulate policy. As Congress developed more-coherent views and gained experience with its own procedures for organizing and expressing those views, it became less inclined to accept executive leadership, regardless of partisan affiliations. By the end of the Jeffersonian period, the policy-making initiative had clearly passed into the hands of Congress.

### The Federalist Era

George Washington generally left the routine workings of executive and Congress to Treasury Secretary Alexander Hamilton, who used his position to carve out a leadership role for the presidency. Hamilton drafted bills for Congress, both on his own initiative and at Congress's request. When department secretaries were prevented from appearing before Congress to propose government action and answer questions, Federalists from the two branches met regularly as a caucus to determine party positions on issues before Congress. Hamilton used meetings of the congressional caucus to convey administration positions to Congress and secure their adoption (Binkley, pp. 32–33). At the same time, Hamilton successfully undertook to lead the other government departments. Thus, through Hamilton, a well-coordinated policy-making process based on executive initiative took shape.

This arrangement did not last long. The very act of proposing an agenda to Congress encouraged the formation of coalitions for and against it. Although Washington won unanimous reelection by the electoral college, the opposition, styling itself "Republican," gained the upper hand in the House of Representatives. As the majority, they worked to end Hamilton's leadership of Congress. The development of standing committees aided that effort by providing a base for challenging the recommendations of the executive and for launching investigations into executive activities.

Conflict in 1795 over Jay's Treaty helped further polarize the Federalists and Republicans during Washington's second term. Congressional Republicans sought to defeat the treaty with Great Britain and, later, to block its implementation. Although they failed, Congress had made it clear that it was not a willing tool of the executive. It would play an independent role.

With the election of John Adams in 1796, the Federalists regained majority status in both houses of Congress. However, Congress was not inclined to resume the close relationship that had prevailed during Washington's first term. In part, this was due to Republican strength in the House and the role of Vice President Thomas Jefferson, Adams's chief political rival, as presiding officer in the Senate. Internal divisions within the Federalist party also accounted for part of the failure. Many Federalists supported Hamilton against Adams. Without a united party, Adams could not avail himself of the party caucus or play the leadership role as Hamilton had. These conditions left Adams in a weak position. Consequently, most laws, including the controversial Alien and Sedition Acts of 1798, were enacted by the Federalists in Congress without Adams's direct involvement.

The Federalist era saw a clear transition in the relationship between the executive and legislature. At the outset, their relations resembled an integrated process directed by the executive. Once the opposition broke the Federalists' hold on the House of Representatives, the relationship became more competitive. With their own agenda and a mistrust of the executive in general, Jeffersonians sought to establish Congress as the executive's coequal. Once the Federalist party returned to majority status in the House under Adams, relations were less combative, but Congress continued to pursue its own independent course.

## The Jeffersonian Era

Once Thomas Jefferson was elected to the presidency in 1801 with supportive majorities in both houses of Congress, he faced a quandary—how to lead without reverting to the Federalist mode of executive leadership against which he had argued for the previous eight years. Jefferson's solution was to defer to Congress formally in his institutional role as president and to lead in practice through his

informal role as head of the Republican party. Thus, he traded off the potential of formal institutional power derived from his office for the personal power that he could exercise as leader of his own party.

Jefferson used a variety of means to achieve his legislative goals. He enlisted members of Congress to lead his party's faction in Congress and to act as his personal emissaries (Young, p. 162). The president also revived, and Congress accepted, the Federalist practice of using department secretaries as sources of information and advice. He assiduously courted individual members of Congress, notably by inviting them to small dinner parties at the White House (Young, pp. 168–170). Another important element of Jefferson's legislative success was the "essentially conservative" nature of his agenda (Young, p. 179). Jefferson's key issues concerned foreign policy, national expansion, and government retrenchment. None of these gave Congress reason to resist Jefferson. However, when Jefferson sought to impose an embargo on France and Britain in 1807, his own party members abandoned him in favor of their constituents' demands, resulting in Jefferson's defeat (Young, p. 180). Thus, by a variety of means, Jefferson led the Republicans into accepting a de facto, if not de jure, form of presidential leadership that might have otherwise seemed more natural among the Federalists. However, his three Republican successors were less inclined to exercise personal or institutional leadership and were confronted by an increasingly hostile Congress.

James Madison and James Monroe concurred with Jefferson's formal view of the circumscribed nature of the presidency's role in the legislative process. However, neither chose to exercise Jefferson's informal party leadership (Young, pp. 191–192). As a result, these presidents lacked influence and their proposals were repeatedly defeated. John Quincy Adams initially sought to lead Congress, as evidenced by his efforts to pass an internal-improvements bill during his first year in office. However, he was unable to overcome congressional resistance to executive initiative (Young, p. 188) and shortly thereafter lost any influence with Congress.

Even if Madison or Monroe had attempted to influence Congress, it is doubtful that they would have had any more success than John

Quincy Adams. For a number of reasons, Congress was increasingly resistant to executive direction. First, congressional caucuses came to control the nomination of presidential candidates, meeting to choose their respective parties' nominees. Congressional control of the nomination process undermined the presidency's independence, because presidents who depended on their party in Congress for nomination and renomination were hesitant to contest Congress's policy preferences. Second, after Jefferson, other sources superseded the presidency as the primary source of Congress's agenda. Ideological disputes remained an important point of division. Despite the label of the one-party "Era of Good Feelings" (1815–1829), Congress remained ideologically divided, split into discernible blocs of voters. Local constituency interests also affected the issues that Congress addressed, for the westward expansion of the country brought into office members of Congress who were more responsive to local interests than to presidential concerns. Third, Congress continued to develop its committee system. Under the direction of party leaders, committees provided alternative sources of coherence and direction to the legislative process. As a result, the presidents found it increasingly difficult to secure members' loyalty or support.

As a result of these factors, Congress clearly dominated the presidents of this period. It increasingly intruded into the presidents' responsibilities over foreign affairs. The Senate refused to confirm Madison's choice for secretary of state, and congressional Republicans used their control over Madison's renomination to pressure him into recommending what became the War of 1812. The two key pieces of domestic legislation considered during Monroe's presidency were the Missouri Compromise of 1820 and a protective tariff in 1824–1825, and both bills passed with very little presidential involvement. Given this unfavorable climate for presidential leadership, it is understandable that the Monroe Doctrine was simply "announced" rather than submitted to Congress. John Quincy Adams, though he sought to enact a significant domestic agenda, secured congressional support for virtually none of it and "could not have had a less significant role if he had been absent from Washington altogether" (Young, p. 188).

The Jeffersonian era ended with Congress possessing both the will and ability to disregard presidents on matters of mutual concern. The presidents lacked the requisite inclination and resources to contest that situation. These inadequacies were not to last for long.

## THE JACKSONIAN ERA

The relationship between the presidency and Congress shifted dramatically following Andrew Jackson's election in 1828. Changes in the presidential-selection rules democratized the office, giving Jackson the legitimacy needed to use powers in ways that had previously been unacceptable. This enabled him to force Congress to address his preferences.

Three major changes in the election system helped strengthen the presidency. First, the congressional-caucus nominating system was replaced by national party conventions. Presidential candidates and sitting presidents were no longer dependent on the legislative branch for the right to compete for the office. This electoral independence from Congress gave presidents greater freedom to pursue their goals in the legislative arena. Second, by 1828, most states had revised their system for choosing electors to the electoral college. In prior elections, state legislatures had chosen the electors, but by 1828, they were chosen by the voters. This created a more direct connection between the voters and their presidents, thereby legitimating presidential claims to leadership. Finally, the 1828 election was the first to be contested under conditions of widespread white male suffrage, which broadened the president's constituency and therefore his legitimacy. Thus, the presidency under Jackson enjoyed a greatly enhanced stature. His desire to lead Congress was legitimated by his status as the one official elected with a truly national constituency.

Public endorsement of Jackson as the "voice of the people" enabled him to use three powers that his predecessors had possessed but not used in a comparable fashion. First, he made extensive use of the veto power. While Jackson's six predecessors together issued only ten vetoes, Jackson vetoed twelve bills. His predecessors usually justified their vetoes on constitutional grounds, but Jackson explicitly used the veto to block legislation because it did not conform to his policy preferences. Most important, Jackson used the threat of the veto to attempt to shape legislation while it was still in Congress.

The second set of powers that Jackson employed in his battles with Congress were those of appointment and removal. The magnitude of personnel turnover during the Jackson presidency, while not a "clean sweep" of the executive branch, was without precedent (Fisher, p. 67). By one count, Jackson removed 10–20 percent of all federal employees during his term of office, and among higher-level "presidential offices" the rate of removal was even higher— 252 out of 612 (White, 1954, p. 308). Jackson's predecessors usually retained cabinet-rank appointees from the previous administration. Before the Adams-Jackson transition, incoming presidents had replaced only 6 of 19 incumbent secretaries, excluding the secretary of state, which was a stepping-stone to the presidency itself. In contrast, Jackson replaced all 5 of Adams's cabinet secretaries. Jackson used his appointment powers for patronage purposes and justified vigorous use of the removal power on democratic grounds. By rotating personnel into and out of government with changes in administration, the bureaucracy would be made more representative of the people. Additionally, by creating so many job openings, Jackson made patronage a valuable political resource in his dealings with party members in and out of Congress.

Finally, with Jackson's election, the presidency attained a position of leadership within the party. During this time, parties began to develop a formal organizational structure. With the emergence of the new party-oriented nomination procedures, the presidency became a natural focal point for party leadership. The mutual self-interest of the state parties and the presidency served to bind them together, with the president taking the lead on national issues. Jackson was able to use this relationship to further his interests in Congress (White, 1954, pp. 44–46).

The dominant issue of the Jackson presidency concerned the Bank of the United States. It occasioned some of his most controversial actions. He vetoed the bill that would have rechartered the bank. He removed Treasury

Secretary William J. Duane for refusing to withdraw federal funds from the bank. That action brought a vote of censure on Jackson. Nonetheless, his decisions stood: the bank was not rechartered, federal funds were withdrawn, and the bank was subsequently closed. Later, Congress revoked its vote of censure, which legitimated Jackson's actions as powerful precedents for his successors.

Throughout the Jacksonian era, Congress resisted presidential leadership. Having acquired significant powers in the early 1800s under Speaker of the House Henry Clay, Congress would not defer to a resurgent presidency. The members who had been leaders in the House during the Jeffersonian period had graduated to the Senate. Thus, while the House of Representatives tended to be more supportive of the Jacksonian presidents, the Senate consistently challenged presidents seeking to lead Congress.

Jackson's pre–Civil War successors varied considerably in their conception of the presidential role. Some presidents had clear goals and pursued them in the face of congressional opposition. John Tyler was elected vice president on the Whig ticket, but returned to his Democratic tendencies when he assumed the presidency on the death of William Henry Harrison. He used the veto to block Whig policy. Twice he vetoed attempts to charter a new national bank. Later, he vetoed a tariff bill not to his liking. Through his actions, Tyler blunted Whig efforts to assert congressional supremacy.

James K. Polk went further, assembling a four-point legislative agenda and securing its passage. He faced considerable Whig opposition to all his efforts and a Whig majority in the House during his last two years in office.

Other Jacksonian presidents, though inclined to pursue an active role, had less success. Martin Van Buren, Jackson's immediate successor, deadlocked with Congress, with neither side achieving significant gains. Zachary Taylor and Millard Fillmore, though both Whigs, adhered in practice to an independent presidential role and worked to achieve their goals. Their most important actions concerned the Compromise of 1850. Taylor's opposition jeopardized its passage. On Taylor's death, Fillmore gave the bill his support, which aided in its eventual passage (Binkley, pp. 108–110).

Other presidents, especially those of the 1850s, were content to let Congress take the initiative. William Henry Harrison's brief tenure gave every indication that he would accept congressional supremacy. Franklin Pierce and James Buchanan, fearful of the slavery issue, avoided leadership responsibilities, and so Congress was again allowed to take the initiative.

The dominant issues of the period shifted from banking and other financial matters to the future of slavery. Slavery was closely intertwined with the nation's westward expansion, since the key question surrounding the admission of each new state was whether it would be free or slave. This issue led eventually to the demise of the Whig party and the formation and success of the Republican party of Abraham Lincoln.

## THE REPUBLICAN ERA

By any standard, legislative-executive relations during Abraham Lincoln's administration were unique. The exercise of power by Lincoln in the conduct of the Civil War remains the highwater mark of presidential power in relation to Congress and government as a whole. Lincoln knowingly and repeatedly overstepped the constitutional boundaries of executive power. Once in office, he expanded the size of the military without the constitutionally mandated authorization of Congress. He formulated rules of order for the military, again contravening constitutional language, which placed that duty with Congress. Acting without congressional authorization, Lincoln had $2 million withdrawn from the Treasury to purchase military equipment. With Congress out of session in 1862, Lincoln issued a proclamation unilaterally suspending habeas corpus. Despite his own Whig background, Lincoln exercised presidential leadership and initiative on a scale beyond the imagination of his predecessors.

Lincoln's actions were taken in the face of strong congressional opposition. The Civil War had virtually eliminated the Democrats as a meaningful opposition party in Congress. The Republicans had a commanding majority, and despite internal divisions between radicals and conservatives, they had a clear sense of objectives that lent coherence and direction to their actions.

Congressional Republicans advocated an extreme form of legislative supremacy. Senator Charles Sumner (R.-Mass.) claimed that the president "is only the instrument of Congress under the Constitution of the United States," while Senator Lyman Trumbull (R.-Ill.) went further, asserting that "he is just as much subject to our control as if we appointed him, except that we cannot remove him and appoint another in his place" (quoted in Binkley, pp. 121, 122).

Congress challenged Lincoln repeatedly. For instance, early in his term, Congress appointed the Joint Committee on the Conduct of the War. Composed of three senators and four representatives, it oversaw military affairs and conducted investigations as it saw fit. It contested Lincoln's authority over the military and pushed him into more-aggressive military action against the Confederacy. Later, Radical Republicans tried unsuccessfully to force Lincoln to reorganize his cabinet by replacing his own supporters with theirs.

Despite these challenges, Lincoln held the upper hand throughout the course of the war. His success was facilitated by two factors. First, as commander in chief in time of war, Lincoln was well positioned to act on his preferences. Many of his decisions consisted of unilateral actions that Congress had few opportunities to contest. Moreover, Congress's recourse against actions that it deemed illegal or unconstitutional—impeachment and conviction—were unthinkable under conditions of civil war, so Congress had to accept what it otherwise might have challenged. Second, Republican opposition to Lincoln focused on his failure to prosecute the war with sufficient vigor. This put them in a difficult position, for Congress had few means available to force Lincoln to do more. They could criticize and complain, but not direct or even effectively contest the president's actions. Thus, Lincoln was able to act relatively freely in the face of congressional opposition.

As these conditions diminished in importance and eventually disappeared, Congress increasingly gained influence over government policy. This was most evident in the dispute over Reconstruction. Lincoln issued a proclamation in 1863 claiming Reconstruction as an executive process, with no significant role for Congress. Congress responded with the Wade-Davis bill, which sought to reverse that situation. Lincoln pocket-vetoed the bill and viewed his reelection in 1864 as vindication of his approach (Binkley, p. 133). However, he was assassinated without a conclusive resolution to the dispute.

The contest over presidential leadership of Congress continued during Andrew Johnson's term. Johnson pursued his own independent course of action. Once in office, he acted swiftly and without congressional consultation to enact Lincoln's Reconstruction plan, but Congress rejected Johnson's attempts to take the lead. It refused to seat southern legislators who had been selected under that plan, and moved to dismantle Johnson's programs. It created the Joint Committee of Fifteen on Reconstruction, which produced a version of Reconstruction that was enacted over repeated vetoes. Congress then moved to limit Johnson's powers of appointment and removal. Johnson had been a Jacksonian Democrat before the war, and Republicans feared that he would use the appointment power both to ensure executive loyalty to his objectives and to create a political resource for use against Congress. In response, Congress enacted the Tenure of Office Act of 1867. It prevented presidents from removing an appointed official until Congress had approved a successor. When Johnson violated the act by removing Secretary of War Edwin Stanton, the House impeached him. Though saved from conviction by a single vote, Johnson was left without influence. Congress made decisions without presidential involvement.

Legislative-executive relations throughout the remainder of the nineteenth century reflected congressional—particularly senatorial—supremacy. Most presidents deferred to Congress, their efforts limited to attempts to protect the office from further decline.

Ulysses S. Grant complied completely with congressional wishes (Galloway, p. 312). His submissiveness was captured in the remarks of one representative, who claimed that members of the Senate "would have received as a personal affront a private message from the White House expressing a desire that they should adopt any course in the discharge of their legislative duties that they did not approve. If they

visited the White House, it was to give, not to receive, advice" (quoted in Binkley, p. 162).

Rutherford B. Hayes took the first steps to redress the balance between the legislature and the executive. He successfully defended his right to exercise his appointment powers independent of the Senate. Further, he repeatedly used the veto to defeat House attempts to use its appropriations power to direct the executive (Galloway, p. 313). Though his actions were primarily defensive in nature, they broke with the previous decade of presidential deference.

The next five presidencies, encompassing those of James Garfield, Chester Arthur, Grover Cleveland, Benjamin Harrison, and Cleveland again, subscribed to the doctrine of separation of powers. This doctrine legitimized presidential efforts to defend the office in the use of the veto and appointment powers, as when Cleveland persuaded Congress to repeal the Tenure of Office Act. However, this doctrine did not authorize presidents to venture into areas of congressional jurisdiction. As a result, few proposals emerged from the executive, and those that did were not pushed for adoption. The initiative remained with Congress.

While the executive refrained from providing direction to the legislative process, Congress was unable to do so. Congress had decentralized its power into committees. By the 1880s, Congress was unable to direct the committees' power into a coherent agenda effectively (Galloway, pp. 313–314). Pending legislation created a vast backlog on the House's calendar. Most floor activity was conducted under the suspension of the rules or by unanimous consent. The House often had trouble establishing a quorum. Thomas Reed (R.-Maine) revitalized Congress after he became Speaker of the House in 1889. He centralized power into the Speaker's office, using it to streamline the House's operation (Peters, pp. 66–69). Similar reforms occurred in the Senate. As a result, by Benjamin Harrison's term, party-directed action in Congress set the nation's agenda and enacted its policies.

During William McKinley's administration, Congress and the president worked together with a high degree of cooperation to achieve mutual goals. McKinley respected congressional prerogatives, but was the "gentle but undoubted leader of Congress" (Binkley, p. 207). The combination of a mild form of presidential leadership and a congressional party structure that enabled the Speaker to create coherence within Congress led to a fairly productive and peaceful relationship. With McKinley's administration, the balance of power began to tip back toward the president, making him a co-equal with Congress.

## FROM PROGRESSIVE PRESIDENTS TO CONSERVATIVE CALM

The first third of the twentieth century exhibited dramatic contrasts in the character of the relations between presidents and Congress. Presidential behavior varied from the activist leadership of Theodore Roosevelt and Woodrow Wilson, to the more passive presidencies of William Howard Taft, Warren G. Harding, Calvin Coolidge, and Herbert Hoover. Over the same period, Congress ranged from a willing acceptance of presidential leadership to strong resistance to it. Congress also experienced periods of strong party leadership and periods when authority was dispersed among its many committees.

Theodore Roosevelt was a progressive Republican, and espoused a "stewardship theory" of presidential power. That theory claimed for the president any power that was not explicitly prohibited by the Constitution or statute, on the grounds that the president was the direct representative of the people. Roosevelt refused to wait for congressional initiatives or to recommend legislation and then defer to congressional judgments. Rather, he claimed presidents should propose and advocate the passage of laws that were in the interests of the public that had elected them.

During Roosevelt's presidency, Congress was dominated by Speaker Joseph Cannon (R.-Ill.). Cannon further centralized control over House operations in the Speaker's office and used that control to impose order and coherence (Peters, pp. 76–80). Roosevelt and Cannon worked to reach agreements on much of Roosevelt's agenda during his first term. When conservative opposition in Congress developed during his second term, Roosevelt brought the pressure of public opinion to bear on Congress to obtain his ends (Galloway, p. 315).

William Howard Taft took office intending to consolidate Roosevelt's achievements. Several factors limited his success. First, his own philosophy of the presidency and his lack of political experience deterred him from playing Roosevelt's activist role. Taft felt that presidents should not act in the absence of explicit legal authorization. Thus, while he proposed a legislative agenda, he did not lobby for its adoption, instead deferring to Congress's decisions. Second, Taft's relations with Congress were undermined by the effects of Roosevelt's presidency. Roosevelt had exacerbated ideological divisions within the Republican party, pitting Progressives against the conservative "Old Guard." This split limited the party's value to Taft. Moreover, after the progressive and Democrat-led revolt in 1910 against Speaker Cannon, Congress's institutional power devolved on the committees. Thus fragmented along ideological and partisan grounds and lacking the institutional structure needed to impose order, Congress was neither willing to support President Taft nor able to offer its own agenda. When the Democrats gained control of the House following the 1910 elections, Taft's ability to work with Congress was ended.

The 1912 elections brought to office Woodrow Wilson and Democratic majorities in both houses of Congress. Given his party's control of Congress, Wilson tried to operate as a prime minister in a parliamentary democracy. The key to success rested in strengthening and exploiting his partisan attachments to the Democrats. "The Democratic party . . . became the hyphen that joined, the buckle that fastened, the legislature to the executive" (Galloway, p. 317).

Wilson took many steps to enhance congressional support for his proposals. He believed that his copartisans would be more loyal to his program if they dealt with him in person. Therefore, he reinstated the practice, dormant since Jefferson, of delivering his State of the Union message in a speech before a joint session of Congress. Wilson also appeared repeatedly on Capitol Hill to lobby individual members of Congress. Wilson was also one of the first presidents who regularly mobilized public opinion behind his legislative proposals. His public appeals grew out of his conception of the presidency as the representative of the people, a conception he incorporated into his basic strategy for securing congressional support. When public opinion supported Wilson, he achieved great success with Congress. For example, early in his first term he secured tariff reforms, the creation of the Federal Reserve System and the Federal Trade Commission, and passage of the Clayton Antitrust Act. However, when public opinion turned against him, his influence with Congress suffered.

Even though Wilson was frequently challenged by Congress on foreign policy matters, he still enhanced the presidency's influence and reduced Congress's role in this field (Galloway, p. 317). The scope of the powers he lawfully exercised during World War I was unprecedented. Lincoln had acted without regard for constitutional or statutory limitations, but Wilson sought and received congressional endorsement of his actions, notably in the Lever Act of 1917, which gave him vast regulatory powers over the economy for the purpose of directing the nation's war effort.

Support for Wilson eroded during his second term. In 1918, Republican majorities were elected to Congress. This ended his cooperative relations with Congress and set the stage for his eventual defeat on the treaty establishing the League of Nations. Nonetheless, Wilson's actions and successes contributed to the growing national perception that leadership in the legislative-executive relationship lay with the presidency.

The decade following Wilson was the last hurrah for the nineteenth century's passive presidential philosophy. The presidents of the 1920s had legislative agendas of some sort for Congress to consider, but none felt it appropriate to lead or influence Congress in its deliberations. Congress, for its part, resisted presidential leadership during the decade. The Republican Senate, in particular, defended its prerogatives and frequently opposed those presidents' proposals. But while Congress was quick to resist any suggestion of presidential initiative, it did not fill the leadership vacuum. Republican majorities decentralized power within Congress, and its leaders had no significant or coherent agendas (Peters, pp. 98–106). Thus, the 1920s was a period of policy drift.

Warren G. Harding and Calvin Coolidge were philosophically disinclined to lead Congress. In the absence of executive leadership, Congress dominated the relationship. The Budget and Accounting Act of 1921 gave the chairman of the newly consolidated House Appropriations Committee many significant powers, which the committee used to enact its preferences over Harding's requests. Congress regularly enacted its own agenda, resulting in the frequent defeat of Harding and Coolidge on those occasions when they proposed legislation.

Herbert Hoover was committed to improving the country's social and economic conditions. On taking office, he called a special session of Congress and proposed a wide range of initiatives. However, his belief in legislative independence prevented him from lobbying for his proposals. Hoover's major opposition came from the Senate. For instance, on the issue of tariff reform, Hoover was one vote short of securing Senate adoption of his preferred revisions in 1929. However, he failed to take any steps to gain that additional vote, and was defeated. In 1930 his proposal was replaced by the Senate's protectionist Smoot-Hawley tariff bill. Despite his personal opposition to the bill, he did not try to defeat it, and signed it into law (Binkley, pp. 252–254).

Confronted with increasing criticism for his lack of congressional leadership, Hoover took a more active role in setting the course of his administration. However, the onset of the Great Depression, coupled with the loss of Republican control of Congress in 1930, prevented him from seizing the initiative. Thus, his later relations with Congress were punctuated with frequent conflicts and defeats. According to Sidney Milkis and Michael Nelson, "Hoover put traditional, nineteenth-century American political practices and principles to their greatest test. But his unalterable commitment to preserving these traditions even in the face of national calamity served only to diminish, if not to discredit, them" (p. 255).

## THE MODERN ERA

Franklin D. Roosevelt institutionalized expectations for presidential leadership of Congress that had been foreshadowed by Theodore Roosevelt and Woodrow Wilson. By the end of his term, the activist presidency model was so firmly established that even his Republican successors adhered to it.

## Inaugurating the Modern Presidency

Roosevelt followed Wilson's strategy of leading Congress as his party's leader. He consulted frequently with party and committee leaders to coordinate their actions. He actively sought congressional support and revived Wilson's practice of delivering the State of the Union address in person. Roosevelt used patronage to cultivate support, and he spent many hours lobbying individual members on the telephone to secure their votes on key bills. Finally, he was a master of shaping public opinion on behalf of his goals (Galloway, p. 322).

At first, Congress eagerly accepted Roosevelt's leadership. The comments of House Minority Leader Bertrand Snell (R.-N.Y.) capture congressional sentiments: "The house is burning down, and the President of the United States says this is the way to put out the fire" (quoted in Galloway, p. 323). Roosevelt's presidency is best remembered for its first one hundred days. In that short time, Roosevelt proposed and Congress enacted fifteen major laws, including the Agricultural Adjustment Act, the National Industrial Recovery Act, and the acts creating the Civilian Conservation Corps and the Tennessee Valley Authority. In addition, many important bills either originated in Congress or were undertaken by Roosevelt under pressure from Congress. The methods and successes of Roosevelt's first term have become the defining criteria for modern presidential leadership of Congress.

The cooperative relationship between Roosevelt and Congress began to sour during his second term. They competed for influence over the increasingly important bureaucracy. Many New Deal programs delegated important rule-making powers to executive agencies, and both branches wanted to retain control over those agencies. This contest formed "one of the most intense political controversies of FDR's presidency" (Milkis and Nelson, p. 268).

A second conflict grew out of Roosevelt's 1937 attempt to increase the size of the Supreme Court. He hoped that an expanded Court would overturn decisions unfavorable to the New Deal agencies. The effort accelerated the emergence of a conservative coalition of Republicans and conservative southern Democrats in Congress to oppose Roosevelt on a wide range of issues. This conflict was exacerbated by the president's attempts in 1938 to defeat those Democrats who did not support the New Deal. His effort failed and greatly curtailed his ability to lead Congress on domestic affairs. By his third term in office, Roosevelt's New Deal programs were under attack by the conservative coalition. Congress used its appropriations powers to eliminate or cut back several programs. Roosevelt's leadership of Congress on domestic matters was effectively at an end.

The growing threat of war enabled Roosevelt to regain the initiative in foreign affairs. He was assisted by Supreme Court decisions authorizing the unilateral exercise of presidential power. Congress further contributed to Roosevelt's authority by passing the Lend-Lease Act of 1941. However, during the course of the war, Congress reverted to its stance of opposition and criticism, culminating in the resignation of the Senate Majority Leader Alben Barkley (D.-Ky.) over the president's veto of a revenue bill. Roosevelt's death, shortly after beginning his fourth term, cut short the conflict.

## Institutionalizing Presidential Ascendance

Congressional expectations of presidential initiative became increasingly pronounced during the period 1945–1969. Congress in the late nineteenth century would have rejected out of hand presidential efforts to set Congress's agenda, but by the 1960s, presidential leadership had come to be routine (Sundquist, 1981, p. 35). This does not mean that Congress would automatically accept the president's proposals, but rather that Congress expected the president to provide the major proposals over which legislative battles were then fought.

Harry Truman took office committed to following Roosevelt's conception of presidential activism. He attempted to institutionalize the New Deal with his "Fair Deal" proposals, but he deadlocked with Congress on domestic policy. Truman's liberal agenda provoked increasingly powerful opposition. The conservative coalition had come into its own and could now defeat Truman's core of northern Democratic support. Opposition increased when Republicans gained control of Congress following the 1946 midterm elections. Congress then rejected most of Truman's Fair Deal proposals and sought to overturn much of the New Deal itself. Truman defended those programs with his veto power, but was often overridden.

Congress strengthened its ability to oppose Truman by passing the Legislative Reorganization Act of 1946. This law streamlined the committee system of Congress and strengthened the committees' independence from the executive branch by allowing them to increase their staff support significantly. These changes enabled Congress to develop its own information and expertise, thereby reducing its dependence on the president and executive-branch agencies. Truman and Congress were caught in an impasse on domestic policy. Each could block the other, but neither was able to take constructive action.

Truman and Congress worked together more effectively on foreign policy. Despite occasional points of conflict, (e.g., the "Great Debate of 1951" on national security policy), foreign and national security policy-making reflected broad bipartisan cooperation (Galloway, pp. 326–327). Rather than trying to impose their will on one another, both branches sought compromise. As a result, Congress enacted many important pieces of legislation designed to contain the Soviet Union. Truman exercised more-direct leadership following the outbreak of hostilities in Korea, using his powers as commander in chief to commit U.S. troops and conduct combat without congressional authorization.

Dwight Eisenhower governed during a period of national calm. This was reflected in the relations between the presidency and Congress as well. Eisenhower had only modest legislative goals. For example, he had no comprehensive legislative program to urge on Congress in 1953. Although he provided agendas for Congress's consideration in subsequent years, throughout his two terms he remained committed to maintaining past policies while limiting growth in existing programs. Moreover, he employed a "hidden hand" political strategy, which relied on quiet diplomacy and indirect means of influence to achieve his goals. Modest policy aspirations and nonconfrontational political strategies limited the level of conflict between the two branches.

Democrats controlled Congress for the last six years of Eisenhower's presidency. Congressional power resided in the chairs of important committees and the party leaders of both houses. These leaders lacked the influence of the turn-of-the-century Speakers of the House. Instead, they operated as brokers, negotiating among blocks of members for support on important legislation. Eisenhower met regularly with these leaders to reach agreement with them on pending legislation. The leaders would then work to secure passage of those bills. This approach was particularly effective on matters of foreign policy and national security.

Eisenhower initiated an important institutional change in legislative-executive relations by creating the White House–based Office of Congressional Relations (OCR). This small staff was charged with providing liaison between the president and Congress. Although Eisenhower used the OCR primarily to shield himself from congressional pressures, his successors used it in a more constructive manner.

The Eisenhower era was not without conflicts, nor did Eisenhower's nonconfrontational tactics mean he was a passive, Taftian president. When he felt it was necessary, Eisenhower directly addressed congressional challenges to his office. For example, Eisenhower made active use of "executive privilege" to protect executive-branch officials from having to testify at the McCarthy-Army hearings in 1953. While the tradition of confidentiality within the executive branch dates back to George Washington's presidency, Eisenhower was the first to label it as executive privilege. The dispute over the "Bricker amendment" in 1954 also reveals Eisenhower's willingness to contest congressional assertions of power. The amendment sponsored by Senator John W. Bricker (R.-Ohio) required Senate ratification of executive agreements. It constituted the most serious congressional threat to presidential power during this period. Eisenhower personally lobbied senators to oppose the amendment and won by a single vote. Bricker himself claimed that the amendment's defeat was due to "Dwight Eisenhower—nobody else!" (quoted in Reichard, p. 67). Such conflicts notwithstanding, in the context of modern presidents the Eisenhower presidency represents a unique period of balance and cooperation between the two branches of government.

John F. Kennedy sought to reestablish assertive presidential leadership in a reinvigorated government. His "New Frontier" agenda built on the legacy of Franklin Roosevelt's New Deal and Harry Truman's Fair Deal. Kennedy, while personally ill disposed to lobby Congress, used his well-regarded OCR staff to smooth the way for his legislative program. This staff, unlike Eisenhower's, employed an aggressive partisan strategy to seek passage of Kennedy's agenda. Ultimately, Kennedy's narrow base of partisan support in Congress constrained his legislative aspirations. Southern Democrats chaired many important committees and used those positions to bottle up Kennedy's proposals. Those bills that did make it to the floor had to face the conservative coalition, which held the key to legislative success. While Kennedy achieved some successes and Congress began to be more responsive in 1963, he made little headway on his most significant agenda items (Sundquist, 1968, pp. 473–484). He was looking ahead to a reelection accompanied by an increase in the number of liberal Democrats in Congress as the means to realizing his goals. This dream went unfulfilled when he was assassinated in November 1963.

Lyndon Johnson used Kennedy's death to generate momentum for Kennedy's legislative agenda. Congress passed Kennedy's tax cut and civil rights legislation in 1964. Johnson won a landslide election in 1964, and Congress reconvened with Democratic margins in both houses of 2–1 over the Republicans. The expansion of the northern Democratic contingent greatly weakened the conservative coalition, which opened the way to passage of a wide-ranging legislative agenda.

Viewing the 1964 election as a historic opportunity, Johnson proposed his "Great Society" program, a massive package of domestic legislation. His success was equally historic. After one year, Congress had adopted eighty of his proposals and rejected only three (Berman, 1987, p. 252). Congress passed additional domestic legislation in 1966, but the window of opportunity was fast closing. The 1966 elec-

tions cut Johnson's majorities, and he spent the remainder of his term protecting the advances he had already achieved.

Presidential-congressional relations in foreign policy focused on Vietnam. Johnson used the 1964 Gulf of Tonkin Resolution to justify expansion of the war under his authority as commander in chief. Not until 1966 did Congress begin to claim that the president was overstepping his constitutional boundaries. Although Johnson faced several challenges to his conduct of the war during the remainder of his term, he generally continued his war policies with few obstructions.

## Congress Reins in the Presidency

Relations in the most recent period reflect a significant weakening of the presidency's leadership role with Congress. This development can be traced to a number of factors. First, the presidents since Johnson have been less able to rely on partisan connections as a foundation for leadership. Parties have always been a weak basis for alliances between Congress and the presidency. However, after 1968, the parties began to shift from state conventions and caucuses to primaries as the predominant method of selecting delegates to the national conventions. Primaries were introduced at the start of the twentieth century as part of the Progressive Era's reform agenda. Primaries played only a peripheral role through the 1968 elections. However, the turmoil at the Democratic National Convention of 1968 associated with Hubert Humphrey's nomination led the party to adopt rules requiring participation in the nominating process of groups that had previously been excluded. Many states met the party's criteria for selecting delegates by adopting primaries. Since 1972, a majority of delegates from both parties have been chosen through primaries. This shift made the voters, rather than the party organizations, the key to winning the nomination. As a result, presidents have depended less on their party organizations during the nomination and general election campaigns and after they took office.

At the same time, members of Congress have distanced themselves from their national parties. In the pursuit of reelection, members attended to local constituents' wishes, at the expense of loyalty to the national party. As members of Congress gained electoral security, they felt less dependent upon presidential coattails for their electoral success. Thus, the party-based sense of a "shared fate" that bound the president and members of his party in Congress has been undermined. As these partisan ties have weakened, the gap between the two institutions has grown. Parties are less able to help Congress and the president establish and achieve common objectives. Thus, although expectations for presidential leadership have increased, one of the important tools available to presidents has been diminished.

Second, Congress has increasingly resisted presidential efforts at legislative leadership. Motivated by its inability to influence the conduct of the Vietnam War, Congress enacted a series of laws (described below) to challenge presidential leadership in foreign affairs and domestic policy making.

Third, there have been changes in the centralization of authority in Congress. During the first half of this period, Congress fragmented its authority structures by adopting rules that strengthened subcommittees at the expense of committees, weakened party leaders, diluted seniority, and enhanced the staffing support for individual members. The result was greater autonomy and potential for independent action by individual members of Congress. These changes undermined Congress's ability to act as a unified, coherent body in its relations with the presidents, thereby limiting the utility of traditional modes of bargaining between presidents and Congress. Thus, while Congress was inclined to challenge presidential initiatives, it was institutionally incapable of providing its own clear alternative agenda. This trend appears to have been reversed in the later years of this period, as institutional authority has been recentralized in the hands of the Speaker of the House and the party caucuses. Party unity has also improved as southern Democrats' constituencies have more closely approximated traditional northern Democratic districts. The result has been a rise in party unity for both parties.

Richard Nixon's presidency marked an important turning point in modern relations between Congress and the presidency. More than three decades of expanding presidential influence over Congress, often encouraged by Congress itself, ended during Nixon's term in a series of confrontations between the two branches, culminating in congressional moves toward impeachment that precipitated Nixon's resignation.

Nixon faced large Democratic majorities in both houses. His two major proposals were to reform both federal aid to state and local governments and national welfare programs (Nathan, p. 17). He had partial success with the former and failed with the latter. Nixon's other conflicts with Congress centered on his attempts to cut the funding of Great Society programs. Nixon also met with unusual senatorial opposition to his attempts to name justices to the Supreme Court when his first two nominees were rejected by the Senate.

In the face of repeated rebuffs, Nixon moved to accomplish his legislative goals by unilateral means. In *The Administrative Presidency* (New York, 1983), Richard Nathan characterized Nixon's adjustment as an "administrative strategy" (p. 7), which enabled Nixon to circumvent Congress by controlling policy implementation by the executive branch from the White House. He impounded funds to block congressional appropriations to Great Society programs, and pocket-vetoed bills during congressional recesses to avoid the possibility of a congressional override. Nixon also took unilateral action to achieve his foreign policy goals, particularly with regard to the Vietnam War. He invoked national security to expand the war into Cambodia without congressional knowledge or approval.

For its part, Congress enacted a series of laws designed to reclaim its role in making domestic and foreign policy and to constrain the president's discretion. The Case Act of 1972 sought to limit the president's ability to make executive agreements without Congress's knowledge. The War Powers Act of 1973, passed over Nixon's veto, laid out conditions under which the president was required to seek congressional approval of the deployment of military forces. The Budget and Impoundment Control Act of 1974 created institutional mechanisms by which Congress could establish its own spending priorities. Thus, in the early 1970s, Congress actively sought to strengthen itself in its relations with the presidency.

Nixon's conflicts with Congress came to a head over the Watergate affair (the concealment by the executive branch of knowledge of the break-in at the Democratic National headquarters in 1972). Congress was supported in its investigation of the affair by the Supreme Court, which ruled that Congress possessed the authority to subpoena tape recordings of conversations held in the White House. Ultimately, the House Judiciary Committee voted articles of impeachment, leading to Nixon's resignation.

In combination, Watergate cover-up and the war in Vietnam undermined the prevailing consensus on the value of presidential leadership. A powerful presidency was now seen as a potential threat to policy in the public's interest, rather than a source of it. Congress was increasingly viewed as a more reliable representative of the public.

Gerald Ford had little success with Congress. He had no electoral mandate to justify a legislative agenda, he faced a Democratic Congress that was hostile to any attempts at presidential leadership, and his pardon of Nixon alienated many potential sympathizers. Congress blocked almost all of Ford's domestic and foreign policy initiatives, and he was reduced to using his veto power to block appropriations bills that exceeded his spending targets. Congress, while regularly opposing Ford, lacked the institutional coherence needed to provide an agenda of its own. The decentralization of power to subcommittees and individual members precluded the creation of an institutional consensus on the major issues facing Congress. Thus, each branch used its powers to block the actions of the other, but was unable to enact its own preferences.

Jimmy Carter was a majority-party president, but had considerable difficulties in his relations with Congress. In many ways, Carter represented the culmination of the trends identified at the beginning of this section. First, his party was not of much value to him in the legislative process. Since he was elected without the active endorsement or assistance of the Democratic party organization, the party had little stake in his success, and this weakened his ability to generate loyalty from the Democrats in Congress. From Congress's side, Democrats were not inclined to accept presidential leadership. They were constituency-oriented representatives of local interests. Party-based appeals were not particularly persuasive. Second, most Democrats had come into office as

members of the opposition and so were accustomed to opposing, not following, presidents (Berman, 1987, p. 317). The fact that the new president was a Democrat was of little consequence. Finally, Congress as an institution was fragmented, which made it difficult for Carter to strike effective bargains with congressional leaders like the Speaker Thomas P. O'Neill (D.-Mass.).

Some of Carter's problems can be attributed to his personal style and strategy for working with Congress. Carter's congressional liaison office broke with the operating principles used by all prior administrations. Rather than assigning each staff member to work with a subset of members of Congress, Carter made each staffer responsible for a particular policy issue and expected each to work with all members of Congress on that issue. This disrupted the traditional pattern of personal relationships that had existed before and provoked a storm of criticism from Congress. Within two years, Carter reverted to the earlier pattern, but the damage to the comity of the relationship had already been done.

Carter also submitted a large agenda and refused to establish priorities among its proposals. He tried to persuade Congress on the merits of his proposals rather than to engage in the usual politics of self-interest. Congress did not understand his philosophy and was not persuaded by his approach. Moreover, Carter was inclined to take on issues that had little public appeal, but that he felt were important and needed to be addressed. This meant Congress had less incentive to be receptive to his initiatives.

Party leaders in Congress were willing to work with Carter. However, their cooperation was not sufficient to overcome the other obstacles that he faced. As a result, Carter and Congress failed to achieve a mutually supportive, cooperative relationship. The presidency was again unable to provide effective leadership in the relationship. Ten years earlier, the office had been viewed as an "imperial presidency," too powerful and in need of restraint. By the end of Carter's term, the office was considered "imperilled," and presidential leadership was an obsolete concept.

In his first year in office, Ronald Reagan appeared to overturn the conventional wisdom about presidential weakness. He focused on a small number of legislative objectives—tax cuts, domestic budget cuts, and a defense buildup—and secured their adoption in that first year. He succeeded by mobilizing public support to sway undecided members of Congress and by gaining the votes of a small number of others through bargaining.

One reason for Reagan's success in leading Congress can be found in the favorable circumstances under which he began his term. Republicans had regained control of the Senate for the first time in almost thirty years, and Reagan had a working majority in the House as a result of support from conservative southern Democrats and unusually high levels of party unity among Republicans. In addition, the Democrats in Congress failed to organize a significant opposition during Reagan's first year. These conditions changed over the course of Reagan's two terms. The cooperative relations with southern Democrats broke down, and moderate Republicans began to defect from Reagan's positions. Democrats began to recentralize power in their party leaders, enabling them to challenge Reagan more effectively and to offer their own alternatives. Reagan's success in his first year had created the impression that presidential leadership was once again ascendant. In retrospect, that year appears to have been an exception to the prevailing pattern of weak presidential leadership of Congress. By the end of his eight-year presidency, Reagan's support in Congress, as measured by *Congressional Quarterly,* was at historic lows.

In foreign affairs, Reagan often compensated for his inability to lead Congress by acting unilaterally, relying on secrecy to circumvent Congress. Notable examples include the secret operations of the Central Intelligence Agency (CIA) in Nicaragua, covert assistance provided to the Nicaraguan Contras in the face of legislative mandates forbidding such aid, and the sale of weapons to Iran in exchange for hostages. All of these actions were taken either in the absence of informed congressional assent or even in the absence of congressional knowledge. Congress tried to limit these executive actions as they became known. For example, when Congress learned that the CIA had played a role in mining Nicaraguan harbors, it passed the Boland Amendment, which cut off all government aid to the Contras. When the

Iran-Contra affair came to light, Congress instigated hearings, seeking to uncover the role played by the president and his aides. The weaknesses of these responses rested in their reactive character. As a result, the Reagan presidency was able to pursue its policies over an extended period of time, despite significant congressional opposition.

George Bush was never able to assume a constructive leadership role with Congress. He was limited in that regard by four factors. First, he was personally predisposed to attend to foreign rather than domestic policy issues. His successes, such as relations with the fractured Soviet Union, and the conduct of the Gulf War, were in foreign affairs. In contrast, he had no clear vision for the United States' domestic agenda. Second, he was the first president to be elected from the incumbent president's party since Herbert Hoover. Proposing major new initiatives would have appeared to criticize his popular predecessor, Ronald Reagan. Third, a decade of large budget deficits meant the government lacked the financial resources to fund new programs that the president might want to propose. Finally, congressional Democrats had been the opposition party for 16 of the preceding 20 years, and been the majority party in the Senate for 12 and in the House of Representative for all 20 of those years. Thus, they were experienced in contending with Republican presidents, and had developed the ability to seize control of the national agenda. They were able to defeat Bush's initiatives while passing their own. These four factors left Bush in a very weak leadership position. He had less success with Congress than virtually any of his predecessors in the era of the modern presidency. Significantly, his major accomplishment was negative in nature: he vetoed 46 bills over his four years, and had only one—his last—overridden. Thus, Bush continued the trend of weak presidential leadership of Congress.

## Summary

This review of legislative-executive relations demonstrates above all the variability present in the relationship. At some times, Congress clearly dominated the relationship, while at other times the president prevailed. On occasion, the relationship was one of close cooperation between the branches. More often, the relationship was competitive, sometimes approaching open warfare.

Characteristics of the individual branches have also varied widely over time. Congress's internal structures ranged from weak authority hierarchies to a fairly strong party government. Some presidents were content to let Congress make its own decisions unencumbered by presidential pressure, while others struggled mightily to get Congress to enact their proposals. For the foreseeable future, presidents will probably remain the main source of important legislative proposals, though they will not necessarily be successful in achieving their goals.

Finally, it should be noted that parties proved capable of unifying members in both branches behind common goals. However, when parties were weak or when opposing parties controlled the two branches, coordination and cooperation was much more difficult to achieve. The recent trend toward a weakening of party ties bodes ill for future prospects of cooperation and coordination between the president and Congress.

## STATE-LEVEL RELATIONS

Drawing broad conclusions about state legislative-executive relations is a difficult exercise, but one general trend can be recognized: there has been a gradual transfer of power over time from the legislature to the governor. Governors were circumscribed in their powers in the earliest state constitutions, those of the late eighteenth and early nineteenth centuries. However, as the country grew in population and modernized during the nineteenth century, both governors and state legislatures shouldered increasingly greater burdens. Governors made further gains in their political power at the beginning of the twentieth century when they became populist leaders in the wake of the financial scandals associated with the rule of party bosses. In the first half of the twentieth century, the national government took the lead in addressing domestic problems. State governments were seen as largely inattentive to those problems and ineffective when they attempted to deal with them. However, beginning in the 1960s, the states underwent significant govern-

mental reform, with governors emerging as the leaders of state government. By the 1980s, governors were generally ascendant in state legislative-executive relations.

Today's strong, popularly elected governor holds an office that bears little resemblance to the office created by the infant states. Popular dislike of the executive carried over in the establishment of the governor's office. Governors were popularly elected in Massachusetts, New York, Rhode Island, and Connecticut, but in all other states, the governors were appointed by the legislatures. Each state constitution also used the legislature to limit gubernatorial power. For example, only the governors of New York, Massachusetts, and, for a short period, South Carolina could veto legislation (Kallenbach, p. 24), and in no case did the governors have appreciable removal or appointment power. Whenever the governors did wield power, the legislatures forced them to seek the advice of executive councils prior to exercising those powers (Kallenbach, p. 18). The framers of the state constitutions appeared to have learned from the colonial experience that strength in the executive was tantamount to illegitimate authority over the population. States would come to learn harder lessons about the corruption brought on by legislative tyranny.

A governor with limited power did not seem to matter quite so much in the early history of the United States, for the states were not given a great many duties to perform. States were responsible for creating their own transportation infrastructures and a favorable climate for business. They did not possess the elaborate social-welfare and regulatory structures that exist today. With the passage of time, states began to give governors greater authority. For example, states admitted to the Union, after the original thirteen, created stronger governorships. The election of Andrew Jackson to the presidency catapulted governors to prominence, on the basis of the new philosophy that elected executives and not legislatures best represented the public's wishes. However, this did not necessarily assure governors of greater power in relation to their state legislatures. Governors gained broader powers of veto, appointment, and pardon, but they were not able to administer their departments. Paradoxically, this weakness resulted from reforms intended to strengthen the executive. The governorship and other state executive-branch officials were democratized through their popular election. The main beneficiaries of this arrangement were the legislatures. Direct election weakened gubernatorial control over the executive branch because the people, not the governor, controlled the fate of the other executive-branch officers.

Diffusion of executive authority hurt the state governments' ability to enforce their laws. This problem became more apparent as America began to industrialize following the Civil War. In the absence of gubernatorial leadership, the legislatures tried the familiar pattern of creating and placing power in agencies of their own creation and under their auspices. Leslie Lipson described three major problems resulting from this continued decentralization: duplication of duties, waste in performance of duties, and irresponsible discharge of duties. The overriding problem was one of accountability and coordination. State government found itself unable to cope with the problems of urbanization and industrialization.

In the last quarter of the nineteenth century, legislative dominance over state government gave way to the influence of state party bosses. The legislatures abdicated rule in favor of the majority-party's state leader, who dispensed patronage and remained in power while governors came and went. Famous state party bosses of this era included Roscoe Conkling and Thomas C. Platt in New York and Charles Ray Brayton in Rhode Island.

The incentive to reorganize state government came from both the expansion of the nation, which required more governing by state government, and from the corruption of the state party bosses. The Progressive movement favored more-effective administration and less-corrupt state government. It believed that strengthening the governors would satisfy these twin demands. The states were out in front of the national government in such tasks as ensuring safety in the workplace; regulating the insurance, banking, and railroad industries; and protecting the environment. In the wake of the financial crisis of the late nineteenth century, brought on in part by the activities of the party bosses, the governors even emerged as advocates for the average citizen. Since governors had not played a meaningful role in state

government at the time of the crisis, they could claim to be a viable alternative.

Thus, the Progressive movement had important influences on the reorganization of state government. Such noted Progressive figures as Theodore Roosevelt, Woodrow Wilson, and Robert La Follette were among the governors who had instituted reforms in their states. As governors, they set their states' agendas. This came to be accepted as a proper function of the governors rather than the legislatures or party bosses. Control over executive agencies was also reconcentrated in the governorships in the interests of administrative efficiency. Consolidating control over state governmental operations made sense during a time (1890–1919) when total state expenditures increased sevenfold (Lipson, p. 76).

As support for the Progressive movement waned, states and their governors became less-important political actors. The two world wars and the Great Depression all confronted the states with problems that they could not hope to address on their own. State governments declined in power as they turned to the national government for assistance, particularly during the New Deal period, when governors in the declining states were usually mediocre politicians. State governments were generally viewed as incompetent and corrupt. Observers even feared that state governments would eventually be transformed into little more than administrative agents of the national government.

Fortunes changed for the states in the 1960s, and governors emerged as the main beneficiaries of massive reforms. Governors acquired increased powers of appointment, which, along with a decline in patronage powers, allowed for an increase in the number of competent officials and for more-unified gubernatorial control at the highest levels of the executive branch. The reapportionment of state legislative seats mandated by the Supreme Court decision in *Baker* v. *Carr,* 369 U.S. 186 (1962), increased urban representation in the state legislatures. This created a closer mirroring of the governors' and legislatures' electoral constituencies and gave the governors' supporters more influence in the legislatures. State legislatures became more centralized and more professionalized. This improved their ability to deal with the more intractable problems of today's society.

Finally, the "New Federalism" of the 1970s brought greater power to the states and governors. This program shifted the types of grants made to the states from categorical grants to block grants and general revenue sharing. As a result, there was a devolution of power from the national government to the states during the Republican presidential administrations of the 1970s and the 1980s.

The primacy of gubernatorial leadership is thus a recent phenomenon. Governors are expected to take the lead in proposing legislation and to veto measures with which they disagree. Even in states with ostensibly "weak" governorships, the governor can still use personal prestige to push an agenda through the legislature. The governors' expanded place in state government has clearly altered the dynamics of state legislative-executive relations, resulting in a much more prominent role for the governors.

## RECENT SCHOLARLY RESEARCH

Studies of the relationship between the legislature and executive have burgeoned in recent decades. Most address whether and how presidents affect the legislative process. This body of scholarship could be described in a number of ways. One approach is to classify it along two dimensions: the substantive foci of the studies and the methods used to study the relationship.

### Substantive Focus

In terms of substance, studies of legislative-executive relations cluster in two groups. The first examines the process by which the relationship is conducted. These studies describe how presidents have gone about achieving their legislative goals. The most important and theoretically grounded of these is Richard Neustadt's *Presidential Power* (1960). Working from an exchange-theory perspective, Neustadt sees the president at the hub of government activity. Presidential influence depends on the president's ability to persuade other political actors, which is in turn conditioned by the president's reputation with Washington elites and the public's support for the president. Neustadt's approach gave the presidency a prominence that continues to inform both scholarly and journalistic accounts of the presidential-congressional relationship.

Any listing of other important process-oriented works is necessarily incomplete. However, the following works exemplify studies using this perspective. In *Legislative Liaison* (1970), Abraham Holtzman used a systems-theory perspective to define the positions, roles, strategies and activities of executive liaison officers. Stephen Wayne's *The Legislative Presidency* (1978) describes the structure, operation, and evolution of the presidency's liaison apparatus. The nature of the interactions among the White House, Congress, the public, and political interest groups inform such studies as Barbara Kellerman's *The Political Presidency* (1984) and Samuel Kernell's *Going Public* (1986). Each of these studies emphasizes the need to examine and understand events or patterns of events as a means of accounting for the successes of some presidents and the failures of others.

The second focus emphasizes the impact of context on the relationship. Contextual studies examine how factors exogenous to the relationship affect the outcomes. Two of the best studies in this vein are George Edwards's *At the Margins* (1989) and Jon Bond and Richard Fleisher's *The President in the Legislative Arena* (1990). These studies emphasize the impact of changes in Congress's partisan and ideological composition and in the public's support for the president, on presidential success in Congress, as measured by votes cast and bills passed by Congress. Mark Peterson's *Legislating Together* (1990) expands the focus by examining not only the outcomes of the legislative process but also the level and types of conflict found in it and by assessing the character of the presidents' legislative agendas as an influence on both outcomes and types of conflict. Despite these differences, however, these studies share a common disregard for the actual workings of the relationship. They leave the process unspecified and instead ask how external factors affect it.

### Methodological Approach

Studies of the presidential-congressional relationship tend to employ one of two methodologies. The historical-narrative method focuses on describing what each president and Congress did. Research from this perspective attempts to develop generalizations about individual presidencies and even across presidencies. Among the sources described earlier, some employ fairly explicit theoretical frameworks (e.g., Neustadt, Kellerman, and Kernell), while others are more flexible in their analytical perspective (e.g., Holtzman, Wayne).

The quantitative-aggregate analysis method typically subjects numerical indicators of relevant concepts (e.g., presidential popularity and congressional support for the president) to statistical analysis. Research cited above that illustrates this approach includes Bond and Fleisher, Edwards, and Peterson.

## An Evaluation

Integrating the two dimensions generates a fourfold classification of research on legislative-executive relations: (1) historical-narrative research with a process orientation; (2) historical-narrative research with a contextual orientation; (3) quantitative-aggregate analysis research with a process orientation; and (4) quantitative-aggregate analysis research with a contextual orientation.

Most studies tend to fall into either the first or last category. Studies employing a historical-narrative approach usually examine the actual interactions between the president and Congress, attempting to explain why each actor behaves as it does and with what consequence. Studies using a quantitative-aggregate analysis approach tend to examine the impact of contextual factors on legislative outcomes without investigating the process by which those factors work.

The most interesting point of comparison between these two schools of study is the difference in their findings. The process-oriented studies tend to emphasize the impact of the president on the legislative process and its outcomes. Neustadt (1960) and those following him have generated a great body of findings making such claims. Most of the studies employed in this review fall into this category.

In contrast, the context-oriented studies find that the president is a peripheral element in the legislative process, with only a marginal impact.

The context-oriented studies point out the methodological flaws of the process-oriented school. Quite correctly, they note that even the most systematic of these studies do not lend themselves to falsifiable propositions or generalizations beyond their particular cases. The context-oriented studies insist on using data that are susceptible to empirical hypothesis testing. Unfortunately, most of these studies have failed to generate data that address questions of process. The process goes empirically unobserved and conceptually unexplored. Thus, the inferences they draw about the presidents' marginal role are without systematic empirical grounding in the actual behaviors of the presidents or Congress. In the absence of models and data about such behaviors, any conclusions these studies offer must be considered extremely tentative.

## Looking Ahead

One cannot speak to the issue of whether or how presidents influence legislative outcomes until one begins to think systematically about the mechanisms and procedures by which presidents and Congress interact. Then one needs to develop ways of measuring these phenomena, even if only indirectly. Generalizations (however intuitively plausible) cannot be sustained on the basis of case studies whose conclusions are not susceptible to falsification. Nor can one attend only to the contextual inputs and voting outcomes of the legislative process and claim to make authoritative statements about behaviors. Studies must turn their attention to generating hypotheses and data that lead to inferences about what presidents actually do in their efforts to influence members of Congress and the outcomes of those efforts. Only then can one begin to speak authoritatively about whether, and how, presidents and Congress affect the legislative process.

## BIBLIOGRAPHY

### General Accounts

Broad treatments of the presidential-congressional relationship over extended periods of time can be found in WILFRED BINKLEY, *The Powers of the President* (New York, 1937), and GEORGE GALLOWAY, *History of the House of Representatives,* 2d ed. (New York, 1976). SIDNEY MILKIS and MICHAEL NELSON, *The American Presidency: Origins and Development 1776–1990* (Washington, D.C., 1990), provides a comprehensive and updated depiction of the relationship.

### Establishing the Presidential-Congressional Relationship

The basic work on colonial legislative-executive relations is EVARTS B. GREENE, *The Provincial Governor* (New York, 1898; repr., 1966). An assessment of presidents carving out power for themselves under the Articles of Confederation, laying the groundwork for today's presidency, is RICHARD B. MORRIS, "The Origins of the Presidency," *Presidential Studies Quarterly* 17:4 (1987). A brief but effective treatment of legislative-gubernatorial relations under the Articles of Confederation is ROBERT F. WILLIAMS, "Evolving State Legislative and Executive Power in the Founding Decade," *Annals of the American Academy of Political and Social Science* 496 (March 1988). A statement on the Whig political philosophy that permeated this period can be found in BARRY SCHWARTZ, "George Washington and the Whig Conception of Heroic Leadership," *American Sociological Review* 48:1 (1983). For more on THOMAS PAINE, see PHILIP S. FONER, ed., *The Complete Writings of Thomas Paine,* 2 vols. (New York, 1969). A discussion of the relevant issues raised at the Constitutional Convention can be found in CHARLES THACH, *The Creation of the Presidency* (Baltimore, 1923). In *Constitutional Conflicts Between Congress and the President* (Princeton, N.J., 1985), LOUIS FISHER identifies and traces the development of the many constitutional disputes between these two branches of government.

### The Pre–Modern Presidency Era

LEONARD D. WHITE provides detailed accounts of the formation and early workings of the United States government in *The Federalists* (New York, 1948) and *The Jeffersonians* (New York, 1951). JAMES S. YOUNG, *The Washington Community: 1800–1828* (New York, 1966), is the classic treatment of the Jeffersonian period. For more detailed treatments of developments within Congress as they influenced its relations with the presidency, see JOHN F. HOADLEY, "The Emergence of Political Parties in Congress, 1789–1803," *American Political Science Review* 74:3 (1980); J. R. POLE, *Foundations of American Independence: 1763–1815* (Indianapolis, 1972); and JOEL H. SILBEY, "The Incomplete World of American Politics, 1815–1829: Presidents, Parties and Politics in the 'Era of Good Feeling'," *Congress and the Presidency* 11:1 (1984). LEONARD D. WHITE, *The Jacksonians* (New York, 1954), describes the conflicts and developments of this period. The period of Republican dominance from the Civil War into the twentieth century is captured in LEONARD D. WHITE, *The Republican Era, 1869–1901* (New York, 1958), and WOODROW WILSON, *Congressional Government* (1885; repr., New York, 1956). RONALD M. PETERS, JR., *The American Speakership: The Office in Historical Perspective* (Baltimore, 1990), conveys the nature of the relationship during this period from the perspective of Congress.

### The Modern Presidency Era

Any discussion of the presidential-congressional relationship in general must begin with RICHARD NEUSTADT, *Presidential Power: The Politics of Leadership* (New York, 1960). This classic formulation of how modern presidents interact with other political institutions, particularly Congress, views these interactions as a bargaining process. BARBARA KELLERMAN, *The Political Presidency* (New York, 1984), updates Neustadt's argument with examples drawn from presidents Kennedy through Reagan. In contrast, SAMUEL KERNELL, *Going Public: New Strategies of Presidential Leadership,* 2d ed. (Washington, D.C., 1993), claims that since the 1970s the bargaining approach has been superceded by presidential appeals to the public as a means of influencing Congress. Persuasive statistical analyses that emphasize the importance of Congress in the relationship can be found in

GEORGE C. EDWARDS III, *At the Margins: Presidential Leadership of Congress* (New Haven, Conn., 1989), JON BOND and RICHARD FLEISHER, *The President in the Legislative Arena* (Chicago, 1990), and MARK A. PETERSON, *Legislating Together: The White House and Capitol Hill from Eisenhower to Reagan* (Cambridge, Mass., 1990).

Many books describe and explain the relations between specific presidents and Congress. An excellent (though now somewhat dated) account from Roosevelt through Carter is found in STEPHEN J. WAYNE, *The Legislative Presidency* (New York, 1978). LARRY BERMAN, *The New American Presidency* (Glenview, Ill., 1987), includes a discussion of the interactions with Congress of every president from Franklin Roosevelt through Reagan. JOSEPH COOPER and DAVID W. BRADY provide a historical assessment of the role of congressional leadership in working with presidents from the early 1900s to the 1960s in "Institutional Context and Leadership Style: The House from Cannon to Rayburn," *American Political Science Review* 75:4 (1981). KENNETH A. SHEPSLE updates that line of inquiry in "The Changing Textbook Congress," in JOHN E. CHUBB and PAUL E. PETERSON, eds., *Can the Government Govern?* (Washington, D.C., 1989). The landmark role of Franklin Roosevelt in shaping the relationship is discussed in WILLIAM E. LEUCHTENBURG, *Franklin D. Roosevelt and the New Deal* (New York, 1963). The relationship as it evolved from the president's side through the Truman and Eisenhower presidencies is the focus of RICHARD NEUSTADT, "Presidency and Legislation: Planning the President's Program," *American Political Science Review* 49:4 (1955). FRED I. GREENSTEIN's study of Dwight Eisenhower, *The Hidden Hand Presidency: Eisenhower as Leader* (New York, 1982), provides important insights regarding his legislative strategy, and GARY R. REICHARD, *The Reaffirmation of Republicanism* (Knoxville, Tenn., 1975) offers a more detailed study of Eisenhower's relations with Congress during his first term. In *Legislative Liaison: Executive Leadership in Congress* (Chicago, 1970), ABRAHAM HOLTZMAN examines organizational developments during the 1960s that took place within the executive branch to facilitate presidential influence in Congress. JAMES L. SUNDQUIST, *Politics and Policy: The Eisenhower, Kennedy, and Johnson Years* (Washington, D.C., 1968), describes the relationship through the 1960s, and his *The Decline and Resurgence of Congress* (Washington, D.C., 1981) continues the analyses into the Carter years. MORRIS P. FIORINA, "The Presidency and Congress: An Electoral Connection?" in MICHAEL NELSON, ed., *The Presidency and the Political System,* 2d ed. (Washington, D.C., 1988), details how changes in the electoral linkage between presidents and Congress during the 1970s and 1980s have weakened congressional loyalty to the presidents. Two outstanding biographies of Jimmy Carter emphasize his congressional connections: ERWIN C. HARGROVE, *Jimmy Carter as President: Leadership and the Politics of the Public Good* (Baton Rouge, La., 1988), and CHARLES O. JONES, *The Trusteeship Presidency: Jimmy Carter and the United States Congress* (Baton Rouge, La., 1988). Ronald Reagan's relation with Congress is described in CHARLES O. JONES, "Ronald Reagan and the U.S. Congress: Visible-Hand Politics," in CHARLES O. JONES, ed., *The Reagan Legacy: Promise and Performance* (Chatham, N.J., 1988).

### State-level Relations

The basic text on governors from the colonial to pre–World War II days is LESLIE LIPSON, *The American Governor from Figurehead to Leader* (New York, 1939; repr., 1968). More recent work includes LARRY SABATO, *Goodbye to Good-Time Charlie: The American Governorship Transformed* (Washington, D.C., 1983), and JOHN D. BUENKER, "State Government," in the *Encyclopedia of American Political History* (New York, 1984). A comparative study of governors and presidents is JOSEPH E. KALLENBACH, *The American Chief Executive: The Presidency and the Governorship* (New York, 1966). Bringing the legislative-gubernatorial relationship up to date is ALAN ROSENTHAL, *Governors and Legislatures: Contending Powers* (Washington, D.C., 1990).

SEE ALSO Congress, the Executive, and Foreign Policy; Congress, the Executive, and War Powers; The Executive Veto; AND The Legislative Veto.

# CONGRESS, THE EXECUTIVE, AND WAR POWERS

## *Duane Tananbaum*

One of the most bitterly disputed issues in the United States in recent decades has been whether Congress or the president has the power to take the nation into war. The U.S. Constitution gives Congress the power to declare war and designates the president as commander in chief of the armed forces, but it does not detail where one of these powers stops and the other begins. By the middle of the twentieth century, Congress's power to declare war seemed an anachronism as presidents used the armed forces in hostilities all over the world, including major wars in Korea and Vietnam, without any congressional declaration of war.

American involvement in Vietnam finally led Congress to reassert its authority over the war-making power by passing the War Powers Resolution in 1973. But, despite the hopes of the bill's sponsors that it would restore Congress to its preeminent role in deciding when the United States should go to war, presidents have continued to send American armed forces into combat in foreign lands without congressional approval.

## THE CONSTITUTIONAL SETTING

In writing the Constitution, the founders of the United States paid special attention to the question of how the new nation would go to war. The United States was created by a revolutionary war in an era in which wars were common. Under British rule, the American colonies had been involved in numerous wars against the Indians and in the various imperial wars among the European powers. The nation's leaders hoped to establish a system in which American involvement in war would become the exception rather than the rule.

The delegates at the Constitutional Convention in 1787 believed that the executive was the branch of government most predisposed to involve a nation in war. They understood that in Europe monarchs decided unilaterally whether their nations went to war. Even in England, as Sir William Blackstone noted in his *Commentaries on the Laws of England,* the king enjoyed "the sole prerogative of making war and peace." But Americans were determined that in the United States no one person would have the authority to take the nation into war.

Pierce Butler of South Carolina was the only delegate at the Constitutional Convention who spoke in favor of giving the president the power to decide when the nation would go to war. Elbridge Gerry of Massachusetts spoke for most of the delegates when he exclaimed that he "never expected to hear in a Republic a motion to empower the Executive alone to declare war." The first drafts of the Constitution reflected Gerry's views, stipulating that "the legislature of the United States shall have the power . . . to make war" (Farrand, vol. 2, pp. 182, 318).

But Gerry and James Madison of Virginia recognized the potential problem in vesting in Congress the power to make war. What would happen if the nation were attacked while Congress was not in session? To deal with that possibility, they moved to substitute *declare* for *make.* This would leave Congress with the power to initiate or decide on war, but it would give the president "the power to repel sudden attacks." Rufus King of Massachusetts also preferred *declare* to *make* because he feared that giving Congress the power to make war might be interpreted as giving the legislature the authority to conduct a war once it had begun. Most of the delegates approved the new wording, which was adopted by a vote of eight states to one (Farrand, vol. 2, pp. 318–319).

The Constitution also vests in Congress other powers closely related to the war power.

Article I, Section 8, gives the legislature the power to

> grant Letters of Marque and Reprisal, and make Rules concerning Captures on Land and Water;
>
> To raise and support Armies . . . ;
>
> To provide and maintain a Navy;
>
> To make rules for the Government and Regulation of the land and naval Forces;
>
> To provide for calling forth the Militia to execute the Laws of the Union, suppress Insurrections and repel invasions; [and]
>
> To provide for organizing, arming, and disciplining, the Militia, and for governing such Part of them as may be employed in the Service of the United States.

Moreover, Congress's power of the purse—the requirement in Article I, Section 9, that "no Money shall be drawn from the Treasury, but in Consequence of Appropriations made by Law"—strengthens the legislature's control over whether the nation goes to war, since a war cannot be fought if Congress refuses to appropriate funds for it.

Although the Constitution vests in Congress alone the power to declare war, it also provides in Article II, Section 2, that "the President shall be Commander in Chief of the Army and Navy of the United States." But this was never intended to mean that the president could initiate war. The nation's founders wanted the president to have the authority to use military force to repel sudden attacks against the United States and to conduct a war once it was declared by Congress. Even Alexander Hamilton, a fervent supporter of broad executive power, conceded in *The Federalist,* no. 69, that the president's authority in this area

> would be nominally the same with that of the king of Great Britain, but in substance much inferior to it. It would amount to nothing more than the supreme command and direction of the military and naval forces, as first general and admiral of the Confederacy; while that of the British king extends to the *declaring* of war and to the *raising* and *regulating* of fleets and armies—all which, by the Constitution under consideration, would appertain to the legislature.

Some have asserted that the president can use the armed forces as he deems necessary as part of his obligations under Article II to "pre-serve, protect and defend the Constitution of the United States" and to "take Care that the Laws be faithfully executed." But the records of the Constitutional Convention make it clear that these provisions were intended as general descriptions of the president's duties, not as grants of authority. The nation's founders were confident that they had lodged in Congress, not the president, the power to take the United States into war. As Thomas Jefferson emphasized in a letter to Madison in 1789, "We have already given in example one effectual check to the dog of war by transferring the power of letting him loose from the Executive to the legislative body" (Julian Boyd, ed., *The Papers of Thomas Jefferson* [Princeton, N.J., 1950–], vol. 15, p. 397).

## THE EARLY REPUBLIC, 1789–1845

Congress and the president began sparring almost immediately over the power to use the armed forces in hostilities short of war. George Washington and most of his successors took an expansive view of their authority to employ the armed forces, and Congress often acquiesced in, rather than challenge, the president's actions. In those few disputes that reached the courts, the judiciary upheld Congress's power to authorize war or hostilities short of war, but nonetheless, the general trend in the early years of the Republic was increasing presidential control over the armed forces and the war powers.

Questions concerning the war powers of Congress and the president's authority first emerged in the debate over George Washington's Neutrality Proclamation in 1793. When war erupted in Europe, Washington asked his cabinet for advice. Hamilton asserted that the president had the power to determine whether America's treaties with France obligated the United States to enter the war, but Jefferson argued that since the president could not declare war on his own, he could not unilaterally choose neutrality either. Jefferson believed that Congress alone had the power to decide whether the United States should remain neutral or go to war. Washington agreed with Hamilton, and the president issued his proclamation on 22 April 1793.

# CONGRESS, THE EXECUTIVE, AND WAR POWERS

Over the next few years, relations between the United States and France deteriorated to the point where the two nations waged an undeclared naval war—the so-called Quasi-War—from 1798 to 1800. This conflict raised the question of whether the executive or the legislature could order hostile actions against other nations in the absence of a declaration of war.

President John Adams believed Congress's approval was required even for measures short of war and so he sought permission in 1797 to arm American merchant ships. But Congress rejected the president's request. After the XYZ affair, however, when French officials demanded bribes before they would negotiate with American diplomats, the legislature readily acceded to the president's requests and authorized hostilities against France. Congress established the U.S. Navy Department and authorized the president to use the navy against French privateers and raiders, to retake captured American ships, and to seize armed French vessels. The lawmakers also agreed to raise an army of ten thousand men.

The undeclared naval war with France resulted in a series of cases in which the Supreme Court ruled that the war power was clearly vested in Congress and that the legislature was the branch of government to decide when and how the United States would wage war or enter into hostilities. In *Bas* v. *Tingy,* 4 Dallas 37 (1800), the Supreme Court ruled that Congress could authorize hostilities or "imperfect war" without a formal declaration of war. In *Talbot* v. *Seeman,* 1 Cranch 1 (1801), the Court ruled that various naval actions were legal because they had been authorized by Congress. In his decision for the Court, Chief Justice John Marshall emphasized that "the whole powers of war being, by the Constitution of the United States, vested in Congress, the acts of that body can alone be resorted to as our guides in this inquiry. . . . Congress may authorize general hostilities . . . or partial war" (p. 28). In *Little* v. *Barreme,* 2 Cranch 170 (1804), the Court concluded that once Congress had established its policy in a statute, the president and the navy were bound to carry out that policy and any orders or actions that exceeded what Congress had authorized were illegal. Thus, in all three cases, the Supreme Court ruled that it was Congress, not the president, which had the authority to decide whether and to what extent the United States would wage war or engage in hostilities, even in the absence of a declaration of war.

While the courts were upholding the legislature's control over the war power, President Thomas Jefferson was using the armed forces against the Barbary pirates without the consent or even the knowledge of Congress. The Barbary pirates had long preyed on American ships in the Mediterranean, and in May 1801, Jefferson dispatched a naval squadron to the Mediterranean to protect American commerce. If the Barbary states had declared war or commenced hostilities against the United States, the American forces were to "chastise their insolence—by sinking, burning, or destroying their ships and vessels wherever you shall find them." The president and the secretary of the navy issued these orders even though Congress had not authorized any hostilities against the Barbary states (U.S. Office of Naval Records and Library, *Naval Documents Related to the United Sttes Wars with the Barbary Powers,* 6 vols. [Washington, D.C., 1939–1944], vol. 1, pp. 466–467).

Jefferson chose not to call Congress into special session to deal with the situation in the Mediterranean. When the legislature finally convened in December 1801, the president reported that Tripoli had declared war against the United States, and that a Tripolitan ship had attacked the USS *Enterprise,* which had defended itself and captured the enemy vessel. Jefferson explained that the Tripolitan ship had then been disabled and released, because American forces were "unauthorized by the Constitution, without the sanction of Congress, to go beyond the line of defense." Jefferson now asked the legislature to authorize offensive actions which would "place our force on an equal footing with that of its adversaries." He would provide Congress with all the relevant information so that it could make an informed judgment "in the exercise of this important function confided by the Constitution to the Legislature exclusively" (Richardson, vol. 1, p. 315).

Like a number of later presidents, Jefferson told Congress less than the whole story. He omitted important information concerning his orders to "chastise" the Barbary states, and he misrepresented the *Enterprise*'s engagement with the Tripolitan ship. In fact, as ordered by the president, the navy had already taken offensive actions, although one could argue that such actions were warranted once Tripoli had declared war against the United States. Jefferson tried to have it both ways, however. Even after Tripoli had declared war, the president maintained in his message to Congress that only the legislature could authorize offensive military actions. But Jefferson's orders had clearly included plans for offensive operations.

The Jeffersonians enjoyed a comfortable majority in Congress, and in February 1802 the lawmakers authorized the president to take all measures he deemed necessary to deal with Tripoli. Congress accepted as sincere and legitimate Jefferson's request that the legislature decide whether the United States should go on the offensive against Tripoli, not knowing that the president had already authorized the navy to do so. Despite his rhetoric acknowledging the power of Congress to declare war and authorize hostilities short of war, Jefferson had established the precedent of a president using the armed forces as he saw fit without the knowledge or permission of Congress.

In 1812 it was Congress rather than the president that was eager for war. Henry Clay of Kentucky and the "War Hawks" in Congress desired war with England to add Canada and Florida to the national domain. Jefferson's and Madison's attempts to use embargoes and other economic pressures to force Britain and France to end their interference with America's neutral trade had resulted in a serious depression in the South and West, which producers and planters blamed on Great Britain. Americans also blamed Britain for inciting the Indians on the frontier. The Democratic-Republican majority in Congress preferred war to the humiliation of submission to British impressment of American sailors and restrictions on American trade.

Ever since 1787, James Madison had argued that the legislature should be the ultimate arbiter when the nation had to choose between peace and war. Madison now believed that the national interest demanded war, but in his message to Congress on 1 June 1812 he emphasized that the Constitution vested in Congress the power to decide whether the United States should go to war. Congress debated the matter

for eighteen days before the House of Representatives approved a declaration of war by a vote of seventy-nine to forty-nine, and the Senate concurred, nineteen to thirteen.

After the War of 1812, many Americans still coveted Florida, and in 1818, General Andrew Jackson brought the situation to a head when he led an American force into Florida in pursuit of Seminole Indians, who had been harassing Americans in Georgia. President James Monroe had instructed Jackson to do whatever was necessary to bring the conflict with the Seminoles to a successful conclusion. Jackson encountered few Indians in Florida, but he captured three Spanish forts and executed two British citizens for aiding the Indians.

Monroe and his advisers recognized that Jackson's incursion into Florida raised the question of whether the president could authorize such actions on his own, or if they required congressional approval. Secretary of the Treasury William Crawford and Secretary of War John Calhoun both argued that Jackson's capture of Spanish forts was an act of war against Spain and was unconstitutional because it had not been authorized by Congress. Secretary of State John Quincy Adams asserted, however, that the president could authorize defensive measures to protect American citizens against the Indians, as Monroe had done in this instance, and that everything that had followed had been incidental to that conflict, not acts of hostility against Spain. Monroe accepted Adams's view that Jackson's actions, including the capture of the Spanish forts, could be justified as self-defense, but the president believed that retaining the forts would constitute an act of war against Spain, which required congressional authorization. Therefore, he decided to return the forts to Spain as soon as possible.

When Congress reconvened in November 1818, special committees were appointed in both the Senate and the House of Representatives to investigate Jackson's actions in Florida. The House committee recommended that Jackson be censured, and the Senate committee emphasized that Congress, not the president, and certainly not General Jackson, had the power to decide if Spain's inability to control the Indians was sufficient cause for war. But the full House and Senate declined to take any formal action against Jackson, whose aggression hastened the Adams-Onís Treaty of

1819, whereby Spain ceded Florida to the United States.

## POLK AND LINCOLN, 1845–1865

In 1845–1846, President James K. Polk demonstrated how a president could use his authority as commander in chief of the armed forces to create a situation in which Congress had little choice but to declare war. In the closing days of his administration, President John Tyler had proposed, and Congress had approved, a joint resolution annexing Texas, with the stipulation that the boundary dispute between Mexico and Texas was to be settled by negotiations. Polk then sent an envoy to Mexico to try to use the boundary dispute and American financial claims against Mexico as leverage to purchase California.

In 1846, Polk ordered General Zachary Taylor and his troops to move to the Rio Grande, occupying all of the disputed territory. American and Mexican forces soon clashed, and Polk immediately asserted that "Mexico has passed the boundary of the United States, has invaded our territory and shed American blood upon the American soil." Accordingly, he asked Congress to recognize that war now existed between the United States and Mexico and to place at his disposal the means of fighting the war (Richardson, vol. 3, p. 2292).

Many in Congress were skeptical about Polk's account of events. American claims to the disputed area were weak, and the clash had occurred at the southernmost end of the contested territory. Polk's critics wanted to see evidence supporting the president's contention that the battle had occurred on American soil. They charged that it was the president's unilateral decision to order Taylor's forces to the Rio Grande that had led to hostilities. But Polk's fellow Democrats, who controlled Congress, embedded the declaration of war in the preamble of a bill to provide supplies for the troops in the field. They limited debate on the measure, demanding its immediate passage, and refused to allow enough time to examine the various documents Polk had sent to Congress. Legislators were reluctant to vote against supplies needed by troops who were under attack, and thus the House approved the bill declaring

war by a vote of 174–14, and the Senate followed suit, 40–2.

As the war continued and Congress learned more about the circumstances of the initial clash of forces, Polk's support dwindled. Legislators resented the way in which Polk had positioned Taylor's forces to make war almost inevitable, and they were angry over the way in which he had misled them about the beginning of hostilities.

One of Polk's chief critics was Abraham Lincoln, then a young congressman from Illinois. Time and again, Lincoln demanded to know the spot on American soil where American blood had been shed. Lincoln explained his position in a letter to a friend in 1848. The friend had defended Polk's decision to send American troops into the disputed area to prevent a possible invasion by Mexican forces. Lincoln's response is worth quoting at length:

> Allow the President to invade a neighboring nation, whenever *he* shall deem it necessary to repel an invasion, and you allow him to do so, *whenever he may choose to say* he deems it necessary for such purpose—and you allow him to make war at his pleasure. . . .
>
> The provision of the Constitution giving the war-making power to Congress, was dictated, as I understand it, by the following reasons. Kings had always been involving and impoverishing their people in wars, pretending generally, if not always, that the good of the people was the object. This our Convention understood to be the most oppressive of all Kingly oppressions; and they resolved to so frame the Constitution that *no one man* should hold the power of bringing this oppression upon us. But your view destroys the whole matter, and places our President where kings have always stood. (Roy Basler, ed., *The Collected Works of Abraham Lincoln,* 9 vols. [New Brunswick, N.J., 1953–1955], vol. 1, pp. 451–452)

In 1861, however, when Lincoln was president and faced the crisis of the Civil War, he chose repeatedly to act unilaterally, exercising authority that was clearly vested by the Constitution in the legislature, not the executive. Congress was not in session when Confederate forces fired on Fort Sumter, and although Lincoln called for a special session of Congress, he set 4 July as the date for the legislature to convene. That left the president with three months to deal with the crisis on his own, without seeking Congress's advice or approval. Lincoln immediately called out the militia, which he was authorized to do by various statutes, proclaimed a state of insurrection, and declared a blockade against the seceding states. The president also suspended the writ of habeas corpus; expended funds for military supplies and ships, even though no such moneys had been appropriated by Congress; and increased the size of the regular army, a violation of Congress's authority to raise and support armies.

When Congress finally did meet in July 1861, Lincoln sought legislative approval for the steps he had taken. Lincoln conceded that many of his acts fell within the jurisdiction of Congress, not the president, and so he asked Congress to ratify the measures he had taken to meet the emergency. Many in Congress believed that Lincoln's actions represented an unconstitutional usurpation of powers rightfully belonging to the legislature, but they accepted his contention that the crisis created by the Civil War required him to take extraordinary steps to preserve the Union. Consequently, Congress enacted a resolution validating all of the president's actions with respect to the army, navy, and the militia, giving them "the same effect as if they had been issued and done under the previous express authority and direction of the Congress of the United States."

Lincoln's actions were challenged in the courts in the *Prize Cases,* 2 Black 635 (1863), in which the Supreme Court upheld the president's imposition of a blockade, even though Congress had not declared war. The Court ruled five to four that even though the Constitution gave Congress alone the power to declare war, in this instance the war had begun with the Confederate shelling of Fort Sumter. Once hostilities had started, the president had the authority and the obligation to respond to attacks against the United States, even in the absence of a declaration of war. The Court also noted that Congress had retroactively approved the blockade, thereby eliminating any constitutional defects that might have applied to the president's actions.

Both Polk and Lincoln contributed significantly to the trend toward the president, rather than Congress, determining when the United States went to war or engaged in hostilities. Polk acknowledged that only Congress could declare war, but he used his authority as commander in chief to position the armed forces in such a way as to make war almost inevitable. Lincoln exercised powers that belonged to Congress, and even though he sought and received subsequent legislative endorsement for his actions, future presidents would cite them as precedents when they encroached on Congress's powers and decided unilaterally when and where to use the armed forces.

## FROM CIVIL WAR TO WORLD WAR, 1865–1917

By the end of the nineteenth century, the generally accepted rule seemed to be that presidents could use the armed forces on their own initiative in minor instances, especially in Latin American and the Far East. Congressional approval was required, however, for using the military against any of the European powers.

Events during William McKinley's presidency illustrate this dichotomy. In the spring of 1898, McKinley concluded that uncertainty stemming from a revolution in Cuba was preventing the American economy from recovering fully from the panic of 1893. Consequently, on 11 April 1898, McKinley recommended to Congress that the United States intervene in Cuba to stop the bloodshed, protect American citizens and their property, and end the war's deleterious effects on the United States. He asked Congress "to authorize and empower the President ... to use the military and naval forces of the United States as may be necessary for these purposes" (Richardson, vol. 9, p. 6292).

Congress responded by passing a joint resolution on 20 April in which the legislature tried to specify the goals for which it was allowing the president to use the armed forces. Congress supported the independence of Cuba, demanding that Spain relinquish the island, and authorized the president to use the armed forces to achieve that objective. The legislators also adopted an amendment sponsored by Senator Henry M. Teller (R.-Colo.), disclaiming any intention of acquiring or annexing Cuba. Spain severed relations with the United States on 21 April, and four days later, at the president's request, Congress declared that a state of war with Spain had existed since 21 April.

Once the war began, the president, as commander in chief of the armed forces, directed the military endeavors. McKinley dispatched American forces to Cuba, and he ordered Admiral George Dewey to proceed to the Philippines to engage the Spanish Pacific fleet in battle. There was no mention of the Philippines in the joint resolution of 20 April or the declaration of war, but nonetheless, the war was fought both in Cuba and in the Philippines. The Spanish were quickly defeated on both fronts and were forced to relinquish Cuba and to cede the Philippines, Puerto Rico, and Guam to the United States. After an acrimonious debate, the Senate narrowly approved the peace treaty, and a war begun over Cuba resulted in the United States acquiring the Philippines, Guam, and Puerto Rico.

The people of the Philippines originally welcomed American forces as allies in their war for independence from Spain. But once they realized that the United States intended to retain control, the Filipinos began a bitter three-year struggle against the occupying American forces. The fighting began on 4 February 1899, two days before the Senate approved the peace treaty with Spain.

During the Philippine Insurrection, McKinley made all the decisions concerning peace or war on his own, without consulting Congress. A few legislators raised questions concerning the president's authority to conduct a war against the Filipinos without congressional authorization, noting that the war had begun prior to the Senate's approval of the peace treaty with Spain and thus prior to the time when the Philippines were formally under American jurisdiction. McKinley's supporters countered that American troops in the Philippines were defending themselves against Filipino attacks. The president consistently misled Congress and the American people, falsely claiming that the Filipinos had struck the first blow, and the military censored reports from the battlefront to prevent the truth from becoming known. The belief that American soldiers had been attacked effectively stifled debate in Congress over the legality of the war in the Philippines.

When Americans in China were threatened by the Boxer Rebellion in 1900, McKinley decided to send five thousand American troops to participate in a combined military operation to rescue Westerners stranded in Beijing. Most legislators supported this use of the armed forces to safeguard American citizens, but a few congressmen warned that the president was straining his power to its limits by acting unilaterally instead of asking Congress to authorize such actions.

Presidents used the armed forces without congressional consent more and more frequently in the early twentieth century, especially in Latin America. Theodore Roosevelt, William Howard Taft, and Woodrow Wilson sent American forces into Panama, Cuba, Haiti, the Dominican Republic, Nicaragua, and Mexico to preserve order, protect American lives or property, put down rebellions, prevent European intervention, and build the Panama Canal. As Roosevelt explained in his famous corollary to the Monroe Doctrine, the United States was exercising "an international police power" in the western hemisphere. The Constitution does not authorize the president to use the armed forces for these purposes, but presidents did so nonetheless in dealing with the Latin American states. The power of the United States was so much greater than that of the Latin American nations that there seemed little risk that war might result from American military actions. For the most part, the president decided on his own when to intervene militarily in Latin America (cf. Richardson, vol. 10, p. 7053).

The most serious incident involving the United States and Latin America during these years occurred in Mexico during the Wilson administration. Mexico could not be treated in such a cavalier manner as were the Caribbean and Central American states, so in this instance Wilson sought congressional approval before using the armed forces to teach the Mexicans a lesson.

After Victoriano Huerta seized power in Mexico in February 1913, President Wilson refused to recognize the new government. Then, in April 1914, American sailors were arrested in Tampico, Mexico, for going ashore without permission from the Mexican authorities. The Mexican commander immediately released them and apologized when he learned what had happened, but the American captain also demanded a twenty-one-gun salute to the American flag. When the Mexicans refused, Wilson decided to use the incident as an excuse for military action against Huerta. On 20

April 1914, Wilson asked Congress to approve his use of the armed forces to teach the Mexicans to respect the rights of the United States. Wilson asserted that he already possessed the necessary authority under the Constitution to deal with Huerta, but he preferred to work with Congress on such an important matter.

The House of Representatives approved the president's request the next day, but senators objected to Wilson's contention that he could employ the armed forces without the consent of Congress. Senators also preferred to justify American intervention as necessary to protect American lives and property rather than as a response to the insult to the American flag. Consequently, the measure was still pending in the Senate when the fighting began. When Wilson learned that a German ship laden with munitions was about to land at Veracruz, he immediately ordered American marines to prevent the arms from reaching Huerta's men. American forces took control of Veracruz, but in the process nineteen Americans and hundreds of Mexicans were killed. All factions in Mexico condemned American intervention, and Wilson quickly accepted when Argentina, Brazil, and Chile offered to mediate the dispute. American forces withdrew from Veracruz on 23 November 1914.

Two years later, however, Wilson ordered General John J. Pershing and six thousand American troops back into Mexico in pursuit of Pancho Villa and his men, who had murdered Americans on both sides of the border. The president took this action without consulting Congress. The American forces did not find Villa, but they moved more than three hundred miles into Mexico, remained there for eleven months, and clashed with the Mexican army. Only when the war in Europe required Wilson's full attention in early 1917 did he withdraw American forces from Mexico.

## THE TWO WORLD WARS, 1917–1945

Events leading to American involvement in World Wars I and II showed once again that even though Congress has the power to declare war, presidents could set policies and position the armed forces to involve the nation in hostilities without congressional approval. Most of the important decisions preceding American entry into these wars were made unilaterally by Woodrow Wilson and Franklin Roosevelt, but both presidents did eventually go to Congress for formal declarations of war.

In dealing with the war in Europe, President Wilson could not ignore Congress the way he usually did in Latin American affairs, but he was able to persuade the legislators to go along with his policies most of the time. Wilson and the State Department made the key decisions and interpretations of American neutrality. In 1916, when Congress threatened to pass the Gore-McLemore Resolutions prohibiting Americans from traveling on belligerent ships, Wilson insisted that Americans not give up any of their neutral rights, and he was able to prevent the measures from passing.

When Germany resumed unrestricted submarine warfare in February 1917, Wilson severed diplomatic relations with Germany. The president still hoped that Germany would refrain from attacking American ships and that American entry into the war could be avoided, but he promised that if American property and lives were lost, he would ask Congress for the authority "to use any means that may be necessary for the protection of our seamen and our people in the prosecution of their peaceful and legitimate errands on the high seas" (*Congressional Record* 54 [1917], p. 2550).

When Germany did attack American ships, Wilson first sought congressional approval for a policy of "armed neutrality." Wilson explained that even though he already possessed the authority to implement such a policy, he preferred to work with Congress. But when a Senate filibuster prevented passage of a resolution authorizing the president to arm American merchant ships, Wilson announced that he would arm the ships anyway, citing an old antipiracy law as his statutory basis for doing so.

Wilson called for a special session of Congress to convene on 2 April, at which time he asked the legislators to recognize that a state of war existed between the United States and Germany. There were serious decisions to be made, Wilson emphasized, and "it was neither right nor constitutionally permissible" for the president to make these decisions unilaterally. Wilson had realized the impracticality of armed neutrality, and he had concluded that American entry into the war was necessary if he were to play a major role in shaping the peace settlement. At the same time, the sinking of American ships and the publication of the Zimmerman Telegram, in which Germany promised to help Mexico regain the land it had lost to the United States if Mexico would go to war against the United States, had turned American public opinion against Germany. On 4 April 1917, the Senate voted 82–6 to declare war, and the House of Representatives agreed on 6 April by a vote of 373–50.

For most of the 1920s and 1930s, Congress used its prerogatives in foreign affairs to protect its authority to declare war. The Senate rejected the Treaty of Versailles in part because the legislators feared that the League of Nations Covenant impinged on Congress's power to declare war. As the world situation deteriorated in the 1930s, Congress sought through neutrality legislation to prevent American involvement in war. The Neutrality Acts of 1935, 1936, and 1937 were designed to avoid the economic ties with the Allies and the kind of incidents at sea that many believed had led the United States into World War I.

Once World War II broke out in Europe, President Franklin Roosevelt tried to aid Britain and the Allies. In the process, he exceeded his authority as president, but he believed that it was necessary to do whatever he could to prevent a German victory. Roosevelt and his advisers frequently justified their actions by citing the Supreme Court's decision in *United States v. Curtiss-Wright Export Corporation*, 299 U.S. 304 (1936), in which Justice George Sutherland had asserted that the president is "the sole organ of the federal government in the field of international relations." As such, according to Sutherland, the president's authority in foreign affairs does not have to be based on acts of Congress, and the president can make decisions and implement policies unilaterally so long as he does not violate any specific provisions of the Constitution.

It should be noted, however, that most of Sutherland's opinion was obiter dictum—excess verbiage not necessary to the ruling in the case. Moreover, a distinction must be made between Congress's power to declare war, a power vested explicitly and exclusively in the legislature, and authority in foreign affairs in general, which is divided between Congress and the president. When John Marshall origi-

nally referred to the president as "the sole organ" of the nation in foreign affairs in 1798, he meant that it was the president alone who communicated with other nations on behalf of the United States. In 1801, Marshall clearly stated in *Talbot* v. *Seeman* that the Constitution vested in Congress "the whole powers of war." Even according to Sutherland's formula, presidential exercise of the war power would be unconstitutional because that authority is expressly given to Congress.

Prior to America's formal entry into World War II, Roosevelt used an executive agreement to transfer fifty American destroyers to Great Britain in exchange for the right to build bases on British territories in the Western Hemisphere, sent American troops to protect Iceland against a possible German occupation, and used the German attack against the American destroyer *Greer* to justify ordering American ships to shoot at German warships and submarines as soon as they were sighted. Roosevelt took these actions unilaterally, citing both his authority as president and commander in chief and the *Curtiss-Wright* decision. Although Senator Robert A. Taft (R.-Ohio) and a few others criticized Roosevelt's actions, most members of Congress did not challenge what Roosevelt had done. The legislature even passed the Lend-Lease Act in March 1941, authorizing the president to transfer military supplies to other nations on whatever terms he chose to set.

By mid-October 1941, the United States and Germany were engaged in an undeclared naval war in the Atlantic. But this time, in contrast to the 1790s, when the undeclared naval war against France had been authorized by Congress, American lives were being lost in hostilities without the consent of Congress. Roosevelt had stretched his authority beyond previous limits.

In November 1941, Roosevelt finally asked Congress to repeal the last vestiges of the Neutrality Acts. As American opposition to Germany rose with the news of German attacks on American ships, Congress authorized the president to arm American merchant ships and allowed American vessels to carry munitions to Britain.

But Roosevelt still shied away from asking Congress to declare war against Germany, and Adolf Hitler chose not to proclaim formal hostilities against the United States. But four days after the Japanese attack on Pearl Harbor on 7

December 1941, Germany supported its ally by declaring war against the United States, which responded in kind that same day. Congress, of course, had already reacted to the Japanese attack at Pearl Harbor by declaring war against Japan on 8 December.

As the end of World War II approached, Roosevelt and the State Department focused on the plans for a postwar United Nations. They remembered how concern that the League of Nations Covenant infringed on Congress's power to declare war had helped defeat the Covenant, and they were determined not to make the same mistake with the U.N. Charter. At the same time, legislators believed that America's failure to join the League had contributed to World War II, so they were more willing to compromise this time. The executive branch worked closely with Congress while the charter was being drafted, and senators and representatives were included in the American delegation to the San Francisco conference at which the charter was approved in 1945. Article 43 of the charter, designed to allay congressional concern, stipulated that agreements making armed forces available to the United Nations had to conform with member nations' constitutional processes. The Senate approved the charter overwhelmingly, and Congress soon passed the United Nations Participation Act authorizing the president to negotiate such an agreement with the United Nations and submit it to Congress. Once an agreement was adopted, the president would be able to make American forces available to the United Nations without further congressional approval. These provisions became moot, however, as the United States has never concluded such an agreement with the United Nations.

## THE COLD WAR AND THE IMPERIAL PRESIDENCY, 1945–1973

In the years after World War II, American presidents further expanded their authority as chief executive and commander in chief, deciding unilaterally where and when to send American forces into hostilities. In the nuclear age, when the United States might have to respond instantaneously to a Soviet challenge, Congress's power to declare war seemed more and more like a relic from a bygone era. Presidents, legislators, and the American people recalled, too, that Congress had been wrong in rejecting American membership in the League of Nations and thinking that the Neutrality Acts would keep the nation out of war. As the United States bounced from crisis to crisis in the Cold War years, Congress generally acquiesced in the erosion of its authority.

In creating the North Atlantic Treaty Organization (NATO) in 1949, the Truman administration paid special attention to legislators' fears that the treaty would encroach on Congress's power to declare war. To meet that concern, Article 5 of the NATO treaty provided that each nation would respond to a Soviet attack by taking "such action as it deems necessary, including the use of armed forces." This would leave each nation free to decide for itself if it would respond militarily. Moreover, Article 11 of the treaty specifically stated that member nations would carry out their obligations "in accordance with their respective constitutional processes." These provisions protected Congress's authority to declare war, and helped the NATO treaty win Senate approval by a vote of eighty-two to thirteen.

When North Korean forces attacked South Korea in June 1950, President Harry Truman committed American forces to a full-fledged war without congressional approval or authorization. The president relied on his authority as commander in chief and on U.N. resolutions as his basis for sending American troops to fight in Korea. Truman and his advisers made all the key decisions without consulting Congress. The president met twice with delegations from Congress during the first week of the conflict, but both meetings were to inform the lawmakers of decisions he had already made, not to seek their opinions or advice.

Most legislators supported the president's firm response to what they perceived as Communist aggression in Korea, but Senator Taft and a few other Republicans condemned Truman's failure to seek congressional approval for sending American forces to Korea. They charged that the president had usurped Congress's power to declare war, and they suggested that Truman at least seek congressional approval for his actions after the fact. After some consideration, Truman decided not to seek a congressional resolution supporting his actions in Korea. Secretary of State Dean Acheson advised that such a measure was unnecessary, and a State Department memorandum listed eighty-five previous instances when presidents had supposedly used the armed forces overseas without congressional authorization or approval. The State Department maintained that "the President, as commander in chief of the armed forces of the United States, has full control over the use thereof" ("Authority of the President to Repel the Attack in Korea," *Department of State Bulletin* 23 [31 July 1950], pp. 173–179).

The State Department had raised executive claims for control over the war powers to new heights. Previous incidents of presidential war-making had usually involved minor skirmishes, and even then presidents had generally asserted that their actions were based on various statutes or treaties and, as such, were authorized by Congress or were in self-defense in response to attacks against Americans. Truman's predecessors had never claimed any unilateral authority to commit the nation to war. But now the executive branch was asserting for the first time that the president, as commander in chief of the armed forces, could involve the nation in a major war without congressional approval.

Actually, President Truman denied that the United States was involved in a war in Korea, accepting a reporter's characterization of the American role in Korea as a "police action" under the auspices of the United Nations. But as the conflict in Korea bogged down and American casualties rose, more and more people complained that Truman had violated the Constitution by unilaterally involving the nation in an undeclared war.

Truman exacerbated concern over presidential usurpation of the war power when he announced in late 1950 that he was sending four divisions of American soldiers to western Europe. A "great debate" ensued, focused on whether the president had the authority to dispatch troops overseas without the consent of Congress. Truman asserted that as commander in chief he had the authority to send American troops "anywhere in the world." The Senate disagreed, however. The legislators eventually adopted a resolution approving the president's plan to send the troops to Europe, but they insisted that no additional troops should be sent to Europe without further congressional approval.

President Dwight Eisenhower made sure not to repeat Truman's mistakes. When Eisenhower considered using American forces to assist the French in Vietnam in 1954, to defend Formosa (now Taiwan) in 1955, and to stop the spread of Communism or pro-Nasser, pan-Arab sentiment in the Middle East in 1957, he sought prior congressional authorization each time. Congressional leaders rejected any use of the armed forces in Vietnam in 1954 unless certain conditions were met, but Congress approved the Formosa Resolution in 1955 and the Middle East Resolution in 1957. Senator Wayne Morse (D.-Oreg.) warned that Congress should never delegate its power to declare war by giving "blanket approval to the President of the United States to proceed to commit an act of war against another nation," but most legislators saw Eisenhower's efforts to work with Congress as a major improvement over Truman's unilateral decisions to deploy American forces overseas. Eisenhower used the Middle East Resolution to send American troops to bolster the pro-Western government of Lebanon in 1958.

Although Eisenhower consulted with Congress concerning Vietnam, Formosa, and the Middle East, he bypassed the legislature completely by using the Central Intelligence Agency (CIA) to train refugees and mercenaries to overthrow governments in Iran, Guatemala, and Cuba. These operations, planned and financed by the United States, constituted acts of war, but they were never approved or authorized by Congress. President John F. Kennedy's attempt to carry out the plan to topple Fidel Castro's regime in Cuba resulted in the Bay of Pigs fiasco in April 1961.

As relations with Cuba deteriorated, Kennedy and Congress debated the president's authority to use the armed forces to deal with Castro. Republican leaders proposed in 1962 that Congress adopt a measure similar to the Formosa Resolution, one that would authorize the president to use the armed forces if necessary to counter the threat posed by Cuba. Kennedy and his supporters, however, wanted the legislature to approve a very different resolution, one declaring that the president already possessed the authority to do whatever was necessary, including using the armed forces, to prevent Cuban aggression or subversion or a military buildup in Cuba. But a number of senators objected to Kennedy's contention that he could initiate military action on his own authority, so Congress approved a measure that conformed more closely with the resolutions adopted in the 1950s. The final bill proclaimed America's determination to do whatever was necessary, "including the use of arms," to prevent Cuba from threatening the United States or any other nation in the western hemisphere. But the resolution did not stipulate whether the president could use the armed forces for such purposes under his own authority or if he needed congressional approval to do so.

Congressional resolutions notwithstanding, Kennedy showed during the Cuban missile crisis that the president now controlled the war powers. As the United States and the Soviet Union went to the brink of war, Kennedy and his advisers in the executive branch made all the important decisions without any input from Congress. Kennedy met with congressional leaders just a few hours before he announced publicly that he had ordered a "quarantine" to prevent the delivery of offensive weapons to Cuba. He later conceded that stopping and searching all ships bound for Cuba was an act of war. But even though only Congress can declare war or authorize hostilities short of war, Kennedy never asked Congress to authorize or approve his actions during the crisis.

Presidential use of congressional resolutions to wage war culminated in the Gulf of Tonkin Resolution and the war in Vietnam. President Eisenhower had sent seven hundred military advisers to help train the South Vietnamese army in 1954, and President Kennedy had increased the number of American advisers in Vietnam to more than fifteen thousand in the early 1960s. But even with advisers and billions of dollars in American aid, the South Vietnamese were losing the war. In early August 1964, President Lyndon Johnson informed Congress and the nation that North Vietnamese patrol boats had fired on American ships on routine patrol in the Gulf of Tonkin. Johnson ordered retaliatory air strikes against North Vietnamese bases and oil depots, and he asked Congress to pass a resolution approving and

supporting his determination "to take all necessary steps, including the use of armed force," to repel any further attacks against American forces, to prevent further aggression, and to assist any members or protocol states of the Southeast Asia Treaty Organization (SEATO). Believing that American ships had been the victims of an unprovoked attack, legislators rallied to support the president and his policy in Vietnam. On 7 August, Congress approved the Gulf of Tonkin Resolution by votes of 416–0 in the House and 88–2 in the Senate.

In 1965, President Johnson cited the Gulf of Tonkin Resolution as authority for ordering extensive bombing raids against North Vietnam and sending the first of 525,000 American combat troops to South Vietnam. When questioned about his authority to wage war in Vietnam without a congressional declaration of war, Johnson time and again pulled the Gulf of Tonkin Resolution out of his pocket and reminded legislators that they had approved it overwhelmingly. Under Secretary of State Nicholas Katzenbach expressed the administration's view when he told the Senate Foreign Relations Committee in 1967 that the Gulf of Tonkin Resolution, combined with the SEATO treaty and congressional appropriations for military operations in Vietnam, were the "functional equivalent" of a declaration of war.

Johnson exacerbated concern over the executive's usurpation of Congress's authority when he dispatched twenty-one thousand troops to the Dominican Republic in April 1965 to protect American citizens and to prevent leftist rebels from overthrowing a military junta. Congressional leaders were informed of the president's plans just a few hours before the troops landed.

By the late 1960s, Senator J. William Fulbright (D.-Ark.) and others in Congress had begun to challenge the view that the president could commit American forces to hostilities anywhere in the world without the consent of Congress. When the Senate Foreign Relations Committee learned that presidents considered executive agreements, letters to heads of state, or even the presence of U.S. bases in various countries as American commitments to defend those nations, the Senate declared in 1969 that a national commitment by the United States to use the armed forces to assist another nation could only be made by the president and Congress acting together through a treaty or specific legislation.

When Richard Nixon became president in 1969, he asserted that as commander in chief of the armed forces he could do whatever was necessary to protect American forces in Vietnam. Congress responded by trying to use its control over appropriations to prevent the president from expanding the war in Southeast Asia. In December 1969, Congress passed the Cooper-Church amendment prohibiting the expenditure of funds to introduce American ground troops into Laos or Thailand. Unfortunately, Congress specified the wrong countries, for in April 1970, Nixon ordered American forces into Cambodia to destroy Vietcong bases and sanctuaries there. The Senate immediately passed an amendment cutting off funds for American troops in Cambodia after 1 July 1970, but Nixon withdrew American forces from Cambodia while the bill was still pending in the House.

Over the next three years, Congress debated numerous measures calling for the withdrawal of American forces from Vietnam by a specified date or cutting off funds for the war. The legislature repealed the Gulf of Tonkin Resolution in December 1970, but Nixon relied on his authority as commander in chief to continue the war. After the Paris peace accords finally ended America's role in the fighting in Vietnam in January 1973, American planes continued to bomb Communist positions in Cambodia until Congress cut off all funds for American military involvement in Southeast Asia unless specifically authorized by Congress. Congressional and public sentiment had restrained Nixon's actions in Vietnam all along, and they finally forced him to end American military involvement in all of Southeast Asia by 15 August 1973.

## CONGRESS RESURGENT? 1973–1993

Nixon's incursion into Cambodia in 1970 led Senator Jacob Javits (R.-N.Y.) to introduce the first version of the War Powers Resolution. For Javits and others, the Cambodian incursion clearly demonstrated the need for Congress to restore the balance originally intended by the nation's founders by reasserting the legislature's authority to decide where and when the United States would engage in war or in lesser hostilities. As the Watergate scandal and revelations of Nixon's misconduct weakened the presidency, Congress adopted the War Powers Resolution over Nixon's veto in November 1973.

Many of the problems with the War Powers Resolution stem from the fact that the final bill represented a compromise between different versions favored by the House and the Senate. The Senate had attempted to define and limit the president's power to use the armed forces in the absence of congressional authorization to do so, while the House had focused more on consultations and reports to Congress in such situations. As finally enacted into law, the resolution requires the president to consult with Congress "in every possible instance . . . before introducing United States Armed Forces into hostilities or into situations where imminent involvement in hostilities is clearly indicated." The president must also report to Congress within forty-eight hours whenever he introduces American forces into hostilities or situations where hostilities are likely, sends troops "equipped for combat" to a foreign nation, or substantially increases the number of American forces so equipped in a foreign country. In subsequent years, there would be considerable disagreement over whether consultations were possible, hostilities were imminent, and American forces were equipped for combat in specific situations.

The most controversial aspects of the War Powers Resolution have been the provisions concerning the termination of American involvement in hostilities. The bill requires the president to withdraw American forces from hostilities within sixty days, unless Congress specifically authorizes him to continue military operations. The president can extend this deadline for an additional thirty days if he certifies that more time is necessary to preserve the safety of American forces while they are being withdrawn. The resolution also allows Congress to order the return of American military forces to the United States at any time by concurrent resolution, a measure not subject to the president's veto, and it sets forth special procedures to ensure that bills approving or rejecting a president's use of the armed forces are not buried in committee or blocked by filibusters in the Senate. Senator Thomas Eagleton

(D.-Mo.), an early proponent of the War Powers Resolution, voted against the final bill because he believed these provisions gave the president the authority to wage war on his own for ninety days.

Presidents from Nixon through George Bush have questioned the constitutionality of the War Powers Resolution, asserting that Congress cannot by statute limit the president's authority under the Constitution as commander in chief of the armed forces. But the Supreme Court has never ruled directly on the resolution; rather, the courts have held that disputes between Congress and the president over the use of American troops are political questions to be settled between the legislature and the executive. In *Immigration and Naturalization Service* v. *Chadha,* 462 U.S. 919 (1983), however, the Supreme Court struck down the legislative-veto provision in an unrelated statute, calling into question the constitutionality of a concurrent resolution ordering the president to remove American troops from hostilities.

During his presidency, Gerald Ford complied with the War Powers Resolution grudgingly and to the least extent possible. He transmitted the required reports to Congress when he used the armed forces to evacuate Americans and South Vietnamese nationals from Southeast Asia in April 1975 and to rescue the crew of the American merchant ship *Mayaguez* when Cambodia seized it in May 1975, but he merely informed congressional leaders of his decisions to use the armed forces instead of engaging in meaningful consultations with them before determining his course of action. Ford did at one point ask Congress to clarify his authority to use the armed forces to evacuate people from Saigon, but he did so only because of various statutes that prohibited the use of funds for military operations in Southeast Asia, not because of the War Powers Resolution. In each of these instances, Ford reported that he had acted under his authority as president and commander in chief.

Jimmy Carter pledged to comply with the letter and the spirit of the War Powers Resolution, but when he used the armed forces to try to rescue Americans held hostage in Iran in 1980, he did not even inform the congressional leaders until the rescue mission had been abandoned. Initially there was some criticism of Carter's failure to consult with Congress, but the nature of the crisis in Iran, the need for secrecy in such an operation, and Carter's explanation that this was a rescue mission rather than a military operation against a foreign nation dissuaded most members of Congress from making the War Powers Resolution an issue in this instance.

In the 1980s, President Ronald Reagan asserted that the War Powers Resolution did not apply in most situations. Carter had sent nineteen military advisers to El Salvador in January 1981, and Reagan later sent thirty-five more. When some legislators questioned whether these actions fell within the purview of the War Powers Resolution, the Reagan administration maintained that the statute did not apply because the advisers were not being introduced into hostilities or situations where hostilities were imminent, they were not equipped for combat, and they would not be accompanying Salvadoran troops on combat missions. But some in Congress disagreed, and they filed suit to force the administration to comply with the War Powers Resolution. In *Crockett* v. *Reagan,* 558 F. Supp. 893 (D.D.C. 1982), the Federal District Court dismissed the case, ruling that Congress itself had to determine whether the War Powers Resolution applied to the situation in El Salvador.

When Reagan sent American forces into Lebanon in August and September 1982, he claimed that the War Powers Resolution did not apply because American forces were part of a multinational peacekeeping force that would not be involved in hostilities. In 1983, however, American forces in Lebanon came under hostile fire, and the president ordered a naval task force to Lebanon, approved air strikes against forces shelling American positions, and authorized the use of American air power and artillery to assist the Lebanese armed forces.

Members of Congress protested that American forces in Lebanon were now engaged in hostilities that had not been authorized by the legislature as required under the War Powers Resolution, and they argued that the time limits specified in the resolution had begun when American marines had first been fired on. When some legislators proposed cutting off funds to force the withdrawal of American troops from Lebanon, the Reagan administration reluctantly entered into negotiations with House Speaker Thomas P. O'Neill (D.-Mass.), which resulted in congressional approval of the Multinational Force in Lebanon Resolution. This bill explicitly stated that the War Powers Resolution applied to the situation in Lebanon and authorized the use of American forces there for eighteen months. Reagan signed the bill into law, but he still challenged the legality of the War Powers Resolution. He emphasized that his signing of the measure should not "be viewed as any acknowledgment that the President's constitutional authority can be impermissibly infringed by statute" (*New York Times,* 13 October 1983).

On 25 October 1983, two days after a terrorist attack killed 241 American marines in Lebanon, President Reagan sent American forces into Grenada, a small island nation in the Caribbean. Like most of his predecessors, Reagan did not really consult with Congress; he informed the congressional leaders of the operation after he had already issued the orders for it. The president reported to Congress and the nation that American forces were being sent to Grenada to protect and evacuate American citizens and to assist in restoring order and constitutional government in Grenada, but Reagan's primary goal was to prevent the Marxist government of Grenada from establishing a military base for Cuba or the Soviet Union.

The War Powers Resolution was designed to apply automatically whenever the president reported or was supposed to report to Congress concerning his use of the armed forces. But having seen presidents deny that the statute applied in Iran, El Salvador, and Lebanon, legislators were determined to enforce it in Grenada, and the House and the Senate approved separate measures formally declaring that the War Powers Resolution's time limits had been triggered by the landing of American forces in Grenada. The Reagan administration insisted, however, that no such measures were needed because the troops would be removed before the sixty-day limit was reached, and so Congress agreed to drop the matter. American combat forces were withdrawn from Grenada by 15 December.

When Reagan increased American involvement in the Persian Gulf in the spring of 1987,

he again ignored the War Powers Resolution. Iran and Iraq were at war when the president agreed to reflag and protect Kuwaiti tankers and to increase the American naval presence in the gulf. Reagan made this decision without consulting Congress. Even after thirty-seven Americans were killed by an Iraqi missile and American personnel in the gulf began receiving "imminent danger" pay bonuses, the administration still maintained that the War Powers Resolution did not apply, because hostilities in the gulf were sporadic rather than constant. Reagan finally reported to Congress in September 1987 when American helicopters fired at Iranian vessels laying mines in the gulf, and he reported on five subsequent occasions concerning American involvement in hostilities in the gulf.

Many in Congress believed that Reagan had violated the War Powers Resolution, because he had not consulted with the legislature, because Congress had not authorized the use of American forces in hostilities in the Persian Gulf, and because the time limit for such involvement without congressional approval had expired. But once again Congress was unable to enforce the Resolution. More than a hundred members of Congress filed suit, trying to invoke the War Powers Resolution, but the court dismissed the case, emphasizing that the judiciary could not step in when Congress itself was divided over whether the resolution applied to the situation in the Persian Gulf (*Lowry* v. *Reagan,* 676 F.Supp. 333 [D.D.C. 1987]).

The invasion of Grenada in 1983 had shown that the best way for presidents to avoid problems with the War Powers Resolution was to win quick military victories and withdraw American forces before the time limits specified in the measure became an issue. George Bush demonstrated in Panama that he had learned this lesson well. On 20 December 1989, Bush ordered American forces into Panama to protect American citizens there, restore democracy, uphold the Panama Canal treaties, and capture General Manuel Noriega. Bush briefed congressional leaders just hours before the invasion began, and he reported to Congress on 21 December. The operation proceeded successfully, Noriega surrendered, and the invasion forces were all withdrawn by 13

February 1990. Some members of Congress complained about the lack of real consultation before the invasion, but as had been the case in Grenada, the operation's quick success helped it win the support of the American people.

When Iraq invaded Kuwait in August 1990, President Bush ignored the War Powers Resolution when he sent two hundred thousand American troops to Saudi Arabia immediately and then again when he sent an additional two hundred thousand troops to the region in November. In both instances, the president deployed the troops without consulting with or seeking the approval of Congress. He met with members of Congress on numerous occasions, but these sessions were to brief them on decisions already made, not to seek their advice. During the fall of 1990, as war seemed more and more likely, legislators sought assurances that the president would comply with the War Powers Resolution and obtain authorization from Congress before going to war, but the Bush administration insisted that the president had the authority under the Constitution to use American military forces as he deemed necessary.

The United Nations set a deadline of 15 January 1991 for Iraq to withdraw from Kuwait, and as that day approached, Congress considered whether to authorize the president to use the armed forces against Iraq. Many legislators believed that such authorization was necessary under the War Powers Resolution, and they introduced a measure modeled after the Formosa Resolution of 1955. President Bush then reversed his earlier position, declaring that he welcomed such a resolution because it would send a clear message to Iraq. Once American forces were already positioned in Saudi Arabia, some legislators believed they had little choice but to authorize the president to use them. Others, however, were determined to exercise their right and prerogative to decide whether the United States would go to war. A momentous debate ensued as the House and the Senate considered a resolution that would authorize the president to use all necessary means, including armed force, to expel Iraqi forces from Kuwait. On 12 January 1991, the Senate approved the resolution 52–47, and the House adopted it 250–183. On 16 January, President Bush ordered American air units to attack Iraq, and ground forces moved in a few weeks later. American troops quickly defeated the Iraqis and drove them out of Kuwait.

## CONCLUSION

For the most part, the War Powers Resolution has had little effect on how the United States goes to war or engages in hostilities with other nations. The measure has not had the major impact its sponsors had hoped and its opponents had feared. It has not restored to Congress its authority under the Constitution to determine when the United States engages in war or lesser hostilities against other nations. The resolution may have restrained President Reagan from getting more deeply involved in El Salvador and from using American forces directly against the Sandinistas in Nicaragua, but presidents continue to question its applicability and legality. The executive branch has rarely consulted with the legislators in a meaningful way; most of the time, congressional leaders are informed of military operations just a few hours before they begin, after the decisions have been made and the orders have been given. In El Salvador in 1981, Lebanon in 1982, and the Persian Gulf in 1987, presidents have argued that the War Powers Resolution did not apply at all. And in Grenada and in Panama, military operations were concluded, and American forces withdrawn, before the sixty-day period specified in the War Powers Resolution had expired. Only in Lebanon in 1983 and in the war against Iraq in 1991 did Congress have any real input and an opportunity to approve or reject the use of American forces, and even in these instances the president's prior deployment of American troops was a major factor in Congress's decision to authorize their use. Thus, even after the adoption of the War Powers Resolution, presidents have still decided unilaterally in most cases where and when to go to war or engage in hostilities. And while both Congress and the executive branch have expressed unhappiness with the resolution, there is no consensus on how to change it, so the measure will likely remain in effect—a minor irritant to presidents rather than the real check and balance that Congress hoped the resolution would provide.

## BIBLIOGRAPHY

Historians, political scientists, and legal scholars have all contributed to the voluminous literature on Congress, the president, and the war powers. Many of these works take a strongly partisan view, arguing that either the president or Congress has the exclusive authority to take the nation into war.

### Primary Sources

Students of the war powers controversy should begin with the debates at the Constitutional Convention, which are reported in MAX FARRAND, ed., *Records of the Constitutional Convention,* rev. ed. (New Haven, Conn., 1937). Presidential messages and statements to Congress through the early twentieth century can be found in JAMES RICHARDSON, ed., *A Compilation of the Messages and Papers of the Presidents* (New York, 1911). More recent presidents' speeches are published in the Public Papers of the Presidents series.

### Congressional Sources

Congressional hearings and reports on the War Powers Resolution detail the conflict between Congress and presidents over the power to commit the nation to hostilities, as well as the arguments for and against strengthening Congress's authority in this area. See, for example, U.S. CONGRESS, COMMITTEE ON FOREIGN RELATIONS, *War Powers Legislation, Hearings,* 92d Cong., 1st sess., 1971; *War Powers,* S. Rept. 220, 93d Cong., 1st sess., 1973; and *The War Power After 200 Years: Congress and the President at a Constitutional Impasse, Hearings* before the Special Subcommittee on War Powers, Senate Committee on Foreign Relations, 100th Cong., 2d sess., 1988. The pending war against Iraq led the SENATE JUDICIARY COMMITTEE to hold a hearing in January 1991, which has been published as *The Constitutional Roles of Congress and the President in Declaring War, Hearing* before the Senate Judiciary Committee, 102d Cong., 1st sess., 1991. The HOUSE COMMITTEE ON FOREIGN AFFAIRS has compiled important documents in its periodic editions of *The War Powers Resolution: Relevant Documents, Correspondence, Reports* (Washington, D.C., 1988–).

### Secondary Sources

EDWARD S. CORWIN, *The President: Office and Powers,* 5th rev. ed. (New York, 1984), and CLINTON ROSSITER, *The Supreme Court and the Commander in Chief,* expanded ed. (Ithaca, N.Y., 1976), remain classic descriptions of the powers of the presidency. ARTHUR M. SCHLESINGER, JR., *The Imperial Presidency* (Boston, 1973), and WILLIAM GOLDSMITH, ed., *The Growth of Presidential Power: A Documented History,* 3 vols. (New York, 1974), trace the tremendous expansion of presidential power from 1789 to the 1970s. JAMES SUNDQUIST, *The Decline and Resurgence of Congress* (Washington, D.C., 1981), focuses on the legislature's efforts to reassert its authority in the 1970s; and RICHARD BARNET, *The Rockets' Red Glare: War, Politics, and the American Presidency* (New York, 1990), shows how presidents have tried to manipulate public opinion, which can be an important restraint on their ability to take the nation into war.

In their book *To Chain the Dog of War: The War Power of Congress in History and Law,* 2d ed. (Urbana, Ill., 1989), FRANCIS D. WORMUTH and EDWIN B. FIRMAGE argue that the nation's founders intended that Congress, not the president, decide where and when the United States would go to war or engage in hostilities. W. TAYLOR REVELEY III, *War Powers of the President and Congress: Who Holds the Arrows and Olive Branch?* (Charlottesville, Va., 1981), points out how usage and practice in committing the nation to hostilities quickly diverged from what the framers of the Constitution had expected, and he proposes a compromise in which Congress would exert less control over the war powers than the founders intended, yet more authority than Presidents would like.

JACOB JAVITS, *Who Makes War* (New York, 1973), relates how presidents from George Washington through Richard Nixon usurped Congress's power to declare war, while THOMAS F. EAGLETON, *War and Presidential Power: A Chronicle of Congressional Surrender* (New York, 1974), details the congressional debate over the War Powers Resolution. MICHAEL BARNHART, ed., *Congress and United States Foreign Policy: Controlling the Use of Force in the Nuclear Age* (Albany, N.Y., 1987), contains a number of important essays on the War Powers Resolution and on Congress and foreign affairs in general.

Two former congressional staffers have written important works on the War Powers Resolution. PAT M. HOLT, *The War Powers Resolution: The Role of Congress in U.S. Armed Intervention* (Washington, D.C., 1978), and JOHN H. SULLIVAN, *The War Powers Resolution* (Washington, D.C., 1982), describe the fight over the bill and its effects once enacted.

### Legal Sources

LOUIS HENKIN, *Foreign Affairs and the Constitution* (Mineola, N.Y., 1972), examines these issues from a legal perspective. ABRAHAM SOFAER, *War, Foreign Affairs, and Constitutional Power* (Cambridge, Mass., 1976), and HENRY BARTHOLOMEW COX, *War, Foreign Affairs and Constitutional Power: 1829–1901* (Cambridge, Mass., 1984), were commissioned by the American Bar Association to provide lawyers, statesmen, and the general public with a better understanding of the roles Congress and presidents have historically played in shaping American foreign policy. Another important work that approaches this issue from a lawyer's point of view is JOHN NORTON MOORE, *Law and the Indo-China War* (Princeton, N.J., 1972).

### Specialized Sources

Numerous monographs shed light on particular instances of presidential use of the armed forces or congressional assertions of authority. Some of the more important works are A. B. C. WHIPPLE, *To the Shores of Tripoli: The Birth of the U.S. Navy and Marines* (New York, 1991); J. C. A. STAGG, *Mr. Madison's War* (Princeton, N.J., 1983); CHARLES SELLERS, *James K. Polk: Continentalist, 1843–1846* (Princeton, N.J., 1966); JOHN SCHROEDER, *Mr. Polk's War: American Opposition and Dissent* (Madison, Wis., 1973); LEWIS GOULD, *The Spanish-American War and President McKinley* (Lawrence, Kans., 1982); RICHARD WELCH, JR., *Response to Imperialism: The United States and the Philippine-American War, 1899–1902* (Chapel Hill, N.C., 1979); ARTHUR LINK, *Woodrow Wilson: Revolution, War, and Peace* (Arlington Heights, Ill., 1979); WILLIAM LANGER and S. EVERETT GLEASON, *The Challenge to Isolation, 1937–1940* (New York, 1952) and *The Undeclared War, 1940–1941* (New York, 1953); DAVID PORTER, *The Seventy-sixth Congress and World War II, 1939–1940* (Columbia, Mo., 1979); ROBERT DIVINE, *Second Chance: The Triumph of Internationalism in America During World War II* (New York, 1967); GLENN PAIGE, *The Korean Decision* (New York, 1968); WILLIAM GIBBONS, *The United States Government and the Vietnam War: Executive and Legislative Roles and Relationships,* 3 vols. (Washington, D.C., 1984–1988); JOHN GALLOWAY, *The Gulf of Tonkin Resolution* (Rutherford, N.J., 1970); JOHN LEHMAN, *The Executive, Congress, and Foreign Policy: Studies of the Nixon Administration* (New York, 1976); P. EDWARD HALEY, *Congress and the Fall of South Vietnam and Cambodia* (Rutherford, N.J., 1982); and JAMES NATHAN, "Salvaging the War Powers Resolution," *Presidential Studies Quarterly* 23:2 (Spring 1993): 235–268.

SEE ALSO Congress, the Executive, and Foreign Policy.

# CONGRESS, THE EXECUTIVE, AND FOREIGN POLICY

## *Walter LaFeber*

Since 1789, the powers of the executive and legislative branches of government have seldom been separated, have often been shared, and have nearly always been vigorously contested. The winner of the various contests has been determined by complex forces, but among the most important have been the changing institutional makeup of Congress, the nature of the party system undergirding the two branches, the type of issue being contested, and the geographical context (continental, Atlantic, global) framing the issue. Viewed from these perspectives, four eras emerge since 1789. The first had its roots in the revolutionary war years and ran to 1808. The second, dominated by the House of Representatives, lasted from 1808 to approximately 1820. The third, in which the Senate primarily shaped foreign policy, extended from 1820 until around 1900. The fourth, almost encompassing the twentieth century, can be called the presidential era.

## FOREIGN-POLICY MAKING IN THE NEW REPUBLIC

This last stage holds considerable irony for the nation's founders. Between 1775 and 1787 their loathing of King George III's (and some colonial governors') abuse of executive power led them to create a congressional system of government. A Committee of Secret Correspondence, formed in 1775, initially oversaw foreign policy; two years later it became the Committee for Foreign Affairs (with Thomas Paine acting as its secretary). As the postwar peace began to be hammered out in 1781, the Congress, now operating under the Articles of Confederation (which provided for no executive), named Robert R. Livingston of New York

as the first secretary for foreign affairs. Livingston, a strong, accomplished person, left his post in June 1783; the divisive politics of a Congress in which each state was both sovereign and insecure had contributed to his decision to resign. He was replaced by fellow New Yorker John Jay. In 1786 Jay tried to resolve an economic crisis by proposing to give up U.S. rights to the Mississippi River for twenty-five or thirty years in return for entry into Spain's markets. Amid howls of protests and threats of secession from southern states holding vast western lands, Jay's request to negotiate a treaty was granted, seven states to five, but because nine were needed to ratify any agreement that might result, his proposal was a dead letter. The crisis, political as well as economic, worsened.

Jay's failure was pivotal in leading him, Alexander Hamilton of New York, and James Madison of Virginia, among others, to move to amend the Articles. At the Constitutional Convention in 1787, however, the government itself was transformed. Behind closed doors in a sweltering Philadelphia summer, the delegates, selected by each state, stripped the states of their power to impose tariffs on imports and to regulate exports. A new bicameral Congress received that right, as well as the power to tax for the purpose of raising armies for the national defense; the power to govern territories that had resulted (and might result) from American expansion; and the authority to appropriate funds. The convention created an executive branch, but in theory it was to work closely with Congress. The president, according to Article II, Section 2, of the Constitution, could make treaties "by and with the advice and consent of the Senate . . . provided two-thirds of the senators present concur." This two-thirds provision protected the South against the possibility of legislation unfavorable to it, such as the 1786 Jay plan, from being passed. The Senate was given power to approve presidential appointees, including ministers who dealt with other nations. The president received only two powers that could be used unilaterally in foreign affairs: the right to receive ambassadors from other countries and the authority to act as commander-in-chief of the army and navy—this last only after both houses of Congress declared war. The convention indeed killed an attempt to give the executive war-declaring powers; Elbridge Gerry of Massachusetts declared he "never expected to hear in a republic a motion to empower the Executive alone to declare war."

Although Gerry won that fight, he ultimately refused to sign the Constitution. He feared it gave Congress the power "to raise armies and money without limit." Many so-called anti-Federalists joined him in opposition. They warned that the president could become an elected monarch; that the House of Representatives (the only branch elected directly by the people), had been "entirely excluded" from treaty making; and that the commander-in-chief clause might allow the executive to wage wars without the legislature's approval, much as had the British king. In *The Federalist,* Hamilton, Madison, and Jay vigorously responded that the president would actually have less power than the British king or even the governor of New York. Hamilton emphasized that any overly ambitious executive would "be subjected to the control of a branch of the legislative body. What more can an enlightened and reasonable people desire?"

Hamilton received an answer just months after the new government met in 1789. Led by Madison in the House, Congress exploited its fresh powers by passing mercantile acts to protect U.S. shipping and exports. When, however, Madison tried to impose import tariffs for the protection of nascent manufacturers, Secretary of the Treasury Hamilton raised objections. His financial plans required British capital and trade for development and funding the national debt. The Federalists who had pushed through the Constitution now began to divide, as Madison feared (correctly) that Hamilton intended to use the new executive power (embodied in the venerated George Washington) to control foreign policies. The argument was not between political parties but between personal cliques, or "factions," as Madison had called them with great distaste. Washington, however, threatened to split Madison's faction by appointing fellow Virginian Thomas Jefferson as the first secretary of state, a position that had been created by Congress in mid-1789. It was Jefferson who accepted the French minister's credentials in 1790 with the words, "the transaction of business with foreign nations is Executive altogether."

As Madison's and Hamilton's factions fought over trade policy, the executive created a new crisis in April 1793 when Washington declared that the United States would remain a neutral in the growing Franco-British war. Because the Americans remained linked to France by the 1778 alliance, Madison condemned this proclamation of neutrality as both pro-British and a usurpation of Congress's power to decide questions of peace and war. In a historic debate waged in the newspapers, Hamilton, writing as "Pacificus," declared that the Constitution gave the president all foreign affairs powers unless the document specifically said otherwise. Madison countered that the president could not exercise even a specified power without Congress's authority if the exercise made war more likely. Madison has rightly been called the father of the Constitution for his role in 1787, but Hamilton won this argument. U.S. policy remained friendly to the British (and opposed to the French Revolution) even as London's navy seized more than 250 American ships that traded with the French. In late 1793, Jefferson resigned as secretary of state and worked with Madison to organize a party that would fight Hamilton's program.

In the Third Congress (1793–1795), identifiable party conflict appeared for the first time as two voting blocs emerged. The Madison-Jefferson bloc threatened to pass anti-British acts over Federalist opposition. A group of influential northeastern Federalist senators finally saved Hamilton by suggesting that Supreme Court chief justice John Jay be sent on a peace mission to London. Jay had a weak hand to play, and Hamilton further weakened it by sending secret assurances to the British. Jay returned with a treaty that infuriated Madison, especially because it further restricted the rich U.S. trade with the West Indies. But it did promise both more trade with the British and that the British would finally leave the northwest forts they had promised to evacuate in 1783. Despite massive public demonstrations against Jay, Washington forced the treaty through the Senate. Madison then made a historic decision; he decided to argue that because of the House's power over appropriations it, like the Senate, could reject treaties by refusing to grant the funds. He demanded (and was supported by a 62–37 vote) that Washington submit all relevant papers. The president refused to accept either the argument or the demand. After two months of bitter debate, the House decided by three votes to give Washington the money needed to carry out the Jay Treaty. The precedent was set and since then the House has not failed to provide funds to meet treaty obligations. Following this decision, Madison left the House to help create a Jeffersonian party to throw the Federalists from power.

The second president, John Adams, found relations improved with Great Britain but souring with France. Hamilton and his congressional followers wanted war with the French. They finally had to settle for an undeclared war fought largely on the oceans. Congress used the crisis as an opportunity to pass the Alien Acts and the Sedition Act, which were used to try to cripple the Jeffersonians. The legislature also enacted the Logan Act in 1799, which protected the executive's power by making it a federal crime for individuals to conduct diplomacy with other nations. The Logan Act remains law two centuries later. It was finally President Adams who courageously decided to avert war (a conflict that might have united the Federalists and won him a second term), by making peace with France in 1800.

Jefferson won the presidency that year and Madison became secretary of state, but as one frustrated senator noted, the Jeffersonians developed the Federalists' affection for presidential power: "I hoped after so long a course of pork that our diet would be changed, but I find it is pork still with only a change of sauce." Jefferson even extended those powers by becoming the first president-as-party-leader who dominated congressional proceedings. At his command, Congress passed some of the most controversial foreign-policy measures in the nineteenth century: the Louisiana purchase in 1803, secret appropriations to pressure Spain out of the Floridas, and the embargo of 1807 that tried to force the British to recognize U.S. maritime rights by cutting off Anglo-American trade. One congressman complained during the Louisiana debate, "We know nothing, we are permitted to know nothing. We sit here as mere automata." The Senate accepted the vast empire of Louisiana, 24 to 7. The embargo, however, backfired as the nation's economy sunk into depression and Jefferson's popularity plummeted. Madison won the presidency in 1808, but he found himself, not involuntarily, facing another war with Great Britain.

## AN ERA OF HOUSE DOMINANCE

By 1811, Madison was dealing with a different kind of Congress. The Senate, as it had with few exceptions since 1789, remained willing to follow executive initiatives, especially in the realm of appointments. Elected by the state legislatures until 1913, debating behind closed doors until 1795, allowing little press coverage until 1802, the Senate received slight public attention or support. It used inefficient, evanescent select committees rather than permanent standing committees. The House, on the other hand, was more vibrant, representative, and powerful than the Senate. In late 1810, Madison acquired a new ally in carrying out his anti-British policies when Henry Clay of Kentucky won election to the House (after having served part of an unexpired term in the Senate), and immediately moved into the Speaker's chair. Clay won support from other new members elected from the South and the West in 1810. They were intent on forcing the British to respect U.S. rights on the seas and the western frontier. (With good reason, the Georgetown boardinghouse where they lived and plotted became known as the "War Mess.") Clay and his supporters captured the Republican caucus, excluded dovish representatives from the leadership, and then ditched the select committees to create standing committees that Clay packed with fellow "war hawks."

Highly sensitive to the Constitution's provisions giving Congress the authority to declare war, Madison was pleased. He and Clay could count on seventy to eighty votes for most war measures in 1811 and early 1812. With middle-state, southern, and western Republicans at its core, the House voted 79–49 for war in the spring of 1812. The seventy-nine Republicans were opposed by all thirty-seven Federalists and twelve Republicans. The Senate approved the war measure, 19–13, again along party lines. The resulting war led to the burning of Washington, D.C., in 1814 and the threatened secession of some New England states. But adept U.S. diplomacy and their more dangerous problems in Europe led the British to agree to peace in 1814.

Americans now turned westward. Nationalism, expansion, and democratization accelerated more rapidly. The House, reflecting many of these changes, moved quickly as Clay determined to expand U.S. influence southwest, even to Latin America, and to tie together this empire with a mercantilist "American System" of government-sponsored tariffs, banks, and internal improvements. Utilizing the new standing committees, Clay whipped through bills to help shippers and new industrialists, and led the way in forcing a highly reluctant secretary of state, John Quincy Adams, to recognize the new Latin American nations in 1822 after their revolt against Spanish control. That same year, the House, led by New England mercantile interests, opened a debate on U.S. claims to the Pacific Northwest that twenty-four years later climaxed in the annexation of the Oregon Territory. The executive, Supreme Court Justice Joseph Story believed in 1818, "has no longer a commanding influence. The House of Representatives has absorbed all the popular feelings and all the effective power of the country."

## AN ERA OF SENATE DOMINANCE

The power was shifting, however, even as Story wrote. Post-1815 expansion created new states, and when the slave territory of Missouri asked for statehood, a fight over slavery began ("a title page to a tragic volume," as John Quincy Adams called it) that during much of the next three decades centered on the Senate. Viewed as a closed, clubby Federalist bastion in 1800, the upper house grew to forty-six members in 1820 and sixty-six on the eve of the Civil War. It opened its doors to reporters who told of the great oratory and shrewd parliamentary maneuvers displayed especially by the "great triumvirate" of Clay (who moved to the Senate in

1831), Daniel Webster of Massachusetts, and John C. Calhoun of South Carolina. As a flourishing two-party system appeared in the 1830s, moreover, the Senate became less insular and more representative. With Clay and Webster at the fore, the Senate became the arena in which the Whig Party attacked claims to executive power made by "King Andrew" Jackson and his Democratic party.

The Whigs fought for an expanded governmental role at home (as Clay's American System implied) but opposed the Democrats' foreign policies that centered around virtually unlimited landed expansion and fear and dislike of Great Britain. Advocating a more friendly approach to obtaining badly needed British trade and capital, and desiring commercial (not landed) expansion, Whigs found the Senate to be a superb sounding board for their foreign policies. The upper house simultaneously imitated the lower house and developed an effective committee system for the first time. Foreign Relations became one of twelve new standing committees in 1816, although a powerful chair of Foreign Relations did not appear until 1834. The Senate was becoming the preferred body; as Senator Thomas Hart Benton (D.-Mo.) believed, "Composed of the pick of the House of Representatives, [the Senate] gains doubly—by brilliant accession to itself and abstraction from the other [body]."

In 1835 the acute French visitor, Alexis de Tocqueville, wrote in *Democracy in America* that American democracy had admirable strengths, but in conducting foreign policy it was far inferior to European aristocratic systems that could keep secrets, be consistent over time, and be untroubled by frequent elections. In 1787 many founders had hoped the Senate would, as Gouverneur Morris phrased it, "show us the might of aristocracy." The Senate never worked closer to Tocqueville's and Morris's standards than between the 1820s and 1900. Executive power remained impressive; the president's 1823 annual address to Congress outlined the Monroe Doctrine, the climax of nearly eight years of diplomacy conducted by Secretary of State John Quincy Adams, perhaps the most successful foreign-policy initiative in the nation's history. The doctrine's three principles—no further European colonization in the Western Hemisphere, no extension of the Europeans' "system" to the Americas, and

U.S. abstention from strictly European quarrels—shaped more than a century of U.S. foreign policy. In almost every case, however—the 1817 Rush-Bagot Agreement demilitarizing the U.S.–Canadian boundary (the nation's first important executive agreement), the 1818 convention maintaining equal American rights in Oregon with the British, the Transcontinental (Adams-Onís) Treaty of 1819 giving the nation Florida and the first clear title to the Pacific Coast, the 1822 recognition of the new Latin American governments, and the Monroe Doctrine itself—the executive worked closely with the Senate or submitted its handiwork to the Senate for approval. The Whig party simply assumed the need for the president to accede largely to congressional wishes, although this assumption never received its ultimate test of a Clay presidency.

In June 1844 Secretary of State John C. Calhoun moved to annex the proslavery nation of Texas that had been independent of Mexico since 1836. The Senate destroyed the treaty, 16 for and 35 against. Within a year, President-elect James K. Polk, Democrat of Tennessee, cut a private deal with pivotal senators that allowed the annexation of Texas by a joint resolution requiring only a majority vote in each house. Polk's deal opened an incredible three years of war fever and expansion that by 1848 increased American territory by more than 50 percent. With strong support from exporting interests in all sections, the president obtained a low-tariff bill in 1846 that strengthened relations with Great Britain. When, however, he tried to please western landed and northeast mercantile groups by pushing for Oregon, he overplayed his hand against the British, approached the brink of war with the world's greatest power, and finally turned the explosive issue over to the Senate where cooler (especially Whig and southern Democrat) heads prevailed. In 1846 a boundary agreement was accepted by the British. Webster bragged that the process reversed the Constitution's treaty-making provision: "Here is a treaty negotiated by the Senate and only agreed to by the President." The second important Senate filibuster (the first occurred in 1841) developed during this debate and lasted for two months. The measure finally was brought to a vote through the use of a unanimous-consent agreement, apparently for the first time. It was during these heated debates that *manifest destiny* became a household phrase.

Polk had meanwhile ordered U.S. troops into land claimed by both Mexico and Texas. Mexican troops opened fire. Determined in any case to obtain California from Mexico, Polk used the incident to force a war declaration through Congress in May 1846 despite last-ditch opposition from the unlikely team of Calhoun and John Quincy Adams. Later that year, however, Polk asked for money to end the conflict and buy land from Mexico. The bill was amended in the House with the Wilmot Proviso which, much to Polk's disgust, provided that no money could be used to acquire land for slavery. Although blocked in the Senate, the proviso fractured party unity on the slave issue and tied up the president's diplomacy for months. As war continued and frustration grew on all sides, an all-Mexico movement, led by northern Democrats, demanded annexation of the entire country. This spread-eagleism was stopped when U.S. diplomat Nicholas Trist negotiated the Treaty of Guadalupe Hidalgo. The agreement was not totally acceptable to Polk, but the weary Senate happily ratified it. In truth, the treaty gave Polk most of his major objectives: California, New Mexico, and the Rio Grande boundary.

The upper body, under Clay's and Webster's guidance, then moved to resolve the central questions arising from the war. The Compromise of 1850 brought in newly acquired California as a nonslave state; allowed the freshly conquered territories of Utah and New Mexico to enter as slave or free states, depending on their inhabitants' preferences; abolished the slave trade (but not slavery) in Washington, D.C.; and passed a fugitive-slave law that required federal authorities to capture and return runaway slaves. The compromise only temporarily quieted the slavery controversy; it reopened in 1854–1855 over the issue of whether free-state or slave-state interests would rule the new territories. As the South realized it was outnumbered, Democratic presidents tried to seize fresh territory for slavery, especially in Cuba, only to be stopped by the Senate where, with California's admission in 1850, the free states now enjoyed a majority.

A major cause of the Civil War can be traced to the South's belief that it had to have fresh territory for slavery, gained through either diplomacy or conquest, and the North's determination not to allow such expansion. The Republican party, which appeared in the mid-1850s, embodied this free-soil principle, and it also advocated a program of high tariffs, a national banking system, plentiful immigrant and contract labor, cheap lands, and vast subsidies to a new transcontinental railroad system. These measures built a foundation for an industrial power that, in just forty years, grew into the world's mightiest. After the Civil War, American foreign policy turned from expanding continental boundaries to expanding overseas markets and finding naval bases for this economic behemoth.

Although the House played a major role, especially as it originated bills for tariffs and subsidies, the Senate remained more important in foreign affairs. Under the control of Republicans in all but two Congresses between 1868 and 1900, producing such powerful committee chairs as Charles Sumner of Massachusetts, and cemented by a deep, stable partisanship throughout the era that produced both supporters in record numbers and unsurpassed party discipline, the Senate by the 1890s was tightly run by Senators William B. Allison of Iowa and Nelson Aldrich of Rhode Island. They regularly met with several friends to play poker and decide arbitrarily who was to serve and chair the committees. Working with state party machines, and intimately involved with the new economic interests, these leaders saw the Senate as a career, a treasure chest, and a coequal with the president in foreign affairs.

## A NEW EMPIRE, A NEW EXECUTIVE

In 1867 Secretary of State William Seward outmaneuvered Senate opponents and—in part because he confronted them with a fait accompli, in part because the Russian minister apparently bribed some doubters—Congress accepted and paid for the purchase of Alaska from Russia. It marked the last major executive foreign-affairs victory for thirty years. In 1870 Sumner led the fight to stop President Ulysses S. Grant from annexing strategic Caribbean areas that Grant (and some questionable friends) coveted. Between 1870 and 1897 the Senate rejected, stalled, or forced major changes in treaties with Great Britain, Mexico,

China, and Hawaii, among others. In 1879 young political scientist Woodrow Wilson defined American government as "the absorption of all power by a legislature which is practically irresponsible for its acts."

Twenty-nine years later Wilson wrote that presidential control over foreign policy was "very absolute" and "without any restriction whatsoever." The sea change between 1879 and 1908 did not involve fundamental differences that occurred in Congress's, especially the Senate's, institutional structure. That structure remained much as it was in the late nineteenth century when the Speaker's power and the Allison-Aldrich faction ruled. The roots of a century of presidential domination in making foreign policy lay in four other areas.

First, the arena for American politics became global in the 1890s as U.S. producers searched out world markets and the country suddenly became enmeshed militarily and politically in crises in Asia and Europe. Foreign relations, which as recently as the 1840s meant American settlers dealing with affairs across an adjacent river or mountain range on the continent, now meant elite officials dealing with transoceanic cultures about which most Americans knew nothing. If the pressures of farmers and land speculators were crucial in shaping policy toward Louisiana, Texas, and Oregon, then a relatively few business leaders, military officers, and, above all, the president shaped policy toward China, Latin America, and North Africa. "The President," John Marshall had declared during House debates in 1799, "is the sole organ of the nation in its external relations, and its sole representative with foreign nations." This generalization had not been strictly true as millions moved on their own across the continent during the next ninety years, but it became increasingly true thereafter as the arena for, and the participants in, U.S. policy-making became transformed.

Second, the issues changed. Before the 1890s Congress wielded power in foreign policy because the questions involved territorial settlement and (especially in the 1790s, 1840s, and 1870s–1890s) external trade relations conducted through tariff debates. The Constitution gave Congress authority over such questions. After 1897, however, the issues revolved around the use of military power overseas, close calculations of the changing European and Asian balance of power, and the protection of U.S. economic interests abroad. These issues could best be handled by the president, especially in his constitutional guise as commander-in-chief.

Third, a new, more ambitious executive arose to deal with these new issues. William McKinley's tenure (1897–1901) marked the beginning of the modern presidency. A veteran of the House and a consummate Ohio politician, McKinley, in the words of one friend, survived those political jungles by combining "the virtues of the serpent, the shark, and the cooing dove." After early 1898 he dominated Congress as had no other president since Jefferson. This success was partly due to his understanding of the new communications revolution, especially the telephone, worldwide cable networks, and the mass-circulation press. Partly it was due to his talent for outflanking congressional critics by centralizing foreign policy information in the White House and establishing the first presidential press staff to ensure that his views were spread through the newspapers.

Finally, the 1894 and 1896 elections, occurring during a terrible economic depression while a Democratic administration was in power, resulted in a critical electoral realignment that ushered in nearly forty years of Republican presidential rule. Instead of the closely fought elections of the previous thirty years that had attracted as many as 80 percent of eligible voters, one-party states appeared (largely Republican in the north, Democrat in the less populous south) that increasingly discouraged partisanship and encouraged voter apathy. Republican presidents frequently worked with Republican majorities in Congress and with committees whose members held unthreatening views. The first modern chief executives could assume legislative support; partisan voting in the House, for example, reached a high in the 1890 to 1915 years before beginning a transition to the decline of partisanship after 1940. Presidents, indeed, began to take congressional support so much for granted that beginning in 1897 they usually appointed as secretary of state not a major party figure who could deal with partisan friends (Monroe in 1811–1812, James Buchanan in the 1840s, William Seward during the Civil War were such models), but instead filled the post with less partisan, sharp administrators (such as Elihu Root, Robert Lansing, Dean Acheson, and

Henry Kissinger), who could efficiently operate the new overseas empire.

A turning point in the executive-legislative struggle over foreign policy occurred in mid-April 1898. McKinley, after many months of holding back congressional war hawks who wanted to use U.S. military force to end Spain's brutal repression of revolutionaries in Cuba, decided the time had arrived when the nation (and the Republican party) could go to war safely and with a strong consensus. Congress declared war with pleasure, but the Senate resolved that McKinley should recognize the Cuban revolutionary regime. The president refused; he mistrusted any revolutionaries, suspected that some members of Congress were financially involved with the Cubans, and was determined in any case to keep his options open after the war. In a week-long, brutal political struggle, McKinley faced down a leader of the Senate's recognition forces, Henry Cabot Lodge of Massachusetts (the political descendant, symbolically, of Charles Sumner, who had stunned Grant in 1870), and forced Congress to accept his approach. Two months later the president determined to annex Hawaii. Senate foes had thwarted his annexation plan the year before, but he now easily obtained the islands through a joint resolution. In February 1899 McKinley forced through a Senate sharply divided between pro- and anti-annexationists the peace treaty with Spain that gave Americans colonial responsibilities in the distant Philippine Islands. Opposition senators were trapped, for on the eve of the vote Filipinos opened fire on U.S. troops who, on the orders of Commander-in-Chief McKinley, had disregarded Filipino rights (much as Polk had disregarded Mexican claims in 1846). During the next two years, the president protected U.S. interests, as he defined them, by landing five thousand American troops on the mainland of China to deal with both a growing Chinese revolution and the military intervention of the world's leading powers. McKinley did so without consulting Congress. In 1899 the powerful Speaker of the House, "Czar" Thomas B. Reed of Maine, disgustedly resigned his House seat, in part because of his repeated and unsuccessful opposition to McKinley's proposals in Cuba, Hawaii, and the Philippines.

Theodore Roosevelt continued McKinley's policies, but more publicly through what he termed the "bully pulpit" of the White House. In 1903 he helped foment a Panamanian revolution against Colombia (which had long controlled the valuable isthmus), prevented Colombian troops from landing, and then began to construct a U.S.–owned-and-operated transoceanic canal that transformed world shipping routes and the ability of U.S. military power to move across the globe. When Democrats tried to stop such blatant colonialism, Roosevelt and his fellow Republicans defeated them in Congress and the 1904 presidential campaign. "I took the Canal Zone and let the Congress debate," Roosevelt trumpeted. In 1907 he asked Congress for funds to send the U.S. fleet around the world. He especially wanted to impress, if not intimidate, the Japanese who had struck out on their own expansionist course in Asia. When Congress refused, Roosevelt dispatched the fleet with the announcement that he had the money to move the navy halfway around the world; Congress would have to appropriate additional money if it wanted the fleet to return. It did.

Perhaps Roosevelt's most lasting contribution to presidential supremacy in foreign affairs was made in 1904 when as commander-in-chief he landed troops in Santo Domingo, then seized the all-important customs house to protect U.S. commercial and strategic interests. The president asked the Senate to ratify a treaty that codified his actions, but the upper house refused to support the imperialism. He then obtained the same result by making an executive agreement with friendly officials in Santo Domingo. The Rush-Bagot pact of 1817 had been the first important executive agreement, and the term *executive agreement* itself would not be commonly used until after 1930. But Roosevelt's determination to circumvent congressional opposition began an era when such pacts became more important than treaties. In her superb study in the *Encyclopedia of American Foreign Policy,* Diane Clemens observes that between 1789 and 1840, an average of .54 executive agreements were concluded annually; between 1889 and 1939 the figure rose to 10.5 (or about two such pacts for each formal treaty), and after 1940 the number began doubling every five years. Between 1946 and 1972, 368 treaties were ratified, but at least 5,590 executive agreements were made. Some of these

implemented congressional legislation or were authorized by Congress. Many of the most important, however, rested on the president's exercising his power independently of, and sometimes contrary to, the wishes of Congress. The founders would probably have been surprised. In 1787 they had expressly defeated a motion in the Constitutional Convention to give the president sole power in making treaties.

Roosevelt and Woodrow Wilson grew to hate each other because of personality and policy differences, but they agreed on the need of the president to reign over Congress in the foreign policy realm. Wilson concluded in 1908 that the American "ownership of distant possessions and [the] many sharp struggles for foreign trade" had created the need for a new type of president who "must stand always at the front of our affairs." In 1910 he condemned the reticent William Howard Taft by declaring that the people "long to see someone . . . put upon Congress itself the pressure of opinion of the whole United States."

For five years after becoming president in 1913, Wilson enjoyed the support of a Democratic Congress, in part because of a Republican split in the 1912 election. He controlled his party in Congress and dominated the legislature, not least by becoming the first president since Thomas Jefferson to deliver his messages personally before Congress, and by repeatedly lobbying legislators in the President's Room on Capitol Hill. Idolizing Britain's parliamentary system, Wilson saw himself as an active, eloquent prime minister who was assured of support from automatic legislative majorities. He rapidly won from Congress a historic low-tariff measure, the Federal Reserve Act of 1913, and the Federal Trade Commission Act of 1914, all of which he correctly viewed as enhancing the ability of U.S. industries and banks to compete in foreign markets. In early 1917, as he slowly led the nation into World War I, his bill to arm neutral U.S. ships was filibustered to death by eleven senators. Wilson condemned them as "a little group of willful men, representing no opinion but their own, [who] have rendered the great government of the United States helpless and contemptible." He called the Senate into special session. A group of stunned Republican and Democratic leaders quickly pushed through the Senate's first cloture rule by a vote of 76 to 3, and then gave Wilson his armed neutrality bill.

## THE CLASH OF 1919–1920 AND ITS AFTERSHOCKS

As a war leader in 1917–1918 the president dominated Congress until he made the fatal error of asking Americans to vote for Democrats in the 1918 congressional elections because, he claimed, they could best help him make the postwar world "safe for democracy." Angry Republicans damned Wilson for impugning their patriotism and captured the Senate. The Foreign Relations Committee first acted on the Treaty of Versailles and the League of Nations Covenant, that Wilson had helped draw up in Paris during 1919, before the two pacts went to the full Senate. The Committee, however, fell under the control of Henry Cabot Lodge, who despised the president. A combination of Lodge-led Republicans, who wanted a sharply amended covenant that would protect U.S. freedom-of-action, and so-called irreconcilables who wanted no foreign commitments at all, defeated Wilson. With their once powerful leader broken by a stroke in late 1919, and his visionary foreign policy in shambles, keen American observers such as journalist Walter Lippmann and banker Thomas Lamont of J. P. Morgan Bank asked what had gone wrong. Their answer rested on Lippmann's analysis that the mass of the people lacked knowledge and were unfit for influencing foreign policy; consequently their representatives in Congress were also less fit than had been thought in the nineteenth century when foreign policy had been simpler.

In the 1920s, Republican officials therefore rested their foreign policies on several assumptions. As the world's strongest economic power and potentially its greatest military force, the United States required minimal commitments and maximum freedom of action. Congress had destroyed Wilson in 1919, but the Republican-dominated legislature now cooperated with the Republican presidents or was circumvented. In some cases, of course, Congress could not be ignored. In 1924 it endangered U.S. interests in Asia by passing the Immigration Act that barred Japanese and other Asians from entry into the United States. The executive led, however, in other areas. In 1921–1922 Secretary of State Charles Evans Hughes shaped the Washington naval conference treaties that outlined a working relationship with Japan and western European powers, while destroying a large part of the world's navies. The Senate quickly ratified the pacts. With these ground rules set, the Republicans allowed key foreign policies (such as the reconstruction of Germany after 1924) to be made by private U.S. business and/or informal, behind-the-scenes direction by the executive. In 1926–1927, peace groups demanded that Congress act on a French proposal that France and the United States agree to outlaw war. The Department of State, fearing it was a trap to entice Americans into France's European alliances, reformulated the proposal to invite dozens of other nations who would pledge to outlaw war (but, notably, permit "defensive" war). The Senate was then allowed to appease the peace groups by ratifying this meaningless "international kiss," as the Kellogg-Briand Pact became known.

A foreign policy that rested on direction by private elites and relatively little congressional influence turned out disastrously. As the business community's power buckled in the 1929 stock market crash, and as the world economy crumbled, Congress reasserted itself in 1930 by passing the Smoot-Hawley Tariff, the highest in American history. The tariff only worsened the crisis as other nations retaliated against American goods. The world broke down into compartmentalized trading blocs that soon waged economic, and then military, war against each other. Congress responded with a series of neutrality acts between 1935 and 1939 that were designed to prevent Americans from being sucked into the next conflagration.

President Franklin D. Roosevelt's administration had suggested neutrality legislation in 1933, but Roosevelt wanted the discretionary authority to decide when the laws would be invoked. In a bitter fight over the first act in 1935, members of Congress, especially from the Midwest, argued that authority must never be centralized "in one man," and that Congress must never "surrender . . . to the Chief Executive" the war-declaring power. When these opponents threatened to filibuster, Roosevelt backed down so that his domestic legislation would not be blocked. In 1937, however, he obtained a "cash and carry" provision that allowed belligerents to purchase strategic goods so long as they did not use U.S. ships or credit. The president received the power to decide which items were to be included and when the law was to be invoked.

As Congress gave this authority to the executive, it also granted him new power over the legislature's cherished jurisdiction over trade. In the 1934 Reciprocal Trade Agreements Act, Congress, after another knockdown struggle in which Republicans warned that President Roosevelt was being given dictatorial powers, authorized the president to cut Smoot-Hawley rates by a maximum of 50 percent over three years. Proponents argued that Congress could no longer micromanage trade. When Republicans later proposed that the resulting treaties at least be presented to the Senate for ratification (as had the reciprocal tariff treaties negotiated by McKinley), they were defeated—largely because Democrats recalled that special congressional interests had killed nearly every one of McKinley's pacts. Unable to say no to local blocs, the more parochial Congress had little choice, given that the United States' prosperity depended on the vagaries of a complex world market, but to assign some of its historic power to the more cosmopolitan and efficient executive. The Reciprocal Trade Agreements Act continued to be basic U.S. trade policy as it was regularly updated throughout the post-1945 era.

As exemplified in the neutrality acts, congressional leadership in the 1930s proved to be no more adept at avoiding catastrophe than had been executive-business leadership in the 1920s. Repeated attempts to insulate the country against the world war that erupted in 1939 gave way initially to silent acquiescence to Roosevelt's pro-British policies (such as his sending London fifty destroyers in 1940 in return for rights to British bases), and then highly reluctant cooperation (most notably in the 1941 Lend-Lease Act when after three months of vicious debate Congress gave Roosevelt the power to provide military goods to any nation "whose defense the President deems vital" to American defense). In truth, Congress's leadership in foreign affairs had been largely discredited by 1940–1941. Roosevelt ex-

ploited that weakness and used to the full his own commander-in-chief power after Americans entered the war in December 1941. The geographical outlines of the early postwar world were largely decided by Roosevelt, Winston Churchill, and Joseph Stalin in secret discussions at Tehran (1943) and Yalta (1945), and then by President Harry Truman when he met in July 1945 with Soviet and British leaders at Potsdam.

Congress, however, was vital in establishing both the United Nations and the most important international economic organizations, the World Bank and International Monetary Fund. Having learned from Wilson's self-destruction in 1919, Roosevelt encouraged Congress to take the lead on the U.N. By 1943 both Republicans (led by Senator Arthur Vandenberg, a onetime isolationist from Michigan), and Democrats (guided by Representative J. William Fulbright of Arkansas) had committed themselves to a postwar organization. In 1945 Vandenberg and other congressional leaders helped write key provisions of the U.N. Charter. Americans possessed the greatest power of any nation in history, but the legislators were unsure how to use that power, or whether to use it if it cost large amounts of their constituents' taxes. A $3.75 billion loan to the war-ravaged British passed in 1946 only after Congress learned not of the economic dangers, but of the threat that Britain might otherwise swing sharply to the left. The transition would not be smooth. As one member recalled, the House Foreign Affairs Committee now had immense global power, but not too many years earlier its most heated debate was over a $20,000 appropriation for an international poultry show in Oklahoma.

## THE COLD WAR TRIPOD

Facing a series of world crises, President Truman and his advisers, led by a top Department of State official, Dean Acheson, created global foreign policies between 1945 and 1951 that shaped the entire Cold War era. Those policies depended on solid congressional support, or at least acquiescence. Truman and Acheson built that support on a tripod composed of an ideological leg of anticommunism, a political leg of strong presidential leadership, and a bureaucratic leg of the National Security Council and covert operations.

The ideological leg was brilliantly constructed. In early 1947 Truman requested $400 million to bolster Greece (where leftists threatened to overthrow a right-wing regime), and Turkey (long the target of Soviet pressure). He had to obtain funds from a pinch-penny Republican Congress that had been stunningly swept into power by the 1946 elections. Undersecretary of State Acheson drafted, and Truman delivered before Congress, a message warning that the world was now divided between the free and enslaved peoples. The president required money and power to protect the free. Congress must quickly decide which side it was on. The Truman Doctrine gave Congress little alternative; the money was soon appropriated. In 1948 Truman reiterated the doctrine when he requested $13 billion for a Marshall Plan to rebuild western Europe, and again Congress appropriated the funds.

Vandenberg, the ranking Republican on the Foreign Relations Committee, became the symbol of the bipartisanship that shaped these postwar foreign policies. During sixteen of the thirty years between 1947 and 1976, including the seminal era of 1947 to 1949, bipartisanship was essential because the president's party did not control Congress. Bipartisanship, however, could be misleading. Congress was not coequal with the president. In constructing the Marshall Plan, as one observer noted, the legislature was only the "modifier and legitimator" of executive initiatives. When the United States entered its first peacetime alliance since 1778 by joining the North Atlantic Treaty Organization (NATO) in 1949, the State Department consulted closely with Vandenberg, and even supported the so-called Vandenberg Resolution that tried to reconcile NATO to the U.N. Charter. However, the NATO treaty ratified in 1949 by the Senate, 82–13, was created in European and American executive offices. In 1949–1950 bipartisanship faltered when Republicans and Truman split over policy toward China. By then even Vandenberg, now terminally ill with cancer, privately expressed doubts about whether bipartisanship served national, especially congressional, interests. He worried that it "inevitably collide[d]" with the two-party system that underlay American democratic government. The anticommunism expressed in the Truman

Doctrine nevertheless created the consensus needed for the executive's foreign policies, with few major exceptions, from 1945 until the late 1980s.

The second leg of the tripod was presidential power and, more specifically, the commander-in-chief authority. It was the president who controlled ultimate power; he could order the dropping of atomic, and after 1952, hydrogen bombs. Truman most notably exercised his authority in June 1950 by committing U.S. forces in the war between North and South Korea. He did so without consulting Congress. Truman acted on Secretary of State Acheson's advice that his commander-in-chief power was sufficient, and that it was better both politically and militarily to define the conflict as a police action rather than an all-out congressionally declared war. Truman further claimed that he acted under U.N. authority, although legal experts denied such authority existed to send U.S. troops into action; in any case, the president committed forces before the appropriate U.N. Security Council resolution passed on 27 June. At first, no one in Congress publicly objected. Then, on June 28, Senate Republican leader Robert Taft of Ohio blistered Truman for seizing Congress's war-declaring power and warned that a precedent had been set for other presidential wars in "Indonesia or Iran or South America." Democratic and internationalist Republican members of Congress supported Truman: "The speed of modern war requires quick executive action," a liberal Democrat declared. Truman's support splintered after he made tragic errors that led to China's entry into the war, and after he had to recall General Douglas MacArthur for insubordination, but never did he have to retreat from his June 1950 claims of presidential war power.

President Dwight D. Eisenhower (1953–1961) refined those claims. When Republican John Bricker of Ohio proposed a constitutional amendment requiring that executive agreements and other international accords (such as those made at the U.N. for protecting human rights) could become U.S. law only after congressional approval, Eisenhower vigorously responded. Helped by Senate Democrats who venerated a strong presidency in the Roosevelt-Truman mold, the president finally, but barely, beat back the Bricker amendment in 1954. Later that year Eisenhower asked Congress to pass a resolution that delegated to him the power to deal as he saw fit with a crisis involving China in the Formosa Strait. Congress quickly agreed. Three years later the president repeated the tactic for a Middle East problem. Congress again complied, although the Senate, under Fulbright's leadership, forced changes in the White House–drafted resolution. The peak of postwar bipartisanship probably occurred in 1958–1959 when both parties in Congress supported four-fifths of the foreign policy–defense measures Eisenhower favored. In 1954 and 1957 the legislature had, as well, willingly surrendered its power to declare war.

In the Cuban missile crisis of 1962, President John F. Kennedy regularly consulted only his handpicked group of fourteen advisers as he took the world to the brink of nuclear war with the Soviet Union. His victory seemed so complete, however, and presidential powers were now so unquestioned, that no congressional voice raised the issue of possible obliteration without representation. In 1964 President Lyndon B. Johnson repeated Eisenhower's approach by claiming that U.S. ships had been fired on in the Tonkin Gulf by Communist North Vietnamese ships, and he asked Congress to pass a resolution supporting his response. Fulbright, sponsoring the Gulf of Tonkin Resolution in the Senate, recognized that the language could also allow Johnson to wage a full-scale war, but he denied the president intended to do so. The measure passed overwhelmingly in both houses.

Johnson then built up a 550,000-troop force in South Vietnam that Congress paid for by regular appropriation bills. In 1965 he landed approximately 22,000 troops to control what he claimed was a possible communist uprising in the Dominican Republic. When that claim was soon discredited, Fulbright turned against Johnson, as did increasing numbers of legislators who began to try to recover the war-declaring authority. They were met by the executive's claim that declaring war was "outmoded phraseology." The Vietnam tragedy and the growing weakness of Richard Nixon's presidency caused by its criminal acts (especially in the Watergate scandal) allowed Congress in 1973 to pass, over Nixon's veto, the War Powers Act that tried to rein in the commander-in-chief power. No succeeding president, however, recognized the restraints as constitutional, and in

1983 a Supreme Court decision undermined a key provision of the act.

The third leg of the tripod on which executive power rested in the Cold War was a vast bureaucracy that the president could use, especially in secret, to carry out his policies. It was rooted in the National Security Act of 1947, which unified the War and Navy departments into the Department of Defense; created the National Security Council through which the president could efficiently coordinate foreign policy; and streamlined intelligence operations under the executive's direction. The act tightened the president's monopoly over information, the lifeblood of foreign policy. It also created the Central Intelligence Agency (CIA), which under White House direction was soon carrying out covert operations against other governments. In passing the 1947 act, Congress seemed willing to abdicate even its responsibility for overseeing national-security policy. The Senate Foreign Relations Committee had only several clerks and secretaries in the mid-1940s, and the 1946 Reorganization Act did little to build up congressional expertise and information gathering that compared with the executive's. When the CIA covertly helped overthrow governments in Iran (1953) and Guatemala (1954), several brave legislators proposed some congressional oversight only to be stopped by Eisenhower's alleged response, "Over my dead body." Not until the exposure of widespread, secret CIA activities in the mid-1970s did Congress create intelligence-oversight committees. Nearly all of the oversight was done behind closed doors. In 1947 some legislators had assumed they could control security policy through the appropriations process. By 1949, however, Truman had already successfully defied that process by refusing to build an aircraft carrier mandated by Congress. "Military policy is made by the Department of Defense," a supposedly powerful member of the House Armed Services Committee observed in the 1950s. "Our committee is a real estate committee."

A Senate staff member later noted that "a proposal to close a navy base in Brooklyn excited far more interest . . . than building one in [Vietnam]." Such traditional sensitivity to parochial interests grew as the political parties weakened, power decentralized, and interest groups flooded over Capitol Hill. Foreign affairs legislation was becoming shaped less by the public partisan divisions that had molded the late-nineteenth-century policies than by lobbyists employed by farm organizations, the American-Israeli Public Affairs Committee (AIPAC), Greek Americans who fought aid to Turkey, or defense contractors. The new television media encouraged legislators to act more individually and seize headline-grabbing topics, although the president, not Congress, more successfully used television to increase his branch's power. Jealous of their political turf, legislators diluted their influence further by demanding that their various committees be consulted on money issues; by the 1950s at least twelve of the nineteen standing House committees had some authority over foreign economic policy. Eisenhower exploited these changes by creating a special executive office to lobby Congress. Kennedy and Johnson refined the operation so congressional factions could be more easily divided and conquered. *Congressional Quarterly* estimated that between 1948 and 1964 the presidents won 70 percent of their foreign policy-defense proposals, as against only 40 percent of their domestic policies.

The rate of presidential successes, however, dropped dramatically in the 1970s. In perspective, the drop was an aberration in the post-1890 presidential era. Its causes were especially the reaction against defeat in Vietnam; Nixon's determination to expand military action in Southeast Asia, impound appropriated funds, and withhold information; and the cover-up of criminal acts climaxing in Nixon's resignation in 1974. Congress meanwhile expanded its staffs to catch up with executive expertise; the Foreign Affairs committee staff alone grew from twenty-four in the late 1960s to seventy-nine by 1979. The Supreme Court had held as early as 1942 in *United States* v. *Pink,* 315 U.S. 203, that executive agreements were equivalent to treaties; after a flurry of such agreements in the 1950s and 1960s Congress passed the Case Act in 1972 requiring presidential notification within sixty days of such new pacts. When Nixon returned from the 1972 Moscow summit with wide-ranging political and economic agreements, Congress destroyed much of his work by linking trade expansion to the demand that the Soviets allow dissidents, especially Jews, to emigrate freely

(the Jackson-Vanik amendment), and by capping government credit to the U.S.S.R. Both Jewish emigration and U.S.–Soviet trade plummeted over the next four years. Congress, led by Tom Harkin (D.-Iowa) in the House and James Abourezk (D.-S.D.) in the Senate, rebelled against Nixon-Kissinger's realpolitik by barring foreign aid to nations found to be grossly violating human rights; an entirely new dimension was added to traditional U.S. foreign policy. In 1976 the legislators, over Kissinger's protests, barred sending military aid into Angola's civil war. Three years later, the Senate was about to kill President Jimmy Carter's arms limitation treaty with the Soviets (the second Strategic Arms Limitation Treaty, or SALT II), when Moscow's invasion of Afghanistan made the issue moot.

Remarkably, however, Carter—considered one of the weaker post-1890s presidents—pushed through over determined Senate opposition a historic treaty that promised to give the isthmian canal to Panama in the year 2000; brokered the Camp David agreements for an Egyptian-Israeli peace; secretly dispatched an unsuccessful military mission to rescue fifty-three American hostages held in Iran, a mission that could have accelerated into a military crisis; inserted the United States into the middle of bloody Central American revolutions; and, in 1980, without consulting Congress, announced the Carter Doctrine that committed the United States to contain, if necessary by force, Soviet power in the Middle East. Even a weaker president could exercise enormous powers, especially after the Cold War worsened in the late 1970s.

Ronald Reagan (1981–1989) enjoyed much greater popularity than Carter and similarly expanded executive power when he nearly tripled the Pentagon's budget; invaded Grenada and bombed Libya without consulting Congress; and kept the nation committed to the anticommunist "Contra" forces in Nicaragua despite congressional and public disapproval. Reagan's sharply ideological policies, however, led to a partisan division in Congress that produced the post-1945 nadir in bipartisanship on foreign policy issues. By 1986 he received support on only one of every seven issues he backed. When Congress temporarily blocked aid to the Contras in 1984, William Casey, director of the CIA, and Lieutenant Colonel

Oliver North of the National Security Council, secretly sold arms to Iran and illegally diverted proceeds to Contra forces. As their diversion was being discovered in late 1986 by investigations carried out by the press and the executive itself, North tried to cover up the illegalities by destroying government documents. Congress roused itself to hold hearings on the debacle, but it was through an independent prosecutor that several of the conspirators were convicted of minor crimes. North escaped jail on technicalities and Casey died before the scheme was fully exposed.

The Iran-Contra scandal encapsulated key themes of the post-1890 presidential-congressional competition over the control of foreign policy. North claimed that the president had the power to commit the nation against communists, and that the executive had the inherent power to "authorize and conduct covert operations with nonappropriated funds"—a claim that denied both congressional oversight and budget-appropriation authority. North and Casey worked in the bureaucratic structure created out of the 1947 National Security Act, the power of which was greatly expanded by later presidents. North, in a complaint anticipated by Kissinger and reiterated by Reagan and other members of the executive, condemned Congress as too fragmented and inefficient to be trusted with foreign-policy making. Due partly to the disappearance of party discipline, partly to the growth of interest groups, and partly to the reorganization rules of 1970 to 1975 that weakened chairs, decentralized responsibility, and opened House legislation to virtually limitless numbers of amendments, Congress could endlessly debate and amend legislation, but the executive usually either obtained the essence of what it wanted or simply did not consult the legislators. Important exceptions often were related, significantly, to economic issues, such as Congress's imposition of economic sanctions in 1986 against South Africa's apartheid (segregationist) policy, and the passage of a tough 1988 trade bill, despite some executive opposition.

Even in those two cases, however, the president received wide discretionary powers in lifting and implementing the economic measures. And as commander-in-chief he continued to dominate the most crucial realm of war powers. In 1991 President George Bush did ask Congress for its explicit support before he began warring against Iraq's dictator, Saddam Hussein, who had invaded oil-rich Kuwait. Congress narrowly voted its support for war, but the president actually gave it little choice. Six months earlier he had dispatched nearly one hundred thousand U.S. troops to the region, and in November 1991 he raised the number to more than four hundred thousand. Either such a large force had to be used quickly or, as the world watched, Congress publicly had to undercut both the president's credibility and American men and women on the battlefield.

The Cold War was ending. In his 1989 inaugural address, Bush declared that "a new breeze is blowing—and the old bipartisanship must be made new again." As U.S. foreign policy became increasingly concerned with economic issues and order in the newly emerging, post–Cold War world, however, few signs indicated that these problems would weaken presidential domination of Congress. That domination predated the communist threat and the appearance of nuclear weapons. It began in the 1890s, when the United States claimed new global responsibilities.

## BIBLIOGRAPHY

*Overviews*
See Lee Benson, Joel H. Silbey, and Phyllis F. Field, "Toward a Theory of Stability and Change in American Voting Patterns: New York State, 1792–1970," in Joel H. Silbey, Allan G. Bogue, and William H. Flanigan, eds. *The His-* *tory of American Electoral Behavior* (Princeton, N.J., 1978); Allan G. Bogue, Jerome M. Clubb, Carroll R. McKibbin, and Santa A. Traugott, "Members of the House of Representatives and the Processes of Modernization, 1789–1960," *Journal of American History* 63

(September 1976); CONGRESSIONAL QUARTERLY, *Origins and Development of Congress,* 2d ed. (Washington, D.C., 1982); EDWARD S. CORWIN, *The President: Office and Powers, 1787–1957: History and Analysis of Practice and Opinion,* 4th rev. ed. (New York, 1957); LOUIS FISHER, *Constitutional Conflicts Between Congress and the President* (Princeton, N.J., 1985); MICHAEL J. GLENNON, *Constitutional Diplomacy* (Princeton, N.J., 1990); JAMES A. ROBINSON, *Congress and Foreign Policy-Making; A Study in Legislative Influence and Initiative* (Homewood, Ill., 1967); ARTHUR M. SCHLESINGER, JR., *The Imperial Presidency* (Boston, 1973); JOEL H. SILBEY, ed., *To Advise and Consent: The United States Congress and Foreign Policy in the Twentieth-Century,* 2 vols. (Brooklyn, N.Y., 1991); JOEL H. SILBEY, "Congress at the Bicentennial: A Comment," *Legislative Studies Quarterly* 14 (February 1989); BARBARA SINCLAIR, *The Transformation of the U.S. Senate* (Baltimore, Md., 1989); and JAMES L. SUNDQUIST, *The Decline and Resurgence of Congress* (Washington, D.C., 1981).

### The Nineteenth Century
Relevant works include GERALD GAMM and KENNETH SHEPSLE, "Emergence of Legislative Institutions: Standing Committees in the House and Senate, 1810–1825," *Legislative Studies Quarterly* 14 (February 1989); JAMES W. GOULD, "The Origins of the Senate Committee on Foreign Relations," *Western Political Quarterly* 12 (September 1959); W. STULL HOLT, *Treaties Defeated by the Senate: A Study of the Struggle Between President and Senate over the Conduct of Foreign Relations* (Baltimore, Md., 1933); JOHN MANLEY, "The Rise of Congress in Foreign Policy-making," *The Annals* 397 (September 1971); WILLIAM G. SHADE, STANLEY D. HOPPER, DAVID JACOBSON, and STEPHEN E. MOILES, "Partisanship in the United States Senate: 1869–1901," *Journal of Interdisciplinary History* 4 (Autumn 1973); and ELAINE K. SWIFT, "Reconstitutive Change in the U.S. Congress: The Early Senate, 1789–1841," *Legislative Studies Quarterly* 14 (1989).

### The Twentieth Century
See DAVID BRADY, RICHARD BRODY, and DAVID EPSTEIN, "Heterogeneous Parties and Political Organization: The U.S. Senate, 1880–1920," *Legislative Studies Quarterly* 14 (May 1989); DAVID W. BRADY, JOSEPH COOPER, and PATRICIA A. HURLEY, "The Decline of Party in the U.S. House of Representatives, 1887–1968," *Legislative Studies Quarterly* 4 (August 1979); PHILIP J. BRIGGS, *Making American Foreign Policy: President-Congress Relations from the Second World War to Vietnam* (Lanham, Md., 1991); HOLBERT N. CARROLL, *The House of Representatives and Foreign Affairs,* rev. ed. (Boston, 1966); RALPH G. CARTER, "Congressional Foreign Policy Behavior: Persistent Patterns of the Postwar Period," *Presidential Studies Quarterly* 16 (Spring 1986); DIANE SHAVER CLEMENS, "Executive Agreements," in ALEXANDER DECONDE, ed., *Encyclopedia of American Foreign Policy: Studies of the Principal Movements and Ideas* (New York, 1978); MELISSA P. COLLIE, "Electoral Patterns and Voting Alignments in the U.S. House, 1886–1986," *Legislative Studies Quarterly* 14 (1989); STEVEN L. ELKIN, "Contempt of Congress: The Iran-Contra Affair and the American Constitution," *Congress and the Presidency* 18 (Spring 1991); SAMUEL HUNTINGTON, "Congressional Responses to the Twentieth Century," in DAVID B. TRUMAN, ed., *Congress and America's Future,* 2d ed. (Englewood Cliffs, N.J., 1973); JAMES M. LINDSAY, "Congress and Defense Policy: 1961–1986," *Armed Forces and Society* 13 (Spring 1987); JAMES M. McCORMICK and EUGENE R. WITTKOPF, "Bipartisanship, Partisanship, and Ideology in Congressional-Executive Foreign Policy Relations, 1947–1988," *Journal of Politics* 52 (November 1990); and CHARLES W. WHALEN, JR., *The House and Foreign Policy: The Irony of Congressional Reform* (Chapel Hill, N.C., 1982).

SEE ALSO Constitutional and Political Constraints on Policy-Making: A Historical Perspective; The Contemporary Congress, 1930–1992; Legislative-Executive Relations; The Modernizing Congress; AND The Role of Congressional Parties.

# EXECUTIVE PRIVILEGE

## Richard M. Fried

The term *executive privilege* refers to the power claimed by the executive branch to withhold information, usually in the form of documents or testimony on the part of its officials, from other branches—most commonly, the legislative. The concept is mentioned nowhere in the Constitution, but its defenders assert that it is implicit in the notion of separation of powers. Some also have argued that it can be read into Article II, Section 3's injunction that the president "shall take Care that the Laws be faithfully executed."

## THE NATURE OF THE ARGUMENT

That the Constitution does not refer to executive privilege is no more conclusive of its nonexistence than the similar omission of the power to investigate forecloses the legislative branch from that activity. The only mention of an authority to bar disclosure of information is Article I, Section 5's injunction that Congress shall keep and publish a journal "excepting such Parts as may in their Judgment require Secrecy." (The Articles of Confederation gave discretion to Congress to exclude from its published journal information about diplomatic and military matters. The Constitutional Convention of 1787 debated how much latitude in this regard to grant the legislative branch of the new government.) The Constitution's failure to allot the executive a similar power was taken by Raoul Berger, the leading authority on executive privilege, as a sign that the framers meant to deny it.

On the other hand, a tradition of expedient secrecy was well established by 1787. Initially the Continental Congress kept its proceedings to itself, but moved toward greater openness, except on sensitive military and diplomatic matters. The Constitutional Convention also met behind closed doors to still, said Alexander Hamilton, "clamours of faction" and "inflamatory declamation." (An "abominable precedent," Jefferson termed it.) Not until 1794 did the Senate make its proceedings public. Such framers of the Constitution as John Jay, in *The Federalist,* no. 64, and James Madison, in the Virginia ratification debates, indicated that secrecy, in the context at least of national security, was among the attributes of the executive branch and indeed a key advantage in having a unitary executive. Moreover, secrecy had long served to enhance the *mystères d'état* (state secrets), and as the sociologist Max Weber noted, secrets proliferate naturally in bureaucracies, for which they provide an instinctive defense against importunate lawmakers.

The secrecy that undergirds executive privilege has never been easy to justify in the United States. It has always seemed to clash with the framers' republican ideology, and as Daniel Hoffman indicated, the political theorists on whom the framers relied viewed secrecy pragmatically but ambivalently. Traditionally secrecy has carried an aura of sin. Moreover, the secrecy inherent in executive privilege struggles uphill against the prevailing value system of an open society. One critic of George Washington's administration complained that its use of secrecy "throws a splendour around the Executive." A half century later, President James K. Polk adverted to "the strong and correct public feeling which exists throughout the country against secrecy of any kind in the administration of the government." Woodrow Wilson (as a candidate) avowed that "government ought to be all outside and no inside."

Defenders of executive privilege assert that its constitutional basis is rooted in the separation of powers. In 1973, Attorney General Richard Kleindienst termed the privilege "squarely founded in the separation-of-powers doctrine. The core principle . . . has been universally accepted." As this statement hints, proponents also find the prerogative anchored in precedents starting with Washington and scattered through the next two centuries. Yet the history of executive privilege that its advocates have concatenated is faulty. Many precedents offered to prove executive privilege a time-honored practice are ambiguous, if not highly dubious.

While the premise that the executive is empowered to withhold information from Congress is rooted in hoary precedent, the term *executive privilege* itself is recent. Raoul Berger stated that the coinage was first used in 1958, but others discovered an occurrence of the term in a 1950 Supreme Court case, and a computer search by Fred R. Shapiro found the phrase, though not used in its present context, embedded in a 1940 ruling of the U.S. Court of Appeals of the District of Columbia.

The doctrine of executive privilege directly confronts the power of Congress to investigate. As such, it is a rampart for the executive in its ongoing contention with the other branches. At the Constitutional Convention, the legislative branch was referred to as the "grand inquest" of the nation. In *Watergate and the Constitution,* Philip Kurland argued that the phrase applied only to the House of Representatives and solely in the exercise of its exclusive impeachment power—not to a broad power to probe. Although the Constitution is silent on Congress's investigative authority, the colonial legislatures and the framers of the Constitution used as a model the plenary power of inquiry long asserted by England's Parliament. Congressional inquiry has not lacked advocates. Woodrow Wilson said that "the informing function of Congress should be preferred even to its legislative function." As for the executive branch's duty to respond to inquiries by Congress, the Constitution's requirement that the president "from time to time give to the Congress Information of the State of the Union" (Article II, Section 3) does not end with the annual State of the Union message.

As with other constitutional boundary disputes, the varied reactions evoked by executive privilege have depended on the prevailing political context. Sometimes a wielding of executive prerogative meets with general approval; in other instances, Congress's objections win greater support. Often responses depend on

whose political ox is being gored. Executive privilege seemed at least a tolerable notion in times when the presidency was exalted, as in the afterglow of Franklin D. Roosevelt's stewardship and when Dwight D. Eisenhower battled with Senator Joseph R. McCarthy (R.-Wis.). Then again, when the presidency was deemed to have waxed too "imperial," as in the Vietnam and Watergate era, executive privilege struck many observers as a menace to the constitutional fabric. In 1974, as the Watergate crisis neared its climax, constitutional authority Raoul Berger declared executive privilege a constitutional "myth." Other authorities, not least the Supreme Court, saw more substance than myth.

Given the Constitution's silence, advocates of executive privilege have relied heavily on usage and precedent. In 1949, Herman Wolkinson, a government lawyer, published in the *Federal Bar Journal* an extensive but misleading list of cases of the executive's refusal to supply information to Congress. As the practice proliferated in the 1950s, Congress grew testy, and attorneys general recycled the Wolkinson study to answer them. Thus, in 1958, Deputy Attorney General William P. Rogers addressed to the Senate Subcommittee on Constitutional Rights a memorandum, "The Power of the President to Withhold Information from the Congress," which engulfed Wolkinson's article without attribution while supplementing it with more-recent instances.

This use by Rogers and a Republican administration of the work of an employee of a prior Democratic administration reveals both the continuities and ironies that surround the issue of executive privilege. Bipartisan borrowing should come as no surprise, given the immutable, supra-partisan institutional interests of the executive branch. In 1948, Representative Richard M. Nixon (R.-Cal.) inveighed on behalf of a Republican-controlled Congress against Truman's use of executive privilege, and Rogers, as counsel for a pesky Senate committee, goaded the Justice Department to commission the Wolkinson memorandum. Yet for the Eisenhower administration in 1958, Rogers offered a spacious, Wolkinsonian version of the same privilege against demands from a Democrat Congress.

Political vicissitudes often explain a zeal for executive nondisclosure. The fact that the executive and legislative branches were controlled by opposing parties in eleven of the twenty-three Congresses between 1946 and 1992 and one house of Congress was at partisan odds with the president in three more Congresses surely helped raise the salience of the issue of executive privilege in modern American politics. Conversely, some of the periods of undivided government, notably during the John F. Kennedy and Lyndon B. Johnson presidencies, saw a diminution, though not a disappearance, of concern about this question.

The debate over executive privilege occasionally produced odd ideological bedfellowship. In recent decades, liberals, usually opposing use of the privilege by conservative presidents, have relied heavily on arguments based on their concept of the "original intent" of the framers to refute the doctrine. In defending it, conservatives have often resorted to claims of almost mystical constitutional inherency. Too much, perhaps, should not be made of this reversal: it is a surprise neither that many liberals resort to constitutionalism nor that ideological boundaries have often blurred. Thus, in two major controversies that pitted Congress's investigative power against executive privilege, the issue was resolved when conservatives perceived that a point of excess had been reached. McCarthy's political fall came when (Republican) conservatives decided he had transgressed. Eisenhower's imposition of executive privilege was a turning point of the Army-McCarthy hearings. Similarly, while Nixon, conservative guardian of the privilege, had more than enough liberal enemies, his downfall arrived when conservatives concluded that he had gone too far. Nixon's nemesis, Senator Sam J. Ervin (D.-N.C.), was no liberal, and he assailed the inflation of executive privilege.

Executive privilege is but one aspect of the broader issue of secrecy in government; there are other ways to conceal and other groups than Congress from whom to do so. There are obvious parallels between executive privilege and government denial of information to the press and, through it, to the people. As executive privilege thrived in the Cold War years, so did "news management." That phrase was applied with particular acerbity to practices of the Kennedy administration, but the journalist James Reston is credited with coining it in 1955 in regard to manipulation of news flow by the Eisenhower regime. (The term *managed* *news* has been traced as far back as 1949.) It is noteworthy that while Presidents Kennedy and Johnson made minimal use of executive privilege, the former elicited criticism for news management and the latter, noted for secretiveness, was scored for creating a "credibility gap."

It is also a mistake to assume that executive privilege and the interbranch conflict of which it is a symptom have been the norm over the more than two hundred years of the nation's existence. Presidential compliance with congressional calls for information has been far more common than recalcitrant. Some presidents have supplied requested data a score or even a hundred times and refused it rarely or not at all. Andrew Johnson granted a congressional committee the freedom to question his staff and peruse both his official files and such private materials as his bank records—all pursuant to an effort to impeach him.

Justifications for executive privilege generally fall into the following categories:

1. Premature or sensitive disclosures to Congress would compromise the secrecy essential to carrying out military and diplomatic policies.

2. Some materials sought by Congress consist of investigative reports, which are often "raw" and of dubious veracity. Revelation would do injustice to the subjects of such files and might also reveal secret sources.

3. Ill-timed disclosure might compromise pending enforcement or litigation efforts: the guilty, forewarned, could elude punishment; the innocent, defamed by premature allegations, would suffer.

4. Advice to presidents must remain confidential: otherwise, advisers could no longer feel secure in giving counsel, and advice offered with knowledge that an audience outside the Oval Office might someday hear it would no longer be reliable.

5. The privilege has also been applied to papers of a preliminary or "predecisional" nature, the disclosure of which would have a similarly chilling effect on advisers.

Presidents have offered each of these caveats from the Republic's early years; the second, fourth and fifth have attained a somewhat increased usage since World War II.

The clash between the two tendencies of executive secrecy and congressional inquisitiveness has produced some of the sharpest conflicts concerning the claim of executive privilege. Here, in particular, is an issue ripe for the expression of situational ethics. Changing perspectives on the disputed turf have produced telling ironies. When President Harry S. Truman refused to disclose loyalty information sought by the House Un-American Activities Committee in 1948, Representative Nixon decried the danger this policy portended to republican government. Twenty-five years later, as president, he took precisely the opposite position, invoking Truman's shade on behalf of a policy of "stonewalling."

The caveat that disclosure might prejudice enforcement or litigation policy in the making has been used less commonly. John Tyler first employed it in connection with bruited land frauds. Ronald Reagan invoked the same principle in seeking to defend the Environmental Protection Agency and the Interior Department from congressional oversight.

Presidents have frequently resorted to the fourth argument for executive privilege—that advisers must be able to offer advice confidentially. In *United States* v. *Nixon,* 418 U.S. 683 (1974), Chief Justice Warren Burger called this argument a fruit of "human experience." The underlying premise seems commonsensical, but relies on a somewhat hypothetical reasoning not always borne out in real life. The Nixon administration made such a case for confidentiality, yet Nixon himself routinely resisted critical or jarring advice under any circumstances.

## EARLY PRECEDENTS OF EXECUTIVE PRIVILEGE

Traditionally, George Washington's response to the lower house's 1792 inquiry into the rout of General Arthur St. Clair's expedition against the Indians has been cited as the first instance of the application of executive privilege. Although it is the earliest formal legislative-executive tussle over information policy, the episode does not bear the weight placed on it by modern advocates of the privilege.

The committee established to examine the causes of St. Clair's defeat was instructed by the House of Representatives to "call for such persons, papers . . . as may be necessary to assist their inquiries" (*Annals of Congress,* vol. 3, p. 493). Washington and his cabinet wrestled to shape a response which they knew would serve as an important precedent. They agreed that Congress was an "inquest" and was thus entitled to call for papers from the executive branch. In future cases there might, they surmised, be papers whose disclosure would not be in the public interest. However, Washington, laying no claim to executive privilege, transmitted all relevant documents, enjoined St. Clair to explain himself, and allowed two cabinet officials to give testimony—in all, not much of a precedent for twentieth-century stonewalling.

The St. Clair episode's chief relevance to the case for executive privilege was the cabinet's agreement on the general principle that the president could reserve those papers whose disclosure "would injure the public." The executive branch would make the judgment. Despite the affair's sensitivity, they found no such papers. The cabinet also concluded, according to Jefferson, that any calls by Congress for information should be directed to the president, not heads of departments. (In this case, the House had made its request of the secretary of war.) This tenet, too, would be invoked in subsequent quarrels.

In 1792, in a context of nascent partisanship, the House of Representatives considered charges against Alexander Hamilton's administration of the Treasury, specifically his handling of certain foreign loans. After his first report was derided as inadequate, Hamilton submitted a more extensive, albeit combative and partisan, response, keeping back no information. The sniping continued. Proposals of censure were introduced, but Hamilton was eventually exonerated. The grounds for censure had included a charge that Hamilton had failed to keep Congress fully informed—the first instance of a formal claim that the executive branch had withheld information. Hamilton, significantly, made no assertion of a right to executive privilege.

A new investigation of Hamilton began in 1794. It canvased the legal basis for Hamilton's credit transactions and with it the issue of whether President Washington had authorized them and thus the issue of executive privilege. Congress, Hamilton averred, could not inquire into his relationship with the president "without interfering with the province of the Chief Magistrate." Here was a bold assertion of privilege that confronted the House's constitutional and statutory oversight of fiscal policy. Congress renewed its inquiry, and Hamilton retreated. The committee persisted, asking him to relay the president's views of his activities. This request, as Daniel Hoffman (p. 123) put it, was "tantamount if not identical to a call for testimony" by the president—an equally bold maneuver in the legislative-executive skirmish. Washington's reply gave wan support to Hamilton but none to the secretary's assertion of executive privilege. Though arguments had been made on behalf of executive secrecy, the thrust of the episode was toward disclosure.

In 1794 the issue of executive privilege also arose in a controversy surrounding Gouverneur Morris, American minister to France. Senate critics of administration policy, suspicious that Morris was hostile to the revolutionary regime, sought access to his diplomatic correspondence. Secretary of State Edmund Randolph searched for rationales to rebuff or vitiate the call for information. Perhaps the demand was too broad, or perhaps the Senate, if acting in an executive capacity, had less authority to investigate than in a legislative mode. In the end, Washington sent the requested papers, but with sensitive portions omitted. The principle of disclosure was maintained. However, Washington had sanitized the documents, and both sides accepted the premise that the president was entitled to hold back materials whose publication he deemed contrary to the public interest.

Debate in 1796 over Jay's Treaty with Great Britain occasioned a weightier precedent for executive privilege. From its beginnings in 1794, the controversial Jay mission had stimulated the growth of partisanship. Senate debates concerning ratification of the treaty in 1795 were conducted in secret, a fact on which its foes placed a strongly negative interpretation.

The diffuse quarreling about secrecy crystallized into a debate over executive privilege in 1796, when Washington sought an appropriation to carry out the treaty. Edward Livingston proposed that the House be permitted to see Jay's diplomatic instructions and correspondence (save any affecting current negotiations). The resolution passed after strenuous debate.

Washington rejected the request not on the basis of an absolute executive privilege but because the House had no constitutional role in the treaty process. (He had submitted all relevant documents to the Senate.) Moreover, the House did not specify a purpose for which it sought the papers, let alone one that satisfied Washington—a discretion he claimed was his. Given the need for secrecy in diplomacy, granting the House access to such papers would be a "dangerous precedent."

The issue stirred lengthy debate. Members of the House claimed to be entitled to information pertinent to the functioning of the government in general—an authority so broad as to surmount any cavil about the treaty-making power. Secrecy claims were deflated by the fact that knowledge of the papers' contents had already spread to thirty senators—and to those congressmen who had visited the Senate chamber to read them. Moreover, in the past the president had shared sensitive diplomatic information with both houses. Subsequent commentators would cite the episode as a demonstration of congressional acquiescence in executive privilege. Washington had made a large claim, but the House's deliberations showed anything but concurrence. Two years later, in connection with the XYZ affair, President John Adams seemingly undercut the precedent. Congress made a broad assertion of its right to see diplomatic papers concerning the mission to France, and Adams, while maintaining he had authority to censor the materials (exercised in a limited fashion, to conceal the identities of X, Y, and Z), acceded to it.

The Burr conspiracy of 1805–1806 brought another confrontation over executive privilege, particularly vis-à-vis the judicial branch. Chief Justice John Marshall presided over Burr's 1807 trial in Richmond. Supporting a defense request for correspondence that might help its client, Marshall issued a subpoena calling on Jefferson to provide pertinent documents and to give testimony. Thus rose the question of whether a president was reachable by the judicial process. The defense especially sought a letter Jefferson had received from General James Wilkinson, once Burr's ally. Jefferson demurred that to divulge its contents might endanger national security and that service of a subpoena on the president derogated the dignity of the office. Giving these claims short shrift, Marshall asserted, "That the president of the United States may be subpoenaed, and examined as a witness, and required to produce any paper in his possession, is not controverted" (*United States* v. *Burr,* 25 Fed. Cas. 187 [No. 14694] [Cir. Ct. Va. 1807]).

While champions of executive privilege have depicted Jefferson as resisting the subpoena, the story is more complex. Despite privately expressed grumblings, Jefferson transmitted the Wilkinson letter to U.S. District Attorney George Hay, trusting him to hold back those portions not directly bearing on the case; Hay himself stood ready to give the entire letter to the court and to let Marshall decide which portions were not material. Marshall's ruling hefted the justifications for the president's withholding of correspondence but determined that they were outweighed by the needs of the defense.

Jefferson also objected privately that attending the trial would set a precedent that would bedevil future presidents, who might be haled inconveniently into courts hither and yon. Yet, however unhappy he was with Marshall's assertions of judicial supremacy (in this case and *Marbury* v. *Madison,* 1 Cranch 137 [1803], wherein the secretary of state had been required to give testimony), he did not claim to be beyond the court's reach. While he did not respond publicly to the subpoena, he offered to execute a deposition. Though cited as another validation of executive privilege, the Burr case offers better precedent for the position that the president is not above the judicial process.

Jefferson also withheld files dealing with the Burr episode from Congress. He reserved papers in which were collected "a mixture of rumors, conjectures, and suspicions" and which came from confidential sources, thus invoking executive privilege to protect both sources and innocent victims of their intelligence. In its request for data Congress had exempted materials that might run against the public interest if published. Consequently, this, too, was a rather equivocal precedent on which to base future claims of executive privilege.

In 1825, James Monroe declined a congressional request for information regarding charges against Navy officers posted to the Pacific. His motive was to protect them from being "censured without just cause," before a proper review of the charges could enable them to defend their own conduct. As with Jefferson, Congress had granted Monroe discretion to retain materials whose disclosure might harm the public welfare. Arthur M. Schlesinger, Jr., pointed out that a subsequent House committee stated that because Monroe used such discretion "where it *was* conferred upon him" did not mean he would have done so "in a case where it *was not* conferred" (p. 44).

## FROM JACKSON TO THE MODERN ERA

Subsequent presidents, either assertive executives or those facing assertive Congresses, had recourse to the privilege. Andrew Jackson, not surprisingly, dueled with the legislative branch over access to information. He once "cheerfully conceded" Congress's right to investigate wrongdoing in the executive branch, and he usually met its requests, but in 1833 he turned down a Senate request for a copy of the document he had read to his cabinet to justify removing federal deposits from the Bank of the United States. He did so on grounds that cabinet deliberations must remain confidential—even though he had given the same item to a newspaper. In 1835 the Senate asked to know on what basis Jackson had removed the surveyor general from office, claiming it needed the information both to confirm a successor and to inquire into fraud in the sale of public lands. Jackson refused. He argued that the charges would be considered secretly and the ousted official thus denied a public opportunity to confront them; he also claimed Congress had no authority to probe the grounds for an official's ouster. Jackson also based his refusal on a novel ground; he would resist "to the utmost any further encroachment on the rights of the Executive" in the form of the inconvenience that the "continued repetition" of such requests for information imposed on him.

John Tyler, marooned in the White House with scant political mandate, was a jealous guardian of executive prerogatives. In 1842, when the House sought a list of recent members of Congress who had applied for federal offices, Tyler respectfully declined. While presidential appointments were matters of public record, applications were not; if they were revealed, an "implied confidence" would be "wantonly violated" and to no useful end. Moreover, it would constitute an "encroachment" on executive authority, specifically the appointing power.

In 1843, Tyler objected to the House's call for certain documents pursuant to an investigation of land frauds perpetrated on the Cherokee. He asserted broad authority to deny such requests on the basis of the potential harm to the reputations of those who might be wrongly accused, safekeeping of the identities of confidential informants, and separation of powers. Using a novel approach, he compared congressional inquiries and court proceedings, and seeking to safeguard the process that would eventually bring the guilty to justice, he reasoned that in both "certain communications and papers are privileged [e.g., against self-incrimination] and that the general authority to compel testimony must give way in certain cases to the paramount rights of individuals or of the Government." Tyler defined executive privilege as broad but not absolute. Moreover, after stating his objections, he provided the key documents on the controversy. Congress, however, did not accept his invocation of the evidentiary privilege. Evidence injurious to the nation could not be introduced in judicial proceedings, but to apply that practice to legislative inquiries was an invitation to tyranny.

The assertive James Polk also resorted to the privilege. In 1846 the House asked for an accounting of President Tyler's use of $5,460 from his secret, discretionary contingency fund during diplomatic negotiations with Great Britain. Though the politics of the query favored his party, Polk offered a classic rationale for veiling intelligence matters with secrecy. Experience taught "that emergencies may arise in which it becomes absolutely necessary for the public safety or the public good to make expenditures the very object of which would be defeated by publicity." He also thought it an ill-advised precedent for him "to break the seal of confidence imposed by the law" and invoked by a predecessor. Yet, in asserting the privilege, Polk admitted Congress's right to pursue cases of suspected malfeasance in office (or impeachments).

The outbreak and prosecution of war with Mexico stirred critics in Congress to demand information and Polk again to stand on executive prerogatives. As Schlesinger pointed out, a distinction between foreign and domestic affairs had by then evolved. By tradition, Congress "directed" departments other than State to submit information; in matters affecting foreign relations, it "requested" that the president provide information "if not incompatible with the public interest." However, in seeking the instructions given to the American minister to Mexico and to naval and military commanders in the region, the House had not included that discretionary formula.

Polk chided the House for its "unconditional" call for information. He did pass along a number of documents, but withheld the instructions to his minister plenipotentiary to Mexico. In defense of this omission, he cited as precedent Washington's message denying the House's request for materials relating to Jay's Treaty. Citing Washington's homily about the need for "caution and secrecy" in diplomacy, Polk found it even more germane in 1848 because, unlike 1796, treaty negotiations had not yet been completed; to make these prewar instructions known to America's adversary would cause "serious embarrassment to any future negotiation."

Polk was prepared to make even more spacious definitions of the need for secrecy in diplomatic engagements. In July 1848, in a request for the instructions he had provided to a subsequent set of peace commissioners, the House included the saving reservation about "public interest," but Polk again invoked the privilege. Though the treaty had now been negotiated and ratified, it was unwise, he said, "to publish the instructions to our ministers until some time had elapsed after the conclusion of such negotiations." However, in February 1849, he now included the instructions along with other materials the House had sought. He still feared adverse consequences from revealing the instructions but believed it his "duty" to transmit them—as well as to make them part of a lengthy defense of his policy.

Representative John Covode (R.-Pa.) sponsored an inquiry into corruption in the Buchanan administration that Republicans hoped would pay dividends in the 1860 election, but it also raised the issue of executive privilege. Buchanan compared the probe to a star-chamber proceeding, a Robespierrean tribunal, and "the lion's mouth at Venice, into which secret denunciations were dropped." The Covode Committee both violated his rights as a citizen and "pursued a course not merely at war with the constitutional rights of the Executive, but tending to degrade the Presidential office itself." Should such a precedent stand, the framers' "worst fears . . . in regard to the usurpations of the legislative on the executive and judicial branches will then be realized." Seeking to bring to light Buchanan's maneuvering to impose the proslavery Lecompton Constitution on "Bleeding Kansas," the committee particularly sought a letter he had written Robert J. Walker, the territorial governor of Kansas.

The Civil War called forth vast exertions by the presidency as well as strenuous efforts by Congress to wrest control over policy in a number of areas. Yet, despite Abraham Lincoln's extraordinary arrogation of wartime powers and running battles with congressional critics, neither admirers nor critics of executive privilege have had much to say about him. He did withhold from Congress the dispatches of Major Robert Anderson, the commandant of Fort Sumter, and other materials whose disclosure he deemed contrary to the public interest. The postwar political tableau was filled with close interparty competition, presidents with narrow mandates, and divided government. The legislative remained the dominant branch until the dynamic presidents of the twentieth century and the national needs they addressed tipped the balance again.

Congressional requests for information were part of the political infighting of the Gilded Age and one area where presidents might battle to maintain executive prerogatives. Thus, in 1876, Ulysses S. Grant parried a partisan thrust by the Democrat-controlled House, which asked what official business he had transacted at his seaside vacation hideaway. Grant denounced the inquiry. It had no legislative purpose; if aimed at impeachment, it asked him to incriminate himself; as for where he performed his duties, the Constitution put no geographical limits on the executive, and Congress had no authority to set any. A bit broadly, Grant claimed to find no constitutional authority under which the House might demand of the executive "an account of his discharge of his appropriate and purely executive offices, acts, and duties, either as to when, where, or

how performed." Moreover, a memorandum on presidential absences (and duties carried on while away) showed that every previous president but Harrison (who died early) and Lincoln (who was immersed in war) had spent time away from Washington—Jefferson for 796 days.

Grover Cleveland clashed with the Republican-controlled Senate when he removed hundreds of Republican holdovers from executive posts. When he named replacements, Senate committees asked department heads for the reasons for removal and for supporting documents. Cleveland ordered these withheld because they related to purely executive acts and disclosure did not serve the public interest. After Cleveland named a U.S. attorney in Alabama in 1886, the Senate Judiciary Committee scored the attorney general's refusal to transmit papers regarding the incumbent's dismissal. Cleveland responded that while eager to inform Congress, he would not surrender the constitutional point that papers related to dismissals were "purely unofficial and private" and the removal power wholly executive. (In 1877, Rutherford Hayes had made the latter point in withholding information about his ouster of the collector of the port of New York.) Cleveland won; his nominee was confirmed. Proponents of executive privilege claim the episode as proof of presidential authority to decide what executive papers do not belong in the public eye. Yet despite such disputes as those involving Grant and Cleveland, according to Schlesinger, "disagreements were absorbed in the political process," Congress usually got the information it asked for, and ultimately "the spirit of comity prevailed" (p. 77).

Twentieth-century activist presidents also contended with Congress concerning the latter's right to know. In 1909 the Senate asked why the Justice Department had not prosecuted the United States Steel Corporation for taking over the Tennessee Coal and Iron Company. Theodore Roosevelt sent papers to Congress bearing on the deal and his role in it, but he ordered the attorney general not to provide explanation, because he deemed it beyond the Senate's authority "to give direction of this character to the head of an executive department." The Senate Judiciary Committee called the director of the Bureau of Corporations and threatened to hold him in contempt if he did not provide the data. Roosevelt theatrically took the papers into his custody, declaring that only by impeachment would Congress lay hands on them. The Senate debated a resolution asserting its right of access to executive-branch documents, but no vote took place. With a similarly grand sense of the executive prerogative, William Howard Taft ordered all department heads to transmit to him any troublesome congressional requests for information.

Calvin Coolidge asserted executive privilege over a 1924 Senate investigation of the Bureau of Internal Revenue. The committee sought a list of companies in which Treasury Secretary Andrew Mellon had interests so that it could check their tax returns. Coolidge informed the Senate that it was his well-established prerogative not to reveal confidential information and that he must "bring to the attention of the Senate [the] serious consequences" of intrusions such as the present one.

Herbert Hoover became embroiled in a dispute over access to foreign policy information. Secretary of State Henry Stimson complied with a Senate Foreign Relations Committee request for materials concerning the London Naval Conference of 1930, but held back portions whose exposure, in the president's view, would not serve the public interest. The committee asserted the countervailing need to have all relevant data in order to pursue its constitutional role in treaty ratification. Hoover responded that while senators were welcome to examine in confidence the materials in question, the traditional convention of diplomatic confidences allowed for no further concession to the Senate. The Senate ratified the treaty with a grudging expression of its assumption that no secrets had been withheld from it.

## THE MODERN ERA

Presidential manipulation of information (not to mention public opinion) expanded notably under Franklin D. Roosevelt. The Great Depression emergency, which he likened to war, prompted him to seek commensurately broad powers, but the alarms raised by an ongoing foreign crisis and the coming of a real war occasioned his most vigorous assertions of control of information. Over the next quarter century, the internal-security issue stimulated especially frequent claims of executive privilege.

The trend toward secrecy began in the mid-1930s. The triggering incident may have been Roosevelt's instruction to Federal Bureau of Investigation (FBI) director J. Edgar Hoover to keep tabs on Communists, Nazis, and other groups with foreign ties whose activities posed a danger to internal security. These surveillance activities were covert, and Hoover undertook additional efforts that he did not always disclose to the attorney general or the president. In the field of internal security, secrecy thus became susceptible to delegation, so that some secrets were concealed even from those who had ultimate executive responsibility for them.

In the late 1930s, increasingly powerful conservative foes of Roosevelt's New Deal on Capitol Hill began to raise the issue of internal security, with emphasis on anti-Communism. The 1938 debut of the House Special Committee on Un-American Activities, chaired by Martin Dies (D.-Tex.), signaled this right-wing counterattack. It also opened a period of intense partisan rancor concerning the issue of Communism in government. Though Dies was a Democrat, anti-Communism was a natural issue for Republicans. The coming of the Dies committee also marked a new phase of legislative-executive conflict about access to information, a phase that would culminate in the McCarthy era.

The threat from the Right and the emergence of the Communist issue made a close-mouthed policy on internal-security matters a fixture of executive-branch strategy. Yet considering how deeply the refusal to disclose data on loyalty roiled the politics of anti-Communism in later years, it was remarkable how little the Roosevelt-Dies relationship was affected by the issue. The president's early policy toward the Dies panel was an ad hoc mixture of cajolery and recrimination. Dies never got the cooperation he sought from the executive branch, but he could call a wealth of self-styled experts on Communism as witnesses and obtain information in other ways. Perhaps for this reason, access to executive-branch files did not become a salient question in his committee's early years; although, it is true, in

1940, Attorney General Robert H. Jackson reproved Dies for insinuating that they had mapped out an arrangement by which he would receive FBI data.

In 1941, Jackson provided a foreshadowing of what would become White House policy. The House Naval Affairs Committee asked to see FBI reports concerning strikes and sabotage in plants producing for the navy. With the president's approval, the attorney general refused. He offered a list of precedents of presidential denials of information and court decisions that, he claimed, though with dubious accuracy, "have repeatedly held" that the president need not surrender papers whose "production is contrary to the public interest." His definition of the public interest encompassed the negative impact that disclosure would have on law enforcement, on the confidentiality of FBI sources, and on the reputations of those who might be falsely accused.

In 1943–1944, a House select committee probe of the Federal Communications Commission (FCC) also ran afoul of executive secrecy. To conservative critics, the FCC represented a noxious New Deal holdover. The committee, led by Eugene Cox (D.-Ga.), sought to question Harold Smith, the director of the Bureau of the Budget, about sensitive FCC foreign-broadcast intelligence activities. Smith was not forthcoming, citing the attorney general's 1941 response to the Naval Affairs inquiry. FCC chairman James L. Fly also refused to bring records the committee subpoenaed. When the secretaries of war and the navy and several officers were asked to testify, they answered that the president, invoking the public interest, refused to allow the committee to have the documents and forbade the officers to testify for the same reason.

In 1944, the Cox Committee issued a subpoena summoning J. Edgar Hoover to testify and bring certain records. He refused to produce either the latter or the directive from the president ordering him not to testify on various sensitive matters (including some touching on Pearl Harbor). The attorney general declared it his view that to waive the "privilege" covering confidential communications between the president and attorney general would "establish an unfortunate precedent." The committee formally "directed" Hoover to answer the questions so as to establish a record on which to

proceed further, but seems not, in this wartime context, to have pressed the issue.

For Harry S. Truman, the loyalty and security programs often occasioned use of executive privilege. Franklin Roosevelt had launched rudimentary loyalty and security programs, but Truman greatly broadened them. In 1947 he established a loyalty program for federal employees, partly to preempt the anti-Communist zeal of the Republican Eightieth Congress. Conflict was inevitable.

Executive policy on access to loyalty-security data was mixed at first. One committee's staff was allowed to sample State Department loyalty files, with the cases numbered and names removed so they could be discussed anonymously. However, push came to shove concerning the case of Edward U. Condon, the director of the National Bureau of Standards, whose politics disenchanted House conservatives. The House Un-American Activities Committee (HUAC), permanently established in 1945, pursued Condon; a subcommittee report termed him "one of the weakest links in our atomic security."

In 1947, J. Edgar Hoover had sent a letter to the secretary of commerce raising questions about Condon. A HUAC employee had managed to copy part of the letter before a Commerce Department official called him off. J. Parnell Thomas (R.-N.J.), HUAC's chairman, demanded the full text, parts of which he had already published. Truman took custody of all copies. On 13 March 1948 he ordered that any future requests from Congress for loyalty files be declined and referred to the White House. National security and welfare required the step "to preserve the confidential character and sources of information furnished, and to protect Government personnel against the dissemination of unfounded or disproved allegations." Republicans glimpsed visions of a promising issue for the coming presidential campaign. HUAC's chairman offered a resolution ordering delivery of Hoover's letter. On 22 April 1948 the House overwhelmingly backed the demand, many members voting to uphold institutional prerogative. Congressman Nixon avowed that Truman's nondisclosure order "cannot stand from a constitutional standpoint." If in effect in the 1920s, it would have blocked the Teapot Dome inquiry. The secretary of commerce cited Truman's order in withholding the letter. A subsequent measure to require all executive agencies to surrender documents when Congress sought them passed the House but died in the Senate.

The loyalty issue continued to embroil Truman and Congress. Charging that Communists infested the State Department, Joseph R. McCarthy goaded Senate Democrats into launching a probe in 1950. Republicans insisted that the investigating panel be authorized to subpoena loyalty files. Chairman Millard Tydings (D.-Md.) tried to cajole the president to release the files. Truman publicly stood by his 1948 order, but privately he told Democratic leaders he would wait and see. The attorney general and the FBI director testified that releasing loyalty files would endanger precedent, future FBI sleuthing, and the reputations of the innocent. For the record, Tydings issued subpoenas. Truman disregarded them. Political hemorrhaging from the Communist issue moved him to lay aside constitutional scruples in May and allow the Tydings Committee to see the loyalty files of the eighty-one State Department employees McCarthy claimed to have on his list (counting his omissions, repeats, etc., the number was actually seventy-six)—at the White House, without aid of staff, with no notes to be removed from the room. This concession was made easier by the fact that four committees of the Eightieth Congress had seen the same files, before Truman's 1948 order. Political benefits from the shift were minuscule.

Truman denied congressional access to loyalty files at other times. He also withheld cryptanalytic materials sought in a 1945 probe of Pearl Harbor, had his adviser John R. Steelman disregard subpoenas seeking his appearance before a House subcommittee in 1948, and had General Omar Bradley decline to testify about a confidential meeting regarding the dismissal of General Douglas MacArthur in 1951. (In 1953, as ex-president, Truman rejected a HUAC subpoena to testify about his handling of alleged Communist Harry Dexter White.)

As noted earlier, in 1949 an employee of Truman's Justice Department, Herman Wolkinson, worked up an elaborate justification for such refusals, including a recitation of precedents. "For over 150 years," he claimed, presidents had established by precedent "that they

and members of their Cabinet have an undoubted privilege and discretion to keep confidential, in the public interest, papers and information which require secrecy." Moreover, courts "have uniformly held" this to be "an uncontrolled discretion [with which] they will not interfere." The Justice Department apparently found Wolkinson's legal citations and memorandum a weak reed, but its use had only begun.

Rampant McCarthyism finally provoked Truman's successor, Dwight D. Eisenhower, to assert executive privilege of unprecedented breadth. In the 1954 Army-McCarthy Hearings, it emerged that McCarthy's adversaries within the administration had held a strategy session on 21 January 1954. Participants in the hearings, not least McCarthy, expressed interest in that meeting, but on 17 May, President Eisenhower ruled it beyond the bounds of inquiry. His letter to the secretary of defense ordered that no one was to testify about advice given within the executive branch, whose employees must be "completely candid in advising each other." (It made no mention of the president.) He acted to "maintain the proper separation of powers." A supplementary memo from the attorney general cited separation-of-powers doctrine and precedents of past refusals of information—Wolkinson's list, plus those of Truman.

McCarthy and others protested, but the president's action, a stick to beat an unpopular dog, generally was lauded. The *Washington Post* declared executive privilege "altogether beyond question." However, Eisenhower's letter opened a Pandora's box. In 1971, Senator J. William Fulbright (D.-Ark.) said that the "evil" of executive privilege, "in its modern form, was born of honorable intent," the effort to muzzle McCarthy. "The 'cure,' however, has proven to be as deadly as the disease." Schlesinger noted the irony that Eisenhower, with his "Whig" conception of the presidency, asserted this prerogative so regally. Under Eisenhower it was applied to conversations and documents anywhere in the executive branch.

As a 1950s fad, executive privilege rivaled the hula hoop. Within two years, more than twenty agencies had employed it. Between 1954 and 1960, Eisenhower's ukase was cited some forty-five times. Several officials used it in 1955 to avoid testimony about a power contract that had been awarded to the Dixon-Yates utilities group. This dispute arose when Congress learned that a man served as consultant to the Bureau of the Budget at the same time he was an officer of the company brokering the interests before government agencies of the Dixon-Yates combine, which was seeking a contract to build a plant to feed power into the Tennessee Valley Authority system. The privilege was cloaked with the claim that preliminary advice and "working papers" must remain confidential. Some critics cited Atomic Energy Commission chairman Lewis L. Strauss's liberal use of the privilege as a reason for rejecting his nomination as secretary of commerce in 1959. In 1958, Eisenhower had denied the Senate access to the Gaither Report on defense preparedness on similar grounds. Attorney General Herbert Brownell cited the privilege to justify taciturnity regarding settlement of an antitrust suit against AT&T.

The practice stirred concern and led to two inquiries. In 1955, John E. Moss (D.-Calif.) headed up the new House Special Subcommittee on Government Information to scrutinize the ways in which the flow of information was stanched. Seven years later, Moss initiated an exchange of letters in which President John F. Kennedy agreed to limit recourse to executive privilege and to let be used only with "specific Presidential approval." Thomas C. Hennings's (D.-Mo.) Senate Subcommittee on Constitutional Rights also studied executive privilege. His 1957 query elicited a memorandum from Deputy Attorney General William P. Rogers, largely a reprise of Wolkinson's, defending the privilege. In 1958, after becoming attorney general, Rogers argued a broad reading, extending the privilege even to heads of independent agencies and making the first widely noted use of the phrase itself. Hennings's plans to draft a "Code on Executive Privilege" were forestalled by his death in 1960.

Use of executive privilege dropped sharply under Kennedy and Johnson; that the Democrats controlled both houses of Congress helped account for the harmony. Kennedy, who had agreed to limit recourse to executive privilege and to use it only with "specific Presidential approval," invoked the privilege to conceal the identities of Pentagon employees who vetted certain department speeches. In addition, the Food and Drug Administration held back data on the drug MER-29, and General Maxwell Taylor declined to testify about the Bay of Pigs incident. (Some scorers credit Kennedy with only one real use of executive privilege.) Under Lyndon B. Johnson, the Defense Department denied the Senate Foreign Relations Committee a copy of its study of the Gulf of Tonkin incident, and a Treasury official refused to testify on the nomination of Abe Fortas to be chief justice (Fortas was excused from discussing confidential advice given to Johnson). Johnson himself, however, never invoked executive privilege. Critics of the privilege were heartened by the decline in use, but other means to hide information evolved. Thus, some agencies held back information because it fell into one or another of the categories excluded from coverage of the Freedom of Information Act, even though that 1966 measure, enacted in part through the efforts of the Moss Committee, stipulated that it was not to be used to deny information to Congress.

## WATERGATE AND BEYOND

Under Nixon, use of executive privilege metastasized. In a by-then-traditional exchange with Representative Moss in 1969, Nixon pledged to invoke the privilege only with "specific Presidential approval"—and then sparingly. However, a Library of Congress study listed fifteen instances of use by administration officials and four by Nixon himself in his first term. Items denied to Congress included reports by the FBI on scientists nominated to Department of Health, Education, and Welfare advisory panels, by the Agency for International Development on aid to Cambodia, and by the Pentagon on military operations in Vietnam. In 1969 (two years before their revelation), the secretary of defense kept the Pentagon Papers from the Senate Foreign Relations Committee, but not on grounds of executive privilege.

The tug-of-war over the privilege was part of a wider conflict with Congress over Nixonian arrogation in such areas as impoundment and executive agreements. Novel kinds of nondisclosure and assertions of executive prerogative flourished. Presidential counsel John Dean used the privilege to block a General Accounting Office request for logs of flights made for campaign purposes and data on the extent to which

Nixon's reelection committee had paid for them. Some officials ducked testimony before Congress on claims that various reasons made it "inappropriate." The Senate Foreign Relations Committee, which had repeatedly been denied copies of a five-year plan for the Military Assistance Program, finally voted to invoke a clause of the Foreign Assistance Act that cut off funds in precisely such cases—only to have Nixon employ executive privilege. For a time in 1970, the Agriculture Department held back a list of hotdog makers who failed to meet the 30 percent fat limitation. In 1973, Attorney General Richard Kleindienst told a Senate panel that "if the President so commands," executive privilege could deny Congress information from any executive-branch employee. The privilege covered even former members of his staff, Nixon claimed.

Congress responded with inquiries and proposals. In 1971, Sam J. Ervin's (D.-N.C.) Senate Subcommittee on Separation of Powers held hearings. Exasperated by the experience of his Foreign Relations Committee, Senator Fulbright offered a bill forbidding executive-branch employees to plead executive privilege to avoid appearing before Congress or, once appearing, to cite it without the president's written authority. The bill was intended to make agencies supply any information Congress sought unless, within thirty days, executive privilege was invoked; the privilege would be honored only if the president put it in writing and stated his reasons; funding would be cut off if an agency violated these rules. Fulbright hoped thus to halt de facto applications of the privilege that merely omitted "the forbidden words." Former Secretary of State Dean Acheson opposed the bill, saying that it might prompt "recollection of both Robespierre and the late Senator Joseph McCarthy." No floor action was taken on it.

By 1973, interest in executive privilege had quickened. Its use emerged as an issue at the confirmation hearings on L. Patrick Gray's ill-starred nomination as FBI director. Nominated attorney general, Elliot Richardson was grilled on the topic at his confirmation hearing. The subcommittees on Intergovernmental Relations (Government Operations Committee), Separation of Powers, and Administrative Practice and Procedure (the last two, both Judiciary) held hearings on the privilege and other

secrecy issues. Attorney General Kleindienst testified unyieldingly that even in impeachment proceedings the president could use the privilege to prevent testimony by a member of his staff. In December 1973 the Senate passed a bill (S. 2432) authorizing committees to subpoena information withheld under the privilege and lodging jurisdiction concerning enforcement of the subpoena in the District of Columbia federal district court. The House Government Operations Committee split on the bill, some members fearing it gave too much recognition to executive privilege. No floor action was taken. Ervin's panel held more hearings in 1974, but Watergate preempted attention from legislative curbs.

Watergate produced many things, including the first real reading of the constitutionality of executive privilege. Nixon initially ordained that under the privilege none of his staff would testify before the Ervin Committee, but public opinion prompted him to give way. In July 1973 the Ervin Select Committee on Campaign Activities learned of the Oval Office taping system. The panel first requested, and then subpoenaed, the tapes. The Watergate grand jury, at the behest of Special Prosecutor Archibald Cox, subpoenaed them too. Nixon riposted with a defense of presidential confidentiality, asserting that the privilege gave absolute presidential discretion and that the presidency was beyond compulsory process of the courts.

Both Cox and the committee sued. Federal District judge John J. Sirica ruled against the committee. It had offered the court no jurisdictional basis for its suit. He found for Cox: executive privilege was not absolute and did not shield the White House from criminal proceedings, and the courts could determine how far it extended. The Court of Appeals upheld Sirica, rejecting Nixon's argument that surrender of the tapes imperiled "the continued existence of the Presidency as a functioning institution." Claims that the president was immune to legal process "are invitations to refashion the Constitution, and we reject them." Nor was executive privilege absolute. The "general confidentiality privilege must recede before the grand jury's showing of need."

Eschewing an appeal, Nixon offered a compromise (as the Appeals Court urged); he would make a summary of the tapes to whose accuracy Senator John Stennis (D.-Miss.) would attest; he also ordered Cox to cease trying to obtain more tapes. When Cox refused and was fired, a "firestorm" of outrage forced Nixon to yield; he complied with Sirica's order and named a new special prosecutor.

Pressing its own hunt for the tapes, the Ervin panel proposed, and Congress passed, a bill to confer jurisdiction over its controversy on the federal courts. In his February 1974 ruling, Judge Gerhard Gesell found Nixon's claim of executive privilege and the committee's claim of investigative power overbroad. He would not enforce the committee's subpoena because it showed no "pressing need" for the tapes and its interest would have to yield to those of pending criminal trials, which further hearings might prejudice. On appeal, the committee again lost, its need for the tapes now found uncompelling, since the House Judiciary Committee, weighing impeachment, then had some of them (courtesy of the special prosecutor, not the courts).

As the new special prosecutor, Leon Jaworski, sought ever more tapes, Nixon balked. Jaworski obtained a subpoena, the White House appealed, and the case went to the Supreme Court. A unanimous 24 July 1974 decision in *United States* v. *Nixon,* by Chief Justice Warren Burger, resolved the executive-legislative quarrel by asserting judicial supremacy. As for executive privilege, Burger saw the need for confidential communications between advisers and leaders "too plain to require further discussion." But he found no basis for "an absolute, unqualified presidential privilege of immunity from judicial process under all circumstances." The "presumptive privilege" must yield to "our historic commitment to the rule of law."

The *Nixon* case sank Nixon's presidency, but dragged a somewhat weakened doctrine of executive privilege to safety. Opinions of the decision vary. Alan F. Westin termed it "one of the Supreme Court's 'better' exercises of judicial statecraft" (Friedman, ed., p. xii). Philip Kurland likened the ruling to "the description of a tennis match. First the Court is on one side of the privilege and then on the side of the subpoena . . . until ultimately it is game, set, and match—to the referee" (p. 66).

A later case disposed of Nixon's assertion of executive privilege to retain his presidential papers. The Supreme Court upheld a law giving control of the papers (including tapes) to Congress and the administrator of the General Services Administration. Executive privilege could follow a president beyond the White House, but its force was vitiated by other interests.

The Nixon years had elevated concern over access to information. In the post-Watergate atmosphere, Congress overrode President Gerald Ford's veto of the 1974 Freedom of Information Act, which caulked loopholes in its 1966 predecessor. Under Presidents Ford and Jimmy Carter, fewer episodes of executive privilege arose, but a still testy Congress discovered the utility of the threat of contempt of Congress. In 1975, Secretary of State Henry Kissinger was nearly cited for contempt of Congress for refusing papers about covert operations to the House Central Intelligence Agency oversight panel. Ford invoked executive privilege, but after several members were briefed on the documents, committee chair Otis Pike (D.-Calif.) declared that to be "substantial compliance." In 1975, Secretary of Commerce Rogers Morton flouted a subpoena seeking data about the Arab boycott of Israel, but relented when Congress brandished the contempt weapon. In 1980, Energy Secretary Charles Duncan faced a similar threat until he released papers relating to President Carter's oil-import fee (but not those directly involving presidential confidentiality).

Under Ronald Reagan, the executive privilege issue revived. In 1981, Interior Secretary James Watt defied a House Energy and Commerce subcommittee subpoena for documents regarding Canadian takeovers of American energy firms and use of federal leasing rights. Reagan invoked executive privilege, stressing that the papers dealt with delicate foreign policy matters. In February 1982 the subcommittee and parent committee voted (on mostly partisan lines) to cite Watt for contempt, but committee chair John D. Dingell (D.-Mich.) worked out a deal with the White House. The documents were made available under guard for four hours to subcommittee members only (no staff or photocopying). A vote by the full House was thus averted.

Less fortunate was Anne Gorsuch, head of the Environmental Protection Agency, whom the president ordered to withhold from two House committees seventy-four documents about enforcement of the Superfund toxic waste cleanup program. Release, it was argued, would hamstring future enforcement. In December 1982 the House voted Gorsuch in contempt, but the Justice Department would not prosecute, filing a suit claiming that executive privilege made the subpoena unconstitutional. A House countermotion to dismiss prevailed, but as the judge urged, a compromise was reached. The committee (and staff) gained access to the documents; the contempt citation was rescinded. As the Justice Department began probing charges of misdeeds, Reagan said he would no longer stand on executive privilege. Gorsuch resigned in March 1983.

The Iran-Contra controversy, erupting in 1986, skirted the edges of executive privilege. Reagan waived the privilege, allowed White House aides to testify, plied Congress with reams of documents, and did not block trials of the Iran-Contra figures. This agreeableness even prompted Representative Henry Hyde (R.-Ill.) to fear for "the eroding of executive privilege."

The trial of Oliver North raised complications. North subpoenaed the president and other high officials to testify; the Justice Department argued that executive privilege shielded Reagan and, in 1989, still covered him as ex-president. Judge Gerhard Gesell ruled that Reagan remained "subject to call" if North showed his testimony to be essential. When North failed to do so, Gesell excused Reagan on nonconstitutional grounds. During the 1990 trial of former national security adviser John Poindexter, Reagan invoked executive privilege when ordered to turn over diary entries, but he agreed to a subsequent order to testify by videotape, thus finessing the issue of haling a chief executive, former or otherwise, into court.

## CONCLUSION

Out of the controversies of the 1980s emerged an executive privilege that was constitutionally established but far from absolute in scope. Congress, the usual target of the privilege, emerged from the Watergate litigation as something of a stepchild, for its claims were shrugged off while those stemming from criminal litigation were satisfied. The courts' entrance into the fray, itself a crucial result of executive-branch assertiveness, is an action that calls for discretion. Judicial surgery may appear to involve a mere stitch here and a tuck there, but as a solution to any "political" question, it is an invasive procedure.

Congress, often frustrated by executive arrogance and unsure of a legislative solution, has found in the contempt power a way to prevent promiscuous and capricious use of the privilege. It is a messy, quarrelsome approach, but one that has led to compromises of the sorts that the courts, in disposing of cases involving executive privilege, have endorsed. If divided government continues, executive privilege will continue to beguile chief executives. The fight over Judge Clarence Thomas's nomination to the Supreme Court suggests that control of information may persist as an issue in confirmation battles. It is also quite possible that the Rehnquist Court of the 1990s will interpret executive privilege in a manner different from that of the Burger Court of the 1970s. Senator Ervin's homily that "we are going to have to have a little oil of mutual understanding poured on the joints of the Constitution where one of the powers begins and another ends" may point to the only peaceable solution to this legislative-executive impasse.

## *BIBLIOGRAPHY*

### *1970s Controversies*
Controversies of the 1970s spawned many works on executive privilege. RAOUL BERGER, *Executive Privilege: A Constitutional Myth* (Cambridge, Mass., 1974), offers a historical review of the privilege's use and tart criticism of arguments as to its constitutional basis. More favorable is ADAM CARLYLE BRECKENRIDGE, *The Executive Privilege: Presidential Control over Information* (Lincoln, Nebr., 1974). HENRY BARTHOLOMEW COX, *War, Foreign Affairs, and Constitutional Power: 1829–1901* (Cambridge, Mass., 1984), has useful coverage. LOUIS FISHER, *Constitutional Conflicts Between Congress and the President* (Princeton, N.J., 1985), has a chapter on the privilege and a longer-lens

focus on Watergate than most works on this subject. Indispensable on the origins of the privilege is DANIEL N. HOFFMAN, *Government Secrecy and the Founding Fathers: A Study in Constitutional Controls* (Westport, Conn., 1981). ARTHUR M. SCHLESINGER, JR., *The Imperial Presidency* (Boston, 1973), treats the privilege in the wider context its title indicates and reflects second thoughts about the wisdom of some aspects of a strong presidency. ABRAHAM SOFAER, *War, Foreign Affairs, and Constitutional Power: The Origins* (Cambridge, Mass., 1976), studies the early years up to 1829. The Sofaer and Cox volumes were commissioned by the American Bar Association.

## Legal Aspects

Law review articles are a major locus of discussion of executive privilege. RAOUL BERGER, "Executive Privilege v. Congressional Inquiry," *UCLA Law Review* 12 (May–August 1965), is an early study for his subsequent book. His "Executive Privilege: A Presidential Pillar Without Constitutional Support," *Villanova Law Review* 26 (January 1981), gives a post-Watergate perspective. ARCHIBALD COX, "Executive Privilege," *University of Pennsylvania Law Review* 122 (June 1974), offers a timely review that distinguishes uses of the privilege from other sorts of withholding of information. JEAN V. D'OVIDIO, "Executive Privilege: Historic Scope and Use in the Watergate and Environmental Protection Agency Hearings," *University of Richmond Law Review* 18 (Fall 1983), takes analysis of court cases into the Reagan era. COLLEEN GRZESKOWIAK, "Executive Privilege and Non-Presidential Actors: The Distress of 'Tidy-Minded Constitutionalists' Continues," *Syracuse Law Review* 38 (Fall 1987), is a specialized examination of an aspect of the privilege. HERMAN WOLKINSON, "Demands of Congressional Committees for Executive Papers," *Federal Bar Journal* 10 (April, July, October 1949), marks the first attempt at synthesis of the political and judicial history of executive privilege. The article's pro-privilege bias undercuts the history it presents. Compare the more critical symposium in volume 19 (January 1959) of the same publication.

## Information Policy

Articles on other aspects of information policy and executive privilege include JAMES HAMILTON and JOHN C. GRABOW, "A Legislative Proposal for Resolving Executive Privilege Disputes Precipitated by Congressional Subpoenas," *Harvard Journal of Legislation* 21:1 (Winter 1984), a discussion of solutions to the executive privilege impasse. WILLIAM J. HAGENS, "The Moss Committee and Freedom of Information," *Michigan Academician* 4:2 (1971), treats that early response to executive secrecy. FRED R. SHAPIRO, "A Computer Search for the Origin of Executive Privilege," *American Speech* 59 (Spring 1984), contains a small surprise. STEPHEN W. STATHIS, "Executive Cooperation: Presidential Recognition of the Investigative Authority of Congress and Courts," *Journal of Law and Politics* 3 (1986), has the great virtue of dealing with constitutional cats that did not get caught in trees.

Numerous books cover wider issues of secrecy. A chapter on executive privilege by NORMAN DORSEN and JOHN SHATTUCK appears in NORMAN DORSEN and STEPHEN GILLERS, eds., *None of Your Business: Government Secrecy in America* (New York, 1974). MILES BEARDSLEY JOHNSON, *The Government Secrecy Controversy* (New York, 1967), has some value as a look at the issue prior to the embroilments of the Nixon era. In *Presidential Secrecy and Deception: Beyond the Power to Persuade* (Westport, Conn., 1980), JOHN M. ORMAN covers a neglected aspect of the busy topic of "presidential leadership." A collection with an essay on executive privilege by ARTHUR S. MILLER is HAROLD C. RELYEA, ed., *The Presidency and Information Policy* (New York, 1981). FRANCIS E. ROURKE, *Secrecy and Publicity: Dilemmas of Democracy* (Baltimore, 1961), is another early glimpse at the issue with some attention to executive privilege.

Watergate itself produced a gusher of books and inspired many of the works cited above. HOWARD BALL, *"We Have a Duty": The Supreme Court and the Watergate Tapes Litigation* (New York, 1990), is useful. LEON FRIEDMAN, ed., *United States v. Nixon* (New York, 1974), has texts of key legal rulings and other documents of Watergate litigation. PHILIP B. KURLAND, *Watergate and the Constitution* (Chicago, 1978), provides important analysis of executive privilege. STANLEY I. KUTLER, *The Wars of Watergate: The Last Crisis of Richard Nixon* (New York, 1990), is a thorough, scholarly, up-to-date study of the subject; executive privilege punctuates the book, but does not emerge as a central theme. JAMES HAMILTON, a member of the legal staff of the Ervin Select (Watergate) Committee, offers a broad legal and historical perspective in *The Power to Probe: A Study of Congressional Investigations* (New York, 1976).

SEE ALSO Legislatures and Impeachment.

# LEGISLATURES AND EXECUTIVE REORGANIZATIONS

## Peri E. Arnold

The executive branch is the locus of administrative power within the American system of government. At the federal level its main components are the great executive agencies such as the State Department, the Defense Department, and the Treasury Department (there are currently fourteen such departments). These, in turn, are composed of large numbers of specialized, subordinated agencies.

As government's role expanded over time, the development of these large agencies dictated that bureaucratic efficiency and economy would become central concerns for government. In the late nineteenth century, executive reorganization emerged as a process for addressing economy and efficiency within the executive branch. Executive reorganization is a process through which government plans and implements reforms within its administrative organizations and is best exemplified in a series of comprehensive reorganization episodes over the last century. Executive reorganization's reforms may aim to improve either structural or procedural aspects of administrative agencies.

In the separation-of-powers model on which the American federal and state constitutions are based, both the legislative and executive branches have constitutional powers vested in them which infer authority over executive organization. One cannot understand executive reorganization through a legislative perspective alone. This essay will study the relations between the legislature and the chief executive in the process of executive reorganization.

The federal experience with executive reorganization has shaped state reorganization efforts and also illustrates in the most general way the character of executive reorganization in a separation-of-powers constitutional system. This essay will give primary attention to the federal experience with reorganization, and in closing, will offer an overview of the history and practice of state executive reorganization. While one notes strong parallels to the federal experience within the state experience, it is important to note variations among the states in their experiences with executive reorganization.

## CONSTITUTIONAL AUTHORITY OVER EXECUTIVE ORGANIZATION

The U.S. Constitution distributes authority over executive-branch organization to both the Congress and the presidency. Scholars debate the amount of power over the executive branch that the Constitution distributes to Congress and the president, respectively. Some argue that the Constitution's intent was to create a presidency with the authority to act as chief manager of the executive branch. This view became commonplace after the presidency of Franklin D. Roosevelt and the formation of what is often called the "modern presidency." Its proponents, among them political scientist Leonard White and administrative expert Louis Brownlow, cite language and actions surrounding the Constitution more than the specifics of the document itself. They bring into evidence items such as Alexander Hamilton's expansive depiction of the presidency in *The Federalist,* nos. 68–75, and the First Congress's decision to grant to the president the right to remove appointees.

On the other hand, there are those who argue that the Constitution favors Congress in the allocation of powers over the executive branch. Proponents of this view cite as support for their position the Congress's ultimate power over finances and the creation of governmental organization. The political scientist James Sundquist is among the leading proponents of this view.

Consider the balance of power over the executive branch in the language of the Constitution itself. Turning first to the presidency, one must review Article II, which constitutes the office and specifies its powers. Article II opens, "The executive power shall be vested in a President." Might this phrase, "the executive power," comprise a grant of significant power to the president? Few commentators until the mid-twentieth century would forward that interpretation of the vesting clause.

Article II contains four specific grants of power pertaining to the executive branch. First, the president is commander-in-chief of the armed forces; this has become an awesome power, but one that is dependent on Congress's power to appropriate monies and raise an army. Second, the president can require the opinion in writing of principal officers of the executive departments. This is nothing more than a right of consultation and implies little about authority over executive-branch organization. Third, the president nominates major officials of government, but their appointment is dependent on concurrence by the Senate. Article II, Section 2, further specifies that through legislation Congress may locate the appointment of lesser officials in persons other than the president, for example, in department heads. Fourth, Article II, Section 3, states that the president must "take Care that the Laws be faithfully executed." Whatever powers might derive from that injunction, the presidential role here is totally dependent on a congressional function, the passage of law.

Throughout Article II, presidential powers are tied to congressional powers and are dependent on them. Turning to Article I and to the Constitution's specification of legislative authority, one encounters those powers that are central to the establishment and conduct of the executive branch: the powers to raise revenues and appropriate funds, the power to legislate governmental actions, and the power to create organizations. Thus, the fundamental authority over the executive branch lies in congressional power.

However, locating the sources of constitutional power over the executive branch is only a starting point for examining the history of Congress's role in executive reorganization. There is an equally important functional dimension to this history. Which branch is more capable of initiating reform of the executive branch? In fact, the history of executive reorganization is a dialectic between constitutional power and institutional efficacy.

## EXECUTIVE ORGANIZATION AND REFORM IN THE NINETEENTH CENTURY

Executive-branch growth during the later nineteenth century placed executive reorganization on the legislative agenda. Thus, it is appropriate to review the nineteenth-century expansion of the executive branch before turning to early efforts at reorganization.

### The Growth of the Executive Branch

For most of the 1800s, Congress's major concerns regarding the executive branch entailed the expansion of agencies and public employment. Between 1789 and the opening of the twentieth century, Congress created seven cabinet-level departments. Federal civilian employment grew from 4,837 in 1816 to 239,476 in 1901.

In 1789 Congress established three departments: State, Treasury, and War. In the same year Congress created the post of attorney general to serve as the government's chief attorney, although the Department of Justice was not established until 1870.

The Department of the Navy was established in 1798, after a long battle in Congress over the issue of whether the new country needed a permanent navy. The Department of the Interior was created by Congress in 1849 after several earlier attempts and long debate over whether this department, which would incorporate already existing governmental activities, represented an undesirable expansion of government. The Department of Justice was created in 1870 to cope with the growing need for attorneys and the expansion of litigation in the work of government. Finally, the Department of Agriculture was raised to full cabinet status in 1889 (it had been created as a noncabinet agency in 1862). This was the first department created to serve a specific economic interest within society (both Commerce and Labor would follow in 1903).

## Executive Reorganization in the Nineteenth Century

As a responsibility that flows from its power to create governmental programs and organization, Congress has authority to oversee the administrative activities of the executive branch agencies. Throughout the early nineteenth century the Congress exercised that role through recurring committee investigations into misconduct in the executive branch. In 1842 a House select committee on retrenchment chaired by Representative Thomas Gilmer (Whig-Va.) approached the executive branch with a broader agenda, to reduce expenditures by eliminating activities and positions.

The broader perspective that had characterized the Gilmer committee became the approach of congressional investigations at the end of the nineteenth century. The increasing size of the executive branch presented Congress with problems it had never before addressed, the costs and efficiency of the expanding governmental apparatus and its corps of public servants.

The late-nineteenth-century Congress was almost continually concerned with the operation of the executive branch. Congress conducted comprehensive investigations of the operations of the executive branch agencies through three select committees in this period. The Joint Select Committee on Retrenchment, chaired by Senator James W. Patterson (R.-N.H.) conducted investigations between 1869 and 1871. Its work comprised a search to economize by identifying wasteful activities, but the committee was without staff and its investigation was unsystematic. No noteworthy reforms were produced in the wake of its investigation.

The second investigation was that of a Senate select committee to inquire into the methods of the executive departments, created in 1887 and chaired by Senator Francis M. Cockrell (D.-Mo.). The Cockrell committee requested voluminous reports from executive branch agencies. It accumulated a wealth of raw data, but the committee had no staff and was without the ability to draw general patterns from its mountain of information. Its final report focused on the possibilities of economizing through the details of work processes and office management in the agencies.

In 1893 Congress established what it called a joint commission with three members from each house and chaired by Representative Alexander M. Dockery (D.-Mo.). Unlike its predecessors, the Dockery joint commission was supplied with an expert staff. The commission appointed three cost accountants to serve as staff experts. The Dockery commission's main accomplishment was to recommend improved accounting techniques for government, but in its other recommendations it did not move above the search for specific instances of waste.

During the nineteenth century, congressional attention on the executive branch shifted from specific scandals to administration more generally. But these congressional investigations did not comprehend the management of the executive branch as a whole. Nothing in these congressional reports recognized that the problem posed by the growth of the executive branch might entail more than retrenchment. There was as yet no recognition that the organization of the executive branch would need overall direction and coordination—that is, modern management.

## EXECUTIVE REORGANIZATION IN THE EARLY TWENTIETH CENTURY

In the nineteenth century, presidents had no part in congressional executive reorganization. That state of affairs would change, beginning with the presidency of Theodore Roosevelt.

### Executive Reorganization in the Progressive Era

The question of responsibility for executive reorganization raises two issues: constitutional powers and functional efficacy. Early in the twentieth century, influential intellectuals and reformers argued that it was the presidency and not Congress that had the greatest capacity for leadership. These Progressives, as they are called, argued that a modern society required more focused and effective government than had characterized the congressionally dominated government of the nineteenth century.

Theodore Roosevelt succeeded to the presidency after William McKinley's assassination in 1901. After being elected to his own term in 1904, Roosevelt established the first presidentially initiated effort at executive reorganization. In June 1905, President Roosevelt named five executive-branch officials to a commission to reform the executive branch, with Assistant Secretary of the Treasury Charles Keep serving as chair. Congress's only role in this effort was to receive Roosevelt's request for an appropriation of $25,000 for the already-organized study. Congress approved only $5,000 for the study, however.

The Keep Commission focused on the details of administration and not on the overall conduct of the executive branch. The commission's recommendations ranged from the management of records to the use of window envelopes. There was nothing in the recommendations to offend Congress. But it was Roosevelt's presumption of the power to act without express congressional authorization that irritated the legislators. Congress attempted to limit such initiatives with the Tawney amendment to the 1909 supplemental appropriation act, stipulating that appropriated funds could not be used to support presidential commissions unless appropriated for that purpose.

William Howard Taft was inaugurated president in March 1909, and he continued Roosevelt's interest in executive reorganization. But whereas Roosevelt had attempted to circumvent Congress in initiating his effort at executive reorganization, Taft had little choice but to work with Congress because of the constraint posed by the Tawney amendment. In 1909 Congress considered creating another congressional study of the executive branch, driven by the federal deficit that appeared after 1904.

It was Congress's inclination to address the deficit by launching yet another search to reduce expenditures in the executive branch. However, President Taft proposed that instead, Congress empower the president to organize an investigation. Congress assented and appropriated $100,000 to fund a presidentially guided study to "attain greater efficiency and economy" in the executive branch. Taft's initiative represented a compromise between the earlier congressional approach to executive reorganization and President Roosevelt's presumption of presidential prerogative over executive reorganization. Taft's approach rested on legislative delegation of authority but incorporated presidential initiative in the conduct of the reorganization study.

To design his reorganization study, President Taft consulted with a number of public administration experts and eventually appointed a prominent academic specialist, Dr. Frederick Cleveland, as his assistant for executive reorganization. In March 1911 Taft established the President's Commission on Economy and Efficiency, composed of six academic specialists and practitioners of public administration. Frederick Cleveland served as the commission's chair.

The recommendations of the president's commission mark a divide in the history of American executive reorganization. Until then, executive reorganization had focused on the executive branch as a universe of isolated, minute activities. But the president's commission conceived of the executive branch as a whole and offered recommendations to improve the capacity of government to direct it as a system of organizations and activities. The commission saw the president as responsible for the management of the executive branch because the presidency represented coherence and singular responsibility, while the Congress was by its nature fragmented.

In 1885, Woodrow Wilson's classic *Congressional Government* portrayed (and decried) the presidency's subservience to Congress. A quarter of a century later, the reports of the president's commission envisioned a very different presidency from that which was lamented by Wilson. In the commission's view, an independent and effective presidency was central to the operation of modern, large-scale government.

The commission's budget recommendation reflected its transformation from a congressional to a presidential view of reorganization. At this point there was no overall plan of spending presented to Congress as a basis for appropriations. The commission concluded that a central budget was crucial to the possibility of overcoming deficits, and it proposed that the president annually present to Congress a budget, setting priorities in government spending. It also recommended the creation of a presidential-staff agency to support presidential budgetary responsibilities.

As bold as the budget recommendation was, Taft's effort at implementing it speaks even more plainly for a changing conception of the president's role over the executive branch. In September 1911 the president directed his commission to create a parallel system for processing appropriations requests from the executive branch agencies. Traditionally, these would be passed through to Congress by the Treasury Department. But now the commission would use those requests to produce a demonstration presidential budget to be delivered to Congress. Recognizing a threat to its authority, Congress passed an amendment to the Sundry Civil Appropriations Act of 1912 (sec. 9) that required executive branch agencies to submit their estimates for appropriations "only in the form and at the time now required by law, and in no other form." President Taft fought back, asserting in a public statement to the heads of executive branch departments on 18 September 1912 that "it is entirely competent for the President to submit a budget, and Congress cannot . . . prevent it. . . . And this power I propose to exercise." But Taft had little ability to oppose Congress. The Republican party had lost seats in the 1910 election, and in the fall of 1912 Taft was involved in a desperate campaign for reelection in which the party was torn in half; by contrast, the Democrats had in Wilson their strongest candidate in two decades.

The president's commission died in early 1913. While he was sympathetic to its general work, the newly inaugurated president, Woodrow Wilson, had his own full agenda of policy proposals, and there was no place for the commission's work in the new administration. But Congress acted to retain a capacity for the kind of technically sophisticated research that it had conducted. In 1913 Congress directed the U.S. Civil Service Commission to continue the commission's work on classification systems in government service. In 1916, Congress expanded the capacity for research on administration by creating the independent Bureau of Efficiency, which operated as an agent of Congress.

## Executive Reorganization in the 1920s

In the aftermath of World War I, Congress again took up executive reorganization, its interests in this area taking two forms. First, Congress finally adopted the idea for an executive budget that had met congressional rejection in 1912. Between 1916 and 1920 the federal debt expanded twenty-fold. Now Congress agreed that government required a more disciplined budget system than it could itself organize. The Budget and Accounting Act of 1921 directed the president to prepare and submit an annual budget. What the act implied was that for reasons of institutional competence, the president could be more effective at formulating a budget than could Congress.

Congress's concern with executive reorganization after World War I was also expressed in the formation of a select committee for the reorganization of the executive branch. In December 1920 the Republican Sixty-sixth Congress created the Joint Committee on Reorganization. It would have six members, three from each house (two being Republican and one a Democrat). The joint committee was created during a vacuum in the presidency. The Democratic lame duck, Woodrow Wilson, was incapacitated by a stroke, and the Republican president-elect, Senator Warren Harding of Ohio, would not be inaugurated until March. Furthermore, it was not expected that Harding would become an advocate for expanded presidential responsibilities.

Could Presidents Roosevelt's and Taft's initiatives in executive reorganization be aberrant, with the nineteenth century precedent of congressional-reorganization studies taken as normal practice? The Sixty-sixth Congress seemed to be answering that question in the affirmative. But after his inauguration, President Harding surprisingly challenged that assumption. He requested that a place be added to the joint committee for a presidential appointee and that this person serve as the committee's chair, replacing Senator Reed Smoot (R.-Utah) in that role. Congress acquiesced, and Harding appointed Walter Brown to the committee. Brown was a prominent Ohio Republican who played an unusual dual role. He chaired a congressional joint committee while not being a member of Congress. At the same time, he served as President Harding's assistant for planning executive reorganization.

In 1921 the joint committee agreed to an administration proposal that the president be made responsible for developing a plan of executive reorganization, and the committee went into hibernation. Walter Brown organized the reorganization plan, working with the department secretaries of the administration.

The plan the Harding administration presented to the joint committee in 1923 took a distinctly presidential perspective. It recommended unifying activities within new Departments of Defense and Welfare. It proposed centralizing governmental financial controls under the president, moving the General Accounting Office from its status as a congressional agency into the Treasury Department. Finally, the plan observed that reorganization is essentially an ongoing presidential responsibility, and it suggested that the president have discretion to order reorganizations within the executive branch.

Congress specified that the joint committee's purpose would be to reorganize agencies to achieve "the largest possible measure of efficiency and economy." In 1921 Senator Smoot had promised to achieve a savings of $300 million. Yet the administration's plan aimed not at economy but at enhanced presidential direction of the executive branch. The plan's prospects were weakened further when President Harding died in August 1923 and was succeeded by Calvin Coolidge, who was not committed to the reorganization planning effort. The joint committee passed on to Congress most of the Harding plan, deleting only the recommendation for merging the Departments of War and Navy. But between 1924 and 1927, only a few of the plan's recommendations were passed into law.

From 1870 through the 1920s an unresolved tension developed over differing conceptions of the appropriate locus of responsibility for executive reorganization in the federal government. There is significant constitutional weight to support the claim of congressional responsibility, but the twentieth century brought an increasingly insistent claim that it was the presidency that exhibited greater institutional capacity to plan for and manage reform within the executive branch.

By the late 1920s there were some signs of a resolution of those competing claims between constitutional authority on the one hand and institutional efficacy on the other. In the Economy Act of 1932, passed in June 1932, Congress gave to the president a qualified authority to effect reorganizations within the executive branch by executive order. A notable feature of this legislation was the first appearance of the legislative veto. This is a device whereby through a simple resolution of either house (one-house veto) or concurrent resolution of both Houses (two-house veto), Congress can disapprove the president's proposed action (neither requires presentation to the president for signature or veto). The Economy Act incorporated a one-house veto. Combining the legislative veto with the delegation of reorganization authority to the president, Congress was able to balance its claim to constitutional authority with the president's claim to great capacity for overseeing the executive branch.

## THE NEW DEAL AND THE BROWNLOW COMMITTEE

In response to economic crisis and war, the government under Franklin Roosevelt grew dramatically in size, range of programs, and costs. From the perspective of an activist president, the governmental growth that Roosevelt had stimulated raised pressing concerns for mechanisms through which government could be more effectively managed. But growing and more costly government also raised concerns in Congress that were rooted in the older, congressional perspective on executive reorganization as a search for economy in government.

### Executive Reorganization on Parallel Tracks

Beginning in 1936, these two concerns produced parallel and ultimately conflicting efforts. In March 1936 President Roosevelt established the Committee on Administrative Management, with the goal of improving the president's capacity to manage the executive branch. The committee was composed of three experts on public administration, Luther

Gulick, Charles Merriam, and its chair, Louis Brownlow. Supported by a staff of twenty-seven political scientists, the Brownlow Committee worked through the year and reported in January of 1937.

Parallel to the Brownlow Committee, two congressional select committees were assigned to study reorganization of the executive branch. The House committee was chaired by Representative James Buchanan (D.-Tex.), and the Senate committee was chaired by Senator Harry Byrd (D.-Va.). Instead of conducting research through congressional staffs, the congressional committees contracted the Brookings Institution to conduct their reorganization investigation.

Initially, there was an agreement to cooperate between the presidential committee and the congressional committees. The Brownlow Committee would focus on overall administrative management of the executive branch. The congressional committees, through the Brookings Institution's study, would focus on duplication and overlap of functions within the executive branch. But that agreement collapsed after President Roosevelt presented the Brownlow Committee's recommendations to the Congress in January 1937, urging that they be adopted into law.

The Brownlow Committee aimed at two results. It sought increased central authority within the executive branch. For example, it recommended that most of the financial-control functions of the General Accounting Office (an agency of Congress created by the Budget and Accounting Act of 1921) be moved into the Treasury Department and made subject to presidential rather than congressional authority. It also recommended the abolition of the independent regulatory commissions and inclusion of their regulatory missions within executive departments. Second, the recommendations specified mechanisms for enhancing the president's managerial capacity over the executive branch. It recommended the addition of six administrative assistants to the president's office. It also proposed several new presidential staff organizations that would be incorporated within a new organizational support system for the presidency, an executive office. Among these new staffs would be an expanded planning agency for social and eco-

nomic policy and a presidential assistant who would serve as head of the civil service, replacing the multiheaded Civil Service Commission. The committee also recommended that the Bureau of the Budget be relocated from Treasury into this new executive office.

In contrast to the Brownlow Committee's recommendations, the congressional recommendations stressed the combination and curtailment of activities aimed at reducing spending. Senator Byrd, chair of the Senate select committee, emerged as one of the leading critics of the Brownlow recommendations. Byrd insisted that reorganization's fundamental purpose was to economize, and he found no promise of economy within the Brownlow recommendations

## The Effort to Pass a Reorganization Bill: 1937–1939

Between 1937 and 1939 the Brownlow Committee's recommendations were caught in tensions between the president and Congress. Added to the problems caused by Senator Byrd's attack on the recommendations was the almost simultaneous presentation to Congress by President Roosevelt of his so-called court-packing plan through which he aimed to overcome the Supreme Court's opposition to New Deal policies. The opposition to this highly contentious proposal spilled over into opposition to Roosevelt's reorganization plan. In the eyes of many of President Roosevelt's opponents, both bills aimed at granting unwarranted powers to the president.

In 1937, bills that incorporated many of the recommendations of the Brownlow Committee succeeded in the House, but the Senate reorganization bill did not come up for a vote during the year. In January 1938, the Senate took up a new version of the reorganization bill. This time it came to a vote and passed, after opponents of the president's plan substantially weakened its provisions through amendments. In April 1938 the House addressed the reorganization issue, essentially in the same form as the bills that it had passed in 1937. But this time leading members of the House attacked the bills as infringing on congressional authority. Amendments also weakened the bills, making them less attractive to their proponents. Finally, in a recommital vote on 8 April, the House killed the reorganization bills.

## The Reorganization Act of 1939

At the beginning of the Seventy-sixth Congress, in early 1939, Representative Lindsay Warren (D.-N.C.) introduced to the House a reorganization bill that was stripped of the controversial Brownlow Committee proposals that had been points of contention over the past two years. Gone were reforms that would put the civil service and financial controls under the president. Gone were centralizing reorganizations of executive branch departments.

Warren's bill contained only two central features. First, it created six positions for administrative assistants to the president. Second, it gave the president authority to order reorganizations of the executive branch, subject to a veto by both houses of Congress through a concurrent resolution. Although the Democrats had lost seventy-one House seats in the 1938 election, there was relatively little opposition to Warren's reorganization bill. The bill passed the House on 8 March 1939, receiving overwhelming support among Democrats and some Republican votes.

The Senate's consideration of the House reorganization bill was also relatively uncontentious. Senator Byrd insisted that economy in government be specified as the purpose for presidential reorganization authority, and his amendment won unanimous support. The Senate passed the Reorganization Act and President Roosevelt signed it on 3 April 1939.

## The Executive Office of the President

Although the Reorganization Act of 1939 was emptied of most of the Brownlow recommendations, it gave to the president the capacity to order reorganization, requiring that it would take majorities in both houses to veto the president. Indeed, in his first use of the reorganization authority President Roosevelt implemented a central Brownlow Committee recommendation by creating the Executive Office of the President.

In late April, Roosevelt issued Reorganization Plan No. 1 of 1939, creating the Executive Office and placing into it the already existing Bureau of the Budget and National Resources Planning Board. In Executive Order 8248, which followed the reorganization plan, the president specified the organization and operations of the Executive Office in more detail. In full, it would include the White House Office, the Bureau of the Budget, the National Resources Planning Board, the Liaison Office for Personnel Management, and the Office of Government Reports.

The creation of the Executive Office of the President launched a new era in American government. Never before did the president have available the resources presented by the Executive Office, and those resources would grow as time passed. In the late 1940s both the Council of Economic Advisers and the National Security Council were added to the Executive Office by congressional action. Along with an expanding White House staff, these became instruments through which activist incumbents could expand the activities and powers of the presidency, in executive reorganization as well as in other policy areas. It is for this reason that many scholars identify the birth of the modern presidency with the creation of the Executive Office.

## THE HOOVER COMMISSIONS

As of early 1993, Congress's last initiatives in executive reorganization planning took the form of two commissions, both chaired by Herbert Hoover. The first was created by the Eightieth Congress in 1947, and the second was created by the Eighty-third Congress in 1953. Relevant to an explanation of the Hoover Commissions is the fact that the Eightieth and Eighty-third Congresses shared the unusual distinction for a modern Congress of having Republican majorities in both houses.

### The First Hoover Commission, 1947–1949

In January 1947 Senator Henry Cabot Lodge (R.-Mass.) and Representative Clarence Brown (R.-Ohio) sponsored a Commission on the Organization of the Executive Branch of the Government to seek economies in government. In congressional testimony, a Bureau of the Budget representative recommended against the bill, stating a preference for continuing attention to reorganization through presidential reorganization authority.

Underlying the Lodge-Brown bill was more than the traditional congressional search for economy in government through executive reorganization. The Eightieth Congress was the first with a Republican majority in both houses in a quarter of a century. For the Republicans, the target of executive reorganization was not just economy in general but what Republicans saw as the bloated bureaucracy created by Democrats in government.

The Lodge-Brown bill specified that the commission would be appointed by three officials. The Speaker of the House, the Senate president pro tempore, and the president would each appoint four members, two of whom would be Republican and two, Democrat. Upon passage of the bill, it was negotiated that former president Herbert Hoover would be appointed by the Speaker of the House and the other appointees would elect him chair. Thus the commission's popular title became the Hoover Commission. Four of the commission's twelve appointees were from Congress, two representatives and two senators.

The Hoover Commission undertook its work by creating twenty-two task forces composed of outside experts. Hoover assigned to himself the first of the commission's study topics, "General Management of the Executive Branch." It was understood that part of the commission's mission was to prepare a set of recommendations for the next Republican president, who was expected to be elected in 1948. The minority of liberal appointees to the commission attempted to uphold at least a neutral administrative perspective in the commission's work, but they were a minority against a majority dominated by Hoover. Despite the party balance in the membership of the commission, the Republican majorities in both houses of the Eightieth Congress meant that eight members of the commission were appointed by Republicans (the Senate president pro tempore and the House Speaker) who sought conservative Democrats for their appointees.

Hoover's initial design of the commission's work was that besides considering administrative structure, it would delve into governmental policies to determine whether they were appropriate subjects of governmental activity. However, the unexpected reelection of President Truman and the Democratic congressional victory in 1948 upset the Hoover Commission's plans.

But the commission adjusted to the change in the political landscape. The Truman administration communicated to Herbert Hoover that it would cooperate with the commission if the commission would restrict itself to problems of administration. Hoover accepted that redirection and the result was a very influential set of reports. The commission's initial report, "General Management of the Executive Branch," written by Hoover, was a reaffirmation of the spirit of the Brownlow Committee perspective that the president was general manager of the executive branch. Twenty-two reports followed, most of which offered precise recommendations for changes in organization and process, and a large proportion of these were adopted through either actions by Congress or the executive. Congress renewed and extended the president's authority to initiate reorganization through the Reorganization Act of 1949.

## The Second Hoover Commission

In 1952, Republicans swept to victory, electing Dwight Eisenhower president and winning both houses of Congress. Even before the start of the Republican Eighty-third Congress, some senior Republican members were planning for the creation of another Hoover Commission to achieve what the first commission had not, a critique of the public policies that had been initiated by Democrats since 1933.

Without any encouragement from the Eisenhower White House, Congress created a new Commission for the Organization of the Executive Branch in early 1953. The bill took the exact form of the act creating the first Hoover Commission with the following important exception. This time the bill specified the purposes of the commission specifically as concerned with governmental activities in public policy. The new commission's goal was to identify possible savings through the elimination of activities and to define the responsibilities of executive branch officials, in an apparent challenge to presidential authority over the executive branch.

In many respects the second commission seems identical to the first. It was chaired by

Herbert Hoover, had twelve members appointed through a tripartite arrangement, and conducted its work through task forces. Like its predecessor, the second commission's membership included two representatives and two senators. However, the commission differed in two important respects. Its membership was more conservative than that of the earlier commission, and there was no pressure such as that posed by the election of 1948 to change the course of the second commission.

By the time the second commission reported in 1955 it found neither Congress nor the president likely to be receptive to its most ideological recommendations, such as reducing the federal government's role in the development of water resources. The Eisenhower White House had not encouraged the commission and conducted its own reorganization efforts, wholly separate from the Hoover Commission. As for Congress, it had changed partisan balance in the 1954 election; new Democratic majorities in both houses were not receptive to attacks on past Democratic policy initiatives.

The commission's eighteen reports issued in 1955 fall into two categories. Those that were technical in perspective and politically neutral, such as "Research and Development" or "Budget and Accounting," had a substantial portion of their recommendations accepted by the Congress and president. Those that focused on substantive policy, such as "Water Resources" and "Legal Services," had few recommendations accepted.

## EXECUTIVE REORGANIZATION BY PRESIDENTIAL INITIATIVE

After 1955 the president became the dominant actor in executive reorganization. Since that time, Congress has not initiated a major reorganization effort. At the same time, the presidency proved more capable than Congress of focusing expertise and information on the problem of reforming the federal executive. In the post-1955 period, Congress's dual role has been to facilitate presidential initiative by delegating reorganization authority to presidents, subject to specified subject qualifications and time limitations, and to check presidential use of that authority through the legislative veto.

With the exception of President Jimmy Carter's Reorganization Project, these presidential reorganization activities were supported from discretionary funds available within the modern presidency. Presidents Eisenhower, Johnson, Nixon, and Carter each initiated major executive reorganization efforts, and each will be outlined below.

### Eisenhower's Advisory Committee on Government Organization

As part of his transition apparatus, President-elect Eisenhower created a committee on government organization to recommend reforms in the executive branch. Its three members were moderate Republicans with extensive Washington experience: Nelson Rockefeller (the chair), Milton Eisenhower (the president-elect's brother), and Arthur Flemming (former civil service commissioner and defense-mobilization official). By April 1953, the committee had given the president twenty memorandums, each addressing a specific organization or aspect of the executive branch. In 1953 Congress renewed presidential reorganization authority, extending for four more years the authority granted in the Reorganization Act of 1949. Armed with that authority and his committee's recommendations, President Eisenhower developed an ambitious reorganization agenda, presenting ten reorganization plans to Congress in 1953. Among other things, these plans created the Department of Health, Education, and Welfare and wrought major changes in the Departments of Agriculture, Defense, and Justice.

In January 1953 President Eisenhower made his advisory committee official as the President's Advisory Committee on Government Organization, incorporating it within the Executive Office of the President. The committee continued to work closely with Eisenhower, addressing organizational problems of the presidency itself as well as reorganization of the executive branch. The President's Advisory Committee represents the beginning of an era in which executive reorganization planning is incorporated within the expanding presidential establishment.

### The Johnson Task Forces

In the mid-1960s some members of Congress, particularly Senator Abraham Ribicoff (D.-

Conn.), sought another congressional reorganization effort, like the Hoover Commissions. But the Johnson administration claimed priority in this area, organizing two task forces to plan for reorganization between 1964 and 1968.

In 1964 President Johnson created his Task Force on Government Reorganization, with ten members, chaired by Don K. Price of Harvard's School of Government. With staff support from the Bureau of the Budget, the task force completed a report to the president in November 1964. Its recommendations had two goals. First, it proposed organizational changes to make the executive branch more efficient in implementing policy. These reforms included a number of changes in cabinet-level departments and proposals for three new departments: transportation, education, and housing. The task force's second goal was to make the executive branch more responsive to presidential leadership. To this end it recommended strengthening the capacity of the Executive Office of the President for systematic analysis of policy and increased presidential control over the upper levels of the civil service. With the exception of its recommendations for departments of transportation and urban affairs, few of the Price task force's recommendations were adopted by the administration.

In September 1966 President Johnson created another reorganization effort, the Task Force on Government Organization. He designated Ben Heineman, a Chicago businessman, to chair the task force, and appointed to it eleven other members. This task force's membership was more influential than the first one. The Price task force was composed primarily of academics, but the Heineman task force included such key Johnson administration figures as Secretary of Defense Robert McNamara, Undersecretary of State Nicholas Katzenbach, Budget Director Charles Schultze, and former national security adviser McGeorge Bundy. It also had its own staff and was independent of the budget bureau.

President Johnson asked the Heineman task force to address problems of management in his Great Society programs as its first job. In December the task force presented to Johnson its recommendations for Great Society programs, several of which were included in the Economic Opportunity Act of 1967. Between early 1967 and mid-1968 the Heineman task force produced reports addressing broader issues, including the consolidation of the existing cabinet-level departments into several "superdepartments," the organization of foreign affairs, and the absence of policy analysis in the president's organization. These proposals emerged in the last days of the Johnson administration and none was adopted.

## Nixon's Ash Council

In 1969 President Richard Nixon created a reorganization planning entity titled the Advisory Council on Executive Organization. It was chaired by Roy Ash of Litton Industries and composed of five others with extensive backgrounds in business. The council's work in the Nixon administration was overwhelmingly focused on means for creating a managerially more effective Executive Office of the President and centralizing the executive branch departments to make them more controllable by the president.

At the end of 1969 the Ash Council presented to President Nixon recommendations for the creation of a Domestic Council in the Executive Office and a bold reorganization of the budget bureau to bring greater stress on its managerial role, renaming it the Office of Management and Budget. President Nixon implemented both recommendations in March 1970 through Reorganization Plan No. 2 of 1970. The Ash Council next presented a report on regulatory commissions that was not approved by the president. Finally, the council presented to Nixon a grand program for reorganizing the executive branch departments. In the spirit of an earlier Heineman task force proposal, the council proposed creating new superdepartments that would unify coherent sectors of public policy by folding together related departments. For example, a department of natural resources would be created from the current Departments of Agriculture and the Interior.

President Nixon embraced the Ash Council's vision of a new executive branch. Since the early 1960s, Congress had included in recurring reorganization acts a prohibition on the use of presidential reorganization authority to create new departments. Thus, in his 1971 State of the Union address, Nixon called for legislation to establish these new entities. Congress subsequently rejected legislation enacting the

Ash Council departmental recommendations, and President Nixon attempted to use presidential administrative resources to achieve similar ends. Increasingly resistant to President Nixon's unilateral actions, Congress did not renew the presidential reorganization authority when it lapsed in 1973.

## President Carter's Reorganization Project

Jimmy Carter initiated a massive reorganization program at the start of his presidency. To plan reorganization, Carter created a new division within the Office of Management and Budget (OMB) called the Reorganization Project. Including volunteers and people on loan from other agencies as well as OMB employees, the Reorganization Project employed almost three hundred people.

The Reorganization Project's work was conducted by study teams focusing on the organization of specific policy areas of government such as national security, economic development, and human resources, as well as functional areas such as paperwork reduction. The project's added cost to the OMB budget was supplied by Congress through a supplemental appropriation of $2,172,000.

To arm himself for reorganization, in February 1977 President Carter requested that Congress restore the presidential reorganization authority that had lapsed in 1973. Congress responded with a three-year grant of authority. A new feature of the Reorganization Act of 1977 was the provision that before an up or down negative vote, Congress could amend a presidential reorganization plan.

The Reorganization Project's major recommendations addressed the reorganization of cabinet departments. At the president's request, it formulated plans for new departments of energy and education. With strong presidential support, these proposals were enacted into law by Congress, energy in 1977 and education in 1979. The Reorganization Project also produced recommendations for four new departments that would result from reorganizations of current departments, departments of natural resources, developmental assistance, trade and technology, and food and nutrition. President Carter chose to seek a department of natural resources and pursued that goal through most of 1979, but the proposal failed to be adopted by Congress.

The Carter administration's leading accomplishment in reorganization was planned through a parallel operation to the Reorganization Project, titled the Personnel Management Project and staffed by 160 people. It produced recommendations for a more flexible personnel system for upper-level civil servants, the Senior Executive Service, along with recommendations for replacing the Civil Service Commission with a streamlined Office of Personnel Management. These recommendations were endorsed by Carter and passed into law by Congress in 1979.

Between the Eisenhower and Carter administrations, executive reorganization was incorporated as a presidential concern and manifested as an element of the modern, organized presidency. But even as executive reorganization appeared to have become a routine part of the expanded powers of the modern presidency, the presidents that followed Carter from 1981 through 1992 showed no interest in expansive reorganization activities. Instead, as some analysts have noted, the Reagan and Bush administrations were primarily concerned with the political orientation of those who were appointed to official positions within the executive branch as a means for effecting the conduct of the executive branch.

While it does not explain the recent decline of presidential interest in large-scale reorganization planning, a 1983 decision of the U.S. Supreme Court complicates the longstanding arrangement whereby Congress delegated reorganization authority to presidents, subject to a congressional check. In *Immigration and Naturalization Service* v. *Chada,* 462 U.S. 919, the Supreme Court declared the legislative veto unconstitutional because it violated the constitutional provisions for legislative action, majority decisions by both houses followed by presentment to the president.

The history of executive reorganization reveals a dialectic between Congress and the president in which each branch has a perspective on, and interest in, reorganization. Despite the current lull of interest in reorganization, one can say that congressional and presidential interests in the executive branch are strong enough so that at some future point, both branches will again wrestle over the issue of which of them will influence executive reorganization.

## EXECUTIVE REORGANIZATION IN THE STATES

Because all state constitutions incorporate a separation-of-powers model, state executive reorganization presents the same fundamental problems of interbranch tensions that have already been observed in the federal government. However, because the states present fifty possible cases of executive reorganization, as a body of governments they constitute a source of observations about different approaches to executive reorganization and their causes.

### The Waves of State Executive Reorganization

There have been four waves of state executive reorganization in the twentieth century. These have followed upon major episodes of executive reorganization planning at the federal level, suggesting the diffusion of reorganization ideas from the federal government to the states.

Following upon Taft's Commission on Economy and Efficiency, thirty-nine states initiated one or more efforts at executive reorganization in the period 1914–1936. From 1936 through 1946, in the wake of the Brownlow Committee, ten states initiated one or more efforts at executive reorganization. A third wave followed the Hoover Commissions, and thirteen states conducted executive reorganization between 1947 and 1965. The fourth wave of state reorganization parallels the extensive reorganization activity of the Johnson, Nixon, and Carter administrations, and twenty-two states initiated executive reorganizations between 1966 and 1987.

### Legislatures vs. Governors in State Executive Reorganization

Like the trend in national executive reorganization toward strengthening the president, the general trend in state executive reorganization has been toward strengthening the governors. However, the situation of the governor in state constitutions differs from that of the president. Governors lack the president's stature and range of formal powers. Thus, state executive reorganization has been slower to strengthen the chief executive than was national executive reorganization.

In the last wave of state reorganization, the governor was central to initiation in eighteen of the twenty-two state efforts, and the governor and legislature jointly initiated reorganization in three states. In only one state, Colorado, was executive reorganization initiated solely by the legislature. Most of these state reorganization plans of the last wave were centralizing and executive enhancing.

State reorganization plans can be characterized in terms of the degree of centralization they impose on the executive branch. Traditional type plans leave government with large numbers of functionally narrow major departments, twenty or twenty-five, with many of them headed by commissions or elected officials. In cabinet type plans, there are ten to fifteen relatively broad departments in the state government, and the governor has power of appointment over the department heads. Secretary-coordinator type plans place existing narrow departments into functional groupings, each headed by a coordinating secretary who is appointed by the governor. The last two types strengthen governors, but the traditional type plan provides significantly less managerial authority to the governor.

Until the last wave of state executive reorganization, the largest proportion of plans produced in state executive reorganization were of the traditional type, although states that were more industrialized and economically advanced were more likely to propose and adopt executive-centralizing executive-reorganization plans.

Finally, the relative disadvantage of the governors in executive reorganization compared to the president can be seen in the distribution of executive reorganization authority to the governors. As of 1970, only eight states gave their governors the authority to initiate reorganization plans, subject to legislative veto. By 1990 twenty-four states gave this authority to their governors, in a slow process through which the states were paralleling, if only partially, the federal government's experience of shifting authority over administration from the legislature to the chief executive.

## BIBLIOGRAPHY

### Federal Reorganization

PERI E. ARNOLD, *Making the Managerial Presidency: Comprehensive Reorganization Planning, 1905–1980* (Princeton, N.J., 1986), treats the role of executive reorganization in the development of the presidency and examines efforts at federal executive reorganization from Theodore Roosevelt's administration through the Carter efforts. BARRY KARL, *Executive Reorganization and Reform in the New Deal: The Genesis of Administrative Management, 1900–1939* (Cambridge, Mass., 1963), analyzes the work of the Brownlow Committee and traces its intellectual origins, offering fine insight into the political context of reorganization in the New Deal. OSCAR KRAINES, "The President Versus Congress: The Keep Commission, 1905–1909," *Western Political Quarterly* 23 (March 1970), describes the origin of the Keep Commission and traces its work, giving detailed attention to its recommendations. RONALD MOE, *The Hoover Commissions Revisited* (Boulder, Colo., 1982), examines the recommendations and accomplishments of the two Hoover commissions. RICHARD POLENBERG, *Reorganizing Roosevelt's Government: The Controversy over Executive Reorganization, 1936–1939* (Cambridge, Mass., 1966), is a study of the aftermath of the Brownlow Committee's report; Polenberg traces Roosevelt's efforts to gain reorganization legislation after 1936, culminating in the Reorganization Act of 1939.

### Executive-Branch Management

LARRY BERMAN, *The Office of Management and Budget and the Presidency, 1921–1979* (Princeton, N.J., 1979), traces the development of the budget bureau from its beginning, offering a good account of Congress's purposes in creating the executive budget and a balanced analysis of the bureau's problems in addressing issues of executive management. JOHN HART, *The Presidential Branch* (Elmsford, N.Y., 1979), examines the growth of presidential power in the executive branch since the 1930s, giving particular attention to the Executive Office of the President and the growth of the White House Office. STEPHEN HESS, *Organizing the Presidency* (Washington, D.C., 1988), studies the use of presidential staff and approaches to the executive branch by presidents from

Franklin Roosevelt through Reagan. RICHARD NATHAN, *The Administrative Presidency* (New York, 1983), analyzes the efforts by the Nixon and Reagan administrations to effect policy goals through administrative tools, circumventing Congress. HAROLD SEIDMAN and ROBERT GILMOUR, *Politics, Position and Power: From the Positive to the Regulatory State* (New York, 1986), examines the executive branch and its management in the context of institutional tensions between the presidency and Congress. LEONARD D. WHITE, *The Republican Era, 1869–1901: A Study in Administrative History* (New York, 1958), details the growth and conduct of the executive branch during the period of congressional dominance. This is the final of four volumes on the history of the executive branch, all of which are indispensable for understanding the evolution of the executive branch in the nineteenth century. The others are *The Federalists* (New York, 1948), which covers the period 1789 to 1801; *The Jeffersonians* (New York, 1951), covering 1801 to 1829; and *The Jacksonians* (New York, 1954), covering 1829 to 1861.

### Congress and the Presidency

LAWRENCE C. DODD and RICHARD L. SCHOTT, *Congress and the Administrative State* (New York, 1979), treats the changing relations of Congress to the executive branch over the last hundred years, analyzing the formal powers and informal means that Congress retains for influencing the executive-branch agencies. LOUIS FISHER, *Constitutional Conflicts Between Congress and the President* (Princeton, N.J., 1985), is a comprehensive treatment of the constitutional powers of Congress and the presidency and the resulting points of tension; it includes a very clear treatment of the legislative veto. MORTON KELLER, *Affairs of State* (Cambridge, Mass., 1977), is a far-reaching study of national politics in the last thirty-five years of the nineteenth century, providing an account of congressional dominance of government in that period. JAMES L. SUNDQUIST, *The Decline and Resurgence of Congress* (Washington, D.C., 1981), treats the decline of Congress in relation to growing presidential power and focuses on Congress's institutional revival after 1973. Along with Seidman and Gilmour above, this is an excellent source for studying the relative power and advantages of the Congress and the presidency over the executive branch. WOODROW WILSON, *Congressional Government* (Boston, 1885), is the classic late-nineteenth-century critique of the dominance of Congress and the weakness of the presidency in American government.

### State Reorganization

JAMES K. CONANT, "In the Shadow of Wilson and Brownlow: Executive Branch Reorganization in the States, 1965 to 1987," *Public Administration Review* 48 (September/October 1988), analyzes the characteristics of fourth-wave state reorganization efforts, assessing a number of variables, such as how they were initiated, the character of their proposals, and their rate of success or failure. COUNCIL OF STATE GOVERNMENTS, *The Book of the States* (Lexington, Ky., annual), contains a section describing state executive reorganizations in the preceding year. JAMES L. GARNETT, *Reorganizing State Government: The Executive Branch* (Boulder, Colo., 1980), catalogs and analyzes all efforts at state reorganization through 1975, seeking to understand why reorganizations occur, how they are conducted, and how they reshape state executive branches.

SEE ALSO Legislative-Executive Relations.

# THE EXECUTIVE VETO

## *Robert J. Spitzer*

The veto power exercised by American executives traces its roots to the Roman Republic of the sixth century B.C., when Roman tribunes used a veto (called *intercessio*) to protect the interests of the plebeians against the encroachments of the patricians. During the Middle Ages, British monarchs exercised an absolute veto—one not subject to override—over acts of Parliament. After the Norman Conquest, the monarchs possessed primary lawmaking power. Gradually, however, Parliament pressed for a greater share of the lawmaking power. By the sixteenth century, the crown was reduced to either accepting or rejecting acts of Parliament. Thus, the monarchical veto was soon all that was left of the crown's once-extensive power over legislation. The last royal veto of a parliamentary act was exercised by Queen Anne in 1707.

In the American colonies, the veto was directly felt, as British monarchs and their colonial governors continued to exercise an absolute veto over colonial legislation. American resentment of this odious power was reflected in the first two complaints lodged against the British king in the Declaration of Independence, both of which protested the arbitrary use of the veto power by the king and his governors. Once the colonies broke free of Britain, their initial reaction was to create state governments with weak executives dependent on state legislatures. The first state to experiment with the veto was South Carolina in its temporary constitution of 1776. Yet when the state's governor actually attempted to use his absolute veto powers, the outcry forced his resignation and the elimination of the veto in 1778.

Portions of this article first appeared in Robert J. Spitzer, *The Presidential Veto* (Albany, 1988). Reprinted by permission of State University of New York Press.

The first state to bestow a gubernatorial veto permanently was New York in its constitution of 1777. This veto was subject to a two-thirds override by the state legislature and was to be exercised by the governor jointly with the judges of the state supreme court and the chancellor of the court of chancery. This group was referred to as the Council of Revision, which continued to operate until 1821, when veto powers were transferred to the governor alone. The significance of the New York gubernatorial veto lay not only in the model that it provided for framers of the Constitution but also in the fact that the veto power was an integral component of America's first strong, independent state executive. Massachusetts followed New York's lead by giving its governor sole veto powers in 1780. The relative success of the New York model became even more clear when compared to the ineffectual, executiveless governing system of the Articles of Confederation.

By the time the Constitution's founders met in Philadelphia in 1787, support for a new governing system with an executive who exercised a veto was widespread among the delegates, despite disagreement over the shape and extent of the veto power. Alexander Hamilton and James Wilson argued that the new executive should exercise an absolute veto—a proposal that was repeatedly and overwhelmingly defeated because of its obvious monarchical implications. The convention agreed that Congress should be able to override a presidential veto with a significant majority vote but waffled on whether this majority should be two-thirds or three-fifths; the delegates finally settled on the former. James Madison and others argued for the veto to be exercised by the president jointly with the members of the Supreme Court, following the New York Council of Revision. Madison also argued vigorously for a congressional veto over state laws, and Pierce Butler proposed an executive power of suspension that could hold legislation in abeyance for some fixed period of time.

The presidential veto was understood to be a legislative power that served to bring the president into the law-making process. This understanding is reflected in the inclusion of the power in Article I rather than Article II of the Constitution. In addition, the Constitution imposed no limits on the circumstances or frequency of use of the regular veto, despite vigorous arguments to the contrary that appeared in veto debates in the nineteenth century. The only limitation on the veto power pertained to the pocket veto, a presidential absolute veto that may only be used if "Congress by their Adjournment prevent its [a bill's] Return" (Article I, Section 7). That the founders would give the president an otherwise odious absolute veto is explainable by concerns at the time that Congress might attempt to avoid a veto by simply adjourning after enacting a bill, thereby preventing return of the bill to Congress. Without this return, there is no veto, absent the pocket-veto provision.

## THE EVOLUTION OF THE PRESIDENTIAL VETO

As with virtually every power enumerated in the Constitution, the veto power evolved over time as experimentation, circumstance, and cumulative precedent combined to give the power its actual shape, frequency, and other conditions of use. Exercise of the veto power contributed to the expansion of executive power, particularly over the legislative realm, and this change occurred primarily in noncrisis domestic circumstances.

Although use of the veto has expanded the presidency, the delicate politics of that power are demonstrated by the fact that vigorous use of the veto has usually been politically detrimental to the presidents involved. Presidents who relied significantly on the veto (thus defending and often extending the accepted use of the power) suffered politically. They were casualties in the struggle to strengthen and enhance presidential powers, but they succeeded in rolling back the perceived limitations on the veto power.

The veto has not by any means been the sole vehicle for the well-recognized expansion of presidential power. But it is vitally important to understand that presidential expansion has occurred not only in times of crisis and through the actions of such forceful presidents as Abraham Lincoln, Theodore and Franklin Roosevelt, and Woodrow Wilson but also in noncrisis times under presidents not generally perceived as dynamic, forceful leaders. In general, these unspectacular presidents are considered less successful or less important because they lost support, failed to resolve problems, and otherwise seemed to lack adroit leadership skills. While such assessments may be correct, it is fallacious to presume that since these presidents somehow failed to lead, they therefore contributed little or nothing to the strong modern presidency. As the story of the veto illustrates, even "failed" presidencies, such as those of John Tyler and Andrew Johnson, helped to advance the accepted bounds of presidential prerogative.

## The First Vetoes

As with so many facets of the presidency, institutional precedent was set by the first chief executive. George Washington was keenly aware of the precedent-setting nature of his actions, and as the presiding officer at the Constitutional Convention, he had been a party to the debates, including consideration of the veto power.

At the start of his first term, Washington considered withholding his signature from a tonnage bill as an expression of displeasure. Although not a veto, it aroused enough concern that members of the Senate promised to accommodate the president's objections in a subsequent bill in exchange for his signature. A few days after this, Washington indicated in a letter to James Madison, then a member of the House of Representatives, that he was considering a veto of a pay bill for the members of Congress. The bill set equal salaries for members of both chambers, but Washington was of the opinion that senators should receive higher pay. He asked Madison his opinion of such a veto in correspondence marked "confidential." Madison's response is not known, but Washington signed the bill in question on 22 September 1989. He may have felt the bill too trivial to warrant the first presidential veto, or he may have decided to refrain from interfering with an essentially internal matter of congressional pay.

In February 1791, Washington seriously considered a veto of the Hamilton-inspired bill to establish a national bank. This major bill was, in the view of many, an unconstitutional intrusion by Congress into fiscal affairs. The president solicited advisory opinions from Attorney General Edmund Randolph, Secretary of State Thomas Jefferson, and Madison, all of whom recommended veto. Washington even asked Madison to draft a possible veto message. Finally, he solicited the opinion of Hamilton, who presented a memo to Washington (on the ninth day after passage of the bill) that made a case for the bank based on the doctrine of implied powers. Hamilton's arguments were so compelling and important that they eventually made their way into Justice John Marshall's opinion in the landmark Supreme Court case of *McCulloch* v. *Maryland*, 4 Wheaton 316, (1819). On the last day of the ten-day period, Washington signed the bill.

The first actual veto occurred on 5 April 1792. The bill in question dealt with congressional reapportionment. The Constitution called for an apportionment in the House based on the ratio of one representative for every thirty thousand people. Yet the bill passed gave more representation than this to some of the larger states in an effort to compensate for the remainder of these states' populations over the thirty thousand multiple (so that the total number of representatives in the House would equal the total population of the country divided by thirty thousand). Jefferson objected strenuously to Washington, as the bill seemed plainly unconstitutional; Jefferson added his concern that, after four years in office, the veto might never be used. Washington was sympathetic to Jefferson's arguments, and on the tenth day after passage, the president met with Jefferson to discuss the bill. The men discussed the bill's primary political problem—that the reapportionment scheme would benefit mostly northern states and that a veto might appear to be a sop to the South—but noted that it had passed by a bare majority in both houses, indicating that a veto override would be unlikely. At the conclusion of the meeting, Washington sent for Randolph and Madison, who, with Jefferson, drew up a veto message, whereupon it was sent immediately to the House. The underlying rationale for the veto was clearly a constitutional question. The House considered a motion to override, but it fell far short of the necessary two-thirds. Congress soon thereafter passed a substitute bill with a new apportionment scheme; this was passed and signed without problem.

Washington's second and final veto occurred four days before the end of his presidency, and it involved a bill that included a provision to reduce the size of the already small army by disbanding two dragoon companies. Acting essentially on his own this time, Washington argued in his veto message that the dragoons were needed and that the move to disband the companies was unfair to the men involved. This time, the veto justification had nothing to do with the Constitution; it was purely and simply a disagreement over policy. The House failed in its attempt to override the veto. It then proceeded immediately to pass the same bill, this time with the offending provision excised. Washington signed the new bill on 3 March 1797, his last day in office. Interestingly, Washington's second veto had the effect of an item veto insofar as Congress removed the provision in question in response to the veto message identifying the objectionable portion.

Already, the first presidential administration had exemplified many of the accepted features of the veto. Its two applications provided cases of both constitutionally and policy-justified vetoes. The legitimacy of the president's mature judgment in deciding whether to veto was accepted. The use of the veto as a positive policy-shaping tool was also demonstrated.

Neither of Washington's two successors, John Adams and Thomas Jefferson, applied the veto in their collective twelve years in office. In the case of Adams, this is something of an irony, as he had been a proponent of absolute veto powers for the president. Despite Jefferson's eagerness to have Washington use the veto, he seemed to share the first president's sense of restraint and gravity when it came to actual veto use.

The first president to use the veto with vigor, and who therefore received national attention for its use, was James Madison. Of the seven bills he vetoed in office, he relied on a constitutional justification for five. The other two bills, relating to naturalization and bank incorporation, were vetoed on policy grounds. The most controversial veto was that of the Bank of the United States bill. Yet the controversy was not based on the absence of a constitutional justification for the veto. Madison acknowledged at the start of his veto message that such a proposal was, in his view, constitutional. Rather, the bank issue was simply one of the most controversial questions of the time. Madison was criticized harshly by members of Congress and various newspapers around the country in what was part of a vigorous national debate over the precarious economic situation of the country. Yet for all the controversy and criticism surrounding this veto, it was sustained, as were all of Madison's vetoes.

Madison was also the first president to employ the pocket veto. The first of two occurred in July 1812. When Congress reconvened in November, Madison worked with Congress to iron out the disputed provisions, and the revised bill was then passed and signed. Madison's second pocket veto occurred in 1816 and aroused little attention.

Despite Madison's more vigorous use of the veto, he was still working within the veto logic established by Washington. Similarly, Madison's critics also limited debate to the issues at hand and did not question the constitutional basis of the manner in which the veto was being employed.

Madison's successor, James Monroe, employed the veto but once, in 1822. He had laid the groundwork for that one veto in his first annual message to Congress, delivered on 2 December 1817. The matter in question involved an issue raised by Madison—the constitutional right of the Congress to establish and finance internal improvements, primarily roads and canals. In his message, Monroe sought to inform Congress clearly from the outset that he did not believe Congress possessed such power.

Monroe went on to suggest passage of a constitutional amendment to grant Congress the right to undertake such internal improvement projects. In his 1822 veto message, Monroe reiterated these arguments. He appended to that message, however, an extremely lengthy, detailed document summarizing his views on the subject of internal improvements; his veto was upheld.

In the aftermath of Monroe's clear threat to use the veto, stated in his 1817 message, a House committee was set up, chaired by Henry Tucker of Virginia, to review the portion of the message relating to Monroe's views on public works. In its report, issued 15 December 1817, it stated the view that the president's expression of opinion should have no influence over congressional actions whatsoever. It further proposed that should a presidential statement announcing a possible veto be made and have the effect of deterring Congress from enacting a measure it might otherwise pass, the veto would then exceed its proper limits. The fear that a veto threat would retard congressional lawmaking never materialized in the dire form predicted. The use of the veto threat has admittedly become an important ancillary power of the veto; it has not, however, transformed the veto into a dictatorial device. Ironically, within thirty years, members of Congress would be criticizing presidential vetoes when they occurred without prior warning from the president. An even more interesting irony about the veto threat is that it was understood by the Founding Fathers to be an acceptable and even useful component of the veto itself, as Alexander Hamilton observed in *The Federalist*, no. 73.

Four months after the committee report, the Virginia congressman William J. Lewis introduced a series of five related constitutional amendments. The first called for the president to be stripped of his approval power over legislation, which effectively meant loss of the veto. This was the first recorded instance of an attempt to strip the president of his veto powers. It would certainly not be the last.

Monroe's successor, John Quincy Adams, exercised no vetoes. He shared the opinion of his predecessors that the veto should be exercised with reserve. After his presidency, Adams served many years as a member of the House, where he played an active role in many veto controversies.

## The Jacksonian Veto

Andrew Jackson's presidency marked a turning point for the veto and for the presidency itself.

Jackson vetoed more bills (twelve) than all of his six predecessors combined. Despite the greater number, the form of these vetoes was not unique. Of the twelve, seven were pocket vetoes; Madison had used the pocket veto twice. Seven of the bills involved public works; Jackson not only based these on constitutional grounds but relied on the logic and precedent of similar Madison and Monroe vetoes. Jackson's most controversial veto, involving a Bank of the United States bill, also followed in the footsteps of the bank-bill veto by Madison.

Several factors did, however, distinguish Jackson from his predecessors. He had announced prior to his first two vetoes that he would in fact veto these public-works bills, should they cross his desk. Like Madison and Monroe, Jackson felt that public works were necessary and important but that Congress did not have the constitutional authority to enact many of the projects it promoted. When Monroe had announced his reservations about a bill before it reached his desk, the action prompted outcry. When Jackson did the same, it had a similar but more forceful consequence. Viewing such a statement as a kind of prior restraint on the legislature, many of its members reacted with outrage, arguing that such statements were an improper, even unconstitutional attempt by the president to regulate the legislative process by discouraging action that might otherwise result in legislation. Nevertheless, Jackson was to do this often, usually through his annual messages to Congress.

Although all twelve of Jackson's vetoes contained constitutional justifications, the logic of the public-works vetoes was considered inconsistent, as Jackson vetoed some, but encouraged other legislation of a like nature. This apparent inconsistency emerged with great force with his 1832 veto of the bank bill, referred to by one historian as "the most celebrated veto in American history" (Jackson, p. 29). In it, President Jackson argued that some of the powers granted to the national bank were unconstitutional. While acknowledging that the Supreme Court had previously ruled favorably on the bank, such precedent need not—even ought not—be the criterion for the president's judgment on the issue. Each branch of government was entitled to judge for itself the constitutionality of important issues. Simply

because the Court had ruled the bank constitutional did not perforce mean that the president could not veto the bill, on constitutional or other grounds, if he felt the necessity to do so. Thus, supplementing the constitutional rationale was a loudly broadcast subtext—that the president need only rely on his political judgment in making a veto decision. Although this conclusion was not inconsistent with the intent of the framers or even with the vetoes of Jackson's predecessors, it was a view that had never been so broadly and baldly articulated by a sitting president.

Jackson's veto message provoked a storm of debate. Transcripts of the debate consumed seventy-five pages of fine print in the *Register of Debates in Congress*. The most long-winded speaker was, not surprisingly, Daniel Webster. In a speech highly critical of Jackson's veto, Webster labored to illustrate the inconsistencies and faults in the veto message. As with many of Jackson's critics, Webster alluded to the seemingly monarchical nature of Jackson's views toward legislation and the veto. This use of the veto was, in Webster's view, as bad as the absolute, arbitrary, and malicious use of the veto during the Tudor and Stuart eras in England.

Webster's discontent, unlike some critics', was not founded in the underlying motive of expedience in Jackson's veto, but rather primarily on Jackson's expansive definition of his own prerogatives. The notion of presidential involvement in legislative drafting and modification, so much taken for granted today, was almost revolutionary during this time; yet it flowed directly from the logic of the veto power. If a veto was to be avoided as a strong action against legislation, an obvious way to do so would be to take the president's wishes into account while the bill was in its formative stages. Jackson shocked many by asserting this boldly.

In his speech against the veto, Henry Clay fell back on the argument—then frequently cited but more suspect by today's standards—that the veto was considered by the founders to be an unusual power to be used only occasionally. Surely, though, the bank veto was no ordinary case. Clay went on to state incorrectly that Madison had used the veto only two or three times and to argue that Jackson's apparently more frequent use contradicted the intent of the founders. Clay then asserted his broader objection to the veto—that it was a power inconsistent with representative government. Clay also questioned whether the founders would have condoned a veto involving an issue so long debated. Clay condemned, too, and at some length, the president's request for prior consultation. The override motion was finally put to a vote, and the veto was sustained, 22–19.

Jackson's bald statement of executive power combined with another aspect of Jackson's veto use that surfaced initially in his 6 December 1830 annual message. The previous May, Jackson had pocket vetoed two public-works bills after Congress had adjourned *sine die* (literally, "without a day," as when Congress adjourns without setting a day for reconvening). The bills were not, however, given an absolute veto; Jackson told the Congress six months later that he had not had sufficient time to consider the bills properly at the rushed end of the session terminating in May. He then returned them to Congress in December. To his critics, this unprecedented retention of bills resembled the manner in which British kings had exercised their veto powers, giving rise to the criticism from Clay and others that Jackson was attempting to establish a de facto monarchy. This retention of bills appeared in no other presidency and was clearly swept aside by the Supreme Court in *The Pocket Veto Case* (1929).

One final factor adding to the Jacksonian stew pot was the changing nature of the country. As the nation grew, so too did sectional and partisan splits. The consequently sharper differences evidenced themselves in Washington and did much to fan the disputes about Jackson's policies and approach to governing. Such issues as the bank and internal improvements, the principal subjects of Jacksonian vetoes, engendered strong sectional feelings.

Jackson's aggressive use of the veto and his attendant controversial approach to governing prompted the Senate to consider and approve a motion to censure the president on 28 March 1834. During debate, Clay alleged that Jackson had claimed powers greater than European kings. Clay had considered a move to impeach, but cast it aside as nearly impossible, since, according to him, any marshal or civil officer des-

ignated to serve a summons on the president could be simply dismissed by the president, and Jackson had control not only of governmental officers but of the army and navy as well. It is also likely that Clay would never have succeeded in getting articles of impeachment passed through the House (where impeachment proceedings must begin), as it was more strongly allied with Jackson. The motion to censure passed the Senate by a vote of 26–20.

On 15 April, Jackson issued a lengthy response to the Senate. In it, he said that the Senate's resolution was unauthorized by the Constitution and included in his rebuttal to the Senate the texts of resolutions from the state legislatures of Maine, New Jersey, and Ohio, all of which affirmed their support of Jackson's vetoes as being both wise and constitutional. Jackson also pointed out that four senators from these states voted for his censure, clearly contrary to the sentiments of the bodies that elected them.

Three times during Jackson's presidency (1833, 1835, and 1836), members of Congress introduced constitutional amendments to change the veto override to a simple majority. After Jackson's presidency, at least nine similar constitutional amendments were proposed in the nineteenth century (in 1838, twice in 1841, three times in 1842, and once each in 1849, 1850, and 1884).

Despite the sentiments of Jackson's opponents, many people supported his actions. Indeed, Jackson's reelection was widely seen as a referendum on his 1832 bank-bill veto. Popularity aside, such contemporary observers as Supreme Court Justice Joseph Story found no constitutional impropriety in Jackson's actions.

## Harrison and the Tyler Crisis

The veto controversy lay dormant throughout the term of Jackson's handpicked successor, Martin Van Buren, who applied the veto only once, in the form of a pocket veto. The nation's first full-scale economic depression did much to bring an end to the Jackson–Van Buren era, allowing for the election of the Whig party candidate William Henry Harrison in 1840. The Whig antipathy to Jackson's executive style found full expression in Harrison, as seen, for example, in his pledge to serve only a single term in office. In President

Harrison's inaugural address, he outlined the features of a Whiggish presidency. The centrality of the veto to executive power is seen in the fact that one-eighth of his address—the longest ever given—was devoted solely to discussion of the veto, including his pledge to use the power sparingly.

Harrison's most lengthy inaugural was followed by the nation's briefest presidency. With Harrison's death a month later, Whig Vice President John Tyler was elevated to the presidency. The bank issue continued to be a preeminent political concern, and, with a Whig in the White House, most assumed that passage was assured. Yet on 16 August 1841, Tyler vetoed the bank bill, citing constitutional reasons relating to states' rights and his own consistent opposition to such a proposal. Although there had been some indications of his opposition to a national bank earlier in his career, Tyler had mostly kept his views to himself and gave no hint that a veto was impending before it occurred. In fact, in his inaugural address of 9 April, Tyler assured Congress that he would sign such a bill.

In the veto's aftermath, the president was congratulated by Democrats, scorned by Whigs, and subjected to unprecedented public signs of disapproval. For example, when the veto message was read in the Senate, some spectators in the gallery hissed. Senator Thomas Hart Benton (D.-Mo.) protested until an arrest of a hisser was made and apologies were extended to Benton. That night, a mob of about thirty gathered in front of the White House after midnight, making a loud disturbance that unsettled the occupants. The following night, a figure of Tyler was burned in effigy near the presidential residence.

In the Senate, bank supporters sought to delay reconsideration of the vetoed bill in the vain hope of winning enough support to clinch an override. But finally, debate and a vote were held on 19 August. Henry Clay led the attack on Tyler. The Senate voted to uphold the veto, 25–24. The next day, members of the Senate briefly debated the nature of the veto power, a debate that would escalate in subsequent months.

After the veto, an effort was made to accommodate the views of the president in a new bank bill. Whigs sent a representative to see the president, who gave his approval to a compromise plan. Two days later, Tyler told his cabinet that a new bank bill could be ready within two days. Congress obliged him; yet on 9 September he again vetoed the bill. Tyler paid dearly for his politically maladroit actions.

Tyler's vacillation on the bank issue, especially after the first veto, infuriated members of Congress and much of the country. In response to the veto, Tyler's entire cabinet resigned, with the exception of Secretary of State Daniel Webster. On 10 September, Congressman John Minor Botts (Whig-Va.) took the floor after an unsuccessful attempt to interrupt House consideration of the veto by considering first a constitutional amendment to lower the veto override to a simple majority. Botts spared little in his vituperation against Tyler, charging him with, among other things, "perfidy and treachery." When the House finally voted, it upheld Tyler's veto, 103–71. Tyler's two vetoes rubbed a nerve still tender from the Jacksonian period.

From February through August 1842, the Senate and House engaged in periodic, lengthy discourses on the veto power. The transcripts of these speeches and debates consume hundreds of pages in the *Congressional Globe*. This debate was prolonged by two more controversial vetoes in June and August of the same year.

On 29 June, Tyler issued his third veto, this time of a provisional tariff bill. Unlike his first two vetoes, Tyler justified this veto on the basis of his substantive objections to the bill itself. Although the veto was expected by members of Congress, it set off a howl of protest and a flood of debate. One Whig newspaper, for example, openly called for Tyler's assassination. Debate in Congress was only slightly less scathing, including for example an invidious comparison of Tyler with Judas Iscariot. Despite, or perhaps because of, the strident rhetoric, Tyler carried the day. On 4 July, the override vote was called. The veto was upheld, 114–97.

A month later, Tyler issued his fourth veto by rejecting for the second time a permanent tariff bill, passed after the failure of the last vetoed bill. If Tyler was consciously seeking a way to whip his opponents into a fury, he could have hardly picked a more effective means. Tyler must have known that this fourth veto would infuriate Congress, given the near-obsequious tone of his veto message. He returned the bill "with unfeigned regret....

Nothing can be more painful to any individual called upon to perform the Chief Executive duties under our limited Constitution than to be constrained to withhold his assent from an important measure adopted by the Legislature." The public outcry was substantial.

After return of the bill to the House, Congressman John Quincy Adams took the floor to propose that the bill be sent to a select committee for consideration and recommendation. Such an unusual action was warranted, said Adams, by the state of civil war that existed between president and Congress. Several objected, pointing out that it was the job of Congress as a whole to reconsider vetoed bills. Adams's motion was, however, approved, 108–84. Of the thirteen committee members (including committee chairman Adams), eleven were anti-Tyler Whigs.

On 16 August 1842, Adams delivered the majority report of the committee, endorsed by ten of thirteen committee members. It was highly critical, emphasizing the executive's dependence on the legislature, and it alluded to the availability of impeachment as a possible remedy for Tyler's alleged abuse of the veto power. The report recommended that the veto override be reduced to a simple majority.

With the submission of the report, the House was faced with two issues: the veto override itself and the proposal to amend the Constitution. The former question was dealt with the following day, with the House voting to uphold the veto. Debate on both questions persisted for several days.

A final constitutional card was played against the president on 10 January 1843. Tyler's archenemy, Congressman Botts, had made it clear during an exchange on the House floor on 6 July 1842, that he was considering a formal move to impeach Tyler. John Minor Botts made good his promise the following January, during the third session of the Twenty-seventh Congress. Botts proposed a series of nine charges dealing with a laundry list of accusations. The two central charges were "withholding his assent to laws undispensable [*sic*] to the just operations of government" and "an arbitrary, despotic and corrupt abuse of the veto power." An additional count condemned Tyler for his so-called fifth veto, referring to Tyler's placing in State Department records his

objections to part of a law, otherwise duly passed and signed, as an apparent circumvention of his presidential responsibility of seeing to the faithful execution of all laws. After some parliamentary maneuvering, the House voted on whether to refer the impeachment resolution to committee for consideration and recommendation. The vote failed, 83–127, killing the proposal. After the vote, several congressmen took the floor to condemn those Tyler critics who failed to support the move to impeach.

In the course of his administration, Tyler issued a total of ten vetoes, including four pocket vetoes. His last regular veto occurred on 20 February 1845, less than a month before he left office and long after the Whig party had chosen another standard-bearer. This final veto, involving a bill relating to revenue cutters and steamers, was historically significant because it was the first to be successfully overridden and enacted into law. Yet the override's political impact was, at best, inconsequential. Tyler's first four vetoes of bank and tariff bills were important because they cut the legs out from under the Whig political program.

By all accounts, Tyler did not set out to either expand the bounds of his office or subordinate congressional will. Rather, he was a staunch supporter of states' rights, and this fact guided his important veto decisions. As to the bank issue, he had in fact made his views known before the 1840 election, although the desire of the Whigs to gain control of the government in that year resulted in the sublimation of this and other issue concerns. Tyler's states'-rights orthodoxy combined with his artless political approach to produce the whirlwind surrounding the Twenty-seventh Congress. This turbulence was greatly enhanced by the manner of Tyler's ascension to office (and the attendant absence of an electoral mandate) and the fact that his use of the veto was inconsistent with the dominant philosophy of his own party. All of Tyler's vetoes, especially the first four, were knives in the side of the Whiggish philosophy.

## Polk and the Maturing Veto

The relatively unpopular and stymied presidency of John Tyler was followed by the more popular and successful one of James K. Polk.

Polk used the veto on three occasions. The first veto, delivered on 3 August 1846, was applied to a rivers and harbors bill. Like Jackson and other presidents, Polk questioned whether Congress had the constitutional authority to approve such internal improvements. He also found the bill inexpedient, especially as the country was at war with Mexico and needed its resources for this purpose. Debate in the House was relatively brief. Ironically (given past controversy over the veto), Polk was criticized for not announcing his intention to veto the bill before the fact. The veto was sustained, 96–91.

Polk's second veto came five days later, involving a bill to allow citizens to recover damages from French spoliations incurred during hostilities with the French before 1801. This issue had been a long-standing irritant. In his veto message, Polk made clear that this veto was rendered solely on the grounds of expediency, a fact that provoked some modest congressional criticism. This veto, too, was upheld, 27–15.

Polk's final veto, a pocket veto, also involved internal improvements; like the first veto, constitutional justification was invoked. Although not required to do so, Polk sent to Congress on 15 December an explanation for this 3 March 1847 veto. The message provoked debate in the House, including a proposal that a special committee by appointed to examine the veto. No action was taken on the proposal, but the debate in Congress over internal improvements and the veto continued.

Democrat Polk was succeeded by two Whigs, Zachary Taylor and Millard Fillmore. During the 1848 campaign, the veto was a major issue. Taylor made it clear that he believed that the veto should be applied rarely and only under unusual circumstances. After Taylor's death in 1850, Fillmore became president. In their collective four years in office, both subscribed to Whig principles by refraining from any use of the veto.

The veto returned in the presidencies of Franklin Pierce and James Buchanan. Most of the vetoes by both presidents involved internal-improvements bills. Yet Pierce's argument that such measures were unconstitutional met with ever more forceful resistance because of the country's accelerating commercial expansion.

This single trend primarily explains the fact that five of Pierce's nine vetoes were overridden. The overrides also support the assertion that successful vetoes on policy grounds must, at least in the view of Congress, be backed by popular support.

Unlike vetoes of the previous decade, relatively little debate on the nature of the veto followed Pierce's applications of the power. Pierce's first veto, however, did engender a lengthy discussion of how soon an override vote needed to be taken after a bill was returned by the president. During consideration of two public-works vetoes on 7 July 1856, the chair of the Senate resolved the long-standing ambiguity of whether a successful veto override vote required two-thirds of all chamber members or two-thirds of a quorum, by ruling that the latter was appropriate (two-thirds of a quorum had been acceptable when Congress approved the Bill of Rights). The chair's ruling was upheld by the Senate, which overrode one of the vetoes by two-thirds of a quorum but less than two-thirds of the Senate's membership.

Buchanan's seven vetoes were similarly conservative in conception. The fact that three were pocket vetoes probably prevented at least one of these from being overridden, and several of the bills vetoed by Buchanan were later enacted during Lincoln's term. The most damaging of Buchanan's vetoes was probably that of the popular homestead bill (enacted in 1862 under Lincoln), which caused many northern farmers and laborers to turn away from the Democrats and support the new Republican party.

The Civil War–era presidents produced a large number of vetoes—seven by Lincoln and twenty-nine by Andrew Johnson. Although the majority of these stirred some controversy, they had little impact on the conception of the veto power itself and were overshadowed by national crisis, which therefore saw the circumvention of routine, noncrisis politics. One new twist emerged with Lincoln's first veto. Up to that time, the prevailing interpretation had been that Congress was required to vote on a returned bill. Thereafter, Congress would often dispense with override attempts. Lincoln's relative restraint in his use of the veto may be attributed to his willingness to compromise with Congress, the expanded powers he was able to exert during the Civil War, and perhaps his own Whig background (as a congressman, Lincoln had embraced the Whiggish view of rare veto use).

Andrew Johnson's twenty-nine vetoes set a numerical record. Like Tyler, Johnson ascended to the presidency through the death of the president. Also like Tyler, he was a high-minded constitutionalist who prided himself on his invocation of constitutional principles and precedents. Like Tyler, he lacked basic political instincts. But unlike Tyler, he faced a Congress willing, able, and even eager to override his vetoes. If anything, the frequency of overrides accelerated the erosion of Johnson's political base. Of Johnson's twenty-one regular vetoes, fifteen were overridden. Most of these vetoes reflected Johnson's effort to void congressional attempts to influence Reconstruction.

By the end of Johnson's term, Congress was overriding his vetoes without debate and literally within minutes of their return to Congress. It was also true of Johnson that his vetoes helped fan the flames of impeachment. Unlike Tyler's case, however, the vetoes were themselves a relatively small component of the Radical Republicans' grudge against Johnson; they came into play only because Johnson was impeached for violating provisions of laws he had initially vetoed. No charge of misuse of veto powers was made against Johnson in the articles of impeachment against him.

## The End of the Veto Controversy

The increasing use of the veto in the wake of the Civil War was paralleled by a decline in objections about the basis of its use. Few of the many vetoes applied by presidents from Grant on aroused a level of controversy comparable to that surrounding controversial vetoes before the Civil War. And in the controversies that did arise there was a critical difference: interpretations of the veto power rarely questioned the right of the president to veto any given bill if he considered it inappropriate to be a law. Presidential judgment continued to be questioned, but not the power that gave rise to the judgment.

Several other important changes in the veto occurred after the Civil War. Aside from the vast increase in use (eighty-eight vetoes through 1868; over two thousand from then to 1990), most vetoed bills were no longer subject to override attempts by the Congress. Some considered this a violation of the Constitution, but it saved much time and effort in the case of bills that did not possess adequate support. Presidents used the pocket veto more frequently, also without serious objection. Presidents began to rely more on cabinet officers and others for advice on whether to veto and for veto messages. Similarly, vetoed bills were more often referred to committees in Congress, where they often died. Finally, the principal cause for the increase in vetoes after the Civil War was the proliferation of private-pension and related private relief bills, of which more will be said.

Ambiguities over the precise nature of the veto power continued to give rise to problems. For example, in August 1876, President Grant vetoed two bills but then informed Congress that he wished the bills returned to him, as he had changed his mind and now wished to sign them into law. In the instance of the first bill, a private relief measure, his request was ignored, and no other action was taken on it. In the case of the second bill, involving a sale of Indian lands, the Senate openly rejected his request for return. This is one of many such questions about the veto that has never been fully resolved.

The president and Congress came to political blows over the veto-related issue of attaching riders to legislation. The practice had occurred at least as early as the 1840s, but became far more frequent during the term of Rutherford B. Hayes. Several of Hayes's vetoes involved appropriations bills (of which he approved) to which Congress had attached provisions politically objectionable to him. In his veto messages, Hayes made his reasoning explicit. According to Hayes, the attachment of riders "strikes from the Constitution the qualified negative of the President." Yet, as if to undercut his own assertion that riders rendered the veto ineffective, Hayes gained the upper hand in his struggle with Congress; he succeeded in forcing Congress to alter or strike out offending provisions by vetoing the bills that carried them. All of the bills with objectionable riders that he vetoed were sustained.

At the same time, he lost support within his party and became a one-term president.

## Pensions, Pork, and Presidents

As mentioned, the largest number of vetoed bills after the Civil War fell in the category of private-pension bills. The pension system was widely (and correctly) perceived as corrupt. There was little incentive for members of Congress to reform the system, as they derived useful political capital by sponsoring the private-pension requests of their constituents, whether these were enacted or not. Indeed, congressmen often expected vetoes of suspect requests yet could be relatively sanguine about the outcome, as blame could be foisted on the president. Thus, the numerous private-pension vetoes represented an intriguing political subsystem of request and refusal.

Presidents Chester Alan Arthur and Grover Cleveland won reputations as protectors of the national purse through their use of the veto against private-pension and other pork bills. Both were also extolled in Thomas Nast cartoons of the time. Although Arthur's vetoes amounted to only twelve, he was considered handy with his veto. Arthur was also handicapped politically with the lack of an independent electoral mandate, because he ascended to the presidency through the death of James Garfield. Arthur's vetoes probably hurt his popularity, but they also served to extend the reputation of the president as the truest spokesman of national interest and as protector of the purse. This public vision of the presidency found its fullest expression in the administration of Grover Cleveland.

In his first term of office, Cleveland vetoed exactly twice as many bills (414) as all of his predecessors combined. He vetoed another 170 bills in his second term. Of all these, only 7 were overridden. On a single day in the summer of 1886, he was sent almost 240 private-pension bills. In the month of June 1886, he vetoed 56 bills. According to one account, Cleveland was sent a total of 2,042 private-pension bills in his first term. Of these, most were signed by the president, some were vetoed, but 284 became law without Cleveland's signature, indicating his unwillingness to affix his signature to bills he considered suspect.

Cleveland not only was handy with his vetoes but exercised some of them with a degree of sarcasm that enraged his opponents. In one case, a man who had served in the army for nine days during the final months of the Civil War contracted measles, was hospitalized, and then was released from the military. He applied for relief in 1880, claiming the measles had affected his eyes and back. Cleveland's veto message described the case this way: "Fifteen years after this brilliant service and this terrific encounter with the measles . . . the claimant discovered that his attack of the measles had some relation to his army enrollment."

The significance of Cleveland's prolific use of the veto should not be construed as merely a quantitative anomaly. First, the vetoes represented a major political preoccupation for the president and Congress. Second, the vetoes illustrated in the most public way possible the president's commitment to sound legislation and his advocacy of prudent use of national resources. Third, Cleveland's vetoes reflected his philosophy that the veto was, and should be, an integral component of his affirmative involvement in the legislative process.

Cleveland's politically aggressive use of the veto occurred in a period of political contentiousness, and all three of his presidential races were close contests. As with Hayes and Arthur, the veto clearly did not offer a ticket to instant political popularity. In fact, Cleveland's veto use probably cost him the election of 1888. Yet the cumulative effect of these vetoes aided the advance of the strong presidency, in large part because of the very fact that this legislation involved "distributive," particularized benefits. According to one account of the time, most members of Congress lacked the influence to get legislation through Congress, as both chambers were controlled by a small clique. Thus, the best most members could hope for in terms of legislative accomplishment was to push through private-pension bills for constituents. Congressmen labored to enact such bills, only to have many of them cut down by veto. The vetoes hurt congressmen of both parties, although they could still garner some benefit for having promoted such bills. This left the president as the de facto defender of the national treasury. The numerous vetoes provided ready evidence that the president was far more fiscally trustworthy than the Congress. In this way, the private-pension struggles led to one of the most important single acquisitions of presidential power: the granting to the executive of budget-making authority in the Budget and Accounting Act of 1921.

Without doubt, use of the veto in the late nineteenth century engendered controversy. But also without doubt, opposition to the veto was now based on political opposition arising from the particular issues of the time, rather than on the questioning of presidential authority. Concomitant with the rising acceptance of the legitimacy of expansive use of the veto came recognition of its popular appeal.

Cleveland's successor (and predecessor), Benjamin Harrison, was somewhat more Whiggish in his attitude toward the presidency; he was also much more willing to accommodate himself to the wishes of Congress. Harrison's view of the veto was that it could be used on anything but should be used parsimoniously and mostly on legislation possessing serious faults or if the president wished to set precedent. Still, Harrison vetoed forty-four bills in four years; nearly all were distributive, private-pension bills, as was also true of the vetoes of McKinley and Theodore Roosevelt.

## The Twentieth-Century Veto

For American institutions, the twentieth century has been the century of the presidency. Yet the veto power seemed to recede in importance, eclipsed by new powers, prerogatives, responsibilities, and crises. The same could essentially be said of the administrations of the next two presidents, William Howard Taft and Woodrow Wilson. Each used the veto without suffering serious criticism. Yet these two presidents are noteworthy for their thoughtful commentary on the veto power—and on the presidency generally—when not in office.

Taft took pride in his legal acumen and became chief justice of the United States after his term as president. In a series of lectures originally published in 1916, he rejected the narrow interpretation of veto exercise, asserting instead its essential nature as part of the lawmaking process and what he saw as the close connection between the veto power and the presidential claim to being the people's first delegate.

Before his presidency, Wilson, a political scientist and former president of the American Political Science Association, rendered his thoughts on governmental powers in numerous writings. In *Congressional Government*, for example, Wilson called the veto the president's "most formidable prerogative," whereby the president "acts not as the executive but as a third branch of the legislature." For Wilson, the president "is no greater than his prerogative of veto makes him."

The last president whose use of the veto seemed in some sense extraordinary was Franklin Roosevelt, who vetoed more bills (635) than any other president, although his average per year was less than that of Cleveland. As in Cleveland's case, the largest number of Roosevelt's vetoes dealt with private-pension or relief bills. Unlike Cleveland, however, Roosevelt dealt with Congresses that were generally supportive of his actions in a time when the president's menu of prerogatives was larger and still growing. Roosevelt's prolific use of the veto can be explained quite simply by the fact that as one of history's greatest presidential activists, he used all of the tools available, including the veto. The intriguing irony of his use of the veto is that although it was usually a weapon of last resort, he could afford to use it more often precisely because he was dealing with a friendly and even submissive Congress. His famed "send me a bill I can veto" approach illustrates his recognition that the power has a positive, as well as a negative, function.

Roosevelt's appreciation of this facet of the veto was illustrated when, in 1935, he announced with great drama that he would deliver his veto of a veterans' bonus bill personally to a joint session of Congress. This unprecedented act was pure theater, designed to sway congressional, as well as popular, sentiment (Roosevelt also delivered the veto address over national radio). The Senate voted to uphold the veto. Roosevelt also relied heavily on the veto threat as a device for molding congressional action. As important as the veto was to him, it was by now one of many powers. It was still important to modern presidents, but like a petunia in a bed of roses, it no longer attracted special notice.

Harry Truman found the veto to be an important tool when he faced a hostile Republican-controlled Congress in 1947 and 1948.

# THE EXECUTIVE VETO

His most famous veto was that of the controversial Labor-Management Relations Act of 1947, known more popularly as the Taft-Hartley Act. Vetoed in June, the bill was reconsidered and the veto overridden within three days of its return. Dwight Eisenhower relied on the veto as well when he faced Democrat-controlled Congresses from 1955 to 1960. Both presidents applied most of their vetoes to suspect private-pension and other private-claims bills.

Presidents John F. Kennedy and Lyndon Johnson found little need for veto use, as they worked with Democrat-controlled Congresses. None of their vetoes were overridden during their collective eight years in office.

Richard Nixon did not rely on the veto as a primary weapon against Congresses controlled by the opposition party for most of his term. In 1972, however, he vetoed seventeen bills in six months in an effort to launch a broad attack on congressional spending. Nixon aides were acutely aware of the potency and minimum effort involved in a veto, but also of the potential backlash that could result from overuse of the power.

In contrast to later presidencies, that of Gerald Ford relied heavily on the veto as a primary means for influencing the course of legislation. Ford's aides found that the means by which Ford became president, under the shadow of Watergate and absent a popular mandate or an opportunity to develop Ford's own policy proposals, impelled the administration to rely on a veto strategy to influence legislation. The politically adverse consequences of sixty-six vetoes during his two-and-one-half years in office likely contributed to Ford's defeat in 1976.

Jimmy Carter's presidency found a return to the Kennedy-Johnson pattern of little veto use. Despite Carter's many reputed problems with Congress during his four-year term, the veto was neither a cause nor a consequence of these difficulties.

Ronald Reagan used a different kind of veto strategy. While Reagan's actual veto use was relatively modest—an average of fewer than ten vetoes per year—he relied heavily on symbolic veto politics. For example, he repeatedly and loudly proclaimed that he would veto "budget-busting" appropriations bills that exceeded his spending targets, despite the fact that he rarely did so. Quoting a line from a Clint Eastwood movie, Reagan dared Congress to "Make my day" by sending him a bill exceeding his spending guidelines so he could then veto it. He revived past presidential requests that the president be given item-veto powers, and he advanced a broad interpretation of pocket-veto powers that had been rejected by Ford and Carter. Reagan's greater success with Congress during the early part of his administration demonstrates that he did not face a Ford-like situation where the veto must become a primary policy tool.

George Bush's administration followed that of Reagan, in that he continued to call for item-veto powers and to promote an aggressive interpretation of pocket-veto powers. In his first two years in office, Bush used his veto power prudently and effectively, vetoing twenty bills; none of these vetoes were overridden.

# THE GUBERNATORIAL VETO

Despite the fact that New York and Massachusetts successfully adopted veto powers before the formulation of the modern federal Constitution, other states were slow to follow suit. Of the original thirteen states, only three adopted a Massachusetts-style veto in the early years of the new nation (the New York veto was exercised jointly between the governor and the Council of Revision until 1822): Georgia in 1789, Pennsylvania in 1790, and New Hampshire in 1792. Other states adopted some form of the veto, but by 1812, only eight of the eighteen states had adopted the veto. Even by the middle of the nineteenth century, four of the original thirteen states—Maryland, Virginia, North Carolina, and South Carolina—had not adopted an executive veto. From the time of Louisiana's admission in 1812 to the present, however, every new state (except West Virginia in 1863) provided for some form of veto when it joined the nation. The increased willingness to grant the gubernatorial veto stemmed from the diminution of mistrust of state executive power. This trend was enhanced by the fact that Congress gave veto powers to territorial governors, allowing them to block the measures of territorial legislatures. After the Civil War, however, gubernatorial veto powers began to grow and diversify beyond those of the president.

Only one state, North Carolina, has still not adopted any kind of executive veto.

## The Item Veto

The power to veto items or parts of legislation first appeared in the Confederate Constitution of 1861, which gave the Confederate president the power to veto items in appropriations bills. President Jefferson Davis never exercised these powers, but he did exercise his regular veto thirty-eight times. After the war, the item veto was adopted by Georgia in 1865 and Texas in 1866. The idea spread rapidly to most of the other states, so that by 1920, thirty-seven states had adopted such powers. The rapidity of the spread of this power also prompted calls for a presidential item veto. As early as 1873, President Ulysses S. Grant called for such a power, as have many presidents since, including Reagan and Bush.

The primary purpose of the gubernatorial item veto was to provide an enhanced means for state executives to block unconstitutional, inappropriate, or excessive expenditures—a serious concern, especially in the late nineteenth and early twentieth centuries, when state legislatures possessed justifiable reputations for ineptitude (enacting hastily written, ill-conceived legislation) and corruption (given their susceptibility to bribery, greed, and graft). Yet according to one analysis from the 1920s, the item veto encouraged legislative irresponsibility, as state legislatures would foist responsibility for state budget balancing and fiscal integrity on the governor by rushing through ill-considered legislation at the end of a session. The governor would then be left to sort out the legislative wheat and chaff. Moreover, virtually all studies of the impact of the gubernatorial item veto conclude that this power has not resulted in appreciably more frugal state spending, but has been important in enhancing the governor's arsenal of political weapons to use against state legislatures.

These practices encouraged the accretion of gubernatorial powers that marked an important difference between governors and the president. Taken as a whole, state governors came to possess a far wider array of powers, such that state governments are, by history, law, and politics, more executive-centered. This fact helps to explain the wide acceptance of the item veto in the states and its rejection at the federal level, where Congress's role in budgeting and other elements of policy-making is far greater. In 1991, forty-three state governors possess item veto powers. Those without such powers are the governors of Indiana, Maine, New Hampshire, New Jersey, North Carolina, Rhode Island, and Vermont.

## Veto Variations

Contemporary veto practices vary across the states. In 1991, for example, thirty-seven of the forty-nine states with veto provisions provided for a two-thirds legislative override; six states allowed a three-fifths override, and six allowed for a simple majority override. Fifteen states granted their governors power of "executive amendment" or "amendatory veto," which allows a vetoed bill to be returned to the legislature with suggested amendments or other bill language. Such bills can then be repassed by a simple majority vote. In addition, ten states granted governors item-reduction veto powers, allowing them to reduce the dollar amount of specific appropriations. These veto variations giving governors greater power emerged during the Progressive Era in the early part of the twentieth century as part of the general movement toward "scientific management," which accepted the principle that greater governmental efficiency could be achieved by giving governors added powers.

A strong veto—one with a higher override threshold (from a simple majority to three-fifths or two-thirds majorities), allowance for item-veto powers, and a greater consideration period for the governor—is usually consonant with stronger governors. Yet the trend toward strong governors and stronger veto powers in the twentieth century has applied across most of the states. The impact of this power is seen in the few successful legislative overrides of gubernatorial vetoes. For example, in California from 1900 to 1956, only twenty-eight gubernatorial vetoes were overridden out of thousands issued during this period. From 1938 to 1956, only four vetoes were overridden in Iowa. From 1909 to 1947, only thirteen vetoes were overridden in Michigan. And in New York, no vetoes were overridden from 1877 to 1977. The rarity of override applies in roughly equal proportion to item vetoes as well.

# THE EXECUTIVE VETO

From the 1950s through the 1980s, according to several studies, governors vetoed on average about 5 percent of all bills presented to them—a rate that has remained relatively constant since the early 1900s. During the same period, however, the average percent of overrides has increased from about 1 percent to almost 9 percent, indicating a resurgence of state legislative assertiveness since the 1950s. This rise in legislative contentiousness is attributed to an increase in divided party control of state governments and enhanced professionalization of state legislatures characterized by longer legislative sessions, increases in legislative staff, a rise in average years of legislative service, and cutbacks in governmental revenue and spending that have emphasized the necessity of difficult policy choices.

## BIBLIOGRAPHY

### Historical Perspectives

CHESTER J. ANTIEAU, *The Executive Veto* (New York, 1988), emphasizes legal and court interpretations of veto powers of state, national, and international executives. CARLTON JACKSON, *Presidential Vetoes, 1792–1945* (Athens, Ga., 1967), provides detailed descriptions of most vetoes up to the end of Franklin Roosevelt's administration. EDWARD C. MASON, *The Veto Power* (Boston, 1890), is a dated but still important systematic description and analysis of the veto power. *Presidential Vetoes, 1789–1976* (Washington, D.C., 1978), with updates, is produced by the U.S. SENATE LIBRARY and is the authoritative compendium of all presidential vetoes. ROBERT J. SPITZER, *The Presidential Veto: Touchstone of the American Presidency* (Albany, N.Y., 1988), summarizes constitutional, historical, legal, and political perspectives of the presidential veto, arguing that the rise of the veto is symptomatic of the rise of the modern strong presidency; the book includes treatment of the pocket veto and item-veto controversy. WOODROW WILSON's classic work, *Congressional Government* (New York, repr. 1956), emphasizes the key role played by the veto power in expanding the president's prerogatives in legislative affairs. CHARLES J. ZINN, *The Veto Power of the President* (Washington, D.C., 1951), was an important report prepared for the House Judiciary Committee on the history and reform possibilities for the veto power.

CHARLES F. HOBSON, "The Negative on State Laws: James Madison and the Crisis of Republican Government," *William and Mary Quarterly* 36 (April 1979), provides a fascinating account of Madison's belief that a congressional veto of state laws was vital to the new Union. RONALD C. MOE, "The Founders and Their Experience with the Executive Veto," *Presidential Studies Quarterly* 17 (Spring 1987), is an excellent, detailed discussion of forces leading up to the inclusion of a veto in the federal Constitution. FRANK W. PRESCOTT and JOSEPH F. ZIMMERMAN, *The Politics of the Veto of Legislation in New York State*, 2 vols. (Washington, D.C., 1980), is an extremely detailed examination of New York's strong executive veto exercised with a council of revision. HARRY C. THOMSON, "The First Presidential Vetoes," *Presidential Studies Quarterly* 8 (Winter 1978), is a definitive account of formative vetoes. RICHARD A. WATSON, "Origins and Early Development of the Veto Power," *Presidential Studies Quarterly* 17 (Spring 1987), is a useful historical overview of the formation of the veto.

### Empirical Analysis of the Presidential Veto

GARY COPELAND, "When Congress and the President Collide: Why Presidents Veto Legislation," *Journal of Politics* 45 (August 1983), applies empirical analysis to observe the impact of such factors as party, electoral mandate, and economic conditions on vetoes. JONG LEE, "Presidential Vetoes from Washington to Nixon," *Journal of Politics* 37 (May 1975), was the first modern analysis of empirical factors influencing the likelihood of presidential vetoes.

### The Gubernatorial Veto

THOMAS R. DYE, "Executive Power and Public Policy in the States," *Western Political Quarterly* 22 (December 1969), concludes that the veto is an important policy-shaping tool for governors. JOHN A. FAIRLIE, "The Veto Power of the State Governor," *American Political Sci-*

ence Review 11 (August 1917), provides a useful overview of the evolution of the gubernatorial veto. ERIC B. HERZIK and CHARLES W. WIGGINS, "Governors vs. Legislatures: Vetoes, Overrides, and Policy Making in the American States," *Policy Studies Journal* 17 (Summer 1989), conclude that the explanations for vetoes and overrides at the state level are largely idiosyncratic to each state. FRANK W. PRESCOTT, "The Executive Veto in American States," *Western Political Quarterly* 3 (March 1950), amasses considerable data on gubernatorial veto powers and patterns of use.

### The Item-Veto Debate

Analysis and debate over the item veto overlaps between studies of state gubernatorial powers and controversy over whether the president should possess such powers. GLENN ABNEY and THOMAS P. LAUTH, "The Line-Item Veto in the States," *Public Administration Review* 45 (May/June 1985), concludes that the fiscal consequences of the item veto are far less than its political consequences. LOUIS FISHER and NEAL DEVINS, "How Successfully Can the States' Item Veto be Transferred to the President?", *Georgetown Law Journal* 75 (October 1986);

DAVID C. Nice, "The Item Veto and Expenditure Restraint," *Journal of Politics* 50 (May 1988); and ROGER H. WELLS, "The Item Veto and State Budget Reform," *American Political Science Review* 18 (1924), reach similar conclusions. VERNON L. WILKINSON, "The Item Veto in the American Constitutional System," *Georgetown Law Journal* 25 (November 1936), traces the legal development and implications of an item veto.

Arguments favoring extending the item veto to the president include JUDITH A. BEST, "The Item Veto: Would the Founders Approve?" *Presidential Studies Quarterly* 14 (Spring 1984), which asserts that the founders *would* have approved, and RUSSELL M. ROSS and FRED SCHWENGEL, "An Item Veto for the President?" *Presidential Studies Quarterly* 12 (Winter 1982), which provides both historical and contemporary analysis. Arguments against extending the item veto to the president are advanced by THOMAS E. CRONIN and JEFFREY J. WEILL, "An Item Veto for the President?" *Congress and the Presidency* 12 (Autumn 1985), and ROBERT J. SPITZER, "The Item Veto Reconsidered," *Presidential Studies Quarterly* 15 (Summer 1985).

SEE ALSO Legislative-Executive Relations AND The Legislative Veto.

# THE LEGISLATIVE VETO

## *Louis Fisher*

The legislative veto has been used regularly by Congress for more than sixty years as an effective control on delegated power. State governments also experiment with this technique. The legislative veto is best thought of as a condition that a legislature places on authority it delegates, allowing it to maintain control over the authority without having to pass another law. For example, in 1932, Congress delegated authority to the president to reorganize the executive branch. Either house of Congress could disapprove the president's reorganization proposal within a sixty-day review period. If neither House disapproved, the proposal was to become law just as if it had been considered and passed by Congress. Depending on the statute delegating the authority, legislative control can be exercised through a one-house veto ("simple resolution"), a two-house veto ("concurrent resolution"), or a committee veto.

In the landmark case of *Immigration and Naturalization Service* v. *Chadha,* 462 U.S. 919 (1983), the Supreme Court struck down a one-house veto in an immigration statute because it violated two principles of the Constitution: bicameralism (requiring action by both houses of Congress) and the presentment clause (requiring that all bills be presented to the president for his signature or veto). In response to the Court's ruling, Congress revised a number of statutes by deleting legislative vetoes and requiring action by a "joint resolution," which requires action by both houses and must be presented to the president for his signature or veto.

However, Congress continues to rely on the legislative veto by allowing committees to control agency actions. Despite the Court's ruling, the legislative veto survives because it is useful to both Congress and the executive branch. Congress can more safely delegate its power by relying on committee control; executive officials gain important discretion and authority through the delegations. To upset this accommodation, perfected over the years, would be costly to both branches.

## ORIGIN OF THE LEGISLATIVE VETO

There is no claim by supporters of the legislative veto that Congress can make law without following the constitutional requirements of bicameralism and presentment. Article I, Section 7, of the Constitution clearly provides that "every Order, Resolution, or Vote to which the Concurrence of the Senate and House of Representatives may be necessary (except on a question of Adjournment) shall be presented to the President." Without adhering to the constitutional process for lawmaking, the legislative veto could have no possible legal force. It would merely express the opinion of the two houses, a single house, or a single committee. Nevertheless, when Congress acts in conformity with this constitutional procedure, suppose it places in a bill submitted to the president a condition that authorizes the legislative veto. By signing the bill, would the President sanction the legislative veto?

The Constitution permits some exceptions to the presentment clause. Congress may adopt constitutional amendments in the form of resolutions and refer them directly to the states for ratification. These resolutions need not be submitted to the president. This procedure is sanctioned by Article V of the Constitution, which states that two-thirds of each house may propose amendments to the Constitution and three-fourths of the states must ratify a proposed amendment. Article V does not mention the president. In *Hollingsworth* v. *Virginia,* 3 Dallas 378 (1798), the Supreme Court agreed that Congress could bypass the president and submit amendments directly to the states.

It was also recognized that Congress could pass resolutions for internal housekeeping matters without submitting the resolutions to the president. These resolutions were not "legislative in effect" or legally binding outside Congress. Many of them were adopted pursuant to congressional powers included in Article I of the Constitution, giving Congress the power to determine its own procedural rules and to expel members. A Senate report in 1897 concluded that what was "legislative in effect" depended not on the mere form of a resolution but on its substance. If it contained matter that was "legislative in its character and effect," it had to be presented to the president (S. Rept. 1335).

Congressional resolutions can take several forms. Either house of Congress may pass a simple resolution (a Senate resolution or a House resolution). A concurrent resolution must be adopted by both houses. Neither simple resolutions nor concurrent resolutions go to the president. A joint resolution passes both houses and must be presented to the president. A joint resolution is identical to a bill in the sense of complying with bicameralism and presentment.

By the middle of the nineteenth century, it had become obvious that simple or concurrent resolutions, if placed in a law, could be used to control the executive branch. Executive officials recognized that the coercive and binding effect of these resolutions changed when their use was sanctioned by a public law. In 1854, Attorney General Caleb Cushing stated that a simple resolution could not coerce a department head "unless in some particular in which a law, duly enacted, has subjected him to the direct action of each; and in such case it is to be intended, that, by approving the law, the President has consented to the exercise of such coerciveness on the part of either House" (6 Op. Attorney Gen. 680, 681, [1854]).

Thus, Congress passed legislation in 1903 providing that either house, by simple resolution, could direct the secretary of commerce to make investigations and issue reports. Two years later, a statute authorized Congress, by concurrent resolution, to direct the secretary of war to make investigations in rivers and harbors matters. Congress even found ways to control the executive action by committee action. Legislation in 1867 added the following restriction on the appropriation of funds for public buildings and grounds: "To pay for completing the repairs and furnishing the executive mansion, thirty-five thousand dollars: *Provided,* That no further payments shall be made on any accounts for repairs and furnishing the executive mansion until such accounts shall have been submitted to a joint committee of Congress, and approved by such committee."

An attempt by Congress to rely on a committee veto provoked a veto by President Woodrow Wilson in 1920. Legislation passed by Congress provided that no government publication could be printed, issued, or discontinued unless authorized under regulations prescribed by the Joint Committee on Printing. Wilson objected that Congress had no right to endow a joint committee or committee of either house "with power to prescribe 'regulations' under which executive departments may operate."

In that same year, Wilson also vetoed a budget and accounting bill because it allowed Congress by concurrent resolution to remove the comptroller general and assistant comptroller general. Wilson stated in his veto message, "It has, I think, always been the accepted construction of the Constitution that the power to appoint officers of this kind carries with it, as an incident, the power to remove. I am convinced that the Congress is without constitutional power to limit the appointing power and its incident, the power of removal derived from the Constitution." After Congress replaced the concurrent resolution with a joint resolution, President Warren G. Harding signed the Budget and Accounting Act of 1921.

The executive branch issued other critiques of the legislative veto. In 1933, Attorney General William DeWitt Mitchell gave his views about the constitutionality of a bill that authorized the Joint Committee on Internal Revenue Taxation to make the final decision on any tax refund that exceeded $20,000. The procedure, he said, was unconstitutional. In previous years, the executive branch had accepted as valid a statute that allowed the committee to decide all tax refunds above $75,000. Why did an apparently constitutional procedure come under attack simply because the threshold for committee action dropped from $75,000 to $20,000? If the limit of $20,000 was unconstitutional, would a dollar figure closer to $75,000 be found valid? At precisely what point on the continuum between the two dollar figures did the constitutional issue emerge?

## EXECUTIVE REORGANIZATION

The first major, sustained use of the legislative veto came in 1932 when Congress delegated to President Herbert Hoover the authority to reorganize the executive branch, subject to a one-house veto. The history of this statute provides a valuable insight into the executive-legislative dynamics that drive the accommodation for a legislative veto.

Beginning in 1929, Hoover advocated executive reorganization powers as a useful "economy and efficiency" measure that would help cut federal spending. In his 1929 annual message to Congress, he requested authority to submit reorganization proposals subject to some form of congressional disapproval, suggesting that the president might act "upon approval of a joint committee of Congress." Economy and efficiency becames catchwords during the 1932 presidential campaign. Both parties called for drastic reductions in federal spending. The mood in Congress favored some grant of authority to the executive as a way to avoid the delays and compromises of the regular legislative process. Senator David Reed (R.-Pa.) expressed the frustration with the prevailing procedures in Congress:

> Mr. President, I do not often envy other countries their governments, but I say that if this country ever needed a Mussolini it needs one now. I am not proposing that we make Mr. Hoover our Mussolini, I am not proposing that we should abdicate the authority that is in us, but if we are to get economies made they have to be made by some one who has the power to make the order and stand by it. Leave it to Congress and we will fiddle around here all summer trying to satisfy every lobbyist, and we will get nowhere. The country does not want that. The country wants stern action, and action quickly. (*Congressional Record,* 75th Cong., 9644, 1932)

Hoover received reorganization authority in the form of an amendment (Part II) to the Legislative Branch Appropriations Act for fiscal 1933. Title IV of Part II, known as the Economy Act of 1932, authorized the president to reorganize the executive branch. The president could transfer the whole or any part of any independent executive agency, or the functions thereof, to an executive department or another independent executive agency, and he could transfer the whole or any part of any executive agency, or the functions thereof, to another executive department. The president's proposal would be submitted to Congress as an executive order and lie there for sixty days. Congress could shorten the period by passing a concurrent resolution of approval. The entire executive order, or any part thereof, would become null and void if either house, during the sixty-day period, passed a resolution of disapproval.

President Hoover issued eleven executive orders consolidating some fifty-eight governmental activities. By that time, however, Hoover had been defeated overwhelmingly in the general election, and it was the intention of Congress, in the closing hours of a lame-duck session, to leave reorganization changes to the incoming president, Franklin D. Roosevelt. The House of Representatives passed a resolution of disapproval by voice vote.

Despite this disappointment, the procedure for reorganization clearly favors the president. It is not necessary to obtain the approval of both houses, which is required of the regular legislative process. Instead, a president's proposal becomes law within a fixed number of days unless one House disapproves. Moreover, Congress cannot offer amendments to a reorganization proposal. It has to be voted with a simple yes or no. Similarly, the president's proposal cannot be buried in committee or filibustered in the Senate. Congress must act to stop it.

In 1933, Congress granted President Roosevelt wide-ranging powers of executive reorganization without the check of a legislative veto. That authority lasted for two years. In 1937, Roosevelt asked Congress to renew his authority to make executive reorganizations. He argued that Congress could defeat a reorganization proposal only by passing a joint resolution of disapproval. Any action short of a bill or joint resolution, such as by simple resolution or concurrent resolution, would have no binding legal force. It would merely be "an expression of congressional sentiment."

Members of the House of Representatives refused to give Roosevelt the authority he wanted. There were disturbing signs that he wanted to concentrate too much power in the president's office, especially after his attempt in 1937 to pack the Supreme Court by adding as many as six new justices. The call for action by bill or joint resolution seemed like another power grab. In effect, Congress would delegate reorganization authority to the president and could recapture it only by passing a joint resolution of disapproval, which could be vetoed by the president. Congress would then need a two-thirds majority in each house to override the president. Given this scenario, the president would prevail by maintaining one-third plus one on his side in a single house to prevent an override.

Realizing that the House would not delegate to him the reorganization powers he wanted, Roosevelt relented within a few days and accepted an amendment that gave Congress a two-house legislative veto. Congress could reject any executive order by passing a concurrent resolution of disapproval. Creative rationalizations were offered to justify Roosevelt's switch in constitutional principles. It was now argued that the president would be acting as an "agent" of Congress, subject to the conditions established by the legislative branch. Congress would be able to use the legislative veto to announce that the president had violated or misused his power of agency. Furthermore, defenders of the amendment distinguished between the invalid use of a legislative veto to control past laws and the valid use of a legislative veto to control laws "in the making."

The Reorganization Act of 1939 authorized the president to submit reorganization plans, which would take effect after sixty days unless Congress, within that time, passed a concurrent resolution of disapproval. When the statute was extended in 1949, Congress insisted that it have the power to disapprove by a single house. Subsequent extensions, including one in 1977, kept the one-house veto. After *Chadha,* Congress switched to a joint resolution of approval, but that step will be explored in detail later.

## THE PROLIFERATION OF LEGISLATIVE VETOES

With the reorganization statute operating as a precedent, Congress and the executive branch entered into a number of other accommodations that relied on the legislative veto. Each statute had similar features: Congress delegated authority and flexibility to the executive branch. In return, the executive branch agreed that Congress could control the delegated authority by exercising some form of legislative veto. Although executive officials often voiced misgivings about the constitutionality of the legislative veto, they acquiesced because they knew that Congress would not delegate such authority without attaching a string to it.

The Lend-Lease Act of 1941 delegated important authority to President Roosevelt on the condition that Congress could terminate the president's authority by passing a concurrent resolution of disapproval. Roosevelt signed the bill and withheld any constitutional objection, because an objection would have been politically imprudent at the time. His political enemies regarded the concurrent resolution as unconstitutional, and Roosevelt did not want to lend them any strength or encouragement. Nevertheless, he used a confidential memorandum to record his constitutional objections to the bill, telling Attorney General Robert H. Jackson to publish the memo after Roosevelt's death. Jackson published the president's legal memo in the *Harvard Law Review* in 1953, explaining Roosevelt's dilemma: "To make public his views at that time would confirm and delight his opposition and let down his friends. It might seriously alienate some of his congressional support at a time when he would need to call on it frequently."

During World War II, Congress and the executive branch entered into a number of other quid pro quos that depended on a legislative veto. Because of the volume of wartime construction and the need for emergency action, it was impracticable for Congress to follow the customary practice of authorizing each defense installation or public-works project. Beginning with an informal system in 1942, all proposals for acquisitions of land and leases were submitted in advance to the Naval Affairs Committee for their approval. With this informal understanding in place, Congress agreed to pass authorizing statutes with lump-sum dollar amounts without identifying the specific projects. Two years later, Congress placed that understanding into law. Before carrying out certain actions, executive agencies were to "come into agreement" with designated committees.

Those provisions flourished under Presidents Harry Truman and Dwight Eisenhower, prompting both presidents to express constitutional objections. In 1955, Attorney General Herbert Brownell issued an opinion that the committee veto of "coming into agreement" provisions violated the Constitution by permitting congressional committees to share in administrative decisions. A similar opinion was released two years later, again calling attention to congressional infringement of executive duties.

Congress retaliated by changing its rules and procedures. It drafted bill language to provide that the Appropriations Committees could not fund certain real estate transactions unless the Public Works Committees had first approved the contracts. Brownell advised President Eisenhower that this new procedure satisfied the Constitution because Congress had the authority to adopt rules for its own internal operations. There was nothing unconstitutional about one committee controlling another. A constitutional problem, said Brownell, emerged when one committee controlled an executive action. Congress was satisfied because the Public Works Committees retained an indirect veto over certain executive activities.

A number of new legislative vetoes appeared in the 1970s. The War Powers Resolution of 1973 provided that Congress could adopt a concurrent resolution requiring the president to withdraw troops engaged in hostilities. The Congressional Budget and Impoundment Control Act of 1974 gave Congress a one-house veto over presidential proposals to "defer" (delay) the spending of funds appropriated by Congress. The Arms Export Control Act of 1974 extended to Congress a two-house veto over arms sales proposed by the president. The National Emergencies Act of 1976 permitted Congress to pass a concurrent resolution to terminate emergency authorities delegated to the president.

These legislative vetoes created some concern within the executive branch, but the step that threatened the executive-legislative accommodation in place since 1932 was the extension of legislative vetoes to agency rule making. In 1974, Congress adopted a one-house veto over rules issued by the General Services Administration regarding the papers of President Richard Nixon. In that same year, it enacted a two-house veto over regulations of the commissioner of education, a two-house veto over passenger restraint rules by the National Highway Traffic Safety Administration, and a one-house veto over regulations by the Federal Election Commission. A statute in 1978 relied on a one-house veto to disapprove incremental pricing regulations proposed by the Federal Energy Regulatory Commission (FERC). A 1980 statute used a one-house veto to control rule making by the Federal Trade Commission.

Members of Congress threatened to replace this piecemeal approach with a generic statute that would subject every rule and regulation adopted by the federal agencies to a legislative veto. In 1976 the House of Representatives voted 265–135 for the Administrative Rule-Making Reform Act. This legislation would have allowed Congress, by concurrent resolution, to disapprove all agency rules. Although the margin far exceeded a majority, it was insufficient under the special procedure adopted by the House (action by suspension of the rules, which requires a two-thirds majority). In 1982 the Senate voted 65–27 for a two-house veto over agency regulations.

These initiatives by Congress ruptured the decades-long accommodation over a legislative veto. In 1978, President Jimmy Carter released a statement in which he examined the growth of legislative vetoes and concluded that they were unconstitutional. Henceforth, he said, all legislative vetoes in statutes would be regarded as "notice-and-wait" provisions. Executive agencies would notify Congress of an intended action and wait a specified number of days before implementing the action. Any legislative veto adopted by Congress during that period would be regarded as purely advisory and nonbinding on the executive branch.

This strict policy had some holes in it. On the very day that President Carter issued his statement, a press conference was called by Attorney General Griffin Bell, White House adviser Stuart Eizenstat, and Justice Department official John Harmon. Reporters asked Bell if President Carter would feel bound if Congress adopted a two-house veto to disapprove the administration's pending Mideast arms-sales package (the procedure authorized by the Arms Export Control Act of 1974). Bell replied,

> He would not be bound in our view, but we have to have comity between the branches of government, just as we have between nations.

And under a spirit of comity, we could abide by it, and there would be nothing wrong with abiding by it. We don't have to have a confrontation every time we can.

Eizenstat added,

I think the point the Judge [Bell] is making is that we don't concede the constitutionality of any of [the legislative vetoes] yet, but that as a matter of comity with certain of these issues where we think the Congress has a legitimate interest, such as the War Powers Act, as a matter of comity, we are willing to forego the specific legal challenge and abide by that judgment because we think it is such an overriding issue.

## TAKING THE ISSUE TO COURT

From 1976 to 1981, court decisions on the legislative veto were highly cautious statements limited to the particular issue challenged. Often the courts avoided the substantive issue by using a procedural reason. By 1982, the courts appeared ready to invalidate all legislative vetoes, a step the Supreme Court took with *Chadha.*

The legislative veto was mentioned tangentially in *Buckley* v. *Valeo,* 424 U.S. 1 (1976), a campaign-finance case that reached the Supreme Court. The Federal Election Campaign Act had been challenged on a number of grounds, especially the limits placed by Congress on individual campaign contributions and the participation by Congress in the appointment of members to the Federal Election Commission (FEC). The statute also allowed either house of Congress to disapprove regulations proposed by the FEC. The Court did not decide the issue over the legislative veto, but Justice Byron White suggested in a separate opinion that the legislative veto might have constitutional support.

A year later, a federal appellate court in *Clark* v. *Valeo,* 559 F.2d 642 (1977), ruled that the dispute over a one-house veto of FEC regulations was not ripe for judicial determination

*From the Office of the White House Secretary, Briefing by Attorney General Griffin B. Bell, Stuart E. Eizenstat, Assistant to the President for Domestic Affairs and Policy, and John Harman, Office of Legal Counsel, 21 June 1978, p. 4.

because Congress had yet to exercise its legislative veto. In that same year, the Court of Claims in *Atkins* v. *United States,* 556 F.2d 1028 (1977), considered a challenge to a one-house veto used to disapprove federal salary increases. The court held that the legislative veto did not bypass the president because the bill authorizing the legislative veto was presented to the president.

The Supreme Court also reviewed a statute that allowed either house of Congress to disapprove regulations issued by the General Services Administration concerning the public papers of President Nixon. Although not ruling directly on the legislative veto, the Court, in *Nixon* v. *Administrator of General Services,* 408 F. Supp. 321 (1976), stated, "Whatever are the future possibilities for constitutional conflict in the promulgation of regulations respecting public access to particular documents, nothing in the Act renders it unduly disruptive of the Executive Branch and, therefore, unconstitutional on its face."

In all of these cases, the courts treated the legislative-veto issue with great sensitivity and caution. They deliberately avoided abstract and sweeping judgments on the legislative veto, preferring to treat it case by case and subject by subject. Similarly, the Ninth Circuit in 1980 struck down a one-house veto in an immigration case (634 F.2d 408), but the court was careful to circumscribe the reach of its decision. It decided only the issue before it: individual, adjudicative-type determinations made by immigration judges. The Ninth Circuit specifically pointed out that it was not faced with other types of legislative vetoes, such as the two-house veto in the Nuclear Nonproliferation Act or the variety of legislative vetoes used to control agency rule making.

This incremental, case-by-case approach to legislative vetoes came to an abrupt halt in 1982 when the D.C. Circuit struck down a one-house veto of FERC rules, a two-house veto of FTC rules, and a committee veto of Department of Housing and Urban Development reorganizations (*Consumer Energy Council of America* v. *FERC,* 673 F.2d 425 [1982]; *Consumers Union, Inc.* v. *FTC,* 691 F.2d 575 [1982]; and *AFGE* v. *Pierce,* 697 F.2d 303, 308 [1982]). From these decisions it appeared that any congressional control over agency actions would have to follow the full legislative process: action by both houses of Congress and presentation of a bill or joint resolution to the president for his signature or veto.

In the *Pierce* case, two federal appellate judges with prior experience in the legislative and executive branches warned their brethren about the dangers of deciding the constitutionality of the legislative veto too broadly. Patricia Wald, who served in the Justice Department during the Carter years, and Abner Mikva, a former member of Congress from Illinois, asked that an earlier case decided by a panel of three judges be reheard by the entire D.C. Circuit "because vitally important issues of executive-legislative relations are articulated too broadly and explored inadequately in the panel opinion" (697 F.2d 303, 308 [1982]). They urged the D.C. Circuit to avoid a black-and-white treatment of unique accommodations that had proven useful for both the executive and legislative branches, such as the Reorganization Act, the Impoundment Control Act, and the Federal Salary Act.

## THE *CHADHA* CASE

The immigration case decided by the Ninth Circuit in 1980 was appealed to the Supreme Court, where it was twice argued before the Court's decision was released in 1983. The case involved Jagdish Rai Chadha, an East Indian born in Kenya and bearing a British passport. He had outstayed his student's visa and was threatened with deportation. Following statutory procedures, he presented his case to an administrative hearing and argued that deportation would result in "extreme hardship." He received a favorable decision from an immigration judge. His name was among those of 340 individuals that the U.S. attorney general sent to Congress, recommending suspension of deportation. Pursuant to statutory authority, the House of Representatives disapproved six names from the list, Chadha's among them.

Attorneys representing the House and the Senate explained to the Supreme Court that the one-house veto marked an accommodation between members of Congress and executive officials. Under the previous system, if the administration wanted to suspend the deportation of an alien, it had to convince Congress to pass a private bill for the individual. These bills, like public bills, had to pass both houses and be presented to the president. The administration persuaded Congress in 1940 that the existing system was too cumbersome and slow to protect the rights of aliens. It was proposed that the attorney general be authorized to suspend deportations subject to some kind of legislative veto. Over the years, Congress relied on both one-house and two-house vetoes.

The Court released its *Chadha* decision on 23 June 1983, declaring that the one-house veto in the immigration statute was unconstitutional because it violated both the principle of bicameralism and the presentment clause. Two-house vetoes satisfied bicameralism, but failed the test of presentment. By this two-part requirement, all legislative vetoes—one-house, two-house, or committee—were unconstitutional. Chief Justice Warren Burger wrote the opinion for the Court, announcing that whenever congressional action had the "purpose and effect of altering the legal rights, duties, and relations of persons" outside the legislative branch, Congress must act through both houses in a bill that is presented to the president. He was joined by five justices. Justice Lewis F. Powell concurred in the judgment, but stated his preference for a more narrowly drawn holding that would be confined to cases (like Chadha's) where Congress tried to override adjudicatory decisions.

Justice White issued a lengthy dissent, condemning the majority for adopting a rigid, formalistic model of separation of powers. He claimed that the decision "sounds the death knell for nearly 200 other statutory provisions in which Congress has reserved a 'legislative veto.'" He argued that "without the legislative veto, Congress is faced with a Hobson's choice: either to refrain from delegating the necessary authority, leaving itself with a hopeless task of writing laws with the requisite specificity to cover endless special circumstances across the entire policy landscape, or in the alternative, to abdicate its lawmaking function to the Executive Branch and independent agencies." In fact, Congress and the executive agencies would think up a number of middle-ground options that now serve many of the same objectives as the supposedly forbidden legislative veto. Those options will be identified later.

In the second dissent, Justice William Rehnquist objected that the one-house veto could not be severed from the discretionary authority given to the attorney general to suspend deportations. If the legislative veto was invalid, the authority should fall with it. The legislative history of the immigration statute persuaded Rehnquist that Congress delegated the authority on the condition that it would retain a legislative veto to control the administration. Chief Justice Burger and the majority held that the legislative veto could be stricken without affecting the attorney general's authority.

The Court's decision contains many deficiencies. First, the decision to sever the legislative veto while retaining the balance of the statute meant that the attorney general would have unchecked authority to suspend deportations. The legislative history provides convincing evidence that Congress and the executive branch had entered into a clear quid pro quo: We give you the authority you want if we can control by legislative veto. Instead of the careful accommodation that was intended to satisfy both legislative and executive interests, the executive branch now had a one-sided advantage.

Second, the Court stated that it was insufficient for Congress to argue that the legislative veto was "efficient, convenient, and useful in facilitating functions of government." That defense of the legislative veto, standing alone, "will not save it if it is contrary to the Constitution. Convenience and efficiency are not the primary objectives—or the hallmarks—of democratic government." The majority opinion acknowledged that the legislative veto may be a "convenient shortcut" and an "appealing compromise," but claimed that it is "crystal clear from the records of the Convention, contemporaneous writings and debates, that the Framers ranked other values higher than efficiency."

What those "higher values" were the Court failed to say. Its comments on convenience and efficiency are false. The historical record from 1776 to 1787 provides abundant evidence that the framers were very much concerned with making government more efficient and effective. The Articles of Confederation had not provided an effective framework for government. The operation of the Continental Congress was regularly condemned for slowness, indecision, and inefficiency. George Washington, James Madison, Thomas Jefferson, John Adams, John Jay, Alexander Hamilton, and other contempo-

raries pressed eagerly for reforms that would yield a more efficient form of government.

Third, the Court misconceived the relationship between the presentment clause and the president's veto power. It stated correctly that the veto was intended to check "oppressive, improvident, or ill-considered measures," but it was misleading to suggest that the legislative veto, by evading the president's veto, necessarily threatened the independence of the president's office and invited ill-considered measures. The legislative veto operated within a very narrow realm. It could defeat only those proposals initiated by the president, such as an executive reorganization plan, an arms-sales proposal, or a request to defer the spending of appropriated funds. If Congress used its legislative veto to disapprove those proposals, the president's office was not threatened. The reorganization of the executive branch remained as before, an arms sale to a foreign government did not go forward, and appropriated funds would have to be spent in accordance with an enacted statute. The president did not need his veto power to protect himself against these legislative vetoes.

Fourth, the Court insisted that the Framers wanted congressional power exercised "in accord with a single, finely wrought and exhaustively considered, procedure." According to the Court's analysis, the records of the Constitutional Convention and the state ratification debates provide "unmistakable expression of a determination that legislation by the national Congress be a step-by-step, deliberate and deliberative process." Here the Court vastly oversimplified the legislative process. There is no constitutional requirement that each exercise of the legislative power be finely wrought, exhaustively considered, step-by-step, deliberate, and deliberative. That often occurs, but the House of Representatives can also suspend its rules to pass a bill without allowing any amendments. The House Rules Committee can report bills that prohibit floor amendments or allow only for specified amendments. The Senate, under its unanimous-consent procedure, can do just about anything it wants. Either house can pass bills that have never been sent to committee or been the subject of congressional hearings. For example, in 1991, President George Bush received an extension of "fast-track" authority that enabled him to negotiate a free trade agreement with Mexico. For the implementing bill needed to effectuate that agreement, amendments are prohibited and deadlines are established for committee and floor action.

Fifth, it is not clear whether the House of Representatives altered the legal rights of Chadha when it disapproved the suspension of his deportation. The attorney general's suspension was conditioned on the availability of a one-house veto. The House acted pursuant to a statute. It did not alter Chadha's legal rights; it was fulfilling the statutory procedure. Moreover, by the time of the Court's decision, Chadha had married an American woman and was no longer subject to deportation. His legal rights were not at issue, either before the Court's decision or afterward.

Sixth, the Court was incorrect in stating that Congress cannot alter the legal rights and duties of persons outside the legislative branch unless it complies with bicameralism and presentment. Each house may command witnesses to appear before congressional committees and may apply sanctions to those who refuse to cooperate. Committees have the power to issue subpoenas. Each house has the power to hold individuals in contempt. Subpoenas and contempt citations do not require bicameralism or presentment.

Seventh, the Court declared that no constitutional provision allows Congress "to repeal or amend laws by other than legislative means pursuant to Art. I." When the House adopted a one-house veto disapproving Chadha's suspension, it was not repealing or amending a law. It was following the procedure already enacted into law. It was the Court, in *Chadha,* that effectively repealed or amended the immigration law by striking the legislative veto and allowing the balance of the statute to remain in force.

The Court's misreading of history and congressional procedures would prove costly to its own prestige. It never understood executive-legislative relations or the original purpose behind the legislative veto. Its theory of government was too much at odds with the practices developed over the years by the political branches. Neither agency heads nor members of Congress want the static model advanced by the Court. Executive officials still seek substantial discretion in administering delegated authority; legislators still want to control delegated authority without having to pass another law. Under those conditions, compliance with the Court's decision would be modest at best.

## COMPLIANCE WITH *CHADHA*

The Court's invalidation of legislative vetoes seemed an unqualified victory for the executive branch. It proved not to be so. When the Court's decision came down, Congress amended the executive reorganization statute to require that the president's reorganization plans be approved by a joint resolution. A joint resolution must be passed by both houses and be presented to the president. Therefore, it complied with *Chadha*. However, the executive branch was now worse off than before. Under the previous system, a reorganization plan would take effect after a specified number of days unless one house of Congress disapproved. The burden was on Congress to act. The new procedure shifted the burden. The president now had to obtain the approval of both houses within a specified number of days. Otherwise the plan would fail. The Reagan administration considered those hurdles so onerous that it did not seek reorganization authority after this procedure expired in 1984.

Congress also fixed some other statutes that contained legislative vetoes. To replace the concurrent resolution used to disapprove the president's emergency powers, Congress switched to a joint resolution of disapproval. It followed the same course in amending the D.C. home-rule statute and legislation on export administration, replacing legislative vetoes with a joint resolution. Congress repealed a legislative veto used in the past to disapprove federal salary increases. The new law required Congress to pass a joint resolution of disapproval.

Because of *Chadha,* Congress could not use its one-house veto to disapprove deferrals of appropriated funds. This inability might have given the administration an unfair advantage, enabling it to defer funds and forcing Congress to pass a public law to disapprove these actions. For a few years, however, the administration agreed not to abuse its authority and entered into an accommodation with Congress: deferral authority would be exercised lightly, and Congress could disapprove by adding language to omnibus appropriations bills. However, when Congress passed the Gramm-Rudman-Hollings Act in 1985, requiring new steps to control the deficit, the administration turned to deferral authority as a method of restricting spending.

The city of New Haven, Connecticut, accompanied by other plaintiffs, went to court to argue that the one-house veto for Congress and the deferral authority for the President were inseverable. If the legislative veto was unconstitutional, the deferral authority could no longer be exercised. In *City of New Haven* v. *United States*, 809 F.2d 900 D.C. Cir. (1987), a district court and the D.C. Circuit agreed with that argument. As a result, presidents would no longer have the authority to defer funds for policy reasons. They could not defer funds merely because they did not ask for them and disagree with the spending priorities enacted by Congress. Deferrals would have to be submitted only for routine and nonpolicy reasons, such as the achievement of management savings or the inability to spend funds because of factors outside the control of the administration.

In response to *Chadha,* Congress considered repealing the concurrent resolution in the War Powers Resolution and replacing it with a joint resolution that would require the president to withdraw troops engaged in hostilities. As the debate continued, however, it was decided to leave the War Powers Resolution untouched. Instead, Congress passed a freestanding statute to authorize an expedited procedure for adopting a joint resolution that would require the president to remove American forces engaged in hostilities outside the United States.

## NONCOMPLIANCE WITH *CHADHA*

Supposedly stripped of the legislative veto, Congress, along with executive agencies, proceeded to fashion various accommodations that were in some cases the functional equivalent of the legislative veto. In other cases, they selected remedies that were identical to the legislative veto. Congress no longer passes one-house or two-house vetoes to control the executive branch. Instead, congressional control has shifted to its committees and subcom-

mittees. From the date of the Court's decision to the end of 1992, Congress placed more than two hundred legislative vetoes in bills that were signed into law by presidents Reagan and Bush. All of those legislative vetoes relied on disapproval mechanisms at the committee and subcommittee level.

Most of the post-*Chadha* legislative vetoes are easy to spot in public laws. For example, construction grants by the Environmental Protection Agency are subject to approval of the Appropriations Committees (97 Stat. 226). The approval of the Appropriations Committees is required before certain amounts in the National Flood Insurance Fund can be exceeded (97 Stat. 227). With the approval of the Appropriations Committees, up to 5 percent may be transferred between designated accounts of the National Aeronautics and Space Administration (NASA) (97 Stat. 229). Reimbursement of certain funds for the Ventura Marina project, administered by the Corps of Engineers, requires the prior approval of the Appropriations Committees. Although the statutory language calls for approval by the Appropriations Committees, that decision is delegated to the subcommittees with jurisdiction over those agencies.

Other legislative vetoes enacted after *Chadha* are more difficult to locate. One statute provided that foreign assistance funds allocated to each country "shall not exceed those provided in fiscal year 1983 or those provided in the budget estimates for each country, whichever are lower, unless submitted through the regular reprogramming procedures of the Committees on Appropriations" (97 Stat. 736). Reprogramming allows agencies to shift funds from one program to another, but these statutory procedures require the prior approval of the Appropriations Committees (actually, the subcommittees on foreign operations). The D.C. appropriation bill prohibited funds from being obligated or spent by reprogramming "except pursuant to advance approval of the reprogramming granted according to the procedure set forth" in two House reports, both of which require approval by the Appropriations Committees.

President Reagan challenged some of these post-*Chadha* legislative vetoes. In 1984 he received an appropriations bill that contained about a half dozen legislative vetoes giving congressional committees final control over certain agency actions. His signing statement, chastising Congress for continuing to place legislative vetoes in bills submitted to the president, stated, "The time has come, with more than a year having passed since the Supreme Court's decision in *Chadha,* to make clear that legislation containing legislative veto devices that come to me for my approval or disapproval will be implemented in a manner consistent with the *Chadha* decision" (H.Rept. 916). The message to Congress came through clearly: the administration did not regard the legislative vetoes as legally binding. Agencies would be free to notify their review committees on pending decisions and proceed independently, regardless of how the committees reacted.

The response from Congress was swift and effective. The House Appropriations Committee reviewed an agreement that it had entered into with NASA four years previously. Congress enacted legislation with dollar caps on various NASA programs, allowing NASA to exceed those caps if it obtained the approval of the Appropriations Committees. The House Appropriations Committee believed that the procedure had worked well, but in view of Reagan's signing statement, the accommodation between Congress and the executive branch apparently had come to an end. The committee said it would repeal the committee veto, to satisfy the administration, but would at the same time repeal NASA's authority to go beyond the dollar caps. In the future, NASA would have to do what the Supreme Court called for in *Chadha:* get a new public law whenever it wanted to spend in excess of the dollar caps. NASA, like Congress, would have to satisfy bicameralism and presentment.

Neither NASA nor the Appropriations Committees wanted this administrative rigidity. Within a matter of weeks the administrator of NASA, James M. Beggs, wrote to the Appropriations Committee and proposed a compromise. His letter reveals the pragmatic sense of give-and-take that is customary between executive agencies and congressional committees. It also underscores the impracticality and unreality of the constitutional doctrines announced in *Chadha.* Beggs began by describing the system of committee approval as "workable," fearing that the repeal of the committee veto would leave "inflexible, binding funding limitations on several programs." He explained,

> Without some procedure for adjustment, other than a subsequent separate legislative enactment, these ceilings could seriously impact the ability of NASA to meet unforeseen technical changes or programs that are inherent in challenging R&D programs. We believe that the present legislative procedure could be converted by this letter into an informal agreement by NASA not to exceed amounts for Committee-designated programs without the approval of the Committees on Appropriations. This agreement would assume that both the statutory funding ceilings and the Committee approval mechanisms would be deleted from the FY 1985 legislation, and that it would not be the normal practice to include either mechanism in future appropriations bills. Further, the agreement would assume that future program ceiling amounts would be identified by the Committees in the Conference Report accompanying NASA's annual appropriations act and confirmed by NASA in its submission of the annual operating plan. NASA would not expend any funds over the ceilings identified in the Conference Report for these programs without the prior approval of the Committees.**

What Beggs proposed was to take the legislative veto out of the public law and place it in an informal, nonstatutory setting. *Chadha* does not prohibit this. NASA is not legally bound by Beggs's agreement, but apparently neither was it legally bound (according to Reagan's signing statement) by the procedure enacted into law. Although the agreement in Begg's letter is not legally binding in the same sense as a statute, NASA knows that violating it would incur the wrath of Congress and subject the agency to stringent statutory limitations in the future. Bad faith on the part of NASA would provoke Congress to place the ceiling caps back in public law and force the agency to seek another public law whenever it needs to exceed a specific ceiling.

---

**James M. Beggs, Administrator of NASA to Congressman Edward P. Boland, 9 August 1984, in Louis Fisher and Neal Devins, *Political Dynamics of Constitutional Law* (St. Paul, Minn., 1992), p. 139.

A similar result developed from a 1987 confrontation between the administration and Congress. For a decade, the following language had appeared in the appropriations bill that funds foreign assistance: "None of the funds made available by this Act may be obligated under an appropriation account to which they were not appropriated without the prior written approval of the Committees on Appropriations." In 1987, Office of Management and Budget (OMB) director James C. Miller III wrote to the Appropriations Committees and said that the committee veto violated constitutional principles announced in *Chadha.*

The response from Congress was predictable. David Obey (D.-Wis.), chairman of the subcommittee that funds foreign assistance, told OMB that he would delete the committee veto and also eliminate the discretion of executive officials to obligate funds under a different account. He said that OMB's position "means we don't have an accommodation any more, so the hell with it, spend the money like we appropriated it. It's just dumb on their part." The ranking minority member, Mickey Edwards (R.-Okla.), agreed. He noted that OMB "has not had a history of being very thoughtful or for consulting people." He regarded the statutory provision as an example of "the spirit of cooperation between the executive and legislative branches, which the administration is not very good at."

Realizing that it had shot itself in the foot, OMB retreated and allowed the language to remain in the bill that became law. But it returned the next year to battle the same issue, and this time Congress made good its word. The entire provision was stricken, the legislative veto as well as the discretionary authority. The two branches worked out a compromise in 1989. Congress deleted the legislative veto, but required the administration to adhere to "the regular notification procedures of the Committees on Appropriations" before transferring funds from one account to another. Those procedures require the administration to notify the committees of each transfer. Although not spelled out in the law, the administration agreed that if the committees objected to a transfer during a fifteen-day review period, it would not transfer the funds. Legally, the administration could ignore the committee objec-

tions, but the cost would be heavy, if not prohibitive.

## INFORMAL LEGISLATIVE VETOES

The arrangements worked out with NASA and the foreign-assistance subcommittee are typical of executive-legislative relationships. These agency-committee accommodations existed before *Chadha,* and they exist after it. In fact, as these examples indicate, the Court's decision serves as a stimulus for additional informal arrangements.

A "reprogramming" procedure has been followed for about four decades, allowing agencies to shift funds within an appropriation account, provided that they notify congressional committees and, in many cases, seek their approval. This quid pro quo offer benefits to Congress and the agencies. Without such an understanding, Congress would have to appropriate with far greater itemization, directing agency actions in minute detail. With the understanding, Congress can appropriate in lump sums and monitor significant deviations of funds through the reprogramming procedure. Agencies like lump-sum funding. They do not want line-itemization. Neither branch can forecast with sufficient accuracy precisely how funds should be spent within a given fiscal year. Good management requires flexibility and the opportunity to shift funds as the fiscal year unfolds.

Reprogramming is called "informal" in the sense that the procedures are rarely included in public laws. Generally, they are explained in committee reports, committee hearings, and correspondence between the agencies and the committees. Agencies then place these understandings in their instructions, directives, and financial management manuals, alerting agency personnel to the types of reprogrammings that can be done internally with only periodic reports to Congress and the reprogrammings that require prior approval from the committees.

The lower courts have recognized the need for informal clearance procedures between agencies and congressional committees. In one case, a statute required the General Services Administration (GSA) to notify certain committees of Congress in advance of any negotiated sale of surplus government property in excess of $10,000. Agency regulations further provided that in the "absence of adverse comment" from a committee, the agency could sell the property on or after thirty-five days. In litigation shortly after *Chadha,* the U.S. Claims Court, in *City of Alexandria* v. *United States,* 3 Cl. Ct. 667 (1983), found "compelling similarities" between the GSA procedure and the legislative veto struck down by the Supreme Court. The combination of the statutory language, agency regulation, and agency deference to committee objections seemed to the Claims Court the functional equivalent of a legislative veto.

A bipartisan brief signed by Representatives Jack Brooks (D.-Tex.) and Frank Horton (R.-N.Y.), the chairman and the ranking minority member, respectively, of the House Government Operations Committee, rejected the analysis by the Claims Court, pointing out that it would render unconstitutional all of the notification procedures presently found in federal statutes. The Court of Appeals for the Federal Circuit reversed the trial court, concluding that there was nothing unconstitutional about the decision of agencies to defer to committee objections:

> Committee chairmen and members naturally develop interest and expertise in the subjects entrusted to their continuing surveillance. Officials in the executive branch have to take these committees into account and keep them informed, respond to their inquiries, and it may be, flatter and please them when necessary. Committees do not need even the type of "report and wait" provision we have here to develop enormous influence over executive branch doings. There is nothing unconstitutional about this: indeed, our separation of powers makes such informal cooperation much more necessary than it would be in a pure system of parliamentary government. (737 F.2d, 1022, 2026, [1984])

In the first year of the Bush administration, executive officials wanted Congress to appropriate humanitarian assistance to the Contras in Nicaragua. Because of the deceptions and lying of the Reagan administration, Congress was not prepared to take at face value the Bush administration's new promises. It feared that money appropriated for humanitarian aid would find its way in some fashion to provide lethal weapons to the Contras. Secretary of State James A. Baker III realized that Congress was in no mood to believe the promises of the administration. Consequently, he agreed that Congress could appropriate $50 million for the Contras and withhold a portion to see if the administration kept to its word. If the administration behaved properly, the withheld funds would be released with the approval of certain congressional committees and party leaders.

White House counsel C. Boyden Gray objected to the plan because it would allow Congress to be involved in the administration of foreign policy, relying on what seemed to be a clear case of a legislative veto. Former federal judge Robert H. Bork regarded the "Baker Accord" as "even more objectionable" than the legislative veto struck down in *Chadha* because it permitted control by committees instead of a one-house or two-house veto. Nevertheless, Baker (with the blessing of President Bush) went ahead with the plan. The administration proceeded to demonstrate its good faith by spending the funds for humanitarian assistance and the balance of the money was released by party leaders and the designated committees.

The *Chadha* decision does not affect these nonstatutory legislative vetoes. They are not legal in effect. They are, however, in effect legal. Agencies are aware of the penalties and sanctions that can be invoked by Congress if they decide to violate understandings and agreements with their review committees.

## STATE LEGISLATIVE VETOES

At the state level, variations of the legislative veto emerged in an effort to maintain control over executive actions. Some of the states followed the federal model and delegated reorganization authority to the governor on the condition that reorganization plans could be rejected by a legislative veto. In 1950, three out of five justices of the Supreme Court of New Hampshire issued an advisory opinion that the delegation of such authority was constitutional but reliance on a legislative veto (in this case a concurrent resolution) was unconstitutional. Released in the form of an advisory opinion, the views of the justices were not binding on the government.

The Supreme Court of New Jersey reached the opposite conclusion in *Brown* v. *Heymann,* 297 A.2d 572 (1972). Under that state's procedure, the governor could submit a reorganization plan, and it would take effect within sixty days unless the two houses of the legislature passed a concurrent resolution of disapproval during that period. Although the procedure was challenged as a violation of the regular legislative process, the court concluded that "there is no bar to cooperative action among the branches of government. On the contrary, the doctrine [of separation of powers] assumes the branches will coordinate to the end that government will fulfill its mission."

By the 1970s, more than half of the state legislatures conducted some kind of review of administrative rules and regulations. Review ranged from a mere advisory role that allowed the legislature to comment and object, but not nullify, a rule, to more-coercive measures. Some states allowed the repeal of an objectionable regulation by review committees, a single house, or both houses acting through a concurrent resolution. A few states required action by joint resolution or bill. Another variation was to allow a review committee to suspend a regulation for a certain period of time during which the full legislature would have to act to nullify the rule permanently. Of the states that permitted review of agency rules by committee, most relied on a single joint committee.

The record of state courts in deciding the constitutionality of these review mechanisms was decidedly mixed. In *State* v. *A.L.I.V.E. Voluntary,* 606 P.2d 769 (1980), the Supreme Court of Alaska held that a state statute authorizing a two-house veto over agency regulations violated the state constitution. In *State ex rel. Barker* v. *Manchin,* 279 S.E.2d 622 (1981), the Supreme Court of Appeals of West Virginia ruled that a statute authorizing legislative committees to veto rules and regulations marked a violation of the separation-of-powers doctrine embodied in the state constitution. Unlike the federal Constitution, the state constitution contained explicit and strict language separating the branches: "The legislative, executive and judicial departments shall be separate and distinct, so that neither shall exercise the powers properly belonging to either of the others; nor

shall any person exercise the powers of more than one of them at the same time, except that justices of the peace shall be eligible to the legislatures."

In 1981 the justices of the Supreme Court of New Hampshire released an advisory opinion regarding the use of legislative vetoes to control agency regulations. They concluded that the creation of a legislative veto by the full legislature was "not *per se* unconstitutional." However, the legislature could not shift the power of disapproval to smaller groups within the legislature, such as committees or party leaders.

In *General Assembly of State of New Jersey* v. *Byrne,* 431 A.2d 449 (1982), the Supreme Court of New Jersey struck down a legislative veto over agency rules, but this decision was less sweeping than in West Virginia. The New Jersey Constitution requires that "the powers of the government shall be divided among three distinct branches. . . . No person or persons belonging to or constituting one branch shall exercise any of the powers properly belonging to either of the others, except as expressly provided in this Constitution." The New Jersey court held that a legislative veto over agency rules excessively interfered with the functions of the governor in faithfully executing laws and contravened the presentment clause. However, the New Jersey court cautioned that its holding did not foreclose all legislative veto provisions. It pointed to *Brown* v. *Heymann,* which had upheld the constitutionality of an executive reorganization statute authorizing the governor to submit reorganization plans to the legislature subject to a two-house veto. Although New Jersey governors vetoed the legislative veto over agency rule making, they made no objection to the two-house veto over executive reorganization. The New Jersey court acknowledged that in some areas the legislative veto "might serve an important function consistent with the separation of powers." If legislative action is necessary to further a statutory scheme requiring cooperation between the two branches and the action does not represent a substantial potential for interfering with exclusive executive functions, "legislative veto power can pass constitutional muster."

On the same day that the New Jersey court handed down this decision, it also upheld a legislative review mechanism over building projects and lease agreements proposed by the New Jersey Building Authority. To begin any project with an estimated cost exceeding $100,000, the Authority had to obtain a concurrent resolution from the legislature within forty-five days. Moreover, every lease agreement between the Authority and a state agency required the approval of the presiding officer of each house of the legislature. In upholding these legislative vetoes in *Enourato* v. *N.J. Building Authority*, 448 A.2d 449, the court explained that separation of powers "leaves room for some legislative oversight and participation in executive actions. Not every legislative input into law enforcement impermissibly interferes with the Executive's law enforcement power." The court reasoned that the legislative vetoes in this statute advanced the important purpose of developing legislative support. The statute made certain that every Authority project received a legislative imprimatur by allowing it to reject a proposed project at its inception. A failure to veto a project carried a message that the legislature would later vote the necessary appropriations. Furthermore, the legislative veto mechanism "can foster close cooperation between the Legislature and the Executive in this area of mutual concern" and encourage the Authority to act "prudently."

After *Chadha* was decided in 1983, state governments began to rethink their legislative veto mechanisms. They did not have to accept the reasoning or the result of the Supreme Court's decision. The language of separation of powers in state constitutions is different from the federal model, and customs and practices at the state level provide additional justification for unique variations. Nothing in *Chadha* compelled state governments to abandon the legislative veto.

In a decision that came after *Chadha*, the Supreme Court of Kansas declared a two-house veto over agency regulations to be unconstitutional. Announcing its ruling in *State ex rel. Stephan* v. *Kansas House of Representatives*, 687 P.2d 622, the court held that the legislative veto violates not only the separation-of-powers doctrine but also the presentment required by the state's legislative process.

The combination of state and federal court decisions in the 1980s resulted in a decline in the legislative veto at the state level. Proposals to authorize the legislative veto by amending state constitutions were rejected by some voters but approved by others. Even in states where the legislative veto had been upheld, state legislatures relied less on the legislative veto and turned to other methods of controlling administrative agencies. Some states have created advisory committees to review agency regulations. If these committees cannot persuade the agency to alter or rescind the regulation, they may introduce legislation to compel action. Other states have placed greater responsibility on the governor for supervising agency regulations, requiring the governor to either sign them to become effective or veto them.

## BIBLIOGRAPHY

### Veto Critiques

An early, prominent critique of the legislative veto is HAROLD H. BRUFF and ERNEST GELLHORN, "Congressional Control of Administrative Regulation: A Study of Legislative Vetoes," *Harvard Law Review* 90 (1977): 1369. Other influential critiques were done by ROBERT G. DIXON, JR., "The Congressional Veto and Separation of Powers: The Executive on a Leash?" *North Carolina Law Review* 56 (1978): 423 and H. LEE WATSON, "Congress Steps Out: A Look at Congressional Control of the Executive," *California Law Review* 63 (1975): 983.

More sympathetic to the origin and purpose of the legislative veto are studies by HARVEY C. MANSFIELD, "The Legislative Veto and the Deportation of Aliens," *Public Administration Review* 1 (1941), JOSEPH and ANN COOPER, "The Legislative Veto and the Constitution," *George Washington Law Review* 30 (1962): 467, and LOUIS FISHER, "A Political Context for Legislative Vetoes," *Political Science Quarterly* 93:2 (Summer 1978).

BARBARA HINKSON CRAIG, *Chadha: The Story of an Epic Constitutional Struggle* (New York, 1988), describes the personalities and issues behind this court case. "Controversy over the Legislative Veto," *Congressional Digest,* (December 1983), covers the dispute using a pro-and-con analysis. E. DONALD ELLIOTT, "*INS* v. *Chadha:* The Administrative Constitution, the Constitution, and the Legislative Veto," *Supreme Court Review* (1983): 125, provides a sophisticated examination of the Court's decision within the framework of the administrative state of the twentieth century. Other close analyses are PETER L. STRAUSS, "Was There a Baby in the Bathwater? A Comment on the Supreme Court's Legislative Veto Decision," *Duke Law Journal* (1983): 748; and LAURENCE H. TRIBE, "The Legislative Veto Decision: A Law by Any Other Name?" *Harvard Journal on Legislation* 21 (1984): 1.

### The Chadha Decision

The effect of *Chadha* on the War Powers Resolution is treated in G. SIDNEY BUCHANAN, "In Defense of the War Powers Resolution: *Chadha* Does Not Apply," *Houston Law Review* 22 (1985): 1155. Whereas Buchanan sees no application, the contrary point is made in DANIEL E. LUNGREN and MARK L. KROTOSKI, "The War Powers Resolution After the *Chadha* Decision," *Loyola of Los Angeles Law Review* 17 (1984): 767.

The survival of the legislative veto after *Chadha* is explored by LOUIS FISHER, "Judicial Misjudgments About the Lawmaking Process: The Legislative Veto Case," *Public Administration Review* 45 (Special Issue, November 1985). See also FREDERICK M. KAISER, "Congressional Control of Executive Actions in the Aftermath of the *Chadha* Decision," *Administrative Law Review* 36 (1984), and DANIEL PAUL FRANKLIN, "Why the Legislative Veto Isn't Dead," *Presidential Studies Quarterly* 16:3 (Summer 1986). Articles supportive of the legislative veto include WILLIAM WEST and JOSEPH COOPER, "The Congressional Veto and Administrative Rulemaking," *Political Science Quarterly* 98:2 (Summer 1983), and JOSEPH COOPER and PATRICIA A. HURLEY, "The Legislative Veto: A Policy Analysis," *Congress & the Presidency* 10:1 (Spring 1983).

### State-Level Veto Studies

For studies on the legislative veto at the state level, see STEPHEN F. JOHNSON, "The Legislative Veto in the States," *State Government* 56 (1983); and H. HAROLD LEVINSON, "Legislative and Executive Veto of Rules of Administrative Agencies: Models and Alternatives," *William and Mary Law Review* 24 (Fall 1982), and "The Decline of the Legislative Veto: Federal/State Comparisons and Interactions," *Journal of Federalism* 17 (Winter 1987).

SEE ALSO Congress, the Executive, and Foreign Policy; Congress, the Executive, and War Powers; Legislative-Executive Relations; AND Legislatures and the Judiciary.

# MEDIA COVERAGE OF LEGISLATURES

## *Donald A. Ritchie*

Despite recurring clashes with the press, American legislatures have customarily been open and hospitable to media coverage. Legislative bodies at national as well as state levels generate and consume vast amounts of news. Legislators expect newspaper and broadcast journalism to keep their names and endeavors before their constituents, as a means both of arousing public opinion on behalf of their legislation and of improving their chances of reelection. In the wake of the American Revolution, it was for such reasons, and the belief that citizens of a republic need to know what their representatives were saying and doing in their name, that state legislatures admitted journalists to their proceedings. Similarly, the United States Congress made accommodations available for reporters long before the White House did so.

Legislative bodies are more divided in opinion than their counterpart executive branches, which tend to try to speak in a single voice. Consequently, although legislatures regularly offer dramatic and newsworthy contests, it is more difficult for journalists to portray them as institutions than executive branches as such. A president or governor personifies an entire executive branch, whereas a legislative branch is usually a mass of discordant parts. Executives generally prefer to release news only after policies have been set and major decisions reached; legislatures, on the other hand, typically open almost all of their lengthy and convoluted lawmaking process to coverage. Despite this openness, though, the media often neglect the day-to-day processes of legislative drafting, negotiation, and consensus-building. With few exceptions, the print media tend to cover the personalities, politics, and last-minute dramatics—a form of distortion that television news often magnifies.

Although investigative reporting has on occasion destroyed legislative careers, relations between legislators and reporters have been more "symbiotic" than adversarial. In the late eighteenth and nineteenth centuries, journalists readily accepted patronage from legislatures, and in return provided highly partisan coverage. In the twentieth century, after changing economic circumstances and ethical standards made the press less dependent on politicians, the relationship grew more subtle and complex. Reporters came to depend upon legislators and their staffs for much of the information they gathered—information about not only legislation but also the inner workings of the executive branch. On the one hand, this dependency of the press has sometimes worked to mute criticism and allow politicians to shape news reporting; on the other, though, reporters have also exerted considerable influence over legislative agendas through the stories they choose to follow and the issues they champion.

## COLONIAL LEGISLATURES

Secrecy prevailed in the legislatures of colonial America. Most legislatures conducted their debates behind closed doors and released information only after editing it for publication. News of the New York Assembly, for instance, could be published only with the approval of the Speaker. Colonial legislatures granted newspapers permission to publish the laws and reports of their debate "by authority"—meaning they were licensed, and could be fined for publishing without legislative authority. For the most part, as far as strife with royal governers was concerned, legislators enjoyed support from colonial newspapers. Despite this sympathy, legislators showed little tolerance of press criticism or unauthorized publication of their own proceedings. While colonial juries tended to acquit printers of libel, colonial legislatures frequently sought to discipline vexatious printers.

British common law offered no guaranteed right to publish the remarks of public officials. Until 1771, the British House of Commons imprisoned those printers who dared to publish its proceedings. In British North America, legislatures took similar action against newspaper violations of their "parliamentary privilege." Colonial legislatures broadly interpreted any criticism of themselves, either collectively or individually, as seditious libel. Repeatedly, colonial legislatures summoned printers to their chambers to answer questions about allegedly libelous publications, and defiant journalists were sometimes jailed for contempt or for breach of legislative privilege. As late as 1774, the upper house of the South Carolina legislature incarcerated a printer for publishing an accurate but unauthorized account of its proceedings.

The larger conflict between the colonies and Great Britain eventually overshadowed the conflicts between the legislatures and the press. Legislators recognized the useful role that newspapers played in rallying public support, and in serving as a check on the abuse of government power. The exposé had become a staple of American newspapers, with royal governors as their most frequent targets. Yet none of the new state governments abandoned the old common laws on criminal defamation or seditious libel that jeopardized printers; part and parcel with this was the state legislatures' continued censure of newspapers for printing "scandalous" accounts of their proceedings. Printers, though, began to call for the lifting of restrictions on a free press and demanded the right to publish without fear of censorship or reprisal.

## FIRST NATIONAL LEGISLATURE

The Continental Congress conducted its proceedings in secret throughout the revolutionary war, having resolved that "the doors be kept shut during the time of business, and that the members consider themselves under the strongest obligations of honor, to keep the proceedings secret, until a majority shall direct them to be made public" (*Journals of the Continental Congress,* vol. 1, p. 10). As if to demonstrate its resolve, the Congress fired Tom Paine as secretary to the committee on foreign affairs after he confessed to leaking reports to a newspaper that France was providing clandestine aid to the American cause in advance of a formal alliance. However, the Continental Congress cited freedom of the press as its reason for not acting against newspapers that had violated congressional privileges.

Americans showed an ambiguous attitude toward newspapers during the Revolution. Patriots championed freedom of the press so long as the press supported their cause, but they censured, mobbed, and tarred and feathered those printers who did not. As newspapers gradually became the voices of the newly developing factions and parties, various members of the state legislatures, the Continental Congress, and the Constitutional Convention used newspapers to broadcast their views and attack their opponents, usually writing under pseudonyms taken from classical Greece and Rome. (Press anonymity continued well into the nineteenth century; journalists generally adopted pen names, for protection both from libel suits and from physical retribution.) Political factions found it advantageous to sponsor newspapers in which they could write and which would promote their views. They supported these papers with patronage, and shielded them from political persecution. Over time, the freedom of the press to criticize the government was written into many state constitutions, and it was added as the First Amendment to the Federal Constitution in 1791.

## EARLY CONGRESS AND STATE LEGISLATURES

After the Revolution, secrecy remained an option for legislative bodies; only two state constitutions mandated that legislative doors be opened to the public. The Constitutional Convention itself met in secret, and required only that the new federal Congress keep records in the form of minutes and publish them "from time to time." The United States Senate chose to conduct its debates behind closed doors, but a major breakthrough occurred when the House of Representatives threw open its doors to the public and press in 1789. "Making the debates public will establish the National Government or break the Confederation," Vice President John Adams commented privately. "I can conceive of no medium between these extremes" (Ritchie, p. 8).

When Congress met in New York and Philadelphia, local newspapers hired stenographers to report on the proceedings of the House of Representatives. Their first reports were generally abbreviated and occasionally inaccurate. Representative James Madison (D./R.-Va.) grumbled that one of these reporters "sometimes filled up blanks in his notes from memory or *imagination*." Meanwhile, Philip Freneau, editor of the *National Gazette,* led a crusade to open Senate proceedings to public scrutiny. The Federalist members generally preferred closed sessions, while the Jeffersonian Republicans argued for public accountability. In 1794, when Federalist senators challenged the seating of Albert Gallatin (D./R.-Pa.), they temporarily admitted the public and press to avoid the appearance of a "Star Chamber" proceeding. Bowing to the inevitable, the Senate ordered construction of a public gallery. Once inside, however, newspapers found the Senate's decorous proceedings far less engaging than the boisterous House, to which they continued to devote the greatest share of their attention and column space.

Even after the Senate opened all of its legislative sessions in 1795, executive sessions (dealing with treaties and nominations) remained closed until the twentieth century. Throughout the nineteenth century, the press regularly penetrated the secrecy of the executive sessions to publish full accounts of many debates and votes. On numerous occasions the Senate sought unsuccessfully to plug leaks and to discover which members were divulging confidential information until 1929, when it finally abandoned the practice of closed-door debates in all but a few rare instances where it discussed information that might affect national security.

## REPORTERS AND CORRESPONDENTS

When Congress moved to the newly created District of Columbia in 1800, Samuel Harrison Smith, publisher of the *National Intelligencer,* assumed the chores of reporting Senate and House debates. Smith's paper served as the "official organ" of the Jefferson administration, and the Republican majorities in Congress granted floor privileges to Smith and later to his successors, Joseph Gales and William Seaton, as quasi-official reporters. Gales and Seaton recorded the debates themselves and hired additional stenographers, publishing the proceedings in the *National Intelligencer.* Federal law permitted them to mail the paper postage-free to other newspapers, which in turn edited and reprinted excerpts from the debates. Starting in 1825, Gales and Seaton also published their reports in the *Register of Debates,* a forerunner of the *Congressional Record.*

The *National Intelligencer* enjoyed a relative monopoly on congressional reporting until the 1820s, when such sectionally divisive issues as tariff legislation prompted newspapers in other cities to send their own representatives to Washington to cover the news from a local or regional perspective. Working before the advent of the telegraph and train transportation, these reporters dispatched their news by mail, and became known as "letter writers" or correspondents. Soon members of Congress came to distinguish between the reporters on the floor and those in the gallery. In 1839, Senator James Buchanan (D.-Pa.) defined reporters of debate as those "who gave a faithful historical account of the proceedings of this body," and letter writers as those who gave "partial and piquant accounts of such proceedings and debates as struck their own fancy" (*Congressional Globe,* 25th Cong., 3d sess., 94).

The steadily increasing number of letter writers frequently petitioned the House and Senate for the same floor privileges as were granted to the Washington reporters. Concerned that this would disrupt the business on the floor, the Senate in 1841 reserved a press gallery exclusively for the use of reporters and correspondents (although some reporters continued to enjoy floor privileges). Located immediately above the presiding officer's chair in the chamber, the press gallery affording a panorama of the legislative debates. Senate and House press galleries still operate from that vantage point, and the lobbies behind them provide the central working quarters for congressional correspondents whenever Congress is in session.

At first, the vice president and the Speaker of the House judged reporters' credentials for admission to the press gallery. It was Vice President Millard Fillmore who admitted the first woman to the press gallery, Jane Gray Swisshelm, who reported for the *New York Tribune* during the debates over the Compromise of 1850. Later in the nineteenth century, when certain members of the press began to lobby and certain lobbyists posed as reporters, the correspondents volunteered to supervise their own galleries. In 1879 the House adopted rules that transferred press gallery accreditation to a Standing Committee of Correspondents, whose members the correspondents themselves elected; the Senate followed suit in 1884. The new rules required that to be admitted a reporter must telegraph dispatches to daily newspapers, must have no personal interest in legislation before Congress, must derive all income from reporting, and must not be employed by an executive agency. However, the rules made an exception for clerks of congressional committees, posts which many nineteenth-century correspondents held to supplement their incomes.

The rule requiring telegraph dispatches indicated how fundamentally that instrument had come to define Washington correspondence. In 1844 Samuel F. B. Morse first tested the long-distance potential of the telegraph by running wires between the Capitol building and a railroad depot in Baltimore. The wires immediately began carrying political news between those two cities. The telegraph especially benefited smaller newspapers that could not afford to hire their own correspondents to cover the state and national capitals. Previously, editors had relied on exchanges of news between papers, through which they clipped and reprinted news of the legislatures. In 1846, ten upstate New York newspapers organized the first wire service; they pooled their resources to hire a correspondent to telegraph a regular column of news from the state capital at Albany. By 1848, the major New York City papers had formed the Associated Press and sent reporters to the U.S. Capitol to telegraph daily news about the House and Senate. When the new House chamber was constructed in the 1850s, the House made provision for a spacious press gallery equipped with a telegraph office. "By this means," a House committee predicted, "the report of an hour's speech might be completely set up in New York within fifteen minutes of its delivery" (*Congressional Globe*, 35th Cong., 1st sess., 32).

By the mid-nineteenth century, newspapers began freeing themselves from party control. Prior to the Civil War, political patronage underwrote newspapers on both state and national levels. Legislatures paid newspapers to print state laws and elected journalists as their official printers. Editors as prominent as Gales and Seaton, Francis P. Blair, Duff Green, and John W. Forney battled to make their papers "official organs" and thereby to collect government largess. Newspaper editors and reporters went on legislative payrolls as clerks, postmasters, librarians, and messengers. Since newspapers generally paid legislative correspondents only for the months that the legislature met—less than half the year—the correspondents augmented their incomes by clerking for legislative committees or serving as members' secretaries, all while they filed their dispatches.

In the late nineteenth century, however, increased advertising revenues enabled newspapers to free themselves from dependence on various political parties, and eventually to pay annual salaries that freed their correspondents from political moonlighting. The telegraph further contributed to the movement toward more objective reporting. During the Civil War, the Associated Press's Washington correspondent, Lawrence Gobright, experienced far less trouble with the government's telegraph censors than did many other reporters. Since his news went to papers of all different editorial hues, he avoided partisan commentary and aimed for impartiality. "My despatches are merely dry matters of fact and detail," he explained (U.S. Congress, Judiciary Committee, *Telegraph Censorship*, H. Rept. 64, 1862, 3).

After the Civil War, the press exposed a succession of embarrassing congressional scandals, causing reporters and members of Congress to adopt, in the words of one correspondent, a "warlike attitude" toward each other. Further friction mounted when the press leaked sensational information from the secret sessions of the Senate. In 1848 and again in

1871 the Senate held newspaper reporters as prisoners in Capitol committee rooms in unsuccessful attempts to force them to divulge how they obtained still-secret texts of treaties. In each case the reporters were eventually released without having revealed their sources. "The truth is," Senator Henry Wilson (R.-Mass.) pointed out to the Senate during one such investigation, "we have talked too much; we have not learned to close our own lips. . . . These gentlemen of the press know everything that is going on quite as well as we do" (*Congressional Globe,* 42d Cong., sp. sess., 867). It was largely to improve relations between legislators and the press that reporters established the above-mentioned Standing Committee of Correspondents and founded the Gridiron Club, which provided an opportunity for reporters and politicians to mingle socially. "The invitations of this club to the highest in power and influence are seldom declined," noted correspondent Henry Boynton, one of its founders. "This has brought about social relations which are of mutual benefit to each of these influential parties in public affairs" (Henry V. Boynton, "The Press and the Public Man," *Century Magazine* 42 [October 1891]: 855).

These comfortable working arrangements between Washington newspaper correspondents and members of Congress were again disrupted, during the first decade of the twentieth century—this time by muckraking magazine exposés. Correspondents depended upon congressional sources for reliable information, and in return, they offered favorable publicity by the proliferating muckraking magazines. Magazine writers, by contrast, had no need to cultivate regular sources in the legislature and could therefore raise new questions about legislators' behavior. Muckrakers such as David Graham Phillips portrayed Congress as the corrupt tool of corporate interests. Phillips's lurid series, "The Treason of the Senate," appeared in nine monthly installments in *Cosmopolitan* magazine during 1906, contributing to the movement toward direct election of senators, as well as to a more skeptical and critical treatment of Congress in the newspaper press. One newspaper correspondent pledged that the press gallery would serve as a "people's lobby," to weigh, doubt, scrutinize, and suspect every congressional action.

## PRESS COVERAGE OF CONGRESS AND THE PRESIDENCY

Throughout the twentieth century, press coverage in Washington has shifted away from Congress and toward the presidency. By observing Theodore Roosevelt and Woodrow Wilson, Washington correspondent Richard Oulahan noted how easily the public could visualize the president, while Congress as a body presented "no identifying human characteristics" to incite affection or admiration. Theodore Roosevelt was the first to perceive the advantages of a colorful presidential personality over the "aggregation of humanity" in Congress, and he encouraged the press to create a climate of public opinion that would force Congress to follow.

Editorial cartoonists, too, found presidential likenesses easier to capture. Nineteenth-century cartoonists such as Thomas Nast and Joseph Keppler filled many of their cartoons with prominent senators and representatives—often assuming that a literate public would recognize these legislators without identifying labels. More flamboyant members, like Roscoe Conkling (R.-N.Y.) with his "turkey-gobbler strut" and "Hyperion curl," made themselves irresistible targets, as did those like Charles Sumner (R.-Mass.), whose pomposity lent itself to caricature. The most consistent attention to Congress and its members appeared in the cartoons of Clifford Berryman and his son Jim, whose realistic, and generally sympathetic likenesses of senators and representatives appeared on the front page and editorial pages of the Washington *Evening Star* from the first years of this century through the 1960s. More critical congressional images by Herbert L. Block (Herblock) became a similarly long-running feature of the *Washington Post.* For the most part, though, presidential politics predominated in editorial cartoons. Cartoonists seized upon presidential emblems from Theodore Roosevelt's "big stick" to Franklin Roosevelt's cigarette holder, while they too often resorted to depicting Congress through some variation on the Capitol dome or a generic legislator attired in frock coat and string tie.

The trend toward presidential dominance of the news accelerated with the election of Franklin Roosevelt in 1932 and the emergence of national radio broadcasting. The media devoted even more attention to presidential actions and even less to legislative developments. Yet paradoxically, as Congress declined as a subject of news, it remained a chief source of news in Washington. Reporters can often learn more about activities inside the executive branch from their sources on Capitol Hill than from within the White House itself. Members of Congress often reveal what they discussed at White House meetings, and the members and staff of congressional committees alert the press about executive-branch activities they intend to investigate and defend presidents who belong to their respective party.

Members' press relations grew more sophisticated when they began to hire former journalists to handle their media relations and work to shape their press coverage. Press secretaries have worked to make their members accessible and quotable; competing for media attention for their employers against some five hundred other members of Congress, they seek to anticipate what reporters will want. They issue press releases, schedule press conferences, and arrange television appearances with the aim of producing news stories and favorable public impressions. A press secretary stands as guardian of his or her employer's credibility with reporters, and their success requires that the two work in close concert. However, the expansion of the congressional staff has increasingly pitted press secretaries against those other staff members who, when it comes to matters of their own legislative specialization, prefer to deal directly with the press.

Each legislator's office provides a steady flow of news releases and inside information, especially to the "regional" reporters who cover their respective state. Members of Congress value a front-page story in their home state or district newspapers as much if not more than a notice in the *New York Times* or *Washington Post*. Although always appreciative of national news coverage, which contributes toward greater visibility and influence in Washington, members find that local coverage counts more toward reelection. Most regional reporters work for news services or newspaper syndicates. Although regional reporting has a fairly low status among Washington correspondents, it nevertheless accounts for some two-

thirds of the reporters on Capitol Hill. The increase in regional reporting helped incumbent members, correspondent David Broder has argued, because the "regionals" tried hard to stay on "the good side" of the members they covered: "They have no better clearinghouse or source of information than the Congressional office."

In his 1937 study *The Washington Correspondent,* sociologist Leo Rosten found that despite the immense growth of the executive branch during the New Deal, Congress remained the primary source for most correspondents' reporting. Close alliances with influential legislators allowed reporters to delve more deeply into stories than official agency press releases would otherwise permit. Senate Finance Committee chairman Pat Harrison (D.-Miss.), as just one example, provided a regular source of news about the Roosevelt administration to the *New York Times*'s Mississippi-born correspondent Turner Catledge—much to the chagrin of President Roosevelt, who frequently voiced his displeasure. Alternatively, members of Congress have floated trial balloons to the press for the administration; just as often, though, they have leaked information so as to scuttle presidential initiatives they did not want to oppose openly.

Legislators' efforts to ingratiate themselves with the press took on ominous dimensions during the anticommunist furor that followed World War II. Senator Joseph R. McCarthy (R.-Wis.) proved exceptionally adroit in manipulating the press by leaking information to cooperative journalists, exploiting the competition between the wire services, and by taking advantage of reporters' "objectivity"—the problematic ideal that requires journalists to report what authority figures say, without interjecting personal opinions as to the merits of what is said. Initially during McCarthy's rampage, newspapers devoted banner headlines to his accusations without pressing for substantiation or giving equal attention to the protests of the accused, thereby uncritically and unfairly destroying reputations and careers. Eventually, when reporters and columnists began to collect information rebutting many of the senator's sensational charges, his credibility among both the press and the public slowly eroded. Although he befriended many reporters, Senator

McCarthy attempted to intimidate those he could not persuade, most notably executives in the emerging television news business. Ironically, television ultimately contributed to McCarthy's downfall by broadcasting the Army-McCarthy hearings in 1954, which exposed his brutality before a national audience.

## DIFFERENCES IN REPORTING ON STATE AND NATIONAL LEGISLATURES

Just as many members of Congress previously served in their state legislatures, many legislative correspondents began their careers at a state capital before being transferred to Washington. Although able to build on their state-level experiences, these journalists have encountered unanticipated differences in reporting on the national legislature.

In February 1892, when an anonymous *New York Times* correspondent moved from covering the state legislature at Albany to the Congress in Washington, he noted that his working environment changed substantially. "To the newspaper man accustomed to the methods that obtain in Albany in legislative sessions," the reporter wrote, "there comes a decidedly lonesome feeling when he first essays the task of keeping track of the doing of Congress." In Albany, a legislative reporter could gain easy entrance to the legislative chambers, sit among the lawmakers on the floor, and question them on the business of the day: "He has most of the rights accorded to members, except those of addressing the House or Senate, or wielding the gavel, or drawing pay from the public Treasury." At Albany, committee rooms were usually open to the press, and even after executive sessions a reporter had no trouble learning what had transpired. "When he retires at night he is reasonably sure that all the news and gossip of the day has been caught in his nut." In Washington, by contrast, the reporter was banished to the galleries, denied floor privileges, and was kept at length from imperious members.

During the 1930s, reporter Griffing Bancroft made a similar move from covering the California legislature to covering Congress. In Sacramento, he had been the sole representative of a wire service, the International News Service, so he covered both houses of the legislature, the governor's press conferences, and all other state functions. As a Washington reporter, though, he found that "you get into a little cubbyhole and cover just one small part. That's the essential difference." Early in his assignment to report on the House of Representatives, Bancroft was teamed with a veteran Senate reporter to cover a joint session; when the newcomer raised some questions about House operations, the Senate reporter replied, "You know more about the House than I do." (Griffing Bancroft, interview by Ritchie, 1990), p. 3). Bancroft came to doubt whether Senate reporters even knew the House existed.

Even in 1990, when the *Tulsa World* sent Jim Myers to report on Congress after covering the Oklahoma state legislature, these contrasts were still evident. He observed that, on one level, House and Senate members in the Oklahoma legislature adopted patterns of behavior that mirrored the two bodies in Congress; House members at both levels were more blunt and their proceedings more chaotic than the tempered, polite behavior of senators. And, not surprisingly, he found state legislators more accessible. In Washington, a reporter had to deal more with the staff who formed protective layers around senators, and to a lesser degree around representatives.

The different atmospheres of the state and national legislature grew more noticeable after World War II, when Congress shifted to year-long sessions while state legislatures continued to meet for a few months, sometimes only every other year. For legislative sessions of limited duration, legislators and reporters were mere transient visitors to the capital, living bachelor lives in hotels and fraternizing after hours. An intimacy developed that led some state legislative reporters to become participants in the political process, rather than mere observers of it, by offering advice to members and helping them to steer legislation to passage. Moreover, statehouse reporters often held their assignments for their entire careers, for their editors reasoned that only a seasoned reporter could follow the arcane practices of a state legislature. This longevity further fostered familiarity. A common result was that reporters ignored and excused legislators' questionable behavior. "When you know the system too well, you're no longer shocked by things," one state capital reporter commented. "You're anesthetized and numbed to things that go on, and so you overlook them sometimes" (Gurwitt, p. 30).

However, in the wake of the publicity and tightened ethical standards that emerged during the Watergate scandal of the early 1970s, the press and the state legislators grew mutually wary of each other and more distant. The trend toward lengthier legislative sessions dissolved the prior hotel-living camaraderie, as reporters and legislators rented apartments, brought their families with them, and settled into the capital for a protracted residence. In addition, the presence of women legislators and reporters further eroded the "old-boy" fraternal atmosphere of the state capitals. Nevertheless, statehouse reporting conditions will likely remain more open and informal than Washington correspondence.

## EVOLUTION OF THE LEGISLATIVE PRESS CORPS

While the press corps at most state capitals has remained relatively stable in number, the Washington press corps multiplied steadily throughout the twentieth century. Among the most notable changes in this respect has been the growing number of women reporters. Of 167 correspondents accredited to the congressional press galleries in 1879, twenty were women; most of them wrote social news and personality sketches of members, which they mailed to their papers. When the new press gallery rules went into effect in 1880, they initially left no women in the press galleries, since none of the women journalists filed daily dispatches by telegraph. Editors would not pay telegraphic tolls for social news, nor would they assign women to cover political news, because they believed, as one editor put it, "their sex prevents them from gathering in hotels, clubs, cafés and places of like character, where men find it convenient to sit and discuss all sorts of topics" (Ritchie, *Press Gallery,* p. 52).

After 1880, occasionally a woman qualified for press gallery accreditation, but few remained for long. By the 1920s, though, women reporters had become more conspicuous in Washington, but few received political assignments. Not until World War II, when many of the men in the press galleries went overseas as war correspondents, did newspapers begin to hire women to cover political news from Congress. With the end of the war, some women were displaced from these jobs, but others continued, and their numbers grew in the postwar years. During the 1980s, women reporters' membership in the congressional press galleries jumped from slightly less than one quarter to more than one third of the total five thousand accredited journalists; broadcast media reporters, the most visible of these positions, accounted for the largest share of the women's gains.

The Senate and House press galleries were integrated by race more slowly than by gender. In the 1870s, Frederick Douglass and his sons received accreditation to the press galleries for their Washington-based paper, the *New National Era.* After the paper folded in 1874, however, no African American reporters occupied the press galleries until 1947. The white press hired no black reporters, and the black press, which sought to cover Washington "from the Negro viewpoint,"* consisted almost entirely of weekly papers—so black reporters could not meet the press gallery requirement of filing daily telegraph dispatches. The question wasn't purely procedural, though; even after World War II, when reporters from the black-owned *Atlanta Daily World* filed for accreditation, the Standing Committee of Correspondents delayed action until the Senate Rules Committee ordered them to admit a black reporter. For decades, black reporters remained noticeably underrepresented on Capitol Hill: by the 1980s, African Americans constituted only 5 percent of reporters in Congress, with the largest share in radio and television. The number of Latino reporters similarly lagged behind. In a 1988 survey, Stephen Hess described the average Washington regional reporter as a middle-aged white male, from the Middle West, with a degree in journalism from a good university.

In other respects, the twentieth century saw decidedly more progress toward openness in congressional proceedings. In 1911, Sena-

---

*Charles Barnett to Ulrie Bell, 15 January 1942, *From a Negro Viewpoint,* Barnett Papers, Chicago Historical Society.

tor Robert La Follette, Sr., invited the press to witness a conference committee meeting on the tariff, the first open conference since 1789. However, conference committee doors immediately closed again, and they remained so until the enactment of "sunshine" legislation in the 1970s, which required Congress to conduct most of its business in public. The reforms also changed floor procedures to create a more public record of the votes that members cast, and they opened to the press both conference committee meetings and the "mark-up" sessions of the various standing committees. Where 40 percent of all congressional committee meetings had been closed to the press during the previous decade, open hearings were the rule and closed ones, the exception. Although the press had lobbied for such reforms, reporters did not always take full advantage when they were enacted; thus, when certain committees began to close controversial mark-up sessions, there were few protests from the press. Nor were there many protests from members of Congress, for many had grown impatient with the sunshine laws, finding that their colleagues made more speeches for home consumption and avoided tough decisions in open sessions. Senator Lawton Chiles (D.-Fla.) noted, in a 1937 article, that a lot of reporters preferred to "just work through their sources and feel like open meetings just open it up so everybody's got the same shot at the information." Albert Hunt, a correspondent for the *Wall Street Journal,* agreed that reporters "did better when meetings were closed because we knew the Hill, we worked it hard. . . . We got more stories."

Many reporters lack the time and inclination to sit through long and technical sessions in small, crowded rooms, so they rely instead on wire services to cover the general substance of most hearings. In the case of closed hearings, though, reporters typically turn to their inside sources to summarize the substance of a meeting. During the 1980s, when such committees as the House Ways and Means Committee once again began to close more executive hearings, few journalists complained.

The press also came to rely on congressional leadership for assistance in evaluating the daily agenda. Each day before the Senate convenes, reporters crowd around the majority and minority leaders on the floor for a briefing on the expected business of the day. This period gives the leadership an opportunity to "float" news items that would promote their party's programs. When the session convenes, the reporters return to the press gallery. In the House, the Speaker meets with the press in his office before the day's session. The minority leadership holds separate briefings for the press.

## RADIO AND TELEVISION

Radio reporters appeared on Capitol Hill as early as 1923, when they broadcast the opening of the Sixty-eighth Congress and President Calvin Coolidge's State of the Union message. However, through the 1920s and 1930s, radio reporters could be admitted to the press gallery only if they reported for a daily newspaper as well. After a campaign led by radio commentator Fulton Lewis, Jr., Congress established separate radio galleries in the House and Senate in 1939; Lewis himself was elected the first president of the Radio Correspondents Association. Thereafter, the U.S. Congress alone among the world's national legislatures divided its press galleries between print and broadcast media. Radio broadcasting was prohibited in the Senate and House chambers, so radio reporters got their news by cornering members of Congress in the corridors and having them repeat portions of their floor speeches on tape.

Congress did not warmly welcome the broadcast media. At first, members did not bother to send news releases to the radio gallery, and radio reporters had to fight the newspaper reporters for seats to cover committee hearings. The first live radio broadcast from the radio gallery came the day after President Franklin Roosevelt's death. After World War II, Congress installed soundproof booths near its chamber for on-the-spot reporting, which facilitated the next live broadcasts, which followed the end of the war.

Radio eased the way for the new medium of television, which broadcasted President Truman's State of the Union message in 1947. Initially, television coverage of House and Senate committee hearings proved controversial, especially when the House Un-American Activities Committee opened its hearings to cameras.

In 1953, Speaker Sam Rayburn banned television from House committees for the remainder of his long tenure. Although the "Rayburn rule" blacked out House committee hearings, television cameras nevertheless became a standard component of Senate hearings, particularly those of major investigations. During the Senate's investigation of organized crime in 1950, witness Frank Costello objected to television coverage of his testimony, and Chairman Estes Kefauver (D.-Tenn.) ordered the cameras turned away from the witness's face; they focused instead on Costello's hands, which he wrung nervously throughout his testimony, creating a memorable image. Television also captured a national audience for the Army-McCarthy hearings in 1954, as well as for the special investigation of the Teamsters Union and labor racketeering in the late 1950s, hearings which first brought to national prominence Senators John F. Kennedy (D.-Mass.) and Barry Goldwater (R.-Ariz).

When the new Senate office building opened in 1958, its committee rooms were specifically designed for television broadcasting. Senators and witnesses no longer sat around the same table; instead, senators sat at a raised circular dais with witnesses facing them many feet away. Legislators attempted to master and manipulate the new media in various ways. In the 1950s, for example, Senator Karl Mundt (R.-S.Dak.) appeared in "Your Washington and You on the Air," for broadcast in his home state. The show featured the senator answering questions posed by a "Washington correspondent" who, in reality, was a Senate Recording Studio employee.

Although the Capitol quickly became a familiar backdrop for nightly news broadcasts, after CBS correspondent Roger Mudd broadcast the first television reports from the Capitol steps during the 1964 Civil Rights Act debates, cameras remained prohibited from both chambers and from House committee hearings. Live coverage of Senate committee hearings remained a rarity, and in 1966 CBS news executive Fred Friendly resigned when his network, for marketing reasons, declined to broadcast live the Senate Foreign Relations Committee's hearings on the Vietnam War. This changed drastically in 1974, though, when live broadcasts of the Senate Watergate Committee and of the House Judiciary Committee's impeachment proceedings riveted a national audience. Not only did the extended televised coverage of the hearings erode public support for the Nixon administration and pave the way for the president's resignation, but they contributed to a sharp rise in Congress's approval level in public opinion polls. These factors helped break down congressional resistance to live broadcasts of House and Senate floor proceedings. Radio broadcasts of Senate debates were permitted in 1978 during deliberations over the Panama Canal treaties. Some newspapers speculated that radio coverage prolonged the debate because each side wanted as many members as possible to argue their case before the "unprecedented audience."

The House eventually approved regular televising of its chamber proceedings in 1979, and the Senate followed in 1986. Congressional employees operated the cameras and provided tape for the broadcast networks in general, and in particular for C-SPAN (Cable Satellite Public Affairs Network), which began broadcasting gavel-to-gavel proceedings of the House and Senate, along with with numerous committee hearings and press conferences. The Senate and House chambers were redecorated to improve their television appearances. Representative John Anderson (R.-Ill.) dismissed televised proceedings as "one more incumbent protection device at taxpayer's expense," but the experiment nevertheless proved popular with members as well as with television viewers.

In the House, where tight time restrictions have prohibited lengthy speeches, the one-minute addresses that members make during "morning business" were a perfect length for television consumption. The House also provided for "special orders," which allotted time to a few members to speak before an entirely empty chamber, for the benefit of home viewers. Special orders were quickly embraced by members who otherwise had little control over regular floor debates. At first, the cameras showed only the speakers during the special orders, but on one occasion, Republican speakers so irked Speaker Thomas P. "Tip" O'Neill (D.-Mass.), that he ordered the cameras to show the empty chamber to television viewers, and that practice has continued.

State legislative proceedings are covered only by local television. Outside of closed-circuit television, no networks provide gavel-to-gavel coverage of the state legislatures; instead, daily coverage has taken the form of edited programs showing excerpts from floor proceedings and committee hearings, often on public-access channels. The Florida legislature, for example, funds a "Today in the Legislature" program for one hour each evening on public television, which draws a small but ardent audience; many other state legislatures are featured on weekly programs. Unlike the tightly controlled camera work in the Congress, the media operate the cameras in each state legislature, under whatever specific rules the legislature has determined. Observers have credited television coverage with improving the attendance, attentiveness, and appearance of state legislators, but fault it for encouraging members to grandstand.

As a dynamic, visual medium, television has significantly affected the legislative bodies that it covers. Candidates now campaign for office via television news and advertisements, and telegenic qualities have became one of the criteria for choosing party leadership. However, some legislators object to the constraints that television imposes upon them. Representative Lee Hamilton (D.-Ind.) has called television unfair to serious members of Congress, who might work for months on a complex bill only to have television reporters ask them to sum up their case "in 20 seconds or less," forcing them to resort to catchy metaphors, sound bites, and visual aids rather than a thorough discussion of the issues. "Politicians must play the game by the rules of television," Hamilton complained, "so they cannot delve into the subtleties and nuances of issues" (Ritchie, *Press Gallery,* p. 226). Political scientists have also noted the broadcast media's uneven legislative coverage, particularly of committee hearings in which celebrity witnesses (such as film stars) often distract television attention from more substantive deliberations.

Senator J. William Fulbright (D.-Ark.) was vexed whenever the media declined to cover what he considered important hearings of the Senate Foreign Relations Committee, or reported only fragments of the testimony. "If you can produce something colorful, scandalous, turn it into a confrontation with an administration official, then you have a chance with the media," he complained. "But if you try to interest them in an idea, a thoughtfully expressed viewpoint, a reasonable rebuttal to a highly controversial presidential speech, nothing comes of it" (J. William Fulbright, *The Price of Empire* [New York, 1989], p. 97).

On the other hand, television reporters who cover Congress complain about the lack of lively film footage that causes editors to cut their congressional stories. Before cameras were permitted in the chambers, the networks employed artists to sketch members debating, a technique that video clips eventually replaced. Yet even after television cameras were installed, network attention to Congress continued to shrink. Surveys conducted in 1975 and 1985 revealed a progressive decline in the amount of networks' congressional coverage. This shift was part of the networks' general effort to de-emphasize Washington in favor of more community-based news, although television news continued to devote extensive attention to the presidency even as it shifted away from the capital to the countryside. One exception to this trend was cable news broadcasting, which made prominent use of videotaped floor proceedings and committee hearings to fill its twenty-four-hour schedule.

Political parties have also hired their own camera crews to cover hearings and to provide members of Congress with edited tapes for satellite transmission for local news programs in their home states. In a sample month in 1990, for example, Democratic television crews filmed twenty-five Senate hearings and Republican crews twenty hearings, in contrast to fifteen hearings covered by cable news, fourteen by C-SPAN, and less than ten by the three major network news programs collectively.

## CONCLUSION

Legislators recognize that their political influence, impact, and longevity generally require getting their message across in the media. As a result, they assiduously compete with each other for press attention, hire press secretaries, issue news releases, hold press conferences, and otherwise make themselves available to the media—even as they regularly criticize their press coverage as negative and unbalanced. Legislators worry that negative reporting evokes cynicism and skepticism about government effectiveness, and that it erodes public confidence in the legislative process. However, the high rate of reelection of incumbents suggests that they overestimate the negative aspects of press coverage.

Legislative reporters, for their part, celebrate the passing of the "sycophantic relationships" that once characterized relations between the press and the legislators. However, they also note some new problems with legislative coverage. Congress, like the state legislatures, has become less of an exclusive assignment for issue-oriented reporters; consequently, they tend to range more broadly through government agencies rather than limit themselves to a single branch. When journalists' attention is diverted or spread too thin, many legislative hearings and debates go unreported. Congressional correspondents have also observed that many of their editors and news directors have never covered Congress and therefore do not understand how to handle legislative news. Whatever the systemic problems with this coverage, though, Congress and the state legislatures remain vital sources of news, assuring that press relations with legislatures, at both the national and state levels, will likely remain more collaborative than adversarial.

## BIBLIOGRAPHY

General historical overviews of the Congress and the media include RALPH O. BLANCHARD, ed., *Congress and the News Media* (New York, 1974); F. B. MARBUT, *News from the Capital: The Story of Washington Reporting* (Carbondale, Ill., 1971); and DONALD A. RITCHIE, *Press Gallery: Congress and the Washington Correspondents* (Cambridge, Mass., 1991). Important additional sources on the early reporting of legislatures can be found in LEONARD W. LEVY, *Emergence of a Free Press* (New York, 1985), THOMAS C. LEONARD, *The Power of the Press: The Birth of American Political Reporting* (New York, 1986), and CULVER H. SMITH, *The Press, Politics, and Patronage: The American Government's Use of Newspapers, 1789–1875* (1977).

SUSAN HEILMAN MILLER, *Reporters and Congressmen: Living in Symbiosis* (Lexington, Ky., 1978), presents a case study of the mutually beneficial relationships that develop between legislators and the press; while EDWIN R. BAYLEY, *Joe McCarthy and the Press* (New York, 1981), assesses Senator McCarthy's abuse of that relationship. DAVID S. BRODER, *Behind the Front Page: A Candid Look at How the News Is Made* (New York, 1987), offers an astute "view from Capitol Hill" of media problems in covering Congress. STEPHEN HESS, *The Washington Reporters* (Washington, D.C., 1981), and *The*

*Ultimate Insiders: U.S. Senators in the National Media* (Washington, D.C., 1986), evaluates the power, influence, and functioning of the Washington media. Other useful analyses include BILL HOGAN, "The Congressional Correspondent," CHERYL ARVIDSON, "The News Manager," and KATHERINE WINTON EVANS, "The News Maker," *Washington Journalism Review* 3:6 (June 1981), and PAUL WEST, "Competing for Coverage in Congress," *Washington Journalism Review* 8:6 (June 1986).

An informative exchange between members of Congress, correspondents, and media analysts appeared in the BIPARTISAN TASK FORCE ON ETHICS, *Hearing on Congressional Ethics and the Role of the Media,* 101st Congress, 1st sess. (20 September 1989).

### On State Legislatures

Sources on reporting are less abundant. A helpful comparison between covering nineteenth-century legislatures in Albany and in Washington appeared in the *New York Times,* February 7, 1892. Other information was drawn from my interviews with GRIFFING BANCROFT and JIM MYERS; and from ROB GURWITT, "In the Capitol Pressroom, the Old Boys Call It a Day," *Governing* 3:10 (July 1990), 27–30.

# LEGISLATURES AND THE MEDIA

## Clayton R. Koppes

In regulating the media, the American legislative system must continually reconcile two competing goals: freedom of expression in a democracy, and the maintenance of social order. The resulting conflicts have been especially acute in national-security crises and when socially stigmatized groups have been affected. For much of American history, Congress and state legislatures assumed broad authority to regulate the media, but since the 1930s, legislatures have operated in a climate that, with certain important exceptions, has sanctioned greater freedom for the media. As constitutional scholar Ronald Dworkin put it: "The United States stands alone, even among democracies, in the extraordinary degree to which its constitution protects freedom of speech and of the press" (Dworkin, "The Coming Battles over Free Speech," *New York Review of Books* 39 (11 June 1992): 55–64). Yet faced with new media technologies—film, radio, television, and cable—Congress has perpetuated a two-tier system with less restraint for the traditional print medium, and sometimes considerable regulation for electronic media.

The relationship between legislatures and the media has been affected perhaps as much as any area of American legislative history by judicial interpretations of the Constitution, especially since World War I. An understanding of legislatures and the media thus requires considerable attention to the dialogue between legislatures and the courts. This is peculiarly a national subject; state legislatures and courts, where media legislation was focused from 1809 to World War I, have regrettably attracted relatively little study.

## CONSTITUTIONAL ISSUES AND EARLY CRISES

The point of departure for defining the relationship of legislatures and the media is the First Amendment to the Constitution, adopted in 1791, which provides that "Congress shall make no law ... abridging the freedom of speech, or of the press." Nine of the original thirteen states wrote similar provisions for freedom of the press into their constitutions (though not necessarily for freedom of speech); many states admitted later followed suit. However, despite the absolutist language of the Bill of Rights and state constitutions, laws restricting the freedom of expression through the media have been a notable feature of American political life. This divergence between constitutional expression and legislative action reflected the ambiguous legacy of the colonial period.

Debate has raged over how much freedom the framers meant to give the media, which then was synonymous with the press. Historian Leonard Levy has argued that the framers "could only have meant to protect the press with which they were familiar and as it operated at the time. They constitutionally guaranteed the *practice* of freedom of the press" (p. 272). The press the framers knew was a vigorous, combative, at times irresponsible medium. It had been instrumental in the colonies' winning of independence. And the republican ideology of the late eighteenth century, heavily influenced by Radical Whig thought in England, laid great stress on the press's necessary role in informing the people and affording a check on government. Freedom of the press was thus to the framers an indispensable element in democratic government.

Yet they also had qualms about how far press freedom should go. The common law of seditious libel was well known. Notoriously difficult to define, seditious libel applied, strictly speaking, to criticism of the government, its officers, and policies; but the concept could be extended to almost any comment that tended to bring the government into disrepute. An editor who transgressed this floating boundary could be subject to criminal prosecution. The consensus of historians appears to be that the framers did not explicitly repudiate the notion of seditious libel. In that sense the press was not as free as the absolutist language of the Bill of Rights suggested. Constitutional scholar Lucas A. Powe, Jr., has concluded that while the framers favored a press that was free to criticize the government, they also believed that "there was a point at which malicious criticism of government went so far beyond the pale as to be criminally punishable" (1991, p. 50). Writing in broad strokes, they did not try to define seditious libel; that was to be worked out in the legislative and judicial arena, under the shifting influence of crisis.

The first such crisis occurred during the undeclared naval war with France in the late 1790s. In that case, as in many subsequent instances, perceptions of media accountability during a national-security crisis brought the issue of media rights to the fore. The Federalist-dominated Congress passed four Alien and Sedition Acts, thereby plunging the new republic into its first major constitutional crisis. The Sedition Act of 1798 had a direct bearing on the press, for it made it illegal for anyone to write, print, or publish "any false, scandalous and malicious writing" against the government, Congress, or president "with intent to defame . . . or to bring them . . . into contempt or disrepute; or to excite against them . . . the hatred of the good people of the United States." Virtually unlimited in scope, the Sedition Act revived the English tradition of seditious libel. Federalists argued that the First Amendment only incorporated the English common-law understanding as expounded by the influential legal commentator Sir William Blackstone—that freedom of the press meant only freedom from prior restraint (that is, government review and banning of publication). They also pointed out that the Sedition Act advanced two safeguards absent in the English tradition—truth was a defense (that is, only false statements could be prosecuted) and jury trials were assured.

Enforcement of the Sedition Act was blatantly partisan; it was used to silence critics and maintain Federalist dominance. Several prominent Republican newspapers ceased publication, two permanently. Neither the defense of truth nor jury trials protected the defendants in times of crisis.

Republicans mustered a defense that significantly furthered the legitimacy of media freedom as an arm of popular government. They argued that an unfettered press was crucial in the coalescence of opinion, and hence simply a refinement of the sovereignty of the people that was the foundation of republican government. They also distinguished between words, which were to be allowed even if inflammatory, and overt acts, which the government had the right to repress. Finally, they doubted the usefulness of "truth as a defense" in politicized matters. As Albert Gallatin, the House Republican leader, presciently queried: "And how could truth of *opinions* be proved by evidence?" (quoted in Powe, p. 61).

The Sedition Act was timed to expire along with John Adams's administration, in March 1801. But in an indication of how tenuous free-press guarantees in fact were, the triumphant Republicans, under President Thomas Jefferson, harassed Federalist editors with prosecutions for seditious libel in state courts. As partisanship dissipated and international crises subsided, the immediate controversy faded. The Sedition Act came to stand for the misuse of the seditious-libel doctrine for partisan advantage. As the episode suggested, however, periods of perceived national crisis would create the conditions in which legislatures—both state and national—would try to circumscribe media boundaries.

## SLAVERY, MORALITY, AND FREEDOM OF THE PRESS

### Abolitionist Literature

The growing national debate over slavery brought the media question to a head over a new issue: the right to disseminate printed material. President Andrew Jackson asked Congress in 1835 to give the U. S. Post Office the power to seize mail that the department considered seditious. His action was triggered by the mailing of abolitionist newspapers, notably William Lloyd Garrison's *The Liberator,* to the South. In Charleston, South Carolina, a mob burned the mailbag containing abolitionist literature. Senator John C. Calhoun argued for the bill's passage, but the Senate was swayed by the appeals of Daniel Webster and Henry Clay, among others, that the measure was unconstitutional; the following year, the Senate rejected it, twenty-nine to nineteen. Congress indirectly solidified the media's right of dissemination later that year when it imposed severe penalties for withholding delivery of mail.

In that era when federal supremacy was still the subject of debate, however, Southern legislatures contravened this putative guarantee. Beginning with Georgia in 1835, all Southern legislatures by the time of the Civil War made it a crime—in extreme cases punishable by death—to possess abolitionist literature. The press might be free to print abolitionist material in one part of the country, but that freedom was effectively nullified in another by bans on dissemination and possession. The media's right to distribute its products was a recurrent issue, especially with the rise of antivice crusades in the late nineteenth century and the development of electronic transmission in the twentieth.

Although war often provides a pretext or necessity for censorship, the media experienced relatively little interference in the North (other than on military plans) during the Civil War. (In the South the near unanimity of opinion in support of the "lost cause" made the issue moot.) In 1863 General Ambrose Burnside suppressed a Copperhead paper, the *Chicago Times,* and banned circulation of the antiwar *New York World* in areas under his control. President Abraham Lincoln, who had suspended the right of habeas corpus, nonetheless reversed Burnside's order, after much thought.

## Obscene Materials

Meanwhile the focus of attention shifted from patriotism to morality. Here too the issue of distribution was central. The Tariff Act of 1842 prohibited the importation of "all indecent and obscene prints, paintings, lithographs, engravings, and transparencies." This provision provoked little debate and no definition. The act established an important precedent that, while not directly bearing on the media, reinforced the state's power to stop distribution.

The potent combination of war fervor and moral anxiety brought an extension of this principle to the distribution of media produced at home as well as abroad. Alarmed that Union soldiers were acquiring great numbers of obscene books and pictures, postal inspectors began seizing such materials. The Postmaster General sought legislative authority for these actions, which Congress granted in 1865 with a sweeping, vaguely worded statute specifying that "no obscene book [or] pamphlet . . . shall be admitted to the mails." Out of respect for citizens' privacy, postal officials were told not to break seals but to make their decisions on a package's external appearance.

*Comstock Laws*  These early efforts at controlling the media were consolidated in the Comstock legislation of 1873 and 1876, named for Anthony Comstock, head of the New York Society for the Suppression of Vice from 1873 to 1915. In 1873 he scandalized Congress with accounts of "sexual materials" (much of it birth-control devices and abortion tools), which he claimed abetted a growing national immorality. Comstock tapped a vein of public anxiety about mounting social unrest, labor agitation, and political corruption as the nation experienced a headlong rush toward industrialization and urbanization. Congress responded by making many different objects, most with sexual implications, illegal to mail. In 1876 the law was extended to books and pictures. The Post Office hired special agents to ferret out offending materials, and Comstock took a starring role. "Comstockery" became a synonym for zealous prudery.

Although state legislatures had passed few antiobscenity measures before this time, they now actively sought to regulate the media. State versions of Comstock laws, first enacted in New York in 1873, eventually spread to every state except New Mexico. Some states tried to curb what was perceived as press licentiousness. In 1891 the Kansas legislature banned papers "devoted largely to the publication of scandals, intrigues, and immoral conduct." California required the press to obtain permission to publish pictures or caricatures of any living person, unless they were public officials or convicted criminals. After the assassination of President William McKinley by an anarchist in 1901, several legislatures imposed restrictions on anarchist newspapers. Most of these press restrictions, including the vague Kansas measure, appear to have survived such state constitutional challenges as were mounted.

The Comstock laws had a pronounced effect. Comstock claimed in his suggestively titled *Death Traps by Mail* (1884) that under federal and state laws, agents had by 1882 seized and destroyed the printing plates for 163 books in New York and Brooklyn (the centers of pornographic publishing), confiscated 204,539 obscene pictures along with great quantities of printing materials, secured the convictions of 311 people, and compiled a list of 979,010 people who might be interested in forbidden material.

The constitutionality of such laws was not so much argued as assumed. They remained intact until 1957. State legislatures were not inhibited by the First Amendment since the Supreme Court had ruled, in *Barron* v. *Mayor and City Council of Baltimore,* 32 U.S. 243 (1833), that the Bill of Rights applied only to the federal government. In 1878, the Court held (*Ex parte Jackson*) that since the government owned the mails it could determine what might be excluded. The vise tightened around the media as the courts, stepping in where Congress had not attempted to tread, borrowed Great Britain's expansive *Hicklin rule,* which held that an entire work could be ruled obscene if *any* portion of it—not the contents taken as a whole—was deemed obscene and if it tended to corrupt *any* member of the community. Artistic merit and authorial intent made no difference. The scope of this common understanding is suggested by the Supreme Court's ruling, in *Patterson* v. *Colorado,* 205 U.S. 454 (1907), that freedom of the press did not extend to publishing "such as may be deemed contrary to the public welfare." The opinion was written by Justice Oliver Wendell Holmes, Jr., who later reversed course and helped fashion the foundations of twentieth-century understanding of the First Amendment.

***Other Constraints*** The tight Victorian corset that late nineteenth-century legislatures and courts stitched imposed significant constraints on the media which went well beyond the "sex devices" that Comstock had been incited to suppress. Literary classics were not immune. The postmaster general deemed Leo Tolstoy's *Kreutzer Sonata* unmailable in 1890. As late as 1930, Theodore Dreiser's *An American Tragedy* and D. H. Lawrence's *Lady Chatterley's Lover* were ruled obscene in Massachusetts. American authors, particularly those of the naturalist school, were forced to bowd-

lerize their works. The chilling effect throughout the media was incalculable but no doubt substantial. Ironically such laws also inhibited the circulation—and hence publication—of reform literature if it strayed into suspect realms. The Post Office even seized an issue of the *Smasher's Mail,* the mouthpiece of Kansas prohibitionist Carry A. Nation, in which she inveighed against masturbation.

Vice societies were pleased. The Boston Watch and Ward Society, whose work made the phrase "banned in Boston" famous throughout the nation, reported in 1885 that obscene books had been largely suppressed. This genre of legislation both reflected and was reinforced by a widespread consensus in the publishing world about the boundaries of permissible public expression. Historian Paul Boyer has pointed out that book censorship in the late nineteenth century was not simply brought about by legislatures or vice societies, but also reflected "the sum total of countless small decisions by editors, publishers, booksellers, librarians, [and] critics" who shared "a common conception of literary propriety" (p. 20).

## The Movies

Other forms of media were restrained more severely than was print. The theater, long suspect not only for its plays but also for the sometimes scandalous conduct of its performers and clients, had been suppressed altogether in some American colonies. Thereafter, theaters in most states operated under tight restrictions, which were generally upheld by state courts as necessary for the maintenance of public order. In 1850, for instance, Ohio legislators delegated the power to license shows to local officials, as did a number of other states. Significantly, these regulations usually involved prior restraint. Such laws echoed Blackstone, who had excluded the theater from the print medium's freedom from prior restraint.

The emergence of motion pictures in the early twentieth century presented a challenge to legislatures intent on upholding public morality. Heralded as the "democratic art" by the *Nation* in 1913, the movies quickly developed a mass following. Their enormous popularity alarmed many reformers and legislators, who feared films would corrupt the masses, particularly the millions of new immigrants. In 1912, Congress forbade the interstate distribution of any prizefight film. The hasty passage of this measure, enacted after black boxer Jack Johnson pummeled the "great white hope" Jim Jeffries, testified to the fear of this new medium's power, especially in the troubled area of race relations. (Often evaded, the law was repealed in 1940.) By 1922, six state legislatures (New York, Pennsylvania, Ohio, Maryland, Kansas, and Virginia) passed laws establishing state censorship boards. Following the lead of Chicago in 1907, a number of municipalities did likewise. These laws typically authorized the boards to review all movies before exhibition in the state, to demand cuts before licensing their presentation, and to ban offensive pictures altogether.

Film censorship was upheld by a unanimous Supreme Court in *Mutual Film Corp.* v. *Industrial Commission of Ohio,* 236 U.S. 230 (1915). This appears to be the first instance in which a medium other than print appealed for First Amendment protection before the nation's highest court. Writing for the Court, Justice Joseph McKenna tartly dismissed the claim, labeling the movies a business "pure and simple," not a part of the press. He went on to say that the state's police power was sufficient to regulate other forms of entertainment, such as the theater and circuses. The cinema did not come under the First Amendment's umbrella until 1952.

After defeating a censorship referendum in a key battle in Massachusetts in 1922, the movie industry set up internal policing organs, which eventually grew into the Production Code Administration (PCA), formed in 1934. It continued to operate until 1968, when it was replaced by a rating system. The PCA, which was often more restrictive than the state boards, averted further film censorship legislation at the state and federal levels.

## NEW UNDERSTANDINGS OF THE FIRST AMENDMENT

The assertion of press-freedom claims in the *Mutual Film* case reflected increasing ferment about First Amendment issues. By the 1910s the issue of freedom of expression engaged not only growing numbers of civil libertarians, but also corporations eager to advance the First Amendment as a barrier to governmental intervention in business matters. Both proprietary interests and civil-libertarian principles helped forge new understandings of the First Amendment, with monumental consequences for legislatures and the media.

## Wartime Legislation

World War I provoked the most important crisis in media legislation since the 1790s. The Espionage Act, passed by Congress in 1917, made it a crime to convey false reports in order to assist the enemy or to foster dissension in the military services or obstruct armed-forces recruitment. The war-inflamed Congress went even further with the "Sedition Act" of 1918 (amendments to the Espionage Act), which made virtually any antiwar activity or statement criminal. The Wilson administration had sought an American equivalent of the British Official Secrets Act, which would have allowed the president to censor any defense-related information, but was blocked when newspapers and members of Congress rallied against it. Nonetheless, as historian Paul Murphy has pointed out, "Not since the infamous Alien and Sedition Acts of 1798 had the federal government launched so vigorous a campaign to curtail dissent and attack critics of wartime government" (p. 22). As the war gave way to the Red Scare of 1919–1920, thousands of war critics, aliens, and radicals—among them the Socialist Party's presidential candidate, Eugene V. Debs—were jailed or deported.

In three landmark cases that directly involved the press, the U.S. Supreme Court made its first serious examination of First Amendment claims. The Court upheld the Espionage and Sedition acts, employing Justice Oliver Wendell Holmes's famous "clear and present danger" test, in *Schenck* v. *United States,* 249 U.S. 47 (1919); press and speech freedoms could constitutionally be curtailed in an emergency. "Clear and present danger" was used initially to sustain restrictions.

The media were significantly affected by these developments. Many publications, generally German-language or of radical persuasion, saw their issues seized. In some cases, mailing permits were revoked. Among the most famous was the revolutionary *The Masses,* whose August 1917 issue was banned from the mails. Two cases involving the German-language press made their way to the Supreme Court, where convictions of editors were sustained for printing articles that called the draft unconstitutional and criticized the war (*Frohwerk* v. *United States,* 249 U.S. 204 [1919]) and for printing "antipatriotic" material (*Schaefer* v. *United States,* 251 U.S. 466 [1920]). Abraham Lincoln's Civil War–era support for press freedom proved unavailing in the crusade to "make the world safe for democracy."

The excesses of the period put the First Amendment under closer scrutiny, led by the American Civil Liberties Union and Harvard law professor Zechariah Chafee. This ferment reached the Court as Holmes and Justice Louis Brandeis began, after the war, to reconsider their support for war-induced curbs on First Amendment freedoms. Brandeis, joined by Holmes, dissented in the Schaefer conviction, calling for a "rule of reason" by which the "clear and present danger" test was applied more narrowly. Both Holmes and Brandeis staked out key positions for press freedoms that were eventually adopted and exceeded. The wartime legislation and resulting prosecutions highlighted the dangers of political expression in wartime and propelled the First Amendment to the forefront of constitutional controversy.

## Antiunion Laws

The boundaries that legislatures were prepared to draw around free-speech guarantees when they feared labor radicalism became apparent during and after the war with a wave of criminal syndicalism laws, which outlawed the advocacy of violence to effect political or industrial change. Following an Idaho model, at least twenty legislatures adopted such codes, mainly in the West and Midwest, where the Industrial Workers of the World (IWW) was strongest. These statutes effectively established an ex post facto censorship of the press by forbidding dissemination of material advocating syndicalism. Prosecution was vigorous in some states until the IWW waned as both an effective force and a politically tempting target in the late 1920s.

## Radio

By the 1920s another technological development—radio—posed fresh legislative challenges. Two factors about radio that distinguished it from the press and the movies heavily influenced early legislation: radio waves were both public property and a finite resource. Following the first commercial broadcast in 1920, radio stations proliferated in a mad scramble for frequencies; the ether bore an unbearable cacophony of floating and interfering radio signals. In 1927 Congress finally stepped in to organize the chaos and wrote the law which, with later revisions, has remained the basic framework for radio, and eventually television, broadcasting.

Ownership and control of all channels was vested in the federal government. The new Federal Radio Commission—after 1934 the Federal Communications Commission (FCC)—was to grant licenses to radio stations to operate in the public interest. The law reflected contemporary understanding of the First Amendment's reach. It prohibited governmental censorship but nonetheless banned obscene, indecent, or profane language; the potential conflict between these two parts of the law was scarcely glimpsed by the Congress of 1927. The law also had serious gaps: it skirted the question of growing network broadcasting, scarcely mentioned advertising, and ignored education. Congress had taken an unprecedented step with governmental regulation and licensing, which inevitably invited scrutiny of program content. This intervention was justified by the Supreme Court in *National Broadcasting Co.* v. *United States,* 316 U.S. 447 (1942), because of the scarcity of the resource. But determining the boundaries of such scrutiny triggered continuing controversies before the FCC and the courts.

## Strengthening the First Amendment

Beginning in the late 1920s the Supreme Court embarked on a fundamental revision of First Amendment interpretations, which was to have major consequences for how legislatures dealt with the media. A crucial first step was the application of the First Amendment to the states. In *Gitlow* v. *People of New York,* 268 U.S. 652 (1925), the Court asserted that the First

Amendment applied to state legislation. This doctrine's significance became clear six years later, when the Court for the first time declared a portion of a state statute to be unconstitutional because it contravened the First Amendment (*Stromberg* v. *California,* 283 U.S. 359 [1931]). This trend strengthened the Court's hand when it ruled for the first time on a case of prior restraint of the press. In 1925 the Minnesota legislature passed what became known as the "Minnesota Gag Law," which allowed a judge, without a jury trial, to issue an injunction against any future publication by a "malicious, scandalous, and defamatory" periodical. The measure was paradoxically supported by the state's major newspapers, who believed it would enhance the reputation of the fourth estate by suppressing disreputable periodicals. In *Near* v. *Minnesota ex. rel. Olson,* 283 U.S. 697 (1931), Chief Justice Charles Evans Hughes ruled, for a Court divided five to four, that such prior restraint was unconstitutional.

A legislature's ability to punish political opponents in the media received a decisive veto from the Court in 1936. At the behest of then-Senator Huey P. Long, a Democrat, the Louisiana legislature imposed a heavy tax on the state's larger newspapers—all of them opponents of the "Kingfish." The Court unanimously found this novel exercise of legislative reprisal to be unconstitutional in *Grosjean* v. *American Press Co.,* 297 U.S. 233 (1936).

The implication of this judicial trend was incongruously spelled out in the fine print of a footnote in *United States* v. *Carolene Products Co.,* 304 U.S. 144 (1938). Writing for the Court, Justice Harlan Fiske Stone said that legislation interfering with the Bill of Rights might be subject to tougher tests of constitutionality than were other statutes. Stone was attempting to explain why the Court gave great deference to New Deal economic legislation but less and less to First Amendment restrictions. For the next half-century the "preferred position" accorded the Bill of Rights, though sometimes compromised, marked out a vital zone for freedom of expression.

## World War II

The nationalization of the First Amendment contributed to the relative restraint that legislatures showed toward the media during World War II. In part because of the reaction against the excesses of World War I, but also because of the virtually unanimous support for the American war effort after Pearl Harbor, legislative intrusions on the media were rare from 1941 to 1945. State attorneys general decided in 1941 that, since sedition was a national offense, legislatures should not enter that arena. Congress revived the World War I Espionage Act in 1940, but prosecutions were rare. In the only such case to reach the Supreme Court—*Hartzel* v. *United States,* 322 U.S. 680 (1944)—Justice Frank Murphy set aside the conviction of a racist, anti-Semitic, and anti-British pamphleteer. The court thus averted a replay of the *Schenck* convictions and offered wartime media much latitude, had they chosen to use it.

As a concomitant of the war, the federal government exercised considerable control over the media. This occurred largely without congressional action. By executive order, President Franklin D. Roosevelt established both a propaganda agency known as the Office of War Information (OWI) and the Office of Censorship. News organizations and movie studios accepted the need for government control of military information. But they resisted government efforts to influence the content of their products. Some Hollywood studio heads were particularly offended by what they saw as OWI officials' attempts to insinuate New Deal themes into feature films. Influenced by such criticism, Congress sharply curbed OWI's domestic operations in 1943.

## ISSUES SINCE WORLD WAR II

In the postwar period the relationship of legislatures and the media was dominated by national security issues, shifting definitions of obscenity, and efforts to cope with the problems of access and scarcity in a rapidly changing media environment.

### The Smith Act

Although not primary targets of Cold War national security legislation, the media were inevitably affected by statutes enacted to deal with the pervasive fear of communism. The Smith Act, which Congress passed in 1940, markedly affected the media. Painting with a broom instead of a brush, Congress made it criminal not merely to conspire to overthrow the government but to advocate or conspire to advocate its overthrow. The act was upheld by the Supreme Court in *Dennis* v. *United States,* 341 U.S. 494 (1951) as necessary for the preservation of society—this during a period when the Court tacked to the right in response to Cold War anxieties. As domestic anticommunist campaigns waned in the late 1950s, the more liberal Court presided over by Chief Justice Earl Warren significantly extended First Amendment guarantees. An important step in this direction occurred in 1957 when, based in part on the Court's reading of *The Daily People's World,* a West Coast communist paper, Justice John Marshall Harlan sharply cut back the Smith Act's reach (*Yates* v. *United States,* 354 U.S. 298 [1957]).

## Libel

The freedom of the print medium was notably expanded in an unprecedented series of court rulings, which were derived from the burst of civil rights activism in the 1960s and the corrosive disillusionment with the Vietnam War in the late 1960s and early 1970s. Libel law—one of the media's principal fears—had traditionally been the domain of state legislatures and courts. But in *New York Times Co.* v. *Sullivan,* 376 U.S. 254 (1964), which grew out of the civil rights movement in Alabama, a unanimous Supreme Court dramatically wrapped national First Amendment standards around libel law. The "preservation of society" argument took a back seat. All First Amendment cases, wrote Justice William Brennan for the Court, must be weighed "against the background of a profound national commitment to the principle that debate on public issues should be uninhibited, robust, and wide-open." To reinforce his point Brennan revived the Sedition Act of 1798, whose constitutionality had never been adjudicated, only to point out that "the restraint it imposed upon criticism of government and public officials" rendered it inconsistent with the First Amendment. The need for robust discussion required greater freedom for the media to criticize public officials than state legislatures had typically afforded. The Court threw out what had been a staple of libel law in Alabama and most other states; instead of proving the media

had merely made erroneous statements, plaintiffs now had to demonstrate *actual malice,* defined as willful knowledge that statements were false or exhibited reckless disregard for accuracy. (Kansas and a few other states, influenced by *Coleman* v. *MacLennan,* 78 Kan. 711 [1908], had given the media greater protection.) Brennan feared the old legislative standard requiring proof of accuracy created a chilling effect on public debate, not only because truth was often elusive but because it might prove impossible to convince a jury in times of social crisis. No other decision had gone so far as *Sullivan* in recognizing the media's claim to a special role in furthering the process of democratic government.

The reach of the *Sullivan* doctrine was underscored in *Brandenburg* v. *Ohio,* 395 U.S. 444 (1969), when the Court announced what Powe has called "the most speech-protective test" in its history (1991, p. 96). Overturning the conviction of a Ku Klux Klan member, the decision voided the Ohio Criminal Syndicalism Statute of 1919. Henceforth a state could not proscribe "advocacy of the use of force . . . except where such advocacy is directed to inciting or producing imminent lawless action and is likely to incite or produce such action." Had such a standard been in place, the World War I–era editors Frohwerk and Schaefer would have gone free, the anticommunism boundaries of the 1950s would have looked quite different, and legislatures' abilities to curb media freedom would have been markedly cut back.

***Public and Private Figures*** Although the media relished its greater freedom from fear of libel, the *Sullivan* decision left many questions unresolved. The distinction between public and private figures, and the remedies that should be available if a private party were libeled, continued to trouble legislatures and the judiciary. In *Gertz* v. *Robert Welch, Inc.,* 418 U.S. 323 (1974), the Court drew a distinction between public officials, candidates, and public figures—for whom the *Sullivan* standard was required—and private citizens, who did not need to demonstrate malice in order to collect actual damages. Private plaintiffs now had to prove some degree of media negligence in order to collect punitive damages. The boundaries of defamation law were murky for all concerned—victims, the media, courts, and legislatures. But indicating a scope for media operations that would have been inconceivable at many points in American history, Justice Lewis Powell, echoing Gallatin, averred for the Court, "Under the First Amendment there is no such thing as a false idea" (ibid., at 339).

## Prior Restraint

As this line of rulings was being developed, the issue of prior restraint appeared in the celebrated Pentagon Papers case in 1971. This was not a replay of the *Near* case of 1931 involving a marginal Minnesota weekly offending local officials, or a small-circulation socialist newspaper uttering general criticism of a war, but a case of the nation's two leading newspapers—the *New York Times* and the *Washington Post*—publishing stolen secret national-security documents in wartime. The Pentagon Papers, the collection of secret Defense Department documents on the origins of American involvement in the Vietnam War, were leaked to the two newspapers by Daniel Ellsberg, a former Pentagon official. There had been no comparable instance of publication of secret government documents against the government's wishes in wartime. Asserting that publication compromised national security and violated the Espionage Act of 1917, the government persuaded a federal judge to issue a temporary injunction, which the *Times* obeyed—the first such instance of prior restraint in the nation's history. The Supreme Court ruled six to three that publication could proceed (*New York Times Co.* v. *United States,* 403 U.S. 713 [1971]). But the justices' opinions also suggested that if the case involved something more immediate than a history, such as war plans, the outcome might well have been different. Although a future suit would turn on an assessment of the likely effect on national security, the Pentagon Papers case reinforced the presumption against the constitutionality of prior restraint.

## Obscenity

The Supreme Court's activism on First Amendment issues after World War II opened another realm of legislative activity to scrutiny—the determination of obscenity. Unlike national-security cases, which involved speech that was clearly political, the obscenity issue raised questions that, though not without political im-

plications, were personal and private in character. Legislatures had been relatively quiet on this issue since passage of the comprehensive Comstock laws. Those monuments to Victorian morality seemed anachronistic in urbanized postwar America, especially as attitudes toward sexuality grew more liberal.

Legislatures' assumptions about their ability to control motion pictures were jolted in 1952 when the Supreme Court nonchalantly extended the First Amendment to motion pictures, thus implicitly reversing its position from 1915. In *Joseph Burstyn, Inc.* v. *Wilson,* 343 U.S. 495, the Court rejected a ban on *The Miracle,* which the New York State censors had found to be sacrilegious. State and municipal courts had occasionally reversed movie censors' decisions, but this marked the first time the nation's highest tribunal had reversed a censorship decision for any type of artistic expression. The scope of legislative action in censorship cases for both print and film media was now in doubt.

The key question was the definition of obscenity. Obscenity has never been protected by the First Amendment (*Chaplinsky* v. *New Hampshire,* 315 U.S. 568 [1942]). Supreme Court decisions dating back to 1896 had held that items that were merely vulgar or tasteless were not obscene. But obscenity is extremely difficult for legislatures or courts to define in a country with diverse moral views, sexual mores, and sexual orientations. The ineradicable subjectivity of defining pornography was captured by Justice Potter Stewart's memorable line: "I know it when I see it."

The Supreme Court began to cut back legislative discretion about obscenity—the Comstock laws were still in place—with *Roth* v. *United States,* 354 U.S. 476 (1957). Justice William Brennan's opinion for the Court marked the abandonment of the Hicklin rule. The contents of a work now had to be considered as a whole, not just a singular passage, and an estimate of its effects had to be based on the perceptions of an average member of the community, not anyone who might be susceptible. In 1962 Justice John Marshall Harlan added the test of "patent offensiveness" when he ruled that the postmaster general had erred in banning gay magazines from the mails (*Manual Enterprises, Inc.* v. *Day,* 370 U.S. 478, 482 [1962]). The Court's efforts reached a climax in the tripartite test Brennan laid down in *"John Cleland's Memoirs"* v. *Attorney General of Massachusetts*, 383 U.S. 413, 418 (1966): "(a) the dominant theme of the material taken as a whole appeals to a prurient interest in sex; (b) the material is patently offensive because it affronts contemporary community standards relating to the description or representation of sexual matters; and (c) the material is utterly without redeeming social value." Since even minimal social value could be advanced for many works, it seemed only hard-core pornography remained unprotected.

The changing concept of obscenity greatly circumscribed legislative action in this area. State movie censorship boards were either abolished by legislatures or held to be unconstitutional by state supreme courts; the last film board went out of existence in 1981, when the Maryland legislature declined to renew its charter. *Memoirs of Hecate County,* a 1946 novel by Edmund Wilson—arguably the most distinguished literary critic of his generation—was banned in New York as late as 1948 because of its enthusiastic descriptions of sexual intercourse. Two decades later, works with even marginal social value in almost any medium circulated largely free of legislative or judicial intervention, although commercial considerations and citizen actions often imposed their own limitations.

But the struggle to recast standards of obscenity continued. The more conservative Supreme Court of Chief Justice Warren Burger invited state legislatures to impose stricter obscenity measures in *Miller* v. *California,* 413 U.S. 15 (1973). Departing from *Memoirs,* Burger fashioned an obscenity test that seemed to give primacy to community standards: "(a) whether 'the average person, applying contemporary community standards' would find that the work, taken as a whole, appeals to the prurient interest, . . . (b) whether the work depicts or describes, in a patently offensive way, sexual conduct specifically defined by the applicable state law; and (c) whether the work, taken as a whole, lacks serious literary, artistic, political, or scientific value." By 1975 eighteen state legislatures accepted the Court's invitation, many of them adopting *Miller*'s language verbatim. In ten other states and the District of Columbia, the *Miller* test was incor-

porated by judicial construction. Thirteen states retained the *Memoirs* standard of "utterly without redeeming social value," while the remaining nine forbade the distribution of obscene materials only to minors or nonconsenting adults. Though *Miller*'s "serious" value promised to be tougher than the *Memoirs* standard, its "patently offensive" prong proved almost equally difficult to meet. For the most part, serious literary and artistic work was unaffected. Zealous prosecutors used *Miller*-inspired legislation against pornographers in some states, chiefly in the South. Hard-core pornography remained widely available in many jurisdictions, however, as law enforcement officers assigned its suppression low priority, fearing the unpredictable subjectivity of juries deciding they knew pornography when they saw it.

## ACCESS TO MEDIA IN THE "INFORMATION AGE"

### The Fairness Doctrine

Although the growth and sophistication of motion pictures eventually brought that medium within a qualified orbit of the First Amendment, radio and its postwar cousin, television, continued to operate within the conceptual boundaries crafted in the late 1920s and early 1930s. Many of these new issues were fought out before the Federal Communications Commission and the courts, but they had strong implications for the legislative branch. One of the most important was the vexing question of access. In 1959, Congress ratified thirty years of FCC practice by enacting the *fairness doctrine,* which required stations to discuss controversial issues and to allow opposing sides to be represented. The Supreme Court upheld this notion in *Red Lion Broadcasting Co.* v. *Federal Communications Commission,* 395 U.S. 367 (1969), relying on the scarcity principle and arguing (too optimistically, to many critics) that government muscle behind the fairness doctrine would enhance the public's right to know. At various points concentration of ownership in the same market (for example, a television station by the dominant or only newspaper in the market) was restricted. The antitrust laws were seldom directed against the media, although in 1948 the Supreme Court found the major motion picture companies' control of both production and distribution to be an antritrust violation.

## Newspapers

By the 1970s the shrinking number of newspapers yielded, paradoxically, the same problem of access that colored any discussion of radio and television. Competing daily newspapers had once been ubiquitous; by 1970 only a handful of large cities enjoyed such diversity. The growing importance of newspaper chains also evoked concern. Indeed, many media watchers argued that the earlier conditions of access had been inverted, with a multiplicity of electronic channels in a given market but often only one newspaper. The keynote of liberal First Amendment interpretation, however, has been state neutrality; neither legislatures nor courts have devoted much attention to the problem of unequal access caused by economic inequalities.

Two measures illustrate the restricted scope of approaches to the problem of media access. One was the Newspaper Preservation Act of 1970, which ostensibly tried to insure continued diversity of ownership in a given market through the device of joint operating agreements. These arrangements permitted sharing of facilities and a variety of practices—among them, price-fixing, profit pooling, and market control—which were otherwise illegal under the antitrust laws. The act was criticized, however, as more likely to kill newspaper competition than preserve it, since a stronger paper has little incentive to forgo the greater profits it would enjoy from a monopoly by prolonging the life of a weaker competitor.

The other was an effort to apply the logic of broadcasting's fairness doctrine to newspapers by giving citizens the right to reply in the paper. Critics pointed out that the huge cost of starting a daily newspaper effectively makes newspaper ownership as scarce a resource as does the limited number of broadcast channels. The Progressive Era Florida legislature enacted a reply law, as did Ohio in 1930. Clinging to the time-honored distinction between print and electronic media, however, the Supreme Court in 1974 unanimously held newspaper reply statutes are unconstitutional.

## CONCLUSION

Whether such distinctions could hold in the face of the information revolution of the 1980s and 1990s, in both its technological and commercial forms, was one of the major issues facing legislatures and the media. New media technologies, particularly cable television, offered the promise of plenty, not scarcity. Congress attempted to solve the cable conundrum with the Cable Communications Policy Act of 1984. Cable operators were allowed to set their own rates (a freedom revoked in 1992 after accusations of rate gouging). In return for granting an operator a monopoly, cities were able to claim a percentage of the company's revenues. The First Amendment received little discussion. By analogy with broadcasting, the company had to provide a certain number of public access channels. Cable systems could not transmit speech that was "obscene or otherwise unprotected by the Constitution"—no further definitions were provided—and devices had to be made available to control children's access to the television set. The hybrid nature of cable seemed certain, however, to provoke continuing legislative and judicial revision.

The issue of obscenity also promised to attract legislative and judicial attention. Attempting to reinscribe "traditional values," conservatives in 1991 sought legislation placing restrictions on the content of federally funded work at the National Endowment for the Humanities and Corporation for Public Broadcasting. Goaded by Senator Jesse Helms (R.-N.C.), the late-twentieth-century analogue of Anthony Comstock, Congress became embroiled in continuing controversy over whether to restrict federal funding of art projects that were deemed by some to be indecent or obscene. Helms also spearheaded legislation to restrict the use of telephone lines for commercial sex talk. Believing that pornography degraded women and encouraged violence against them, some feminists also supported legislation against pornography. But the few such laws to be enacted, notably antipornography ordinances in Minneapolis and Indianapolis, were struck down by the courts. Meanwhile, other groups called for the enactment of speech codes that would protect minorities from being the recipients of hostile expression, such as "hate speech"—measures the courts usually viewed skeptically. By trying to put state power behind a particular point of view, these arguments call into question the principle of state neutrality, which had been the bedrock of First Amendment construction since the 1930s.

Whatever changes legislatures attempt for the media will take place against a background that has been markedly altered by social, legislative, and judicial currents since the 1930s. Legislatures have, with some important exceptions, found their ability to regulate media content cut back, although in the two-tier system that has evolved, the electronic media remain under tighter restrictions than print or film. As political controversies continue to swirl around obscenity and mere indecency, legislatures and courts face ongoing struggles to demarcate media boundaries. The marked changes in the media's technological and economic structure pose important problems of access and diversity that legislatures must address, especially if the media's unique role in furthering democratic government is taken seriously by the media and the citizenry. For civil libertarians the history of the fragility of First Amendment protections in times of social stress underscores the need for unflagging scrutiny of media-restricting legislation.

## BIBLIOGRAPHY

### General Works

On legislatures and the media, books on freedom of expression are important. ZECHARIAH CHAFEE, JR.'s classic *Free Speech in the United States,* 2d ed. (Cambridge, Mass., 1941), should be read in conjunction with more recent works. A worthy successor is HARRY KALVEN, JR., *A Worthy Tradition: Freedom of Speech in America,* edited by JAMIE KALVEN (New York, 1988). Enlightening revisions of the development of the modern understanding of the First Amendment are found in DAVID M. RABBAN, "The First Amendment in Its Forgotten Years," *Yale Law Journal* 90 (1981): 514–595, and his "The Emergence of Modern First Amendment Doctrine," *University of Chicago Law Review* 50 (1983): 1205–1355; and JOHN WERTHEIMER, "Free-Speech Fights: The Roots of Modern Free-Speech Litigation in the United States" (Ph.D. diss., Princeton University, 1992).

General works on the Constitution are helpful, especially PAUL L. MURPHY, *The Constitution in Crisis Times, 1918–1969,* The New American Nation Series (New York, 1972); and LOREN P. BETH, *The Development of the American Constitution, 1877–1917,* The New American Nation Series (New York, 1971). A diverse sourcebook is WALTER M. BRASCH and DANA R. ULLOTH, *The Press and the State: Sociohistorical and Contemporary Studies* (Lanham, Md., 1986). Crucial for understanding legislation affecting the press in the colonial period and early republic are the many works of LEONARD W. LEVY, especially *Emergence of a Free Press* (New York, 1985), which should be read in conjunction with DAVID M. RABBAN, "The Ahistorical Historian: Leonard Levy on Freedom of Expression in Early American History," *Stanford Law Review* 37 (1985): 795–856.

### Specific Subjects

For libel, see NORMAN L. ROSENBERG, *Protecting the Best Men: An Interpretive History of the Law of Libel,* Studies in Legal History (Chapel Hill, N.C., 1986). For censorship of books, see PAUL S. BOYER, *Purity in Print: The Vice-Society Movement and Book Censorship in America* (New York, 1968). For the press, see LUCAS A. POWE, JR., *The Fourth Estate and the Constitution: Freedom of the Press in America* (Berkeley, Calif., 1991); ANTHONY LEWIS, *Make No Law: The Sullivan Case and the First Amendment* (New York, 1991); and NORMAN L. ROSENBERG, "Another History of Free Speech: The 1920s and the 1930s," *Law and Inequality: A Journal of Theory and Practice* 7 (1989): 333–366.

On film, see EDWARD DE GRAZIA and ROGER

# LEGISLATURES AND THE MEDIA

K. Newman, *Banned Films: Movies, Censors, and the First Amendment* (New York, 1982); Clayton R. Koppes and Gregory D. Black, *Hollywood Goes to War: How Politics, Profits, and Propaganda Shaped World War II Movies* (New York, 1987); Richard Randall, *Censorship of the Movies* (Madison, Wis., 1968); and the special issue of *American Quarterly* (December 1992). For broadcasting, see Lucas A. Powe, Jr., *American Broadcasting and the First Amendment* (Berkeley, Calif., 1987); and Erik Barnouw, *A History of Broadcasting in the United States,* Vol. 1, *A Tower in Babel* (New York, 1966). For discussion of obscenity and pornography, see Edward de Grazia, *Girls Lean Back Everywhere: The Law of Obscenity and the Assault on Genius* (New York, 1992); Frederick F. Schauer, *The Law of Obscenity* (Washington, D.C., 1976); Donald Alexander Downs, *The New Politics of Pornography* (Chicago, 1989); and Downs, "An Empirical Inquiry into the Effects of *Miller* v. *California* on the Control of Obscenity," *New York University Law Review* 52 (1977): 810–939.

# CONGRESS AND OTHER LEGISLATURES

## *Philip R. VanderMeer*

The connections between Congress and other American legislatures have been both direct and indirect, the result of general American beliefs about legislatures, government, and politics, and the product of specific personal and institutional interactions. Congress began as the product of Anglo-American legislative traditions and new theories about legislatures and government. Over the next two centuries, the role and status of the legislative branch of government, both state and federal, changed dramatically. In part, this stemmed from changing notions about legislatures—their structures, procedures, and operations, as well as legislative representation and districts. This also reflects changing ideas about government generally—about political careers, policy-making, administration, and efficiency. Thus, American political culture stimulated common developments in both Congress and state legislatures, but their similarities also resulted from mutual observation and imitation. Such borrowing was fundamental to all new state legislatures and common in all periods, but it was especially frequent during the early national period, the Progressive Era, and the 1960s and 1970s.

Congress has also been directly connected with other legislatures. Many of its members had prior experience in state or territorial legislatures, and there have even been a few state lawmakers who previously served in Congress. An even more direct influence on membership was the selection of U.S. senators by state legislatures. This institutional link had significant consequences for both sides and grew increasingly complex until its elimination in 1913. The legislatures have also been directly and significantly connected by policy-making. The interactive component of this process has become more significant over the years, while the balance in the relationship has changed. Thus, state legislatures have continued to recom-

mend and request congressional actions, but state legislative instructions to members of Congress have ceased, and formal petitions by state governments are relatively infrequent and unimportant. Since the 1930s, Congress has had the lead in policy-making, enacting measures that require or prompt action by state legislatures.

Obviously, the expansion of government powers generally and of the federal government in particular has substantially altered the interaction of Congress and state legislatures. This is an important part of the changes in federalism during the last two centuries, but it is not the entire story. That includes a wide variety of matters, such as increases in presidential executive orders, lobbying of Congress and the executive branch by agents of state government, and the responsibilities of state bureaucracies or municipalities in administering revenue-sharing funds. Such developments are properly part of the history of federalism, but because they are not legislative relationships, they are not part of this study.

## INSTITUTIONAL ORIGINS

The institutional similarities between Congress and other American legislatures stem from their function, origins, and efforts at imitation. Colonial legislatures were guided by British parliamentary tradition. This provided basic notions of representation, legislative organization, parliamentary procedure, and legislative rights, such as the right of each legislative chamber to judge the elections and qualifications of its members. Colonial and state legislatures modified and developed this heritage in various ways, such as specifying methods of committee organization and cooperation between two houses. In turn, the Continental and Confederation congresses built on this tradition while also attempting to deal with matters unique to national legislatures.

Thus, the federal Congress drew on a rich legislative tradition, but it was also part of a determined effort to devise new patterns of government. This was apparent in both the structures of new state governments and the creation of Congress as a bicameral legislature, chosen at biennial elections, with one house having two-year terms and the other having staggered six-year terms. This rejected the British model of indeterminate terms and the Confederation expediency of a unicameral legislature. While resembling the colonial arrangement, it more directly imitated the bicameral structure of new state governments. It also followed the precedents of Virginia, Delaware, and New York for a senate with staggered multiyear terms, but this was not the norm, for all states had annual elections and most provided annual terms for legislators.

The most difficult structural issue, on both theoretical and practical grounds, was determining the rationale for each of the chambers and the relationship between them. There was a consensus concerning the house of representatives (at both the national and state levels) which had obvious antecedents in the House of Commons and the lower house of colonial governments. This was the popular house, the initiator of financial measures, and the more powerful chamber. By contrast, the second chamber had a less clear purpose in the new republican governments. The product of colonial experience, political theory, and a politically necessary compromise, the national Senate was pulled in different directions. Traditionally, upper houses were largely chambers of the elite—either the hereditary aristocracy or appointive officials having greater wealth, status, and experience. Although no one envisioned a House of Lords, the colonial system of elite advisers had some support. Toward this end, New Jersey, Maryland, and South Carolina included property qualifications for senators, and many states set a higher minimum-age requirement. Initially, this model also influenced the federal Senate. Structurally, this is reflected in the higher age requirement for senators, and in practice, it is evidenced in President George Washington's disastrous visit to the Senate to seek counsel on an Indian treaty and in the Senate's debate over titles of address. However, various practical and ideological considerations relating to the separation of powers, plus the availability of cabinet officials to advise the president, soon led to the rejection of this model and its presumptive standards for Senate membership and behavior.

A second model for the Senate was as a chamber whose members represented their own states' interests. To at least some extent, this was what political theory and the practical need for compromise had devised in 1787, both in the allotment of two senators to each state and in the selection of those members by state legislatures. In practice, however, the Senate struggled to expand beyond such a narrow definition. From its beginning, some members adopted a national vision; many expressed a republican belief in representing people, not states, and saw common interests with the people of other states. Given these divisions over its role and the contrast between its presumed representation of limited or even special interest and the House's national purpose, the Senate began as a distinctly subordinate chamber.

Changes in the status of the Senate, its position relative to the House, and its relationship with state legislatures became evident by the 1830s. The transition began in the 1790s, when the Senate opened its sessions to the public and began publishing its debates. Population growth and the admission of new states had even more effect. By 1832, the House had more than doubled in size, from 100 to 240 members, while Senate membership had increased only by half, to 48. Because of the House's increased size and the resulting changes in its organization and procedures, service in that chamber lost some of its attraction for ambitious politicians.

Also important were the Senate's inherent advantages, such as the six-year term and the capacity to confirm or deny presidential appointments, a power enhanced by the rise of the spoils system. Furthermore, although the state basis of the Senate was commonly irrelevant to policy divisions, it was directly related to the state-based conflict over slavery. Thus, the Senate emerged as the major arena for national debate and the focus of institutional and partisan conflict with the president. It kept this status, despite organizational innovations that strengthened the House, because it remained a relatively manageable size (especially compared to the House) and because the growing role of foreign policy enhanced its advice-and-consent powers.

The relationship between upper and lower state legislative chambers developed in similar but not identical fashion. Even though state legislatures lacked the foreign policy responsibilities of Congress, they were influenced by congressional example. The admission of new states and the greater ease of amending state constitutions encouraged a shift of some power to state upper houses. By the 1830s, almost all states had eliminated wealth qualifications for their upper houses, while most still retained a federal-like higher age standard. By the mid-nineteenth century, the basic outline of federal and state legislatures was similar: most state senates resembled the U.S. Senate in having fewer members, longer terms, an elected outsider as presiding officer, and the power to confirm appointments, while state houses of representatives retained their power as the initiator of financial measures.

## REPRESENTATION, APPORTIONMENT, AND DISTRICTS

State and federal legislatures have also shared concerns and had more significant interaction over the basis of representation and the construction of legislative districts. The principles for determining congressional districts were clearly established in the Constitution: geography for the Senate and population for the House. Such simplicity did not determine representation in states, particularly in the original thirteen states, which used three standards (cf. Haynes, "Representation in State Legislatures"). Geography was the primary basis; using local communities and existing boundaries satisfied tradition and the desire for recognizable districts. Population was a second consideration, and together with geography, it justified new legislative districts in the western parts of these thirteen states. More important, it was used to modify the traditional geographical basis of representation in state lower houses. Thus, New England states used towns, and other states used counties, as house districts, with the more populous districts receiving one or more additional representatives.

Such modifications did only a little to equalize representation in state lower houses, but far greater inequities existed (often for many years) in the senates of the original states, which ignored population. Some states used simple geography as the basis: Rhode Island allocated one senator per town, and New Jersey, one per county. Others relied on a third factor, wealth: New Hampshire used tax receipts and counties; Massachusetts apportioned senators by county, based on the total amount of property taxes paid; and New York established districts based on the number of freeholders with an estate of at least one hundred pounds. Some changes were made in these systems during the next century, as when New York and Massachusetts abandoned wealth-based districting in 1821 and 1840. Nevertheless, such systems were increasingly inequitable and attracted growing criticism.

States admitted after 1800 created systems that were more democratic. They typically used counties as the basis of representation for both houses, but often without guaranteeing a legislator for each county. They also provided multiple representatives for areas with greater population, but they more closely approximated the population differences. Furthermore, some states provided additional representation for larger counties by creating "joint" districts, which combined a county meriting more than one but not two seats with one or more smaller counties. Such methods improved on those of eastern states, but the reliance on county boundaries made it impossible to create truly equal districts and equal representation. Only some midwestern states that divided the more populous counties into districts were able to create systems of roughly equal representation.

Designing legislative districts grew even more difficult during the nineteenth century. Population growth and redistribution, particularly the growing disparity between county populations, created increasingly serious dilemmas for all legislatures, especially for states that guaranteed a representative for each county. They also complicated calculations for states that limited the size of their legislatures. Even the advantages and relative equity of multi-member districts were reduced when a winner-take-all system included districts of ten or more members, as did Washington, Oregon, Montana, and Colorado in the 1890s. Finally, even when the districting system was flexible, it still demanded that states accept new population realities and changes in power.

Legislative debates over reapportionment and redistricting, both national and state, started with the federal Constitution, which requires using the census for apportioning congressional seats among the states. Most states included a similar provision in their constitutions, and some required either a state census or an enumeration of voters. The major political problem, as Congress first discovered, was that maintaining equal representation without reducing the representation for a state or county (and thus stimulating their opposition to the entire plan) meant continuously expanding the size of the legislature. Congress did this until 1840 and again from 1870 to 1920, but many state legislatures were constrained by constitutional limits on their size.

Except during Reconstruction, Congress has not acted to influence the composition of state legislative districts. However, it has tried to instruct state legislatures about constructing congressional districts. From the beginning, a substantial majority of states believed that members of Congress should be elected from districts. Seeking to establish this system everywhere, twenty-two state resolutions between 1816 and 1822 proposed this as a constitutional requirement; the Senate passed an amendment to that effect three times, but each time it failed in the House. As late as 1840, six states still did not use districts. Finally, the Reapportionment Act of 1842 required contiguous single-member districts. Thereafter, despite occasional tardiness by states that gained additional seats, members of Congress were chosen from districts.

Reapportionment and redistricting always generated difficult political struggles for Congress and for state legislatures, but by the early twentieth century the battles had become much more intense. This conflict took particular form in the South, where racial exclusion encouraged ossification of the political system, but fear and criticism of urban growth and political machines mounted across the nation. One consequence was slow congressional redistricting after 1910, most obviously in the six states in 1915 and four in 1917 that still elected their additional representatives at large, includ-ing two from Illinois and four from Pennsylvania. Various states also failed to reapportion their legislatures.

Conditions worsened in the 1920s, when Congress was unable to agree on a reapportionment plan. Although complicated by the decision not to expand the size of the House and by debates over statistical methods for apportionment, the urban-rural conflict was the fundamental cause for failure to act. Congress resumed reapportioning seats in 1929, but the apportionment law of that year, unlike others since 1842, did not require or even discuss districts. Partly as a consequence, a number of states, notably Illinois, New York, and Ohio, failed to redistrict completely before the mid-1940s, and in 1957 four states still elected one or more at-large members of Congress.

By 1960, the refusal of many states to accommodate the enormous population changes since the late nineteenth century, plus the crudeness of the apportionment and districting systems, had produced unacceptable inequities in state legislative representation. In Connecticut, one-quarter of the voters, living in the five largest cities, elected only 10 of 294 representatives. A majority of Florida's population elected only 6 of 38 senators. California had one senatorial district with fourteen thousand voters and another with over six million. In *Baker* v. *Carr,* 369 U.S. 186 (1962), the U.S. Supreme Court overturned Tennessee's apportionment law, and in *Reynolds* v. *Sims,* 377 U.S. 533 (1964), it elaborated on its ruling. Endorsing the principle of one-person, one-vote and explicitly rejecting any analogy with the federal government, the Court required that both houses of each state legislature have districts of equal population. The Court took a similar position on congressional districts, and in 1967, Congress required districts to be of equal population.

The Court rulings prompted vigorous opposition. The most concerted attempts sought a constitutional amendment allowing states to apportion one house on grounds other than simply population. Led by Senator Everett Dirksen (R.-Ill.), the Senate in 1965 and 1966 passed such measures, but by less than the required two-thirds. Failing this, thirty-two states (including twenty-six with malapportioned legislatures) requested a constitutional convention to pass such an amendment. Ultimately, rising opposition, particularly from newly apportioned legislatures, and the death of Senator Dirksen in 1969 ended these efforts.

The more recent discussions of districting have focused on the general underrepresentation of racial minorities, especially in Congress. Proceeding partly through direction from federal courts and from the U.S. Justice Department, districts have been substantially redrawn, especially following the 1990 census. As a result, the number of minority representatives has grown and is expected to rise still further. These districts have been criticized, but not on grounds that Senator Dirksen would have appreciated. Instead, critics have complained—justly—that such districts violate the previous reform standard of compact and contiguous districts. A final issue is the widespread and continuing complaints about the gerrymandering of state and federal districts for partisan advantage.

## LEGISLATIVE PROCEDURES AND STRUCTURES

Even more than basic structural characteristics and far more than matters of apportionment, the initial procedures and internal structures of American state and federal legislatures derived from colonial and British precedents and models —and for a longer time resembled them. Because the lower house originated as the "popular" chamber and became the larger house and because the presiding officer of the upper house was not chosen by that body, the lower house led in organization innovations.

The organization of a lower house began with the selection of a Speaker, who appointed the few standing and many select committees. Legislating was a complicated ritual in which a member asked permission of the house to introduce a measure or a standing committee referred a petition to the house, a select committee then framed a bill, and, finally, the house debated the measure as a committee of the whole. Legislation concerned both general and special, or private, matters; debate was governed largely by British precedents, which were modified slightly and codified by Vice President Thomas Jefferson as *Jefferson's Manual of Parliamentary Practice,* which quickly became the bible of parliamentary procedure for American legislatures.

These conditions changed by the 1820s and 1830s, first in Congress and then in various state legislatures. The U.S. House increased its standing committees from four in 1795 to fourteen by 1810, and to twenty-five by 1820; its use of select committees declined by more than 80 percent during this period. Beginning in 1811, the House allowed a majority to end debate and establish an order of business, and in 1827, it adopted the simple method of asking unanimous consent to introduce a bill and having it referred to a standing committee. Various Speakers of the House, especially Henry Clay, shaped these developments as they expanded the powers of that office. Changes came more slowly in the Senate, but it had fifteen standing committees by 1822, and its procedures also matured.

States followed a similar pattern, although the timing depended on a state's age and its level of economic development. In New York, one of the more advanced states, the assembly in 1800 had only seven committees, which merely reported on petitions, and it worked primarily in committee of the whole. By 1830, it included twenty-nine committees, which could introduce bills based on petitions, and by 1850, it used select committees only for specialized subjects. The same development occurred in Pennsylvania. Introduction of bills from the floor by individual members began in the New York Senate in 1808; by the 1830s, both New York and Pennsylvania routinely accepted this practice and referred such measures to standing committees.

Political parties existed in Congress and some state legislatures from the beginning of the national period, for they had roots in the opposition groups in the colonial and British legislatures. But although these parties fulfilled many of the functions of modern parties, they differed, in that only a few legislators were strong partisans and some members did not identify with any party. This was apparent in electoral campaigns, legislative organization, and voting on policy questions. Thus, even though the most intense Federalist-Republican conflict of the 1790s did produce relatively high levels of party behavior in Congress and some states, this was atypical of most legislatures before the 1830s. Creation of the second party system transformed most factional and geographical conflicts into partisan struggles, provided a clear basis for organizing legislatures, and introduced a major—though not the only—determinant of voting behavior on public policies.

Legislative organization and procedures had changed greatly by the late nineteenth and early twentieth centuries. As contemporaries often noted, Congress and state legislatures had important similarities in status and operation, but they also had major structural differences, which limited their connections. Legislatures were partisan institutions, and the most powerful legislative leader in each was the house speaker, the leader of the house majority party. By the 1890s, speakers appointed committee members and chairmen, interpreted rules, and recognized members wishing to speak (sometimes using their discretion). In state lower houses, the speakers referred bills to committees. Speakers of the U.S. House, however, had the greater power of serving on the Rules Committee, which determines not only the committee to which bills are to be referred but also the conditions of debate for each bill.

The increased amount and complexity of legislative business forced Congress and state legislatures to change their operations in certain ways. Beginning by the middle of the nineteenth century and increasingly during the succeeding decades, they both reduced the amount of private and special legislation they considered, either through state constitutional limits or by internal decisions. Such measures were time-consuming; they were also special pleading at best and wasteful or corrupt at worst. Efforts to gain exemptions from Civil War pension requirements or special appropriations for county courthouses brought the legislature into disrepute. New ideas about government and administration let bureaucracies administer pensions and courts decide on personal disputes (such as divorces) or claims on government programs (such as Indian depredations claims). Rather than write separate laws for each county, township, or city, state legislatures increasingly devised general laws with subcategories for areas of different population sizes. Finally, both Congress and the states developed separate calendars for minor measures.

The U.S. House, all state lower houses, many state senates, and finally, in 1917, the U.S. Senate permitted some method of closing off debate. This limited filibusters and improved the efficiency of legislative debate to some extent. However, its effects were less than they would have been some decades previously, for as many observers noted, American legislatures were no longer places of debate. Open discussion in committee of the whole had been replaced by closed party caucuses, but especially by committee deliberation.

State legislatures obtained assistance from legislative manuals, or "blue books." These publications included legislative rules and procedures, biographical information on state officials, and often a compilation of various data concerning the state. The *Congressional Directory* and other materials served similar functions for Congress. Legislative reference bureaus were even more helpful. Charles McCarthy developed the first such bureau in Wisconsin in 1901, and by 1911 he had a staff of twelve who assisted legislators in writing legislation, did research for the legislature, and exchanged data with other states. By 1920, more than half the states had such an institution. The congressional Legislative Reference Service (the Congressional Research Service from 1970) was established in 1914 as a result of legislation introduced by Senator Robert La Follette (R.-Wis.) and Representative John Nelson (R.-Wis.).

These similarities represent a shared condition and a conscious imitation by Congress and state legislatures, but at the same time, their different constituencies and constitutional positions meant that they would not be identical in their patterns of leadership or methods of operation. In the U.S. House, opposition to the concentration and use of power by the Speaker grew. In the 1890s, Democrats bitterly criticized "Czar" Thomas B. Reed (R.-Maine) and his rule changes; thereafter, complaints mounted over the Speaker's interference with the seniority system in making committee appointments. Finally, in 1909–1910 a group of insurgent Republicans joined the Democratic minority to "overthrow" Speaker Joseph Cannon (R.-Ill.) by taking away the Speaker's power of appointment and removing him from the Rules Committee. The House also established a consent calendar for noncontroversial measures and a rule enabling members to discharge bills trapped in committee.

Critics of state speakers sometimes borrowed the rhetoric of congressional reformers. Although some of the parallels they drew were accurate, the conditions in state legislatures and Congress, as well as the demands on their leaders, differed in several important respects. Congress adopted a seniority system to structure its committees, but state legislatures could not develop such a system. First, the level of experience in state legislatures was very low: roughly half to three-fourths of the members were freshmen, virtually none of the members served more than three or four terms, and speakers usually served only one term in that office. Second, the membership of both state chambers was much smaller than that of Congress. Thus, state legislatures were simply unable to implement a committee-based seniority system. Instead, they were forced to employ a system that rewarded experience in the legislature but also allowed considerable opportunity for talented freshmen. Given the complexity of this process and the brevity of sessions, the best way to structure the legislature and pass legislation was to consolidate power in the hands of the speaker. He was constrained not by a seniority system but by a need to form a majority coalition. This was done by bargaining committee chairmanships to allies before the session began—a system much like that which the U.S. House had employed until the late nineteenth century.

Both Congress and state legislatures had additional leadership posts and structures. Sometimes they were similar, as with party caucuses; yet, because of differences in legislative tenure and session length, most differed in important ways. Although a number of state legislatures developed the formal position of floor leader shortly after, and in imitation of, Congress, they kept other functions informal and often linked them with important committee chairmanships. States had rules, steering, or "sifting" committees that directed legislative business, but these often functioned only near the end of the session and as a means of speeding up the passage of legislation. Of course, some parallels did exist. Critics charged the Rules Committee of the New York Assembly with abuse of power and in 1913 limited its authority. More important, state legislatures, like

Congress, allowed the discharge of bills trapped in committee.

Even more significant as evidence and cause of the differences between Congress and state legislatures was the major disparity in the frequency and length of legislative sessions. Beginning in the mid-nineteenth century, all but a few states changed from annual to biennial legislative sessions. In addition, roughly three-fourths of the states (i.e., all but New England as well as some Middle Atlantic and midwestern states) restricted the length of those sessions. Most adopted a limit of sixty days, but Kansas allowed only thirty days, while Oregon, Wyoming, and South Carolina set a forty-day limit. There was also a financial incentive to leave legislative work. New York and Illinois paid the top session salaries in 1900 of $1,500 and $1,000, respectfully, but eleven states paid only $200 or less (with Rhode Island offering a meager $1 per day), and the median state legislative pay was $383 (Luce, pp. 138–145, 528–535; Haynes, "Representation in State Legislatures," pp. 105–108, 214–218, 251–253, 411–415). By contrast, congressional office was becoming a full-time post; the Fifty-fifth through the Sixty-fourth Congresses were in session an average of 190 days per year. Partly as a consequence, congressional salaries were set at $5,000 in 1866 and raised to $7,500 in 1907.

Despite the importance of these differences, they cannot override the fact that Congress and state legislatures were bound by similar functions, common traditions, and especially a shared public perception. The reputation of legislatures began declining in the early nineteenth century, partly because it had begun so high, but also because of changing ideas about government. Suspicion of governmental and particularly executive power, an important part of republican thought, declined substantially during the nineteenth century. It was replaced by a respect for executive authority, which contrasted with a growing perception of legislative inefficiency. This was reflected not only in various proposals for changing legislative procedures but also in the fact that between 1912 and 1920 seven states considered proposals for a unicameral state legislature.

Respect for the institution also declined because of negative views of those who served. The most extreme case is the U.S. Senate's reputation as the "Millionaire's Club," but many other bodies were also damned as havens for the rich, hicks, "boodlers," and other unworthy sorts. A belief in legislative corruption was fed by actual instances of illegal, unethical, or inappropriate actions. This led to useful remedial legislation, such as limiting access to the legislative floor and requiring lobbyists to register. However, the perception of corruption grew far out of proportion to the reality of the problem. Allegations of bribery or influence peddling, though sometimes real, frequently amounted to anger at the effective presentation of information by industry lobbyists or frustration with the changing combination of interests and participants in legislative decision-making. Complaints about excessive legislative staff were probably legitimate concerning doorkeepers or janitors, but not—given the increasing legislative work load—for clerks and stenographers. Finally, the indictment of legislators for removing supplies at the end of the session or even ordering an excess of penknives (as the 1911 Minnesota legislature was accused of) seem less serious today.

Various restrictions were placed on legislative action, especially by states, and many involved policy choices. Beginning in the mid-nineteenth century, states began using laws and especially new constitutions to specify and limit legislative action, on finances or elections, for example, or even on legislative procedure. The Progressive Era measures of initiative, referendum, and recall represented efforts to bypass the legislature. For their part, both Congress and state legislatures sought to become more efficient by streamlining their procedures, by innovations such as the electric voting system pioneered in Wisconsin, and by reducing the number of their committees.

Since the early 1950s, American legislatures have changed considerably. Congress has altered in some major ways, but the transformation of state legislatures has been even greater and has produced more similarity between Congress and at least some state legislatures. The most striking development is the increased length of legislative sessions. After 1960 the length of congressional sessions increased by roughly 25 percent, and the hours per day increased as well. These and other measures suggest that the congressional work load nearly doubled between 1960 and 1980.

Even though state legislatures had less freedom than Congress to extend their sessions, they too met more frequently. By 1964, the legislatures of nineteen states had annual sessions, and by 1978 the number had jumped to forty-three. In addition, many states raised the maximum number of days per session, and special sessions were called with increasing frequency (257 in the 1960s alone). These changes followed from mounting demands on the legislatures; the number of bills increased sixfold from the 1950s to the 1970s, while the number of laws and resolutions enacted grew by more than 300 percent (*Book of the States, 1970–1971*, pp. 52-53, 66-67; *1980–1981*, pp. 104-109; Jewell and Patterson, p. 117).

Congress and state legislatures responded to the demands on them by revising their structures and expanding their support systems. In 1946, most state lower houses had from thirty-one to fifty committees and senates had from twenty-one to fifty. This was an excessive number, given the membership size of these institutions, and resulted simply from adding new committees over the years. In the post–World War II era, legislatures reorganized their committee structures to reflect more accurately the number of legislators and the distribution of legislative business. Thus, by 1973, most houses and senates had from eleven to twenty committees. In the Legislative Reorganization Act of 1946, Congress reduced its committees by half and increased their staff. During the 1970s, besides modifying the seniority system, it further expanded staff support and substantially boosted the number of subcommittees. The result was a near quadrupling of personal staff between 1946 and 1972, with even greater increases—mainly in the 1970s—for committee staff. Congress also created and enlarged such agencies as the Congressional Budget Office and the General Accounting Office.

Driven by their serious need and guided by congressional example, state legislatures dramatically expanded their resources and staff support. By 1971, nearly all states gave secretarial assistance to legislators; by 1990, nearly all provided some office space. The number of staff members also grew substantially, understandably reaching greater levels in states like New York and California (almost 2,000 in the mid-1970s). By the 1970s, nearly all states, like

Congress, had staff for fiscal analysis and auditing. For the broader range of policy questions, many states created legislative councils—bipartisan joint committees assisted by a research staff that by the mid-1970s ranged up to 250 persons in Pennsylvania. Finally, to compensate for continuing restrictions on the length of sessions, some legislatures allowed committees to meet when the legislature was not in session. Thus, even though the salaries for most state legislatures remained very low compared to Congress, the activity and expertise of state legislatures rose dramatically.

## POLITICAL RECRUITMENT AND CAREERS

A main connection between American legislatures has been the nature of their membership. Their similar function and the general prominence of legislators—especially before the creation of numerous other elective and appointive offices—encouraged members to shift between chambers and from state legislatures to Congress. By modifying and expanding the political structures of their states (within constitutional constraints, of course), legislators defined the paths of political experience and mobility. The establishment and definition of political methods, such as direct primaries, also shaped the prospects of would-be lawmakers. They influenced the selection of individuals more clearly through redistricting. Finally, the most direct connection was the election of U.S. senators by state legislatures. This system provided substantial linkages, as well as difficulties, between the different levels of government; its elimination had various consequences.

In the late eighteenth century, most legislators developed some tenure in their institution and had legislative experience at a lower level. In New York, for example, a session average of 90 percent of the senators and two-thirds of the assembly members had prior legislative experience; two-thirds of the Connecticut lawmakers were also veteran lawmakers. Members of the first Congresses also had legislative backgrounds; more than three-fourths of the senators had previously served in the Continental or Confederation Congresses, and almost as

high a proportion of representatives had been state legislators. But, despite their similar levels of experience and prominence, representatives and senators did not have the same types of career experience in Congress.

The House, being the more powerful chamber, attracted the more ambitious and successful politicians. It was also able to retain them; despite political turmoil in the 1790s, two-thirds of the members stayed for the following session. The Senate's record is quite different: more than a third of the senators resigned before completing their terms, and another third did not seek reelection. Such a plague of resignations and short-term appointments was disruptive and indicated limited chamber loyalty; it also reflected the nature of political careers in a new era and political system. Office-holding was typically intermittent, and men were often draftees. Furthermore, in a new federal polity, with attractions on state and national levels, careers were often not linear, moving along some local-national continuum, but often circular. Thus, some politicians left national office voluntarily; some later served in state office—even the legislature. For example, Michael Leib (Dem.-R.-Pa.) first served in the state lower house (1795–1798) and then moved to the U.S. House, serving from 1799 until his resignation in 1806; elected to the U.S. Senate in 1808, he served until resigning in 1814 and concluded his political career in the state lower house (1817–1818). George Baer (Fed.-Md.) bounced around even more, serving in the state lower house (1794), the U.S. House (1797–1801), the state lower house again (1808–1809), and the U.S. House again (1815–1817), finally holding the office of mayor of Frederick in 1820, the year in which he died.

The nature of political recruitment and careers began changing by the 1830s, influenced by the changing relationships of the U.S. House and Senate and of the federal and state governments and by new ideas about holding political office. The greater size of the House and the necessary procedural changes diminished the allure of that chamber, while the longer term, inherent powers, and national view of the Senate enhanced its status. New ideas about "public service" and "professional politicians" led to longer and more continuous political careers, greater competition for office, and a demand for rotation in office. As a result, although the prior political experience of House members remained high, their tenure in that office declined. By contrast, the Senate became better able to attract and retain capable men. The proportion of resignations from the Senate fell to one-quarter, and many resulted from presidential appointment to another federal office, not a desire for state office or simply for retirement. State legislatures showed a pattern much like that of the House, with the proportion of experienced members falling dramatically to 20 percent in New York and Connecticut. In other states, such as Indiana, the drop was less precipitous, but even there veterans made up less than half of the legislators.

Office-holding in the later nineteenth century reflected an emerging hierarchy of offices and a further shift in views on political careers. Congressional membership stabilized; typically, freshmen constituted less than 40 percent of the House and less than 20 percent of the Senate. The proportion of members with state legislative experience remained high: 60 percent in the Senate, declining a bit more to 42 percent in the lower chamber. The political careers of state legislators ranged widely, depending on the socioeconomic circumstances, populations, districts, and levels of political competition in their states. Still, a basic pattern emerged. Turnover remained at high levels during the late 1800s, with freshmen constituting roughly 75 percent of each legislature. During the next several decades, a shift began, started by a core of legislators who stayed roughly four to seven terms. During the 1920s and 1930s, a larger group of lawmakers remained for a second term, reducing the proportion of freshmen to less than half in most legislatures. This figure fell still further, to about one-third, during the post–World War II era, when there was a rise in all levels of experience.

Increased levels of experience also characterized Congress during the twentieth century. This was particularly true of the House, where the proportion of freshmen declined to roughly one-quarter until the mid-1920s, when it dropped below 20 percent, where it has generally remained. Senate membership, though fluctuating periodically with electoral forces, has also remained at high levels of experience.

The proportion of members with state legislative experience has stayed relatively constant at one-third in the House, but in the Senate it dropped to 40 percent in the Progressive Era, to less than 30 percent in the 1930s, and to 20 percent in the post–World War II era. This decline in legislative experience reflects the increased number of state offices, the closer correspondence between the size of congressional districts and that of cities, and the rise of nonpolitical means of gaining prominence—working in the media, for instance, or involvement by businessmen in public affairs. Equally important, it follows a basic change in the process by which senators are selected.

## SELECTION OF SENATORS

One of the most important direct connections between American legislatures was the selection of U.S. senators by state legislatures. This system lasted until 1913, when the Seventeenth Amendment established the direct election of senators. The original process established a relationship that greatly influenced federalism and political patterns but also caused increasing problems. Initially, when a Senate seat was less of a prize, the primary problem was replacing the men who resigned. By the 1830s, factional and partisan considerations had begun to complicate the process. Although the decision was still made by the legislature, the campaign for a Senate seat could sometimes be popularized, somewhat like the growing interest in campaigns for the presidency despite the intermediacy of the electoral college. Thus, when both parties' candidates were widely known, they sometimes sought direct, public confrontation, as first seen in a race for a Senate seat from Mississippi in 1834 (cf. Riker). The most familiar example of a "public canvass" for the office is the debates between Abraham Lincoln and Stephen Douglas in the 1858 race in Illinois. However, many other senatorial contests during this decade, and some in previous years also, had seen candidates confront each other publicly and appeal to voters.

After the Civil War, political developments, both in government and in party organization, transformed the connection between senators and state legislatures. The great increase in the number of federal jobs created an expanding currency for political power. Many senators, perhaps most notably Roscoe Conkling (R.-N.Y.), struggled with the presidents for control of these appointments. They sought to obtain government positions in Washington, D.C., and these went disproportionately to men from politically important and competitive states. Far more important were government offices at home. Senators such as John Logan (R.-Ill.) and Matthew Quay (R.-Pa.) skillfully used federal appointments to sustain their state political machines, rewarding supporters and withholding favors from opponents. Competition between and within parties intensified the need for senators interested in survival to remain current with all facets of state politics, especially the legislature.

Political campaigns became increasingly integrated during the late nineteenth century, as the expansion of transportation and communication created new opportunities and responsibilities for party managers. Basing highly structured state parties on local, grass-roots organizations, these managers worked to obtain support for the full range of party candidates. As a result, the public canvass for U.S. Senate seats became more common and more important. Incumbent senators, de facto nominees, and potential senatorial candidates traveled to legislative districts around the state to speak for the entire party ticket, including the local legislative candidate, whose vote was necessary for their own election. It was, in other words, a process that tied together the various levels of the political system—when it worked. In fact, plagued by inherent inequities and vulnerable to subversion, it increasingly faltered.

The potential for difficulty had been illustrated in 1791, when Pennsylvania's inability to agree on a successor to Senator William Maclay left the seat vacant for two years. Thereafter, such instances were relatively rare, with any vacancies typically brief and while Congress was not in session. The political turmoil of the 1850s—particularly the birth and death of political parties—created much greater problems. In 1855, Pennsylvania, Missouri, Indiana, and California were all unable to fill vacancies, which lasted for twenty-two months in each of the latter three states. The dispute in Indiana grew even more complicated, first paralyzing the legislature and then leading the next session to select a substitute pair of senators—whom the Senate refused to seat. Mindful of these conflicts, in 1866 the Senate sought to clarify the process by specifying the mode of election: a voice vote of a joint legislative session, with only one ballot per day. This measure did eliminate several causes of disagreement, but the potential for division and questions about the equity and efficiency of this system remained.

The process was simple when a clear party majority united behind a single candidate, for legislative minorities had limited power. These conditions existed in most states at most times, but not all. The most obvious exceptions occurred during the 1890s, with the appearance of the Populists and splinter groups like the Silver Republicans. A more serious and continuous problem was factionalism. Contrary to the view of many contemporaries, the "political machines" of this era were less like centralized corporations—with uniform rules and power flowing down from the top—than like feudal relationships, with hierarchies of mutual dependence based on traditions, personal relationships, and local variations. Party leaders, or "bosses," certainly tried to create integrated machines, and they used patronage, money, new organizational skills, and partisan appeals to accomplish this, but their successes were incomplete and never final. Issues were sometimes factors in senatorial elections, but power, pique, and prominent individuals were traditionally the more important elements. The balance shifted by the early twentieth century, however, as factional opponents, like progressives, were more likely to focus on specific policy agendas.

This senatorial election system involved three types of problems. First, it had deleterious effects on state legislatures, which often wasted valuable time and energy, voting dozens, even hundreds, of times. Such disputes sometimes extended legislative sessions and even required special sessions, which were costly. In the most divisive cases, this interfered with necessary legislative operations, producing deadlock or, in the extreme case of Oregon in 1897, preventing the legislature from convening. Police and troops were involved in Kentucky in 1896 and Colorado in 1903. Even without involving violence or causing such obstruction, election contests frequently intruded into legislative operations, affecting the selection of legislative leaders and influencing legislative decisions on issues.

The most serious consequence for state legislatures was the creation of opportunities for bribery and corruption. Between 1866 and 1901, the Senate investigated nine cases of alleged election bribery. The evidence was substantial in two cases, but both senators resigned before conviction. However, the second man, William Clark (D.-Mont.), sought and won reelection to his seat by the next legislature. The most striking case involved William Lorimer (R.-Ill.), who was elected in 1909 on the ninety-ninth ballot after a five-month stalemate. After two Senate investigations uncovered evidence that ten Illinois legislators had been bribed to vote for Lorimer, he was expelled from the Senate in July 1912.

A second category of difficulties were those which plagued the U.S. Senate. Election challenges, especially those alleging bribery, required substantial efforts by the Senate, but even the rejection of attempted gubernatorial appointments took away from normal legislative business. Furthermore, accusations of electoral corruption, especially those associated with seated members such as Senator Lorimer, diminished the Senate's reputation. Even more disturbing, because they diminished the institution's legitimacy, were the numerous vacancies resulting from state legislative deadlocks; from 1891 to 1905 there were fourteen such vacancies, and another six occurred by 1913. The worst state was Delaware, which had no Senate representation at all from 1901 to 1903 and only one senator for five of the other years between 1897 and 1906.

A third weakness with the system of election by state legislatures was that it was indirect. This would not have been so great a problem if state legislatures had been less malapportioned, which seriously distorted the real balance of interests and powers within a state. The greater problem, however, was that ideas regarding the role of senators had changed substantially by the late nineteenth century. Increasingly, senators were viewed as representing not a state, but a state's people. Thus, the indirect and inexact nature of this system came under increasing criticism.

Proposals for change began appearing before the Civil War, and by the 1890s, they were

being made constantly. Petitions and resolutions from state legislatures clearly showed public support for change. A majority in the House voted for a constitutional amendment five times between 1893 and 1902, but the Senate always refused to act. In the face of this intransigence, states devised their own systems to provide popular control, starting with party-convention declarations and moving to preferential and then binding primary elections. Thus, by 1912, when the Senate finally agreed to submit the direct-election amendment to the states, twenty-nine had already established some system for directing the legislature's decision. States rapidly ratified the Seventeenth Amendment, and it went into effect in 1913. Thus, it became apparent that the original method of senatorial selection was badly flawed. However, that system had provided a vital link between local, state, and national politics, and removing that link was to have serious consequences for the American political system.

## PROTECTION OF STATE INTERESTS

A third form of direct legislative interaction has been the states' efforts to influence policies that affected them. One such effort, the instruction of political representatives, was familiar during the eighteenth century to New England towns and to colonial and state legislatures. Similarly, representatives to the Confederation Congress had been instructed by their state legislatures. Debates over instruction involved several different issues, especially who could issue instructions and what such instructions meant. When Congress began considering the Bill of Rights amendments to the new Constitution in 1789, one proposal would have guaranteed to the people the right to instruct their congressmen. Proponents, like Elbridge Gerry, claimed that support for this measure followed necessarily from a belief in popular sovereignty. Critics argued that instructions would obstruct legislative agreements and, with James Madison, held that rights of speech, petition, and assembly gave people sufficient protection. The measure failed after it provoked considerable discussion in the House but found virtually no support in the Senate. This settled the matter of popular instruction and effectively rejected the theory that representatives were simply and directly delegates of the people.

A second matter was whether state legislatures could issue instructions. They often tried to influence or direct their states' congressional representatives, and during the first several decades of the nation's history, some specifically claimed the right and periodically tried to issue binding instructions. In nearly all cases, however, the representatives asserted the right to speak for their constituents and themselves. Thus, legislatures generally came to petition or "request" that their congressional delegates support a particular policy.

The idea of instructing senators created far more debate, for it involved theories not only about the nature of representation, but also about the nature of the Senate. Although the Senate was established partly to protect state interests, a number of Federalist senators in the early sessions echoed the sentiments of Alexander Hamilton during the constitutional debates that senators were national agents and that legislatures had no right to instruct. For example, Senator Benjamin Hawkins (Fed.-N.C.) resisted instructions in 1791, pointing out that senators took an oath to support the Constitution. On the other side, the Virginia Assembly firmly and frequently instructed its senators, who accepted that position. In general, Jeffersonian Republicans argued that state legislatures could instruct their senators on policy directives, but Republican senators sometimes claimed direct responsibility to the people, particularly when the legislature was controlled by opponents.

After a flurry of discussions during the first several Congresses, debate over the matter of instructing senators subsided. The practice continued, however, most notably in 1798, as the Kentucky and Virginia legislatures instructed their senators to support a set of resolutions on state authority, and later over the War of 1812. The issuance of instructions increased thereafter, especially in southern states, peaking during the 1830s and 1840s. The most concentrated—and least creditable—use involved efforts in the 1830s to expunge from the congressional record a resolution from 1834 censuring President Andrew Jackson.

During the next decade instructions were used for other, specifically partisan reasons, particularly by Democrats, while Whigs sought to distinguish between constitutional and policy matters. In the late 1840s nearly all states issued instructions concerning the Wilmot Proviso. This was an important substantive issue on which states and parties had good reason to take a stand, but binding instructions limited Congress's ability to construct a compromise on the territorial issues—just the problem that critics in the 1790s had warned about. Recognizing this difficulty, some senators, such as Lewis Cass (D.-Mich.), successfully pressured their respective legislatures to rescind instructions.

Because of this experience and the increasing unwillingness of senators to honor such demands, the practice of legislative instruction had declined substantially by 1860. A final effort to revive instructions came in the impeachment trial of President Andrew Johnson, but both public and personal opinion played a greater role than legislative instructions in shaping senatorial decisions. Finally, L. Q. C. Lamar (D.-Miss.) showed how much opinions about this practice had changed by defying firm legislative instructions on several issues and, after defending his judgment and independence, winning reelection in 1883.

In attempting to enforce their instructions and to control the actions of senators, some legislatures talked of being able to recall these officials. State legislatures had held this power under the Articles of Confederation; but the Constitution did not grant it, and only two state ratifying conventions had proposed it as a constitutional amendment. In the absence of legal authority to remove, the real disciplinary threat against senators was formal and explicit disapproval by their constituents and party. Thus, when the Massachusetts legislature expressed its displeasure with the decisions of Senator John Quincy Adams by electing his successor six months early in 1808, Adams felt compelled to resign.

This type of forced resignation became more common during the following decades, as the institutional and partisan conflict between senators and legislatures continued. When facing odious instructions and unwilling to oppose a clear legislative directive, some senators considered it honorable and necessary to resign—and some legislatures counted on this view. A number of senators quit in the Jackson-censure battles of 1834–1837, but fewer did so during the following decade; the last such forced resignation came in 1846. Further evidence of the changing balance of power between senators and legislatures came in 1850, when Cass's threat to resign rather than follow an unacceptable policy caused the Michigan legislature to rescind its instructions. Thereafter, senators either emphasized their role as public representatives and accepted legislative resolutions as indicating public opinion or, like L. C. Q. Lamar, defended the independence of their office and the wisdom of their views.

Far more common than instructions to their congressional delegates, and of continuing importance, have been the petitions and resolutions that state legislatures have sent to Congress. The most important of these have taken the form of constitutional amendments. The Bill of Rights is the end product of the constitutional ratification debates: they generated state petitions that were sent to Congress in 1789, reduced from eighty to twelve proposals, and ratified as the first ten amendments. (One of those which "failed," the one prohibiting a pay raise for congressmen until after the next election, finally received endorsement by the "statistically necessary" number of states in 1992, although the lapse of two centuries from first to last adoption may prevent ratification.)

All subsequent amendments, plus other measures not adopted or ratified, appeared partly in response to state petitions, but some measures resulted more directly from state action than did others. The Seventeenth Amendment, providing for direct election of senators, was most clearly the product of state action; it was introduced several times after continual state demands, and the Senate finally approved it only after receiving petitions from thirty-one states and after realizing that the states would otherwise call a constitutional convention. Two other Progressive Era amendments—the Eighteenth, which enacted prohibition, and the Nineteenth, which enfranchised women—followed state legislation and demands, while the Twenty-first Amendment, repealing Prohibition, also came after considerable legislation, referenda, and petitioning in many states. State petitions and demands were also factors in several of the amendments that failed, notably the

effort to prohibit federal interference with slavery in 1861 and the proposed child-labor amendment in the 1920s and 1930s.

State legislatures have been involved in constitutional amendments not just in initiating proposals but also in ratifying or rejecting proposed amendments. In the case of the Twenty-first Amendment, the sole instance in which legislatures were not the ratifying bodies, they determined the procedures under which the state ratifying conventions were called. Furthermore, various states have periodically called for a new constitutional convention. Such efforts came close to success in two cases: first, over Senate resistance to the direct election of senators, and then when many malapportioned state legislatures in the 1960s sought to overturn the Supreme Court's decision on districting.

State legislatures have also petitioned the federal government on a wide range of important issues, and this has been a continuing though changing feature of federalism. During the nation's early decades, it was common to channel demands for or against federal action through state legislatures to Congress. The most dramatic early instance of such an effort were the Kentucky and Virginia resolutions in 1798, which declared the Alien and Sedition Acts unconstitutional and claimed the right to void those measures, asserting that states, not people, had been the compacting parties to the Constitution. Foreign policy, especially developments that preceded or were part of the War of 1812, also produced considerable memorializing by states. State legislatures denounced taxes on a continuing basis, from criticism of the excise taxes of the 1790s through opposition to various tariff measures, most notably the "Tariff of Abominations" in 1828.

Certainly, the greatest amount of petitioning concerned slavery. Although formal statements by state legislatures were only a small part of the massive and growing expression of opinion on slavery by petition during the first half of the nineteenth century, they played a vital and visible role in the debates. After early protests over slave treatment, slave trade and colonization, and the denial of petitioning rights to Congress, by the 1840s states were increasingly demanding that Congress prohibit the expansion of slavery into new territories (as in the Wilmot Proviso), ban the interstate commerce in slaves, and, ultimately, abolish slavery altogether. And, of course, Southern state legislatures petitioned against these issues and in support of slavery. After the Civil War, because ideas about state authority had changed, petitions from state legislatures more often expressed opinions rather than requesting specific action. Increasingly, congressional policymaking was influenced directly by the actions of individual senators and representatives, by the platforms of political parties, and by the lobbying of countless private groups and associations.

## SOURCES AND TYPES OF FEDERAL LEGISLATION

Direct legislative connections have also been important in the development of national policies. National and state legislative actions have been intertwined since the nation's very beginning, starting with Congress's requesting, and then accepting, state cessions of western land claims and with one of the first actions of the new federal government in 1790—the assumption of state revolutionary war debts. Although this relationship has remained significant over the centuries, its context and the impetus for action have changed substantially. A vast increase in interpersonal connections and interstate commerce was brought by revolutions in transportation and communications, economic development, and urbanization. The governmental consequence of these developments were accepted fitfully by the public and often somewhat grudgingly by the Supreme Court.

The impetus for national legislation has always come from both state and federal levels, but the balance between them has changed. Congressional actions have always represented some reaction to real or potential constituency concerns, but over time they became less often a response to state legislation than to public opinion, lobbies, or other pressures. In addition, state legislation was increasingly prompted or required by federal laws. Although it is difficult to summarize such a complex relationship, the years from the 1880s to 1933 may be viewed as a transitional era; the New Deal established federal dominance in the relationship, and the 1960s saw a greater emphasis on national standards and an increase in direct contact between the federal and local governments. (This latter connection and the increased role of other branches of government are outside the scope of this essay, which deals with interactions.)

Federal legislation largely prompted by state action falls into three categories. The first and clearest instances involved congressional adoption of state laws—notably in the 1790s and early 1800s—on issues like quarantines and the slave trade or on more technical matters like harbor pilotage or workers' compensation for sailors. A second category includes federal laws that complemented a virtual unanimity of state laws on, for example, prohibiting lotteries, white slavery, auto theft, or drug use. Finally, and more generally, Congress has followed state attempts at regulation. These efforts have, of course, been shaped by changing technologies and Supreme Court rulings, as in the creation of the Interstate Commerce Commission in 1887 after the Court invalidated state measures. Subsequent legislation reflected a growing awareness of the changing realities of a complex national business. State efforts to deal with problems of labor and industrialization during the late nineteenth and early twentieth centuries led to struggles for national legislation on issues like child labor, minimum wages and maximum hours, and workers' compensation—struggles that finally began coming to fruition in the 1930s.

While the particular problems of interstate commerce and the explicit constitutional justification prompted congressional action in this area, a concern with equity and efficiency—in the face of substantial and frequently conflicting state actions—prompted congressional legislative efforts to establish national uniform standards in many areas. For example, the U.S. Securities Act of 1934 built on, and effectively replaced, three decades of state regulation. State legislative action also stimulated Congress in other areas. Efforts to evade national policy on matters, such as race, have prompted congressional action, such as the civil rights laws of the 1860s, 1870s, and 1960s, and attempted measures like the Lodge force bill of 1890; this bill (sometimes referred to as the Lodge election bill) would have provided federal supervisors for registration and elections for federal offices in cities and in districts where voters petitioned for such services (i.e., in the South). Similarly, in various eras state legislation on elections led eventually to attempts, successful or not, to respond with federal legislation. This included constitutional amendments (the Fifteenth and Twenty-fourth), efforts to pass a federal anti–poll tax law in the 1930s and 1940s, and the Voting Rights Act of 1965. This interest in national standards has been confronted not only by individual states but also, in some instances, by regional blocs seeking to influence Congress: the South on race, the midwestern farm bloc on agricultural issues, and western states on federal land policy and water rights.

Congress has always originated legislation that has affected state legislatures, but over time, the number of measures and the complexity of the relationship grew enormously. In the nineteenth century, Congress established various programs, many involving the distribution of federal resources. Such programs were typically not central to the concerns of state or federal governments (as noted by critics of the theory of "cooperative federalism"), but they were useful and established important precedents. Since the early twentieth century, the volume and importance of federal legislation have grown dramatically, responding less to state legislative demands or initiatives and more often stimulating or even requiring action by state legislatures. Because this essay is intended to clarify patterns rather than catalog all policies, and given the size of this legislative output, it is most useful to discuss congressional measures as they fit into the following three general categories.

One type of congressional action can be termed *enabling legislation.* Especially common for areas of acknowledged federal dominance, such as commerce, it usually involves issues affected by technological change or about which the Supreme Court has changed its interpretation. The effect of such legislation has been to clarify or encourage state action (which sometimes was, and other times was not, the intent). One instance of this concerned regulation of the liquor trade, where the Wilson (1890) and Webb-Kenyon (1913) acts permitted states to control the interstate trade. The Pure Food and Drug Act of 1906 led all but one state to enact complementary legislation; the related federal measure that was passed in 1938 prompted action within a few

years by thirteen states. Federal legislation concerning labor unions also stimulated state actions. The Wagner Act (1935), which outlined the rights and protections for unions, was followed by the passage of "little Wagner Acts" in nearly a dozen states; the Taft-Hartley Act (1947) restricted the powers of unions, and by 1955, seventeen states had passed right-to-work laws.

Because of the growing size and importance of the federal government, its decisions have shaped state actions. One example of this is that congressional decisions on deductions and rate levels for the federal income tax increasingly influenced how states determined their own taxation policies. Thus, the federal decision in 1926 (and continued thereafter) to allow an 80-percent deduction for state inheritance tax encouraged all states, except Nevada, to adopt such a tax. Similarly, the growing complexity of the federal tax code and the growing demands on federal and state government have led an increasing number of states to link the calculation of their income taxes with the federal tax. As a consequence, changes in federal policy, such as those in the 1986 tax-reform act, have required states to act, even if they wished only to maintain the status quo.

A second type of congressionally initiated action, *reward legislation,* gives cooperating states some sort of benefits. The most important, most familiar, and longest-lasting of these are federal grant-in-aid programs. Such programs have been part of a broad pattern of congressional activity—imitated by state legislatures—in distributing economic benefits to individuals or groups (including corporations), to local governments, and to states. Certain cases have had effectively no restrictions on the "gifts," as in the allocation of "surplus" money to states in 1837, in land grants to new states, and in revenue sharing in the 1970s. In the nineteenth century other, more numerous grants were given to encourage a specific purpose. They were occasionally provided in cash, as for the militia, starting with an act in 1808, and for agricultural experiment stations, starting with the Hatch Act of 1887. More frequently, Congress provided land—to promote various forms of transportation and especially to support common-school education—starting with the Northwest Ordinance in 1787 and continuing with various additional grants, as in 1802, 1848, and 1850. Other grants required not only selling land, but also a specific action, like the Morrill Act of 1862, which provided land to any state that established a college to teach agriculture and mechanical arts. During the twentieth century, such general grants were replaced by a more restrictive approach, but the older approach regained some approval in Congress during the 1960s, as shown by the passage of block grants such as the Omnibus Crime Control and Safe Streets Act of 1968. However, beginning in the 1960s, more federal grants went directly to local governments or state agencies, bypassing state legislatures.

The third category of federal action, *conditional legislation,* includes several types, but all have offered benefits to any states willing to accept certain conditions. Proliferating during the New Deal and growing even more rapidly since 1960, legislation of this type attempted to establish greater uniformity, efficiency, and activity. Programs providing matching funds— that is, allocating federal funds dependent on states appropriating a fixed amount of funds— were created during the nineteenth century (for example, in 1887, funds were provided to support military veterans living in state soldiers homes).

Matching programs remained relatively minor until the passage of three measures led to a major increase in federal expenditures: the Smith-Lever Act (1914), providing money for agricultural extension services; the Federal-Aid Highway Act (1916); and the Smith-Hughes Act (1917), providing for vocational training in agriculture and home economics. These three programs were modified and extended during the next several decades, especially during the 1930s. Since World War II, there has been a tremendous proliferation of such programs, dealing with many types and levels of education, with public health and hospitals, with airport construction and mass transit, and with housing and slum clearance, to mention only some of the areas.

Some federal programs required changes in the structure of state government. For example, the 1916 Highway Act demanded that states organize highway departments, and the Social Security Act (1935) required the creation of a single state agency dealing with welfare. In addition, changes in procedures or other aspects of state law have sometimes been requirements for receiving federal moneys. New Deal legislation often included such provisions, as in establishing a merit system for handling Social Security, redefining conditions of municipal debt and bankruptcy, revising educational standards, or passing soil-conservation measures. Federal programs since World War II have often mandated actions directly related to the particular measure, such as requiring hospital licensing in return for funding. The number of such requirements has grown considerably, and some general restrictions, such as nondiscrimination, were routinely added. While measures of this sort have often caused dissatisfaction, state legislatures have been even more critical of federal threats to adopt a punitive option, such as the threat during the 1970s to withhold federal highway funds from states that refused to reduce speed limits on highways.

## TERRITORIAL LEGISLATURES

Another aspect of the American legislative experience both resembles, and is distinct from, the relationship between state legislatures and Congress. Territorial governments have occupied a unique position: derivative and subordinate, but transitional and in the process of becoming equal. While these governments were created by Congress, their perceptions and policies were also shaped by the experiences of other states and by the understanding that they would eventually achieve statehood. Thus, the territorial-congressional relationship resembled in certain ways the basic state-congressional pattern, but it also differed in development because the national governmental context changed so significantly over time.

The basic expectations of territorial government were shaped in the 1780s by the transformation of state-held western lands into federal territory and an understanding that the subdivisions of this territory would eventually become states equal in rights and authority to the original thirteen. The Ordinance of 1784 and especially the Northwest Ordinance of 1785 defined the process of obtaining statehood, by prescribing three stages of governmental development and establishing the presumption that admission to the Union would follow rather routinely after a territory reached a population of sixty thousand. This established a context, a set of expectations, and a process, but political realities were much more complicated. The prescribed development of government by stages was disrupted by several factors, such as subdivision of existing territories, and statehood increasingly involved disputes between Congress and territories.

Territorial government began with appointed officials—governors, secretaries, and judges—many of whom had served in Congress and were familiar with the national government. Elected local government also came with the earliest settlers, although its form varied somewhat from place to place. Initially, territorial legislatures were to be created in the second stage, and the prescription was for a bicameral legislature with an elected lower house and appointed senate. In the early nineteenth century, however, several territories had unicameral legislatures, and some had legislatures from the time of their organization. The pattern simplified after 1827 and was set by the 1836 law establishing the Wisconsin Territory: popular election of a bicameral legislature at the earliest opportunity. These legislatures followed the procedures, and frequently adopted the policies, of those states from which the members had come. Their powers were more limited than those of state legislatures, but after 1839 some of them were permitted to override gubernatorial vetoes. They also expended the most public funds in the territory, paying for education, welfare, and justice and sometimes supplementing their own salaries or those of other territorial officials. Legislatures frequently struggled with those officials, in part because they were appointed and were implementing federal policies. Because of this subordinate status, territorial legislatures directed far more petitions to Congress than did state assemblies, especially after the Civil War.

The territorial delegate was the primary conduit for presenting these petitions. Initially chosen by legislatures in the second stage of governmental development, direct popular election began in Mississippi in 1809, and in 1817 it became the standard method of selection. As a nonvoting member of the House, a delegate could speak on the floor. He served to provide information and advice, to influence details, and to explain the desires of his territory. Although Congress did not have to grant these requests, congressmen knew from observation that territories would become states and that delegates would become their colleagues in Congress.

Congressional control of territories was delegated to a committee of the House in 1825 and of the Senate in 1844. In 1871 the territorial delegates began gathering as a group, and one of their members served as a nonvoting member of the House committee. Potentially, Congress had almost total control over territorial legislatures, being limited mainly by its desires to follow previous policies and to abide by the few constitutional provisions. It had the power to overturn territorial legislation, and in the 1830s it disallowed banks and transportation companies. It could also legislate for territories, as it did in defining their governmental structure. It was effectively limited by practical politics in one area, slavery, but it abolished slavery in the territories in 1862, and after the Civil War it passed greater levels of legislation than before.

The major areas of legislative interaction concerned congressional expenditures on territories and the question of statehood. Congress paid salaries of appointed officials (which were increasingly inadequate after the Civil War), the costs of printing, the expense of erecting capitol buildings and prisons, and miscellaneous expenses like judicial libraries. It also paid territorial legislators an amount for mileage and a per diem, which remained at roughly $3 to $4 throughout the nineteenth century. Its desire to reduce expenditures was a major reason why Congress generally limited the membership of territorial legislatures to roughly twenty-four in the lower house and twelve in the upper chamber. Predictably, these issues produced substantial interaction and disagreement.

Statehood was, of course, one of the most important matters that bound Congress and the territorial legislatures. Although the early national experience suggested that statehood was achieved by an automatic process, resulting primarily from population growth, it was always part of the political process. Boundary disputes were one political element of statehood struggles (notably for Michigan and Utah), and occasionally the nature of state government became an issue, as it did for Arizona. National political considerations were a much more common and important part of the admission process, however, and this became most apparent beginning in 1820 with the efforts to balance the number of slave and free states. Territorial policy and the actions of territorial legislatures became even more important during the 1850s. The admission of Minnesota, Oregon, Kansas, West Virginia, and Nevada were thus part of sectional and Civil War politics. The long delay in admitting the remaining western territories reflected increasing disparities between state and territorial populations and their greater distance from national population centers, but it also resulted from a different national political system, one that found advantage in territories. The admission of six states in 1889–1890 resulted primarily from Republican electoral calculations. Finally, Congress resisted the requests from Utah, Oklahoma, Arizona, and New Mexico because of fears concerning the populations of those territories. With the admission of the last two of these in 1912, all of the contiguous territories had become states, and the interaction between Congress and the remaining territorial legislatures became a matter of only peripheral importance.

## CONCLUSION

Congressional interaction with legislatures, whether territorial or state, has been shaped by developing notions of governmental and legislative responsibilities. The major shifts in federalism have been especially evident in legislative relations. The declining powers of state government have been reflected in the consensus that senators are national rather than state officials, in the ending of instruction for senators, and in having senators (like territorial delegates) chosen directly by the people. The increased authority of the federal government is shown by the transformation of policymaking, with state legislatures less often petitioning or leading Congress and more often responding to congressional initiatives. Finally, the declining importance of the legislative branch has been evident in political careers, as the legislature has become less important as either a means or an end of political ambition.

Despite these substantial changes in the relationship between legislatures, they have remained closely connected. In structure and procedure, for example, American legislatures have continued to imitate each other. After Congress began by adopting the traditions of states, as well as those of other national assemblies, it fairly soon became the major source of innovation, but the more advanced state legislatures continued to provide new ideas. This interdependence resulted not only from observation or from legislatures' similarity of functions but also from their overlapping membership. Individuals moved from one legislature to another, bringing to each their political values, ideas about procedures and political behavior, and experiences with certain types of issues or political environments. Despite some decline over time, service in state or territorial legislatures has always been the single most common political experience for anyone in Congress. Finally, although Congress became the dominant party in policy-making, state legislatures have always devised policies that can attract or compel congressional action. Thus, the purpose and character of American legislatures have been fundamentally shaped by their interconnection.

## BIBLIOGRAPHY

*Contemporary Legislatures*
The starting point for any analysis is GERHARD LOEWENBERG, SAMUEL C. PATTERSON, and MALCOLM E. JEWELL, eds., *Handbook of Legislative Research* (Cambridge, Mass., 1985), a collection of essays about literature on legislatures; historical studies are mentioned in some of the essays and are the focus of MARGARET SUSAN THOMPSON and JOEL H. SILBEY, "Historical Research on Nineteenth-Century Legislatures." See also SILBEY, "'Delegates Fresh from the People': American Congressional Legislative Be-

havior," *Journal of Interdisciplinary History* 13 (Spring 1983): 603–627.

MALCOLM E. JEWELL and SAMUEL C. PATTERSON, *The Legislative Process in the United States,* 3d ed., (New York, 1977), is an insightful comparative analysis of American legislatures. ROBERT LUCE, *Legislative Assemblies* (Boston, 1924), provides a valuable historical analysis of many aspects of legislatures.

### Historical Studies of Congress
*Congressional Quarterly's Guide to the Congress of the United States,* 3d ed. (Washington, D.C., 1982), is the most comprehensive book on Congress. Two basic studies are GEORGE BARNES GALLOWAY, *History of the House of Representatives,* rev. ed. (New York, 1976); and GEORGE H. HAYNES, *The Senate of the United States,* 2 vols. (Boston, 1938), a source of considerable information and insight, although it is a bit dated in some respects. An insightful and thorough study is ROY SWANSTROM, *The United States Senate, 1787–1801* (Washington, D.C., 1985). The relationship between the Senate and the states is discussed in WILLIAM RIKER, "The Senate and American Federalism," *American Political Science Review* 49 (June 1955): 452–469. JAMES S. YOUNG, *The Washington Community, 1800–1838* (New York, 1966), explains the social context of congressional behavior. JOEL H. SILBEY, *The Shrine of Party* (Pittsburgh, 1967), explains congressional voting behavior and sectional conflict from 1841 to 1852. DAVID J. ROTHMAN, *Politics and Power: The United States Senate, 1869–1901* (Cambridge, Mass., 1966), a very useful analysis of the upper house, is complemented by MARGARET SUSAN THOMPSON, *The "Spider Web": Congress and Lobbying in the Age of Grant* (Ithaca, N.Y., 1985). DAVID W. BRADY, *Congressional Voting in a Partisan Era: A Study of the McKinley Houses and a Comparison to the Modern House of Representatives* (Lawrence, Kans., 1973), usefully discusses structure, personnel, and policymaking. DONALD R. MATTHEWS, *U.S. Senators and Their World* (New York, 1960), offers valuable insights into the upper house and its members during the 1950s.

### State Representation
GEORGE H. HAYNES published a four-part article in Annals of the *American Academy of Politi-*

*cal and Social Science,* generally entitled "Representation in State Legislatures," appearing in 15 (March 1900): 204–235; 15 (May 1900): 405–425; 16 (July 1900): 93–119; and 16 (September 1900): 243–272. H. W. DODDS, "Procedure in State Legislatures," *Annals of the American Academy of Political and Social Science* 77 (1918), Suppl., offers an excellent analysis of the historical development of procedures. JUSTIN E. WALSH, *The Centennial History of the Indiana General Assembly, 1816–1978* (Indianapolis, 1987), is unique—a comprehensive and insightful study of a single legislature. L. RAY GUNN, *The Decline of Authority: Public Economic Policy and Political Development in New York, 1800–1860* (Ithaca, N.Y., 1988), offers useful information on procedure and politicians. BALLARD C. CAMPBELL, *Representative Democracy: Public Policy and Midwestern Legislatures in the Late Nineteenth Century* (Cambridge, Mass., 1980), presents a compelling view of legislative life, while PHILIP R. VANDERMEER, *The Hoosier Politician: Officeholding and Political Culture in Indiana, 1896–1920* (Urbana, Ill., 1985), details the patterns of political recruitment and legislative structure in the succeeding decades.

The controversies over reapportionment are studied in CHARLES W. EAGLES, *Democracy Delayed: Congressional Reapportionment and Urban-Rural Conflict in the 1920s* (Athens, Ga., 1990), while the extent and consequences of malapportionment are discussed in PETER ARGERSINGER, "The Value of the Vote: Political Representation in the Gilded Age," *Journal of American History* 76 (June 1989): 59–90.

### Legislators
The innumerable sources include *Book of the States* (Lexington, Ky., 1935–), for recent legislatures; *The Biographical Directory of the American Congress, 1774–1961* (Washington, D.C., 1961); state-sponsored collections of legislative biographies; and state legislative manuals, or "blue books," which include biographical data and sometimes a historical index of legislative membership, as well as information on legislative structure and rules.

### Political Recruitment and Careers
A starting point for analysis is ALLAN G. BOGUE, JEROME M. CLUBB, CARROLL R. McKIBBIN, and

# CONGRESS AND OTHER LEGISLATURES

SANTA A. TRAUGOTT, "Members of the House of Representatives and the Process of Modernization, 1789–1960," *Journal of American History* 63 (September 1976): 275–302. NELSON W. POLSBY, "The Institutionalization of the House of Representatives," *American Political Science Review* 62 (March 1968): 144–168, is a seminal study linking legislative structure and changes in personnel. KWANG S. SHIN and JOHN S. JACKSON III, provide a useful collection of data and some analysis in "Membership Turnover in U.S. State Legislatures, 1931–1976," *Legislative Studies Quarterly* 4 (February 1979): 95–104; and several essays in *Annals of the American Academy of Political and Social Science* 195 (January 1938): 21–52, discuss the pattern of legislative recruitment in individual states.

### "Cooperative Federalism"
Studies that present a case for "cooperative federalism" in terms of policy-making include MORTON GRODZINS, *The American System: A New View of Government in the United States* (Chicago, 1966); W. BROOKE GRAVES's compre-

hensive analysis, *American Intergovernmental Relations* (New York, 1964); and DANIEL J. ELAZAR, *The American Partnership* (Chicago, 1962). A readable and thoughtful study of New Deal legislatures is JAMES T. PATTERSON, *The New Deal and the States* (Princeton, N.J., 1969), while several essays in *Annals of the American Academy of Political and Social Science* 207 (June 1940): 1–36, present valuable specifics about the development of intergovernmental relations during the New Deal.

### Legislators and Delegates
JACK ERICSON EBLEN, *The First and Second United States Empires: Governors and Territorial Government, 1784–1912* (Pittsburgh, 1968), explains the context of legislatures and delegates. PETER S. ONUF, *The Origins of the Federal Republic* (Philadelphia, 1983), analyzes the early development of territorial politics. An excellent analysis is EARL S. POMEROY, *The Territories and the United States, 1861–1890* (Philadelphia, 1947), while HOWARD R. LAMAR, *The Far Southwest, 1846–1912* (New Haven, Conn., 1966), provides a fine case study.

SEE ALSO Federalism and American Legislatures; The Historical Legislative Career; Legislative Records and Publications; Local Legislative Institutions; Measuring Legislative Behavior; The Modern Legislative Career; The Origins and Early Development of State Legislatures; The Social Bases of Legislative Recruitment; Territorial Legislatures to 1862; AND Territorial Legislatures Since 1862.

# LEGISLATURES AND THE JUDICIARY

## Samuel Krislov

The closest the Constitution comes to embracing any separation of powers is the opening grant of authority in each of its first three articles. Though these "vesting clauses" were last-minute flourishes added by the Convention of 1787's Committee on Style, they have proven sufficient to establish not merely separation but also some notion of rough equality of the branches. This has been achieved in the face of a tradition of subordination of judges exemplified by Hamilton's somewhat condescending characterization of the judiciary as "the least dangerous" branch (*The Federalist,* no. 78).

The attitude of the framers, in short, was close to that of nineteenth-century Europeans, who regarded the judiciary as an elegant and prestigious type of bureaucracy. Policy formulation was a monopoly of legislatures as extensions and expressions of the popular will. Frank Goodnow's classic dichotomization of government into policy formation ("will") and policy application ("administration") was, in fact, a succinct statement of continental theory. Such an approach not only denies even approximately coequal status to the judiciary but consigns it to the level of medium- or even low-level bureaucracy. Executives are linked to policy formation through participation in legislation and are allowed some leeway in implementation. Judges are merely expected to adapt a policy to a concrete situation.

The American judiciary soon was vaulted to a higher role than that, although initially it was unimportant enough for John Jay to resign as chief justice to become governor of New York. And it was vulnerable to, but surmounted, Jeffersonian attacks on its power. However, the acute leadership of John Marshall brought the courts to the center stage of power.

Other key clashes with legislative and executive power have occurred since then, the most serious one being the Civil War period of reaction to the Supreme Court's disastrous decision in *Dred Scott* v. *Sandford,* 19 Howard 393 (1857). But the Court bobbed and weaved its way to even greater prominence in the last part of the nineteenth century, assuming the role of protector of a nascent industrialism from populist regulation at both the national and state levels.

It was this period that witnessed negative European reaction to America's system of government, which was characterized especially by the French as "a government of judges." In particular, judicial review of legislation was seen as antimajoritarian. Even in the United States, strong attacks upon "judicial usurpation" were predicated upon its antidemocratic, nonrepresentative character.

Perhaps more unexpected was the simultaneous decline of judicial power in England. While up to colonial times the judiciary there had flirted with asserting an authority that appealed to a "higher law," it withdrew from such a role in the nineteenth century and embraced parliamentary supremacy with a vengeance. In effect, it even abandoned much of the notion that the common law was an evolutionary system. The "Law Lords" (the highest court in England) took the position for half a century before 1966 that it had no power to alter its own precedents. Except for new legislation, English law was as theoretically immutable as the laws of the Medes and the Persians.

Paradoxically, judges in the continental civil law tradition, aspiring to few claims to prominence or authority, have always been more creative than that. This has become more pronounced in the post–World War II era. Shocked by the ease of the Hitlerian seizure of legal institutions, continental countries introduced judicially enforced constitutional restraints into their systems. Further, because commitment to the European Economic Community involves judicial enforcement of community norms, the Continent has become more receptive to judicial activism.

Ad hoc explanations of this pattern abound, though systematic treatment is rare. Though rejected at home, judicial review has largely flourished in former British colonies, and some writers think that important. But it has been repudiated in South Africa and was routed in India. There is rather more diversity than parallelism between the United States, Canada, Australia, New Zealand, and other present or former British colonies.

A more persuasive explanation points to the influence of federalism. When this is reinforced by ethnic tension between a nation's federal units (rather than within a component), courts often gain a policy role, one that goes beyond preservation of the balance between national and state legislatures. The growing authority of the Canadian courts in the late twentieth century supports this, as does the increasingly stronger role of the judiciary in Germany as compared to such a nation as France. But South Africa and India remain exceptions to this trend.

It is even more likely that traditional explanations have mistaken conditions merely conducive to formation of this pattern with its real cause. A much simpler and more powerful explanation is that the principal determinant of judicial creativity is the expectation of quick and decisive legislative action in retaliation. Judicial creativity would then be expected to be negatively correlated with cabinet government, and especially so in a two-party system with strong party discipline. Cabinet government merges executive-legislative functions and facilitates prompt responses to judicial action. Because response is diluted in a weakly disciplined cabinet system, the fears of judges would lessen. That would encourage creativity, particularly in less salient matters.

The emergence of a highly disciplined two-party, cabinet-dominated system in Great Britain would explain the almost total subordination of a judiciary once quite willing to exert policy influence. One-party dominance in India and South Africa set the stage for the eclipsing of judicial authority in those countries, but the new competitiveness in India may presage a revival there. In the United States, rivalry between president and Congress, coupled with weak party discipline, would maximize judicial daring by minimizing threatened response.

In a sense, this approach subsumes a hypothesis on American judicial review put forth by Robert Dahl. He suggested that in the face of a durable national majority, defined as attitudes shared by president and Congress, a contrary-minded Supreme Court decision will be, and always has been, reversed within two decades of the offending decision. Jonathan Casper's important and convincing critique does not really gainsay the central point of Dahl's argument.

The approach here suggested would reduce Dahl's argument to a specific implication of a more general observation. In those instances where the American system approximates cabinet governments of a disciplined nature, it performs in ways approximating them.

## THE PATTERN OF LEGISLATIVE-COURT INTERACTION

The specific points of interaction between American legislatures and courts are numerous and often subtle. But they may be not too crudely grouped into a small number of categories: (1) Courts influence legislative policies by their inevitable need to construe legislation and—in those systems which, like the American, involve legislative participation—treaties. (2) Where the courts have the power of judicial review—that is, the right to invalidate legislation as being forbidden by the Constitution—a qualitative change occurs in the relationship. For example, such courts have the power to "save" statutes from constitutional infirmity by reinterpreting them, sometimes in heroic ways. (3) Courts influence legislative practice and procedures by, for example, adjudicating election results and membership of legislatures and occasionally by limiting prerogatives, especially personal benefits, within the legislature. They also deal with criminal procedures and the exemptions of legislators. (4) Legislative operations may rest on legal enforcement. The efficacy of investigations can depend on contempt proceedings, which, at least in the American system, are often impractical for a busy legislature. (5) Finally, the very nature of the separation of powers may rest on court delineation of the line of authority of executive and legislative. This is generally an issue of constitutional law, but the proliferation of legal confrontations between president and Congress in recent decades is a striking phenomenon.

The legislative powers over courts are even less bounded: (1) Courts are established, and their jurisdiction defined, by legislative action. (2) Numbers and perquisites depend on continuous legislative action. (3) The appointment or reappointment of individual judges in many systems requires approval by the legislature, and judges may be subject to scrutiny or removal by the legislature. (4) Legislatures may, through legislation or constitutional amendment, reverse the policy implications (though generally not the verdict) of court decisions. Often there is a sense of rebuke or challenge when such action occurs.

## COURTS AND INTERPRETATION

It is difficult to draft regulations devoid of ambiguity. Even the most careful draftsmanship cannot anticipate all of the intricate variations real life can contrive to develop. Thus, common law judges have generally been allocated a fair amount of freedom in interpreting statutes. As Sir William Blackstone, the great British legal commentator, observed, judges may err in construing the will of the lawgiver, but the rules of interpretation help provide a stability that continuous assertion of shifting preferences by a lawgiver does not. The civil law countries persist in the fiction that only written codes constitute law. While the common law accepts construction of a statute as "precedent," civil law judges regard such decisions merely as helpful indications of what has been thought about the statute.

Probably the most influential formula for interpretation of statutes in Anglo-American jurisprudence is that in *Heydon's Case*, 3 COKE 72, 76; *Eng. Rep.* 637 (1584):

> 1st, what was the common law before the making of the Act? 2nd, what was the mischief and defect for which the common law did not provide? 3rd, what remedy the Parliament hath resolved and appointed to cure the disease of the Commonwealth and 4th the true reason of the remedy.

This somewhat folksy observation involves three major components unranked and of course unweighted: the text of the ordinance, the historical context of its passage, and the intent. As in much of the common law, the categories are loosely articulated and the judge is left with considerable freedom, particularly where ambiguity is present in the text.

American courts generally pay heed to context and intent when the text does not lead to an obvious result or one that does not comport with their view of good policy. However, "intent" of the legislators is not a Freudian matter of internal purpose. Aesopian language by a drafter with a hidden private purpose does not constrain, or even interest, judges. Rather, it is the expression of purpose in a lawmaking context that is important; for example, what the chair of a committee steering a bill through the minefields of enactment says on the floor of the enacting body is of great moment.

Justice Antonin Scalia has argued for less reliance on legislative history, given the propensity of American legislatures—especially Congress—to permit tampering with the record of debate. That practice allows legislative sponsors to convey to courts a clarity never proffered to legislators. Scalia rather would fall back on the "objective" circumstances and the text itself.

In the American system, the existence of multiple arenas makes intent particularly malleable, especially with respect to constitutional amendments. Congressional debates will be a starting point, but state ratifying conventions permit different arguments to be raised. Popular discussion prior to such conventions is a third obvious source of evidence.

The most thoroughly researched and least helpful historical efforts concerning legislative intent have been those relating to the Fourteenth Amendment. Prodigious scholarship, some of it with an ideological purpose, has produced strongly opposed views of the amendment's purpose and scope. The historical methods pursued are themselves varied, including study of congressional debates, ratifying sessions of the states, and popular discussions. But Charles Fairman also analyzed the behavior of ratifiers when voting on bills in Congress or in state legislatures in the years after passage of the amendment, and other scholars have examined the behavior of Reconstruction administrations as an indicator of what was assumed to be a federal, authoritative interpretation. In short, scholars were looking into a historical kaleidoscope, and when a particular view was not to their liking, they could, with a twist of the wrist, alter the arrangement of facts until it presented a view they did like.

American courts have assumed that they have a freer hand with constitutional texts than with statutes, at least since Chief Justice John Marshall brilliantly adumbrated that proposition in *McCulloch* v. *Maryland,* 4 Wheaton 316 (1819), when he wrote, "We must never forget, that it is a constitution we are expounding." The "commerce clause," for example, the chief vehicle of national regulatory power, has historically been interpreted in widely different ways by the Supreme Court, permitting federalist concepts to shade into states'-rights interpretations and back to a view of Congress as "exercising plenary power." Of course, such clearly nonself-defining constitutional terms as "unreasonable search and seizure," "due process of law," and "cruel and unusual punishment" cry out for contemporary, rather than fixed, meanings. However, there are provisions of the Constitution that are truly wide open for legal interpretation and that the courts have refused to utilize precisely because the judges would be nonbounded. Among the most conspicuous are the requirement of a "republican form of government" for the states and the Ninth Amendment, which reserves an undefined body of freedom to the people.

In recent decades much ink has been spilled over whether constitutional law should be "interpretative" (i.e., based on the constitutional text) or "noninterpretative" (i.e., based on a tradition involving extraconstitutional principles and values). Broadly speaking, on policy questions, interpretivists tend to be conservatives (though Justice Hugo Black broke that mold), and noninterpretivists, mainly liberal (though there is a considerable group of natural-rights, conservative noninterpretivists). Interpretivists claim they are much more deferential to Congress and legislatures. But their critics point out that deference is usually not extended to broad congressional authority under the Fourteenth Amendment. (This anomaly becomes even odder when one notes that Congress is specifically given power by the Fourteenth Amendment to pass legislation.)

Some interpretivists, like the former attorney general Edwin Meese, insist on enforcing a "plain meaning" of the Constitution. Others, like Judge Robert H. Bork, emphasize the "original intent" of the framers without regard to later glosses or precedents, though not limiting themselves to the text. It is not clear that original intent is easily ascertainable in practice, as former justice William J. Brennan suggested when he labeled the approach "judicial dogmatism masquerading as humility." Justice Black demonstrated that novel approaches could be imputed to the framers by the magic of "lawyer's history." And one of the most formidable and effective of conservative thinkers and judges, Richard Posner, has protested against eradication of judicial creativity in an essay entitled "What Am I, a Potted Plant?"

In any event, sitting judges do not openly embrace either of these positions. Neither do judges generally espouse "activism" or nonlegalistic interpretivism, if only because they would weaken their effectiveness as judges by doing so. The official doctrine remains Marshallian: there must be a constitutionally based peg for authority. But the realities of a constitution require looseness in the joints. After all, judicial review and separation of powers are nowhere explicit but permeate all approaches, interpretativeist or noninterpretativeist. The elasticities of "necessary and proper clauses" and injunctions "to take care that the laws be faithfully executed" permit judges to ply their craft without undue exposure to popular or legislative criticism.

## COURTS AND LEGISLATIVE OPPORTUNITY

To a large degree, the Constitution insulates Congress from the control of the other two branches. Each house is a master of its own rules and judge of the qualifications of its members. Only when they disagree on adjournment may the president set such a date. Qualifications for voters are indirectly set when states define eligibility to vote for the most numerous branch of the state legislature. Members may not be questioned in the courts for their votes in Congress, are immune from criminal or civil processes in conducting legislative affairs, and may not be arrested on other charges while in Congress or on the way to or from such business.

The courts have respected the need for such independence. In *Fletcher* v. *Peck,* 6 Cranch 87 (1810), Marshall refused to permit inquiry into the integrity of a statute, even in the face of strong evidence of bribery. State courts have invalidated laws as not being passed "for a public purpose," but they generally base this on direct inspection of the legislation rather than on an inquiry into how it passed. During the heyday of Supreme Court control of economic policy (roughly 1897–1937), congressional actions were often invalidated under interpretations of the commerce clause and the Tenth Amendment, and similar state efforts were invalidated under the due process clause. Those approaches were largely dismantled in Supreme Court decisions of 1937–1944. Some writers are pressing for a revival of such inquiries where "special interests" have had "inordinate" influence. But the Supreme Court has uniformly rejected such a role. To the judges, political outcomes are self-justifying, and the cure for bad policy is popular reaction—majority correctives—especially where economic policy is involved.

It would also appear that the courts will not attempt to control or define the amendment process, leaving that to Congress and appropriate executive officers. This is not a certainty, since only a plurality in the leading case of *Coleman* v. *Miller,* 307 U.S. 433 (1939), took that position, and the trend has been to limit, not expand, the domain of the "political questions" doctrine.

The courts have stringently construed the language exempting members of Congress from being answerable for votes. While members of Congress may be convicted of bribery, their votes or voting patterns cannot be use in evidence. This was, in part, offered as justification for an elaborate Federal Bureau of Investigation ABSCAM "sting" operation, begun in 1978, which resulted in convictions. Conversely, the courts have liberally interpreted congressional immunity to include speeches given on the floor of Congress and other official communications. Staff members and congressional employees also have immunity commensurate with their official duties. However, direct communications to the public do not come under the special immunity.

The most important judicial involvement with congressional process is in the field of investigations and is in consequence of legislative invocation of the courts to punish contempt. Each house of Congress could punish on its own, but only during the session involved. To assure uniform punishment and to avoid tying up the body in a hearing, Congress has chosen to employ the courts.

As investigations have multiplied, so have problems of abuse of rights of witnesses. The courts have required that a witness be apprised of the purpose of an investigation and the pertinency of questions. Congress has also been forced, or has moved on its own, to require fairer treatment, including permitting continuous advice of counsel to witnesses.

In *Powell* v. *McCormack,* 395 U.S. 486 (1969), the Supreme Court dealt with the question of denial of admission to a seat by an elected member. Adam Clayton Powell, Harlem's flamboyant African American representative in Congress, was found to have misused funds in his official capacity. The resolution denying him membership invoked both a denial of seating and expulsion, the former process under the Constitution requiring a majority and the latter a two-thirds vote. Though two-thirds of the House voted against Powell, the Court held that the members could vote to exclude but could do so only if judging qualifications. A chamber may not add to the constitutional requirements by, for example, excluding an elected representative who had an unpopular view, such as Victor Berger's opposition to World War I. Though some writers have suggested that this means the courts must rule on other legislative proceedings, such as impeachment, the lack of further Court intervention suggests that the Powell decision was based solely on the very explicit constitutional wording.

In a sense, this is supported by the Court decision in *Immigration and Naturalization Service* v. *Chadha,* 462 U.S. 919 (1983), which in a single decision doubled the number of laws held unconstitutional in all the nation's history. At issue was the "legislative veto," so-called because it provided for administrative regulations to go into effect subject to a congressional negative. This inventive form of delegation of power allowed policy to be set or action to be taken by the executive and then reported to Congress, which had varying periods to veto the said policy or action. Another question was whether both houses had to negate the action or only one house. The effect was to delegate power to the executive with strings attached, which the legislature could unilaterally pull back, bypassing any threat of presidential veto. The Court invalidated these arrangements in *Chadha,* heavily emphasizing the constitutional text which itself is heavily studded with qualifications about how bills must be enacted. The Court rejected Justice Byron White's minority view of the legislative veto as a functional equivalent of enacting new law where any of the three participants could refuse to approve the new action. The majority focused on the impermissible bypassing of the president and the requirement of bicameralism.

In yet another major way the courts have influenced Congress by accepting supervision of apportionment. In the landmark case of *Baker* v. *Carr,* 369 U.S. 186 (1962), the Supreme Court held such matters were justiciable and not closed to review merely by calling them "political questions." Though Justice Felix Frankfurter asserted the contrary, the precedents for judicial inaction were not very substantial, and Justice Brennan's careful opinion suggested standards as to when judicial action is appropriate or to be avoided. The Court subsequently accepted the "one person, one vote" standard, holding that substantially equal districting is required by the equal protection clause. In districting for the House of Representatives, the political unit being directly controlled is the state, but the consequences of unequal size are inflicted on voters. Federal protection of all voter rights, qualifications, and the electoral process, of course, have consequences for the outcomes in both chambers.

Finally, court decisions have significantly influenced efforts at reform of campaign financing. The problem is to avoid a restriction on freedom of expression under the First Amendment, while trying to limit expenditures and excessive reliance on large contributors. Congress has sought to handle this by establishing a campaign fund for presidential candidates that makes availability of funds dependent on acceptance of restrictions on amounts and types of contributions and expenditures. The courts' decisions in this area sustain these efforts, but emphasize the right of others not in control of the candidate to expend funds. The effect is to all but eviscerate the regulatory scheme, even when candidates elect to receive government funds, which not all do (see *Buckley* v. *Valeo,* 424 U.S. 1 [1976]).

## THE NEW AGE OF JUDICIAL ACTIVISM

The most important sea change in American constitutional decision-making came in 1937. Contemporaneous with the defeat of Roosevelt's "Court-packing" bill, this change gave Roosevelt a legal triumph even as he suffered a drastic political defeat. Roosevelt had proposed adding new justices if older ones did not retire. Ostensibly this was to add youthful vigor to the Court, but obviously this was a calculated effort to give him the opportunity to appoint justices more sympathetic to the New Deal.

After 1937 the Supreme Court withdrew from active and extensive supervision of economic policy, viewing itself as undemocratic and poorly constituted to be wise, effective, or authoritative in that domain. But its entry into a new domain of authoritative action was foreshadowed in a famous footnote to *United States* v. *Carolene Products,* 304 U.S. 144 (1938). Justice Harlan Stone suggested that there might be more-rigorous Court review of legislation (1) where expressly granted constitutional rights were infringed; (2) where the corrective political means were themselves thwarted, as in censorship regulations that cannot be criticized; (3) where racial or religious minorities were denied guaranteed rights; or (4) where "insular minorities" were unable to express themselves effectively. In essence, the *Carolene Products* footnote represented the heart of a new judicial sensitivity to "nonpersons" in American law and assumes a role for the Court in coping with "political breakdowns" analogous to economists' "market breakdowns."

The Court has also opened itself to a greater role under the Fourteenth Amendment and authorized an even greater expansion of congressional authority under the enforcement clauses of the Fourteenth and Fifteenth Amendments. Its protection of criminal process, the illegitimate, and women's rights is part of this approach, though in each instance is based on specific constitutional provisions. The expanded approach has been most dramatic in the area of expression. The decision in *New York Times* v. *Sullivan*, 376 U.S. 254 (1964), opted for "robust" public discussion of public issues by allowing critics of public officials to remain immune from libel unless there is "reckless disregard for the truth."

Sharply curtailed, but by no means buried, was the "political questions" doctrine, by which the Court avoided ruling on matters which might cause it to be confrontational with the "political branches." Basic to the doctrine of political questions is the truism that some matters are inherently immune to legal resolution and require expertise not readily available to jurists. At its height, the doctrine was invoked broadly to protect the prerogatives of state legislatures—for example, to allow them to control apportionment—as well as both presidential and congressional prerogatives.

Beginning with *Baker* v. *Carr* and *Bond* v. *Floyd,* 385 U.S. 116 (1966), the latter requiring Georgia to seat a legislator critical of the Vietnam War, the Supreme Court clearly indicated that its power over state agencies is not limited by the political-question doctrine, though respect for federalism remains. And, at the national level, matters once not reviewed involving congressional and executive processes are now dealt with, subject to analysis under a truncated political-questions doctrine. Matters explicitly designated as discretionary by the Constitution (e.g., recognition of foreign governments and the raising of revenue), matters inherently requiring a single policy, and matters about which the judiciary is incompetent or unable to enforce a judgment are still subject to the doctrine. But as Louis Henkin has masterfully shown, this answer comes after analysis rather than as a knee-jerk reaction to a label.

Some of the most significant decisions of recent decades have been made in cases that would probably have once been rejected for consideration, without explanation. The ruling that President Richard Nixon could be compelled to turn over confidential recordings of consultations with his aides was vital to providing the evidence of his having obstructed justice that was necessary to force his resignation. Still later, a congressional requirement that he surrender his presidential papers for scholarly and other examination of his claimed misdeeds was upheld. But the *Chadha* decision limited

congressional power to attach conditions to the delegation of power, and *Bowsher* v. *Synar,* 478 U.S. 714 (1986), limited Congress's authority to delegate law enforcement to its own agents. This trend of construing separation of powers to the advantage of an all-embracing executive branch has, however, been limited by *Morrison* v. *Olson,* 487 U.S. 654 (1988). Congress's establishment of special prosecutors, largely independent from presidential control, to investigate executive misconduct was sustained.

## LEGISLATIVE CONTROL OF COURTS

Courts generally impact on legislatures in subtle ways, but legislatures control courts much more obviously. The direct, even brusque nature of legislative action conflicts with an American proclivity to see political responses to judicial action as "interference with the umpire" and, as such, unconstitutional or even anticonstitutional. As Thomas Schelling has demonstrated, in confrontations strength can be a weakness and weakness a source of strength.

Congress possesses a number of weapons that could severely and directly control courts. They include the power to determine jurisdiction, impeach judges, and alter their numbers. In the 1950s the American Bar Association sought constitutional amendments to insulate the courts from such constraints, but to no avail. There are strong arguments that these constraints have not been abused by Congress; in any event, they should be available to apply the brakes to a truly runaway court, should it develop.

### Congress and Jurisdiction

While suits between states and suits involving ambassadors are constitutionally assigned to the Supreme Court, jurisdiction "in all other cases" is subject to definitions and rules set down by Congress. Over the years, Congress has passed legislation defining and redefining jurisdiction in terms of almost every imaginable category—time of suit, subject matter, dollar amounts, source of the law. Its plenary power is basically incontestable.

The most dramatic example came in the Reconstruction period in *Ex parte McCardle,* 7

Wallace 506 (1869). While the Supreme Court was hearing a claim to habeas corpus by an alleged Confederate sympathizer, Congress repealed the section of the Judiciary Act authorizing the Court's jurisdiction in this case. The Supreme Court promptly dismissed the case, though carefully noting habeas corpus could still be sought under other provisions.

On the practical level, any such removal of jurisdiction from the Supreme Court threatens to denationalize American law, since each court of appeals could potentially establish its own set of precedents for its circuit. On the political level, changing jurisdiction as punishment is also disdained. For example, in the 1950s, diehard southerners sought to strip the Warren Court of jurisdiction over schools. Not only did this fail, but their efforts to back punitive legislation in matters of criminal justice, economic policy, and Communist control also failed precisely because these efforts were seen as driven by segregationists.

There remains the possibility of establishing a "junior Supreme Court," as suggested by Richard Nixon and Warren Burger in response to the problem of Supreme Court overload. The proposal became instantly suspect to a liberal Senate. Ultimately, a compromise was reached establishing in 1982 the Court of Appeals for the Federal Circuit, with jurisdiction over many legally picayune matters that formerly fell to the Supreme Court. The court's potential for use as a weapon by Congress remains untested.

Ostensibly, Congress may not use its jurisdictional authority to alter a court ruling (though it may sometimes be able to do so in practical terms, such as appropriating money to a claimant who lost in the courts). Thus, when Congress was considering prohibiting busing as a remedy in segregation cases, most legal authorities doubted its right to do so, though they noted that suggesting to judges a preference to use busing only as a "last resort" might be constitutional. Most ingeniously, Henry Hart has argued that Congress's power to redistribute jurisdiction cannot impair the status of the Supreme Court, which constitutionally must be "one Supreme Court" with "such inferior Courts as the Congress should establish." Of course, the Supreme Court itself would probably have the last word on the matter.

## Salaries, Numbers, and Impeachment

Despite occasional blips, the constitutional provision that judges' salaries may not be diminished in their lifetimes has operated quite adequately to protect their independence. Congress does from time to time respond to unwanted judicial decisions by not raising judges' salaries commensurate with other federal employees, but ultimately it has not diminished the attractiveness of such service by continuous punitiveness. Indeed, when Congress in 1987 approved an unpopular pay raise (including itself in the package) and repealed it under pressure a few days later, the judges' increase could not be withdrawn.

Historically, the power to alter the number of Supreme Court justices was utilized, sometimes to control decisions. The original number, six, was altered to five to prevent the selection of a replacement, but the justices stayed in office long enough for a later Congress to restore the original number. Subsequent years witnessed changes, with the number gradually inching up to ten before settling on the current number of nine, which has prevailed for more than a century and now would be politically difficult to alter. Chief Justice Charles Evans Hughes took a strong line in his letter for the Court opposing Roosevelt's Court-packing bill, insisting that the requirement of "one Supreme Court" in the Constitution meant the Court could not decide cases in panels of three or more—as most multimember courts in the world do—so additional members would obviously complicate, rather than facilitate, case consideration. The argument is hardly unanswerable, but would complicate efforts to raise the number.

Recalling the break of the power of the British House of Lords by a threat to create enough life peers to pass a bill and thereby end that chamber's veto power, observers have considered the potential of creating new justiceships, the most vulnerable spot in the Court's armor. Roosevelt, of course, moved in that manner in 1937 and was soundly rebuffed. But that does not preclude another move.

Impeachment has been regarded as a "broken reed" ever since Jefferson so labeled it. Efforts to convict Justice Samuel Chase for his almost vicious conduct toward Jeffersonians under the Alien and Sedition Acts of 1798 failed by a slender margin in 1805, and no other serious effort has since been mounted against Supreme Court justices. Billboards calling for the impeachment of Chief Justice Earl Warren were part of the harassment of the Court in the late 1950s and early 1960s, and the threat of impeachment against Justice Abe Fortas for fiscal greediness secured his resignation, though it is doubtful the Senate would finally have removed him. When Justice William O. Douglas defied the Nixon administration's threats on similar but less-widely publicized activities, the Nixonites backed down. However, such a move right on the heels of their Fortas success might have boomeranged and been seen as a political vendetta.

Congress does occasionally impeach lower-court judges, but is usually willing to spend the time only on matters involving major criminal misbehavior. The most common infirmities among judges, senility and alcoholism, are usually dealt with by pressure to retire or containment tactics. Congress has provided for generous full pay to judges who take "senior status," relieving them of all obligatory service. They can also, by mutual consent, be given limited assignments to hear cases and may earn per diem expenses, making the status quite attractive.

The power of Congress to control rules and regulations has on occasion been employed as an effective weapon. For example, early in 1802 the Supreme Court, which had adjourned in December 1801, was legally forbidden by Congress to meet until February 1803. Such an action would be politically impossible today under normal political conditions.

## Confirmation

The Senate has a strong role in the selection of federal judges; under Article II, Section 2, of the Constitution judges are to be chosen with the "Advice and Consent of the Senate." But this understates the case drastically. By the loose understanding that came to be quaintly labeled "senatorial courtesy," senators will not ordinarily vote for a judicial appointee from a state when objected to by the senior senator of that state if he or she is a member of the president's party. By this means, the choice of judges had historically become, as Joseph Harris has suggested, nomination by the senators, subject to consent of the president. But "senatorial courtesy" is an inexact practice. Because some senators have been extremely unpopular, like the egregious Theodore Bilbo (D.-Miss.) in the late 1930s, their opposition has been ignored by their colleagues. Generous (or weak) senior senators may share selection with junior colleagues of the same or, more rarely, the other political party. For example, Alphonse D'Amato (R.-N.Y.) allowed Daniel P. Moynihan (D.-N.Y.) one of three nominations, gaining reciprocity from Moynihan after Democrat Bill Clinton's election as president in 1992. Similarly, Senator Everett Dirksen of Illinois, a Republican minority leader, was accorded significant minority leader, was accorded significant patronage by Democratic presidents. Such Senate pillars as Sam Nunn (D.-Ga.) and Clinton P. Anderson (D.-N.M.) even effectively opposed presidents of the opposing party in the selection of cabinet officers, an area in which the Senate usually concedes virtually untrammeled executive choice. In short, the prestige and power of a senator has much to do with the rejection or acceptance of a nominee. But normally, a senator can expect to prevail on a federal district judgeship, still one of the most prized patronage positions in the system.

At the level of the courts of appeals, the fact that an appointment can be made from several states, even when counterbalanced by expectations or custom as to allocation, allows the president a more dominant role. The administration enjoys a particularly free hand with the prestigious U.S. Court of Appeals for the District of Columbia, the leading administrative law court of the country. And, of course, no particular senator may claim a prerogative over any Supreme Court vacancy.

So long as justices rode circuit and heard cases as part of the appeals courts, they were invariably selected from the geographic area they were to serve. (Riding circuit was an onerous task for middle-aged as well as elderly justices, even if part of their duties involved their home state.) The senators from the region—sometimes a specific state—had expectations and therefore considerable leverage on nominations. The Senate was not limited to the less flexible thumbs-up, thumbs-down of the confirmation process.

Presidential freedom to select Supreme Court justices has grown over time. As the number of states increases, presidential power to play one senator against the others increases. The liberation of the justices from circuit riding in 1891 means that since then, there has been no great reason to choose inhabitants of any particular state or region, especially when nine justices must in any event supervise eleven circuits.

Hand in hand with the diminished role of the individual senator in selecting lower-court nominees went a decline in rejection of presidential choices for the Supreme Court. In the early years of the nation, simple partisan issues were the main reasons for rejection, particularly in the waning months of an administration. One-third of all rejections were during the enfeebled administrations of John Tyler and Millard Fillmore. Lame-duck considerations were involved also in rejections of choices by James Madison, James Buchanan, Rutherford Hayes, and Lyndon Johnson. During Grover Cleveland's presidency, Senator David Hill (D.-N.Y.) successfully invoked senatorial courtesy to defeat two New York choices; Cleveland outmaneuvered Hill by choosing Senator Edward White (D.-La.). Personal qualities and ethics were at issue in a half dozen instances, and specific political stands, often involving nonlegal matters, such as Jay's Treaty and civil service reform, were behind a number of rejections. The "postponement" of Roger B. Taney's nomination to be an associate justice in 1835 was part of the temporary anti-Jackson position of the Senate; his nomination as chief justice came later the same year, and he was confirmed almost precisely a year after his initial rejection. Of the first eighty-seven Supreme Court nominations submitted to the Senate by 1900, twenty-one were effectively rejected. Since that time, only John J. Parker, Abe Fortas (as nominee for chief justice), Clement Haynsworth, G. Harrold Carswell, and Robert H. Bork were rejected (and Douglas Ginsburg withdrawn) out of fifty-eight names submitted to the Senate. This 10-percent rate of rejection compares to just short of 25 percent in times past. The relative decline of the Senate has also been evident in fewer senators becoming Supreme Court justices.

Traditionally, Senate review took place without the appearance of a nominee before the Senate. Even a nominee's contact with the president was handled gingerly and decorously, in accordance with Lincoln's maxim that one may not ask how a judge might decide cases and that "we would despise" a candidate who answered. This changed in 1925 because a key issue in the confirmation of Harlan Fiske Stone was his record as attorney general, particularly his refusal to drop charges against Senator Burton Wheeler (D.-Mont.) that had been brought by Stone's predecessor at the Justice Department. Stone appeared before the Judiciary Committee and convinced members that the investigation was nonpolitical and would, by clearing the senator, be in Wheeler's best interests. The unusual nature of the charges seemed to justify an unusual event.

When Frankfurter's name was submitted in 1939, his reputation as a "radical" led him to agree to appear before the Judiciary Committee. He answered personal questions freely, but refused to delve into legal or ideological positions at all. His participation became a precedent that subsequent nominees have had little choice but to follow. All nominees insist on their right—really obligation—not to answer questions inhibiting their future vote on legal issues, but in fact, some do answer quite searching probes when they deem it useful to do so. Such hearings (now televised) have become more onerous, and indeed grueling, though they vary with the degree of controversy surrounding the nominee. There is little doubt that the hearings played a major part in the rejection of Robert Bork and, conversely, in the confirmation of David Souter.

After his rejection, Bork, a former solicitor general, Yale law professor, and court of appeals judge, penned a best-selling book that argued his defeat constituted a watershed in Supreme Court appointments and would result in a decline in the quality of nominees. Essentially, he and his supporters argued that (1) it has been a norm of American politics, at least since the fight to confirm Louis Brandeis in 1916, that the Senate's role be limited to inquiry as to the character and fitness of a nominee; (2) ideological and programmatic considerations are solely the prerogative of the president, acting on a public mandate; and (3) it is unseemly and improper to have judicial confirmation become a routine part of interest-group politicking.

The textbook argument that after the Brandeis confirmation a norm was agreed on to limit the scope of Senate responsibility does not stand up to much scrutiny and appears Pollyannaish in the light of history. The Opposition to Brandeis was embarrassingly open in its anti-Semitism, but premised on his supposed lack of "judicial temperament." His acknowledged subsequent greatness as a justice discredited the acumen of his detractors, especially the paladins of the American Bar Association.

But that embarrassment does not prove that burnt senators learned lessons. Only fifteen years after the Brandeis affair the superbly equipped Charles Evans Hughes was vigorously opposed on the grounds that, as a conservative, he would aggravate problems caused by a conservative Court. The subsequent treatment of nominees, including intentionally insulting questioning of Thurgood Marshall by southern senators, suggests neither progressive New Deal senators nor Dixiecrat conservatives felt constrained by any post-Brandeis norm. The Constitution suggests broad Senate participation. Active involvement in all aspects seems more nearly in accordance with "original intent."

The Reagan administration set out on a crusade to restaff the judiciary. It sought out youthful jurists of conservative hue, especially to secure a Supreme Court majority. Given a liberal Senate majority, the administration's expectations were perhaps provocative. But other patterns also motivated Senate reaction. Beginning with the Kennedy administration, White House involvement in all appointments, including those to the judiciary, increased dramatically. The growth in the number of judgeships and the decline of much other patronage triggered more-systemic scrutiny by both the Department of Justice and White House headhunters. The techniques of investigation and selection sharpened by successive presidents of different views necessarily lessened senatorial influence on the selection process. As senators found themselves with less influence in the selection stage, they turned inevitably to searching scrutiny at the confirmation stage. The mitigation of presidential authority that once manifested itself in the blending of senatorial with other advice at the nomination stage now required enforcement at the approval stage.

The growing role of the Senate Judiciary Committee in developing a public record on judges almost precisely parallels the growth of the presidential power of selection. The seeds were sown in the Truman and Eisenhower years, but blossomed during the Kennedy administration. A partnership with such groups as the American Bar Association was shrewdly formed to help buttress Senate claims.

It is difficult to see why the Senate is precluded from exercising ideological judgments. As Senator Joseph Biden (D.-Del.) noted in indicating his support for Justice Souter, senators ultimately cannot force presidents to make nominations repugnant to them. But senators also have public mandates, so it is not clear why they must accept repugnant appointments either. Even so powerful a president as Franklin Roosevelt, with his own party in firm control of the Senate, carefully modulated his judicial appointments and consulted widely.

The role of the judiciary in the American system is complex, as with every authority based on expertise. The use of television advertisements urging nonconfirmation based on simplified characterizations of complex decisions and attitudes is demeaning to both the process and the nominees. Yet much the same can be said of a good deal of Senate participation. Oversimplification and amateurism are inherent in the democratic process. Demagoguery in the American system was not confined to the Bork hearings. Certainly a Supreme Court that plays a major role in the system must expect some scrutiny from both the legislative branch and the public. Confirmation hearings have focused attention on the Court, but as defenders point out, they have also educated the public in remarkable ways.

## HISTORICAL OVERVIEW

The Supreme Court was a slow starter in the governmental sweepstakes. The nature and extent of its interaction with Congress have varied enormously over time, though on the whole, the Court has moved toward more nearly co-equal status with the other branches. Within that pattern, some sharp defeats and important triumphs define both periods of power and periods of decline. While theoretically Court power over national affairs is separable from its relations to state powers, the ebb and flow of the two is historically closely related.

## The Early Period: 1789–1835

The Court was seen as of little consequence in the early life of the nation. Turnover was high, and many who were offered a justiceship refused. Only one nomination, that of former Justice John Rutledge to succeed John Jay as chief justice in 1795, was rejected, mainly over Rutledge's opposition to Jay's Treaty.

A few major cases were decided, notably *Calder* v. *Bull,* 3 Dallas 386 (1798), and *Ware* v. *Hylton,* 3 Dallas 199 (1796). In the latter, the power of the Court to declare laws unconstitutional was at least implicitly involved. Two decisions by justices functioning as circuit judges helped develop the separation-of-powers doctrine: *Hayburn's Case,* 2 Dallas 409 (1792), on judicial independence, and *United States* v. *Yale Todd* (decided in 1794, but not reported until 13 Howard 52 n. [1852]), which may have been the first judicial invalidation of an act of Congress. In *Hylton* v. *United States,* 3 Dallas 171 (1796), such a claim was explicitly rejected.

The most important constitutional issue was raised by the Alien and Sedition Laws of 1798. The Virginia and Kentucky Resolutions, written to protest these laws, constituted an instance of state legislatures claiming the power of constitutional interpretation, a power that John Marshall later seized for the Court. The role of Federalist judges—especially Justice Samuel Chase—in enforcing and interpreting those laws became a political issue in the election of 1800. In the last month of the Adams administration, the Federalists passed the Judiciary Act of 1801, which would have expanded the federal courts and limited Jefferson's ability to appoint new justices. The new Republican majority repealed the offensive parts of that effort in 1802. A Jeffersonian attempt to impeach Chase succeeded, but the judge was acquitted in 1805.

Meanwhile, in the waning hours of his presidency, Adams had appointed what came to be called "midnight judges," including the Federalist William Marbury as justice of the peace

for the District of Columbia. When a Republican Congress legislated against the commissioning of these Federalist appointees, Marbury sued Secretary of State James Madison.

Marshall, authored the decision in *Marbury* v. *Madison,* 1 Cranch 137 (1803), which established the power of judicial review and constituted its first explicit exercise by the Supreme Court. What is noteworthy about Marshall's performance in Marbury is the dazzling way he advanced the power of the Court but avoided any action that directly challenged the power of potential enemies. Marbury, to be sure, declared the president at fault and invalidated an act of Congress, but ultimately did nothing for the plaintiffs, precisely what the Jeffersonians wanted. And Marshall was just as cautious in later years, avoiding any other finding of unconstitutionality at the federal level.

Marshall's great decisions advanced national power and congressional authority. *McCulloch* v. *Maryland* 17 U.S. 315 (1819), for example, sustained national power over state action under the supremacy clause and tax immunity for federal instruments over state impositions. But it was also important for its explicit development of a method for interpreting legislative power (largely synonymous with national power).

In Marshall's later years, the slow but steady stream of Democratic (i.e., Jeffersonian Republican) justices began to erode his dominance. Congress in the 1820s considered a whole series of proposals to alter the jurisdiction of the Court, limit tenure of justices, require individual opinions, and require unanimity on matters invalidating state law or acts of Congress. The high-water mark was an attempt to repeal Court authority over state courts in 1831.

## The Taney Period: 1836–1864

With a Democratic chief justice joining a Supreme Court with an underlying antifederalist majority, many expected the undoing of Marshall's major doctrines. Instead, Taney's leadership was cautious and consolidating, modifying and perfecting Marshallian decisions rather than overturning them. Thus, the great decision in *Cooley* v. *Board of Wardens,* 12 Howard 299 (1852), reconciled opposing views of the commerce clause in a masterful way, while the decision in *Charles River Bridge* v. *Warren River Bridge,* 11 Peters 420 (1837), mitigated the holding in *Dartmouth College* v. *Woodward,* 4 Wheaton 518 (1819), without completely undermining Marshall's assumption that a governmental grant to private persons is protected by the contract clause. The modifications generally strengthened states' rights, but some were quite vigorously federal in import. The Taney Court had a good feel for the pulse of opinion and was exceptionally popular. While the rejection of nominees by the Senate was at its maximum in the Tyler, Fillmore, and Buchanan administrations, it was presidential-congressional antagonisms that were at issue, not Taney Court decisions.

However, the Taney Court's normally sure touch was completely absent in its most famous and most disastrous decision, the 1857 *Dred Scott* decision, which was also its only use of judicial review. The invocation of this power—previously used only in rather trivial ways—to deal with the most difficult social issue the nation has historically faced proved foolhardy. Charles Evans Hughes listed the *Dred Scott* decision as among the most severe "self-inflicted wounds" of the Supreme Court. But in fact, it wounded the nation even more. The prestige of the Court was drastically undermined by the decision, which was later explicitly overruled by the Fourteenth Amendment, which declares all persons born in the United States to be citizens and establishes national citizenship as dominant over state citizenship. The Court was all but ignored by the Lincoln administration, and observers feared a move to abolish it. The Court trimmed its sails to the wind, largely upholding efforts to support the Civil War. But animosity toward the Court was to dissipate with surprising ease.

## The Chase and Waite Years: 1864–1888

The Supreme Court made a remarkable comeback. The conflict between the president and Congress that persisted throughout the Reconstruction period probably created the opportunity for this, for the Court was an institution capable of resolving and minimizing acrimony. The problems of the reintegration of the southern states and of new forms of financing and taxation arising from the Civil War also presented legal problems of immense importance.

The Court basically waited until the Civil War was nearly over to rebuke the Lincoln administration for violations of the Constitution. The decision in *Ex parte Milligan,* 4 Wallace 2 (1866), is a landmark of constitutional government asserting civil law dominance over martial law. But in *Ex parte McCardle,* 6 Wallace 318 (1868) and 7 Wallace 506 (1869), congressional authority over Court jurisdiction was acknowledged in perhaps the strongest way in American history. The most important Reconstruction decision, in *Texas* v. *White,* 7 Wallace 700 (1869), also gave Congress a strong hand in Reconstruction, especially acknowledging its power to control the reseating of the delegations of the rebellious states.

Probably the most significant decision of the era came in the *Legal Tender Cases* (*Hepburn* v. *Griswold,* 8 Wallace 603, [1870]; *Knox* v. *Lee,* 12 Wallace 457, [1871]). In effect, the Court invalidated making paper money legal tender, but President U. S. Grant, in appointing two new justices, effected an immediate reversal.

Five nominations were rejected or withdrawn during this period, largely a product of party discord between president and Senate. The personal ethics and political stands of the nominees were also at issue. But Stanley Kutler reported that criticism of the Court itself was surprisingly muted, especially so in the light of the increasing activity of the federal courts. More than a dozen acts of Congress were declared unconstitutional during this period, for example.

## The Fuller, White, and Taft Eras: 1888–1930

By the turn of the nineteenth century, the Supreme Court had developed great power over state legislation through the due process clause of the Fourteenth Amendment and the "negative implications" of the commerce power. National legislation could be sustained by invoking enumerated powers, especially the power to regulate commerce, or invalidated as an invasion of states' rights under the Tenth Amendment. Constitutional doctrine emphasized "dual federalism," the notion that each level of government must be confined to protect the other. The Court was seen as the guardian of this balance.

As a national economy emerged, the Court grudgingly permitted congressional regulatory power to grow. It did so by developing dual lines of precedents, one to permit national power to deal with some problems, one to strike down other efforts. Liberals like Oliver Wendell Holmes, Louis D. Brandeis and, later, Harlan Fiske Stone, who wished to sustain broad congressional power, condemned this as hypocritical. So did rock-ribbed conservatives, like George Sutherland and Willis Van Devanter, who would rather have sharply curtailed all such legislation. The balance of power was held by conservative pragmatists like Charles Evans Hughes, Joseph McKenna, and even William Howard Taft, and the Court exercised something close to a policy veto over economic legislation during this time.

The Court's apex (or nadir) came in 1896 when it declared the income tax unconstitutional; ruled that the Sherman Antitrust Act, which prohibited monopolies, did not stop a company from acquiring ownership of its rivals (because stock purchases were strictly local); and sustained Cleveland's dispatch of troops into Illinois to break the Pullman strike over the objections of the governor of the state. The Court, never popular with majoritarian forces, was now viewed as suspect by populists and later by progressives. Such liberal forces were, however, not strong enough to resist confirmation of conservative appointees, though they did mobilize effectively to protect Brandeis against a sustained conservative contention that his liberal policies meant he lacked judicial temperament.

Theodore Roosevelt reflected progressive discontent with the Court in his 1912 campaign for the presidency. The hold the Court had over the public is perhaps best illustrated by the fact that while he in fact criticized the Supreme Court, his timid operative remedy was the recall of state judges.

## The Hughes, Stone, and Vinson Years: 1930–1953

The 1920s had witnessed increasing conflict between two visions of American life. Running as a third-party, Progressive candidate in 1924, Senator Robert La Follette (R.-Wis.) was the first presidential candidate to campaign suggesting limiting Supreme Court power. When the formidable Charles Evans Hughes, a former Supreme Court justice, candidate for president, and secretary of state, was nominated for chief justice, the Progressives mounted a credible though ineffective attack on his confirmation. They had better luck with a more vulnerable candidate, Judge John J. Parker of North Carolina.

The Taft Court, though stolidly conservative, had made many pragmatic concessions to the country's demand for socially responsive measures. The 1930s threatened basic change and stiffened the Court, so that during the Hughes years it was less willing to support new policies.

As the New Deal of Franklin Roosevelt unfolded, with its sometimes desperate efforts to cope with the Great Depression, the justices became increasingly alarmed. The pragmatists, Hughes and Owen Roberts, increasingly sided with the conservatives; even Brandeis was shocked by what he saw as collectivist and antifederalist moves. The Court struck down a whole series of New Deal programs almost on the eve of the 1936 elections, which gave Roosevelt a sweeping political endorsement.

The president sought revenge with his court-packing bill in 1937. Alarmed, the justices sought to avert institutional defeat by overturning states'-rights doctrines and by retiring from the Court, thereby allowing new views to be considered. Roosevelt was to appoint more justices than any president since Washington and to see his constitutional doctrines triumph.

The new judges were unsure of the path the Supreme Court should take and were highly fearful of conflict with Congress. They began to build on the Holmes-Brandeis-Hughes-Stone commitment to civil liberties, but by the 1950s had become timid in the face of a nascent McCarthyism. They dismantled economic due process, but as they cautiously protected Jehovah's Witnesses and supported claims of blacks at the state level, they endlessly debated their role and worriedly looked back to the lessons of the Court-packing attempt.

## The Activist Era: 1953–1969

President Eisenhower's choice of Earl Warren as chief justice proved momentous. The most important item before the Supreme Court was the issue of segregation in schools, and the new chief justice was able to lead his colleagues to a unanimous decision undermining the "separate but equal" decision of *Plessy* v. *Ferguson,* 163 U.S. 537 (1896). The cautiously courageous decision in *Brown* v. *Board of Education of Topeka,* 347 U.S. 483 (1954), was to restore to the Court its lost honor and to propel it to new heights of power. Warren, less than a great legal craftsman, was to retire to the plaudits of some as the greatest chief justice since John Marshall.

The Warren Court plunged enthusiastically into a new role that Justices Stone and Black had advanced only tentatively—the development of an expansive and aggressive protection of individual rights. This had been advocated even earlier by the first Justice Harlan and Brandeis, but now gained momentum as a major function of the Court with respect to both national and state governments. Judicial control over criminal law, emphasis on the rights of underprivileged groups under the equal protection clause, and unprecedented expansion of rights of expression and privacy were all part of the legacy of the Warren years.

Critics, including congressional figures, argued that the Court was abandoning old law for their own predilections. The justices were accused of coddling criminals and being preoccupied with technicalities rather than issues of guilt and innocence. By turning over precedents at an unprecedented pace, they were, it was suggested, contributing to the social turbulence of the 1960s. And by their willingness to ignore legal forms, it was suggested, they were destroying the boundaries between the judiciary and the legislature.

Richard Nixon, while a presidential candidate, directly criticized the Supreme Court as fomenting crime; his solution was to appoint justices who would "obey the law" rather than create it. The hue and cry against Warren Court criminal decisions was clearly sincere on the part of prosecutors and police, among others, but it was also utilized as an acceptable cover for segregationists. Congress, as noted above, considered a raft of bills to limit the jurisdiction of the Court, some only narrowly rejected, and used the power of confirmation to harass prospective nominees and to make public the senators' criticisms.

The Court pressed its policies with vigor, though it tried to avoid needless confrontation.

It was backed on desegregation somewhat reluctantly by the Eisenhower administration and with only a bit more enthusiasm in the early months of the Kennedy administration. Though the latter was generally more sympathetic to the Warren Court efforts on criminal justice, religious freedom, and social programs, it took time for the Kennedy administration to commit vigorously to civil rights.

Congress itself provided the breakthrough. Federal aid to education was transformed into a major instrument of desegregation by denying such funds to segregated systems. Desegregation, which had dwindled to a trickle in the early 1960s, suddenly experienced new life. The Civil Rights Act of 1964 and the Voting Rights Act of 1965 buttressed even more-basic protections. With congressional ratification of equal protection, the area of Court-Congress conflict became more limited, rational, and focused. It did not, however, disappear.

## The Burger and Rehnquist Eras

Comparisons of the Court in the post-Warren era with the Taney Court's efforts to reverse John Marshall's aachievements seem inevitable. Successive presidents—Nixon, Reagan, and Bush—made the courts a political issue and selected justices with a view to altering the jurisprudence of the time. As regards the Court, Jimmy Carter was, as in most matters, unlucky: he did not see a single vacancy. In contrast, Republican presidents made eleven unanswered appointments to the Supreme Court from 1969 to 1993. Clinton's 1993 designation of Judge Ruth Bader Ginsburg to replace Justice Byron White was the first Democratic nomination in a quarter of a century, and this was a replacement for the only swing Democratic justice.

The verdict on the Court under Chief Justice Warren Burger is that it constituted "the counterrevolution that wasn't." The Rehnquist Court decisions, dealing with abortion and flag burning, have simply produced additional bones of contention for both public and Congress. In the fields of criminal justice and the Fourteenth Amendment, there was considerable backtracking but no clear resolution satisfying to either conservatives or a liberal Congress. Indeed, in many ways, some decisions in those areas expanded asserted rights. Prayer in the schools is still contested legislatively and politically, though a constitutional amendment in favor of it no longer seems in the offing. Ultimately, Burger failed to achieve his primary goal, cutting back the Warren Court criminal decisions.

Only in respect to the pornography issue was the Burger Court able to achieve a significant victory for conservatives, but that was little more than a Taney-like tinkering, rather than a sharp ideological coup. By substituting "local standards" of obscenity and pornography for a national standard and requiring a "redeeming" purpose of the material when "judged as a whole," the Burger Court modified the older Warren Court formulas, in an effort to halt the trend toward making it almost impossible to prosecute vendors. (Ironically, Warren himself favored a "local community" standard.) In any event, the Burger Court change was largely cosmetic, especially after it established a floor for community standards in *Jenkins* v. *Georgia,* 418 U.S. 153 (1974). It was Congress that made such prosecutions effective instruments by passing the Racketeer-Influenced and Corrupt Organizations (RICO) Act (1970), which, under the theory that organized pornography is racketeering, made vendors' assets seizable, but sidestepped difficult First Amendment issues.

The most potent difference between the Taney era and the Burger and early Rehnquist eras was that in Taney's time Congress was in the same partisan hands as the presidency. This has had an effect on the confirmation process, resulting in some moderate nominees being selected. But there has also been intervention by Congress on other matters, notably in the area of affirmative action. In general, while Congress is still somewhat critical of busing, it shows no inclination to legislatie any further against the practice. More important, when the Court has interpreted statutes to limit affirmative action, Congress has enacted the broader concepts rejected by the Court, as in the Civil Rights Restoration Act of 1988. Similarly, Congress in 1989 passed a civil rights bill to undo Court interpretations on employment discrimination, but failed to override a presidential veto by only one vote in the Senate.

Under Chief Justice William Rehnquist, however, a conservative majority has promulgated significant exceptions to Warren Court principles: (1) The "good faith" exception to the exclusionary rule permitted materials improperly seized to be placed in evidence if the police had not deliberately misbehaved. (2) The "harmless error" doctrine was applied to coerced confessions. (3) A limitation has been placed on criminal appeals in the absence of new evidence—a favorite Burger proposal. These "exceptions" can be construed broadly or narrowly, so only time will truly tell whether they are minor modifications or "exceptions that devour the rule." As of 1992, no wholesale revision of the Warren Court vision of justice seemed in the offing.

Congress continues to express unhappiness with the school-prayer issue. Abandoning the 1960s effort to constitutionalize prayer through the amendment process, Congress has indicated support for "uncoerced" voluntary prayer in the schools. Most significant in this regard was the Equal Access Act of 1984, which required schools receiving federal funds and opening its facilities to extracurricular programs to permit religious groups to meet on school premises. Voluntary prayer under these circumstances is facilitated, but problems of faculty supervision and the appearance of coercion have yet to be successfully defined. But Congress has weighed in heavily in this area.

The most enduring and divisive issue has ironically been the Burger Court decision in *Roe* v. *Wade,* 410 U.S. 113 (1973). Its holding that abortion in the crucial first trimester is a matter between a woman and her physician has been challenged mostly by ingenious state legislative incursions, some finally sustained in *Webster* v. *Reproductive Health Services,* 109 S.CT., 3040 (1989). Congress has given right-to-lifers small victories with numerous prohibitions and restrictions, notably in the passing of the Hyde Amendment, which forbids use of federal funds for abortion.

Efforts to "interpret" the *Roe* decisions by such measures as congressional definition of the persons protected by the Fourteenth Amendment have been buried in the halls of Congress. Such a measure would have violated judicial strictures that legislatures can not define the beginning of life without accepting a religious view (though no such objection seems to be made to a definition of death by the same means). It is obvious, though that legislative-judicial interaction will continue to be intense on these issues for some time.

The limit of conservative erosion of Roe was reached in *Planned Parenthood of Pennsylvania* v. *Casey,* 112 S.Ct. 2791 (1992). A moderate-conservative group—O'Connor, Kennedy, and Souter—joined the liberal remnant of the Court—Blackmun and Stevens—to reaffirm the "right to privacy" basis of abortion. The moderates argued *stare decisis* demanded such a stance, even though they modified the trimester division of Roe, substituting O'Connor's more pliable "undue burdens" test, which could allow considerable state regulation of the abortion process.

The retirement of Justice White and the election of Bill Clinton suggest a shift in direction back to reaffirmation of this right. Congressional action to strengthen abortion rights and even permit federal funding were widely discussed in the first year of the Clinton administration.

The temporary emergence of a new majority on the Court changed the nature and direction of public criticism. The conservatives were charged with activism and usurpation of legislative authority. For example, when the Court moved to abridge multiple appeals in felony cases, the minority claimed bad faith. Such appeals, particularly with respect to felons awaiting execution, have been prolix, driving the legal costs of the death penalty well beyond the costs of life imprisonment. Chief Justice Rehnquist spent months lobbying in Congress to relieve the burden on courts by restricting the right to appeal. Dissenters argued that the majority was enacting by decision what Congress had refused to enact by legislation. Similarly, when the Rehnquist Court rule that Oregon could prohibit peyote use in religious ceremonies simply because the statute was a generally drawn prohibition against use of drugs, religious groups were alarmed over Justice Scalia's casual assumptions that religion had no special protection. They turned to Congress for a restoration of religious entitlement that would reaffirm the court's liberal jurisprudence, requiring a showing of a compelling state need for a law restricting religious freedom.

The effect of a temporarily conservative Supreme Court has been to exacerbate congressional problems. The Civil Rights Restoration Act, in effect, repudiates the Court's narrow construction of a number of statutes. The success of that effort has encouraged liberal Court critics to turn to Congress to order changes in Constitutional decision-making. Congress can either pass new legislation or clarify old laws when it dislikes Court implementation. But congressional "correction" of Supreme Court errors on constitutional interpretation is of doubtful validity and creates deep separation-of-powers problems, at least as our system has evolved. Such efforts by conservatives were denounced by scholars in the 1960s and 1970s and no doubt the O'Connor-Kennedy-Souter opinion in *Planned Parenthood* v. *Casey* was written, in part, to caution their colleagues against provoking such a challenge, as well as avoiding its need.

Presumably the opportunity by President Clinton to make appointments that bring the Court closer to the mainstream of American political life will diminish the appetite of the Congress to consider itself a committee for correction of Court error. If not, it is likely we will again be shown that the founders of our nation created a much more flexible system than has been appreciated.

## BIBLIOGRAPHY

The closest approximations to a theory of legislative-judicial relations are the classics of separation of power. Probably the most germane is SIR WILLIAM BLACKSTONE, *Commentaries on the Laws of England* (4 vols., 1765–1769), which seems persistently to be on the verge of saying profound things about the relationship, but inevitably withdraws into platitudes. The much-reprinted *Federalist Papers* of James Madison, Alexander Hamilton, and John Jay are stronger and more consistent on the legislature and executive, but the discussion of the judiciary is rewarding in its own right and has exerted enormous influence as well. ALEXIS DE TOCQUEVILLE, *Democracy in America* (2 vols., 1835, 1840), is shrewd and thoughtful on the judiciary and, it is known, draws heavily on the wisdom of Supreme Court Justice Joseph Story. CHARLES MCIWAIN, *The High Court of Parliament and Its Supremacy* (New Haven, Conn., 1916), suggests court roots are legislative and Frank Horack, *Cases and Materials on Legisla-*

*tion* (Chicago, 1940, 1950), draws ingenious legislative judicial parallels. FRANK GOODNOW, *Politics and Administration* (1900; repr., New York, 1967), suggests that functionally courts are part of administration. THEODORE LOWI, *The End of Liberalism* (New York, 1969), sees law and policy flexibility as antithetical. JESSE CHOPER, *Judicial Review and the National Political Process* (Chicago, 1980), is magisterial and lucid in summarizing both legal and political analyses of the political relationship between the Supreme Court and Congress. His proposal that the court give up power to delcare congressional acts unconstitutional on the basis of state authority is not only provocative but also very close to current Court doctrine. JOHN SCHMIDHAUSER and L.L. BERG deal with the topic, especially through a case-study approach, in *The Supreme Court and Congress* (New York, 1972). Another authoritative work with strong historical emphasis is D. L. MORGAN, *Congress and the Constitution* (Cambridge, Mass., 1966).

DONALD HOROWITZ, *The Courts and Social Policy* (Washington, D.C., 1977), tries to delineate a precise and more limited role for courts and his work has spawned a whole literature in response. HENRY HART has treated the Constitutional authority of Congress in "The Power of Congress to Limit the Jurisdiction of the Federal Courts," *Harvard Law Review* 66 (April 1953).

Though perhaps not as comprehensive as its title suggests—about 75 percent of the volume deals with the Warren Court era—WALTER MURPHY, *Congress and the Court* (Chicago, 1962), is a good treatment of that conflict and its first brief pages constitute a useful introduction to legislative Supreme Court conflicts. C. HERMAN PRITCHETT, *Congress Versus the Supreme Court, 1957–1960* (Minneapolis, 1961), is also useful for Warren Court attacks. The best-detailed treatment of such troubles in CHARLES WARREN, "Legislative and Judicial Attacks on the Supreme Court," *American Law Review* 47:1 (1913), which principally chronicles efforts to alter section 25 of the Judiciary Act. A broader, more uneven, but gripping account of court-legislative confrontation is ROBERT JACKSON, *The Struggle for Judicial Supremacy* (New York, 1941). ROBERT BORK, *The Tempting of America*

(New York, 1990), reviews much the same ground from a different perspective, but the sections on the Senate's role in confirmation are more urgent and compelling.

Other works of importance deal with smaller issues or more discrete time sequences. JOSEPH PRATT HARRIS, *Advice and Consent of the Senate* (1953; repr., Westport, Conn., 1968), remains the standard work, though much has since changed. STANLEY KUTLER, *Judicial Power and Reconstruction Politics* (Chicago, 1968), is illuminating about the resurgence of the Supreme Court during Reconstruction. The volumes of the *Oliver Wendell Holmes Devise History of the United States Supreme Court* (New York, 1971–) provides greater depth and detail than Charles Warren's history; see especially the volumes by CARL SWISHER, CHARLES FAIRMAN, and EDWARD WHITE. A good technical treatment of an important aspect of relations is to be found in "Congressional Reversal of Supreme Court Decisions," *Harvard Law Review* 71 (April 1957). A. T. MASON, *Harlan Fiske Stone* (New York, 1956), and LEONARD BAKER, *Back to Back: The Duel Between FDR and the Supreme Court* (New York, 1967), deal well with the Court-packing proposal.

There have been considerable attempts to study the political relations systematically. Particularly influential is Robert Dahl, "Decision Making in a Democracy," *Journal of Public Law* 6:2 (1957), and a critique by JONATHAN CASPER, "The Supreme Court and National Policy-Making," *American Political Science Review* 70:1 (1976). RICHARD FUNSTON, "The Supreme Court and Critical Elections," *American Political Science Review* 69:3 (1975), is closely related.

LOUIS HENKIN, "Is There a 'Political Question' Doctrine?" *Yale Law Journal* 85:5 (1971) is a gem, as is CHARLES FAIRMAN, "Does the Fourteenth Amendment Incorporate the Bill of Rights?" *Stanford Law Review* 2 (December 1949). The literature on the Fourteenth Amendment, though maddeningly inconclusive, has drawn writers of great skill and authority, including ALEXANDER BICKEL and RAUL BURGER and younger writers such as MICHAEL KENT CURTIS and MICHAEL ZUCKERT. A good starting point is WILLIAM NELSON, *The Fourteenth Amendment* (Cambridge, Mass., 1988).

SEE ALSO Federalism and American Legislatures; Legislative Power Over Appointments and Confirmations; AND The U.S. Congress: The Era of Party Patronage and Sectional Stress, 1829–1881.

# LEGISLATURES AND BUREAUCRACY

## Barry D. Karl

The avoidance of the term *bureaucracy* by Americans and its assignment to a category of pejorative aspects of government can be traced in part to Anglo-American conceptions of continental governments. English and American proponents of democratic or representative theory perceived the managers of European governments as authoritarian figures committed to the following of rules. Using powers delegated to them by the nonelected rulers who appointed them, they could stay within the confines of specific authority when required to or substitute their own judgments when allowed to, but in either case remain free from responsibility to the public at large. From such perspectives, bureaucracy and legislative democracy could come to be understood as being in direct opposition to one another. Even though it might be difficult from time to time to distinguish a "civil servant" from a "bureaucrat," both popular and professional literatures saw in such a distinction one of the identifying characteristics of Anglo-American democracy. Contemporary efforts to introduce a more acceptable understanding of bureaucracies stem from the influence in American political science and sociology of the writings of Max Weber. The failure of that understanding to move from academia to practical politics can be demonstrated by the continuing use in political campaigns of bureaucracy and bureaucrats as antidemocratic elements to be condemned and, if possible, rooted out.

It is nonetheless true that bureaucracies and bureaucrats have been essential parts of the American political scene and continue to be, whether one calls them "civil servants," "public administrators," or "staff members" of an executive or, much more recently, legislative branch of government. Nor is it altogether easy to explain why an essay on the relation between bureaucracies and legislatures should begin with a focus on the executive branch, even though the reasons are simple.

As Senator Robert Byrd (D.-W.Va.) says in his brief history of the Legislative Reform Act of 1946, for a large part of the nineteenth century most members of Congress "enjoyed sufficient leisure to do their own research, draft their own legislation and write their own lengthy speeches." He goes on to explain, "Most members had no other office space than their desks in the Senate chamber or in their boarding house quarters near the Capitol Building." Again for much of the last century, members who required staff paid for it out of their own pockets, and from what is known of the personal wealth of some of them, that was not so unusual. Again, virtually until 1946, the term *staff* meant clerical or secretarial services.

This does not mean that a bureaucracy did not exist or that its relation to Congress was not close. That it was often an adventitious (in the sense of being unstructured and unplanned), even adversarial relation can be summed up in a quote attributed to Harry Truman: "The business of a good legislator is not to get things done quickly or efficiently, as a good administrator has to do but to prevent, if possible, the enactment into the law of the land many crazy and crackpot measures." A brief history of the developing relationship between bureaucracies, by whatever name they are acceptably understood, and legislatures might help to set the scene for discussion of the relationship in more recent times.

## EARLY HISTORICAL BACKGROUND

Inherent in the colonial disputes over the power of executives was the assumption that, ideally at least, executives ought to be the servants of legislatures and totally subject to their will. The concept was as revolutionary as any aspect of American government as individuals who would once have been considered ministers of the king gradually became ministers of the people, executives charged with the responsibility of executing public will. According to James Madison's notes on the Constitutional Convention of 1787—and according to many scholars who have reexamined constitutional theory in the late twentieth century—that was at least partly the intention of the framers of the U.S. Constitution. Wherever one chooses to begin the elaboration of independent executive authority—with the era of Andrew Jackson or with Woodrow Wilson as some contemporary scholarship has insisted—the growth of an executive branch staffed by a bureaucracy that mediates between the president and Congress has a long history in American government. That history remains outside the design of the Constitution, however much constitutional debate it may have generated.

It is thus difficult to find the beginnings of bureaucracy in American history beyond the gradual extension of departmental staffs that grew up around the legislature established by the Articles of Confederation, to which the president as chief executive was somewhat crudely attached. Those involved in the formulation of those articles and the subsequent Constitution had much reason to believe that the departments served their purposes. The issue of whether those purposes were to be articulated by Congress or by the president has never been wholly resolved. That very irresolution contributes to the difficulty of defining a legislative bureaucracy that is in any real sense distinct from the administrative branch. One might better see it as a tug-of-war between the two branches, with the various bureaucracies that join them serving as the rope.

One can begin with the cabinet, whose members, while appointed with the advice and consent of the Senate, are selected by the president and are subject to his administrative will, although both their selection and their relation to the Senate have periodically been disputed, as the bitter, post–Civil War battles over so-called tenure of office demonstrate. The potential for serious conflict was there early and unexpectedly. With the development of political parties in the early years of the Republic, a development the framers of the Constitution had sought to avoid, the selection of cabinet officers and their power to appoint bureaucratic officials in the states took on a partisan dimension. The term *spoils* as associated with the administration of Andrew Jackson meant that the party in power would have the authority to redistribute those offices which were under federal control. Whether or not that was in fact the evil that reformers took it to be has been questioned by scholars of the period, but nonetheless the appointment of cabinet members to departments such as the Post Office, with its postmasterships; the Department of the Interior, whose control of land distribution gave it offices of considerable importance; and the Department of State, whose consular appointments were coveted, gave members of Congress reason to interest themselves not only in the choice among job applicants but also in the policies they would be called on to carry out.

The evolution of the cabinet to the point where it has become the focal point of a managerial bureaucracy has given the president a set of informal options to consider when he chooses those who will be his link with the departments and Congress. He can choose a figure from one of the congressional bodies who will help him negotiate programs and their legislative outcomes. He can choose someone who is particularly well versed in the administrative specialization represented by a department and who may also reflect the interests with which that department deals. Finally, he may select someone with whom he has worked closely throughout his own career and whom he can trust to carry out his own programs in a department. The growth of bureaus and agencies has, even from the beginning, forced sometimes difficult negotiations between the president and Congress on issues of policy and its execution by the federal bureaucracy.

It seems clear from George Washington's use of his original cabinet that he intended it to function as bureaucratic staff to the presidency. But it is also clear that as partisan politics began to affect the formulation of public policy, the role of the cabinet became more complex. Increasingly, presidents would find it difficult to depend on the cabinet for rigorous loyalty as cabinet officers chose to use their possible influence in Congress to express disagreement with presidential policies. The battle between Alexander Hamilton and Thomas Jefferson in the Washington administration was the first of such confrontations. Complex though it was, it represents an early form of the bureaucratic infighting that has continued to characterize the American form of bureaucratic politics.

How those bureaucracies actually functioned has been the subject of a certain amount of historical dispute. The Federalists began in a mood of what historians call republican virtue, applying a term borrowed from English political thought. The decline of such practices by the early nineteenth century and their replacement by a democratic moralism helped support a side of Jacksonian practice that was less the result of partisanship than the need to find new, Benthamite representative virtues in administrative practices bound by accurate applications of justice.

The boundaries set by federalism gave the primary responsibility of government to the states, which served not only the needs of citizens but the very definition of citizenship itself. Suffrage was determined by the states, which also had other roles to play in the selection of national leaders. The major exception lay in the function of territorial legislatures, which established a now-forgotten but nonetheless important relation between such legislatures and the federal bureaucracy in an era when the United States consisted of large areas of unorganized territory.

The frontier life dramatically memorialized by Frederick Jackson Turner had closer relations with the War Department and its various offices and with the Department of the Interior and such subsidiary agencies as the Geological Survey than it did with any other governments until statehood carved out new governmental forms closer to home. The almost forgotten territorial legislatures and other territorial agencies, federal marshals, and the post offices had a great deal to do with the shaping of the states of the West. The northern boundaries of Illinois and Indiana, for example, were shifted further north than originally planned in order to give both new states lake ports to prevent their permanent attachment to the southern channeled waterways of the Ohio and Mississippi rivers. Such manipulative planning—and one should certainly include the Lewis and Clark survey of the Louisiana Purchase among them—are examples of the federally directed

bureaucratic management that ended with the admission of states to the Union.

All such manipulation came to be governed by the promise of opportunity held out by the availability of land, the freedom of water transportation, the maintenance of lines of communication protected from the unwanted presence of Indian tribes, and management by government officials who were classical bureaucrats in many respects and subject to criticism, as all bureaucracies were. The bureaucratic treatment of the American Indian is a case in point. Originally Native American–white relations were managed by the Department of State according to treaty obligations. As the Indian population ceased being viewed as a foreign entity and became a military threat, relations tended to be managed through the War Department. The establishment of the Department of the Interior in 1849 and the placement of the Office (later, Bureau) of Indian Affairs therein acknowledged that the federal government would now treat Indians as de facto wards.

Such officers were in a sense the opportunistic warriors who led from their desks the opening of the West. Theodore Roosevelt's work *The Winning of the West* could better—and less heroically—have been called *The Opportunistic Management of the Western Lands,* for it was such management that utilized meager knowledge of the technological possibility and natural resources of the vast western plains to encourage potential farmers of wheat, corn, meat, and wool to chance the same risks being taken by the British in Canada, Australia, and New Zealand. Revolutions in the technology of communication and transportation, again masterminded in part by a federal bureaucracy operating with congressional oversight that was scandalous at times, supported the expansion of a system of exploiting natural resources and the adventurism of new classes of entrepreneurs. John D. Rockefeller's oil explorations had little initial connection to the combustion engine but more to kerosene for heating and lighting. Andrew Carnegie's experiments with steel had less to do initially with the rail wheels and roadbeds than with the utility of iron as a building material. Innovation turned discovered materials to new uses, and new uses gave unanticipated value to further discovery.

The role of bureaucrats and legislatures

complicated matters to the degree that members of both were also seeking advantage for themselves, as indeed they always had. The Crédit Mobilier scandal of the early 1870s arose out of the manner in which a post–Civil War Congress undertook the distribution of vast western land tracts for the building of transcontinental rail lines. Without agreed-on guidelines for covering the relation between, on the one hand, a necessary generation of entrepreneurial gamblers and, on the other, federal legislators and bureaucrats attempting to manage a system as mysterious to them as to those engaged in the gamble, scandal was destined to result. Whether that conception of the behavior was as accurate as historian Henry Adams thought when he surveyed his own family's financial difficulties in attempting to get protection from men like Jay Gould and Jim Fisk, may be true, but is beside the point. Civil service reform seems a frail protection, although it is certainly one that the Adams brothers looked to as the salvation of their own conception of an entrepreneurial system that was also publicly responsible.

Earlier, President Lincoln had come to resent the annoyance of job seekers, however virtuous their intention, but also to respect the need to meet congressional pressures for constituents. Yet, the efforts on the part of Congress to manage the war was the precursor of a battle that would reach an even more serious confrontation in the management of Reconstruction, but by then the president was Andrew Johnson, not Lincoln.

## LEGISLATURES AND BUREAUCRACY IN THE POST–CIVIL WAR ERA

In January 1867, Congress called itself into special session for the express purpose of depriving Johnson of authority, which he considered, as do contemporary scholars, an unconstitutional encroachment on executive power. The Command of the Army Act required that he issue all military orders through General of the Army Ulysses S. Grant. The Tenure of Office Act of 1867 forbade him from dismissing from office any government official appointed with the advice and consent of the Senate without returning to the Senate for its consent in the removal. This and other legislation, vetoed by the president and passed over his veto, marked the beginning of confrontations over appointments and management that would end, finally, in the impeachment of Johnson.

The failure of Congress to convict Andrew Johnson of high crimes and misdemeanors for his refusal to obey the Tenure of Office Act did not remove all provisions of the act from the books; that did not happen until 1887, when Grover Cleveland asserted the independent right of the president to select his staff and to remove them according to his own judgment. To be sure, the drama of the Johnson impeachment trial had made the act more or less irrelevant in the intervening years. Presidents had found various methods of sustaining their appointments, even against Senate disapproval. Cleveland's assertion was in many ways more a confirmation of a fact than a new interpretation of presidential independence; but it did point to the expanded bureaucratic authority of the president and to the increasing inability of the Senate or Congress as a whole to exercise administrative authority on its own.

Nonetheless, the continuing battle between the president and Congress over the exercise of bureaucratic power took on new shapes in the 1880s as the administrative responsibilities of the federal government grew. Along with that growth came the necessity of determining where such responsibilities would be placed, who would exercise them, and how Congress would decide its own need to oversee the exercise of those responsibilities and hold the growing administrative bureaucracy accountable to its will.

The mid-1880s was a remarkable era so far as the formulation of the problem of the relation between Congress and the bureaucratic staffing of the executive branch was concerned. The assassination of President James Garfield in 1881 by what has always been described as a disappointed office seeker gave sudden energy to the civil service reform movement, which had existed for more than twenty years, the pet project of largely WASP reformers who resented what they saw as the takeover of American politics by manipulative party politicians. The assumption of the presidency by Vice President Chester A. Arthur, a man the reformers saw as precisely the kind of partisan politician they had fought, led nonetheless to the passage of the nation's first civil service reform legislation, the Pendleton Act of 1883. The act called for competitive examinations and, although it applied only to a small number of federal employees, empowered the president to expand the list subject to such examination. It also forbade the demand for political contributions from federal employees.

Limited though it was, the Pendleton Act—and the public pressures that brought it in to existence—moved the older Civil Service Reform Association into position as a national influence for the first time and raised a political issue that would press politics at all levels, local as well as national, to consider. Civil service and its counterpart efforts to reform corruption and political-campaign funding would remain at the center of American politics for the next three decades, to reemerge as issues even up to the present.

The subject of bureaucracy was brought to the fore academically by Woodrow Wilson, who, in an 1887 essay in the *Political Science Quarterly* gave it its first acceptable name. "The Study of Administration" was destined to serve as the beginning point of the field of public administration. In it, Wilson took a term that in English usage had been applied narrowly to the carrying out of provisions of wills and the more specific aspects of legal rulings and enlarged it to cover the entirety of the management of government. Wilson's essay established a Whiggish, if not downright romantic, difference between authoritarian continental bureaucracies, who executed royal commands, and British legislative limits on executive power, which he envisaged stretching back to Henry II.

That same year, 1887, the Senate created a committee, headed by Senator Francis Marion Cockrell (D.-Mo.), to study the executive branch. The report of the committee is as important for what it does not say as for what it does say. It is, for example, the first attempt to provide detailed information on the size and cost of an executive branch that would, by 1887, have tripled in the years since the presidency of James Madison. It is also a virtual litany of inefficiency and behavior that would have been called "corrupt" had anyone chosen to define it that way. "Inefficiency" encompassed such unprofessional conduct as the failure to answer letters, the loss of documents, and other examples of poor record keeping.

"Corruption" involved such activities as the hiring of substitutes by employees whose hold on a job gave them the opportunity to engage others at the same or even lesser salaries without losing their own prior rights of employment. While not prohibited by statute, the substitute system indicated the degree to which civil service reform had found ways of transferring abuses rather than ending them.

The most notable omission from the Cockrell report is the absence of discussion of the chief executive or even the acknowledgment of his office as the nation's chief administrative office. The omission is somewhat more complex than it appears at first glance. While it is clear that the report is built on the assumption that the various executive offices are responsible primarily to Congress, the steps leading up to the appointment of the committee were shadowed by the concerns then felt by the Republican minority in the Senate that Grover Cleveland, as a reforming Democrat, would use administrative change to gain control over the executive branch. Since that comes close to being what Cleveland attempted to do through his use of the veto to end one of the major administrative abuses of the post–Civil War era, politicization of veterans' pensions, there may be reason to credit his opponents with a significant degree of foresight.

The fact that the appointment of another congressional investigating committee, the so-called Cockrell-Dockery Commission, coincided with Cleveland's return to office in 1893 also suggests both the growing consciousness of the need for more effective administrative controls and the continuing unwillingness of Congress to admit its own inability to exercise those controls itself. This time, however, the White House was included in the discussion of the executive branch, even though the details of that inclusion are themselves rather startling.

Out of a total of 17,622 federal government employees paid $13,364,196.10, the Executive Office of the President operated with a budget of $93,200 for a staff of 23. Of that sum, $50,000 went to the president and $8,000 to the vice president, with the remainder divided among two secretaries, two executive clerks, four general clerks, one usher, one steward, five doorkeepers, four messengers, one engineer, and one watchman. Even so, the inclusion of the White House in the executive branch did little to change the view that the departments of the executive branch were responsible to Congress. Thus, the significance of the repeal of the Tenure of Office Act as a device for indicating a new conception of presidential control may be debatable. Congress still asserted its authority.

In some respects, the presidency of William McKinley is a turning point, even more so than that of Theodore Roosevelt, long labeled the first "modern" presidency. McKinley took a number of traditional steps to expand his immediate staff, but more important, he routinized functions by giving individuals the responsibility for dealing with the national press, congressional leaders, and the growing national and international business and banking communities. Keeping his own role behind the scenes, he operated as an effective national symbol above the increasingly complex battles being waged around him.

McKinley may thus have been what Leonard White has called "the last Jacksonian," just as he may also have been the first of a new kind of executive leader, managing the administrative office with what Fred Greenstein has called a "hidden hand" and influencing national public opinion from front stage. Perceiving himself the servant of congressional will, he nonetheless accepted responsibility for manipulating that will. His successors in the office, even today, have been faced with the same parallel alternatives.

## THE FIRST "MODERN" PRESIDENCY

What may indeed be modern about the presidency of Theodore Roosevelt was his use of the adversarial administrative presidency. Also new was his willingness to confront the issue of administrative control in a curiously oblique fashion, to acknowledge the need for, and to demand, presidential control of the administrative branch, but to limit himself as to the method. Roosevelt's concerns did not involve the elaboration of administrative theories as later administrative theorists would understand them. He was concerned with searching for new ways of accomplishing old tasks. That fact in itself touches on the tendency of later theorists to see in many Progressive writers and articulators of new conceptions of industrial order the harbingers of executive management.

Herbert Croly, Frederick Winslow Taylor, and Mary Parker Follette were all leading proponents of various forms of new management; but that group included people, like Louis Brandeis, whose commitment to decentralized forms of democratic control illustrated the degree of disagreement with advocates of strengthened centralized authority that could enflame their opposition to one another. What is important is that their common support of direct leadership over the disarray and social dislocation they saw in the industrial disorder around them led them to question not democracy but its reflection in the self-interested partisan groups that seemed to stand in the way of a nonpartisan national interest. The failure of the new executive leadership to build a "state" in the modern sense was reflected in its inability to build a bureaucratic system that would provide the state with its administrative underpinnings. That failure, in turn, was the product not of accident but of the inability of Congress and successive presidents to resolve the issue of who would exercise control over the executive branch.

It may be worth pointing out that the issue is not an abstract one, even though administrative theorists ever since Wilson have worked to put it that way. The federal government is the chief distributor of the nation's resources. Those resources have been central to the mobility of those citizens able to take advantage of them. That was true of land in America's nineteenth-century history. It was also true of jobs in the first half of the twentieth century, and it has become true of education today. Congress represents the local and regional system of such distribution. To give up that control, to rationalize—even nationalize—that control, could threaten the local base on which local political power rests before it comes to be represented in Congress. It could threaten the maneuverability of individual representatives after they are elected. That threat is one of the reasons item veto is sought by presidents and rejected by Congresses.

In the course of the modernization of American national government, the administrative bureaucracy has become the means through which the president and Congress arrive at the behind-the-scenes compromises that, however irrational they may be as examples of logrolling and pork barrel politics, enable the system to work from one session to the next, from one presidency to the next. The irrationality of it has led successive presidents to try to rationalize it and successive administrative theorists to work out those rationalizations and to provide presidents with justifications for them. None of them has succeeded, at least for long, unless one excepts the Keep Commission, appointed by Theodore Roosevelt, who seems to have known better than to try.

Whether the Keep Commission or the commission appointed by William Howard Taft and headed by Frederick A. Cleveland was the first essentially presidential reorganization commission has been the subject of some debate between those who see Taft and the Cleveland Commission as the product of an interest in administrative theory rather than in particular methods of governmental management. Both Taft and Roosevelt came to the White House from strong backgrounds in administration. Taft's experiences were entirely bureaucratic, however; his only essentially political experience had come from appearances before Congress as a representative of the McKinley and Roosevelt administrations.

A strict constitutionalist, by contrast with Roosevelt, Taft insisted that any commission studying the executive branch be under the control of the president, not Congress, thereby revealing a political naïveté that would characterize all of his efforts to establish White House conferences without authorization from Congress. A congressional attempt in 1909 to stop such presidential practices met with the rebuff of silence from the White House, and a practice was begun that would characterize every presidency thereafter. The presidential search for expert advice on which to base presidential policy-making became an independent element of American public policy, with funding from various private sources.

Central to the difference between Roosevelt and Taft is a distinction the new administrative theorists were finding attractive. In 1900, Frank J. Goodnow published *Politics and Administration,* a book that helped establish an ideal that went considerably further than Goodnow intended. The Anglophiliac dream of an administrator who could be free of political influence had been part of the American civil service reform movement. Whether it could be made part of American political reality was an-

other matter. Nonetheless, the creation of schools of public administration and research institutes to examine government behavior from outside government were all part of an effort to objectify and de-politicize the study of bureaucracy. Roosevelt's political realism and tactical skills contrasted sharply with Taft's political innocence and constitutional rigidity. Taft, like Herbert Hoover after him, was a victim of Progressive conceptions of bureaucratic management.

Nor was policy advice the only—or even the central—source of conflict between the president and Congress over the administrative management of the federal government. One might well put the question in its most general terms: Why since 1887 and at very regular intervals did presidents and Congresses find themselves wrestling over the authority to run the government? Had the Constitution of 1787 not designated their separate powers in the first place?

The simplest answer to such questions can be adduced from what has already been said. The assumption that the president would act as the chief bureaucratic agent of the Congress was part of constitutional understanding for the first century of American government. That assumption rested on the belief that all but a few of the regulatory powers of the state would be carried out by the states themselves. By the end of the nineteenth century, the growth of national business and industry and the need for a national banking and currency policy, shortly to be followed by the necessity of a national tax policy that appeared to spring unexpectedly from a Treasury surplus that turned into a deficit, placed on the federal government what can only be called a managerial overload. The assumption of congressional control of the management of government and the consciousness of the need for modernized executive skills and techniques in all forms of national enterprise were on a collision course. Congress saw no alternative to its own control. Presidents, even one as conservative as Taft, were attracted to the new management of the industrial state.

The crisis was diverted by a compromise that some experts have seen as so completely unconstitutional as to defy explanation. Beginning with the Interstate Commerce Commission, Congress created a system of regulatory bodies that collapse in various ways the tradition of separation of powers. Under full control of neither the executive nor the legislature, these regulatory bodies create and execute rules. Although they are often accused of having dangerously close relationships with the interest groups they are charged with regulating, one could just as well say that they rely on the regulated for the information they need, for help in establishing uniform rules of providing such information, and for the expertise required to interpret industry behavior. Although weak and ineffectual in their early years by operating primarily as gatherers of information rather than enforcers of policy, the agencies ultimately took on considerably more power to influence economic development.

The relationships between Congress and the regulatory agencies and between the White House and the regulatory agencies are the subject of periodic attack as accusations of influence are used to explain the relaxation of rules when the agency acts as executive or the decisions handed down by hearings when the agency acts as a court of law. Yet, despite the fact that such agencies seem to defy the fundamentals of separation of powers and of checks and balances, suggestions that they become part of the particular executive departments that manage cognate issues have been rejected each time they have been raised. The only answer has been deregulation, the abandonment of regulation as a whole.

Where one wants to place the entirely new bureaucracy established by the development of the regulatory agency remains something of a puzzle as modern theories of state bureaucracies go. Though presidential appointments to commissions are for specific and not necessarily consistent terms from agency to agency, presidential control is no greater than that over appointments to the courts. Presidents can attempt to read track records of appointees, but their ability to manage is limited to the initial selection. The same is true of congressional control unless, of course, Congress abolishes the agency entirely. As will be shown, congressional efforts to affect specific agency rulings have run into difficulties with the courts.

All in all, the management crisis was resolved by compromise. The confrontations with Congress and the banking community initiated by Theodore Roosevelt and brought to a disastrous peak by William Howard Taft reached a temporary ending that pleased no one but left in place a new and strange bureaucratic instrument that could be used both by presidents and by Congresses in nonthreatening ways. The fact that the threat would remain, however, became clear in Woodrow Wilson's first administration and by his management of World War I.

A less peculiar compromise took the form of what ultimately became the federal budget. Nowhere was the battle for control waged more vociferously than in the efforts on the part of presidents to gain control over fiscal planning and the reluctance of Congress to relinquish that control. Presidents, prior to Warren G. Harding, were forced to accept the appearances of executive department heads before relevant congressional committees to plead for allocations and to negotiate with those committees for their funding. Taft attempted to gain control of the overall executive budget by executive order, hoping to coerce his own cabinet into accepting his leadership; but neither the congressional committees involved nor, apparently, the departments were willing to give up what was, after all, significant independence from the White House.

Taft's efforts were, in a sense, part of a wave of Progressive reform energy that had been sweeping state houses and businesses alike and would soon reach every level of government. Budgeting opened public expenditure to public view, applying "scientific" judgment to expert analysis. It also revealed the negotiations between legislative bodies and the bureaucracies that executed popular will. When the first Wilson administration, for example, wanted to extend the nation's highway system in an effort to prepare the country for automobile travel, particularly in the quiet anticipation of American entry into the war in either Mexico or Europe, the building of highways required the efforts of the Army Corps of Engineers, which in turn required the support of the so-called rivers and harbors bloc in Congress. The relation between the War Department and such blocs in Congress was, in a significant sense, closer than that between the president and either of the others.

A similar need for negotiation characterized much of the wartime relationship between the executive branch and Congress. What is remarkable about the passage of the Budget and

Accounting Act of 1921 is really how long it took to bring it into being, particularly in view of the rapid development of technological advances in electric power, air transportation, and radio that followed the war. The only thing remarkable about the wartime management of the railroads is the fact that they were returned to private ownership after the war. On every other scale, wartime technology proved the need for federal management, and both proved the essential necessity of a federal budget.

## NEW INSTRUMENTS OF MANAGEMENT

Three pieces of prewar legislation illustrate the new range of bureaucratic creation that Progressivism generated. The Clayton Antitrust Act, while in some respects a classic piece of regulatory legislation, nonetheless laid out guidelines for bureaucratic judgment that deviated from tradition. Where labor was concerned, for example, the Clayton Act exempted unions from antitrust coverage and gave labor a special role in the regulatory process. Asserting somewhat ambiguously that labor was not to be considered a commodity in exchange and implying that a living wage was close to being a right to which laborers were entitled, the Clayton Act seemed to be an effort to reach for a bureaucratic standard of measuring practical behavior.

The legislation establishing the Federal Reserve System created a partnership between the private banking system and the Treasury's concern with interest rates and what today would be called the "money supply" to stabilize fluctuations in the availability of private resources for investment. Yet the Treasury and the White House had no control over the decisions of the Federal Reserve, which based its actions on its own specialized perceptions of the needs of the economy, whether or not those needs were understood by the nation's political leaders as expedient. Although William Jennings Bryan, one of the architects of the original legislation, saw the division into regional banks as a way of preventing creation of a central banking system controlled from Washington, practice and the character of American banking quickly made the New York bank first among equals, still without giving Treasury or Congress the authority that a central system needed. Nonetheless, a new generation of economists came into being to advise and to form a new nongovernmental bureaucracy influencing government policy.

To be sure, even though Congress could not control interest rates, legislation could influence the banking process by what came to be a routinization of the practice of setting the content of the currency, the relative proportions of gold and commercial paper that backed the dollar. Again, that took time. Not until the early 1960s did the currency in circulation consist entirely of Federal Reserve notes, and by then, no one seemed to notice the difference. Finally, the establishment of a national income tax in 1913 produced a quiet revolution in the relation between the citizen and the state. Here, however, Congress and the president shared a high degree of power by being able to agree on the various changes possible in a tax code that initially affected relatively few people and only those at the higher income levels. Still, the administration of the tax code by a bureaucracy charged not only with enforcing that code but interpreting it where legislation left congressional intent unclear required both a large national bureaucracy and a court system to adjudicate its meaning. Only the Post Office had the potential of affecting the citizen in his daily life, but the Post Office was perceived as a benign, even admired service. Citizens had long debated the role of the tariff as "the mother of trusts," but the tariff was chiefly metaphoric in its invasion of the household. No one seemed concerned with the officers who enforced it. No punishments were levied on citizens for their failure to pay it, assuming such a failure could even be defined.

While one could point to the bureaucratic consequences of other pieces of legislation from Wilson's New Freedom, with the important exception of the Budget and Accounting Act, which Wilson pushed but which was not passed during his administration, they fall into one or the other of the categories suggested above. All suggest the movement toward the establishment of a bureaucratic state, but all, again, reflect differences between the president and Congress about who would manage it. The character of the legislation reflects those differences, and the character of the state underscores them. That character, oddly enough, requires one to separate the peacetime Wilson presidency from the war presidency, even though the distinction may seem artificial. For what may most reflect the difference between the two is the fact that the war administration was intended to be temporary by both Wilson and Congress. Both seemed to fear the construction of a bureaucratic state, which they saw as "militaristic" and defined as the very "Teutonic" evil they were fighting.

## THE PRESIDENT AND CONGRESS AT WAR

What most characterizes Wilson's organization for war was his insistence that the war be a citizen war, that its managers be citizens drawn from the various industrial professions that war organization required. While that may seem a fine idealization of the practice of bringing farmers from their plows—and returning them home after victory was won—it had some very practical defects. It worked, for example, at the very top, where men like Herbert Hoover, Bernard Baruch, Joseph Kennedy, John D. Rockefeller, Jr., and Newton Baker had personal resources—or could tap resources—that would enable them to leave their careers and work for the much-praised "dollar a year." But it did not work for those who could not, and particularly for the many who also had to fund the often sizable and necessary "expert" staffs, staffs they required as much as their wealthier colleagues did.

*Voluntarism,* the term they continued to use to describe what they were doing, meant just that. The president had no money for them, and Congress apparently saw no need to provide it. After all, Congress had never seen the need to support administrative staffing. College president and federal fuel administrator Harry Garfield complained about the difference between the staffing, beyond, secreatarie, clerks, and doorkeepers, and those he could afford and the staffing he saw around him in the offices of more affluent "volunteers." Since most of the wartime agencies had state offices, the problem was multiplied around the country.

Where the system did work was in the private agencies funded and run by foundations, the Red Cross, and religious missionary associations. The professional social-work groups founded during the Progressive Era were im-

portant in the shift to government war work. But the fear that war administration would have a permanent influence on bureaucratic management and future legislation had a curiously unintended effect. The war produced the first national administrative system since the Civil War, but on a much greater scale. Late in the war, through the Overman Act of 1918, Congress gave the president limited authority to reorganize wartime agencies by using executive orders, which could be vetoed by Congress. Congress's interest, however, was primarily economy and efficiency, as well as the avoidance of duplication and overlap, considerations that for years to come would serve as the basis for presidential requests for more effective administrative authority.

One of the unintended side effects was in part the result of the emerging social sciences, wherein data collecting and the application of statistical study revealed new understandings of the actual state of the industrial system. The interest in everything from overproduction and needless duplication to illiteracy, poor health, and unemployment as national phenomena, while long part of the academic interest in economics and statistics and of the professions of public health and social work, now assumed a more prominent position among the nation's policymakers. Similar results came from the wartime draft, the psychological testing for which revealed problems of regional educational differentials that were destined to occupy the nation's educators for decades to come.

Among the many interesting attitudes to come out of their experience of wartime volunteer public servants was a sometimes romantic revival of self-government, the belief that Americans did not really need complex bureaucracies. On a scale that ranges from Herbert Hoover's *American Individualism* (1922) to John Dewey's *The Public and Its Problems* (1927), with Robert Staughton Lynd and Helen Lynd's *Middletown* (1929) somewhere in between, American intellectuals were asking how much government they needed. The picture is a troubled and troubling one. New attitudes toward the relation between local and national government, the nation's police forces, and the ambiguity of a federal police force for managing the growing number of policies requiring federal governance—chief among them Prohibition—were given a disturbing emphasis by the federal government's engagement in the identification and deportation of presumably radical aliens: the Red Scare and the related and dramatically new concern with civil liberties were part of that brief postwar hysteria.

The corruption associated with the postwar redistribution of resources taken over by the government for military planning—some of the oil fields of the West, for example—and the postwar activities of the offices dealing with veterans' affairs and the veterans' hospitals embodied the classic problem of new administrative functions for which precedents did not exist. The resulting occasions for opportunism could be as crude as the illegal sale of the Teapot Dome oil fields, which sent one cabinet member to jail, or the disagreements about postwar income tax, which continued to cloud the reputation of Secretary of the Treasury Andrew Mellon.

The decade of the 1920s was nonetheless an era of continued expansion of the professionalization of local administrative bureaucracies begun in the Progressive Era. The city manager movement was paralleled by the growth of professional organizations for planners, state government officials, police and fire officials, engineers, and other groups whose political status was under attack when politics could be proven to have subverted scientific knowledge, and often little proof was needed. The replacement of partisan legislative debate by management was a phenomenon of much of the industrialized world, as Mussolini's Fascism and Lenin's one-party system of planning took often specific stands against nineteenth-century liberalism. Max Weber's conceptions of bureaucracy took a middle ground, suggesting both scientific professionalization and rational-legal commitments capable of modernizing democracy without necessarily replacing it.

As both an engineer and a firm believer in individualist democracy, Herbert Hoover reflected an American ambivalence—perhaps even a contradiction—that was characteristic of the decade. A master manager with a clear understanding both of the uses and abuses of bureaucratic authority, he nonetheless believed that state control was not necessary for the creation of an administrative utopia. His understanding of voluntarism and the voluntary state was a step further in the Progressives' vision of a society that could be persuaded to act on the

basis of facts presented to it by experts whose prescriptions would become self-evident. Yet even he reflected the growing understanding of the need for bureaucracies that could act when squabbling, self-interested legislatures produced ineffective legislation. His problems in dealing with the Great Depression were as much an inability to manage the politics of his relationships with Congress as an unwillingness to use even the bureaucratic powers available to him to engage in what he would have called "demagoguery" or "gesticulation." His hostility to politics and politicians only underscored the separation he and many in his generation of business leaders were coming to see in their version of the Progressive's distinction between politics and administration.

## ROOSEVELT THROUGH EISENHOWER, 1933–1961

For most of his first two terms in office, Franklin Roosevelt used politics as his method, persuading and cajoling Congress to produce programs that his sometimes chaotic administrative methods could manage. Aware of the fact that, between the traditional cabinet and the rapidly growing agencies being created by New Deal legislation, he was losing presidential control over the management of the administrative branch, he appointed a committee in 1936 to advise him on what he and his committee were now calling "administrative management." The President's Committee on Administrative Management, better known as the Brownlow Committee after its chairman, Louis Brownlow, created what many consider the first modern plan for executive reorganization.

The original plan effectively proposed attacking the major problems of bureaucratic management to give the president control over the selection of personnel, the operation of the budget, and a board that would coordinate planning operations in what were envisaged as the major regions of the country. In addition, the president was to have a staff of administrative assistants in the White House who would help him remain informed of programs being managed by the departments. There was also a proposal to abolish the regulatory commissions as independent agencies and turn their functions over to the relevant departments. The president would have the power to shuffle administrative agencies and bureaus from one department to another through the submission of reorganization plans that would go into effect if not vetoed by both houses of Congress within sixty days.

Even though Congress gutted much of the original plan when it finally passed the Reorganization Act of 1939, the principles established by the report remained in place—chiefly, the guarding of administrative organization from persistent legislative intervention and the increase of the president's ability to manipulate bureaucratic organization—until the administration of Richard Nixon when Congress, stung by what it considered the usurpation of its administrative oversight, sought to clamp down on executive independence.

Yet, *executive independence* is in some respects too strong a term for defining the New Deal's effects on bureaucratic legislative relationships, while in other respects it may not be strong enough, for the New Deal's contribution to federal management lay not in executive reorganization or in the "alphabet agencies" created to cope with the problems of the Great Depression. It lay in the growing power of government administrators to use the authority given them by the regulatory commissions to engage in rule making, a process that one of the leading administrative minds of the New Deal era, James M. Landis, considered a more workable and certainly more rational substitute for the awkward legislative process. Following the model established by the Internal Revenue Service, the regulatory agencies could interpret legislative injunctions through rules that operated as laws, subject to the gradually expanding involvement of the courts in administrative affairs. Like the courts that interpreted tax laws on a case-by-case basis, often utilizing the judge's opinion where legislative intent was unclear or even where, although clear, irrational or, again in the judge's opinion, unjust, the federal courts affirmed or rejected agency rules. Such opinions were effective until Congress, in subsequent legislation, spoke to the issues involved.

New Deal agencies and those employed by them nonetheless awakened congressional opposition as Congress, suspicious that men such as relief administrator Harry Hopkins were using their resources to assure support for the New Deal by the expanded bureaucracy through political contributions, passed the Hatch Act of 1939, which forbade the participation in political campaigns of federal workers below top policy-making levels and the soliciting of funds from workers employed by such agencies as the Works Projects Administration. The act in fact underscored a dispute that had run throughout the New Deal between old Progressives like Secretary of the Interior Harold Ickes, who was willing to hold up the assignment of government contracts until he was sure that patronage was not involved, and Hopkins, who felt that the reviving of the local political system could be useful if it put people to work.

Executive reorganization and agency rule-making between them expanded the administrative authority of the president by giving him initiatives that were more flexible than legislative proposals and less subject to congressional tinkering. Although such initiatives were not subject to logrolling or other forms of direct manipulation by Congress, they could be vetoed by Congress through procedures set up by various pieces of reorganization legislation. The role of the White House staff and its relation to both the cabinet and Congress underscored implicitly the fact that whatever the original intention of creating the cabinet, the cabinet no longer served the purpose of staff to the president, if indeed it ever had. Yet, perhaps because of other preoccupations, Roosevelt did not make full use of the system he had created. That was left to Harry Truman.

It is quite likely that the Legislative Reform Act of 1946 is the most revolutionary piece of bureaucratic legislation in American history precisely because it directs its attention to the central topic of this essay. The sense that the fall of democratic governments in Europe had contributed to the rise of Fascism was attached to several other, perhaps more realistic issues, even if they are related. Conscious of the greater control over expertise then available to the executive branch and unwilling to depend on knowledge it did not itself independently generate (an issue that went back to Washington and Jefferson's seeming misinterpretation of the president's relation to the Senate on treaty-making powers), Congress sought to create its own legislative information devices, chiefly the employment of specialists in legislative policy. On the eve of the Japanese attack on Pearl Harbor in 1941, Congress had rejected Librarian of Congress Archibald MacLeish's request for funding for his badly understaffed legislative reference service in the institution originally intended as research staff for Congress. The new method was a shrewd, if ultimately more expensive, compromise, in that it gave each member the right to hire "experts."

By 1946, despite opposition within Congress itself from those who saw reform as an attack on patronage, a new mood in favor of establishing expertise was in the air, although there were those opponents who continued to insist that they did not need experts, partly because they associated the very term with the supposed radicalism of the New Deal. Yet there was other evidence of the new mood. In 1945 the *Congressional Quarterly*, which continues to provide high-level information about the activities of Congress, was founded. There was another side to the coin of executive domination, but it required a genuine alternative. Congress revamped the committee structure, reducing not only the number of committees but also the number on which any member could serve. It also took steps to gain control of autocratic chairs and to require reports and establish rules for open hearings.

Given the events of the next decade, chiefly the role of Senator Joseph McCarthy (R.-Wis.) and his subversive-activities subcommittee, the revolution may not now seem so great, but the openness of committee hearings and their reporting by television and the press may require rethinking. The funding of investigative staff was a significant step forward, even when it was misused, and the expansion of congressional information gathering has been an important and growing factor ever since. In a very real sense, legislative bureaucracy had been placed on a new footing.

President Truman's sense of administrative reorganization within the executive branch was unusually acute not only because of the methods involved but because of his sensitivity to congressional politics and his selection of former President Herbert Hoover as the head of the Commission on Organization of the Executive Branch of the Government, which recommended the plans. Hoover's revived reputation not only among Republicans but in public opinion in general lent him an authority he had lost by the end of his presidency. His

ability to lobby his conservative constituency proved to be enormously important, as did his reputation as an administrator among business leaders and journalists. The Hoover Commission, as it came to be known, was significantly influenced by the academics and practitioners who had been protégés of those who had created the Brownlow Committee's report, such as Don K. Price, who followed Brownlow, directing the Washington office of the Public Administration Clearing House.

Among the most significant of the 277 proposals recommended by the Hoover Commission was the establishment of a White House secretariat to provide the president with a greatly enlarged formal staff system. One can see in this proposal, nonetheless, the beginning of the problem that subsequent presidents have faced: the growing interface between the presidency and the departments through the creation of a White House bureaucracy over which Congress has no control and a congressional staffing system with which the White House bureaucracy must learn to deal, and very quickly. An example of the potential for misunderstanding inherent in the system occurred in the 1990 budget-planning conferences when the director of the Office of Management and Budget and the White House chief of staff told the members of the House Budget Committee that they could not bring staff to the joint conferences. They had to be reminded by committee members that they, too, were staff.

President Eisenhower's use of a second Hoover Commission and subsequent reorganization plans also included the use of executive orders to bring about such changes as the transformation of the Department of Defense through a diminution of the powers of the Joint Chiefs of Staff and the expansion of the authority of the civilian secretary of defense begun during the Truman years. Eisenhower was able to deal with congressional opposition to such change, even within his own party, where it was strongest, by pointing to his own military experience.

Thus, both Truman and Eisenhower extended the administrative authority granted the presidency by the depression and World War II, but their uses of that authority were confined by Congress to acts of consolidation rather than obvious expansions of presidential power. A good example of the political ambiguities such consolidations led to can be seen in the creation of the Council of Economic Advisers (CEA) in the Employment Act of 1946. Originally intended as an expansion of governmental responsibility for jobs foreseen in Roosevelt's inclusion of a right to a job in a new, postwar bill of rights, the legislation was reduced by Congress from the "full employment" of its original title to "employment" and gave the president the CEA to help him prepare a report on the state of the nation's economy. The act also forbade the president from naming academics to the CEA, a slap at Roosevelt's use of academics in his brains trust and his planning agency, but one that, by the Eisenhower administration, presidents could feel free to ignore.

It is important to point out that despite congressional controls on domestic policy, the introduction of a vastly expanded, and expanding, Department of Defense, and the increased responsibilities of the Department of State for foreign policy produced changes in the relation between the bureaucracy and Congress that were destined to have long-term effects. Both defense policy and foreign policy required levels of secrecy that, at extremes represented by the Central Intelligence Agency (CIA), virtually negated congressional oversight. Efforts on the part of congressional leaders to establish controls, beginning with the activities of Senator Joseph McCarthy but by no means confined to his more dramatic hearings, ranged from the successful attempt by Senator Patrick McCarran (D.-Nev.) to control travel in and out of the United States by legislating rules for the passport and immigration offices, to the development of blocs within Congress whose interest in defense contracting depended either on their own experiences in World War II, which gave them a certain willingness to support the services of which they had been part, or on a simple eagerness to win lucrative projects for employment in their states and districts.

In the Cold War years the question of control could be hedged by the fears generated by the Soviet Union. Regions of the United States, the Northwest for example, developed single industries that Congress could bail out, when necessary, in return for concessions involving labor relations and management conditions. The trade-offs that were intended to cushion transformations—or to prevent them altogether—remain to be applied to other areas of the economy under present circumstances.

While the point has probably been exaggerated, such practices did lead to what are sometimes called "iron triangles" or "cozy" relationships between and among defense contractors, legislative groups, and the bureaucracies established for dealing with them. Despite efforts at the outset to keep armaments and defense matters open to the public—the battle to subject nuclear development to civilian control is perhaps the chief example—the emergence of what came to be known as the Cold War imposed a secrecy that was sometimes short of wartime emergency controls but considerably less than public. In the absence of emergency rulings, the practices of the various agencies involved in defense and foreign policy seemed sometimes to have been reduced to individual judgments supported by congressional backing for administrators who served various specific purposes. The Loyalty Review Board of 1947 reflected an inquisitorial process of information gathering and quasi-judicial procedures that failed to protect bureaucrats called to defend themselves even with the most fundamental of rights beyond the right to remain silent under the Fifth Amendment. Not until the Nixon administration would the issues of information begin to be protected by law, and then only by virtue of what were perceived as executive violations of new conceptions of citizen rights to information.

By the 1960s, a growing awareness of crises in domestic affairs led to what some have perceived as a shift from foreign policy to domestic policy, even in the era of the Vietnam War. Poverty, civil rights, the degeneration of cities, urban crime and rioting, education, and environmentalism all seemed to require massive federal intervention. With programs often initiated by private foundation funding, the federal government moved into every area of public life, including the natural sciences, the social sciences, and even the arts and humanities. The mixture of federal and local funding and management was not always easy to see and to accept, particularly when federal funding came to influence the hiring practices of private institutions that received federal money or the determination of standards of taste and morals by bureaucrats who perceived themselves as subject to congressional control.

Ever since the 1920s, concepts of regionalism had been used to justify the maintenance of cultural differences from one part of the country to another. By the end of World War II, it was becoming clear that the repression of African Americans—rapidly becoming the only identifiable "race" because "ethnicity" was replacing the prewar concept of race—was not confined to the southern states. Often excluded from social-reform programs put in place by the New Deal, African Americans were coming to see federal legislation and court decisions as potential protections for the first time. Yet, various approaches to what was called a "new federalism" or "revenue sharing" could act as protections of older attitudes by allowing state and local governments to determine for themselves how programs would be administered. Such programs managed out of Washington tended to carry with them the reformist intentions of those who had created them, while efforts by those same reformers to introduce local control by local citizen groups could, if they bypassed politically established local governments, be perceived as unwarranted interventions.

## THE BUREAUCRACY SINCE 1961

In any case, the new social programs generated by the Kennedy and Johnson administrations led to a vast expansion of the payrolls of state and local governments, an estimated 40 percent more than federal additions during the same period. New forms of administrative expertise reflected in the participation of academics and philanthropic foundation personnel in the planning and execution of programs extended what had been a sporadic involvement of such people in previous eras. The expansion of the professional field of public administration and the growth of schools of what was being called "public policy," to which must be added the management of information represented in the infusion of electronic data gathering and analysis, generated an explosion of new services that transformed both the executive and the legislature as each branch sought to adapt itself to a sometimes disturbing array of new tools.

One such tool was known as the planning, programming, and budgeting (PPB) system. Worked out in the Department of Defense in

the late 1950s, it was something of an ideal of advanced planning. Designed to coordinate the three basic elements of planning, it called for five-year forecasts and the spelling out of objectives and alternatives, and utilized new techniques of analysis: cost-benefit analyses, strategic planning, and systems analysis. President Johnson envisioned it as the mechanism that would control the Great Society programs and in 1965 required all federal agencies to utilize it. By 1971, it was clear to the Nixon administration that PPB was not working, although the reasons are not clear. Criticism in academic circles, from agency administrators overburdened with the work load placed on them by the process, and, quite possibly, from legislators who simply could not relate such complex processes and techniques to the politics they understood and the demands of their constituents all helped bring PPB to an end for the federal government, or at least to limit its use. One might also consider it the first major skirmish in the battle of the bureaucracies—executive and congressional—over the availability and accuracy of information, a battle exacerbated by the Vietnam War.

That process of adaptation ultimately came to threaten both Congress and the executive branch as each, from its own perspective, came to view the bureaucracy as independent of its own responsibilities as representative of the public interest. By the late 1960s and early 1970s, even iron triangles seemed systematic but outdated as first Johnson and then Nixon attempted to gain control of the government that their programs had created or had sought unsuccessfully to destroy. In a report presented to him by the industrialist Ben Heineman, Johnson saw the opportunity to rationalize the relation between the White House and the bureaucracy through the establishment of subpresidencies that would mediate between the White House and the cabinet departments, as well as state and local governments. Johnson's departure from the presidency stopped the idea from developing beyond the drawing board, but a Nixon-appointed committee, under the chairmanship of Litton Industries executive Roy Ash, began its report with a quotation from the Heineman report.

While no one can be certain what Johnson would have done with Heineman's advice, one has a better idea of what Nixon sought to do with Ash's. His creation of White House councils under presidential assistants was a remarkable revolution against the Brownlow tradition of leaving the functions of command to the president and his cabinet, with assistants serving as bridges of communication. Nixon's White House councils put authority for command in the White House staff, an authority formalized clearest by the naming of Henry Kissinger as both secretary of state and national security adviser. Nixon's transformation of the Office of Management and Budget into an arm of political policy-making, his effort to purge a bureaucracy that sophisticated studies by political scientists acknowledged was opposed to the president's policies, and his interest in centralizing intelligence services in the White House, while all explicable as parts of the "siege mentality" that critics saw the Nixon White House as displaying, are also explicable as attempts to regain presidential control of administrative management.

It is difficult to get beneath the layers of hostility and turmoil, much of it attributable to the growing public reaction to the Vietnam War, in order to reveal the conflict between Congress and the president for control over the federal bureaucracy during the Nixon years. Both Nixon's full term and his partial term were dominated in a sense by the partisan division over White House and congressional control, which was to become more or less the norm for the next several years as the voting public elected Republican presidents and Democratic Congresses. Efforts by the president to scale back federally funded programs or to return their control to the states could easily face opposition from groups within Congress who saw them as threats to constituent interests and from federal bureaucrats who saw them as damaging to programs they were committed to protecting. Whether that protection stemmed from an intellectual perception of social needs that the government should meet or from the kind of bureaucratic intransigence that critics in the press and in academic circles were beginning to write about still made "bureaucrats," "Washington," and "the government on our backs" useful enemies for political leaders to target.

Again, the war and the War Powers Act of 1973, which attempted to limit presidential authority for the sending of troops into war zones, overshadow the multiple conflicts between Nixon and his Congresses. The act is the most visible and dramatic example of the steps Congress took to limit the authority of administrators to control the policies of their presidencies. The American tendency to exclude foreign policy from direct legislative oversight leads to problems in discussing administrative-legislative relationships at their most historically complex—the authority of the the chief executive to make war.

When Congress refused President Nixon's attempts to reorganize his administration with congressional help, he attempted to resort to executive orders, something he surely knew Eisenhower had done. His impoundment of funds, while a practice used by some of his predecessors, led to calls in Congress for a resolution forbidding such actions. The administration's argument that it was the only way of preventing the overloading of spending legislation with congressional additions unwanted by the administration cast impoundment as a substitute for item veto. The passage of the Congressional Budget and Impoundment Control Act of 1974 gave Congress a budget office of its own for the first time. It served, in a sense, as a counter to the politicization of the Office of Budget and Management, but set the White House and Congress at partisan sword points over budgetary issues that fifty years of reform had been designed, at least in principle, to avoid and created sizable bureaucracies for the management of both agencies. At the same time, both offices were systematic acknowledgments of the revolutions in economics, economic forecasting, and the complex relations between monetary and fiscal policies that had been part of the revolution in government financing since World War II. Both, too, recognized the bureaucratic complexities occasioned by the expanded role for experts, whose positions on government boards and commissions gave them a visible authority, if not actual power, that both Congress and the president would find difficult to control.

At one extreme, one could find in the writings of former White House staff members accusations of deliberate mistrust, even misguidance, by staff of the previous president—in this case, Johnson in the aftermath of the Kennedy assassination and Ford in the aftermath of the Nixon resignation—or confusions created by agency heads ignoring presidential orders. At the other extreme, one could find much more of an attempt at systematic analysis of the problems inherent in the new bureaucracy. Zero-based budgeting was introduced as a concept in 1974 to describe a process by which each program would be required to justify its continued existence before reauthorization. A revolution against the previous practice of incremental budgeting, whereby programs would be assumed to be continuing with greater or lesser funding, the zero-based idea had a certain popular attractiveness to it and was used by Jimmy Carter as part of his campaign argument in 1976, although he dropped it shortly after becoming president. Despite a certain amount of professional ridicule at the time, the principle remains to be tested.

What is understood today as deregulation began during the Carter administration under the leadership of economist Alfred Kahn, then of the Civil Aeronautics Board. In a pattern that would form the basis for an odd bipartisan congressional support, deregulation could be defended by Republicans as a way of ending bureaucratic interference with industry and by Democrats as a way of lowering prices by short-circuiting industry influence on publicly controlled private services. In either case, the effort to reduce bureaucratic power was complicated by Supreme Court rulings that limited the authority of Congress to use its legislative veto power to affect administrative rules and by rulings that forced agencies to abide by rules already established. The Supreme Court's intervention seemed to create an administrative no-man's-land that protected branches of the government from one another, as well as the bureaucracies that carried out their policies, without clearly protecting the public.

The greatest and most systematically effective attack on the federal bureaucracy since the founding of civil service reform was completed by President Carter in the Civil Service Reform Act of 1978. Unionization had already had its influence on civil service regulation, and Carter attacked it, as he attacked all of the protections that he felt favored incompetence. The act divided the U.S. Civil Service Commission into two agencies, the White House Office of Personnel Management and the independent Merit System Protection Board. The Federal Labor Relations Authority was established to deal with labor-management issues.

Perhaps the most far-reaching effect of the Civil Service Reform Act of 1978 was its creation of the Senior Executive Service. While all kinds of protections were built in to assure what was, in effect, the top management corps of the federal government's independence—only 10 percent of staff could be noncareer employees and 45 percent of the positions were to be reserved for career managers—the initial effort to provide freedom for imaginative and flexible intellectual interventions in the bureaucratic process was complicated by a performance management system with bonus awards that opened up the possibility of a variety of influences from the executive branch, where the politics of personnel issues continued to play the role it had always played. But now what President Nixon had been forced to do up front, or at least before congressional critics, President Reagan could accomplish behind the scenes, quietly shifting managerial staff rather than imposing them. Whether the problems seen in some of the housing and banking agencies of the Reagan administration are the result of such personnel management, combined with deregulation, has been obscured for the moment by more recent international events. It seems quite likely that in time they will return to center stage.

If there is a center of a stage, then, what is the drama being played out on it? The efforts to avoid the creation of a bureaucratic state to govern American society have not been successful: it has one. If it is not a very good one in administrative terms, in the sense that it is neither managerially efficient nor socially scientific, it is a very good one in political terms, in that it remains responsive to the pressures it may originally have been created to respond to—the legislature, the executive, and the public. One might well ask in what order the three groups are responded to or what parts of each get the responses they demand. The answer would be a complicated historical one indeed. Experiments in bureaucratic reordering were an essential part of American history in the 1970s and 1980s. There have been ardent proponents of more-systematic and more-efficient bureaucratic decision-making such as PPB and zero-base budgeting, but there have also been expert defenders of "muddling-through" and "adhocracy," who argue for immediate responsiveness rather than long-range plans that have to be dropped or distorted as circumstances shift. Periods of unanticipated economic stringency, whatever their cause, create demands for new priorities that Congress and the executive must determine.

The order shifts, not always in response to the most rational reasons. A charismatic leader, dramatic events, and public perceptions can all influence the shifts. As long as the present form of government remains what it is, the bureaucracy itself cannot shift it. The bureaucracy remains imprisoned by the character of the political order, for better or for worse, and it may well be either one.

## *BIBLIOGRAPHY*

Generally speaking, and perhaps as a consequence of the barriers between politics and administration erected almost a century ago by Progressive Era administrative and political theorists, historians have not been inclined to be interested in public administration or administrative theory, and when administrative theorists move into history, they rarely approach the problems that historians find important. The literature of public administration provides a history oriented more toward the executive branch than toward the legislative. Congress is more often seen as an usurper of executive prerogatives than a supporter of them. Nonetheless, a perusal of the back issues of the *Public Administration Review,* the *Journal of Politics,* and the *Political Science Quarterly* will provide more background than one might expect. It does, however, require a good deal of historical redigestion. The emergence of a historical literature on bureaucracy and state building is headed in a direction that might prove fruitful, but it may be too soon to tell. STEPHEN SKOWRONEK, *Building a New American State* (New York, 1982), remains the best example.

The fullest account of the first century of American administrative history remains the four volumes by LEONARD WHITE, *The Federalists* (New York, 1948), *The Jeffersonians* (New York, 1951), *The Jacksonians* (New York, 1954), and *The Republican Era, 1869–1901* (New York, 1958). MATTHEW CRENSON has revised White's view of the Jacksonians in *The Federal Machine: The Beginnings of Bureaucracy in Jacksonian America* (Baltimore, 1975). One should also note the writings of LOUIS BROWNLOW and DON K. PRICE as examples of a very historically oriented administrative commentary. NELSON POLSBY's unusual historical sensitivities have been most helpful in preparing this essay. OSCAR KRAINES has made a continuous and deeply committed effort to draw attention to the early years of executive reorganization in his studies of the years of the Cockrell and Dockery investigations, *Congress and the Challenge of Big Government* (Cambridge, Mass., 1958). MORTON KELLER's two volumes, *Affairs of State* (Cambridge, Mass., 1977) and *Regulating a New Economy* (Cambridge, Mass., 1990), offer a necessary background of detail on which many of the problems of bureaucratic history depend. One can also see in the kind of business history written by ALFRED D. CHANDLER and THOMAS K. MCCRAW aspects of management that can help provide categories for a governmentally oriented bureaucratic history. CHANDLER's *Strategy and Structure: Chapters in the History of the Industrial Enterprise* (Cambridge, Mass., 1969), and *The Visible Hand: The Managerial Revolution in American Business* (Cambridge, Mass., 1977), are primary examples, as is MCCRAW, *Prophets of Regulation: Charles Francis Adams, Louis D. Brandeis, James M. Landis, Alfred E. Kahn* (Cambridge, Mass., 1984). PERI ARNOLD, *Making the Managerial Presidency* (Princeton, N.J., 1986), is a study of the history of executive reorganization and management up to 1980. WILLIAM PEMBERTON has studied the uses of the reports of the Hoover Commission in his *Bureaucratic Politics: Executive Reorganization During the Truman Administration* (Columbia, Mo., 1979), and EMMETTE S. REDFORD and MARIAN BLISSETT, *Organizing the Executive Branch* (Chicago, 1981), is part of a series on the Johnson administration. The best collection of materials is LOUIS GALAMBOS, ed., *The New American State: Bureaucracies and Policies Since World War II* (Baltimore, Md., 1987).

# LEGISLATIVE POWER OVER APPOINTMENTS AND CONFIRMATIONS

## Richard Allan Baker

The U.S. Constitution provides that the president "shall nominate, and by and with the Advice and Consent of the Senate, shall appoint Ambassadors, other public Ministers and Consuls, Judges of the Supreme Court, and all other Officers of the United States, whose Appointments are not herein otherwise provided for" (Article II, Section 2). This provision, like many others in the Constitution, was born of compromise, and over the more than two centuries since its adoption, it has inspired widely varying interpretations. Also, like other federal constitutional provisions, it has fostered similar language in state constitutions.

At the federal level, the president nominates all judges in the judicial branch and specified officers in cabinet-level departments, independent agencies, the military services, the foreign service, uniformed civilian services, and U.S. attorneys and U.S. marshals. In 1989, 320 positions in fourteen cabinet agencies and 117 positions in independent and other agencies were subject to presidential appointment. During the 101st Congress (1989–1991), President George Bush's administration submitted 93,368 civilian and military nominations. Of that number, 88,078 were confirmed. Only one, that of John G. Tower as defense secretary, was rejected. The remainder were withdrawn or not acted upon.

The importance of the position, the qualifications of the nominee, and the prevailing political climate influence the character of the Senate's response to each nomination. Views of the Senate's "proper role" range from a narrow construction that the Senate is obligated to confirm unless the nominee is manifestly lacking in character and competence, to a broad interpretation that accords the Senate power to reject a nominee for any reason that a majority of its members deem appropriate. As the president is not required to explain why he selected

a particular nominee, so the Senate is not obligated to give reasons for rejecting a nominee.

Executive-branch appointments customarily end with the departure of the president who made them. Judicial appointments, on the contrary, are for life and can be terminated only through the time-consuming impeachment process. Historically, Supreme Court nominations, in great disproportion to their number, have attracted the close attention of senators, the media, and scholars. While the Senate explicitly rejected fewer than 2 percent (9 of more than 500) of all cabinet nominees between 1789 and 1989, it blocked 20 percent (28 of 146) of all Supreme Court nominations. (During the nineteenth century the Senate killed one-third of all Supreme Court nominations.)

Generally, when the president and the majority of the Senate belong to the same political party, the Senate tends to approve the president's choices. The exceptions to this well-established pattern occur in the final year of a president's term and in cases in which the nominee obviously lacks competence or personal integrity.

Throughout the nation's history, appointments to judicial posts below the Supreme Court have generated little controversy. This has been so in part because of the large number of such appointments and the tradition of "senatorial courtesy," which defers to the preferences of those senators belonging to the president's party who represent the nominee's home state. Lower court judges have been considered less potentially mischievous because they are more closely constrained by precedent than are Supreme Court justices, and they do not have the final judicial say on significant issues.

Except in the case of nominations to cabinet departments and the Supreme Court, most rejections in modern times have taken place at the committee level, either by vote not to send to the Senate floor for consideration or through inaction. Before the 1860s, the Senate considered most nominations without referring them to the committee holding jurisdiction over the vacant post. The Senate rules of 1868, for the first time, provided for the referral of nominations to "appropriate committees." Not until the middle of the twentieth century, however, did those committees routinely require nominees for major positions to appear in person. Presidents have occasionally circumvented the confirmation process by making "recess appointments" when the Senate is in adjournment between sessions or in recess within a session. As provided by the Constitution, such appointments expire at the end of the following congressional session, but may expire earlier in certain specified circumstances.

The appointment process at the state level reflects the diversity of the individual states, with no consistent pattern evident. Only eighteen of the fifty states directly follow the national model, dividing appointment power between the governor and state senate. In Alaska and Virginia, both legislative chambers participate in the confirmation process, while other states provide for some legislative involvement. The eleven states in which legislatures have virtually no role in the process are Alabama, Arkansas, Indiana, Kentucky, Massachusetts, Nevada, New Hampshire, North Carolina, Tennessee, Texas, and Washington. Among these states, governors exercise unfettered appointment power in Arkansas, Kentucky, Massachusetts, and Nevada. In the remaining seven states of this group, the appointment process is entrusted variously to the electorate, commissions, boards, and agency heads.

Nomination and confirmation of key officials at the state level has rarely generated much controversy. Where state legislatures are involved, by constitutional mandate or statutory provision, the pattern has been to refer nominations to a standing committee with jurisdiction over the specific position, although several legislatures rely on a special administrative committee. Chamber operating rules seldom provide specific procedural guidance. This is the case, for example, with the conduct of public hearings. Most legislatures leave to their respective committee chairs the decision on whether to hold a hearing and how to proceed.

Hearings are most likely to be held if the legislature lacks adequate information on the nominee, if the nominee is considered controversial, if the post is viewed as one of major importance, or if a member insists on a thorough examination of a nominee. A few legislatures specifically do not hold confirmation hearings.

Legislatures also differ widely in the extent of background information about a nominee that they provide their members. A few chambers, imitating the U.S. Senate's custom of senatorial courtesy, require approval by the nominee's senator before beginning deliberation. Committee staff usually undertake background investigations, but in some states this task is left to the governor's staff, to a standard questionnaire, or even to committee members. If the inquiry develops adverse information, governors usually withdraw the nomination to avoid a legislative floor fight. Withdrawn candidates have on occasion been resubmitted and approved in later sessions. When a committee reports a nomination back to its parent chamber, that body is required to act, with either a simple majority or a two-thirds vote necessary for approval. Few candidates are denied confirmation once the nomination has been reported to the full chamber, but the threat of legislative refusal is considered an ever-present danger. In most states, reflecting the relative pro forma nature of the confirmation process, nominees take office at the time the governor appoints them and step down only if the legislature fails to act or specifically rejects them.

## HISTORICAL BACKGROUND

The earliest colonial charters provided for divided responsibility in the appointment of key officials. The Massachusetts charter of 1691 gave that colony's governor the power to nominate officers "with the advice and consent" of his council. Early state constitutions included a reference to council "advice," but omitted "consent." South Carolina was the first to depart from this practice, by entrusting key appointments to the legislature. Virginia specified that its legislature would elect judges, but the governor would appoint justices of the peace with the advice of the privy council. In Delaware the state president and general as-

# LEGISLATIVE POWER OVER APPOINTMENTS AND CONFIRMATIONS

sembly were to appoint justices, while the president and privy council were to select various specified officials. The assembly alone would appoint justices of the peace.

When the federal constitutional convention assembled at Philadelphia in 1787, delegates of the twelve states represented could refer to no generally accepted principle for selecting judges and executive officials. These men were well versed in the mechanics of legislative operation, as most of the fifty-five had served in state or local governments. At that time, state constitutions granted the appointment power to their legislatures or to a council that the legislature appointed. Under the government of the existing Articles of Confederation, which lacked a separate executive, the unicameral Congress made all appointments, based on recommendations of the delegates from the state involved.

At the convention, initial plans for organizing the new government split the appointment power, with Congress filling judicial appointments and the president selecting executive officers. The framers eventually agreed to confine the congressional role to the Senate, as they believed its smaller size would promote the desired secrecy and efficiency of the process.

The greater debate centered on whether the Senate or the president would be best able to identify suitable candidates. In the convention's final days, following Massachusetts's century-old practice, delegates divided responsibility between the two. In so doing, the framers addressed the fears of certain influential delegates that entrusting the appointment power exclusively to the president would encourage monarchical tendencies. As the Senate was to represent each state equally, its role offered security to the small states, whose delegates feared they would be overwhelmed by appointees sympathetic to the larger states. Even Alexander Hamilton, who wished to strengthen the executive against legislative interference, supported the concept of dual responsibility, believing that the president's authority to nominate was sufficient to control the appointment process, for the Senate could do no more than accept or reject his choices. In placing the legislative role in the Senate, which was intended to be relatively immune from political pressure, and by requiring joint action with the president, the framers hoped to minimize corrupt bargaining for appointments.

## THE WASHINGTON ADMINISTRATION

President George Washington was aware that his every action would have significant consequences for the success of the new government, and he predicted that the making of appointments would be among his most difficult duties. In selecting nominees, Washington turned to his closest advisers and to members of Congress, but the president resolutely insisted that he alone would be responsible for the final selection. He shared a common view that the Senate's constitutionally mandated advice was to come after the nomination was made. (This differed from some existing state constitutional arrangements in which the governor was to seek the advice of his council before making a nomination.)

Washington sent his first nomination to the Senate on 15 June 1789. He named William Short to oversee American affairs in Paris during the absence of minister Thomas Jefferson. For the first and only time, Washington offered to send to the Senate "papers which will acquaint you with his character" (Harris, p. 38). Secretary of Foreign Affairs John Jay presented Short's papers on 17 June, and the Senate, after deciding that the vote should be by secret ballot, quickly confirmed him.

The method of Senate voting sparked a vigorous debate. Vice President John Adams, the presiding officer, sought to put administration supporters and opponents on record and urged a voice vote. William Maclay (Anti-Fed.-Pa.) won the day with his argument against an open vote, which he contended would subject those in the Senate who opposed a nominee to a loss of presidential "sunshine."

### The First Rejection

On 5 August 1789, the Senate, for the first time, rejected a nomination and in so doing, established the tradition of "senatorial courtesy." Two days earlier, Washington had submitted the names of 102 nominees as collectors, naval officers, and surveyors to seaports. The Senate readily agreed to all but one—Benjamin Fishbourn of Georgia. Earlier in his career,

Fishbourn had offended James Gunn, who in 1789 had become one of Georgia's two senators. This seemed to have been Fishbourn's only shortcoming. In rejecting him, the Senate shared the view of some of the Constitution's framers that senators were best qualified to judge the fitness of nominees from their states. The president submitted a replacement, and a tactful letter of protest. He noted that the Senate probably had its reasons for rejecting Fishbourn, but he urged members who might question future nominations "to communicate that circumstance to me, and thereby avail yourselves of the information which led me to make them and which I would with pleasure lay before you" (DePauw, p. 24). In later years, as the tradition of senatorial courtesy evolved, presidents would routinely survey senators of their party before formally submitting candidates from their states to fill major executive and judicial positions.

Immediately after the Senate rejected Fishbourn, a motion was introduced "that it is the opinion of the Senate that their advice, and consent to the appointment of Officers should be given in the presence of the President" (DePauw, p. 24). Washington decided that this arrangement could embarrass both the president and the Senate by forcing their silence or their argumentation. He concluded that as he had the right to nominate without specifying his reasons, so did senators have the right to dissent without detailing theirs. The Senate accepted the president's decision and then reversed its earlier agreement to vote in secret on nominations and treaties. For both types of "executive" business, the Senate decided that a voice vote would be required, whether or not the president was present. Although executive sessions of the Senate would remain closed to the press and public until 1929, members' votes would be publicized in the Senate's executive journal.

The First Congress addressed many issues left unsettled at the Constitutional Convention. Among those related to appointments was the power of removal. Representative James Madison (Va.), who had been the convention's guiding spirit, introduced a bill in the House to establish a cabinet department of foreign affairs, with a provision explicitly acknowledging the president's power to remove the "principal officer of the department." This language emerged from a five-day debate that thoroughly explored the framers' intentions. Members had advanced the following constitutional interpretations: the president alone had power of removal; the president shared it with the Senate; an officer could be removed only by the impeachment process; and Congress could resolve this issue because the Constitution was silent on it. Madison vigorously supported sole executive responsibility. He acknowledged the Senate's confirming role, but he warned that he would not "extend or strain that qualification beyond the limits precisely fixed for it" (Harris, p. 32).

## Washington's Supreme Court Nominations

The first president holds the record for the most Supreme Court nominations. He made fourteen selections for ten vacancies on the six-member court between 1789 and 1796. One associate justice declined to serve after confirmation in 1789, one nominee was rejected in 1795, and one associate justice turned down a promotion to chief justice in 1796. Washington named only men he knew well, and he measured them against specific criteria, including the fitness of their character and health, rigorous training, and public recognition. He expected outspoken support for the Constitution, an exemplary military record, and distinguished prior political and judicial service.

Washington nominated John Jay of New York as chief justice. When Jay resigned in 1795, the president selected South Carolina's John Rutledge, who had served briefly as an associate justice, to replace him. His nomination raised questions about the order of succession to the chief justiceship. Some argued that the appointment should have been made from the ranks of the sitting associate justices, with preference given to the senior justice. Others contended that the best available man should be found for the job and that "dull seniority and length of service should be considered as nothing." As the Senate was in recess until winter, Rutledge received only a temporary commission.

Several weeks after his appointment, Rutledge delivered a speech highly critical of Jay's Treaty, which the administration and Senate had supported. Many in the administration cited this ill-timed speech as evidence of Rutledge's advancing mental incapacity. Ignoring this swirling controversy, Rutledge arrived at the capital in August 1795 and took his seat. When the Senate convened in December, it promptly rejected his nomination. Rutledge thus became the first Supreme Court justice to be rejected and the only one among the fifteen who would gain their offices through recess appointments not to be subsequently confirmed. In rejecting Rutledge, the Senate made it clear that an examination of a nominee's qualifications would extend beyond his personal qualifications to his political views. Those who differed substantively from the majority of senators could expect rough going.

## Washington's Cabinet

The first president applied to the choice of his first cabinet criteria similar to those he used for his first judicial nominees. His major appointments were to the Departments of State, Treasury, and War. Washington's closest adviser was Alexander Hamilton, whom he named secretary of the Treasury in recognition of the New Yorker's superior administrative skills and sparkling intellect. Thomas Jefferson, who would rather have remained as minister to France, accepted leadership of the tiny State Department, and Secretary of War Henry Knox and Attorney General Edmund Randolph continued the assignments they had held under the Articles of Confederation. Washington also named Timothy Pickering to be postmaster general. The Senate readily confirmed all five appointees.

## THE ADAMS, JEFFERSON, AND MADISON ADMINISTRATIONS

Despite expectations, political partisanship quickly became a factor in the organization and operation of the new government. Washington had asserted that he would consider political loyalty as a factor in selecting key officeholders, but he vowed that subordinate posts would be filled only on merit. Despite this laudable aim, his later appointments and those of his immediate successors took on a strong political coloration. John Adams pledged to be more careful than Washington in avoiding the ap-

pointment of vigorous partisans and promised to respect men of principle and competence, regardless of their political views. Adams encountered resistance to the free exercise of his nominating prerogatives from a number of forces, including holdover appointees, who felt no obligation to resign; from the influential Alexander Hamilton; and from the Senate, which insisted on an active role far beyond screening out only those nominees who were demonstrably unfit for service. Adams thus continued the practice of consulting members of the Senate, as well as the House, on appointments within their individual states, and he gave more weight to congressional recommendations than did his predecessor.

Thomas Jefferson enjoyed strong support in the Senate for most of his eight years as president and worked closely with state delegations in selecting appointees. He removed very few holdover appointees and carefully examined every nomination, from Supreme Court justice to lighthouse keeper. He maintained Washington's firm control of the nomination process, refusing requests to share with the Senate letters of recommendation for individual nominees. The third president viewed the Senate's role as being only to counterbalance any undue favoritism that the chief executive might be tempted to extend to his family or friends. Near the end of Jefferson's second term, however, the Senate inflicted an embarrassing defeat. He appointed as minister to Russia his friend William Short, who had been George Washington's first nominee. Opposing establishment of permanent missions in other countries, the Senate unanimously rejected Short.

While the Senate gave Jefferson little difficulty with his nominations, it responded vigorously to those of his successor, James Madison. The first battle occurred when Madison announced his intention to appoint Albert Gallatin, Jefferson's Treasury secretary, as secretary of state. Three senators, including Samuel Smith (R.-Md.), immediately informed the president that Gallatin would not be confirmed. Smith hoped to have his brother Robert, then secretary of the navy, appointed to that post. By way of compromise, they agreed to support Gallatin if Robert Smith were named to replace him as Treasury secretary. Gallatin refused to participate in such a deal and requested to remain at Treasury. Madison then appointed Smith to the State Department post, despite serious doubts about his competence. John Quincy Adams later observed that the War of 1812 would never have occurred if Gallatin had been secretary of state.

During that war, Madison appointed Gallatin to a peace commission. This energized Gallatin's enemies in the Senate, who blocked his confirmation on the grounds that his duties in both posts were incompatible. When a Senate committee called on the president to discuss the nomination, Madison turned them aside, contending that the Senate had not formally authorized their visit. When a committee returned with Senate authorization, Madison sent a protest message to the Senate insisting on executive independence from Senate influence in appointments. In Madison's opinion, the Senate was welcome to ask for the information on which the president based his nomination and was welcome to reject the nomination. A committee of the Senate, Madison argued, was not coequal to the executive and therefore lacked standing for such a meeting. The Senate committee persisted and eventually received a chilly presidential reception. Madison subsequently obliged Gallatin's enemies by replacing him at Treasury and resubmitting his nomination to the peace commission. The Senate promptly confirmed Gallatin.

Madison suffered additional major rejections—one to the Supreme Court and one to his cabinet. In 1811 he selected, as his first nominee to the Supreme Court, Alexander Wolcott, a Connecticut customs collector. Convinced that Wolcott lacked appropriate legal training and experience and angered by his strident partisanship, the Senate decisively killed his nomination by a 9–24 vote.

In 1815, Madison named Henry Dearborn secretary of war. Dearborn had held that post in Jefferson's administration, but subsequently had come under attack for his poor military record during the War of 1812. Realizing that Senate rejection was inevitable, Madison moved to withdraw the nomination the day after its submission. His action came too late, as the Senate voted to reject Dearborn. Realizing that Madison was about to rescind the nomination, the Senate quietly erased from its journal the record of these proceedings. Al-

though not formally credited with this distinction, Dearborn in effect became the first cabinet nominee rejected by the Senate.

In 1820, Congress passed the Four Years Act, which limited the terms of federal officers such as district attorneys and customs collectors. This legislation was intended to relieve pressures on the president and the Senate by assuring a regular supply of vacancies. Thomas Jefferson predicted, to the contrary, that the act would create great mischief by keeping job seekers constantly agitated. Presidents James Monroe and John Quincy Adams, refusing to comply with the act's intent, reappointed most who fell under its provisions. Its impact was first felt in the political sea change that followed the 1828 election of Andrew Jackson.

## THE JACKSON ADMINISTRATION

More than any other president since George Washington, Andrew Jackson defined the relations between the executive and Congress. From the start of his administration in 1829, he intruded into congressional operations. And the Senate responded. Dramatic nomination fights erupted almost immediately and resulted in the first open rejection of a cabinet secretary, the third defeat of a Supreme Court nominee, and the making of a vice president.

Among Jackson's first set of nominations were a "batch of editors" who had supported his presidential campaign and were clearly being rewarded for their political services. Most were selected while the Senate was out of session and thus assumed their assignments under recess appointments. When the Senate returned to session, Jackson's political foes responded with a "massacre of the editors," rejecting ten nominees. When the Senate rejected New Hampshire editor Isaac Hill's appointment to a key Treasury office because of his attacks on the previous administration, he returned home and successfully ran for the Senate, thus gaining satisfaction at being able to sit among those who had spurned him. Of the 319 Jacksonian nominations, the Senate actually rejected only a small number, and the administration subsequently was able to overturn several of these. Coming at the start of a new administration and considering the passion that these fights unleashed, this clash was unprecedented. The struggle might have been even more intense, had not Jackson been so popular.

In 1831 as part of a scheme to allow Jackson to reshuffle his cabinet, Secretary of State Martin Van Buren resigned and accepted an appointment as ambassador to Great Britain. Administration opponents in the Senate, fearing that Van Buren was being positioned as Jackson's successor, moved to block his confirmation. Although the opposition had sufficient votes to reject Van Buren, they arranged a tie vote so that so that Vice President John C. Calhoun, a bitter enemy of Van Buren, would have the satisfaction of casting the decisive ballot. Administration ally Thomas Hart Benton (D.-Mo.) doubted the wisdom of this strategy, accurately predicting that in defeating a minister, the opposition had guaranteed the election of a vice president.

By the summer of 1834, relations between the Senate, which stood evenly divided between anti-Jackson men and administration supporters, were at an all-time low because of the president's attack on the second Bank of the United States. The Senate, demonstrating its capacity for combat in instances where the president's party lacked a firm majority, rejected four of the bank's government directors. When Jackson renominated them, the Senate again rebuffed them by an even larger margin, leading Senator John Tyler (Whig-Va.) to warn that renominations should be made only in "very clear and strong cases." In the final week of the congressional session, Jackson nominated Attorney General Roger B. Taney as secretary of the Treasury. Taney had been the architect of Jackson's plan to dismantle the bank. A day later, a pro-bank majority in the Senate, including both senators from Taney's Maryland, voted 18–28 to deny Taney the post, making him the first cabinet nominee to be openly rejected.

The following year, Jackson named Taney associate justice of the Supreme Court, but opponents blocked a Senate vote on the last day of that session and tried unsuccessfully to eliminate one seat from the Court. When the Senate reconvened in December 1835, under a slim margin of Democratic control, it received a new Taney nomination, this time to fill a vacancy for chief justice. Following extended maneuvering and bitter debate, the Senate confirmed Taney. On departing office a year later, Jackson wrote to a friend that he was looking forward to seeing Van Buren, once rejected by the Senate, sworn into office as president by Chief Justice Taney, who also had been rejected by the Senate.

## ANTEBELLUM PERIOD

With the departure of the overbearing Jackson, the Senate quickly reasserted its prerogatives over appointments and maintained its dominance throughout the nineteenth century. One of the most dramatic confirmation struggles occurred in the administration of John Tyler, who had fallen out with the Senate's Whig majority shortly after he succeeded to the presidency in 1841. These troubles further emphasized the capacity for struggle between a Senate and administration of differing political orientations. On 3 March 1843, the final day of a contentious congressional session, the Senate considered Tyler's nomination of Caleb Cushing to be secretary of the Treasury. Cushing had deeply antagonized administration foes in the Senate with his strident defense of the president. For the second time in history, the Senate formally rejected a cabinet nominee. Signing last-minute legislation in a room adjoining the Senate chamber, Tyler quickly resubmitted his nomination of Cushing, contradicting his own earlier views against renominations. Minutes later, by an even greater margin the Senate again rejected Cushing. Not deterred, Tyler again sent in Cushing's name. And again, with only two affirmative votes, the Senate dismissed the nominee, demonstrating the power of institutional loyalty over partisan allegiance. Following this pattern, the Senate subsequently twice rejected Tyler's nominee as minister to France and turned down appointees for the posts of minister to Brazil, secretary of the Treasury, secretary of the navy, secretary of war, and four Supreme Court nominees. Hopes among Whig senators that their former colleague Henry Clay would be the next president accounted for the Senate's refusal to move on any Supreme Court nominations until after the 1844 election.

Tyler's successor turned out to be Democrat James K. Polk, who complained bitterly of pressure from members of Congress to influence appointments. On one occasion he appointed a surveyor to the port of Saint Louis. When that nomination was defeated at the request of the very senator who had recommended the candidate, Polk asked for an explanation. The senator replied that he was obligated to recommend any constituent who might apply. From 1844 to 1853, eight of thirteen nominees failed to secure confirmation, with most defeats coming in the final months of the appointing president's term.

## THE CIVIL WAR AND RECONSTRUCTION

President Abraham Lincoln, following the practice of his predecessors, used patronage appointments to solidify his power base. Only to the highest posts did he apply a standard of competence for officeholders. Otherwise, he left to Congress the choices for the many positions that had become available as the spoils of his party's ascendancy. Republicans in the House of Representatives were allowed to recommend candidates for minor offices such as postmasterships, while Republican senators were given a fairly free hand in choosing nominees for major offices.

The end of the Civil War and the ensuing disputes over Reconstruction policies reopened traditional animosities between the executive and Congress. With the leadership of the House and Senate intent on pursuing a harsher policy than Lincoln's successor, Andrew Johnson, the entire appointments process became subject to thorough reexamination.

The fundamental issue involved authority to remove officeholders. During Lincoln's administration, Congress passed, and the president signed, a law stipulating that Senate permission would be required to remove the controller of the Treasury. Other statutes curbed the president's removal power over consular clerks and military officers. Andrew Johnson reacted to congressional attacks on his policies by removing officials originally appointed at the request of those who had become his opponents in Congress. In response, Congress passed, over Johnson's veto, the Tenure of Office Act. This bold statute, enacted on

2 March 1867, prohibited the president from removing civil officials appointed with the Senate's advice and consent without first obtaining Senate approval. Congressional supporters of Secretary of War Edwin Stanton intended this law to insulate him against removal. Five months later, while the Senate was in recess, Johnson suspended Stanton and appointed General Ulysses Grant. On reconvening in December, the Senate and House passed resolutions asserting that the president had violated the Tenure of Office Act. This test failed when Grant relinquished his post to Stanton; but the House then approved articles of impeachment against the president and the Senate conducted the trial, which came within one vote of removing Johnson. Attorney General Henry Stanbery had resigned his office to serve as Johnson's counsel during the impeachment proceedings. On the conclusion of the trial, Johnson reappointed Stanbery to his former post, and the Senate immediately rejected him 11–29. (The Supreme Court declared the Tenure of Office Act unconstitutional in *Myers* v. *United States*, 272 U.S. 52 [1926], preserving presidents' rights to dismiss all appointees except regulatory commission members and other fixed-term officeholders whose independence would be violated by removal.)

From 1894 to 1968 the Senate would reject only one Supreme Court nomination. Prior to 1895, however, the Senate had rejected, or had otherwise caused to be blocked, twenty-two nominations to the High Court. The greatest series of rejections came in the years immediately following the Civil War, at a time of intense partisan conflict when the majority of senators viewed the Court as a political institution whose members should represent geographical regions and hold "acceptable" political views. Radical Republicans feared that a hostile Court would undermine the results of the Civil War and Reconstruction.

The Court had taken a sharp decline in public esteem following its 1857 *Dred Scott* decision. During the Civil War, the Lincoln administration viewed the Court as unsupportive of its efforts to preserve the Union and sought to fill vacancies with politically reliable allies. In 1866, Congress passed legislation to preserve Lincoln's amicable Supreme Court, which had increased to ten in 1863, by reducing its membership through attrition to seven. The Court soon proved unfriendly to the aims of the Radical Republicans in Congress, and those members considered plans to limit the Court's powers, such as requiring a two-thirds vote to invalidate an act of Congress. Through the remainder of the 1860s and 1870s, justices repeatedly acted in an overtly partisan manner.

The 1866 act reducing the size of the Court blocked President Andrew Johnson's appointment of Henry Stanbery and removed his opportunity to fill the next two vacancies. When the politically more palatable Ulysses Grant became president, Congress reversed itself and set the Court's size at its current nine members. In 1869, Grant named Ebenezer Hoar to the Court. As attorney general, Hoar had offended many senators by insisting on highly qualified judicial appointees—a standard that left little room for political-patronage considerations. Hoar's stinging criticism of several candidates was not soon forgotten by their senatorial patrons. When Grant nominated Hoar to the High Court, his Senate foes ensured his defeat, despite wide popular endorsement, by an unambiguous 24–33 margin.

Hoar's nomination marked a break with the practice of selecting justices from the judicial circuit of the previous incumbent. This arrangement had minimized controversy by allowing appointment of a candidate popular with the legal community of a specific circuit. But Grant was unwilling to name a southerner, in part because southern opposition had provided the margin to reject Hoar's confirmation. Several years later, Grant nominated the former senator George H. Williams to be chief justice. Unlike the Hoar appointment, this selection stimulated widespread public condemnation. The New York Bar Association charged that he lacked the experience, intellect, and reputation essential for Supreme Court service. Williams subsequently withdrew his nomination.

Grant then named Caleb Cushing as chief justice. Thirty years earlier the Senate had rejected Cushing three times as Tyler's Treasury secretary. Although he was a well-regarded jurist, Radical Republicans forced his withdrawal on the overblown charge that he had corresponded with Confederate president Jefferson Davis in the early days of the Civil War. Beneath this, they feared that he would not be a firm partisan and that he was a man of "unstable character." During Grant's administration, the Senate rejected nine of fifty-eight contested executive and judicial nominations.

In the following administration of Rutherford Hayes, the Senate disapproved fifty-one of ninety-two contested nominations. Hayes's successor, James Garfield, tried to accommodate all major factions in his relations with the Senate. However, deciding to attack the custom of "senatorial courtesy," he soon became embroiled in a dispute over appointments to federal posts in New York with that state's Republican senators, Roscoe Conkling and Thomas Platt. In the course of the struggle, he declared that the issue at stake was whether the president was to be the registering clerk of the Senate or the nation's chief executive. He warned that senators who dared oppose him would no longer be welcome at the White House. When Garfield, over Conkling's and Platt's vigorous objections, refused to withdraw his controversial appointment for collector of the port of New York, both senators resigned in hopes of gaining a moral victory over the president through reelection. With those hostile senators gone, the Senate approved the nomination. Neither senator succeeded in his reelection bid, and the concept of senatorial courtesy, carried to its extreme, suffered a severe blow.

The assassination of Garfield by a demented job seeker hastened passage of the Pendleton Act of 1883, which reformed the civil service by removing many lower-level federal positions from patronage control, thereby reducing opportunities for friction between Congress and the president. By 1891, Republicans had abandoned their efforts to improve the lot of southern blacks and instead followed accommodationist policies that eliminated war-related issues as sticking points in the confirmation process. Nominees who were Confederate veterans moved easily to confirmation in the 1890s. After the Reconstruction era, Supreme Court nominees were selected without respect to their geographical base or narrow political views. In 1891, Congress recognized the Court's growing work load—a reflection of the country's economic expansion. The difficulty of justices covering geographical circuits was solved by creating a new circuit court system and relieving justices of circuit-riding duties. Nominees tended to be businesslike, legal technicians who experienced little difficulty in being confirmed and who raised the Court's public esteem. During this period and until 1916, the Senate and the chief executive maintained relatively harmonious relations in dealing with appointments. Presidents appeared unwilling to allow patronage considerations to erode support for their broader legislative agendas.

## THE TWENTIETH CENTURY

The twentieth century brought a significant shift in the balance of power between Congress and the presidency. As the nation moved to world-power status, the chief executive assumed greater authority. This shift became apparent in the smaller number of appointments contested in the Senate, particularly when its majorities were of the same party as the president. From 1897 to 1955, the presidency and the Senate were in the hands of the same party for all but four years (1919–1921 and 1947–1949). During the century's first nine decades the Senate would reject only three cabinet nominees and five Supreme Court justices. Of these nine rejections, five occurred during periods of divided party control.

President Theodore Roosevelt asserted presidential leadership in his appointments by selecting justices according to his view of their character, competence, and philosophical compatibility. His successor, William Howard Taft, expected an "avalanche of abuse" from fellow Republicans when he named as chief justice Edward Douglass White—a Democrat, a Catholic, and a Confederate army veteran. The Senate surprised Taft by confirming White quickly and unanimously, signifying how times had changed. Taft's nomination of Charles Evans Hughes also brought nearly universal praise, despite the New York Republican governor's highly partisan role in the recent presidential campaign.

When Woodrow Wilson entered office in 1913, returning the Democratic party to power for the first time in sixteen years, a large number of appointment choices awaited him. He occasionally ran afoul of senators of both parties who expected their wishes to be considered seriously for positions within their states,

and he suffered minor rejections for choosing individuals whose business interests seemed too closely tied to the position to which they were nominated.

Like Roosevelt and Taft, Wilson sought men he believed would implement his political ideology. In January 1916, Wilson named Louis D. Brandeis, the progressive "People's Lawyer" from Boston, to the Supreme Court. The Brandeis nomination ended the quiescent period by sparking a bitter and passionately waged confirmation fight. Brandeis deeply antagonized the nation's conservative legal establishment with his advocacy of "sociological jurisprudence." Brandeis had become famous in legal circles for the "Brandeis brief," which downplayed constitutional issues and precedents and focused instead on such social and economic issues as the health and welfare of workers. The American Bar Association, for the first time, attempted to kill the nomination, charging that Brandeis was unfit. Buried amidst charges that he lacked "judicial temperament" was a deep vein of anti-Semitism. Despite the Senate Judiciary Committee's slim two-vote margin in his favor, Brandeis secured confirmation by a comfortable 47–22 margin and became one of the Court's greatest justices.

Fourth Circuit chief judge John J. Parker, a prominent and distinguished North Carolina Republican, was the first Supreme Court nominee in the twentieth century to be rejected. The battle focused on the nominee's judicial record, rather than his personal competence. Powerful opposition from the American Federation of Labor and the National Association for the Advancement of Colored People, portraying him as unfriendly to labor and minorities, caused his defeat by a two-vote margin on 7 May 1930.

In 1925 the Senate for the first time summoned a Supreme Court nominee to testify before its Judiciary Committee. Harlan Fiske Stone's appearance was brief, but the senatorial questioning was vigorous. The next five nominees escaped this personal interrogation, but in 1939 the committee requested Felix Frankfurter to appear. Although he eventually complied, Frankfurter complained that his views were a matter of public record. Since the 1955 nomination of John Marshall Harlan, all Supreme Court appointees have appeared before the Judiciary Committee.

# LEGISLATIVE POWER OVER APPOINTMENTS AND CONFIRMATIONS

Of the twenty-four Supreme Court nominations between John Parker's rejection in 1930 and that of Abe Fortas in 1968, seventeen were confirmed unanimously, while only six stimulated significant Senate opposition. This pattern changed with President Lyndon Johnson's June 1968 nomination of Associate Justice Fortas to be chief justice. His rejection reflected the difficulty of gaining confirmation in the final year of a presidential administration and the special challenge that confronts associate justices named to be chief justice (being the difficulty sitting justices face whose established records inute senatorial scrutiny).

The Senate's refusal to confirm Fortas was also attributable to two tactical errors of the Johnson administration. The president had antagonized Senator Richard Russell (D.-Ga.), the most influential senator of the day, by delaying action on a Russell protégé for a federal judgeship. Moreover, the president—a former Senate majority leader—failed to calculate Senate irritation at being considered a rubber stamp for the president's wishes. At the time he submitted Fortas's nomination, Johnson, assuming that Fortas would be easily confirmed, also named a political crony of modest ability to fill the expected associate justice vacancy. Although the Judiciary Committee recommended favorable action, Republican senators, with a view to their party's brightening chances to capture the presidency in the approaching election, launched a filibuster to stall action. They expressed disapproval of Associate Justice Fortas's activities as a de facto presidential adviser, despite similar relationships in presidencies from Wilson's through Truman's, and of his tangled financial dealings. When his supporters were unable to end the marathon debate, Fortas asked Johnson to withdraw his nomination. He continued as an associate justice until the early months of the Nixon administration, when deepening evidence of financial misconduct forced his resignation.

President Richard Nixon nominated appeals court judge Clement F. Haynsworth, Jr., to the vacancy. The conservative South Carolinian, who was recognized by those who knew him as distinguished and able, quickly ran into conflict-of-interest charges similar to those directed at Fortas. He also encountered the hostility of labor and civil rights organizations for alleged insensitivity to their interests. Ulti-

mately the Senate rejected his nomination on a 45–55 vote because Republicans who had recently opposed Democratic nominee Fortas on ethical and moral grounds believed consistency dictated a similar stance against Haynsworth. Deeply angered, Nixon responded spitefully by nominating appeals court judge G. Harold Carswell, an undistinguished Florida jurist considered far less qualified than Haynsworth. The Senate seemed initially disposed to confirm Carswell, but evidence of his racial biases and mediocre intellect shifted sentiment against him. Seeking to save the nomination, floor manager Roman Hruska (R.-Nebr.) delivered an assessment that proved to be fatal: "Even if he is mediocre there are a lot of mediocre judges and people and lawyers. They are entitled to a little representation, aren't they, and a little chance? We can't have all Brandeises, Cardozos, and Frankfurters, and stuff like that there" (quoted in Abraham, pp. 6–7). After four months, the Senate rejected Carswell, triggering a statement from Nixon that he considered the Senate's confirmation responsibilities under the Constitution only pro forma. Abandoning his efforts to place a strict-constructionist southerner on the High Court, he turned to appeals court judge Harry Blackmun, a Minnesotan whom the Senate quickly approved.

Reagan administration experience with its Supreme Court nominees in its first six years reinforced the view that court nominees stand the best chance of approval when the Senate and presidency are in the hands of the same party and when appointments are made prior to the final year of a presidential term. The Senate unanimously confirmed the appointments of Sandra Day O'Connor in 1981 and Antonin Scalia in 1986. In the three-month-long confirmation proceedings of 1986 that led to the elevation of Associate Justice William Rehnquist to chief justice by a 65–33 vote.

In 1987, when control of the Senate returned to the Democrats and with less than two years remaining to the increasingly beleaguered Reagan administration, the Senate took special interest in the nomination of federal appeals court judge Robert Bork. A richly qualified, highly intelligent, and outspoken jurist, Bork responded to his critics in a manner that sparked one of the most acrimonious confirmation battles in Senate history. Bork's doctrinaire conservative judicial views, along with his untelegenic personal appearance, undermined his initial support. Intense media coverage, including strident advertising campaigns by supporters and opponents, created strongly negative impressions among senators and the general public. The Judiciary Committee adversely reported his nomination to the Senate, which rejected Bork by a 42–58 vote. Bork subsequently contended that the aggressive questioning about basic constitutional issues to which he was subjected would limit future selection of judges to those who had written little and whose views were noncontroversial.

President George Bush's successful 1990 appointment of Judge David H. Souter, a virtually unknown federal jurist, seemed to corroborate Bork's view. Bush continued in this pattern in 1991, nominating Judge Clarence Thomas, a conservative black of little judicial distinction, to fill the seat of retiring Justice Thurgood Marshall, the Court's first black member. The administration, wary of the perils of divided political control, despite its belief that Senate Democrats would have trouble opposing a black nominee, carefully coached the nominee to avoid extended discussions of his judicial philosophy and delayed hearings until it believed Thomas had gained sufficient support. As an evenly divided Judiciary Committee sent the nomination to the Senate floor without a recommendation, a committee source leaked to the news media information that a former professional associate, Anita Hill, had charged that Thomas had sexually harassed her ten years earlier. The Senate, minutes from its scheduled vote and under pressure from a swelling national outcry, returned the nomination to the committee for further investigation. Demonstrating the immense power of the news media to shape the modern confirmation process, the committee's three-day proceeding became a weekend television spectacle as a transfixed nation divided its sympathies between the nominee and his accuser. Although Thomas was eventually confirmed by the closest margin in a century, the proceedings, with their unremitting public inquiry into the nominee's personal life, triggered a vigorous debate on the Senate's conduct of the confirmation process.

During the twentieth century, the Senate generally adhered to its tradition of confirming cabinet and other key executive nominees on the principle that presidents should be allowed a free hand in choosing their closest advisers. On only three occasions (1925, 1959, and 1989) did the Senate reject proposed cabinet officers, while other major executive nominees were specifically rejected fewer than thirty times.

In 1925, President Calvin Coolidge named the ultraconservative Detroit lawyer and politician Charles Warren to be attorney general. Progressive Republicans, recalling that Warren had aided the sugar trust in extending its monopolistic control over that industry, believed this appointment was a further example of the president's policy of turning over government regulatory agencies to individuals sympathetic to the interests they were charged with regulating. Despite Coolidge administration efforts to delay Senate action until a majority could be built for Warren, the progressive Republicans combined with Democrats in March 1925 to defeat the nomination narrowly. Outraged, Coolidge resubmitted Warren's name. As with the Caleb Cushing renomination eight decades earlier, even administration supporters in the Senate took offense at this failure to recognize that the Senate had spoken, and they joined to produce a larger margin of defeat. The president then nominated an obscure Vermont lawyer, whom the Senate immediately confirmed.

President Harry Truman recognized the difficulty of getting nominations approved by a Senate controlled by the opposition party. When the Senate passed to Republican hands in 1947, bringing divided government for the only time in the century since 1919–1921, Truman sought to avoid controversy by selecting individuals he thought would be readily acceptable to the Senate. As a result the Senate did not reject any of his appointees, but in 1948 it failed to act on 11,122 nominations in the misplaced hope that a Republican would be elected president that year and would fill the positions with Republicans in 1949.

On 13 October 1949, the Senate, back under Democratic control, voted 15–53 to reject Truman's nomination of Leland Olds to a third term on the Federal Power Commission. Olds, a ten-year veteran of the commission and an outspoken advocate of strict federal regulation for privately owned utilities, had become the target of powerful oil and gas interests.

Freshman senator Lyndon B. Johnson (D.-Tex.), seeking to ingratiate himself to those interests and to shed his New Deal reform image, led the attack on the liberal Olds. Johnson eagerly gained chairmanship of the hostile Commerce subcommittee that conducted the confirmation hearings. The subsequent proceedings demonstrated the difficulty of reconfirming a controversial public figure with powerful enemies eager to settle old grievances. At a time of intensifying national paranoia about communism, Johnson abandoned any pretense of fairness and allowed witnesses to pillory Olds for communistic sympathies on the basis of articles he had written more than two decades earlier. Following the subcommittee's unanimous vote of rejection, Truman sought to make this contest a matter of party loyalty. Democratic senators angrily opposed the president's interference in the confirmation process and provided the votes to bring about this rare rejection of an incumbent official.

On 19 June 1959, by a dramatic 46–49 roll-call vote, the Senate rejected President Dwight Eisenhower's nomination of Admiral Lewis Strauss to be secretary of commerce. Strauss was a seasoned administrator who expected quick approval to this essentially noncontroversial post. Like Leland Olds, however, he had accumulated powerful enemies as the outspoken head of a regulatory commission. Consequently, Eisenhower was unwilling to risk a defeat by renominating him to that agency. Several factors evident in hotly contested Supreme Court nominations existed in the Strauss case. It occurred in the seventh year of a Republican presidency with Democrats in control of both Houses of Congress. The 1958 elections, reflecting public dissatisfaction with Eisenhower administration policies, shifted thirteen Senate seats—a record number—from Republican to Democratic control. This gave the Democrats a 64–34 majority as party leaders laid their plans to regain the White House in the 1960 presidential election. In a gesture of defiance reminiscent of its performance in the Olds nomination, the Senate Commerce Committee delayed considering the nomination for two months. When the hearing began, the nominee immediately fueled the committee's antagonism by his evasive responses to members' questions and his demand to cross-examine hostile witnesses—including senators. Strauss's repeated

expressions of disdain and condescension antagonized key senators and fatally eroded his support. Appearing to question the Senate's constitutional prerogatives, the imperious Strauss personified the worst elements of executive-branch domination at precisely the time that the Senate was seeking to cast off such control and had acquired the Democratic majorities to do so.

Three decades passed before another cabinet nominee suffered an identical fate. John Tower (R.-Tex.) had served twenty-four years in the Senate when he retired in 1985. During those years his Senate colleagues came to resent his abrasive manner. But when President George Bush nominated Tower as secretary of defense in January 1989, few guessed that defeat lay ahead. During an investigation by the Senate Armed Services Committee, which Tower had chaired less than five years earlier, his opponents among the Senate's Democratic majority built a case against his character rather than his competence. Confronted with evidence of Tower's "womanizing," abuse of alcohol, and questionable financial dealings with defense contractors, the Senate engaged in one of the most rancorous debates in modern times before killing his nomination by a largely party-line vote of 47–53. Tower became not only the first nominee of a new president's initial cabinet to be rejected but also the first former member to be turned down by his former colleagues for a cabinet post. Tower subsequently died in a plane crash while promoting his book *Consequences,* attacking the Senate's role in his defeat.

## CONCLUSION

Throughout the nation's history, the Senate and the president have maintained a guarded relationship in their joint constitutional responsibility for appointments to major executive and judicial positions. Contrary to recurring claims that traditionally a nominee's philosophy and ideology have not been legitimate sources of Senate attention, senators have routinely considered these matters, even if they veiled their concerns in more-acceptable objections over the nominee's ability and character. Among all appointments, those to the Supreme Court have assumed a far greater significance than those to lower judicial posts and executive positions. For these other posts, at both the national and state levels, the major value of the confirmation process has been to provide an airing of the nominee's views, and to serve as a reference point against which to measure his or her future performance. Only in the most blatant instances of unsuitability have these lesser nominees been rejected.

For all nominees, perhaps the best advice was that of veteran political consultant Tom Korologos. "Model yourself after a bridegroom at a wedding: Be on time, stay out of the way, and keep your mouth shut. Between the day of nomination and the day of the confirmation, give no speeches, write no letters, make no public appearances. . . . The Senate expects you to be suitably humble and deferential, not cocky. There is no subject on earth that the Senate is not free to probe. Be ready with polite and persuasive answers" (*New York Times,* 18 August 1986).

## *BIBLIOGRAPHY*

### General Studies

The major historical study of the appointments process is JOSEPH P. HARRIS, *The Advice and Consent of the Senate* (Berkeley and Los Angeles, 1953). There is no work that comprehensively updates HARRIS's forty-year-old classic, although three important studies include coverage of the post-1950 period: G. CALVIN MACKENZIE, *The Politics of Presidential Appointments* (New York, 1981), which concentrates on major executive branch nominations for the years 1964 to 1978; HENRY J. ABRAHAM, *Justices and Presidents: A Political History of Appointments to the Supreme Court,* 3d ed. (New York, 1985); and LAURENCE H. TRIBE, *God Save This Honorable Court: How the Choice of Supreme Court Justices Shapes Our History* (New York, 1985). Three significant bibliographies include the most significant modern studies of judicial selection; they are NANCY CHINN and LARRY BERKSON, *Literature on Judicial Selection* (Chicago, 1980), with sections on state, federal, and foreign practices; MICHAEL J. SLINGER, LUCY SALSBURY PAYNE, and JAMES LLOYD GATES, JR., "The Senate Power of Advice and Consent on Judicial Appointments: An Annotated Research Bibliography," *Notre Dame Law Review* 64:1 (1989), for works published since 1980, and LIBRARY OF CONGRESS, CONGRESSIONAL RESEARCH SERVICE, *Senate Confirmation of Supreme Court Nominees: Selected References* by GEORGE WALSER (Washington, D.C., 1991).

### On Supreme Court Nominations

For an account of proceedings during the precedent-setting First Congress, see LINDA GRANT DEPAUW, ed., *Documentary History of the First Federal Congress of the United States of America,* Volume II: *Senate Executive Journal and Related Documents* (Baltimore, 1974). Writings on this topic vastly outnumber all others related to the appointments process. Despite their focus on the High Court, they are useful in explaining relations between the Senate and presidency that apply to the appointments process for other posts. The most comprehensive general work in this category is ABRAHAM, noted above. Supreme Court confirmation battles of the late 1960s, early 1970s, and late 1980s produced many well-researched and insightful law-review contributions. Three excellent collections of essays appear in the *Harvard Law Review* 101 (April 1988), the *Kentucky Law Journal* 77 (Spring 1989), and the *Northwestern University Law Review* 84:3,4 (1990). Important articles not included in the Slinger et al. and Walser bibliographies are CHARLES BLACK, "A Note on Senatorial Consideration of Supreme Court Nominees," *Yale Law Journal* 79 (March 1970), and PHILIP B. KURLAND, "The Appointment and Disappointment of Supreme Court Justices," *Law and the Social Order* (1972).

There are many studies of individual Supreme Court nominations. A classic among these is DAVID J. DANELSKI, *A Supreme Court Justice Is Appointed* (New York, 1964), on the 1922 confirmation of Pierce Butler. Another useful account is ETHAN BRONNER, *Battle for Justice: How the Bork Nomination Shook America* (New York, 1989). Printed congressional hearings offer rich insights into the process; in this respect, see U.S. SENATE, COMMITTEE ON THE JUDICIARY, *Nomination of David H. Souter to Be Associate Justice of the Supreme Court of the United States,* Serial J-101-95 (Washington, D.C., 1991).

### Other Federal Judicial Nominees

Although Harris and Mackenzie, noted above, provide the best substantive discussion of the appointments process for non–Supreme Court nominees, a more encyclopedic and up-to-date account appears in CONGRESSIONAL QUARTERLY, *Guide to Congress,* 3d ed. (Washington, D.C., 1982). For a major twentieth-century cabinet rejection, see RICHARD ALLAN BAKER, "A Slap at the 'Hidden-Hand Presidency': The Senate and the Lewis Strauss Affair," *Congress and the Presidency* 14 (1987).

### State-level Appointments

Significant writings on the appointment process at the state level are virtually nonexistent. The best source of state constitutional provisions is COLUMBIA UNIVERSITY, LEGISLATIVE DRAFTING RESEARCH FUND, *Constitutions of the United States: National and State* (Dobbs Ferry, N.Y., 1974—), and the best survey of current state practices is the COUNCIL OF STATE GOVERNMENTS, *Book of the States* (Lexington, Ky., 1935—). In 1988 the Nebraska Legislative Research Division surveyed other legislatures on their confirmation practices. Its brief report is NEBRASKA LEGISLATURE, LEGISLATIVE RESEARCH DIVISION, *Legislative Confirmation of Gubernatorial Appointments* (1988).

SEE ALSO Federalism and American Legislatures AND Legislatures and the Judiciary.

# LEGISLATURES AND IMPEACHMENT

## *Peter Charles Hoffer*

Impeachment is a legislative enactment by a lower house or assembly that certifies charges against an individual or individuals for trial in the upper house of a legislative body. The verb *impeach* means to accuse or to challenge the credibility of another and is commonly used in civil and criminal proceedings to confute testimony or deposition. Impeachment by a lower legislative body is not a trial, but a hearing. It may be likened to a grand-jury indictment in a criminal proceeding, but the charges need not amount to a crime and the procedural guarantees may or may not include a right to counsel, a right of cross-examination, and other rights familiar in criminal trials.

Impeachment by the assembly may be based upon precedent, as in English parliamentary practice, or statutory and constitutional provisions, as in the various states of the United States and in the U.S. Congress. In the former case, the right to impeach was a privilege accorded the House of Commons by the crown and later developed according to the usages of the House of Commons and the guidance of the House of Lords. In the latter case, impeachment is based on the text of constitutions, but is susceptible to periodic reinterpretation, much like all provisions of constitutions. History demonstrates that the rules of impeachment are neither logic nor text, but experience.

## IMPEACHMENT AND THE AMERICAN POLITICAL SYSTEM

Most impeachments are politically charged events—the defendants hold political office, the prosecutors ("managers") are politicians, the offenses involve political acts as well as crimes—and the public perceives impeachment as highly partisan. The check on such partisanship in systems like America's is the formal separation of powers among three branches of government, but impeachment poses problems for the doctrine of separation of powers. Impeachment blurs separation of powers between the legislative and the judiciary. Insofar as impeachment may reach any civil officers, it extends to sitting judges and executive incumbents, giving to the legislative branch the authority to remove members of the other two branches, as well as members of the legislature. Moreover, in impeachment and trial the legislative branch mimics many of the investigatory and trial procedures of the judicial branch.

American appellate courts have not limited or challenged impeachment, even impeachment of judges, despite the fact that judicial independence is a concept as deeply rooted in constitutional language as impeachment. Spokespersons for the executive branch have been far less amenable to the idea of impeachment. In the inquiry into the Watergate break-in and cover-up (1972–1974), for example, defenders of President Richard Nixon tried to limit the scope of impeachment inquiries.

The inquiry into President Nixon's involvement in the Watergate burglary and the subsequent cover-up supported the claims of critics of impeachment that the process was not only violative of separation of powers but also time-consuming and cumbersome. Defenders of the process responded that impeachment was limited to cases of great moment and to the great offices of state, a view neither historically nor textually grounded. In fact, there is nothing in the textual provisions for impeachment that limits it to great crimes or to great offices, but ironically, modern impeachment has become so time-consuming precisely because impeachment has come to resemble the modern criminal trial, with its time-consuming guarantees of procedural fairness.

## IMPEACHABLE OFFENSES

Impeachment and trial are not criminal procedures per se, but merely the means to remove misbehaving officials and, perhaps, disqualify them from future office-holding. Despite the absence of criminal penalties or, indeed, guarantees of procedural rights for defendants in the textual provisions for impeachment, case after case has revived a controversy over whether a defendant must violate existing criminal law to be impeachable. Misdemeanor in office is grounds for impeachment, but the term *misdemeanor* has two meanings in American constitutional discourse: it may mean, first, a crime or, second, maladministration, misconduct, or some other misuse of the powers of office.

Historically, impeachable offenses—that is, acts for which officials have faced impeachment—fall into one of three categories. The first, most common, and most likely to result in impeachment and trial is financial misconduct. Misuse of public funds, receiving or extorting monies, or felonious theft by an official is grounds for impeachment. The offenses may be crimes (misdemeanors or felonies) or some species of maladministration or malfeasance.

The second category is much vaguer and may now be outmoded by alternative statutory provisions for removal of sitting judges: incapacity, inability, or unwillingness to perform an office. These charges are not so important when lodged against an elected official, for she or he may simply be denied reelection. Appointed officials, particularly those holding office during good behavior (e.g., federal judges), are proof against electoral removal, and to this day, such officials can only be removed through impeachment and trial. Federal district and circuit court judges, who throughout the nineteenth and early twentieth centuries were veritable barons on their own estates, were likely targets of such impeachments. In fact, few were ever removed for incapacity.

The final and invariably the most controversial category of impeachable offenses is political misconduct. The extremity of political misconduct is treason, but only one official has ever been impeached for treason—federal district judge West H. Humphreys of Tennessee. He declared himself for the Confederacy in 1861 and was impeached, tried, and convicted in absentia in 1862 (by which time he was serving in the Confederate judiciary). Commonly, political charges involve extreme partisanship—using one's office to further the interests of one's party or faction, or to harass and demean one's political opponents. In much fiercely partisan democratic political systems there is no clear line separating the unscrupulous campaigner from the impeachable official. In this setting, impeachments may verge upon bills of attainder, although the term *misdemeanor* has a civil as well as criminal connotation and includes gross misconduct partisan in origin.

## RULES AND PRECEDENTS

The U.S. federal system permits the sovereign states and the federal government to impeach, try, and remove offending officials. There are two sets of impeachment provisions and precedents. The first arises from the colonial experience and expresses itself in the constitutions of the states. The majority of them wrote rules for impeachment and trial into their fundamental laws, and a goodly number engaged in some form of impeachment and trial activity. States entering the Union after 1787 modeled their provisions on those of the U.S. Constitution, but retained earlier states' provisions for impeachment upon proof of maladministration.

The second set of provisions and cases is federal, resting on the various portions of the U.S. Constitution regarding impeachment. There have been far fewer federal impeachments than state cases, although the former have attracted the bulk of scholarly attention. Historically, federal impeachment practices and law are distinct from, but related to, the cases and provisions in the various states. The federal constitutional rules were based on state rules, not English precedent, and throughout the experience of the Congress with impeachment, changing state precedent has influenced congressional conduct. In part, this is because there is such a paucity of congressional impeachment precedent, but even more important is the fact that congressmen and women are first and foremost representatives of their states, and as state politicians, representatives bring with them to the federal government vast experience in state politics and respect for their own state traditions. Congressional adoption of state attitudes toward impeachable offenses is an example of what may be called "corresponding powers."

Formal provisions for impeachment in the state and federal constitutions are capable of widely varying constructions. Although this vagueness may seem an invitation to politicization of the process, in practice impeachment charges are followed by thorough investigation. Even when the lower house moves forward with prosecution, the upper house checks abuses of the procedure. Although the rules of impeachment in the United States are quite different from those in England's Parliament, the American precedent strongly resembles the English experience in the allotment of functions to the lower and upper houses. Partisanship may bend rules, but the trial requirement in the upper house bars conviction of all but the most palpable misusers of power.

Impeachment voters and managers in the lower houses and triers of impeachment in the upper houses have relied for guidance not only on the formal text of the rules but also on prior cases. American lawmakers, unlike English lawmakers, regard the legislative record as a legitimate source of law. Thus, the arguments of prosecutors and counsel for the defense in impeachment cases are often cited by one side or the other in later cases. Scholars have found in these legislative debates and trials fertile sources of controversy.

In the course of a two-century-long controversy over who may be impeached for what offenses, a controversy thoroughly merging substance and procedure, the U.S. Congress has agreed on certain rules to govern proceedings in impeachment and trial. Although these rules have the appearance of evenhandedness, they are not neutral. They favor the better-financed and legally better-educated defendant over officers who are poorer and have no legal training. In the House of Representatives, these rules are matters of custom, not law. They include a guarantee that the defendant will be informed of the charges and the evidence and may be present at the hearings of the Judiciary Committee and the House sitting as a committee of the whole. In the twentieth century, defendants have been allowed counsel from the first stages of investigation of charges. The House has retained the right to accept, amend, and reject specific articles and to bring them to the Senate at a time of the House's own choosing. The House also may determine the managers of the impeachment, who in turn may select their own chairperson, a power implied in the House's right to exercise the "sole power" over impeachments but not mentioned in the Constitution.

The Senate rules for trial were originally matters of custom. The only constitutional requirements were that the senators be under oath, the chief justice preside when the president was a defendant, and the verdict have a two-thirds majority. To these, the Senate added twenty-five more rules on 3 March 1868, the eve of the trial of President Andrew Johnson. A twenty-sixth rule was added on 28 May 1935. The majority of the rules concerned housekeeping matters—who was to notify the Senate that the trial was to begin; that trials were to take place on the afternoons of weekdays; and that the presiding officer would render all legal judgments, but that the Senate as a body issued writs, summonses, and subpoenas. Defendants were allowed counsel, the right to produce and cross-examine witnesses, and the right to examine senators. The rules also provided for record keeping and roll-call voting on each article of impeachment. The rule approved in 1935 allowed the Senate to name its own investigatory committee to take depositions and seek out additional evidence away from the Senate chamber and report such evidence back to the Senate. In 1993 the U.S. Supreme Court reminded federal courts not to interfere with the Senate's "sole power" to make these housekeeping rules.

## THE HISTORICAL RECORD

The main stream of impeachment cases has involved financial misconduct or simple disability, but sudden surges in political impeachments in the states and Congress have pulsated to the ebb and flow of other major political shifts in American history. In periods of intense partisanship, when party structures are in flux and the rules of the game of politics are changing, impeachment became more prominent. Surges of impeachments in these eras follow the contours of the changing political ideas and activities. Thus, a portion of the first wave of state cases, from 1776 through 1787, attempted to bring the judicial and financial agents of the new republics under control. In particular, impeachment curbed old-style English financial misconduct of the sort that imperial officers had practiced quite freely before independence and state-appointed collectors of customs and sheriffs attempted to duplicate during and after the Revolution.

The second rush of state and federal cases, marking the struggle between the Hamiltonian Federalists and the Jeffersonian Republicans, took the shape of a debate over the very legitimacy of party organization and public opposition to government. Impeachments tested the limits that the leaders of this first party system were willing to give to partisan campaigning and patronage.

A third surge of impeachments, in the Reconstruction era, measured party leaders' and dissenters' ability to manage internal party discipline. These cases were followed shortly by a burst of impeachments in the Progressive Era, marking reformers' efforts to use legislative action when courts seemed indifferent to political corruption.

A series of post–New Deal impeachments has pit the branches of government against each other, with Congress and state legislatures wielding impeachment to curb the excesses of officials in the other branches. Most recently, statutes providing for alternatives to impeachment to remove incapacitated executive and judicial officials, notably the federal Judicial Conduct and Disability Act of 1980, have reduced the need for legislative impeachments, but even more recently, three federal district judges have suffered impeachment and removal on charges of bribery, peculation, and income tax evasion.

It is because impeachment and trial is so closely connected to larger movements in American politics, rather than standing alone as an autonomous body of pure law, that the vast majority of motions to impeach never even reach the stage of investigation or, if investigated, do not result in a vote to impeach by the lower house. Impeachment can be as much a tool to express disagreement with a policy or to libel an opponent, as a tool to get at covert misconduct among those charged with a public trust. In the 1870s, land speculators lobbied Congress to impeach territorial judges who stood in the way of pet projects. Nearly a cen-

tury later, the demand that Chief Justice Earl Warren be impeached was periodically introduced in Congress after Warren read the Supreme Court's opinion in *Brown* v. *Board of Education,* 347 U.S. 483 (1954). Warren's most radical colleague, Justice William O. Douglas, was investigated in 1970 on Representative Gerald Ford's (R.-Mich.) motion, but was entirely exonerated. Ford may or may not have believed that the charges were true or, if true, that they amounted to impeachable offenses, but the thrust of his and others' assault was that Douglas's opinions were too far off center. There is little other way to curb the independence of an official who holds office during good behavior.

## The English Experience

In one sense, the first English impeachments mirrored the attack on Justice Douglas. To his accusers, he was obnoxious, and impeachment promised a way to remove him from political power. The first English impeachments, in the fourteenth century, were just such efforts to oust great men from positions of all but unreachable height. Revived in the seventeenth century, impeachment became a method by which the lower house of Parliament could curb corrupt ministers and councillors. Parliament was a court as well as a legislative body, and its power to impeach and try rested upon its judicial authority. The House of Lords sat to hear impeachment managers prosecute the case, although even in the heyday of impeachments, very few actually got this far. Punishment upon conviction was not limited to loss of office or disqualification, and included prison, fines, and forfeiture of lands. The death penalty was meted out once in the seventeenth century and six times in the eighteenth, invariably for treason. Anyone could be impeached; indeed, private citizens were tried upon impeachments for libeling the government. All the cases were political in some fashion, but the impeachments were not merely political acts. There was always some breach of law or misuse of the public trust.

There were nearly two hundred impeachments in England between 1615 and 1715, leading scholars to believe that the lower house strove to find charges against the king's friends and thereby increase the power of the most representative branch of government, but this is far too simple an explanation. Like so many other controversies in that much-troubled period of English politics, impeachment was often a tool by which powerful factions vied for dominance of the polity. After 1715, impeachment and trial fell into relative desuetude. Only a handful of cases were brought in the eighteenth century, and only two, of Lord Chancellor Macclesfield in 1725 and Warren Hastings, governor general of the colony of India, in 1786, were for corruption. The cabinet system had evolved to the point where other means could be used to remove erring ministers of state.

## American Colonial Impeachments

Colonial American assemblies had no legal right to impeach anyone, but assumed that right in the process of reconceptualizing themselves as miniature parliaments. The first impeachment, in all but name, occurred in Virginia in 1635, with the thrusting out of Governor John Harvey. Later cases in Maryland, Virginia, Massachusetts, Pennsylvania, South Carolina, North Carolina, and New Jersey marked colonial assemblies' attempts to oust corrupt officials, appointees, and magistrates. The colonial impeachments were, like the parliamentary impeachments, highly political, but unlike Parliament, the assemblies only went after sitting officeholders and limited (by necessity rather than choice) punishment to removal from office.

By the end of the colonial experience, impeachment had all but ceased to be a quasi-criminal proceeding and had become a step by which assemblies could protect themselves from crown officials and, ultimately, from the crown itself. The last of the colonial impeachments, that of Chief Justice Peter Oliver (1774), did not come to trial, but did greatly aid the revolutionaries in their effort to destabilize the royal government. In the process, the leaders of the impeachment movement, notably John Adams, developed a conception of public accountability of officials that carried over into the framing of the first Massachusetts state constitution.

## Impeachment in the New States

There were serious obstacles to the reception of impeachment law in the new American republics. Impeachment was a parliamentary sanction, based upon Parliament's inherent authority as a high court. American legislatures were not courts—the very idea violated separation-of-powers doctrine—and Parliament itself was much hated in the new states for the Intolerable Acts of 1774. Impeachment seemed to give to the new American legislature the very untrammeled power that the revolutionaries had resisted when exercised by the crown.

These reservations to the contrary notwithstanding, impeachment had proven itself in certain of the colonies and was adopted when those colonies became states. Impeachment was republicanized; defendants had to be sitting officials, offenses were defined (albeit vaguely), and punishment was restricted to loss of office and disqualification. The first state constitutions included among offenses maladministration or malconduct (Delaware, Massachusetts, New Hampshire, North Carolina, Pennsylvania, South Carolina, Virginia), misdemeanor (New Jersey), and crimes or misdemeanors (New York), or gave no definition of offenses at all (Georgia). Impeachment and trial was designed to remove erring, incompetent, or corrupt officials, not to prove that they were criminals.

A series of impeachments of corrupt purchasing agents, sheriffs and other inferior law officers, and tax collectors proved that impeachment and trial could be swift and effective checks on greedy officials. Impeachments of officials for misusing their powers of office followed. A number of impeachments were launched simply to upbraid or harass high officials for failing to perform their duties. Thomas Jefferson, while governor of Virginia, faced down such an inquiry in 1781. Although his conduct in the face of advancing British troops was hardly exemplary, there was little he could have done to prevent them from despoiling Richmond, even had he stayed and led the militia into battle.

The states' successful experience with impeachment and trial encouraged the framers of the federal Constitution to adopt the procedure. The prime movers behind the addition of impeachment provisions came from states with impeachment precedent and were themselves connected with earlier state cases. The final shape of federal impeachment law resembled that of the states, not England. The Senate was given the power to convict on impeachments made by the House of Representatives, but conviction required a two-thirds vote, to ensure deliberation and certainty (Article I, Section 3). Impeachments were not criminal indictments, although impeachable offenses were limited to "Treason, Bribery, or other high Crimes and Misdemeanors." Impeachment was confined to "the President, Vice-President and all civil Officers of the United States," which the framers took to mean appointees and electees (Article II, Section 4). Ordinary crimes were impeachable offenses, at least by implication, for trial by jury was guaranteed to criminals, except in impeachments, where trial by the Senate was prescribed (Article III, Section 2). The president could not pardon an official removed through impeachment and trial (Article II, Section 2). There was little attempt to lay out procedure for impeachment trials. The only stricture was that, should the president be impeached, the president of the Senate (the vice president of the United States, who would become president if the incumbent were removed) was replaced by the chief justice of the Supreme Court as presiding officer of the Senate (Article I, Section 3).

All of the states that entered the Union or revised their impeachment and trial procedures after 1789 adopted some version of the federal requirement of a two-thirds vote for conviction and limitation of punishment to removal, but almost all cleaved not to the federal standard for impeachable offenses, "high Crimes and Misdemeanors," but to pre-1787 state language. Only Colorado (constitution of 1876) and Indiana (1816) adopted the substance of the federal formula and refused to go beyond it. Of those states that provide for impeachment and trial of officials, most allowed impeachment on "any misdemeanor," maladministration, corrupt conduct in office, or malfeasance (Alabama [1819], Arizona [1912], Arkansas [1836], California [1849], Florida [1838], Illinois [1818], Iowa [1846], Kansas [1859], Kentucky [1792], Louisiana [1812], Minnesota [1857], Mississippi [1817], Missouri [1920], Montana [1889], Nebraska [1866], Nevada [1864], New Mexico [1910], North Dakota [1889], Ohio [1802], Tennessee [1796], Utah [1895], Vermont [1793], Washington [1889], West Virginia [1870], Wisconsin [1848], and Wyoming [1889]). Oklahoma's constitution (1907) was more specific: impeachment would lie for "wilful neglect of duty, corruption in office, habitual drunkenness, incompetency, or any offense involving moral turpitude committed while in office." A number of states did not define impeachable offenses (Alaska [1956], Connecticut [1818], Hawaii [1959], Idaho [1889], Maine [1819], Maryland [1851], Michigan [1835], Rhode Island [1842], and Texas [1845]).

## The Dangerous Tendencies of Party

The appearance of the first organized, disciplined opposition parties in the United States led to a series of impeachments. From 1795 to 1815, Federalists and Republicans struggled for control of the national government. Denied dominance of the executive and legislative branches after Jefferson's victory in 1800, Federalists found refuge in the judiciary. Newly expanded under the Judiciary Act of 1801 passed by a lame-duck Federalist majority in Congress and signed into law by outgoing President John Adams, the federal judiciary provided a home for many Federalist partisans. Federalists already occupied the entire Supreme Court bench. Republicans in Congress repealed the act in 1802 and used impeachment to harass the Federalist judiciary.

The models for impeachment of Federalist judges were a series of cases in Pennsylvania, in which a Republican majority in the legislature removed a state court judge, Alexander Addison, in 1803 and harried Federalists on the state supreme court. Taking their cue from these cases, in 1803 Republicans in Congress impeached and tried Federalist district court judge John Pickering of New Hampshire. Pickering was incapable of performing his duties—his son admitted as much—and impeachment and trial was the only way to remove him.

Heartened by their success in this relatively straightforward case, the Republicans took on Supreme Court Justice Samuel Chase in 1804. At one time an antifederalist, Chase had become an intemperate Federalist by 1801. In a series of charges to grand juries during his circuit duties, he directly attacked the Republican party. There was no question of his partisanship, and his conduct on the bench certainly did not befit a judge. Chief Justice John Marshall, perhaps the next target of the Republicans, told Chase to mend his ways, but Chase could not curb his own tongue. Impeached in the House, he escaped conviction by a narrow margin when some Republicans in the Senate broke ranks and voted to acquit him.

The Republicans who voted to acquit had agreed with their Federalist colleagues that acts that were dangerous in their tendency were not of themselves impeachable offenses. Together, the nay voters in the Senate erected a precedent against conviction on grounds of mere partisanship. Chase had not violated any criminal laws, and his assault on the Republicans had been within the framework of the Alien and Sedition acts of 1798. He had not misused federal funds and had neither sought nor extorted bribes. He had bullied counsel, witnesses, and jurors in court, but these actions, at that time, had much precedent within the Anglo-American tradition of judicial conduct.

Meanwhile, state legislators in South Carolina, Vermont, New Jersey, Massachusetts, Tennessee, and Georgia brought impeachments against well-documented malfeasants throughout the 1790s and early 1800s. The defendants included peculating appointees of the state and judges who took bribes, led riots, violated law, or took law into their own hands. Impeachments were fair, went expeditiously, and led to convictions in upper houses.

In Congress, Senator William Blount of Tennessee was impeached in 1797, but he was almost simultaneously expelled by the Senate and left Philadelphia. His offense, never clearly established, may have been treasonous conspiracy with Britain to create an empire in the Old Southwest or merely a speculative scheme to refloat his own fortune, which he had dissipated. There was no question that he used his office to further his own ends, a violation of his oath, but not of any statute.

In 1830 a similar charge of violation of the oath of office was brought against James H. Peck, a federal district judge in Missouri. In 1825, outraged at a newspaper article on a case that he had heard and later commented on in the press, Peck fined and barred the lawyer who wrote the article from practicing in the federal court for eighteen months. The contempt citation was well within Peck's powers, but hardly fitted the offense. A year later, U.S. Representative John Scott of Missouri moved to impeach Peck, but the lower house was not sure how to proceed. Abuse of the contempt power had been one of the charges made in the Pennsylvania Supreme Court impeachment cases of 1803 and the Chase impeachment, but Peck's misconduct was limited to a single episode. In the end, he escaped conviction by a slim majority. The precedent was bifurcated: impeachment might proceed for a noncriminal act, but the Senate was not satisfied that Peck, an otherwise mild-mannered man, had any intent to violate his oath or the law. In sum, he had bent, but not broken, the standard of good behavior under which he held office, and the Senate refused to abandon that constitutional standard in favor of the much looser one of "during pleasure."

## The Reconstruction Era

The spate of impeachments during the Reconstruction period resembled a flotilla of small vessels proceeding and surrounding the greatest of all American impeachment trials, that of President Andrew Johnson in 1868. It was an era of real and reputed corruption, particularly in the reconstructed South, but most of the impeachments did not arise from gross corruption, much less violation of criminal law. Instead, the issue was who would control the highly volatile Reconstruction governments.

The best example of a struggle between branches, within a party, and between parties for control of the political process was the impeachment and trial of President Johnson. Radical Republicans became dissatisfied with Johnson's views on Reconstruction soon after he replaced the assassinated Abraham Lincoln. In part, the dissatisfaction was grounded in Johnson's apparent betrayal of the interests of the newly freed slaves. He resisted the Civil Rights acts and vetoed the freedmen's bill of 1866. His opposition to the Fourteenth Amendment, though he could not prevent its passage, was palpable and vocal.

In part, the Radical Republicans in Congress resented Johnson because he was at heart a southern Democrat and did not favor the Republicans entrenching their party in the South. Johnson had been reared in eastern Tennessee and matched his hatred of the wealthy planters with a virulent racism. His support for quick and easy reconstruction of state governments may have arisen as much from his indifference to the fate of former slaves as from any commitment to continue Lincoln's wartime policies of leniency. Johnson planned to abandon the Republican party standard and pull together a party of Democrats and conservative Unionists, denying the Republicans the political fruits of their electoral victories. To them, he was a dangerous man.

Republicans watched Johnson hinder military governors and their courts, use his patronage power to build a personal following, ignore the provisions of the Test Oath Act of 1865, allow southern states to pass virulent "black codes" that virtually reenslaved the freedmen and women, and veto the Civil Rights and Freedmen's Bureau acts with mounting disgust and fear. He did not violate law, but frankly confuted the aims of the Republican majority in Congress.

Conservatives in the Republican party and Democrats in Congress continued to resist any open attack on Johnson, but Radicals did not want to wait until 1868, when the Republicans could abandon him for another candidate. Meanwhile, Johnson, always a stubborn man, replaced military commanders who favored the Civil Rights Act of 1866 with others who supported his own policies, infuriating the Radicals.

Just as in the state cases, substantive questions of economic policy intermingled with the issues of party control and patronage, and joined with partisan animosities in Johnson's case. Fearing the President's program was undermining the Radicals at the polls (a fear the local elections of 1867 seemed to bear out) and wishing to maintain their power against their most conservative colleagues in the party (who wanted to run General of the Army U. S. Grant for the presidency in 1868), the Radicals forced the issue. By the end of 1867, a Radical majority in the House had fashioned eleven impeachment articles, revolving about Johnson's refusal to obey or enforce the Reconstruction Acts of 1867. No crime was alleged, save the violation of an oath of office. Divided by issues of economic policy and championing different candidates for the presidency, the Republicans divided themselves, and the first motion to impeach failed to gain a majority.

Ironically, it was Johnson, after a period of relative quiet in 1867, having weathered the first thrust of his enemies, who resuscitated the impeachment effort. Convinced that he had a chance to win election in 1868, he pushed ahead with his program to replace Radicals in federal office. He suspended Secretary of War Edwin Stanton, and though he explained his actions to Congress, as required by the law, his opponents there regarded his actions as a violation of the Tenure of Office Act of 1867.

At stake were political questions as well as legal ones, but the mixture of the two led not to the lawsuit Johnson hoped Stanton would file but to another round of impeachment hearings. On 24 February 1868, the House voted the impeachment of President Johnson. Every Republican present supported the resolve; no longer were conservatives, moderates, and radicals divided on the question, for Johnson had driven away his potential friends in the Republican ranks. The Democrats voted nay, to little avail.

The trial lasted almost twelve weeks, from 5 March through 26 May. Chief Justice Salmon Chase, a presidential hopeful, presided, but the proceedings were raucous and sometimes disorganized. The Radicals called for speed; Johnson's counsel wanted more time. Throughout the trial, the senators engaged in political maneuver and speculation concerning what would happen if the succession passed to Benjamin Wade, president of the Senate, who would become president of the United States if Johnson were removed. Wade, a Radical from Ohio, led the impeachment movement that would bring him to the highest office in the land.

The issues were political, but a trial in the high court of the Senate was a legal affair, requiring the production of evidence, its assessment, and rulings on law and fact. Despite Chief Justice Chase's efforts to prohibit mere hearsay, the Senate opted for a broader rule of admissibility of evidence. Historians divide sharply on the legality of the charges. Some find the articles of impeachment mere subterfuges for political ambition and animus, with the resulting trial at best a farce and at worst a descent into demagoguery. Not all of these scholars agree with William M. Evarts, one of Johnson's counsels, that only proven acts of criminality were impeachable offenses. Other scholars concede that the charges were not sufficient to warrant removal, but cite the leading contemporary treatises on the Constitution by James Kent, John Norton Pomeroy, William Rawle, and Joseph Story, in support of impeachment for misfeasance or malfeasance in office. These scholars find the trial itself remarkable for its attention to strictly legal questions, although the rulings the Senate made can be questioned.

Johnson escaped removal when seven Republican senators joined their Democratic counterparts on the crucial issue of Johnson's violation of the Tenure of Office Act. There was little support to remove Johnson for bringing the Senate into disrepute, one of the articles, or for using his power as head of the army to transfer military commanders. Quietly, Johnson had promised the defectors among the Republicans that he would serve the rest of his term without giving them offense. He kept his word.

The impeachment and trial of Johnson should be seen as the denouement of an era of political vitriol, the last act of a gruesome and prolonged Civil War. In this light, the assault on Johnson can hardly be regarded as monstrous—not when so many had died so recently to save the Union from dismemberment. Indeed, before, during, and after his trial, the system of checks and balances remained in place. Congress had overridden Johnson's vetoes; Johnson had used his power of appointment and his position as commander in chief to undermine congressional reconstruction; and the battle at the trial continued the contest by other means. Impeachment and trial were constitutional; the acquittal was a proof of that, if nothing else.

Johnson's narrow escape may have established an enduring legal precedent that intransigence and prolonged refusal of a chief executive to obey another, equal branch of government was not impeachable, but at the time, his case set precedent for the opposite principle— that impeachment could harass and disable otherwise powerful political opponents in the executive and judicial branches. Throughout the Reconstruction era, with its sharply diver-

gent party views on civil rights for the freedmen, impeachment flourished. The civil rights issue, rather than the accusations of corruption that flew from every direction, underlay many impeachment contests.

Thus, in 1867–1868, two judges in Arkansas, Elias Harrell and Augustus Hargrove, were impeached by the conservative Democrats who controlled the state under President Johnson's lenient policy of reconstruction and escaped punishment after a new state government was fashioned according to congressional reconstruction plans. Governor Powell Clayton, elected under the new constitution with strong freedman, Unionist, and Republican support, was about to be impeached, but used his influence (and perhaps some promises of monetary rewards) to avert the wrath of the impeachment investigatory committee. In Georgia, the governor arranged for an impeachment of the state treasurer as the treasurer was trying to induce the lower house to impeach the governor. Governors in Mississippi, North Carolina, and Louisiana were impeached in sharp intra-party struggles, in part disputes over the division of the spoils of office, in part attempts to force independent-minded mavericks to knuckle under to party discipline. Throughout Reconstruction, impeachment motions were common items of business for southern legislatures to ponder.

Many of these impeachments were directly influenced by the Johnson case. The southern constitutions written under Republican congressional supervision often included a provision that an impeached officer be temporarily suspended from his office until the charges were dismissed or brought to trial and a verdict was given. Had this provision been part of the federal Constitution, President Johnson would not have had the ability to influence the dissidents among the Republicans that he did, a fact the Republican impeachment managers knew well.

The two impeachments, in 1868 and 1872, of Governor Harrison Reed of Florida were typical of the cases in this period. The charges in the Florida case involved a series of state bond issues. States throughout the Union were competing for railroad routes and other capital improvements, all financed by floating bonds. When these sank, as so many did, one faction of politicians, usually those who did not share in the spoils, went after the politicians who had gotten something from the deal. Reed was accused of juggling the state books, taking state money for his own use, exceeding his authority to involve the state in private enterprises, and paying out state money without permission. He was never tried, although the state senate sat twice as a court on his case, and served out his term.

Upon showing of similar patterns of high-handedness, suspected corruption, and partisan infighting, William Holden, governor of North Carolina, was removed from office in 1871. He had suspended the writ of habeas corpus in his efforts to curb the violence of the Ku Klux Klan. David Butler of North Carolina was impeached and convicted for misusing school funds in the same year, although the conviction was erased from the record later and Butler returned to sit in the governor's chair again. Alexander Davis of Mississippi was removed in 1876, and Henry Warmoth, governor of Louisiana, like Reed, narrowly escaped trial. As in Reed's cases, these impeachments were highly partisan, and the evidence the prosecution produced was sometimes simply fabricated for the occasion. In all of the cases, the underlying issues included internecine party conflict and interbranch competition having little to do with the letter of the charges.

Most of the Reconstruction-era cases thus leave a very confused precedent behind them. There is no question that misfeasance or malfeasance was grounds for impeachment and removal in the Reconstruction era. At the same time, the factual content of the charges was so unreliable that the definition of misfeasance or malfeasance cannot be precisely ascertained and therefore does not fit any clear pattern. The content of the charges aside, one can only say that impeachment functioned as a mechanism for removing officers who had lost the support of their parties.

In the end, no one was safe from the wrath of the lower house. Vice President Schulyer Colfax was investigated in 1873 for his involvement in the Crédit Mobilier scandal, but he proved that he had purchased his stock in the company before he became vice president. In 1874, Democrats whispered to one another— and Republicans feared—that President U. S. Grant would be impeached, if only for allowing corruption and perhaps forgiving it. Two years later, the ax fell instead on Grant's friend William Belknap, secretary of war. Deeply in love with a wife who arranged for her family and friends to benefit from federal posts as Indian agents, Belknap should have paid more attention to the monetary returns his family pocketed from these appointees. He resigned before trial and was subsequently acquitted in the Senate, many voting not guilty on the technical grounds that he was no longer an officer of the United States.

Standing alongside these highly partisan cases was a series of entirely different impeachments aimed at judges and magistrates. In these cases, the charges always involved an alleged misuse of office, sometimes connected to criminal acts, but often no more than a lack of a judicial temperament. Despite the acquittal of Samuel Chase on such charges, state judges such as James T. Magbee of Florida resigned in 1871 for less cause. Judge George G. Barnard, a crony of the Boss Tweed Ring in New York, was impeached and removed for vulgar and arbitrary proceedings on the bench in 1872. Other officials resigned when lower houses marshaled evidence that the officials were incompetent or had exceeded their authority, as in the case of the federal judge Mark Delahay in 1873. In other cases, such as that of Judge Philander Lucas of Missouri in 1872, impeachment charges, investigated and disproved or dropped, cleared the air and the accused remained in office, as had Judge Peck.

## The Progressive Era and the New Deal

At the beginning of the twentieth century, populist and progressive legislatures became more and more estranged from a conservative bench and bar over the latter's resistance to regulation of the railroads and public utilities, working people's wages, and working conditions. At the same time, the unprecedented growth of corporate wealth and independence of action multiplied the opportunities for graft and corruption among public officials. Impeachment of executive and judicial officeholders again became popular as legislatures sought to gain preeminence in government and curb misconduct in the other branches of government.

Governors William Sulzer of New York (1913), James Ferguson of Texas (1917), and Huey Long of Louisiana (1929), impeached for usurpation of power, headlined a veritable explosion of impeachments almost equaling the heyday of impeachment in the Reconstruction era. Sulzer, a politician elected with Tammany Hall support who turned on his supporters, was thrown out of office for peculation. "Farmer Jim" Ferguson, a self-made man who took on himself the firing of University of Texas professors not to his liking, was found guilty on ten of the twenty-one articles and resigned the day before the verdict was announced. Long, the "Kingfish," whose political career was marked by personal and partisan excesses as well as achievements, was spared a trial when the bulk of the Senate announced that it would vote to acquit him, whatever case the managers made. Long was assassinated six years later.

Oklahoma led the country in frequency of impeachment in these years, failing by one vote to impeach Governor J. B. A. Robertson in 1916, and also impeaching and removing Governor J. C. Walton in 1928 on a charge of malfeasance. His lieutenant governor barely escaped removal himself at the same time. The next year, Governor Henry S. Johnston was impeached and removed, while three of the judges of the state supreme court who ruled that the legislature was out of order in bringing charges against Johnston also faced impeachment. Oklahoma's lower house sent thirteen impeachments to its upper house in the 1891–1930 period.

Congress was also an active impeachment tribunal in this period. In 1904, Judge Charles Swayne, of the Northern District of Florida, was impeached on charges of misusing public funds. Additional charges, centering on his arbitrary behavior out of court, won even stronger support, but none of the articles was persuasive at trial. Swayne was acquitted, in part because the Senate insisted that criminal conduct be proven beyond a reasonable doubt, the standard for matters of fact in a criminal proceeding.

Swayne's case was followed in 1912 by the impeachment and trial of Robert W. Archibald. Archibald, chief judge of the Commerce Court, an institution that did not survive his impeachment and removal, lost by a 223–1 vote in the lower house. He was charged with profiteering, collusion with counsel, influencing the outcome of cases, soliciting and accepting bribes, and unduly involving himself in government purchasing and leasing contracts. Archibald was

convicted on five of the thirteen counts on 13 January 1913.

Faced with similar charges of undue influence in pending cases and additional misconduct on the bench, Judge George W. English of the Eastern District of Illinois resigned in November 1926. The evidence suggested that English had arranged to transfer federal bankruptcy funds to certain banks in return for favors.

Harry Daugherty, President Warren G. Harding's attorney general and a close personal friend of the president, faced an impeachment inquiry for his involvement in the Teapot Dome scandal in 1922. The impeachment move was sidetracked by a general congressional investigation, at the conclusion of which President Calvin Coolidge forced Daugherty to resign.

Archibald, Daugherty, and English were forced out of office because they misused their official position in matters outside their official duties; Swayne, alleged to have abused his power on the bench, remained in office. The pattern continued with the impeachment and acquittal of Judge Harold C. Louderback of the North District of California. In March 1933 the House of Representatives impeached Louderback for favoritism and partiality in the conduct of his duties. A majority of senators agreed that the judge had shown some degree of partisanship, but the vote fell short of the two-thirds necessary to convict. Other articles were voted down by substantial majorities. Misconduct on the bench was an impeachable offense as far as the lower house was concerned; a majority of the Senate agreed, but the two-thirds provision stymied the impeachment.

Judge Halstead L. Ritter, of the Southern District of Florida, was impeached in 1936 for practicing law while on the bench, having taken a retainer from a former law partner. A majority of the Senate believed that this was a removable offense, but the only article on which two-thirds of the Senate voted to convict Ritter was a catchall seventh article, accusing Ritter of bringing his court into scandal and reprobation. Without avail, Ritter's counsel argued that the Senate ought not to convict on a general article when the prosecution could not muster a two-thirds vote on any of the particular articles. Again, it was off-the-bench conduct that doomed Ritter, proving that the Senate was more sensitive to misconduct away from official duties than misfeasance in them.

The federal cases from Swayne through Ritter had induced in the Senate an increasingly legalistic conception of procedure. Counsel for the defendants continued to insist that their clients were only liable for removal on charges of criminal actions and that these had to be proved beyond a reasonable doubt. The Senate did not cleave to this line, but did lay down more-complex rules for admissibility of evidence and cross-examination of witnesses approaching those in a criminal trial. The Senate regarded its duties as a court of impeachment as an invitation to adopt more and more of the procedural rigor of a regular court of law. Increasing numbers of lawyers occupied seats in state legislatures and Congress, and brought with them a concern for the procedural rigor of civil litigation and the procedural guarantees of criminal prosecutions.

The lower houses, including the U.S. House of Representatives, developed no such hard-and-fast internal rules in the first half of the twentieth century. In the English impeachment, two representatives came near to blows when one, Ogden Mills, a New York Republican, thought another, John E. Rankin, a Democrat from Mississippi, was trying to slow or stall the vote on impeachment. Any member of the lower house could still bring a motion to impeach a sitting official, a tradition that harked back to the origins of impeachment and carries on to this day. The lower house acts as a collector of claims of wrongdoing. For example, the House of Representatives heard motions to impeach President Herbert Hoover for failure to act decisively during the Great Depression.

## The 1950s and 1960s

While lower houses continued to entertain all manner of impeachment motions, the seriousness with which twentieth-century upper houses came to regard impeachment procedure had established itself by the 1950s. In 1957 the impeachment trial of a Miami circuit court judge, George E. Holt, occupied the upper house of the Florida legislature for a month. Holt was accused of violating the judicial code of ethics by borrowing money and accepting gifts from lawyers practicing before him. By a margin of three votes, the prosecu-

tion failed to gain the two-thirds majority needed to convict Holt.

A year later, the Tennessee lower house impeached a criminal court judge, Raulston Schoolfield of Chattanooga, for taking bribes from criminals. The vote was 89–7 in the lower house. Despite claiming that he had been victimized by prointegration political opponents, Schoolfield was removed by the Senate for racketeering. In 1964 the Arizona Senate cleared E. T. Williams and A. P. Buzzard of charges that they misused their powers as tax commissioners. A newspaper attack on them had led to their impeachment, but the commissioners won in the Senate and vowed to submit themselves for reelection.

These state trials were full and fair and were well reported, and no battery occurred during their progress. An even fuller trial led to the ouster of Justice Napoleon Bonaparte Johnson of the Oklahoma Supreme Court in 1965. The managers convinced the state senate that over a long course of time Johnson had received bribes to favor parties before him in court.

## The Case of President Richard M. Nixon

The most celebrated impeachment in modern American history never even reached a vote on the floor of the House of Representatives. It did, however, bring together the popular demand for revealing hidden corruption and misconduct, with close attention to procedures for gathering evidence and determining guilt, which are the two major features of modern impeachment.

Richard M. Nixon was a veteran Republican politician when he was elected president in 1968. Suspicious of his opponents' motives and angered at their criticism of his handling of the Vietnam War, he instigated programs of domestic surveillance of antiwar groups, including illegal wiretapping. Drawing a small circle of administrative aides about him and demanding absolute loyalty from them, he conceived a plan to undermine rival Democrats through "dirty tricks" that ultimately led to the wiretapping of the Democratic National Headquarters in the Watergate apartment complex, in Washington, D.C. This first conspiracy unraveled when the four men sent to the office to remove the evidence of wiretapping were caught, indicted, and tried for burglary. The four were convinced to remain silent about their employer, the Committee to Reelect the President, but one of the planners of the burglary, James McCord, refused to remain silent when faced with a prison term. He struck a deal with prosecutors in John Sirica's federal district court, and early in 1973 testified to the Senate Select Committee on Presidential Campaign Activities, chaired by Sam Ervin (D.-N.C.), about the connection between the White House and the burglary. The floodgates began to open, revealing a second conspiracy to conceal the first conspiracy.

The impeachment inquiry into the activities of President Richard M. Nixon during the Watergate burglary trials continued for more than a year and a half and rarely left the front pages of the nation's newspapers. Before 1973, impeachment and trial had been common in American legislatures and had often aroused great popular attention, but had never dominated the entire process of government. Even the impeachment and trial of President Andrew Johnson was more a public referendum on Johnson's policies than a challenge to the presidency itself. Johnson's refusal to curb his temper or moderate his internal Reconstruction policies led to his ultimate impeachment, and his personal assurances to do both averted conviction. The movement to impeach Nixon had a more fundamental quality, a test not of policy or even of wills but of the rule of law itself.

By the spring of 1973, the House of Representatives and the Senate foresaw that an impeachment inquiry was forthcoming. Presidential aides had revealed that a system to tape-record conversations in the White House had been installed by President Nixon, and the first Watergate special prosecutor, Harvard law professor Archibald Cox, and the Senate committee counsel, Samuel Dash, had asked the White House for key tapes. A number of the tapes were thought to contain "smoking guns," evidence implicating the president himself in the cover-up. At first, the president released a portion of the tapes requested. Then he refused to release any more, save those that he edited and prepared himself. When Cox persisted, President Nixon fired him. The firing, dubbed "the Saturday Night Massacre," fanned the popular belief that Nixon had something truly heinous hidden on the tapes. Subpoenaed

successively by the Senate, the House Judiciary Committee, and the second special prosecutor, Leon Jaworski, a Houston lawyer, the tapes not only proved that the president had conspired with his aides to use various branches of the government to conceal the practices of the Committee to Reelect the President but that Nixon himself used foul language, had little concern for the everyday issues of government, and exhibited contempt for his political opponents only slightly greater than his contempt for those who did not sacrifice themselves to protect him.

Although the House Judiciary Committee did not rush to begin its impeachment inquiry of President Nixon, when its chairman, Peter Rodino (D.-N.J.), opened the proceedings in March 1974, the evidence led the committee to begin to vote on articles of impeachment on 27 July 1974. By 30 July, three articles had been drafted and approved. The committee refused to impeach President Nixon for decisions about the Vietnam War, believing that these came within the scope of his discretionary powers as commander in chief. The committee resolutions focused instead on the burglary and the cover-up.

The first article of impeachment alleged that President Nixon had delayed, impeded, and obstructed the investigation of the burglary by withholding evidence, counseling witnesses to lie under oath in court, lying about his own involvement, interfering with the Department of Justice as it sought to inquire into the Watergate burglary, paying hush money to the defendants, leaking Department of Justice information to the defendants, and misusing the Central Intelligence Agency to cover up the entire affair. Six Republicans joined all twenty-one Democrats in voting for this article.

The second article claimed that President Nixon had engaged in a more far-reaching subversion of the government. He supposedly used the Internal Revenue Service to harass his political foes, engaged the Federal Bureau of Investigation in illegal surveillance of citizens, created a secret investigative unit (the "plumbers") within the executive branch, and generally failed to take care that the laws be faithfully executed, a breach of his oath of office. The second article did not rest on criminal charges, but nonetheless received one more vote than the first, an additional Republican joining the twenty-one Democrats and six Republicans who had voted the first article.

Finally, a third article accused President Nixon of refusing, against law, to deliver papers and tapes to the House Judiciary Committee, thus violating his trust and undermining the laws, "to the manifest injury of the people of the United States." The last article clearly rested on the concept of maladministration, not criminality. It gained only twenty-one votes, two Democrats, both southerners, bolting the majority of their party, and joining fifteen Republicans to vote nay.

Ironically in the light of the extensive legal quarrels about impeachable offenses and admissibility of evidence of wrongdoing that the House committee aired on television for more than three months, President Richard M. Nixon was not impeached. All of his close aides (notably John Haldeman, John Ehrlichman, John Dean, and Charles Colson), their aides, and much of the Committee to Reelect the President had been indicted, tried, and convicted for their part in the many plots that surrounded his presidency, but he had vowed to fight to the end. Although Republican stalwarts feared the effect of Nixon remaining in office, he recruited a new staff and subjected it to the same demand for loyalty that he had imposed on his previous advisers. Asked to surrender the tapes, he first produced a much-edited version and introduced into American political jargon the phrase "expletive deleted." When the House committee and the special prosecutor's office persisted, his lawyers carried the case to the Supreme Court. Citing the extratextual doctrine of "executive privilege," lawyers for the president resisted demands for full disclosure of the tapes. The U.S. Supreme Court, in *United States* v. *Nixon,* 418 U.S. 683 (1974), unanimously ordered the president to produce the voice recordings requested by special prosecutor Leon Jaworski and the House Judiciary Committee, but left to the lower courts the power to determine whether particular future requests might be denied on grounds of executive privilege. While he waited to hear whether the Court would decree that he must turn over the tapes, he was still tinkering with plans to erase the tapes.

By the end of July 1974, the public knew what the President had revealed on 23 June 1972 to John Dean and H. R. Haldeman—that he had known, approved, and intended to conceal the illegal activities of his staff and supporters. Then and only then, when his popular support had vanished and few in his party spoke in his defense, did Nixon agree to resign. On 8 August 1974, at 9:00 P.M., Nixon announced his resignation, effective at noon on the next day.

The Nixon case set all manner of precedent in the areas of interbranch relations, but technically none in impeachment law. The House Judiciary Committee regarded his attempt to prevent full investigation of the Watergate burglary as an impeachable offense, but the battle between President Nixon and the Senate and House committees focused not on the limits of impeachable offense but on the accessibility to Congress and the courts of documents and tape recordings generated in the executive branch. The tangled skein of political ambition, disregard for law, and open conspiracy to use his power as president to thwart the courts and Congress led to Nixon's downfall.

## The Limits of Impeachment
## After Watergate

When President Nixon resigned, he commented that his own partisanship may have given rise to the partisanship of his opponents in Congress. This somewhat disingenuous description of the events surrounding Watergate and the cover-up implied that his chief crime was an excess of party zeal, but his case and succeeding impeachments demonstrated that mere partisanship or favoritism is never enough to convict a defendant. The cases of two governors faced with impeachment in the 1980s, the Democrat William Sheffield of Alaska and the Republican Evan Mecham of Arizona, demonstrate this rule.

In May 1985 a grand jury investigating the award of government leases raised questions about Sheffield's conduct. The state senate intervened before the lower house could begin its hearings, and voted that such charges did not amount to an impeachable offense. The case was dropped. The Alaska Senate had not quite duplicated the actions of the Louisiana Senate in the Long case, but its early intervention raised a question of whether impeachment remained the sole preserve of a lower house. Could a state senate effectually bar an impeachment by refusing in advance to hear the case? The issue remains unresolved. The Sheffield case may be a hard one precisely because the charges were so weak. Sheffield's partisanship, if such it was, did not exhibit self-serving corruption or avarice.

When a governor diverted public funds or funds earmarked for a public purpose to his own use, impeachment was not barred by upper houses. In Arizona, the lower house voted, and the state senate agreed, to remove Governor Evan Mecham for turning campaign contributions to personal use. The vote to remove Mecham was overwhelming, for his abusive public conduct and disrespect for the legislature was too blatant even for his own Republican party leaders to stomach.

Mecham was indicted for criminal activities in the regular courts, but such indictments—and even convictions on them—are not automatic grounds for impeachment. Only after independent investigation did Congress act to remove judges convicted of crime in the regular courts. In the case of Harry Claiborne, a district judge in Nevada convicted of income tax evasion in May 1986, Congress waited until the judge's last appeal was denied, and then moved to impeach him. Claiborne had refused to resign, and for five months of his prison term between May and October 1986 collected his federal salary in prison. Claiborne was removed on 6 October 1986.

In the same year, Walter L. Nixon, chief judge of the District Court for the Southern District of Mississippi, was convicted of perjury, but like Claiborne, he refused to resign. He claimed that the perjury charges were an attempt to railroad him because he was an opponent of civil rights litigation. An independent congressional investigation revealed additional instances of perjury, and the House impeached Judge Nixon. After a three and a half day trial, the Senate removed him from office in 1989.

At the end of the 1980s, impeachment inquiries entered a new and complex legal stage. Disturbed by the time and effort such inquiries demanded, now that they had come fully to resemble trials at law, members of Congress proposed alternatives to traditional means of impeachment and trial. In Walter Nixon's case, the Senate impaneled a committee to conduct the trial, reserving to the whole body rulings on matters of law and the final vote on guilt or

innocence. In addition, the size and complexity of the federal judiciary had grown so great that Congress considered administrative hearings and dismissals. Alarmed at the threat to judicial independence, lawyers and judges proposed an internal judicial mechanism to identify and examine suspicions of judicial misconduct. The Judicial Councils Reform and Judicial Conduct and Disabilities Act of 1980 gave to the circuit judicial councils the power to investigate wrongdoing and incapacity among federal judges. Advocates praised the act for allowing the judiciary to supervise and correct its own failings expeditiously. Critics complained that the act's inquisitorial approach to suspected malfeasance denied those it investigated the rights and privileges that any common criminal had in the regular courts. The judicial councils lacked the power to remove judges, and some opponents of impeachment suggested that three-person panels of appellate courts, chosen by the chief justice, ought to have the power to remove a sitting judge when he or she was charged with a felony. Critics retorted that any such move required a constitutional amendment.

The 1990 Judicial Discipline and Removal Act gave to the Judicial Councils the authority to recommend impeachment hearings without first carrying on an investigation. The act went further in its expression of concern for the inefficiency of impeachment by creating a thirteen-member commission to study alternatives to impeachment and trial for removal of federal judges. The commission is actively sponsoring research and discussion in furtherance of this goal.

A test of all the new procedures arose when Alcee Hastings of the Southern District of Florida was accused of soliciting bribes in 1983. He was cleared by a grand jury, but two of his brethren on the court asked the judicial council for the Eleventh Circuit to carry on its own investigation under the act. During the course of a three-year investigation by a committee of the council, Hastings and his judicial clerks protested against the subpoena of evidence of confidential meetings and the requirement of testimony to the investigating committee, using arguments similar to those advanced by James St. Clair, President Nixon's counsel, in *United States* v. *Nixon*. On appeal, the Eleventh Circuit found the investigatory procedures fully warranted by the letter of the act.

Evidence obtained through the circuit council's investigation led to a motion in Congress to impeach Hastings for lying repeatedly about the bribery charges. After its own exhaustive investigation, lasting more than a year and a half, the House in 1989 voted 413–3 to impeach Hastings on seventeen articles. Although Hastings, an African American, complained that the prosecution was racially motivated, leading members of the Black Caucus in the House joined in the prosecution. Hastings's trial lasted for eighteen days in the Senate, during which another specially named committee of senators heard testimony from sixty witnesses on 364 exhibits, and generated a transcript of more than thirty-five hundred pages. The Senate voted 69–29 to convict Hastings for corruption in office and removed him from the bench. Efforts by judges Hastings and Nixon to gain judicial review of their trials in the Senate failed in 1993. Chief Justice William Rehnquist, writing for a majority of his Court, decided that federal courts could not intervene in these cases.

## CONCLUSION

In the letter of impeachment law and the great variety of impeachment precedent, three themes emerge. The first is that impeachment still works as it was designed to work, to give to the legislative branch a check on the other branches of government when officials in them exceed or misuse their powers. From the inception of the new American republics, the legislative branch, the representative of the people, has always claimed for itself the status of first among equals. There are many checks and balances in the constitutional system of separation of powers; impeachment is one of these.

The provisions for impeachment and trial recall this original understanding of checks and balances, but do not rest upon original arrangements alone. The course of impeachment practice over two hundred years has demonstrated that impeachment is a highly accessible and public ratification of the popular will. Unlike the activities of the executive branch, often shrouded in secrecy, and the operation of the courts, governed by technical rules and artificial language, impeachment and trial are highly visible, direct, and relatively easy to understand.

Second, impeachment is a legal proceeding, not a political one. If the rules for impeachment are not written in the texts or in the debates over the adoption of those texts, they have emerged from precedent. The lessons continue, but their general outline has become clear. To be successful, impeachment charges cannot rest on mere partisanship or bad temper. There must be intentional harm to the public weal, measured by damage suffered by individuals who were mistreated. When laws are broken or not enforced or unfairly enforced, impeachment is available.

The triers of fact in these cases, the upper houses, are always more stringent in their definition of the legal basis of impeachment than the lower houses. This is as it should be, for the upper house is a deliberative body, and the lower house, a more representative body. The requirement that impeachment convictions rest on at least a two-thirds majority while impeachment itself needs only a majority vote underlines this distinction between representation and deliberation. The vote to convict does not have to be unanimous, as do jury verdicts in criminal trials, for the trial on an impeachment is not a criminal proceeding. Some upper houses have set a precedent for themselves that purely criminal charges impose a special burden on the prosecution managers. They must be proved beyond a reasonable doubt. Other upper houses have not insisted on this rule.

Potentially, the power of the lower house to bring impeachment as a check on the other branches knows no limitation. While a member of the House, Gerald Ford told that body during the investigation of Justice William O. Douglas, "An impeachable offense is whatever a majority of the House of Representatives considers [it] to be at a given moment in history" (*Congressional Record,* vol. 116 [15 April 1970], p. 11912). Legally, the breadth of this claim is restricted not only by the text of the Constitution but by the rulings of successive senatorial courts. Ford implied that the Senate might simply follow the lead of the lower house and impose its capricious will at any particular trial, but the U.S. Senate and the state senates have acted in entirely different fashion, moving toward increasing rigor in their regard for the

# LEGISLATURES AND IMPEACHMENT

legal rights of the accused and a precise and consistent definition of offenses. In a number of cases, the upper houses have even intervened before the prosecution was brought to them, in order to ensure a fair hearing of the case.

The self-consciousness of the upper houses notwithstanding, impeachment remains first and foremost a means of removal of public officials rather than a political analogue of a criminal indictment. From this large understanding, the third theme of American impeachment emerges. The long-term effectiveness of impeachment is inseparable from Americans' firm adherence to the concept of the accountability of government, in which erring officials are removable for misuse of the trust placed in them. Impeachment and trial by

a representative legislature provides a mechanism for removal short of revolution or assassination, the problem that has plagued government throughout recorded history. Abuse of public trust rests on this broad base of the trusteeship character of office-holding in America. Trustees who violate their sworn duties or ignore the best interests of the beneficiaries of the public trust—the American people—must be removed from office. The charges may range from outright criminality to abusive conduct toward the public and maladministration, but the penalty is limited to removal and disqualification. For this reason, despite the time and effort impeachment consumes, it remains a central and distinguishing feature of American legislative activity.

## BIBLIOGRAPHY

**General Studies**
General works on legislatures and impeachment include RAOUL BERGER, *Impeachment: The Constitutional Problems* (Cambridge, Mass., 1973); CHARLES L. BLACK, *Impeachment: A Handbook* (New Haven, Conn., 1974); IRVING BRANT, *Impeachment: Trials and Errors* (New York, 1972); STEPHEN B. BURBANK, "Alternative Career Resolution: An Essay on the Removal of Federal Judges," *Kentucky Law Journal* 76 (December 1989–January 1990); CONGRESSIONAL QUARTERLY, *Impeachment and the U.S. Congress* (Washington, D.C., 1974); MICHAEL GERHARDT, "The Constitutional Limits to Impeachment and Its Alternatives," *Texas Law Review* 68 (November 1989); MICHAEL HONEY, ed., *Milestone Documents in the National Archives: Records of Impeachment* (Washington, D.C., 1987); JOHN R. LABOVITZ, *Presidential Impeachment* (New Haven, Conn., 1978); MELISSA H. MAXMAN, "In Defense of the Constitution's Judicial Impeachment Standard," *Michigan Law Review* 86 (November 1987); RONALD J. ROTUNDA, "Discipline and Impeachment," *Kentucky Law Journal* 76 (December 1989–January 1990); MORRIS B. SCHNAPPER, ed., *Presidential Impeachment: A Documentary Overview* (Washington, D.C., 1974); and WILLIAM F. SWINDLER, "High Court of Congress: Impeachment Trials, 1797–1936," *American Bar Association Journal* 60 (April 1974).

**Early Impeachment Cases and States Cases**
See JAMES W. ELY, "'That No Office Whatever Be Held During Life of Good Behavior': Judicial Impeachments and the Struggle for Democracy in South Carolina," *Vanderbilt Law Review* 30 (March 1977); JOHN DUNNE and MICHAEL BALBONI, "New York's Impeachment Law and the Trial of Governor Sulzer," *Fordham Urban Law Journal* 15:1 (1987); ROBERT JEROME GLENNON, "Impeachment: Lessons from the Mecham Experience," *Arizona Law Review* 30:3 (1988); PETER CHARLES HOFFER and N. E. H. HULL, *Impeachment in America, 1635–1805* (New Haven, Conn., 1984); FREDRICK B. KARL and MARGUERITE DAVIS, "Impeachment in Florida," *Florida State University Law Review* 6 (Winter 1978); and STEPHEN A. SMITH, "Impeachment, Address, and the Removal of Judges in Arkansas," *Arkansas Law Review* 32 (Summer 1978).

**The Impeachment and Trial of Andrew Johnson**
Works about the seventeenth president's ordeals include MICHAEL LES BENEDICT, *The Impeachment and Trial of Andrew Johnson* (New

York, 1973); MILTON LOMASK, *Andrew Johnson: President on Trial* (New York, 1973); ERIC MCKITRICK, ed., *Andrew Johnson: A Profile* (New York, 1969); GENE SMITH, *High Crimes and Misdemeanors: The Impeachment and Trial of Andrew Johnson* (New York, 1977); and HANS L. TREFOUSSE, *Impeachment of a President: Andrew Johnson, the Blacks, and Reconstruction* (Knoxville, Tenn., 1977).

### The Richard M. Nixon Case
See SAMUEL DASH, *Chief Counsel* (New York, 1976); JOHN W. DEAN, *Blind Ambition* (New York, 1976); JOHN D. EHRLICHMAN, *Witness to Power* (New York, 1982); SAM J. ERVIN, *The Whole Truth: The Watergate Conspiracy* (New York, 1980); H. R. HALDEMAN, *The Ends of Power* (Boston, 1978); LEON JAWORSKI, *The Right and the Power: The Prosecution of Watergate* (New York, 1976); STANLEY I. KUTLER, *The Wars of Watergate* (New York, 1990); RICHARD M. NIXON, *RN: The Memoirs of Richard Nixon* (New York, 1978); JOHN SIRICA, *To Set the Record Straight* (New York, 1979); THEODORE H. WHITE, *Breach of Faith: The Fall of Richard Nixon* (New York, 1975); and two works by BOB WOODWARD and CARL BERNSTEIN—*All the President's Men* (New York, 1974), and *The Final Days* (New York, 1976).

SEE ALSO Recall and Expulsion of Legislators.

# LEGISLATURES AND CORRUPTION FROM COLONIAL TIMES TO THE PRESENT

## Gary W. Reichard

The incisive French observer Alexis de Tocqueville, reflecting on the nature and sources of democracy in the United States in the early decades of the nineteenth century, suggested that a tendency to corruption was inherent in the nature of the young American society. Because Americans enjoyed relatively equal circumstances, he argued, they were "naturally urge[d] . . . to embark in commercial and industrial pursuits"—an urge that could easily tempt them to corrupt the nation's democratic institutions. The connection was easily enough imagined, since an individual could rapidly attain economic benefits through the purchase of special favors from government. Similarly—and perhaps even more threatening to the health of democratic institutions—one could hope to profit more directly by achieving public office and misusing the position for private gain.

The tendencies to corruption against which Tocqueville warned were well understood by Americans in the early years of the Republic. Indeed, the issue of political corruption, and legislative corruption in particular, has struck deep chords in the American psyche since colonial days. A central criticism of the British regime that led to the American Revolution was that it had been corrupted by the king. The colonists objected especially to the presence of royally controlled members in the House of Commons; as the popularly based house of Parliament, Commons held the potential of being a counterweight to bribery and control by the crown. By the late eighteenth century, however, the entire British government—notably including the Commons—seemed to be built on corruption, including bribery, the purchase of political power, and other dishonest practices. The colonists' great fear was that the Stamp Act of 1765 and other

such enactments would spread this corruption to America (Kelley, p. 276). Thus, from the beginning, Americans resolved that their government, in particular the popularly based legislative branch, should be free from corruption.

Some colonial leaders believed that the colonies could protect themselves from the corruption of the mother country by securing a separate American legislature within the British imperial system. Others, such as Patrick Henry, feared that if a colonial legislature were created within the empire, it, too, would soon be "polluted." Henry and like-minded colonists therefore believed the best solution was a clean break from England and the establishment of their own version of the House of Commons. The doctrine of separation of powers underlying the new American government established after the successful revolution was partially intended to ensure that the corruption of Parliament could not be replicated in the United States; the new "more perfect Union," by its very design, would be immune to the corrupting influence of an overweening executive branch.

Constitutional provisions were carefully drawn to guard against corruption in the executive and judicial branches, where history seemed to teach that dishonesty was a great threat, but the legislative branch was apparently assumed to be immune from such evils. Impeachment as a remedy for corruption, for example, was provided for only in the case of the executive branch and possibly for the judiciary (Noonan, p. 431). The reason for exempting the legislature from suspicion of corrupt tendency was summed up by James Madison in 1787: "Besides the restraints of their personal integrity and honor, the difficulty of acting in concert for purposes of corruption was a security to the public. And if one or a few members only should be seduced, the soundness of the remaining members would maintain the integrity and fidelity of the body." There was a certain illogic in this rationale, given the history of corruption in the House of Commons, where individuals of corrupt tendency had had little difficulty in sustaining their dishonest practices. Nonetheless, Madison's view prevailed, and Americans launched their new experiment secure in their faith in the inherent integrity of the legislative branch.

Accordingly, the only constitutional barrier to corruption in the national legislature was a relatively mild and narrow one. Article I, Section 6, provides that "no Senator or Representative shall, during the Time for which he was elected, be appointed to any civil Office under the Authority of the United States, which shall have been created, or the Emoluments whereof shall have been increased during such time; and no Person holding any Office under the United States shall be a Member of either House during his Continuance in Office." No specific penalty was set for violation of this ban, nor was any other type of legislative misbehavior defined in the new instrument of government. While the president and judges could be removed for malfeasance, apparently there was no need to plan for such an eventuality in the legislative branch.

## TYPES OF LEGISLATIVE CORRUPTION

If legislative corruption has proved exceptionally difficult to guard against in the American system, there may be good reasons for the problem. As already noted, since it was not a problem Americans envisioned when they founded a democratic republic, no clear definitions of it were set forth in the Constitution. As the American political system has evolved, it has remained very difficult to define legislative corruption with clarity or certitude, mostly because the nature and functions of American representative institutions seem to invite behaviors that can be confused with the two most likely types of such corruption, bribery and conflict of interest. Moreover, throughout most of American history, legislatures have avoided drawing up specific rules or codes of ethics that would obligate them to punish misbeha-

vior on the part of their members. Rather, legislators have chosen to rely on the courts to define and punish "corruption" and have largely failed to impose additional sanctions on offending legislators, even in instances when the courts have established their guilt.

Bribery, which had been such an obvious offense in Parliament, was generally regarded as corrupt behavior at the time the new government was founded. Defined precisely enough in the U.S. Federal Criminal Code as "offer[ing] or promis[ing] anything of value to any public official ... with intent ... to influence any public act," bribery has nonetheless often been hard to identify, let alone prove. The problem is that, in the American system, bribes can be almost indistinguishable from campaign contributions. For example, a contributor is likely to believe that his contribution should guarantee that his views will receive a hearing from the legislator if ever an issue arises where the contributor's interests are directly involved. It is a short step from the concept of such guaranteed "access" to the legislator, to an expectation that the grateful legislator will support the contributor's position in such cases. If, in such a circumstance, the legislator so favored does support the position advocated by the donor, the explanation can easily be that the two merely share a common viewpoint—else why would the contribution have been made in the first instance? A legitimate question remains as to whether such a contribution constitutes a bribe, punishable as corruption, or not. Common sense can help in making this distinction; generally, it is reasonable to assume that the greater the size of the contribution and the greater the secrecy surrounding it, the more likely is the donor to expect favorable action and the more likely is the legislator to give it— that is, that a bribe has been given and received (Noonan, p. 698). One final complication in cases of bribery has been the repeatedly demonstrated propensity to blame the giver rather than the recipient, treating the legislator in such a case almost as a victim of the unethical behavior of outsiders.

A second type of behavior among legislators that is commonly considered to be corrupt, conflict of interest, has also proved very difficult to define because of the nature of American representative government. Since, under the Constitution, the legislator is supposed to represent the interests of his or her local constituency and since the legislator is likely to share those broad interests, how can it be determined whether the lawmaker is acting from self-interest or representing the legitimate interests of his or her constituency (Benson, p. 138)?

The difficulties of distinguishing clearly when legislative corruption has occurred and the sometimes contradictory forces that characterize capitalism and democracy, respectively, as suggested by Tocqueville, have combined to make the issue of legislative corruption in the United States particularly complex and difficult to deal with. The reluctance of legislators to prescribe and punish the behaviors of their colleagues has only added to the problem.

## LEGISLATIVE CORRUPTION IN THE NEW REPUBLIC

The first notable instance of legislative corruption in the new nation was the "Yazoo case." This episode had its origins in 1795, when the Georgia legislature sold the so-called Yazoo lands, thirty-five million acres that stretched west to the Mississippi and south to the Gulf of Mexico, to several speculator groups at bargain-basement prices (about 1.5 cents per acre), after these groups had generously distributed shares in their companies to many of the legislators. Among the speculator-agents who had helped to persuade the legislature to sell the lands was at least one member of Congress, James Gunn.

When, in response to public outcry at this flagrant demonstration of conflict of interest, the legislature rescinded the land sale, the original speculators took their case to Congress. There, through the purchased services of Postmaster General Gideon Granger, they successfully lobbied for a federal buy-out of the disputed lands in 1798 and their redistribution to the claimants at a somewhat higher but still ridiculously low price. When controversy continued, the Supreme Court ultimately entered into the dispute, ruling in *Fletcher* v. *Peck*, 6 Cranch 87 (1810), that notwithstanding ethical arguments against such a federal "bailout" of the original speculators, the original contract had to be respected; the Georgia legislature

could not rescind its original grant and the congressional deal must stand.

The outcome of the Yazoo case gave little reason for hope that legislative corruption in the form of conflict of interest would be easily prosecuted in the United States. In upholding the original contract, the Court legitimized the corrupt vote-buying scheme of the original investors, as well as the legislators' behavior in voting to sell the Yazoo lands at prices that benefited themselves. Although the complicated Yazoo affair did not immediately serve as a precedent for other greedy speculators or opportunistic legislators, it nonetheless demonstrated a dangerous ethical permissiveness that belied the confidence the framers of the Constitution had placed in legislatures.

One aspect of the young American system that clearly invited legislative corruption, especially in the form of conflict of interest, was that most federal and state legislators considered their public service as only a sideline to their private careers. Rather than believing that their "real" careers ought to be interrupted by their public service, legislators and other public officials seemed to feel that it was justifiable to advance their private interests through their public positions. Perhaps the most famous example of this attitude in action was Daniel Webster, who, throughout a congressional career that spanned most of the four decades up to 1850, continued to provide legal representation to numerous clients who stood to benefit by his actions as a public official. Webster did nothing to try to hide this association, nor did any but his political enemies condemn him for it. Webster's important clients included the Bank of the United States, but he had plenty of company in delivering "services" for the bank; in an 1837 memorandum, the bank's president, Nicholas Biddle, revealed that it had issued "loans" to more than fifty other members of Congress (Berg, Hahn, and Schmidhauser, pp. 17–18). Another well-known senator of the period, Thomas Hart Benton (D.-Mo.), similarly served as a paid representative of John Jacob Astor and the American Fur Company throughout the Jacksonian period, drawing a hefty retainer for his legal services while a member of the Senate (Noonan, p. 444).

The dispensation of subsidies and special privileges such as franchises also led to instances of legislative corruption in the early nineteenth century. As one midwestern Jacksonian congressman put it, "A rich Government ever has been, and ever will be, a corrupt Government" (quoted in Summers, p. 173). Such an argument, of course, could be—and was—put to partisan use by Jacksonian Democrats, since it conveniently reinforced their opposition to the ambitious program of internal improvements and government subsidies favored by the Whigs. As they argued, such projects and subsidies as those advanced by Henry Clay and his fellow Whigs merely served to multiply the opportunities for corruption by greedy politicians and developers. As the activities of Benton and many other Democratic legislators of the time indicated, however, conflict of interest was not the exclusive preserve of Whigs.

During the Jacksonian era, a number of types of legislative corruption began to appear with greater frequency. Ethical problems attached, for example, to the granting of patent renewals, charters, and special franchises of all types, at both the state and national levels. The rise of lobbyists (or "borers," as they were then called), a number of which were functioning in Washington and state capitals by the 1850s, was closely connected to such matters. Indeed, these agents for special interests began to be perceived as an essential ingredient of the lawmaking process; one lobbyist offered the opinion in testimony before a House committee in the 1850s that "there is nobody who knows the organization of Congress who expects to carry anything through it merely from love of justice" (quoted in Summers, pp. 6–7). Prominent among the most successful of lobbyists in this period were former members of Congress and former state legislators, who could apply their specialized institutional knowledge and personal contacts for the profit of their private clients.

The renewal of the 1836 patent for the Colt revolver provided an excellent example of corruption connected with patent renewals. Lobbyists for manufacturer Samuel Colt reportedly spent more than $60,000 on lavish entertainment and gifts (including large numbers of Colt pistols) for members of Congress in order to win their support for his continued exclusive control of the patent. In this instance, the money spent was not enough; although the House, after an investigation of Colt's lobbying

efforts, passed the patent extension, the bill died in the Senate. Rather than proving that corruption did not pay, however, the failure of the Colt lobby's efforts could just as easily be attributed to the reality that more than $60,000 would have been needed to produce victory in both houses.

Similarly, the granting of government subsidies for services such as overseas mail delivery afforded great possibilities for the trading of stocks, money, and other favors to legislators in return for their support for a given special-interest group. Sharp competition among entrepreneurs for this government business fanned corrupt tendencies. In the first six months of 1852 alone, for example, no fewer than seventeen shipping firms competed for an estimated $80 million in government subsidies to carry the mails to California and overseas; in such a market, unethical members of Congress eager to profit could trade their votes for company shares, cash, or both (Summers, p. 103). Similarly, banks that sought to become depositories for federal funds proved a lucrative source of outside income for opportunistic legislators. Too, the granting of corporate charters invited corruption. Even though by the early decades of the nineteenth century the practice of granting individual charters had been replaced by a less easily manipulated system of general incorporation laws, companies still frequently sought "special charters" with privileges built into them. The only available cure for this was to make general incorporation mandatory, and by the 1870s most states had done so (Summers, pp. 99–100).

Land speculation, too, continued to produce deals of questionable propriety between private interests and legislators, even if few cases were as spectacular as the earlier Yazoo case. The rapid national expansion of the 1840s and 1850s, marked by feverish competition to build a network of railroads in the newly settled lands, gave rise to numerous activities that, though often not considered corrupt by the standards of the day, would likely be judged so today. After victory in the Mexican War increased the nation's land holdings by nearly one-third, the sale and assignment of federal land became a big business. In the flurry of land grants that were given to lure speculators and private corporations to develop the newly acquired territories, many members of Congress found ways to enrich themselves. Senator John Slidell (D.-La.), for example, engineered passage of a bill giving him title to a large grant that had previously been held up in the courts, and another senator, David Yulee (D.-Fla.), pressed successfully for a land grant to the Florida Railroad, of which he was a director (Summers, p. 153). The fact that actions such as Slidell's and Yulee's were not adjudged as corrupt by Congress or the public at the time would suggest that Tocqueville had been right to suspect the possibly corrosive effects of entrepreneurial capitalism on the young nation's democratic institutions.

## MID-NINETEENTH-CENTURY CORRUPTION

Although lobbyists were not new to the American scene in the middle of the nineteenth century, their large numbers and the obviousness of their methods seemed to many to pose a particular danger to the Republic in the decade before the Civil War. The nature of the lobbying business disposed most private interests to encourage secrecy where the business of their borers was concerned. This veil of secrecy allowed clients to express "naive outrage" if their lobbyists were found to be engaging in illegal activities, but it also fostered public suspicion about the legitimacy of lobbying generally (Summers, p. 87).

Not all lobbyists were corrupt and self-interested, of course; in many cases, they served legislators as needed sources of information on the technicalities of businesses such as mail shipment, railroad construction, and the like. Moreover, what was described as "lobbying" could include a wide range of activities, only some of which were corrupt. While all might agree on the basis of modern standards that outright bribe-giving was a corrupt behavior, was it necessarily "corruption" if a lobbyist entertained legislators or provided other unsolicited favors or gifts, unconnected to any particular piece of legislation? In any case, the public perception of borers was becoming highly negative by midcentury, a trend reflected even in literature of the time. In an 1856 poem, for example, Walt Whitman characterized "lobbyers" as "crawling serpentine men, the lousy combings and born freedom sellers

of the earth" (quoted in Thompson, p. 54). Press accounts, too, were beginning to reinforce such an image.

In response to rising criticisms of the behaviors of lobbyists and some legislators, Congress took its first steps to define and provide sanctions against corruption. In 1853 it enacted the first antibribery law, making it a crime to offer "money, goods, right in action, bribe, present, or reward . . . or any other valuable thing whatever" to any public official, including members of Congress, in order "to influence his vote, opinion, or decision." While this law applied only to the offering of bribes, three years later it was amended to make the accepting of bribes a federal offense as well. The Senate, however, tacked on a rider clarifying that "Conviction of bribetaking would not automatically deprive a member of his seat in Congress" (Noonan, pp. 451–453). In 1862, yet a third anticorruption measure made its way through Congress, establishing a maximum penalty of $10,000 and two years in prison for "any member of Congress" or "any officer of the government of the United States" who accepted money, property, or anything else of value in exchange for a "contract, office, or place" in government or, in the case of members of Congress, in return for "his attention, service, action, vote, or decision" (Noonan, p. 454).

In the political environment that produced such laws, the most flagrant instances of legislative corruption could be expected to lead to exposure and condemnation, as when an 1857 House investigation into alleged bribe-taking resulted in the resignations of three members and the expulsion of a fourth, Orsamus Matteson (Whig-N.Y.), by a vote of eighty to seventeen. But it remained relatively easy for legislators and lobbyists alike to circumvent the new laws. One common maneuver was to mask bribes as gambling debts, with "unlucky" lobbyists losing hand after hand at the gaming tables, for which misfortune they would soon "owe" their legislator-opponents large debts, which could then be paid off without breaking any laws.

Other questionable practices also appeared in this period. Reimbursements for mileage between a member's home district and the capital, for example, were insufficiently (or not at all) audited, with predictable results. The most egregious abuse of this type was the so-called "constructive mileage"—reimbursement accepted by many senators in both 1849 and 1851 for imaginary travel to their homes and back between the formal adjournment of one session of Congress and the beginning of a second later in the same day; again in response to public criticism, this practice was specifically outlawed by the Senate in 1852.

Corruption in Congress was a major public issue in the 1850s. In 1855 the *New York Tribune* complained that a Congress "so corrupt and profligate—a Congress so prodigal and unfaithful—[had] never before assembled in this country" (Summers, p. 202). But as is so often the case, this phenomenon occurred in a larger context. The Buchanan administration itself was rife with corruption, and behaviors at the state level were little better. In many states, the composition of the legislature was virtually indistinguishable from the membership of the boards of directors and executives of the most important industries of the state—particularly the railroads. The legislatures of New York and Pennsylvania provided perhaps the most glaring examples of conflict of interest and outright corruption in the form of vote-selling and "strike bills" (measures specially designed to hamper a particular economic interest), but they were by no means unique. Within this web of corruption, businesses were generally less guilty than the politicians, many of whom actively sought payment for their services.

Two main explanations for the apparent growth of corruption in this period are persuasive. First, it is clear that the sudden economic boom of the 1840s and 1850s intensified the quest for acquisition and wealth, producing a mad scramble for subsidies, charters, and other favors from legislatures. Second, the expanded size and capabilities of the media by the middle of the nineteenth century ensured that much greater light was shed on dealings in Congress and the state capitals, suggesting the possibility that the problem was not that there was more dishonesty than before but only that it was being reported more thoroughly (Summers, p. 17).

## THE "GREAT BARBECUE": THE LATE NINETEENTH CENTURY

It is the period after the Civil War, however, that is most associated with rampant government corruption. The failings of the Grant administration bear special responsibility for this negative image, but Congress, too, shared in the behaviors that produced such epithets for the period as "the Great Barbecue," "the Gilded Age," and "the Age of the Robber Barons." It was an era of colorful, swashbuckling entrepreneurs—men such as Jay Gould, Jim Fisk, and Collis Huntington—and a period that saw more money pass between businessmen and public officials and larger numbers of legislators apparently participate in the largesse than had been true in earlier eras. The Congress of the mid-1870s, according to Collis Huntington of the Southern Pacific Railroad, was "the hungriest set of men that ever got together" (Benson, p. 83).

The Crédit Mobilier scandal was easily the most significant instance of governmental corruption in the late nineteenth century. This episode featured creation in the 1860s of a dummy construction company, Crédit Mobilier, to siphon off the funds that had been provided to the Union Pacific Railroad by way of government subsidy. Specifically, stockholders in Crédit Mobilier—basically the same individuals who held stock in the railroad—contracted for their company's services and then arranged to pay themselves excessively large dividends (profits as high as 600 percent annually) from moneys supplied by the railroad for track construction. The broad involvement of members of Congress came in the form of bribery by Crédit Mobilier's stockholders; stocks were distributed at par (that is, well below face value) to nearly twenty members and former members of Congress, in order to forestall any possible future legislation that might hamper the companies' activities or, worse yet, bring about an investigation.

The key figure in these dealings was U.S. Representative Oakes Ames (R.-Mass.), who was himself a stockholder in both companies. Ames distributed Crédit Mobilier stocks shrewdly; among the beneficiaries in the House were Speaker James G. Blaine (R.-Maine); the Democratic leader, James Brooks of New York; the chairman of the Ways and Means Committee, Henry L. Dawes (R.-Mass.); and the chairman of the Appropriations Committee, James A. Garfield (R.-Ohio). A brief investigation by the Justice Department in 1869, which had been prompted by the Union Pacific's rival, the Central Pacific, came to naught. In 1872, however, a disgruntled promoter, H. S. McComb, released to the press a series of damaging letters that had been written by Ames, detailing the bribery scheme; the resulting publicity led to the dreaded congressional investigation. When the verdict came in 1873, the established tendency to blame the giver, but not the recipient, was reinforced. Ames was censured, as was Brooks; other implicated House members went unpunished. In the Senate, James W. Patterson (R.-N.H.) was targeted for expulsion as a result of his involvement, but since he was then in the last days of a lame-duck term, no action was taken. For all the publicity surrounding Crédit Mobilier, however, it did not seem to mobilize the electorate against corruption in government; in the 1874 elections, nearly all of those directly involved escaped unscathed, and one, Garfield, was later elected president.

Much has been written on the corruption that pervaded American political life in the post–Civil War years. In general, the problems that had marked the years prior to the 1860s simply intensified in this period. The continued prevalence of bribery and other types of corruption, in the context of more numerous and more aggressive lobbies, heightened public concern and was reflected in the press and the arts. In 1873, for example, Mark Twain and Charles Dudley Warner produced a novel entitled *The Gilded Age,* in which a number of congressmen (one of them named Trollop) were engaged in a fraudulent business enterprise and one of the more unsympathetic characters was clearly modeled on Oakes Ames. (Twain had earlier served as secretary to a Nevada senator, William Stewart, who had helped to expose the Crédit Mobilier scandal.) Similarly, *Democracy,* a novel published anonymously by Henry Adams in 1880, focused on the harsh realities of corruption in Washington. Such attacks in literature were echoed in political campaigns of the time as well. In the wake of Crédit Mobilier, government corruption was a much talked-about issue in the 1876 elections, and in each of his three presidential campaigns (1884–1892), Grover Cleveland came across as being virtually obsessed with the issue of cleaning up government. Ironically, only a century after the Americans had successfully thrown off the shackles of what they perceived as a thoroughly corrupt British system, the term "American-style politics" had come to be equated in England and elsewhere with dishonesty in politics (Kelley, pp. 277–278, 331–332).

In these last decades of the nineteenth century, there were some attempts at reform. One investigation into alleged bribery in connection with a mail-carrying subsidy in the mid-1870s, for instance, produced an effort to require all lobbies to register with Congress. This measure was the first lobby-registration bill ever to pass in either house of Congress—in this case, the lower house—but it died for lack of action by the Senate. As should have been clear at the time, lobbyists were not the main problem, even though they made good scapegoats. Nor, perhaps, were officeholders themselves uniquely lacking in ethical standards; indeed, in holding lobbyists and politicians up to such ridicule in the period, the press and the public may have been blaming a few for what was wrong with politics as a whole (Thompson, pp. 54–55). The basic problem seems to have been the convergence in the Gilded Age of three powerful forces: economic prosperity, rapid modernization (placing on government new burdens and responsibilities for which it was institutionally unprepared), and an unusually assertive capitalist ideology that seemed to encourage maximum profit at any cost.

## THE PROGRESSIVE ERA

The Progressive movement of the early twentieth century, which drew strength from dramatic journalistic exposés ("muckraking," in the colorful term coined by Theodore Roosevelt), took on the evils of legislative corruption as one of many public iniquities in the period. Just as Lincoln Steffens's *The Shame of the Cities* (1904) provided grist for the mills of those who wished to reform municipal government, David Graham Phillips's *The Treason of the Senate* (published serially by *Cosmopolitan Magazine* in 1906) passionately attacked the many sorts of corruption that characterized the upper house, including bribery and intimidation of state legislatures by powerful business interests in the process of selecting senators, as well as the tendency of senators to grow rich as a result of their continued association with those powerful interests. In all, Phillips muckraked more than twenty sitting senators, half of them powerful committee chairmen. Additional articles critical of the Senate appeared in the daily press and in such popular magazines as the *North American Review, Atlantic Monthly,* and *Century.*

At least indirectly, such muckraking helped lead to ratification of the Seventeenth Amendment, requiring direct election of senators. Significant reforms affecting the election of legislators were also enacted. The Tillman Act of 1907 prohibited banks and corporations from contributing to either congressional or presidential campaigns, and a 1910 law required candidates for Congress and their political committees to report all campaign contributions and expenditures.

During the Progressive Era, the frequency with which Congress and state legislatures utilized both standing and special committees to investigate instances of corruption connected to trusts and lobbies increased appreciably, though such investigations did not always produce significant results. The most notable example of this activity at the state level was the New York legislature's 1905 investigation of the insurance companies of New York City, which eventually resulted in a large number of prosecutions of corporations for illegal campaign contributions and such other offenses as proffering bribes and prostitutes to members of the legislature. In Congress, the much-publicized Elkins Committee probe into the railroads went nowhere, but a House Judiciary Committee investigation into alleged improprieties by Representative James McDermott (D.-Ill.) led it not only to denounce McDermott's activities but also to condemn the National Association of Manufacturers (NAM) for "engaging in systematic secret and disreputable practices against the honor, dignity, and integrity of the House." McDermott was not censured, instead being permitted to resign; he was subsequently reelected and served an additional four years in Congress. Neither was the NAM penalized in any way for its actions (Wilson, p. 27). Again, as so often had been the case, Congress seemed unwilling to punish its own.

The growing impatience of Progressive reformers with legislative corruption was reflected in the more frequent intrusion of the executive and judicial branches into cases of alleged wrongdoing by lawmakers. Theodore Roosevelt's Justice Department, for example, successfully used the 1853 antibribery law to prosecute first-term Senator Joseph R. Burton (R.-Kans.) for taking $2,500 to stop a mail-fraud investigation, as well as a Democratic ex-congressman from Brooklyn, Edmund H. Driggs, for accepting $12,500 in exchange for helping to secure a contract for government purchase of business equipment (Noonan, p. 602). At the state level, too, the executive branch—a favored instrument of Progressive reformers—frequently took the lead in attacking legislative corruption, as in California, where reform governor Hiram Johnson was able to break the Southern Pacific Railroad's hold over state politics. State courts were also active; in Missouri and Ohio, grand-jury investigations in the early 1900s led to the convictions of several incumbent legislators.

The Progressive assault against legislative corruption, while obviously much needed, carried within it an inherent problem. Speaking from the perspective of one who supported the reforms, Theodore Roosevelt underscored the continuing problem of the unenforceability of such laws in an address to Congress in December 1907. "There is," he said, "always danger in laws of this kind, . . . the danger being lest they are obeyed by the honest, and disobeyed by the unscrupulous, so as to act only as a penalty upon honest men." This risk notwithstanding, it is clear that the Progressive Era produced a reduction of overt corruption in legislatures, as elsewhere in government.

## A PERIOD OF INATTENTION: THE MID-TWENTIETH CENTURY

After the brief flurry of the Progressive years, little sustained attention was paid to problems of legislative corruption for nearly fifty years, as the preoccupations of economic boom and bust, total war, and Cold War helped to divert the attention of the public and the media from such issues. Continuing its long-established pattern, Congress in several cases between the 1920s and the 1960s passed up opportunities to discipline members who had been found to have violated the law and who in some cases had been convicted in the courts. In the 1920s and 1930s, for example, two sitting members and two individuals who had recently left Congress were tried on various charges of corruption. One, Representative John Wesley Langley (R.-Ky.), was successfully prosecuted by the Coolidge administration for taking bribes in exchange for helping to obtain permits for whiskey shipments; a decade later, two recently defeated representatives and a second-term House member were convicted on counts of appointment-selling and coercing political appointees to make financial contributions. No action was taken by Congress against any of the four.

Congress continued to evidence an unwillingness to punish its own even while the pace of legislative corruption—or at least the rate of its exposure—increased in the 1940s and early 1950s. In the 1940s four Democratic House members, Eugene Cox (Ga.), John M. Coffee (Wash.), Andrew Jackson May (Ky.), and James Michael Curley (Mass.), were each found by their colleagues to be in violation of federal statutes, yet none was formally disciplined by the House. Cox, who had accepted stock from a radio station whose licensing request he expedited, was even described by the Democratic majority leader in the floor debate following hearings on his offense as being "beyond reproach" for his "honesty and integrity" (Wilson, p. 65). Coffee, who defended taking payments to aid a local contractor as evidence of his office's efforts "to build up a reputation as gogetters," was not disciplined by either the Senate investigating committee or the Justice Department, though he did pay the price of electoral defeat in 1946. And Curley, having been reelected mayor of Boston in 1945 while still a member of the House of Representatives, continued to hold both offices until 1947, even after being convicted in federal court for mail fraud. Similarly, Representatives J. Parnell Thomas (R.-N.J.) and Walter Brehm (R.-Ohio), who in 1949 and 1951, respectively, were convicted of receiving salary kickbacks, escaped punishment at the hands of their colleagues; Thomas even postdated his resignation after conviction so that he would receive additional salary while in prison. At least one member of Congress who was "condemned" for his habit of taking gifts from prospective government contractors, Senator Theodore Bilbo (D.-Miss.), was barred from taking his seat—perhaps more a result of his personal unpopularity rather than of Congress's "getting religion"—but he suffered no further penalty.

Immediately after World War II, as part of the effort to reform a number of congressional procedures, Congress passed yet another measure designed to bring the activities of lobbies under better control. This measure, the Federal Regulation of Lobbying Act (Title III of the Legislative Reorganization Act) of 1946, required registration and financial reporting by all lobbies seeking to influence legislators. The law represented an important and useful step, but even if rigorously enforced it could not fully control those interested in giving or taking financial favors. Nor was it any simpler than it had ever been to distinguish between illegal payments by lobbyists and other private interests for legislative favors, on the one hand, and legal payments received by legislators for valid outside professional services performed by them or their personal business associates, on the other. For example, the law firm of Senator George Smathers (D.-Fla.) regularly received large retainers from a railroad line that could (and did) benefit from Smathers's actions as a member of the Senate Commerce Committee, and Senator John Bricker (R.-Ohio) similarly drew salary from a Columbus law firm that served the Pennsylvania Railroad (Benson, p. 138). Obviously, in an institutional environment where not even certifiably illegal actions were acted on by Congress, such situations went unremarked by colleagues.

In the affluence-oriented 1950s and early 1960s, a long-established tradition of congressional "influence peddling" flourished and apparently hit new heights of profitability as well. The offices of both Speaker John McCormack (D.-Mass.) and Senate Majority Leader Lyndon Johnson (D.-Tex.) were among those whose office space, telephone, and stationery—not to mention their influence—were used by "fixers" to deliver favors to special interests whose gratitude was manifested in the form of generous contributions to the legislator and to the fixer himself. Bobby Baker, the wheeler-dealer who used Johnson's office, reportedly amassed a fortune of over $2 million in this manner, though in the partisan Democratic-controlled investigation that brought down Baker, Johnson himself escaped condemnation. "We're not investigating Senators," the chair of the investigating committee snapped when asked if the panel intended to try to shed light on Johnson's activities (Garment, p. 24).

By the mid-twentieth century, the continuing pattern of revelations of legislative wrongdoing, with no follow-up in the form of sanctions against the perpetrators, made it clear that an overhaul of ethics legislation was still much needed. While Congress had frequently displayed a willingness to investigate cases of alleged corruption and had even arrived at some guilty verdicts, it almost always left the imposition of sanctions to the courts or opted to let the voters mete out punishment, if they wished, in the next election. This strategy frequently led to the ouster of the guilty legislator, but it did not serve to induce much feeling of accountability among lawmakers. What seemed to be needed were the catalysts of media scrutiny and heightened public indignation, such as had produced the reforms of the 1850s and the Progressive Era.

## THE DODD CASE AND AFTER

In early 1966, journalists Drew Pearson and Jack Anderson published some thirty newspaper columns detailing the alleged corrupt practices of a second-term Democratic senator from Connecticut, Thomas J. Dodd. In assembling their accusations, including misdeeds ranging from expense padding to the appropriation of campaign funds for personal use, the two reporters had the advantage of active assistance from disgruntled former members of Dodd's staff. Their information was therefore well documented and, as it turned out, persuasive to the special Senate committee that investigated Dodd's case. In April 1967, this committee unanimously recommended censure, and the Senate voted, ninety-two to five, in favor of that recommendation.

Dodd's fate was not exclusively the result of the Pearson-Anderson revelations, nor was it unduly influenced by his personal unpopularity or the strong hostility that some felt toward his strident anti-Communism, though all of these factors were relevant to the outcome. More significant, however, were certain systematic changes that were occurring in Congress in the 1960s. One of these changes was the increased size of congressional staffs due to the Legislative Reorganization Act of 1946; the relative impersonality of the substantially enlarged staff setting tended to make staff members less likely than in earlier times to develop the sort of personal loyalty that might have kept them from "blowing the whistle" on inappropriate or illegal behavior on the part of their employer. In Dodd's case, an additional important factor in his staff members' collective decision to expose his actions was the atmosphere of heightened moralism that existed during the era of protest against the Vietnam War. In such an environment, principled adherence to a "higher morality" could, and did, lead insiders to break from congressional folkways that had long served as at least partial protection for those who bent or broke the law (Garment, pp. 33–34). In the 1970s, the Watergate crisis and its resolution reflected and further reinforced this increased tendency to allow a higher morality to supplant politics as usual.

These developments of the Vietnam-Watergate era help to explain the spate of revelations of legislative corruption in the 1970s and 1980s, and the renewed attention paid to ethics legislation in the period. Even so, legislative bodies proved only slightly more willing than before to take disciplinary action against sitting members. During the 1970s, a number of Senate and House members were convicted in the courts of bribery and/or conspiracy to receive bribes, and in some of those cases, Congress also acted, meting out penalties ranging from a reprimand to expulsion. The most notable episode was the "Koreagate" scandal of 1977, in which more than a hundred members of Congress were initially alleged to have taken gifts totaling between $500,000 and $1,000,000 per year from a South Korean lobbyist, Tongsun Park; the public and press furor surrounding these charges was intense, but only three members ultimately received House reprimands for their actions. The issuance of reprimands rather than censure reflected the continuing hesitancy of the House to take strong action against its members, since by the rules of the lower house a reprimand did not even require those being punished to be physically present, as did censure.

Other instances of suspected corruption in the 1970s produced no formal congressional action at all. For example, an investigation into the political financing operations of Gulf Oil, which developed from revelations in the Watergate hearings, suggested a pattern of illicit giving and taking (perhaps totaling $5 million over ten years) that involved some of the most highly placed members of the Senate and House. Claiming that it was too difficult to determine the exact nature of Gulf's transactions, however, the investigating committee recommended no punitive steps and none was taken by Congress. One unfortunate recipient was eventually indicted in the courts as a result of the findings, however, and Gulf itself cleaned up its questionable lobbying procedures.

One congressional response to the wave of corrupt activities uncovered in the Vietnam-Watergate era was enactment of stricter legislation on both campaign spending and outside earnings by legislators. In 1977, both houses adopted new, more explicit codes of ethics, including limitations on, and required disclosure of, outside income; restrictions on gifts; prohibitions on unofficial office accounts in which personal and campaign funds could be commingled; and a ban on government-reimbursed foreign travel by lame-duck members. Perhaps equally valuable was a 1978 law to protect whistle-blowers, which, though directed more at the executive branch than at Congress itself, could serve to protect those, like Dodd's former assistants, who might choose to reveal legislative corruption in the future.

Perhaps the most dramatic example of legislative corruption revealed in the early 1980s was the episode known as Abscam. Having begun as an Federal Bureau of Investigation (FBI) follow-up to Justice Department allegations of widespread corruption among federal officials, Abscam quickly concentrated on the legislative branch. The operation took its name from Abdul Enterprises, a dummy corporation set up with a $1-million account in the Chase Manhattan Bank to serve as a source of payoffs to pliant members of Congress who expressed willingness to do special favors for the supposed agents of the company. In 1979 and 1980, the Abscam operation caught six House members, John Jenrette (D.-S.C.), Richard Kelly (R.-Fla.), Raymond Lederer (D.-Pa.), Michael ("Ozzie") Myers (D.-Pa.), John Murphy (D.-N.Y.), and Frank Thompson (D.-N.J.), and one senator, the powerful Harrison Williams (D.-N.J.). Despite the defendants' claims of entrapment and violation of due pro-

cess, all were convicted and sentenced to jail terms, and their convictions were upheld in appellate courts. Three of the convicted members resigned (Jenrette, Lederer, and Williams), and three were defeated for reelection; the House was left to deal with only one of the miscreants, Myers, who suffered the penalty of expulsion.

Legislators were not alone in criticizing the spirit behind Abscam, which seemed motivated by a deep-seated distrust of officeholders; even if the courts failed to accept the defendants' claim of entrapment, both the media and the public at large evidenced unhappiness with the methods the FBI had used. By contrast, in the best-publicized instances of financial corruption in Congress in the years after Abscam, there could be no doubt that the accused had acted on their own initiative. Among the offenders were two of the top-ranking Democrats in the House of Representatives, Speaker Jim Wright (Tex.) and whip Tony Coelho (Calif.), and several prominent senior senators in both parties.

Wright's fall was rooted in bitter partisan warfare. In mid-1988, Republican House whip Newt Gingrich (Ga.), a bitter foe of Wright, convinced more than seventy fellow Republicans to join him in a complaint that the Speaker had accepted and failed to report gifts in violation of House ethical standards and that he had exceeded the House-imposed outside-income limitations. The public-interest lobby Common Cause, a creation of the corruption-conscious 1970s, joined in the call for an investigation, and the resulting Ethics Committee probe found that Wright had indeed disguised thousands of dollars in speaking fees (which had been limited by the 1977 ethics laws) as book royalties (on which there were no limits). In addition, the investigation found that Wright had taken gifts from a Fort Worth, Texas, associate who had a clear interest in federal programs over which Wright had influence. On a potentially more damaging charge, that Wright had directly intervened in savings-and-loan regulations to aid particular banks, the committee took no stand. Once again, as had happened so often before, the House managed to avoid taking action against one of its own, as Wright—protesting the "mindless cannibalism" of such repeated ethics probes—announced on 31 May

1989 that he would resign from the House. Only one year after Wright's case, Senator David Durenberger (R.-Minn.) was found guilty of a similar violation of the income limitations of the 1977 ethics law under the "cover" of book royalties and of taking unreported gifts. A Senate investigation of Durenberger's misdeeds resulted in his being formally denounced (the near equivalent of censure) by a 96–0 vote of his colleagues in July 1990.

The case of Democratic House whip Tony Coelho, which coincided with Wright's case in 1989, was like the latter in reflecting the intellectual and spiritual fabric of the materialistic 1980s, a decade that seemed to spawn some of the most unrestrained legislative corruption since the Gilded Age. Coelho was an appropriate symbol of the times, since his rise to prominence in the House was due to his mastery of the post-Watergate campaign financing practices created in the 1970s. His phenomenal success, while chair of the Democratic Congressional Campaign Committee in the early 1980s, in raising money from a myriad of political action committees (PACs) had in fact been the subject of a 1988 book by journalist Brooks Jackson suggestively entitled *Honest Graft*. It was not Coelho's wizardry with PACs that got him in trouble, however. Rather, in early 1989, the press exposed his participation in a junk-bond-selling scheme in which his financial risk had been underwritten by the securities firm Drexel Burnham Lambert, which was itself under investigation, and he had gone on to make a large profit from the sale of his stock. Coelho's certifiable offense was his failure to report the sale and his subsequent underpayment of taxes on the resulting profits, but the probe into his affairs revealed an additional possible conflict of interest in that he had continued to hold an interest in a dairy-management farm while helping to pass a dairy-subsidy bill. This offense, ironically, was not so different from scores of earlier cases. It was enough, however, to bring Coelho down. Like Wright, he chose to resign rather than to risk punishment. His House colleagues, relieved of the obligation of taking action against him (which they might or might not have done), instead feted him with dinners and parties in the days before his departure. Shortly thereafter, Coelho assumed a lucrative position directing a private investment firm—presenting a symboli-

cally appropriate denouement to this typically 1980s-style scandal.

The cases of Wright, Durenberger, and especially Coelho seemed to reflect a continuing tolerance within Congress for abuses of the system. Only when feeling forced to act because of media and public pressure was Congress likely to take action against abusers. As the round of parties for the "disgraced" Coelho emphatically indicated, despite the strengthening of formal procedures to deal with legislative corruption in the years after Watergate, the members' hearts were not in the pursuit and punishment of such misdeeds.

The glare of media publicity, however, reinforced by the growing disgust of the American electorate where the misbehavior of public officials was concerned, made it increasingly impossible for legislators to cover up the corrupt behavior of their colleagues. This truth was vividly demonstrated in the two most dramatic episodes involving congressional corruption that unfolded in the early 1990s. The first of these two cases, centered in the Senate, took its name from the key outside perpetrator, Charles Keating, head of the Lincoln Savings and Loan Company of California. The so-called Keating Five—Democratic senators Alan Cranston (Calif.), Dennis DeConcini (Ariz.), John Glenn (Ohio), and Donald Riegle (Mich.), and Republican senator John McCain (Ariz.)—were accused of accepting large campaign contributions in payment for their active intervention in the regulation process on behalf of Keating's operations. This case was all the more sensitive because of the financial scandal surrounding the savings-and-loan industry as a whole, a story of gross mismanagement and corporate greed that threatened to cost the American public millions of dollars in bailout funds.

The months-long Senate ethics investigation of the Keating Five (begun only after the 1990 elections) let two of the accused off very lightly (McCain and Glenn), was slightly more critical of two others (DeConcini and Riegle), and singled out one (Cranston) for "an impermissible pattern of conduct." Ill and having already announced plans to retire in 1992, even Cranston escaped with a light rap on the wrist. In November 1991, the Senate Ethics Committee "reprimanded" him "on behalf of and in the name of the U.S. Senate." This was an extremely mild sanction, given the committee's certification of Cranston's misconduct. Unlike other recent cases where the Senate had finally acted against corruption in its midst (the cases of Dodd, Williams, and Durenberger, for example), the full Senate took no action at all and the offender was even permitted to deliver a rebuttal on the floor. Denying his guilt to the end, Cranston took full advantage of the opportunity, telling his accusers defiantly, "Here, but for the grace of God, stand you."

To those who viewed the legislative corruption of the 1970s and 1980s as evidence of a systemic disorder, the scandal that broke in the House of Representatives in October 1991 seemed the final proof that corruption was no longer the exception in Congress, but had indeed become the norm. The "House Bank scandal," as it was known, originated—as had become common—in a partisan effort to embarrass the opposition. In this case, several Republican House freshmen raised questions about a number of Democratic colleagues who were revealed by a government audit to have written large numbers of bad checks on their accounts in the House of Representatives bank. Although the bipartisan House leadership acted swiftly to try to contain the scandal by obtaining passage of a resolution closing the House bank and calling for an ethics inquiry, neither the Republicans nor the media would let the issue alone. By the spring of 1992, the scandal had widened to include 325 current and former members of the House, including Speaker Thomas Foley, Republican Whip Newt Gingrich, and many other powerful members.

Although the House bank was a strictly inhouse venture, using no public funds, the public was outraged at the vision of legislators writing bad checks with impunity, having those checks honored by the bank (which covered thousands of such checks by using other House members' deposits, in a classic "shell game"), and suffering no penalty. Since 1992 was an election year, the fallout from the bank scandal threatened to produce a massive purge of incumbents, offenders and nonoffenders alike. Although there may have been other reasons operating as well, this threat led to a wave of retirement announcements by House members, including some of the most notorious check-bouncers. Meanwhile, with the House leadership resisting each escalation of media and public pressure to expose (and perhaps pun-

ish) those who had misused the bank, the Bush administration's Department of Justice entered the fray, appointing a special prosecutor to determine whether criminal violations had occurred.

Since all signs suggested that the Democrats would suffer far more than the Republicans from further publicity and prosecution of the bank scandal, it was obvious that partisan motives were partially behind the Justice Department initiative. Moreover, as many House members objected, the appointment of the special prosecutor constituted a possible violation of the separation of powers. Nonetheless, to a public grown contemptuous of legislative corruption and eager for full disclosure, investigation from the outside was a welcome prospect. Recognizing that fact, the House voted overwhelmingly to comply with the prosecutor's subpoena of all House bank records, rejecting the plea of Speaker Foley and others to block such an unconstitutional intrusion into the private affairs of legislators. By the end of 1992, with the Democrats again safely in control of both Congress and the White House, the investigations had come to little; all but twenty of the transgressors had been totally exonerated by letter from the special prosecutor, and the remainder—mostly already gone from Congress—seemed unlikely to be prosecuted further.

As the House bank investigation came to a close, two things were clear. First, it demonstrated that the American public had grown impatient with the long-standing reluctance of Congress to clean its own house. Although the House bank scandal was an instance where no public trust had been breached (since no funds other than the members' own funds had been involved), such a distinction no longer seemed to matter to outsiders. Second, the willingness of the public—and even the House members themselves—to equivocate on such important matters as separation of powers in their eagerness (finally) to get the scandal behind them in an election year—pointed to the likelihood that Congress would feel a need to give further attention to the issues of legislative ethics and corruption in the immediate future. The question remained, however, as to whether such renewed attention to these problems would appreciably change the established pattern of reluctance to police and refusal to define precisely what constituted behavior that did not "reflect creditably" on the legislative branch.

## CONCLUSION

The spate of legislative conflict-of-interest and corruption cases in the late 1980s and early 1990s revealed not only a continuity in the way legislators tended to handle the problem of corruption in their midst (that is, to avoid punishing any but the most flagrant wrongdoing) but also a new determination in the public and the media to do the necessary housecleaning and policing of legislative behavior if the legislators themselves failed to act.

While the lack of clarity in the definition of conflict of interest and other types of legislative corruption that has persisted over the years seems to have served to protect transgressors from punishment, in the House bank scandal the reverse seemed to be true: frustrated and disgusted by repeated examples of questionable ethical behavior by legislators and other public officials, American voters and the media appeared intent by the early 1990s on punishing any questionable behaviors, as an example to others. This point was effectively made by the prosecution during the hearings on Speaker Jim Wright's case. Defending the Speaker before the House Ethics Committee in 1989, his attorney quoted Oliver Wendell Holmes's dictum that "the very meaning of a [dividing] line in the law is that you intentionally may go as close to it as you can if you do not pass it." Not so, replied the prosecutor; foreshadowing the public outcry that greeted the bank scandal two years later, he argued that lawmakers should stay as far away from that line as possible to avoid even the suggestion of misconduct (quoted in Garment, pp. 238–239).

Even if Congress were to make a genuine effort to define carefully where the "line" between legal and illegal conduct lies, it may not be a simple task. As Senator Cranston stated in his rebuttal to the reprimand by the ethics committee in 1991, "The present system makes it virtually impossible . . . for a senator to avoid what some will assert is a conflict of interest. There is no Senate rule stating when you can and when you can't help a contributor. I don't see how one could be formulated" (*Congressional Quarterly Weekly Reports,* 23 November

1991). Whether or not Senator Cranston's comments were self-serving, there is truth to his statement. Senator Paul H. Douglas (D.-Ill.), who was much concerned about the problem of corruption in Congress, observed in his 1952 book *Ethics in Government* that sometimes even the most well-intentioned legislator is hard-pressed to make such distinctions, and may genuinely believe "that there is no causal connection between the favors he has received and the decisions which he makes" (p. 44).

Despite the considerable publicity given to instances of legislative corruption in the Reagan and Bush years—particularly situations of conflict of interest—there is little evidence to suggest that corruption has become more widespread than in the past. In fact, the effective investigative techniques of the media have presented a considerable deterrent to misbehavior by public officials. Although such media attention may in part be a response to a stronger public fascination for scandal in recent times, it is clear that Watergate heightened public sensitivity where the conduct of public officials is concerned and that the scandals of the late 1980s and early 1990s intensified that sensitivity (Garment, pp. 2, 6).

If scrutiny by the media affords one protection against the grossest excesses of legislative corruption, strengthened party discipline and, by extension, more energetic party competition can have a similar restraining effect. In the mid-1970s, empirical research by Neal Peirce suggested that political corruption occurred less frequently in those states with a high degree of party competition and thus greater accountability to the public (cited in Benson, p. 131). The partisan origins of such well-publicized scandals as that involving Speaker Wright and the House bank abusers underscores the effectiveness of the "partisan deterrent."

There is reason to hope, then, that in the future American legislatures will continue to try to improve their own ethical standards and will demonstrate greater willingness to place sanctions on those who violate them. At the state level, such developments may be further encouraged by the continuing movement to professionalize legislatures by increasing the pay of legislators, thereby attracting higher-quality individuals and reducing the temptations to seek outside compensation through

# LEGISLATURES AND CORRUPTION

unethical or illegal conduct. But, as already noted, it will continue to be difficult to distinguish precisely that which constitutes conflict of interest from that which constitutes legitimate representation of interests within the electorate.

A more fundamental obstacle to satisfying the public where the issue of legislative corruption is concerned lies in the ambitiousness of the American vision of politics. As Lord Bryce observed in 1888, "in America men [have been] inclined to apply an ideal standard, because she is a republic, professing to have made a new departure in politics, and setting before her a higher ideal than most European monarchies" (quoted in Louis Hacker, ed., *The American Commonwealth*, 1959, p. 229). In the end, such a vision may prove elusive. As Tocqueville pointed out, the forces underlying capitalism and democracy are to a degree internally inconsistent. In all likelihood, cycles of public concern will continue to force periodic housecleanings by legislatures, but it is unrealistic to believe that legislative corruption will ever be eliminated in American legislatures or in the political system as a whole.

## BIBLIOGRAPHY

**General Works**
The subject of American legislative corruption is most frequently treated in the context of general political corruption. Useful studies of this larger subject include GEORGE C. S. BENSON, with STEVEN A. MAARANEN and ALAN HESLOP, *Political Corruption in America* (Lexington, Mass., 1978); ABRAHAM S. EISENSTADT, ARI HOOGENBOOM, and HANS L. TREFOUSSE, eds., *Before Watergate: Problems of Corruption in American Society* (New York, 1979); and LARRY L. BERG, HARLAN HAHN, and JOHN R. SCHMIDHAUSER, *Corruption in the American Political System* (Morristown, N.J., 1976). An even broader work, which examines political corruption from ancient times through the 1980s, is JOHN T. NOONAN, JR., *Bribes* (New York, 1987). An informative treatment of state-level corruption is GEORGE AMICK, *The American Way of Graft: A Study of Corruption in State and Local Government, How It Happens, and What Can Be Done About It* (Princeton, N.J., 1976).

**The Early National Period**
Anticorruption as a revolutionary theme in America is analyzed in BERNARD BAILYN, *The Origins of American Politics* (New York, 1968). Although little scholarly attention has been paid to corruption in the first decades of the federal government, Noonan, cited above, presents a thorough discussion of the important Yazoo case. MARK W. SUMMERS, *The Plundering Generation: Corruption and the Crisis of the Union, 1849–1861* (New York, 1987), is an excellent study focusing on the magnitude and significance of corruption in Washington (Congress and presidency alike) and state legislatures during the critical decade before the Civil War.

**The Post–Civil War Era**
Especially valuable on corruption in the years after the Civil War is SUSAN M. THOMPSON, *The "Spider Web": Congress and Lobbying in the Age of Grant* (Ithaca, N.Y., 1985), an evenhanded treatment of both the good and bad side of legislative lobbies. A much more polemical treatment of corruption in this era is MATTHEW JOSEPHSON, *The Politicos: 1865–1896* (New York, 1938). MAURY KLEIN, *The Life and Legend of Jay Gould* (Baltimore, 1986), examines the life of one of the most notorious political "corrupters" in the period. An interesting, complementary view of American politics during the Gilded Age is provided by ROBERT KELLEY, *The Transatlantic Persuasion: The Liberal-Democratic Mind in the Age of Gladstone* (New York, 1969), which emphasizes opposition to corruption as a unifying political force in the period.

**The Progressive Era**
For the Progressive Era, when concern with corruption in government was a major political force, DAVID GRAHAM PHILLIPS's 1906 muckraking articles, later published as *The Treason of the Senate* (Chicago, 1964), edited by GEORGE E. MOWRY and JUDSON A. GRENIER, remain the

most useful source on congressional misdeeds. ROBERT C. BROOKS, *Corruption in American Politics and Life* (New York, 1910), is a useful and representative reformist study of the period, but it does not focus specifically on legislative corruption. H. R. WILSON, *Congress: Corruption and Compromise* (New York, 1951), picks up the story where Phillips leaves off, presenting detailed vignettes of congressional corruption in the years from 1913 to the early 1950s, and emphasizing that Congress very infrequently took action against those accused of corrupt behavior in the period.

## The Recent Period

Accurately reflecting the renewal of widespread public concern with political corruption, a spate of studies has appeared on the subject since the mid-1960s. DREW PEARSON and JACK ANDERSON, *The Case Against Congress* (New York, 1968), while concerned primarily with the case of Senator Dodd, presents a modern-day indictment of Congress as damning as Phillips's Progressive Era critique. Another informative work on the Dodd case is JAMES BOYD, *Above the Law* (New York, 1968), the author of which was one of the former staffers who "blew the whistle" on the senator. The influence-peddling scandal involving Bobby Baker is thoroughly described by BAKER, with LARRY L. KING, *Wheeling and Dealing: Confessions of a Capitol Hill Operator* (New York, 1978).

The issues of campaign financing, PACs, and conflict of interest have produced a rather sizable body of literature. Among the more useful studies of these subjects are ELIZABETH DREW, *Politics and Money: The New Road to Corruption* (New York, 1983); AMITAI ETZIONI, *Capital Corruption: The New Attack on American Democracy* (San Diego, Calif., 1984); BROOKS JACKSON, *Honest Graft* (1988; rev. ed., Washington, D.C., 1990); and MICHAEL J. MALBIN, ed., *Money and Politics in the United States: Financing Elections in the 1980s* (Chatham, N.J., 1984). On the 1980 Abscam episode, see MARTIN MAYER, *The Greatest-Ever Bank Robbery: The Collapse of the Savings and Loan Industry* (New York, 1990). An especially interesting, somewhat broader study of recent legislative and executive scandals is SUZANNE GARMENT, *Scandal: The Crisis of Mistrust in American Politics* (New York, 1991), which develops the theory that the contemporary focus on political behavior is the product of public intolerance with conventional politics, coupled with the efforts of sensationalist media.

SEE ALSO Legislatures and Impeachment; PACs and Congressional Decisions; AND Pressure Groups and Lobbies.

# CONTRIBUTORS

**Joel H. Silbey, *Editor in Chief.*** President White Professor of History, Cornell University. Author of *The Shrine of Party: Congressional Voting Behavior, 1841–1852; A Respectable Minority: The Democratic Party in the Civil War Era; The Partisan Imperative: The Dynamics of American Politics Before the Civil War;* and *The American Political Nation, 1838–1893.* Editor of *The Congress of the United States, 1789–1989,* 10 vols. in 23, a collection of the outstanding scholarly articles about the history of Congress. THE HISTORIOGRAPHY OF THE AMERICAN LEGISLATIVE SYSTEM

**Alan I. Abramowitz.** Professor of Political Science, Emory University. Coauthor of *Senate Elections* and author of articles on voting behavior and American congressional elections. ELECTIONS TO THE U.S. HOUSE OF REPRESENTATIVES

**Thomas G. Alexander.** Lemuel Hardison Redd, Jr., Professor of Western American History, Brigham Young University. Former president, Utah Academy of Sciences, Arts, and Letters. Author of *Things in Heaven and Earth: The Life and Times of Wilford Woodruff, A Mormon Prophet;* and *Mormonism in Transition: A History of the Latter-day Saints, 1890–1930.* STATE LEGISLATURES IN THE TWENTIETH CENTURY

**Howard W. Allen.** Professor of History, Southern Illinois University at Carbondale. Author of *Poindexter of Washington: A Study in Progressive Politics;* coeditor of *Illinois Elections, 1818–1990: Candidates and County Returns for President, Governor, Senate, and House of Representatives.* INSURGENCY AND THIRD PARTIES IN THE U.S. CONGRESS

**Eugene J. Alpert.** Associate Professor of Political Science, Texas Christian University. Former American Political Science Congressional Fellow. Author of "A Reconceptualization of Representational Role" and "Conventional Wisdom: A Television Viewer's Guide to the National Political Conventions." THE RESPONSIBILITY OF THE REPRESENTATIVE

**Glenn C. Altschuler.** Dean, School of Continuing Education and Summer Sessions, and Professor of American Studies, Cornell University. Author of five books, including *Race, Ethnicity, and Class in American Social Thought, 1865–1919* and *Andrew D. White—Educator, Historian, and Diplomat.* LEGISLATURES AND SOCIAL WELFARE POLICY

**R. Bruce Anderson.** Ph.D. candidate, Political Science Department, Rice University. Assistant editor, *Legislative Studies Section Newsletter,* American Political Science Association. POLITICAL PARTIES IN STATE LEGISLATURES

**Peri E. Arnold.** Professor of Government and International Studies, University of Notre Dame. Author of *Making the Managerial Presidency: Comprehensive Executive Reorganization, 1905–1980* and articles on the presidency, public administration, and American political development. LEGISLATURES AND EXECUTIVE REORGANIZATIONS

**Stanley Bach.** Senior Specialist in the Legislative Process, Congressional Research Service, Library of Congress. LEGISLATING: FLOOR AND CONFERENCE PROCEDURES IN CONGRESS

**Richard Allan Baker.** Historian of the United States Senate. Author of *Conservation Politics: The Senate Career of Clinton P. Anderson* and *The Senate of the United States: A Bicentennial History;* coeditor of *First Among Equals: Outstanding Senate Leaders of the Twentieth Century.* LEGISLATIVE POWER OVER APPOINTMENTS AND CONFIRMATIONS

**Gordon Morris Bakken.** Professor of History, California State University, Fullerton. Author of *The Development of Law on the Rocky Mountain Frontier; Rocky Mountain Constitution Making;* and *Practicing Law in Frontier California.* THE TERRITORIAL SYSTEM SINCE 1862

# CONTRIBUTORS

**Richard Franklin Bensel.** Professor of Government, Cornell University. Author of *Sectionalism and American Political Development, 1880–1980* and *Yankee Leviathan: The Origins of Central State Authority in America, 1859–1877.* CONGRESS, SECTIONALISM, AND PUBLIC-POLICY FORMATION SINCE 1870

**Jo Tice Bloom.** Lecturer in American history, Sierra College (Rocklin, Calif.); author of articles on the territorial delegate and frontier history. TERRITORIAL LEGISLATURES TO 1862

**Allan G. Bogue.** Frederick Jackson Turner Professor of History (Emeritus), University of Wisconsin, Madison. Author of *The Congressman's Civil War* and many other publications on American political and economic history. THE U.S. CONGRESS: THE ERA OF PARTY PATRONAGE AND SECTIONAL STRESS, 1829–1881

**David W. Brady.** Bowen H. and Janice Arthur McCoy Professor of Political Science, Business, and Environment and John M. Olin Faculty Fellow, 1988–1989, Graduate School of Business; and Professor of Political Science, Stanford University. Author of five books including *Critical Elections and Congressional Policy-Making* and *Congressional Voting in a Partisan Era: A Comparison of the McKinley House to the Modern House.* CONSTITUTIONAL AND POLITICAL CONSTRAINTS ON POLICY-MAKING: A HISTORICAL PERSPECTIVE

**Charles Spencer Bullock, III.** Richard B. Russell Professor of Political Science, University of Georgia. Former president, Southern Political Science Association. Coauthor of *Runoff Elections in the United States; The Georgia Political Almanac; Forest Resource Policy; Implementation of Civil Rights Policy;* and *Public Policy and Politics in America.* COMMITTEE SELECTION IN CONGRESS

**Ross E. Burkhart.** Ph.D. candidate, Department of Political Science, University of Iowa. LEGISLATIVE-EXECUTIVE RELATIONS

**Bruce Edward Cain.** Professor of Political Science and Associate Director of the Institute of Governmental Studies, University of California, Berkeley. Author of *Reapportionment Puzzle* and coauthor of *Congressional Redistricting* and *Personal Vote: Constituency Service and Electoral Independence.* LEGISLATIVE REDISTRICTING

**Ballard C. Campbell.** Professor of History, Northeastern University, Boston. Author of *Representative Democracy* and *The Growth of American Government.* FEDERALISM AND AMERICAN LEGISLATURES

**David T. Canon.** Assistant Professor of Political Science, University of Wisconsin, Madison. Author of *Actors, Athletes and Astronauts: Political Amateurs in the U.S. Congress* and articles on political careers, congressional elections, and party leadership in Congress. THE SOCIAL BASES OF LEGISLATIVE RECRUITMENT

**Aage R. Clausen.** Professor of Political Science, Ohio State University. Former president, Social Science History Association. Author of *How Congressmen Decide: A Policy Focus* and articles on roll-call research and methodology. MEASURING LEGISLATIVE BEHAVIOR

**Jerome M. Clubb.** Senior Research Scientist and Professor of History, University of Michigan. THE HISTORICAL LEGISLATIVE CAREER

**John F. Cogan.** Senior Fellow, Hoover Institution. Author of *The Great Budget Puzzle.* THE CONGRESSIONAL BUDGET PROCESS AND FEDERAL BUDGET DEFICIT

**Melissa P. Collie.** Associate Professor of Government, University of Texas at Austin. Book Review Editor, *American Political Science Review.* Former editorial board member, *American Journal of Political Science, Legislative Studies Quarterly,* and *American Politics Quarterly.* LEGISLATIVE STRUCTURE AND ITS EFFECTS

**Joseph Cooper.** Provost and Professor of Political Science, Johns Hopkins University. Author of several works on the development of the committee system. THE ROLE OF CONGRESSIONAL PARTIES

**Cary R. Covington.** Associate Professor of Political Science, University of Iowa. Coauthor of *The Coalitional Presidency* (with Lester Seligman). Author of articles regarding how presidents build coalitions in Congress and how presidents try to shape Congress's legislative agenda. LEGISLATIVE-EXECUTIVE RELATIONS

**Gary W. Cox.** Professor of Political Science, University of California, San Diego. Author of *The Efficient Secret: The Cabinet and the Development of Political Parties in Victorian En-*

*gland*; coauthor of *Legislative Leviathan: Party Government in the House.* PARTY COHERENCE ON ROLL-CALL VOTES IN THE U.S. HOUSE OF REPRESENTATIVES

**Heinz Eulau.** William B. Munro Professor of Political Science Emeritus, Stanford University. Former president, American Political Science Association. Associate Director, Inter-University Consortium for Political and Social Research. Author of *The Legislative System; The Behavioral Persuasion in Congress; Labyrinths of Democracy;* and *Politics, Self, and Society.* LEGISLATIVE NORMS

**Phyllis F. Field.** Associate Professor of History, Ohio University. Author of *The Politics of Race in New York: The Struggle for Black Suffrage in the Civil War Era.* LEGISLATURES AND SLAVERY

**Morris P. Fiorina.** Professor of Government, Harvard University. Author of numerous works on Congress and elections, including *Representatives, Roll Calls, and Constituents; Retrospective Voting in American National Elections; Congress: Keystone of the Washington Establishment;* and (with Bruce Cain and John Ferejohn) *Personal Vote: Constituency Service and Electoral Independence.* LEGISLATIVE INCUMBENCY AND INSULATION

**Louis Fisher.** Senior Specialist in Separation of Powers, Congressional Research Service, Library of Congress. Author of *American Constitutional Law;* and *Constitutional Conflicts Between Congress and the President.* Coeditor of the *Encyclopedia of the American Presidency.* THE LEGISLATIVE VETO

**Linda L. Fowler.** Professor of Political Science, Syracuse University. Author of *Political Ambition: Who Decides to Run for Congress; Candidates, Congress, and the American Democracy;* and articles on congressional politics. CONSTITUENCIES

**Wayne L. Francis.** Professor of Political Science, University of Florida. Author of *Legislative Issues in the Fifty States; The Legislative Committee Game; American Politics: Analysis of Choice;* and articles on state legislatures. FLOOR PROCEDURES AND CONFERENCE COMMITTEES IN STATE LEGISLATURES

**Richard M. Fried.** Professor of History, University of Illinois, Chicago. Author of *Men Against McCarthy* and *Nightmare in Red: The McCarthy Era in Perspective.* EXECUTIVE PRIVILEGE

**Christian G. Fritz.** Associate Professor of Law, University of New Mexico School of Law. Author of *Federal Justice in California: The Court of Ogden Hoffman, 1851–1891.* CONSTITUTIONAL CONVENTIONS

**Joyce Gelb.** Professor of Political Science, City College of New York and Graduate Center, CUNY. Director, Program in Public Policy, City College of New York. Author of *Women and Public Policies* and *Feminism and Politics* and articles on urban and feminist politics and policy. WOMEN IN LEGISLATURES

**Anthony Gierzynski.** Assistant Professor of Political Science, University of Vermont. Author of *Legislative Party Campaign Committees in the American States* and coauthor of articles on campaign finance in state legislative elections. ELECTIONS TO THE STATE LEGISLATURES

**Lori D. Ginzberg.** Associate Professor of History and Women's Studies, Penn State University. Author of *Women and the Work of Benevolence: Morality, Politics, and Class in the Nineteenth-Century United States.* LEGISLATURES AND GENDER ISSUES

**James J. Gosling.** Professor of Political Science and Dean of Continuing Education, University of Utah. Author of *Budgetary Politics in American Governments; Politics, Policy, and Management in the American States* (with Dennis L. Dresang); and articles on state politics and public budgeting. BUDGET PROCEDURES AND EXECUTIVE REVIEW IN STATE LEGISLATURES

**Hugh Davis Graham.** Holland McTyeire Professor of American History, Vanderbilt University. Author of *Civil Rights and the Presidency* and *The Civil Rights Era.* LEGISLATURES AND CIVIL RIGHTS

**Virginia Gray.** Professor of Political Science, University of Minnesota, Minneapolis. Coauthor of *American States and Cities; Feminism and the New Right;* and *The Organizational Politics of Criminal Justice.* Author of articles on state politics, policy innovation, and public policy. STATE LEGISLATURES AND POLICY INNOVATORS

# CONTRIBUTORS

**Jack P. Greene.** Andrew W. Mellon Professor in the Humanities, Johns Hopkins University. Author of *Peripheries and Center: Constitutional Development in the Extended Polities of the British Empire and the United States, 1607–1788; All Men Are Created Equal: Some Reflections on the Character of the American Revolution;* and *The Quest for Power: The Lower Houses of Assembly in the Southern Royal Colonies, 1689–1776.* COLONIAL ASSEMBLIES

**David Roy Hall.** Ph.D. candidate, University of California, Santa Barbara. STATE LEGISLATURES IN THE TWENTIETH CENTURY

**Richard L. Hall.** Associate Professor of Political Science and Public Policy Studies, University of Michigan. Former American Political Science Association Congressional Fellow. Author of *Participation in Congress.* AGENDA SETTING, ACTORS, AND ALIGNMENTS IN CONGRESSIONAL COMMITTEES

**Keith E. Hamm.** Associate Professor of Political Science, Rice University. Editor of *Legislative Studies Section Newsletter,* American Political Science Association. Author of articles on state legislatures. COMMITTEES IN STATE LEGISLATURES and POLITICAL PARTIES IN STATE LEGISLATURES

**Susan Webb Hammond.** Professor of Political Science, American University. Editor of *Congress & the Presidency: A Journal of Capital Studies.* Coauthor of *Congressional Staffs: The Invisible Force in American Lawmaking* and articles on informal caucuses and congressional staffs, organization, change, and reform. CONGRESSIONAL STAFFS

**Ronald D. Hedlund.** Vice Provost for Research and Professor of Political Science, University of Rhode Island. Author of *The Job of the Wisconsin Legislator, Representatives and Represented* and articles on state legislatures, especially legislative organization and structure. COMMITTEES IN STATE LEGISLATURES and POLITICAL PARTIES IN STATE LEGISLATURES

**John R. Hibbing.** Professor and Chair, Department of Political Science, University of Nebraska, Lincoln. Former coeditor of *American Politics Quarterly* and *Legislative Studies Quarterly.* Author of several books and articles on legislatures and legislative careers. MODERN LEGISLATIVE CAREERS

**Barbara Hinckley.** Professor of Political Science, Purdue University. Election consultant, ABC News. Author of *Stability and Change in Congress; Congressional Elections;* and *The Symbolic Presidency.* ELECTIONS TO THE U.S. SENATE

**Peter Charles Hoffer.** Research Professor of History and Adjunct Professor of Law, University of Georgia. LEGISLATURES AND IMPEACHMENT

**Thomas R. Huffman.** Adjunct Professor of History, St. John's University/College of St. Benedict, Minnesota. Author of *Protectors of the Land and Water: The Origins and Rise of Environmentalism in Wisconsin, 1961–1968.* LEGISLATURES AND THE ENVIRONMENT

**Patricia A. Hurley.** Associate Professor of Political Science, Texas A&M University. Author of articles on partisanship, representation, and realignment in Congress. ELECTORAL REALIGNMENTS

**Barry D. Karl.** Norman and Edna Freehling Professor of History, University of Chicago. Author of *The Uneasy State: The United States from 1915–1945; Charles E. Merriam and the Study of Politics;* and *Executive Reorganization and Reform in the New Deal.* LEGISLATURES AND BUREAUCRACY

**Clayton R. Koppes.** Professor of History, Oberlin College. Author of *Hollywood Goes to War: How Politics, Profits, and Propaganda Shaped World War II Movies* (with Gregory D. Black) and *JPL and the American Space Program: A History of the Jet Propulsion Laboratory.* LEGISLATURES AND THE MEDIA

**Samuel Krislov.** Professor of Political Science, University of Minnesota, Minneapolis. Former president, Law in Society. Author of *The Supreme Court and American Politics* and coauthor of *American Constitutional Law* (with Malcolm Feeley) and *Representative Bureaucracy* (with David Rosenblum). LEGISLATURES AND THE JUDICIARY

**Marc W. Kruman.** Associate Professor of History, Wayne State University, Detroit. Author of *Parties and Politics in North Carolina, 1836–1865.* LEGISLATURES AND POLITICAL RIGHTS

# CONTRIBUTORS

**Walter LaFeber.** Noll Professor of American History, Cornell University. Author of *The American Age, 1750 to the Present; America, Russia, and the Cold War, 1945–1992; Inevitable Revolutions: The United States in Central America;* and *The American Search for Opportunity, 1865–1913.* CONGRESS, THE EXECUTIVE, AND FOREIGN POLICY

**Burdett A. Loomis.** Professor of Political Science, University of Kansas. Directed the Congressional Management Project. Author of *The New American Politician;* coauthor of *Setting Course: A Congressional Management Guide;* and coeditor of *Interest Group Politics.* THE MOTIVATIONS OF LEGISLATORS

**M. Philip Lucas.** Associate Professor of History, Cornell College. Author of articles on antebellum southern politics. LEGISLATIVE RECORDS AND PUBLICATIONS

**Mathew D. McCubbins.** Professor of Political Science, University of California, San Diego. Coauthor of *Legislative Leviathan: Party Government in the House* and *The Logic of Delegation: Congressional Parties and the Appropriations Process.* PARTY COHERENCE ON ROLL-CALL VOTES IN THE U.S. HOUSE OF REPRESENTATIVES

**Gary J. McKissick.** Ph.D. candidate, Department of Political Science, University of Michigan. AGENDA SETTING, ACTORS, AND ALIGNMENTS IN CONGRESSIONAL COMMITTEES

**L. Sandy Maisel.** Charles A. Dana Professor of American Democratic Institutions, Colby College. Author of *From Obscurity to Oblivion: Running in the Congressional Primary;* and editor of *Political Parties and Elections in the United States: An Encyclopedia.* LEGISLATIVE WORK LOAD

**Michael J. Malbin.** Professor of Political Science, State University of New York, Albany. Director, Center for Legislative Studies, Rockefeller Institute of Government, SUNY. Member, National Council on the Humanities. Author of *Unelected Representatives;* editor of *Money and Politics in the U.S.;* and coeditor of *Limiting Legislative Terms.* LEGISLATIVE ETHICS

**Jack H. Maskell.** Legislative Attorney, American Law Division, Congressional Research Service, Library of Congress. Instructor, Graduate School, Catholic University, Washington, D.C. RECALL AND EXPULSION OF LEGISLATORS

**David R. Mayhew.** Alfred Cowles Professor of Government, Yale University. Author of *Party Loyalty Among Congressmen; Congress: The Electoral Connection; Placing Parties in American Politics;* and *Divided We Govern.* PARTIES, ELECTIONS, MOODS, AND LAWMAKING SURGES

**Sarah McCally Morehouse.** Professor Emeritus of Political Science, University of Connecticut. Author of *State Politics, Parties, and Policy* and articles and chapters on governors and their political conditions. EXECUTIVE LEADERSHIP AND PARTY ORGANIZATION IN STATE LEGISLATURES

**Milton D. Morris.** Joint Center for Political and Economic Studies. Author of *Blacks and the Nineteen Eighty-eight Republican National Convention; 1985 Immigration: The Beleaguered Bureacracy;* and coauthor of (with Albert Mayio) *Illegal Immigration.* AFRICAN AMERICAN LEGISLATORS

**Edward Muir.** Bradley Fellow and Ph.D. candidate, Department of Politics, New York University. Adjunct Professor, George Washington University. ELECTIONS TO THE U.S. SENATE

**Garrison Nelson.** Professor of Political Science, University of Vermont. Editor of many works including *Encyclopedia of the U.S. Congress; Leaders of the American Congress, 1789–1993; Encyclopedia of American Political History.* THE MODERNIZING CONGRESS, 1870–1930

**Walter J. Oleszek.** Senior Specialist in the Legislative Process, Congressional Research Service, Library of Congress. THE CONGRESSIONAL BUDGET PROCESS

**Peter S. Onuf.** Professor of History, University of Virginia. Author of *The Origins of the Federal Republic: Jurisdictional Controversies in the United States, 1775–1787* and *Statehood and Union: A History of the Northwest Ordinance.* Editor of *The New American Nation, 1775–1820,* 12 vols. THE ORIGINS AND DEVELOPMENT OF THE STATE LEGISLATURES

**Bruce I. Oppenheimer.** Professor of Political Science, Vanderbilt University. Author of *Oil and the Congressional Process;* primary contributor and editor of *A History of the Committee on Rules;* and coeditor of *Congress Reconsidered.* THE RULES COMMITTEE: THE HOUSE TRAFFIC COP

**Glenn R. Parker.** Distinguished Research Professor, Florida State University. John Adams Chair in American Studies (the Netherlands) by the Fulbright Scholar Program. Author of *Institutional Change, Discretion, and the Making of Modern Congress: An Economic Interpretation; Characteristics of Congress; Homeward Bound: Explaining Changes in Congressional Behavior;* and coauthor of *Factions in House Committees.* THE FRAGMENTATION OF POWER WITHIN CONGRESSIONAL COMMITTEES

**Samuel C. Patterson.** Professor of Political Science, Ohio State University. Former managing editor, *American Political Science Review.* Coauthor of *The Legislative Process in the United States, Representatives and Represented* and *Comparing Legislatures;* coeditor of *Handbook of Legislative Research.* REPRESENTATION

**Timothy S. Prinz.** Assistant Professor of Government and Foreign Affairs, University of Virginia. Author of studies of congressional careers and the mass media in congressional elections. LEGISLATIVE INCUMBENCY AND INSULATION

**Jack N. Rakove.** Professor of History, Stanford University. Author of *The Beginnings of National Politics: An Interpretive History of the Continental Congress* and *James Madison and the Creation of the American Republic;* editor of *Interpreting the Constitution: The Debate over Original Intent.* THE ORIGINS OF CONGRESS

**Gary W. Reichard.** Professor and Chair of History, Florida Atlantic University. Author of *The Reaffirmation of Republicanism: Eisenhower and the Eighty-third Congress* and *Politics as Usual: The Age of Truman and Eisenhower.* Coeditor of *Reshaping America; American Choices;* and *American Issues.* LEGISLATURES AND CORRUPTION FROM COLONIAL TIMES TO THE PRESENT

**Leroy N. Rieselbach.** Professor of Political Science, Indiana University at Bloomington. Author of *The Roots of Isolationism; Congressional Politics;* and *Congressional Reform.* Editor of *The Congressional System: Notes and Readings* and *Legislative Reform: The Policy Impact.* Coeditor of *Policy Change in Congress.* CONGRESSIONAL REFORM

**Norman K. Risjord.** Professor of History, University of Wisconsin, Madison. Author of *The Old Republicans: Southern Conservatism in the Age of Jefferson and Chesapeake Politics, 1780–1800.* CONGRESS IN THE FEDERALIST-REPUBLICAN ERA, 1789–1828

**Donald A. Ritchie.** Associate Historian, United States Senate. Author of *Press Gallery: Congress and the Washington Correspondents;* editor of the *Executive Sessions of the Senate Foreign Relations Committee* (Historical Series). MEDIA COVERAGE OF LEGISLATURES

**David W. Rohde.** University Distinguished Professor of Political Science, Michigan State University. Former editor, *American Journal of Political Science* and former chair, Legislative Studies Section, American Political Science Association. Author of *Parties and Leaders in the Postreform House* and coauthor of *Change and Continuity in the 1992 Elections.* THE CONTEMPORARY CONGRESS, 1930–1992

**Alan Rosenthal.** Professor of Political Science, Eagleton Institute of Politics, Rutgers University. Consultant for legislatures in thirty-five states. Author of *Legislative Life, Governors, and Legislatures* and *The Third House: Lobbyists and Lobbying in the States.* REFORM IN STATE LEGISLATURES

**Catherine E. Rudder.** Executive Director of the American Political Science Association in Washington, D.C. Worked for two members of the House Committee on Ways and Means. Author of articles on Congress and on tax-policy making. THE HOUSE COMMITTEE ON WAYS AND MEANS

**Paul S. Rundquist.** Specialist in Congressional Operations and Procedure, Congressional Research Service, Library of Congress. Adjunct Professor of Government, American University and Catholic University of America. CONSTITUTIONAL REQUIREMENTS FOR LEGISLATIVE SERVICE

**Harry N. Scheiber.** Stefan Risenfeld Professor of Law and History, University of California, Berkeley. Author of *Ohio Canal Era: A Case Study of Government and the Economy; The Wilson Administration and Civil Liberties;*

# CONTRIBUTORS

*American Economic History* (with H. Faulkner and H. Vatter); and *American Law and the Constitutional Order* (with L. Friedman), as well as more than one hundred articles related to legal history, economic history, and law. LEGISLATURES AND AMERICAN ECONOMIC DEVELOPMENT

**William G. Shade.** Professor of History, Lehigh University. Author of *Banks or No Banks: The Money Issue in Western Politics, 1832–1865* and well as other books and articles on political and social history. AMERICAN STATE LEGISLATURES IN THE NINETEENTH CENTURY

**Barbara Sinclair.** Professor of Political Science, University of California, Riverside. Author of *Congressional Realignment; Majority Leadership in the U.S. House;* and *Transformation of the U.S. Senate.* EXECUTIVE LEADERSHIP AND PARTY ORGANIZATION IN CONGRESS

**Steven S. Smith.** Professor of Political Science, University of Minnesota. Associate staff member, Brookings Institution. Coauthor of *Congress: Managing Uncertainty* and *Call to Order: Floor Politics in the House and Senate.* THE CONGRESSIONAL COMMITTEE SYSTEM

**Robert J. Spitzer.** Professor of Political Science, State University of New York, Cortland. Author of *The Presidency and Public Policy; The Right to Life Movement and Third Party Politics; The Presidential Veto;* and *President and Congress;* editor of *Media and Public Policy.* THE EXECUTIVE VETO

**Charles Stewart III.** Associate Professor of Political Science and MacVicar Faculty Fellow at the Massachusetts Institute of Technology. Author of *Budget Reform Politics: The Design of the Appropriations Process in the House of Representatives, 1865–1921* and numerous articles on congressional history, budgetary and tax policy, and congressional elections in *American Journal of Political Science, Journal of Politics* and other journals and edited collections. CONGRESSIONAL APPROPRIATIONS COMMITTEES

**Duane Tananbaum.** Associate Professor of History, Lehman College, City University of New York. Author of *The Bricker Amendment Controversy: A Test of Eisenhower's Political Leadership* and articles on the War Power Resolution and congressional-presidential relations in foreign affairs. CONGRESS, THE EXECUTIVE, AND WAR POWERS

**Jon C. Teaford.** Professor of History, Purdue University. Author of *The Unheralded Triumph: City Government in America, 1870–1900* and *The Rough Road to Renaissance: Urban Revitalization in America, 1940–1985.* LOCAL LEGISLATIVE INSTITUTIONS

**Athan G. Theoharis.** Professor of History, Marquette University, specializing in federal surveillance policy and executive-legislative relations. Author of *The Boss,* a biography of J. Edgar Hoover, and *Spying on Americans,* a survey of federal surveillance policy from 1936 to 1978. LEGISLATURES AND CIVIL LIBERTIES

**Gregory S. Thielemann.** Professor of Political Economy, University of Texas, Dallas. Director, Texas Legislative Surveys. Author of articles on Texas politics and legislative decision-making. STATE LEGISLATIVE SUPPORT STAFFS AND ADMINISTRATION

**John T. Tierney.** Associate Professor of Political Science, Boston College. Author of *Organized Interests and American Democracy* and other books and articles on American politics, government organization, and public policy. PRESSURE GROUPS AND LOBBIES

**Philip R. VanderMeer.** Associate Professor of History, Arizona State University. Author of *The Hoosier Politician: Officeholding and Political Culture in Indiana, 1826–1920;* coeditor of *Belief and Behavior: Essays in the New Religious History.* CONGRESS AND OTHER LEGISLATURES

**Daniel S. Ward.** Assistant Professor of Political Science, Rice University. Author of articles in *Legislative Studies Quarterly, Comparative Politics,* and other political science journals. PACs AND CONGRESSIONAL DECISIONS

**William F. West.** Associate Professor of Political Science, Texas A&M University. Author of *Administrative Rulemaking: Politics and Processes.* CONGRESSIONAL OVERSIGHT

**Rick K. Wilson.** Associate Professor of Political Science, Rice University. Specialist in the usage of formal models and historical data to understand legislative institutions. THE ROLE OF CONGRESSIONAL PARTIES

# INDEX

# INDEX

Arizona House of Representatives, committee system, decision-making role, 672

Arizona Progressive party, 272

Arizona (territory)
capital location battle, 276–277
lawmaking and, 271
mining taxation and, 272
partisan politics in, 268–269

Arkansas
Reconstruction era, impeachments in, 1629
state election districts in, 439
state legislative retirees in, 507

Arkansas legislature
executive-budget development, 768
reforms, 841

Arkansas (territory), slavery question and, 1226

Armey, Dick, 419

Arms Export Control Act (1974), legislative-veto provision, 1509

Armstrong, John S., 277

Armstrong, William W., 217

Army Corps of Engineers, General Survey Act and, 1199

Army-McCarthy hearings, 1465
television coverage of, 1527, 1530

Arnold, Douglas, *The Logic of Congressional Action*, 582

Arnold, R. Douglas, 1009

Arrears of Pensions Act (1879), 1261, 1366

Arrington, Russell, 839

Arthur, Chester Alan
civil service reform and, 1590–1591
separation of powers doctrine, 1406
veto use, 1499

Articles of Confederation
on appointment powers, 1607
Continental Congress under, 55–58, 72
on executive power, 1399, 1588
failure to amend, 191
foreign policy provisions, 1439
on legislative representation, 9–10
Madison on, 61
promoting centralized government, 873
protections for naturalized citizens, 305
qualification for delegates, 304
recall provisions, 555
state constitutionalism and, 176, 178–179
on terms of service, 487

Ash, Roy, 1483, 1601

Ash Council, 1483

Asher, Herbert, 592

Asian-American legislators, in U.S. Congress, 317, 500

Aspin, Lee, on federal budget, 735

Aspinall, Wayne N., 1322
on House Interior Committee, 504

Assemblies, colonial. *See* Colonial assemblies

Associated Press, established, 1524

Association of Medical Superintendents of the Insane, 1258

Astor, John Jacob, 1641

Astor, Nancy, Lady, 316

Asylums, antebellum era, 1258

*Atkins* v. *United States* (1977), 1510

*Atlanta Daily World, The,* 1528

Atlantic Ocean, British control of, in Jeffersonian era, 1127

*At the Margins. See* Edwards, George

Attorney general, U.S., authority to suspend deportations, 1511

Auditor's office, 805

Austin-Boston connection, 333

Australian ballot, in party power reduction, 492

Authorization bills
appropriations bills and, 734–735
types of, 736–737

Autobiographies, as historiography, 281

Automobile ownership
1920s, 220
1940s, 228

Autonomous committees model, 643
mid-twentieth century, 648
1920s, 648

AWSA. *See* American Woman Suffrage Association

Axelrod, Robert, 586

Bach, Stanley, 1063

"Backdoor spending," 1027
controls on, 740
defined, 737

*Badham* v. *Eu* (1989), 390

Baer, George, 1555

Bailey, Stephen K., *Congress Makes a Law,* 285–286

Baker, Bobby, 1161, 1647

Baker, Edward, 313

Baker, James A., III, 1517

Baker, Ross, 590

Baker Accord, 1517

*Baker* v. *Carr* (1962), 16, 52, 164, 227, 388, 438, 802, 838, 1416, 1574
legal constituency definition and, 402

Balanced Budget and Emergency Deficit Control Act (1985), 423, 741–743, 827, 1514
amendments, 1029

Balanced-budget requirements, interstate variation, 779

Balance of power
over executive branch, 1474
states, 849

Ballinger, Richard A., Pinchot and, 1135–1136

Bancroft, Griffing, 1527

Bankhead, William B., 940, 1055

Banking system
antebellum, 1200, 1204, 1642
Civil War era, 125, 1205
federal bureaucracy and, 1595
Federalist-Republican era, 196
Populist proposal on, 1132
Progressive Era, 1208

territorial chartering, 252
*See also* Savings-and-loan industry

Bank laws, publication of, 864

Bank of the United States
bill vetoes, 1491–1493, 1495
controversy over establishment of, 75, 1198
rechartering of
Brent and, 103
vetoed, 890
Supreme Court cases, 1158
D. Webster and, 1641
*See also* Second Bank of the United States

Bank of the United States, Second. *See* Second Bank of the United States

Bankruptcy, proposed federal legislation on, 96

Banks, Nathaniel P., as Speaker of U.S. House, 1131

Banner, James, Jr., 198

Barbour, James, 100

Barbour, Phillip Pendleton, 102

Barden, Graham, vs. L. B. Johnson, 1005

Barkley, Alben, 1409

Barnard, George G., 1630

Barnard, Henry, dismissed, 1259

Baron, David, 596

*Barron* v. *Mayor and City Council of Baltimore* (1833), 1536

Base budget reallocation, 767

Bashford, Coles, 271, 278

"Bastardy" laws, colonial Virginia, 1381

*Bas* v. *Tingy* (1800), 1423

Bateman, Ray, 840

Battin, James, 313

Bayard, James A., 94, 96

Bayh, Birch, 477

Beckley, John, 95

Beeman, Richard R., 197

Beggs, James M., 1515

Behavior
definition, 581
vs. structure, 572, 581–582

Behavioral theory
legislative historiography and, 285–291
legislators' motivations and, 323

Belgian legislative norms, 593

Belknap, William W., 558, 1630

Bell, Griffin, 1509–1510

Bell, Rudolph, 1224

Bennett Law (Wisc.), 1262

Bensel, Richard, 1205

Benson, Egbert, 183

Benson, Lee, 203

Benton, Thomas Hart, 105, 109, 122, 1442, 1495, 1611, 1641

Berger, Victor L., 311, 1157, 1282, 1573

Berkowitz, Edward, 1270

Berkshire County (Mass.), Revolutionary-era constitutionalism in, 182

Bernard, Francis, 177

Berryman, Clifford, 1525

Berryman, Jim, 1525

# INDEX

# INDEX

Gramm-Rudman-Hollings
amendment and, 742
legislation arising from, 741
legislative-executive relations
and, 1414
political gridlock over, 619
state tax revolts and, 1212
reduction techniques, 827
World War I era, 734
Budget deficit, state
antebellum constitution-making
and, 48, 1203
Hamilton's proposals on, 1198
1920s, 220–221, 1209–1210
Budget Enforcement Act (1990),
739, 743–744
Budget office, state
budget development role, 767–768
size of staff and, 768
controlling budget execution,
771
transferring budget funds, 771
veto-deliberation process, 770
Bullock, Charles S., III, 995–996
Bundling (PAC strategy), 1098,
1102
Bundy, McGeorge, 1483
Bureaucracy.
early twentieth century, 1592–1597
expansion during the Great Depression, 1369
historical background, 1587–1590
1933–1961, 1597–1601
policy innovations and, 1355
post-1961, 1601–1603
post–Civil War, 1590–1592
scandal and, 1590
*See also* Civil service; Executive
branch
Bureaucrat, civil servant distinguished from, 1587
Bureau of Efficiency, 1477
Bureau of Immigration and Naturalization, creation of, 145
Bureau of Indian Affairs, 1589
Bureau of Land Management
(BLM), appropriations, 1021
Bureau of the Budget (BOB)
established, 613, 734
Kennedy-Johnson era, 614
program budgeting, 776
Burger, Warren
*Chadha* opinion, 760
civil rights rulings, 1310
on executive privilege, 1458
"junior Supreme Court" concept
and, 1576
legislative-veto rulings, 1511
on obscenity, 1542
U.S. Supreme Court service of,
1583–1584
women's rights and, 1389
Burke, Aedanus, 95
Burke, Edmund
on legislators' roles, 420
on representatives' roles, 4
on virtual representation, 5
Burleigh, Walter A., 278
Burnett, Henry C., expelled from
House, 552

Burns, Hugh, 1291
Burns, Lucy, 1247
Burr conspiracy, executive privilege
issues, 1459
Burton, Joseph R., 1646
*Burton* v. *United States* (1906), 555
Bush, George
appointments by, 1616
Budget Enforcement Act (1990)
and, 743–744
Gulf War, 1435, 1452
humanitarian aid to Contras, 1517
in 1988 election, 454–455, 461–462
in 1992 election, 451
Noriega capture, 826
Panamanian invasion, 1435–1436
U.S. Congress relations with, 1414
veto use, 1501
Bush administration
budget deficit proposal of,
463–464
civil rights policy, 1311
corruption under, 1652
deregulation under, 85, 1211
environmental policy, 1328
House Bank scandal and, 1651
nominations by, 1605
state tax revolts under, 1212
Tower nomination and, 1617
women's rights and, 1390
Businesses, territorial chartering of,
252
Business-Industry Political Action
Committee, 1094
Business interests. *See* Commercial
interests
Businessmen, in state legislatures,
in twentieth century, 498
Business PACs. *See* Corporate PACs
Business Roundtable, 1113
Busing, U.S. Supreme Court and,
1584
Butler, Andrew Pickens, 110
Butler, David, 1630
Butler, Marion, Populist party and,
1132
Butler, Pierce, 1421, 1490
Butler, Roderick, 1159
Buzzard, A. P., 1632
Byrd, Harry, 476, 1479
amendment to Reorganization Act,
1480
Byrd, Robert C., 1164
Democratic party organs and, 662

Cabinet, presidential, 1598
history of, 1588–1589
reorganization of departments,
1484
Cabinet officers
Jefferson administration, 98
judiciaries and, 1570
selection of, 1577
twentieth century, 1616
Washington era, 1609
Cable Communications Policy Act
(1984), 1542
Cable-news broadcasting, 1531
Cable Satellite Public Affairs Network, 1530

U.S. congressional proceedings,
824
Calendaring, of state legislation,
724–725
Calendar Wednesday, adoption of,
142
Calhoun, John C., 1424, 1442
on "concurrent majority," 215
as House Foreign Affairs Committee member, 101
property rights, resolutions of,
1229
slavery question and, 1226
on Texas annexation, 1228, 1443
Van Buren ambassadorial nomination and, 1611
as vice president, 105
vs. Whigs, 1230
California
Compromise of 1850 on, 1129
divorce legislation and, 1350
environmental policy, 1327–
1328
First Amendment and, 1539
Great Depression era, 222
labor legislation of, 218–219,
226
late twentieth century
divorce law in, 1389
social welfare legislation in,
1274
legislation on obscenity, 1535
PAC expenditures, 632
political innovation diffusion and,
1356
post–World War II era, party caucuses in, 954
Progressive Era, 217–218, 1646
property taxes in, 85, 229
racist legislation in, 219
recall provisions, 554
World War II era, 226
California Board of Fish Commissioners, 1316
California constitutional convention
(1849), 44
California Legislative Counsel
legal opinions on bills, 867
reform, 805
California legislature
bill files, 864
campaigns
competitiveness of, 443
financial expenditures, 446
Republican contributions to, 439
espionage and sedition acts, 1282,
1291
Fact-Finding Committee on Un-
American Activities, 1286, 1291
Massachusetts General Court and,
1274
New Hampshire legislature and,
1151
news coverage of, 1527
policy innovations and, 1355
reform, 837
staffing system, 805–806
term limitations, 523
term of office, 442, 444, 506
turnover in, 507

# INDEX

California legislature. Assembly, 498, 501
  chief clerk, 805
  Office of Information Services, 806
  reforms, 839
  Rules Committee, 806
California legislature. Senate, 968
  committee system, decision-making role, 672
  districts, 436
  secretary, 805
California Office of the Legislative Analyst, 805
California Supreme Court, Reuf and, 218
Cambodia, American forces in, 1433
Cameron, Simon, 209, 952
Caminetti, Anthony, 1317
Campaign committees, in state legislative elections, 446–447
Campaign contributions
  bribery and, 1640
  ethical issues, 852
  gubernatorial races, 622–623
  incumbency advantage and, 521–522
  to incumbent U.S. legislators, 542
  judiciary and, 1574
  law of diminishing returns, 521–522
  by PACs, 1091–1104
  party funding in state elections, 631–632
  political access and, 522
  by pressure groups, 1110–1112
  public, 523
  reforms, 523, 825, 831, 1163
  regulation of, 447
    Ford administration, 889, 1649
    Progressive Era, 1646
    Taft administration, 887
    to state legislative candidates, 439, 446, 978
    to third parties, 1125
    U.S. Congress, 520–522
    sources of, 521t
    U.S. House candidates, 458–459, 461
    U.S. Senate candidates, 460
  See also Fund-raising
Campaign contributions, corporate. See Corporate political campaign contributions
Campaigning. See Electioneering
Campaign spending
  excessive, 309
  incumbents vs. challengers, 521–522
  limitations on, 523
  1974–1988, 521
  Senate elections, 478
  state legislative seats, 631–632
  See also Fund-raising
Campbell, Angus, 461
Campbell, Ballard C., 17, 210, 485, 951
Campbell, George Washington, 95, 100
Campbell, Philip, 1054, 1057
Camp David agreements, 1451

Canada. Parliament. House of Commons, 591
Canal projects
  federal encouragement of, 1199
  in Old Northwest, 1204
Candler, Ezekiel, on consumer protection legislation, 1265
Cannon, Clarence
  centralized spending control, 1027
  committee appointments, 1026
  HAC leadership, 1018
Cannon, George Q., 310
Cannon, Joseph G., 142, 1034
  centralization of control, 1407
  "Insurgent Revolt" against, 492, 611, 647, 819, 1050, 1052–1053, 1056, 1134–1135, 1407
Canon, Martha Hughes, 353
Canwell, Albert, 1291
Capital cities, in Revolutionary era, 187–188
Capitalism
  corruption and, 1643, 1645
  early nineteenth century, judicial shaping of, 1202
  Progressive Era, 1263
Careerism in politics, 851–852
  as legislator's motivation, 344
  U.S. Congress, 520, 526
Careers. See Occupations
Careers, legislative. See Legislative careers
Caribbean sugar colonies, slavery in, 1217–1218
Carlisle, John G., 1024–1025, 1033, 1052
Carnegie, Andrew, 1589
Carpetbaggers, 206
  modern, 471
Carr, Frank, 1288
Carroll, Charles, 183
Carroll, John J., 591
Carson, Rachel, *Silent Spring*, 1322
Carswell, G. Harold, nomination denied to, 1615
Carswell Air Force Base, closing of, 419
Carter, Jimmy, 1043
  Better Jobs and Income Program and, 1273
  Democratic ideological heterogeneity and, 616
  federal management and, 1603
  foreign policy actions, 1451
  Iran hostage rescue, 1434
  on legislative veto, 1509–1510
  vs. Reagan, 453, 462
  Reorganization Project, 1483–1484
  U.S. Congress relations with, 168, 1413
  U.S. Supreme Court and, 1583
  veto use, 1501
Carter, Landon, 30
Carter administration
  deregulation under, 85, 894
  energy policy, 1062–1063, 1326
  federal legislation passed under, 889
  fiscal policies of, 229
  public mood under, 895

zero-base budgeting, 777–778
Cartoonists. See Editorial cartoonists
Case Act (1972), 1412, 1451
Casework, 412–413
  as response to constituency, 409
  as substantive representation, 422
Casey, William, in Iran-Contra affair, 1451–1452
Casper, Jonathan, 1570
Catastrophic Health Insurance Act (1988), 407
Catholicism, legislative recruitment and, 329–330
Catholics
  antebellum, Protestant response to, 1260
  late nineteenth century, birthrate of, 1263
  mid-nineteenth century, American party and, 1130
Catledge, Turner, 1526
Catt, Carrie Chapman, 1247, 1385
Caucus campaign committees. See Campaign committees
Caucus Club, 9
Caucus committees, PAC funding, 632
Caucuses
  African American, 375–376
  categories of, 634
  minority parties, 634
  sectionalism and, 1366
  state, 725–726, 965, 968–970, 973
    origins of, 949
    post–World War II era, 954
    Reconstruction era, 951
    speaker selection and, 961
    state legislatures, 634–635
  U.S. Congress
    committees and, 641
    Federalist era, 1401
    late twentieth century, 662
    mid-nineteenth century, 119
    nomination of presidential candidates, 1403
  U.S. House
    early twentieth century, 647
    1970s, 165
    1980s, 170
  U.S. Senate, mid-nineteenth century, 116–117
  women's, 359, 362
  See also Democratic Caucus; King Caucus
Cause groups, 1107
  agendas of, 1108
Cavanagh, Thomas, 796
CBS News–*New York Times* polls
  on congressional performance, 464
  on party identification, 451
CEA. See Council of Economic Advisors
Celler, Emanuel, 998, 1162
Censorship, in Civil War, 1535
Censorship, Office of, 1539
Censure of legislators, 549
  for financial misconduct, 1159–1162
  nineteenth century, 1158–1160
  for past misconduct, 551–552

# INDEX

U.S. Congress, 1157–1160
Census, U.S.
  1830–1910, 108
  established (1787), 11
  state legislative districts and, 438
Census data
  constituencies and, 401
  legislator response to constitu-
    ency and, 410–411
  reapportionment and, 387
  redistricting and, 394
Center for Political Studies (University of Michigan). *See* University of Michigan Center for Political Studies
Central clearance, defined, 604
Central economic policy-making
  Civil War era, 1205
  constitutional ratification debates
    on, 1195
  disengagement from, 890
  New Deal era, 1210
  partisan response to, 538
Central Intelligence Agency (CIA)
  acts of war, 1431
  covert operations, 1414, 1450
  Nixon and, 1633
  U.S. Congress oversight, 1450
Centralization
  of budget process, 823
  Colonial assemblies, 1399
  executive-branch, 1581
  state legislative staffs, 812
  U.S. Congress, 828, 1407
Central Pacific Railroad, 1644
Centrism
  during the Great Depression, 1369
  sectionalism and, 1367–1368
*Chadha, Immigration and Naturali-
  zation Service v.. See Immigra-
  tion and Naturalization Serv-
  ice v. Chadha* (1983)
Chadha, Jagdish Rai, 1511
Chafee, John H., 1327
Chairmanships. *See* Congressional
  committee chairmanships; Leg-
  islative committees, chairper-
  sons of
Chamber-dominated committees
  model, 643–644
  early Congresses and, 645
Chamberlain, George, 469
Chamber rules. *See* Parliamentary
  rules
Chambers, Whittaker, 1286–1287
Change, studies of, 295–296
Chappell, Harry, 1101
Charitable institutions, colonial era,
  1256
*Charles River Bridge* v. *Warren
  River Bridge* (1837), 1581
Chartered commercial trading com-
  panies, English. *See* English
  trading corporations
Charters, colonial. *See* Colonial
  charters
Charters of incorporation. *See* Cor-
  porate charters
Chase, Salmon P., 126
  Free-Soil party and, 1129

A. Johnson and, 1628
Chase, Samuel, 183, 558
  Alien and Sedition acts and,
    1576–1577, 1580
  impeachment of, 1626–1627, 1630
Chase Manhattan Bank, 1649
Chattel. *See* Personal property
Chavez, Dennis, 317
Check-kiting scandal, congressional
  elections and, 508
Checks and balances
  policy-making and, 874
  political parties and, 876
  power of the purse, 1015
  in the Senate, 468
Cherokee Nation, Arkansas
  Territory's petition to Congress
  regarding, 252
Chestnut, James, Jr., 552
Cheyenne, Wyo., as territorial capi-
  tal, 276
Chief executive officers, corporate.
  *See* Corporate chief executive
  officers
Child labor legislation
  Great Depression era, 224
  *Hammer* v. *Dagenhart* (1918)
    and, 81, 220
  late nineteenth century, 1262
  Progressive Era, 218–219
Children
  antebellum era, guardianship of,
    1383
  colonial era
    of mixed races, 1381
    social welfare policy on,
      1256–1257
  guardianship of
    late twentieth century, 1389
    mid-twentieth century, 1387
  of slaves, 1218, 1221
  social welfare policy, late nine-
    teenth century, 1262–1263
  *See also* Abortion
Children's Bureau, U.S., established,
  1265
Child Support Enforcement amend-
  ments (1984), 1390
Chiles, Lawton, 841, 1529
Chiltern Hundreds, stewards of, 312
China, U.S. troops in, 1427, 1445
Chinese Exclusion acts (1882, 1884,
  1892), 139
Chipman, Nathaniel, 192
Chisholm, Shirley, 316
Chu, Chi-Hung, 997
Church, Frank, 1290
  recall petitions, 556
Churches
  as political opportunity, 326
  *See also individual religions;*
  Religion
Churchill, Winston, 1448
Church of Jesus Christ of Latter-day
  Saints
  in Idaho Territory, 268
  members of in Congress, 310
  in Utah Territory, 260–261
Cigarette Labeling and Advertising
  Act (1965), 85

CIO. *See* Congress of Industrial
  Organizations
CIO-PAC, 1093
Circuit-riding
  elimination of, 1613
  judge selection and, 1577–1578
Circular letters, Federalist-
  Republican era, 96
Circumvention conventions
  antebellum period, 48
  defined, 42
  early national period, 43, 47
*CIS U.S. Congressional Committee
  Prints Index*, 858
Citizen legislatures, 801, 851
  term limitations and, 525
Citizens Conference on State Legislatures (CCSL), 724, 839–840
  Legislative Evaluation Study, 841
  recommendations for reform,
    842–843
  evaluations of, 846
Citizens' groups, 1107
Citizenship
  requirements for legislators,
    305–306
  as territorial legislative service re-
    quirement, 254
City government
  city-manager plan, 240–241, 244
  commission plan, 239–240, 244
  early twentieth century, 239–242
  late twentieth century, 244
  nineteenth century, 236
  separation of powers and, 233
*City of Alexandria* v. *United States*
  (1983), 1517
*City of Mobile, Ala.* v. *Bolden*
  (1980), 1310
*City of New Haven* v. *United States*
  (1987), 1514
Civil Appropriations Act (1912), 1477
Civil codes, territorial establishment
  of, 251
"Civil death." *See* Feme covert status
Civil law
  European, 1569–1570
  judicial interpretation of, 1571
Civil liberties
  Civil War and Reconstruction,
    1279–1281
  colonial period, 1277–1278
  legislation
    1930–1945, 158
    World War I, 149
  legislative restrictions on
    Cold War era, 1286–1292
    hearings and investigations, 1277
    Lusk hearings, 1282–1283
    Vietnam War, 1290
    World Wars and the Great De-
      pression, 1281–1286
  modern issues, 1292
  national era, 1278–1279
Civil rights
  antebellum period, 1296
  definition, 1295
  enforcement, 1301–1302
    judicial approach, 1303–1304
      (*continued*)

# INDEX

# INDEX

Congress members (*continued*)
late nineteenth century, 1133
mid-nineteenth century, 108–110
state loyalties of, 1622
term of office, 10–11
work load of, 1143–1149
Civil War era, 733
*See also* Congressional elections;
Incumbent U.S. legislators;
Legislative turnover, in U.S.
Congress; Senators; Term
limitations
Congress members, state, committee
assignments, 682
continuity of membership, 684
*Congressmen in Committees. See*
Fenno, Richard F.
Congress of Industrial Organizations (CIO)
AFL-CIO and, 1094
CIO-PAC and, 1093
*See also* AFL-CIO
Congress of Racial Equality
(CORE), 1304
Congress on Administrative Management, 1478–1479
Conkling, Roscoe, 952, 1525, 1613
Connecticut
apportionment, in post-
Revolutionary state legislature, 8
Great Depression era, 221–222
late eighteenth century, emancipation in, 1221
late nineteenth century, moral
legislation in, 1262
late twentieth century, 961
post–World War II era, 228
redistricting process, 395
World War II era, 225
Connecticut Asylum for the Deaf
and Dumb, 1258
Connecticut Colony
charter of, 45
divorce law in, 1380
electorate of, 187
Revolutionary-era transition in,
182
voting qualifications, 1236
Connecticut Compromise (1787),
10, 12
Connecticut legislature
abortion policy of, 1391
espionage and sedition acts, 1291
joint-committee system, 674–675
Legislative Office Building, 847
public education policy of, 1259
records, 868
reforms, 841
gubernatorial opposition to, 842
Connecticut legislature. Senate, 973
Conness, John, 1316–1317
Consensus, on legislative norms,
592–593
"Consent" calendars, 819
defined, 724
Conservation legislation
Progressive Era, 219, 1208–1209
*See also* Environmental policy;
Wildlife conservation

Conservation movement
legislative response, 1315
New Deal program, 1320–1321
origin, 1315–1319
park preservation, 1316
economic considerations,
1317–1318
legislative participation, 1317
Progressive Era, 1319–1320
Conservation of natural resources
energy, 1326
forest, 1315, 1318
game laws, 1316
new, 1322
Taft era, 1135
Conservatism
among congressional committee
chairs, 649
U.S. Supreme Court and, 1582,
1584–1585
Conservative coalition. *See* Southern
Democrat–Republican coalition
Consolidated Gas Company, 217
Constituencies
defining, 400–408
diversity of, 406
educating by legislators, 426, 430
identifying, 427–428
impact on policy, 428–430
studies of, 406–407
influence on representatives,
16–17
legislator service to, 422–423
national interest and, 415–416
political interests of, 405–406
preferences of
legislators' perceptions of, 407
ordering of, 424
party attachments and, 410
religious background and, 331
representation of
Constitutional Convention on, 12
vs. political party representation, 16–17
responsiveness to, 409
tradition of, 399–400
U.S. Congress, growth in size of, 18
Constituent-representative relations, 4
colonial period, 28–30, 177, 181
defined, 3–5
direct lobbying and, 1113
Federalist-Republican era, 96
grass-roots lobbying and, 1112
measurement of, 1176
Revolutionary era, 185–190
U.S. Congress, 505
communication technology and,
1146
critical elections and, 537
factionalism and, 1073–1074
parties' roles and, 917–918
social choice theory of, 932
*See also* Electioneering; Political
parties, constituencies of
Constituents. *See* Constituent-
representative relations; Instructions, constituents'
Constitution, U.S.
ambiguities of, 71
on appointments, 1605

apportionment and, 387–388
Article I, 701
balance of powers, 1474
checks and balances, 468
color-blindness, 1306
Confederate constitutions and, 49
constituencies and, 399
corruption safeguards in, 1640
distribution of powers, 1400
executive-branch authority, 1473,
1588
expulsion of legislators, 549–550
expulsion power of legislature, 548
on federal judge selection, 1577
fiscal provisions of, 732
on House of Representatives, 452
impeachment procedure, 557,
1625–1626
judicial interpretation of, 1572
legislative detail in, 40
legislative ethics
disciplinary actions, 1156–1157
electoral vs. internal control,
1156
legislative service requirements,
303–308
on legislators' motivations, 343
legislators' social backgrounds
and, 322
media and, 1533–1534
national bank proposal controversy and, 75
naturalization standards, 305
on patents, 1197
presentment clause, exceptions
to, 1505–1506, 1512
on presidential veto, 603, 1490
public vs. private interests,
1155–1156
qualifications for legislators, 555
accepting incompatible offices,
311–314
religious tests, 310
recall provision, 555
revision of, state constitutional revision and, 38
on separation of powers, 1569
speech or debate clause, 549
state constitutions and
nineteenth century, 40, 43
Revolutionary era, 46, 191–192,
1625–1626
on State of the Union messages,
610
taxation powers of, 1197
U.S. congressional committees
and, 641
U.S. congressional self-
government, 701
Virginia legislature and, 196–197
war powers provisions, 1421–1422
*See also* Judicial review
Constitutional amendment
procedures
federal, judiciary and, 1573
state
in Confederacy, 49
early demands for, 47
Constitutional amendments, U.S.,
1505

# INDEX

# INDEX

Dawes, Henry L., 1644
Dawes, Thomas, on slave population and state representation in Congress, 13–14
Dawes Severalty Act (1887), 139, 1261
Dawkins, Pete, 332
Dawson, John, 94
Dawson, Robert, as committee chair, 369
Dawson, William L., 315, 368
Day, William R., 81
Day-care legislation, Nixon era, 1389
Dayton, Jonathan, 92–93
Deadlock, 415
Deaf and dumb institutions, antebellum era, 1258
Dealignment concept, congressional parties' roles and, 901
Dean, John, 1466, 1634
Dearborn, Henry, 1610
Death penalty
for treason, 1624
U.S. Supreme Court and, 1585
Debate rules
collective debate controls, 703
House of Representatives, 702–703
minority-majority party balance, 702, 704
power to end, 703
speech limitations, 703
in U.S. Senate, 703–704
Debates, congressional, records of, 856
Debates, state legislative, records of, 863
*Debates and Proceedings in the Congress of the United States*, 856
DeBats, Donald A., 949–950
Debs, Eugene V., in election of 1912, 1134
Debt. *See* Budget deficit
Debt, state
antebellum constitution making and, 48
1920s, 220–221
Decentralization
of Congress, 824, 1406
in committee system, 877
modern era, 1412
staffing changes with, 786
constituencies and, 400
of state legislatures, 816
problems resulting from, 1416
Decision making
institutionalization and, 1175
*See also* Collective decision-making
Decision making, legislative
committee role in, state level, 670–672
in standing committees, 848
uncertainty in, 577, 579
Declaration of Independence
on executive veto, 1489
monarchical sentiment and, 180
on slave trade, 1223

"Declaration of Sentiments" (Seneca Falls Convention), 1384
DeConcini, Dennis, 1166
DeCrow, Karen, 1389
Defense, U.S. Department of
appropriations for, Aspin on, 735
program budgeting, 776
Defense Base Closure and Realignment Act (1990), 423
Defense contracting, 1600
Defense Department, U.S.
PPB system and, 1601
reorganization of, 1599–1600
Defense legislation
1980s, 171
*See also* Foreign policy
Deferential political culture
in colonial assemblies, 29
in European parliaments, 593
*See also* Senatorial courtesy
Deferral authority, legislative veto and, 1513–1514
Deferred expenditures, federal, 740
Deficiency Appropriation Act (1943), 1285
Deficit. *See* Budget deficit
DeGregorio, Christine, 796
Delahay, Mark, 1630
Delaney, James
career longevity of, 502
as U.S. House Rules Committee chairman, 1061
Delaware
appointment powers in, 1607–1608
Senate representation, 468
Delaware (colony)
colonial assembly, religious tests for members, 309–310
Loyalist sentiment in, 182
Delaware constitution, popular ratification of, 46
Delaware legislature, gradual emancipation and, 1222
Delegate (type of legislator)
defined, 420
perception of constituency preferences, 425
response to constituency and, 411
role of, 424
view of constituencies, 427–428
Democracy, representative, in American colonies, 6
*Democracy in America. See* Tocqueville, Alexis de
Democrat and Greenback party. *See* Greenback party
Democratic Caucus
choosing committee chairs, 823, 828
committee chairs and, 655–656, 824
early twentieth century, 1053
instruction of Rules Committee, 823
loss of autonomy in, 662
majority sentiment expressed in, 606
party leadership elected by, 605
Rules Committee membership and, 616

subcommittee bill of rights, 824
subcommittees reduced by, 656
Democratic Congressional Campaign Committee, Coelho and, 1650
Democratic moralism, 1589
Democratic National Convention, Hubert Humphrey nomination, 1411
Democratic party
administration cleavages and, 1083
African American legislators and, 383
agenda of, 939–940
all-white primary elections, 1299
antebellum era, social welfare policy of, 1258
in Arizona Territory, 269
civil rights policy, 1300
in Colorado Territory, 267
committee assignments, 985–986, 988
effect of term limitations on, 525
fiscal redistribution programs and, 1887–1932, 80
in Hawaii Territory, 268
in Idaho Territory, 268
ideological cleavages and, 1071–1072
impact of constituency and, 429
increase in committee seats, 984
Kennedy-Johnson years, 1411
late twentieth century, party unity in, 933
leadership votes in, 941
legal constituency definition and, 402–403
northern vs. southern wing, 876
Progressive Era, in Wisconsin, 953
reform, Congressional committee assignments and, 1034
response to constituency and, 410
responsiveness to African Americans, 327
slavery issue, 880
spending reform and, 1916, 1337
under Wilson, 1407
in U.S. Congress
1946–1960, 160
1967–1976, 164–165
1977–1980, 168
1981–1990, 169–170
U.S. congressional reforms of, 1970s, 1068
in U.S. House
1870–1895, 136
1895–1911, 140–142
1911–1919, 145–146
1919–1931, 149–151
U.S. House Ways and Means Committee and, 1038, 1040
reforms and, 1042
in U.S. Senate, 1895–1911, 143
white male suffrage and, 1240
*See also* Bourbon Democrats; Democratic party vs. Republican party; Democratic party vs. Whig party; Jacksonian
*(continued)*

# INDEX

Edwards, Mickey, 1516
Ego compensation, as legislator's
motivation, 344–345
Eisenhower, Dwight D., 160, 1481
executive-branch reorganization,
1482, 1599
federal control over suffrage and,
1249
grants authorized by, 83
intergovernmental relations and,
227–228
legislative role of, 613–614
Reagan and, 618
Strauss nomination and, 1617
U.S. Congress relations with, 1410
use of executive privilege, 1457,
1465
veto use, 1501
voting-rights bill, 1303
war powers claims, 1449–1450
war powers exercised, 1431
Warren and, 1582
Eisenhower, Milton, 1482
Eisenhower administration
Federal-Aid Highway Program
and, 228
social welfare policies of, 1269
U.S. House Rule Committee of,
1058
Eizenstat, Stuart, 1509–1510
Elazar, Daniel, 86
Election districts, congressional,
1549–1551
Republican U.S. House losses
and, 461
"safe," 454
size of, 15–16
state responsibility for, 16
Election districts, state, 435–441
Electioneering
candidate's political experience
and, 338
contributions for
regulations on, 166
sources of, 167
costs of, 293, 349
for women, 328–329
detachment from party organization, 165
learning of constituency preferences and, 426
nineteenth century, 1556–1557
by state legislators, 436–437
underrepresentation of women
and ethnic groups in, 408
See also Constituent-
representative relations
Elections
colonial era, 27–28
influence of money on, 308–309
local government
changes in early twentieth century, 240–241
late twentieth century, 244
political innovations and,
1353–1354
procedure, and legitimacy of representation, 4
run-off, African American representation and, 326

See also Campaign contributions;
Congressional elections; Direct primaries; Legislatures,
state, elections to; National
elections; Political participation; Presidential elections
Election statistics, in state legislative election research, 435
Electoral accountability, one-party
rule and, 463–464
Electoral calendar, altering, 525–
526
Electoral campaigns. See
Electioneering
Electoral college
choosing electors, 1403
Constitutional Convention debate
on, 68
Electoral Commission, election of
1876 and, 127
Electoral realignments, 529–545
cross-cutting issues, 880–882
legislative surges and, 893
party voting and, 881–882
policy changes during, 879–883
Sundquist on, 953
third parties and, 1124
turnover and partisan control following, 881
U.S. congressional committees
and, 536–537, 644
Electoral realignment theory, legislative historiography and, 292
Electoral system, single-member
plurality, 875–876
Electoral turnover
with decrease in uncertainty,
516
following electoral realignments,
881–883
Electorate. See Suffrage
Electronic media, 1529–1531
in state legislative elections, 441
U.S. congressional incumbents
and, 457
See also Communication technology; Radio; Television
Electronic voting
in state legislatures, 723
in U.S. House, 660–661
Elementary and Secondary School
Education Act (1965), 1270
Elements of the Law and Practice
of Legislative Assemblies. See
Stearns, Luther
Elites
colonial, 28–29
corruption fears and, 32
decline of, 195–196
metropolitan traditional politics
and, 33–34, 175
transformed by imperial arrogance, 177
in Congress, anticipated by Constitutional Convention delegates, 68
Federalist-Republican era, in Virginia legislature, 197
Elizabethan Poor law. See Poor
laws, English

Elkins Committee, 1646
Elliot, Carl, 1059
Ellsberg, Daniel, 1541
Ellsworth, Oliver, 62, 89
on citizenship requirement for
legislators, 305
El Salvador, U.S. military advisers
in, 1434
Emancipation
New England, 1220–1221
Northern states, 1221–1222
West Indies, 1226
See also Manumission
Emancipation Proclamation, issu-
ance of, 125, 1232
Embargoes
Jefferson era, 1127
of War of 1812, 100–101
Emergency appropriations. See Sup-
plemental appropriations
Emergency Banking Relief Act,
158
Emergency Price Control Act
(1942), 1371
Emergency Relief and Construction
Act (1932), 888
Emigration and immigration
antebellum
of blacks, 1225
federal policy on, 1198–1199
Protestant response to, 1260
public health and, 1202
civil liberties issues, 1280
Civil War era, 1205
Constitutional Convention debate
on, 64
legislation
1870–1895, 139
legislative veto, 1511
1919–1931, 153
Locke on, 25
mid-nineteenth century, American
party and, 1130
Progressive Era, 1209
World War II era, 225
Eminent domain
nineteenth century
state constitutions on, 51
state law on, 1202
water laws and, 273
Empathy, response to constituency
and, 409–410
Employment
Federal government, civilian,
1945–1947, 160
See also Discrimination, employment; Labor conditions; Labor
supply; Unemployment
Employment Act (1946), 160–161
Enabling legislation, 1562
See also Statehood, process of
Endangered Species Act, 1327
Energy policy, 1326
legislation in Carter administra-
tion, 1062–1063
sectionalism and, 1374–1375
U.S. House Ways and Means Com-
mittee and, 1044
Enforcement Acts (1870–1875). See
Force Acts

Enforcement mechanisms, norms and, 586

English, Arthur, 591

English, George W., 1631–1632
impeachment, 558

English common law. See Common law

English families, in state legislatures, Federalist-Republican era, 197

English judiciary, 1569

English-language instruction, late nineteenth century, 1262

English political rights
colonial emigration and, 25
property ownership and, 24
voting qualifications and, 1235–1236

English poor laws. See Poor laws, English

English representative government.
American constitutionalism and, 37, 176
colonial elections and, 27
colonial franchise and, 26
colonial governance and, 25, 31–32, 95, 175–177
constituent-representative relations in, 30
corruption suspected in, 32
See also British government

English trading corporations, colonial assemblies and, 23–24

Enjoyment, as legislator's motivation, 349

Enlightenment, the, slave codes and, 1219

Enourato v. N.J. Building Authority, 1519

Entertainment, censorship of, 1537

Entitlement programs, 738, 1016, 1339–1340
Budget Enforcement Act (1990) and, 744
eligibility changes, 1343
federal deficit and, 742
jurisdiction for, 1343
"scorekeeping" and, 739

Entrepreneurship, business. See Private companies

Entrepreneurship, policy. See Policy entrepreneurship

"Enumerated articles." See Exports, colonial

Environmental Action (organization), 1111

Environmental-impact reports, introduction of, 1211

Environmentalism, 1322
U.S. congressional committees and lobbying, 1012

Environmental issues, territorial expansion and, 265

Environmental policy
committee role in, 1318, 1321–1322
dual federalism approach, 1313
economic considerations, 1317–1318, 1322

efficiency ethos, 1320
exploitation ethic, 1314
federal-state interaction, 1316, 1320–1321, 1325, 1327
global problems, 1328
hazardous wastes, 1327
history and development, 1313–1314
integrated approach, 1325
legislative reformers, 1322–1323
lobbying efforts, 1322–1323
national pattern, 1326
new conservation laws, 1322
Nixon era, 889, 891
pollution-control measures, 1323
Progressive Era, 1319–1320
Reagan-Bush administrations, 1326–1328
reform era
congressional role, 1325–1326
origins, 1321–1324
state role, 1324–1325
regionalism, 1324, 1326
speculative laws, 1324
state and national parks, 1316–1319
state legislation, 1314, 1316, 1319–1321, 1324–1325
superfund laws, 1327
U.S. congressional activism, 1315, 1319–1323, 1325–1326
hearings and investigations, 1320
See also Conservation legislation; Conservation movement; Wildlife conservation

Environmental pollution, territorial lawmaking and, 274

Equal Access Act (1984), 1584

Equal Employment Opportunity Commission (EEOC), 1388
enforcement of women's rights, 1307
prosecuting authority, 1305

Equality League of Self-Supporting Women in New York, 1247

Equal Pay Act (1963), 1307, 1388

Equal Rights Amendment (ERA), 356, 889, 1307, 1386, 1388
as disinnovation, 1351

Equal Rights Association, 1243

Equilibrium, preference-driven, 578

Equilibrium, structure-induced, 576–577

ERA. See Equal Rights Amendment (ERA)

Era of Good Feelings (1815–1829), 1403
defined, 199

"Era of No Decision," 534

Erie Canal project, success of, 1203

Ershkowitz, Herbert, 202, 950

Ervin, Sam J., 1633
on executive privilege, 1457
Select Committee on Campaign Activities, 1467
Senate Subcommittee on Separation of Powers, 1467

Espionage Act (1917), 311, 1281, 1537

Espionage Act (1940), 1539

"Essex Result." See Parsons, Theophilus

Ethics in Government Act (1978), disclosure provisions, 1164

Ethics in Government. See Douglas, Paul H.

Ethics Reform Act (1989), 1116

Ethics standards
nonpartisan cleavages and, 1085
state offices, 852
See also Legislative ethics

Ethnic demographics
Midwest, 210
Nebraska, 211
state constitutions and, 44

Ethnic groups
constituency definition and, 404
factor in legislative recruitment, 325–327
proportional representation and, 401

Ethnic identification, as force in politics, 325

Ethnic minorities
civil rights legislation, 1278–1292
in congressional staff positions, 794
discrimination, nineteenth century, 1295–1296
federal legislation and, 1870–1895, 139
in U.S. Congress, 314–317

Ethnic-minority employment
World War II era, 226
See also Affirmative-action programs

Ethnic-minority legislators, 511
in U.S. Congress, 500
See also African American legislators; Latino legislators

Ethnic-minority preferences, 1307–1308
Dirksen compromise, 1305
set-aside program, 1309–1310

Ethnic representation. See Proportional representation

Euchner, Jonathan, 974, 976

Eulau, Heinz, 672

European civil law, 1569–1570

European consumers, U.S. consumer legislation and, 1265–1266

European Economic Community, judicial activism and, 1569–1570

European governments, influence on American bureaucracy, 1587

European parliaments, norms in, 593

European political theory, nineteenth century, 1569

European social welfare policy, 1256
Progressives and, 1264

European trade, Jefferson era, 1127

Eustis, William, 101

Evangelical revivals. See Religious revivals

Evarts, William M., 1629

Everett, Edward, 105

Excess-profits tax legislation, Eisenhower administration, 1058

Excise tax, Civil War era, 1205

slave codes and, 1218
supposed threat of, 1222
Freedmen's Bureau, 1260–1261, 1297
established, 125
A. Johnson and, 126
Freedom March, 1249
Freedom of assembly, First Amendment debate over, 12
Freedom of Information Act (1966), 1290, 1466
Freedom of Information Act (1974), veto of, 1468
Freedom of speech, 1533
*Buckley* v. *Valeo* (1976) on, 1095
colonial era, 1277–1278, 1521–1522
labor radicalism and, 1538
legislative restrictions on, 1283–1284
*New York Times* v. *Sullivan* (1964) and, 1575
pornography and, 1393
Freedom of the press. *See* Freedom of speech; Libel
Free-for-all multimember state-election districts, 441
Freehold property
colonial franchise and, 26
colonial Virginia franchise and, 195
Free labor, eighteenth century, 1220
"Free rider" concept
M. Olson on, 1109
virtual representation and, 5
Free-Soil party, 258–259, 1128–1130, 1138
campaign expenditures of, 1125
potential constituency of, 1230
Free Staters, 258–259
Freeway construction. *See* Highway construction
Frèmont, John Charles
American party and, 1131
as governor of Arizona Territory, 269
Frendreis, John, 1102
Freneau, Philip, Senate proceedings publication and, 1523
Friendly, Fred, 1530
Friends (Quakers). *See* Quakers (Society of Friends)
*Frohwerk* v. *United States* (1919), 1538
Frontier. *See* Western frontier
Fugitive Slave Act (1793), 1224
proposed revision of, 1229
Fugitive Slave Act (1850), 314, 1129
Fulbright, J. William, 163
challenges presidential war powers, 1432
on executive privilege, 1465, 1467
postwar organization, 1448
on television coverage, 1531
Full Employment Act (1946), 285–286
Fuller, Melville W., U.S. Supreme Court service of, 1581–1582
*Fullilove* v. *Klutznick* (1980), 1310
Functionalism, structural. *See* Structural-functionalism

Fund-raising
ethical issues, 852
incumbents, 632
advantages of, 474, 476–477
U.S. Senate elections, 478, 526
*See also* Campaign contributions

Gage, Thomas, 177
Gag laws (1836), 1279
Gag rule, 116
U.S. House, 116, 1054, 1228
Gain, private, as legislator's motivation, 347–348
Gains-in-trade politics, congressional parties' roles and, 907–908
Gales, Joseph, 1523
Gallatin, Albert
House Ways and Means Committee and, 92
the "Invisibles" and, 99
news coverage of, 1523
nominated by Madison, 1609–1610
social life of, 98
Yazoo land scandal and, 1126–1127
Gambling debts, 1643
Garand, James C., on incumbent state legislators, 443
*Garcia* v. *San Antonio Metropolitan Transit Authority* (1985), 87
Garfield, Harry, 1596
Garfield, James A.
appointments by, 1613
Crèdit Mobilier scandal and, 1644
as House Appropriations Committee chair, 135–136
as secretary of the interior, 1135
on self-government, 74
separation of powers doctrine, 1406
Garn, Jake, 1022–1023
Garner, John Nance ("Cactus Jack"), 151
Garrett, Finis, 151, 1055
Garza, Kika de la, 317
Gasoline taxes, 1920s, 220, 1209
"Gatekeeping" power, in U.S. Congress, 650
Geary, John, 258
Gender discrimination, twentieth century, 1388, 1393
Gender issues. *See* Sexuality; Women
General Accounting Office (GAO), 793
creation of, 1027
established, 615, 734
oversight function, 749
strengthened, 823
General appropriations bills, defined, 736
*General Assembly of State of New Jersey* v. *Byrne* (1982), 1518
General-benefit norms, defined, 597
*General Electric Co.* v. *Gilbert* (1976), 1307
General-fund revenue, 778
budget deficits and, 1334
deficits and, 1342
1950–1984, 1341
trust-fund taxes and, 1341

General-revenue sharing, state, 780
General Revision Act (1891), Section 24, 1318
General Services Administration (GSA), sale of government property, 1516–1517
General Survey Act (1824), 1199
Geographical constituency, 401, 427
Geographical unit
as basis of legislator selection, 1549
as basis of representation, 18, 332–333
George, Walter, 316
George III, King of England
John Adams on, 179
slave trade and, 1223
Georgia
budgetary process, 727, 773
Federalist-Republican era, Yazoo land-speculation scandal and, 94
floterial election districts of, 440
Reconstruction era
impeachments in, 1629
military rule in, 127
Washington era, slave question and, 1223
zero-base budgeting, 777
Georgia Colony
bicameralism in, 182
colonial assembly, property qualification, 308
Georgia legislature
African Americans in, 206
antebellum
party activity in, 949–950
public education policy of, 1259
mid-twentieth century, *Bond* v. *Floyd* and, 1575
number of committee positions, 677
railroad regulation and, 216
Yazoo land question and, 1126–1127, 1641
Gephardt, Richard, 459
Geren, Pete, 419
Germaneness rule, in U.S. House, 651
appropriations bills and, 736
Germany
proportional representation and, 401
in World War II, 1429–1430
Gerry, Elbridge, 1421, 1440, 1558
at Constitutional Convention, 64–65
Gerrymandering, 16, 389–390
legal constituency definition and, 402–403
1980s, 438–439, 461
racial, 1551
redistricting and, 396
*Gertz* v. *Robert Welch, Inc.* (1974), 1540
Gesell, Gerhard, 1468–1469
G.I. Bill of Rights, 1269
*Gibbons* v. *Ogden* (1824), 75

Harrison, William Henry, (*continued*)
Northwest Territory and, 250
veto use, 1494–1495
Whig victory and, 532
Harrison administration (B.
Harrison), federal legislation
passed under, 890
Hart, Henry, 1576
Harvey, John, 1625
Hastings, Alcee, 1635–1636
impeachment, 559
Hastings, Warren, 1625
Hatch Act (1887), as grants-in-aid
prototype, 79
Hatch Act (1939), 1284, 1598
campaign regulations of, 1093
Hate-crimes legislation, 1392–1393
Hate speech, 1543
restrictions on, 1292
Hawaii, annexation of, 1445
Hawaii (territory)
constitutional conventions of, 269
partisan politics in, 266–267
women's rights and, 275
Hawes, Harry B., 1320
Hawkins, Augustus, 316
Hawkins, Benjamin, 1558
Hawkins, Paula, 476
Hay, George, 1460
*Hayburn's Case* (1792), 1580
Hayden, Charles Trumball, 277
Hayes, Rutherford B.
appointments by, 1613
appropriations bill riders and, 112
southern states and, 127
use of appointment powers, 1406
use of executive privilege, 1462
veto use, 1498
Hayne, Robert Y., 105
Haynes, George H., 18–19, 444, 469
Haynsworth, Clement F., Jr., nomina-
tion denied to, 1615
Hays, Wayne, 1163
Hazardous-waste control, 1326–1327
Health, Education and Welfare, U.S.
Department of, Office of Bilin-
gual Education, 1309
Health care, reforms, as example of
policy innovation diffusion, 1359
Health insurance
Progressive Era, 1264
Truman era, 1269
Health legislation. *See* Public
health legislation
Hearings, congressional
consequences of, 855
records of, 860–861
Hearings, state legislative, records
of, 866
Hebert, F. Ted, 586, 590–592
Hedlund, Ronald, 677
"Organizational Attributes of Leg-
islative Institutions," 569
Heineman, Ben, 1483, 1601
Heinz, John, 471
Helena (Mont.) as territorial capital,
276
Helms, Jesse, 477
freedom of expression and, 1542

Hemphill, John, 552
Henderson, David B., 141
Henkin, Louis, 1575
Hennings, Thomas C., 1466
Henry, Patrick
on corruption, 1639
on virtual representation, 13
Henry, Robert, on U.S. House gag
rule, 1054
Hepburn, William, consumer pro-
tection legislation and, 1265
Hepburn Act (1906), 886
*Hepburn* v. *Griswold* (1870), 1581
Herblock. *See* Block, Herbert L.
Herzberg, Donald G., 840
Hess, Stephen, 1528
Hetch Hetchy Valley incident
(1901–1913), 1320
*Heydon's Case* (1584), 1571
Hicklin rule of obscenity, 1536, 1541
High-technology industry, as inter-
state policy innovation, 1349
Highway Beautification Act (1965),
230
Highway construction
antebellum, 1199
executive/legislative compromise
and, 1594
federal funding for, 1563
Eisenhower administration, 83,
85, 228
Sixth Congress, 93
state compliance and, 230
as trust fund, 1341
Minnesota, 221
Progressive Era, 1209
state funding for, 220
Highway Trust Fund, 228
Hill, Anita, 1616
Hill, David, Cleveland and, 1578
Hill, Isaac, 1610
Hillhouse, James, on Louisiana slav-
ery, 1225
Hinds, Asher, 1051–1052
Hiss, Alger, 1286–1287
*Hiss* v. *Bartlett* (1855), 553
Historiography, legislative
behavioral era (1950s–1970s),
286–291
data available for, 297
descriptive-formalist era (1900–
1950s), 283–286
Hoar, Ebenezer, 1613
Hoar, Roger Sherman, 44
Hoey, Clyde, 1288
Holden, William, 1630
Holding companies, 1920s, 1209
Holding Company Act (1935), 1055
Holliday, Frederick W. M., 207
*Hollingsworth* v. *Virginia* (1798),
1505
Holman, William S., 112
Holman Rule, 1025
Holmes, Oliver Wendell, 1652
on antiwar activity, 1537–1538
Holt, George E., 1632
Holt, Michael F., 202
Holtzman, Abraham, *Legislative Li-
aison*, 1417

Home rule
for city governments, 241–242
for county governments, 242
Home Rule (Ireland), 934
"Home rule" (municipalities). *See*
Municipalities, "home rule" for
Home Rule party (Hawaii territory),
266
Home-state ties, of U.S. senators, 471
Homestead Act (1862), 1201, 1205,
1314, 1366
Home style
assumptions of, 431
defined, 420
response to constituency and, 409
studies of, 292
Homosexuality, 1392–1393
in government, Hoey committee
investigations, 1288
*Honest Graft. See* Jackson, Brooks
Honoraria, 1115–1116
Hoover, Herbert, 880
bureaucracy and, 1597
executive branch reorganization
and, 1480–1482, 1507, 1599
Great Depression and, 81, 534,
1267
impeachment motions against,
1632
on-year elections, 519
U.S. Congress relations with, 1408
use of executive privilege, 1463
Hoover, J. Edgar
Condon letter, 1464
covert surveillance activities, 1463
HUAC assistance, 1287
"Responsibilities Program," 1292
"Sex Deviates" program, 1288
subpoenaed by Cox Committee,
1464
Hoover administration
federal legislation passed under,
888
legislative activity of, 612
Hoover Commission. *See* Commis-
sion on the Organization of the
Executive Branch of the
Government
Hopkins, Harry L., 223, 1268, 1598
Hornaday, William T., 1320
Horton, Frank, 1517
Hospitals, lobbying by, 1106–1107
Hours of labor
antebellum era, Massachusetts,
1383
Progressive Era, 1386
House Appropriations Committee
(HAC). *See* House of Represen-
tatives, U.S., Appropriations
Committee
*House at Work, The. See* Cooper,
Joseph, and MacKenzie, G. Calvin
House Bank scandal, 1651–1652
House Calendar, 704, 709
House Commission on Administra-
tion Review, 796
House Committee on Standards of
Official Conduct, expulsion of
members, 552

# INDEX

# INDEX

Inaugural addresses, program articulation in, 624

Incapacity. *See* Disability

Incentives, as legislator's motivation, 343–347

Income guarantees. *See* Annual guaranteed income

Income maintenance programs. *See* Public welfare

Income tax
Civil War era, 1205
early twentieth century, 1209
federal, bureaucracy and, 1595
federalism and, 81
state, 1920s, 220
World War II and, 83

Incorporation. *See* Corporate charters

Incumbency
gerrymandering and, 390
strategic behavior, 518
studies of, 293
women and
in Congress, 361
in state legislatures and, 356

Incumbency advantage, 516–518
in campaign finance, 474, 476–477, 521–522, 632
changes in voting behavior affecting, 517–518
electoral responsiveness and, 520
redistricting and, 517
reelection and, 474, 476–477, 517*t*, 630–631

Incumbent state legislators, reelection of, 443–446, 506, 955

Incumbent U.S. legislators
advantages of, 517
electoral realignment and, 541–542
information control by, 453–457
news coverage of, 1526
PACs and, 1098–1101, 1103
party-line voting decline and, 452–453
presidential unpopularity and, 462
public opinion and, 894
reelection of, 508, 1174

Indentured servants, in colonial Virginia, 1217, 1381

Indenture laws, 256–257
*See also* Slavery

Independent regulatory commissions
civil rights enforcement, 1302
early twentieth century, 1612, 1616
federal management and, 1598
late twentieth century, 1212
in local government, nineteenth century, 236
New Deal era, 1210
separation of powers and, 1593–1594
U.S. congressional factionalism and, 1072

Independent Treasury scheme, 1200

Independent voters, party response to, 978

Independent Voters Association (N.D.), 953

Index of party cohesion/disagreement, defined, 203

India, judicial system of, 1570

Indiana
Bayh-Quayle race, 477
legislators
nineteenth century, 201–202, 210
twentieth century, 491, 493
reapportionment, 390
gerrymandering claimed in, 439
senator selection problems, 1557
state boundary of, 1589
state election districts in, 439–440

Indiana constitution (1816), 1626

Indian Affairs, Office of. *See* Bureau of Indian Affairs

Indian agents, Belknap and, 1630

Indiana legislature, journals, 863

Indiana (territory)
boundary disputes and, 256
slavery and, 256–257
*See also* Northwest Territory

Indians. *See* Native Americans

"Individualistic fallacy," 596

Individualistic state culture, 1353

Industrial accidents, Pennsylvania, 1264

Industrialization
civil liberties issues, 1280
government growth and, 1887–1932, 78
late nineteenth century
vs. agricultural interests, 535–536
corruption and, 1645
mid-nineteenth century, American party and, 1130
political effects of, 880
Progressive Era, 1263
sectionalism and, 1368
U.S. congressional changes and, 132
U.S. House committees and, 114

Industrial policy, 1860–1929, 1205–1210

Industrial Workers of the World (IWW), 1538

Industry, World War II mobilization and, 1371

Infancy and Maternity Act (1921), 1265

Infant mortality, Progressive era, 1265

Inflation (finance)
Continental Congress and, 58
late nineteenth century, third-party support for, 1132
late twentieth century, Social Security benefits and, 1271

Information
access to, 1468
for committee members, 1180
for legislators, from lobbyists, 1113, 1643
reforms in, 827
staff access to, 787–788
U.S. congressional committee power and, 652
U.S. House incumbent control of, 453–457
about U.S. senators, 459–460
*See also* Communication networks; Communication technology; Journalistic coverage; Mass media

*Information and Legislative Organization. See* Krehbiel, Keith

Infrastructure. *See* Internal improvements

Ingersoll, Charles J., 860

Inheritance tax, state, 1562

Initiative and referendum procedure, 554
in local government, early twentieth century, 241
pressure groups and, 1111–1112
state legislator policy congruence and, 410

Innovation in politics. *See* Political innovation

Innovative states, defined, 1352

Inouye, Daniel, 317, 737, 1029

*Inquiry into the Nature and Causes of the Wealth of Nations. See* Smith, Adam

*In re Chapman* (1897), 551

Institutional capacity, state legislatures, 847–848

Institutionalism, legislative historiography and, 296

Institutionalization, 1174–1175
apprenticeship and, 1182
of Congress, 820

"Institutional kinship," in U.S. Senate, 590

Institutional loyalty, research on, 1182

Institutional structure
causes and effects of, 566
nonrandom evolution, 570
rational choice perspective, 578
role of party system, 580
study of, 565

Instructions, constituents'
controversy over, 118
Madison's opposition to, 16–17
to members of Congress, 12
to state legislators, post-Revolutionary, 8–9

Instrumental representation, 1

Insurance, social. *See* Social insurance

Insurance industry, New York State, 217, 1646

Insurgency, 1123–1141

"Insurgent Revolt" (1910). *See* Cannon, Joseph G., "Insurgent Revolt" against

Integration, racial. *See* Desegregation

Intelligence agencies, congressional oversight, 1290

Intelligence congressional committees, permanence of, 643

Interest (finance), proposed withholding of, 1112

Interests
representation of, 19
*See also* Private interests

Intergovernmental lobby, 1108

Intergovernmental relations
Eisenhower administration, 227–228
Revolutionary era, 189–192

Interior, U.S. Department of the
appropriations, 1021

(continued)

Jefferson, Thomas (*continued*)
　as secretary of state, 1440
　U.S. Congress relations with, 98–99
　use of presidential power, 1441
　veto use, 1491
　on Virginia constitution, 45
　in Washington cabinet, 1609
Jefferson administration
　House standing committees and, 94
　news coverage of, 1523
　Old Republicans and, 1126, 1139
　party affiliations in, 1123
　state constitutional conventions and, 43, 47
Jeffersonian Republicans. *See* Republican party (Jeffersonian Republicans)
Jencks law, 1289
*Jencks* v. *United States* (1957), 1289
*Jenkins* v. *Georgia* (1974), 1584
Jenner, William, 1289
Jennings, Jonathan, 256
Jenrette, John W., Jr., resigns from Senate, 553
Jewell, Malcolm E., 953–954, 970–971, 997
　*See also* Loewenberg, Gerhard
Jews
　elected to Parliament, 309
　legislative recruitment and, 329–330
　in U.S. Congress, 310
Jim Crow laws, 1280, 1299
Job Opportunities and Basic Skills Program, 1273
*"John Cleland's Memoirs"* v. *Attorney General of Massachusetts* (1966), 1542
Johnson, Andrew
　appointments by, 1612–1613
　bureaucracy and, 1590
　Freedmen's Bureau and, 1260
　impeachment of, 126, 558, 1498, 1612, 1627–1629, 1633
　joint congressional action against, 114
　legislative surge despite, 891
　readmission of southern state governments, 1297
　repudiated by party, 118
　Southern constitutional revision and, 50
　U.S. Congress relations with, 122, 126, 134
　use of presidential power, 1406
　veto use, 1498
Johnson, Hirum, 219, 1646
Johnson, Lyndon B., 468
　in 1964 election, 540
　action on Jenner Bill, and 1289
　Bobbie Baker and, 1647
　vs. Barden, 1005
　biographies of, 350–351
　Civil Rights Act of 1957 and, 161
　committee assignment process and, 988
　domestic policies of, 162
　executive reorganization, 1482–1483

federal control over suffrage and, 1249–1250
federal management and, 1601
foreign policies of, 163
Fortas nomination and, 1615
legislative role of, 614
motivations of, 350–351
news management, 1457
Olds nomination and, 1617
Texas joint senatorial-presidential races and, 509
U.S. congressional career of, 648
use of executive privilege, 1466
Vietnam War and, 1432, 1450
voting-rights bill and, 1306
*See also* Great Society programs
Johnson, Napoleon Bonaparte, 1632
Johnson, Richard M.
　on House Military Affairs Committee, 101, 105
　U.S. congressional pay proposal of, 103–104
Johnson, Robert Underwood, 1317
Johnson, Waldo P., 552
Johnson administration (A. Johnson), legislation passed under, 886
Johnson administration (L. B. Johnson)
　civil rights legislation during, 1303
　environmental policy during, 1322
　legislation passed under, 888–889
Johnson-Reed Act (1924), 1209
Johnson Rule, 989, 1018
　defined, 503
Johnston, Henry S., 1631
Joint committees
　state, 726
　U.S. Congress, 642–643
　*See also* Congressional committee system; *under* Congress, U.S., Joint Committees
Joint districts, 1549
Joint resolutions, 1505–1506
　to approve reorganization plans, 1513
Joint staffing, state legislatures, 806
Jones, Charles H., 116–117
Jones, J. Glancy, 116
Jones, Woodrow, 1102
Jordan, Winthrop D., 1217
*Joseph Burstyn, Inc.* v. *Wilson* (1952), 1541
Journalistic coverage
　of corruption
　　antebellum era, 1644
　　Progressive Era, 1646
　legislative, 1521–1532
　of T. Roosevelt, 612, 1525
　of U.S. House, 95
　of U.S. Senate, 96, 99
　*See also* Mass media
Judges
　county court appointments and, colonial era, 234
　impeachment of, 559, 1624, 1630, 1635
　selection and appointment of, 1605
　antebellum state constitutions on, 49

state, recall, 554–555
U.S. Supreme Court, 1576–1579
　presidential impeachment and, 1626
Judicial Conduct and Disability Act (1980), 1624, 1635
Judicial Councils, 1635
Judicial Discipline and Removal Act (1990), 1635
Judicial oversight, 759
　shortcomings, 761
Judicial review
　vs. amendment, 38
　antebellum state constitutions on, 49
　in British colonies, 1570
　in early Republic, 75, 1580–1581
　legislative-court interaction and, 1570
　separation of powers and, 1572
　Harlan Stone on, 1574
　of U.S. Constitution, vs. amendment, 38
Judicial supremacy, 1460, 1468
Judiciary. *See* Courts; Judges
Judiciary, federal. *See* Courts, federal
Judiciary Act (1801)
　Federalist judiciary and, 1626
　passage of, 1580
　on U.S. Supreme Court jurisdiction, 1576
*The Jungle. See* Sinclair, Upton
Junk-bond–selling scheme, Coelho and, 1650
Jury service, mid-twentieth century, 1387
Justice, U.S. Department of
　ABSCAM affair and, 1649
　Administrative Index, 1290
　Civil Rights Division, 1249, 1303
　creation of, 1474
　Crèdit Mobilier scandal and, 1644–1645
　House Bank scandal and, 1651
　Nixon and, 1633
　T. Roosevelt era, 1646
　Woodruff-Johnson Resolution and, 1054
Justices. *See* Judges
Justices of the peace, territorial, 251
"Justification books," 736
Juvenile offenders, in Colorado, 218

Kalanianaole, Jonah Kuhio, 317
Kammen, Michael, 6
Kanowitz, Leo, 1390
Kansas
　admitted to union, 125
　legislation on obscenity, 1535
　party voting, 476
Kansas-Nebraska Act (1854), 124
　American party and, 1131
　Stephen A. Douglas and, 1230–1231
Kansas Supreme Court, legislative veto ruling, 1519
Kansas (territory)
　partisan politics and, 255
　slavery and, 257–259

# INDEX

Land grants (*continued*)
  Civil War era, 1205
Landlord and Tenant Act (North
    Carolina), 207
Landon, Alf, 471
Langley, John Wesley, 1647
Language issues, Hawaii territory, 266
Lanterman, Frank, 1355
Lasswell, Harold D., 343
Lathrop, Julia, 1265
Latin America
  recognition of new governments,
    1442–1443
  U.S. forces in, 1427
Latino legislators, 408
  state, 851
  in U.S. Congress, 317, 500
Latinos
  African American legislators and,
    369
  civil rights movement, 1309
  constituency definition and, 404
  legislative recruitment of, 325
  New Mexico Territory legislature
    and, 259
  Latino legislators in U.S. Con-
    gress, 500
Laughlin, Gail, 1387
Lauth, Thomas, 727, 773
*Lau* v. *Nichols* (1974), 1309
Law codes. *See* Civil codes; Crimi-
    nal law
Law-enforcement officers, in U.S.
    Congress, 335
"Law Lords," 1569
Lawmaker (type of legislator), 345
Lawmaking. *See* Legislation
Law of diminishing returns, in cam-
    paign finance, 521–522
Lawyers
  on Judiciary Committees, 993
  in legislatures, twentieth century,
    1632
  in New York Assembly, mid-
    nineteenth century, 204
  Reconstruction era, in Alabama
    legislature, 208
  as southern legislators, mid-
    nineteenth century, 201–202
  in state legislatures, 851
    twentieth-century, 486, 498
  in U.S. congressional staff posi-
    tions, 794
  in U.S. Congress, 334–336, 483–
    484, 500
    mid-nineteenth century, 119–120
    twentieth century, 500
  in U.S. Senate, 470
Leadership
  studies of, 296–297
  *See also* Political leadership
Leadership, legislative
  executive-budget development,
    768
  including policy in budget, 766
  reforms enhancing, 844–845
Leadership Conference on Civil
    Rights, 1303, 1310
League of Nations, congressional re-
    jection of, 1408

League of Nations Covenant, 1429–
    1430, 1447
League of Women Voters, 1387
  legislative-reform movement, 840
  women's campaigns and, 359
Lear, Tobias, 97
Lebanon, American forces in, 1431,
    1434–1435
Lecompton Constitution, 258
Ledbetter, Cal, 841
Lederer, Raymond, resigns from
    House, 553
Lee, Charles, 311
Lee, Richard Henry
  in First Congress, 89
  opinions solicited by, 96
Legal constituency, 400–404
*Legal Tender Cases* (1870–1871),
    1581
*Legislating Together. See* Peterson,
    Mark
Legislation
  introduced by women, 360
  studies of, 291
  in territories, 270–271, 278
  *See also* Initiative process; Legis-
    lative intent
Legislation, federal
  agenda control, 705–706
  amendments
    late twentieth century,
      1063–1064
    mid-nineteenth century, 113
  attaching riders to, 1498
  attempts to evade by states,
    1561–1562
  bicameral, 716
  effect on state legislatures,
    1562
  1870–1895, 139–140
  1895–1911, 144–145
  Federal-Republican era, House
    passage of, 102
  "in the House," 708, 714–715
  moving from committee to floor
    House of Representatives,
      704–705
    U.S. Senate, 705–707
  multiple referral, 828
    late twentieth century, 662–663
  1911–1919, 148–149
  1919–1931, 153
  passing, 711
  placing holds on, 706
  privileged status, 704
  process of consideration, 707–713
    House of Representatives,
      708–711
    U.S. Senate, 711–713
  publication of, 856
  sources of, 859, 1561–1563
  state legislative influence on,
    1561–1563
  studies of, 284
  types of, 1561–1563
  U.S. congressional committees
    and, 641, 650, 655–656, 1012
  volume of, mid-nineteenth cen-
    tury, 120–121
  *See also* Legislative amendments

Legislation, private, 1552
Legislation, state
  adopted by Congress, 1561
  assigning to committees, 690, 692
  authorizing constitutional conven-
    tions, 43
  chamber acceptance, 693, 695
  Constitutional Convention (1787)
    and, 46, 66
  expansion of, 1887–1932, 79
  federalism and, 72, 84–85
  floor activity on, 722–726
  incorporated in constitutions, 41
  publication of, 864
  routinization of, 803
  screening, 693
  shaping of, 692–693
  social welfare, 1920s, 1266
Legislative amendments
  in committee, 711
  complete substitutes, 712–713
  direct up or down votes, 712
  first-degree, 710, 712
  germaneness requirement, 707,
    715, 766
  House of Representatives, 707,
    709–711
  lobbying and, 1118
  by minority-party members, 711
  perfecting, 710, 712
  pro forma, 710
  recommittal motions, 711, 713
  restrictive rules, 714
  second-degree, 710
    perfecting, 712
  specialization and, 1181–1182
  tabling, 703, 712
  U.S. Senate, 707, 712–713
  *See also* Legislation, federal,
    amendments
Legislative behavior measurement,
    1171–1191
Legislative Branch Appropriations Act
  amendment to raise Senate sala-
    ries, 1164
  staff funding provisions, 791–792
Legislative campaign committees,
    fund-raising, 632
Legislative candidates, state, party
    funding, 631–632
Legislative careers
  historical, 481–496
  measurement of, 1175–1176
  modern, 497–512
  private careers and, 1641
  U.S. Congress, 520
  *See also* Careerism in politics;
    Professionalization
Legislative committees
  in bill sponsorship, 723
  chairpersons of, 971
  decision-making in, 970–973
  Fenno on, 589, 596
  investigations by
    antebellum era, 1258
    Progressive Era, 1646
  norms in, 1181–1182
  pressure groups and, 1113
  research on, 1177–1181
  seniority and, 1175

Lincoln, Abraham (*continued*)
federalism-liberty link and, 76
on judge selection, 1578
legislative initiatives of, 610
nominations by, 1612
party support for, 122
proclamation of 1863, 1405–1406
vs. Radical Republicans, 125
Reconstruction plans of, 126, 1406
on states' rights, 74
U.S. Supreme Court and, 1581
use of executive power, 1405
use of war powers, 1425–1426
veto use, 1497–1498
Lincoln, Levi, Yazoo land scandal and, 1126–1127
Lincoln-Douglas debates, 468
Lincoln Savings and Loan scandal, 1166
Lindsey, Ben, 218
Lippmann, Walter, 1447
Liquor-prohibition legislation. *See* Prohibition
Literacy tests, 1245–1246
Literary theory, 816
Literature, censorship of, 1536
*Little* v. *Barreme*, 1423
Livingston, Edward, 1459
Livingston, Robert R., 1439
Lloyd, Henry Demarest, *Wealth Against Commonwealth*, 208–209
Lobbying, 1105–1121
antebellum era, 1642–1643
federalism and, 72
industrial development and, 78
late nineteenth century
Midwest, 210
Pennsylvania, 209
registration of, 1645
regulation of, 952
late twentieth century, PACs and, 1092, 1099
mid-nineteenth century, 119–120
regulation of, 1647
public interest, 822
state level, 852
substantive representation and, 423
*See also* Interests
Local Fiscal Assistance Act, 1271–1272
Local government
administrative units
colonial period, 26, 233–235
nineteenth century, 235–239
constituencies of, 405
early twentieth century, 239–244
1887–1932, expansion of, 78–79
federal regulation of, mid-twentieth century, 889
Great Depression era, 81
late twentieth century, 244–246
reapportionment and, 387
revenue sharing and, 84
Revolutionary era, New England, 182, 190
state financial assistance, 780
suburbanization and, 244
*See also* City government; County court; County government;

Municipal corporation; Town meeting
Localism
legislative recruitment and, 332–333
of U.S. legislators, 464
*Lochner* v. *New York* (1905), 1262
Locke, John, *Two Treatises of Government*, 25
Lodge, Henry Cabot, 152, 1447
Commission on the Organization of the Executive Branch of the Government, 1480–1481
M. Poindexter and, 1125
Lodge-Brown bill. *See* Commission on the Organization of the Executive Branch of the Government
Lodge force bill (1890), 1561
Loewenberg, Gerhard, 593
Loewenberg, Gerhard, Patterson, C. Samuel, and Jewell, Malcolm, *Handbook of Legislative Research*, 298, 566–567
Loftus, Tom, 632
Logan Act (1799), 1441
*Logic of Congressional Action, The. See* Arnold, Douglas
*Logic of Delegation, The. See* Kiewiet, D. Roderick
Logjams, legislative. *See* Legislative logjams
"Logrolling" (vote trading), antebellum, 1199
London Naval Conference (1930), executive-privilege issues, 1463
Long, Gillis, 1061
Long, Huey P.
First Amendment and, 1539
impeachment proceedings against, 559, 1630–1631
oath of office, 312
F. D. Roosevelt and, 1268
Long, Jefferson F., 315, 365
Long, Russell, on WIN Program, 1271
Longworth, Nicholas, 151, 873
Loomis, Burdett, 597
Lore, Charles, 733
Lorimer, William, 1558
Los Angeles (city), charter (1903), recall provisions, 554
Los Angeles County, home-rule charter (1912), 242
Lott, Trent, 989
Lotteries, as example of policy innovation diffusion, 1356
Louderback, Harold C., 1631
impeachment of, 558–559
Louisiana
African American legislators, 379
antebellum, banking system of, 1204
Federalist-Republican era, slavery in, 1225
First Amendment and, 1539
*See also* Orleans Territory
Louisiana constitution (1898), voting requirements of, 51

Louisiana constitution (1921), U.S. Constitution and, 40
Louisiana legislature, railroad regulation and, 216
Louisiana Purchase
slavery question and, 1226
west Florida and, 1127
Lovett, Robert Morrs, 1285
Lowell, A. Lawrence, 209, 211, 282, 951
Lowenthal, Max, *The Federal Bureau of Investigation*, 1288–1289
*Lowry* v. *Reagan* (1987), 1435
Loyalists. *See* Whig Loyalists
Loyalty oaths
Civil War era, by federal officeholders, 112
colonial period, 1278
during Civil War and Reconstruction, 1280
for federal employees, 1280, 1284
for schoolteachers, 1282–1283, 1285, 1292
southern states, 1279
state legislatures, 1285
suffrage and, 1238
Loyalty Review Board (1947), 1600
Lucas, Philander, 1630
Luce, Robert, 735, 952
Lukens, Donald E. ("Buzz"), scandalous behavior of, 508
*Lusitania*, 1053
Lusk, Clayton, 1282–1283
Lynch, John R., 368
Lynching, 1299, 1372
federal antilynching laws, 1300–1301
Lyon, Caleb, 265

Maass, Arthur, *Congress and the Common Good*, 582
MacArthur, Douglas
dismissal of, 1465
recalled, 1449
McCain, John, 1166
McCarran, Patrick, 1600
McCarran Act (1950), 1287
internment program authorization, 1289–1290
McCarthy, Charles, 1552
McCarthy, Eugene
FAP and, 1272
FECA amendments and, 1095
McCarthy, Joseph R.
bureaucracy and, 1599
condemnation of, 1157
federal government investigations, 1287–1288
political fall, 1457
press and, 1526–1527
Senate censure, 551
State Department investigation, 1465
television coverage of, 1530
Macclesfield, Thomas Parker, Lord Chancellor, 1625
McCluggage, Vera, 672
McComb, H. S., 1645
McCord, James, 1633

# INDEX

*Marbury* v. *Madison* (1803), 75, 1460, 1580
Marginalized classes
  Civil Rights Act (1964) and, 1212
  early twentieth century, 1386
  judiciary and, 1574
  *See also* Ethnic demographics; Poverty; Vagrants
Margolis, Larry, 840–841
Market. *See* National market
Marriage laws
  colonial era, 1380–1381
  post–Revolutionary era, 1382
  territorial establishment of, 252, 270
"Married persons clauses" (labor law), 1387
Married Women's Property Act (Mississippi), 1382
Married Women's Property Act (N.Y. State), 1382
Marsh, George Perkins, *Man and Nature*, 1315
Marshall, John
  Samuel Chase and, 1627
  executive-veto rulings, 1491
  federalism and, 75
  on *Fletcher* v. *Peck* (1810), 1573
  *McCulloch* v. *Maryland* (1819) and, 1572, 1580
  *Marbury* v. *Madison* (1803) and, 1580
  on presidential powers, 1429, 1444, 1459–1460
  state constitutional interpretation and, 1580
  on war powers, 1423
Marshall, Thurgood
  retirement of, 1616
  Senate hearings on, 1579
Marshall, William. *See* Weingast, Barry
Marshall Plan, 161, 1449
Martin, Joseph, 1055
Martin, Luther, 63, 555
Martineau, Harriet, 108
Maryland
  budgetary process, 768
  Ober Law, 1291
  U.S. congressional delegates of, 104
Maryland Colony
  commercial legislation in, 1196
  constitutionalism in, 183
  ministerial corruption in, 33
  senatorial property requirements in, 186
  voting qualifications, 1236
Maryland constitution, Plumber on, 735
Maryland constitutional convention (1850), Dorr's Rebellion and, 48
Maryland constitutional convention (1967), 42
Maryland legislature, reforms, 841
Mason, George, 304
  on citizenship requirement for legislators, 305
  at Constitutional Convention, 64, 66–67

Mason, James M., 552
Masonic Lodge (N.Y. State), 1128
Massachusetts
  antebellum era
    reform movement in, 1383
    social welfare in, 1258–1259
    Texas annexation issue and, 1229
  apportionment, in post-Revolutionary state legislature, 8
  colonial legislators' instructions regarding Stamp Act, 8
  divided government, 879
  expulsion of legislators, 553
  federal district court orders against, 86
  Federal-Republican era, legislators of, 197–198
  Great Depression–era, 1268
  gubernatorial veto, 1489
  late twentieth century
    pornography control in, 1393
    social welfare in, 1273–1274
  legislators of, nineteenth century, 201, 210
  1920s, social legislation of, 220
  political innovation diffusion and, 1356
  Progressive Era, unemployment insurance proposed in, 1264
  senator apportionment, 1549
  woman labor legislation in, 218
  *See also* Shay's Rebellion
Massachusetts Assembly, social welfare investigations of, 1257
Massachusetts Bay Colony
  boundaries secured by, 190
  British Coercive Acts and, 55
  charter of, on nomination powers, 1606
  colonial assembly, religious tests for membership, 309
  commercial legislation in, 1196
  constitutionalism in, 182–183
  divorce law in, 1380
  executive-legislative cooperation in, 33
  proportional representation in, 186–187
  proposed senate for, 187
  slavery in, 1220–1221
  social welfare policy of, 1256
  Townshend duties and, 177
Massachusetts Board of Education, antebellum era, 1259
Massachusetts Colony
  boundaries secured by, 190
  British Coercive Acts and, 55
  constitutionalism in, 182–183
  executive-legislative cooperation in, 33
  proportional representation in, 186–187
  proposed senate for, 187
  Townshend duties and, 177
  voting qualifications, 1236
Massachusetts constitution
  executive power in, 59
  popular ratification of, 45
  U.S. Constitution modeled on, 38

Massachusetts constitutional convention (1780)
  guiding principle of, 39
  as pioneering effort, 45
Massachusetts constitutional convention (1820–1821), ideological division in, 47
Massachusetts General Court
  bill files, 864
  joint-committee system, 674–675
  Know-Nothings and, 204
  partisanship in, 952
  public education policy of, 1259
  reforms, 840
  War of 1812, speeches on, 863
Massachusetts General Court. House, 965, 1383
Massachusetts legislature. *See* Massachusetts General Court
Massachusetts State Board of Health, 1262
Massage, regulation of, 1107
Mass media
  accountability, 1790s, 1534
  constituency definition and, 404
  corruption coverage by, 1650, 1652
  dissemination right, 1534–1535
  electronic, 1542–1544
  fairness doctrine, 1542–1543
  freedom of expression and, 1542
  legislative coverage by, 1521–1532
  legislative historiography and, 293
  lobbyist-legislator coverage by, 1115–1116
  presidential coverage by, 612–613
  prior restraint and, 1541
  in Reagan era, 616–617
  role in Senate elections, 477–478
  senatorial coverage by, 459–460
  in state legislative elections, 437
  U.S. congressional election coverage by
    incumbency rates and, 454
    minimal, 455, 457
  voter participation and, 165
  women candidates and, 328
  World War I and, 1537–1538
  World War II and, 1539
  *See also* Electronic media; Journalistic coverage
Maternity leave, 1394
Mathematics, legislative historiography and, 294–295
Matsunaga, Spark, 1060
Matteson, Orasmus B., 1643
  resigns from House, 553
Matthews, Donald R., 586, 588, 597, 599, 995–996
Mattingly, Mack, 476
Maw, Herbert, 226
May, Andrew Jackson, 1161, 1647
May, Erskine, 304
*Mayaguez* rescue, 826
Mayhew, David R., 455, 589, 594
  *Congress: The Electoral Connection*, 578
  histograms, 517, 519
Mayors
  colonial era, 235
  early twentieth century, 241

# INDEX

Missouri
  grand-jury investigations, early twentieth century, 1646
  impeachment provisions, 559
  legislators of, twentieth century, 491, 494
  U.S. Senate election of 1905, 18–19
Missouri Compromise (1820), 1403
  Stephen A. Douglas and, 1230–1231
  Era of Good Feelings and, 199
  passage of, 1226
  Senate role in, 99
  on slave trade, 1225
Missouri constitution, amendment procedures of, 47
Missouri Organic Act (1812), 254
Missouri (territory)
  partisan politics and, 255
  slavery and, 257
  slavery question in, 1225–1226
Mitchell, Arthur W., 315, 368
Mitchell, Charles B., 552
Mitchell, George
  Democratic party organs and, 662
  television skill of, 502–503
Mitchell, Parren, 383
Mitchell, William DeWitt, 1506
Mitchill, Samuel Latham, 98–99
Mixed corporations, advent of, 200
Model Cities program, 414
Mohr, James, 1391
Molinari, Susan, 317
Monarchy
  American constitutionalism and, 179–180
  See also British monarchy
Moncrief, Gary, 772
Mondale, Walter, vs. Reagan, 453
Mondell, Franklin, 150
Monetary policy. See Economic issues
Monetary question. See Currency
Monroe, James
  Clay and, 100–101
  in First Congress, 89
  Four Years Act (1820) and, 1610
  Non-Importation Act and, 1127
  Old Republicans and, 1126
  Seminole conflict, 1424
  Senate relations with, 99
  use of executive privilege, 1460
  veto use, 1492
  view of presidency, 1402
  Virginia gubernatorial election and, 197
Monroe Doctrine, 1403
  principles of, 1442–1443
  Roosevelt corollary, 1427
Monroney, Mike, drafts Legislative Reorganization Act, 789
Montana
  old-age pensions in, 220
  party voting, 476
Montana legislature, espionage and sedition acts, 1282–1283
Montana (territory)
  capital location battle, 276
  partisan politics in, 268
Montgomery, G. V. ("Sonny"), Veter-

ans Committee and, 503
*Monthly Checklist of State Publications*, 867
Moral issues
  abolitionism as, 1227
  opinion-policy congruence on, 540–541
  in state legislatures, 1115
  teenage sexuality as, 1393
  U.S. congressional corruption and, 1648
  See also Corruption; Ethics standards
Moralistic state culture, 1353
Moral reform legislation, 1255
  antebellum era, 1259–1260
  early twentieth century, 1386
  late nineteenth century, 1262–1263
Moral reforms, antebellum era, 1383–1384
Morgan, Edmund S., 1220
Morgan, William, 1128
Mormons. See Church of Jesus Christ of Latter-day Saints
Morrill Act (1862), 1260
Morris, Gouverneur, 1459
  on property qualifications, 308
  on religious tests for legislators, 310
  on Senate foreign policy–making, 1442
  on Senate terms, 467
*Morrison* v. *Olson* (1988), 1575
Morse, Samuel F. B., 1524
Morse, Wayne, 468, 1431
Morton, Rogers, 1468
Morton, Thurston, on successful Senate contests, 467
Moseley-Braun, Carol, 369, 470
Moss, John E., 1466
Mothers' Aid legislation, as example of policy innovation spreading, 1348
Mothers' pensions. See Pensions, for mothers
Motion pictures, censorship of, 1536–1537, 1541
Motions to proceed, 705–706
  filibustering, 706
Motivation-displacement-rationalization theory, 344
Moynihan, Daniel P.
  D'Amato and, 1577
  Family Assistance Plan and, 1264
Muckraking, 1645–1646
  in magazine journalism, 1525
Mudd, Roger, 1530
Mugwumps, electoral reforms and, 1124
Muhlenburg, Frederick A.
  as House Speaker, 91
  House Ways and Means Committee appointed by, 92
  Sedgwick and, 92
Muir, John, 1317
*Muller* v. *Oregon* (1908), 1385
Multicandidate committees, federal regulation of, 1092
Multi-issue groups, agendas of, 1108
Multimember districts, 439–441

racial gerrymandering and, 379
  women running in, 356
Multinational Force in Lebanon Resolution (1983), 1435
Multiple-box balloting, 1245
Multiple legislative referral, 573
  in U.S. House, 662–663, 1062–1063
  lobbying and, 1114
Multiyear appropriations, 736
Mundt, Karl, television appearances of, 1530
Munger, Michael C., 998, 1102
Municipal corporation
  colonial era, 235
  nineteenth century, 236
Municipal government reform. See Urban government reform
Municipalities
  "home rule" for, 1207–1208
  See also Metropolitan areas
Murder law, antebellum, southern states, 1219
Murdock, Victor, 1052
Murphy, Nathan O., 272
Murray, Charles A., 1273
Murray, John, 197
Murray, William ("Alfalfa Bill"), 222
Murray, William Vans, 98
Muscle Shoals water-power project, Farm Bloc and, 1138
Muskie, Edmund S., 1323
*Mutual Film Corp.* v. *Industrial Commission of Ohio* (1915), 1537
Myers, Jim, 1527
Myers, Michael J. "Ozzie," expelled from House, 552
*Myers* v. *United States* (1926), 1612
Myrdal, Gunnar, *An American Dilemma*, 1302

NAACP. See National Association for the Advancement of Colored People
Nader, Ralph, 1322
  traffic safety legislation and, 1006
Nance, John, federal public works and, 1267
Nash, Gary B., 27
Nast, Thomas, 1525
Nathan, Richard, *The Administrative Presidency*, 1412
National Academy of Public Administration, 1151
National Aeronautics and Space Administration (NASA), appropriations, 1515
National American Woman Suffrage Association (NAWSA), 1246–1248
National Archives, original bills stored in, 856
National Association for the Advancement of Colored People (NAACP), 1300, 1614
  suffrage and, 1248
National Association of Colored Women, 1248
National Association of Letter Carriers, 1112

Panama, American forces in, 1989, 1435–1436
Panama Canal
  foreign policy issues, 1446
  return of, 1451
Panama Canal treaties, Senate debates on, radio coverage of, 1530
Panics, financial. *See* Financial panics
Paper currency
  of Continental Congress, 58
  *Legal Tender Cases* on, 1581
Paradigmatic modeling, legislative historiography and, 298–299
Parental leave, 1394
Park, Tongsun, 1163, 1648
Parker, John J.
  Progressive party and, 1582
  U.S. Supreme Court nomination denied to, 1614
Park preservation movement. *See* Conservation movement
Parliamentary government. *See* Canada. Parliament; European parliaments; Great Britain. Parliament; Representative government
Parliamentary privilege, violations of, 1522
Parliamentary procedure, 1551
Parliamentary rules
  on congressional committees, 641
  defined, 1049
  U.S. congressional majority leadership and, 607
  in U.S. House, 661
  *See also* Suspension of the rules
Parliament (Great Britain). *See* Great Britain. Parliament
Parsons, Theophilus
  "Essex Result," 181
  on proportional representation, 190
  on representation, 7
Partisan politics
  antebellum era, land policy and, 1200–1201
  in budget process, 772
  colonial era, 33–34
  committee integration and, 1179–1180
  in congressional elections, 451, 457, 508
  in constitutional ratification campaign, 192
  corruption and, 1652
  declining
    Clubb on, 538
    in congressional elections, 541
    voter turnout and, 463
  early twentieth century, electoral reforms and, 492
  electoral realignments of. *See* Electoral realignments
  in European parliaments, 593
  Federalist-Republican era, 196
  Great Depression era, 221
  impeachment and, 1621
  late nineteenth century, 489
  in legislative staff structure, 804–806, 808, 812

measurement of, 1184–1185
mid-nineteenth century, 118
  Pennsylvania, 209
1967–1976, 166
presidential legislative aims and, 609–610
Reconstruction era, in state legislatures, 951
research on, 900–901
  relation to policy outcomes, 903–904
Revolutionary era, 188–189
sources of factionalism, 1070–1074
state chamber seating arrangements and, 972
state conference committees and, 728
state legislative elections and, 439, 445
state legislative redistricting and, 438
in territories, post-1862, 266–268
in U.S. Congress, 931–945, 1445
  legislative surges and, 892–893
U.S. congressional change and, 158–159
U.S. congressional power fragmentation and, 1069
in U.S. House
  committee appointments, 606
  legislative activity, 608
in U.S. House elections
  incumbency and, 452
  split-ticket voting replaces, 454
  *See also* Bipartisanship; Political parties; Straight-ticket voting
Partisan representation, in electoral realignments, 539–540
Party agendas, 937–941
  party cohesion and, 944
  party-leadership votes and, 936–937
Party caucuses. *See* Caucuses
Party cohesion
  lax, position-taking and, 455–456
  measurement of, 1185–1186
  in state legislative committees, 974
  in U.S. House, 931–945
Party conventions, nomination of presidential candidates, 1403, 1411
Party-dominated committees model, 643
Party leadership
  committee assignment responsibility, 986
  Eisenhower administration, 1410
  electoral function, 852
  late twentieth century
    news reporters and, 1529
    PAC contributions to, 1100
  mid-nineteenth century, New Jersey, 949
  PAC funding of committees, 632
  party-enhancing reforms, 828
  presidential role in, 1404
  *See also* Majority-party leadership; Roll-call voting
Party leadership, state, 961–967, 973, 975–976

committee appointments, 635
decline in, 853
influence on committee policy, 689–690
Party-line politics. *See* Partisan politics
Party loyalty. *See* Partisan politics
Party platforms, realignment eras, 881
Party politics. *See* Partisan politics
Party system
  committee domination by, 580
  rational choice perspective, 578–579
Party voting
  electoral realignment eras, 881–882
  state legislatures, 636–638
  in U.S. Senate elections, 475–476
  vs. incumbency voting, 518
Pascoe, Peggy, 1381
Passman, Otto E., 1164
Patent law, early, 1197–1198
Paterson, William, at Constitutional Convention, 62, 64
Patriotism, Revolutionary era, 61
Patronage
  Jacksonian era, 1404
  Roosevelt's use of, 1409
  state-level, 628
Patterson, Elizabeth, 317
Patterson, James Thomas, 222, 224–225, 1056
Patterson, James W., 1160, 1475, 1645
Patterson, Samuel. *See* Loewenberg, Gerhard
Patterson, Samuel C., 796, 972
*Patterson* v. *Colorado* (1907), 1536
Paul, Alice, 1247
Paupers. *See* Poverty
Pay-as-you-go financing, 744, 827
Payne, James, on legislators' motivations, 343–344
Payne-Aldrich tariff, 1135–1136
Payson, Lewis E., 1318
PCA. *See* Production Code Administration
Peabody, Robert L., 597, 1059
Pearson, Drew, 1161, 1648
Peck, James H., 558, 1627, 1630
Peffer, William A., Populist party and, 1132–1133
Pelosi, Nancy, 317
Pendleton, Edmund
  on electioneering, 189
  property qualifications and, 187
Pendleton Act (1883), 139, 1591, 1613
Penner, Rudolph, 731
Pennington, William, 115
Pennsylvania
  corruption in, nineteenth century, 208–209
  Federal-Republican era
    emancipation in, 1224
    federal politics and, 199
    impeachments in, 1626
    legislators of, 198
  Great Depression era, 221
                     *(continued)*

# INDEX

Pole, J. R., 26
"Police powers." *See* Regulatory
legislation
Policy congruence, 410–412
measuring, 412
as response to constituency,
409
as substantive representation,
422
Policy-dimensional analysis, 1187
Policy entrepreneurship
business lobbies and, 1117
presidential legislative aims and,
617
U.S. congressional committees
agendas and, 1004–1006
coalition-building and, 1010
jurisdiction and, 1003
Policy formation. *See* Policy-making
Policy-making
choice-consequence relationship,
579
committee role in, 876–877
constitutional context, 873–875
effect of coalitions on, 876
executive influence, records of,
857–858
gubernatorial responsibility,
623–626
implementation
task environment, 763
U.S. Congress oversight, 757–
759, 1022
incrementalist, 873, 879
lack of major changes in, 878
legislative-executive interaction,
849–850
as legislator's motivation, 347
by little government, 875
localized elections and, 875
localized interests affecting, 877,
880
majority preference and, 575–
576
nonparticularistic, 582
party role in, 875–879
state-level, 635–638
party vs. committee dominance,
635
rational choice analysis, 574
representation in context of, 3–4
sectional diversity and, 874
state, impact of reforms on,
846–847
U.S. congressional organization
and, 876–879
Policy networks, 1357
Policy stalemate. *See* Political
gridlock
Policy subgovernments. *See*
Subgovernments
Policy window, 1354
Political action committees (PACs),
1091–1104, 1110
campaign expenditures
caucus and leadership committee funding, 632
congressional races, 521
contribution to incumbents, 831

effect on voting behavior, 522
Coelho and, 458, 1650
fundraising, 478
growth of, 521
in 1970s, 167
purposes of, 1009
U.S. congressional campaigns
and, 458, 542
women campaigning and, 356–
357
Political campaign contributions,
corporate. *See* Corporate political campaign contributions
Political campaigns. *See*
Electioneering
Political communication
in grass-roots lobbying, 1112
in state legislative elections, 446
U.S. Congress, 1146–1147
Political corruption. *See* Corruption
Political culture concept, women in
legislatures and, 353
Political experience, value of for
candidates, 337–338
Political gridlock
conditions for, 619
U.S. congressional work load and,
1149
Political innovations
adoption stage, 1352
defined, 1352
British colonies and, 24
defined, 1351–1352
diffusion process, 1352
defined, 1352
disinnovation, 1349, 1351
economic resources and, 1353
electoral competition and,
1353–1354
entrepreneurs, 1355
external determinants, 1356–1358
defined, 1352
federal, 1349–1351
institutional capacity and, 1354
internal determinants, 1353–1356
defined, 1352
interstate, 1349–1350
national diffusion, 1356
partisan politics and, 903–904
policy process and, 1351–1358
problem recognition, 1352
professional networks and,
1356–1357
regional diffusion, 1356
solution formulation, 1352
state culture and, 1353
state legislatures and, 1348, 1547
Political leadership
colonial era, 28–29
institutionalization and, 1175
state appointive powers, 687
in state legislatures, 961
training opportunities, for women,
355
women and, 356–361
*See also* Party leadership; Leadership, legislative
Political machines.
immigrant recruitment and, 325

senator selection and, 1557
*See also under* Political parties
Political participation
colonial era, 27, 29
declining, 462–463
expectations and, 1990s, 171
expectations of representatives
vs. legislature as whole,
416
impact on policy, 428
legislator response to constituency and, 410
in local government, early twentieth century, 241
media and,
165
party loyalty and, 403
Revolutionary era, 187–188
sources of information for, 165
southern states, late nineteenth
century, 51
state constitutions and, nineteenth century, 41–43, 47
Political parties
African American legislators and,
383
in American colonies, 17
budgetary influence, 828
campaign financing role, 523
campaigns and, nineteenth century, 1557
coalitions of, New Jersey, 217
colonial era, 34
constituencies of
critical elections and, 535–536
differences across, 405
early nineteenth century, 104–105,
530
effects of federal system on,
875–876
electoral realignments, 879–883
endorsement of candidates, state
level, 631
executive and legislative dominance, 635–636
executive-branch control and, 1085
factionalism and, 1070–1071
federalism and, 72, 77
fragmentation of, 875–876
heterogeneous membership, 878
industrial development and, 78
influence of, studies, 290, 293
influence on representatives,
16–18
late twentieth century, declining
influence of, 541
legislative historiography and, 288
legislative surges and, 890–893
legislator responsibility to, 425
legislator's ambition and, 349
legislature organization and, 1551
loyalty to, voting behavior and,
406–407
policy-making role, 635–638
preprimary endorsements, 621–
622, 631
presidential cabinet and, 1588
Progressive historians on, 196
*(continued)*

Political parties (*continued*)
  proportional representation and, 401
  Reconstruction constitutional conventions and, 50
  representative function in Congress, 17–18
  research on congressional role
    conceptualization, 915–916
    criticism of, 909–914
    deemphasizing, 912
    emphasizing, 913–914
    empirical, 923–925
    external relationships and, 902–903
    ignoring, 912–913
    institutional issues, 907–908
    linkage issues, 906–907, 916–920
    narrative approaches, 901–902
    nontraditional, 905–908
    normative issues, 923–925
    operational issues, 920–923
    operations and, 903–905
    theory construction, 914–925
    theory needs, 909–914
    traditional, 900–905
  response to constituency and, 410
  rotation of legislators, 514
  spending reform and, 1916, 1337
  statehood struggles and, 262
  state legislatures, 633, 947–981
    characteristics, 879
    committees and, 358
    committee size and, 680
  state/local, 87
  PACs and, 1098
  television crews of, 1531
  in territorial legislatures, 255
  U.S. congressional roles of
    contemporary research, 899–908
    increasing power, 828
    limits on, 921–922
    party leaders and, 922–923
    power fragmentation and, 1068
    reform and, 827–828
    U.S. House Ways and Means Committee and, 1038
    U.S. Senate, 878
    weakness of, 1411–1412
  women in legislatures and, 356
  *See also* Bipartisanship; British parties; Campaign contributions; Constituent-representative relations; Electoral realignments; Insurgency; One-party rule; Partisan politics; Party agendas; Party cohesion; Party discipline; Party leadership; Party system; Third political parties
Political philosophy, on nature of representation, 420–421
*Political Presidency, The. See* Kellerman, Barbara
"Political questions" doctrine, 1575
  *Baker* v. *Carr* (1962) and, 1574
Political realignments. *See* Electoral realignments
Political reforms
  1887–1932, 79

late nineteenth century, 952
  Populist party proposals for, 1132
  Progressive Era, 217–218
Political representation. *See* Representative government
Political rights. *See* English political rights; Suffrage
Political science
  legislative historiography and, 284
  legislators' motivations and, 322
  U.S. congressional parties' roles and, 899
Politico (type of legislator), defined, 421
Politics/administration dichotomy, 757
Polk, James K.
  against secrecy in government, 1455
  annexation of Texas, 1443
  expansion crisis and, 123
  on federalism-liberty link, 74
  nominations by, 1611–1612
  on Tariff Reduction bill lobbying, 119
  as U.S. House Ways and Means Committee speaker, 115–116
  use of executive power, 1404
  use of executive privilege, 1461
  veto use, 1496–1497
  war with Mexico, 1425, 1514–1521
  Wilmot and, 1229
Polk, Trusten, 552
Polling places, Revolutionary era, 188
*Pollock* v. *Farmers Loan and Trust Company* (1895), 81
Polls, use of, 430
Poll tax, 1245
  elimination of, 1248–1249, 1372
  Mississippi, 51
Polsby, Nelson W., 108–109, 289, 592–594, 651, 837
  "The Institutionalization of the U.S. House of Representatives," 570
Polygamy, 260–261
  election to Congress and, 310
Pomeroy, Samuel C., 113
Poorhouses, antebellum era, 1258
Poor laws
  English, colonial social welfare policy and, 1256
  *See also* Social welfare legislation
Poor relief. *See* Public welfare
Popular sovereignty
  colonial independence movement and, 178
  constitutional conventions and, 37, 39, 42–43, 45
  federalism and, 71
  A. C. Hanson on, 183
  Pennsylvania constitutionalism and, 184
  state constitutionalism and, 38–40, 46, 180–181, 190
Population
  as basis for apportionment
    Constitutional Convention on, 10–11
    Continental Congress debates over, 9

"one person, one vote," 16
  in post-Revolutionary U.S., 9–10
  Three-fifths Compromise for slaves, 13–14
  under Northwest Ordinance (1787), 10
  U.S. experiments with, 14–16
  as basis for legislator selection, 1549
  representation and, in post-Revolutionary legislatures, 8
Population changes
  African American legislators and, 369, 379
  1860–1930, 132
  local government and, late twentieth century, 245
  reapportionment and, 387, 1549–1550
  redistricting and, 391
  sectionalism and, 1373–1374
  statehood struggle and, 1565
  U.S. congressional changes and, 1981–1990, 170
Populism
  Nebraska, 211
  political representation and, in nineteenth century, 14
  in post-Revolutionary U.S., 7, 12
  Reconstruction era, 208
Populist party, 880, 1132–1133, 1139, 1365
  founded, 534
  G. W. Norris and, 1125–1126
  Progressivism and, 1137–1138
  sectionalism and, 1367
  suffrage and, 1245
  in U.S. House of Representatives, 1870–1895, 135
Pork barrel appropriations, 773
  *See also* Resource allocation
Pork barrel legislation, 829
  Shepsle and Weingast on, 595
Pornography. *See* Obscenity
Pornography-control legislation, 1393
  late nineteenth century, 1262, 1390–1391
  late twentieth century, U.S. Supreme Court and, 1584
  Rohde on, 1394
Porter, John, expelled from House of Burgesses, 309
Port regulation. *See* Shipping regulation
Position-taking, by U.S. representatives, 455–456
Posner, Richard, 1572
Post Office, U.S.
  bureaucracy and, 1595
  media's right of dissemination and, 1534–1535
  obscene materials and, 1535
Potter, David, 1131
Poverty
  legislator attitudes toward, 1255
  New Deal legislation and, 1269
  Nixon era legislation and, 1272
  *See also* Poor laws
Powell, Adam Clayton, Jr., 315, 368, 998, 1157, 1629

reforms, 838, 846
state legislatures, 1416
computerization of data, 804
*Red Lion Broadcasting Co.* v. *Federal Communications Commission* (1969), 1542
Red squads, 1292
Reece, B. Carroll, 1289
Reed, David, 1507
Reed, Harrison, 1629–1630
Reed, Thomas (fl. 1918), on Sheppard-Towner bill, 1265
Reed, Thomas B. (1839–1902), 137, 819, 1051
resignation of, 1445
Reed, Thomas, 1406
Reed, W. Robert, 516
Reeder, Andrew, 258
Reed Rules, U.S. House Speaker power and, 610
Reelection
committee selection and, 990, 994
impact on policy position, 568
incumbency advantage and, 517*t*
as legislator's motivation, 346–347
rates of, 524
response to constituency and, 413, 416, 425
of state legislators, 852
U.S. Congress oversight and, 754–756
of U.S. senators, 474
Reelection constituency, 406–408, 427
Reference bureaus, 1552
Reference services, for state legislatures, 837
Referendum procedure. *See* Initiative and referendum procedure
Reform. *See* Administrative reform; Political reforms; Reform, congressional; Reform, legislative
Reform, congressional, 832
in accountability, 824–825, 830–832
agency staff increases, 793
budgetary, 823
consequences of, 820
defined, 815
examples of, 818–825
history, 822–825
to improve responsiveness, 823–824, 828–830
internal and external imperatives, 815–816
1967–1976, 165–166
political incentives, 822
promoting visibility, 824, 830–831
in response to public pressure, 816
for responsibility, 822–823, 825–828
results of, 825–832
revolt against Cannon, 1910–1911, 819–820
theories of, 816–817
in U.S. House, 1967–1976, 165–166
in U.S. Senate, 1967–1976, 166
vs. change, 815–816
*See also* Executive branch, reorganization

Reform, electoral, Progressive Era, 1124–1125, 1139, 1646
Reform, legislative
characteristics of, 842–845
citizens' campaigns, 840
consequences of, 845–853
in frequency and length of sessions, 843, 847
in functional performance, 849–851
funding for, 839
historiography and, 285, 289–290
improving operations, 844
incentives for, 1416
increasing governmental power, 848–849
increasing space and facilities, 844, 847–848
institution and process, 851–853
internal and external impetus, 838
national organizations supporting, 839
obstacles to, 841–842
outside vs. inside strategies, 840
public policy, 846–847
reducing size of legislature, 843
requiring amendments to constitutions, 841
salary increases, 843
in standards of conduct, 843
variety of recommendations for, 842
Reform legislation
Progressive Era, 1207–1210
state, Reconstruction era, 950–951
*See also* Moral reform legislation; Political reforms; Social reforms
Refugees, Freedmen and Abandoned Land, Bureau of. *See* Freedmen's Bureau
Regionalism
antebellum era, 1228
defined, 1361
Democratic party agenda and, 939
Democratic party leadership support and, 942
electoral realignment and, 535–536
legislative historiography and, 282
new federalism and, 1600–1601
policy-making and, 874
political ramifications of, 1361–1364
state constitutions and, 44
statehood struggles and, 1565
tariff policy and, 1201
U.S. congressional voting and, 118
Regional planning, Great Depression era, 224
*Register of Debates in Congress*, 856, 1523
Regular appropriations bills. *See* General appropriations bills
Regulations, state, legislative review, 850
Regulatory agencies. *See* Independent regulatory commissions
Regulatory legislation
antebellum, 1199, 1202–1203
bureaucracy and, 1595

Congress following states' examples, 1561
1895–1911, 144
mid-twentieth century, 83–85, 889
New Deal era, of states, 1211
1911–1919, 148
1930–1945, 158
nineteenth century, U.S. Supreme Court and, 1582
Progressive Era, 216–217, 1207–1210
radio and, 1538
by state legislatures, 1347
states burdened by, 86, 230
*See also* Commercial regulation; Deregulation; Economic regulation; Food and drug regulation
Rehabilitation Act (1973), 1309
Rehnquist, William
dissent in *Chadha* case, 1511–1512
impeachments and, 1636
U.S. Supreme Court service of, 1584–1585, 1615
Reid, John W., expelled from House, 552
Reilly, William, 1328
Reinsch, Paul S., 680
*American Legislatures and Legislative Methods*, 675
Relief (aid). *See* Public welfare
Relief Appropriation Act (1939), 1284
Relief legislation. *See* Social welfare legislation
Religion
ERA and, 1351
legislative recruitment and, 329–331
studies of, 330–331
suffrage and
early Republic, 1239
Revolutionary era, 1238
as voting qualification, 1236
*See also individual religions*
Religious affiliation
Federal-Republican era, Middle States, 198
late twentieth century
freedom of, 1585
schools and, 1584
nineteenth century
Midwest, 210
Nebraska, 211
New England, 202
*See also* School prayer
Religious revivals
abolitionism and, 1220
moral legislation and, 1259–1260
Reluctant (type of legislator), 345
Removal of appointees, 1624
Constitutional Convention debate on, 1608
from judiciary, 1577
*See also* Impeachment; Presidential powers
Reorganization Act (1939), 1480, 1598
Reorganization Act (1946). *See* Legislative Reorganization Act (1946)

Representation
American ideas and practices of, 5–14
concept of, 3–5, 420–421
constituency support and, 4
debates over, in Continental Congress, 9
geographical unit at center of, 18
of interests, 19
legislative composition and, 4
in nonlegislative systems, 4–5
political parties and, 14
types of, 421–424
See also Actual representation; Compositional representation; Constituent-representative relations; Instrumental representation; Proportional representation; Symbolic representation
Representational constituency, 427
Representational role, defined, 424
Representative
as delegate, in post-Revolutionary era, 8
determining status of, 3
political role of, 4
responsiveness of, 3–4
sources of influence on, 16–18
See also Constituent-representative relations; Legislators
Representative assembly
functions of, 3
See also Legislature
Representative-constituent relations. See Constituent-representative relations
Representative democracy
constituencies, 400
legislators' social backgrounds and, 322–323
Representative government
ethical issues, 1156
Adam Smith on, 23
See also Apportionment; British government; Constitutions; Elections; Proportional representation; Suffrage
Representative government, English. See English representative government
Reprimanding legislators, 549
Reprogramming, 1516
Republicanism
bicameralism and, 59–60
in constitution making
eighteenth century, 59, 72
popular sovereignty theory and, 37, 45, 47
federalism and, 71, 176
freedom of the press and, 1534
Old Republicans and, 1126
slavery issue and, 1229
suffrage and, 1237
Republican National Committee, state legislative elections and, 439
Republican National State Elections Committee, state legislative elections and, 439

Republican party (GOP)
administration cleavages and, 1083
African American suffrage and, 1242, 1297–1298
antebellum era, 1231
American party and, 1131
public lands policy of, 1201
birth of, 124, 204, 533
in Colorado Territory, 267
committee assignments, 986–989
control of Congress, 1918, 1027
in Dakota Territory, 267
Great Depression era, 221
Dred Scott decision and, 76
during Great Depression, 1369
early twentieth century
insurgency in, 1134–1137
U.S. House Rules Committee and, 1054
effect of term limitations on, 525
foreign policy, 1447
free-soil principle, 1444
in Hawaii Territory, 266–268
House Committee on Committees and, 986–988
ideological cleavages and, 1071–1072
impact of constituency and, 429
industry and, 1365
late nineteenth century
presidential nominations and, 1613
Senate controlled by, 647
late twentieth century, in state legislative campaigns, 959–960
leadership votes in, 942
legal constituency definition and, 402
legislative-executive relations, under Lincoln, 1405–1406
mid-twentieth century
southern Democrats and, 618
U.S. House Rules Committee and, 1058
in 1964 election, 163
1920s, presidential legislative roles of, 612
in Oklahoma Territory, 267
post–World War I, control of U.S. Senate, 1447
vs. presidents, 122
Progressive Era, in Wisconsin, 953
Progressives vs. Old Guard, 1407
Reconstruction era, 365
legislative surge of, 890
southern constitutional revision and, 50
state legislatures and, 205–207
U.S. congressional changes and, 132
reform, Congressional committee assignments and, 1034
replaced Whig party, 880
response to constituency and, 410
sectionalism and, 1364
spending reform and, 1916, 1337
in the South, 1306

in U.S. Congress, 159–160
1946–1960, 159–160
1967–1976, 164–165
1981–1990, 169–170
two-house majority, 1480–1481
in U.S. House
1870–1895, 135–136
1895–1911, 140–142
1919–1931, 149–151
U.S. House Ways and Means Committee and, 1038, 1040
in U.S. Senate
1870–1895, 138
1895–1911, 143
1919–1931, 152
U.S. Senate Committee on Committees and, 989
in Washington Territory, 267
See also Democratic party vs. Republican party; "Gypsy moth" Republicans; Radical Republicans; Southern Democrat–Republican coalition; Southern Republicans
Republican party (Jeffersonian Republicans)
Albany Regency and, 948
executive relations, 1401
vs. Federalists. See Federalists, vs. Jeffersonian Republicans
See also Old Republicans
Republican principle, constituencies and, 399
Republican progressive–Democratic party coalition. See Democratic party–Progressive Republican coalition
Republican virtue, 1589
Rescissions, defined, 740
Research institutions, 297
Resolutions, congressional
concurrent, 1506, 1508, 1518
simple, 1506
See also Joint resolutions
Resource allocation, 413–414, 1592
legislator responsibilities and, 419
as response to constituency, 409
as substantive representation, 423
Resource Conservation and Recovery Act (1976), 1327
Responsibility, congressional
evaluation criteria, 817
reforms for, 822–823, 827
results of, 825
Responsible party theory, 816
Responsiveness
as redistricting criterion, 393
of representative, 3–4, 20
Responsiveness, congressional
committee chairs and, 1068
evaluation criteria, 817–818
reforms for, 823–824, 828–830
U.S. House Ways and Means Committee and, 1037
Restrictive rules, 714
Retirement, voluntary. See Voluntary retirement
Retirement rate, U.S. senators, 474
Retirement slump
among state legislators, 446

among U.S. representatives, 454
Reuf, Abraham, 218
Revels, Hiram R., 315, 365
Revenue. *See* General-fund revenue; Trust fund taxes
Revenue Act (1918), 1036
Revenue Act (1932), 888
Revenue estimating
 executive prerogative, 775
 political aspects, 775
"Revenue-only principle," 1201
Revenue raising. *See* Tariff legislation; Taxation
Revenue sharing
 1972, 229
 1973–1986, 84
Revivals. *See* Religious revivals
Revolutionary war. *See* American Revolution
Revolutionary war veterans
 federal support of, 1257
 House Committee of Claims and, 91
Revolution of 1800. *See* National elections, 1800
Reward legislation, 1562–1563
*Reynolds* v. *Sims* (1964), 438, 802, 838
RFC. *See* Reconstruction Finance Corporation
Rhode, Deborah, 1382, 1386, 1389, 1393–1394
Rhode Island
 emancipation in, late-eighteenth-century, 1221
 Revolutionary-era transition in, 182
 white male suffrage and, 1240
 *See also* Dorr's Rebellion
Rhode Island Colony
 charter of, 45
 electorate of, 187
 embryonic political parties in, 34
Rhode Island Colony Assembly, 1257
Rhode Island legislature, reforms, 841
Ribicoff, Abraham, 1482–1483
 FAP and, 1273
Rice, Henry M., 255
Rice's coefficient of cohesion, 933*n*
Rich, Michael, 86
Richardson, Elliot, 1467
Richmond (Va.), Revolutionary era, 1625
Riddick, Floyd, 1054
Riding circuit. *See* Circuit-riding
Riegle, Donald, 1166
Riffe, Vern, 965
Rights Revolution, 1970s, 1308–1311
Right to appeal. *See* Appeal rights
Right to privacy. *See* Privacy rights
Right to vote. *See* Suffrage
Riker, William H., 294, 905–906
Riparian rights. *See* Water laws
Ripley, Randall, 610
Risjord, Norman, 197
Ritter, Halstead L., 1631–1632
 impeachment, 559
Rives, John C. *See* Blair, Francis P.

Roberts, Brigham H., 310, 1157
Robertson, J. B. A., 1631
Robinson, John, Jr., 30
Robinson, Joseph, 152
Rockefeller, Jay, oath of office, 312
Rockefeller, John D., 1589
Rockefeller, John D., IV, 471
Rockefeller, Nelson, 1482
 public relations efforts, 628
Rodino, Peter, 998, 1633
*Roe* v. *Wade* (1973), 1392, 1584
Rogers, William P., on executive privilege, 1456, 1466
Rohde, David, 597, 599, 932–933
Role analysis, 1181–1183
Role conflict, for women in legislatures, 354
Roll-call divisions, in voting measurement, 1184
Roll-call voting
 ADA ratings of, 1189
 committee success measured by, 1178
 in congressional committees, 1009, 1011
 constituency impact on, 406–407
 dimensional analysis of, 1186–1188
 in legislative careers, 505
 legislative historiography and, 282
 legislative surges and, 892
 in North Carolina legislature, Reconstruction era, 951
 recording of, 165, 863
 religious background and, 331
 response to constituency and, 410–411
 scorecards of, 1111
 in state legislatures, nineteenth century, 949
 studies of, 288
 in U.S. Congress, growth in, 1144
 in U.S. House, party coherence in, 931–945
Rolph, James, 222
Roman Catholics. *See* Catholics
Romero, Trinidad, 317
Roosevelt, Eleanor, 1307
Roosevelt, Franklin D.
 bureaucracy and, 1597–1598
 Congressional relations with, 1408–1409
 executive reorganization, 1478–1480, 1507
 vs. Hoover, 534
 HUAC relationship, 1463
 Japanese-American internment and, 226, 1285
 Huey Long and, 1268
 media control and, 1539
 news coverage of, 1525–1526
 as New York State governor, 221
 postwar organization, 1448
 pro-British policies, 1448
 United Nations plans, 1430
 U.S. Supreme Court and, 1574, 1576, 1579, 1582
 court-packing plan, 1479
 use of executive privilege, 1463
 veto use, 1500

war powers exercised, 1429
 *See also* New Deal
Roosevelt, Theodore, 144
 administrative control and, 1592–1593
 appointments by, 1614
 armed forces in Latin America, 1427
 conservation efforts, 1319
 on corruption, 1646
 in election of 1912, 1133
 executive reorganization, 1476
 foreign policy issues, 1445–1446
 governorship, 1416
 Hepburn Act and, 886
 insurgent Republicans and, 1052
 legislative aims of, 611, 892
 mass circulation press and, 612, 1525
 Monroe Doctrine corollary, 1427
 "muckraking" coined by, 1645
 Panama Canal, 1446
 Progressivism inaugurated by, 894
 vs. Taft, 1136
 U.S. Supreme Court and, 1582
 use of presidential power, 1407
 *Winning of the West, The*, 1589
Roosevelt (F. D.) administration
 civil rights policy, 315, 1301
 environmental policy, 1320–1321
 legislative activity of, 612–613
 neutrality legislation, 1447–1448
Roosevelt (T.) administration, Republican cohesion in, 1134
Rose, Ernestine, 1382
Rosenthal, Alan, 498, 721, 972
Rosten, Leo, 1526
Rostenkowski, Dan, as U.S. House Ways and Means Committee chair, 1046–1047
Rotation in office. *See* Legislative turnover
Rothschild, Lionel, 309
*Roth* v. *United States* (1957), 1541
Royal colonies, assemblies in, constitutional status of, 31
Royal councils, state constitutionalism and, 179
Royal governors. *See* Colonial governors
Rudman, Warren, 1166–1167
Rules, parliamentary. *See* Parliamentary rules; Suspension of the rules
Rules committees
 states, 725
 *See also* House of Representatives, U.S., Rules Committee; Senate, U.S., Rules Committee
"Rules of the game." *See* Norms
Rundquist, Barry, 727, 1009
Rural districts
 Great Depression era, 536
 late nineteenth century, 535
 legislative recruitment and, 333
 post-World War II era, party competition in, 954
Rural-urban conflict, legislative historiography and, 289

established, 134, 733, 1026–1028, 1335
full jurisdiction restored, 1922, 1027
size of, 1019
Armed Services Committee
legislator response to constituency and, 414
Tower nomination and, 1617
Astronautical and Space Sciences Panel, eliminated, 821
Banking and Currency Committee, Huitt's research on, 587–588
Budget Committee
established, 739, 821
member requirements, 1028
censure of Jackson, 1494
censure of members, 551
checks and balances, 468
cloture rule, 1447, 1552
codes of ethics, 824–825, 831, 1161, 1163
Commerce Committee
Nader and, 1006
Smathers and, 1647
Strauss and, 1617
committee assignments, 995
Democrats, 988
motivation, 992–993
Republicans, 989
Committee on Committees, late nineteenth century, 647
committees
agendas in, 1004–1005
antebellum era, 646
early twentieth century, 1529
Federalist-Republican era, 89–90, 645
late twentieth century, 649–651, 655–656, 658–659
mid-twentieth century, 1144–1145
presidential nominations and, 1606
publication of reports, 861
committee structure
1870–1895, 139
1895–1911, 144
1911–1919, 148
1919–1931, 153
composition of established (1787), 11
conference committees, 716–718
Constitutional Convention debate on, 63–65, 67–68
diplomatic nomination rejected by, mid-nineteenth century, 122
direct public election of members, 322
District of Columbia Panel, eliminated, 821
early nineteenth century, 99–100, 104–105
early twentieth century
decentralized leadership in, 611
presidential relations with, 1614
elections to. See Senators, U.S., election of

electoral patterns, 473–478
electoral politics
1870–1895, 138
1895–1911, 143
1911–1919, 146–147
1919–1931, 152
1946–1960, 160
1967–1976, 164–165
1981–1990, 168–169
elite character of, 468
equal representation of states provided for, 12
Ethics Committee, 419
Cranston and, 1650–1651
expulsion of members, 552
executive reorganization bill, 1479
expulsion of members, 549–553
failure to ratify SALT II, 826
Fair Employment Practices Board, 794
Federalist-Republican era
committees of, 89–90
presidential nominations and, 1609
public interest in, 96
Washington and, 97
filling vacancies, 469–470
Finance Committee
Civil War era, 117, 646, 733
Federalist-Republican era, 100, 732
fiscal responsibilities, 1023, 1335
Nixon era, 1272
relation to House Ways and Means Committee, 1034, 1036
Taft era, 1135
folkways of, 588, 590, 598
foreign policy role, 1440, 1442–1444
nineteenth century, 1441–1442
Foreign Relations Committee, 426
establishment of, 1442
Federalist-Republican era, 100, 105
mid-nineteenth century, 116
mid-twentieth century, 1530
Governmental Affairs Committee, 652
history, 467–470
impeachment
New Deal era, 1631–1632
powers of, 557
individuality tolerated in, 644
Internal Security Subcommittee (SISS), Communism in publishing investigation, 1288–1289
Jackson era, 1610–1611
Judiciary Committee, 114
hearings transcripts, 860
in judge selection, 1578–1580
lawyers in, 334–336
leadership
1870–1895, 138
1895–1911, 143
late nineteenth century, 611
mid-nineteenth century, 117
1911–1919, 147
1919–1931, 152
staff, 793

legislation
moving to floor, 705–707
multiple referrals, 706
process of consideration, 708–713
records of, 857
Legislative Assistance Allowance, 793
length and nature of terms, 467
Madison era, 1610
Majority Caucus, mid-nineteenth century, 117
majority leader, 608–609
making motions to proceed, 706
membership
1870–1895, 138–139
1895–1911, 143–144
1911–1919, 147–148
1919–1931, 152–153
Military Affairs Committee, 100, 105
minorities in, 470
motions to proceed, 705–706
Naval Affairs Committee, 100, 105
nomination confirmation by, 1605
organization, 878–879
partisan voting in, 538–539
party organization
1870–1895, 138
1895–1911, 143
1911–1919, 147
1919–1931, 152
1967–1976, 166
perceptions of constituency preferences, 425, 430
petitions to, 859
Post Office and Civil Service Panel, eliminated, 821
power fragmentation, sources of, 1068
presidential veto discourse, 1495
Progressive Era, corruption in, 1645–1646
Public Lands Committee, 1318
public perception of, 1558
public proceedings, 1455
rationale for, 1548
redefining committee jurisdictions, 823
reelection, incumbency advantage, 474, 476–477
reforms, 828
rejection of Treaty of Versailles, 1429
Republican dominance, late nineteenth century, 646–647
Resolution 266, 1283
restrictions on civil liberties, 1282
retirement rates, 474
Rules and Administration Committee
assignment to, 993
House Standing Committee of Correspondents and, 1528
staff funding levels, 791
Select Committee on Campaign Activities, 1467

*(continued)*

legislative-court interaction and, 1570–1571

legislative veto and, 1519

limitation on congressional oversight, 760

in local legislative institutions, 233

*Morrison* v. *Olson* and, 1575

policy-making and, 874

political parties and, 876

presidential adherence to, 1406

regulatory agencies and, 1593–1594

Revolutionary-era interest in, 189

in state constitutions
  antebellum, 48–49
  early, 45, 59
  Parsons on, 181

state governments, 879

studies of, 291

Sequestration, 423, 742–743
  *See also* Minisequesters

Session laws, publication of, 864

Sewall, Samuel, 93

Seward, William, anti-Masonic movement and, 1125, 1128

Sexuality, 1379, 1390–1394
  antebellum era, 1384
  colonial era, southern states, 1381
  early twentieth century, 1386
  late twentieth century, 1389–1390

Sexual stereotyping, 328

Shade, William G., 202, 950

Shadow constitutional conventions.
  *See* Staunton Conventions

*Shame of the Cities, The. See* Steffens, Lincoln

Shapp, Milton, 775

Share the Wealth program, F. D. Roosevelt and, 1268

Sharkansky, Ira, 772

Shay's Rebellion, 189, 468

Sheffield, William, 1634–1635

Sheppard-Towner Maternity and Infant Protection Act (1921), 1265, 1386

Shepsle, Kenneth A., 595, 797, 931, 984, 1004
  disequilibrium theory, 576–577

Sherman, Roger, 62
  on religious tests for legislators, 310

Sherman Anti-Trust Act (1890), 81, 140, 1206, 1208–1209, 1582

Shipping, Atlantic Ocean, Jefferson era, 1127

Shipping firms, government subsidies for, 1642

Shipping regulation
  colonial, 1196
  Federal-Republican era, 1197

Short, William, nominations of, 1607, 1609

Sibley, Henry H., 255

Sierra Club
  environmental lobbying, 1322
  Yosemite recession campaign, 1317

Sikes, Robert L.F., 1163

Silbey, Joel H., 17, 948

*Silent Spring. See* Carson, Rachel

Silver coinage
  Democratic national convention (1896) and, 534
  Populist party and, 1132–1133

Simmons, James F., 120, 1159

Simon, Paul, 476

Simpson, Alan, 471

Simpson, Milward, 471

Sims, Kimberly, 1102

Sinclair, Barbara, 538, 597–599
  *The Transformation of the U.S. Senate*, 582

Sinclair, Upton, *The Jungle*, 1265–1266

Single-issue groups. *See* Cause groups

Single-member, simple plurality rules
  reapportionment and, 391
  redistricting and, 392

Single-member districts
  constituencies and, 400–401
  in states
    incumbent reelection in, 955
    multimember districts and, 441
    third parties and, 1124, 1139
    women running in, 356

Sirica, John J., 1467–1468, 1633

Sisk, B. F., 1059

Slaughterhouse cases, 1298–1299

Slavery, 1217–1233
  abolished, 125, 886
  civil rights issues, 1279, 1296
  colonial, 1196
  Confederate constitutions on, 49
  Constitutional Convention debates on, 64–65, 67
  electoral realignment and, 533
  federalism dispute and, 39, 76
  Native American, 259
  southern courts and, 1202
  southern legislators and, 202, 205, 485
  in Southwest Territory, 251
  state legislative influence on federal policy, 1560
  tariff policy and, 1201
  territorial legislatures and, 1564
  in territories, 256–259, 1225
    Compromise of 1850 and, 1129, 1230
    congressional response to, 123
  Three-fifths Compromise for counting state populations (1787), 13–14
  U.S. congressional debate, 1405, 1442
  U.S. Constitution on, 40
  U.S. Senate debate on, 1548
  *See also* Abolitionism; African Americans; Gag rules; Indenture laws; Peonage

Slidell, John, 1643

Smalls, Robert, 368

Smathers, George, 1647

Smith, Adam, *Inquiry into the Nature and Causes of the Wealth of Nations*, 23, 34

Smith, Al, 1283

Smith, Frank L., 309

Smith, Harold, 1464

Smith, Howard Worth, 1056–1060

Smith, Marcus Aurelius, 269

Smith, Margaret Chase, 317, 468–469

Smith, Melancton, on size of Congress, 11

Smith, Robert, 99, 1609–1610

Smith, Samuel Harrison, 95–96, 99, 100, 1523, 1609

Smith, Sir Thomas, on consent through Parliament, 5

Smith, Steven S., 985, 1063

Smith, William, on colonial representative assemblies, 6

Smith, William, Jr., 28

Smith, William Loughton, 91–93, 96

Smith Act. *See* Alien Registration Act

Smith-Connally Act. *See* War Labor Dispute Act

Smith-Hughes Act (1917), 1563

Smith-Lever Act (1914), 1563

Smoot, Reed, 310, 1477

Smoot-Hawley Tariff (1930), 1035, 1408, 1447–1448

SMSP. *See* Single-member, simple plurality rules

Smyth, Alexander, 105

Snell, Bertrand, 1055, 1409

Snyder, Simon, 198–199

Social-choice theory, legislative historiography and, 294

Social hygiene, World War I era, 1386

Social insurance, 1255
  *See also* Social Security system

Social issues, mid-nineteenth century
  in Pennsylvania legislature, 204
  in state legislatures, 203

Socialist party
  Progressive Era, 1134
  representatives denied seats, 1282

"Social" lobbying, 1114–1115

Social mobility, legislative recruitment and, 325

Social movements, legislative surges and, 895

Social norms. *See* Legislative norms; Norms

Social order, maintenance of, 1533

Social programs, bureaucracy and, 1601

Social Purity Alliance, 1391

Social reforms
  antebellum era, 1257
  by state legislatures, 1347
  *See also* Moral reforms

Social regulatory policy
  state control of, 74
  U.S. Congress oversight, 753

Social sciences, bureaucracy and, 1596

Social Security Act (1935), New Deal programs under, 82, 1268

Social Security Administration, old age and survivors insurance, 1016

Social Security system
  introduction of, 223–224

(continued)

sectionalism and, 1361
  black suffrage and, 1372
  suffrage and, 1245–1246
  *See also* Confederate states
Southwest Ordinance (1790), 251
Southwest states, slavery in, 1129
Southwest Territory, 250–251
Sovereignty
  antifederalists on, 191
  *See also* Popular sovereignty
Soviet Union, U.S. trade with, Jewish immigration issues, 1451
Spain
  Cuban independence war and, 1445
  Florida ceded to U.S., 1424
  West Florida and, 1127
Spanish-American War, 1426–1427
  members of Congress serving in, 313
  presidential elections and, 144
Spatial analysis, 1187
Speakers of British House of Commons, 91
Speakers of colonial assemblies, 30
Speakers of House of Representatives
  appointing conference committee members, 717
  bill-referral power, 828
  centralization of power, 1406
  committee appointments, 986
    criteria for, 1024
  control of floor schedule, 705
  control of House proceedings, 819
  early twentieth century
    Cannon "Insurgent Revolt" and, 492, 611, 647
    under Cannon, 1407
  1870–1895, 135–137
  1895–1911, 141–142
  Eisenhower era, 614
  Federalist-Republican era, 91–95, 102, 105
  late nineteenth century, 610–611, 646
  late twentieth century
    ad hoc committees appointed by, 38
    enhanced power of, 662–663
    floor activity and, 661
    multiple referral power of, 1063
  majority leadership and, 607
  mid-nineteenth century, 111, 113–116, 118–119
  motions to suspend the rules, 705, 711
  news reporters and, 1524
  1911–1919, 145–146
  1919–1931, 150–151
  nineteenth century, third parties and, 1125
  power of, 1552
  Rules Committee and, 606, 610–611, 616, 646, 649, 1050–1053, 1061, 1135
  nominations, 705
  selection by party caucuses, 134
  Senate majority leaders and, 609
Speakers of state houses, 633–634
  committee appointments, 635, 639

selection of, 961
Special charters, antebellum, 1204, 1642
Special congressional committees. *See* Select committees, congressional
Special districts, late twentieth century, 245
Special elections
  to fill Senate vacancies, 469–470
  to recall legislators, 547
Special interests. *See* Private interests
Specialization
  by legislative scholars, 1190
  by legislators, 1181–1182
  in state legislative committees, 673–685
    committee continuity and, 683–684
    member evaluations, 685, 687*t*
  by state legislative staff, 802
  U.S. congressional staff, 792
Special orders
  in U.S. House, 111, 1530
  U.S. House Rules Committee and, 1051–1052
  in U.S. Senate, 113
Special prosecutors
  separation of powers and, 1651
  U.S. Congress, 1575
Special rules
  U.S. House of Representatives, 714–715
  U.S. Senate, 715–716
Spectator (type of legislator), 345
Speculators, land. *See* Land companies
Speech, freedom of. *See* Freedom of speech; Press, freedom of
Speech codes, freedom of expression and, 1543
Speech freedoms. *See* Freedom of speech
Speed limits, 230
Spending. *See* Public expenditures
Split-ticket voting, 519–520
  divided government and, 541
  New Deal era, 953
  in U.S. House districts, 454
  *See also* Straight-ticket voting
Spoils system, 1588
  late nineteenth century, attempted reforms of, 952
Spooner, John, consumer protection legislation and, 1265
Sprague, John, 996
Staff, congressional
  accountability, 787
  allowances for, 787
  chronology, 789–791
  current status, 791–794
  distribution, 786, 790, 796
  duties, 787
    contextual effects, 796
    duties and communication patterns, 795
  employment discrimination, 794
  equal access to, 787
  growth of, 787–791
  House-Senate equity, 787–788

impact and contributions, 797–798
increased flexibility in, 788
as information processors, 797
institutional values and structures affecting, 786–787
leadership, 793
legislation affecting, 789
legislative support agencies, 793
members' use of, 796
minority party, 787, 790
numbers, 785–786, 789
office organization, 794
pay and benefits, 793
personal office, 787, 792–794
policy positions, 792
previous occupations of, 794–795
records and regulations, 788
reforms, 829–830
  catalysts for, 788
specialization, 792
state and district ties, 795
studies on, 795–797
turnover, 795
U.S. congressional characteristics affecting, 785
women and minorities in, 794
*See also* Committee staff
Staff, legislative
  increasing number and competence, 844
  professionalization of
    effects of reform on, 848
    public policy impact, 847
Staff, state legislative
  amalgam model, 808–811
  centralization, 812
  distribution of resources, 852
  evolution, 802–804
  fiscal duties, 769
  legislative council model, 804, 811–812
  partisanship issues, 804, 806, 808, 812
  permanent vs. part-time, 803
  policy analysis, 806
  procedural contributions, 803
  professionalization, 803
  size of, 803
  system modeling, 804–812
  technical expertise, 803–804, 806
  traditional nonpartisan model, 805–806
  traditional partisan model, 806–808
Stafford, Robert T., 1327
Stagflation, 1043
Staggered selection system, 469
Stalemate. *See* Political gridlock
Stalin, Joseph, postwar organization, 1448
"Stalwarts" (Wisconsin faction), 953
Stam, Colin F., 1036
Stamp Act (1765), 1639
Stamp Act Congress, resolutions of, 55
Stanbery, Henry
  appointment denied to, 1613
  Johnson impeachment and, 1612
Standard Oil Company, Pennsylvania legislature and, 208–209

# INDEX

ing Act (1965) and, 85
colonial regulation of, 1196
Tocqueville, Alexis de
on corruption, 1639, 1643, 1653
*Democracy in America*, 108, 1091, 1442
"Today in the Legislature" (TV program), 1531
Toledo War (1835–1836), 255
Tonnage regulation. *See* Shipping regulation
Tower, John G., confirmation denied to, 1605, 1617
Town meeting
colonial era, 234
early twentieth century, 243–244
late twentieth century, 244
Townshend duties, denounced in Massachusetts, 177
Townshend Plan, F. D. Roosevelt and, 1268
Townships, nineteenth century, 237
Townsmen. *See* Selectmen
Trade associations
lobbying by, 1107
membership of, 1109
Trade PACs, 1093
Traders, sole. *See* Sole traders
Trade unions. *See* Labor unions
Trading companies, English. *See* English trading corporations
Traditionalistic state culture, 1353
Transcontinental railroad construction
antebellum attempts to establish, 1199–1200
Civil War era grants for, 1205
Transcontinental Treaty (1819), 1424, 1443
*Transformation of the U.S. Senate, The. See* Sinclair, Barbara
Transportation Act (1920), 1209
Transportation facilities
government encouragement of, 74
antebellum era, 1199–1200
regulation of, 1368
U.S. congressional changes and, 1860–1930, 133
*See also* Highway construction; Railroad construction
Traugott, Sandra, 935
Travel expenses, fictitious, 1643–1644
Treason
death penalty for, 1624
impeachment for, 1622
*Treason of the Senate, The*, 1645–1646
Treasury, U.S. Department of the
antebellum era, 1200
creation of, 1023
Lincoln era, 1612
outlays of, 734–735
relation to U.S. House Ways and Means Committee, 1036
spending authority and, 1339
Washington era, 97
Treaties
legislative-court interaction on, 1570
post–World War I, 153

*Treatise on Constitutional Conventions. See* Jameson, John A..
Treaty of Guadalupe Hidalgo, 1443
Treaty of Versailles, Senate rejection of, 1429, 1447
Trimble, James, 1060
"Triple alliances." *See* "Iron triangles"
Tripoli, declares war on U.S., 1423–1424
Trist, Nicholas, 1443
Truancy laws, late nineteenth century, 1262
Truman, David, 288, 587
Truman, Harry S.
appointments by, 1616–1617
on bureaucrats, 1587
executive-branch reorganization, 1481, 1599
Fair Deal proposals, 1409–1410
forces sent to Korea, 1430–1431
foreign policy, 1410, 1448–1449
health-care proposals of, 1269
loyalty files, 1458, 1464–1465
NATO negotiations, 1430
television coverage of, 1529
use of executive privilege, 1456, 1464–1465
veto use, 1500–1501
Truman Doctrine, 1449
Trumbull, Jonathan, 91
Trumbull, Lyman, 1405
Trustee, Burke's concept of representative as, 4
Trustee (type of legislator)
defined, 420
perception of constituency preferences, 425
response to constituency and, 411
role of, 424
view of constituencies, 427–428
Trust-fund taxes
budget deficits and, 1334–1335, 1342
creation of, 1340–1341
1950–1984, 1341
Trusts. *See* Antitrust legislation
Tucker, Harvey J., 442–443, 724, 955, 958–959
Tucker, Henry, 1492
Tucker, Thomas Tudor, 185
on freedom of assembly, 12
Tucson (Ariz.), as territorial capital, 277
Tullock, Gordon, 906
"Why So Much Stability?" 576
Turner, Frederick Jackson, 282
Turner, George, 1132
Turnover, legislative. *See* Legislative turnover
Twain, Mark, 1645
Tweed ring. *See* Boss Tweed ring
Twenty-one day rule, 821–822, 1058–1060
Twilight, Alexander Lucius, 376
Two-party system, ideological division underlying, 1278
*Two Treatises of Government. See* Locke, John
Tydings, Millard, 1465

Tyler, John
cabinet of, 122
impeachment resolution, 1496
A. Johnson and, 126
nominations by, 1611
party repudiation of, 118
Texas annexation and, 1228, 1425
use of executive privilege, 1458, 1460–1461
veto use, 1404, 1495–1496
Whigs and, 123

Udall, Stewart, 1322
Ullman, Al, 1045
Unanimity
incentives for, in U.S. House, 934
norms research on, 594, 1184
requests for
in U.S. House, 1060
in U.S. Senate, 595, 609
Unanimous consent agreements, 703, 713
to avoid filibusters, 706
partial, 716
in setting floor schedules, 706
*See also* Time agreements
Uncertainty postulate, 579
Understanding clause, 1246
Underwood, Oscar W., 146, 152, 1034
U.S. House posts of, 1053
Underwood Tariff (1913), 1035, 1209
Unemployment
Depression era, 1266
Nixon era, 1272
Unemployment compensation systems, 1256
Great Depression era, 224–225, 1268
Progressive Era, 1264
Uniform state law campaign, 79
Union Calendar, 704, 709
Union Pacific Railroad, 1644
Unions. *See* Labor unions
United Brethren of the War of 1812, 119
United Nations
charter, 1430
U.S. congressional role in establishing, 1448
United Nations Participation Act (1945), 1430
United Negro College Fund, 1152
United States Sanitary Commission, 1262
*United States Statutes at Large*, 856
*United States* v. *Ballin* (1892), 314
*United States* v. *Brewster* (1972), 550
*United States* v. *Burr* (1807), 1460
*United States* v. *Butler* (1936), 82
*United States* v. *Carolene Products Co.* (1938), 1539, 1574
*United States* v. *Cruikshank* (1876), 1299
*United States* v. *Curtiss-Wright Export Corporation* (1936), 1429
*United States* v. *E. C. Knight Company* (1895), 80–81
*United States* v. *Nixon* (1974), 1458, 1468, 1634–1635
*United States* v. *Pink* (1942), 1451

# INDEX